A HISTORY
OF SOUTHERN AFRICA

A HISTORY OF SOUTHERN AFRICA

by

ERIC A. WALKER

*Fellow of St. John's College, and Emeritus
Vere Harmsworth Professor of Imperial
and Naval History in the University of
Cambridge; sometime Professor of History
in the University of Cape Town*

1724

LONGMANS

LONGMANS, GREEN AND CO LTD
48 Grosvenor Street, London W.1
*Associated companies, branches and representatives
throughout the world*

*First Published (under the title 'A History of South
Africa')* 1928
Reissue with Extensive Additions 1935
Second Edition 1940
New Impression 1941
New Impression (with minor corrections) 1947
*Third Edition (published under the title 'A History
of Southern Africa')* 1957
Reissue with corrections 1959
New impression with corrections 1962
New impressions 1964 *and* 1965

MADE AND PRINTED BY OFFSET IN GREAT BRITAIN BY
WILLIAM CLOWES AND SONS, LIMITED
LONDON AND BECCLES

PREFACE TO THE THIRD EDITION

EUROPEANS have dwelt on the coasts of Southern Africa for more than four hundred years. During most of that period they have steadily penetrated the continent from the south-west. If the inception of the Portuguese settlements be taken as the starting-point, European Southern Africa has a history as long as that of Latin America; if time be reckoned from the more fruitful Dutch occupation of Table Bay, it has a history almost as long as that of the United States.

Until recent times Southern Africa was a little world to itself within a ring-fence marked out by Ocean and the vast bulk of Darkest Africa. It has experimented with almost every conceivable type of polity from tribal chieftainships to a latter-day Dominion; but its social foundations are even more diversified than its constitutional superstructure. Southern African humanity ranges from Stone Age man to Professors of Anthropology. A few Bushman hunters lurk in the shadows, Hottentot pastoralists survive in outlying parts, sturdy Bantu agriculturalists everywhere outnumber all the other racial groups. In the south-western region are the Cape Coloured Folk, the progeny of Africans of all kinds, of Asiatics and, in some cases, of Europeans also, a few of them good Moslems, who point with pride to traces of Malay blood. Indians are numerous in the south-eastern parts. The Europeans are Afrikaners descended in the main from Dutch, Belgian, West German and French ancestors, men of various British stocks, a considerable number of Jews principally from Central and Eastern Europe, Germans in South-West Africa, and Portuguese in Mozambique Province.

In essaying to tell the story, I have broken away from traditional methods in two main respects. First, I have made no attempt to give an account of each of the component parts of the Southern African state system as a thing by itself, but rather to trace the interplay of those parts, which has always been much more significant than the doings of any one of them. Secondly, I have made neither the struggle between British and Afrikaners nor the achievement of self-government or closer union the main theme. At times these

a*   v

things fill the stage, but they do so at the cost of pushing the principals into the wings. Those principals are Western civilisation, tribal Africa and, to a less degree, theocratic Asia.

The humane adjustment of the mutual relations of these three cultures in the plural societies that extend from the shores of Table Bay to the borders of Abyssinia is one of the outstanding problems facing the world and especially the British Commonwealth. The history of Southern Africa, the largest and longest-established of those societies, is of far more than local importance, because it accounts for, even if it be not held to justify, the ideas on the 'proper relations' of Whites to Non-Whites held by the vast majority of European Southern Africans. Those ideas and the experience behind them must at least be understood before the necessary adjustment can be made on a continental scale—perhaps an adjustment on an even grander scale, since the course of events in Southern Africa throws a revealing light on the working of world-wide forces. Everywhere Western peoples, a minority in our crowded world, are seeking to defend their high standard of living against the competition of spare-living alien folk. They can, if they will, see that struggle in all its nakedness in Southern Africa, where the competitors live, not at different ends of the earth, but on adjoining farms, in adjacent streets or even in the same house. It was fitting, therefore, that I should have ended the first edition of this book in June 1924, when a Union ministry compounded of rural Afrikaners and predominantly British Labour men took office to safeguard 'White South Africa' and, partly as a means to that end, to seek the 'fullest self-determination for the Union.'

In a subsequent edition I carried the story on till the outbreak of the Axis War in 1939. In this present edition, I have not only revised the text and brought the select bibliography up to date, but made extensive changes in that text and the scope of the book. The chief changes have been in the chapters dealing with the Great Trek, the eighteen-sixties and 'seventies, the Jameson Raid and, generally, the events leading up to the South African War. Further, I have added so much of the history of the Two Rhodesias and Nyasaland that I have re-named the book *The History of Southern Africa*.

Many more friends have helped me than I can mention here; but there are some to whom I owe special debts. Chief among these are the late Professor Leo Fouche and Professor W. M. Macmillan, both formerly on the staff of the University of the Witwatersrand, the late Professor R. Coupland, sometime Beit Professor of British Imperial History in the University of Oxford, Professor H. J. Mandelbrote, my successor in the University of Cape Town, the late Mr. P. Ribbink, Union Parliamentary Librarian, Mr. C. G.

Botha and Mr. P. J. Venter, successive Keepers of the Cape Archives, the late Mr. A. C. G. Lloyd and Mr. D. Varley, successive Librarians of the South African Public Library, Cape Town, Mr. V. H. Hiller, Keeper of the Central African Archives, Salisbury, and the High Commissioners for the Union of South Africa, for the Federation of Rhodesia and Nyasaland in the United Kingdom. While writing *Lord de Villiers and His Times* and *W. P. Schreiner. A South African*, I was privileged to see the papers of these two statesmen, besides the unpublished *Materials* of the late Lord Loch and some of the papers of the late Mr. John X. Merriman. Taken together, these are a mine of political information covering the years 1870–1919. In addition, the late Dr. J. G. Gubbins of Ottoshoop, Transvaal, Mr. J. A. I. Agar-Hamilton, then of the University of Pretoria, and the late Sir Drummond Chaplin lent me many documents ranging from the eighteen-thirties to the late 'nineties, and the executors of the late Mr. J. G. R. Lewis, sometime Director of Education in South-West Africa, put at my disposal the completed portion of his history of that territory. I acknowledge in the select bibliography my many obligations to the unpublished theses of post-graduate students.

ERIC A. WALKER

St. John's College,
Cambridge,
April 1961

CONTENTS

ix

CONTENTS

CONTENTS

LIST OF MAPS

ABBREVIATIONS USED IN THE FOOTNOTES

Bas. Rec. = *Basutoland Records*, compiled by G. M. Theal.

Bird = *The Annals of Natal*, compiled by J. Bird.

C.H.B.E. VIII. = *Cambridge History of the British Empire*, vol. VIII.: *South Africa, Rhodesia and the High Commission Territories*.

Eybers = *Select Constitutional Documents* . . . *1795–1910*, compiled by G. W. Eybers.

Misc. Bas. Rec. = Unpublished *Miscellaneous Basutoland Records* (Cape Archives).

Nat. Not. = *Voortrekker Wetgewing. Die Notule van die Natalse Volksraad, 1839–45*, edited by G. S. Preller.

Rec. C.C. = *Records of the Cape Colony*, compiled by G. M. Theal.

Rec. S.E.A. = *The Records of South-Eastern Africa*, compiled by G. M. Theal.

Theal, I*a*, etc. = *History and Ethnography of Africa South of the Zambesi before 1795*, vol. I., etc., by G. M. Theal.

Theal, I*b*, etc. = *History of South Africa since 1795*, vol. I., etc., by G. M. Theal.

V.R. Soc. I. = Publications of the Van Riebeeck Society, vol. I.

Voort. Argief. = *Voortrekker-Argiefstukke, 1829–1849*, edited by H. S. Pretorius and D. W. Kruger.

A. 6–96 (Cape) = Document published by order of the Cape House of Assembly, No. 6 of 1896.

G. 2–84 (Cape) = Document published by order of the Cape Government, No. 2 of 1884.

S.C. 9–89 (Cape) = Report of Select Committee, No. 9 of 1889.

U.G. 4–16 = Document published by order of the Union Government, No. 4 of 1916.

LIST OF EXECUTIVE OFFICERS

DUTCH EAST INDIA COMPANY, 1652–1795

UNITED PROVINCES. *Government of the United Provinces* and *The Council of Seventeen (Die Heeren Superiores in Patria).*

EAST INDIES. *Governor-General and Council of India, Batavia, Java.*

CAPE COLONY. *Commanders:* Johan Anthonie van Riebeeck, April 7, 1652–May 6, 1662; Zacharias Wagenaar, May 6, 1662–Sept. 27, 1666; Cornelis van Quaelberg, Sept. 27, 1666–June 18, 1668; Jacob Borghorst, June 18, 1668–March 25, 1670; Pieter Hackius, March 25, 1670–Nov. 30, 1671. *Council of Policy,* Nov. 30, 1671–March 25, 1672. *Acting Commander:* Albert van Breugel (Secunde), March 25–Oct. 2, 1672. *Governors:* Isbrand Goske, Oct. 2, 1672–March 14, 1676; Johan Bax, March 14, 1676–June 29, 1678. *Acting Commander:* Hendrik Crudorp (Secunde), June 29, 1678–Oct. 12, 1679. *Commander:* Simon van der Stel, Oct. 12, 1678–May 31, 1691. *Governors:* Simon van der Stel, June 1, 1691–Feb. 11, 1699; Willem Adriaan van der Stel, Feb. 11, 1699–June 3, 1707. *Acting Governor:* Johan Cornelis d'Ableing (Secunde), June 7, 1707–Feb. 1708. *Governor:* Louis van Assenburgh, Feb. 1, 1708–Dec. 27, 1711. *Acting Governor:* Willem Helot (Secunde), Dec. 28, 1711–March 28, 1714. *Governor:* Mauritz Pasques de Chavonnes, March 28, 1714–Sept. 8, 1724. *Acting Governor:* Jean (Jan) de la Fontaine (Secunde), Sept. 8, 1724–Feb. 25, 1727. *Governor:* Pieter Gysbert Noodt, Feb. 25, 1727–April 23, 1729. *Acting Governor:* Jean de la Fontaine, April 24, 1729–March 8, 1737. *Governors:* J. de la Fontaine, March 8–Aug. 31, 1737; Adriaan van Kervel, Aug. 31–Sept. 19, 1737. *Acting Governor:* Daniel van den Henghel (Independent Fiscal), Sept. 20, 1737–April 14, 1739. *Governors:* Hendrik Swellengrebel, April 14, 1739–Feb. 27, 1751; Ryk Tulbagh, Feb. 27, 1751–Aug. 11, 1771. *Acting Governor:* Joachim van Plettenberg (Secunde), Aug. 12, 1771–May 18, 1774. *Governors:* J. van Plettenberg, May 18, 1774–Feb. 14, 1785; Cornelis Jacob van der Graaff, Feb. 14, 1785–June 24, 1791. *Acting Governor:* Johan Isaak Rhenius, June 24, 1791–July 3, 1792. *Commissioners-General:* Sebastiaan Cornelis Nederburgh and Simon Hendrik Frykenius, July 3, 1792–Sept. 2, 1793, Abraham Josias Sluysken, Sept. 2, 1793–Sept. 16, 1795.

FIRST BRITISH OCCUPATION, 1795–1803

GREAT BRITAIN AND UNITED KINGDOM. *British Sovereign:* George III, Oct. 25, 1760–Jan. 29, 1820. *Committee of Trade and Plantations* and *Secretary of State for War:* Henry Dundas, July 11, 1794–March 16, 1801. *Secretary of State for War and Colonies:* Lord Hobart, March 17, 1801–May 11, 1804.

CAPE COLONY. *Commanders:* Admiral Sir George Keith Elphinstone, Major-Generals Alured Clarke and James Henry Craig, Sept. 16–Nov. 15, 1795. *Commandant:* Major-General J. H. Craig, Nov. 15, 1795–May 5, 1797. *Governor:* Earl Macartney, May 5, 1797–Nov. 20, 1798. *Acting-Governor:* Major-General Francis Dundas, Nov. 20, 1798–Dec. 9, 1799. *Governor:* Sir George Yonge, Dec. 10, 1799–April 20, 1801. *Acting-Governor:* Maj.-Gen. F. Dundas, April 21, 1801–Feb. 20, 1803.

BATAVIAN REPUBLIC, 1803–6

NETHERLANDS. *Government of the Batavian Republic* and *Batavian Council for the Asiatic Possessions.*
CAPE COLONY. *Commissioner-General:* Jacob Abraham de Mist, Feb. 21, 1803–Sept. 25, 1804. *Governor:* Lieut.-Gen. Jan Willem Janssens, March 1, 1803–Jan. 18, 1806.

SECOND BRITISH OCCUPATION, 1806–71

UNITED KINGDOM. *British Sovereigns:* George III, Oct. 25, 1760–Jan. 29, 1820; George IV, Jan. 29, 1820–June 26, 1830; William IV, June 26, 1830–June 20, 1837; Victoria, June 20, 1837–Jan. 22, 1901.

Secretaries of State for War and Colonies: Viscount Castlereagh, June 10, 1805–Feb. 13, 1806; William Windham, Feb. 14, 1806–March 31, 1807; Viscount Castlereagh, March 31, 1807–Sept. 8, 1809; Earl of Liverpool, Oct. 11, 1809–June 10, 1812; Earl Bathurst, June 11, 1812–April 29, 1827; Viscount Goderich, April 30–Aug. 16, 1827; William Huskisson, Aug. 17, 1827–May 29, 1828; Sir George Murray, May 30, 1828–Nov. 21, 1830; Viscount Goderich, Nov. 22, 1830–April 2, 1833; Edward George Geoffrey Smith-Stanley (Lord Stanley), April 3, 1833–June 4, 1834; Thomas Spring-Rice, June 5–Nov. 14, 1834; Duke of Wellington, Nov. 14–Dec. 19, 1834; Earl of Aberdeen, Dec. 20, 1834–April 17, 1835; Charles Grant (Lord Glenelg, May 1835), April 18, 1835–Feb. 19, 1839; Marquess of Normanby, Feb. 20–Aug. 30, 1839; Lord John Russell, Aug. 30, 1839–Sept. 3, 1841; Lord Stanley, Sept. 3, 1841–Dec. 23, 1845; William Ewart Gladstone, Dec. 23, 1845–July 2, 1846; Earl Grey, July 3, 1846–Feb. 27, 1852; Sir John Somerset Pakington, Feb. 27–Dec. 7, 1852; Duke of Newcastle, Dec. 8, 1852–June 10, 1854.

Secretaries of State for the Colonies: Sir George Grey, June 10, 1854–Feb. 7, 1855; Sidney Herbert, Feb. 8–22, 1855; Lord John Russell, Feb. 23–July 21, 1855; Sir William Molesworth, July 21–Nov. 16, 1855; Henry Labouchere, Nov. 17, 1855–Feb. 26, 1858; Lord Edward Henry Stanley, Feb. 26–May 31, 1858; Sir Edward George Earle Lytton Bulwer-Lytton, May 31, 1858–June 18, 1859; Duke of Newcastle, June 18, 1859–April 4, 1864; Edward Cardwell, April 4, 1864–July 6, 1866; Earl of Carnarvon, July 6, 1866–March 8, 1867; Duke of Buckingham, March 8, 1867–Dec. 10, 1868; Earl Granville, Dec. 10, 1868–July 6, 1870; Earl of Kimberley, July 6, 1870–Feb. 21, 1874.

CAPE COLONY. *Acting Governors:* Maj.-Gen. Sir David Baird, Jan. 10, 1806–Jan. 17 1807; Lieut.-Gen. Henry George Grey, Jan. 17–May 21, 1807. *Governor:* Du Pré Alexander, Earl of Caledon, May 22, 1807–July 4, 1811. *Acting Governors:* Lieut.-Gen. H. G. Grey, July 4–Sept. 5, 1811; Maj.-Gen. Robert Meade, Oct. 18, 1813–Jan. 7, 1814. *Governors:* Lieut.-Gen. Sir Francis Cradock, Sept. 6, 1811–April 6, 1814; Lieut.-Gen. Lord Charles Henry Somerset, April 6, 1814–March 5, 1826 (resigned in England, April 1827). *Acting Governors:* Maj.-Gen. Sir Rufane Shawe Donkin, Jan. 13, 1820–Nov. 30, 1821; Maj.-Gen. Richard Bourke, March 5, 1826–Sept. 9, 1828. *Governor:* Lieut.-Gen. Sir Galbraith Lowry Cole, Sept. 9, 1828–Aug. 10, 1833. *Acting Governor:* Lieut.-Col. Thomas Francis Wade, Aug. 10, 1833–Jan. 16, 1834. *Governors:* Maj.-Gen. Sir Benjamin D'Urban, Jan. 10, 1834–Jan. 20, 1838; Maj.-Gen. Sir George Thomas Napier, Jan. 22, 1838–March 18, 1844; Lieut.-Gen. Sir Peregrine Maitland, March 18, 1844–Jan. 27, 1847. *High Commissioners and Governors of the Cape Colony:* Maj.-Gen. Sir Henry Eldred Pottinger, Jan. 27–Dec. 1, 1847; Maj.-Gen. Sir Henry George Wakelyn Smith, Dec. 1, 1847–March 31, 1852; Lieut.-Gen. the Hon. George Cathcart, March 31, 1852–May 26, 1854. *Acting Head of the Government:* Lieut.-Gov. Charles Henry Darling, May 26–Dec. 5, 1854. *Governor:* Sir George Grey, Dec. 5, 1854–Aug. 15, 1861. *Lieutenant-Governor and*

Acting Administrator: Lieut.-Gen. Robert Henry Wynyard, Aug. 20, 1859–July 4, 1860, and Aug. 15, 1861–Jan. 15, 1862. *Governor:* Sir Philip Edmond Wodehouse, Jan. 15, 1862–May 20, 1870. *Lieut.-Governor and Acting Administrator:* Lieut.-Gen. Charles Crawfurd Hay, May 20–Dec. 31, 1870. *Governor:* Sir Henry Barkly, Dec. 31, 1870–March 31, 1877.

CAPE COLONY. *Lieutenant-Governor:* Andries Stockenstrom, July 25, 1836–Aug. 31, 1839. *Acting Lieutenant-Governor:* Lieut.-Col. John Hare, Aug. 9, 1838–Sept. 1839, and then *Lieutenant-Governor* till Sept. 1846. *Secretary of Government, Capetown,* Sept. 1846–April 9, 1847. *Lieutenant-Governor:* Sir Henry Edward Fox Young, April 9–Nov. 4, 1847.

NATAL. *Commandants-General:* Andries Willem Jacobus Pretorius, Nov. 23, 1838–Aug. 9, 1842; Gerrit Rudolf, Aug. 9, 1842–May 10, 1843. *Special Commissioner:* Henry Cloete, May 10, 1843–May 1844. *Lieutenant-Governors:* Martin Thomas West, Dec. 4, 1845–Aug. 1, 1849; Benjamin Chilley Campbell Pine, April 19, 1850–March 3, 1855; John Scott, Nov. 5, 1856–Dec. 31, 1864; Lieut.-Col. John Maclean, Dec. 31, 1864–July 26, 1865; *Acting Administrators:* Lieut.-Col. John Wellesley Thomas, July 26–Aug. 26, 1865; Lieut.-Col. John Jarvis Bisset, Aug. 26, 1865–May 24, 1867. *Lieutenant-Governor:* Robert William Keate, May 24, 1867–July 19, 1872.

BRITISH KAFFRARIA. *Chief Commissioners:* Lieut.-Col. George Henry Mackinnon, Dec. 23, 1847–Oct. 1852; Lieut.-Col. John Maclean, Oct. 1852–Oct. 26, 1860; became *Lieutenant-Governor,* Oct. 26, 1860–Dec. 24, 1864. *Governor's Deputy:* Robert Graham, Dec. 24, 1864–April 17, 1866.

ORANGE RIVER SOVEREIGNTY. *Residents:* Major Henry Douglas Warden, March 8, 1848–July 23, 1852; Henry Green, July 23, 1852–March 11, 1854.

ORANGE FREE STATE. *Provisional Government of Seven,* March–May 1854. *President:* Josias Philip Hoffman, May 15, 1854–Feb. 1855; *Provisional Government of Four,* Feb.–Aug. 27, 1855. *Presidents:* Jacobus Nicolaas Boshof, Aug. 27, 1855–June 25, 1859; Marthinus Wessel Pretorius, Feb. 8, 1860–April 15, 1863. *Acting President:* Jacobus Johannes Venter, June 17, 1863–Feb. 2, 1864. *President:* Jan Hendrik Brand (knighted, 1886), Feb. 2, 1864–July 16, 1888.

TRANSVAAL (SOUTH AFRICAN REPUBLIC). *Local Commandant-General,* then *President:* Marthinus Wessel Pretorius, Jan. 5, 1857–Sept. 10, 1860. *Rival Acting Presidents:* Stephanus Schoeman, Oct. 9, 1860–Jan. 20, 1863; Willem Janse van Rensburg, April 2, 1862–Oct. 24, 1863, then *President* Oct. 1863–May 10, 1864; *President:* M. W. Pretorius, May 10, 1864–Nov. 16, 1871.

SELF-GOVERNMENT, 1872–1910

UNITED KINGDOM. *British Sovereigns:* Victoria, June 20, 1837–Jan. 22, 1901; Edward VII, Jan. 22, 1901–May 6, 1910; George V, May 6, 1910–Jan. 20, 1936.

Secretaries of State for the Colonies: Earl of Kimberley, July 6, 1870–Feb. 21, 1874; Earl of Carnarvon, Feb. 21, 1874–Jan. 22, 1878; Sir Michael Edward Hicks Beach, Feb. 4, 1878–April 28, 1880; Earl of Kimberley, April 28, 1880–Dec. 11, 1882; Earl of Derby, Dec. 11, 1882–June 24, 1885; Col. Frederick Arthur Stanley, June 24, 1885–Feb. 6, 1886; Earl Granville, Feb. 6–Aug. 1, 1886; Hon. Edward Stanhope, Aug. 3, 1886–Jan. 14, 1887; Sir Henry Thurstan Holland (Lord Knutsford, 1888), Jan. 14, 1887–Aug. 16, 1892; Marquess of Ripon, Aug. 17, 1892–June 28, 1895; Joseph Chamberlain, June 28, 1895–Sept. 18, 1903; Alfred Lyttelton, Oct. 9, 1903–Dec. 5, 1905; Earl of Elgin, Dec. 11, 1905–April 16, 1908; Earl of Crewe, April 16, 1908–Nov. 7, 1910.

CAPE COLONY. *Governors and High Commissioners:* Sir Henry Barkly, Dec. 31, 1870–March 31, 1877; Sir Henry Bartle Edward Frere, March 31, 1877–Sept. 15, 1880. *Officers Administering:* Maj.-Gen. Henry Hugh Clifford, Sept. 15–27, 1880;

Sir George Cumine Strahan, Sept. 27, 1880–Jan. 22, 1881. *Governor and High Commissioner:* Sir Hercules George Robert Robinson, Jan. 22, 1881–May 1, 1889. *Officers Administering:* Lieut.-Gen. Sir Leicester Smyth, April 30–Aug. 1881, and April 25, 1883–March 26, 1884; Lieut.-Gen. Sir Henry d'Oyley Torrens, April 7–July 7, 1886; Lieut.-Gen. Henry Augustus Smyth, May 1–Dec. 13, 1889. *Governor and High Commissioner:* Sir Henry Brougham Loch, Dec. 13, 1889– May 30, 1895. *Officer Administering:* Lieut.-Gen. Sir William Gordon Cameron, Jan. 14, 1891–Dec. 1, 1892, and May–July 1894. *Governor and High Commissioner:* Sir Hercules Robinson (Lord Rosmead, 1896), May 30, 1895–April 21, 1897. *Officer Administering:* Lieut.-Gen. Sir William Howley Goodenough, April 21–May 5, 1897. *Governor and High Commissioner:* Sir Alfred Milner, May 5, 1897–March 6, 1901. *Officer Administering:* Lieut.-Gen. Sir William Francis Butler, Nov. 2, 1898– Feb. 14, 1899. *Governor:* Sir Walter Francis Hely-Hutchinson, March 6, 1901–May 31, 1910, and *Acting High Commissioners,* June 17– Sept. 21, 1909; Maj.-Gen. Sir Henry Jenner Scobell, Sept. 21, 1909–May 31, 1910.

SOUTH-EAST AFRICA. *High Commissioners for South-East Africa:* Maj.-Gen. Sir Garnet Joseph Wolseley, June 28, 1879–April 27, 1880; Maj.-Gen. Sir George Pomeroy Colley, July 2, 1880–Feb. 27, 1881. *Acting High Commissioner:* Maj.-Gen. Sir Evelyn Wood, Feb. 27–Aug. 8, 1881.

TRANSVAAL AND ORANGE RIVER COLONY. *Governors and High Commissioners:* Sir Alfred Milner (Baron, 1901; Viscount, 1902), March 1901–April 1, 1905; Earl of Selborne, April 2, 1905–May 31, 1910 (ceased to be Governor of the Orange River Colony, June 7, 1907).

CAPE COLONY. *Prime Ministers:* John Charles Molteno, Dec. 1, 1872–Feb. 5, 1878; John Gordon Sprigg, Feb. 6, 1878–May 8, 1881; Thomas Charles Scanlen, May 9, 1881–May 12, 1884; Thomas Upington, May 13, 1884–Nov. 24, 1886; Sir Gordon Sprigg, Nov. 25, 1886–July 16, 1890; Cecil John Rhodes, July 17, 1890–Jan. 12, 1896; Sir Gordon Sprigg, Jan. 13, 1896–Oct. 13, 1898; William Philip Schreiner, Oct. 14, 1898–June 17, 1900; Sir Gordon Sprigg, June 18, 1900– Feb. 21, 1904; Dr. Leander Starr Jameson, Feb. 22, 1904–Feb. 2, 1908; John Xavier Merriman, Feb. 3, 1908–May 31, 1910.

GRIQUALAND WEST. *Triumvirate:* Oct. 1871–Jan. 9, 1873. *Administrator:* Richard Southey (Sir, 1891), Jan. 10–July 17, 1873, then *Lieutenant-Governor* till Aug. 3, 1875. *Administrator:* Lieut.-Col. William Owen Lanyon, Aug. 4, 1875– Feb. 1879; thereafter *Acting Administrators* till Oct. 15, 1880.

NATAL. *Lieutenant-Governor:* Anthony Musgrave, July 19, 1872–April 30, 1873. *Officer Administering:* Lieut.-Col. Thomas Milles, April 30–July 22, 1873. *Lieutenant-Governor:* Sir Benjamin Chilley Campbell Pine, July 22, 1873–April 1, 1875. *Officer Administering:* Maj.-Gen. Sir Garnet Joseph Wolseley, April 1– Sept. 3, 1875; *Lieutenant-Governor:* Sir Henry Ernest Bulwer, Sept. 3, 1875– April 20, 1880. *Officers Administering:* Lieut.-Col. William Bellairs, April 20– May 5, 1880; Maj.-Gen. Henry Hugh Clifford, May 5–July 2, 1880; Lieut.-Col. Henry Alexander, Aug. 17–Sept. 14, 1880. *Governor:* Maj.-Gen. Sir George Pomeroy Colley, July 2, 1880–Feb. 27, 1881. *Officers Administering:* Lieut.-Gen. Sir Evelyn Wood, Feb. 27–April 3, 1881; Lieut.-Col. Redvers Henry Buller, April 3–Aug. 9, 1881; Lieut.-Col. Charles Bullen Hugh Mitchell, Dec. 22, 1881– March 6, 1882. *Governors:* Sir Henry Bulwer, March 6, 1882–Oct. 23, 1885; Sir Arthur Elibank Havelock, Feb. 18, 1886–June 5, 1889; Sir Charles Mitchell, Dec. 1, 1889–July 1893. *Officer Administering:* Francis Seymour Haden, July–Sept. 27, 1893. *Governors:* Sir Walter Francis Hely-Hutchinson, Sept. 28, 1893–March 6, 1901; Sir Henry Edward McCallum, May 13, 1901–June 7, 1907; Sir Matthew Nathan, Sept. 2, 1907–Dec. 23, 1909; Lord Methuen, Jan. 17–May 31, 1910.

NATAL. *Prime Ministers:* Sir John Robinson, Oct. 10, 1893–Feb. 14, 1897; Harry Escombe, Feb. 15–Oct. 4, 1897; Sir Henry Binns, Oct. 5, 1897–June 8,

1899; Sir Albert Henry Hime, June 9, 1899–Aug. 17, 1903; George Morris Sutton, Aug. 18, 1903–May 16, 1905; Charles John Smythe, May 15, 1905–Nov. 28, 1906; Frederick Robert Moor, Nov. 28, 1906–April 28, 1910.

ORANGE FREE STATE. *President:* Jan Hendrik Brand (Sir, 1876), Feb. 2, 1864–July 16, 1888. *Acting President:* Friedrich Kaufmann Höhne, Aug. 31–Oct. 4, 1872. *Committee:* William Collins, Friederich Pieter Schnehage and Gerhardus Johannes du Toit, Oct. 4, 1872–June 16, 1873. *Presidents:* Francis William Reitz, Jan. 11, 1889–Nov. 1895; Marthinus Theunis Steyn, Feb. 21, 1896–May 31, 1910.

ORANGE RIVER COLONY. *Lieutenant-Governor:* Sir Hamilton John Goold-Adams, Jan. 1901–June 7, 1907; *Governors:* Lord Milner, June 21, 1902–April 1, 1905; Earl of Selborne, April 2, 1905–June 7, 1907; Sir Hamilton Goold-Adams, June 7, 1907–May 31, 1910. *Prime Minister:* Abraham Fischer, Nov. 27, 1907–May 31, 1910.

SOUTH AFRICAN REPUBLIC. *Acting President:* Daniel Jacobus Erasmus, Nov. 16, 1871–June 30, 1872. *President:* Rev. Thomas François Burgers, July 1, 1872–April 12, 1877.

TRANSVAAL. *Administrators:* Sir Theophilus Shepstone, April 12, 1877–March 4, 1879; Lt.-Col. Owen William Lanyon (Sir, 1880), March 4, 1879–Aug. 8, 1881. *Governor:* Sir Garnet Wolseley, Sept. 29, 1879–April 27, 1880. TRANSVAAL STATE. *Triumvirate:* Stephanus Johannes Paulus Kruger, Petrus Jacobus Joubert and Marthinus Wessel Pretorius, Aug. 8, 1881–May 8, 1883.

SOUTH AFRICAN REPUBLIC. *President:* S. J. P. Kruger, May 8, 1883–May 31, 1902.

TRANSVAAL. *Governors:* Lord Milner, June 21, 1902–April 1, 1905; Earl of Selborne, April 2, 1905–May 31, 1910. *Lieutenant-Governors:* Sir Arthur Lawley, Sept. 29, 1902–Dec. 3, 1905; Sir Richard Solomon, Dec. 4, 1905–Oct. 2, 1906. *Prime Minister:* Gen. Louis Botha, Feb. 4, 1907–May 31, 1910.

RHODESIA. *Directors of the British South Africa Company:* Second Duke of Abercorn, President 1889 onwards; Duke of Fife, 1889–Feb. 1896; Cecil John Rhodes, 1889–June 1896, April 1898–March 1902; Lord Gifford, 1889 onwards; Alfred Beit, 1889–June 1896, July 1902–1906; George Cawston, 1889–1908; Albert Henry George Grey (Earl, 1894), 1889–1903; Horace Farquhar (Sir, 1892), 1889–Feb. 1896; Sir Sidney Shippard, 1898–1902; James Rochfort Maguire, 1898 onwards; Philip Lyttelton Gell, 1899 onwards; Dr. Leander Starr Jameson, 1902 onwards; Sir Lewis Loyd Michell, 1902 onwards; Henry Birchenough, 1905 onwards; Marquess of Winchester, 1907 onwards; Otto Beit, 1910 onwards.

MASHONALAND. *Acting Resident Commissioner:* Archibald Ross Colquhoun, June 29, 1890–Sept. 17, 1891. *Chief Magistrate:* Dr. Leander Starr Jameson, Sept. 18, 1891–Sept. 9, 1894. *Acting Chief Magistrate:* Andrew Henry Farrell Duncan, Oct. 8, 1893–May 1894.

SOUTHERN RHODESIA. *Administrator:* Dr. L. S. Jameson, Sept. 10, 1894–Feb. 1896. *Acting Administrator:* Col. Francis William Rhodes, Oct. 28, 1894–April 1, 1895. Judge Joseph Vintcent, June 1895–May 2, 1896. *Administrator:* Albert, Earl Grey, May 2, 1896–July 23, 1897. *Acting Administrator of Matabeleland:* Arthur Lawley, Nov. 1896–Feb. 1897. *Deputy Administrator of Matabeleland:* A. Lawley, Feb. 1897–Dec. 4, 1898. *Acting Administrator:* William Henry Milton, July 24, 1897–Dec. 4, 1898. *Acting Administrators of Mashonaland:* Sir Thomas Charles Scanlen, Dec. 5, 1898–Jan. 1899; A Lawley, June 22–Dec. 5, 1899. *Administrator of Mashonaland and Senior Administrator of Southern Rhodesia:* W. H. Milton, Dec. 5, 1898–Jan. 24, 1901. *Administrator of Matabeleland:* A. Lawley (Sir, 1901), Dec. 5, 1898–March 1901. *Administrator of Southern Rhodesia:* W. H. Milton, Jan. 24, 1901–Oct. 31, 1914.

NORTH-EASTERN RHODESIA. *Administrator:* Major Patrick William Forbes, July 1, 1895–June 1897. *Acting Administrator:* Capt. Henry Lawrence Daly, June, 1897–July 10, 1898. *Deputy Administrator:* Robert Edward Codrington,

July 11, 1898–May 31, 1900, and then *Administrator* till April 24, 1907; Lawrence Aubrey Wallace, April 24, 1907–Jan. 1909. *Acting Administrator:* Leicester Paul Beaufort, Jan. 1909–May 16, 1911.

NORTH-WESTERN RHODESIA. *Resident in Barotseland:* Robert Thorne Coryndon, April 8, 1897–Sept. 18, 1900, and then *Administrator* till April 8, 1907; R. E. Codrington, April 8, 1907–Dec. 16, 1908. *Acting Administrators:* Hugh Marshall Hole, April 8–Oct. 20, 1907; Lieut.-Col. John Carden, Oct. 20, 1907–Feb. 1908; L. A. Wallace, Jan. 1909–Aug. 16, 1911.

NYASALAND (BRITISH CENTRAL AFRICA). *Commissioner and Consul-General:* Harry Hamilton Johnston (Sir, 1896), Feb. 1, 1891–April 15, 1896. *Acting Commissioner and Consul-General:* Alfred Sharpe (Sir, 1903), April 16, 1896–July 14, 1897, and then *Commissioner and Consul-General* till March 31, 1907. *Acting Commissioner and Consul-General:* Major Francis Barrow Pearce, April 1–Sept. 6, 1907. *Governor:* Sir Alfred Sharpe, Sept. 6, 1907–March 31, 1910. *Acting Governor:* F. B. Pearce, April 1–July 3, 1910.

UNION, 1910–55

UNITED KINGDOM. *British Sovereigns:* George V, May 6, 1910–Jan. 20, 1936; Edward VIII, Jan. 20–Dec. 11, 1936; George VI, Dec. 11, 1936–Feb. 6, 1952; Elizabeth II, Feb. 6, 1952, onwards.

Secretaries of State for the Colonies: Earl of Crewe, April 16, 1908–Nov. 7, 1910; Lewis Harcourt, Nov. 7, 1910–May 27, 1915; Andrew Bonar Law, May 27, 1915–Dec. 11, 1916; Walter Hume Long, Dec. 11, 1916–Jan. 10, 1919; Viscount Milner, Jan. 10, 1919–Feb. 12, 1921; Winston Leonard Spencer Churchill, Feb. 14, 1921–Oct. 19, 1922; Duke of Devonshire, Oct. 25, 1922–Jan. 23, 1924; James Henry Thomas, Jan. 23–Nov. 7, 1924; Lieut.-Col. Leopold Charles Maurice Stennett Amery, Nov. 7, 1924–June 8, 1929; Lord Passfield, June 8, 1929–Aug. 26,, 1931; J. H. Thomas, Aug. 26–Nov. 9, 1931; Sir Philip Cunliffe-Lister, Nov. 9, 1931–June 7, 1935; Malcolm John MacDonald, June 7–Nov. 22, 1935; J. H. Thomas, Nov. 27, 1935–May 22, 1936; William George Arthur Ormesby-Gore (Lord Harlech, 1938), May 29, 1936–May 16, 1938; M. J. MacDonald, May 16, 1938–May 10, 1940; Lord Lloyd, May 12, 1940–Feb. 4, 1941; Lord Moyne, Feb. 8, 1941–Feb. 22, 1942; Lord Cranborne, Feb. 22–Nov. 22, 1942; Oliver Stanley, Nov. 22, 1942–Aug. 5, 1945; George Henry Hall, Aug. 5, 1945–Oct. 4, 1946; Arthur Creech-Jones, Oct. 4, 1946–Feb. 28, 1950; James Griffiths, Feb. 28, 1950–Oct. 27, 1951; Oliver Lyttelton, Oct. 27, 1951–July 28, 1954; Alan Tindal Lennox-Boyd, July 28, 1954, onwards.

Secretaries of State for Dominion Affairs: L. C. M. S. Amery, July 7, 1925–June 8, 1929; Lord Passfield, June 8, 1929–June 8, 1930; J. H. Thomas, June 13, 1930–Nov. 22, 1935; M. J. MacDonald, Nov. 27, 1935–May 16, 1937; Lord Stanley, May 16–Oct. 31, 1937; M. J. MacDonald, Oct. 31, 1937–Jan. 28, 1939; Sir Thomas Walker Hobart Inskip (Viscount Caldecote, 1939), Jan. 28–Sept. 3, 1939; Anthony Eden, Sept. 3, 1939–May 10, 1940; Viscount Caldecote, May 14–Oct. 3, 1940; Lord Cranborne, Oct. 3, 1940–Feb. 19, 1942; Clement Richard Attlee, Feb. 19, 1942–Sept. 24, 1943; Lord Cranborne (Marquess of Salisbury, 1947), Sept. 24, 1943–Aug. 5, 1945; Viscount Addison, Aug. 5, 1945–July 3, 1947.

Secretaries of State for Commonwealth Relations: Viscount Addison, July 3–Oct. 7, 1947; Philip John Noel-Baker, Oct. 7, 1947–March 1, 1950; Patrick Chrestien Gordon Walker, March 2, 1950–Oct. 27, 1951; Lord Ismay, Oct. 27, 1951–March 12, 1952; Marquess of Salisbury, March 24–Dec. 15, 1952; Viscount Swinton, Dec. 15, 1952, onwards.

UNION OF SOUTH AFRICA. *Governor-General and High Commissioner:* Viscount Gladstone, May 31, 1910–July 17, 1914. *Acting Governor-General:* Lord de Villiers, July 17–Nov. 11, 1912, and July 11–Sept. 2, 1914. *Acting High Commissioners:*

Sir Reginald Clare Hart, July 17–Nov. 22, 1912; Sir James Wolfe Murray, July 11 –Sept. 8, 1914. *Governor-General and High Commissioner:* Viscount Buxton, Sept. 8, 1914–July 17, 1920. *Acting Governor-General:* Sir James Rose-Innes, July 17–Nov. 20, 1920. *Acting High Commissioner:* Brig.-Gen. Beresford Cecil Molyneux Carter, Sept. 3–Nov. 20, 1920. *Governor-General and High Commissioner:* Prince Arthur of Connaught, Nov. 20, 1920–Dec. 5, 1923. *Acting Governor-General:* Sir J. Rose-Innes, Dec. 5, 1923–Jan. 21, 1924. *Acting High Commissioner:* Rear-Adm. Sir Rudolph Walter Bentinck, Dec. 10, 1923–Jan. 21, 1924. *Governor-General and High Commissioner:* Earl of Athlone, Jan. 21, 1924–Dec. 21, 1930. *Acting Governor-General:* Jacob de Villiers, Dec. 21, 1930–Jan. 26, 1931.

Governors-General: Earl of Clarendon, Jan. 26, 1931–March 17, 1937; Sir Patrick Duncan, April 5, 1937–July 17, 1943. *Acting Governor-General:* Nicolaas Jacobus de Wet, C.J., July 17, 1943–Dec. 31, 1945. *Governors-General:* Gideon Brand van Zyl, Jan. 1, 1946–Dec. 31, 1950; Ernest George Jansen, Jan. 1, 1951, onwards.

High Commissioner: Sir Herbert James Stanley, April 6, 1931–Jan. 6, 1935. *Acting High Commissioner:* Vice-Adm. Edward Ratcliffe Garth Russell Evans, Aug. 1–Dec. 1, 1933. *High Commissioner for Basutoland, the Bechuanaland Protectorate and Swaziland:* Sir William Henry Clark, Jan. 7, 1935–Jan. 3, 1940. *Acting High Commissioner:* Sir Walter Clarence Huggard, Jan. 3–May 24, 1941. *High Commissioner:* Lord Harlech, May 24, 1941–May 13, 1944. *Acting High Commissioner:* Harold Eddy Priestman, May 13–June 23, 1944. *High Commissioners:* Sir Walter Huggard, June 23–Oct. 27, 1944; Sir Evelyn Baring, Oct. 27, 1944–Oct. 1, 1951; Sir John Helier le Rougetel, Oct. 2, 1951–Feb. 2, 1955; Sir Percivale Liesching, March 4, 1955, onwards.

Prime Ministers: Gen. Louis Botha, May 31, 1910–Aug. 27, 1919; Gen. Jan Christian Smuts, Sept. 3, 1919–June 29, 1924; Gen. James Barry Munnik Hertzog, June 30, 1924–March 30, 1933 (Pact Ministry), and then March 31, 1933–Sept. 5, 1939 (Coalition and Fusion Ministries); Gen. J. C. Smuts, Sept. 5, 1939–Nov. 26, 1945 (Coalition Ministry), and then Nov. 26, 1945–May 26, 1948 (United Party Ministry); Dr. Daniel François Malan, June 3, 1948–Nov. 30, 1954; Johannes Gerhardus Strydom, Dec. 2, 1954, onwards.

SOUTH-WEST AFRICA. *Administrators:* Sir Howard Gorges, Oct. 30, 1915–Sept. 30, 1920; Gysbert Reitz Hofmeyr, Oct. 1, 1920–March 31, 1926; Albertus Johannes Werth, April 1, 1926–March 31, 1933; David Gideon Conradie, April 1, 1933–April 1, 1943; Col. Petrus Imker Hoogenhout, April 5, 1943–Dec. 5, 1951; Dr. Johannes Roux van Rhyn, Dec. 6, 1951–Sept. 7, 1953. *Acting Administrator:* Johannes Neser, Sept. 8–Dec. 1953. *Administrator:* Daniel Thomas du Plessis Viljoen, Dec. 1953, onwards.

RHODESIA. *Directors of the British South Africa Company, 1910–25:* Second Duke of Abercorn, President, d. 1913; Lord Gifford, d. 1911; James Rochfort Maguire, President 1923, d. 1925; Philip Lyttelton Gell, President 1920, res. 1925; Dr. Leander Starr Jameson (Baronet, 1911), President 1913, d. 1917; Sir Lewis Loyd Michell, d. 1928; Sir Henry Birchenough, President 1925, d. 1937; Marquess of Winchester, 1907 onwards; Sir Otto Beit, d. 1930; Baron Emile Beaumont d'Erlanger, 1913 onwards; Henry Wilson Fox, 1913–1921; Brig.-Gen. Everard Baring, 1913 onwards; Dougal Orme Malcolm (Sir, 1938), 1913 onwards; Third Duke of Abercorn, 1913 onwards; Major Percy Sidney Inskipp, 1913–1922.

SOUTHERN RHODESIA. *Administrator:* Sir William Milton, Jan. 24, 1901–Oct. 31, 1914. *Acting Administrator:* Sir Francis James Newton, Nov. 2–Dec. 24, 1914. *Administrator:* Francis Drummond Percy Chaplin (Sir, 1917), Dec. 24, 1914–Feb. 16, 1921. *Acting Administrators:* Clarkson Henry Tredgold (Sir, 1922), Oct. 15–Dec. 14, 1919; Ernest William Sanders Montagu, Sept. 10–Dec. 10, 1920, and Nov. 15, 1922–May 10, 1923.

SOUTHERN AND NORTHERN RHODESIA. *Administrator:* Sir Drummond Chaplin, Feb. 17, 1921–Sept. 20, 1923. *Acting Administrator:* Percy Donald Leslie Fynn, Sept. 21–23, 1923.

SOUTHERN RHODESIA. *Governor:* Sir John Robert Chancellor, Oct. 1, 1923–May 30, 1928. *Acting Governor:* Sir Murray Bissett, June 15–Nov. 24, 1928. *Governor:* Sir Cecil Hunter Rodwell, Nov. 24, 1928–June 30, 1934. *Acting Governor:* Sir Alexander Fraser Russell, July 1, 1934–Jan. 8, 1935. *Governor:* Sir Herbert James Stanley, Jan. 8, 1935–Jan. 6, 1942. *Acting Governor:* Sir Alexander Russell, Jan. 8, 1942–Dec. 10, 1942. *Governor:* Sir Evelyn Baring, Dec. 10, 1942–Oct. 26, 1944. *Acting Governor:* Sir Robert James Hudson, Oct. 26, 1944–Feb. 20, 1945. *Governor:* Admiral Sir Campbell Tait, Feb. 20, 1945–Feb. 2, 1946. *Acting Governors:* Sir A. Russell, Feb. 2–July 19 1946; Sir R. Hudson, July 19, 1946–Jan. 14, 1947. *Governor:* Sir John Noble Kennedy, Jan. 14, 1947–Nov. 21, 1953. *Acting Governors:* Walter Eric Thomas, Oct. 17–Nov. 13, 1950; Sir Robert Clarkson Tredgold, Nov. 21, 1953–Nov. 26, 1954. *Governor:* Vice-Adm. Sir Peveril Barton Reiby Wallop William-Powlett, Nov. 26, 1954, onwards.

Prime Ministers: Sir Charles Patrick John Coghlan, Oct. 1, 1923–Aug. 28, 1927; Howard Unwin Moffat, Sept. 2, 1927–July 5, 1933; George Mitchell, July 5–Sept. 11, 1933; Godfrey Martin Huggins (Sir, 1941), Sept. 12, 1933–Sept. 7, 1953; Reginald Stephen Garfield Todd, Sept. 7, 1953, onwards.

NORTHERN RHODESIA. *Acting Administrator:* Hugh Charlie Marshall, May 9–Aug. 17, 1911. *Administrators:* Lawrence Aubrey Wallace (Sir, 1918), Aug. 17, 1911–March 17, 1921; Sir Drummond Chaplin, March 17, 1921–Sept. 20, 1923. *Acting Administrator:* Richard Allmond Jeffrey Goode, Sept. 20, 1923–March 31, 1924. *Governor:* Sir Herbert James Stanley, April 1, 1924–July 25, 1927. *Acting Governor:* R. A. J. Goode, July 25–Aug. 31, 1927; *Governors:* Sir James Crawford Maxwell, Aug. 31, 1927–Nov. 30, 1932; Sir Ronald Storrs, Dec. 1, 1932–March 20, 1934; Sir Hubert Winthrop Young, March 20, 1934–Aug. 31, 1938; Sir John Alexander Maybin, Sept. 1, 1938–April 9, 1941. *Acting Governor:* William Marston Logan, April 9–Oct. 15, 1941. *Governor:* Sir Eubule John Waddington, Oct. 16, 1941–Oct. 15, 1947. *Acting Governor:* Richard Christopher Stafford Stanley, Oct. 16, 1947–Feb. 18, 1948. *Governor:* Sir Gilbert McCall Rennie, Feb. 19, 1948–March 8, 1954. *Acting Governor:* Alexander Thomas Williams, March 8–May 24, 1954. *Governor:* Sir Arthur Edward Trevor Benson, May 25, 1954, onwards.

NYASALAND. *Acting Governor:* Henry Richard Wallis, July 4, 1910–Feb. 6, 1911. *Governors:* Sir William Manning, Feb. 6, 1911–Sept. 23, 1913; George Smith (Sir, 1914), Sept. 23, 1913–April 12, 1923. *Acting Governor:* Richard Sims Donkin Rankine, April 12, 1923–March 27, 1924. *Governor:* Sir Charles Calvert Bowring, March 27, 1924–May 30, 1929. *Acting Governor:* Lieut.-Col. Wilfred Bennett Davidson-Houston, May 30–Nov. 7, 1929. *Governors:* Sir Thomas Shenton Whitelegge Thomas, Nov. 7, 1929–Nov. 22, 1932; Major Sir Hubert Winthrop Young, Nov. 22, 1932–April 9, 1934. *Acting Governor:* Kenneth Lambert Hall, April 9–Sept. 21, 1934. *Governors:* Sir Harold Baxter Kittermaster, Sept. 21, 1934–Jan. 14, 1939; Sir Henry Charles Donald Cleveland Mackenzie-Kennedy, March 10, 1939–Aug. 8, 1942; Sir Edmund Charles Richards, Aug. 8, 1942–March 27, 1947. *Acting Governors* March 27, 1947–March 30, 1948. *Governor:* Sir Geoffrey Francis Taylor Colby, March 30, 1948–May 31, 1951. *Acting Governors* May 31, 1951–Nov. 11, 1954; *Governor:* Sir G. Colby resumed duty, Nov. 11, 1954, onwards.

FEDERATION OF RHODESIA AND NYASALAND. *Governor-General:* Lórd Llewellin, Sept. 4, 1953, onwards. *Prime Minister:* Sir Godfrey Huggins, Sept. 4, 1953, onwards.

CHAPTER I

THE DISCOVERY

Pharaoh Necho, 1; Hanno, 2; ancient knowledge of the East Coast, 2; Arabs and Persians on the East Coast, 5; Bushmen, Bantu and Hottentots, 6; Zimbabwe, 8; Portuguese on the road *ad Indos*, 13; Portuguese Empire in East Africa and the Indies, 17; Missionaries and Monomotapa, 19; Abambo and Amazimba, 20; the Spanish Annexation of the Portuguese Empire, 20.

MEN hailed Bartholomew Diaz as a pioneer when he rounded the Cape of Storms, and a later generation stood amazed when a ship passed down de Lesseps' Suez Canal; but long ago the disillusioned Preacher had asked whether there was anything whereof it might be said 'See, this is new,' and old Herodotus, the remembrancer of former things, had recorded that both these things at least were 'already of old time, which was before us.'

Six hundred years and more before the birth of Christ, Pharaoh Necho tried to re-open the Nile-Red Sea Canal, 'the channel leading to the Erythrean Sea' first cut by Seti seven hundred years earlier, the channel whose length was 'a voyage of four days, and in breadth it was so dug that two triremes could go side by side driven by oars . . . and in the reign of Necos there perished while digging it twelve myriads of the Egyptians.' So said the Egyptian priests, adding that 'Necos ceased in the midst of his digging, because the utterance of an oracle impeded him.'

A less pious age may well suspect that the death of myriads weighed more with the divine and imperial engineer than did the oracle; but, in any case, Necho left the task to be completed almost in Herodotus's own day by Darius the Persian. Nevertheless, as South African history bears witness, where the direct road is blocked, there is usually a way round. And so it was on this, the earliest occasion on which the curtain half rises on that history. Necho was determined to put his Mediterranean fleet of Greek warships in touch with his Red Sea squadron. Accordingly, believing doubtless that 'Libya' did not extend very far to the southward, he sent *Circa* 'Phœnicians with ships, bidding them sail and come back through 600 the Pillars of Hercules to the Northern Sea and so to Egypt. The B.C. Phœnicians therefore set forth from the Erythrean Sea and sailed through the Southern Sea. . . . In the third year they turned through the Pillars of Hercules and arrived again in Egypt. And they reported

1

a thing which I cannot believe, but another man may, namely, that in sailing round Libya they had the sun on their right hand.'[1] So Herodotus, who was as near in time to Necho as we are to George Washington, doubted where he should have believed. The Phœnicians' story rings true. If light coir-sewn Arab barks could in after years venture as far as Cape Correntes, substantial biremes might have braved the Agulhas swell still further south; the voyagers tell us that they landed each year to grow corn for the next stage of the journey, the very thing that the Greek, Eudoxus, proposed to do on his disastrous attempt to sail from Gades to India round by the Cape of Good Hope about 125 B.C. and that the wrecked crew of the *Haarlem*, Dutch East Indiaman, did in Table Bay in A.D. 1647; above all, they say they saw the sun to the north at midday on their right hand as they coasted westward round the Cape of Good Hope. No Phœnician sailor, 'splendaciously mendacious,' ever invented a yarn like that in the seventh century B.C.

News of the West Coast is meagre for the next two thousand years. Eighty years after the return of Necho's argosy, Hanno the Carthaginian sailed with a large squadron to found Punic factories in those parts. He had a scuffle with 'wild men wearing the skins of beasts' on the Senegal, rounded Cape Verde and pushed on as far as Sierra Leone. There he turned back taking with him one or two of the inhabitants, 'wild men and women covered with hair.' But because space on a trireme was limited these luckless chimpanzees never saw Carthage, for their fellow-voyagers slew them and merely kept their skins to hang in the temple of Ashtaroth. So Hanno blazed the trail for Prince Henry the Navigator's captains. No civilised man, as far as we know, made the voyage again till A.D. 1446, and none made the complete run to India for another fifty years thereafter.[2]

Our knowledge of the East Coast is more substantial and continuous. That is as it should be, for not only does the valley of the Nile, which is Egypt, link tropical Africa to the Mediterranean world but the East Coast itself looks out upon Arabia Felix and India, homes of ancient and seafaring civilisations. Egyptians, never great sailors, went down the Red Sea in the days of the Middle Kingdom from about 2250 B.C. onwards, and further on still to Somaliland, the Land of Punt, during the reign of the great XVIIIth Dynasty Queen, Hatshepsut, about 1400 B.C.; Necho's shipmen were even more venturesome than they, and subjects of the early Ptolemies traded vigorously at least as far south as Cape Guardafui. Presently,

---

[1] Herodotus, II. 158; IV. 42. *C.H.B.E.* VIII. 56, suspends judgment but inclines to disbelief in the Circumnavigation.

[2] Citizens of Gades (Cadiz) said they made the run to India repeatedly during the second century B.C.

during the first and second centuries after Christ, *Rumi*, Greek-speaking merchants of the early Roman Empire, sailed regularly to India and down the East Coast, possibly as far as the Comoro Islands, and made Zingis (Zanzibar) known to Ptolemy, the famous Alexandrian geographer of the mid-second century. Later on, Byzantine Emperors reopened the traffic for a time.

Meanwhile, Indians and Sabaeans from Yemen in South Arabia had long been active in the Indian Ocean and on the East Coast of Africa, for how long no man can say. The Portuguese found 'Arabs' and Indians in possession of much of the East Coast at the end of the fifteenth century A.D.; the Moslem, Massoudi, knew that both 915 those peoples were in Mozambique in the early tenth century; the A.D. customs of the Makaranga in Southern Rhodesia, customs fast dying out, point to intercourse with an Arabia that knew not Mohammed; a certain King Kharabit of Sabaea (Sheba) had interests far down the East Coast in the days of Trajan; the customs of the Comoro islanders suggest a connection with Arabs or kindred Idumaean Jews of the time of Solomon.[1] It is also recorded that that wise ruler of Israel joined with Hiram of Tyre to send expeditions southward and that 'once in three years came the navy of Tarshish bringing gold and silver, ivory and apes and peacocks . . . great plenty of almug trees and precious stones . . . and incense and the sweet cane from a far country.'[2] In their day, moreover, the wealthy Queen of Sheba herself went to see the palace and temple Solomon was a-building in Jerusalem. Genesis takes the story still further back, for it tells us that the grandsons of Shem, father of 'Yellow Asia,' were none other than Sheba and Ophir and Havilah, while the grandsons of Ham, parent of 'Black Africa' were, once more, Seba and Havilah.[3] All of which suggests that light-skinned Asiatics and dark-skinned Africans were intermingling a very long time ago in those parts of Africa which almost touch Arabia.

What is certain is that those subjects of Pharoahs, Ptolemies, Roman and Byzantine Emperors who thrust their way spasmodically into the Indian Ocean had entered an Indo-Arabian *mare clausum*. It was a preserve which Islam was destined to make more inaccessible than ever for close on nine hundred years till the latter-day Portuguese broke in at the close of the fifteenth century. In the seventh and early eighth centuries A.D., Arabia burst its bounds; the banners of the Prophet swept up to the Oxus, the Taurus and the Pyrenees, and were hardly stayed by the walls and fleets of Constantinople and the valour of the Christian hosts of Frankish Gaul. While Leo the Isaurian and Charles Martel were thus grimly winning a future for Western Christendom, Zaide, great-grandson of Ali the son-in-law

[1] Hall, *Great Zimbubwe*, p. xxxvii, and *Pre-Historic Rhodesia*, p. 361.
[2] Kings I. x. 11, 22.   [3] Genesis x. 7, 29.

Circa 740 A.D. of Mohammed, led a group of Moslem heretics out of Arabia. These Emozaide came down the well-worn East Coast trade-route as far as the Equator, mixing with the natives as they came. Hard on their heels came three ship-loads of true believers driven out of Central Arabia by hostile neighbours. These men founded Brava and Magadoxo and drove the Emozaide, doubly obnoxious as trade rivals and heretics, into the interior to become middlemen between

Circa 950 A.D. the tribesmen and themselves. Presently a party from Magadoxo reached Sofala and, finding that there was gold to be had, made a settlement.

915 A.D. A much-travelled Moslem, Massoudi of Baghdad, then appeared on this scene of petty bickering and, like so many later visitors to Africa, wrote a book about it. In his famous *Meadows of Gold* he tells of Arabs and Persians passing along the ancient monsoon trade-route from Madagascar and East Africa to the Malabar Coast and Ceylon; of the coming and going between the Red Sea and the Persian Gulf and Sofala; of the little Bushmen, the Wak-wak, in the parts around Sofala, and of the Zendjs, the Bantu, who were already pushing southward bartering gold and ivory, panther skins and tortoiseshell with Arab traders for the markets of India and China.[1]

Two generations passed and the world of Islam was once more on the move. Moslems crossed the Khyber Pass to add a further complication to the problems of India; Seljuk Turks trooped down from Turkestan to turn the line of the Taurus and overthrow the Byzantines at Manzikert; the green-flag Fatimites seized Egypt; Arabian zealots rallied the Berbers at Tunis and pushed thence across North Africa as far as Lake Chad, Wadai and Darfur; the Tuareg Almoravid, Yussuf, set up the first of the Mahdis, the figure-head of a Moslem revival, conquered Senegambia and Morocco and, crossing

1086. the Straits of Gibraltar, crushed the rising Christian power of Castile at Zallaca in the year that William the Conqueror finished his

Circa 1020. Domesday survey. This energy radiating in all directions did not leave the East Coast of Africa unscathed. Persian Moslems from Ormuz, bitterly hostile to the Arabs, settled at Quiloa. Here their power grew till, by 1314 (in that year the Bruce stood victorious at Bannockburn), their city had become the leading power on the coast. Quiloa controlled Sofala and Melinde, Mombasa, Pemba and Zanzibar, Mafia and Mozambique; it had stations in Madagascar and the Comoros; its sailors knew of the rivers of Sena and Quilimane, the mouths of the great Zambesi.[2]

Ibn Batuta of Tangier, in the course of travels as wide as those of Marco Polo, noted what this Semitic trading empire was like in the

[1] Hall, *Pre-historic Rhodesia*, pp. 72 ff.; Dos Santos quoted by Hall, *P. R.*, p. 83; *ibid.* chapter 3, on Arab gold trade.
[2] Rec. S.E.A., I. 12.

early fourteenth century. The towns, like Tyre of old or Carthage, *Circa* were perched either on islands or on easily defended promontories. $\begin{smallmatrix}1330\\A.D.\end{smallmatrix}$ The wood and mud hovels of an earlier day had given way to stone houses with flat roofs and stoeps which overhung the narrow, winding alleys; the fortified palace of the sultan stood upon the sea-front; above the flat roofs rose the minarets of the mosques; around the huddled whitewashed houses stretched the gardens and the palm groves. Aristocrats, who still kept something of their Asiatic blood, and men of wealth moved slowly along the streets in long flowing robes; Moslems of all colours were privileged to wear the turban and the sword even though the rest of their apparel was limited to a loin-cloth.

The sword was much in evidence. The coast was full of war: orthodox Arabs and Persians against heretic Emozaide, Arabs against Persians, and, on occasion, the infidel 'Kaffirs' against all three. Nevertheless, the Semites mixed freely with the Bantu; they traded with them in the intervals of warfare; sometimes these tribesmen brought alluvial gold down to the coast ports, but as a rule the half-breeds, with whom the ports abounded, went inland to fetch it.[1] Of settlement inland there was none. The Arabs clung to the coast and exploited the interior, Carthaginian fashion, by levying incredible dues, the perquisite of the powers-that-be in all the East, upon the goods that came into their towns.[2]

The goods thus won were passed on far and wide by sea. Little *zambucos*, mere half-decked boats, were good enough for the river and harbour traffic; the more ambitious *pangayos* served for the coasting trade to Ormuz and Yemen; but it was only the large *dhows*, 'the great birds from heaven,' which dared to run before the monsoons to Calicut. These vessels were manned as a rule by half-breeds; but at Calicut, the middlemen were once again 'Arabs' or Rumi, renegade Greeks, and there too were men from the Far East who had come in their blundering, square-bowed junks with the spices of the Moluccas and the scented woods and silks and pottery of China and Japan. What though the 'Arabs' presently established an outpost at Malacca, the yellow men still came on in Arab dhows to Calicut.

The ships in which the 'Arabs' fared forth were flimsy enough. Even the *dhows* were built of roughly split planks fastened together with coir rope and wooden pegs, and driven by great lateen sails of closely woven matting. The Moors might use the levantine compass, quadrants and marine charts while European sailors still hugged the shore and pinned their faith on Ptolemy, but the fact remained that they dared not trust themselves to the grip of the Mozambique

---

[1] Hall, *Pre-historic Rhodesia*, pp. 73 ff.
[2] Rec. S.E.A., III. 93 ff.

current south of Cape Correntes because they feared the whirlpools and sirens with which, they were persuaded, those far southern seas were infested.[1]

What, now, did civilised Mediterranean folk know of the interior of the vast unbroken continent that lay to the southward of the forbidding Sahara? Truth to tell, little enough until almost our grandfathers' time. Pharaohs of the New Empire conquered parts of Nubia, 'the miserable land of Cush,' some distance up the Nile. Their Macedonian and Roman successors were less ambitious, though the imaginative Nero did indeed send one expedition up-river only to learn that it had been stopped by the *sudd*. Probably neither pagan Greeks and Romans knew anything of what lay in the interior beyond the present-day Khartum, except perhaps a learned man like Ptolemy the geographer, who had heard of the Great Lakes from which the life-giving Nile was said to rise and made a good guess at the far-distant Niger. Christian Egyptians knew somewhat *Circa* more, for their Alexandrian missionaries converted the Nubians and *330* Abyssinians far up the great river. But did any of them know of the *A.D.* Bushmen, those relics of the Stone Age, the dwarfs who had delighted long-dead Pharaohs with their dancing? Maybe they did, though possibly those dancers were ancestors of the tiny folk even more backward than they, who, lacking even the knowledge of fire, still survive in the depths of the Congo forests. Be that as it may, once upon a time the Bushmen probably wandered over all Africa south of the Sahara till stronger peoples drove them from their hunting-grounds. At all events, Massoudi found these little Wak-wak with their clicking speech living in the early tenth century A.D. just south of Zenj, 'the black man's land' off which lay Zanzibar, and already he found that the black men aforesaid, sturdy Bantu herdsmen and rough-and-ready agriculturalists, were hunting them as 'baboons' who had been in the world when the Great Spirit had brought men out of the rock. And so it has gone from that day to this.

Perhaps Massoudi's Wak-wak included Hottentots as well as Bushmen, for pastoralists though the former were, they were not much bigger than Bushmen, they were of much the same colour, they too clicked in their speech, and to the casual observer were so indistinguishable from them that the seventeenth-century Dutch settlers at Capetown at first saw no difference between the two peoples. Some there be who hold that both peoples were sprung from the same stock. The orthodox account of their coming to Southern Africa put forward by Stow and hallowed by the conservative South African historian, Theal, is that a thousand years or so before the landing of the Dutch in 1652 the Hottentots had

[1] Rec. S.E.A., I. 12; III. 77, 93 ff.

lived around the Great Lakes in Central Africa, that they had then trekked away gradually, possibly through a gap in the advancing Bantu, and that having hastened across the Zambesi valley to escape the deadly tsetse fly, they had drifted down the south-west coast into the Cape Peninsula, whence they dispersed themselves eastward as far as the western frontier of Natal, mixing with the Bushmen as they went. On the other hand, Massoudi's statement that the Wakwak lived in what is now Tanganyika gives some support to Orpen's belief that the Hottentots really came down the East Coast moving away from the oncoming Bantu whose Xosa vanguard mingled its blood and speech with theirs.

Today, Bantu tribesmen are scattered over all Africa south of a line drawn from the Gulf of Guinea right across to the East Coast.[1] They were certainly in Tanganyika in Massoudi's day, but how much further south they then extended we do not know. Assuredly, however, they were not yet in Southern Africa, for in some parts of the present-day Union and Southern Rhodesia their occupation is not much older than that of the Europeans, and in the western half of the Cape Colony it is more recent than theirs. It is commonly held that there are two main types of Bantu: the light-skinned Nilotic peoples who are said to have come from North-East Africa, and the dark-skinned folk from the forests of the Congo. In any event, the Bantu moved gradually into Southern Africa by way of the Great Lakes. They came, as a rule, slowly and in comparatively small groups, but they came on a wide front. Some of them, probably ancestors of the present-day Bakalahari, were already south of the Zambesi well before the end of the fourteenth century, for had there been no native inhabitants other than the profitless Bushmen, the Arabs would hardly have troubled to found Sofala in that region. Others of these Bakalahari had by that time pushed on further south-west into what are now the western Transvaal and eastern Bechuanaland. Presently, fresh Bantu invaders from the north, notably the Leghoya or Bataung, came in upon them all along the line, slaying them or mixing with them in the Rhodesia-Sofala region, and in the Transvaal-Bechuanaland area slaying them, enslaving them unto this day, or else driving them into the Kalahari desert. Still further to the westward, Bantu pioneers had entered what is now South-West Africa; but they fared ill, for the Hottentots conquered them and reduced them to leading a miserable half Hottentot, half Bushman existence as Berg Damaras. Meanwhile, yet other invaders, the

[1] On the Bantu in Southern Africa, *vide* Theal, Ia. 5 ff.; IIIa. 64 ff.; Stow, *Native Races*, pp. 256 ff., chapters xxi–xxvi; J. Maclean, *Compendium of Kafir Laws and Customs*; C. Brownlee, *Reminiscences of Kaffir Life and History*; D. Kidd, *The Essential Kafir* and *Kafir Socialism*; M. S. Evans, *Black and White in South-East Africa*; Molema, *The Bantu, Past and Present*; C.H.B.E., VIII. 34 ff.

Makaranga, a Bantu people with a strong infusion of Arab blood, had made themselves dominant in the parts behind Sofala. There, they formed a strong confederacy which even in the day of its decline was dignified by the Portuguese with the title of the Empire of Monomotapa.

Possibly the Bantu predecessors of the Makaranga, and certainly the Makaranga themselves and kindred later comers whose modern descendants are the Barotse, mined gold in the lands that stretch from the Zambesi southward into the northern Transvaal. That huge expanse is dotted with workings: quartz-mining with regular pits and galleries which had been abandoned only when the water rose upon. the miners. From first to last—and Bantu sought gold in their own fashion thereabouts as late as the first quarter of the nineteenth century—many million pounds worth of gold has been taken from those pits. But was it they who also constructed the dry-stone buildings and irrigation works which are found in the same region? These monuments to past ingenuity and energy are many and various. There is, for instance, one great group of buildings at Khami near Bulawayo, remains of irrigation channels in many parts, terraced hillsides at Mount Fura and in the Inyanga district towards the Zambezi, and lines of blockhouses running from the port of Sofala to the greatest and most famous piles of all, the temple and fortress standing on adjacent hilltops at Zimbabwe in the centre of a mass of ruins covering four square miles. Throughout this vast territory the buildings are of different dates and the work of different peoples. Much of the work is crude enough, but some of it is of a high order. This is especially true of the Zimbabwe temple, whose main mass is well constructed but whose western wall has obviously been rebuilt later and much more roughly on a foundation of ash, slag and up-turned earth left by goldsmelters. As it stands now, the temple is a huge elliptical building whose grey stone looks lovely against the background of green foliage on a 'saft day.' A passage-way, presumably for processions, passes between an outer and an inner wall of stone blocks through three gateways to the principal altar near the centre; another altar platform stands near a conical tower on the east side, and close by rises a great baobab tree. Once upon a time soapstone birds, perched upon shafts, stood upon the outer wall facing east; the eastern wall is adorned with a row of chevron pattern; the floors are of stone and a kind of cement; there are no inscriptions. Débris tell of a long-continued occupation; ashes, moulds and gold itself tell of gold-smelting; but there are no signs of mining in the immediate neighbourhood of Zimbabwe. The fruitful land around was obviously used for agriculture to support the men who held the temple and fortress on the boulder-strewn hill-tops.

Archæologists have long argued over the origins of these famous

Zimbabwe ruins, some dating them as early as the tenth century B.C. and others as late as the fifteenth century after Christ.[1]

There are those who say that Zimbabwe is the work of mediæval Bantu, others of ancient Sabæans, others again of Dravidian Indians. MacIver, an early upholder of the Bantu theory, points to the undoubted facts that the Makaranga occupied the Zimbabwe ruins, repaired them and mined in a fashion; that the Mashona, close kinsmen of the Makaranga, at least used them as cattle kraals; that the Barotse also occupied the buildings, and that both Barotse and Makaranga are famous among Bantu for their stone-work. But authority, as far as numbers go, was long opposed to the Bantu theory.

The sixteenth-century Portuguese believed that the mines, which they diligently sought, and the ruins, the chief of which they never saw, were 'the Ophir where the Queen of Sheba had her riches, when she went to Jerusalem,' for, after all, there were, according to old Moorish and native tradition, 'certain ancient ruins said to have been the factory of the Queen of Sheba or of Solomon,' and 'the mountain called Fura,' Afura, or Aufur sounds very like Ophir.[2] Learned philologists in modern times have built wilder theories on less substantial foundations; besides, anything might be believed of a land where gold was said to be found not only in stones but growing up inside the bark of trees. Again, if cargoes could go from Sofala to India in the sixteenth century, why should they have not gone thence in the days of Solomon? Be that as it might, the idea that Rhodesia was the home of 'King Solomon's mines' long held the field.

These conjectures have been carried further in our own day by men who did see the ruins, notably by Keane and Hall. They held that the mines and most ancient buildings were the work of Sabæans from Yemen who probably used Indian and Bantu labourers, that 'the whole land of Havilah where there is "gold" was Southern Rhodesia, that Tarshish was Sofala, and that Ophir was the depôt in Yemen whence came Sheba's Queen.'[3] And, to be sure, Southern Rhodesia can supply all the products listed in the Book of Kings except the peacock, for which highly decorative bird it must substitute the sober bustard. Van Oordt, again, has made out a plausible case for Dravidian Indian origins; but latterly the weight of authority

---

[1] Vide J. T. Bent, *Ruined Cities of Mashonaland*; A. Wilmot, *Monomotapa*; A. H. Keane, *The Gold of Ophir*; R. N. Hall and G. W. Neal, *The Ancient Ruins of Rhodesia*; R. N. Hall, *Great Zimbabwe* and *Pre-historic Rhodesia*; D. Randall-MacIver, *Mediæval Rhodesia*; J. F. Van Oordt, *Who were the Builders of Great Zimbabwe?*; S. S. Dornan and J. F. Schofield, *S.A. Journal of Science*, 1915 and 1926; G. Caton-Thompson, *The Zimbabwe Culture*; L. Fouche, *Mapungubwe*.
[2] Rec. S.E.A., I. 22; VII. 275 ff.
[3] Hall, *Pre-historic Rhodesia*, pp. 3, 364.

1*

has swung back decisively in the direction of Bantu origins and a comparatively recent date.

Two Rhodesian investigators, Dornan and Schofield, have traversed the Sabæan and, *a fortiori*, the Dravidian theories at all points. The Zimbabwe temple, they claim, was the great place of a Bantu priest-chief; the double walls were for defence; the cement is a mixture of dagga and dung such as modern Bantu use; the phallic cones are cairns to mark the graves of dead chiefs; the eagles were mere totems which once stood at the door of the witch-doctor's house; the baobab is indigenous. Schofield insists that Zimbabwe and other edifices are typical Bantu ovals and too badly built at that to have a really ancient history; Dornan adduces native tradition to show that Makaranga were mining gold and occupying some of the Rhodesian ruins when the Matabele, last of a series of invaders, burst in upon them about 1840, and points to late nineteenth-century Bantu buildings elsewhere which exhibit all the architectural features of Zimbabwe. These conclusions have been powerfully supported by the researches of Caton-Thompson in Southern Rhodesia, and of Fouche in the north-western Transvaal. It may now be taken as fairly established that the Zimbabwe culture was Bantu, that its origins date back possibly to the seventh century A.D., that it received its original stimulus from Arabs who traded with India whither most of the gold mined by the Bantu was exported, and that, having reached its zenith in the eleventh century, it gradually declined. On one point, however, all the bickering pundits are agreed and that is that the Rhodesia and Transvaal ruins were already ruins when the Portuguese arrived at Sofala at the end of the fifteenth century after Christ.

Intercourse and Moorish pressure had long ago forced the Iberians, Goths and Sueves in the western parts of the Spanish peninsula to make terms with one another. The county of Portugal gradually took shape, fought its Christian and Moslem neighbours indiscriminately, but on the whole the Moslems more vigorously, and won its capital of Lisbon with the help of a body of Crusaders, Englishmen for the most part, who were on their way to the Holy Land. Thereafter, the Moslem revival headed by the Berber Almohades threatened Portugal in common with the other Iberian principalities; but, by the middle of the thirteenth century, the Almohad empire had broken up and Portugal, a full-blown kingdom now, had conquered the Moorish Algarves to the extreme southern tip of her territory.

The enlarged kingdom of Portugal was still small and mountainous and much of its land was in the hands of the king, the Church and the military Order of Christ who by no means made full use of it; nevertheless, by the middle of the fourteenth century, she had

developed her abundant fisheries somewhat; her Jews and conquered Moors gave her some little wealth with their wool and silk;
a Genoese, Pessanha, had organised her navy; her commerce, widespread for so small a state, put her in touch with Italy, Flanders and
England. Under the glorious House of Avis, her people became
conscious that they were a nation; but still more were they conscious
of the neighbourhood of the Shereefian sultans of Morocco, whose
pirate barks harried their coasts and whose continued independence
was an affront to inveterate Crusaders. Their king, reviving St. Louis'
great dream of a Tunis dependent on France, determined to conquer
Morocco. Accordingly what time the English archers were smiting 1415.
the French chivalry at Agincourt and Christendom assembled at
Constance was burning John Hus, the Portuguese took Ceuta. The
European exploitation of Africa had begun.

Among those who distinguished themselves at the taking of Ceuta
was Prince Henry, grandson of John of Gaunt and second son of the
Portuguese king, half Portuguese, half Anglo-Frenchman, a very
typical product of the West.[1] Knighted for his valour and appointed
Grand Master of the Order of Christ, he, a Renaissance Cecil
Rhodes, used the revenues of the corporation he now controlled to
finance exploring ventures. For, being minded to see how far the
power of the Infidels extended in Africa and to set a limit to it 'for
the glory of God and the profit of Portugal,' he retired to the pro-
montory of Sagres, built himself a house, a chapel and an observatory, studied navigation and shipbuilding, and planned those
voyages which, after his death, opened the sea-road from the West
to India.

The Navigator's motives were mixed, for he was only human.
There was the crusade against the Moroccans; there was missionary
zeal and the hope of making touch with that potent Christian
monarch, Prester John, wherever he might be—perhaps in Abyssinia;
there was the acquisition of gain, for it was notorious that Moslem
caravans crossed the Sahara southward to Bilhad Ghana, the land
of wealth which we call Guinea. Had not Edrisi the Moor shown *Circa*
that land on the map he drew long ago for Roger II, the Norman 1150.
king of Sicily? There was growing confidence, for knowledge was
reviving in the West. The Church Fathers might hold fast to Ptolemy
and vote:

> Anyone doubting him sold to the demon.
> Their observations were formally noted;
> Still—better maps could be got from the seamen.[2]

---

[1] C. R. Beazley, *Prince Henry the Navigator*; R. H. Major, *Life of Prince Henry
of Portugal.*
[2] *Saturday Westminster*, July 11, 1914.

Genoese sailors and Balearic islanders had ferreted about beyond the Pillars of Hercules for many years past; their *portulani* showed many things that did not appear with the Land of Nod and Ultima Thule in the orthodox atlases; one good map of 1351—it is still preserved in the Laurentian Library at Florence—showed Madeira; Portuguese and Spaniards, the latter fortified by a Papal Bull, were actually competing for the Fortunate Isles, the Canaries, and, in the

1415. very year of the taking of Ceuta, the Spaniards made good their claim to Tenerife, 'wonderful among islands of the earth.' More to

Circa the point, Prince Henry knew that Marco Polo, the Venetian, had
1294. heard tell of 'Madageiscar' even though he had confused it with

Circa Zanzibar, that Ibn Batuta had written of the gold, iron and skins of
1330. Sofala, and, finally, a full generation before that widely-travelled Moslem had given the West its first reliable non-Ptolemaic idea of the East Coast as far south as that city, the Genoese brothers, Ugolino and Guido Vivaldi, had been cast away in a vain attempt to get round Africa from the west. If Genoese could try, why should not Portuguese succeed?

Doubtless Prince Henry's plans took more definite shape as the navigation proceeded. Could his captains but find the West Nile, the river which watered Ethiopia 'as the East Nile doth water Egypt,' they could join hands with Prester John and take the Moslem world from the rear. But gradually the scheme grew bolder. The Laurentian map showed something else besides Madeira. In spite of Ptolemy's South Land which made the Indian Ocean a land-locked sea, it showed the southern horn of Africa and an open road to the East, the land of jewels and silks and spices, desirable wares which were still in the hands of the Infidels and only reached the West through the Italians—at a price. Might not the Portuguese find their way to these lands for themselves, circumvent the grasping Venetians and, rounding the Cape, fall on the Ottoman Turks from behind? It did not look such a very long voyage on the map and these Ottomans were a growing peril; already they had conquered most of the Balkan peninsula; Byzantium alone held out against them; it would be an act worthy of a Christian prince to overthrow the Great Soldan.

From whatever motives and with whatever end in view, Prince

1418– Henry sent his captains forth.[1] They colonised Madeira, planting
1419. there the vines and sugar-cane of Cyprus; far out in the Atlantic

1427. they settled the Azores, with Flemings for the most part; bold Gil
1434. Eannes rounded Cape Bojador into a sea of 'darkness and ghosts';

---

[1] On the Portuguese discoveries and conquests *vide* Rec. S.E.A. I. 1–46; II. 26 ff.; III. 67 ff.; V. 349 ff.; VI. (De Barros) 147 ff.: Scott Keltie, *Partition of Africa*; W. C. Abbott, *The Expansion of Europe*, I.; Acton, *Lectures on Modern History*; E. Prestage, *The Portuguese Pioneers*; *C.H.B.E.* VIII. 77 ff.

a little later, Antonio Gonsalvez and Nuno Tristan ventured past
Cape Blanco and brought back gold dust from the Rio d'Ouro as 1442.
well as ten slaves, 'real Guinea natives,' who were duly 'converted
to the true way of salvation.' Thus did the Renaissance Portuguese
revive in Europe the domestic institution of slavery which had died
out during the Middle Ages.

They did so under the most exalted patronage. Popes Nicholas V
and Calixtus III granted remission of sins to all who took part in
this new crusade, gave Portugal the sole privilege of seizing and converting the peoples of Darkest Africa, and conferred on the Order
of Christ spiritual jurisdiction over all lands south of Cape Blanco
ad Indos. Many erring souls would be brought to God by the dis-
coverers; black ivory would help to pay the cost of the discoveries,
and the Portuguese Government buttressed the Bull with a charter
granting Henry the monopoly of the African trade and one-fifth of
its profits. The idea of reaching India was thus fully formed, and
'philanthropy and five per cent.' began to play their part in the
opening-up of Africa.

In the course of the next few years a full thousand slaves were
landed at Lisbon under licences issued by the Navigator, and soon
Diniz Diaz was able to report that he had rounded Cape Verde and 1448.
passed Sierra Leone, old Hanno's furthest south. It was the Navigator's furthest south also. It is true that the good Italian, Giovanni
Cadamosto, cheered him with the news that he had been far up the
'West Nile' (Senegal) and gathered authentic news of Moslem Tim-
buctoo from the local inhabitants, 'tawny Moors . . . a filthy race,
all of them mean and very abject, liars and traitorous knaves.' Evidently Cadamosto fared better at the hands of the negroes, 'well-built,
noble-looking men, with an Emperor so honest that he might well
have been an example to any Christian,' which, in the mid-fifteenth
century, did not imply a high standard; but Cadamosto added
nothing to Prince Henry's knowledge of the road to the East. The
Portuguese had reached the Gold and Slave Coasts; discovery and
the crusade paled before the delights and profits of commerce. So 1460.
in due time there died Prince Henry the Navigator, 'a Prince so
mighty who had sent so many fleets and won so much from Negro-
land and had fought so constantly against the Saracens for the
Faith.' [1] And Prester John was still to seek and the Great Soldan was
now enthroned at Constantinople.

Exploration was presently resumed at the price of giving one,
Fernan Gomez, the monopoly of the slave trade for five years provided he discovered one hundred leagues of coast each year. The
bargain was kept. Dahomey, Bornu and the mouths of the Niger
were found, the equator was crossed and, on an average, a thousand

---

[1] Beazley, *op. cit.*, pp. 269, 273, 305.

Negroes were imported annually to mix their blood with that of the
Portuguese peasantry. Ten years later the energetic young king,
John II, secured a base on the Gold Coast by fortifying São Jorge
de Mina (Elmina) and then sent Diego Cão southward to discover
the Congo estuary and plant a stone pillar (*padrão*) at Cape Cross in
South-West Africa.

With the road to the Indies thus visibly opening before him, King
John determined on a great effort. Ships and methods of navigation
had improved markedly. It is true that there was no means of fixing
the longitude, and the great wooden astrolabes would only give a
fair reading of the latitude on dry land; but John got the best expert
advice available from Rodrigo and Joseph, a Jew, and Martin
Behaim of Nuremberg, a disciple of Johan Müller of Königsberg,
Regiomontanus, 'an astronomer renowned.' These men gave him
'tables of the declination of the sun' which made his captains independent of the stars and astrolabes;[1] nevertheless, John's chosen
captain, Bartholomew Diaz, still clung to the coast as far as Angra dos
Voltas, presumably the mouth of the Orange river. He was then blown
far out to sea, but, tacking back, made landfall after many days at
Angra dos Vaquieros. The inhabitants of Mossel Bay, almost certainly Hottentots, did not wait to be interviewed; they fled inland
with their herds of cattle and left Diaz to push on eastwards to
Algoa Bay. There he set up a cross on a little island and a pillar at
Cape Padrone on the mainland a few miles further on. He must have
known from the trend of the coast and the warm current that flowed
down against him that he was heading straight for the Indies, but
at the Infante river, probably the Fish, his men refused to go further.
'And being about returning' he discovered the 'Cabo de Boa
Esperança,' and planted the last of his *padrões* thereon. Whether
it was his King or he himself who named the Cape thus, the name
was well chosen for 'the great hope it gave of discovering the
Indies.'[2]

Hope might spring eternal in the royal breast, but for a time faith
seemed to be lacking in the hearts of the royal councillors. It is true
that shortly before the departure of Diaz they had sent two
messengers overland to find India and Prester John. One emissary,
Paiva, died, and though the other, Pedro de Covilhan, reached
Calicut and Goa, he was held in honourable captivity in Prester
John's Abyssinia to the end of his days.[3] Covilhan did, however,
send a message home by Joseph of Lamego, a Jew: 'If you persist
to the Southward, Africa will come to an end. When the ships come

1482–
1485.

1487.

[1] Rec. S.E.A., VI. 165.
[2] *Ibid.*, I. 2; VI. 152; Prestage, *op. cit.*, p. 225; *C.H.B.E.*, VIII. 82. Probably
Diaz gave the Cape its present name.
[3] Rec. S.E.A., I. 2; VI. 154.

to the Eastern Ocean, let them ask for Sofala and the Island of the Moon (Madagascar) and they will find pilots to take them to Malabar.'[1] The message can hardly have reached Lisbon before Diaz had reported that there was in truth an end even to Africa; nevertheless, many of John's councillors were averse to taking further action 'as it would be greatly envied by all the kings and republics of Europe, as also by the Sultan of Babylon and the kings and lords of India themselves.'[2]

So Leopold of Belgium must have felt when he, the least of *Circa* Western monarchs, proposed to acquire the coveted Congo basin, 1879. moreover John's advisers feared that the search for India would damage the prospects of conquests in North Africa and their cherished Guinea trade. But a greater fear and the king's urgency at last forced their hand. The Genoese Columbus sailed westward 1492. under the Spanish flag and found the 'Indies'; at least, he said he had, and the most disreputable of Popes, Alexander Borgia, divided the world between Spain and Portugal. Those Powers prudently 1494. interpreted the Papal Bull by treaty; even so, Portugal must be quick if she wished to make good her monopoly over the road *ad Indos*. Wherefore, on the death of John, Manuel the Fortunate took action, spurred thereto by the news that another Italian, John Cabot, had 1497. sailed westward on behalf of Henry Tudor, King of England.

Manuel chose Vasco da Gama for the venture.[3] Da Gama was equipped with improved brass astrolabes, which he distrusted, and the knowledge that Diaz, after drifting far out of sight of land, had been brought safely to the Cape by the westerly winds and currents. He, therefore, struck out to sea from the Cape Verde islands and 1497– sailed southward in a wide sweep for no less than ninety-three days. 1499. He sighted land at St. Helena Bay, doubled the Cape, passed up the coast of Natal at Christmastide and named it, and reached Arab Mozambique. His reception and his own behaviour there were not altogether happy; but at Melinde, farther up the coast, he fared better and acquired the services of a Gujarati pilot, one Malemo Cana, who was 'so expert in navigation that being shown an astrolabe he took little notice of it, as one who was used to more considerable instruments.'[4] Under Cana's guidance the Portuguese ran before the monsoon, and on May 16, 1498, 'with great rejoicing and with the sound of trumpets after dinner . . . they cast anchor two leagues from the city of Calicut.'[5]

Early in 1499 da Gama was back once more in Lisbon. He had left an unsavoury reputation behind him at Calicut and 115 of his original company of 170 dead on the way; but he brought with him

---

[1] Quoted by Abbott, *Expansion of Europe*, I. 95.
[2] Rec. S.E.A., III. 68.   [3] *Ibid.*, III. 70 ff.; VI. (de Barros) 149 ff.
[4] *Ibid.*, I. 6, 7.   [5] *Ibid.*, III. 86.

definite news of Bombay, Ceylon and Sumatra, and a cargo of spices which paid the cost of his expedition sixty times over. In his joy Manuel the Fortunate assumed the style of 'Lord of the Conquest, Navigation and Commerce of Ethiopia, Arabia, Persia and China.'[1] Pharaoh Necho of famous memory, King of Upper and Lower Egypt, Lord of the Two Lands, Son of the Sun, Beloved of the Gods, Lord of Diadems, triumphant, could hardly have done better.

Da Gama's trumpets at Calicut echoed round the globe. And well they might, for they proclaimed the confirmation of ancient history and the outflanking of the Turk, and heralded the opening up of one-third of the world to Christianity, the ruin of the trade of Venice, and the transference of the balance of power at sea from the Mediterranean to the Atlantic.

The rise of the Portuguese empire in the East was very rapid. True, in spite of the profits of a second voyage, da Gama was forbidden to return to the Indies for more than twenty years, possibly because of his violence at Calicut; but his successors carried all before them. They came at a fortunate time. The Arabs were divided against themselves; their ships were feeble and, though the European cannon were more remarkable for noise than efficiency, the Portuguese were vastly superior to the Moslems in body armour, discipline, and the great good luck which at first attended them and on which they regularly counted. Conditions in India were equally favourable. As Christians they were welcomed by the Indian Nestorians, upon whose aid Prince Henry had once counted; they found that the Zamorin of Calicut was merely *primus inter pares* of a host of petty Malabar rajahs accustomed to men of divers faiths, keen to trade and hampered by a chivalrous mode of warfare of which they took full advantage. There was no strong government in all India. A quarter of a century was to pass before Baber, first of the Great Moguls, placed his foot in the stirrup of resolution and his hand on the reins of the confidence of God and marched against the dominions of Hindustan.

At first, Portugal's policy was mainly commercial, not to say piratical, her seamen merely seeking to secure one or two bases for trade. Pedro Cabral, sailing far westward, annexed Brazil in the name of His Most Faithful Majesty; then, pushing on, he and de Neuva sank a Moorish squadron at Calicut. Presently Duarte Pacheco drove out the Moorish middlemen and established the Portuguese arms in Cochin and Cannanore; but Saldanha made no attempt to hold the watering-place under the shadow of Table Mountain, though men called Table Bay by his name for more than a hundred years to come. Then came a change. The losses in the

1502–
1503.

1500–
1503.

---

[1] Abbott, *Expansion of Europe*, I. 105.

trade might be heavy—Cabral lost seven of his thirteen ships—but the gains were enormous and the damage to Venice grievous. The Bride of the Adriatic tried to come to terms with the Lord of the Atlantic and Indian Oceans. She was snubbed for her pains and promptly sought revenge. The Sultan of Egypt was anxious for his customs revenue from the Indian traffic—£290,000 a year, no less—which was threatened by the Portuguese, 'Crusaders coming the other way, and robbing the Moslems of their resources.'[1] Jealous Venice egged on the Sultan, who proposed to sweep the newcomers off the Eastern seas.

Portugal prepared for the coming storm. She sent Francesco de Almeida to win and hold a series of naval bases as a sure foundation for economic predominance. St. Helena was occupied as a post- 1505-house on the road; everywhere on the East Coast the Arabs were 1509. crushed or overawed and forts raised at Sofala and Mombasa, Quiloa and Mozambique; a footing was made in Ceylon, and Almeida was granted his crowning mercy when he destroyed a great 1509. Arab and Egyptian fleet at Diu.[2]

Almeida thus made the Indian Ocean a Portuguese sea for a hundred years; but already the ground had been cut from under his feet by that royal ingratitude and official jealousy which was to be the bane of the rising Portuguese empire. Almeida stood for a naval policy: command of the sea and as little responsibility for the land as possible; his successor, Affonso de Albuquerque, was a conscious imperialist whose aim was to found self-sufficing colonies and extend Portuguese authority in the East. Albuquerque harried the East 1507. Coast on his way out, seized Brava and Socotra, thus hampering the Arab Red Sea traffic, and was greeted with imprisonment on his arrival in India. But at last Almeida had to release him and sail home. Almeida never saw Portugal. He landed in Table Bay, and 'as it is always the character of the Portuguese to endeavour to rob the poor natives of the country,' a quarrel arose with the Hottentots, who 1510. slew him and many of his companions as they struggled towards their boats through the heavy sand of Salt River beach.[3]

Albuquerque was the real builder of the Portuguese Indian empire. 1510-He seized Goa and made it the capital; he occupied Malacca to 1515. control the Far Eastern trade; he took Ormuz and thus closed the gates of the Persian Gulf, and narrowly failed to repeat this success at Aden. Before his death, he had 20,000 men holding fifty-two stations scattered along 15,000 miles of coast.

Few important additions were made to this imperial Jonah's

[1] Acton, *Lectures on Modern History*, p. 56.
[2] Rec. S.E.A., I. 13, 14, 62, 99; II. 43; III. 113, 122; V. 382; VI. 246, 288; VII. 187.
[3] *Ibid.*, II. 45.

1538. gourd thereafter. Diu was secured; two years later the Portuguese appeared in Japan, but their hold there was of the slightest; they
1556. then occupied the poor harbour of Macao, and finally seized the
1564. rich Moluccas, the plum of the spice-trade. In Africa, their hold was confined to the coasts and islands even more rigidly than in the Indies. At first they made good progress on the West Coast; they occupied the islands and San Salvador, whence Christianity made such headway that there was soon need for a negro bishop in this Kingdom of Congo; but Christianity failed to come to terms with polygamy, the Bula Matadi headed a pagan reaction, and the ferocious Jagga burst in upon the 'land of war and trade.' With experience sailors gave up hugging the shore and the islands ceased to be of much importance; on the mainland European influence was confined to the purlieus of S. Paulo de Loanda in Angola and Kabinda, sole remnant of Congo, where alone the slave-trade made it worth while for the Portuguese to hold on.[1]

The East Coast settlements were equally unsuccessful. By 1520, the Portuguese held Quiloa, Zanzibar, Mombasa, Sofala, Mozam-
1531– bique, Brava and other minor posts. They then spread southwards,
1535. settled at Sena and Tete in the lower Zambesi valley, took Quilimane
1544. at its mouth and occupied part of Delagoa Bay, the Rio de Lagoa, 'now called Espirito Santo, since Lourenço Marques visited it.'
1558. Mozambique, hitherto a town of small importance, supplanted Sofala as the local capital and, about the same time, Portuguese ships began to call at Inhambane.[2]

In spite of this fair show, the Portuguese occupation of the East Coast was a long-drawn-out, expensive failure.[3] Set on a fever-sodden coast with a barbaric hinterland, the settlements had no chance till the development of the interior from the south in the course of the nineteenth century gave them something from which to draw sustenance. There was no real colonisation for lack of women; the posts were expensive to maintain; Arab rulers like the Sultan of Zanzibar might pay tribute, but Bantu chiefs had to be subsidised, for it was to them that the Portuguese looked for the gold and silver which were at first all that they desired. The influence of the Portuguese on the interior was trifling. They neither mined nor traded themselves, though, like the Arabs, they occasionally induced natives to dig gold for them; their jealousy of the Arabs was such that they refused to have them as middlemen; they merely ousted them and waited at the ports for the streams of gold to flow in. Such gold as was forthcoming was dust, and it was in miticals, a given weight of dust, that the

---

[1] Johnston, *Colonisation of Africa*, p. 33; *C.H.B.E.*, VIII. chap. IV.
[2] Rec. S.E.A., I. 14, 62; III. 33, 94, 122; VI. 265.
[3] *Ibid.*, III. 103. On trade and colonisation *vide* Rec. S.E.A., I. 22, 80 ff.; II. 405; III. 216, 223, 464, 489; IV. 2, 35, 39, 213, 279, 423; VI. 268; VII. 186, 218, 366; VIII. 364. 406, 478.

currency was reckoned; but there was little enough of it, and from the first men lamented that the Sofala trade was 'a great expense for so little revenue and profit.'[1] Already, Mozambique was running on its persistent annual deficit.

Twice there were promises of better things. There was a Bantu potentate in the interior, the Monomotapa, whom the Portuguese dignified with the title of Emperor and whose realm even mid-seventeenth-century map-makers showed stretching southward from the Zambesi to the Fish river. As a matter of fact he was paramount chief of the Makaranga, ruling from his wattle and daub capitals, the *zimbaoes* of N'Pande and Mount Fura, territory which ran some 750 miles inland along the south bank of the Zambesi. His power was not what it had been, for the chiefs of the Sabi country and Quiteve behind Sofala and Manica, where Umtali now stands, had all broken away; but many chiefs still owed him allegiance and he was a power to be reckoned with.[2]

Jesuit fathers presently arrived to preach the Gospel to the Bantu. Da Silveira and Fernandez went first to the Batonga near Inhambane; 1560. thence da Silveira went to Mount Fura where he speedily baptised the complacent Monomotapa and many of his followers. Da Silveira's success was short-lived; Moorish jealousies destroyed his hopes; he was martyred, and the effort ended.[3] Nearly twenty years later the Dominicans arrived, fixed their headquarters at Mozambique and soon set up branch stations at Sofala, Sena and Tete. 1577. Most of their energies were perforce expended on the European and half-breed inhabitants of the towns; such as they could spare for the tribes were long unavailing as the hinterland was being ravaged by fierce bands of Bantu invaders from the north. This terror past, the rivalry between the Hounds of the Lord and the Company of Jesus seriously hampered the work of evangelisation, and it was not until 1630 that the Dominicans were established in any strength up the lower Zambesi valley.

Missionary effort, then, was comparatively speaking a failure. The search for gold, the other lodestar of the conquistador stage of European expansion, was a failure *sans phrase*. Dom Sebastian, the young King of Portugal, determined to give substance to an empire in South-East Africa which should rival that of Spain in the Americas by finding and conquering the gold-mines. He therefore divided his Indian dominions into three parts: 'Malacca,' stretching from China 1571. to Pegu; 'India,' from Ceylon to Cape Guardafui; and 'Mono-motapa,' from Guardafui to Cape Correntes. Over this last he appointed Francesco Barreto as 'captain-general and conqueror of the

---

[1] Rec. S.E.A., I. 80 ff.; Scott Keltie, *Partition of Africa*, p. 57.
[2] *Ibid.*, III. 353 ff.; VI. 390 ff.; VII. 273 ff.
[3] *Ibid.*, II. 73, 94 ff.

kingdoms,' with instructions to conquer first Manica, the gold-fields
that lay nearest to Sofala.[1]

Barreto and his officers proposed to take the shortest route inland
but Father Monclaros, a strong-minded Jesuit, insisted on marching
up the pestilential Zambesi valley. Monclaros had his way; it was
summer and, at Sena, horses, cattle and men began to die. Monclaros
put the blame for the sins of the tsetse fly upon the Moors, who, he
said, were poisoning the grass, and, though Barreto was justly
sceptical, he induced the captain to slay some of the Moslems on the
ground that they meant to poison the water supply. The ill-fated
expedition plodded on. It reached the court of the Monomotapa,
helped him to defeat a rival on the Mazoë river, and then staggered
1572.   back to Sena.[2] Next year, Barreto tried again, but at Sena 'this great
man, having escaped so many bullets . . . fell by the words of a
religious man,' dying broken-hearted at the revilings of Monclaros.[3]
One, Homem, succeeded him and reached Manica by marching
straight inland from Sofala; but he soon came away in despair; the
fort he had built as a base for the search for the reputed silver-mines
1574.   of Chicova was destroyed, and King Sebastian suppressed the cap-
tain-generalship of Monomotapa.[4]

It was almost the last act of the restless young king, for a year or
two later, in a valiant attempt to conquer Morocco, he ended his life
and dreams of African domination on the stricken field of Alcazar-
Kebir. His successor soon died and with him the House of Avis.
Philip II of Spain, whose claims were reinforced by power and
propinquity, annexed Portugal and thus ushered in the long half-
century during which her empire languished under the dead hand of
the Hapsburgs of Madrid.

As if to break the hearts of the handful of Portuguese marooned
in East Africa there came waves of Bantu invaders from the north,
the Abambo and Amazimba, fierce men, cannibals on occasion and
at all times slaughterers of the peaceful Makaranga. Nor did they
spare the white men, for though they were beaten off at Melinde,
they destroyed Quiloa, sacked Mombasa and took Tete. At last,
however, they stormed away southward, leaving the dishevelled
Portuguese to seek a revenue from ivory, amber, wax, ambergris and
such little gold as found its way to the coast. Little enough gold in
all conscience, however much the authorities might still expect of
the reputed gold and silver mines in the interior and, in that hope,
maintain three markets inland, all furnished with Dominican
churches and one of them with a Portuguese judge, who dispensed
Portuguese justice by grace of the Monomotapa. On the coast, the
captain of Mozambique held the monopoly of the trade 'towards

[1] Rec. S.E.A. VI. 266, 357; VII. 281.   [2] Ibid., III. 204 ff., 223; VI. 358 ff.
[3] Ibid., I. 28.   [4] Ibid., I. 27 ff.; VI. 383, 386.

the Cape' and fitted it easily into one small ship each year; the ivory revenue of Sofala was eaten up by the fort and its garrison; a three years' lease of all Cuama and Monomotapa yielded no return; the opening of the gold and silver trade in East Africa to Portuguese subjects on payment of the royal fifth simply gave rise to contraband trade in the ivory, tar and other products which were still reserved for the officials; soon the captain of Sofala, who had bought his position from the Viceroy, was spending his own money on the defences of his town. Meanwhile, the hope of silver at Chicova had 1635. proved to be only a hope, and the Portuguese had abandoned their efforts to conquer Monomotapa.[1] Prestige and the hope of better things alone induced them to hold on to their decaying East Coast settlements.

That decay was part of a general decay. Signs of troubles to come had shown themselves in the army and navy before ever Manuel the 1521. Fortunate was dead. The soldiers intermarried with the natives of India and Africa, for Albuquerque and his successors preferred married to unruly single soldiers; but the effect was to relax discipline and reduce the troops to the level of an armed mob. Discipline slackened in the navy also; the government sacrificed the seaworthiness of their ships to mere size and sent great floating castles, such as *Revenge* shattered at Flores in the Azores, to face the winds and 1598. currents of the Cape. The luck departed; the candid de Couto soon had to lament that his countrymen were not nearly such good sailors as the Dutch and English interlopers, and Linschoten noted that the Portuguese marvelled that 'the Englishmen being . . . heretics and blasphemers of God, with so small and weak vessels,' passed the Cape so easily.[2]

The corruption of the civil service was as bad as that of the armed forces. The spoils system was in vogue almost from the first; good men like Almeida and Barreto were broken by slander and jealousy; the effort to check the corruption which flourished under a system of royal monopoly leased out to swarms of officials, the morally halt and lame of Portugal, killed da Gama; the sale of the royal monopoly 1524. of trade to a company merely ruined the company, which sank under 1580. the weight of short-term officials with a truly Chinese conception of the meaning of 'the squeeze'; the fate of Portuguese India was sealed when the King bade the Viceroy auction all commands of 1614. fortresses, official posts and profits of voyages. Thereafter government and commerce became a mere organised robbery by an orientalised, semi-European ruling caste whose work was done by slaves and wealth produced by peoples whose very languages they *Circa* never tried to understand. St. Francis Xavier was of opinion that 1545.

[1] Rec. S.E.A., I. 23; II. 405; III. 412; IV. 2, 35, 39, 213, 279; VII. 270, 282.
[2] *Ibid.*, IV. 423; VI. 392; Linschoten, *Voyage*, II. 246.

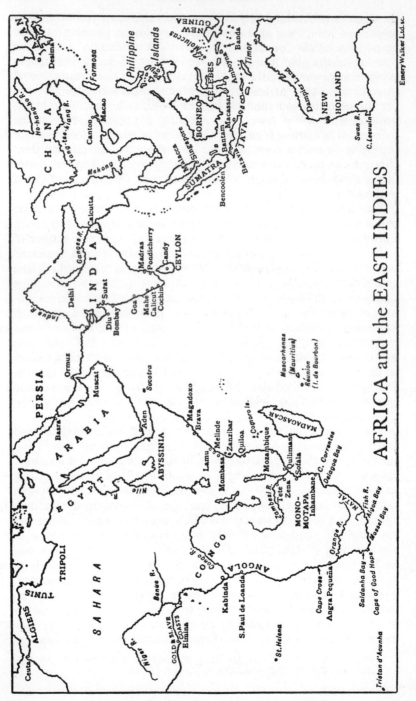

AFRICA and the EAST INDIES

no Portuguese official in India could save his soul, and de Couto frankly admitted that all the world, even the Kaffirs, despised the Portuguese as barbarians.[1]

The record of the Church was little better than that of the State. Saints like Xavier in India and Japan and less-known heroes in the back-blocks of East Africa shine like stars upon a dingy background. The clergy destroyed the Hindu temples in Goa, introduced the Inquisition to harry Jews who had sought refuge in India from persecution in Portugal, and finally tried to force the Gospel on the native Goanese. The Indians, who already despaired of justice at the hands of their lay rulers, abandoned the capital of Portuguese India. It was small consolation to the Viceroy that the religious orders flourished so vigorously that they became a serious drain on his dwindling resources.

The reaction of the Indian trade on Portugal itself was disastrous. Portugal at the end of the fifteenth century was a state of 3,000,000 inhabitants averse to exporting silver and possessed of few products which Indians desired. In the early days, when the trade was more a matter of buccaneering than anything else, huge profits were made; but these soon ceased; the locking up of capital in ships and cargoes for long periods was inconvenient; the shipping losses were grievous and the loss of life appalling. For a full hundred years, one in nine of the ships that sailed from Lisbon *ad Indos* never came back, and sixty per cent. of the men who set out never saw India.[2] Yet royal and clerical excitement flogged Portugal on to a task beyond her economic strength, a strength sapped in advance by the expulsion of her Jews. 1497. Lisbon trebled in size in eighty years, other towns grew vastly and the importation of slaves set men free for overseas ventures; but slave-holding gave rise to miscegenation, the growth of big, ill-developed estates, the elimination of the peasant, and all the social and economic evils of the servile state. Honest work was despised as fit only for Jews and Moriscoes; the poor sponged upon the rich and the rich on the government; the price of necessities rose; famine and disease stalked; the total population declined, and at last 1609. Portugal expelled her industrious Moriscoes.

[1] Keller, *Colonization*, pp. 117 ff.; Rec. S.E.A., VI. 392.
[2] Acton, *Lectures on Modern History*, p. 58.

CHAPTER II

THE DUTCH OCCUPATION OF THE CAPE, 1581–1679

The United Provinces, 24; the Dutch East India Company, 27; English and Dutch in Table Bay, 29; Foundations (1652–62), 30; Bushmen, 33; Hottentots, 34; Slaves and Free Burghers, 37; Hottentot war and exploration, 40; marking time, 42.

THE annexation of Portugal by Spain was an almost unmixed evil for the Portuguese empire overseas. Spain ruled in the East, but her interests were in the West; the Spanish system of administration was even more rigid and centralised than that of Portugal; worst of all, Spain's enemies became Portugal's, and Spain's foes were many. The Portuguese, by reason of their own exclusive commercial policy, could expect no mercy from trade rivals, and now their ill-defended possessions lay open to attack by every French Huguenot, English sea-dog or Dutch sea-beggar who saw fit 'to singe the King of Spain his beard.' All these people were finding their way into Eastern

1580–1591. waters: Sir Francis Drake rounded the Cape, that 'most stately thing'; van Linschoten followed in a Portuguese ship; five years later came Sir Thomas Cavendish, and, in 1591, James Lancaster, first of all Englishmen, set foot ashore in 'the goodly bay' at the base of Table Mountain.[1]

The French and English, however, busied themselves as a rule in Spain's *mare clausum* in the West. Competition in the East was most likely to come from the Dutch who had long had an indirect interest in the Eastern trade. The lordly Portuguese had scorned the retail trade; it was sufficient for them if they brought the spices to Lisbon and there passed them on to humbler folk for distribution throughout Europe. Lisbon thus became the meeting-place of men of divers nations, who listened eagerly to tales of 'all the wealth of Ormuz and of Ind.' None had listened more eagerly than the Dutch; but now that Philip ruled at Lisbon, the Dutch came there no more. For the northern provinces of the Netherlands had revolted. Holland, Zeeland, Guelderland, Utrecht, Gröningen, Overyssel and Friesland had banded themselves together in the Union of Utrecht and, led

1579. by William of Orange, had thrown off their allegiance and offered the sovereignty of the Netherlands to the French Duke of Anjou. Philip's answer came short and sharp. He outlawed William and set

1581. a price upon his head. Then, having annexed Portugal, he closed the port of Lisbon to Dutch shipping.

Philip's embargo forced the Dutch to go to the East themselves.

---

[1] Hakluyt, *Principal Navigations*, XI. 132, 342; Hakluyt Society's publications, LVI., LIX.; Linschoten, *Voyage*.

Spain's road to the Indies lay south-west and Portugal's south-east; the English were diligently seeking a north-west passage; the Dutch therefore decided to go by way of the north-east and planted a 1584. factory at Archangel. Their first efforts were necessarily tentative, but, once the combined artillery of God and Queen Elizabeth had shattered Philip's Invincible Armada, they bestirred themselves in 1588. good earnest. De Moucheron pushed on through the ice to Nova Zembla, but the road was too hard and, in the following year, Cornelis Houtman found a more excellent way. With four ships he 1595. challenged the Iberian monopoly and sailed round the Cape to Java. Three years later, a score of Dutch ships, equipped by a number of small trading companies, made the voyage to India. Thus, long before the weary struggle with Spain was ended in 1609, the Dutch were fairly embarked on the East Indian trade.

Economically, the United Provinces were well equipped for the work. The country was small but it had many resources. Safe behind their ships and dykes, an industrious people relied on dairy and wool-farming, the cultivation of root and grass crops, and the intensive horticulture which rose to such strange heights in the tulip mania of the sixteen-thirties. There was cloth weaving and good linen at Leyden; the spoils of the sea were taken by the hardy fishermen of Holland and Zeeland; Amsterdam itself, men said, was built on herring barrels. Geography made the Dutch a nation of middlemen set at the crossing of the sea, rivers and roadways of Western Europe; the coasting trade of the West and the Baltic corn-trade brought them wealth; their financial power increased. The Spanish Terror had ruined Antwerp in the south; war and, presently, treaties closed 1576. the Scheldt; Philip broke the Italian bankers and the Fuggers of Augsburg and Antwerp by repudiating his debts; his successor persecuted the Jews. Amsterdam reaped the benefit of all this wild sowing. Financiers, Belgian refugees, and Jews fled to the northern port as to 'their great new Jerusalem,' and Amsterdam became the banking centre of Western Europe.[1]

Ships and men and capital were thus available for the Indian voyages. Politically, the Dutch were not so well equipped. The United Provinces were organised as a loose federation of sovereign provinces, each with its estates and stadtholder, who jointly controlled finance and foreign policy. Each province was itself a collection of towns and each town was ruled by a council, elected in Gröningen and Overyssel but co-opted elsewhere. The central government was cumbrous. Delegates from the provincial estates formed the States General, the national legislature, which controlled peace and war, alliance and taxation, but had little power to act effectively without the concurrence of the provincial authorities. A

[1] Sombart, *The Jews and Modern Capitalism*, p. 15.

council of state, a captain-general and an admiral formed a shadowy central executive.

It was a constitution in keeping with the centrifugal traditions which had survived the centralising efforts of Burgundian dukes and Spanish kings. The wealthy mercantile western provinces had interests other than those of the eastern; each maritime province had its own navy; sacrifices for the common good were apt to be made only in emergency, and even then, as in the English North American colonies later on, each province had a very human desire for its neighbours to show their hands first. The provinces themselves could not always count on the local patriotism of their inhabitants, for there was much truth in the saying that the Netherlander recognised no Fatherland but only a father city.

Nevertheless, there were forces which helped the Lion of the Netherlands to hold the seven arrows fast in his paw. There was external pressure, by Spain first and afterwards by France; there was a concentric system of government whereunder members of the republican burgher class, jealous of the House of Orange and, as Arminians, hostile to the Calvinistic clergy, controlled the town councils, the provincial and central estates, and the great East and West India Companies; there was the House of Orange, strong in the support of the Reformed clergy and the mass of the people, stronger still in the fact that until 1650 the heads of the house, Maurice of Nassau, Frederic Henry and William II, were as a rule captains-general, admirals and stadtholders in five of the seven provinces and at all times worthy descendants of William the Silent; there was, lastly, the great weight of the province of Holland. There lay The Hague, the seat of the national government, and Amsterdam, the commercial capital; there also were ·Dordrecht, Rotterdam, Delft, and Leyden. Holland paid as much in taxes as the other provinces put together; its shareholdings in the East and West India Companies were in proportion; it alone sent ambassadors to Paris and Vienna. Politically and economically, the United Provinces were Holland writ large, and Holland was Amsterdam.

The political and constitutional structure of the United Provinces was faithfully reflected in the Dutch East India Company. There were at first four rival companies in Amsterdam trading with India, two in Rotterdam, and others in Middelburg, Delft, Hoorn and Enckhuisen. Naturally, 'they sailed . . . the shoes off each other's feet.'[1] Cut-throat competition in a trade which demanded large capital and, east of Suez, found safety only in numbers was the hangman's whip that drove the companies towards union. Pressure by

---

[1] Keller, *Colonization*, p. 389, quoting de Reus, p. xii. On the Dutch East India Company *vide* Keller, chapters 10, 11.

Maurice of Nassau, his rival Jan van Oldenbarneveldt, advocate of Holland, and the States General at last induced the rival companies to come together. It was hard work to achieve so much, for, apart from local patriotisms, the Dutch were suspicious of monopoly and inclined to favour individual as opposed to corporate enterprise. Nevertheless, the thing was done and the East India Company 1602. received its charter.

It was the day of chartered companies. The States General nominally claimed sovereignty over the prospective possessions of the Company eastward from the Cape and westward from the Straits of Magellan; the Company's servants were bound by oath not to set up an absolutely independent government in the sphere of the charter; short of that the government leased to the Company, for twenty-one years, all that sovereignty implied, especially the monopoly of trade as far as Dutch subjects were concerned. The connection between the great commercial corporation and the State was close: the government took a large block of shares, 20 per cent. of the loot of Spanish and Portuguese shipping, and customs dues on certain classes of goods; it looked to the Company for independent action at sea in case of war; it charged it heavily each time the charter was renewed. But during the long intervals between these renewals, the amount of control exercised by the Estates General was trifling. The leaders in the legislature were also directors of the Company, and Dr. Jekyll could hardly be expected to catechise Mr. Hyde too closely in public. Before long, the directors dared to tell the States General that, while recognising its authority, the East Indies were their own to sell to the King of Spain if they chose.

The connection between the Company and the nation was equally close. Only Dutchmen were allowed to hold shares, but small subscribers were encouraged so that the Company might become as wide as the Dutch nation. The Company was to be the nation in one of its commercial manifestations and, to increase public confidence, a regular account of its doings and financial condition was promised. The report was as regularly postponed and, to the end, the true state of the Company was known only to its directors.

'Jan Compagnie' itself, like the United Provinces, was a federation. The original companies survived in the Chambers into which it was divided and, had it broken up, each of its component parts was quite capable of functioning on its own account. There were four Chambers. Each had its own directors elected by the estates of those provinces which had subscribed at least 50,000 florins. These *Bewindhebbers* numbered some sixty or seventy, and of them twenty were allotted to Amsterdam, twelve to Zeeland (Middelburg), and fourteen each to the Chambers of the Maas (Delft and Rotterdam) and the North Quarter (Hoorn and Enckhuisen). The predominance of Amsterdam was deserved, for that chamber supplied half the original capital of 6,440,200 gulden (by 1672 it had furnished three-fourths) and equipped half the fleets. Hence Amsterdam had eight of the seats on the governing Council of Seventeen which were filled by the States General from lists sent up by the *Bewindhebbers* of the various Chambers. Zeeland, which supplied a quarter of the capital and the ships, had four seats; the smaller Chambers had two each, and the seventeenth member was chosen by Zeeland and the smaller Chambers in turn. Conduct of policy lay with the mighty Seventeen, subject, from 1650 onwards, to review by a Vigilance Committee of eight directors at The Hague.[1] It was to the Seventeen, the *Heeren Majores in patria*, that, by the space of a hundred and fifty years, the rulers of the Cape Colony were destined to give an account of themselves.

1602–
1604.   The Company thrust its way into Portuguese waters with vigour. Within two years of its foundation it possessed itself of Bantam,
1604– the coveted Moluccas and Java; seized Amboyna and half Timor in
1608.   due course, and made a series of unsuccessful attempts upon Mozambique.[2] A regular government was soon organised in the
1609.   East; Pieter Both became first governor-general with five and, presently, nine officials to advise him, and, a little later, this Council
1619.   of India was stationed at Batavia in Java, the capital henceforward of the Dutch East Indian empire.

These years of growth were trying. There were no dividends forthcoming in thirteen several years between 1611 and 1634, and the attacks of one, Willem Usselincx, caused the directors much anguish. For Usselincx shared Bacon's opinion that 'merchants have gain for a pole-star and greed for a compass and are unfit to rule,' and, even though he was driven to take his outrageous plans for a colony of free men innocent of slavery and commercial monopoly to Gustavus
1621.   Adolphus of Sweden, not all the efforts of the Seventeen could prevent the issue of a charter to a Dutch West India Company whose sphere ate into their own as far westward as New Guinea, or persuade
1624.   the government to grant them a renewal of their own charter on what they considered reasonable terms. Nevertheless, the East India Company's men found their way to Siam and Japan; they built
1613– factories at Pulicat on the Coromandel coast and at Surat; they
1617.   failed indeed to exclude the English from Bantam, but drove them
1623.   out of Amboyna, not without bloodshed for which Oliver Cromwell made the Netherlands pay dearly at a later day; they occupied Formosa to strengthen their hold on the China tea-trade, and, even when Japan closed her gates to foreigners, they alone of Europeans

---

[1] V.R. Soc., IV. 43; Déherain, *Le Cap de Bonne Espérance au XVIIe Siècle*, p. 7 (*n*).
[2] Rec. S.E.A., VII. 333.

were allowed to carry on a precarious traffic from the barren isle of Desima off Nagasaki harbour. In that same year the Company *1638.* occupied Mauritius and then seized Malacca, where all the sea-roads of the Far East meet, founded a refreshment station at the Cape and *1641–* offset their expulsion from Formosa at the hands of Chinese pirates *1662.* by the conquest of coastal Ceylon. Meanwhile Dutch sailors had haunted the forbidding western shores of Australia and one of them, Tasman, found the island which now bears his name, skirted *1643–* New Zealand, Fiji and Tonga, and narrowly missed anticipating *1644.* Captain Cook's discovery of the fertile eastern shore of the great 'Southland.'

Thus, when the golden age of the independent Netherlands was *Circa* drawing to its close, the Governor-General and Council of India *1660.* controlled seven sub-governorships: Amboyna, Banda, the Cape, Ceylon, Macassar, Malacca and the Moluccas. Of these the youngest and, from the official point of view, the least desirable was the Cape. A full century and a half had passed after its discovery before a permanent European settlement was made there. The Portuguese had given it a wide berth. There was no gold to be had; the Hottentots were reported to be killers of all strangers; there was no doubt that the Cape itself, 'the Lion of the Sea,' surpassed its inhabitants in ferocity towards Portuguese mariners; besides, the Portuguese had St. Helena as a posting-house to India on one side of Africa and Mozambique on the other. But it soon became tolerably certain that either the Dutch or English would occupy the halfway house to India. The course their vessels took to and from the Indies decided that. The course from Europe lay southward in Hanno's tracks to a point off Sierra Leone, then south-westward along the coast of Brazil, and thence on the prevailing westerly winds to the Cape. Portuguese vessels crept up the Mozambique channel to Goa, but the rest ran far out towards the coast of Australia and then on the South-easter to the Spice Islands. The homeward course lay southward of Madagascar to the Cape once more, and so home by way of St. Helena. The Cape was the one point, coming and going, at which ships could conveniently make landfall.[1]

The English Company very nearly anticipated its Dutch rival. Sir Thomas Roe put into Table Bay with four ships on which were *1615.* 'some Japonezas returning to their own country,' and also eight 'lewd malefactors' to whom King James, least bloodthirsty of monarchs, had granted their lives on condition that they went exploring and thereby gained much-needed time for repentance. These men were set ashore at Table Bay. One was killed by the outraged Hottentots; four others were swept out to sea on a raft; the

[1] S. F. N. Gie, *Geskiedenis van Suid-Afrika*, l. 43 ff.

survivors were rescued and taken home to England, where they promptly stole a purse and were hanged for their pains. In the following year three more gaol-birds were landed, but a tender-hearted captain took them off and carried them to Bantam. Then, four years later, a much more definite attempt was made to secure the halfway house to India. Andrew Shilling and Humphrey Fitz-Herbert of the English Company's service 'took quiet and peaceable possession of the Bay of Saldania' in King James's name; but that canny sovereign declined the gift and Table Bay still waited for a master.[1]

June, 1620.

It waited for full thirty years while Dutch and English ships put in more and more regularly for fresh water and the letters which they left for one another under the 'post-office stones' which now adorn South African museums. Meanwhile the Dutch East India Company took St. Helena and notably increased its holdings in the Indies, and the West India Company strengthened the grip of the Netherlands on the West Coast of Africa at Goree, Elmina, and Axim. Then, the Indiaman, *Haarlem*, was wrecked in Table Bay. The crew reached shore and remained there, growing their own food in the style of Necho's mariners, till they were rescued by the return fleet twelve months later. They were glad to go and gladdest of all was their sub-factor, Leendert Janssen, who had had much trouble with his men. No one had a good word to say for the Cape. The admiral of the return fleet cursed it because there were so few supplies available that he had to put into St. Helena, and one of the ship's surgeons, Johan van Riebeeck, who spent much time ashore, gave a most uncomplimentary description of the Hottentots, 'a faithless rabble.'[2]

1617– 1645.

March, 1647– March, 1648.

Yet when Janssen was asked to report, he and Nicolaas Proot, another member of the crew of the *Haarlem*, couched their *Remonstrantie* in such glowing terms that, after much debate, the Chamber of Amsterdam was instructed to make the Cape a strongly-held rendezvous in place of St. Helena, where dogs were sadly ravaging the game.[3]

1649.

1650.

The task of founding the refreshment station on Table Bay was entrusted to the aforementioned van Riebeeck, a thick-set, determined little man of thirty-three, tanned by the sun of the West Indies, Siam and China, and hard-bitten with the winds of Greenland. His instructions were precise. He was to build a fort 'to bear the name of the Good Hope' capable of housing some eighty men, to plant a garden 'in the best and fattest land,' and to keep on good terms with the natives for the sake of the cattle-trade.[4] Perhaps, as Janssen and Proot had suggested, 'if God bless the work,' many souls would be

---

[1] E. Terry, *A Voyage to East India*, pp. 24 ff.; Harris, *Collection of Voyages*, I. 149; *Letters received by the East India Company*, III. 119, 317; IV. 122; *The English Factories in India, 1618–21*, p. 215; Barrow, *Travels* (1801), I. 2.
[2] *Journal 1651–62*, I. 8.   [3] *Lett. Rec.*, 1649–62, I. 1 ff.
[4] *Ibid.*, I. 28 ff.

'brought to the Christian reformed religion and to God' (these things still looked well in a prospectus); but, in any case, the new commander must make sure of the water-supply and the meat, vegetables and fruit which were to save the lives of many who must otherwise die of scurvy. Captains could put off their sick to recover in the pleasant Mediterranean climate of the Cape, take on fresh hands and still earn their bonus of £50 by making the run from the Texel to Batavia within six months. The Cape then was to be occupied as 'a depot of provisions for the ships.' The directors were insistent on that score. For that purpose alone, they told a later governor, was the place kept up at great expense.[1]

So on April 6, 1652, the three ships, *Goede Hoop*, *Dromedaris* and *Reiger*, dropped anchor in Table Bay after a run of four months from the Texel with only two deaths and one birth. It was a good omen. Next day, van Riebeeck stepped ashore to begin the history of the Cape Colony.

Van Riebeeck ruled the Cape for ten years, not without reproachful appeals to the Seventeen to 'think of our removal and promotion . . . in India.' Nevertheless, he did his duty by his employers.[2] His first business on landing was to build his little fort of the Good Hope, a humble erection of earth and timber on a site near the present main line railway station. Having thus guarded the water-supply, he set his master-gardener, Hendrik Boom, to lay out the Company's garden, and himself organised a government for the new settlement.

The machinery of government was easily organised: indeed, it had been in a great measure in existence before van Riebeeck landed. In the background were the *Heeren Majores*, the mighty Seventeen. Instructions might reach the Cape from them or from one or other of the Chambers, usually the all-pervading Chamber of Amsterdam; the Cape reported and requisitioned on them in the same way; a copy of the Commander's journal had to go to Holland each year, where it might or might not be read, for certainly some of the Chambers never received copies. But Amsterdam was far away; *instans tyrannus* was the Governor-General at Batavia. The Commander must take the oath of obedience to His Excellency; appeals lay to him and his Council of India; the books must be sent to him annually for inspection and reports on the state of trade at intervals; from Batavia came orders to curtail expenditure, to direct

---

[1] *Lett. Rec., 1695-1708*, pp. 15, 16.
[2] On van Riebeeck's governorship *vide* Godée-Molsbergen, *Jan van Riebeeck and Dagverhael*; Déherain, *Le Cap . . . au XVIIe Siècle*; Leibbrandt, *Précis of the Archives. Letters Despatched, 1652-62; Letters Received, 1649-62; Journal, 1651-62; Rambles through the Archives; Resolutien*; Blue Book, No. 50 of 1835, pp. 9 ff.; D. Moodie, *Specimens of the Authentic Records of the . . . Cape*; C. L. Leipoldt, *Jan van Riebeeck.*

the movements of shipping, and to see to it that the Company's crews were supplied with better food in future.[1]

But even Batavia was three months' sail away to the eastward, and eighteen months might pass before an answer was received to a despatch. Isolation ensured that the powers of the local government at the Cape were very great. That government was vested in the Commander, since for many years the Cape was not sufficiently important to warrant a full-blown Governor, and a Council of Policy. The Council was really a ship's council and might become a Broad Council by the inclusion of officers from ships in the Bay. That was the common practice in the Company's fleets, and van Riebeeck had summoned such a council to his flagship a few days after leaving the Texel when he was faced with heavy weather and the proximity of Prince Rupert's privateers. The Commander took the chair at the Council, be it narrow or broad, unless a superior officer was present. To such he must give way, whether he was an ordinary commissioner or a high commissioner armed with the plenary powers of the Seventeen. But in these early days ordinary commissioners were rare and no high commissioner landed till 1685, when the *heeren majores* were minded to transform their refreshment station into a real colony.

The personnel of the Council of Policy varied; but, whatever its composition, it was Leviathan. It was the executive, though the Commander could, if he wished, utter the magic formula, 'ik neem haet op mij,' and override its advice;[2] it was the legislature, issuing *placaaten* on all manner of subjects from the cattle-trade to the illicit sale of soldiers' clothing; it was also the nucleus of the High Court of Justice. As such its form was somewhat regularised when van
1656.   Riebeeck added the judicial wisdom of the constable of the fort and the two corporals to that of its ordinary members; its scope was
1657–   widened when he summoned first one and then two burgher coun-
1658.   cillors when justice was to be done on the free burghers who presently appeared.[3]

The Company made its own arrangements for the cure of souls. The *Classis* (Presbytery) of Amsterdam licensed ministers and their understudies, the sick-comforters, and throughout it remained the court of ecclesiastical appeal; but it was the Company which installed and paid the minister, gave him a *pastorie* to live in, kept a strict watch on his doings and, when necessary, transferred him like any other of its servants. No minister was stationed at the Cape for the first thirteen years, because the settlement was too small to

---

[1] Till *circa* 1735, when Batavia was forbidden to issue orders to the Cape to avoid confusion.
[2] 'I take it upon myself'; V.R. Soc., IV. 138 ff.
[3] *Resolutien*, p. 110; Theal, IIa. 65, 88.

have a minister of its own for the first thirteen years. It must make shift with such occasional chaplains as landed from the fleets and with the devoted sick-comforter, Willem Wylant, who came out with van Riebeeck, and, after him, Pieter van der Stael. But the sick-comforter's powers were rigidly limited. He might neither administer the sacrament nor marry nor bury; he might indeed read prayers and other men's sermons, but did he presume to use his own words, even in emergency, he was liable to reprimand as poor Wylant found. Marriages in the early days were celebrated by the omnicompetent Council of Policy after the banns had been called thrice by the sick-comforter.[1]

At first this embryo Government had only three classes of persons to deal with: Company's servants, Bushmen and Hottentots. The servants were a mixed party, for the Company recruited Protestants of all classes and nations; but they were under strict discipline and, during the first five years, there were neither free burghers nor slaves to complicate the issue. At first, also, the native problem appeared to be equally simple, for it was not until 1685 that the Netherlanders recognised the distinction between Bushmen and Hottentot.[2] To the early Commanders the natives were just natives, 'dull, stupid, lazy and stinking,' according to van Riebeeck, 'zwarte stinkende Honden' in the eyes and nostrils of the colonists.

The Bushmen were relics of the Stone Age.[3] Their neighbours may be pardoned for doubting whether they were quite human, for they were little sallow folk, barely five feet high, their heads adorned with peppercorn tufts of hair and lobeless ears, their triangular fox-like faces almost innocent of beards. Their twinkling eyes were deep-set beneath upright foreheads, their noses broad and low-rooted, their jaws projecting; and their slender limbs and tiny feet seemed ill-fitted to bear the protuberant stomachs of the men or the pendulous breasts and fat buttocks of the women.

Unprepossessing in appearance the Bushmen were, and every man's hand was against them, for they were hunters, and between Jacob, the tender of flocks and herds, and Esau, the wanderer, there can be no peace. They wandered about in clans of three hundred souls at most, each calling itself by the name of some sacred animal and each under a chief who was little more than a war-leader. Family ties were weak; the older men practised polygamy and the younger men sometimes had to fight for their wives; but even the marriage tie was feeble; parental authority practically ended when the children could shift for themselves, and the sick and aged were

[1] Spoelstra, *Bouwstoffen*, I. 1.; II. 544, 594; *Lett. Rec., 1649–62*; I. 126.
[2] Stow says the Strandloopers constituted a third group of natives more nearly allied to the Bushmen than to the Hottentot (*Native Races of South Africa*, p. 245).
[3] On the Bushmen, *vide* Stow, *Native Races of South Africa*, chapters 1–12; Theal, Ia, chapter 1; *C.H.B.E.*. VIII. 21 ff.

2

abandoned when they could no longer keep up with the party. Their religion, as far as is known, was rudimentary. Fear of violating custom, the use of charms against witches, propitiation of spirits, and a vague belief in immortality were common to all of them; but some believed also in Kaang, the chief of the Sky, and others, it is said, prayed to the moon and stars. Their language, full of queer clicks, was limited in vocabulary and devoid of plurals; their knowledge of numbers stopped short at three; but they made up for linguistic and mathematical shortcomings by great skill in painting and carving. Therein they rivalled the Palæolithic men who produced the marvels of Altamira. Their other artistic accomplishments were a love of story-telling, a genius for mimicry, and a capacity for dancing which seems to be indigenous to the soil of South Africa. For the rest, they had few of the comforts or amenities of life. They procured fire by friction, lived in huts or under reed wind-screens, decked themselves with ornaments of shell and ostrich egg, smoked dagga and, on occasion, made merry on a mead of fermented root-juice and honey; but they had no domestic animals, other than the dog, the first friend of man; they had neither metals nor weaving nor agriculture; their pottery was of the rudest; they relied for their food on the roots and ants' eggs which the women dug up with digging-sticks weighted at the lower end with a pierced round stone, or the game which the men brought down with their little poisoned arrows.

There is a monotony about the story of the dealings of other races with the little hunters. The Iron Age and the Stone could not live side by side. To the Bushmen the cattle of the Europeans and Hottentots were merely fat lethargic game and their owners trespassers on the hunting-grounds; to the Europeans and Hottentots, the Bushmen were a nuisance and, at times, a danger. Van Riebeeck found them in Table Mountain, whence they raided farms at Wynberg as late as 1678; explorers on the way north-eastward to Monomotapa killed some; another party killed a few near Mossel Bay; but, during the first twenty-five years, the main pre-occupation of the Dutch was with the Hottentots rather than the Bushmen.

1660–
1668.

The Hottentots, much later comers than the Bushmen, were thinly scattered in small loosely organised clans from Walvis Bay in what is now South-West Africa to the Umtamvuna river in Natal.[1] Physically they were bigger than the despised Bushmen; *khoi-khoi* they were, in their own eyes, 'men of men' compared with them. Other observers were less laudatory, for though some of the Hottentots were as tall as Europeans and could even boast of beards, all of them were of slight build with backs as hollow and hands and feet as small

[1] On the Hottentots *vide* Stow, *op. cit.*, chapters 13–16; Theal, Ia, chapter 2; J. M. Orpen, *Reminiscences*, pp. 33 ff.; *C.H.B.E.*, VIII. 28 ff.

as the Bushmen's; their eyes were far apart, their cheeks sunken and their chins pointed, their skins a dingy olive-yellow. 'The Hottentots,' wrote John Maxwell, an English visitor to the Cape, '. . . are a race of men distinct both from negroes and European whites, for their hair is woolly, short and frizzled, their noses flat, and their lips thick, but their skin is naturally as white as ours. . . . They besmear their faces and bodies all over with suet or other oleaginous stuff, which together with exposing their bodies to a warm sun, makes their skin of a tawny colour, and causes them so to stink that one may smell 'em at a considerable distance to windward. They adorn their hair . . . with shells, pieces of copper, etc. Both sexes are clad with the skin commonly of a sheep . . . the hairy side outward in summer but inward in winter. . . . They go barefooted, except when they travel they wear a piece of skin fasten'd about their feet. Their weapons are javelins . . . and bows with poisoned arrows. . . . Their houses are hemispherical, made of mats supported with stakes. . . . I believe their ignorance can hardly be parallel'd.' [1]

1708.

It is a sufficiently unflattering picture, but the Hottentots were half-way between the Copper and Iron Ages, millennia in advance of the Bushmen hunters. They used copper freely and could work iron if they chose; above all, they were pastoralists whose main wealth lay in cattle. The beasts were the care of the men, but once the milk, their staple diet, was taken inside the huts, it passed into the keeping of the women. The clans were bound together by no tribal unity; each was ruled by an hereditary chief, whose rule was rarely strong, for riches counted for more than rank and the religious sanctions behind the chieftainship were feeble. Polygamy was practised by the wealthier men; [2] but little care was bestowed on the sick and aged and, from a pastoral people, little could be expected. Their language was much fuller than that of the Bushmen, from whom they had, none the less, borrowed many clicks; they were as fond of story-telling and dancing as they, but they lacked much of their bravery and all their artistic talent, for they neither carved nor painted.

The Hottentot armament was much more varied than the excellent Maxwell thought, for, besides their arrows and assegais, either hardened in fire or tipped with metal, they used clubs, carried small hide-shields and, in the case of the Namaquas, hide breastplates as well, and even trained bulls to act as bovine tanks, a screen in battle. Again, Maxwell held that they were devoid of all religious observance except for 'a custom they have in moonshiny nights of dancing in the fields, of which if you ask 'em the reason all their answer is that

---

[1] J. Maxwell (1708), V.R. Soc., V. 49 ff.
[2] John Ovington (1693) says there was no polygamy except among the chiefs, who might entertain three wives at once (V.R. Soc., V. 104).

it is a custom of the Hottentots, and was so of their forefathers.'[1] Later and more competent students state that all believed in charms and witches, some in the magical powers of the python, and the Namaquas, at least, in a good being who lived in the red sky and a bad being in the black.

Few pure-blooded Hottentots survive today. They have disappeared by death or absorption into the ranks of the multitudinous mixed-breeds of Southern Africa; even in van Riebeeck's time they were not numerous; but such as they were, they constituted his native problem, cheerful, dirty, hospitable to the verge of improvidence and beyond, given to petty larceny, huge eaters of anything available and good starvers in lean times, odoriferous (all authorities are agreed upon that), grateful and true, some said, to anyone who kept faith with them, and incurably indolent. 'Their Native Inclination to Idleness and a careless Life,' laments Maxwell, 'will scarce admit of either Force or Rewards for reclaiming them from that innate Lethargick humour.'[2]

Van Riebeeck found three clans wandering with their sheep and cattle in and about the Cape Peninsula: Herry's Strandloopers or, to give them their full title, Goringhaikonas, a mere eighteen strong; the Kaapmen or Goringhaikuas, some 600 warriors in all, and the Koras, Gorachouquas or tobacco-thieves, 300 fighting-men all told. Explorers and visitors soon taught him of the existence of other clans: the Chainouquas and Hessequas to the east; two groups of Chochoquas, the strongest of all the local clans, under Gonnema and Oedosoa in the neighbourhood of Saldanha Bay; Little Grigriquas on this side of the Olifant's river, and Great Grigriquas and Namaquas beyond.[3]

After a brief experience, van Riebeeck favoured a drastic solution of the native question: the seizure of the Hottentot cattle and the shipping off of their owners as slaves to the Indies.[4] But his instructions stood in the way, and he strove to keep the peace and do business. At first his orders to his men were marked by a certain nervousness: do not molest them even when they steal the very copper buttons from the children's clothes; go armed, but do not stray far from the fort for fear of massacre; do not trade with them privately under pain of dismissal; treat them kindly even after Herry and the 'Watermans' had killed the herdboy, David Jansen, and stolen forty-four head of Company's cattle. This last exploit did, however, impel him to send an armed party under a corporal to 1653. False Bay to recover the cattle by force if necessary.[5] It was the first

[1] V.R. Soc., V. 50.
[2] Ibid., IV. 36,; V. 105.
[3] Theal, IIa. 126–7; Moodie, Records, I. 247.
[4] Journal, 1651–62, I. 51.
[5] XXXIX. No. 50 of 1835, pp. 9, 10; Moodie, Records, I. 10, 16, 36.

such expedition, the first of many. Bickering between the local clans, however, interrupted the all-important cattle-trade; hence, exploring parties were sent inland, the one beyond False Bay, the other 1655. Malmesbury way, to barter with more distant peoples. The desire for knowledge, precious stones and the gold of Monomotapa, the expected discovery of the mythical city of Vigiti Magna and the rumoured river of Cammissa are in no wise to be ignored; but one of the prime incentives to the exploration of Africa from the South was the search for fresh meat.

At this stage, van Riebeeck's responsibilities were immeasurably increased by the appearance of free burghers and imported slaves in the infant colony. The black and white extremes of South Africa's labour problem arrived simultaneously. The Seventeen long hesitated before they permitted any but their own servants to reside at the Cape. Governor-General Coen's scheme for the settlement of Euro- 1619–peans in the tropical East Indies had not been a success; free settlers 1630. would be expensive to send out and would certainly demand slaves, a further source of expense; they might even give rise to the political complications which were afflicting the West India Company in its cosmopolitan settlement of New Amsterdam, where the burghers, 1647–stimulated by immigrants from New England, were making Governor 1664. Stuyvesant's life a burden with their demands for autonomy.[1]

Generally speaking, the Company was against colonisation. That was not its object, though it was prepared to embark upon it for good and sufficient reasons. Its main aim was necessarily profit arising from the trade monopoly. Its whole commercial policy, in common with that of all chartered companies of the day, was monopolistic; competition was simply not permitted. The massacre of Amboyna, the seizure of Malacca, the exclusion of the English from the Spice Islands by the Treaty of Breda, the closing of Java to the English and 1667. French were all stages in the stranglehold which the Dutch Company 1684. acquired upon the spice-trade of the Indies. Coen indeed had used the Chinese as middlemen in the spice traffic and even encouraged private venturers to trade with China and Japan on payment of duties; but, as a rule, the Company guarded the spices most rigorously and strove to destroy all rival traders whether native or European. Coen himself wiped out the people of Banda and allowed 1621. only nutmegs to be grown there and cloves in Amboyna; Ternate 1680. was ravaged; in good years crops were burnt to keep up prices in the narrow European market; native princes were even subsidised to root up redundant spice trees.

Though there was no native industry to be destroyed at the Cape and no spice-trade to guard, the spirit and methods of the Dutch

[1] Keller, *Colonization*, p. 450.

Indian administration were applied there in full force. The Directors meant to keep the trade monopoly, but they also wanted a supply of meat, grain and wine for their ships. So far official farming had not been very successful, and the importation of supplies was expensive. Van Riebeeck and his immediate successor, like so many East Indian officials of their time, would have preferred industrious Chinese; the Seventeen, however, decided to try the experiment of setting free some of its servants to grow cattle, corn and wine for the ships and possibly the Indian stations with due precautions that they did not trench upon the sacred trade monopoly.

1657. Hence, nine free burghers, all of them married men of Dutch or German birth, were established in the Liesbeeck valley on small farms of 13⅓ morgen free of land tax for twelve years.[1] The terms of their freedom were laid down by van Riebeeck and relaxed somewhat by a visiting commissioner, Rykloff van Goens. They were bound to remain for twenty years;[2] they were to take turns in manning the redoubts which the Commander had built to supplement the Fort: Duynhoop overlooking the whale fishery on Woodstock beach, and Coornhoop 'in the middle of the ploughlands,' where now is Mowbray; they were to pay one-tenth of their cattle to the Company in return for pasturage; to sell cattle to the Company, which guaranteed to take all they could offer at a fixed price; to pay no more to the Hottentots for beasts than the Company paid and to have no further dealings with them; to abstain from growing tobacco lest they hurt the Company's importation; to grow no more vegetables than they needed for their own wants and, if there was a surplus after their own and the Company's wants had been supplied, to abstain from selling it to visiting crews for the first three days after their arrival. Purveyors of meat, corn and wine to the Company: that is what the free burghers were by intention. 'I once more recommend you,' wrote van Goens, 'to attend above all to the . . . cultivation of grain. We shall never become noblemen here until we have first become good farmers.'[3]

The process of becoming noblemen at all on such terms was likely to be a long one. Even the limited market on ship-board was precarious. Ships were few and far between, perhaps twenty-five Company's vessels and a stray Englishman or Frenchman, say, 5000 souls annually, each stopping for ten days or so; besides it was not clear whether the Seventeen meant the Cape to be a place of refreshment for foreign ships at all. English ships were well received at first; but,

---

[1] Keller, IIa. 62, 64; *Lett. Desp. 1652–62*, II. 314; III. 260 ff.; *Lett. Rec. 1649–62*, II. 326; *Journal, 1651–62*, II. 48. A morgen is 2·11654 English acres, rather less than one hectare.
[2] By the end of the century the term was fifteen years (*Letter Rec., 1695–1708*, p. 268).
[3] Moodie, *Records*, I. 97.

in 1656, the Seventeen, worried by a shortage of supplies, only permitted foreigners to take in water, catch fish and buy vegetables from such folk as had gardens. As a rule, however, visiting crews could get what they wanted in the way of provisions, and once at least van Riebeeck had to placate some of them with presents to make up for the poor cattle supplied to them. Nevertheless, the free burghers were painfully restricted and, within a year of the issue of their papers of freedom, they presented an ultimatum to the Government.

Van Riebeeck disliked the idea of private trade with the natives. He had forbidden it because the bartering of ivory, rhinoceros horns, ostrich eggs and turtles with his men distracted the Hottentots' 1654. attention from their appointed function of purveying cattle to the Company.[1] Van Goens had overridden him, and at once free burghers had scattered to barter cattle with the clans.[2] Van Riebeeck 1658. checked this diaspora by forbidding them to go far away and persuading the Seventeen to ban the private cattle-barter altogether. He relied on official trading only and sent one expedition to traffic at Saldanha Bay and another to seek for ivory, feathers, gold, 1657– precious stones and cattle among the Chainouquas beyond the 1658. Great Berg river.[3] Meanwhile, he formed a herd of Company's cattle in the Peninsula and of sheep on Robben Island, and, to make matters worse, forbade burghers to board the ships to sell their vegetables because some men had fled from the Cape as stowaways. The burghers in a body presented a list of grievances, adding that the Company's price for grain compared with the cost of labour was 1658. impossible. 'Let a price be fixed,' they wrote, 'for till that is done, we will not cultivate any more ground, for we will not be slaves to the Company.'[4] It was a strike in bad times, the first open move towards real freedom by the burghers. Having talked out their troubles with the Commander, they departed much relieved and were rewarded by a slight increase in the price of corn and the removal of the embargo on selling to visiting crews; but their other woes remained unassuaged.

Van Riebeeck tried to meet the demand for labour by importing slaves. The domestic institution spread almost automatically from the Indies to the halfway house. A dozen slaves from Java and Madagascar were landed in 1657 and proved so useful that two ships, *Maria* and *Hasselt*, were sent into the West India Company's sphere to get more. Meanwhile, *Amersfoort*, Indiaman, came in with the 1658.

---

[1] No. 50 of 1835, p. 10 ; Moodie, *Records*, I. 54.
[2] *Journal, 1651–62*, II. 93; *Rambles*, p. 62.
[3] No. 50 of 1835, p. 10; Moodie, *Records*, I. 108, 112, 119 ff.
[4] *Journal, 1651–62*, II. 195.

170 survivors of 250 slaves she had taken from a leaky Portugee in mid-ocean, so that the demand was met before *Hasselt* returned with 185 picked up on the Slave Coast. The unwanted balance was forwarded to Batavia, and the colony essayed to absorb the rest. The first importation was not a success. The newly imported Angolese were governed generally by the statutes of Batavia issued by Governor-General van Diemen in 1642, but van Reibeeck, mindful of the warning that the world is disquieted for a servant when he reigneth, issued special regulations for their protection and bade the sick-comforter teach them the rudiments of Christianity with tobacco and brandy as prizes. The regulations were of little avail; many of the slaves fled and the burghers concluded that West African negroes were more nuisance than they were worth. Henceforward, the Cape left Angolese severely alone, since they were more dangerous than the very Hottentots, and imported from Madagascar, Delagoa Bay and the Indies. There was a little private speculation, but as a rule the Company undertook the traffic. Some slaves it kept for its own use; others it hired out, and others again it sold at about £6 a head payable in wheat.[1]

The flight of the Angolese served to complicate the non-European problem. Trouble had already begun with the Kaapmen. The colony was growing and the clansmen 'dwelt long upon our taking every day . . . more of the land which had belonged to them from all ages.' Van Goens had proposed a thorough-going scheme of segregation by cutting a canal to sever the peninsula of *De Kaap* from the Flats and Africa, but expense and van Riebeeck were against him. The Commander for his part proposed to set up a line of redoubts within which the Kaapmen's women, children and cattle should be kept while the men were sent out to barter cattle.[2] But for a time, nothing was done beyond telling the Kaapmen that they must keep without the line of the Liesbeeck and Salt rivers. Then van Riebeeck arrested Herry the Strandlooper and some of the Kaapmen to make the others give back the runaway slaves and the murderers of the Company's herdsmen. The result was war.

1658–1660. This Hottentot war was a scuffling affair mixed up with the intertribal bickerings of Namaquas and Chochoquas (Saldanhars); but it had a marked influence on the military system of the little colony. The Company's troops were a cosmopolitan crew, mercenaries of Dutch or German extraction.[3] Their strength varied, for Batavia was always apt to take away drafts; but usually van Riebeeck had

---

[1] Theal, IIa. 79, 238; Déherain, chapter 6; No. 50 of 1835, p. 11; *Lett. Rec., 1695–1708*, pp. 24, 288; Moodie, *Records*, I. 122; W. Blommaert, *Slavernij aan de Kaap.*

[2] Theal, IIa. 71; Moodie, *Records*, I. 205.

[3] *Lett. Rec., 1649–62*, II. p. 241. On the defence system *vide* P. E. Roux, *Die Verdedigingstelsel aan die Kaap . . . 1652–1795.*

anything from 70 to 170 men. The free burghers were called on to
supplement the garrison. From the first they had been obliged to
defend the redoubts in turn. Now, in the midst of the Hottentot war,
they were organised as musketeers, the nucleus of the Cape burgher
infantry,[1] and a council of war (Krygsraad) was created: the captain 1659.
of militia, two burgher councillors, a sergeant, a corporal and a paid
secretary, with a war-chest replenished with fines for dereliction of
duty by able-bodied burghers, all of whom were liable to service at
suitable rates of pay. The members of the Krygsraad were selected
annually by the Council of Policy from a double list presented by the
outgoing raad, an old Netherland practice which ran through Cape
local government in the seventeenth and eighteenth centuries. During
the Kaapmen war soldiers were billeted on the farms; dogs and slaves
armed with spears assisted the burghers and the troops.[2] At last, Nov.
peace was made with the Kaapmen, who had to recognise that the 1660.
Liesbeeck lands were lost to them for ever.

To secure the lands thus won, van Riebeeck gave orders that all
barter was to be conducted at the Fort and that Hottentots must
keep to the road within the colonial borders. He marked out those
borders with a fence of poles and a bitter-almond hedge from Salt
river mouth to the mountain slopes behind Wynberg; along the
line of the Liesbeeck he built three blockhouses: Kyckuyt, Keert de
Koe and Houd den Bul—significant names—and, beyond it, on the 1659–
edge of the sandy flats, stationed a mounted guard at the Ruyter- 1660.
borst. A system of flag signals was arranged to give warning of
impending attack and van Riebeeck sat down behind his hedge, the
last comprehensive frontier the colony was to have till 1798![3]

The insistent demand for beef threatened to trample down the
new frontier. The Hottentots would not stay outside the hedge, the
Europeans could not stay inside it. The Company must have meat,
while war and indiscriminate barter for tobacco, copper and trinkets
had so impoverished the local clans that there was little to be had.
There was joy at headquarters when the Hessequas came in from
distant Caledon; but even that was not enough; van Riebeeck had
to send his men far afield. 'You must,' he told them, 'try every
imaginable means to persuade them to come to the fort or at least
to send some of their people with you,'[4] and, regularly every year, 1657–
exploring parties fared forth to find Monomotapa, Vigiti Magna and 1662.
Cammissa, but also to get in touch with the Namaquas—white
people, it was said, with long hair and rich in cattle, three or four

[1] *Journal, 1651–62*, III., 14; No. 50 of 1835, p. 12.
[2] *Ibid.*, 17, 23; Moodie, *Records*, I. 221 ff.
[3] *Lett. Rec., 1649–62*, II. 274, 309, 340; *Journal, 1649–62*, III. 91, 138. Part of
this hedge survives as a national monument and a witness to the failure of the
first attempt at *apartheid*.
[4] *Rambles*, p. 13; *Journal, 1651–62*, III. 6, 214.
2*

weeks' trek to the northward. Jan Danckearts, Pieter Everaert, Pieter Cruythoff and Pieter van Meerhof all pushed on beyond the Olifants river till drought and Bushmen proved too much for them; nevertheless, the Namaquas were found, Hottentots like the rest.[1] At the last, van Riebeeck, who had already mediated peace between the Saldanhars and Namaquas, intervened once more in high tribal politics and offered to sell the Company's protection to the Cape clans against Oedosoa's Chocohquas. But nothing came of it, and, in 1662, 'the Commander' was allowed to sail for Malacca.

Van Riebeeck sailed east with joy to make his fortune, but his ten years' work at the Cape constitute his claim to remembrance. He had found a sandy shore and a green valley; he left behind him the little village of De Kaap, a mere huddle of houses, it is true, but an unmistakable centre of Western civilisation running back from the Zee Straat or, as men call it now, Strand Street to Longmarket Street. To the east stood the fort; behind the village to the south were the Company's Gardens, a sight for the weary eyes of scurvy-stricken mariners; around lay the gardens of the burghers and officials. The Company had its own farm and orchard at Rondebosch, and, hard by, the big barn which still bears the name of Groote Schuur; the Commander's own farm lay at Wynberg near the Boscheuvel on the southern frontier, and, on either side of the Liesbeeck river, were the farms of free burghers, the foundation members of 'white South Africa.' Bushmen hunters and Hottentot tribesmen might be kept out of the Colony with fair success, but, already, within the narrow confines of the settlement, there were slaves, half-castes and detribalised natives. All the economic and social problems which exercise South Africa to-day had begun to take shape before van Riebeeck's eyes. For, in South Africa at least, there is nothing whereof it may be said 'See, this is new.' It hath been already of old time, which was before us.

Seventeen troubled years passed between van Riebeeck's departure and the arrival of the 'second founder of the Colony,' Simon van der Stel. The European settlement was tiny. There had been 46 free adults and 14 children in 1660; twelve years later there were 64 free men who, with the garrison, gave the Commander a force of 370 all told;[2] but marriageable women were scarce. Van Riebeeck for this 1656. reason, and in keeping with East Indian precedents, had recommended mixed marriages, and Jan Wouter had duly wedded Catherine, a freed woman, daughter of Antonie of Bengal. Then van Meerhof, the doughty explorer, married Eva, a Hottentot. He was

[1] On travels to the northward *vide* E. C. Godee-Molsbergen, *Reizen*, I. (Linschoten Vereeniging).
[2] *Lett. Desp., 1652-62*, III. 273; *Journal, 1671-8*, p. 81.

the first European to marry a Hottentot and received promotion
to the rank of surgeon as a wedding present from the Company. On
his death Eva went to the bad; but as a Christian she was buried in
the Fort and a burgher took her two half-caste children to Mauritius,
where one presently married a European.[1] There were already Bantu
slaves and detribalised Hottentots in the little Colony; now, Asians 1667.
began to arrive, Moslems sent from India to the Cape to expiate their
crimes in servitude for a term of years. Miscegenation of all these
elements began, and soon three-fourths of such slave children as
there were, were half-breeds. The Cape Coloured Folk had emerged.

A flow back from the farms was noticeable; even so in 1660 there
were only sixteen free families in the town: ten mechanics, one
grocer, one baker, and four canteen-keepers. Canteen-keeping
became so popular that the number of licences had to be limited to 1670.
nine for the whole settlement.[2] There was even a flow out of the
Colony, for men smuggled themselves on board ship. 'It is to be
lamented,' wrote van Quaelberg, 'that Your Honour's Colonies . . . 1667.
do not advance . . . because the Colonists as soon as they find they
are not allowed their head, always turn head and ears towards
Fatherland.'[3]

Nevertheless, the settlement grew slowly, and the machinery of
government was elaborated to meet the new needs. Van Riebeeck's
four immediate successors had to be content with his humble title
of Commander; the next two, Goske and Bax, enjoyed the style of 1672–
Governor, for it was war-time and the halfway house to India 1679.
assumed a new importance; but their more famous successor, van
der Stel, was merely Commander till 1691, when he was rewarded
for his services with the higher office. Henceforward the Cape was
ruled by Governors till the hasty arrival of Special Commissioners in
1792 heralded the end of the Company's rule.

The free burghers were given a larger share in the business of
government. Three of them were given seats on the High Court, 1675.
whence they presented a list of grievances to a visiting commissioner;
in other words these burgher councillors, thus early, went beyond
their lawful judicial functions and virtually claimed to speak on
behalf of the whole body of freemen.[4] Burghers were also represented
on two newly created boards: the Matrimonial Court of two officials
and two burghers before whom intending brides and bridegrooms 1676.
had to appear, by no means a hardship in these early days but an
intolerable grievance later on when the confines of the Colony had
disappeared into the waste spaces of Africa, and the Orphan 1674.
Chamber, again of two officials and two burghers under a president
appointed by the Commander. No widow or widower might re-marry

[1] Moodie, *Records*, I. 279, 354.   [2] Theal, IIa. 158, 179.
[3] Moodie, *Records*, I. 191, 300.   [4] Theal, IIa. 224.

without satisfying the latter committee that the rights of their children had been safeguarded; the committee itself invested the orphans' money and thus played a useful part as a loan bank.[1] Half the members of each board retired annually and their places were filled from a double list as in the case of the Krygsraad.

This principle of selection co-optation was also applied to the Church. The first two sick-comforters were satisfactory enough, but the conduct of the third was so scandalous that the Council inter-

1665. preted the appearance of a great shooting star as a direct warning and shipped him away forthwith. They were rewarded by the arrival of a fully qualified predikant, Johan van Arckel, whom they welcomed by putting the state ecclesiastical on a more satisfactory footing. A consistory was formed: the minister in the chair, deacons selected annually by the Council from a double list presented by the consistory, elders elected by the congregation and confirmed by Council, and a councillor as political commissioner to take note of the proceedings. Such was the Erastian system which held good in essentials till 1843. A wooden church was also set up in the midst of

1666. the confusion which marked the beginning of the new Castle and, though van Arckel was buried there all too soon in the year after his coming, the Cape was never afterwards without the ministrations of regular clergy.[2]

The Castle was the centre of the new scheme of defence which the Company undertook on the outbreak of war with England.

1665. Pieter Dombar designed it on the most approved model of Louis XIV's great military engineer, Vauban. Commander Wagenaar laid the first stone; convicts and slaves busily collected timber at Hout Bay and shells for lime on Robben Island till the Peace of Breda stopped the work. In 1672, however, Louis of France attacked the United Provinces, building was hastily resumed and, two years later, the garrison moved into its new quarters; but again peace hindered the work and it was only by dint of commandeering passers-by to

1677. help with the digging of the ditch that Governor Bax more or less finished it. A little later the five bastions were named after the chief titles held by the Prince of Orange: Orange, Nassau, Leerdam, Buuren and Katzenellebogen.[3]

From time to time during these years the Cape promised to become the centre of a scattered group of possessions in southern waters;

1662. but de Lairesse's attack on Mozambique failed; the temporary
1673. seizure of St. Helena ended abruptly with the return of the English

---

[1] The Orphan Chamber was increased to six members in 1699 with an official as president and a burgher as vice-president. From 1711 onwards all wills had to be registered with it, and from 1746 executors had to register inventories of estates (Theal, IIa. 223–3).

[2] *Journal, 1662–70*, pp. 153, 169, 172; Theal, IIa. 149; Spoelstra, *op. cit.*, I. 30.

[3] Theal, IIa. 244.

in overwhelming force.[1] Jan Blank's expedition to Madagascar pro- 1663. duced only a miserable seven head of slaves and nine tons of rice, and, though the Zululand coast was twice explored, no permanent acquisition was made by the Company other than Mauritius, which 1664. was re-occupied after a six years' abandonment.

Knowledge of what lay on the mainland immediately beyond the confines of the Colony increased and, with knowledge, European influence. The valleys of the Groote and Klein Berg rivers were thoroughly explored, Riebeeck's Kasteel and Vierentwintig Rivieren named, and the land of Waveren (Tulbagh) entered; de la Guerre and van Meerhof once more struggled on beyond the Olifants river 1663. and made contact with the Great Grigriqua Hottentots; but, in that direction, there was apparently not much hope of expansion, for *Grundel* sailed along an inhospitable shore as far north as Angra 1669. Pequena and *Bode* skirted a dry and thirsty land where no water was as far as Portuguese territory. Meanwhile, Cruse went eastward 1667. through the land of the Hessequas as far as Mossel Bay, where he heard of the Attaqua clan farther on, and, next year, in the course of an attempt to reach Natal by sea, he landed at Mossel Bay, pushed on to 'George,' found the Attaquas and heard of the still more 1668. remote Outeniquas. Later in the year Cruse went back again and, to the great joy of the Hessequas, defeated some Bushmen and recovered looted Hottentot cattle.[2]

Hitherto the Company's cattle-runs, the Schuur, Steenberg, Bommelshoek and Boerboomen, had all lain within the Peninsula or on Robben and Dassen Islands; but now new stations were opened at Saldanha Bay and Vishoek on the far side of False Bay 1666. and, by 1679, Company cattle and sheep were grazing at the Tygerberg, Eerste river and Hottentots-Holland. At each post there was a handful of soldiers to frighten away the Bushmen and keep an eye on the doings of the free burghers. For the question of the food supply was still the main preoccupation of the authorities. It was on this score that they had their chief difficulties with their subjects and their neighbours.

The one industry on which the burghers and local officials desired to embark was cattle and sheep-rearing, and that was the one industry on which their lords and masters were determined they should not. Competition would mean a rise in the price of cattle bartered with the Hottentots, and the Company did not propose to pay more for its meat than it must. The burghers were still allowed to keep cattle: indeed the Company gave them cattle on credit, van Riebeeck compensated them in live-stock for their losses during the Hottentot War of 1659, and the Directors encouraged them by 1668.

[1] The English E.I. Company had held St. Helena since 1659.
[2] Theal, IIIa. index; Godée-Molsbergen, *Reizen*, I. II. III.

forbidding its officials to keep cattle or to have more land than a mere garden; but the *placaat* against cattle-barter with the Hottentots had to be re-issued sixteen times between 1658 and 1680,[1] a proof that the law was systematically disregarded.

Contact with Europeans, official and unofficial, had serious effects on the loose tribal system of the Hottentots. To put it shortly, the Hottentots began to differentiate into three classes: detribalised natives in and about the Colony, clans which remained in touch with the white men but still kept something of their tribal organisation, and clans which saved themselves by withdrawing into the interior. The Company had advertised its intentions to Christianise the 1663. natives, and in the early days Dominie van der Stael did his best: Hottentots were admitted to the reconstituted school alongside of European and slave children, and, a few years later, the salary of the predikant de Voogt was raised because 'die zwarte natie' had made such progress in knowledge of Christianity and the Catechism.[2] A few urban Hottentots like Herry, Eva and the interpreter Doman adopted a more or less European style of life; Willem Willems, the black sheep of the settlement, found to his cost that it was not safe 1676. to kill a Hottentot, for he was first deported to Robben Island and then, at the request of the outraged natives, to the penal settlement of Mauritius.[3] But as a body the Hottentots were not readily absorbed into the ranks of civilised society. Detribalised men hung about eager for surreptitious arrack and tobacco;[4] the older folk begged or sold firewood; the girls went out to inefficient domestic service. So it was with them as early as 1666.

The later developments of van Riebeeck's native policy had not found favour at headquarters. The Chamber of Amsterdam had censured his treatment of the Kaapmen; his successor, Wagenaar, had ordered the Company's servants to be more tactful, and van Quaelberg had decreed that Hottentots were not to be struck nor punished even when they were guilty of misdoing.[5] But now the Company's men felt themselves strong enough to deal decisively with the neighbouring clans. European diseases were completing the break-up of the Hottentots which loss of their cattle had begun; wherefore the Dutch claimed the Peninsula as 'justly won by the 1672. sword'; but, to regularise their position, they went through the farce of buying it and the lands adjacent to False and Saldanha Bays nominally for £1600 and actually for £9 12s. 9d. in goods.[6] Meanwhile, the Directors had rejected van Riebeeck's proposal to sell the Company's protection to one clan against another, and had bidden

[1] *Rambles*, p. 62.   [2] No. 50 of 1835, p. 13.
[3] *Ibid.*, p. 14; Moodie, *Records*, I. 343, 381.
[4] Sale of liquor to Hottentots was illegal (No. 50 of 1835, p. 13).
[5] No. 50 of 1835, p. 13; Moodie, *Records*, I. 255, 297.
[6] *Ibid.*, 205, 317.

van Quaelberg abstain from intervention in tribal politics; nevertheless, the Cape Government began to give brass-headed staffs' to 1673.
selected chiefs as a recognition of their chiefdom[1] and supported
Klaas the Chainouqua against his enemies. They thereby involved
themselves in serious trouble with Gonnema, the redoubtable
Chochoqua. Bushmen killed three burghers in the Breede river valley
far away from the settlement, and Gonnema, as reputed overlord
of the murderers, was held responsible. Then Kees, Gonnema's son,
slew a party of Europeans and destroyed the post at Saldanha Bay.
Commandos of soldiers and burghers took the field; commando 1674.
service was made obligatory on burghers for the first time; friendly
Hottentots assisted, and the bickering went on to the great damage
of the cattle-barter. At last, a general pacification was made and a 1677.
joint force of troops, burghers and Hottentots made a fruitless
expedition against the Bushmen in the eastern borderlands.[2]

That commando was significant. Henceforward, the Europeans
met with little serious resistance from the Hottentots; rather the
men of the two cattle-owning races worked together against the
common enemy, the Bushmen. Nevertheless, the Koranas have a
tradition that at this time the Gorachouquas, 'the sons of Kora,'
began to trek away inland, clearing off the Bushmen as they went.
The withdrawal of the Hottentots before the face of the white man
had begun.[3]

CHAPTER III

COLONISATION, 1679–1717

THE last two decades of the seventeenth century and the first two
of the eighteenth are the most important in the early history of
Europeanised South Africa. The East India Company experimented
once more with colonisation in its eastern possessions and made a
deliberate effort to transform its refreshment station at the Cape into
a genuine colony. This period of assisted immigration and close
settlement covered the governorships of the van der Stels, father and
son, and saw the arrival of the majority of the ancestors of the

[1] Theal, IIa. 210.
[2] *Journal, 1671–6*, pp. 190, 240 ff.; No. 50 of 1835, pp. 13, 14.
[3] Theal, IIa. 246.

present Afrikaner folk of South Africa. The effort ceased for a variety of reasons in 1707. During the ten years which followed the cessation of immigration, various institutions which had been slowly forming in earlier years took definite shape, and, in 1717, the vital decision was taken to import slaves rather than white artisans. The Colony at the Cape, thus based definitely on servile labour, was condemned to face all the problems of a tropical dependency in a temperate climate.

Fear of the French and the precarious nature of the cattle-trade with the Hottentots were the two main motives which prompted the Seventeen to make this colonising experiment. Towards the close of a long war with Louis XIV, the authorities at the Cape had made great preparations for an expected French attack, entrusting their cherished flocks and herds to faithful Hottentot allies and employing destitute natives on the fortifications in return for their rations.[1] The French peril ended with the Peace of Nymwegen; meanwhile, owing to intertribal quarrelling, the supply of cattle had been highly intermittent and had almost entirely ceased during the war with Gonnema. The Directors were then faced with two problems: first, how could they ensure a steady food-supply at the halfway house without undue expense to themselves, for, assuredly, the Colony was too expensive to be run as a mere vegetable garden with a semi-official, semi-barbarian 'migratory farm' attached; secondly, how could they reduce the costly garrison and yet strengthen their hold on the Cape, again without undue expense, against the Frenchmen, Englishmen and Danes who were finding their way past it in increasing numbers?[2] They found the answer to both puzzles in an increase of free burghers, and sent out Simon van der Stel as Commander to look to it.

Simon was the son of Adriaan van der Stel of Dordrecht, once Governor of Mauritius, and of his Indian wife, Monica of the Coast.[3] Born at Mauritius and educated at Amsterdam, Simon arrived at the Cape in 1679, a dark, cheerful man of medium height, forty years of age, and an ardent Dutch patriot. He at once, as it were, leaped the sandy Flats which cut off the Cape from 'Africa' and founded a new village in the fruitful Eerste river valley at Stellenbosch. There he gave his settlers farms in full ownership as large as they could cultivate, and the use of unoccupied ground for grazing; but the farms were to revert to the Company if they were not worked, the culture of tobacco was forbidden, and one-tenth of

In the left margin:
1672–1678.
1674–1677.
1679.

---

[1] No. 50 of 1835, p. 14.
[2] Shipping, 1662–71: 370 Dutch, 26 French, 9 English, 2 Danes. 1672–1700: 976 Dutch, 170 English, 42 Danes, 36 French.
[3] *Bel. Hist. Dok.*, III. 11.

the grain not consumed by the growers was to be handed over to the Company at the barrier outside the Castle. So far, so good: but the new settlement was a mere skeleton, and if Simon was to extend it as he proposed along the Berg river valley under the purple shadows of the mountains of Africa, he must have immigrants. 'Our colonists,' he reported, 'consist chiefly of strong, gallant, and industrious bachelors'; but the Seventeen regretted that they saw very little chance of sending out suitable settlers, 'because people can at present earn a very good livelihood here.'[1] Even girls from the orphanages of the Netherlands refused to make the voyage, and the appointment of the Cape as a depot for East Indian prisoners of rank was cold comfort to a Commander so keen on 'our people' as was Simon.

The flood of Commissioners which poured in upon the Cape during the next few years witnessed to the interest which the *Heeren Majores in patria* were taking in their southern dependency. First came ex-Governor-General van Goens, followed by his son, an Ordinary Councillor from Ceylon; then Councillor Extraordinary Daniel Heyns to inspect False Bay and tinker with the currency, and, finally, Ordinary Councillor and Admiral of the Fleet Wouter Valckenier to do many things that he should not have done.[2] But the acts of these men with their high-sounding titles could be reversed either by the Seventeen or Batavia or their successors. It was otherwise with Hendrik Adriaan van Rheede, Lord of Mydrecht and Drakenstein, for he was a High Commissioner answerable only to the mighty Seventeen.[3] 1682– 1684. 1699. 1700. 1685.

Van Rheede came with *carte blanche* to set the Dutch East Indian empire in order. He found that, at its most westerly station, Commander Simon had already somewhat improved the machinery of government to meet the needs of the growing colony. At the capital he had set up a Petty Court of two officials and two burghers appointed annually to sit weekly and relieve the High Court by hearing minor civil suits arising from the Cape district, subject to an appeal to the High Court itself. At the same time he had established a court of four Heemraden at newly founded Stellenbosch.[4] These men were burghers, half retiring annually after presenting to the Council the usual double list of names of proposed successors; they were unpaid and limited to hearing petty civil cases, but their powers though ill-defined, were none the less respected from the first. Van Rheede now fixed the fluctuating number of seats on the Council of Policy at 1682.

---

[1] Moodie, *Records*, I. 376, 394.

[2] *Journal, 1699–1732*, pp. 3, 7, 23; *Lett. Rec., 1695–1708*, p. 248; *Rambles*, p. 143.

[3] *Bel. Hist. Dok.*, I.

[4] *Journal, 1699–1732*, pp. 45, 58, 65; Moodie, *Records*, I. 390; C. G. Botha, *Early Inferior Courts of Justice* (S.A. Law Journal, 1921).

eight. The Council could still be expanded into a Broad Council when ships were in the Bay; sometimes to the fury of the Governor, admirals convened Broad Councils on ship-board without consulting him, but henceforward there were never more than eight councillors chosen from among the Governor—*De Edel Heer*, Councillor Extraordinary of India—the Secunde, the two chief military officers, the treasurer, secretary, chief salesman, garrison book-keeper and cashier. Van Rheede also fixed the membership of the High Court at eight officials and two senior burgher Councillors appointed annually with a reminder that relatives could not be permitted to serve together.

Finally van Rheede appointed a Landdrost at Stellenbosch. The primary duties of this official, who would normally be appointed by the Commander, were to look after the Company's farms, cattleruns and other interests; but, as chairman of the court of Heemraden, he also had judicial and administrative work to do. This court was to meet monthly to settle civil suits involving not more than £10, subject to an appeal to the High Court in all but the most trivial cases; to act as a district council for the care of roads, water-supply and destruction of vermin; to levy a paid *corvée* of wagons, slaves and draught animals for public purposes; to raise a local revenue by milling corn and levying a small duty on sheep and cattle, to report applications for land and to spend up to £100 without reference to the central authorities.[1] Such was the basis of local government which survived the Company in the Cape by many years and later on reappeared in all essentials in the republics which arose beyond its borders in the mid-nineteenth century.

One other important addition to the ruling powers in the Colony was made after van Rheede's departure. This was the Independent 1689. Fiscal, who was appointed to watch the finances, regulate the administration of justice and act as public prosecutor. He was responsible only to the Seventeen, who were eager to check the corruption and private trade which were already eating out the heart of the Company; wherefore, since *justitia magnum emolumentum est*, he was stimulated to do his duty by the promise of one-third of the fines levied by the High Court in addition to his lordly salary of £100 per annum.[2]

Meanwhile, the population increased step by step with this increasing weight of governmental machinery. The Directors succeeded in sending out a number of Dutch and German settlers; Company's

---

[1] This court, *e.g.* encouraged wool-growing, organised the Waveren trek (1699) and saw to the carting of fuel to the predikant. A quarrel over its power to levy *corvée* led to the definition of the Cape-Stellenbosch boundary in 1711 (Theal, II*a*. 429). Its summary civil powers were increased in 1716 (*ibid.*, 437).

[2] *Journal, 1699–1732*, p. 152; *Lett. Rec., 1695–1798*, p. 9.

servants and soldiers took their letters of freedom at the Cape; the van der Stels waylaid likely men till the Directors had to protest against 'this habit of disembarking and keeping artisans at the Cape who are destined for India.'[1] But salvation really came indirectly from France. There had long been French-speaking Walloons in the United Provinces who had fled thither from the Spanish terror at the close of the sixteenth century. These refugees were now being joined by Huguenots who abandoned France where that Most Christian King, Louis XIV, was bearing with increasing severity on those of the reformed faith. Some Huguenots betook themselves to Brandenburg, others to England or to her American colonies, but many went to the free Netherlands, especially after Louis had 1685. revoked what was left of the Edict of Nantes. In the Netherlands they were organised as branches of existing Dutch congregations; but their numbers became an embarrassment, and the Seventeen bethought them that here lay a reservoir from which they could draw settlers for their African colony. Some of the Frenchmen knew how to make wine, brandy and vinegar, and the less said of attempts to manufacture these commodities at the Cape hitherto the better; moreover, the young women could furnish desirable wives for Simon's gallant bachelors.

The Directors, therefore, offered such Huguenots and Piedmontese (Dalluyden) as were prepared to take the oath of allegiance a free passage to the Cape and advances for equipment, to be repaid in kind as opportunity offered. They were to undertake to stay at the Cape for at least five years, unless by grace of the Company they were released sooner, and then they might pay their own way home if they wished. The Piedmontese refused to sail after all; but the 1688. Frenchmen began to arrive, 'industrious people, satisfied with little,' who, by command of the *Heeren Majores*, were to be treated as if they were free-born Dutchmen.[2]

This Simon was only too pleased to do, for the Hugenots promised to 'benefit and strengthen the colony in a wonderful degree.' They were never very numerous. The total of the original parties of 1688–1689, together with the families which came in during the next few years, was something under two hundred souls all told, or about one-sixth of the free burgher population of the Cape; but economically and socially their influence was out of all proportion to their numbers. They were of a better social class than most of the Dutch and German settlers who accompanied or preceded them; some of them were skilled vine and olive-dressers or artisans; they were nearly all young and married, real colonists who had no Fatherland towards which

---

[1] *Lett. Rec. 1695–1708*, pp. 183, 301.
[2] C. G. Botha, *The French Refugees at the Cape*, pp. 132 ff.; Moodie, *Records*, I. 422; Spoelstra, *op. cit.*, II. 641 ff.

to turn their head and ears in bad times, for the Netherlands had been at best a city of refuge and *la belle France* was closed to them. Politically, however, there was a certain risk in admitting them. The Dutch were frightened of the French, and with good reason, for Colbert was but newly dead and Louis was still acquisitive; the Huguenots in England and Brandenburg openly said they would go home if they could, and it was doubtful whether those at the Cape would resist or aid a French invading force. Men remembered how

1667. Montdevergue had planted the French lilies at Saldanha Bay, and how Commander van Quaelberg had been dismissed next year for furnishing a visiting French squadron from the Company's stores.[1] Indeed, Simon was not quite certain how far his masters meant him to keep open house for foreigners. At first he was forbidden to supply them with anything more than water; but in response to protests from foreign Powers, the Seventeen permitted their ships to buy anything they liked from burghers except wheat and fuel, which were both running low, and even to have ship's stores in case of absolute necessity. But the position was long uncertain. As late as 1698, Simon was forbidden to give an English East India Squadron any assistance and had to excuse himself for selling them a couple of sails on the plea that the English were allies and both the sails were very bad.[2] But the French were the Company's bugbear at this time. Simon took excessive precautions when Vaudricourt's peaceful

1686. flotilla of six ships put into Table Bay on its way to Siam, and when, a little later, he accepted a medallion from another French visitor,

1690. he was reprimanded by the Seventeen. The du Quesnes were active at Mascarenhas (Mauritius), and the republican *Heeren Majores* disliked medallions bearing the image and superscription of *le Grand Monarque*.

However, here were the Huguenots, and van der Stel made haste to settle them in his new 'colonies' in the Berg river valley. Already he had planted twenty-three Dutch and German families at Draken-stein, each on sixty morgen in full ownership on terms similar to the

1687. grants at Stellenbosch. The Frenchmen were settled mainly at Drakenstein and French Hoek hard by, but, to their dismay, they were interspersed among stout burghers of other nationalities. Some of them declared that they would rather live with their own folk as servants than tolerate such neighbours; but Simon was determined to have no French Quebec at the Cape, and so the French, Dutch and German colonies spread down the Berg river valley, to the Paarl in 1688, to Wagenmakers' Vallei in 1698, and to the Land of Waveren in 1699.[3]

The bulk of the Frenchmen settled at French Hoek and Draken-stein. Difficulties soon arose. Paul Roux, the parish clerk and school-

---

[1] Moodie, *Records*, I. 299. [2] *Lett. Desp., 1696–1708*, pp. 70, 74.
[3] *Ibid.*, pp. 101, 136, 151, 159; *Journal, 1699–1732*, pp. 1, 2, 29, 32. The system of land-tenure was developing at this time. A record of grants wa

master, could speak both French and Dutch, but Pierre Simond, the Frenchmen's pastor, only knew his own tongue; nevertheless, Simond was given a seat on the Stellenbosch consistory. This by no means satisfied his followers. They asked for a consistory of their own; whereat van der Stel lost his temper and railed at 'the impertinence of the French,' who were apparently 'of a mind to have their own Magistrate, Commander and Prince to be chosen from the people.' The distant Seventeen took a more statesmanlike view than the harassed Commander. They consented to a separate consistory of elders and deacons for Drakenstein, 'who, if there are any such to be found, shall be able to understand both the French and Dutch languages,' and promised to send out bilingual schoolmasters to Stellenbosch and Drakenstein specially to teach Dutch to the French children, 'in order to unite our nation by this means.' To further this amalgamation, van der Stel was bidden to 'make them live among one another.' This he was already doing, and he now arranged that Church services should be held alternately at Stellenbosch and Drakenstein.[1]

Amalgamation steadily took place. The Huguenots were few and scattered, and their recruitment speedily ceased. Willem Adriaan van der Stel, Simon's son and successor as Governor, thought little of them, and asked for Zeelanders instead, and the Directors decided 1700. to send out no more Frenchmen. Henceforward, while the colonising experiment lasted, only Dutchmen and Germans were assisted to the Cape; but, on the whole, the Directors handled the Frenchmen at the Cape tactfully. The refugees naturally clung to their own way of life, and the older folk especially found it hard to learn Dutch; hence when Pierre Simond retired, another bilingual minister was sent out, 1702. 'not as we take it to preach in the latter language (French), but only to be of service to the aged colonists who do not know our language . . . in order that in course of time the French language may die out . . . and, with this object in view, the schools are to give in future no other or further instruction than is necessary to let the youth learn to read and write our language.' But the Frenchmen protested; the Chamber of Amsterdam told the Governor to use his judgment, and Willem Adriaan relented sufficiently to permit the new Drakenstein minister, the Rev. Engelbertus le Boucq to preach in French at least every other week.[2]

kept; the cost of survey was paid by the grantee, but no grants were registered till survey had been completed. Sometimes years passed between the actual grant and registration; meanwhile, the holder had to be content with a mere notification of allotment. On Land Tenures *vide* Rec. C.C., VIII. 106; Report of Cape Surveyor-General, G. 30–1876; C. G. Botha, *Early Land Tenures at the Cape* (S.A. Law Journal, May and Aug., 1919); E. A. Walker, *Historical Atlas of South Africa*, pp. 7 ff.).

[1] Botha, *French Refugees*, pp. 152 ff.; Spoelstra, *op. cit.*, II. 599 ff.
[2] Botha, *op. cit.*, pp. 158, 160; *Bel. Hist. Dok.*, III. 2; Spoelstra, *op. cit.*, II. 603.

The policy of the Company was thus to fuse the jarring elements in the Cape population. That fusion was hastened in an unforeseen manner by the irregular conduct of the Governor, for in common opposition to the officials at *De Kaap*, the Frenchmen, Germans and Dutchmen of the Berg river valley learnt to know one another better.

The economic condition of the Cape was thoroughly unhealthy. The settlement had been founded as a supply depot, for the first forty years or so of its career, had failed to meet the demands made upon it. The supply depot had then become a colony and found that the supply, except in the very worst years, outran the demand. The local market was small, restricted, and easily glutted; the burgher population was tiny and in many ways inexperienced; the Cape itself was remote from other parts of the civilised world; the monopolistic policy of the Company accentuated the ills to which South African farming and industry are naturally subject.

Generally speaking, the Seventeen meant well by the burghers so long as their trading monopoly was not touched and prices of supplies were not raised against them. Even so, the burghers found it hard to turn their produce into good money. The Company had first call on their cattle, corn and wine, and claimed a three days' start in the sale of vegetables and other minor commodities to foreigners; foreigners were few; for the rest, the burghers found themselves hopelessly restricted.

Monopoly, engrossing, regrating and all the economic heresies of the seventeenth century were in the blood and bones of 'Jan Compagnie.' Before ever there were free burghers at the Cape, the concession policy had been introduced when Annetje de Boerin acquired a monopoly of the milk supply. By the time of Governor Goske the
1655.   practice of leasing the right to retail spirits, wine, beer, tobacco, oil, vinegar, bread and meat was well established, and the demand of
1673.   the harassed burghers that they might sell their grain, wine and other products freely to anyone on payment of suitable duties was rejected.

1676.   The leases were the simplest means of controlling local trade and raising revenue; indeed, considerably more than half the Cape revenue was drawn from this source, even though the purchase price was rarely paid in full. The leases for the retail trade and the supply of such commodities as the Company chose to buy through the contractors were auctioned annually on the basis of falling bids for supply to the Company, and rising bids for retail to fellow-burghers who must buy and sell through the contractors. These lessees were fairly free to fleece the stranger as God and opportunity might permit, because while prices for the Company and the burghers were fixed, those chargeable to foreigners were left open, and Simon van der Stel privately advised the free burghers to demand from passers-by four or five times the usual prices. As the Cape was the first port of call 1681. for sailors and officials returning home from the Indies with their accumulated pay in their pockets, the prices asked were usually paid; but the Cape earned a bad name among men who went down to the sea in ships.[1]

During the van der Stel period, the oil and vinegar leases were dropped because the return was so small; on the other hand, the Company's salt monopoly was stiffened. The Company owned the pans and allowed anyone to collect salt provided they delivered one wagon-load in every three at the Castle; but so much damage was done by driving wagons into the pans, that fines were presently levied on burghers who collected salt without a permit.[2]

There was continual friction over the beer licences. The European beer lease was trifling, but that for home-brewed beer was a different 1705. matter. The Company furnished one of the burghers with land and boilers, partly on credit; but it only allowed him to sell by the cask lest the European beer licensee suffer and the families who made sugar beer be ruined. These things required nice adjustment by an anxious government; even so, there were the usual complaints of bad beer, the blame for which was thrown on the tapsters. Then the unhappy brewer died, bad harvests starved the infant industry, and the matter ended for the time being when the widow declined, with many 'irrelevant and aggravating expressions,' to pay for the boilers.[3]

After beer, tobacco—naturally. At first, the lessee alone had the right to buy from the Company, but later on anyone was allowed to buy at the same price. The wretched retailer lost heavily on such terms, and the old plan had to be revived, though the Company retained the right to sell wholesale in rolls over the head of the holder. 1700. With the reduction of the garrison—Marlborough and the Allies apparently had the French on the run—the value of the lease fell off, and the Company decided to sell direct to the public at a profit of 1707. fifty per cent. The sanguine expectation was defeated by the smugglers, and the Company had to instruct the landdrost to off-load its unsaleable supplies on the farmers of Stellenbosch at any price, payable in corn![4]

Beer, tobacco, oil, vinegar, these be but toys. The really important products were meat, corn and wine, and it was over the handling of them that the struggle arose between the government and some of its free burghers.[5] The issue at stake was the bread and butter of the

---

[1] *Lett. Desp., 1696–1708*, pp. 69, 188; *Journal, 1699–1732*, p. 87; Theal, IIa. 257.
[2] *Lett. Desp., 1696–1708*, pp. 25, 274; *Journal, 1699–1732*, p. 86.
[3] *Lett. Desp., 1696–1708*, pp. 21, 46, 136, 315; *Journal, 1699–1732*, pp. 31, 99, 109.
[4] *Lett. Desp., 1696–1708*, pp. 319, 393; *Journal, 1699–1732*, pp. 31, 40, 79.
[5] On the van der Stel controversy, *vide* L. Fouche, *The Diary of Adam Tas*.

wine and wheat farmers. Wheat, the staple crop, best tells the story of an African farm of those days. Van Riebeeck had commanded his free burghers to leave cattle-bartering alone, to devote but little time to vegetables and vines, and to concentrate on ploughing. Meanwhile the Company had diligently tried to grow corn for itself; but burghers and Company's men had long failed to supply themselves adequately, let alone the shipping and the East Indian stations, and in bad times rice had had to be rushed in from Java to stave off famine. Borghorst had then ploughed up new lands at Hottentots-Holland, and, to encourage the burghers, had leased the Company's farm at Rondebosch and raised the price which the Company was prepared to pay for grain.[1]

1670.

Cultivation increased; the younger van Goens remitted the tithe for two years; the first small export of grain to Batavia took place, and in the following year van Rheede fixed prices, talked hopefully of a large export, and ordered all available corn to be stored at the Castle with due precautions against fire. Immigrants flowed in; Simon bade his Frenchmen grow vines by all means, but corn at all costs; new corn lands were broken; the Company which had long ago forbidden its officials to farm, began to give up the unnecessary and expensive task of growing its own corn and, while keeping two years' supply in its magazines, soon found that anything up to 2000 muids was available annually for despatch to Batavia.[2] Then, the supply of corn having thus outstripped the demand, Batavia declined to take any more wheat because it was much too expensive and not so good as the Surat variety. The anxious Seventeen admitted that wheat at the Cape cost nearly twice as much as in Holland, but, once more to encourage the colonists, they commanded Batavia to take Cape wheat at Bengal and Surat prices and ordered van der Stel to urge his farmers on to greater efforts. Batavia took a little with a bad grace; Simon replied that his men were set on quick returns and would take no pains; and then came a run of bad seasons which forced him to import Java rice and ration the burghers. Next year the drought broke with such violence that the crops were flooded out in the Berg river valley and disease appeared in what survived.[3]

1685.

1696.

1698–
1705.

The story of Cape wine and brandy is equally depressing. Wine had been made from 1659 onwards; but Batavia disliked it and the wine farmers scorned the suggestion of the Cape Council that they should send their wines to the East and sell them for what they would fetch on payment of freight and duty. Restriction and monopoly had infected them and they rejected the offer of qualified free

[1] Theal, IIa. 178.
[2] Bel. Hist. Dok., I. 21, 42; Lett. Desp., 1696–1708, p. 11; Lett. Rec., 1695–1708, pp. 61-2. A muid is 2·972 bushels.
[3] Lett. Desp., 1696–1708, pp. 11, 18, 37, 54, 93; Lett. Rec., 1695–1708, pp. 68, 86; Journal, 1699–1732, pp. 2, 3, 76; Rambles, pp. 7, 8, 158.

trade. It was not made to them again for many a long day. Meanwhile the Cape tried its hand at brandy. It was of a nature even more 1672. startling than the wine, and van Rheede presently complained that neither wine nor brandy nor vinegar had ever been properly made at the Cape. However, as the Company wanted wine, the High Commissioner prohibited the manufacture of brandy and left Simon 1685. to put wine-making on a sound footing.[1] Wherefore Simon imported new cuttings and Huguenots, forbade pressing till the vines had been inspected by a committee, and himself experimented with success on the farm Constantia which van Rheede had granted to him. Wine was exported to Ceylon, and the Company began to buy from 1688. the farmers at £5 per *legger* for export to Batavia. Alas! Batavia 1694. complained that pork-casks were not fit receptacles for the juice of the grape, and tactfully suggested that the Cape should make brandy or vinegar instead; the Fatherland itself evinced no enthusiasm,[2] and some foreigners were openly rude on the score of Cape wine. ''Tis Colour'd like Rhenish,' wrote the Englishman Ovington, 'and therefore they pass it under that specious name in *India*, but the taste of it is much harder and less palatable; its operations more searching, and the strength of it more intoxicating and offensive to the Brain.'[3] Later comers gave a rather more favourable report. Maxwell could note in 1708 that Cape wines were 'not inconsiderable either for quantity, quality or variety';[4] the Constantia brand was already recognised as good, for the labours of Simon and the Huguenots had not been in vain; nevertheless, the Colony had to face the fact that the only sure outlet for its fast-increasing volume of wine was the Capetown market and the ships. That outlet was jealously guarded. Farmers might not retail their own wines, for the wine lease was the most valuable of all to the Company and the lessees giving the former over five-sixths of the total revenue from leases and the latter a privileged position at a port whose inhabitants were much given to keeping canteens. For a time the wine lease was divided 1699– between four persons, who were supposed to be independent of one 1705. another and who certainly had liberty to buy and sell where and how they pleased.[5]

As with wine, so with brandy. The importation of foreign brandy

---

[1] *Bel. Hist. Dok.*, I. 19.
[2] *Lett. Desp., 1696–1708*, pp. 13, 46; *Lett. Rec., 1695–1708*, p. 32. A legger is four aums or some 133 gallons.
[3] V.R. Soc., V. 107.
[4] *Ibid.*, p. 53. Compare Lady Anne Barnard's defence of Cape wines (*South Africa a Century Ago*, p. 44; also *State of the Cape in 1822*, p. 109). The truth is that Cape wines varied immensely; some brands were good, others bad, and in good seasons the bad were apt to swamp the good and give the whole an unenviable reputation.
[5] *Bel. Hist. Dok.*, I. 13; *Lett. Desp., 1696–1708*, pp. 141, 188; *Journal, 1699–1732*, pp. 5, 6, 12, 13.

was a Company monopoly. The retail trade was duly leased, and to protect the lessee and its own interests the Company first forbade the making of Cape brandy and then divided the lease into four parts to force the lessees to buy only from its stores. For everyone knew that Cape brandy was made; the lessees complained loudly that the folk of Stellenbosch, Drakenstein and other 'do-nothing' people smuggled it to the troops and boarding-house keepers at Capetown. It was in vain that the Fiscal was given inquisitorial powers; the illicit stills and traffic flourished; the very lessees smuggled, and for lack of foreign spirit the Company had first to remit part of the lease money and then allow the lessees to replenish stores from the ships or, in the last resort, to buy the forbidden local product. The Company clung fast to its monopoly, but the value of the lease fell with the size of the garrison; something had to be done with the flood of wine that was pouring forth at the Cape, and at last, after two years' hesitation, it yielded to Willem Adriaan's importunity and allowed 1707. the burghers to make brandy and vinegar. But, perhaps prudently, it would not undertake to buy either.[1]

The Company tried to encourage minor industries, but indigo, olives, coconuts, sugar, cassava, rice and hops failed one after another; Natal millet throve and made good native beer, but that was all, and Simon had to report that the burghers would take no trouble with any intensive kind of cultivation. Simon was unduly hard on the burghers, for climate and soil were against them, and the very seasons of the year fought against his son's attempt to establish a silk industry. The mulberry trees came into leaf at the wrong time of year and the worms, failing to realise that they were now south of the Equator, died. So it went, and the export of a few ostrich eggs to the King of Candy gave no promise of closer settlement and the elaborate farming which goes therewith.[2]

The Cape thus failed to produce many things which the Company desired; conversely, one of the supplies which it had at first furnished in abundance was in danger of exhaustion. Van Riebeeck had found the mountain kloofs of the Peninsula full of trees and had added the oak and the fir thereto; but timber had been cut wastefully, and already in van Rheede's time the very garrison was short of firewood.[3] Simon van der Stel sent an expedition 120 leagues by sea to search for timber on the mythical islands of Dina and Marseveen,[4] but he also took more practical steps nearer home. He planted oaks on the Company's lands, offered oaks to farmers and ordered every man

---

[1] *Bel. Hist. Dok.*, I. 19; *Lett. Disp.*, *1696–1708*, pp. 69, 95, 141, 236, 254, 319; *Lett. Rec.*, *1695–1708*, p. 414; *Journal*, *1699–1732*, pp. 36, 62, 159.
[2] *Lett. Desp.*, *1696–1708*, pp. 28, 153, 176; Theal, IIa. 126, 201, 263, 319, 362, 374.
[3] *Bel. Hist. Dok.*, I. 22.
[4] *Lett. Desp.*, *1696–1708*, p. 115; *Journal*, *1699–1732*, p. 7.

who felled a tree to plant an acorn; he levied *corvée* through the burgher councillors for tree-planting at Wynberg, and gave Stellenbosch and Drakenstein the oaks for which they are still famous. His son carried on the good work; but both father and son did it in the teeth of popular opposition. Farmers complained that there was no room for trees on little farms of 60 morgen, and that, in any case, trees harboured destructive birds, and Willem Adriaan was driven to drawing up regulations to protect the oaks in the very streets of Stellenbosch. So long as the van der Stels ruled afforestation continued, but even they had to confess that the quick-growing local trees were useless for ships' timbers.[1]

Experiments in wool were equally disappointing. The Seventeen wanted wool, and the van der Stels did their best to get it. Simon experimented with woolled sheep alongside of his horses and cattle at Constantia; Willem Adriaan fetched rams from Europe and Persian sheep from Java and ran them at his farm, Vergelegen; under pressure of the Directors and the Governors, a few farmers sheared sheep. The samples were good, but they remained mere samples, and the vast majority of the burghers would not even try to grow wool. They preferred the fat-tailed, hairy sheep of the country, for there was always a demand for mutton at Capetown.[2]

Of the three staple products, corn, wine and meat, the Company bought the first two direct from the burghers if it chose, but the last it bought through a contractor.[3] Since 1668 members of the Council of Policy had been forbidden to keep more cattle than would supply their own needs, but free burghers were able to buy beasts from the Company at little more than cost price and hire breeding ewes on halves. On the other hand, the Company assiduously reared cattle and sheep and, to keep down prices and prevent contact between the burghers and the natives, reserved to itself the cattle-barter with the Hottentots. The difficulty was that cattle had far more attractions for the farmers than had general agriculture; cattle could look after themselves and walk to market; there was a sure return on those that survived the trek. Wherefore, the laws against the trade were deadletters and a new social class began to emerge in the borderlands.

From the very first the farmer, the *boer*, had tended to become a cattle-farmer, a *veeboer*. Now, long before the end of the seventeenth century, the frontier *veeboer* was in process of becoming the *trekboer*, the semi-nomadic frontiersman *sang pur* who was to blaze the trail for civilisation far into the interior of Africa.[4] The original free burghers had all kept cattle, and one of them, Herman Remajenne,

---

[1] *Lett. Desp.*, *1696–1708*, pp. 22, 183, 209; *Journal, 1699–1732*, pp. 10 ff.
[2] *Lett. Desp.*, *1696–1708*, pp. 138, 167, 388; *Lett. Rec.*, *1695–1708*, p. 331; *Journal, 1699–1732*, pp. 13, 15; *Rambles*, chapter 20.
[3] Fouche, *Tas*, p. 189.
[4] *Vide* L. Fouche, *Die Evolutie van die Trekboer*.

had been caught red-handed bartering with the Hottentots; twenty years later, barely one-third of the sixty-two farmer families farmed grain, and an armed party had to go to fetch back three colonists

1679. who were living with Gonnema's people and kill them if they would not come.[1] By Simon's time the frontiersmen were inured to their way of life. Hunting was all in the day's work, for lions and leopards abounded and they looked to game to give them the lean meat which they ate with their fat mutton. The boers were magnificent shots with their heavy guns, and as early as 1681 they had killed off most of the game between the Cape and the Olifants river, ten to twelve days' trek away. Well-to-do farmers had big cattle runs; the young men pushed into the valleys which run among the mountains of Africa, content to live in their trek-wagons or mere hartebeest huts of reeds, content to travel light as men must do who had to pack their wagons in pieces over Roodezand Pass into the Land of Waveren and the Breede river valley. Bread they could do without; they drank neither wine nor beer; meat, milk and honey sufficed them with a pull of honey-beer on Sundays.

It was against such men that the authorities of the Castle launched *placaaten* forbidding barter or trekking beyond the frontiers. It is true that the Company had had to bribe the burghers to go against Gonnema with a promised share in the loot of cattle, and, at the

1677– close of the campaign, had permitted open trade with Gonnema's
1678. people. But it had soon stiffened the rules again. No one was to pay Hottentots in sheep; no one was to give Hottentots money lest they buy tobacco and refuse to barter cattle for that desirable and jealously monopolised commodity; waggons coming to the Cape

1684. were to be searched at Keert de Koe for native wares; finally, a policeman was told off to relieve the Hottentots of their cash and force them to put their goods on the open market.[2]

Van Rheede foresaw a time when the Company would be able to breed enough cattle for itself and could then safely leave the barter to the burghers;[3] but, as the years went by, the Company began to think of giving up cattle-raising. There were continual complaints of the leanness of its beasts; there was no reason why, with reasonable care, the burghers should not supply the meat market at a fixed price. Simon did not share that opinion; he wanted to limit the size of the colony till it was properly colonised and had no intention of throwing the cattle-trade open.[4] But he was himself partly to blame if his colony was bursting its banks, for he had done much to spread know-

1682– ledge of what lay beyond the frontiers. He had thrice sent expeditions
1685. beyond the Olifants in search of Namaqua copper, and, undeterred by their failure, had himself pushed on to the Koperberg at Ookiep,

[1] No. 50 of 1835, p. 15.   [2] *Ibid.*, pp. 14, 15.
[3] *Bel. Hist. Dok.*, I. 17.   [4] V.R. Soc., V. pp. 11 ff.

where he found wealth of copper in the desert and heard of the great Orange river to the north; he had sent another expedition eastward which reached the Inqua Hottentots in the present Prince Albert district.[1] Nevertheless, he was determined to control the colonisation of southern Africa. He held that the free burghers sent up prices against the Company, bullied the natives, took cattle by force pretending to be Company's men, and thereby risked involving Government in war with the Hottentots, exchanged bad beasts for good Company's animals as they passed the cattle-posts, and sold cattle cheap to fellow-burghers. Hence, he offered informers one-third of the cattle taken from illicit traders, ordered all those burghers who were wandering around to report themselves to the landdrost, bade the men of Stellenbosch and Drakenstein go to their homes each night, and laid down limits beyond which owners might not drive their cattle to graze under pain of confiscation and twelve months' hard labour. It was useless; even the threat of penalties falling just short of death failed to stop the barter, and, in 1699, Simon handed over the colony and all its cares to his son, Willem Adriaan, with much good advice in the style of David to the youthful Solomon on the way he should go with the free burghers in general and the cattle-farmers in particular.[2]

Willem Adriaan van der Stel had his virtues. He was energetic, enterprising, and not lacking in courage or self-confidence; but he also had vices which his upbringing in the Company's service had not been calculated to check.[3] He had greater difficulties to face than had any previous Cape Governor. The settlement was growing fast; the Dutch and Huguenots were jealous of one another; there were many undesirables in the colony: heavy droughts had followed the locust plagues of 1695; above all, the food supply had outrun the demand. Times and tempers were alike bad; he himself was an unsympathetic man and, to make matters worse, his father lived on in the great house at Constantia which he had built to shelter the wife who refused to leave the Netherlands, and there gave rein to the acquisitiveness which was the besetting sin of the van der Stels.

Willem Adriaan was also exposed to great temptations. The moral tone of the East India service was thoroughly rotten, the power of its officials each in his own sphere was almost unchecked. Inquiry 1685. had shown that Admiralty officials allowed whole cargoes to be smuggled into the Netherlands because the smugglers were their friends; twenty years later, Abraham van Riebeeck, Director-General 1706.

---

[1] Godée-Molsbergen, *Reizen*, I. 139 ff.; Moodie, *Records*, I. 400, 429 ff.
[2] *Lett. Desp., 1696–1708*, pp. 19, 24; No. 50 of 1835, p. 16; V.R. Soc., V. pp. 11 ff.
[3] Fouche, *Tas*, pp. xxiii, xxv.

in India, could write that 'the gentlemen in the Fatherland regulate matters as they find good there; but we act here according to our knowledge as we judge best.'[1] All these evils were reproduced on a small scale at the Cape. Salaries were small, but the higher officials had substantial allowances, and all officials were allowed various fees and a limited private trade in crockery, calico, and some other Eastern products. These privileges were abused, and the Fiscal, who was supposed to check them, looked to fees and perquisites to make ends meet. Van Rheede had to limit the amount of free board and vegetables from the Company's gardens taken by officials; the Company had to order its servants to buy from its stores at the same prices as ordinary folk, and, in order to check the cluttering of ships with private wares which were off-loaded into lighters before reaching the Texel, limited the quantity of passengers' baggage, directed the Fiscal to search ships on arrival, and commanded all its captains to sail straight to the port of the Chamber to which they were directed.[2]

It was the ambition of every one of the superabundant servants of the Company to make his fortune and retire. Willem Adriaan was no exception, but his opportunities at the Cape were limited. However, he was invested with autocratic powers, and he determined to make the most of such opportunities as did offer. He first bought up wine cheaply, treated it, and sold it at a great profit to the ships. This was straightforward business; but there was no fortune in it. The only fortune to be made at the Cape lay in the supply of meat, corn and wine to the Company. Willem Adriaan and some of the higher officials, therefore, embarked on large-scale agriculture in flat defiance of the law and proceeded to corner this supply in the small Cape market which they, as the government, could regulate as they chose.

Since 1668 the Company, with the avowed intention of helping the free burghers, had forbidden its officials to hold more land than a mere vegetable garden. High Commissioner van Rheede had indeed recommended that officials be allowed to farm and had given Simon Constantia; but the Directors had maintained the rule and only confirmed van Rheede's grant as an exception. Now, Willem Adriaan persuaded Wouter Valckenier, a mere ordinary commissioner, to grant him a considerable farm at Vergelegen just below the Hottentots-Holland pass, a farm which he presently enlarged by purchase.[3] Valckenier granted other farms to the Secunde, the Fiscal, the Captain, the Predikant and even the Surveyor, and gave Father Simon the southern half of the Peninsula as a cattle-ranch. The

---

[1] W. Cunningham, *Western Civilisation*, II. 205; Theal, IIa. 488.
[2] *Bel. Hist. Dok.*, I. 16, 21, 40; *Lett. Rec., 1695–1708*, pp. 117, 224, 227, 242, 254, 314.
[3] *Bel. Hist. Dok.*, I.: *Lett. Desp., 1696–1708*, p. 333; Theal, *Historical Sketches*, pp. 179, 208.

Governor's brother Frans also held a farm near Vergelegen; in other words, the van der Stels and the officials who stood in with them owned one-third of the farming area of the colony, besides the cattle-runs which Willem Adriaan acquired beyond the Hottentots-Holland mountains. The Governor used Company's gardeners, servants, slaves and materials for the building of his house and the laying out of his farm; in time of war, with the fear of the French abroad in the land, he spent long weeks there when he should have been at the Castle; his cattle and sheep kraals were replenished by the landdrost of Stellenbosch and the master gardener, who displayed a passionate interest in the flora—or was it the fauna—beyond the mountains. Nor was he himself above compelling men to purchase his favour with slaves and sheep; Frans, his brother, 'a pest to the colony,' obliged his neighbours to do work for him from fear of government displeasure; worse still, Simon and Adriaan between them soon owned one-third of the vine-stocks in the Colony.[1]

Meanwhile, the Governor took steps to get a strangle-hold on the supply of meat and wine to the Company. He was handicapped at the start by two facts. First, the meat contract which van Rheede 1699. had made with a wealthy burgher, Henning Huising, expired, and at once the free men began to slaughter for themselves without the necessary inspection.[2] Secondly, in the same year, the Seventeen threw the cattle-barter open to burghers, forbade members of the Council and High Court to participate or to supply the Company, ordered the sale of the Company's herds and lands, and merely retained the right to call on the burghers for draught oxen at a price.[3] The first difficulty was apparently overcome when Huising, who was at that time in favour at the Castle, was given the meat contract for five years; the second by sheer suppression till, in response to repeated orders, Willem was obliged to declare the barter 1700. open. At the same time, he stationed guards of mounted men on the frontiers to keep an eye on the dealings of the burghers with the natives.[4]

Evidence of abuses was soon forthcoming. A party of forty-five 1702. Europeans and as many Hottentots, equipped by Jakobus van der Heiden and other well-to-do Stellenbosch burghers, journeyed on a cattle-trading expedition some five hundred miles eastward to the Fish river. There they fell foul of a stray party of Bantu, attacked various Hottentot clans and drove off much cattle. Willem Adriaan promptly closed the cattle-trade pending the decision of the Seventeen, and held an inquiry. At first the *heeren majores* approved of

---

[1] Fouche, *Tas*, pp. 205, 337 ff., 349.
[2] *Lett. Desp.*, *1696–1708*, p. 10; *Journal*, *1699–1732*, p. 11.
[3] *Lett. Desp.*, *1696–1708*, p. 217; *Lett. Rec.*, *1695–1708*, p. 204; *Journal*, *1695–1708*, p. 25; No. 50 of 1835, p. 16.
[4] *Lett. Desp.*, *1695–1708*, pp. 191, 217.

his action, but in the end they reopened the traffic and directed him to push his inquiry no further.[1]

Willem Adriaan now closed in on the vital contracts. He induced the Directors to agree that the meat contract should be granted to four butchers who should not themselves be owners of cattle; on the other hand, after much effort, he got leave to knock down more than one of the four wine leases to the same party. Hence, Huising lost his lucrative meat contract, which went to four creatures of the Governor, and the whole of the wine contract fell to another dubious character who was equally dependent on him. Here, then, were the two principal contracts virtually in the hands of officials who could supply much of the wine, meat and corn required, who had the first entry to the narrow market, paid no tithe and held their subject competitors politically in the hollow of their hands. 'Already a year ago,' the Fiscal noted, 'there was folks did say that within that time there should here be no more burghers requisite.'[2]

The free burghers had also noted that ugly fact. Some of them risked taking action. It is not easy to determine the exact amount of truth in the charges they made against the Governor and his friends. Times were very bad, so bad that the Seventeen had just decreed that foreigners were to be given nothing but fresh water.[3] Admittedly, many of the recalcitrant burghers were jealous of the van der Stel family; being human they made the very most they could of any evidence they had. Some of them were themselves unlovely characters, Huising grudged the loss of his contract and van der Heiden had been the power behind the cattle-rieving expedition of 1702; but when all is said and done, many of the charges they levied were common ground between the two parties and others were partially admitted by Willem Adriaan. Together, the accusations were enough to ruin the official clique.

Adam Tas, a well-educated Stellenbosch burgher, drew up a petition on behalf of Huising, van der Heiden and other leaders. This was signed by sixty-three burghers of whom half were French, and was smuggled away to Batavia. The Indian authorities sent one copy to Amsterdam and another to the Cape. Willem Adriaan acted promptly. He summoned to the Castle the folk of Capetown, who had no particular quarrel with him, entertained them liberally and got them to sign a glowing testimonial to his virtues as a ruler. Numbers signed, including some Asiatics and free blacks, but, to make sure, the names of certain men were added without their knowledge or consent. The landdrost, by show of arms, collected

(marginal note: 1706.)

---

[1] Lett. Desp., 1696–1708, p. 219; Lett. Rec., 1695–1708, pp. 301, 331, 347; No. 50 of 1835, p. 16; Journal, 1699–1732, p. 56; Defence of W. A. v. d. Stel, annexure M.; Fouche, Tas, pp. 335 ff.
[2] Fouche, Tas, pp. xxi, 331.   [3] Lett. Desp., 1696–1708, p. 260.

other signatures at Stellenbosch, and though many there refused to sign, the document in the end bore the names of two hundred and forty out of a total of five hundred and fifty free men.[1]

This done, the Governor arrested Tas without a warrant, threatened to arrest all signatories of malicious petitions, arrested van der Heiden and other leaders, deported one of them to Batavia, and then rashly despatched Huising and three others to the Netherlands, where they duly made trouble for him. Meanwhile, the prisoners in the Castle, thirteen in all, were tried before an irregular court of officials, most of whom were implicated in the misdemeanours complained of by the burghers, with the Governor controlling the proceedings from behind the door of the next room. Some of the prisoners at once gave satisfactory answers to the court's questions, but Tas held out for nearly a month; van der Heiden held out even longer under abominable conditions, and was only released when the Governor feared he would die on his hands; another of the accused held out for four months and a half. Willem Adriaan then talked of further arrests. This, combined with the abandonment of the traditional annual target shooting (and free drinks), led to a riot at Stellenbosch in which the women took an active part. Thereupon the Governor appointed officers to the local militia in an irregular manner and exceeded his powers by dismissing the heemraden and nominating others.[2]

It was almost his last public act. The Seventeen had long been suspicious that all was not well at the Cape. In 1705 they had reminded their officials there that they must take no part in supplying meat to the Company; then had come the burghers' petition by way of Batavia, and now had come a memorial which Huising and his fellow deportees brought with them direct from the Colony. A strong committee of inquiry issued a report, and on that report the Directors acted. Willem Adriaan and some of the other leading officials were recalled; Frans was expelled from the Company's dominions; Constantia was left to Simon, but Vergelegen was broken up and sold in four lots since the Directors desired equality among burghers rather than semi-official model farms; servants were once more forbidden to own or lease land or to trade in cattle, corn, wine and other supplies; burghers were left free to sell cattle subject to the Company's privileges; the wine licence was once more divided into four lots; finally there was to be an end to assisted immigration.[3]

[1] Fouche, *Tas*, p. 215.
[2] *Journal, 1699–1732*, pp. 55, 62, 97 ff., 109; *Lett. Desp., 1696–1708*, pp. 304 ff., 317.
[3] *Bel. Hist. Dok.*, III. pp. 3 ff. The local officials eased the abruptness of the van der Stels' departure as much as possible, for the incoming Governor, van Assenburgh, was a relative of the family. Willem Adriaan and Frans sailed in April 1708, accompanied by their enemies, van der Heiden and Adam Tas. The struggle was thus transferred to Amsterdam. After a fair trial, the ex-Governor and two other officials were dismissed the Company's service.

3

The two outstanding facts in the van der Stel controversy were first that the burghers, the 'bastards of the Company,' had defeated the officials, 'the Company's legitimate children,' and secondly, that the Seventeen were so alarmed that they decided to send no more immigrants to the Cape. The period of settlement was over and there was no more assisted immigration worth speaking of till the coming of the English Settlers in 1820. Throughout the eighteenth century immigration was of the slightest; the main additions to the seventeen hundred free burghers, men, women and children, of 1707 were due to natural increase.[1] Hence the importance of the existing handful of Europeans to the future of South Africa was far greater than their numbers would seem to warrant. They were already differentiated into three groups: the townsmen of *De Kaap*; the grain and wine farmers of the Berg river valley beyond the natural barrier of the sandy Cape Flats, the *boeren* who had successfully resisted the official clique, and the cattle farmers who were already far away behind the mountains of Africa. Each of these classes had their peculiar interests and strongly marked characteristics; all of them were practically marooned at the southern horn of Africa, six thousand miles from anywhere, and already the colonial-born in the outlying parts were calling themselves *Afrikaners* in contrast to the semi-foreign Hollander officials at the Castle.[2]

Circa 1710. The Colony as Willem Adriaan left it has been well described by the English visitor, Maxwell. 'The Dutch,' he wrote, 'have settled for the Convenience of a Rendezvous for their homeward-bound East India fleet, and they have possess'd themselves of the country 60 miles from the place of their first settlement. Beside their principal town in Table Valley . . . where they have a Fort, a Hospital, a supply'd Church, with about 300 families, they have two other small towns in the country call'd Dragenstein and Stellambuss. . . . There are about 120 families, and have one minister between both villages, a Dutchman who speaks French.'[3]

That was all after sixty years; yet the little colony owed much to the energy of the van der Stels. The huddle of houses on the shore of Table Bay had become a presentable little town; Simon, an enthusiastic gardener, and the botanist, Hendrik Oldenland, had beautified the famous Gardens, divided them into four sections 'in each of which grew abundance of the more remarkable vegetables belonging to its corresponding quarter of the world,'[4] and had built a pleasure-house on the site of the present Houses of Parliament. Willem Adriaan, it is true, had let the Gardens decay; but to make

---

[1]   Free burgher
        population.   Adults.   Children.
   1687.   573   342   231   (Theal, IIa. 325)
   1707.   1623   803   820   (*Lett. Desp., 1696–1708*, p. 318).
[2] *Die Huisgenoot*, Sept. 21, 1928.   [3] V.R. Soc., V. 53.   [4] *Ibid.*, p. 54.

up for that he had laid out another garden behind the Devil's Peak
at Newlands. The defence had also been strengthened, for not only
had Simon closed the Castle's old sea-gate and built the existing
handsome gateway, but he had levelled the parade ground in front
of the new entrance and run the Keisersgracht, now Darling Street,
along its inland side to take the place of the old road between the
Castle and the sea. He had also finished the Castle's walls, erected

CAPE COLONY, circa 1710 A.D.

the beautiful Kat and the government offices which lined the central
dividing wall, and built the dividing wall itself to protect the soldiers
on the battlements from plunging fire from neighbouring high ground.
For, though he punished a rash sergeant who blurted out that the
Castle was no good, he and van Rheede knew that it was not such a
strong place as it looked, and his son had to defend the main approach
with ravelins. Simon had also built a new reservoir and a large hospital; his son had built the Groote Kerk; by 1710, the houses of burghers
and officials were spreading along either side of the Gardens.[1]

    [1] *Bel. Hist. Dok.*, I. 6 ff.; *Lett. Desp. 1696–1708*, pp. 3, 22, 223–31, 237; *Journal,
1699–1732*, pp. 34, 63; Theal, IIa. 240, 427, 430; Spoelstra, *op. cit.*, I. 137.

The church had expanded with the settlement and the schools with the churches. The original church of Stellenbosch had become

1699.   too small and another one had been built, the burghers paying the cost of the structure and the Company furnishing the glass and iron; but, as late as 1707, the fiery predikant, Engelbertus le Boucq, could complain that services at Drakenstein had to be held in a shanty. There was the usual elementary school at each church-place, conducted by the parish clerk; for the rest, parents had to teach their own children or rely on wandering *meesters*, who were, as a rule, minor Company's servants on leave of absence. Other educational

1714.   facilities there were none till a certain Lambertus Slicher, who had been in turn ship's chaplain and midshipman, opened a Latin and High Dutch school in Capetown which presently failed for lack of public support.[1]

Church and school were rigidly controlled by Government. Special leave had to be asked for a joint meeting of the Stellenbosch and Drakenstein consistories, and when, in the groundswell of the van der Stel controversy, le Boucq challenged the right of the lay arm to interfere in spiritual matters, the support of the men of Stellenbosch did not save him from being packed off to Batavia. There had been talk of joint meetings of the three consistories as early as 1691, and, in 1710, a visiting minister proposed that they should form a local *Classis*; but Johannes d'Ailly, the minister at the Groote Kerk, was against the idea, the Directors were suspicious, and no such assembly met till 1746. On the other hand, d'Ailly and

1714.   the Secunde were appointed scholarchs to examine prospective teachers in the public schools and, a little later, *meesters* were subjected to a form of licensing.[2]

The system of defence had also grown more elaborate. The strength of the garrison varied from 100 in peace time to 700 at the crisis of the War of the Spanish Succession, but its actual was always below its paper strength by reason of desertion, sickness, and the absence of men at the cattle-posts or on leave of absence. Some of these last worked for the higher civil and military officials; others were *pasgangers* who paid for the privilege of working on their own account; others again were men set free to work as *knechts* or overseers of farms or as *meesters* or both, subject to recall to the colours at a moment's notice.[3]

[1] *Lett. Desp. 1696–1708*, p. 101; *Journal, 1699–1732*, p. 129; *Rambles*, p. 4; V.R. Soc. IV., 165; Theal, IIa. 453.

[2] *Lett. Desp., 1696–1708*, pp. 365, 376; *Journal, 1699–1732*, pp. 130 ff., 155, 227; Theal, IIIa. 453 ff.; E. G. Malherbe, *History of Education in South Africa*, pp. 35 ff.; Spoelstra, *op. cit.*, I. 38; II. 608.

[3] On the defence system, *vide* P. E. Roux, *Die Verdedigingstelsel aan die Kaap*; V.R. Soc. IV. 161 ff.; VI. 57 ff.: also *Journal, 1699–1732*, pp. 16, 31, 42, 55, 62, 98 ff., 109; *Lett. Desp., 1696–1708*, pp. 20, 23, 317.

The soldiers were liable for police work; but the Capetown 1686. burghers were also specially organised for that duty in a burgher watch of six companies, each of them thirty strong under a sergeant and a corporal. These took turns to patrol the town from 4 P.M. to 9 A.M. In the outer districts was the burgher militia, which was kept in touch with the Castle by an elaborate system of flag signals. In 1708 there were two companies of infantry and one of mounted 'dragonders' in the Cape Peninsula, one infantry company at Stellenbosch, another at Drakenstein, and a combined company of dragonders for the two latter centres; in all, 380 infantry and 133 mounted men. Drakenstein and Stellenbosch each had a krygsraad under the presidency of the landdrost, but whereas in van Riebeeck's time officers had been elected by their men, now the *kyrgsraad* appointed them for life with the approval of the Council of Policy. Burghers were liable for picket duty in the Peninsula in time of war; they fell in to receive distinguished visitors; van Riebeeck's Sunday afternoon parades had long ago been made compulsory. Even boys of thirteen drilled with the rest, presented their arms for inspection twice a year, and hated it all as whole-heartedly as their elders and betters. There had been a time when the annual target-shooting at the Castle or on the Papagaaiberg at Stellenbosch had been a day of pleasure; but Batavia had cut off the free drinks at Capetown, the Council had extended the embargo to Stellenbosch and the junketing had departed.

The commando system arose out of this general system of defence under pressure of the exigencies of native policy. Simon had realised that the Obiquas, the Bushmen, were not only distinct from the 1685. Hottentots but so hostile to them that they impeded the cattle-barter. These 'banditti' lifted cattle, killed the owners on occasion and made travel unsafe beyond the borders of the Colony; but, for a time, friction died down as the little hunters withdrew behind the Drakenstein and Hottentots-Holland mountains. Then the 1694. colonists followed them up, and Adriaan van der Stel had to send a Stellenbosch commando to Waveren in pursuit of Bushman murderers and multiply his guard posts along the eastern frontier. 1701.

For a few years thereafter the Bushmen gave little trouble, but at last they raided so heavily that the Company established new military posts at Hex river, Witzenberg and Pikenier's Kloof. It was in response to this raid that the commando took on its characteristically 1715. South African form. Service on the part of the burghers had at first been voluntary, but it had soon been made compulsory and had naturally given rise to discord between the burghers and the regulars. Speed was essential against so nimble a foe as the Bushmen. Van Riebeeck had proved the value of mounted men against the Hottentots, and the mounted burghers felt themselves hampered by the presence of slow-moving, disciplined troops; but for a long time the forces sent against the natives were mixed parties of troops and burghers, sometimes with Hottentot auxiliaries, and always under the command of a regular officer or the landdrost. But occasionally burghers had been given a free hand against the Bushmen, and now, in 1715, a purely burgher commando took the field under a burgher ensign and a *wachtmeester*, forerunner of the later field cornet.[1] Henceforward, commando officers were sometimes elected by their followers, sometimes appointed by the Governor or landdrost; the Company supplied the ammunition; those who took part in each *straf-commando* reported the result to the Castle, and the expenses of each commando were levied on the men of the Cape and Stellenbosch districts by the burggeraaden and heemraden respectively. The meaning of it all was that the central government was leaving the defence of the frontiers to the frontiersmen, even to the extent of withdrawing the newly formed military posts on the extreme frontier.[2]

1716.

The relations of the Europeans with the Hottentots were peaceful on the whole. Bloodshed and cattle-lifting by Hottentots practically ceased after 1689. The tribal system of the neighbouring clans decayed visibly; but the Company still took the chiefs seriously, presented them with staffs of office, recognised successors of chiefs deceased, made no effort to bring them under its own law unless a European or his slave was concerned in the case, helped one clan against another or against the Bushmen, and even talked of giving them reserves. Detribalised Hottentots were steadily drawn into the lowest ranks of Western society; they were not enslaved, for, after the fever epidemic of 1687, they began to come forward readily to work in the harvest fields. The attempt to Christianise them was kept up in a half-hearted way; van Rheede laid down regulations for their admission to the school alongside of white and slave children, and Petrus Kalden, predikant in the time of the younger van der Stel, studied their language. But Kalden departed and the civilising efforts of the Company soon dwindled away.[3]

1685.

Then came disaster. Smallpox appeared for the first time and killed nearly one-quarter of the inhabitants of Capetown in six weeks. An unknown number of Europeans died in the countryside; the slaves suffered heavily, for they lived in dirt; the isolated Bushmen apparently escaped; the Hottentots perished in hundreds. It was they who suffered most severely of all; some of the best-known clans simply disappeared and the farmers were left to look for casual labour in vain.[4]

1713.

[1] No. 50 of 1835, pp. 15 ff.   [2] Theal, IIa. 439.
[3] *Bel. Hist. Dok.*, I. 43; No. 50 of 1835, p. 16; *Rambles*, p. 35.
[4] Theal, IIa. 431 ff.

Slaves were the obvious alternative labour supply. The number owned by free burghers had increased considerably of late years. This increase was mainly due to importation, which took place even in foreign ships in spite of the Navigation Acts, for natural increase was slow and most of the imported slaves were men.[1] Take it all round, slavery at the Cape was not cruel. In Capetown, skilled slaves were allowed to hire themselves out in their spare time and thus earn money with which to buy a substitute and win their own freedom.[2] There was, of course, the crop of crime which always flourishes on servile soil; there were the usual escapes, sometimes of groups of men who obtained arms, pillaged outlying farms, and had to be hunted down by commandos; sometimes there was trouble with the Hottentot clans for harbouring runaways.[3] Slave law, the product of fear, was harsh even by the fierce seventeenth century standards; the whip, chains, branding and the loss of ears were the penalties for such crimes as stealing cabbages from a garden; murderers and rapers were either broken at the wheel or hanged as high as Haman; the High Court did not shrink from torturing slaves if necessary.[4] On the other hand, though van Rheede permitted owners to administer 'moderate punishment,' that is, an ordinary beating at discretion, he forbade them to trice up a slave and flog him without permission of the Fiscal or Governor; burghers were punished for ill-using slaves, and the Company ordered the public sale of a slave who had accused his master of crime as the best means of saving him from domestic vengeance.[5]

Manumission was fairly common, especially as the laws governing it were for a long time vague. As early as 1656 it was recognised, on East Indian analogy, that a black who professed Christianity was the equal of a white man, for though heathens could justly be enslaved, Christians could not. In spite of this rule, the Cape authorities made repeated efforts to Christianise slaves; the scholastic venture which had ended with the flight of van Riebeeck's Angolese was revived; Isbrand Goske decreed that all slave children should be sent to school; next year, a separate school for blacks was organised under a black master; van Rheede ordered all slave children under the age of twelve to attend this school where silver tokens 'and, to slave children in particular, sweet cakes' were offered as prizes

1663.

1677.

---

[1] From 310 in 1687 to 1107 in 1708. In addition, the Company owned about 600 slaves.

	Male Slaves.	Female Slaves.	Slave Children.	
1687.	230	44	36	
1708.	981	166	151	(Déherain, *Le Cap*, p. 211).

[2] *Requesten, 1715–1806*, pp. 1, 3, 669.
[3] No. 50 of 1835, pp. 15, 16: *Journal, 1699–1732*, pp. 144, 272; *Rambles*, p. 32.
[4] *Journal, 1671–6*, pp. 259, 277.
[5] *Bel. Hist. Dok.*, I. 41; *Journal, 1699–1732*, pp. 46, 169; No. 50 of 1835, p. 15.

for excellence in the Christmas Day examinations. Moreover, Goske ordered that slaves were to be married to avoid scandal and reminded owners that no half-breed children should be kept in servitude.[1]

Goske had to deal with a difficult social problem. Pure-blooded blacks who professed Christianity had a good claim to freedom; half-breed Christians could claim freedom by law. Already a fierce 1664. discussion had arisen in India as to whether children of unbelieving parents ought to be baptised. The quarrel spread to the Cape, where visiting chaplains had been in the habit of baptising slave children and urging owners to have them taught the true way. The ecclesiastical court at Batavia and the Amsterdam *Classis* both upheld the custom; but the Council and community at the Cape were long divided on the point. Goske, however, ordered the Christianisation of all slaves, and the Council of Policy decided that children of European fathers and half-caste mothers must be baptised, that children of pagans could be baptised provided their parents also tried to qualify for baptism, and that steps must be taken to bring such children forward for baptism.[2]

The difficulty was that most of the slave children were of mixed breed. There were not many of them, it is true, but, helped by frequent manumissions, the numbers of freedmen increased so fast 1682. that the Directors talked of marking out a reserve for them, especially as at that time they were despairing of attracting European colonists to the Cape. Van Goens the elder gave orders that no more heathen slaves should be freed except for good cause shown, and that heathen freedmen living in idleness might be re-enslaved. Then came van 1685. Rheede. He stiffened the rules considerably. Henceforward Christian, Dutch-speaking half-breeds could claim freedom as of right on attaining the full legal age of twenty-five for men and twenty-one for women, and 'foreign slaves' after thirty years' service. Negroes born in the colony on attaining the age of forty could offer their owners £8 6s. 8d. and ask for freedom as a favour. Finally, to check the production of half-breed children, marriage between whites and full-blooded blacks was forbidden, though marriage between whites and half-castes was still permissible.[3] So the law stood till, in face of 1708. trouble with runaway slaves and the low level of life with which freedmen were content, it was announced that owners must not manumit their slaves unless they gave a guarantee that the new freedmen would not become a charge on the public funds for ten years to come.[4]

---

[1] Theal, IIa., 59, 154; No. 50 of 1835, pp. 14, 16.
[2] *Ibid.*, IIa. 150 ff.; No. 50 of 1835, pp. 14, 15; Spoelstra, *op. cit.*, I. 29.
[3] *Bel. Hist. Dok.*, I. 23, 25, 41.
[4] The term was raised to twenty years in 1783 (No. 50 of 1835, p. 20).

Such was the lot of the colonists, bond and free, white, black, and multi-coloured, when in 1716 the anxious Directors began to ask themselves and the Council of Policy what was wrong with their colony at the Cape.[1] Something was obviously very wrong indeed. Governor van Assenburgh, King Log following the van der Stel King Stork, had been popular enough with the burghers. True, he was a recluse and a toper, but he had left the colonists alone and had therefore been in their eyes the very model of an *edel heer*.[2] The root of the trouble lay deeper than any matter of personality. At the end of the long wars with Louis of France, the Seventeen had looked for 1713. a speedy return to 'normalcy' and more also; they had built new and bigger ships for their Eastern trade; they had supplied the Cape with a new and vigorous Governor, de Chavonnes; in short, they had piped hopefully, but, so far, the Cape had refused to dance.

The Cape seemed to be sliding backwards after the all-too-vigorous push forward administered by the van der Stels. Half the meat contract had been given to Huising, and a rent of £2 10s. had been levied on the great cattle-runs of 3000 morgen and upwards which the burghers held on annual loan from the Company; where-upon a brand-new disease had appeared among the cattle. The wool-growing enterprise had failed, for the farmers had cheerfully bastard-ised the imported sheep till even their samples of wool became unsaleable. The forestry scheme had also been abandoned. Farmers declined to plant trees, many trees were 'missing' from the Stellen-bosch reserves, the timber in the Peninsula kloofs was exhausted, and, after an ineffectual attempt to get wood from the far-distant Zondereind valley, the local authorities had folded their hands. The mixed flood of wine was still pouring forth in such volume that the Council levied a tax upon it for the first time; but the fate of wheat 1715 was more chequered. In good years the Company would not take all that was offered, and farmers were reduced to turning their grain into spirits. The Council, intent on revenue, then demanded a tithe of all grain harvested and not merely, as heretofore, of the grain brought into Capetown for sale, and, when no one would undertake to farm so unpopular a tax, demanded that its share should be delivered by the growers at the Castle. Thereupon, the annual *opgaaf* of the burghers' produce became more unreliable than ever. The crops for 1711 and 1712 were poor; smallpox paralysed all industry in 1713, and when in 1714 a bumper crop was forthcoming all the old troubles arose with Batavia about prices and uncertain quantities. The farmers declined to send their corn to India to be sold for what it would fetch; they still wanted a quick and certain return and said

---

[1] V.R. Soc., I. 85 ff.
[2] Theal, II*a*. 420, 429; Godée-Molsbergen, *Van Riebeeck*, p. 245 ff.

3*

they would be ruined unless the Company, their immanent Providence, took all that they produced; hence, the perplexed authorities took it at a reduced price, refused to give out any more land for wine and sheep, encouraged the burghers to concentrate on peas, beans and barley for the homeward-bound fleets, and passed a Stamp Act.[1]

The new taxes on cattle-runs, wine, stamps and corn helped to swell the revenue already furnished by the transfer duty and, above all, the annually auctioned leases;[2] even so, revenue was, as ever, far behind expenditure. It had been so, it was so, and was to be so to the end. It is hard to count the exact cost to the Company of the Cape as a colony; the system of bookkeeping was archaic and involved; the currency was chaotic; the Cape itself was a mere branch establishment and was charged with many items—such as the cost of ships' stores, the hospital and wages to sailors—which should have been put down to the Company's general expenditure; on the other hand, it was debited neither with the cost of ammunition and transport of ammunition, the cost of materials from Holland, nor various sums paid on behalf of the colony in India or the Netherlands. Roughly speaking, and reckoning the florin at 1s. 8d., the expenditure from 1697 to 1707 ranged from £14,350 to £18,400 and the revenue from £5500 to £6900.[3]

1716. The Directors wanted to fill that gap and promote the prosperity of their little colony; they, therefore, plied de Chavonnes and his Council with questions.[4] Could more people be accommodated at the Cape, and, if so, of what class? Could skilled artisans make a decent living? If no more people could be taken in under existing conditions, could not new means of subsistence be developed, such as the growing of coffee, sugar, cotton, indigo, olives, flax, silk, 'and more especially tobacco'? Would hop-growing encourage the cultivation of grain or should hops be imported for the making of beer? Would it pay better to break up the official cattle-run at Groenekloof into small quit-rent farms or go on leasing it en bloc? Would a tax on provisions sold to foreigners bring in revenue and silence the complaint of the colonists that foreigners knew how to get better and cheaper meat than they themselves? Finally, were European farm-hands and agriculturists likely to be cheaper than slaves; in other words, was the colony to be based on free white or on servile coloured labour?

1717. The Council sent in a gloomy report. They expected nothing in the way of experiments from the farmers, for in all the colony not more

---

[1] *Lett. Desp.*, *1696–1708*, p. 355; *Lett. Rec.*, *1695–1708*, p. 250; Theal, IIa. 420, 428, 436, 446, 485.
[2] *Bel. Hist. Dok.*, I. 35; V.R. Soc., IV. 45; VI. 34.
[3] *Lett. Desp.*, pp. 255, 320; Theal, IIa. 434 ff.
[4] V.R. Soc., I. pp. 85 ff.

than thirty families were wealthy; the rest were mortgaged up to the eyes to the Orphan Chamber, the Poor Fund, or richer neighbours. The wind blew tobacco plants to pieces, the sun scorched what was left, and the shrivelled relics were unsaleable; there was not enough labour for cotton or flax, and folk preferred the East Indian varieties; two coffee plants had been known to struggle to maturity, but neither had borne beans; wool, indigo, olives, and silk had all been tried and had duly failed; wind again damaged hops, which were no good for export, and too much beer would ruin the wine farmers; as it was, no one outside the Cape would drink the local wines unless they had to. As for mining and manufacture, there might be coal at French Hoek, but that was sixty miles away and the cost of transport would be too heavy; one councillor had ideas on the subject of silver mines, but, as the Directors had not asked for information on this head, he kept his knowledge of the local Chicova to himself; one of van der Stel's Frenchmen, Taillefer, had made wool hats, but he had died and the industry with him; the making of woollen gloves and socks had also dwindled away; there was no opening for artisans, and those who were already in the colony were mere handy men with few tools and less skill. As for Groenekloof, that had better be leased as usual.

The one practical suggestion made by honourable councillors was 'that it should please our Lords and Masters to grant us free trade to Madagascar, Mauritius and surrounding islands and the East Coast of Africa, . . . a regular free traffic between this out-of-the-way place and a few other places,' a traffic which could hardly hurt the Company's monopoly and whose freights and tolls would swell the exiguous Cape revenue. Finally, on the vital issue of free *versus* slave labour, all the councillors save one condemned white labour as lazy, incompetent, intractable, liable to drunkenness and, withal, more expensive than slave labour.

One man only spoke up for free men, free industry, and therefore for a large home market.[1] This was the captain of the garrison, Dominique de Chavonnes, brother of the Governor, a soldier who thought in terms of men rather than florins. He insisted that the colony could carry 150 white artisans and, even if a white man cost £12 a year in wages as against £6 down for a slave, two of them could do the work of three slaves; they required less watching and speeding up; they would spend their wages to the benefit of all concerned. Further, free Europeans meant husbands for the women, a numerous body of colonists and a strong defence which would enable the Company to cut down its costly garrison. Pressure of population would force men to seek new means of subsistence, and the very lack of slaves would breed habits of industry; already the Drakenstein

[1] V.R. Soc., I. 97, 101.

children were helping their fathers with good results. Slaves meant conspiracies against masters; worse still, they meant big plantations, and one of the main weaknesses of the colony was the unwieldy size of the farms. Break up the farms, said the captain, and work them properly; break up Groenekloof and give the meat contract to a round dozen competing parties; so three families might learn to live where only one at present existed.

At this crisis of its fate, the Cape Colony took the wrong turning. Captain de Chavonnes was outvoted on all points. Had his advice been taken, the western Colony at least might have become a genuine white man's country, for the climate was Mediterranean; slavery was not deeply rooted; five-sixths of the slaves were men; the feckless Hottentots were dying or retiring, and could never have competed with Europeans in industry; the sturdy Bantu were still far off. As it was, the work of 1707 was completed in 1717. The colony, denied a steady recruitment of European immigrants, was condemned to slave labour and a rigidly restricted market. The history of the eighteenth century was foreshadowed in Dominique de Chavonnes' report: stagnation in the West, dispersion in the East, and intellectual and material poverty throughout.

CHAPTER IV

THE DIASPORA, 1717–78

THE Seventeen had asked what was wrong with their Cape Colony, and Captain de Chavonnes had answered them. *Onze heeren superiores* might well have gone on to ask what was wrong with the East India Company as a whole. The truth was that the Golden Age of the Netherlands and therefore of the Company had ended about the time that van Riebeeck landed at the Cape. The United Provinces, carried forward by the national enthusiasm stirred by the long and victorious struggle with Spain, had made the most of their geographical, financial, and commercial opportunities while their continental neighbours were busied with the dreadful Thirty Years' War and the Franco-Spanish struggle which had arisen therefrom, and their potential English rivals were at each other's throats in the name of King Charles or the Long Parliament. But the Thirty Years' War ended; Cromwell set up strong one-man rule in the British Isles; 1648– France and Spain made peace, and the republican burgher party in 1659. the Netherlands under Jan and Cornelis de Witt clipped the wings of the House of Orange.

The Netherlands had to face growing economic and political pressure at home and abroad. The Baltic trade began to fail in face of Scandinavian and English competition; three Anglo-Dutch com- 1652– mercial wars followed in quick succession; side by side with them 1674. ran Colbert's economic war, which opened out into real war or 1668– rumours of war with the French. The Treaty of Utrecht had indeed 1713. ended the long struggle against Louis XIV, and the Netherlands found themselves on the winning side; but the cost of their victory had been greater than that of many defeats. They had been forced to lavish their money, men and energies on troops and fortifications and to leave the naval side of the war to the English, or rather to the British, since England and Scotland had sunk their ancient animosi- 1707. ties sufficiently to form the strong political and economic union of Great Britain. Naval supremacy had passed from the Dutch to the British; the financial centre of the West had abandoned Amsterdam for London with its new Bank of England; Great Britain, an island secure from attack in a way that the United Provinces were not, was even better placed than they to take the lion's share of the commerce of the growing outer worlds of West and East which must pass up her Channel on its way to Continental Europe. The persistence of the Scots was now added to the cautious enterprise of the English, a dangerous combination; the English had latterly reorganised their East India Company on a much stronger basis than before; in the East they could count on the support of the Portuguese under the 1640. House of Braganza which they had helped to restore and had bound to them by the famous 'port-wine treaty'; the power of the French 1703. Company in the Indies was also growing and was buttressed by strong naval stations in the Indian Ocean at Ile de Bourbon and, since 1715, Mauritius.

The Dutch Company by reason of its obnoxious economic policy could expect no mercy from these rivals, and it was now finding that the spice-trade to which everything else had been sacrificed was not so valuable as it had believed. Tropical goods came in so slowly and at such high prices that it was hard to make a profit; as in Portugal, the excitements of the Indian trade had bred contempt for steady industry; lavishness had appeared in the frugal Netherlands counter-balanced by poverty and discontent among the less successful classes; speculation was rife; all the weaknesses of the chartered company system were coming to light. The Company had done well enough until it took up the responsibilities of ruling on a large scale; but from the first it had been financially unsound and had made matters worse by declaring dividends when there were no profits or even, in the later seventeenth century, when it was deeply in debt. The £250 shares rose and fell in the most amazing fashion from £1720 to £48 and then up again to £1260. *Windhandel*, men called it; but it continued so long as dividends were forthcoming, and this was always the case, anything from 25 to 71 per cent. till 1782, when the Company paid its last dividend.[1]

The policy of the Company showed nervousness and indecision in the late seventeenth and early eighteenth centuries, notably in South-Eastern Africa. There it alternately tightened and relaxed its hold. Simon van der Stel had despatched *Centaurus* as far as the Kei river, and had twice sent *Noord* as far as Delagoa Bay. On the second occasion, the captain of *Noord* had bought Port Natal from a local Bantu chieftain for £1650 on paper and for the odd £50 in actual cash; but on the way home the vessel was wrecked, and though the survivors of the crew struggled home overland to Capetown much harassed by Bushmen, the precious document was lost. Willem Adriaan had sent an expedition to renew the treaty; but the complacent chief's son was then reigning at the Port and blandly replied that his father was dead, 'his skins are buried with him in the floor of his house . . . and as to what he agreed to, it was for himself, and I have nothing to say to it.'[2]

Farther to the east, for fear of the French, the Company had reoccupied Mauritius, which they had abandoned in 1658. This island they ruled as a dependency of the Cape, for the Mauritius Council was subordinate to that at Capetown; appeals from its court lay either to Batavia or the Castle; the Cape Governors, especially the younger van der Stel, used it as a penal settlement, and since the life of the little garrison and the handful of burghers was wretched, deportation thither was regarded as sentence of death. In the space of a few short years, floods wrecked the Governor's house and the magazines, fire destroyed the whole of the Company's premises, and pirates held the garrison to ransom. The island was of little profit to the Company. It produced ambergris, ebony, waggon-woods, and the dodo; but very few ships called, industrial experiments failed, Batavia would not touch Mauritian tobacco, arrack, soap or butter, and the islanders had to eke out a living by traffic with stray English ships. Simon van der Stel had long talked of abandonment, but his son was for holding on to keep out the

1688–
1689.

1664.

---

[1] Keller, *Colonization*, pp. 408, 460; Cunningham, *Western Civilization*, II. 203 ff.; V.R. Soc., IV. 44; Theal, IIa. 488.
[2] Moodie, *Records*, pp. 441, 444; V.R. Soc., V. 54; Godée-Molsbergen, *Reizen*, III.

French and to make ebony pay by supplying proper transport. On Willem Adriaan's fall, the Company abandoned the island, a few of 1710. the families came back to the Cape, the rest went on to Batavia, and the departing officials turned dogs loose to ravage the game.[1] As Willem Adriaan had foreseen, the French snapped up the derelict 1715. island and made it their chief naval base in Eastern waters for nearly a hundred years.

Perhaps repenting of the abandonment of Mauritius, the Company made a determined effort to secure Delagoa Bay. The Portuguese Governor of Mozambique, nominally responsible to the shadowy Viceroy at Goa, still claimed to rule all the East African coast from Cape Guardafui to Lourenço Marques; but in reality the Moslems had reconquered all the forts from Magadoxo to Zanzibar by 1698 and the Portuguese only retained Pemba island and the coasts south of Cape Delgado. The Mozambique administration still bolstered up the feeble majesty of the Christian Monomotapa with a military and ecclesiastical bodyguard; but Bantu chiefs and semi-Portuguese *prazo* holders freely challenged the Governor's authority. The very Portuguese missions were rotten. The Dominicans, for the most part Africans, Asiatics or half-castes, were such a nuisance that the king 1719. withdrew them all except the vicars of churches and the commissioners of the Inquisition, and a few years later threatened to replace even these with Jesuits and secular priests. The trade of the territory was trifling. 'Arabs,' who did what little retail trade and skilled work there was, were severely repressed, forbidden to buy baptised slaves and ordered to sell slaves only to Christians. Clearly the slave-trade was the one hope, and the Portuguese officials meant to engross it.[2]

Early in the eighteenth century English adventurers, and cosmopolitan pirates from their haunt at Libertatia in Madagascar, frightened the Portuguese away from Delagoa Bay. The Dutch East 1721– India Company thereupon occupied it and held it for ten years. 1730. It was a disastrous occupation, first at Fort Lagoa, and then at its more substantial successor, Fort Lydzaamheid. The garrison, German mercenaries for the most part sent thither for their sins, had need of all the patience they could muster; two-thirds of the original party died of fever in the first six weeks, and next year pirates drove the survivors into the bush. Relief came, and the adjacent territory was purchased from the local chiefs; but fever raged; some of the Germans deserted and perished miserably north of Inhambane; others mutinied and were barbarously crushed. Trade was disappointing, merely a little gold, ivory, ambergris, wax and copper, while, if sugar and indigo did well on a small scale, expeditions failed

---

[1] *Letter Desp.* (*v. d. Stel*), pp. 14, 15, 58, 206, 265, 353; *Lett. Rec.*, pp. 24, 26, 50, 284, 414; *Journal*, p. 116; *Rambles*, chapters 15, 16.
[2] Rec. S.E.A., V. 1 ff., 145, 156, 165; Theal, IIIa. 317 ff.

to find the gold and copper mines and the rumoured mountain of iron in the interior; the Portuguese maltreated natives who dared to traffic with the interlopers; the natives destroyed a party of Dutchmen, in self-defence, they said, and judging from the character of the garrison that may well have been so. At last the fort was evacuated, and though Dutch ships hung about for two years to come, the East Coast was finally abandoned in 1732 to the Portuguese, the Bantu, and the pirates.[1] Thereafter, Portuguese East Africa slid steadily downhill, neglected by Pombal, Portugal's great reforming minister, and pillaged by its own officials who appropriated government gunpowder to their own uses and cornered the traffic in slaves and beads which, apart from a little ivory at Inhambane, was the only trade worth having. The Moslems, the real traders of the country lived a harassed life, being alternately driven out and allowed to creep back unarmed; Pombal took the lead in securing the suppression of the Jesuit Order, the Dominicans withdrew to the ruins that bore the name of Goa, and Christianity simply died out among the Bantu. The inland trading and mission stations disappeared, notably the mission station at Zumbo, the furthest up the Zambesi. In short, by the end of the eighteenth century, all that Portugal could show for three hundred years of occupation were some thirteen hundred European and half-caste Christians.

Thus, at the beginning of the second quarter of the eighteenth century, the hold of Western civilisation on Southern Africa was feeble. The Portuguese, representatives of a decaying monarchy in Europe and a falling empire in the East clung to the south-eastern coasts; far away to the south-west the Dutch Company's flag flew over the little depressed and isolated Cape Colony. The Cape Colony of 1730, however, was not without elements of strength. It was more homogeneous than it had ever been before. Time, intermarriage and the stresses of the van der Stel controversy had steadily welded the composite European elements into a single people; newcomers were so few that they were easily absorbed; above all, the Huguenots mingled their blood and identity with that of their Dutch and German fellow-citizens. Official policy helped forward the fusion. In 1708 the Drakenstein consistory had been told that henceforward all official correspondence must be in Dutch; but as late as 1724, on the death of Paul Roux, Amsterdam gave leave for the appointment of another French parish clerk, just this once, for the sake of the score or so of old folk who knew no Dutch.[2] Thereafter such a concession was unnecessary, for French simply died out. But France still lived in the surnames and personal appearance of many of the colonists, and, in so far as the clash of tongues could have that

---

[1] Theal, IIa. 461 ff.; No. 252 of 1835, p. 101; Bel. Hist. Dok., II.
[2] Botha, French Refugees, pp. 149, 159; Spoelstra, op. cit., II. 608.

effect, French had played its part in breaking down the spoken High Dutch of the late seventeenth century into the early · form of Afrikaans.[1]

On the other hand, growing racial homogeneity was tempered by social and economic divisions.[2] Cape society became more and more sharply split up into groups as time went on, and it is this differentiation which relieves the monotony of the short and simple annals of the mid-eighteenth century Cape, a monotony which could prompt Commissioner de Mist to write, in 1802, that the only changes in the polity of the Cape during the last century of Company rule had been in 'the taxes, the number of Company's servants at the Cape, and the cost of living. . . . Regulated at rare intervals, they rose step by step.'[3]

In the Peninsula were the Company's servants; too many of them, some said, too much set on intriguing for pay and promotion, more intent on private trade than on the welfare of the Company, avid of fees and perquisites and precedence, contemptuous of the burgher *canaille*, corrupt themselves and breeders of corruption in others. The story of this period begins with the suspension of the Secunde Helot for diverting Company's property to his own uses; it ends— *quis custodiet ipsos custodes?*—with Fiscal Boers compounding a felony by taking money from a burgher who wanted to import firearms from a Swedish vessel. There were occasional attempts at reform. Van Imhoff visited Capetown on the way to take up the 1743. Governor-Generalship of India in the room of Valckenier, who had been recalled for massacring the Chinese in Batavia and arbitrarily imprisoning van Imhoff himself and other honourable councillors. He was the new broom that was to sweep the Indies clean; in passing he tried to render conditions at the Cape more salubrious.[4] He found

---

[1] The influence of other languages on the formation of Afrikaans has been questioned (Union Year Book, No. 8, pp. 14 ff.: article by J. J. Smith).

[2] There were at the Cape, in 1740, about 4000 free burghers—men, women and children—and 1500 Company's servants and soldiers with their families (Theal, II*q*, 512); in 1778 there were 9867 burghers, 1122 servants and 454 soldiers (*Kaapse Argiefstukken*, 1778, p. 327). Theal states that the church registers show that 1526 men and 449 women arrived between 1652 and 1795 and left descendants:

	Dutch.	French.	German.	Various.
Men . . .	494	74	806	152
Women : .	322	72	48	7

Theal notes the preponderance of Dutch women, the youthful vigour of the French, and the comparative age and physical exhaustion of many of the Germans. H. T. Colenbrander in his *Afkomst der Boeren* reckons a higher proportion of German blood in the Afrikander people than does Theal; but he counts as German all those who came from German-Swiss cantons and parts of Germany along the Dutch border, whereas Theal notes that many of these Germans were descended from sixteenth-century Dutch refugees, and counts as Dutch all those who were members of the Dutch Reformed Church (Theal, III*b*. 427).

[3] V.R. Soc., III. 171.   [4] *Ibid.*, I. pp. 129 ff.

the officials eking out their meagre salaries by juggling with the currency, a chaotic numismatic museum ranging from golden ducats to copper stuivers, trading on their own account and digging by proxy in the gardens of two morgen or so which they had been allowed to have for twenty years past. Most of this he could not alter; but he forbade private trade and, in lieu thereof, allowed the leading officials to take fees on certain kinds of business, such as wine, trading licences, and the drawing up of official documents. So

1751– he passed on to Batavia, and in due course Governor Ryk Tulbagh,
1771. the South African Clive, had to institute a twenty-year-long anti-corruption campaign, forbidding private trade, fixing fees, and setting a good example. But Father Tulbagh died, and before long

1779. the burghers raised their voices against renewed official corruption. So it was to the end. 'If ever venality prevailed in any part of the world,' wrote a British naval officer in 1795, 'it is in the Dutch colonies.'[1]

De Kaap, or Kaapstad as men began to call it in Tulbagh's time, grew steadily. By about 1775 it consisted of some 1200 substantial houses, many of them double storied, stuccoed and either white-washed or painted green, flat-fronted, for the most part flat-roofed also, with a stoep and a garden between each and the road. The Castle, the Company's offices and hospital, and Tulbagh's new burgher watch-house gave the town an air of distinction which was enhanced by the Gardens in the background. The unpaved streets were hard and served their purpose well enough; but the dust blown up by the summer south-easters was trying and cancelled much of the freshness imparted by the oak avenues on either side of the road and the stream of water which flowed down the middle. The people of the town, like the officials, looked to the passing ships for their living; boarding houses and canteens flourished in good times. Visitors were apt to complain that the men were lazy and indifferent except when there was easy money to be made; but in general they held a higher opinion of the ladies, especially the younger ones, who were proud of their knowledge of French and English, passionately fond of dancing, fairly skilled upon the piano and keenly interested in the fashions of Paris and The Hague. Old Admiral Stavorinus might depict the damsels as giddy, de Mist later on could stigmatise the younger generation as indolent and possessed of 'an intense prejudice against exerting themselves mentally'; but, after all, that was only to be expected in a town where life passed placidly, except when the fleets came in, and all classes were much given to gossip over the eternal cups of tea and coffee sweetened with sugar-candy.[2]

[1] Rec. C.C., I. 30. Cf. J. S. Stavorinus, Voyages, II. 131, 275.
[2] V.R. Soc. IV. 65 ff., 95; III. 201; Theal, IIIa. 51, 97; Stavorinus, Voyages, III. chapter ix; A. Sparrman, Voyage to the Cape, I. 10.

Outside the town, in the Peninsula and, still more, beyond the sandy Flats, were the wine and corn farms of the van der Stel settlement. Stellenbosch had rebuilt itself after the fire of 1710, gloried in a handsome new drostdy, and diverted the Eerste river so that it no longer flooded the streets in the rainy season. Substantial farmhouses were the rule in these parts, many of them latterly adorned with the famous Cape-Dutch gables.[1] But agriculture was still very rough and ready. The heavy wooden ploughs were dragged by eight oxen or horses and manned by four men: one to lead and one to drive the team, another to guide the plough, the fourth to scatter the seed in front; for it was mere 'under-furrowing' with but little harrowing and hardly any use of manure. That was kept for fuel in a land where timber was not too plentiful, or for the flooring of the humbler houses. The interests of these *plaas-boers* lay in their farms, each of which was a state in miniature, producing little more than was needed for the maintenance of its inhabitants, but self-sufficing in everything save luxuries, articles of manufacture and a few raw materials. The farmers crossed the Flats as seldom as might be. Physically that barren waste was a great divider; attempts to bind the drifting sands with knot-grass and wild-olive all failed; the absence of a hard road made it impossible for men to grow wine or corn as a commercial proposition more than sixty miles or three days' trek from their only market in Capetown. Spiritually, too, there was a great gulf fixed between the farming centres and the capital; for the memories of the van der Stel struggle lived still, and to the farmer Capetown spelt grasping officials, payment of tithe and arrears of taxes at the barrier, and sharp practice by sophisticated townsmen. The men of the capital might look outwards to the sea, but they themselves took no stock of what happened in the outer world. Did a stranger speak of the advantages of Europe, they would ask him why he had troubled to come to Africa; did he question them on things African, they would show surprise at his ignorance.[2] Their vineyards, ploughlands and beloved oxen were for them a universe that was bounded by the Flats and the Mountains of Africa.

The Peninsula and the Berg river valley together formed 'the West' as distinct from the fast-expanding 'East.' It was the West which, in the course of the eighteenth century, became thoroughly dependent on slave labour; it was the West which suffered most from the strait-jacket of the Company's economic policy. After the famous decision of the Council in 1717, importation of slaves continued steadily till the slaves outnumbered the free burghers and, 1756. until the British stopped the trade in 1807, kept the numerical

---

[1] D. Fairbridge, *Historic Houses.*
[2] V.R. Soc., IV. 11, 54; *Bel. Hist. Dok.*, III. 49; Theal, IIIa, 51, 183.

advantage they had gained.[1] The slaves were still drawn mainly from East Africa and the Indies, though the despatch of Indian criminals to Capetown was stopped in 1767 at the request of the Council of Policy.[2] By that time the slaves were as clearly grouped in classes as were their masters: negroes, the cheapest of all, 'faithful, patient and good servants,' who did the rough work in the fields; Malays, the real skilled workers of the Colony and makers of so many of the lovely Cape-Dutch gables, who ranked themselves above all other slaves and free Hottentots; half-castes or Afrikanders, a growing class, who were household slaves and often the confidants of their masters and mistresses, permanent family servants and almost members of the family.[3]

Even the farm labourers were much better treated than the West Coast negroes, who were still being shipped across the Atlantic to the West Indies; manumission was still fairly common, sometimes by will, sometimes by the marriage of a slave girl to a white man who would buy or give her her freedom, sometimes by a colonist who freed his slaves on returning to Europe.[4] Since 1722, slaves who were taken to the Netherlands became free provided the authorities approved, though slaves who smuggled themselves overseas were liable to be sent back to be prosecuted by the Fiscal. On the other hand, as the numbers of slaves increased, there was a steady stiffening of law and custom against them. The conscious effort to Christianise them died away. Europeans found it hard enough to keep in touch with Church and school themselves without educating their property into the bargain; the Company's slaves, housed in the Slave Lodge which served the purpose of a brothel for soldiers and sailors between the hours of 8 and 9 P.M., were bad workers, and their shortcomings were put down to the official schooling which they still received; above all, in spite of the laws of 1708, there was the belief that conversion must lead to manumission. Slaves had long ago been deprived of their old privilege of standing sponsor to slave children at their baptism;[5] but the Council of India decreed that all slaves must be baptised, that baptised slaves might not be sold, and, borrowing a leaf from the Portuguese, that Moslems might only sell their slaves to Christians. The value of slaves, whose market was thus restricted, promptly fell; owners saw to it that the Christianisation of their slaves did not go beyond attendance at family prayers,

1770.

---

[1]

	Burghers.	Slaves of burghers.	Company's slaves.
1756.	5,123	5,787	600
1793.	13,830	16,767	

(Theal, IIIa. 40; Moodie, *Records*, III. 16; V.R. Soc., III. 175).

[2] Theal, IIIa. 31.

[3] V.R. Soc., III. 252; *State of the Cape . . . in 1822*, pp. 73 ff., 148; W. J. Burchell, *Travels in the Interior*, I. 31 ff.

[4] V.R. Soc., III. 252; *Requesten*, pp. 2, 66, 366, 669, 851.

[5] No. 50 of 1835, pp. 17, 18; V.R. Soc., IV. 116.

and the slaves began to turn a ready ear to the missionaries of the Prophet. 'Some religion they must have,' a later observer noted, 'and they are not allowed to be Christians.'[1]

The slave laws became fiercer, the punishments less discriminate. In the year of our Lord 1732 a murderer was broken at the wheel and left dangling without the *coup de grâce* till sunset, and, alongside of him, hung another slave in like case for stealing a violin. It was a callous age as the criminal records of all Europe witness, but even Cape society shuddered when the wretched Titus of Bengal was impaled for complicity in the murder of his master.[2] Nevertheless, Tulbagh, a humane Governor if ever there was one, codified all the 1753. fierce old slave penalties, including death for a slave who raised his hand against his master, flogging without trial at the bidding of the ministers of justice, and harsh punishments for making a noise at funerals.[3] They at least treated the dead with great respect in the mid-eighteenth century.

Slavery has been defended as one means of introducing a barbarous people to the ways of civilised society; but against these possible advantages must be set the evil effects of the domestic institution upon the slave-owners. Those evils were made manifest in the Cape of the eighteenth century. Van Imhoff did not mince his words on 1743. that score. 'A mason and a carpenter,' he wrote, 'each earns from eight to nine schellingen a day and in addition receives food and drink and withal does not do as much as a half-trained artisan in Europe. . . . I believe it would have been far better had we, when this Colony was founded, commenced with Europeans and brought them hither in such numbers that hunger and want would have forced them to work. But having imported slaves every common or ordinary European becomes a gentleman and prefers to be served than to serve. . . . We have in addition the fact that the majority of the farmers in this Colony are not farmers in the real sense of the word, but owners of plantations, and that many of them consider it a shame to work with their own hands. Such a bad example makes the farm-hands worse.'[4] Here was a Dominique de Chavonnes come to judgment, and nearly a hundred years later an English official could write that 'the power exercised over slaves gives to every Christian man ... so much distinction, that pomp in rags displays its superiority even in the street.'[5]

The economic history of an isolated European community thus based on slave labour and oppressed by a monopolistic trading corporation was necessarily dismal. That shrewd Commissioner- 1802. General, de Mist, summed it up well at the beginning of the

[1] *State of the Cape*, pp. 74 ff., 349.   [2] *Journal, 1699–1732*, pp. 260, 337.
[3] Theal, IIIa. 34.   [4] V.R. Soc., I. 136–7.
[5] *State of the Cape*, pp. 176.

nineteenth century. 'The Colony,' he wrote, 'was fairly prosperous so long as the number of colonists was limited. . . . But this balance was gradually upset and the . . . Company did not allow the colonists sufficient freedom in trade to dispose of surplus produce. At the same time the Company encouraged increased production.' This disciple of Adam Smith and the Physiocrats noted in fairness that the Company had indeed tried to take the surplus at a fixed price and export it itself; nevertheless, he concluded that 'the balance between production and consumption is bound to be upset unless freedom of trade is allowed, and . . . a period of plenty and prosperity is often followed by a period of famine and poverty.'[1]

1717–1719. At the time of the Chavonnes inquiry, the Council of Policy had asked for a limited freedom of trade and the burgher councillors had echoed the request. The demand was refused. The Seventeen decided rather to develop intensive cultivation of semi-tropical products, made elaborate preparations, sent out experts and hoped for the best. All the experiments failed. The experts condemned tobacco; olives failed at once; Persian sheep retained their identity for a decade and were then absorbed in the general ovine community of fat-tailed, hairy sheep; silk promised well but 'the "expert" himself was not so skilful as expected'[2]—'Is there anything whereof it may be said, "See, this is new?" '—and the factory was closed down after producing six pounds of silk. Indigo, a little cotton and the hope of silver mines in the Drakenstein valley were all that remained after 1735, and, in due course, indigo and cotton were given up and the silver was not forthcoming. Meanwhile, government actually discussed the possibilities of overseas trade with the burgher councillors, but these worthies, perhaps dismayed by the Company's costly failure at Delagoa Bay, replied that the enthusiasts of 1719 had either died or changed their minds.[3]

The fortunes of wine, corn and meat, the staple products of the Cape, fluctuated violently. Seeing that the meat supply was more and more provided by the cattle-farmers and Hottentots beyond the mountains, corn and wine were the hope of the West. The Directors **1719.** tried to encourage the official export of wine to Europe and India, but the samples sent to Amsterdam and Batavia were unfit for use; bottled wine fared no better; the Constantia brand alone found favour, and of that there was far too little. As for wheat and cattle, a run of bad harvests drove the garrison back on rice rations, and cattle-disease obliged the Company first to forbid the sale of live beasts to foreigners and then to prohibit all sale of fresh meat and vegetables to them till the Company's own needs had been met at a fixed price. It is true that government had to capitulate and pay the

---

[1] V.R. Soc., III. 173 ff.   [2] *Ibid.*, IV. 117.
[3] Theal, II*a*. 444 ff., 482 ff., 490.

high prices for meat demanded by the burghers and supply the foreigners as of grace; but the dearth and embargo of 1723 gave the Tavern of the Seas a bad name among foreigners which it only gradually lived down.[1]

So it went. A new form of horse-sickness appeared; twenty years 1724. later van Imhoff found that the farmers had had no sale for their 1743. wines for many years. The Directors were willing to help them by taking brandy for the ships instead of wine, if it was drinkable, and van Imhoff proposed to give them leave to export their own wines to India on Company's ships, if there was room for them. The burghers would not have it so; hence, the Governor-General increased the wine-tax, promised to take as much as the Company wanted at a fixed price, and left the farmers free to sell the rest to foreigners; but, as usual, Batavia grumbled at the quality of the 1744. wine, experts failed to improve it and the Council of Policy refused to risk reciprocal free trade with the great Labourdonnais' Mauritius. Meanwhile, the grain harvests varied; sometimes drought and rust called for proclamations to check profiteering, at other times there was a fair amount of corn for export. Van Imhoff made the same arrangements for the export of wheat as for wine; but when the Company tried to reduce the prices the farmers cried out that the cost of labour would not allow it, and the locusts came for the first 1746. time in fifty years. Nevertheless, by 1750 the Cape was exporting 7500 muids of grain supplemented by peas, beans, wine, dried fruit, ivory, skins and ostrich feathers.[2]

It was little enough on which to support a colony whose population was growing fast, thanks to early and frequent marriages and a healthy climate, but whose internal power of consumption was none the less small in proportion to the amounts produced in good years. Then, as now, white South Africa was peculiarly dependent on export, and the exporting channels were sadly choked. The foreigners were the best hope for the ordinary burghers; but, though more ships came to the Cape after the Treaty of Utrecht than ever before, the number was not great. In the 'twenties and 'thirties there had been a marked increase, but by 1750 the average yearly total was down again to what it had been fifty years before, that is, some sixty-eight vessels annually, four-fifths of them Dutch with the English second. The truth was that the Company's trade was not expanding, foreigners resented the prices demanded of them, and Table Bay was not a safe harbour. Efforts to protect the ships by building a breakwater from Mouille Point were unsuccessful, and from 1742 onwards the Company's ships put into Simons Bay, some twenty

[1] Theal, II*a*, 445 ff.
[2] V.R. Soc., I. 131; Theal, II*a*. 1, 7, 8, 16, 17. A muid is rather less than three bushels (2·972).

miles distant, during the winter months when the north-westers raged on the Capetown side of the Peninsula.[1]

1750. The Directors then bethought themselves once more of European immigration as the cure for the present discontents of the Cape Colony. With one accord, the colonists replied that that would only make a bad business worse. Newcomers, the burgher councillors of Capetown declared, would 'merely add to the very serious state of poverty which already exists, for the reason that the major portion of the income of the inhabitants is earned by lodging the passing seafarers,' and now even these *heeren van ses weeken* by reason of their poverty cheated the boarding-house keepers of their 16*d.* a day either by remaining on board or by pitching tents on the seashore. 'With regard to the Artizan,' they added, 'he is obliged to remain idle half the year, owing to lack of materials,' and the only remedy they could suggest was 'free freight,' that is, liberty to trade on their own account. The Stellenbosch heemraden were even more explicit. They considered that the existing population was more than enough. Parents were already anxious about their children's prospects, oppressed by debts, disappointed with the results of stock-farming and agriculture, and more and more driven to trekking because grazing was becoming sour in the low-lying parts of the district. The heemraden of newly established Swellendam were equally despondent; their folk were very scattered, the most distant six weeks' trek away from the capital; there were very few springs; the cattle found it difficult to drink at the steep banks of the rivers. In short, the Colony could barely carry its 4500 free burghers as it was; to add to the number would be disastrous.[2]

This dejected community was now called on to pay 5*d.* in the £ on the value of its property on the analogy of Holland, and when this failed to cause a perceptible shrinkage in the gulf between expenditure and revenue, the Company, as a last resort, levied fresh duties on wine and brandy. Under the circumstances, the application to the Colony of the Indian sumptuary laws was a work of supererogation,

1755. all the more as, in that very year, the smallpox returned in full force. The scattered farmers and Bushmen escaped with small loss; but Capetown suffered heavily, the property market crashed, even plate and jewels became unsaleable, and for months the frightened farmers refused to bring their produce into the stricken capital. As in 1713, the miserable Hottentots suffered most severely of all, and, to add to their woes, leprosy attacked them.[3]

These afflictions brought the Colony to the verge of ruin. The new export duty on wine and brandy sold to foreigners hampered business; Batavia still took as little Cape wine as it could; the outbreak of the

---

[1] Theal, IIa. 521 ff.   [2] V.R. Soc., I. 149 ff.
[3] Theal, IIIa. 28, 36 ff.

Seven Years' War frightened shipping away from South African 1756. waters and drove many Cape wine-farmers into bankruptcy. But in the third year, the very war which thus promised disaster proved to be the economic salvation of the Colony for the time being. The French and English Companies were struggling for control of the trade of India; their ships flocked into Table Bay and, until peace broke out in 1763, the producers of the Cape received whatever prices they chose to ask.

The later 'sixties were again a time of depression, but in the 'seventies there were signs of better things. The Cape was already exporting a little butter and aloes and horses, small and ugly, but indubitably horses. The number of ships touching at Capetown or Simonstown also rose markedly, especially the profitable foreigners, who henceforward outnumbered the Company's own vessels with the British an easy first, then Frenchmen, Danes, and even a few Swedes and Prussians and a solitary Spaniard.[1] The burghers liked it because foreigners were fair game; the Directors were equally pleased, for, by allowing the burghers to fleece the passers-by, their own contractors were able to supply them with cheap meat. The Seventeen then decided to encourage export of general cargoes to 1772. the Netherlands as well as the wine which had gone thither regularly since 1736, for the big new hospital talked of in Tulbagh's time was being built at last and since most of the materials had to be sent from the Fatherland, the best way to keep down the cost of the outward carriage, then as now, was the promise of a return cargo. Hitherto samples—the Cape ran to samples in the eighteenth century—had been expensive and unsatisfactory, always excepting wheat. There was a constant demand for that, and the French in Mauritius were buying at such high prices that the Company had to issue a special *placaat* to secure a small shipload of wheat, rye, barley, wine and tallow for Holland.

During the seventeen-seventies Cape exports to Europe and the Indies increased, but expanding trade did not bring the burghers the prosperity they had expected. The Directors refused to allow them to ship wine on their own account to Holland; the Fiscal declined to buy wheat for despatch overseas till the Company's local needs had been met. The price for local supply was low, and since the price for export to Holland was six rix-dollars per muid less than that to Batavia, the authorities naturally tended to send more of the surplus to Europe than to the Indies.[2] Farmers complained bitterly, for strangers at the Cape were prepared to pay them twice as much as

[1] Yearly average of   1770–9.   1780–9.   1790–3.
      Dutch ships .   .   .   52   49   58
      Foreign ships.   .   .   59   99   97
[2] A rix-dollar was worth about four shillings British.

the Company, and the price of farming necessities was rising against them. Nor was it easy for them to get what they wanted even when they could pay for it. Importations were irregular and the embargo on foreign trade reacted fatally on corn and wine prices. Cash was scarce and men fell back on barter with all the inconvenience and loss that was thereby entailed; merchants had no real security and farmers sometimes stove in their wine-casks in the streets of Capetown to save themselves the thankless task of trekking them and their unsaleable contents home again.[1]

Meanwhile the East, 'the colony of dispersion,' grew rapidly behind the harassed 'colony of settlement' in the West. All the forces which had begun to make the trek-boer in the time of the van der Stels gained momentum as time went on; the children of men living in isolation grew up in isolation and learnt to love it. Geographical conditions favoured the dispersion. The mountains which rise range behind range to the high plateau of the interior were steep on the sea side, but there were plenty of passes, the descent on the far side was short, and though the land was neither rich nor well-watered, it was good enough for cattle and sheep provided their owners did not mind them scattering; the Hottentots played the part of bloodhounds, smelling out the springs and the fertile land, and moving on cheerfully for a small bribe as soon as the inevitable white man pitched his moving camp beside their hovels. Once on the plains of the interior, the Boers had little inducement to return to the coast belt. If Capetown had little attraction for the wine and grain farmers, it had less for them. They might trek in once in a way with a waggonload of butter and soap which they were glad to sell for half its value; they must come in at least once in their lives with their prospective brides to present themselves before the hated matrimonial court; but they were out of their element in the streets of a town, and they knew it. The capital represented to them the seat of an unsympathetic and alien central government which presumed to tax them, gave them little in return, interfered with their cherished cattle-trade with the tribes, and even tried to preserve the game on which they relied for so much of their food. They went to Capetown as seldom as possible and left it as soon as they had bought brandy, coffee, and dress-lengths for the coming year.[2]

There was little to stop the outward movement of the Boers once they had dragged their lumbering tented waggons over the passes with double spans of oxen or taken them to pieces and packed them over. The Hottentots offered no resistance, for the smallpox had to

[1] V.R. Soc., III. 176; Theal, IIIa. 97 ff.; Moodie, *Records*, III. 10 ff.; C. G. Botha, *Prices in the 18th Century* (S.A. Journal of Science, XX. 552 ff.).
[2] V.R. Soc., IV. 36, 149; Lichtenstein, *Travels*, I. 142, 364, *et passim*.

a great extent cleared the country of them; the Bushmen were a nuisance, but they were few and never made a determined stand till the 'seventies, when they had been pushed back to the last great range of mountains which skirted the dry central plateau.

Law and custom alike stimulated the trek. The original free bur-ghers had been given small freehold farms; but quite early farmers had learnt to prefer the *leenings plaatsen*—great cattle runs of 3000 morgen and upwards held on loan from the Company first for six months and then for a year at a time. Legally, the Company could resume the grant at the end of the year, but in practice it rarely did so, and when it did, it compensated the holder. If the holder died, his heirs were by law entitled only to the value of the *opstal*, that is the house and other improvements; but in practice, again, the prices paid for these farms clearly represented the value of the *opstal* and of the land. The loan place was thus to all intents and purposes a free grant of land for which the government made no charge at all till 1714, when it levied an annual rent or recognition of £2 10s. and the usual tithe of grain, if any were grown.[1]

The cattle-farmers thus learnt to look upon the grant of one or more of these great ranches as their birthright. Where possible they held two such farms in different parts of the country, one for the summer and the other for winter grazing. And they needed them. They had passed out of the 'Mediterranean' belt, with its good winter rains, that stretches back for a hundred miles behind Capetown, and they were not yet within the sphere of the summer rains which drench the south-east coasts. They were in the Karoo lands, the dry, inter-mediate country, and there they learnt to move back and forth between their farms like true nomads. They were continually on the move, for there was little to anchor them to any one place. The risk that the loan place might be resumed by the Company deterred any, who were so inclined, from making improvements; their large families of sons, each of whom was by law entitled to his legitimate portion in his father's estate, made it certain that on the death of the father the *opstal* at least would be sold. The sons might then elect to live together as a family group on the paternal farm till pressure of growing flocks and families forced them to disperse; but it was much more likely that the younger sons would push outwards to find fresh farms for themselves in a land where farms were to be had for the asking—or taking. And, in advance of the cattle-farmers, went the ivory-hunters far away into the wilds for eight months at a time, as far eastward as Pondoland, and possibly Natal itself. So popular *Circa* did elephant-hunting become that soon no borderland lass would *1730.* look at a young fellow who had not been once at least *op jagt*.[2]

---

[1] Theal, IIa. 436. On Land Tenure *vide* p. 53 *supra* (n.).
[2] Fouché, *Evolutie van die Trekboer*, p. 9; Theal IIa. 496.

The authorities did not know what to make of this steady and unwelcome expansion of the Colony in the tracks of the trek-waggons. Its traditional policy was monopoly of the cattle-trade for itself and, for its free burghers, non-intercourse with the tribes. From time to time it tried to enforce that policy; more usually it launched placaat after placaat at the heads of its disappearing subjects, in whose eyes then and for long afterwards the law of the central government became a thing of contempt. The need for fresh meat forced the Company to depart from the rigid policy of non-intercourse which it had enunciated after the downfall of the van der Stels. Cattle-disease had appeared in 1714; there were no bids for the meat contract in 1718, and next year a commando had to be called out against the Bushmen, who were plundering border farms in revenge, they said, for injuries done to them by the cattle-barterers. Thereafter there was little trouble with the Bushmen for twenty years to come.[1]

1723. Meanwhile the Company, despairing of its meat supply, gave van der Heiden leave to barter cattle for them from distant clans of Hottentots in spite of his connection with the cattle-rieving expedition of 1702.[2] Presently ugly stories began to drift in, and the Drakenstein consistory accused van der Heiden and his men of atrocious conduct. The inquiry broke down for lack of evidence; but the Company revived the system of guard-posts and planted one in the Zondereind valley and another at Rietvlei on the Buffeljagt's river near Swellendam, forbade the cattle-barter under heavier penalties than before, and modified its system of land-tenure in the

1732. hope of checking the Diaspora. It doubled the rents of the loan farms and offered small farms adjoining them on *erfpacht*—that is, lease for fifteen years at a low rental with the promise of compensation for improvements on resumption.[3] It was no use; the illicit

1737. traffic and the dispersion went on apace in spite of renewed orders, following the massacre of some elephant hunters far to the eastward, that no one was to go beyond the eastern border. That prohibition had to be waived, and for the next few years there was chaos in the eastern borderlands.[4]

It was during these troubled years that the first missionary effort was made on behalf of the Hottentots. The evangelical revival was beginning to stir; Wesleyans were active in England, the Moravian Brethren in Germany, and both in the British North American

1737– colonies. George Schmidt, a Moravian, now came to the far-distant
1744. Cape and set up a mission at Baviaan's Kloof in the Zondereind valley beyond the Hottentots-Holland Mountains. The Council of Policy favoured him, but other classes of the community resented

---

[1] Theal, IIa. 438 ff., 505 ff.   [2] *Vide supra*, p. 63.   [3] *Ibid.*, p. 53 (n.).
[4] No. 50 of 1835, pp. 17, 18; Theal, IIa. 484, 489, 491, 510; *Rambles*, p. 64.

his intrusion. The farmers were hostile, the Dutch Reformed clergy jealous, and when Schmidt, who had never been ordained, baptised five Hottentots, even the Council forbade him to do so again and lodged a complaint with the Amsterdam *Classis*. The jealousy of the clergy was in keeping with the political and religious principles of the day; they had just prevented the Lutherans of Capetown from building a church, and now saw to it that an unlucky parish clerk whom the churchwardens accused of Moravian leanings was despatched to Batavia. Schmidt took the hint, and finding he could do nothing with the unstable Hottentots, departed.[1]

Clearly the day of the evangelical missions in South Africa was not yet, but perhaps Schmidt might have been more successful had the times been quieter. They were anything but quiet. For some years 1719– past the Bushmen had done so little damage that a friendly burgher 1738. had been commissioned by the authorities to come to definite terms with them if he could. It was an isolated attempt at conciliation which duly aroused the wrath and suspicion of the frontiersmen. Nor was it successful. Bushmen and a few Hottentots heavily raided the 1739. cattle-runs round Piketberg and on the Bokkeveld; a panic ensued; farms were abandoned on all sides, and a commando, ill-supported by the burghers, had to fall back. A strong force was then called out, soldiers were stationed at temporary posts, losses were inflicted on the raiders and peace made.[2]

At the same time a petty European rebellion took place, a foretaste of what was to become common on the eastern frontier in later years. It arose out of a breach of the cattle-barter laws. Ten Piketbergers and some Hottentots fell foul of Namaquas near the Orange river; the Namaquas appealed to the Government, and the landdrost of Stellenbosch, at the bidding of the acting-governor, summoned the members of the expedition and other suspected parties to give an account of themselves in court. There was great excitement in all the land from Drakenstein northward at this unheard-of exercise of authority; the accused held the acting-governor to be 'a harsh unsympathetic man' and defied the landdrost. The landdrost thereupon ruled that the Namaquas had been aggrieved, gave them back as many of their looted cattle as possible, and took them under his protection. The accused were then summoned to the High Court. This was too much, and Etienne Barbier, a deserting ex-sergeant of 1739. the garrison who pretended to great influence in Europe, accused the acting-governor and the landdrost of tyranny, corruption, and favouring Hottentots and Chinese above white men,[3] advised the

---

[1] Theal, IIa. 518, 521; No. 50 of 1835, p. 18; J. du Plessis, *Christian Missions in South Africa*, pp. 50 ff.; Spoelstra, *op. cit.*, I. 195, 204; II. 75.
[2] Theal, IIa. 505 ff.; No. 50 of 1835, p. 18.
[3] This was in the year in which Valckenier massacred the Chinese at Batavia.

farmers to pay no more taxes, and raised the standard of revolt at the Paarl. Barbier found a few supporters, but the rising failed and most of them were glad to earn pardon by joining the second and successful commando against the Bushmen. Barbier himself was taken and executed in the ferocious fashion of the day, and the authorities issued a General Placaat against intercourse with natives of all tribes and nations.[1]

1743.
The Company now made another attempt to keep the Colony within bounds. Numbers were still small, for, when all was said and done, there were only about 400 loan places in existence. Van Imhoff suggested that 60 morgen in freehold round each homestead should be offered for sale, cash down, at rates varying from £10 8s. 4d. to £14 13s. 4d., the rest of the loan place being rented as before. It was a well-intentioned effort and van Imhoff was prepared to deal gently with the farmers since 'to some of them it was a hardship when the rent was increased from 12 to 24 rix-dollars.' Wherefore, he told the Councillors that, 'in such cases you, as honest and faithful ministers, must use your discretion and be considerate.'[2] At the same time, a ferry was placed on the Berg river and a heemraden's court was set up at Swellendam in the lower Breede valley. Two years later a landdrost was appointed there to rule all up to the vague line 'where the power of the honourable Company ends.'[3]

1743.
1745.
The State thus followed up its wandering subjects, and, in a measure, the Church did likewise. For many years there had been only three churches in the Colony: the Groote Kerk at Capetown and the churches at Stellenbosch and Drakenstein. Now, two more were built with their attendant schools: one at Roodezand (Tulbagh) at the point where the road to the interior ran out of the Roodezand Pass, and the other nearer the capital at Zwartland in the cornfields of Malmesbury. It was Roodezand which became the church of the frontiersmen, though for many years the only permanent inhabitants were the predikant, the sick-comforter, and the sexton.[4] Meanwhile, there was even some prospect that the unwieldy Colony would be firmly held together ecclesiastically. Hitherto, in spite of proposed reforms in 1691 and 1710, each church consistory had remained isolated, but at last the predikants and representatives of all five

1746.
congregations and the inevitable political commissioner met in a *Classicale Vergadering*.[5] The powers of this incipient synod were limited; nevertheless, there were official heart-searchings, and in deference to the susceptibilities of the Amsterdam *Classis*, the

---

[1] *Bel. Hist. Dok.*, I.; No. 50 of 1835, p. 18.
[2] V.R. Soc., I. 138: *vide* p. 55, *supra* (n.).
[3] Theal, IIIa. 5, 6, 9.
[4] *Ibid.*, p. 514; Spoelstra, *op, cit.*, I. 200: II. 529.
[5] Engelbrecht, *Geschiedenis*, I. 4 ff.; Spoelstra, *op. cit.*, I. 212.

assembly took the title of *Gecombineerde Kerkvergadering*. All went well till an attempt to deal justly with a reverend gentleman of notoriously evil life (it was the period of *Tom Jones*) led to friction with the home authorities, which was made worse when the assembly dared to correspond with the Delft *Classis*. Amsterdam objected and 1759. the assembly desisted; but its opponents on the Council of Policy seized their chance and suppressed it. For many years to come the Cape congregations were destined to remain *disjecta membra* of the Church somnolent.

So the Church lost grip, van Imhoff's new land-tenure failed to attract the Boers, and the Diaspora continued northward and eastward. It was in vain that the Company pursued the cattle-farmers and ivory-hunters with placaaten bidding them stop and, in any 1745. case, not to shoot game without a licence. Farmers were already at the west bank of the Gamtoos river: Beutler, travelling on Com- 1752. pany's service, found farmhouses at Mossel Bay and himself pushed on to the land of the Bantu Tembus beyond the Kei river; already to the north, Boers had established themselves in Calvinia and Little Namaqualand; a few years later Jacobus Coetsee, an elephant- 1760. hunter, first of all known Europeans crossed the Orange river, and cattle-farmers were pushing down the Langekloof or through the Ghoup where Beaufort West now stands.[1]

Such Hottentot clans as still held together gradually withdrew before the European advance. The Great Namaquas crossed the lower Orange into what is now South-West Africa; an expedition presently found the Little Namaquas living in poverty on the further bank of that river. To the south of these was the Bastaard Adam Kok, who had been living near Piketberg till he rashly reported that Bushmen had been raiding the cattle-runs; whereupon the Stellenbosch landdrost had then made inquiry and bidden him take himself off the Bokkeveld. This Kok had done and established himself further north at the Khamiesberg, where he gathered round him half-breed Bastaards and Hottentot Grigriquas, the nucleus of the Griquas who were to play so important a part in mid-nineteenth century South African history. Presently another Hottentot chief, Wildschut, was suffered to occupy land close by, his claim to which the authorities upheld even against a European grantee. Meanwhile, the Koranas steadily drew away north-eastward towards the middle Orange.[2]

The relations of government and burghers with these organised clans were friendly enough. There was brutality on the part of ne'er-do-well whites and coloured men in the borderlands which the

[1] *Bel. Hist. Dok*. II.; Theal, IIIa. 18, 30, 46.
[2] No. 50 of 1835, p. 18; Theal, IIIa. 48; J. M. Orpen, *Reminiscences*; Moodie, *Records*, III. 11; J. S. Marais, *The Cape Coloured People*.

Company did its best to check, but as a rule Government merely tried
to keep the peace, wherein it succeeded, and to prevent the Hottentots
getting guns and horses. Therein it failed. The Hottentots accompanied the elephant and game hunters, became expert shots, learnt
to fight in European fashion, and presently became purveyors of
ivory, ostrich feathers and skins on their own account.[1]

The bulk of the Hottentots remained in the Colony. They were
still nominally tribesmen, beyond the jurisdiction of the courts
unless a European or his slave was concerned in the case. The courts
passed heavy sentences against Europeans convicted of maltreating
them; but for the rest, they were left to shift for themselves. Some
lived as wanderers, others as labourers whose indolence reacted
badly on their employers; arrack and brandy carried on the work of
destruction which the smallpox and leprosy had begun; such claims
to land and *fonteins* as they may have had steadily passed into the
hands of Europeans. Moreover, as a pure-blooded race, they were
steadily disappearing into the ranks of the Coloured population. It
was a slow process, but, as early as 1721, slave-owners in the outlying
parts had asked that the offspring of slave fathers and Hottentot
mothers might be apprenticed 'to the persons bringing them up.'
Nothing was done till at length complaints were made that runaway
slaves were passing themselves off as bastard Hottentots. It was
1775. therefore decreed that the children of slave fathers and Hottentot
mothers who remained in the service of a farmer till the child was
eighteen months old were to be apprenticed in return for their keep
till they attained the age of twenty-five.[2]

If the relations of the Europeans with the Hottentots improved,
those with the Bushmen became worse. It was war to the knife
between the little Stone Age men and the advance guard of Western
civilisation. The Council was much exercised by ugly stories from
the Swellendam frontier. Commandos were said to be shooting
Bushmen regardless of sex and age, but inquiry proved nothing
1754. definite; then the Bushmen raided the Roggeveld and Bokkeveld,
and a burgher was arrested on suspicion of inciting them to plunder.
Raids took place from time to time during the next few years, each
raid answered by a *straf-commando*, which as a rule killed a number
of the raiders and apprenticed captured women and children. The
Circa struggle gradually became more bitter, for the Boers were pushing
1770. their way into the Ghoup and Camdebo and were thus driving their
enemies into the mountains. White *knechts* were killed from time to
time; houses were besieged; once, a family of farmers was massacred.
Field-corporal Adriaan van Jaarsveld came to the front as the ham-
1772. mer of the Bushmen on the north-eastern border; troops had to go

---

[1] Sparrman, *Voyages*, II. 63; Moodie, *Records*, III. 32; Theal, IIa. 53, 104.
[2] No. 50 of 1835, pp. 17, 19; Theal, IIIa. 104; *vide infra*, p. 128.

up to the help of the burghers and, this time, prisoners were taken back to the Castle to be hanged or broken at the wheel or to have their ankle-sinews cut preparatory to serving life-sentences.[1]

It was a horrid, inconclusive business. The white men, exasperated at raids on their cattle and the sniping of isolated fellow-burghers by a treacherous foe, hunted the Bushmen down with Hottentot trackers and virtually enslaved their prisoners; the Bushmen, utterly unable to adapt their style of life to changed conditions, desperately defended their hunting grounds. In the course of it the commando system was developed on broader lines. There were already thirteen field-corporals, each liable to be called out with his men by the landdrost; but to deal adequately with the Bushmen, the Council at length appointed Godlieb Opperman as field-commandant of a joint force of all the local commandos along the northern border from Piketberg eastward to the Sneeuwberg;[2] 250 men with Hottentot auxiliaries scoured three hundred miles of border, lost one man, killed over 500 Bushmen, and took 239 prisoners, who were for the most part apprenticed.[3] It was the biggest effort yet, but it failed of its object. One Bushman captain indeed promised to steal no more and was given presents in return; but he was the exception; the raids continued, the commandos turned out, and the Company supplied ammunition and injunctions to abstain from cruelty with monotonous regularity. 1774.

Meanwhile, the trekkers had come in contact with a foe more worthy of their steel than the half-hearted Hottentot or the puny Bushman. A boundary commission reported that Boer families were moving about just within the Colony and that others were between the Gamtoos and Fish rivers far beyond the most distant loanplaces, paying no rent for their farms and carrying on barter with the Xosa vanguard of the advancing Bantu along a track well-worn despite placaaten as old as 1737. In other words, the cattle-farmers were following their migratory farms round either side of the Great Karoo, the inhospitable Droogeveld. To keep some sort of hold on the borderers, the Council extended the eastern frontier to Bruintjes Hoogte and the Gamtoos; but, within a short two years, Willem Prinsloo, an old elephant-hunter, who had been given leave to pick a couple of farms within the new border, promptly went beyond it and planted himself at the Boschberg which we now call Somerset 1770.

[1] No. 50 of 1835, p. 18; Theal, IIIa. 54 ff., 125; Moodie, *Records*, III. 7.
[2] Sparrman, *Voyages*, I. 198, 202; Roux, *Verdedigingstelsel*, pp. 153 ff.; No. 50 of 1835, p. 19. For a good account *vide* du Plessis, *op. cit.*, p. 265.
[3] The Stellenbosch landdrost ordered Opperman to let captured 'Bushman-Hottentot' women go, but to keep the men and children till the end of the campaign and then either release them 'or divide them in proportion among the poorest of the inhabitants there, in order to continue to serve them for a fixed and equitable term of years, in consideration of their receiving proper maintenance, for which purpose some of them must be brought hither' (Moodie, *Records*, III. 29).

4

East. He ignored commands to come back; friends joined him, and
1775. the frontier had to be carried up to the Bushman's and the upper
Fish rivers. Then, van Jaarsveld, fresh from a campaign against the
1776. Bushmen on the Zeekoe river in the present district of Colesberg,
arrived at Bruintjes Hoogte and made direct and friendly contact
with the Imidange Xosas.[1]

Tidings of this new development, news of incessant Bushman
raids in the Sneeuwberg area, and the request of van Jaarsveld and
his friends for a church and a drostdy brought Governor van
1778. Plettenberg to the frontiers.[2] He found the two races, black and white,
fairly interlocked: the Gunukwebes, half Xosa, half Hottentot, on
the coast lands between the Bushman's and Sunday rivers, and, to
the north, Boers and Xosas on the colonial side of the middle Fish.
He planted a beacon near the site of Colesberg to mark the north-
eastern limit of the Colony, agreed with some petty Xosa chieftains
that the middle Fish river should be the dividing line between
Europeans and Bantu, and returned home naming Plettenberg's Bay
en route. His Council ratified this agreement, but claimed a line along
the whole length of the Fish, thus taking in the Zuurveld, the future
1777- Albany.[3] Meanwhile, far away to the north, Captain Robert Gordon
1779. and his English friend, Lieutenant William Paterson, had named
the Orange river, but no boundary was fixed on that side.[4]

So in the short space of two generations the cattle-farmers had
carried Western civilisation, or as much of it as their trek-waggons
could accommodate, from the valley of the Breede to the Khamiesberg in the north and the Fish river in the east. They lost much of
that civilisation on the way; the farmhouses sixty miles from Capetown were already much ruder than those in the more settled parts
of the Colony, and van Plettenberg noted that there was not a
substantial homestead between Hex River and the Gamtoos;[5] but
whether the Boers lived in houses or in their waggons or hartebeest
huts, they were surrounded by great herds of cattle and sheep and
trains of dependants, slaves in the more westerly parts, Hottentots
and even 'tame Bushmen' in the east. Cattle was their wealth; it
was almost their currency as well, for money was scarce on the
frontiers and both Tulbagh and van Plettenberg were fain to accept
three bullocks in lieu of recognition money for a loan farm.[6] They
lived in isolation and preferred it so; but for the slaves, wrote
Captain Cook, the Cape Colony with its one man to every $5\frac{1}{2}$ square
1776. miles, would be more thinly peopled than any other part of the globe.[7]

[1] No. 50 of 1835, p. 18; Moodie, *Records*, III. 1 ff., 14, 49; Theal, III*a*. 96.
[2] *Bel. Hist. Dok.*, I.; No. 50 of 1835, p. 19; Moodie, *Records*, III. 74; Godée
Molsbergen, *Reizen*, II. 61 ff.
[3] J. S. Marais, *Maynier and the First Boer Republic*, pp. 5 ff.; *vide infra*, p. 156.
[4] Theal, III*a*. 111.   [5] *Bel. Hist. Dok.*, I. 29.
[6] Theal, III*a*. 118.   [7] Cook, *A Voyage to the Pacific Ocean*, I. 41.

They had developed a passion for independence and a restiveness against all forms of government that went beyond the strictly limited powers of the landdrost and heemraden, and most of them had little idea of what even those might mean since the nearest drostdy was far away to the west at Swellendam.

The Boers had drifted away from the organised state; their contact with the organised church and the book-learning that went therewith was hardly closer. They made desperate efforts to keep touch. They did their best to come in on occasion for *Nachtmaal* (Holy Communion); women would travel in to the nearest church at Roodezand, six or seven weeks' trek away, for the christening of their babies; sometimes they brought in their last few children in batches. Many Boers could read or half-read, half-recite the Scriptures; they all knew their Psalms by heart and loved the hymns of Willem Sluyter; some could write, still more could sign their names; but, for the rest, literature and the affairs of the great world outside their veld were closed books to them. Hollander visitors complained that they had begun to lose the cohesion and cleanliness' of the home Dutch; a little later de Mist, conning masses of reports from Company's officials and others, concluded that the extreme frontiersmen, 'these half-wild Europeans,' rebellious and unreasonable in their behaviour, were suffering from 'a complete corruption of their moral sense,' a corruption bred by 'the long distances . . . from Cape Town . . . ; the lack of social intercourse with civilised individuals; the monotonous life of the herdsman . . .; the daily hunt, the continual diet of meat . . .; the war . . . conducted for some years against the Bushmen and Kaffirs,' a war in which some of them had learnt to doubt whether it really were a crime to kill a native. Later on, de Mist and other observers perceived virtues in the frontiersmen: courage, self-reliance, and a natural courtesy; succeeding generations of South Africans have recognised that with all their faults they staked out the claims of Europeans to the sparsely peopled lands between the Tulbagh mountains, the Fish river and the Orange before the Bantu flood could pour in from the East. Nevertheless, they had done it at great cost to themselves. Critical Westerners could complain that many of the rising generation were well on the way to becoming worse than Hottentots.[1] *Circa 1781.*

Such was the society which was growing up in the East, beyond the empty spaces of the Great Karoo, in the last days of Jan Compagnie. The frontiersmen were the fathers or grandfathers of the men of the Great Trek, who from 1836 onwards, carried the frontiers *Circa 1775.*

[1] V.R. Soc., III. 198, 256 ; IV. 149; Engelbrecht, *Geschiedenis*, p. 8; Beyers, *Die Kaapse Patriotte*; Stavorinus, *Voyages*, III. 444 ; Lichtenstein, *Travels*, I. 377 ff. On the eastern districts, 1775–1806, *vide* P. A. C. Wieringa, *De oudste Boeren-Republieken*.

at a bound beyond the Vaal and, by the very rapidity of their dispersion, immeasurably complicated the problems of their relations with the central government, with the tribes, and with each other. All that changed in the course of the nineteenth century was the scene and the scale of these problems. The problems were there long before the British stepped into the shoes of the Company.

CHAPTER V

THE DECLINE AND FALL OF THE DUTCH
EAST INDIA COMPANY

Decline of the Netherlands, 100 ; the Cape Patriots, 101 ; van der Graaff's reforms, 105 ; Nederburgh and Frykenius, 106 ; Bantu expansion and tribal system, 109 ; the first Kaffir war. 115 ; Maynier, 116; the first Boer republic, 119; First British Occupation, 120.

THE great Dutch East India Company entered on the last stage of its decline in the 'seventies of the eighteenth century. It still made an imposing show; dividends were still forthcoming; 20,000 Netherlanders still found employment and the upper classes gained advancement in its service; but deep-seated official corruption sapped its vitality; expensive wars drained its resources; the English Company, victorious over the French, went from strength to strength in Indian waters and took away the China trade, trade in the tea which 1743- darkened Boston harbour in 1773. Bankruptcy crept on; van Imhoff 1779. uttered a warning, shrewd old Stavorinus repeated it thirty years later, and in due time the Company was faced with a deficit of £150,000 on all its stations taken together.[1]

The Netherlands themselves were going downhill. Scientific farming in the England of 'Turnip Townshend' and 'Farmer George,' and the corn of Southern Russia issuing from Czarina Catherine's new conquest of Odessa hit the Dutch corn-traders hard. Growing economic inequalities at home inflamed political differences. There had been a time when the republican burgher oligarchy, the *staatsgezinde* party, had had the upper hand; but the Orangemen had 1747- rallied, restored the Prince to the offices of admiral and captain- 1749. general, made him stadtholder for life, and forced him on the East India Company as director-in-chief and governor-general.

A reaction set in against this budding monarchy. The wind of

[1] V.R. Soc., I.; Stavorinus, *Voyages*, III. chapters vi, vii. On the last years of the Company *vide* A. L. Geyer, *Das Wirtschaftliche System . . . am Kap . . . 1785-95.*

liberalism emanating from England blew strongly in France and stirred the dry bones of Europe. A radical party arose in England; a Joan Derk van der Capellen then formed a democratic Patriot party in the Netherlands and moved on towards alliance with the Gallophile burgher oligarchy. The democrats owed something to Montesquieu and a little to Benjamin Franklin's letters on the state of affairs in British North America; but they, like the French, drew their main stock of ideas from the great British philosophers, Hobbes, Locke, Hume and Adam Smith, or from contemporary English radicals like Price and Priestley. There was much talk in Holland of freedom, of natural law, of the popular will; there was excitement when tidings 1775– came of the revolt of the Americans against King George, who was 1776. held to have broken the social contract between himself as ruler and 'the good people of these colonies.'[1]

The news of all these doings reached the distant Cape by way of the Netherlands. Netherlanders were girding against the Ancien Régime in Europe; Americans were revolting against the old colonial system on the other side of the Atlantic; why should free burghers submit to both combined in Africa? Accordingly a burgher meeting 1779. was summoned secretly at Capetown and four men were empowered to go to Amsterdam as representatives of the Cape burghers to lay their grievances before the mighty Seventeen.

These Cape Patriots were drawn entirely from the West. Some 400 of the 3000 free men of the Colony signed the petition, all of them living within a day's ride of Capetown; the cattle-farmers of Swellendam had neither part nor lot in the movement. They were screwed to the sticking-point by van Plettenberg's free use of his power of deportation. The Company had a legal right to recall free burghers to its service and send them where it chose; indeed, Simon van der Stel had been ordered to pack lazy and unmarried fellows off to the Indies, there to serve the Company at nine florins a month.[2] But as Charles I had learnt to his cost and Edmund Burke had noted in connection with the British Parliament's undoubted right to tax Americans, what matters is 'not what a lawyer tells me I may do but what right and justice tell me I ought to do.' Times were very bad at the Cape; nerves were frayed; the air was charged with the electricity of revolution; yet van Plettenberg deported eighteen men in eight years, whereas Father Tulbagh had been content with ten in more than twice that time. The eighteenth deportee was admittedly a black sheep; but the order of his going was abominable and, to make matters worse, he was acquitted by the Batavian court and died at sea on the way home. This Afrikaner John Wilkes promptly

---

[1] C. Beyers, *Die Kaapse Patriotte*; Theal, IIIa. 112 ff.
[2] *Journal, 1699–1732*, p. 91.

became a popular hero and men began to ask how much longer they were to submit to a vague and arbitrarily administered law. True, 1715. the principle had long ago been laid down that the Courts were to be guided by local *placaaten* in the first instance, and, if these failed, were to have recourse to the Statutes of India and, in the last resort, to the Roman-Dutch law of the Netherlands.[1] So far, so good; but the *placaaten* were in fearful confusion; the judges were for the most part amateurs, and the risk that obsolete laws might be raised from the dead was very great.

The Cape Patriots, therefore, asked that the laws be written down; in other words, like the French and North American Revolutionists later on, they demanded a written constitution. They went further; they demanded a share in the making and administering of the laws and a fuller share in the interpretation of them. It was a new development in Cape politics. Hitherto burgher uprisings had taken place on economic grounds, but now the men of the capital and the old colony of settlement demanded seven seats on the Council of Policy when matters affecting the burghers were to be discussed. Two of these seats were to be vacated annually and filled by men freely nominated by the burgher councillors and approved of by the Governor; the burgher councillors as a body were to have the right to report to the Seventeen on the state of the Colony. Similarly, the petitioners demanded half the seats on the High Court and the right of appeal to Amsterdam instead of to corrupt Batavia.

These were the most epoch-making demands. The rest were a very mixed collection of grievances, big and little: relief from the burden of attendance at the matrimonial court, a fixed scale of official fees, reduction of farm rents, a better price for wine, more churches in the hinterland, liberty to flog slaves without reference to the Fiscal, leave to send a few cargoes to the Netherlands, free-trade with the Indies and slaving in Madagascar, an end to the keeping of shops or doing of business by freed Chinese and Javanese prisoners since these men received goods stolen by slaves, an end also to the right of foreigners to live at the Cape or to buy or hire houses or to drive a 'burgher trade' or to ride inland or to become burghers unless they had first been in the Company's service. Thus were natural rights interpreted in Capetown when the American Declaration of Independence and *The Wealth of Nations* were hardly three years old.

The Patriots accompanied their demands with an unvarnished account of the state of the Colony. They said little against van Plettenberg, for, in spite of his extravagance, he was a just man and popular withal; but they vigorously attacked the Fiscal, Boers, and certain other highly placed personages. The Seventeen, therefore,

---

[1] *Resolutien*, Feb. 12, 1715; J. L. W. Stock, *The New Statutes of India* (S.A. Law Journal, 1915); *C. H. B. E.*, VIII, pp. 832 ff.

ordered the officials to reply. This they did after a long delay. Van
Plettenberg stated his case moderately, pointing out that the vast
bulk of the burghers had taken no part in the agitation and that the
Colony was prosperous enough. This was true, for war had again
come to the rescue and Capetown was full of friendly French soldiers 1781.
and army contractors. It was equally true that most of the burghers
wanted to live on the labour of slaves and Hottentots and the
proceeds of their traffic with foreign crews. But these arguments, as
van Plettenberg well knew, did not go to the root of the matter.
He therefore proposed remedies. He would not hear of burghers on
the Council of Policy; but he recommended that they be given half
the seats on the High Court, that the laws be defined, that officials
be paid decent salaries in lieu of fees and perquisites, and that a
limited private trade be permitted. Finally, he offered to make way
for a newcomer who would have a better hope than he of instituting
these reforms satisfactorily.

Most of the other officials contented themselves with remarking
that the abuses complained of were of long standing, but Fiscal
Boers carried the war into the enemy's country. In spite of the
precedents of a hundred years, he refused to acknowledge that the
burgher councillors had any right to speak for the free men or any
powers other than the limited share in the administration of justice
given them by van Riebeeck; he held that free trade would leave the
Company and the Colony itself denuded of supplies since export
prices were so tempting, and added drily that the smuggling trade
gave the burghers all the free trade they could desire. Grenville had
noted the same fact in North America with unfortunate results.

However, temporary economic salvation had come to the Cape,
not for the last time, by war and, with it, a check to mutual recriminations. The War of American Independence had gradually opened
out into a world war of the old style between Great Britain and the
Bourbon Powers, and the Netherlands had been drawn in on the side 1780.
of France and Spain. The republican party and their democratic
allies had gained the upper hand at The Hague, and Great Britain,
preferring the smiting of an open enemy to the blows of a neutral
friend, had ended her hundred years *entente* with the United
Provinces. At once the Cape was dragged out of the political back-
water in which it had lain for so long. With Warren Hastings fighting
for the life of 'John Company' against Indian princes and their
French allies, it became a question whether France or Great Britain
would occupy the half-way house to India. In the year of Yorktown, 1781.
Commodore Johnstone and Admiral Suffren, both racing for the
Cape, came upon one another unexpectedly at Porto Praya in the
Cape Verde Islands; Suffren broke off the engagement and sailed
southward to be welcomed by the colonial authorities. Johnstone,

arriving too late, solaced himself by seizing some richly laden Dutch Indiamen in Saldanha Bay and sheered off to India.[1]

The Frenchmen virtually occupied Capetown for three years. There was a great coming and going of troops: the regiment of Pondicherry, the regiment of Luxembourg in Dutch pay and, when that sailed east, the regiment Van Waldener. House property, slaves, horses rose 50 to 100 per cent. in value; the demand for produce was so great that the Company had to fix maximum prices to protect itself and its allies; Capetown blossomed forth as 'Little Paris,' with marked effect on the morals of the rising generation. Indeed, that stout Dutch patriot, de Mist, afterwards complained that loyal Netherlanders and fair-minded foreigners alike spoke disparagingly of conditions in the Colony, and that justly. For the French had 'entirely corrupted the standard of living at the Cape, and extravagance and indulgence in an unbroken round of amusements and diversions have come to be regarded as necessities.' It would, he feared, be the work of years to transform the citizens of Capetown once again into *Netherlanders*.[2]

The prosperity was fictitious. The shipping returns told that. Far more ships than ever before put into Table Bay, but the vast and increasing majority of them were foreigners. The British had reasserted their old naval supremacy and were busily sweeping Dutch shipping off the seven seas. The Company paid its last dividend in 1782, and in the same year issued inconvertible paper money at the Cape.[3] True, it promised to redeem it as soon as possible; but meanwhile the paper-flood rose and with it prices. Then came rumours of peace. Luxembourg departed; Van Waldener sailed eastwards almost as soon as it had come; drought set in in the west and did not break till 1787; Pondicherry departed when Holland at last made peace with Great Britain; the trading-houses which had sprung up in Capetown during the war boom wilted visibly; the agitation against the authorities revived. Men remembered that Boers had stopped the local manufacture of coarse cloth and blankets during the war for fear of damaging the industries of Holland and their pockets; the demand for a coasting trade grew louder; the returning Patriot representatives passed on a good deal of the revolutionary French philosophy they had picked up at Amsterdam, and the American version came with the first ship flying the Stars and Stripes to touch at the Cape.[4]

1784.

Meanwhile, the Seventeen had approved of the officials' replies to the original burgher petition and tardily proposed minor reforms. These in no wise satisfied the Patriots; but Boers and other hated

1783.

---

[1] All were taken except the *Middelburg*, which was gallantly blown up by Abraham de Smidt, one of its officers.
[2] V.R. Soc., III. 201.   [3] *Ibid.*, p. 282.   [4] *Ibid.*, p. 170; Beyers, *op. cit.*

officials had departed, a new Governor was expected, and they at
first proposed to await his coming. Then, news that an unpopular man
was to become Fiscal and an attempt to arrest a burgher forced their
hand. A group of Patriots drew up a new list of grievances and
secured the written approval of over four hundred men and women,
and when the new Governor, van der Graaff, arrived to assuage the Jan.
grievances of the Colony and to make Capetown more easily defen- 1785.
sible, his programme of reform failed to find favour with them.
They forthwith commissioned four representatives to lay their
petition before the States General.

The Cape Patriots had thus appealed from the Company to the
Sovereign. The appeal failed. The delegates quarrelled among themselves, the Seventeen made haste to propose further reforms; the
States General considered that these would meet the case, and van
der Graaff was left in peace to carry them out and indulge to the full
his taste for fortification.

Van der Graaff gave the burghers six seats on the High Court, but, 1785–
as the Seventeen had recommended, he limited the right to sit on 1789.
that board and on the Council of Policy to members of the Established Church; he set up a Commission of the High Court, three
officials and three burghers, to care for the roads, fix prices and
suggest new forms of taxation; he carried out his predecessor's intention by appointing a badly needed landdrost near the eastern
frontier at Graaff-Reinet. He also relaxed the restrictions on trade
and industry somewhat, opened a depot for grain at Mossel Bay and
another for timber farther east at Plettenberg's Bay with a military
guard at each, and permitted burghers to send wine on their own
account to Holland on Company's ships. Finally, the Company gave
up exporting European goods and threw open all its trade, save that
with China and Japan, to Dutch subjects.[1]

The long-deferred boon of 'free trade' was more apparent than
real. Trade was burdened with heavy customs duties; it must be
carried on in Cape ships, one-third of whose crews must be Cape
colonists, and the Cape was noted for the fact that it supplied no
sailors to the Company's own ships; there was little to export from
a colony which had had to ward off famine by importing rice from 1786.
Java and flour from Europe. Above all, the boon was granted too
late. The financial condition of the Company at the end of the War
of American Independence was deplorable. The States General had
to come to the rescue, but the Company's debts more than tripled
in the course of seven years and showed no signs of stopping. Of
all its liabilities overseas, the Cape was the most grievous. The
rising tide of foreigners which flowed into Table Bay and out again

[1] Theal, IIIa. 171, 174, 192.

had swelled the proceeds of the wine and liquor licences; stricter collection of the grain tithe increased the revenues for a time; but official staffs were overblown and expensive from the Governor with his sixty carriage horses and yearly allowances of 18,000 florins downwards;[1] there was gross mismanagement at the cattle-posts, and open frauds at the giant hospital where the sick multiplied miraculously for the benefit of the staff; van der Graaff's fortifications sent expenditure up from £25,000 to £120,000 a year.[2] After all, what could be expected when the Governor himself was an engineer officer and 'the engineers who drew up the plans are also in every case the Contractors (*risum teneatis!*), and, being to a large extent residents there, they behave as though the Cape were an African Maastricht or Luxembourg'?[3]

In short, the Colony was costing the embarrassed Directors more than all their other East Indian stations combined. They, therefore, took up the axe and ended the fool's paradise at the Cape. Van der Graaff was recalled; the fortification works were closed down and the new military posts withdrawn from the Swellendam district; most of the Swiss and South German mercenaries, the best customers in the Colony next to the Company, sailed away; in other words, some 1,500 officials, 14,000 burghers and 17,000 slaves were practically left to their own devices. So the miserable Colony awaited the Special Commissioners who were on their way to save, if it might be, the sinking fortunes of the Company in the East.

1791.

July 1792.

Commissioners Nederburgh and Frykenius came with powers to carry out some at least of the reforms which van Plettenberg had advocated. The whole of their policy was, however, coloured by the fact that Nederburgh, for one, was convinced that the Company must go bankrupt sooner or later, and was determined that it should be later rather than sooner.

The situation was grave. True, away in the Netherlands, van der Capellen had died long since and the invading Prussians had recently crushed his Patriot party, while at the Cape that movement had died away after the appointment of a new Fiscal. Again, the leading merchants and most of the civil and military officials in the Colony were good Orangemen, who had been appointed by the Prince of Orange on the recommendation of the Seventeen; but, as against this, any number of the burghers and rank and file of the garrison were pro-French and anti-Orange. They lent a ready ear to the doctrines of Revolutionary France, called themselves Nationals like

1787.

----

[1] A florin was two shillings British.
[2] V.R. Soc. III. 180; A. L. Geyer, *Das Wirtshaftliche System*, pp. 9 ff.; Theal, IIIa. 123, 183.
[3] V.R. Soc., III. 263.

any Frenchmen, professed an undying loyalty to the Republic of the free Netherlands and an equally undying hatred for 'Jan Compagnie,' and, though they talked little of Equality or Fraternity, as was only natural in a mixed society, which de Mist afterwards noted was far more like that of San Domingo than of the United States, they talked much of 'Liberty, liberty,' which they inevitably interpreted in their own way. The Commissioners found 'the large majority of the settlers financially ruined,' the grain farmers sowing only enough for their own needs, with revenue sadly in arrears and like to remain so while everyone was obstinately resolved to refuse payment of the new collateral succession duty. They were soon to be faced with 'open rebellion . . . against the authority of the Government to collect their taxes.'[1]

The burgher councillors demanded to be heard as representatives of the people. The Commissioners took as narrow a view of their functions as Fiscal Boers had done and refused to recognise them as such; but on finding that there were only eighteen days' supply of corn in Capetown and no more likely to come in till the burgher councillors were heard, they gave way. After discussion, the Commissioners reformed the Capetown police and cut down the powers of the Independent Fiscal, who was henceforward to be merely Fiscal and subject like any other official to the local government. Their main work was financial. They gave the officials reasonable salaries and allowed them to retain their statutory fees; but they cut off nearly all their perquisites, and by rigidly limiting other expenses reduced the outgoings by nearly fifty per cent. They then tried to bridge the gulf which still yawned between revenue and expenditure by raising new taxes. Customs duties, ever the resort of political financiers in distress, came first: a £2 duty on every slave imported and a five per cent. *ad valorem* duty on all other goods exported or imported in other than Company ships. Then came an increase of the transfer duty, a carriage and waggon tax, a £2 anchorage fee for non-Company vessels, twelve shillings on every legger of brandy brought into town, five per cent. *ad valorem* on the goods and chattels of all higher officials who left the Colony and failed to return within three years, a share of the percentages charged by the official auctioneers through whose hands so much of the business of the Cape passed in those days, an increase of the stamp duties, and, *horribile dictu*, the demand for a stamp on auction receipts payable by the purchaser. The Commissioners even leased the Gardens and the Company's country seat at Rustenberg and farmed out the salt-pans. And still revenues fell short of expenditure by nearly half.[2]

Nederburgh and Frykenius were, however, not merely content to tax; they were anxious to help the Colony, provided the Company's

---

[1] V.R. Soc., III. 178, 196, 274. [2] *Ibid.*, III. 180; Theal, IIIa. 206.

interests were not damaged thereby. They proposed that the Company should have a call on as much grain as it wanted at a slightly enhanced price and that the farmers should have liberty to export the rest to Holland or India in Dutch ships; they threw open the whale fishery to Dutch subjects; they opened Table Bay, Mossel Bay and Plettenberg's Bay to trade with any part of the Dutch Indies, provided the ships used were Dutch-built and bought their return cargoes from the Company; they allowed Cape burghers to go to Madagascar and the East Indies for slaves. But the Navigation Acts were still as the law of the Medes and Persians; the Commissioners were determined that the trade of the Dutch empire should be carried on solely by Dutchmen, for Dutchmen, and in Dutch ships; they therefore forbade foreign ships to land any goods at the Cape. Finally they experimented with the paper currency. This had soon fallen markedly in value, but the importation of silver and the cancellation of some of the notes had more or less restored it to par except where large payments had to be made to foreigners. Thus emboldened, Nederburgh and Frykenius established a Loan Bank, and financed it with new paper. Then, with the knowledge that the Netherlands and its ally, Great Britain, were at war with Republican

1793. France, they sailed for Java, leaving Abraham Sluysken and a skeleton garrison to hold the discontented Colony as best they might.

Some few of the colonists tried to take advantage of their new opportunities: Sebastiaan van Reenen took over the Spanish sheep which Colonel Gordon had recently imported and ran them for some time with success; Jacobus and Jan Kirsten tried to improve the breed of cattle and horses with New England stock; a few likely bays and islands on the Namaqua-Damaraland coast were annexed for the benefit of the whale-fishers. But it was all on a small scale, a mere flicker of light and hope in the economic darkness. The townsmen had learnt to rely on foreign ships; they could hardly have done otherwise, for, roughly speaking, two foreigners called for every Dutch ship that put into Table Bay; they were furious at the embargo on foreign imports, and to make matters worse, now that war had come, few ships came near the Cape at all. In town and country, men raged against the auction and transfer duties; they found the purchasing power of the paper money falling, and, resting as it did 'entirely upon the good opinion of the people,' it fell still further; they sank deeper and deeper into debt to the new Loan

1794. Bank. And, far away in Holland, the famous East India Company, ten millions to the bad and its credit gone, solemnly declared the bankruptcy which Nederburgh had foreseen. What wonder that men in the western Colony were in a mood to welcome any change that would bring them *novae tabulae*?[1]

[1] V.R. Soc., III. 177, 283; Theal, IIIa. 207 ff., 228, 237.

In the background, the cattle-farmers of Swellendam and Graaff-Reinet drifted steadily towards rebellion, for they and therefore their rulers were in touch with a native problem of a much more searching nature than any that the feckless Hottentots or the exasperating Bushmen had ever presented, a problem with which the decrepit government at Capetown was utterly unfitted to deal. In short, the frontiersmen had made full contact with the advance-guard of the Bantu.[1]

The general situation in Southern Africa about the year 1775 was that after a century and a quarter of dispersion, such white settlement as there was covered little more than the coast-belt of Portuguese East Africa and perhaps half the present Cape Province. The slow outward drift of white folk was still going on, but the Bantu counter-advance was also proceeding apace. Far away to the north-west the survivors of the Makaranga and Mashona had remained in Portuguese East Africa and Southern Rhodesia after the ferocious Abambo and Amazimba had swept away southward. They were presently overrun by the Barotse, who, however, ultimately settled for the most part in Northern Rhodesia on the far side of the Zambesi. Nearer the Cape Colony but not yet in touch with it, during the first half of the eighteenth century, the Bavenda and Bakwena conquered what are now the Transvaal and the Orange Free State as far south as the Caledon river, while the Batlapin and Barolong drove the Leghoya (Bataung) into the north-eastern Free State. The invading Batlapin settled round Old Lithako between the Molopo and Harts rivers in Bechuanaland, the Barolong close by on the banks of the Harts. During those same years, the Ovambo and cattle-rearing Ovaherero *Circa* had streamed into South-West Africa, and the Xosas, the vanguard of *1775.* the coast tribes, had pushed right up to the line of the Fish river.

Thus there were, in the latter part of the eighteenth century, three main groups of Bantu in the hinterland of the expanding Cape Colony. To the north, and as yet beyond the ken of the colonists, were the plateau tribes: Ovaherero and Damaras, blacker, smaller and duller than the rest, and behind them the far superior Ovambo;[2] Batlapin much mixed with Bakalahari and Balala and even with Hottentots and Bushmen; Bechuana and, further east, Bataung. To the north-east in the centre of the Bantu ring were the highlanders: Barotse, Bavenda and Bakwena, big men whose colour ranged from copper to black, with crisply curling hair and small beards, some with the flat noses of the forest dwellers, others with aquiline noses which spoke of East Coast Semitic influences. To the east were the coast

---

[1] On the Bantu in Southern Africa *vide* Theal, I*a*. 5 ff.; III*a*. 64 ff.; Stow, *Native Races*, pp. 256 ff., chapters xxi–xxvi; J. Maclean, *Compendium of Kafir Laws and Customs*; C. Brownlee, *Reminiscences of Kaffir Life and History*; D. Kidd, *The Essential Kafir* and *Kafir Socialism*; M. S. Evans, *Black and White in South-East Africa*; Molema, *The Bantu, Past and Present*; *C.H.B.E.*, VIII. 34 ff.
[2] Stow, *Native Races*, pp. 256 ff.

tribes, the only Bantu as yet to have made contact with the Cape frontiersmen.

These coast tribes had arisen out of the chaos produced by the incursion of the Abambo and Amazimba into what are now Zulu-land and Natal. Early in the seventeenth century, either those invaders or the wrecks of the tribes they had driven before them or all of them had broken up in the neighbourhood of the Tugela river and formed new tribes. All of these had kept the snake as their *siboko* or totem, but each tribe took the name of its chief or some other hero, prefixed it with the word Ama (people) and so became the Ama-Xosa, -Tembu, -Pondo, -Swazi and so on. A few of them pushed over the Drakensberg into the north-eastern Free State and became Basia and Baputi; but the bulk of them either stayed where they were or pushed slowly down the coast belt towards the Colony.

Circa 1623. The Xosas came first, with the Tembus hard on their heels. They killed or chased away the Bushmen—all invaders did that—but the Xosas especially mixed freely with the Hottentots and borrowed much of their clicking speech, and perhaps something of their fickleness. Soon the main body of the Xosas were on the Umzimvubu river, but some of them and even some of the Tembu were already beyond it to the west. In Simon van der Stel's time the Xosas crossed 1702. the Kei and sent out hunting parties beyond the Fish, where they met European and Hottentot cattle-traders from Stellenbosch. Soon the Company included Kaffirs in the list of tribes with whom the burghers might have no intercourse, and, as was to be expected, intercourse between white and black became closer. But for a long time that intercourse was a mere matter of hunting and cattle-barter; the two main streams of migration had not yet met. Meanwhile, in Tulbagh's day, the great Xosa chief Palo ruled in the Amatola mountains, sent his men into the lands between the Kei 1775. and the Fish and, in due time, died. The Xosa clans to the east of the Kei then passed to his 'great son,' Galeka, while those between the Kei and the Fish followed another son, Rarabe.[1] Among the clans

---

[1] This genealogy of the Ama-Xosa chiefs is based on Theal, IIIa. 93:—

Palo, d. 1775 ca.

(Eastern Xosas or Galekas)		(Western Xosas: Rarabes or Gaikas)
Galeka, d. 1790.		Rarabe, d. 1785 *ca.*
Kawuta, d. 1804		
	Umlawu, d. 1780 *ca.*	Ndhlambi, d. 1828
Hintsa, d. 1835		
	Gaika, d. 1828	Dushane, d. 1828
Kreli, ceased to rule, June 1881.		
	Sandile, d. 1878	Macomo, d. 1873

owing allegiance to Rarabe were the half-Xosa, half-Hottentot Gunukwebes who were already established on the western side of the Fish river.

The comprehensive segregation or *apartheid* policy which van Plettenberg had then proclaimed by taking the Fish river as the dividing line between white and black had not the slightest chance of success. 1778. Apart from the fact that such a policy could only have been enforced by officials, troops and numerous white settlers, all of whom were lacking, the policy itself ran dead against the expansive traditions of the trek-boers on the one hand and the whole social and political system of the Bantu on the other.

Bantu tribal customs vary, and it is hard, in our present state of knowledge, to generalise; nevertheless there are certain principles which are common to all tribesmen. The Bantu were in every way more advanced than the Bushmen and Hottentots. Their tribal system, based on religious sanctions, was strong. Each tribe looked to a great or paramount chief. In time of war, the power of the chief was as wide as that of the President of the U.S.A.; in time of peace, its extent depended largely on his own force of character and the strength of the tribal custom interpreted by the *amapakati* or councillors without whose advice he was usually not supposed to act.[1] And behind the *amapakati* sat the tribal council, a veritable African Folkmoot.

Beneath the paramount chief were lesser chiefs. These men were usually his sons or other relatives, for the Bantu had great respect for the blood royal. New clans were continually being formed within the tribe. Great chiefs, like all others who could afford to do so, practised polygamy. The first wife of such a chief was known as the 'wife of the right hand,' and the second the 'wife of the left hand.' But there was also a 'great wife,' married as a rule for political reasons and destined, if all went well, to be the mother of the heir to the throne. As the great wife was often married late in life, it frequently chanced that the heir succeeded his father as a child under the regency of an uncle or an elder half-brother, a fact which by no means added to the tranquillity of the tribe during the regency and still less when the time came for the regent to hand over his authority to the rightful owner. The sons of the right and left hands, meanwhile, were given men and cattle with which to found new clans within the tribe.

Hence, it was rarely easy for Europeans to know precisely where authority lay. They might make a treaty with a chief, as did van

---

[1] The nineteenth century military despotisms of the Zulus under Chaka and his successors, and of the kindred Matabele under Msilikazi and Lobengula, were no more typical of the Bantu system of rule than the Napoleonic empires were typical of the European states of their day.

Plettenberg, and then find that the paramount chief or other minor chiefs were not bound by it; they might make another with a great chief and then discover that it was 'for himself' and in no wise for his successor; they might even find that a treaty with a great chief could not be enforced upon his subordinate chieftains. The history of the dealings of the Dutch and British with the Xosas and, still more, with the Basuto confederacy later on is full of these difficulties. From the Bantu point of view, however, the frequency with which clans could be formed within the tribe and the readiness with which fugitives could be adopted into the clans served as a check upon tyranny. If a chief 'ate up' his men too greedily by confiscating their cattle and other goods in the name of justice, that 'great source of gain,' he might wake up to find them gone over to a milder rival. But only a grinding tyranny would drive warriors away from their lawful chief, for loyalty and patience were and are the cardinal virtues of Bantu tribesmen.

Bantu rule was not and is not, except in rare cases, merely capricious. The tribes had and, in so far as their tribal systems survive, have a well-defined system of courts and customary law. Some of the northern tribes used the ordeal by red-hot iron or emetics; too often the guilty were simply 'smelt out' by the witch-doctor; but a man was held to be innocent until he had been proved guilty, and in many cases an appeal was allowed to the chief paramount. Punishments were two: death or a fine payable in cattle, for tribes who lived in mud and thatch huts could hardly have attained to the refinement of imprisonment. Death and the confiscation of goods was the inevitable penalty of witchcraft, for that was a sin against both Church and State. At the back of Bantu religion was the idea of a Great One, Unkulunkulu, who had brought men and all things living out of the earth—or was it out of the split reed? But Unkulunkulu was a shadowy personage, a kind of Father Adam rather than God the Creator.[1] The foreground was filled with ancestral spirits with whom touch must be kept, and, still more, with evil spirits and goblins who must at all costs be placated. It was with these evil spirits that the witches were supposed to be in league, to the great hurt of man and beast and crops; it was the duty of the chief's witch-doctor to smell out the witches; it was the temptation of the chief to indicate privately the over-wealthy tribesman who was to be smelt out. Nevertheless, smelling-out was always done decently and in order; it was at least part of the law of the land, and the Bantu were not unique in that their law did not always square with essential justice.

The tribal law was carried in the memories of the *amapakati* and other 'elder statesmen,' for writing the Bantu had none. Perhaps for

---

[1] Kidd, *The Essential Kafir*, pp. 96 ff.; Stow, *Native Races*, p. 3.

that reason, they prized the spoken word. A chief must depend to a
certain extent on his eloquence for carrying his council with him;
he would take care to supplement his own gift of tongues with the
services of a *mbongo* or official praiser; his men well understood and
valued the long debates which, in other lands, have formed the basis
of parliaments; the very women were less impatient of male verbosity
than their more civilised sisters elsewhere have been wont. Indeed,
it often fell to the women to enrich the musical language of the tribe;
for, to avoid mentioning the names of their husbands' male relatives,
they had perforce to invent new words. To-day, the Zulu women,
members of the most conservative tribe in the Union, have a private
language of about 5000 words.[1]

Economically, the Bantu were and are cattle-farmers practising
agriculture as a side line. The hoeing of the gardens, the tending of
the mealies, Kaffir corn and pumpkins, and the making of the beer
fell to the women, who were thus an asset rather than a liability;
but the care of the cattle was the man's privilege. Horned cattle were
the wealth and pride of the Bantu, the central facts in their lives.
The beasts were sacred. It was the sacrifice of an ox in the centre
of the cattle-kraal round which the huts were usually grouped that
put the living in touch with the irritable dead; the skinned ox, one
for the tribe, the other for the enemy, that lived longest foretold
success or failure in a coming campaign; it was with cattle that fines
or compensation for injuries were liquidated: the tail hairs of a
selected beast were a sovereign remedy against sickness; cattle were
the chief prize in war and the medium through which 'reparations'
were paid; it was *lobola*, the cattle given by the bridegroom to the
father of the bride, that gave women a dignified position in society
and, what is more, 'begot the children.' Without the cattle the children would have been illegitimate.[2]

Nevertheless, the Bantu system was and is based on land-holding.
'The patrimony of a chief is not cattle. It is land and men.'[3] In
theory, the 'great place,' the kraal of the paramount chief, was the
centre of the tribal state; around it were grouped the lesser kraals,
and around all lay the tribal lands. The frontiers of those lands were
not precisely defined. A chief might, if necessary, point to certain
landmarks well within the lands claimed by his neighbours, who
would certainly do the same; in other words, he and they would
admit that there were belts of debatable land between the ground
actually used by one tribe and another. So long as there was plenty

[1] Verbal information from J. B. Lindley, Esq., son of the Rev. Daniel Lindley,
the missionary to the Zulus and friend of the Trekkers.
[2] Some tribes pay *lobola* in other articles. To-day, in the decay of the tribal
system, men even pay money for their wives.
[3] So Sandile the Gaika told Sir George Grey. Desp. 517. Grey to S. of S.,
Feb. 22, 1855.

of room this land would be left empty; but, if not, men of both tribes would settle there side by side under the rule of their own chiefs. Sovereignty was personal rather than territorial; but, if strife did arise between the interlocking tribes, the one that was defeated lost claim to the debatable lands, and a tribe whose royal family was wiped out in war lost even its right to its fully occupied land.

War, *ultima ratio regum*, was the surest way by which the tribal lands could pass from one tribe to another. The land did not belong to the chief; it was hardly 'owned' in the European sense by the tribe itself; certainly the chief could neither sell it nor cede it. It was precisely on this vital matter of landholding that European and Bantu ideas differed most fundamentally: the European based on contract and the personal, private ownership of a wedge of the universe cutting the earth's superficies and stretching 'from Hell to Heaven'; the Bantu ignorant of contract,[1] holding fast to status and regarding the actual soil as of less importance than the beings that lived upon and above it. Every member of a tribe, simply because he had been either born or adopted into the blood-fellowship of that tribe, was freely entitled to the use of air, water, grass, timber and the game upon the tribal lands, provided he gave the chief the haunch of buck or the tusk of the elephant which custom demanded. All that Bantu chiefs meant to do or could have meant to do when they 'ceded' land by treaty or otherwise to colonists, missionaries or other chiefs was to give these men the same privileges over land as their own tribesmen in return for the payment of a few cattle, sheep, or even muskets as a recognition that the bargain had been made. In the chief's eyes the newcomers thereby became his vassals.

Such a conflict of ideas was bound to lead to trouble when white men came into contact with Bantu. The chief might think that he was granting the use of certain territories; the Europeans naturally held that he was selling them the fee-simple of the land. Even the one kind of land which could, in Bantu law, be held upon individual tenure tended to complicate the issue still further. A tribesman, who, by permission of his chief, broke in a piece of hitherto unused soil, had a perpetual claim to the use of that land, unless indeed the chief gave it to another. Once the crop was reaped, all might drive their cattle into the stubble; but, as soon as the new seed was sown, all must keep off it. Interrupted occupation made no difference; that piece of land was earmarked for the use of the original holder and of his sons' sons after him. Such a practice might work well enough among scattered tribes; it could not fail to lead to friction when Europeans occupied apparently waste land as farms and then found themselves faced by the Bantu claimants returning out of a far country.

In short, there were in 1779 on either side of an ill-defined and

---

[1] Except debt, which never dies. (Evans, *Black and White*, p. 69.)

totally unpoliced border, white men and black, at very different levels of civilisation it is true, but both rough and ready agriculturalists, both essentially cattle-farmers, both migratory and both greedy of land. Land and water and not cattle have been the keys of the problem of the frontiers from that day to this.

While the northern border officials were preparing for a big commando for the extirpation of the Bushmen, news reached them that a Kaffir war had broken out upon the eastern frontier.[1] It was the first war in a century of such wars. Who fired the first shot no man can say, nor what caused the firing. The number of Europeans in the eastern borderlands had increased steadily since Willem Prinsloo had established himself at the Boschberg a few years previously; soon frontiersmen were complaining to van Plettenberg that the Kaffirs were stealing their cattle; then, in 1779, Gunukwebe, Imidange and other Xosa clans spread themselves over the parts that are now Albany and Somerset East and the fighting duly began. Some say Prinsloo was to blame for shooting an Imidange and seizing cattle in revenge for the theft of a sheep; others that his son, Marthinus, had gone with an illicit cattle-trading party beyond the Keiskamma and killed one of Rarabe's men; others again that farmers had driven a Xosa signatory of the van Plettenberg treaty back beyond the Fish river with unnecessary violence;[2] but, from whatever cause, though Rarabe himself was peaceably inclined, Xosas killed some Hottentots and laid hands on European cattle.

The Xosas were organised for war on the usual Bantu lines. They had little of the fierce military discipline which afterwards distinguished the Zulus and Matabele; but they were organised in regiments; those who had killed their man wore the crane's feathers in their head-ring; all were well practised in sham fights and equipped with the ox-hide shield, knobkerry and assegai. Unlike some of the tribes of the inland plateau, they did not use the bow or the iron battle-axe; nevertheless, they were dangerous antagonists to a handful of undisciplined mounted farmers armed with clumsy flint-locks.

The first war, a prolonged series of skirmishes, ended in favour of the colonists. Josua Joubert and his friends took it on themselves to form a commando, killed many Kaffirs and shared the captured cattle among themselves; whereupon the Council of Policy reluctantly allowed the local officials to take action and itself appointed Adriaan van Jaarsveld field-commandant. Van Jaarsveld drove the Xosas back across the Fish, not without one bad display of treachery against the Imidange; the commando shared the 5300 captured cattle, and for a time the eastern border had peace.[3]

1779.

1781.

---

[1] No. 50 of 1835, p. 19; Moodie, *Records*, III. 78 ff.   [2] Theal, IIIa. 128.
[3] No. 50 of 1835, p. 20; Moodie, *Records*, III. 89 ff.

During the 'eighties, times were good in the east. There was drought in the west, but the cattle-farmers were blessed with abundant rains and Capetown's demand for fresh meat was in-
1786. satiable. The long-promised landdrost was sent to Graaff-Reinet, closely followed by a sick-comforter,[1] but from the first it was clear that the control which the central authority hoped to exercise in the east was very limited, for it told even Swellendam that it could give no help in the collection of district taxes, and in Graaff-Reinet it merely organised a *krygsraad* and two mounted companies of burgher 'dragonders' and furnished the usual ammunition and good advice. But the instructions given to the landdrost, Maurits Woeke, showed what was going on along the eastern frontier.[2] He was, of course, to prevent the occupation of Algoa Bay by a foreign Power and collect the recognition money for the cattle-runs ; but he was also to keep the peace with the tribes, check Kaffir robberies, recall all burghers to the colonial side of the Fish and put an end to the practice of going into Kaffirland.[3] It was the same old story: pro-clamations and no police to enforce them. The Company set up no military posts in Graaff-Reinet and never sent the frontier guard which Woeke demanded. So the Boers went freely into Kaffirland bartering cattle, and Xosas worked for them on the farms far to the westward in Swellendam district.

Circa Rarabe was now dead, and his son Ndhlambi ruled in the name
1785. of his little grandson Gaika; wherefore the Xosas who had crossed the Kei before Rarabe held that they owed allegiance to no one but
March the distant paramount, Galeka. Then some minor Xosa chiefs with
1789. their people crossed the lower Fish into the Zuurveld and Boers complained of stock-theft and insecurity. Woeke promptly called out a commando, but van der Graaff, anxious to avoid the risks and expenses of war, advised caution in dealing with the Xosas, and sent Honoratus Maynier as secretary to Graaff-Reinet to co-operate with the retiring secretary, Jan Wagener, in coming to terms with the in-vaders, if necessary by buying up any claims they might have against the colonists.[4] The two secretaries, who had hitherto shared to the full the opinions entertained by Western officialdom on the short-comings of the frontiers, made an analysis of the situation which did not altogether confirm those opinions. Plainly, the predatory Bushmen were, in their eyes, the principal enemy; wherefore, they did all they could to strengthen the commandos against them. On
Aug. the other hand, while admitting that frontiersmen were suffering at
1789. the hands of the Bantu, they sought to keep the peace with the Xosas. Making a virtue of necessity, they told the latter that they might

[1] Theal, IIIa. 151, 174; Spoelstra, I. 574.
[2] Geyer, *Das Wirtschaftliche System*, pp. 23 ff.
[3] No. 50 of 1835, p. 20.   [4] Van der Merwe, *Trekboer*, 291-310

remain on the Zuurveld *quamdiu se bene gesserint* and 'without prejudice to the ownership of Europeans.'[1]

For the next year or two Maynier practically superseded the incompetent Woeke. It has now been established that the view long held, on Theal's authority, about the character and policy of Maynier needs drastic revision. There is no evidence that he accepted Rousseau's views on the virtues of the 'noble savage,' though his 'humanity undoubtedly owes something to the intellectual climate of his age. He hated cruelty and injustice. . . . But he was neither a sentimentalist nor a visionary. He knew what crimes brown and black men were capable of.'[2] Nevertheless, as he learned more of the facts, he began to lay increasing stress in his official reports on the shortcomings of the colonists. In obedience to orders from head-quarters, he strove doggedly to set up 'the rule of law' on the frontier; he tried to do justice to all men, but he lacked the police which were necessary to safeguard liberty. All he could do was to prevent the frontiersmen from taking their own line. He was aware that, owing to the factor of distance, the rule of law could not be completely enforced as between the Boers and their Hottentot servants, but he did his best to prevent gross cruelty and injustice.[3] He would not allow unauthorised commandos to go into Kaffirland and would then only sanction a *wachtmeester's* party in place of a general levy of frontiersmen. Most of the Boers had welcomed his coming and many continued to stand by him; but many others turned away and were soon complaining that the Rev. Jan von Manger, who had arrived at long last in 1792 as predikant, interfered with them instead of confining himself to his clerical duties, and they might also have complained that, since he scarcely ever moved away from the drostdy, he never got to know most of his parishioners. True, they had asked for a landdrost and a predikant, but they had not thought that that would bring them a Maynier and a von Manger.[4]

Meanwhile the bulk of the Cape garrison was withdrawn, the 1791. posts in Swellendam were abandoned, and the Company's new grain store at Mossel Bay was closed to the farmers of Swellendam who had borrowed money wherewith to buy ploughs and oxen on the strength of the Company's offer to take their produce.[5] Discontent and troubles accumulated along the whole frontier. In the north, the Bushmen drove numbers of farmers off their farms; the three land-drosts were summoned to Capetown to concert measures against them, and, when the distant Woeke failed to appear, he was sus-pended. The others agreed with the military command on a great campaign against the Bushmen and offered a reward of £3 for every

[1] Van der Merwe, *Trekboer*, 291–310.
[2] Marais, *Maynier*, p. 36.
[3] *Ibid.*, chaps. III–VI, IX, X.
[4] Rec. C.C., I. 207, 497; IV. 283 ff.
[5] *Ibid.*, I. 173.

Bushman, Hottentot or Bastaard robber of any sex or age delivered alive at Robben Island, there to serve the Company in chains *ad vitam*. The Graaff-Reineters turned out too late, but Jan van der Walt of the Koude Bokkeveld and Jonker Afrikaner, the Hottentot free-booter of the Hantam, did yeoman service killing over 600 Bushmen and taking a few alive. As a reward for all this, van der Walt was given two farms on the Nieuwveld, provided he occupied them, and was empowered to call out commandos whenever he thought fit.[1]

Indecisive bickering with the Bushmen was still going on in the north when hostilities broke out again with the Kaffirs in the east. Maynier had been appointed landdrost in Woeke's place; there was a severe drought which afflicted black and white impartially; the Xosas were short of grain and those on the Zuurveld had eaten or lost most of their cattle; some thirty Boer families had gone in beyond the Fish in search of pasture; west of the lower Fish certain Xosa clans, who seem to have lost much of their cattle in warfare with Ndhlambi, were, the Boers complained, stealing their stock, 'eating up' their pastures, killing their game and enticing slaves and Hottentots to leave their service. On their side the Xosa complained of maltreatment at the hands of Boers, mentioning by name, amongst others, Christoffel Botha, Coenraad Bezuidenhout with other members of that turbulent family, and especially the ruffian Coenraad Buis. Maynier added that the Boers ill-treated Xosa servants. It was the dreary story of no-man's land all the world over, and it presently had the usual sequel. A burgher, Barend Lindeque, raised a commando on his own account, got help from Ndhlambi, seized Xosa cattle and shared the booty with his ally. Thereupon, the Xosas cleared nearly all the farms between the lower Fish and Zwartkops rivers, slew some of the fugitive farmers and their Hottentot retainers, and seized a great spoil of cattle, sheep and horses.[2]

Most of the raiders retired to safety beyond the Fish, Ndhlambi was only too willing to let the rest come over with their plunder, and the chiefs promised Maynier to respect the Fish boundary. But they declined to give up their loot; plundering went on; the central government sent a Swellendam commando to the front, and Maynier took the field himself with a Graaff-Reinet commando.[3] There were wild rumours in Swellendam that the Hottentots meant to rise and massacre the farmers; nevertheless, the Swellendamers joined Maynier and the combined force pushed eastward into Kaffirland as far as the Buffalo river. It effected nothing decisive; most of the cattle it captured had to be either eaten or abandoned on the way

April
1793.

May
1793.

Aug.
1793.

---

[1] No. 50 of 1835, p. 21; Theal, IIIa. 212 ff.
[2] Marais, *Maynier*, chapters II–IV.; Van der Merwe, *Die Kaffer Oorlog van 1793*, p. 17.
[3] Marais, *Maynier*, pp. 43–7.

home, and an attempt to clear the Zuurveld ended in failure. Maynier then tried to come to terms with the Xosas. He was hampered by a burgher, Hendrik van Rensburg, who raised a private commando; but him he dissuaded and at last made peace more or less on the basis of the *status quo*.

The frontiersmen were vastly displeased. They had certainly exaggerated the losses inflicted on them by the Kaffirs at the first onset, for the discrepancies between the losses reported and the previous *opgaaf* were too great to be explained by the customary underestimate for taxing purposes; but their losses had undoubtedly been serious; they had taken comparatively few cattle from their enemies; the Zuurveld was lost and some of them had been reduced to covering their nakedness with sheepskins. Moreover they knew that the officials at Capetown saw the chief cause of the war in their conduct, for the Council of Policy had issued a fearsome *placaat* recapitulating the *placaaten* of 1677, 1727, 1739, 1770, 1774, 1786 and the General Placaat of 1739 against the cattle-barter and inter-course with the tribes, forbidding anyone to go beyond Baviaan's river or the Tarka district, prohibiting the sale of arms to natives or the ill-treatment of Hottentots, who were, in future, not to be separated from their families, and ordering the *wachtmeesters* to arrest all offenders and report them to the Fiscal. In face of this, it was small comfort to the frontiersmen that natives found in arms might be handed over to the landdrost to be dealt with as vagabonds, for so long as Maynier was landdrost they had little hope that this law would be administered as they desired. Worse still, Commis-sioner Sluysken not only refused to recall Maynier at the request of a frontier deputation, but reaffirmed the Fish river frontier and for-bade either colonists or Kaffirs to cross its magic waters, the former without a landdrost's pass, the latter without a copper token.[1]

At last, the eastern borderers determined to submit no longer to a Company which neither defended them nor permitted them to defend themselves in the usual fashion of frontiersmen and diligent students of the more warlike portions of the Old Testament. They would pay neither rent nor taxes to such a government; they meant to go into Kaffirland in search of missing cattle; they would see to it that their Hottentots got none of the teaching which they heard the Moravians were once more giving in the west to those at Schmidt's old mission station; above all, they would have their own locally elected officials. Hence, van Jaarsveld and Jan Trigardt with a party Feb. of forty men mounted the tricolour cockade and drove Maynier out 1795. of his drostdy. Sluysken sent down Commissioners, but they too were expelled and the Graaff-Reinet rebels chose their own pro- June visional landdrost and heemraden. They went through the farce of 1795.

[1] Rec. C.C., I. 167, 174 ; V.R. Soc., III. 256 ; No. 50 of 1835, pp. 21, 22.

asking Sluysken to confirm the elections, but what they had really done was to set up a local republic. Four days later the majority of the Swellendammers followed their example and elected a National Assembly.[1]

June 11, 1795.

In that same week, nine British warships with troops on board cast anchor in Simon's Bay. Their coming had not been entirely unexpected, for half Europe was at war with the French Republic, the Netherlands were in the thick of it on the side of the Allies, and the halfway house to India could not hope to remain unscathed. It was certain that either France or Great Britain would try to secure it as they had done in the last great war. The French, entrenched at the Cape as well as at Mauritius and Île de Bourbon (Reunion), could harry English East Indiamen more grievously than ever and this Great Britain could not afford, all the more as her interests in India had grown vastly since 1783. Moreover, the Netherlands had secretly

1785.

bound herself to both the great antagonists. The Patriots had made an insurance treaty with France; the restored House of Orange had

1788.

then made a reinsurance treaty, whereunder the British and Dutch in the East were to help each other in wartime without waiting for orders from home.[2]

The British now came in terms of this latter treaty. There had been talk of some such friendly occupation at the beginning of the French

Jan. 1795.

war; but no move had been made till Pichegru's invading troops had been welcomed by the republican party in the Netherlands and had sent the Prince of Orange flying across the English Channel. Then the British expedition had slipped away southward in three divisions.[3]

The first two divisions entered Simon's Bay together. The commanders, Elphinstone and Craig, held a letter signed by the Prince of Orange bidding Sluysken admit them peaceably.[4] It was a letter which the princely refugee at Kew had signed as soon as he had been assured that the Cape would be given back to him whenever peace and independence, to wit, himself should be restored to the Netherlands. The British commanders hoped that it would prove an 'Open Sesame.' They had no desire to fight, for they could put less than 1600 men into the field; they had neither cavalry nor guns; the country between Simonstown and Capetown was sandy and difficult, and a direct attack on the capital by sea was out of the question in the teeth of winter north-westers and the batteries.

The Castle was the centre of an elaborate system of defence: the Chavonnes battery begun at the close of the War of the Spanish

[1] Rec., C.C., I. 172, 209, 479.   [2] Blok, *Geschiedenis*, VI. 501, 529.
[3] Rec. C.C., I. 1 ff., 35.
[4] *Ibid.*, 1. 27 ff.; Blok, *Geschiedenis*, VII. 31 ff. Many Dutch possessions besides the Cape were occupied by the British, one or two peaceably.

Succession; Fort Knokke, the Sea Lines and *couvreface* Imhoff built during the War of the Austrian Succession; the New Battery at Salt River, the French Lines from Knokke up the slopes of the Devil's Peak, an unfinished line of redoubts in support, the massive Amsterdam Battery and smaller batteries at Rogge Bay, Mouille Point, Camps Bay and Kloof Nek, fruit of the energy of the French army of occupation and van der Graaff's engineering zeal. Sluysken himself had hurriedly constructed two batteries at Simon's Bay and three at Hout Bay.[1]

The Peninsula bristled with guns, but 3000 men would hardly suffice to man the defences, and Sluysken had barely half that number of even tolerably trained men. He had merely the National Battalion, 571 strong, mercenaries of the usual type; 430 much more reliable gunners, for the most part Dutchmen, supplemented by a few hastily-enrolled Malays, a few odds and ends from the depots of the Meuron and Wurtemberg regiments, Hottentot and half-caste Pandours, and the Pennists drawn from the ranks of the civil service. Behind this first line stood the burgher militia organised on the customary district basis. The Cape could supply four companies of infantry and two of dragoons, Stellenbosch five mounted companies and Swellendam three, and Graaff-Reinet three mounted companies more; in all, 3000 men on paper and, under existing political circumstances, likely to remain largely on paper.[2]

The British commanders did not expect much resistance from such a heterogeneous force, especially as they had reasonable hopes that the mercenaries, 'mostly kidnapped Germans,' ill-paid and ill-led, would have no stomach for a fight and might even be induced to change sides.[3] They themselves were short of money, bread and spirits, and were anxious for a speedy settlement which would free them from their crowded, scurvy-ridden ships. There lay the difficulty. Sluysken himself was pro-Orange; his senior officers, from Commandant Gordon downwards, were more inclined to become 'Great Britainers' than yield to the Nationals ;[4] he and they were willing enough to admit the newcomers; but the latest news from home had hinted that Holland might change sides in the great war, the orders of a dethroned prince were not convincing, and the Francophiles of Capetown were being reinforced daily by burghers from the country, 'totally undisciplined . . . extremely turbulent.'[5] In vain did the British offer good terms and depict the horrors of French republicanism. Sluysken, who had hitherto merely played for time, now learned that his country had become the Batavian

---

[1] Roux, *Verdedigingstelsel*, pp. 9 ff.; E. A. Walker, *Historical Atlas*, p. 13.
[2] No. 50 of 1835, p. 20; Roux, *op. cit.*; Theal, IIIa. 124 ff. From first to last, 1690 burghers turned out. None came from Graaff-Reinet.
[3] Rec. C.C., I. 36, 62, 82, 110, 183, 230.
[4] *Ibid.*, I. 45, 53, 60; II. 191.   [5] *Ibid.*, I. 101.

Republic and might ally with France. He therefore resolved to resist and, to gain time, abandoned distant Simonstown and occupied 'the uncommonly strong post,' at Muizenberg.

Craig had meanwhile sent for General Clarke who was waiting with the main body in Brazil. He now landed his men in leisurely fashion, and made ready to attack under cover of the ships' guns in spite of the Dutch batteries and 1500 burghers, many of whom were on horseback and 'armed with guns that kill at a great distance.'[1] Risking the shallows, the warships stood in, the redcoats advanced, the Company's mercenaries fled, and Muizenberg, the key of the Peninsula, passed into Craig's hands.

A troubled month followed, during which British detachments were worsted at Retreat and the Steenberg; but the burghers began to dribble away homewards and, at the end of the month, Clarke arrived with 5000 men and guns. The British at once made a double move. The warships threatened Capetown, while the troops attacked the Company's forces on Wynberg Hill. Again the mercenaries bolted and, though the rest stood to it for a time, they too had to fall back and the 500 remaining burghers dispersed with cries of 'Treachery.'

Sept. 16, 1795. In view of the Franco-Batavian alliance of May, Clarke had orders to take the Cape in King George's name. This fact governed the capitulation signed at Rustenburg.[2] The Dutch troops surrendered as prisoners of war. Some of the officers were allowed to sail for Holland with Sluysken, who was presently acquitted of all blame for his curious mode of defence, and a fair number of mercenaries enlisted with the British for service in India. The colonists for their part were promised free internal trade for the first time, overseas trade on the best possible terms, no alteration of laws or customs, and, in view of the parlous condition of the Colony, reduction of taxation where possible. The new rulers also undertook to maintain the value of the paper money on the understanding that 'the Lands and Houses the property of . . . the Company in this settlement' should continue the security for such portion as was not lent on private mortgage. That the said property had never been thus pledged and was, in any event, totally inadequate to the task was only discovered by the British two years later.[3] However, disillusionment was still in the future, and as soon as the men of the Cape, Stellenbosch and Swellendam districts had taken the oath of allegiance to George III for so long a time as he should hold the Colony, Clarke and Elphinstone sailed for India, leaving Craig to defend the Cape with 2900 men.

Nov. 15, 1795. The new Government's writ did not run in Graaff-Reinet for nearly a year to come. The Nationals of Graaff-Reinet were not disposed to recognise Craig's Government unconditionally. King George might

[1] Rec. C.C., I. 161.
[2] Ibid., 127 ff., 153; Eybers, p. 3.
[3] Rec. C.C., I. 130.

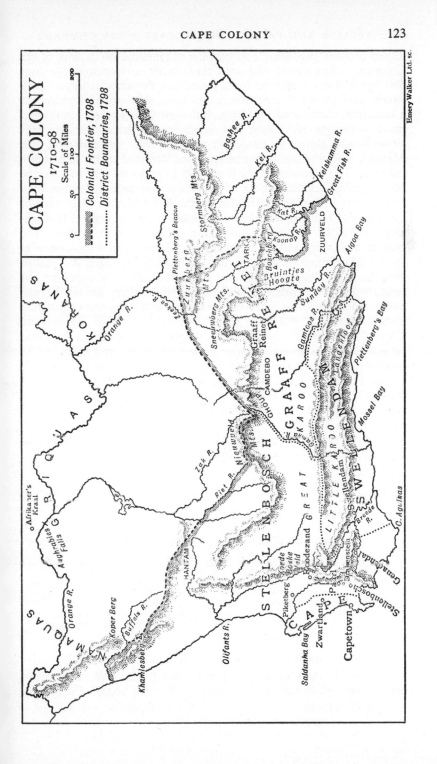

CAPE COLONY
1710-98
Scale of Miles

Colonial Frontier, 1798
District Boundaries, 1798

Emery Walker Ltd. sc.

indeed become 'protector' and supplier of ammunition in place of the Company; they would still send their cattle to Capetown—a hint that the halfway house to India could not do without them—they would obey all reasonable orders and laws, they would even accept a landdrost nominated by Craig, but their own elected heemraden must be recognised.[1] Craig was determined to be master. He sent Frans Bresler thither as landdrost together with the predikant, von Manger, who, the frontiersmen said, had deserted them 'in a subtle manner.' The National officials refused to make way or to take the oath of allegiance. Stirred up by Jan Woyer, an ardent Jacobin, they rallied round Marthinus Prinsloo of the Boschberg as 'Protector of the Voice of the People.' The representatives of the central Government therefore withdrew and Craig prepared to use force. The quieter and more settled burghers of the northern wards were in favour of submission, but the men of Bruintjes Hoogte, Zwartkops river and the Zuurveld held out and even talked of expelling the landdrost of Swellendam. The position was serious, for the French had a strong squadron in the Indian Ocean, and a Batavian squadron under Admiral Engelbertus Lucus was on its way to recover the

Aug. 17, 1796.

Cape. Lucas's ships were, however, captured in Saldanha Bay, and Graaff-Reinet submitted. Craig recalled his troops and promised an amnesty to all save the elusive Woyer, who had gone to seek help of the French in the East Indies. But he refused to suffer elected heemraden or to allow farmers to enter Kaffirland in search of stolen cattle or to permit them to occupy the vacant land beyond the Fish as far as the Koonap 'or, if it could be, unto the Kat.'[2]

Thus did the British discover that the half-way house to India had a hinterland with problems of its own.

CHAPTER VI

THE OFFICIAL OCCUPATIONS, 1795–1823

First British Occupation : government, 124 ; commerce and finance, 127 ; Eastern frontier troubles, 129.—**Batavian Republic :** government, 133 ; frontier policy, 134 ; economic and social reforms, 135.—**Second British Occupation :** Western colonists, 138 ; cession of the Cape, 139 ; administrative reforms, 141 ; economic policy, 142 ; Church and schools, 143 ; Missionaries, 144 ; end of the British slave trade, 146 ; Hottentots and Griquas, 148 ; Dr. Philip, 152 ; Eastern frontier, 153 ; the 1820 Settlers and Commission of Inquiry, 156.

FIRST BRITISH OCCUPATION, Sept. 1795–Feb. 1803

BY occupying the Castle at Capetown the British had made themselves responsible for the governance of some 16,000 Europeans,

[1] Rec. C.C., I. 208. [2] Ibid., 1. 208, 234, 431, 480, 502.

17,000 slaves, and an indeterminate number of Hottentots and Bushmen.[1] The quality of the British administration was on the whole good for the time and circumstances. The Governors, especially Lord Macartney, were upright if somewhat stiff in manner and, like the rest of their class, suspicious of anything that smacked of 'French principles.' Yonge indeed had his faults, but he was at least a man of ideas ranging from experimental farming to vaccination. Government was naturally paternal in the manner of the Roman father. There were occasional deportations, sometimes with and sometimes without sentence of the High Court, but always for 'Jacobinism,' incitement to rebellion or correspondence with the French. Worse things were being done in England and much worse in Ireland, for Great Britain was fighting for her life among the ruins of the European Coalitions. Even so, the Secretary of State curtly told Yonge that deportation 'is a power not to be recurred to for offences cognizable in the Courts.'[2]

Just, on the whole, the Government might be; popular it was not outside the ranks of Orange society in the capital, in spite of the charm of Lady Anne Barnard, the accomplished wife of Macartney's secretary and hostess at the Castle, whose power of 'placing herself in sympathy with those whom she addressed' was invaluable to a temporary administration;[3] in spite, too, of Yonge's innovation of a state ball for 'all the Principal Gentlemen and Ladies which opened at nine o'clock and lasted till four in the morning.'[4] Some of the higher Dutch officials retained their posts; the first appointments after the Occupation were of colonists; colonists throughout supplied the rank and file of the civil service, but the higher posts were filled, as occasion offered, with Englishmen.[5] The Government was expensive. The British taxpayer paid for the squadron and the garrison and made up any deficiencies in revenue, but the colonists had to pay the twelve chief officials £26,000 in sterling—almost as much as the total revenue for 1796 in paper—a real grievance to the public and to the remaining officials who had to put up with the depreciating cartoon-money. Nevertheless, apart from the fact that revenue rose markedly during the first five years without extra taxation, it may well be doubted whether the British officials cost the Colony more than the Company's men with their perquisites, houses, farms, horses, servants, household allowances and fees of office. This last nuisance Macartney stopped. Officials were put upon regular salaries.

[1] De Mist reckoned 13,830 Europeans in 1793; Barrow gave 20,000, including 5000 in Capetown, in 1798 (V.R. Soc., III. 175).
[2] Rec. C.C., III. 201, 353. On the First British Occupation *vide South Africa a Century Ago*; D. Fairbridge, *Lady Anne Barnard at the Cape* (1924); *Bel. Hist. Dok.* III. 13 ff.; V.R. Soc. III.
[3] *South Africa a Century Ago*, p. xxiii.   [4] Rec. C.C., III. 40.
[5] *Ibid.*, I. 184, 199, 297, 319; II. 85; III. 489.

Only the Fiscal as Public Prosecutor and, after something of a struggle, the Judge of the new Vice-Admiralty Court were allowed to draw the fees customary to their offices.[1] Except in the purlieus of Government House in Yonge's time, the administration was purer than it had ever been before, and Yonge, a hoary old jobber more sinned against by his associates than sinning, was speedily recalled in disgrace to the surprise and delight of the colonists.[2]

In spite of the recommendations of the Fiscal, Willem van Ryneveld, a staunch Orangeman, few changes were made in the law or con-

1796. stitution. Craig replaced the Commission of the High Court by a Burgher Senate of six burghers selected by the Governor in the usual fashion from a fourfold list presented by the board as vacancies occurred to do all that its predecessor had done, save in judicial matters. After much opposition from the Judges, he and Macartney abolished the practice of torturing slaves and Hottentots on suspicion, and of breaking at the wheel and the more barbarous forms of capital

1799. punishment hitherto used in the Colony. Macartney made a few other necessary changes. He and the Lieutenant-Governor took the place of the Court at Batavia as the Court of Civil Appeal; a Vice-Admiralty Court, independent of the Colonial Government, was established; the unwieldy High Court was cut down from thirteen members to eight and all the judges were paid; the civil powers of the landdrosts' courts were extended, especially in far-distant Graaff-Reinet. On the other hand, whether Yonge liked it or not, Roman-Dutch law, on the analogy of French law in newly conquered Martinique, was applied even to British-born subjects by special order of the Secretary of State.[3]

The authorities were shaken once, when, in October 1797, news of the mutiny at Spithead inspired some of the seamen in the Cape squadron to 'hoist the jacket.' At Simonstown, the crews returned to duty when Rear-Admiral Thomas Pringle, like 'Black Dick Howe' at home, listened to the men's complaints and promised redress; but the trouble was not ended in Table Bay till Macartney had threatened to open fire on the mutineers from the imposing Amsterdam Battery. Mercifully, all was over before news of the much more dangerous political mutiny at the Nore reached the Cape. For the rest, the administration was in a better position than the Company to further the prosperity of the Colony, for it was a government and nothing but a government. In terms of the Capitulation all monopolies were cancelled, restrictions on the sale of goods to the ships and on internal trade were swept away, coasting trade was permitted even eastward into the sphere of the English East India Company,

---

[1] Rec. C.C., I. 177, 217; II. 35, 291, 294, 433 ff.; III. 42.
[2] *Ibid.*, III. 395 ff., 441, 484 ff.; IV. 107, 221 ff.
[3] *Ibid.*, I. 298, 302, 320 ff., 373; II. 6; III. 329, 481.

and by a most unusual arrangement goods from any part of the British dominions were admitted duty-free.[1] Though this privilege was subsequently limited to goods from the newly United Kingdom,[2] arrears of land rents were remitted up to the beginning of the Occupation and no new taxes were levied till after Yonge's arrival. Some of his taxes caused no complaint; but his game licences and the increased brandy duty raised a storm which did not abate till he had been recalled and the obnoxious imposts cancelled by his successor.[3] Signs of the times and of closer connection with the rest of the civilised world were the opening of a post-office for the ocean mail and the granting of a monopoly for printing. It was a monopoly of which Government speedily repented, for it almost immediately bought it out. Henceforward the *Government Gazette* was produced in the Castle under the watchful eye of Mr. Secretary John Barrow.[4]

Commerce hung fire at first, because neutral ships, on which the Colony was wont to rely in time of war, were discouraged lest they smuggle enemy goods; but British ships soon began to call and the local speculators were made happy.[5] Even Macartney made a venture. Yielding to the persuasion of the Burgher Senate, he imported three ship-loads of mixed goods at government expense; but private merchants refused to buy at the repeated auctions, the small Cape market was already glutted, and his successor, Yonge, was left to foot the bill.[6] In other directions private enterprise made some slight headway. There was a little milling, a few attempts at forestry and a small development in whaling once Craig had taken possession of Angra Pequeña and Walvis Bay in the interests of the fishers; but agriculture remained the chief industry, and a large garrison and squadron held out to the farmers hopes of a prosperity tempered only by the fact that Government, in self-defence in so small a market, fixed the price payable to its contractors for supplies. As it was, 'every other article of life (the three excepted—wine, bread and butcher's meat) is extraordinarily dear . . . and every assistance of labour three times as much' as in London.'[7] Worse still both farmers and administration were unlucky. Craig found the magazines full of corn and the farmers burdened with an unsaleable harvest. He therefore sent away all the corn he could to help to meet the shortage in Great Britain, and was rewarded by a run of bad seasons which went far to ruin the grandiose schemes of Yonge and his master-gardener,

Margin notes: July 1802. Dec. 1799. Aug. 1800.

[1] Rec. C.C., II. 1, 77, 116; *C.H.B.E.*, VIII. 179.
[2] Rec. C.C., III. 421, 463, 483; IV. 106.
[3] *Ibid.*, II. 96, 111; III. 47, 195.   [4] *Ibid.*, III. 198; IV. 80.
[5] Like the excellent Mr. Trail of Simonstown 'who buys up everything the moment the ships come in, and then puts his own price on the goods. *N.B.*—By his office he is debarred from what he practises' (*South Africa a Century Ago* p. 24).
[6] Rec. C.C., II. 283, 286, 319, 420, 497; III. 28, 87, 94, 100, 105, 334.
[7] *South Africa a Century Ago*, p. 7.

William Duckitt, for the encouragement of scientific farming and cattle-breeding, and forced successive governors to import wheat and rice on whatever terms they could.[1]

Closely connected with the problem of supply was that of the paper money. The British found it at 30 per cent. discount: some 614,000 rix dollars ostensibly secured on unrealisable government buildings and a few farms, and 677,000 issued on private mortgage by the Loan Bank. Craig long resisted temptation till the impossibility of paying his troops forced him to issue fresh paper. Macartney tried to check the vagaries of the exchanges by importing silver Spanish dollars (4*s*. 8*d*.) and copper *dubbeltjes*, pence which passed for twopence. Dundas, urged on by the Burgher Senate, set the printing-press to work once more, partly to furnish capital to the bank and partly to finance the purchase of corn and rice. Most of this last issue 1803. was cancelled as the supplies were sold to the public and, later on, property was handed over to the Batavian successors of the British to balance the remainder including part of Craig's small issue. Nevertheless, the British had found 1,291,000 Rd. in circulation, and they left 1,786,000.[2]

Such reforms and mistakes as the British made affected principally the western districts. The problem of the frontier districts remained. It was a problem with which a government experienced only in the conditions of the extreme south-west corner of the Colony was ill-fitted to cope. The West was one thing, the East quite another, and the British had little enough to guide them towards a solution of the questions it presented. So far from having a frontier policy, the Company had never even had a boundary on all sides of the Colony since 1660. Latterly, it had left the Boers to settle their differences with the Bushmen in the customary frontier fashion so long as they reported each *straf commando* after the event. Now, in the north-eastern districts Bushmen were sometimes serving as cattle-herds; 1797. but as a rule they were still being shot or chased away, except in the parts about Tarka, where they were numerous enough to make the scattered farmers withdraw.[3]

The Hottentots presented a less dangerous but more complicated problem.[4] Of recent years, they had been gradually recognised as 1775. humble dependents of European society. Children of slave fathers and Hottentot mothers had been specially provided for as serfs of the owners of the slaves; field commandants and *veldwachtmeesters* had been ordered to make a return to the landdrosts of all Hottentots

---

[1] Rec. C.C., I. 271, 328, 331; II. 62, 418, 428; III. 102, 330, 375, 390, 430, 446, 475; IV. 45, 118, 142 ff.
[2] *Ibid.*, I. 276, 405; II. 70, 91, 116, 189 ff.; III. 26, 31, 323, 393; IV. 135.
[3] *Ibid.*, II. 97.   [4] *Vide supra*, p. 95.

to check the practice of runaway slaves passing themselves off as 1781. Hottentots, for already it was difficult to distinguish one class of Coloured man from another; a Hottentot corps had been raised during the War of American Independence, and though it had been disbanded provisionally on the arrival of the French troops, all Hottentots and Bastaards, except those in the Graaff-Reinet district, had later been called on to assist in the defence of the Colony; 1793. Bastaards who were not in the service of colonists had to enrol, make 1787. *opgaaf* and pay taxes like ordinary burghers. Nevertheless, the pure-blooded Hottentots were still regarded as free men living in the Colony but not of it.

Their tribal system was now far gone in decay; only two petty *kaptijns* and their clans still held land; the rest, and that for the most 1795. part in the East, were either vagrants or miserably paid or unpaid farm-labourers.[1] As such their treatment varied with the nature of their masters. Many hard things have been said of the Boers' treatment of the Hottentots, and the placaaten of the Company show that there was fire beneath the smoke; but the reforming de Mist 1803. could write that 'if a half of what is written is ignored, a fourth considered doubtful, and the rest modified by reforms, it will be seen that the Hottentots are even more favourably situated than the peasant farmers of Meierij.'[2] It may be possible to accept de Mist's dictum without envying the men of Meierij; nevertheless, the fact remains that, whereas the Hottentots had once occupied grazing lands and *fonteins*, now they held none. Such organised tribes as survived were leaving the Colony. The Koranas were seeking refuge round the junction of the Vaal and Harts rivers; the Bastaards and Grigriquas were either holding on with Adam Kok I at Pella on the Lower Orange[3] or following his son, Cornelis, from the Khamiesberg to the middle Orange valley; the Namaquas were drifting northwards into what is now South-West Africa. The Orange River valley to the northward of the Colony thus swarmed with half-breeds, Hottentots, runaway slaves and outlaws, a menace to the border farmers. Notable among them was the Namaqua, Afrikaner, who raided Europeans and Griquas impartially from his impregnable island in the middle of the great river. As for the Kaffirs on the Eastern Frontier, they were a new factor, and beyond proclaiming the Fish as the boundary between white and black and decreeing a policy of non-intercourse, the Company had done nothing at all.

The problem of the borderlands was one, but for many years to come the most pressing difficulties were to arise on the Eastern Frontier. There the Company had done little for its European

---

[1] No. 50 of 1835, pp. 19 ff., 127, 147; Rec. C.C., IV. 90; VIII. 301; Moodie, *Records*, III. 40.
[2] V.R. Soc., III. 254-6.   [3] *Vide supra*, p. 95.

subjects. It had indeed supplied them with ammunition, registered their loan-places, taxed them when they came to Capetown and, latterly, marooned a landdrost and predikant among the mud hovels of Graaff-Reinet. It had never defended them; at the most it had hampered them when they had tried to take the law into their own hands. The upshot had been rebellion.

Finding that there was a border problem, the British faced it as best they could. Craig had already dealt in his own way with the three main issues of frontier politics: local government, land and 1797. relations with the tribes. Now Macartney took up the task. Afrikaner was out in the north; the Bushmen were raiding the Bokkeveld and Tarka; Xosas were ensconced on the banks of the Bushman's river well to the west of the boundary, and Bruintjes Hoogte men were to the east of it on the Koonap. As far as Afrikaner was concerned, Macartney was fain to let ill alone, but for the Bushmen he prescribed humane treatment by the commandos but, if necessary, expulsion to the Kalahari. Meanwhile he distributed breeding cattle to those nearest at hand, cattle which were either eaten by their new owners or stolen by less favoured neighbours.[1] He then sent Landdrost July Bresler, Barrow and a handful of dragoons to Graaff-Reinet with 1798. orders to remit rent for six years to those Tarka and Zuurveld farmers who should reoccupy their farms at once, to bring the Boers back from the Koonap and, generally, to confirm a comprehensive boundary on all sides of the Colony.[2] Farmers living to the north-ward of the new line were not to be disturbed, for no Kaffirs lay in that direction as far as was known. So Bresler enforced as far as he was able the old policy of non-intercourse upon the Europeans; but with the Kaffirs he was less successful. The Rarabe-Xosa clans on the Zuurveld refused to go back behind the Fish for fear of Gaika, and Gaika, their nominal lord, dwelling in the Tyumie valley beyond the Fish, politely washed his hands of them, saying they were no subjects of his.

May Bresler's partial settlement could not stand. A scare of foreign 1797. intervention, it is true, ended with the capture at Delagoa Bay of a brig carrying guns and ammunition from Batavia; the presence of officials and the novelty of dragoons had a calming effect on the frontier. But at the New Year of 1799 all went amiss. Macartney, 'the old lord,' departed, fire destroyed many of the naval and military stores at Capetown, and the veteran troops sailed to India to fight Tippoo Sahib and his French allies. The battalions of youngsters sent in exchange were so weak that the English residents of the capital had to form a volunteer corps to assist the garrison, and the naval squadron was much reduced. All this news and more also reached the frontiers. Matters were brought to a head by the arrest of van

[1] Rec. C.C., II. 99.   [2] Ibid., II. 95 ff.

Jaarsveld, a leading National, for forgery. He was rescued by his neighbours, who blockaded the drostdy and joined hands with some British deserters and Coenraad Buis, a ruffianly outlaw of considerable ability and great physical strength, who had married widely into Gaika's tribe. Relying on Buis's promise of Kaffir help and the hope of raising eastern Swellendam, the rebels demanded the release of van Jaarsveld, the reversal of Buis's outlawry, liberty for farmers to graze their cattle each night beyond the Fish, and permission for field cornets to reclaim runaway slaves and Hottentots from beyond the border. Government, they said moreover, must communicate with the Kaffirs in future through trusty burghers and not through Hottentot messengers.[1]

Tidings of the rising reached the Castle in time to offset the good news that the French frigate *Prudente* had been captured with volunteers on board bound for Algoa Bay. General Vandeleur's dragoons rode post-haste to Graaff-Reinet, infantry and Hottentots followed more leisurely by sea. They found the bulk of the Graaff-Reineters peaceable and a few even ready to help them; but their main recruitment came from the Hottentots, who, seeing their fellows in arms, thought it was a war between them and their white masters. One hundred joined the Hottentot Regiment, and a mixed crowd of men, women and children fled from the farms to tag along behind the troops as they marched to the Boschberg. There van Jaarsveld, disappointed of his expected aid, was arrested, and a few days later Marthinus Prinsloo, the aforetime Protector of the Voice of the People, surrendered with over a hundred followers. Most of these were sent home; but much to their surprise Prinsloo and seventeen others were despatched to the Castle with van Jaarsveld and his son.[2]

The rebellion being over, Vandeleur marched his men down towards Algoa Bay through the Zuurveld, a land troubled by Ndhlambi, who had fled from his nephew, Gaika, rallied all the local clans except the Gunukwebes, and driven out the farmers. Vandeleur hoped to get through unmolested, but he was unexpectedly attacked by the Gunukwebes and only reached his camp near the Bay with serious loss. There most of the remaining rebels surrendered, and Vandeleur called out Swellendam and Graaff-Reinet commandos to deal with the Kaffirs and the handful of Boers and British deserters who had joined them under Buis. Hardly had he done so when he heard that Afrikaner had looted the Hantam, and as soon as he himself tried to disarm some of his newly joined Hottentots, they fled with their arms, formed bands under David Stuurman, Hans Trompetter and Boesak, and joined the Xosas. Well might Vandeleur write that either the Boers and British together must drive the Kaffirs from the Zuurveld or the British must build a fort and watch the

---

[1] Rec. C.C., II. 148 ff., 333 ff., 349 ff., 364 ff.   [2] *Ibid.*, II. 493; III. 49.

Boers and the natives fight it out.[1] Three generations of fluctuating British policy were foreshadowed in that one sentence.

Dundas, the acting Governor, took a middle line. The official view, both Dutch and British, was that the Boers had brought most of their troubles on themselves by virtually enslaving the Hottentots and driving an illicit cattle-trade with the Kaffirs. 'There must,' wrote Dundas, 'be justice for all or there will be trouble.' To secure that justice he appeared on the frontier at the head of a strong Stellenbosch-Swellendam commando, garrisoned Fort Frederick, the nucleus of the future Port Elizabeth, on the south-western shore of Algoa Bay, and appointed Maynier as Resident Commissioner over Swellendam and Graaff-Reinet. But it was, as he himself frankly admitted, 'a withdrawal from war' rather than a peace. The Xosas remained upon the Zuurveld.[2]

Back once more in Capetown, Dundas pressed on with the trial of van Jaarsveld and his friends. Four were released, twelve were variously sentenced, and van Jaarsveld and Prinsloo were condemned to death. These death sentences were, however, referred to Downing Street[3] and were, in the event, never carried out, because Dundas risked a reprimand rather than have the men executed. Meanwhile, in Graaff-Reinet, the Boers were thoroughly discontented. Thanks to war and desertion they were short of Hottentot servants, they were plagued by locusts, and the game on which many of them depended was scarce. Here was fruitful soil for disaffection against a government which used Hottentot troops, punished farmers when they rebelled, and put its trust in Maynier. Poor Maynier's health was failing and his attempts to make friends with Gaika were thwarted by Buis. He outraged frontier opinion by issuing regulations for the registration and better treatment of Hottentot servants, by allowing Hottentots and slaves to worship in the church on Sunday afternoons, by enforcing the law of non-intercourse with the Kaffirs, and by refusing to allow anything larger than a field cornet's party to go in to make reprisals for stolen cattle.[4]

Maynier's position was indeed impossible. He was trying to enforce the rule of law without the police, the magistrates and the circuit courts that could alone give the general security which is the foundation of all law. At last the men of the Zuurveld, Bruintjes Hoogte and Zwartkops laid siege to the drostdy, and even men who had hitherto loyally turned out on commando joined them. In face of this, Dundas withdrew the Commissioner, who was duly cleared of all charges after an official inquiry. Dundas also sent up the troops. They found the farms deserted from Algoa Bay to Graaff-Reinet,

Oct.
1801.

[1] Rec. C.C., II. 384, 399, 458; III. 48 ff.
[2] Ibid., II. 497; III. 3, 8, 16, 49, 52, 56–7.
[3] Ibid., III. 91, 213 ff.   [4] Ibid., IV. 283 ff.; No. 50 of 1835, pp. 27 ff.

bands of Hottentots plundering as they chose, and the rebels
ready to disperse on the promise of pardon. Dundas therefore tried
persuasion as well as force. He allowed the Rev. Johannes van der
Kemp, the first of the newly arrived London Missionary Society
missionaries, to lead such Hottentots as would follow him from
Graaff-Reinet to a temporary location on the Zwartkops river, a
recognition of the fact that the root of the Hottentot trouble was
lack of land. He then called out the commandos once more to deal
with the Hottentot bands and the Xosas. The surly burghers responded but poorly, skirmished for two months, took 13,000 cattle Aug.
and then dispersed. Dundas, knowing that the Cape was about to be 1802.
restored to the Batavian Republic, hurried to the frontier. He was
anxious to hand the Colony over in good order, but it can hardly
be said that he succeeded. Maynier induced a few small groups of
Hottentots to settle alongside the Hottentot Corps at Rietvlei near
Capetown; but that was all. And already the Batavians were waiting
to receive the keys of the Castle. Dundas therefore called out a
commando from all the districts outside the Cape itself to cover the
withdrawal of his troops. So the Great Commando took the field Feb.
to find the Hottentots and Kaffirs quarrelling over the spoil. All 20,
sides were weary of fighting, and at last an arrangement was 1803.
patched up whereby each of the three parties, white, black, and
brown, agreed not to molest the others.[1]

Next day, in terms of the Treaty of Amiens, the British handed
over the Castle and all that it stood for to the representatives of the
Batavian Republic, the successor of the old United Provinces.[2]

The Batavian Republic, February 1803–January 1806

The Dutch East India Company had come to an end in 1798, and
after some preliminary experiments, the task of ruling its territories
had been entrusted to a Council for the Asiatic Possessions. Commissioner-General Jacob Abraham de Mist, a member of this
Council, was now instructed to install Lieut.-General Jan Willem
Janssens as Governor at the Cape.[3]

The period of direct rule by the Batavian Republic is one of the
most tantalising in South African history. Looking back over the
space of a full hundred years, some regard it as the dawn of a
golden age, a dawn all too soon overcast by the second coming of
the British. It may be so; but, since de Mist, a determined though
mild revolutionary of the *Aufklärung*, resigned after eighteen months'

---

[1] Rec. C.C., IV. 98 ff.   [2] *Ibid.*, V. 156.
[3] V.R. Soc., III. 289–90. *Vide* J P. Van der Merwe, *Die Kaap onder die
Bataafse Republick*.

service partly because he was not prepared to abandon reforms which he admitted were far in advance of public opinion, it is permissible to suggest that the dawn would in any case have been overcast by clouds arising in the interior.[1] For what could the Colony make of a man who indeed reprobated 'all so-called revolutionary measures,' but yet held 'that this is perhaps the most important . . . outcome of periods of anarchy . . . that at such times, as if by an electric shock, the whole order of things is changed, and sweeping reforms which have been needed for many years are immediately instituted.' However, the period of Batavian liberalism in a High Tory colony was a mere interlude, for, within four months of its inception, the Batavian Republic was once more at war with Great Britain as a dependent ally of France.[2]

The Batavian representatives were well received in the West by all save the Orange officials. None the less, most of these were suffered to retain their posts, while Duckitt, the enterprising master-gardener, and such other British residents as chose to stay on in the Colony were assured of a welcome. De Mist declared liberty of trade with all Batavian possessions, and then installed Janssens as Governor at a more modest salary than his predecessors with an executive Council of four salaried officials and a secretary to assist him. He also radically reformed the High Court. This now became a body of seven professional lawyers, independent of the executive, with an attorney-general as public prosecutor in place of the Fiscal.[3]

Having reorganised the central government, de Mist and Janssens proceeded to gain first-hand knowledge of the outlying districts. The Governor set out upon his travels first.[4] He might reckon on a good reception from the frontiersmen, for though van Jaarsveld had died in prison, de Mist had released his comrades, and he himself came as the representative of those Netherlands to which the Boers had always professed loyalty. He found the 150 Waldecker mercenaries at Fort Frederick surveying the customary scene of confusion. The Hottentot bands under Stuurman and Boesak were still at large; but they were weary of the whole business, disgusted with their Xosa allies and anxious to have land of their own. Janssens, therefore, agreed to offset their past sufferings against the harm they had done and gave them reserves. He also fulfilled Dundas's intentions by establishing van der Kemp with his congregation at Bethelsdorp near Fort Frederick and, to ensure the good treatment of farm servants, banished two farmers from the frontier for their harsh dealings with their labourers and carried Maynier's registration policy a step further by ordering that Hottentots might enter service only under contract on definite terms recorded by competent

April 1803.

---

[1] Van der Merwe, p. 374; Theal, I*b.* 126. [2] V.R. Soc., III. 170-1.
[3] Van der Merwe, pp. 81 ff. [4] *Bel. Hist. Dok.*, III. 206 ff.

officials.[1] Under this growing rule of law, most of the Hottentots took service, and not only ceased to be a peril to the Colony, but in due course became a reinforcement to it against the Kaffirs.

Janssens had less success with the Xosas. Gaika indeed cheerfully acknowledged the Fish once more as the boundary and even gave up some of the European renegades at his kraals;[2] but the western clans refused to retire from the Zuurveld, the future Albany. All Janssens could do was to repeat the well-worn injunctions against intercourse with the tribes and set out northwards to inspect the Bushmen. Before he could reach them, tidings of the renewed French wars brought him hurrying back to the Castle.

De Mist was even less successful in his dealings with the Kaffirs. In the course of a ceremonious and comprehensive tour of the Colony,[3] he found all quiet except on the Zuurveld, where the bickering chiefs defied the tiny garrison at Fort Frederick and declined even to meet him. The lesson was not lost. He made up his mind that the central Government must be more fully represented on all the frontiers. Taking up one of Macartney's schemes, he set up a new drostdy at Uitenhage on the Zwartkops river in touch with the troubled Zuurveld and the sea. On his return to Capetown, he formed a sixth magistracy, Tulbagh, out of the north-western portion of the huge Stellenbosch district,[4] extended its border to Zak river, and put all the drostdies in touch with the capital by means of a weekly post. *(Oct. 1803. Feb.–April 1804. July 1804–Feb. 1805.)*

De Mist then laid down the lines on which local government was to be reorganised. Much of his work was little more than bringing up to date powers that were already supposed to be exercised; nevertheless, it was destined to form the groundwork of the future Trekker republics. The landdrost was to represent the administrative authority of the central government in his district; he was still to exercise quasi-judicial powers by taking criminal depositions, meting out summary punishment to slaves and settling petty criminal charges out of court. In civil cases, however, he was to be assisted by six unpaid heemraden in the usual fashion. The most notable part of de Mist's instructions related to still humbler officials. The *veldwachtmeester* had accumulated civil in addition to his military duties. All these duties were now regularised and his name changed to *veldkornet*. The landdrost was to recommend and the Governor to appoint one such official in each of the wards, six hours' ride in diameter, into which the district was to be divided. It was to be the

---

[1] *Bel. Hist. Dok.*, III. 207, 218 ff., 235 ff.; Proclamation, May 9, 1803; No. 50 of 1835, pp. 23, 164.
[2] *Bel. Hist. Dok.*, III. 233, 249. *Treaties, 1803–54*, pp. 1 ff.
[3] Godée-Molsbergen, *Reizen*, II. 167.
[4] *Bel. Hist. Dok.*, III. 121; Placaaten, 115 C, pp. 419, 506 (Cape Archives); du Plessis, *Christian Missions*, p. 426.

business of the field cornets to keep the peace, settle petty quarrels, take the census, publish new laws, and generally act as guides, philosophers and friends to the people of their wards. They were to be men-of-all-work like the Tudor justices of the peace, rewarded with prestige, freedom from taxation, a free farm or a small salary, and power according to the strength of their characters and their opportunities.[1]

De Mist also did what he could to encourage the scientific agriculture which Duckitt, Yonge's master-gardener, had begun, by giving a board of commissioners the Groote Post at Groenekloof and a supply of new paper money wherewith to buy merino rams. The Spanish rams duly arrived and bred mightily, but, in spite of the samples of cloth woven from Cape wool in the Netherlands, the vast majority of the farmers clung to their fat-tailed, hairy sheep. The day of the great Cape wool industry was still far off; nor could official encouragement improve the quality of the Cape wines— always excepting the Constantia—or induce the olive to bear its fruit out of due season.

The efforts of the Batavians to raise the level of civilisation at the Cape were hampered throughout by lack of money and skilled labour. The financial difficulty could be surmounted in a measure by means of the printing-press, and de Mist struck off new notes to pay the troops and finance his agricultural experiments, his new drostdies and the rebuilding of Stellenbosch after a devastating fire. But this meant that the 1,786,000 Rd. rose to 2,086,000, and the 4s. rix-dollar fell to 3s. 4d. in English silver. As for labour, de Mist and Janssens both believed that it was not yet too late to substitute freemen for slaves as the basis of society. Given a steady flow of white immigrants and no further importation of slaves, in due time the existing slaves might be segregated in reserves and the rest of the Colony be settled with Europeans. But, like their predecessors, they found the public insistent, and Janssens, who was much more pliable than de Mist, admitted cargoes of black ivory; while as for the European immigrants, it would be hard to say whether they themselves or the enthusiastic Hollander, Gysbert van Hogendorp, a forerunner of Gibbon Wakefield, were most to blame for the failure of the settlement which was to have been at Plettenberg's Bay and whose remnants were actually dissipated at Hout Bay in the Cape Peninsula.[2]

Other measures they carried through were of a still more revolutionary nature. The Dutch Reformed clergy of the day might be apathetic, but visitors noted 'the high pre-eminence' they held over the laity. The quarterly *Naachtmaal* (Communion) was an event, all shops

Dec.
1803.

---

[1] Ordonantie, Oct. 22, 1805.
[2] Theal, *History*, I. 117; Rec. C.C., VI. 136 ff.; Van der Merwe, p. 279; H. M. Robertson, *The Cape . . . and Systematic Colonization*.

closing for the week-end on the Friday evening. And the ministers were jealous of their rights. Anglican clergy might be given the use of the Groote Kerk on occasion; Moslems might worship in private rooms; the Lutherans might even have their own church in Capetown; but, recently, there had been much bickering over the spiritual future of children born of 'mixed' Reformed and Lutheran marriages, and the congregation of the Groote Kerk was as obstinately determined that the Lutherans should not build a spire to their conventicle as the Lutherans were to build it.[1] De Mist and Janssens continued to pay the predikants of the established church; but they reduced their number at Capetown, promised the 'equal protection òf the law . . . to all communities worshipping a Supreme Being for the promotion of virtue and good morals,'[2] and even permitted Roman Catholic priests to celebrate Mass in the Castle. At this stage de Mist resigned, for he must leave the Governor a free hand to prepare for the defence of the Peninsula. Besides, his electric shocks were inducing a storm in the Colony which was by no means allayed when landdrosts and heemraden were allowed to solemnise civil marriages *à la française*, and the new Board of Education met to organise public schools free from clerical control, a system horrifying to a generation whose whole conception of education was closely bound up with the Church and religion.[3] _{Sept. 1804.}

Janssens held on with the shadow of war coming ever nearer. His best troops were taken away to Batavia and he had to fall back on Hottentots and Malay gunners. But his real help in time of trouble would be the burghers. He reorganised the militia, divided the men liable to personal service into three classes according to age, and ordered those who might not be called up by their field cornets to supply transport and food to the others.[4] So he awaited the arrival of the British. _{Oct. 1805.}

The British soon came. Before Napoleon's Boulogne scheme was fully ended, a fleet of sixty-three ships under Sir Home Popham set out with Major-General Baird and 6700 troops on board. Trafalgar, Ulm and Austerlitz were lost and won as they sailed southward narrowly escaping destruction by a French squadron from Rochefort;[5] the map of Old Europe was being rolled up as Pitt lay dying; but Great Britain was at least making sure of the key to India. In spite of the summer south-easters, a landing was effected near Blaauwberg and Janssens' two thousand mixed levies were sent _{July 1805.} _{Jan. 1806.}

---

[1] *State of the Cape*, pp. 61 ff.; Theal, *History*, III. 14, 233. In the end the Lutherans did build a lovely church tower.

[2] *Kaapsche Courant*, Aug. 10, 1805; Engelbrecht, *Geschiedenis van die Hervormde Kerk*, I. 8; Hoge, *Luthersche Kerk aan die Kaap*, p. 160.

[3] Malherbe, *History of Education*, chapter iii.

[4] *Bel. Hist. Dok.*, III. 202 ff.; Ordonantie, Oct. 25, 1805.

[5] L. Turner, *The Cape . . . and the Trafalgar Campaign*.

5*

flying, the Waldeckers leading the way. Half the defeated force fell back on Capetown, where it surrendered under the Capitulation of Papendorp, while Janssens with the remainder retired to the Hottentots-Holland Pass beyond the Flats. There he dismissed the burghers and held out till, weakened by desertions and fearing to be cut off from the interior, he surrendered with the honours of war.[1]

So, in March, Janssens followed de Mist to the Netherlands, commending the colonists to Baird's care. 'Give no credit,' he wrote, '. . . to Mr. Barrow nor to the enemies of the inhabitants. They have their faults, but these are more than compensated by good qualities. Through lenity . . . they may be conducted to any good.'[2]

SECOND BRITISH OCCUPATION, 1806–1823

The British found themselves responsible for a larger colony than that which they had taken over in 1795,[3] a colony whose problems had advanced a further stage towards complexity, especially the problems of the frontiers and, as the end of the British slave trade drew near, of the slaves. The British officials themselves were men of much the same type as those of the First Occupation, a little less fearful of Jacobinism since Napoleon had put the Revolution into uniform, a good deal more war-hardened and fully as hostile to all things French. Some of them were able men, notably the Governors and a few of the army officers; but the rank and file were mediocre, and all were Tories with the virtues and failings of their kind, men who regarded the bluff country gentlemen of the England of the Corn and Game Laws and the Justices of the Peace as the political and social ideal. At the capital they were welcomed by the Orange-men who continued to fill such high posts as were not given to born-subjects of King George; the Batavian officials, who for the most part retained their posts, soon learnt to hob-nob with them at the African Coffee House on the Heerengracht; but the average towns-man still preferred 'French insincerity and politesse' to the stiffness of these shy English and the Anglo-Indians who now came to the Cape to nurse their livers. Nevertheless, many of the British officials and merchants, more especially the adaptable Scots and Irish, found favour with the Cape ladies of marriageable age, though their own womenkind were still slow to bestow their smiles on the young men of the country.[4] Of course, Capetown was not the Colony, and the key to much that follows is that the British officials sometimes forgot the distinction. But the early Governors were popular enough. After

[1] Rec. C.C., V. 261 ff., 299.
[2] Theal, 1b. 150.
[3] Europeans. 25,757. Slaves, 29,545. Hottentots, 20,000 (Van der Merwe, p. 372).
[4] *South Africa a Century Ago* (1910), p. 190; *State of the Cape*, pp. 154, 171

all, they shared the views of most of their white subjects on such matters as personal dignity, the significance of land-owning, and the respect due from the lower classes.

The departure of Janssens ended the Batavian Liberal experiment at the Cape, and British Liberalism still lay in the future. The new officials could be trusted to give a conservative administration suited

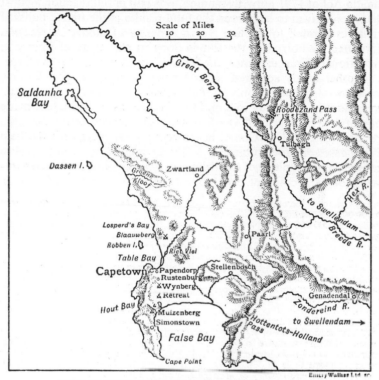

THE BRITISH OCCUPATIONS, 1795 and 1806.

to the tastes of a conservative community; necessarily so at first, for until the Cape was formally ceded to Great Britain under the general peace settlement of 1814,[1] the situation was governed by the terms

[1] The belief is apparently not yet dead that Great Britain bought the Cape. The Allies restored the Prince of Orange in 1813. The Dutch 'colonials,' headed by van Nagell, Secretary for Foreign Affairs, demanded the restoration of all the Dutch colonies, including those ceded under the Treaty of Amiens (1802), and their Government showed itself so exigent that Castlereagh declined any longer to keep the colonial negotiations separate from the general peace settlement (Rec. C.C., X. 130). Little was said about the Cape during the negotiations, the main debates centring upon Guiana.

In terms of the treaty of August 13, 1814, Great Britain restored to the Kingdom of the Netherlands (Holland and Belgium) the rich East Indies and all other Dutch colonies taken by her during the Napoleonic wars, except the Cape and

of the Capitulation which secured the colonists their existing laws, privileges and forms of worship. Even so, few radical changes were made till 1825, when a Commission of Inquiry set to work in earnest.

1807–1808. The Earl of Caledon, the first civil Governor, put the new government on a more regular footing. It was war-time; the Cape had been taken by force of arms; the ruling class in Great Britain, Pitt's liberal Canada Act of 1791 notwithstanding, was still in full reaction against what it conceived to have been the fatal results of the undue political privileges granted to the late North American Colonies, a reaction stimulated by horror of the things done in the name of liberty in revolutionary France. Hence, the form of administration at the Cape, as in other newly acquired dependencies with mixed populations, was autocratic. Subject only to the control of the Secretary of State, three months' sail away in London, the Governor legislated, made appointments, suspended or dismissed all officials other than the President of the High Court, heard criminal appeals with the help of two assessors and, subject to a further appeal in certain cases to the Judicial Committee of the Privy Council, sat with the Lieutenant-Governor as a court of civil appeal. Moreover, he could and, in

British Guiana (Demerara, Essequibo and Berbice). She also agreed to pay up to £6,000,000 'in consideration' thereof. Of this sum, £1,000,000 was to be paid to Sweden, £2,000,000 to the Netherlands for the fortification of the Belgian border against France, and up to £3,000,000 to help to consolidate the position of the Dutch King in his enlarged kingdom (Hertslet, *Treaties*, I. 359, 365; Rec. C.C., X. 170). Each of these financial clauses calls for explanation.

(1) During the later stages of the war, Great Britain had given Sweden French Guadeloupe in exchange for commercial privileges. At the peace settlement, the Allies decided that all the French colonies should be given back except Mauritius, St. Lucia and Tobago. Sweden was offered various Dutch West Indian possessions 'out of the common stock' (Rec. C.C., X. 144) in lieu of Guadeloupe, but she demanded Guiana. Finally she compounded for £1,000,000 of British money.

(2) The second item of £2,000,000 naturally failed to please the Dutch 'colonials,' who had no desire to be saddled with Belgium, especially as the Netherlands must spend a like amount on fortifications. By the end of 1820, the British had spent more than £1,500,000 in strengthening the barrier fortresses (J. H. Clapham, *Economic History of Modern Britain*, I. 330).

(3) The meaning of the third clause was elucidated by the Anglo-Russian-Dutch treaty of May 19, 1815 (Hertslet, IV. 371). The Emperor Alexander had to be reconciled to the Western settlement. He had a large army in France and no money at St. Petersburg. Some time previously, Russia had floated a loan in Holland through Hope and Co. of Amsterdam. Interest was in arrears and likely to remain so. The Netherlands Government now undertook to make itself responsible for part of the capital and arrears of interest, and Great Britain promised to do the same up to £3,000,000. By thus combining the colonial and financial arrangements, hard-pressed British ministers were able to 'hold forth to the public' the Cape and Guiana as an offset to the £6,000,000 which Parliament was asked to vote at the end of two decades of war (Rec. C.C., X. 145). Great Britain paid 6 per cent. interest and 1 per cent. sinking fund on behalf of Russia till 1891, when arrangements were made which extinguished the debt in 1906 (*Economic Journal*, December 1917, article by J. H. Clapham; *Journal of the Royal Institute of International Affairs*, V. No. 3, p. 147). *Vide* also J. E. Heeres, *De Overgang der Kaapkolonie*; H. T. Colenbrander, *Gedenkstukken van Nederland*, XXIII. 26; W. H. Robson, 'New Light on Lord Castlereagh's Diplomacy' (*Journal of Modern History*, June 1931); *C.H.B.E.*, VIII. 211 ff.

Caledon's case, did dispute the control of the troops with the General.[1] Wherefore, H.M. Government appointed no more civilian Governors till it sent out Sir George Grey in 1854.

The High Court reverted to its pre-Batavian amateur condition, the Fiscal once more became public prosecutor, and the independent Vice-Admiralty Court was revived. One valuable judicial innovation was, however, made. After an illuminating visit to the eastern frontier, Caledon at last instituted circuit courts of two judges who, 1811. armed with the full civil powers of the High Court and all its criminal powers save that of passing the death sentence, were to sit twice yearly with open doors. Changes in the actual law were few. Open 1813. doors in all Courts, a modicum of English procedure, permission for British settlers married before their arrival in the Colony to make their wills in English style, a proclamation foreshadowing the use of 1822. English as the official language—that was practically all. The Roman-Dutch law adapted to local requirements still held good, however much true-born Englishmen like the redoubtable Dr. Halloran might protest.[2]

The machinery of local justice and administration remained almost unchanged, though its scope was widened. In Capetown the Burgher Senate still served as a kind of town council and adviser to the Government; a deputy-fiscal dispensed justice at Simonstown, the naval base; the rest of the Cape district was put under a new 1808- landdrost's court, and eight new magistracies were created, for the 1819. most part on the frontiers. All landdrosts' courts were given minor 1817- criminal jurisdiction for the first time, but, though they could still 1819. act as matrimonial courts, they were forbidden to perform the actual 1806. marriage ceremony.[3]

As in the days of the First Occupation the civil establishment was top heavy and expensive. The Governor once more drew his £10,000 a year in sterling, and one of them, Lord Charles Somerset, used to have no fewer than four official residences at a time when revenue was practically stationary and the purchasing power of the paper money falling. The economic condition of the Colony did not warrant this expenditure. The end of the war, as on similar and later occasions, was celebrated by wholesale speculation and 1815. importation on a scale far beyond the countervailing exporting power of the Colony. As for exports, the wine of the western districts held pride of place, but the preference given to it in the British market merely resulted in the production of more wine of a 1813.

[1] Rec. C.C., VI. 6 ff., 115, 362; VII. 296, 369, 435, 493; Eybers, *Select Documents*, p. 102.

[2] Rec. C.C., VI. 32, 331; IX. 211, 239; XIV. 452, 458; *Cape Times*, April 15, 1914, on Dr. Halloran, a most engaging scoundrel; Eybers, *Select Documents*, p. 103.

[3] Rec. C.C., V. 407; VI. 469.

worse quality, in spite of the efforts of an overworked wine-taster.[1] Hides and skins ranked next, drawn mainly from beyond the northern borders. Whaling prospered somewhat, and Somerset did much to further agriculture by taking the Groote Post under his own control and laying out the Somerset Farm at the Boschberg. He was a pretty judge of a horse and, thanks to his energy, the Cape was soon sending excellent mounts to Mauritius and India. Wool was still in its infancy and all Caledon's cajolements and the experiments of a few enterprising farmers, Dutch and British, failed to reconcile the bulk of the stock farmers to the Spanish rams. Cattle rearing and general farming, helped by Duckitt's new ploughs and harrows, remained the hope of the Colony. The presence of four or five thousand troops and a large squadron offered a good market for produce, though there was still a risk that in good years part of the harvest would be left on the farmers' hands and in bad years the certainty that overseas flour and rice would have to be rushed in at any price.[2] Many of the troops were withdrawn at the end of the great war, but for some time to come the troops and ships watching Napoleon at St. Helena kept up the demand.

Many social improvements were effected during the years of seeming prosperity. Hottentot runners supplemented the weekly post-riders, a monthly mail made the voyage to and from England, if all went well, in a hundred days, and the first South African light-house was built at Green Point in the year that H.M. Observatory was founded. The Old Somerset Hospital and the Weeshuis (Orphanage) at Capetown and a leper asylum near Caledon ministered to the sick and the helpless; the new Commercial Exchange at Capetown at least served as a place for public meetings and the dances of which, even in those days, the townsfolk were never tired. The householders provided the two main streets of the capital with oil-lamps at night, and the Burgher Senate, duly financed with new paper dollars, laid down iron pipes with real taps and levied a water rate to meet the cost. Government took over a museum from the explorer, Dr. Andrew Smith, and gave a grant to a public library which was soon enriched with the Dessinian Collection, which Joachim Nikolaus van Dessin, a German settler, had bequeathed to the Colony in 1761 with a fund for its increase.[3]

A caustic observer noted that van Dessin had been unable to bequeath the other thing needful, 'a collection of readers.'[4] Attempts

1824.

---

[1] Rec. C.C., VIII. 241; XI. 274; XIII. 350; XVII. 116, 129, 132; XIX. 389; XX. 114 ff.
[2] Ibid., VI. 73, 472; XII. 43; XIV. 289.
[3] Ibid., VI. 39, 506; IX. 301, 323, 357, 362; X. 372; XIII. 210; XV. 231; XXI. 500; XXII. 227; State of the Cape, p. 151. The Dessinian Collection is now in the South Africa Public Library, Capetown.
[4] State of the Cape, p. 152.

had been made for some time past to remedy the defect. De Mist and Janssens had tried to provide free education, but, in face of poverty, lack of teachers and popular suspicion, had accomplished little outside Capetown. Cradock encouraged the existing schools at the capital and the drostdies and, building on the foundations laid by the Batavians, formed a Bible and School Committee to raise sub- 1813. scriptions for free schools.[1] But, apart from the Tot Nut van't Algemeen school founded under the Batavians and a classical school under the Colonial chaplain at Capetown, there was 'no good school in the Colony beyond mere English and Writing.' Hence Thomas Pringle, the poet and assistant public librarian, bade his friend, John 1822. Fairbairn, bring with him from Scotland 'a copy of Euclid, some of Gray's arithmetic, a few of the more elementary books in Geography, French, Latin and Greek, Mother's Catechism, a pair of small globes, and a good atlas' wherewith to furnish a 'classical and commercial academy.'[2] Meanwhile, Somerset had taken the matter in hand with his usual energy. He projected a system of state schools wherein Scottish schoolmasters should give a good English education free of charge, religious instruction in Dutch, and Latin extra. So, Somerset's Scots came out: James Rose-Innes to Uitenhage, William Robertson to Graaff-Reinet, William Dawson to George, James Rattray to Tulbagh, Robert Blair to Caledon and Archibald Brown to Stellenbosch, the first of the many Lowland Scots who were to do so much for that notable Afrikaner Western Province town and future university centre. One or two of them, being human, were undeniable failures, and none of them, being schoolmasters, perhaps did all that was expected of them; but the rest, and notably Rose-Innes, served their adopted country well by setting education in South Africa more firmly on its feet than ever before.[3]

As with the schools, so with the Church. The Dutch Reformed Church had fallen on evil days. De Mist had found it impossible to fill vacancies; there were no means of training predikants locally; under the new dispensation Hollanders were neither available nor desired. Somerset once more fell back on Scotland. He summoned to his help the Scotsman, the Rev. Dr. George Thom, sometime Superintendent of the London Missionary Society's South African missions and, since 1818, Dutch Reformed predikant at Caledon. Thom recruited the Revs. Andrew Murray, Alexander Smith and William Ritchie Thomson, the first of whom was sent to Graaff-Reinet, the second to Uitenhage, and the third to work in government service under the Rev. John Brownlee among the Hottentots and Gaika's people at the newly founded Tyumie industrial mission on the

[1] Rec. C.C., IX. 69, 216; X. 82; Malherbe, *op. cit.*, pp. 56 ff.
[2] Pringle to Fairbairn, Nov. 24 and Dec. 1822 (Jardine Collection).
[3] Rec. C.C., XIII. 168; XIV. 97, 129; XV. 354; Malherbe, *op. cit.*, pp. 63 ff.

Gwali river some little distance beyond the Eastern Frontier.[1] These three men came to the Colony direct; but Thom's other recruits, the

1822. Rev. Henry Sutherland, George Morgan and Colin Fraser went first to the Netherlands to learn a little Dutch before taking up their respective charges at Worcester, Somerset East and Beaufort West. The fact that these three men took this precaution and that all six newcomers preached or tried to preach in Dutch should acquit Somerset of the charge that he meant to use them, as well as his Scottish schoolmasters, as agents of anglicisation.[2] Rather, let the rapid multiplication of congregations and the number of districts which bear their names recall the solid work these men did for the Colony and the chiefest of its churches.

The clerical element in the population grew steadily. The Lutherans still had their congregation in Capetown; the Church of England held services in the Groote Kerk, in its own church at Simonstown, and in the Wesleyan chapel at Grahamstown; after some difficulty with Somerset, the Wesleyans made good their footing in Capetown and were soon strongly represented on the Eastern Frontier; and

1820. even the Roman Catholic priests, expelled in 1806, were allowed to resume their ministrations in the capital.[3]

The main recruitment of the clergy came through the missionary societies. The Wesleyan movement, the Evangelical revival in Great Britain, and the Lutheran revival in Germany had put new life into Protestantism throughout Western Europe. This 'mickle stirring'

1788. had even affected the far-distant Cape, where the Rev. Helperus van Lier, predikant at the Groote Kerk, and the Rev. Michiel Vos of Roodezand, formed a group of 'serious people,' who carried the Gospel to slaves and Hottentots. After van Lier's untimely death, Dr. Johannes van der Kemp, a Hollander ex-cornet of horse, doctor of medicine and boon companion of Commissioner-General de Mist, enrolled members of this group in his South African Society, a welcome support to the incoming evangelical missionaries.[4]

The missionary stream had begun to flow in the last days of the Company, but, until 1816, only two important societies had entered the field: the Moravian Brethren and the London Missionary Society.

1792. The Moravians had arrived first. They reoccupied Schmidt's old station at Baviaan's Kloof and presently renamed it Genadendal.

[1] R. H. W. Shepherd, *Lovedale*. This station was near the site on which the Rev. John Ross was destined to found in 1824 the Glasgow Mission's notable civilising centre of Lovedale.
[2] Rec. C.C., XIII. 168; XIV. 37, 95, 129, 292, 452; XV. 292; J. du Plessis, *Christian Missions in South Africa*, pp. 139, 141, 155, 182; Theal, 1*b*. 310; C. H. B. E. VIII. 847.
[3] Rec. C.C., XIII. 20, 358, 365 (Catholics); XIII. 175, and *State of the Cape*, pp. 63 ff. (Anglicans); XI. 62; XIV. 31, 38, 192 (Wesleyans).
[4] Du Plessis, *Christian Missions*, pp. 61 ff.

There these plain, sensible German mechanics, unhampered by the 'enthusiasm' which staid critics reprobated in the L.M.S. men, laboured with their wives and families among the semi-civilised Hottentots and half-breeds of the settled western Colony. At first they had been suspect of their European neighbours and had found it prudent to withdraw to Capetown during the upheaval of 1795; but they had soon gone back to their posts, there to win golden opinions as a civilising agency from British and Batavian officials. Presently they were given new stations at Mamre in the West, where 1807. they were equally successful, and Enon near the Eastern Frontier, 1816. where, under much more difficult conditions, their success was markedly less.[1]

Germany, Holland, Denmark and, later on, France did much to swell the missionary flood, but Great Britain did so much more that the Parisian press regarded the whole business as an imperialist plot on the part of *perfide Albion*. 'The Missionary Society,' afterwards 1794. called the L.M.S., was founded expressly to preach the Gospel as interpreted by the Independents to the heathen. Its first emissaries to the Cape went two by two, Dutch and British together, to the 1799. wildest parts, to Gaika's kraal and to the Bushmen on the Zak River.[2] Van der Kemp was the most influential of these early missionaries. He failed at Gaika's; but he founded Bethelsdorp, and though the 1803. site was a poor one and he himself perhaps 'too much absorbed in the idea of conversion' to make a good missionary,[3] his influence was such that, for long years after his death, the Coast Kaffirs regarded all missionaries as 'Jankanna's children' and Bethelsdorp became the Zion of the Hottentots.

The L.M.S. missions spread so rapidly to the Eastern Frontier and beyond the Orange to the Griquas that by 1816 they had twenty men at work. They were now joined by the Wesleyans and the Glasgow 1816– Society in the East, while within the colonial borders the Dutch and 1823. English clergy formed the Bible and Tract Society. The S.A. Society, 1799. founded by van der Kemp, worked among the Coloured folk of many of the dorps, and the pioneers of the Church Missionary Society, fruit of the famous conversation in William Wilberforce's rooms, found their first and truly urgent call no further from Capetown than 1821. Wynberg.[4]

The coming of the missionaries did more than stimulate religious life in the Colony. It interested the organised, semi-educated,

---

[1] No. 584 of 1830, p. 12, and No. 50 of 1835, pp. 23–7; Du Plessis, *op. cit.*, pp. 243, 424: Lichtenstein, *Travels*, I. 152.
[2] Rec. C.C., III. 336 ff.; IV. 366; Moffat, *Missionary Labours*, pp. 22 ff.
[3] Lichtenstein, *Travels*, I. 239. For a good summing up of van der Kemp's strength and weakness *vide* Moffat, *Missionary Labours*, pp. 39 ff.; A. D. Martin, *Dr. Vanderkemp*.
[4] *State of the Cape*, p. 64; Du Plessis, *Christian Missions*.

evangelically-minded and entirely vocal British middle class, which was rising to influence on the wave of the Industrial Revolution, in the peoples of the colonies and above all in the 'aborigines.' Henceforward, to an increasing degree, native policies had to be carried out under watchful eyes at home and in the colonies themselves. Liberalism, driven out of the State by the British Tories, began to return through the Church and, in due time, caused a revolution in the old Cape Colony.

With the abolition of the slave trade, the first stage in this revolution, the missionaries as such had little to do. Britain's share in that *Circa 1680.* traffic had long been condemned. While yet it was only on a small scale, English clergymen had exclaimed against the horrors of the Middle Passage and of slavery itself. English Quakers followed with 1776. protests; Pennsylvanian Quakers took active steps to end slave-owning in their own ranks; the trend of English literature, especially of poetry, began to run strongly in the same direction.[1] And then 1773. the lawyers came to the help of the writers. Lord Mansfield, in Somersett's case, declared that the 'domestic institution' could not live on English ground save under the shelter of a special statute. He thereby set free 14,000 negroes who were living in England with their masters.

Inspired by this famous judgment, Granville Sharp began his 1787. crusade against the Trade. He formed the Anti-Slavery Committee and found allies in Thomas Clarkson and, above all, William Wilberforce, the friend of the young Prime Minister, William Pitt. The reforming Pitt declared in favour of abolition, but could do nothing more than help to carry a private bill which limited the number of slaves who might be carried on a ship of a given tonnage. Then the French Revolution and the rebellion of the hastily enfranchised slaves in Hayti came to strengthen the hands of the 'West Indian' 1792. party in Parliament. In spite of the cautious resolution of Denmark to give up the traffic ten years hence, the hopes of the Abolitionists were ended for many years to come.

Abolition would be a serious matter for British shipping, for unless international action were taken the abandoned trade would simply serve to enrich her rivals. It would certainly damage her slave-owning colonies, and among them the Cape. Slaves at the Cape *Circa* somewhat outnumbered the Europeans and, in the West particularly, 1795. formed the mass of the labouring class. During the First British Occupation, except for illicit traffic in Yonge's time, slaves were landed under permits granted as a rule at the request of the Burgher Senate. The Batavian Republic had contemplated the gradual

[1] On Abolition *vide* R. Coupland, *Wilberforce*; I. E. Edwards, *Towards Emancipation*.

abolition of slavery and its representatives at the Cape had opposed the traffic on principle; but even they had had to give way to popular pressure and permit a limited importation. Baird was in like case,[1] but before the tale of slaves for whom he issued licences was completed, the British Slave Trade was legally a thing of the past. The Abolitionists had begun to press again; Charles James Fox, in office at last, had threatened to wreck the Ministry of All the Talents if the 1807. Abolition Bill were not carried, and carried it was, just as the U.S.A. Congress also decreed the end of the traffic. But, whereas the Stars and Stripes remained the flag most abused by slavers till Lincoln's day, the British, having command of the sea, implemented their promise. At first the penalty for breach of the Act was a fine; then it was changed to fourteen years' transportation; finally it became 1811. a hanging matter, and with that the British slavers went out of 1823. business.

Undismayed by the pious resolution *et praeterea nihil* passed against the Trade by the eight Great Powers at the Congress of 1814. Vienna, the British frigates began their long war against the slavers. Some of the rescued slaves were apprenticed for fourteen years as Prize Negroes at Capetown; for a time also Spanish and Portuguese ships 'in distress' ran slaves ashore at Table Bay and were duly 1821. wroth when they were warned off.[2] The addition to the labour force of the Colony from both these sources cannot have been great, for with the stoppage of the Trade, the free burgher population rapidly outstripped the servile. The price of slaves rose and with it the amount of care bestowed upon them. Domestic slaves have usually been tolerably well treated in all times and places, and the Cape was no exception to the rule. Even predial slavery was not and never had been so harsh at the Cape as in the West Indies, especially in the settled and comparatively well-governed western districts where the vast majority of the slaves dwelt. Somerset waxed almost lyrical over the happy lot of the Cape slave, the less exuberant Cradock admitted that it was better than in any other part of the world he had seen,[3] and, later on, the Commissioners of Inquiry found that most of the complaints of ill usage came from the country districts and that many were groundless. There were, of course, frequent desertions to the Kaffirs or the banditti of the Orange valley, the usual crop of slave crimes: murder, arson, and rape, and once a revolt of over 300 1808. slaves organised by two Irishmen in the Malmesbury district;[4] but on the whole the system worked peaceably. Government was

[1] Rec. C.C., I. 29; II. 39; III. 79 ff., 121, 126, 372, 377; V. 403-4; VI. 49; Cory, *op. cit.*, III. 7.

[2] Rec. C.C., IX. 129; XIII. 26; XIV. 485 ff.; Prize Negroes were landed occasionally till the 1840s, Marais, J. S., *The Cape Coloured People*, p. 161.

[3] *Ibid.*, IX. 143 ff., 451; XVIII. 310; XXI. 448; XXIX. 457; Report of Registrar of Slaves, 1826; V.R. Soc., III. 253.   [4] Rec. C.C., VI. 392, 408 ff.; VII. 7.

benevolent. Craig and Macartney abolished torture and the wheel; Janssens ordered good treatment, and Caledon bade the circuit judges see that it was given; Cradock encouraged owners to Christianise their slaves[1] and limited the lashes that might legally be given to a figure that must have moved British red-coats and men-of-war's men to envy, and Somerset opened schools for slave children and ordered a registration of slaves similar to that of the Hottentots. But avowedly nothing was done to weaken the owners' rights over their human property.[2] That was reserved for a later and more eventful time.

The growing power of the British philanthropists was soon to be dedicated to other peoples who were not slaves but who none the less merited attention. Official knowledge of what lay beyond the frontiers of the Colony had increased greatly since 1795. Truter, 1801– Somerville, Lichtenstein, van der Graaff and Burchell had all 1815. travelled northward of the Orange to the Griquas of Klaarwater and the Batlapin of Lithako. More immediately important were the 1808– official tours of Colonel Richard Collins who went north-eastward 1809. to inspect the Bushmen and then travelled along the upper Orange and so down to Hintsa's kraal beyond the Kei.[3]

Collins recommended leniency towards the Bushmen. The little hunters had ceased to offer serious resistance to the advancing Europeans. Some still hung about in the northern Karoo, others lived as they were to do for many years in the arid plains of Great Bushman Land south of the middle Orange, others were moving away northward to be cut down by the Griquas or to find a refuge in the Kalahari desert. There was little slaughter by Europeans after 1810, though as late as 1823 commandos took the field in Tarka and the Sneeuwberg. The traffic in prisoners and children abandoned by their starving parents still went on, a traffic which Somerset tried to 1817. regularise by insisting that they should be officially apprenticed under written contracts. Such of these apprentices as remained with their masters became good cattle-herds; kindly Boers confessed that no good had come of all the bloodshed and were prepared to wink at a little stealing so long as their Bushmen brought back their cattle in good condition; Andries Stockenstrom senior, landdrost of Graaff-Reinet, vouched for the fact that many a Boer was on good terms with the Stone Age men and occasionally gave them sheep.[4] The L.M.S. missionaries at Tooverberg and Hephzibah also had fair success with the Bushmen; but experience at Zak River and

[1] Eybers, op. cit., p. 18.   [2] Rec. C.C., VIII. 500; IX. 131; XI. 102.
[3] Ibid., VI. 340 ff.; VII. 20 ff.
[4] Ibid., VIII. 306; XI. 365; Thompson, Travels, I. 74, 395, 404; No. 50 of 1835, pp. 119, 133; Moffat, Missionary Labours, p. 4; Du Plessis. op. cit., p. 269.

Bethelsdorp proved that the Hottentots and half-breeds were much more amenable than they to civilised ways.

Unfortunately the L.M.S. stations had from the first been viewed askance by the officials, men of a class which had little sympathy with vagrants or landless men either in Holland or in England. Yonge had suspected the first missionaries of being Jacobins in sheep's clothing: de Mist had regarded the S.A. Society as an interloper; Janssens had bidden missionaries keep well beyond the borders; now Collins recommended the break-up of Bethelsdorp, since it was 'designed for the benefit of the Hottentots rather than that of the Colony.'[1] Nor had most of the Colonists, especially the numerous frontiersmen, any love for mission stations, the only reserves there were in those days. Ignoring the fact that these did, after all, furnish them with many 'hands,' they saw only that they harboured squatters, casual workers, wood-cutters and transport riders, who would rather make shift for themselves than work at low pay for white men. Hence, whether justified or not, the 'almost universal' charge laid at the door of the mission stations by officials and colonists alike was that they were draining off labour at a time when a shortage was threatened by the stopping of the Slave Trade.[2] Caledon, on whom this view was diligently pressed, therefore tried to meet the demand for labour and at the same time protect the Hottentots. He abolished the remains of the tribal system, put the Nov. Hottentots under colonial law, strengthened the old laws providing 1809. for written contracts, and after his visit to the Eastern Frontier 1811. instructed the circuit judges to receive Hottentot complaints. But he also bade the Hottentots find fixed abodes and not move beyond the district boundaries without a pass from the landdrost. Cradock further directed that Hottentot children born while their parents 1812. were in service and maintained by the master to the age of eight were to be apprenticed to that master for ten years to come.[3] The intention was to provide a supply of labour and to encourage farmers to look after whole families of dependants; but it only needed Somerset's permission to landdrosts to *inboek* orphans to reduce the 1819. Hottentots to the level of serfs at the disposal of the local officials.[4] Hardly any of them held land; it was even doubtful whether they could legally do so; did they wander about, they were liable to be treated as vagrants by the nearest field cornet. There was nothing for it but to go beyond the borders, as some did, or to choose

[1] Rec. C.C., III. 114 ff., 336 ff., 391; VII. 109; No. 50 of 1835, p. 163; Proclamation, Feb. 21, 1805; Leyd's, *First Annexation*, p. 24.

[2] Rec. C.C., IX. 350; Macmillan, *Cape Colour Question*, p. 153.

[3] Rec. C.C., VII. 211; VIII. 385; Patterson, p. 9; J. S. Marais, *The Cape Coloured People*, pp. 109 ff.; M. L. Hodgson, *The Hottentots in South Africa*, pp. 494 ff.

[4] Rec. C.C., XII. 249.

between the farms and the mission stations. As for the protection of the law, the Hottentot who ran the gauntlet to the far-distant drostdy was kept in the dark gaol till his case came on before heemraden of the same class as the accused, and then had to face the prospect of punishment if he failed to prove his charge.[1] Granted that some check had to be put on frivolous charges, the situation was still unsatisfactory.

The new circuit court promised some relief, and James Read, van der Kemp's colleague and an over-credulous person, brought 1812. a heavy tale of charges against the frontier farmers. The circuit court duly dealt therewith. Many charges were undoubtedly baseless; many never came into court at all; many could have been paralleled from the annals of the domestic system of industry or of the factory system which was taking its place in England. Of seventeen Boers charged with murder, one was convicted of assault, two cases were postponed and three referred to the High Court, because the Circuit Judges could not pass the death sentence; of fifteen charged with violence, seven were found guilty and the cases of two held over for lack of evidence. But there is another side to the story of this Black Circuit. The charges were difficult to prove, for they covered many years and a wide area; 'Jankanna' had just died, and the difficulty, at all times great, of persuading servants to give evidence against their masters was thereby doubled; a good many charges of illegal detention of wages, cattle and children were established; the violence proved was bad, and one of the accused was condemned to death by the High Court, but was reprieved.[2]

The general effect of the Black Circuit was unhappy. Hundreds of Europeans had been put to inconvenience and even risk by having to travel to court at the close of a Kaffir war; those against whom the charges had broken down were naturally indignant at the mere suspicion; all resented the novel experience of being hauled to court at the instance of a parcel of Hottentots and missionaries. Their growing suspicion and dislike were henceforward focused on Bethelsdorp.

The L.M.S. in South Africa fared badly in the years that followed the Black Circuit. It received scant sympathy from Somerset, who distrusted Nonconformists and believed in work for dependent 1817. people whether in England or at the Cape. He encouraged the local officials to be strict, disbanded the Hottentot Corps partly because he disliked coloured troops and partly because he thought the men and their wives ought to be at work, and approved of the closing down of more than one mission station beyond the borders.[3] His

---

[1] Rec. C.C., IV. 92 ff.; VIII. 301, 308, 380.
[2] *Ibid.*, IX. 328 ff.; X. 1 ff.; *The Critic*, Oct. 1934, article by H. A. Reyburn.
[3] Rec. C.C., XI. 5, 157, 167, 380; XII. 243; XV. 223; J. Philip, *Researches*, II. pp. 165, 280; Moffat, *Missionary Labours*, p. 61.

coolness towards the Society was not altogether unmerited. Its members were widely scattered, independent in every sense of the word, and so jealous of control that even the best of them could protest against anything so 'papal' as a Superintendent. Some of its men had more zeal than knowledge, for, the precedent of St. Paul notwithstanding, the idea that a missionary should be a well-educated man was by no means generally accepted.[1] One or two of them had more knowledge than character; but Somerset's main objection to the extra-colonial stations rested less on the possible short-comings of the missionaries than on the difficulties and dangers of their position. In short, he shared Janssen's fears that these stations might prove Caves of Adullam lacking the Davids essential to their tranquillity.

The danger was especially acute in the stony, sun-baked wastes beyond the northern border. Most of the Namaquas had disappeared *Circa* beyond the lower Orange to conquer the Hereros with their guns; 1823. but the six hundred miles of the Orange valley still swarmed with Hottentots, Bastaards (half-castes), Bushmen and even a few stray Xosas. In this pandemonium there was one growing focus of ordered civilisation. William Anderson of the L.M.S. had induced the mixed 1803. crowd of Bastaards and Hottentots which had followed Barend Barends and the brothers, Adam II and Cornelis II, sons of the first Cornelis Kok,[2] out of the Colony to settle round Klaarwater in what is now Griqualand West. There his unruly protégés had hunted out the luckless Bushmen for a hundred miles around. Another missionary, John Campbell, had then renamed the Bastaards 'Griquas' 1813. and their village 'Griquatown,' appointed Barends and Adam Kok captains, and furnished them with code, law courts and coinage complete. Presently, Andries Waterboer, the ablest of all these semi-civilised chieftains, came up from the Colony and was elected captain of this 'Hottentot Republic under the patriarchal government of missionaries.'[3]

The dauntless Waterboer waged war on the Orange river banditti with mixed success, while Somerset, anxious for the security of the northern border, appointed a deputy-landdrost at Beaufort West 1818. with a reserve hard by under the control of a D.R. Church minister, and a periodical fair to canalise the trade in hides and skins with the hunting Griquas.[4] The Directors of the L.M.S., for their part, alarmed at the ill reports which reached them from the Colony, sent John Campbell to bring back a report, and with him Dr. John Philip not to serve as a missionary, but to remain as superintendent of all their

[1] Du Plessis, *op. cit.*, p. 118.   [2] *Vide supra*, p. 135.
[3] No. 50 of 1835, pp. 126, 129, 133, 211–12; No. 252 of 1835, p. 115; No. 538 of 1836, pp. 608 ff.; Stow, *Native Races*, chapters xvii–xx; Orpen, *Reminiscences*, pp. 184 ff.; Chase, *Natal Papers*, II. 250.
[4] Rec. C.C., XI. 254; XII. 62, 81 ff., 112.

stations in South Africa.[1] So there landed at Capetown the man who, by reason of his force of character and length of service, became one of the most outstanding political figures in the South Africa of his day.

John Philip was the son of a Kirkcaldy weaver, born in 1775, trained at Hoxton and called as Independent minister to Aberdeen. He was stiff in opinions, given to hyperbole, and fully endowed with that love of disputation which Benjamin Franklin noted as the characteristic of lawyers, university men and Scots; nevertheless, Nonconformist though he was, he was well received by Somerset and some of the leading Cape officials. He then set out on his travels with Campbell.[2] Together they reformed the most serious abuses in their Society, though they did not visit the stations beyond the northern border because the Governor had forbidden them to station new men there. Philip, however, made up his mind that the L.M.S. should keep its footing in Griqualand, for that was 'the neck of the bottle' through which the Gospel must pass on its way to Central Africa. He told Somerset that the weakness of the missionaries' position was that they could not expel vagrants. To remedy this defect of power, if only in a measure, Somerset appointed John Melville, a surveyor, as resident at Waterboer's Griquatown,[3] where Anderson was struggling against Buis of Kaffir frontier fame, who, having helped to wreck the station at Tooverberg, had transferred his undoubted abilities still further beyond the pale of the law. It was the first vague extension of British authority beyond the Orange.[4]

Satisfied that the extra-colonial stations were not to be closed after all, Philip turned his attention to the Hottentots within the Colony. As a convinced segregationist, at a time when there was still ample land available to make *apartheid* practicable, he was opposed to the indiscriminate mixing of races which must follow from the complete dispersion of the Hottentots on the farms. He held that they would never become civilised until they stood on a legal equality with Europeans and, as the economic basis of that equality was land, he began to press the authorities for additional grants to the mission stations. Herein he had scant success, but he did convince Christopher Bird, the Colonial Secretary at Capetown, that Jacob Cuyler, landdrost of Uitenhage, was levying forced labour at miserable wages on the Bethelsdorpers.[5] Bird offered him an ordinance protecting
1822. these people. 'Yes,' said Philip, 'with the royal seal upon it.'[6] But

---

[1] Rec. C.C., XII. 55. On Philip *vide* W. M. Macmillan, *Cape Colour Question and Bantu, Boer and Briton*; Philip, *Researches*; No. 538 of 1836.
[2] Rec. C.C., XII. 243; XIII. 185.
[3] John Melvill afterwards joined the L.M.S.
[4] Rec. C.C., XI. 229, 254; XII. 34, 162, 247; No. 66 of 1835, p. 219.
[5] Philip, *Researches*, II. 403 ff.; Macmillan, *op. cit.*, p. 138.
[6] Philip, *Narrative* (unpublished, *circa* 1845).

this Somerset could not give. Philip therefore sent home his first comprehensive report on the L.M.S. stations, made clear to the philanthropic public of Great Britain the distinction between the slave and the Hottentot problems, and got into touch with Wilberforce and Thomas Fowell Buxton, who were girding up their loins for the struggle which was to end slavery within the British Empire.

Trade, finance, slaves and Hottentots all drew attention to the affairs of the Cape. The arrival of a considerable body of British citizens on the Eastern Frontier redoubled the interest of those who remained at home. Conditions on that frontier were precarious. Since the failure of the Great Commando, the Xosas had claimed 1803. all from the Fish to the Sunday river as theirs by right of conquest and occupation, and had even ventured westward of the Gamtoos for a time. The Europeans claimed all as far as the Fish and treated Gaika as paramount chief of the western Xosas, however stoutly he and they might deny the fact. The indefatigable Collins was sent to report. He visited Hintsa, paramount chief of all the Xosas, at his 1809. kraal beyond the Kei, met the poverty-stricken Gaika in the upper valley of the Keiskamma, and recommended that the only way to secure the peace of the Frontier was to carry the border across the empty lands to the Koonap, appoint more magistrates to check intercourse with the tribes, drive Ndhlambi and his allies from the Zuurveld and settle that area with a dense European population.[1]

The clearing of the Zuurveld was carried out by Cradock. A large force of troops and burghers swept 20,000 Ndhlambis and Gunukwebes beyond the Fish, and to hold the frontier Cradock built a March double line of block-houses, garrisoned them with troops and 1812. burghers, placed a deputy landdrost behind each wing of the line at the new villages of Cradock and Grahamstown, and offered quitrent farms of 2000 morgen, two-thirds the usual size of a farm, near each military post.[2]

Cradock's was the most decisive step yet taken to establish the rule of law on the Eastern Frontier. That rule was displeasing to some of the frontiersmen. To the men or sons of the men who had taken part in the disturbances of 1795–1803, landdrosts, heemraden and field cornets were all very well, but High Court judges backed by troops, and often Hottentot troops at that, were anathema. The memories of the Black Circuit were still fresh when the Slachter's Nek rebellion took place. Frederick Bezuidenhout of Baviaan's river on the extreme frontier, by the space of two years, defied the summons of the courts to answer a charge of cruelty to a Hottentot servant. An officer and a dozen Hottentots were sent to fetch him. 1815. He fired on them and was killed. His brother, Johannes, and his

[1] Rec. C.C., VII. 101–3, 136.   [2] Ibid., VIII. 374, 427, 480, 501.

friends swore to avenge him, to drive the British and the Hottentots from the borderlands and to found a republic there. Twice they summoned Gaika to their aid, offering him the Zuurveld and other advantages in exchange for the Kat river lands, and when Hendrik Prinsloo, son of old Marthinus the firebrand of the Boschberg and the only influential man of their party, was arrested, they essayed to rescue him and then tried to raise the countryside. They failed, and most of them surrendered to the troops and their fellow-burghers at Slachter's Nek. A few fled towards Kaffirland, but Johannes was killed and the rest were captured. A special commission of the High Court presently banished thirty-two of the prisoners from the Eastern Frontier and sentenced six others to death. Of these, Somerset reprieved one, but the rest were publicly hanged under more than usually distressing circumstances at Van Aardt's farm.[1]

In later times the event became a symbol of British oppression like the so-called 'Bloody Massacre' of Boston and Peterloo. The execution of white men for rebellion undoubtedly shocked frontier opinion; but the rising in all its details save its conclusion was nothing new on that frontier, and the fact that the judges were either Hollanders or Afrikaners administering the fierce Roman-Dutch law of the day may serve to modify harsh judgments on the conduct of the British. The really significant fact is that the great mass of the frontiersmen either gave the rebels no support or actively helped the authorities. Given security the average frontier Boer of 1815 was law-abiding enough in most respects.

Unluckily, Cradock's settlement failed to make an end of the cattle thefts. His successor, therefore, tried to come to terms with Gaika and his famous son, Macomo. Treating Gaika as paramount chief of the western Xosas, Somerset arranged a reprisal system on a principle well understood in Kaffir law, whereby owners accompanied by small bodies of troops might trace the spoor of stolen cattle to the kraal at which it ended and there either retake their cattle or recoup themselves at the expense of the kraal. Somerset 1817. still further relaxed the system of non-intercourse by permitting a Kaffir fair twice yearly at Grahamstown.[2] Hardly had this arrangement been concluded than the garrison was reduced and Somerset was obliged to make up for the loss of the invaluable dragoons by substituting for the disbanded Hottentot Regiment a mixed cavalry and infantry Cape Corps of Hottentots and Coloured folk.[3] Robberies increased, and then Dushane, son of Ndhlambi, who had hitherto supported Gaika, went over to his father and the prophet, Makana,

---

[1] Rec. C.C., XI. 2 ff., 71; Leibbrandt, *Slachter's Nek Rebellion, 1815*; *The Critic*, Jan. and April 1935, articles by H. A. Reyburn.
[2] Rec. C.C., XI. 296 ff., 313; XII. 121; XIII. 69.   [3] *Ibid.*, XI. 380, 389.

who were seeking to unite the Western Xosas. Together, the new Nov.
allies overthrew Gaika on the bloody field of Amalinde. Gaika called 1818.
on the Governor for help. Troops and burghers crossed the Fish and
returned with many of Ndhlambi's cattle. Ndhlambi retaliated by April
harrying the borderlands and boldly attacking Grahamstown in 1819.
broad daylight. He was beaten off, and after some delay due to
drought and horse-sickness, the Colonial forces broke his power,
advanced to the Kei and returned with all and more than all the
cattle that he had lifted from the Colony. Somerset once more met
Gaika, obliged the other chieftains (Ndhlambi being in hiding) to Oct.
recognise him as paramount, and made a verbal treaty which proved 1819.
a fruitful seed-plot for dragon's teeth. All the country between the
Fish and the Keiskamma, save only the ill-defined Tyumie valley
which Gaika retained, was declared neutral territory. Excepting
Fort Willshire on the Keiskamma, the land was to be kept empty of
all, both black and white, by military patrols.[1]

Troops, magistrates, two rivers in place of one and a vacuum
between would never make the frontier secure unless they were
backed by a dense white population. There had been talk from time
to time of assisted immigration; but nothing was done till the end
of the Napoleonic wars turned men's thoughts towards immigration
as a cure for unemployment, and the need for economy brought home
to ministers the value of a close settlement as a border guard to
supplement the reduced garrison.[2] The first efforts affecting South
Africa were private. Benjamin Moodie brought out three hundred
young Scots under indenture with good success, but another party
failed and the boys from the Refuge of the Destitute were a nuisance.[3]
All these schemes affected only the Western districts. Meanwhile,
Cradock's Zuurveld settlement was dwindling away. Indeed, his whole
quit-rent policy, of which that scheme had been the forerunner, had
failed so far to answer its purpose of fixing the slowly drifting Boers
to their farms. Cradock's scheme was to give out no more Crown lands
on the old loan-place tenure. In future grants were to be of the usual
3000 morgen on quit-rents varying with the value of the land, while
every inducement was to be held out to farmers to convert their
existing loan-places into quit-rent holdings. So would they become
'real landholders.'[4] A Tory Governor could hold out no higher
inducement; but the colonists refused to be converted and the Zuurveld settlers gradually moved away to the north-eastern borders
where the land was better, Bushmen were available to take the place

[1] Rec. C.C., XII. 193, 203, 308, 320, 337 ff.
[2] C.H.B.E., VIII. 219 ff.; Treaties . . . 1803–54, p. 9; Cape Town Gazette,
October 30, 1819.
[3] Rec. C.C., VIII. 219; IX. 183; X. 206, 242; XI. 189, 275, 358, 430; XII. 22,
172, 295 ff., 315, 325; XIII. 28.
[4] Ibid., IX. 204 ff.

of the all too scarce Hottentot servants, and Kaffirs were non-existent.[1]

What wonder then that Somerset, in reply to Downing Street's inquiries, painted a highly coloured picture of the joys of the Zuurveld? Parliament voted £50,000 to pay the passages of 57 parties each organised under a leader, in a few cases half-pay officers, and entitled to 100 acres per man on quit-rent payable after a term of years. These 1820 Settlers were accompanied by others who travelled at their own charges. Altogether, nearly 5000 British landed, a notable addition to the scanty population of the Colony.[2]

March 1820– May 1821.

Somerset was away in England when the first transports arrived. The actual planting of the settlement therefore fell to Donkin, the acting Governor. He interpreted Bathurst's instructions that each nationality should be given land to itself so literally that he drafted the Irish and some of the English to an impossible site near Clanwilliam in the Western Colony; but he soon sent the bulk of them to join the other Settlers and their thirty-eight Dutch neighbours on the Zuurveld, and himself speedily followed them thither. He found them working with a zeal that was not always according to knowledge, the farmers among them grumbling at the smallness of their holdings and the artisans anxious to be off to the towns. Most of their grievances he could not remedy; but he remitted the cost of their transport up-country, appointed a provisional landdrost with wide powers at Bathurst, proclaimed the new district under the name of Albany, and christened the little port below Fort Frederick on Algoa Bay, Port Elizabeth, in memory of his dead wife.[3]

May 1820.

A year later Donkin visited Albany once more. Blight had destroyed the first wheat crop and many of the artisans were gone, but the rest were holding on. He appointed a landdrost to cope with the Kaffirs, who were becoming a nuisance and, in an attempt to check the traders who, in defiance of orders, were already pushing into Kaffirland, permitted a fair at Fort Willshire which soon became something like a permanent market. He still further weakened the policy of non-intercourse by inducing Gaika to allow the formation of an ex-officers' settlement at Fredericksburg in the Neutral Territory, a trespass from the Colonial side which was soon balanced by the return of Macomo to the upper waters of the Kat.[4]

June 1821.

Somerset returned furious with Donkin for having meddled with his frontier policy and dismayed to find the whole Colony sinking

Dec. 1821.

[1] Rec. C.C., XV. 85 ff., 328 ff. Between 1814 and 1821, only 410 out of 2206 loan-places were converted. (*State of the Cape*, p. 361.)

[2] *Ibid.*, XI. 363, 404, 425 ff.; Cory, *op. cit.*, II. 1 ff.; *State of the Cape*, pp. 178 ff.; *Treaties . . . 1803–54*, p. 5.

[3] Rec. C.C., XIII. 224, 297; XV. 73.

[4] *Ibid.*, XIV. 15, 56, 121; Proclamations, 1820–21, p. 29; No. 50 of 1835, pp. 202, 204.

into an economic decline. Napoleon was dead and the St. Helena demand had died with him; a run of bad seasons had set in; the post-war boom had collapsed and his cherished Albany settlement was visibly wilting. The Settlers were heavily in debt to the Government for rations; townsmen were giving up the attempt to learn South African farming; the rest were grumbling like any Boers that they were forbidden to keep slaves[1] and railing at the Somerset Farm as a subsidised state competitor. Some of the Governor's measures made matters worse. He appointed as landdrost a new and unpopular man—any man would have been unpopular under the circumstances—removed the seat of local government and the troops from Bathurst to Grahamstown, and abandoned Fredericksburg. On the other hand, he proposed to issue title-deeds to the Settlers for increased land grants at a very low quit-rent and hoped for the best. Then floods swept the countryside and forced many of the destitute Settlers to fall back on relief funds raised in the Colony, Great Britain and India.[2]

It was the darkest hour before the dawn, but the Albany men could not know that. They sent up a cry of complaint against Somerset and all his works which swelled the chorus of accusation arising from public and private enemies in London and Capetown. But already that chorus, the financial débacle at the Cape and the evangelical pressure of Wilberforce and Philip had impelled the Commons to include the Cape in the list of colonies which were to be visited by commissions of inquiry.[3] Hence, in July 1823, John Bigge, a lawyer who had reported recently on distant New South Wales, and Major William Colebrooke landed at Capetown. They ushered in the period of political, constitutional and economic reform which led up to the Great Trek.

---

[1] Edwards, *op. cit.*, pp. 67 ff., 177.
[2] Rec. C.C., XIII. 133; XIV. 13, 23, 93, 288, 309; XV. 2 ff., 106, 128, 283 ff., 348, 395.
[3] *C.H.B.E.*, VIII. 246.

CHAPTER VII

THE PERIOD OF CHANGE, 1823-36

REFORM, 1823-36

FROM 1823 onwards the fortunes of the thinly peopled, straggling Cape Colony were governed by two factors: poverty and the increasing interest taken in its affairs by the Imperial Government and certain sections of the British public. The arrival of a Commission of Inquiry was an earnest of the former, the task to which the Commissioners immediately addressed themselves was a witness to the latter.

That task was the restoration of the finances as part of a general imperial policy. The Bank of England had recently resumed specie payments and H.M. Government proposed to make British silver current in those of its colonies which had hitherto relied on the Spanish dollar.[1] The Cape, however, was a case for special treatment.[2]

1806
1823.
The purchasing power of its paper rix-dollar had fallen from 3s. 6d. to 1s. 6¼d.; the total of 2,086,275 Rd. left behind by the Batavians had been swelled in response to the exigencies of the troops, the public works department and the Burgher Senate to 3,587,056 (nominally £269,029) of which 484,851 were forged notes. Loan Bank mortgages notwithstanding, the word of the Government was the real security for it all. Efforts to prevent the operation of Gresham's Law had

1816.
been abandoned when Somerset permitted the export of bullion and saw men of means buy up the Spanish dollars imported to pay the troops and sell them at an ever-increasing premium to merchants for

Circa
1820.
remittance to London. During the post-war boom the demand for coin or drafts had been great; but it was clear that the amount of paper in circulation was excessive, as country business was mainly

[1] Rec. C.C., XX. 18 ff.
[2] *Ibid.*, XXII., 141 ff.; No. 438 of 1826. For the reports of the Commissioners on various matters *vide* Rec. C.C. (index) and Blue Books No. 282, 406 of 1826-7; 300 of 1829; 584 of 1830.

a matter of barter and town business of drafts on the Loan Bank, which in 1808 had become a bank of discount and deposit.[1]

The 4s. paper rix-dollar was now fixed at 1s. 6d. in silver, the 1825. average value for the past three years. £56,000 in silver and copper were provided to be paid out to the garrison, which, as the biggest spender in the Colony, could be trusted to put the new money into circulation, and the Commissariat was authorised to issue bills on London against this silver or paper at a steadily reduced discount. With this silver, 1,237,000 Rd. were soon bought in and cancelled; in other words, Great Britain lent the Colony over £92,000 without interest. The balance of the paper was replaced by new notes of English denominations exchangeable at par for the Treasury bills which now formed the security.[2]

The process of wiping out the paper money continued for nearly twenty years and, however much it may have been to the advantage of the Colony to have got rid of it, there is no doubt that the arrangement of 1825 hit creditors hard at the time, especially as the bank, having been too free with credit, suddenly stopped paying interest on deposits.[3] To make matters worse, the revenues of the Colony 1826– during the decade preceding the Great Trek were less than those of 1835. the ten years following the battle of Waterloo; the real value of land revenue fell with the fall of the rix-dollar; the adoption of English methods of business reduced the proceeds of the lucrative auction duty, and heavier taxes and quit-rents failed to fill the gap. Expenditure far exceeded revenue and Lord Charles Somerset was driven to borrow from the Orphan Chamber, the Loan Bank, the Commissariat and the East India Company. At last he helped himself to 1824. an Imperial loan earmarked for the repair of damage done by storm in the Western districts, a loan which had not been needed after all. It was the last straw at a time when conditions were so bad that banks in Great Britain and markets in Latin America were crashing in spite of independence and the Monroe Doctrine. The Imperial 1825. Government did indeed cancel the ration debt of the Albany Settlers and take over the Cape Corps, reduced to 250 mounted men, but it stopped all public works and, after Somerset's retirement, began to retrench official salaries from the Governor's lordly £10,000 a year downwards.[4] Henceforward, until 1843, the Colony had to face the fact that an inelastic revenue and a heavy debt put public

[1] Rec. C.C., VI. 358, 372; XI. 107, 112; XIX. 391; XXII. 123 ff.; *State of the Cape*, pp. 32, 305, 346; P. W. Grant, *Considerations on . . . Currency at the Cape*, pp. 7, 23, 119; E. H. D. Arndt, *History of Banking*, pp. 30, 32.
[2] Rec. C.C., XX. 372; XXI. 476; XXIV. 348 ff.; XXXV. 100.
[3] *Ibid.*, XXIII. 106 ff., 118 ff., 230.
[4] *Ibid.*, XXII. 219, 499; XXIII. 243, 414, 419; XXVIII. 133; XXXI. 179; XXXII. 19; XXXIV. 51; XXXV. 21.

works, assisted immigration, the proper staffing of magistracies and the policing of the frontiers out of the question. Public poverty and private discontent explain much that follows.

Somerset's financial policy had brought him into disfavour in Downing Street, and the outcry against him in the Colony and in London, some of it justifiable and some of it not, waxed louder. He did not fall without a struggle. He stood for a system, the High 1819. Toryism which, during the Peterloo troubles, had passed the famous Six Acts against seditious libels and open-air public meetings. The Young Tories were coming to the front, but the Acts were still in 1822. force in England when Somerset warned the Albany men that he would suffer neither the one nor the other. Now he instituted proceedings against some of his enemies in the High Court.[1] These measures brought him into conflict with Dr. Philip and the advocates of a free press.[2]

Apart from small presses in far distant mission stations, the only active press in the Colony was that in the Castle from which emanated the jejune columns of the *Government Gazette*. Thomas Pringle 1823. and the Rev. Abraham Faure then asked leave to produce a monthly magazine alternately in English and Dutch 'to enlighten South Africa,'[3] and George Greig, a printer, proposed to issue an apparently innocuous periodical 'rigidly excluding personal controversy and all discussion of . . . the policy or administration of the Colonial Government.' Somerset opposed both schemes, for there was a vigour in journalism in the days of Cobbett most unsettling to administrations; but Greig found that, though there was a law against unlicensed magazines, there was none against publishing a Jan. newspaper. He promptly issued the first number of the *S.A. Com-* 1824. *mercial Advertiser* edited by Pringle and Fairbairn and printed on a wooden missionary press borrowed from Dr. Philip.[4] Meanwhile, the Colonial Secretary, Lord Bathurst, had sanctioned a magazine Mar.– which should eschew politics and personalities. Hence, Pringle's April. *Journal* appeared, to be followed by Faure's *Tydschrift*.

Immediately, there were wigs on the green. Pringle was too out- May. spoken on the plight of the 1820 Settlers and had to abandon the *Journal*, while the Governor used all his social influence to ruin that 'seminary of sedition,' the Classical and Commercial Academy, where he and Fairbairn were supposed to teach 'the most disgusting principles of republicanism,'[5] and even threatened to proclaim their

---

[1] Rec. C.C., XIV. 376; XX. 170 ff., 183 ff., 377 ff., 389.
[2] On the Press *vide* Meurant, *Sixty Years Ago, passim*, and Lloyd, *The Birth of Printing in South Africa*.
[3] Pringle to Fairbairn, Nov. 24, 1822.   [4] Rec. C.C., XXI. 6.
[5] Pringle to Fairbairn, March 1825 (Jardine Collection).

Literary and Scientific Society an illegal assembly. Greig was told that he must cease reporting the Governor's libel actions and submit to a censorship for going beyond the limits of his prospectus and, when he refused, was given a month in which to leave the Colony. He therefore published the *Facts* relating to the suppression of his paper and sailed to London, while the Governor bought up his type and press at a valuation and entrusted them to William Bridekirk, who brought out the *S.A. Chronicle* till that estimable organ of Government opinion perished of inanition in the following year.[1]

By annexing Grieg's press, the Governor widened the growing breach between himself and Philip. The Doctor was already suspicious of Somerset's policy towards the tribes and the Albany Settlers, with both of whom he sympathised. He now concluded that he was hostile to all missions and not merely those beyond the borders. Somerset, for his part, erroneously believed that Philip was behind the press agitation and, by censuring him, ranged the L.M.S. side by side with the Settlers and the advocates of a free press. In London, Greig won a qualified victory with the help of Joseph Hume, Henry Brougham, Stephen Lushington and the editors of *The Times* and *Chronicle*. Bathurst gave him leave to publish within the four corners of his prospectus. Thereupon, the *Advertiser* appeared once more, under the guidance of Fairbairn fresh from a gubernatorial scolding for having launched the *New Organ*, the paper of a day, without leave and without excuse.[2] Aug. 1825.

The truth was that Somerset's days as Governor were numbered and with them the days of the existing system of governance at the Cape. Bathurst may have agreed to the appointment of the Commission of Inquiry in the hope that it would whitewash his nominee; but, whatever it might do, he could not wait for its report now that the vindictive Henry Brougham was threatening to impeach Somerset.[3] The Liverpool ministry, ageing towards dissolution, desired nothing less. Bathurst therefore decided to set up an Advisory Council at Capetown similar to that which had recently been established at Sydney. This Council was to consist of the Governor, the Chief Justice, the Colonial Secretary, the Officer Commanding, the Deputy-Quartermaster-General, the Auditor-General and the Treasurer, and was to pass ordinances with more formality than had hitherto been the practice, discuss such points as the Governor might raise, advise on all matters save those of urgency and confirm or even revise the Governor's emergency actions. His Excellency

---

[1] Rec. C.C., XVIII. 288, 347; XXIV. 11.
[2] Greig to Fairbairn, Jan. 25, 1825; Rec. C.C., XXIX. 235, 241; No. 470 of 1827. On Philip's relations with the Settlers *vide* Macmillan, *op. cit.*, pp. 113 ff.
[3] Rec. C.C., XXVIII. 411; London *Times*, Jan. 19, 1826.

6

Mav 4,
1825.

could, however, still act against its advice provided he justified him-self to the Secretary of State. The Council met forthwith.[1]

In due time, the Commissioners of Inquiry gave the Council their blessing and advised the creation of a similar Council for the Eastern districts, to be followed, once the Colony was more settled and slavery had been abolished, by representative assemblies in both provinces. They thus fired the first round in the long-sustained but unsuccessful battle for Separation. There was much to be said for the scheme. Grahamstown was 600 miles distant from the capital; the weekly post, carried on horseback in heavy leather bags, might well take the full seven days to make the journey; travellers must ride the 75 miles from Grahamstown to Port Elizabeth and finish their journey to Capetown in an 80-ton coasting schooner. Distance, the hope of developing an eastern trade with Mauritius, and the need for an authority competent to deal with Kaffirs and local officials all pointed towards Separation. The Ministry was inclined to divide the Colony on the analogy of the Two Canadas, and probably also it wished to cover Somerset's retreat.[2] Bourke was therefore sent out, nominally

March
1826.

as Lieutenant-Governor of the East but really as acting Governor of the whole Colony, and Somerset departed to end his days in com-parative peace in the Brighton of George IV. The need for a resident authority on the frontier was met a little later by a compromise,

July
1828.

when Andries Stockenstrom, the second of that name and landdrost of Graaff-Reinet, was appointed Commissioner-General at Grahams-town to supervise and report to the Governor on the affairs of the Eastern districts including Beaufort West.[3]

From a constitutional point of view, the year 1828 is the *annus mirabilis* of Cape history, for in it the freedom of the press was fully won and the judicial and local administrative systems were revolu-

1827.

tionised. Somerset, in England, had been strong enough to have the *Advertiser* suppressed once more, and Greig had refused to make terms with the acting governor Bourke, that 'blundering, insidious, two-faced Irish hypocrite,'[4] who none the less favoured a free press. Leading Cape citizens thereupon paid Fairbairn's expenses to

April
30,
1828.

London, where, at last, the Colonial Secretary, Sir George Murray, gave leave for a press ordinance based on the law of England. Printers and publishers who were prepared to deposit £300 as personal surety and a like amount guaranteed by friends, might publish newspapers on 1*d.* stamped sheets paid for in advance at the

---

[1] Rec. C.C., XX. 6 ff.; XXI. 184; Kilpin, *When Downing Street Ruled* and *The Romance of a Colonial Parliament.*
[2] Edwards, *1820 Settlers,* p. 127.
[3] Rec. C.C., XXII. 462, 495; XXVII. 342 ff.; XXXIV. 133.
[4] Greig to Fairbairn, March 29, 1827.

Capetown Stamp Office subject to the law of libel as interpreted by the Judges.[1] The *Advertiser* reappeared in triumph and was soon followed by a covey of news-sheets. Some of these died young; but April others, like Christoffel Brand's *Zuid Afrikaan* and Louis Meurant's 1830. *Grahamstown Journal*, were destined to long and influential careers. 1831. Dec.

The press might be printed in both English and Dutch but, between 1823 and 1828, the official language of the Colony became English. Some knowledge of English had long been necessary for 1813. aspirants to the public service; a large British immigration was expected, and Somerset's Scottish schoolmasters introduced a strong leaven of English into the country districts. On the other hand, High Dutch was not the spoken language of the country and the days of Afrikaans as a literary language were far distant. Important notices in the *Gazette* were still issued bilingually and, in the towns, the new policy inconvenienced few save elderly lawyers and civil servants, but, in the country districts, it bore hardly on Afrikaner litigants and witnesses.[2]

The adoption of English as the language of the Courts synchron- 1828. ised with the issue of the First Charter of Justice. The Commissioners of Inquiry condemned the old legal system. The heads of the Executive were the Court of Appeal; they worked slowly; they were guided by English law and, not being as a rule supplied with detailed judgments, often overturned the decisions of the High Court. Latterly, appeals had become little more than private interviews with His Excellency. The judges of the High Court were often part-time amateurs exposed, like the landdrosts and heemraden, to all kinds of social pressure. Naturally, their judgments carried little weight.[3]

The existing judicial system was therefore swept away lock, stock and barrel. The new machinery of justice was set up by the Charter of 1827 and expanded and modified by accompanying proclamations and a Second Charter in 1834. It consisted of a Supreme Court staffed by members of the Bars of the United Kingdom or of the Colony itself holding office *quamdiu se bene gesserint* and subject only to temporary suspension by the Governor. Two judges formed the quorum in civil cases, but a single judge tried criminal cases and conducted the circuit court twice annually. The Chief Justice, Sir John Wylde, took over the duties of the Vice-Admiralty Court, the Attorney-General those of the Fiscal, and, in 1834, the Master those of the Orphan Chamber. A jury of nine or, on circuit, where so many good men and true might not be forthcoming, six only sat beside my lord the King's Justice to hear criminal cases. Civil appeals

---

[1] Greig to Fairbairn, July 15, 1829, and Greig to Under-Secretary for the Colonies, Dec. 31, 1828.

[2] Rec. C.C., IX. 39; XIV. 184–5, 297, 371–3, 452; XXXI. 66; XXXII. 261, 282; XXXIII. 85; XXXIV. 117, 177–8, 238, 250; Eybers, *op. cit.*, p. 23.

[3] Rec. C.C., XXVIII. 1 ff.

from the circuit courts lay to the Supreme Court and from it again in serious cases to the Privy Council.[1]

At the district centres, the courts of the landdrosts and heemraden made way for those of resident magistrates. These officials were armed with minor civil jurisdiction subject in certain cases to an appeal to the Supreme Court or the circuit court, summary criminal powers, and authority to act with their clerks of the peace as matrimonial officers. The powers actually given them were less than those named in the Charter, for the salaries were so low that men of ability were not, as a rule, attracted.[2] The field cornets lost their petty judicial powers other than the mere conducting of inquests and preliminary examinations, while the new justices of the peace who supplemented them were little more than ornamental. The administrative duties of the landdrosts passed to civil commissioners and, at the same time, the Burgher Senate handed over its property to the superintendent of police and its revenues to the Government collector of taxes.[3] There was thereafter no semblance of municipal government in the Colony till 1837, nor in Capetown till 1840.

The Commissioners of Inquiry recommended that English law be introduced throughout as opportunity offered. Their advice was only partially taken. As in Quebec, criminal law became mainly English. No punishment repugnant to the spirit of that law was to be permitted, a great gain to the Colony in view of the criminal law reforms from 1821 onwards and the harsh nature of some of the penalties still prescribed by the Roman-Dutch law; the jury also brought the English law of evidence in its wake; but apart from issuing instructions to the judges to frame the rules of court as far as possible in accordance with those at Westminster and to follow the spirit of English law in submitting ordinances amending colonial laws to the Governor, the British Government was content to allow the Roman-Dutch civil law to remain the law of the Colony.[4]

[1] Rec. C.C., XXXII. 274 ff.; Eybers, pp. 107 ff. A Chief Justice and three Puisne Judges were appointed in 1828, three to form the quorum (Sir John Wylde, C.J. (1828–55), W. Menzies, G. Kekewich and W. W. Burton). The Second Charter reduced the number of Puisne Judges to two (Burton had already gone to New South Wales) and reduced the quorum to two, made members of the Cape Bar eligible for appointment to the Bench, limited the appeal to the Privy Council to cases involving £500 instead of £1000, transferred the patronage of the Supreme Court from the Chief Justice to the Governor, bade the Chief Justice take his turn on circuit, and, to enable him to do so, omitted him from the new Legislative Council, which he joined as President only in 1853.

[2] Rec. C.C., XXXIV. 208, 248 ff., 527; Eybers, p. 109. The Resident Magistrate could hear civil suits involving not more than £10 and terminate those involving less than £2. He could award one month's imprisonment, a private whipping, and a fine up to £5.

[3] Rec. C.C., XXXII. 266, 269; XXXIII. 432; XXXIV. 144, 176 ff., 262.

[4] Ibid., XX. 13; XXVII. 502; Wessels, History of the Roman-Dutch Law, chapters xxxiii., xxxv.; Botha, Early Influence of the English Law (S.A. Law Journal, Nov. 1923); Walker, De Villiers and his Times, chapter v. The Legislative Council was empowered to alter the Charter of Justice in 1844.

The effect of these reforms was to give the Colony greater efficiency at the price of almost all popular share in the work of government. On the other hand, the Dutch Reformed Church had already begun to gain a measure of corporate liberty. De Mist had talked of reviving the experimental Synod of 1746–59, but it was only in Somerset's Nov. time that such a body met. Twelve ministers and ten elders, under 1824. the watchful eye of two political commissioners, then organised the Church into three presbyteries and, in view of the difficulty of ensuring a supply of future predikants, seriously debated union with the Scottish Kirk.[1] The resolutions of the Synod were subject to disallowance by His Majesty and remained so till 1843, but the 1826– political commissioners were at once withdrawn from the church 1828. consistories. As a further sign of approaching ecclesiastical liberty and in keeping with Catholic emancipation in the United Kingdom, full civil privileges were granted to Roman Catholics with the excep- 1830. tion of a few religious orders, and priests were even paid Government salaries like the clergy of so many other churches in the Colony.[2]

The example of the Church, the recent advent of many politically-minded English and Scots, the inclusion of non-officials in the legislature of New South Wales, the assemblies foreshadowed by the 1825. Commissioners of Inquiry and the rising clamour for Parliamentary reform in Great Britain itself gave rise to a demand for representative institutions. The focus of that agitation was the editorial offices of the *Commercial Advertiser*.[3] Two of the Burgher Senators resigned as 1826. a protest against the Government's slave policy, the citizens of Capetown asked leave to elect their successors and, when that was refused, petitioned Parliament for a representative assembly.[4] That request was also refused by a ministry which was having endless trouble in persuading elected legislatures in the West Indies to improve the condition of the slaves and was not minded to set up another such body in the slave-owning Cape Colony. Moreover, the Colony was extensive, poor, badly supplied with means of communication and peopled by a sparse, racially divided and, for the most part, politically inexperienced European population outnumbered by slaves and coloured folk, to say nothing of the Bantu upon the borders. There were not, wrote Bourke, enough men capable of forming a good Assembly in the whole country.[5] Indeed official Britain regarded the British colonists very coolly. There was little of that sentimental regard for colonists as such which marked the early years of the

---

[1] Engelbrecht, *op. cit.*, I. 8–13; Rec. C.C., XIX. 186, 495. The Scottish element in the D.R. Church was very strong. Of the twenty-five ministers in 1837, thirteen were Scots (*vide* Proceedings of the Synod at Capetown, Oct. 1837). The question of union with the Scottish Kirk was debated as late as 1918.
[2] Rec. C.C., XXXI. 204; Eybers, p. 29.
[3] *Vide S.A. Comm. Adv.*, Jan. 9, 13, and April 24, 1830.
[4] Rec. C.C., XXVIII. 208.   [5] *Ibid.*, XXVIII. 454; Eybers, p. 30.

twentieth century. Rather the reverse. As for the Afrikaners, the reports of eighteenth-century Hollander officials had not been flattering nor had subsequent observers of divers nationalities seriously modified their verdict. The main source on which British opinion relied was the *Travels* of John Barrow, at one time Lord Macartney's secretary, now a power at the Admiralty and soon to be the founder of the Royal Geographical Society and a baronet to boot. His conclusions, hostile to the frontier Boers especially, were supplemented in 1828 by Philip's *Researches*, which had little good to say of either Afrikaner or British settlers.

The Cape could hardly expect to be treated differently from the small mixed colonies which formed so large a proportion of the British Empire of the day. Nor was it so treated till the Imperial Government had freed the slaves and given civil liberty to the Hottentots. The whole issue of representative institutions was governed by these two factors. Nevertheless, to make up for the 1827. elimination of the popular share in government by the impending reforms of 1828, two nominated burghers were given seats on the Advisory Council.[1]

No one was satisfied with the concession, for the Council had little power as against a Secretary of State who disallowed ordinances or insisted that laws must be passed before a given date, or against a Governor who blandly announced that he had issued an ordinance himself to save time. Fairbairn, allied with Christoffel Brand, raised the cry of 'No taxation without consent' and bade the Colonists take the U.S.A. as their model.[2] He could and did point to many signs of progress: the rebuilding of houses and the building of 1831. churches in Capetown;[3] the foundation of the first Colonial fire and insurance company and the Good Hope Savings Bank; the free 1829. press and the opening of the South African College with its pro- 1825. phetic name. The *Enterprise*, the first steamship to round the Cape, 1830. had come and gone, the earnest of greater things to come, and a good road over Sir Lowry Pass had at last linked Capetown with the south-western districts. The rapid formation of Dutch Reformed Church congregations pointed towards revival.[4] In the east the 1825. tide had clearly turned. Somerset had visited the Frontier, carried the line eastward to the Koonap and Stormberg spruit, scrapped the hated Somerset Farm, removed the unpopular landdrost, issued the promised title-deeds for larger holdings, and permitted direct trade

[1] Rec. C.C., XXXI. 443; XXXII. 6.
[2] *S.A. Comm. Adv.*, Aug. 21 and Oct. 2, 1830; Jan. 22, 1831.
[3] St. Andrew's (Presbyterian), 1827; Burg Street Wesleyan Church, 1829; St. George's Cathedral, 1830–4; Bree Street Dutch Reformed Church, 1833.
[4] Colesberg (Tooverberg) and Somerset East, 1825; Pampoenkraal (Durbanville) and Clanwilliam, 1826; Wynberg and Glen Lynden, 1829, an increase from ten churches to twenty in less than two decades.

with England from Port Elizabeth and Port Frances.[1] The Settlers' debts to Government were cancelled, and before long Albany was firmly established on the backs of its cattle and sheep. There were *Circa* farmhouses everywhere; the newcomers were intermarrying with the 1830. Afrikaners; Grahamstown and Port Elizabeth, like Graaff-Reinet, were already thriving little towns.

Fairbairn had hoped much from the support of the British settlers; but an Albany petition for an Assembly was rejected and a Cape- 1830– town petition to the King shared a like fate, the new Governor, Sir 1831. Lowry Cole, remarking that an Assembly would fall into the hands of 'demagogues and briefless barristers,' a palpable hit at Fairbairn and his ally, Brand.[2] Then the reformers split on the rock of slavery. Fairbairn had long been interested in native affairs, an interest accentuated by the fact that he attended Philip's church, accom- 1830– panied him on a short visit to the Eastern Frontier and married his 1831. daughter. Philip, for his part, had made up his mind to procure an Act of the Imperial Parliament safeguarding the rights of all races and classes in the Colony. Brand, on the other hand, came of slave-owning stock and had founded the *Zuid Afrikaan* in opposition to the *Advertiser*. He suggested as a compromise that H.M. Government should grant the Colony an Assembly which would then co-operate with it in the abolition of slavery.[3] The cleavage of opinion began to run on racial lines. Matters came to a head when some farmers near Capetown threatened to rebel against fresh slave regulations May and the *Zuid Afrikaan* talked of the 'rights of Dutch burghers' 1832. and 'the length of a Boer rifle.' This was too much for Fairbairn. 'We dislike the despotism of *one*,' he retorted, 'but we think the despotism of fifty Koeberg farmers fifty thousand times worse,' and he wrote no more in favour of representative institutions.[4] He even approved when Cole, fearing 'the new feeling' against the British Government, issued a proclamation against public meetings and improper petitions and claimed power to deport.[5]

But a change was clearly coming now that the great Reform Bill Sept. had become law in England. Cole allowed 2000 people, mostly 1832. slave-owners, to meet in Capetown and petition for an Assembly; the Secretary of State made him cancel his recent proclamation, since British subjects might only be deported after trial or by Act of Parliament;[6] the Reformed Parliament met; slave emancipation 1833. was carried; Cole departed; letters patent were issued providing for

---

[1] Rec. C.C., XX. 403. Originally called 'Port Kowie' and, after 1866, 'Port Alfred.'
[2] C.O. 1444, Cole to S. of S., April 16, 1831.
[3] *Zuid Afrikaan*, July 15, 22, 1831; Macmillan, *op. cit.*, pp. 182, 187.
[4] *S.A. Comm. Adv.*, May 16, 29, June 30, July 11, 1832.
[5] C.O. 1445, Cole to S. of S., June 19, 1832, and Ordinance, June 6, 1832.
[6] C.O. 1320, Goderich to Cole, Nov. 25, 1832.

Jan. 10, 1834. a nominated Legislative Council at the Cape, and Sir Benjamin D'Urban arrived to put the new constitution into force.

Under the new letters patent the Executive Council consisted of the Governor and the four leading officials. The Legislative Council included the same officials, the Attorney-General and from five to seven nominees. Its powers were greater than those of the Advisory Council, for its consent was necessary for legislation, it had freedom of debate and of initiation except on the long list of reserved matters, and its laws could only be set aside if the King-in-Council failed to approve of them within two years. Five citizens, all Westerners, took their seats beside the officials for the first time on April 2, 1834.[1] At first they sat in secret, but in response to popular demand they soon admitted reporters and friends of members to the gallery.

D'Urban came to do much more than institute a legislature. He was the new broom of Whiggish liberalism which was to sweep clean. He was to carry retrenchment still further, consider the possibility of municipal institutions, emancipate the slaves and evolve a satisfactory native policy. Retrenchment was a comparatively simple though necessarily a painful matter. D'Urban himself drew only £5000 a year, for he was the first Governor who had no high family connections; other salaries were reduced in proportion; offices were in some cases combined to the advantage of the Exchequer and the detriment of the public service.

The problem of local government had been simplified by the disappearance of the Commissioner-Generalship of the East.[2] March 1833. Stockenstrom, the holder of that office, had recently gone overseas on long leave, after he had, with a perspicacity rare among Government servants, offered to resign on the ground that there was not sufficient work to be done. Stanley presently abolished his office. Meanwhile, a demand for elective heemraden had arisen and the *Grahamstown Journal* pressed for Separation and a 'resident authority' in the East.[3] H.M. Government declined to accede to either request, but bade D'Urban examine the scheme of municipal government drafted by the magistrate of Grahamstown. In face of this proposal and of the new Legislative Council in being, the agitation for a separate Assembly for the East, which in truth had little genuine support at that time outside the offices of the *Grahamstown Journal*, died away. But, not for the last time in South Africa's history, violence destroyed the immediate prospects of reform. A 1834–1835. serious Kaffir war delayed the grant of municipal institutions, and it was only in 1836 that the necessary ordinance was passed.[4]

---

[1] Governor, General Officer Commanding, Colonial Secretary, Treasurer, Auditor-General, Attorney-General and P. L. Cloete, J. B. Ebden, M. van Breda, C. S. Pillans and J. J. du Toit.
[2] Stockenstrom, *Autobiography*, I. 430.   [3] *Grahamstown Journal*, July 25, 1833.
[4] Ordinance, Aug. 15, 1836; Eybers. p. 78.

This Kaffir war was only the worst of many perplexities that beset the well-intentioned but leisurely D'Urban. Long before he was caught up in it, he had been hard at work reorganising the government of a Colony which was in the throes of a social revolution which had begun in 1828, six years back, with the granting of civil liberty to Hottentots and 'other free persons of colour.' It was his business to carry that revolution a long step further by freeing the slaves.

The slave and Hottentot problems were intimately connected, for the Hottentots were the alternative labour supply to the slaves. The average Colonial official and farmer still looked on the Hottentots as a labour force which ought not to be drained off to the thirty mission stations within or just beyond the borders. The missionaries denied that they were so drawn off, pointed to the fact that most of the inmates of Bethelsdorp, *fons et origo mali*, went out to work, and urged that, given equal opportunity, Hottentots and Kaffirs were potentially equal to Europeans, but for the present stood in need of special protection.[1]

This missionary point of view varied in intensity from Society to Society. It was held most uncompromisingly by the L.M.S. and by none more strongly than Philip. His reasoned policy for the regulation of the relations of white and black in all Southern Africa and his support of the Government during the Kaffir war of 1834–35 prove that he was no enemy of the Europeans; but he had a high opinion of the capabilities of the Hottentots and Griquas, if only they could be given land on which to develop civilisation under missionary or official control and be shielded from the drink pressed upon them by Europeans. Had not Collins as long ago as 1809 fulminated against the tot system of payment, a system which is to this day a gross evil on the wine farms of the Western Cape?[2] At first he had contented himself with championing the Hottentots in the overcrowded reserves at Bethelsdorp and Theopolis, but later he took the whole race under his ægis. If the abolition of the Slave Trade had been followed by the class legislation of 1809–19, what might not Emancipation lead to? The root weakness of the Pass Laws was that the Hottentots outside the mission stations were practically at the mercy of the local officials, themselves farmers, and their friends. As landless men, bound by the pass system to work where they dwelt, they had no opportunity of improving their lot and thereby adding to the prosperity of the Colony. 'The abettors of the present system,' wrote Philip, a disciple of Adam Smith, 'seem never to have contemplated the aborigines of the Colony as consumers.'[3]

[1] Macmillan, *op. cit.*, pp. 139, 153. [2] Rec. C.C., VII. 111.
[3] No. 538 of 1836, pp. 723 ff.; Macmillan, *op. cit.*, p. 176.

6*

It was clear that slave emancipation was coming. Philip therefore sailed for England, petitioned Sir George Murray, the Secretary of State, and published his *Researches*. At times his statements were as wrong in point of detail as they were more often exaggerated in form, and he was presently successfully sued for libel in Capetown; but his attack on the system was irresistible. Murray, with the general support of the Commons, bade Bourke give general freedom and equality before the law to all classes in the Colony. The necessary action had, however, already been taken at Capetown. Stockenstrom had prepared a report on which the philanthropically minded acting-Governor based the famous 50th Ordinance. This measure cancelled the restrictive Hottentot laws of 1809–19 and gave Hottentots, Bushmen and free coloured persons full right to own land if they could get it.[1] All that remained for Murray to do was to secure the addition of a clause forbidding any alteration therein without the consent of the King-in-Council. It was the King's seal which Philip had vainly demanded in 1822.[2]

[margin: 1826–1828.]

[margin: July 1828.]

The civil rights of the free Coloured Folk at the Cape were thus specially entrenched. The turn of the slaves, the servile section of that folk, came next. Post-war problems and the High Tory reaction in England had pushed the question of emancipation into the background, but once the younger Tories led by Canning had risen to power, the Anti-Slavery Committee was formed and Thomas Fowell Buxton began to play Joshua to Wilberforce's Moses. He moved for the immediate emancipation of slave children and the gradual abolition of slavery as a thing 'repugnant to the British constitution and Christianity.' Canning shelved the motion by inviting the nineteen slave-owning colonies, all of them in the West Indies save Mauritius and the Cape, to propose means for improving the condition of their slaves. Members of the Jamaica Assembly promptly talked of secession. Buxton tried again, still moderately advocating a term of apprenticeship for the liberated slaves and compensation for the owners. This time Canning passed the Trinidad Ordinance of 1824 prescribing various reforms in the hope that the other West Indian islands, which, unlike Trinidad, had legislatures of their own, would adopt them. They declined to move and, for two years more, nothing was done—except at the Cape.[3]

[margin: 1822.]

[margin: 1823.]

The Cape Government had continued to care for the slaves and, latterly, as part of the Imperial policy, had limited the extension of slavery. The 1820 Settlers were forbidden to keep slaves, a rule which they resented as a slur on their characters, but a rule which was none the less enforced later on in the mixed Anglo-Afrikaner Koonap

[margin: 1830.]

---

[1] No. 50 of 1835, p. 169; Eybers, p. 26.
[2] Galbraith, J. S., *Reluctant Empire*, pp. 83–4. Philip overestimated his influence in this matter.
[3] On Slave Emancipation *vide* Coupland, *Wilberforce*; Cory, *op. cit.*, III. pp. 27 ff.; *C.H.B.E.*, VIII. 269 ff.

settlement further east. Somerset also issued detailed regulations for the care of slaves and the education of their children, permitted March slaves to own property, and allowed the evidence of baptised slaves 1823. to rank in Court beside that of *Christen mense*.[1] Bathurst, however, was displeased because Somerset's reforms fell far short of what H.M. Government and its philanthropic advisers desired. He therefore obliged Bourke to adapt the Trinidad Ordinance to local condi- June tions. The consequent 19th Ordinance thus provided a registrar and 1826. guardian of slaves, but omitted the prohibition against carrying the whip in the fields as unnecessary and the punishment record book as impossible since many owners could not write.[2] Unluckily times were bad, the value of slaves was falling as the restrictions on their use accumulated, and Somerset's liberal Ordinance of 1823 had been followed by a small slave rising in the Bokkeveld (Worcester district). It was now alleged that that Ordinance had been the cause of the rising. Bourke could hardly get the 19th Ordinance proclaimed in Capetown and Stellenbosch; the president and two members of the Burgher Senate resigned and a Capetown meeting petitioned for a representative Assembly.[3]

Slave-owners, seeing that emancipation was only a question of time, naturally tried to arrange for it in the way that would suit themselves best. There had long been talk of freeing female slaves, a scheme which Somerset had favoured, always provided compensation were given, for slaves, 'the only property of note,' were heavily mortgaged. The folk of Graaff-Reinet, where Bantu were beginning to supply the demand for labour, then proposed the automatic 1826. emancipation of female children at birth, a proposal which would have left the adult slaves and, with them, the 'domestic situation' untouched for an indefinite period, while, in Capetown, a few enthusiasts and a Government grant maintained an ineffective slave redemption society.[4] So the matter dragged on till the Cape became 1830. liable to all the omitted regulations of the Trinidad Ordinance. The men of the capital told Cole they could not and would not keep punishment record books; at the first inspection of the same, Stellenbosch broke into riot and the *Zuid Afrikaan* organised a petition in favour of the emancipation of female children in exchange for the grant of representative institutions. Graaff-Reinet asked Government for some £8,000 annually for ten or twelve years wherewith to buy

---

[1] Proclamation, 18 March 1823; Edwards *op. cit.*, pp. 91 ff., 221 ff.; Rec. C.C., XIII. 136; XIV. 469; XV. 336; XVI. 493; XIX. 161–5; XXI. 295; XXIII. 70. *Vide also* XXX. 352 ff. for history of slavery.
[2] Ordinance 19 of 1826.
[3] Rec. C.C., XX. 66; XXIV. 309; XXVI. 468; XXVII. 89 ff., 184, 208, 303, 389.
[4] A. F. Hattersley, article in *History*, Oct. 1925. The influence of this society was trifling.

1832. the freedom of slave female children and, after the issue of further regulations, Koeberg farmers hinted broadly at rebellion.

The slave-owners used their fears of emancipation to the best of their ability as a lever with which to extort an Assembly; but their fears were none the less genuine. Five Orders in Council and fourteen slave proclamations had been launched at their heads since 1823. Most of these had remained dead letters; but in so far as they were operative, they made slave-owning a harassing undertaking, and now Buxton was forcing the pace in England. Parliamentary reform was near, and with the decline of the sugar trade the power of the 'West Indian party' was not what it had been. Mass meetings condemned gradual emancipation as 'utterly wild and visionary,' and the Commons by a large majority accepted the principle of forthright emancipation. The Whigs took office and at once freed the Crown slaves; whereupon the privately owned slaves in Jamaica, thinking that the boon was universal and that their masters were withholding it from them, sacked some plantations. Though they harmed no white man, they were sternly repressed and Parliament voted compensation to the owners. Then, at the general election of 1832, many members pledged themselves to emancipation.[1] Committees of both Houses decided that it could be effected safely and Buxton, in the day of his strength, once more became moderate and thereby lost the support of his extremists. Under pressure, ministers made emancipation a Government measure; Henry Whiteley's pamphlet on Jamaica with a preface by Pringle, now secretary of the Anti-Slavery Committee, sold in thousands; popular petitions were widely signed and the Bill passed the vital second reading. A few days later Wilberforce died.[2]

July 6, 1833.

Between August and December 1834 eight hundred thousand slaves would be set free throughout the British Empire. The news of this impending event, 'one of the greatest events in the history of the world,' was received quietly in the Cape Colony. After all, the ex-slaves were to be apprenticed to their former masters for four years from December 1, and Parliament was dealing more gently with owners than it had dealt with those who had invested in the rotten boroughs. These had just been swept away without compensation, but £20,000,000 had been voted to recompense slave-owners for their losses. Many Cape Colonists, headed by Fairbairn, held that the British taxpayer must pay up the full value of the slaves; but that was to ignore the fact, which Macaulay had already pointed out, that the colonial publics and, where these existed, colonial legislatures had been eager for slaves and must shoulder their share of the cost of emancipation. In any case, the prospect of some compensation money was welcome at a time when the Cape wine

[1] Rec. C.C., XXXV. 352; vide also No. 335 of 1829; 8 of 1830; 230 of 1831.
[2] Eybers, p. 38; Coupland, Wilberforce, p. 516.

market was in a bad way and men were at last anxious to buy woolled sheep.[1]

Like other slave-owners, the Cape Colonists looked round for an alternative supply of labour. Mauritius and other colonies afterwards found it in indentured Indian coolies, but the Cape hoped to secure it through a vagrancy law. The cry for such a law had gone up for some time past, especially in the East. Vagrancy had increased since the passing of the 50th Ordinance, for of all the drifting peoples of the border districts the Hottentots were the most migratory. Crime had apparently diminished, but this may have been because it was more difficult to trace it among free men than among pass-bound farm labourers. Most of the Hottentots, after a first taste of liberty and dop in the villages, had returned to work on the farms; but some 9000, perhaps a quarter of their total number, were still wandering about, 'eating up' their more industrious relations or robbing the farmers, if only by searching for roots, honey, fruit and game in immemorial Hottentot fashion.[2] The basic trouble was still the same. Outside the mission reserves, the Hottentots were practically a landless folk. Cole and Stockenstrom, like Dundas and Janssens before them, had recognised this fact when they established **1829.** nearly 3000 half-breeds, Hottentots and Kaffirs, round the L.M.S. station at Philipton and the Glasgow mission at Balfour in the Kat River Settlement.[3] Some, like Robert Godlonton in his first contributions to the *Grahamstown Journal*, spoke well of a policy which made possible the moral and material prosperity of these people;[4] but others complained that the Hottentots were becoming lazy and insolent, that they were intriguing with the Kaffirs and that wages were being forced up. Cole had wished to make the Hottentots work, and Wade, the acting-Governor, now promised 'a sufficiency of **Jan.** labourers' and issued a draft vagrancy law.[5]   **1834.**

This measure was narrowly passed by the new Legislative Council soon after D'Urban's arrival. It empowered any official to send suspects to the public works till they either gave surety that they would wander no more or went out to service under contract. The Chief Justice held that the law could not stand against the 50th Ordinance; the Moravians cried out that it would throw them back to the beginning; the Rev. William Boyce, the leading Wesleyan and rival of Philip, admitted the existence of vagrancy, but urged that police and magistrates were the proper cure and not serfdom; Philip roused the missions to protest, and told the Governor that if there must be a vagrancy law, it must be accompanied by grants

---

[1] *S.A. Comm. Adv.*, Feb. 9, May 22 and Aug. 14, 1832.
[2] Boyce, *Notes*, pp. 119–27; No. 538 of 1836, pp. 153, 288.
[3] No. 252 of 1835, pp. 52 ff.
[4] *Grahamstown Journal*, June 8, 1832; Macmillan, *op. cit.*, p. 234.
[5] Meurant, *op. cit.*, p. 93; No. 252 of 1835, p. 77; Chase, *Natal Papers*, I. 44.

of land where vagrants could work under the guidance of picked men armed with magisterial powers and assisted by schoolmasters and missionaries. The land could be bought, if necessary, from the Kaffirs between the Fish and the Keiskamma, and, he added, 'allow *no one* to erect a canteen among them.' Philip, an advocate of *apartheid* ahead of his time, carried his point to this extent—that the revised draft made it possible for Hottentots to acquire small holdings. D'Urban, however, this time suspended the Ordinance in spite of a petition in its favour from the half-breeds of Balfour. It was promptly disallowed in London, but not before the Governor had had to dismiss two or three field cornets for enforcing it prematurely.[1]

Emancipation, then, would find both Hottentots and ex-slaves, in other words, the Coloured Folk, unchecked by a vagrancy law. Fairbairn urged repeatedly that the slave compensation money be paid out without delay, the Governor himself set to work as chairman of the committee which was to apportion the expected funds, and, in due course, some 39,000 slaves embarked upon their four years' apprenticeship. Three weeks later the Xosas came over the Eastern Frontier.

Dec. 1, 1834.

Thus was still another of D'Urban's reforms ruined by war. The slave compensation lists, compiled in the midst of the confusion, were not completed till June 1836. Then came the news that instead of the £2,824,224 assessed in the final lists only £1,247,401 would be forthcoming, and that payable in London partly in cash and partly in $3\frac{1}{2}$ per cent. stock which was somewhat below par and likely to go still lower. It was soon known, moreover, that £12,000, the cost of the valuation, would be deducted. Gladstone in the Commons sneered at the smallness of the compensation. So did the Colonists. Many of them had to face the foreclosing of their mortgages, and even the slave-owners who escaped that fate were hard hit. Townsmen could cash their claims through the banks, but the countrymen were at the mercy of speculators who bought up the vouchers at a heavy discount. Some owners were destined shortly to go out on the Great Trek without claiming their money, for when the claims expired in December 1845, an unclaimed balance of £5900 remained.[2]

Nov. 1836.

'CAPE COLONY' BECOMES 'SOUTH AFRICA'

D'Urban's governorship has rightly been dwelt on at some length in all South African histories, because during it the Great Trek

[1] No. 538 of 1836, pp. 723 ff.; *S.A. Comm. Adv.*, May 31, July 17, Aug. 9, 1834. The way in which the vagrancy law must have worked is well illustrated by C. L. Stretch, afterwards Gaika commissioner. He noted that at the New Year of 1835 a field cornet had arrested thirty Hottentots with their sheep and cattle and marched them into Fort Beaufort, because they would not work. The field cornet thought the Vagrancy Bill had become law. C. L. Stretch, Kingwilliamstown, July 4, 1835; Macmillan, *op. cit.*, p. 244.

[2] *S.A. Comm. Adv.*, Jan. 4, 1837; Cory III. 44; Chase, *op. cit.*, I. 43.

began. But it should be memorable also because it saw the first attempt to face as a whole the problems created by the tribes and the Europeans who were already beyond the borders.

For fifteen years or so before D'Urban's arrival, pandemonium *Circa* had raged among the Bantu of South-eastern Africa. The Bantu 1820– still call those the days of the *Mfecane*, the crushing, for what befell 1834. then was just such another disaster as had accompanied the onslaught of the Abambo and Amazimba two hundred years back. The storm-centre lay between the Mkusi and Tugela rivers. There, Dingiswayo, King of the Abatetwa, had revived the old Bantu practice of arming his impis, circumcised, celibate, beef-fed and fiercely disciplined, with the big ox-hide shield and broad stabbing assegai, and had taught them to fight in crescent formation with the 'bull's head' in the centre, 'horns' on either flank and a massive reserve in the rear. He was succeeded by Chaka, head of the Zulus, at that time a humble little tribe among his cohorts. Chaka still further stiffened the discipline, did away with circumcision, and appointed not hereditary chieftains but whom he chose as captains of regiments. He first drove the Angoni and Shangaans northward to carry desolation through the eastern coastlands behind the helpless Portuguese settlements as far as Lake Nyasa, and then stabbed his way through and through Natal.

Chaka even crossed the Drakensberg mountains, but beyond them the devastation was wrought by others. In his sweep through Natal in 1823, he had driven the Amangwane in upon the Hlubi. These tribes fought each other and, thus fighting, poured northward and smashed every tribe that lay in their path to the westward of the Caledon river in what is now the Orange Free State. Next, Msilikazi, leader of one of Chaka's impis, fell foul of his master. He fled with his men, laid waste the southern and western Transvaal and came to a halt in the Marico river area, whence he raided the Bechuana. These Bechuana had, in many cases, already been smitten by the Mantatis under their terrible Batlokua queen, MaNtatisi, and her son, Sikonyela, a mixed horde that had been set in motion by the Amangwane and Hlubi. These Mantatis had traversed Basutoland, given up all hope of raiding the Cape Colony at sight of the flooded Orange, and then harried the northern Free State and south-western Transvaal. In Bechuanaland, the Bangwaketse of Kanye managed to head them off southward to sack Old Lithako; none the less, their onrush drove another lesser horde under Tswane, Chief of the Bafokeng, down upon the L.M.S. mission station at Kuruman (New Lithako).[1] There, these raiders were boken by Waterboer's Griquas and local Batlapin under the anxious eyes of the missionary, Robert Moffat, and John Melville, Government agent at Griquatown.

[1] *Basutoland Records*, I. 517.

Presently, the Mantati horde broke up. One section, the Makololo, cut their way to the middle Zambesi where David Livingstone found them later on; another, including Sikonyela's Batlokua, straggled back to the Caledon valley; others again drifted southward to take service in the frontier districts of the Colony as far south as newly-settled Albany.

The *Mfecane* did not end with the dispersion of the Mantatis; indeed, it was still going on a dozen years later when the Great Trek was well under way. But, by 1823 or thereabouts, the worst was over with its heavy slaughter and widespread destruction of tribes and their whole way of life. It is, however, easy to exaggerate the numbers of the slain and to forget that there was also much displacement.[1] That displacement should be remembered when men claim that the Trekkers were the first inhabitants of the temporarily empty lands beyond the Orange and the Vaal.

Meanwhile, behind this whirling mass of tribesmen, a few scattered European settlements clung to the south-east coast. The Governor of Mozambique, who had been independent of the Viceroy at Goa since 1807, nominally ruled the coast and the lower reaches of that great river, the river Zambesi; but in truth his authority ended with the range of the guns of the forts at each station wherein a few white, half-caste and negro soldiers overlooked a huddle of huts, a church and the fever-sodden hinterland. His hold on Delagoa Bay had long been intermittent. A party from Mozambique had stayed there in 1755 by leave of the local chiefs; a little later a wrecked crew of Dutch sailors had lived there for two years 1775– and never seen a Portuguese; for a time, William Bolt, late of the 1781. English East India Company, had held his own in the name of Maria Theresa's Asiatic Company of Trieste, but in the end the Austrian government had withdrawn the charter and the Portuguese had driven Bolt away. The Portuguese had then made a serious attempt to occupy the north shore and built a fort at Espirito Santo (Lourenço 1796. Marques), but the French had destroyed the station.

There was, however, at least one energetic man in decadent Portuguese East Africa. This was Dr. Francisco Lacerda, an able scientist and explorer, who set out in 1798 with an expedition equipped by the authorities to travel right across to the West Coast, a feat that had hitherto only been performed by two Goanese named Pereira. Alas, the gallant Lacerda died at Kazembe near Lake Mweru on the present Northern Rhodesia-Congo frontier, and the survivors straggled back to Tete. After this setback, a handful of Portuguese officials planted themselves once more at Delagoa Bay, and, in defiance of their own navigation laws, looked for a living to the slave-

[1] Theal estimated the number of dead at 'nearer two millions than one,' but gave no authority for the estimate. Theal, I*b*. 396.

trade and traffic with the British and American whalers who put into the Bay despite the whaling monopoly granted by His Most Faithful Majesty to an overstaffed and official-ridden Portuguese company. Captain William Owen, R.N., then appeared and was told 1823. by the captain of the fort of Espirito Santo that the natives were none of his subjects. Owen therefore made treaties with some of the chiefs, securing the western and southern shores of Delagoa Bay and Inyaka and Elephant Islands for King George.[1]

In vain did Owen tell his country, somewhat in the style of the immortal Mrs. Jellyby, that Delagoa Bay 'opens all the interior of Africa to her commerce where millions of people are ready to receive clothing (and blankets and woollens are much more valued by them than cottons) and civilisation from her'; in vain did he dwell upon its value as a base for the suppression of the slave trade, and the danger that it might be occupied by the French or Americans or Russians; H.M. Government merely shelved the treaty and took no steps to make good the gallant captain's claims. So Delagoa Bay was left to the Portuguese, the mosquitoes and the tribes.[2] To the tribes especially, for, while Owen was yet at the Bay, the Angoni were slaughtering the tribes around and selling the spoils to the Portuguese. Presently Manikusa the Shangaan came to drive the Angoni north- 1833–ward, to sack most of the Portuguese posts south of the Zambesi, 1836. destroy the unlucky fort of Espirito Santo and make himself master of Gazaland.

On the other hand, it seemed likely that the port which was destined to become the most determined rival of Delagoa Bay would be incorporated in the British Empire. Two Englishmen, Francis Farewell and James King, were given leave by Somerset to trade with 1824. Natal. They bought a block of land round Port Natal, 100 miles by 30, from Chaka, who claimed the whole of Natal as his. There they were joined by a few other British traders and ivory-hunters, who lived, like the Portuguese further north, on sufferance of the native monarch, some of them ruling little groups of natives who had fled to them for protection and all, on occasion, helping the Zulus with their guns.[3] They made touch with the Cape Colony overland; but Farewell was killed on the way back, and, in the same year, the 1829. seizure and sale of their little ship *Elizabeth and Susan* by the customs officers at Port Elizabeth was a forcible reminder that Port Natal was not regarded as a British possession.[4]

However, further unattached Englishmen drifted in; Portuguese

[1] Rec. S.E.A., IX. 17 ff., 117 ff.; C. 1361 of 1875, pp. 14 ff.
[2] Rec. S.E.A., II. 472–3, 477; R. Coupland, *East Africa and its Invaders*, pp. 228, 235 ff.
[3] Bird, *Annals of Natal*, I. 71 ff., 86, 93, 193; Chase, *Natal Papers*, I. 25; Isaacs, *Travels*, p. 311; No. 252 of 1835, p. 25.
[4] Bird, I. 101; Cory, *op. cit.*, II. 366.

half-castes traded with the Natives, and American whalers talked of establishing themselves at the Port. On the other hand, the report

1828. that Chaka meant to attack the coast Kaffirs from behind suggested to the Cape Government that Natal was a point of strategic importance to themselves, and two more scares that the Zulus were about to attack the English at the Port indicated the need for offering them

1833. protection, even though Dingaan, Chaka's successor, on the latter occasion, had withdrawn all his people to the east of the Tugela.[1] At about the same time, the Colonial Secretary, Lord Goderich, discounting reports from Albany that the ubiquitous Yankees had designs in that quarter, bade Cole station an officer there to maintain good relations between the Zulus and the European families that

1832. were settling in their country: but the salary offered was too low, and an appointment which might have had important effects on the course of the Trek that was to come was never made.[2] D'Urban,

1834. however, on his arrival, was petitioned by Cape merchants, by the explorer, Dr. Andrew Smith, who had visited Dingaan two years previously, and by Captain Allan Gardiner, a naval officer turned Anglican missionary, to set up a government backed by a hundred troops at the Port. D'Urban noted that he had no troops to spare, and H.M. Government refused on the score of expense.[3]

Port Natal and Delagoa Bay were far away in the background. A Cape Governor was inevitably more concerned with what lay

1823. immediately beyond the colonial frontiers. Much that concerned
on- him already lay there, for the Colony was throwing out an ever-
wards. thickening fringe of skirmishers: missionaries, traders, trek-boers and ne'er-do-wells. The missionary flood ran strongly. The L.M.S. men established themselves on both sides of the Orange and Eastern Frontier, beyond which the Moravians also ventured; the Wesleyans stretched their line of outposts through Kaffirland to the far-distant Pondos; the Glasgow men and, presently, the Berlin Society went to the Xosas; the Rhenish and Paris Evangelicals arrived, the former to work within the Colony, the latter to go first to the Bechuana and then to the Basuto.[4]

The L.M.S. men and the Paris Evangelicals were thus pushing

[1] Bird, I. 195 ff.; No. 252 of 1835, pp. 57–9; Chase, op. cit., I. 34–5.
[2] C.O. 1318, April 20, 1831; C.O. 1320, May 25, 1832.
[3] V.R. Soc. No. XXXVI, Bird, I. 252, 272; No. 252 of 1835, pp. 93. 102.
[4] L.M.S. at Hankey, Kingwilliamstown, Knapp's Hope and Philipton (1825–1829); Moravians at Shiloh (1828); Wesleyans at Mount Coke, Butterworth, Old Morley, Clarkebury and Buntingville (1825–30); Glasgow Society at Old Lovedale, Balfour, Pirie and Burnshill (1824–30); Berlin Society at Bethal (Stutterheim, 1836); Rhenish Society among the Coloured Folk in various villages throughout the Colony (1829 onwards); Paris Evangelicals to Motito (1832), Morija (1833) and Thaba Bosigo (1837); U.S.A. Zulu Mission to Zululand and Mosega (1835); Church of England to Ungungundhlovu (1837–38) (vide J. du Plessis, Christian Missions).

along the first stages of the 'Missionaries Road' which led to Central Africa. Across that road, just beyond the Orange, lay Griqualand. History was rapidly in the making there. Soon after Andries *Circa* Waterboer had become captain at Griquatown, Barend Barends had 1820. wandered away to be despoiled by the Matabele, young Cornelis 1826. Kok II had gone north to Campbell, and Adam II, his brother, armed with a grant from Philip, had established himself at the abandoned Bushman mission station of Philippolis.[1] There were thus three little Griqua states: Griquatown and Campbell on the lower Vaal and Philippolis further to the east. Such civilisation as the Griquas had—and they had far more than had their poverty-stricken descendants at the time of the Diamond Fields dispute a generation later—they had either brought with them from the Colony or owed to the missionaries. The question was, how long could they and their superficial civilisation stand against the pressure which was being brought to bear from the south?

The tide of European migration, which had for so long swayed to and fro upon the Zuurveld, had swerved north-eastward. In 1824, the Colonial frontier had been carried up to the drifts of the Orange river opposite Philippolis in the wake of the advancing cattle-farmers. A year later, Boer cattle were grazing among the Griqua herds beyond the river; by 1833 at the latest, many Boers were living in Adam Kok II's country on land sold or leased to them by Griquas in defiance of missionary-Griqua law. These Boers regarded themselves as members of the Colony and paid their taxes at Colesberg; but they drove their cattle in dry seasons to Zevenfontein (Beersheba) on the Basuto border, and many of them were asking for the annexation of 'Transorangia' to the Colony.[2]

This prospective annexation was beginning to interest Boers within the Colony itself, for conditions were changing in the eastern parts and many of them disliked the change. From the general point of view of the Colony, the changes were all for the better. Population was denser than it had been when Somerset had made his verbal 1819. treaty with Gaika. A fairly solid block of British were living in Albany, and other groups further north, with scattered farms in between. Graaff-Reinet, thanks largely to the energy of Stockenstrom, could show 300 well-built houses, and Port Elizabeth 1200 inhabitants and two churches, while the 3700 citizens of Grahamstown, 'City of the Saints,' could boast four churches and a newspaper. Flocks and herds had improved in quantity and quality since 1827. Lieutenants Richard Daniell, Charles Griffith and Thomas White, three of those half-pay officers to whom the wool industry in New

---

[1] Chase, *Natal Papers*, II. 250 ff.   *Vide supra*, pp. 95, 129, 151.
[2] No. 425 of 1837, pp. 143 ff.; No. 252 of 1835, p. 77; Cole to Hay, Nov. 15, 1833.

South Wales and the Colony owes so much, had established merino sheep in Albany.[1] It was, indeed, already the stock argument of loyal Easterners in favour of Separation, or at the very least the removal of the capital eastward, that theirs was the richest and most progressive part of the Colony. But the ugly fact stared cattle-farmers in the face that land was less easy to get than it had been. The Kaffirs barred the way eastward, and when Cole offered grants of land along
1831. the Koonap river, Downing Street had decreed that only British and Hottentots were eligible.[2] Much worse was to come. Notice was
May. given that, in accordance with the so-called Ripon Scheme, Crown
1832. lands would no more be granted freely but sold at auction.[3] To the Government the projected new policy promised sorely needed revenue; to the Boers it meant that they and their sons would have to pay for what they had learnt to look on as the birthright of
1832. Afrikaners. Landless men petitioned in vain for leave to occupy land between the Vet and Sand rivers in the future Free State; then, as dissatisfaction with the Government's social policy increased, leading men, like Gerrit Maritz of Graaff-Reinet and Piet Retief of the Winterberg, began to talk of a large scale trek.[4] Though they denied any such intention as a 'calumny on the Boers' when other folk talked about it, they themselves spoke of it so openly that Fairbairn could write as if the Great Trek was actually in progress.[5] Fairbairn was mistaken; nevertheless, in the latter part of 1834, frontiersmen sent three *commissie trekke* to spy out the land: one to the dry and thirsty *Dorsteland* in the present South-West Africa, another to the Zoutpansberg in the far Northern Transvaal, the third and best known under Piet Uys through Kaffirland to Natal. They came back with the news that to the north and east there was fine land well-nigh bare of inhabitants to be had for the taking.

The Great Trek did not take place yet awhile, for the *commissie trekke* came back to find a Kaffir war raging. On the Eastern Frontier, cattle-farming was still the staple industry and cattle-stealing the custom of the Kaffirs. In Somerset's time, the point of friction had been near Macomo's kraal on the Kat river. Macomo robbed and the failure of the Baviaan's river Boers to recover their cattle em-
1821 boldened him. The relaxation of the restrictions on trade with the
on- Kaffirs in Albany had led to quarrels ending sometimes in bloodshed,
wards. and in spite of the increase of the frontier guard, cattle were stolen, sold in Albany and then restolen. According to local officials the colonial losses were heavy and, as a rule, recoveries comparatively small; but as the later history of the Basuto border suggests, both in

---

[1] Cory, II. 427.   [2] No. 252 of 1835, p. 57.
[3] C.O. 1319, S. of S. to Gov., Jan. 10, 1832. In the event, Crown lands were not auctioned till much later (Robertson, *Systematic Colonization*).
[4] Bird, I. 231, 252, 504; Preller, *Voortrekkermense*, I. 275 ff.
[5] *Comercial Advertiser*, June 21, 1834.

Sovereignty and early Free State days, men who claim compensation always 'stand upon their biggest foot.' The losses were certainly not all on one side. Troops and burghers twice read Macomo a lesson; a little later another force crossed the Keiskamma, and similar raids became easier after 1827 when the infantry section of the Cape Corps was disbanded and the cavalry section was renamed the Cape Mounted Rifles. Probably the colonists took as many cattle as they lost; it is possible that they took more, for they rated colonial cattle higher and higher in terms of Kaffir beasts as the quality of their own improved;[1] but what the Kaffirs objected to was that they took land. 1823–
1825.

In describing frontier affairs, it is easy to lay too much stress upon cattle. Cattle-stealing and reprisals were a perpetual harassment and at times a *casus belli*; but land and water were the fundamental factors in the problem of the Kaffir as of the Griqua frontier. On both sides of the Eastern frontier were peoples who to a greater or lesser degree were agriculturists, both wasteful of land and both relying mainly on their cattle. And cattle all the world over demand water and wide pastures. The struggle for the Zuurveld, where both races had been newcomers, had been settled in favour of the white men by Cradock's campaign. The contest had thereby been transferred to the lands between the Fish and the Keiskamma. Gaika had virtually given away this Neutral Territory by a verbal treaty, which was no treaty in the eyes of resident clans who by no means universally regarded him as paramount. There was some show of right for what he had done in the northern half where he himself lived, but the Gunukwebe clans claimed the southern half as theirs. The territory had been steadily occupied from both sides, sometimes by mutual consent, sometimes without. The abortive settlement of Fredericksburg had been more than balanced by Macomo's return to the Kat; then Somerset had allowed farmers to settle as far east as the Koonap river, and allowed the friendly Gunukwebe chiefs, Pato, Kama and Kobe, to graze cattle in their old lands;[2] Bourke had allowed them to reoccupy those lands in what was now called the Ceded Territory, and other chiefs had crept back on sufferance, notably Tyali to the Mancazana next to his brother, Macomo. Meanwhile, Somerset had recognised that Ndhlambi and Dushane were independent of Gaika and had allowed them to come back from the lands east of the Buffalo, where they had been lurking since 1819, to die in peace on the further bank of the Keiskamma.

1812.

1819.

1821.

1825.

1824.

1828.

The restlessness of the Xosas was partly due to the pressure exerted by the Zulus on the tribes piled up in their rear. Tembus

---

[1] No. 538 of 1836, p. 283; No. 50 of 1835, pp. 183, 190 ff.; Cory, III. 331; Theal, IIb. 3; Rec. C.C., XXXI. 282; XXXIV. 51; XXXV. 21.

[2] No. 252 of 1835, p. 139; No. 538 of 1836, p. 52; Rec. C.C., XXV. 230; Cory, II. 215; No. 50 of 1835, p. 177.

1827. were pushed into the Colony and were duly pushed back by the Colonial Government, and in response to an alarm that Chaka was
1828. coming, troops, burghers and friendly Kaffirs, marched beyond the Bashee river, where they overthrew a fierce horde of Amangwane (Fetcani) under the impression that they were Zulus. Chaka duly
1829. raided Pondoland and was presently murdered, while the wrecks of the Amangwane became Fingos, 'the dogs' of the Xosas. These Fingos and many other Bantu from beyond the frontier soon showed how impossible it was to keep the races apart when employers called from one side of the dividing line and labourers responded from the other, for, armed with passes issued by field cornets in terms of Bourke's 49th Ordinance of 1828, they began to seek and find work on farms within the Colony.[1] This intermingling of the races was forcibly hastened by Macomo, who, as Regent for the young Sandile since Gaika's death, chased stray Tembus into the Tarka district. Sir Lowry Cole, the new Governor, took comprehensive measures. Without actually repealing Bourke's Ordinance, he virtually suspended it by forbidding field cornets to issue any more passes and commanding them to see to it that wandering passless immigrant Bantu were sent back whence they had come.[2] He then drove Macomo out, carried the frontier up to the hills west of the Tyumie and a line drawn thence to the Kat below Fort Beaufort, settled Hottentots in the Kat River Settlement on Macomo's lands and warned the other chiefs in the Ceded Territory that they were there on sufferance. At this there was excitement in all Kaffirland as far as
1830. Hintsa's kraal beyond the Kei; but, undismayed, Cole stationed troops at Gwalana Post to overawe the Gunukwebes, though under the guidance of the Wesleyan, William Shaw, they had given Albany but little trouble, and proceeded to grant small farms on the Kat river. Twice thereafter Macomo was allowed to come back from the dry eastern lands to the valleys west of the Tyumie; twice he was
1833. expelled, and with him, as a rule, his brother, Tyali;[3] finally the site of Old Lovedale mission station was annexed to the Colony. Well might Macomo, with all his sins heavy upon him, ask on the eve of the war, 'When shall I and my people be able to get rest?' It was a question that was beginning to trouble other chiefs, for already the men of Albany, Graaff-Reinet and Somerset were driving their herds far into Kaffirland because of the drought, and Louis Trigardt, the future Voortrekker, was firmly established with a group of Boer families on the Indwe beyond the Kei.[4]

---

[1] Theal, IIb. 11 ff.; S. Patterson, *Colour and Culture in South Africa*, p. 27.
[2] Theal, IIb. 11 ff.; Cory, II. 341, 350–61, 367–82; Macmillan, *Bantu, Boer and Briton*, p. 66.
[3] No. 252 of 1835, pp. 21 ff.; 35, 42 ff.; 52 ff.; Proclamation, Aug. 2, 1830.
[4] No. 538 of 1836, p. 555; Campbell to D'Urban, June 27, 1834; Cory, IV. 3.

The Colonial Government was struggling to maintain an impossible system. Police, closer settlement and magisterial control of both Europeans and tribesmen would alone bring peace with security, and most of these were still to seek. The constant changes in Somerset's reprisal system tell the story. Somerset had allowed patrols of troops and aggrieved farmers to take back their own cattle or, if they could not find them, an equivalent in Kaffir stock; Bourke would allow no patrols to enter Kaffirland unless the stolen cattle were in sight; Cole let them go in and recover lifted cattle, but not take Kaffir beasts in lieu thereof. Cole's system was as liable to abuse on this as on any other frontier in recorded history, and the traders who swarmed into Kaffirland as soon as permission to enter 1830. had been given, made matters worse in spite of Wade's efforts to control the sale of gunpowder.[1]

Such was the situation that faced D'Urban on his arrival. He was Jan. under orders to find a substitute for the commando system, 'that 1834. fearful scourge' to the tribes, as Lord Stanley, the Colonial Secretary, called it, though the experienced Stockenstrom begged leave to doubt whether it was so black as it was painted, and Cole had found it so unpopular among the northern farmers at least that he had had to stiffen up the rules of service.[2] D'Urban was also empowered to devote £600 to the payment of 'prudent and intelligent men,' who should act as agents to the most suitable border chiefs and induce them to control their men.

Stanley's plan was a tentative and parsimonious adaptation of Indian methods of government to South Africa. A more comprehensive and ambitious policy was put forward by Philip. Philip had been thoroughly alarmed at what he had seen on a trek through Griqualand in 1832. He had at once urged Wade to annex the Griqua states to the Colony and secure the lands of the Griquas to them on the same lines as at the Kat River Settlement. Thus would the half-Europeanised Griquas, who lived in compact villages and not on scattered farms like the Boers, but who yet fought in Boer fashion, become 'a wall of iron' shielding the Colony from the terrors of the Bantu north and keeping the colonists to the south within the colonial borders. Failing annexation, he recommended that Andries Waterboer, who was well under missionary control, be made commandant of all the Griquas and, in return for a small salary, be called upon to keep the peace from the Caledon to the Atlantic.[3]

Philip spoke with a less certain voice about the Kaffirs. He knew less about them and was less interested in them than in the Griquas;

---

[1] No. 538 of 1836, p. 283; Ordinances 49 of 1826 and 99 of 1833; No. 252 of 1835, pp. 34, 75 ff., 83.
[2] No. 252 of 1835, pp. 60, 64, 66.
[3] No. 538 of 1836, pp. 608, 625–6, 633; No. 425 of 1837, pp. 143 ff.

but he did tell D'Urban that he would not object to his annexing
Kaffirland 'even from the Keiskamma to Delagoa Bay,' provided he
civilised the tribes on their lands 'on the plan adopted by the ancient
Romans.' [1] Presently, acting on a hint from Stockenstrom, he advised
him to settle Hottentots as another wall of iron along the Eastern
Frontier and to treat certain Kaffir chiefs as Government officials,
hold them responsible for cattle thefts and for dealings with the
tribes behind them, and support them, for a time at least, with troops. [2]
D'Urban, who had come to the Colony without any marked leanings
towards philanthropy, was inclined to listen to Philip at this time,
but he had neither men nor money for anything more than Stanley's
'Indian' policy. He decided to apply it to the northern border first.
He repeated the old orders that no one was to go beyond the frontiers without leave, and added that in no wise must slaves, who were
so soon to be freed, be taken across them. Then, ten days before the
Dec.   outbreak of the Kaffir war, he signed a treaty with Andries Water-
1834. boer under which the Griqua chief was to receive a small salary and
some guns, admit the Rev. Peter Wright as Resident to Griquatown [3]
and keep order in the valley of the Orange from Kheis to Ramah
on either side of the Missionaries' Road just beyond the north-
western confines of the Colony.

The sudden outbreak of the Kaffir war prevented similar arrangements being made on the east. Moravians, Wesleyans and L.M.S.
men for some time past had dilated on the peaceful prospects there;
but D'Urban, Philip and Colonel Henry Somerset, the ex-Governor's
son in command of the frontier troops, believed that prompt action
was necessary. There was no immediate fear of a crisis, said Colonel
Somerset, but 'Come quickly,' and he got leave for Macomo and Tyali
to return to their valleys pending a general settlement whose character
should be determined by their behaviour. Between May and July,
Macomo handed back a number of cattle, but his behaviour
Aug.   was less reassuring when he and Tyali retailed their woes at
1834. a meeting of the Ndhlambi clans at Burnshill, where the young men
mustered armed with guns. The Kat River Hottentots were restive
on the score of the proposed vagrancy law; there followed much
coming and going across the border; traders were molested and
Hintsa, head of the Galeka Xosas, left Butterworth to join Trigardt
near the White Kei.

At D'Urban's request Philip visited the border tribes telling them
that the Governor was coming to redress grievances. [4] Doubtless
Philip led the chiefs to overrate his influence with the Governor and

---

[1] No. 538 of 1836, p. 693.   [2] No. 538, pp. 697 ff.
[3] No. 252 of 1835, pp. 115–16; *Treaties . . . 1803–54*, p. 13.
[4] Macmillan, *op. cit.*, p. 240; No. 503 of 1837, pp. 163 ff.

let them see that he himself thought the patrols and the occupation of the Ceded Territory were among their grievances, for he had urged D'Urban to allow selected chiefs to settle in the territory under treaty, there to be civilised by missionaries and well-paid residents; but it was noted that cattle thefts diminished markedly while he was on the frontier. So he waited till he could wait no longer for a Governor who never came, and even before he had set out for Capetown, Somerset, anxious to recover outstanding cattle before D'Urban's arrival, whipped up his patrols.[1] Scuffles ensued; royal blood was shed; Macomo and Tyali, possibly thinking that they were now beyond the pale, called up their warriors to leave their gardens unreaped, and, at the head of 12,000 men, poured into the Colony. Dec. 21, 1834.

For two weeks the Xosas ravaged the country from Algoa Bay to Somerset East. Retief, however, checked them in the Winterberg; Somerset held out in Grahamstown; the Hottentots remained quiet; Colonel Harry Smith raced overland from Capetown to Grahamstown to take command; reinforcements and, at last, the Governor arrived, and the Eastern Frontier folk recovered from their panic so completely that Smith could note that 'those who funked the most formerly' were now the most valiant.[2] Now that the British Tommies were come, the counter-attack was pushed beyond the Kei, for Hintsa and, the authorities had reason to believe, Trigardt also had egged on the Gaika Xosas to war and were acting as 'bush' to the captured colonial cattle and horses. Smith obliged Hintsa to promise a large indemnity in cattle, proclaimed the land between the Keiskamma and the Kei as Queen Adelaide Province, and announced that hostile tribes would be driven beyond the Kei into Hintsa's country 'for ever.' Next day, Hintsa, while trying to escape, was shot by George Southey in self-defence; Macomo was sent to Robben Island, and Kreli, Hintsa's son, was installed as great chief by D'Urban subject to his late father's liabilities. D'Urban then dismissed the burghers.[3] May 10, 1835. June 1835.

Smith fixed his headquarters at Kingwilliamstown and built forts in the new province of Queen Adelaide, but, try as he would, he could not 'exterminate'[4] the Kaffirs. They refused to be sent beyond the Kei and even raided the Colony. So, yielding to the logic of facts and the remonstrances of the missionaries, who were solidly against depriving the tribes of their lands, D'Urban radically modified his policy. He called out the burghers again after the sowing, got into touch with the chiefs through the Wesleyans, William Boyce and

---

[1] No. 252 of 1835, pp. 117, 119; No. 538 of 1836, pp. 550–6; No. 503 of 1837, pp. 75, 212; Boyce, *Notes*, p. 13.
[2] Smith, *Autobiography*, p. 721.
[3] No. 252 of 1835, p. 132; No. 279 of 1836, pp. 11, 41; 48 ff., 51.
[4] 'Exterminate' means 'expel'.

Sept. 1835.   William Shepstone, and made peace with the Xosas. This time the chiefs were promised reserves in Queen Adelaide, provided they gave up their arms, became British subjects under the laws of the Colony, held themselves responsible for cattle thefts, accepted missionaries and Government agents and forbore to enter the Colony in arms or without a pass.[1] This was in many ways the very policy Philip had recommended; but there was this difference: D'Urban still proposed to settle Europeans round the forts and along a broad belt of land across Queen Adelaide and to give out all the Ceded Territory in farms, except where it was occupied by Hottentots and Gunukwebes and the 17,000 Fingos, whom he was bringing out of Kaffirland to a reserve round Fort Peddie with the cattle which their Xosa masters had left in their charge.[2] In this way, helped by a superintending agent at Grahamstown, he hoped to substitute colonial law for tribal custom and to introduce the Kaffirs to industry and civilisation, religion and morality 'by the power of legal coercion . . . humane persuasion and example' behind the presumably defensible barrier of the Kei.[3]

Oct. 1835.   D'Urban rounded off his conquests by annexing the troubled area north of the Stormberg mountains as far as the Kraai river, where some 150 Boer families were living as members of the Colony *in partibus*.[4] But, as the forces of law and order closed in, Louis Trigardt, hearing that there was a warrant out against him, slipped away northwards across the Orange. He was soon joined by Jan van Rensburg's party. The Great Trek had begun, a warning that the affairs of the Colony were passing beyond the control of a mere Colonial Governor.

D'Urban's immediate measures, on his return to Capetown, showed that he was aware of that fact. Busied though he was with the examination of the claims for slave compensation, he found time to consider the relations of the Colony to the chiefs beyond the Orange and to the Englishmen settled on the south-east coast of Africa. During the war, Moshesh, chief of the Basuto, had plundered the Xosas and, though he had lost most of his booty, he was evidently a potentate to be reckoned with. D'Urban, therefore asked Dr. Andrew Smith to come to terms with him and those like him. Smith visited all the chiefs on either side of the Caledon and then crossed the Vaal to the kraals of Msilikazi, King of the Matabele. He gave these rulers medals and reported that since they now looked on

[1] No. 279 of 1836, pp. 95 ff.; No. 538 of 1836, pp. 496, 629, 721 ff.; Boyce, *Notes*, App. II.; No. 503 of 1837, p. 253.
[2] No. 279 of 1836, p. 16; No. 424 of 1851, p. 20.
[3] No. 279 of 1836, p. 102. On D'Urban's policy *vide* D'Urban Papers (Cape Archives); D'Urban-Smith Papers (S.A. Public Library); *The Kaffir War of 1835* (ed. Theal); *Treaties . . . 1803–54*, pp. 17 ff.
[4] No. 503 of 1837, p. 6.

themselves as 'white men under the white King,' it would be well
to enter into treaties with them. Accordingly, a treaty of friendship March
was concluded with the Matabele at their king's request.[1]   1836.

Nor was far-distant Port Natal forgotten. Captain Allan Gardiner
had already gone thither hoping to establish his mission beyond the
Tugela in Zululand itself. Therein he failed, for he had to deal with
the suspicious Dingaan, who had cleared the way to the throne in
1828 by murdering Chaka. On the other hand, Gardiner had soon
taken the lead among the settlers at the Port and made a treaty with
Dingaan under which he promised to hand back Zulu refugees in
future to their lord, but in return secured the promise of the southern
half of Natal. True, Chaka and Dingaan had already ceded that
country either in whole or in part to Farewell, Nathaniel Isaacs and
the Grahamstown trader, James Collis; but since all three beneficiaries were either dead or departed, Gardiner boldly named the
territory the District of Victoria in honour of the young princess on
whom the hopes of all good Englishmen were set, organised the little
settlement at the Port as the township of Durban, and asked Sir
Benjamin to take over the country.[2] The distant Governor appreciated the importance of a base in the rear of the Xosas; indeed, during
the war just ended he had sent embassies to secure the goodwill of
the Tembus and Pondos who lay between those tribesmen and Natal;
besides, now that United States Presbyterian missionaries were on
their way to the Port, it needed no German Emperor to tell him that
'the blood of the martyrs is the seed of the Empire.' He therefore
supported Gardiner's request.[3]

Thus far D'Urban's settlement within and without the borders of
the Colony. He was immensely popular, especially in the eastern
districts, partly by reason of his frontier settlement and partly
because, without encouraging the Separatist agitation which had
been revived in Grahamstown, he had told the Colonial Secretary,
Lord Glenelg, that the capital ought to be removed to Uitenhage or,
failing that, a Lieutenant-Governor be appointed in spite of the risk
of friction with the Governor.[4] The annexation of Queen Adelaide
in May had held out the hope of compensation in land to the
frontiersmen who had suffered most from the Kaffir inroad and
the wastage of the ensuing campaign. That had been the hope of the
Easterners, official and unofficial, throughout the war, and it was to
that point of view that D'Urban had at first conformed. His much
less sweeping September policy had caused something of a chill which

---

[1] No. 503 of 1837, pp. 347–50; *Treaties* . . . *1803–54*, p. 35.
[2] *Treaties* . . . *1803–54*, p. 15; Eybers, p. 143; Bird, I. 307–12; Chase, *op.
cit.*, I. 42.
[3] Bird, I. 198 ff.; No. 503 of 1837, p. 14.
[4] No. 279 of 1836, p. 58; *Grahamstown Journal*, Nov. 5, 1835.

even affected the perfervid columns of the *Grahamstown Journal*; nevertheless, land would still be available and the Governor was besieged with requests for farms in the Ceded Territory, Queen Adelaide and the Stormberg area.[1]

The frontiersmen's attitude was natural. 'Seven thousand of His Majesty's subjects were, in one week, driven to utter destitution'; one hundred Europeans and Hottentots had been killed, 455 farms had been burnt and many thousands of horses, cattle and sheep carried off, and, of the cattle taken or retaken, most had been eaten by the troops and commandos during nine months of war, and now many burghers were too impoverished to buy the remnant at auction even with two months' credit. The total colonial losses amounted to perhaps £300,000. Of course, in proportion to their wealth, the Kaffir losses were much more severe: scores of warriors slain, kraals and gardens destroyed freely and 60,000 head of cattle taken, besides nearly all their goats and the cattle stolen by the Fingos and Basuto. Incidentally, the campaign had cost the British taxpayer £154,000 over and above the usual £96,000 for the expenses of the garrison.[2]

The Kaffirs had struck first and must pay the forfeit of war. But to make the settlement a real one was not an easy matter. For one thing, the Colony had burst its bounds. Louis Trigardt and Jan van Rensburg were well on their way to the Zoutpansberg and other parties were drifting about just within the borders. In spite of the legend which afterwards grew up that cattle thefts had been almost unknown during the D'Urban regime, there were robberies during the post-war confusion in the annexed territories and the parts adjacent. Harry Smith, however, gradually got it under by dint of martial law and 'Smith law,' by dint also of retaining the Hottentots long after their term of service had expired. He had long ago lost caste with the 'Settler party,' for he made no secret of the fact that he held that Grahamstown, by reason of the many alarmist reports that emanated therefrom, 'ought to be called "Necessity" for it is the mother of invention.'[3] The Hottentot soldiery, however, were willing to stay as long as he was there to lead them, his native police recovered considerable numbers of stolen cattle, he himself liked the tribesmen and was liked by them in return. Even Macomo was well-disposed in spite of his frank determination to recover his Kat river lands some day, and Tyali restored stolen beasts and saw to it that the thief was thrashed.[4]

[1] *Grahamstown Journal*, Sept. 25, Oct. 8, 1835; Chase, *op. cit.*, II. 298; *Speeches . . of the late John Mitford Bowker* (1864), p. 264.
[2] No. 279 of 1836, pp. 15 ff., 86 ff.; No. 503 of 1837, pp. 43, 69. The official estimate of 4000 warriors slain was an exaggeration. (Cf. Stockenstrom, No. 1334 of 1851, p. 13.)
[3] Smith, *Autobiography*, p. 725.
[4] Various letters from C. L. Stretch, afterwards Gaika commissioner, July 1835–Nov. 1836.

But everything depended on Smith, and the question was, How long could he hold his own? D'Urban was short of men and money and knew that he was responsible to Secretaries of State who, however rapidly they might succeed one another, were all agreed that respect for the inalienable rights of Natives to their lands was 'the only policy which it becomes this country to observe.'[1] Doubts were soon raised as to the wisdom of the settlement. Was it wise to bring thousands of savages under colonial law? Was it of any real advantage to push the frontier a hundred miles farther away from the base at Grahamstown? Even though D'Urban proposed to make a new base at Kingwilliamstown and the banks of the Kei were less bushy than those of the Fish, the new line to be defended was fully as long as the old and more distant from the main mass of the Colony.

Then there were the missionaries. Most of them held that the war had been forced upon the Colony, and all of them had supported the Government in its conduct of the actual fighting. Philip had called on the mission Hottentots to assist; both he and Fairbairn had insisted as strongly as did Boyce, no great admirer of them and their works, that 'we must be masters'; they had even approved of strong measures against 'good king Hintsa' and did not object to the annexation of Queen Adelaide.[2] Leading missionaries were even numbered among the prophets. 'Our power,' wrote Boyce, 'will advance, and that within a few years, as far as the Tropics', and Philip added that 'an able Governor might in twelve years influence the continent of Africa as far as the Tropics . . . for good, make every tribe to know its limits.' But D'Urban's 'extermination' policy of May set them all against him.[3] That policy was simply Cradock's *refoulement* on a grand scale. It would only relieve the pressure on the Fish-Keiskamma border and allow Colonists to settle along the Kei with the certainty of future trouble with the Kaffirs crowded together on the lands of the unwilling Galekas. If so, was the frontier to be pushed back again to the Bashee or 'if it could be,' to the Umzimvubu?

The Philip party was up in arms at once against D'Urban's original 'extermination' policy. Their protests were laid before Glenelg, who, as the son of Charles Grant, a leading light of the famous Clapham Sect, was philanthropically inclined. On receipt of Oct. D'Urban's despatch announcing that policy, he replied coldly for-1835. bidding him to give away land or to build forts because his annexation might have to be abandoned. D'Urban then maintained a masterly silence for several months, when he announced his second

---

[1] No. 252 of 1835, p. 117.

[2] Boyce, *Notes*, p. 21 and Appendix I.; No. 538 of 1836, p. 554; *S.A. Comm. Adv.*, Jan. 7, 24, and May 23, 1835.

[3] No. 538 of 1836, pp. 57, 496, 631; Boyce, *Notes*, pp. 5, 32. Extermination= rooting or driving out rather than wiping out.

modified policy, still leaving Glenelg to gather that much land was
to be granted to Europeans.[1]

Aug.
1835.
The Secretary of State, however, had more to rely upon than
L.M.S. reports. The Commons had appointed an Aborigines Committee to consider the relations of European subjects of the King
with 'aborigines' in all parts of the Empire. The Committee sat at
once for a month and heard much from Andries Stockenstrom. He
was, in their eyes, the expert witness, the man from the spot, a
colonist born, an official and a landowner on the frontier of twenty-
five years' standing, a man who had led commandos and was
destined to get into trouble for what he was alleged to have done on
one of them. His evidence was damaging to the old reprisals system
and to some of the colonists. Like Harry Smith and other frontier
officials after him, he held that farmers were partly to blame for their
own losses in that they did not look after their cattle on a frontier
innocent of fences, and added that there were men on the frontier,
as on most frontiers, to whom 'peace would be a losing game.' He
censured some of Philip's statements about officials and farmers;
but he also advised that the Bushmen be placed in missionary
reserves, the Hottentots be settled if possible alongside of Europeans
as had been the original intention at the Kat River Settlement, and
'new colonies' for Europeans be founded, if required, among the
Kaffirs on land secured from the tribes by treaty. Such land could be
sold to settlers and the proceeds devoted to the civilisation of the
Kaffirs in the reserves that remained to them. In other words, he
recommended a policy of partial segregation.[2]

In face of this information and still, apparently, in ignorance of
D'Urban's September policy which would leave the Xosas in Queen
Adelaide as British subjects, Glenelg wrote his well-known despatch
of December, 1835, excusing the Kaffirs for their attack in the light
of their past wrongs, warning D'Urban that a Lieutenant-Governor
was coming and bidding him 'prepare the public mind' for the
abandonment of the new province. But he explicitly stated that he
was giving these orders on the assumption that his unofficial information was correct and that, if the Governor knew of facts to the
contrary, it would be his duty to inform him and to suspend any
part of these instructions he saw fit until he should receive 'further
directions.'[3] What followed is almost incredible. Even allowing for
the fact that D'Urban interpreted this long and confusing despatch
as orders to withdraw and necessarily required time to collect data
in support of his apologia, it is hard to understand why he did not
write some sort of defence of his policy till June 1836, nor post it till

[1] No. 503 of 1837, p. 1; No. 279 of 1836, pp. 86 ff.
[2] No. 538 of 1836, pp. 183 ff., 248; No. 503 of 1837, p. 285.
[3] No. 279 of 1836, pp. 59 ff.

the following December.[1] He thereby probably set up a record even for the leisurely official tradition of those days.

Rumour was soon abroad that Queen Adelaide was to be given up. London merchants cancelled sailings; in the Colony, both Afrikaners and British protested against any tampering with D'Urban's modified settlement, and Hendrik Potgieter, the future founder of the Transvaal, trekked. Meanwhile, Stockenstrom was appointed Lieutenant-Governor of the Eastern Province excluding Beaufort West, and the Aborigines Committee met once more. It heard, among others, Colonel Thomas Wade and Captain William Dundas, ex-colonial officials, Shaw, the Wesleyan missionary, and Philip and his followers: James Read and his half-breed son, Stoffles a Hottentot from Kat river, and Jan Tzatsoe a young Kaffrarian chief.[2] The evidence of the first three taken as a whole gave a balanced account of frontier conditions; that of the last five was adverse to the colonists. On the head of policy, Philip repeated his advice to keep Queen Adelaide and secure the Kaffirs their land therein. Unfortunately he did not press the point, and the Committee listened to Strockenstrom and the general body of philanthropists who were for wholesale abandonment and an extension of Stanley's treaty system.

Feb. 1836. Feb.-Aug. 1836.

So the Committee adjourned to draft its massive report, while Philip and his samples of South African humanity became the lions of the United Kingdom's philanthropic season. The Committee's conclusion was that the care of aborigines must devolve, not on colonial legislatures but on imperial officials, who were to regulate labour contracts and the sale of firearms and spirits; then, with an eye on white infiltration into still independent New Zealand, that British subjects going beyond the borders and acquiring land did so at their own risk, and that in any case no new territory was to be annexed without a preliminary Act of Parliament; finally, that, as a general rule, treaties with tribes were to be discouraged because of the disparity of the parties, but that, in view of its peculiar circumstances, the Cape should enter into some such arrangement with the tribes upon its borders.[3]

These conclusions coincided with Glenelg's own opinions. He 'warmly concurred' in the findings of the court of inquiry which exonerated all concerned in the death of 'good King Hintsa,' and naturally approved of Dr. Smith's dealings with the northern tribes and of the Matabele treaty.[4] But he declined to annex Natal and merely permitted D'Urban to send thither a magistrate under the

---

[1] No. 503 of 1837, pp. 54 ff.; Cory, III. 314. There were 254 enclosures to D'Urban's despatch.
[2] No. 538 of 1836, vide index. [3] No. 238 of 1837, pp. 76 ff.
[4] No. 503 of 1837, pp. 269, 351.

Aug.
1835.
Cape of Good Hope Punishment Act, which Parliament had just passed on the half-hearted recommendation of the Aborigines Committee.[1] Disclaiming all sovereignty, that Act rendered British subjects amenable to the Cape courts for crimes committed in uncivilised parts south of the 25th degree of south latitude, provided they and the witnesses could be sent back to the Colony. With these shadowy powers, Captain Gardiner set out for Port Natal in May 1837 as magistrate.

July.
1836.
By that time, Queen Adelaide was a bitter memory. In spite of the protests of the Easterners, Stockenstrom landed at Capetown as Lieutenant-Governor of the Eastern Province. D'Urban had expected that he would bring him fresh instructions; but, since Glenelg was still waiting for the expected official report from the Cape, Stockenstrom brought nothing beyond a hint that the Stormberg area might possibly be retained as a native reserve. The two men therefore agreed to carry on with D'Urban's modified policy till further orders. No sooner, however, had Stockenstrom proceeded to the East to take over from Smith, than D'Urban cancelled the martial law which Smith and Stockenstrom agreed was the sole means by which Queen Adelaide could be maintained.[2]

Aug.
1836.

Stockenstrom had a very mixed reception in the East. The Settlers showed their feelings as boldly as they dared; but the army officers gave him a good reception to atone for Grahamstown's chilly welcome and the Boers declined to join in the outcry against him which, they said, was due to the fact that he, the son of a Swede, was Dutch.[3] Nevertheless, at this stage, Gerrit Maritz set off with a large party of Trekkers, and Smith reported that many other Boers were waiting just beyond the borders to see if Queen Adelaide was to be abandoned before trekking too, Boers who according to Retief, would return if they were assured of security.[4] No such security as they desired was given. Stockenstrom began to concentrate the troops from the forts along the vulnerable Fish frontier. D'Urban tried to stop him, for his idea now was to make the southern part of the old Ceded Territory a kind of Somerset Nomansland. Then, on receipt of another letter from London which conveyed no fresh orders for lack of information on which to base them, but which showed that Glenelg still favoured withdrawal, D'Urban suddenly threw Queen Adelaide to the winds and ordered instant evacuation.[5]

Oct.
1836.

Dec.
1836.
Stockenstrom therefore released the Kaffir chiefs from their allegiance and made treaties with them. The colonial frontier of 1829

[1] Eybers, p. 146; Bird, I. 313.
[2] Eybers, p. 39; C.O. 1447, Gov. to S. of S., Aug. 23 and Dec. 2, 1836.
[3] Stretch, June 14, 1836.   [4] Preller, Piet Retief, pp. 50-1.
[5] No. 503, p. 44.

was maintained, for he had long ago pointed out that farmers could not be expected to go back to the old line of 1819. Beyond Cole's line in the Ceded Territory, the tribes were still to be British subjects and must respect the Fingos at Fort Peddie; but they were to be ruled by their chiefs, the troops were not to 'scour the bush' and cattle were to be watched in future by armed herdsmen. There and in Kaffirland, Government agents were stationed with leading chiefs; elaborate rules were drawn up for the recovery of cattle; patrols were forbidden to enter Kaffirland on the one hand and armed Kaffirs to enter the Colony on the other, and Europeans who ventured into Kaffirland were warned that they did so at their own risk and rendered themselves liable to expulsion by the chiefs.[1]

Thus was Queen Adelaide Province left to God, the missionaries, the new Government agents and the tribes by what Glenelg afterwards called 'this premature abandonment,' the prospect of which had moved Fairbairn and Mrs. John Philip to dismay.[2]

Stockenstrom carried out the abandonment under a running fire of criticism from the Grahamstown men and petitions to Parliament for an inquiry and compensation for their war losses.[3] Friction increased between the Governor and himself. He was jealous and quarrelsome, D'Urban incurably dilatory. D'Urban could only approach the Eastern officials through him, and he himself must write to Downing Street through Capetown, where the Governor stored up his despatches for months at a time and then sent them on in bales to the unhappy Glenelg. He also fell foul of Retief, the leading Boer official on the frontier. Retief complained that the new frontier system was impossible and asked for security and sympathetic government.[4] Stockenstrom, suspicious of Retief's pre-war activities and the nature of the security demanded, would only promise 'strict justice' in stiff and ever stiffer tones, and even warned Retief that he might have to deprive him of his commandantship. At last, Retief decided to trek, and challenged authority by publishing Feb. his reasons for so doing. Stockenstrom, much to D'Urban's annoy- 1837. ance, promptly dismissed him for disturbing the public mind.[5]

So the months passed gloomily and confusedly. It is true that, after the first 'eating-up' of opponents by the Gaika chiefs in the turmoil of the abandonment, the agents were able to report growing peace, very few thefts of European cattle, and the recovery of stolen beasts by Botman and the redoubtable Macomo. On the other hand,

[1] No. 503 of 1837, p. 3; No. 424 of 1851, p. 2; *Cape Govt. Gazette*, June 9, 1837; *Treaties . . . 1803–54*, pp. 37 ff., 73–92.
[2] Mrs. Philip to Philip, Dec. 1836 (verbal information by W. M. Macmillan).
[3] *Grahamstown Journal*, Jan. 28, May 5 and Sept. 8, 1836.
[4] *Ibid.*, Nov. 17, 1836; Preller, *Piet Retief*, pp. 40 ff.; Chase, I. 54 ff.
[5] Stretch to Fairbairn, Feb. 17, 1837; No. 424 of 1851, p. 23; Eybers, p. 143, Cory, III. 396, and *Grahamstown Journal*, Feb. 2, 1837, for Retief's Manifesto.

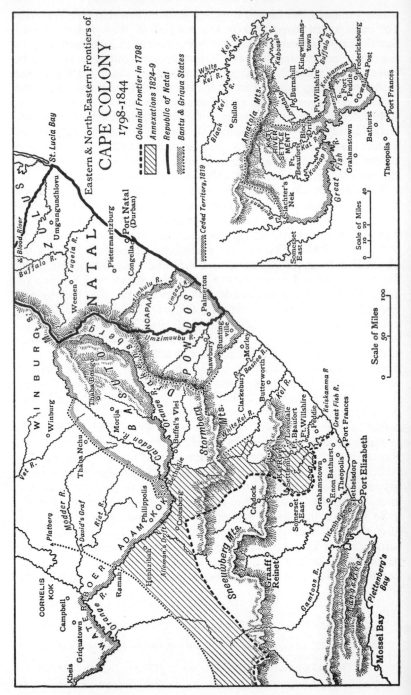

Eastern & North-Eastern Frontiers of
CAPE COLONY
1798–1844

- - - - Colonial Frontier in 1798
///// Annexations 1824–9
▬▬▬ Republic of Natal
\\\\\ Bantu & Griqua States

these very chiefs and Stockenstrom soon had to complain that D'Urban's pass-law against extra-colonial Kaffirs was useless for lack of magistrates and police to enforce it.;[1] attempts to hold Umhela, great chief of the Ndhlambis, responsible for a raid by his followers on the Peddie Fingos failed; some of Stockenstrom's own cattle were taken; the Fingos drifted to and fro; Englishmen in some cases sold their farms and withdrew westward from the frontier since they did not know how to trek, while Boers sold their places, turned their paper money into golden sovereigns and, with their flocks and herds, great still in spite of all, set out northward.[2]

The year of Queen Victoria's accession, 1837, was the great year of the Trek. Pieter Retief, Pieter Uys and Pieter Jacobs all moved off in that year. By September, some 2000 souls, 'the flower of the frontiersmen,' as D'Urban called them, had crossed the Orange river.

CHAPTER VIII

THE GREAT TREK, 1835–48

The Republic of Natal: causes of the Great Trek, 196; organisation, 200; inhabitants of the Trek area, 201; Trigardt, 203; Thaba Nchu Constitution, Mosega and Marico, 204; D'Urban, Napier and the Trekkers, 206; Retief, 207; first British occupation of Natal, 209; Andries Pretorius and Blood River, 209; the Natal Republic, 209; Stockenstrom System on the Eastern frontier, 212; Ncapaai, segregation and second British occupation of Natal, 215.—**British Attempt to Control the Trekkers:** Transorangia, 217; Menzies's annexation and Napier's treaties, 220; Winburg—Potchefstroom, 223; Touwfontein, 224; Eastern frontier, 225; Pondo treaty state, 226; War of the Axe, 228; High Commissionership, 229; annexations of Victoria East and British Kaffraria, 230, along the Orange, 231, Natal, 232, and Orange River Sovereignty, 233.

THE rapid invasion of lands beyond the Orange and the Vaal by the Trekkers extended the old problems of the Eastern Frontier over a large part of South-eastern Africa and, thereby, immeasurably intensified the difficulties of the Cape Governors. Legally the situation was governed by the principle *Nemo potest exuere patriam.* British subjects the Boers were and, like the English traders of Port Natal, British subjects they must remain unless they chose to submit to the jurisdiction of the chiefs in whose territories they settled. H.M. Government would not recognise their independence. Once beyond the frontiers, however, they were out of Government's control except through the Punishment Act, which was almost useless for

---

[1] Ordinance 2 of 1837; Van der Horst, *Native Labour in South Africa,* pp. 13, 15.
[2] No. 424 of 1851, pp. 9, 15; Cory III. 403.

lack of any means of bringing criminals to the Colony for trial.[1] The extension of full British sovereignty over the country occupied by the Trekkers was the logical conclusion to which officials like Stockenstrom and missionaries like Boyce pointed; but though Great Britain, under philanthropic guidance, regarded herself as the trustee for the Natives both against the Boers and 'the most degraded of the English,' she was none the less 'deeply persuaded of the inexpediency of engaging in any scheme of colonisation.'[2]

The Governors of the Colony, short of troops and money, were thus left to struggle with a political situation which was *de facto* radically different from any that had gone before, whatever the position might be *de jure*. Hitherto, the story of European South Africa had been that of the Cape Colony. Now, Boer Republics were set up and, alongside of them, Bantu and Griqua states.

1843– Presently, H.M. Government reluctantly annexed Natal partly to
1845. safeguard the Eastern frontier, partly from fear of foreign intervention and partly in the commercial interests of the Cape. But that was not enough. Difficulties increased in Transorangia, and the War

1846. of the Axe with the Xosas ruined what still remained of the Treaty System. The Governor of the Cape became High Commissioner, a recognition of the new order, and a year later Sir Harry Smith boldly

1847– annexed large blocks of territory south of the Orange to the Colony
1848. and proclaimed the Queen's sovereignty over all, white, black and coloured, between that river and the Vaal. It was a belated attempt to control the Great Trek.[3]

THE REPUBLIC OF NATAL

From one point of view the Great Trek was merely an acceleration of a process which had been going on as long as men could remember: the steady drift of Europeans and half-castes out beyond the proclaimed frontiers of the Colony. The trek spirit was inborn in the Boer frontiersmen of the 'thirties. From the end of the seventeenth century the cattle-farmers had followed their migratory farms eastward till in 1775 they had been checked by the Kaffirs along the Fish. There, a generation of young Boers had grown up all looking forward to farms of their own and fretting against Government restrictions which forbade them to go to the Koonap or, 'if it could be, unto the Kat.' The great effort of 1812 which had cleared the Zuurveld had been followed by a revolution in land tenure, for henceforward new farms were to be obtained only at variable quit-rents. Then, as the second generation grew to manhood, the 1820 Settlers

---

[1] Bird, I. 389; Chase, *Natal Papers*, I. 50, 119.
[2] *Spectator*, May 17, 1834; C.O. 1323, S. of S. to Gov., March 29, 1836.
[3] *Vide* E. A. Walker, *The Great Trek*.

had come crowding into the Zuurveld. The Ceded Territory had offered some relief, but the main tide of migration had already turned north-eastward, when woolled sheep followed the Settlers in and Government threatened to auction Crown lands. With a third 1832. generation of lads soon to be provided for and drought following drought in grim succession, what could cattle-farmers do but look around for a way of escape from changing conditions which promised to make the old style of life, the *lekker leven*, impossible? Farmers began to drift across the Orange and a big trek was talked of; but it was only organised after the return of the *kommissie* treks, which 1835. told the Boers that there were fine and almost vacant lands where to-day are the Free State and Transvaal cattle and mealie farms and the fertile valleys of Natal.[1] A large and steady emigration would, humanly speaking, have taken place had emancipation, the Xosas and Stockenstrom never afflicted the frontiersmen, for, as Retief told Dingaan, the Colony was too small and the Boers were becoming landless.[2] The Kaffir war cut right across the projected trek, and it was not till the fighting was finished that the first two organised Sept. parties crossed the Orange. Even so, Trigardt had been living beyond 1835. the borders for three years past and had very special reasons for his final departure. The movement remained on a small scale till the latter half of 1836; then, helped on by a severe drought, the abrogation of martial law and the fading of all hope of land in Queen Adelaide, the Great Trek began in good earnest.[3]

The Great Trek was however more than a matter of mere belly-need. It was unprecedented in South African history by reason of its organisation, its size and its spirit. The pre-Trek Boers and some of the scattered groups which drifted out of the Colony alongside the Trek parties meant to take the Colony with them as their fathers had done before them. Not so the trekkers of the Trek. Many of them were sons or grandsons of the men of Graaff-Reinet in whom republican ideas had stirred in 1795, and all had grievances. They

---

[1] Bird, *Annals*, I. 231; Preller, *Voortrekkermense*, I. 269 ff.; Cloete, *Great Trek*, p. 62; Cory, III. 401.

[2] Bird, I. 368.

[3] Causes of the Trek: (a) Trekker authorities. J. N. Boshof (Bird, I. 504 ff.); P. Retief (Preller, *Piet Retief*; Chase, *Natal Papers*, I. 100); P. Uys (Preller, *Voortrekkermense*, I.; Theal, *Hist. Sketches*, pp. 280 ff.); J. H. Hatting (Preller, *Voort.*, I.); Anna Steenkamp (Bird, I. 459; Preller, *Voort.*, II.); W. J. Pretorius (Bird, I. 230); Sarel Cilliers (Bird, I. 238 ff.); D. P. Bezuidenhout (Preller, *Voort.*, III.; Bird, I. 367); Louis Trigardt (Preller, *Dagboek*, and *Voort.*, II.); F. P. van Gass and L. C. de Klerk (Preller, *Voort.*, I.); Erasmus Smit (*ibid.*, II); A. H. Potgieter, A. H. Stander, I. J. Breytenbach and A. B. and B. Oosthuizen (*ibid.*, III.); Natal Volksraad (Bird, I. 691); J. G. S. Bronkhorst (Chase, I. 71 ff.); Natalians (Eybers, p. 153).

(b) Non-trekker authorities. H. Cloete, *Great Trek*; Chase, *Natal Papers*, II.; Backhouse and Walker (Bird, I. 614); D'Urban-Smith Papers, IV. 18 ff.; Napier (Bird, I. 394, 606; Chase, II. 48); Charters (Chase, I. 44); Stockenstrom (Bird, I. 498; No. 424 of 1851, p. 22).

moved off inspired by feelings towards H.M. Government ranging from bitter hatred to a mild but firm determination to have nothing more to do with it. 'We quit this Colony,' wrote Retief, 'under the full assurance that the English Government . . . will allow us to govern ourselves without its interference.' [1]

Apart from the general desire for land, the motives of the Trekkers varied almost from family to family. There was the new system of land tenure administered by a haphazard Lands Department. Complaints were frequent of high and unequal quit-rents, of favouritism in the allocation of farms, of delay in the issue of title-deeds after survey, of the possibility that titles would be withdrawn and fresh fees charged. There was profound dissatisfaction with the nature of the Government. Officials representing the central power had never been popular on the Frontier even when checked by local heemraden, and now the heemraden were no more. All the evils, wrote the Natal Volksraad in 1842, arose from the lack of representative government. Perhaps that was an afterthought; nevertheless, as soon as the Trekkers could organise their own states, the first thing they did was to revive the courts of the landdrosts and heemraden and restore the field cornets to all their old powers and more also. Nor was there enough even of this purely official government near the Frontiers. Not only were many of the field cornets incompetent to perform such duties as remained to them, but the magistrates were too few to permit of the farmers complying with the law. Again, Government set limits to the powder trade and forbade reprisals; but it did not protect. Uys is said to have trekked because the mountains near his home were full of Kaffirs armed with muskets, though his enthusiasm for Natal and his indignation that his wife should have been haled to court, there to answer a charge brought against her by a Hottentot, also explain his action. What though Mrs. Uys was acquitted, there was the delay and expense of the journey to the far-distant magistracy, a difficulty which gave a farmer the choice between marching errant servants to court for punishment with all the risk attendant on leaving the homestead unguarded, or of taking the law into his own hands at the risk of incurring the penalty of the law. On all sides the cry went up that there was no security on the Frontier.

There were also financial grievances. Government held that it had done its duty when it had paid and paid heavily for defence and supplies; but two years after the close of the Kaffir war requisition notes were still unhonoured and changing hands cheaply. Moreover the colonists, both Afrikaner and British, had expected that, since there were to be no land grants, Government, which had made them buy at auction their own recaptured cattle during the war, would

Since 1827–1828.

[1] Cory, *op. cit.*, III. 397; *Grahamstown Journal*, Feb. 2, 1837.

make good their war losses. This Glenelg declined to do, in spite of the plea of D'Urban and Napier that it would be worth while checking the Trek at the cost of a bad precedent. Some Trekkers, like Uys, complained that they ought to have been let off the payment of taxes for a year or two; one, Jacobus Boshof, mentions the redemption of the paper money as a grievance.

The loss due to this redemption can hardly have been felt generally, for the Boers did much of their trade by barter, and Boshof, a townsman, was the only man who recorded it. Much more serious were the losses occasioned by emancipation. Nearly all the Trekkers who have left records mention this, as a rule carefully explaining that it was not emancipation as such but the way in which it was carried out that hurt them. This emphasis is strange at first sight, since nearly all the Trekkers came from districts which had contained only a trifling slave population. It is true that, where other labour was scarce, that of even a few slaves would be valued, and yet the owner might not feel it worth while to try to recover compensation on so small a number; but the insistence in their public statements on the compensation grievance suggests that the Trekkers were specially anxious to refute the charge that they were inveterate slavers who were leaving the Colony because they were not allowed to keep slaves. Nevertheless, the pecuniary losses were not the only cause of offence. The 'vexatious laws' which had preceded emancipation and emancipation itself were also felt as real grievances. Anna Steenkamp, Retief's own sister, spoke for many when she deprecated not so much the freedom of the slaves as their being placed on an equal footing with Christians; Trigardt told the sympathetic Portuguese that one of his three reasons for trekking was that the slaves had been set free (his own had run away from him back to the Colony and freedom); Willem Jeremias Pretorius sets emancipation down as a 'chief incentive.' Undoubtedly the social revolution brought about by emancipation so soon after the passing of the 50th Ordinance in the 1828 interests of Hottentots had shocked the Boer's pride of race.

Closely connected with emancipation was the withholding of a vagrancy law. The Trekkers complained that thieves abounded, servants were out of control, always changing their employment and liable to run off to the magistrate with tales of ill-usage which led to court cases where the farmer (or his wife), ignorant probably of English and certainly of the ways of lawyers, was at a disadvantage. 'We are resolved,' wrote Retief in his famous manifesto, '. . . that we will uphold the just principles of liberty; but whilst we will take care that no one shall be held in a state of slavery, it is our determination to maintain such regulations as may suppress crime and preserve proper relations between master and servant.'[1] There would

[1] Cory, III. 396; Macmillan, *Cape Coloured Question*, pp. 78 ff.

at least be none of that 'ungodly equality' between white and black, ex-master and ex-slave, of which Anna Steenkamp complained.[1] If any one cause could be named as the cause *par excellence* of the Great Trek, it was fear of that equality.

There was, of course, the usual crop of wild rumours which had always accompanied any big movement on the frontier, a crop sown, according to Stockenstrom, by speculators eager to buy farms cheaply.[2] Such things have happened. All the land, it was said, was to be given to Hottentots; Government was going to encourage mixed marriages and incite blacks to behave as the equals of whites in church; the Boers were to be forced to become Roman Catholics and pressed into military service, this last canard the result of D'Urban's attempt to revise the commando lists. Over and above all, embittering every other grievance real and imaginary, was the feeling that their case was going by default in Capetown and London. 'A flood of unjustifiable odium' was being poured upon them by 'interested persons,' notably by members of the L.M.S., and when a good Governor had come to make a good settlement, he was recalled and there was apparently no means of letting the King know their side of the case. So wrote Retief and Uys on behalf of their less articulate followers to D'Urban, who perhaps read their last lament with an uneasy conscience.

Had there been no land available outside the Colony there might have been a rebellion even against a government which, as the fate of the Slachter's Nek rebels witnessed, took rebellion seriously. As it was, the Boers trekked. Once the movement had begun, it gathered speed by its own momentum. The knowledge that there was no legal bar, once martial law had been abrogated, decided many;[3] others went because the leading man in their district went or because their neighbours trekked and they feared isolation. Some moved off to help their comrades after the early disasters in Natal; others when victories like Blood River showed them that they could safely do so; others again when Napier, D'Urban's successor, showed that he meant to uphold the treaty system. Nor was 'enthusiasm' wanting. 'We rather withdrew,' wrote Anna Steenkamp, 'in order thus to preserve our doctrines in purity.' 'They fancy they are under a divine impulse,' wrote one observer; 'the women seem more bent on it than the men.'[4] From the start, petticoat influence was strong among the Trekkers.

The parties, drawn almost entirely from the frontier districts, marched as a rule under the leading local official, like Retief, or the

[1] Preller, *Voortrekkermense*, II. 30.
[2] Bird, I. 499.
[3] Eybers, *op. cit.*, p. 145.
[4] A. B. to Fairbairn, Oct. 7, 1836 (*S.A. Comm. Adv.*).

family patriarch, like Jacobus Uys.[1] Fairbairn went too far when he said that they abandoned nothing of value.[2] There were, indeed, no Groot Constantias in the East and families rarely occupied the same farm for two generations, but many of the houses were substantial. He was on firmer ground when he said their wants were few and 'even the luxury of bread is not universal amongst them.' Game was plentiful; the creaking, tilted waggon with its straining team of oxen could carry wife and children and 'the family pot,' while beside the waggon padded cattle and sheep in herds surprisingly great considering the drought and the wastage of the war.[3] Ammunition presented few difficulties to those who had hard money, and the Boers readily changed the paper proceeds of their farms at the rate of 23s. for each English sovereign. Some farms were simply abandoned, but many were sold at reasonable prices, considering that the absence of title-deeds in many cases diminished their value.[4] Prices naturally fell when numbers of farms were thrown on the market; nevertheless, the proverbial exchange of a farm, which had originally been a free grant, for a waggon and span of oxen was not always a bad bargain at a time when waggons and oxen were in great demand.

Once they had crossed the drifts of the middle Orange into Griqua Philippolis, the Trekkers had before them a huge parallelogram of grasslands: the present Free State, half Bechuanaland and two-thirds of the Transvaal. To the west the grass faded away into the Kalahari Desert; on the east it was bounded by mountains; on the north by mountains again and the deadly tsetse fly of the Limpopo valley. Just beyond the Orange were pre-Trek Boers, who by no means welcomed the new arrivals, and Griquas centring round the L.M.S. stations. Abram Kok reigned at Philippolis itself in the room of Adam II, deceased, and away to the west, beyond the lower Vaal, 1835. Andries Waterboer ruled at Griquatown and Cornelis Kok at Campbell. Eastwards on either side of the Caledon river lay Bantu and half-breed clans with their missionaries. The Berliners cared for the Koranas at Bethanie, but on the western bank of the Caledon the Wesleyans held most of the field. They were at Imparani among Sikonyela's Batlokua, at Merumetsu with Taaibosch's Koranas, with Baatje's half-breeds at Platberg, and with the Barolong of Moroko

---

[1] The leaders and localities of the principal parties were (1835–37): Trigardt and van Rensburg (Albany and extra-Colonial); A. H. Potgieter (Tarka); Cilliers and Liebenberg (Colesberg); Maritz (Graaff Reinet); Retief (Winterberg); Uys (Uitenhage); Jacobs (Beaufort West).

[2] *S. A. Comm. Adv.*, Aug. 27, 1836.

[3] 113 folk from Tarka took £60,000 worth (Chase, II. 106). 29 small parties or families from Tarka took 6156 cattle and 96,000 sheep (Cory, III. 404). In 1836, 27 people lost 96 horses, 4671 cattle and 50,745 sheep to the Matabele (Chase, I. 134).

[4] Cory, III. 403; *S.A. Comm. Adv.*, Aug. 27, 1836.

7*

and Tawane at Thaba Nchu. The Paris Evangelicals were with Lepui's Batlapin at Bethulie and with the Bataung at Mekuatling; but their main field was among the Basuto to the east of the Caledon at Morija and, after 1837, at Thaba Bosigo, Moshesh's capital. All these Caledon chiefs, big and little, were *amici* of the Colony, 'white men under the white King.'

On the western side of the grasslands the L.M.S. men had long been with the Batlapin at Robert Moffat's Kuruman. More recently American Zulu missionaries had settled at Mosega with the Matabele. Msilikazi's kraals lay north of the Vaal grouped round Kapain and Mosega.[1] Around them lay a waste of Matabele making, and beyond, on the edge of the Kalahari, lurked the remnants of Gasiyitsiwe's Bangwaketse, Secheli's Bakwena and further north at Shoshong, Sekhomi's Bamangwato. In the mountains of the north-eastern and eastern Transvaal lay the Batlou at Makapans Poort, the Maguamba in the Zoutpansberg, the Bapedi, kinsmen of the Basuto, in the Lulu Mountains and the Swazis on the crest of the Lebombo. To the east and south-east of the Drakensberg the land fell away, step by step, till it flattened out into the narrow tropical coast strip of Zululand and Natal. In what is now Portuguese East Africa Mani-kusa did what he chose, while the Portuguese cautiously reoccupied the posts on the lower Zambesi and the coast which his Shangaans had recently sacked. To the south, from the border of Swaziland to the Umzimvubu river, were lands densely peopled only where Dingaan's Zulus lived between the Mkusi and the Tugela rivers and a few clans huddled in the foothills of the Drakensberg mountains or round the English hunters at Port Natal. Between the Umzimvubu and the colonial frontier were the Pondos and the other coast tribes of Kaffirland.

Had the *Mfecane* not swept so much of the country bare of inhabitants, the tribesmen might have been able to hold the line of the Orange or, in the last resort, the Vaal as doggedly as the Xosas had long held the line of the Fish river. As it was, the only enemies the Trekkers had to fear in the plains immediately north of the Colonial boundary were Griquas armed indeed with firearms and horses like themselves, but a mere divided scattering of folk, and, far away in the background, the Zulu and Matabele impis which, for all their valour, had no missile weapons other than the light throwing assegai and had never even seen a horse. The Trekkers with their heavy muskets, horses and stout waggons soon found that, unless they were cornered or surprised, the odds were all in their favour, and that the country was admirably adapted to their style of fighting except in the wooded hills and valleys of Natal and Zululand and, presently, the mountains of Basutoland. The enemy could be seen far off on the great plains,

[1] Harris, *Wild Sports*, pp. 84 ff.; A. Smith, *Report* (1836), p. 22.

and there was usually time to form laager as in Potgieter's fight with
the Matabele at Vegkop, waggon locked to waggon by the trek- 1836.
chains in a great ring and the space between the wheels filled with
thorn bush. Or, if the men were out unhampered by waggons and
families, there was room to ride up within range, fire, retire to load
and then fire again with the heavy roers (elephant guns) which 'kill
at a great distance,' till the enemy gave way as at the rout of the 1837.
Matabele in the Marico battle. Sometimes, as at the crowning mercy
of Blood River against the Zulus, the two tactics could be combined.[1] 1838.
A very few decisive battles were enough to make the Trekkers masters
of open country which had been cleared of most of its inhabitants
either by death or displacement during the *Mfecane*.[2]

The first two trek parties fared ill. Trigardt and Jan van Rensburg 1835–
journeyed together far into the Transvaal. There they separated, 1839.
Jan van Rensburg's people to be wiped out by hostile tribes in the
lower Limpopo valley, and Trigardt's to find rest in the Zoutpansberg. Presently, sadly reduced by fever, they stumbled on to Delagoa
Bay, whence most of the survivors were brought by sea to Natal in
1839. The later parties followed in their tracks. Potgieter, Carel
Cilliers and Barend Leibenberg joined hands beyond the Orange, and, Feb.
with them went a boy of ten, Paul Kruger, future President of the 1836.
South African Republic. Potgieter, most restless of all the Trekkers,
went north naming many of the Free State rivers and making verbal
treaties of friendship with neighbouring chiefs. From his base camp
in what is now the northern Orange Free State, he pushed on with a
small party to find Trigardt and a road to Delagoa Bay.[3] At the
Zoutpansberg he found Trigardt; but he failed to find the road to
the sea, and on his return home he learnt that the Matabele, who
resented the presence of armed bands in their country in place of the
hunters and the men of God who had always asked the King for
'the road,' had destroyed the Liebenbergs on the northern bank of
the Vaal. He himself was glad to beat the Matabele off at Vegkop
at the price of losing his cattle.[4] Moroko, the Barolong chief, and
his Wesleyan missionary, the Rev. William Archbell, helped him back Oct.
to Thaba Nchu, and there he was joined by a new party of Trekkers 1836.
led by Gerrit Maritz of Graaff-Reinet.

Of the five things needful to the formation of a republic Potgieter
had done one: he had surveyed the land. But it still remained for the
Trekkers to acquire that land, to frame government machinery, to
come to terms with their non-European neighbours and to win
recognition of their independence from H.M. Government. They first

---

[1] Compare the British cavalry charge from the hollow square at Ulundi (Zulu
War, 1879).
[2] Preller, *Dagboek*, and *Voort.*, II. 1 ff.; Chase I. 70; V.R. Soc. XIII.
[3] For Boer attempts to reach the sea *vide* Krüger, *Die Weg na die See.*
[4] Chase, I. 71 ff., 134; *Voort. Argief.*, p. 30; Bird, I. 238 ff.; Preller, *Voort.*, III.

faced the problem of government. It was not an easy task. Unlike the emigrants drawn from all the strata of old-established societies, who went to North America in the seventeenth century or to Australasia and the eastern Cape Colony in the nineteenth, the Trekkers were, with hardly an exception, men of one class only. They were stock-farmers, of all civilised men the least accustomed to common action and the restraints of the law. They lacked political experience; there were few among them who were competent to carry on public business; they were self-reliant to a fault; their leaders were jealous of one another; they had, as yet, no sure abiding place in the great plains. And they must build their state from bedrock upwards. Their first constitution was of such a rudimentary nature that it has since been disputed whether it can be called a constitution at all. At Thaba Nchu, 'Het Volk' (the People) elected Maritz, a man of some education and legal experience, as landdrost, and six other men to act with him as bench, legislature and council of war administering such laws as might be agreed upon by a general meeting of all the men of the trek party.[1] Potgieter and Maritz then led their fighting men and a few Griquas, Koranas and Barolong against the Matabele. They read them a sharp lesson at Mosega, regained captured waggons and cattle and returned to Thaba Nchu with the American missionaries, who despaired of the Matabele after a year's experience and hoped for better success with the kindred Zulus near Port Natal.

Piet Retief then rode in with 400 followers. He was the ablest of the Voortrekkers and, helped by the quarrels of Potgieter and Maritz, soon established his ascendancy. At Vet River, the Thaba Nchu constitution was adapted to the new conditions and confirmed by the Nine Articles of association. Maritz remained President of the Volksraad and the landdrost of that body when it should sit, like the House of Lords, in a judicial capacity; but Retief was elected Commandant-General and Governor with an elected Council of Policy to assist him. Retief's Governorship and the Council of Policy, which was probably the Volksraad in another form, were the nearest approach to a civil as distinct from a military executive that the Trekkers were to have for many years. Thus entrenched as head of the state, Retief organised the church. For lack of a fully ordained minister and in spite of the furious opposition of Potgieter, who would have preferred the ministrations of the Wesleyan, 'Aardspiel' of Thaba Nchu, he appointed the ex-mission teacher, Erasmus Smit, to conduct services.[3] He then turned to deal with the pressing matter

Dec. 1836.

Jan. 1837.

April 1837.

June 1837.

---

[1] *Voort. Argief.*, p. 13.
[2] Preller, *Piet Retief*, p. 96; Chase, I. 87; *Voort. Argief.*, p. 14; *Zuid Afrikaan*, Nov. 10, 1837.
[3] Engelbrecht, *Geschiedenis*, I. 19-20.

of native policy. He bade his commandants shed no innocent blood on patrol nor take Bushman children as apprentices without their parents' consent, and made treaties with neighbouring chiefs, notably with Moroko, the good friend of the Trekkers, and with Sikonyela and Moshesh. None of these treaties survive, possibly because they were verbal; but, on the analogy of treaties concluded soon after-wards, they must have provided for peace, amity and leave for the white man to occupy land, probably in return for a consideration.[1]

At this stage, Jacobus Uys and his famous son, Piet, arrived from Uitenhage, closely followed by Jacobs and his neighbours from Beaufort West. Now that some four to five hundred fighting-men were assembled with perhaps a thousand waggons, Retief felt strong enough to deal decisively with the Matabele. Fear of the Griquas and, more certainly, quarrels among the leaders ruined his plans. Potgieter, who wished to trek north of the Vaal as far away as possible from British influence and find a port on the East Coast, finally parted company with Maritz; Uys with 170 followers formally repudiated Retief's authority and proposed to found a state in Natal at his leisure on U.S.A. principles;[2] Retief himself decided to go to the Promised Land of Natal, the point of contact with the outer world and the vantage ground from which to bargain for independ-ence and friendly relations with the British. So Retief rode down to Oct. Port Natal with a few friends to get into touch with Dingaan, while 1837. Potgieter and Uys with 135 men and a few of Tawane's Barolong defeated the Matabele in a nine days' running fight along the Marico Nov. river without the loss of a man. Msilikazi, who had been roughly 1837. handled a little before by the Zulus, withdrew northwards beyond the Limpopo into what is now Matabeleland, and Potgieter claimed all the lands that had been subject to him from the Vaal to the Zoutspansberg, and the Kalahari to Rhenoster Poort.[3] The Trekkers were thus potential masters of all the open grasslands from the Griqua borders to the edge of the tsetse belt. They hoped soon to be masters of Natal also.

Fairbairn was right in the long run when he wrote that the depar-ture of the cattle-farmers would be no loss to the Colony as British sheep-farmers would take their places.[4] That was the oft-repeated story of the U.S.A. frontier with friction but ultimate economic gain at each stage as the invasion of the interior opened up new markets for established traders. But, at the moment, the loss to the

---

[1] Chase, I. 88, 110; Moodie, *Battles and Adventures*, I. 525; Cloete, *Great Trek*, p. 94.
[2] Chase, I. 103, 110; Preller, *Retief*, p. 117; Theal, *Hist. Sketches*, pp. 283 ff.
[3] Chase, I. 132; Bird, I. 325; II. 203; *Voort. Argief.*, p. 97; J. H. Malan, *Die Opkoms van 'n Republiek*, p. 511.
[4] *S.A. Comm. Adv.*, Aug. 27, 1836.

Colony was serious. The withdrawal of the most readily com-
mandeerable burghers weakened the frontier at the very time that
the weight of the Trek, thrust into a seething mass of tribes, might
well drive dispossessed natives over the colonial border. That danger,
already a preoccupation, now became a nightmare to colonial
Governors. D'Urban tried to kill the Trek by kindness, pressing for
payment of compensation for war losses and requisitions, hastening
the issue of land titles, offering land in Queen Adelaide and the
Stormberg area while it remained to him, appointing new magistrates
on the frontier furnished with bilingual instructions, and stationing
more troops in the Winterberg. But without martial law he could
not stop the movement, and now, with reports before him of the
Mosega fight, the harrying of natives, and the seizure of Bushman
children by stray Boers and, finally, Retief's proposed journey to
Natal, he frankly told Glenelg that the position was impossible.
Was he or was he not to recognise the independence of the
emigrants? [1] Glenelg replied that he must rely on that broken reed,
the Punishment Act, and ask the chiefs to send guilty parties back to
the Colony with proofs. As for Natal, 'that is a foreign land ... and
the Government has neither the right nor the intention to interfere.'
And, he added, after perusing D'Urban's fiery though belated
explanation of his Kaffir policy, the Governor must retire as soon as
he could be relieved. [2]

Jan.
1838

D'Urban therefore handed over his peck of troubles to Sir George
Napier. Most of his comprehensive programme of reforms had been
accomplished; the Legislative Council, the revised Charter of Justice,
retrenchment, emancipation and the beginnings of municipal
government witnessed to that. But a satisfactory native policy had
not been evolved. There is much South African political history
summed up in D'Urban's four years of office.

So far from being solved the native question had been immensely
complicated by the Trek. It was this fact which had to be faced by the
new Governor, Sir George Napier. He was a Peninsular veteran like
D'Urban, but, unlike him, a convinced negrophilist avowedly prepared to make the best of the treaty system and to send on
Stockenstrom's letters promptly to Downing Street. [3] Soon after landing he visited the Eastern Frontier (few Governors were to omit that
formality for many years to come) and found some of the clans stealing
extensively, and the drought, which helped to explain the prevalence of
theft, making the tracing of the spoor and, therefore, recovery difficult.

---

[1] Eybers, p. 145; *Basutoland Records*, I. 15; C.O. 1447, D'Urban to S. of S.,
July 1837.
[2] Bird, I. 327; No. 503 of 1837, p. 278.
[3] No. 424 of 1851, p. 25; J. Philip to Fairbairn, Nov. 1, 1837.

He condemned the bush of the lower Fish river as a boundary, demanded the reinforcements which D'Urban had asked for in vain, tried to move the Fingos back further into the Colony away from the Xosas who still hankered after the cattle stolen by their 'dogs' during the late war, threatened Macomo and the Emigrant Tembus with reprisals if they did not behave themselves and, on the advice of Stockenstrom, made defensive alliances with the friendly Gunukwebes in the Ceded Territory.[1] At that very moment he was robbed of Stockenstrom's services. To the unbounded joy of the Easterners, Sept. the Lieutenant-Governor lost a libel action which he had brought 1838. against one of his critics and sailed for England, leaving Colonel John Hare, an honest man of no great ability, to act in his stead.

Napier, meanwhile, tried to stop the Trek and persuade the Trekkers to return home. He enlisted the help of the border officials and of the D.R. Church clergy, who disapproved of a movement which was taking so many of their flocks beyond the reach of civilisation and the means of grace, pressed for compensation for war losses and security of land tenure, and even had a hurried and unavailing interview with a Boer deputation on the northern border. All he could do was to issue a warning that no ex-slaves might be taken beyond the frontiers as the day of complete freedom was due in December, and to send a field cornet, Gideon Joubert, to bring back smuggled apprentices into the Colony. Joubert returned with forty, having left over a hundred behind at their own request, two of whom were, however, sent back presently by sea from Natal to receive their freedom.[2]

From the time of Napier's visit to the northern border till the middle of 1842, Transorangia was left to take care of itself and Natal became the storm centre of South African politics. Gardiner had taken up his duties as magistrate at the Port and persuaded June Dingaan to cede the southern half of Natal to the Crown,[3] waive 1837. his claim to runaway subjects and receive an Anglican missionary, the Reverend Francis Owen, at his kraal of Ungungundhlovu. On the other hand, Gardiner was powerless to check gun-runners, for he had no prison and no police and, now, the majority of the English defied him, repudiated the Royal claim to Natal and declared their independence. They welcomed Retief to the Port and sent one or Oct.- two of their number with him to interview Dingaan. From him Nov. Retief received the promise of land, presumably the whole of Natal, 1837. provided he recovered Zulu cattle stolen by Sikonyela and, added the King, 'if possible, the thief as well.'[4] So Retief rode homewards

---

[1] No. 424 of 1851, pp. 30 ff., 39; *Treaties . . . 1803–54*, p. 93.
[2] *Ibid.*, p. 35; Bird, I. 415; Chase, II. 17, 43.
[3] *Ibid.*, I. 96; Eybers, p. 149.
[4] Bird, I. 318 ff., 326, 333,-360; Chase, I. 96 ff., 130; Preller, *Retief*, pp. 170–1; Eybers, p. 150.

to be met by his own followers and those of Maritz pouring down the passes of the Drakensberg and forming laager among the rolling hills of northern Natal in breach of their promise to stand fast till he should return. However, he recovered the Zulu cattle, took all Sikonyela's horses and guns, and then, in spite of more than one warning and the entreaties of Maritz, rode off to Dingaan's kraal with seventy followers, thirty coloured attendants and an English interpreter from Port Natal.[1]

Retief and his men rode into a death-trap. For some time past Dingaan had been growing uneasy at the news of the doings of these white men mounted on 'hornless cattle' and armed with the guns he coveted. Retief himself had told him how they had routed his deadly enemy, Msilikazi, at no loss to themselves, and the King had plagued his missionary to teach him 'what he really wanted to know, the use of firearms.' Now the Boers had come 'like an army from the direction of Msilikazi' to build houses in his country, their leader was actually at his kraal with just such a commando as had harried the Matabele at Mosega, and the rest of them were scattered unsuspecting among their tents. It was a chance not to be missed. After a day or two of negotiation, during which he called up reinforcements, Dingaan signed a deed giving Natal to Retief and his followers and, having thus enticed them all into his kraal unarmed, slew them and the Hottentots without the gate.[2]

Dec. 1838.

At first Dingaan thought of making a clean sweep of the white men in his country, but after some hesitation he let the English and American missionaries get away. On the other hand he at once sent his impis to fall upon the Boer laagers. The slaughter at Weenen followed; but the other laagers stood firm, Potgieter and Uys came down from the High Veld and joint action was arranged with the English. Disaster ensued. Neither of the Boer leaders would serve under the other or under Maritz; Uys was trapped by the Zulus and killed; Potgieter, who had never liked the Natal adventure, rode back to the High Veld; one English expedition effected little, a second was destroyed, and the Zulus, storming down to Port Natal, drove the survivors and the missionaries on shipboard.[3]

April 1838.

The fortunes of the Trekkers were now at their lowest ebb, for the Zulus had thus far killed 361 of their number and about 200 of their Coloured servants besides thirteen Englishmen and many of their Bantu followers. Then the tide began to turn. The Trekkers might

[1] Bird, I. 369, 401; *V.R. Soc.*, VII. 157-8; Preller, *Retief*, p. 209; Chase, I. 132.
[2] On the Retief massacre *vide* Owen's Diary (*V.R. Soc.* VII.); Preller, *Retief*; Bird, I. 233, 241, 307, 325, 369, 402, 436, 462, 493, 516, 519; Chase, I. 130; II. 3; Moodie, *Battles*, I. 422. Also articles by J. du Plessis (*Het. Zoeklicht*, Aug. 1923); W. Blommaert (*Die Burger*, July 14, 21, and *Die Huisgenoot*, Sept. 1923); Sir G. Cory (*Cape Times*, July 12, 1923); Walker, *Great Trek*, pp. 147 ff.
[3] Bird, I. 234, 242, 370, 399; Chase, II. 8; Moodie, *Battles*, I. 500; Preller, *Voort.*, II. 51; Bird, I. 355.

hope that Andries Pretorius of Graaff-Reinet, who had visited them before the recent disasters, would give such a good report of Natal in the Eastern districts that many of his neighbours would be tempted to join them, and, then, that the very news of their misfortunes would arouse many more to come to the rescue. It proved indeed to be so. True, Maritz died, but the Natalians founded their capital of Pietermaritzburg. Carel Landman, Maritz's successor, gained possession of the Port with the consent of the few surviving English,[1] and in due time Pretorius came back with a strong following, took the lead and began to plan vengeance on Dingaan. On the other hand, the redcoats came close on his heels. From the first, Napier had wished to send troops to Port Natal to keep order and check the Trek. As confused rumours of strife between Boers and Bantu in various parts of the hinterland drifted in, he had become more insistent and had at last wrung a grudging consent from Glenelg on condition that there was no 'colonisation.' He promptly sent Major Samuel Charters with a hundred men to the Port to restore peace and prevent the importation of warlike stores or the formation of an independent government; but now that he realised that there was no hope of inducing the Trekkers to return to the Colony, he urged Glenelg to set up an administration in Natal subordinate to that at Capetown.[2] Charters meanwhile occupied the Port; but in spite of his efforts to stop Pretorius, the latter marched into Zululand and, on December 16, 1838, overthrew many of Dingaan's impis at the three-hour battle of Blood River.[3] Pressing on, Pretorius occupied the smouldering ruins of Umgungundhlovu and found the deed of cession in Retief's wallet beside his bones on the Hill of Execution hard by.

Though some three thousand Zulus were slain at the cost of three Boers slightly wounded, the victory of Blood River by no means broke the Zulu power. It did, however, clear the way for the organisation of the most elaborate Trekker republic yet attempted around the church which the Natalians built at Pietermaritzburg as a thank-offering for their deliverance.[4] This Republic was a continuation of that founded at Thaba Nchu and Vet River, for six of the seven members of the High Veld Raad had trekked down into Natal, Oct. with instructions drawn up based on existing regulations.[5] These 1838. instructions, with additional rules to meet new circumstances, were now put into force. A Volksraad of twenty-four members, two from each field cornetcy elected annually on adult white male suffrage, served as legislature, court of appeal and, in many respects, executive

---

[1] *Nat. Not.*, pp. 133, 156–7.   [2] Bird, I. 389, 394, 414; Chase, II. 43, 49 ff.
[3] Bird, I. 234, 243, 433, 438, 492.
[4] This church is now a *Volksmuseum.*
[5] On the Natal constitution see *Voortrekker Wetgewing* (*Notulen* of the Natal Volksraad, edited by Preller).

as well.[1] At first it met at irregular intervals and then quarterly,
Feb. while, later still, a *Kommissie Raad* of five carried on between the
1842. sessions subject to the ratification of its acts at the next full meeting.[2]
As at Thaba Nchu, the Volksraad was checked by *Het Publiek*, that
is, such of the electorate as could attend.[3] Apart from the Krygsraad
(Council of War) there was no executive, for, since the Natal constitution marked a reaction against the centralising policy of Retief,
there was no Governor and nothing but a passing reference to a
Council of Policy. True, the Volksraad elected a President at each
session, but he was a mere chairman and, though Pretorius as Head
March Commandant sat in the Volksraad, he had no vote and his office
1840. was presently abolished except in time of war.[4] Subject to review by
the Volksraad, landdrosts' courts administered justice at the capital
and at the new villages of Congella and Weenen,[5] and at each of
Oct. these villages a church consistory was organised, though there was
1839–
April no fully qualified minister in Natal except the devoted American
1840. missionary, Daniel Lindley.[6] In each ward there were field cornets
with the usual powers.

Meanwhile, Captain Henry Jervis, Charters' successor, failed to
exercise his authority under the Punishment Act over the Natalians;
but, however much Pretorius might try to keep the fact in the background, he did succeed in mediating peace between the Boers and
May Dingaan. Dingaan acknowledged the Boer claim to Natal and
1839. promised to surrender all firearms, horses and cattle taken from the
Trekkers, to pay a huge indemnity in cattle, and, by a clause unknown to Jervis, to cede to the Republic the southern half of Zululand, including St. Lucia Bay, and to withdraw his people therefrom.[7]
Lord Normanby, the Colonial Secretary, ignorant of this republican
version of D'Urban's abortive 'extermination' policy, ordered
Napier to withdraw the troops. But Napier held on as long as he could,[8]
because the Trek was proceeding faster than ever, Faku the Pondo
was quarrelling with a Baca chief, Ncapaai, on the southern border
of Natal, Dingaan was fulfilling his side of the treaty but slowly,
and Pretorius himself was in treaty with Panda, Dingaan's brother
and rival.[9] At last he could hold on no longer. The troops sailed,
Dec. wishing the Natalians good luck, the Republicans hoisted their new
1839. flag, and, at that very moment, Lord John Russell, now Secretary of
State, sat down to write under strong commercial pressure that since
the Trekkers would not come home and might look to Holland for

---

[1] *Nat. Not.* pp. 46, 49, 77, 226, 264.   [2] *Ibid.*, pp. 107, 245.
[3] *Ibid.*, pp. 23, 244.   [4] *Ibid.*, pp. 15, 40, 43.
[5] *Ibid.*, pp. xiii. 7, 14, 20, 44, 69, 188; Chase, II. 102.
[6] *Nat. Not.*, pp. 12, 27, 31, 34, 78, 92, 174.
[7] Bird, I. 494, 520; Chase II. 92; *Nat. Not.*, pp. 1–5, 15; Walker, *Great Trek*,
pp. 196, 204, 249.
[8] Bird, I. 523, 534; *Nat. Not.*, p. 26.   [9] Bird, I. 536, 540, 553 ff.

aid, he was prepared to consider the annexation of Natal, provided it entailed neither heavy expense nor injustice to the tribes.[1] Napier's comments on receiving that letter are not recorded.

Pretorius made the most of his opportunity. He ended the Zulu menace by playing off one half of the Zulu monarchy against the other. A campaign in which Panda's men did the fighting and the Boers took the loot ended with the flight and death of Dingaan in Feb. Swaziland. This victory at Magongo was marred by the judicial 1840. murder of two of Dingaan's envoys and by quarrels over the distribution of the captured cattle and apprentices after the battle, but the results were decisive. Panda was recognised as Prince of the Zulus ruling his dominions as a vassal of the Republic, and was held responsible for the huge tale of cattle due from the defaulting Dingaan and more also.[2] No wonder the Natalians called this 'the Cattle Commando!'

Secure at home, Pretorius pressed on with the negotiations which he had begun some time since for closer union with the other Boer republics. There was as yet no semblance of European rule in Transorangia between the Orange and the Vet; but, north of that area, Potgieter claimed the whole Vet River district (afterwards Winburg) as far as the Vaal river in terms of a treaty with Makwana, a petty local Bataung chief. North of the Vaal, he claimed to rule a Nov. vast territory from his new centre at Potchefstroom.[3] The three 1838. republics were now federated loosely. Natal, as much the most Oct. important and populous state, was senior partner. Potgieter remained 1840. Chief Commandant north of the Drakensberg, but had to report his doings to Pretorius as Commandant-General. Similarly, the Vet River–Potchefstroom Raad became a mere adjunct Raad bound to submit its resolutions twice yearly to the legislature at Pietermaritzburg, but entitled to send members to sit there when matters of common concern were to be discussed.[4]

Pretorius, heir to Retief's policy, had thus achieved two of the dead leader's aims: the acquisition of a port and something like the union of all the territories occupied by the Trekkers. The question of independence remained to be settled. He therefore offered to send Sept. delegates to Capetown to treat for independence and the privileges 1840. of British subjects.[5] The auguries were good. Napier indeed had orders from Russell to reoccupy Port Natal or some commanding position hard by in view of the 'deplorable calamities' attendant on

[1] C.O. 2079, Dec. 23, 1839; Chase, II. 111, 115, 131, 134–7; Bird, I. 562.
[2] Bird, I. 375, 562, 576, 583, 595, 627; Chase, II. 120 ff.; Nat. Not., p. 45.
[3] Otherwise called Mooi River Dorp or Vryburg. For boundaries claimed vide Bloemhof Arbitration Blue-book, p. 307; Voort. Argief., p. 317; J. H. Malan, op. cit., p. 511.
[4] Bird, I. 388; II. 203; Nat. Not., pp. 73, 77, 82, 101 ff., 111, 145, 150 ff.
[5] Bird, I. 611, 627; Nat. Not., pp. 65, 88; Eybers, p. 159.

the Magongo campaign; but he was in no hurry to carry out those orders. The reoccupation of the Port must now mean a struggle, and he had no wish to fight; the Natalians seemed to be settling down; the Zulu refugees pouring into Natal away from Panda were docile; since Natal was to be treated commercially as a foreign country and could easily endanger the peace of the Eastern Frontier by pressing on the Kaffir tribes, it would be well to make friends with the Republicans. Napier commented drily that it might be hard to give them the privileges without the liabilities of British subjects, but he was at least prepared to discuss the matter.[1]

The condition of the Eastern Frontier as pictured by Napier in Capetown was such as to make him think kindly of any possible allies. His veteran Highlanders had been withdrawn; Sandile's Gaikas were restive at the prolonged uproar behind them in Natal; British and Afrikaner farmers in the Winterberg, Koonap and Mancazana lands threatened to trek unless the frontier system were changed, and so numerous were the reports of thefts and murders of armed herdsmen by Kaffirs that he concluded that the Stocken-strom treaty system had broken down.[2]

Oct.
1840.

It is easy to condemn the Stockenstrom system. It is much harder to arrive at any just conclusion as to its potential value as a policy, because the complete system was never tried. Stockenstrom's policy had been to make treaties with all chiefs capable of maintaining a settled government with whom the Colony was likely to come into contact, and then to trust to time, peace and commercial intercourse to civilise and Christianise their followers and perhaps ultimately secure their willing incorporation in the Queen's dominions. Elsewhere, he proposed to extend British rule over all areas occupied by British subjects or by natives who lacked strong rulers of their own; in other words, to control the Trek. This ambitious scheme was not attempted. Even in its narrower application to the Eastern Frontier the system never had a chance.[3] It was set up at the end of a wasting war in a drought-stricken land with the Trekkers pouring out of the frontier districts, and Stockenstrom himself so harassed by his enemies and his own brooding nature that he could never give it his undivided attention.

The general aim of this Eastern Frontier part of the system was to do away with reprisals by patrols set in motion by the mere *ipse dixit* of a farmer, and to provide for the legal punishment of thieves when taken or, if neither thief nor stolen stock could be secured, to hold the chief and clan responsible for proved losses—a principle well understood in Bantu law. Many of the chiefs at first carried out

[1] Bird, I. 605 ff., 622. This was before the days of Dominion status.
[2] No. 424 of 1851, pp. 46, 54, 58–62; Chase II. 142–7.
[3] Memorandum on the Treaty System by Stockenstrom.

the terms as long as they saw that the Government was in earnest and itself prepared to hold scrupulously to the treaties. Unfortunately, the force which Stockenstrom held to be essential for the support of the system was not provided, and the fear of causing a fresh war displayed by the authorities encouraged those who might so wish to defy the law.

Towards the close of 1838 Napier had asked for reinforcements to check cattle-stealing. Then, Stockenstrom's departure unsettled the tribes, who saw in it the prelude of a change. Napier himself broke the treaties by entering Kaffirland with a bodyguard of a hundred men.[1] Macomo became a nuisance, and the Emigrant Tembus in the north stole to recoup themselves, as they alleged, for their losses at the hands of Trekkers. With the arrival of the first reinforcements, Hare attacked the Tembus at Shiloh, recovered stolen cattle and overawed Macomo.[2] Thereafter, for a time, Napier received official reports of peace such as even Colonel Somerset in all his long experience had never known; the Kaffir police, hated by the frontiersmen, reproached by their fellows, ill-paid by Government but supported as a rule by the chiefs, recovered cattle properly reclaimable under the treaties as well as others which could not legally be reclaimed; some chiefs did justice to those Europeans who condescended to sue according to Kaffir law, and even Tyali fined a man for horse-stealing. But frontier officials went far to destroy the whole system by demanding the restoration of beasts which could not properly be claimed under the treaties. This 'Not Reclaimable List,' based on reports from the military posts and the newspapers of which the Agents with the tribes knew nothing, grew and grew. Henceforward every hoof lost, stolen or strayed was laid to the charge of the chiefs, who, on the Kat river border, were quite unable to comply with the continual demands. 'Our people,' the chiefs admitted, 'steal oxen and cows, but the Government steals with the pen.' Tyali gave up attending the quarterly meetings for settlement, and the cry of the frontiersmen for a radical revision of the treaties grew louder.[3]

Napier hurried to the frontier in the expectation of war armed with a drastic revision of the treaties drawn up by Judge William Menzies, who had never forgiven Stockenstrom for trying to limit the powers of the Supreme Court in 1828.[4] But once he was actually on the frontier, he learnt, like Harry Smith before him, to take Grahamstown alarms more calmly.[5] He found out for himself what

April 1839.

_1840._

_1840._

---

[1] No. 424 of 1851, pp. 39, 53; Stretch to Philip, July 22, 1839.

[2] No. 424 of 1851, pp. 45 ff.

[3] _Ibid._, pp. 35, 49; Stretch to Philip, July 23, 1839, and to Government Secretary, Oct. 28, 1839; Memorandum by Stretch, 1846; No. 424 of 1851, p. 54.

[4] Stockenstrom to Fairbairn, May 11, 1838.

[5] Napier told Stretch, the Gaika agent, that if all he had heard in Capetown had been true, he would have declared martial law and hanged him! (Stretch's Memo.)

Stockenstrom was finding now that he had returned to his exposed farm in the middle of the area from which the despairing Afrikaner and British memorials had recently emanated. Thefts there were, but not such as to justify recourse to arms. Better face a loss of some £4000 annually than risk a war which might, and, when it came, did cost a round £1,000,000. Any radical change of system must mean war, for the Kaffirs were getting guns from traders and, now that the fighting Boers had trekked, held themselves more than a match for the Settlers. The Boers away from the immediate border-lands, thankful that they had not been called out for four years past, openly said that they would not leave valuable farms again to fight in the bush for the sake of men who had got frontier farms either for nothing or at a very low price and then left their beasts to wander at will day and night. Some even muttered that they 'would rather see all the Englishmen's throats cut than go on commando and face the guns with which they have supplied the enemy.'[1] Above all, there was the question of policy. Was the search for a *modus vivendi* with the 'Caffer Nation' to be continued in the hope of civilising them at long last, or was it to be a matter of rolling them up between 'ten regiments and the republicans of Natal' and then being content to 'civilise the remnants into our herdsmen'?[2]

There was no doubt what one section of frontier opinion desired. Albany was full of men who said that the tribes must be cleared out of the Ceded Territory; Hare himself at his first meeting with the chiefs had blurted out that their proper boundary was the Umzimvubu, far away to the east, and there were even men who held that all Kaffirland must be annexed, since it was already ringed round by Europeans.[3] But Napier knew well enough that Fingos, Hottentots and ex-slaves were responsible for much of the stealing, and that a return to the D'Urban system would not cure this evil. He therefore contented himself with modifying the treaties in detail.

---

[1] The Commando system had not worked well as far back as 1793. It worked ill during the war of 1834–35, still worse in the war of 1846–7, and practically broke down in that of 1850–53. Napier's comments on the proposed changes in the Treaty system in 1840 illuminate both sides of the question. 'I am fully aware of the *whole* of this case, but I must observe that Mr. Hart, by his own admission, was in the habit of turning out his cattle to graze for *three and four months* at a time night and day totally left to themselves, being only counted once in that period, and his cattle might have *strayed* into Caffreland, and did so, I believe. At the same time I think it was very unjust that when he pointed out his stolen cattle in Caffreland he was refused permission to recover them. . . . All that Mr. Menzies says about passes would be strongly opposed by Missionaries and others as against the grand principle of *constant intercourse* between the civilised and savage man. . . . I think the learned Judge views that part of the question, more as regards the preservation of property by preventing Caffres entering the Colony than in respect of Civilisation. In short he takes a lawyer's view of the question, but I may be wrong.' (Napier's notes to Menzies' MSS.; No. 424 of 1851, pp. 65, 67, 85; Stockenstrom to Fairbairn, Oct. 29, 1840.)

[2] Stockenstrom to Fairbairn, Oct. 29, 1840.   [3] No. 424 of 1851, p. 89.

He began, *sub rosa*, to pay half-compensation for irreclaimable losses, allowed small unarmed parties to enter Kaffirland and take additional cattle for their pains, relieved herdsmen of the duty of going armed and thus serving as targets for Kaffirs and others desiring stock or a gun, and warned the chiefs that they must give up murderers. To all of which the chiefs agreed once they were satisfied that 'there was nothing behind it,'[1] and, during the early months of 1841, there was a distinct lull in the depredations.

Meanwhile a crisis had arisen in the danger zone of eastern Kaffirland which ruined whatever slender chance the Natalians had ever had of winning Napier's support for their independence. That chance had been steadily growing fainter, but both Napier and Russell were still prepared to offer the Boers a civil government of their own provided they eschewed slavery and allowed H.M. Government to control the troops.[2] The Natalians, however, had been troubled by cattle-stealing on their southern border and claimed to have traced the spoor to the kraals of Ncapaai the Baca. Pretorius was sent with a commando, which, in excess of its instructions and against the wishes of some of its own members, fell on Ncapaai without warning and carried off 3000 cattle and 17 child apprentices. Pretorius managed to quell the ensuing storm in the Volksraad, but the conduct of the commando brought renewed British intervention a step nearer. Faku the Pondo had recently moved across to the east side of the Umzimvubu and was now the near neighbour both of Ncapaai, with whom he was at war, and of the Republic. He professed to fear that the Boers would attack him next and, on the advice of his Wesleyan missionary, the Rev. Thomas Jenkins, appealed to Napier. Napier regarded Ncapaai as a public nuisance, but Faku was the *amicus* of the Colony. He therefore sent Captain Thomas Smith with 150 men to the Umgazi river to protect Faku and overawe the coast tribes on the one hand and the Boers on the other.[3] *(Dec. 1840.)* *(Jan. 1841.)*

The Boers now sent Napier their precise proposals, plainly relying on the Royal Navy to defend their independence; but Smith was on the march, and, pending further instructions, the Governor declined to discuss the matter.[4] Those instructions arrived piecemeal; first to promise protection to such tribes beyond the Colonial borders as asked for it, placing agents with them but in no wise annexing them, and then to offer the Natalians the commercial privileges of British subjects provided they admitted the troops. Even so Napier made no move till he heard that the Natal Volksraad had, after one or two *(Dec. 1841.)*

---

[1] No. 424 of 1851, pp. 70, 81, 84; Chase, II. 157, 169; Cory, IV. 353 ff.; Stretch to Fairbairn, Dec. 2 and 7, 1840; *Treaties . . . 1803–54*, pp. 97, 126.

[2] Bird, I. 612, 618, 621.

[3] *Nat. Not.*, pp. 76, 86; Bird, I. 249, 622, 631–5, 646; Chase, II. 159; Cloete, *Lectures*, p. 137.

[4] Bird, I., pp. 627, 630, 634.

previous attempts to relieve the Republic of the Bantu who were steadily pouring in from Zululand, decided to draft swarms of super-fluous tribesmen into lands between the Umtamvuna and the Um-zimvubu rivers, parts of which lands were claimed by Faku. Whether they were claimed justly or not, they were hard by his country and the arrival of strangers there might cause the repercussions on the Kaffirland tribes which a Cape Governor must dread above all things.[1] Napier was also convinced that the isolated and bickering Natalians were not to be trusted even with a subordinate government of their own; he was influenced perhaps by Grahamstown meetings which dilated on the coal, lead, indigo, cotton and tobacco of Natal, all the more exploitable now that Dingaan was gone. In any case, he ordered Smith to advance.

May 1842.   Rains delayed the march, but at length the troops reoccupied Port Natal.[2] While they were digging themselves in at Fort Victoria near the Point, Pretorius mobilised his men telling them that the Republic was in alliance with the Netherlands. This he did on the strength of the word of Johan Smellekamp, who posed as a Netherlands envoy although he was only the supercargo of the brig *Brazilia* which the Dutch merchant, George Ohrig, had sent to Natal.[3] Neither Winburg (Vet River) nor Potchefstroom moved officially; but Jan Mocke came down from Transorangia with 300 Modder River Boers, the Natal-ians seized some of Smith's oxen, and, when Smith tried to break up the Boer camp at Congella, Pretorius beat him and laid siege to his

June 1842.   fort. Dick King and his Zulu servant Ndongeni, however, rode over-land for help to Grahamstown, and Colonel Josias Cloete duly arrived by sea to relieve the hard-pressed garrison.[4]

Hardly had the news of the relief reached Capetown than orders came from Lord Stanley, the new Secretary of State, to abandon Port Natal with all speed since H.M. Government could not follow its restless subjects all round the world. Was it not enough that Her Majesty had just been compelled by her venturous and loving subjects to annex New Zealand? Napier, however, flatly though con-fidentially refused to budge now that shots had been exchanged[5] and Cloete pressed the Natalians to return to their allegiance.

The republicans were in a miserable position. Most of them were poor; Mocke's men had withdrawn and, with them, all hope of help from the High Veld; the moderates feared to submit lest this British occupation prove as short lived as the last; but against that fear was the dread of Panda (and already, in the confusion three Boers had

---

[1] Bird, I. 640 ff.; *Nat. Not.*, pp. 110, 135–9.
[2] Bird, I. 658, 660, 687; Moodie, *Battles*, I. 458; Chase, II. 183, 207.
[3] Bird, II. 34; Chase, II. 206; Cloete, *op. cit.*, pp. 144, 212; *Nat. Not.*, pp. 198–202; Stuart, *Holl. Afrik.*, pp. 166 ff.
[4] Bird, II. 14 ff.; Chase, II. 233, 240; D'Urban-Smith Papers, IV. 196 ff.
[5] Bird, I. 700, 705; II. 45.

been killed by Zulus) and the certainty that the British would march on Maritzburg. Pretorius, Landman and Jacobus Boshof, the future President of the Free State and now Voorsitter of the Natal Volksraad, threw their weight on the side of peace, if only to give the seventeenth-century Holland of their imagination time to intervene. Accordingly the Rump of the Volksraad submitted, an amnesty was July granted to all save four men specially named, two of whom had 1842. seized Government stores, and all, white and black alike, were secured in the tenure of their lands pending a final settlement. Pretorius then made way for Gert Rudolph as Commandant-General; the Volksraad continued to function feebly at the capital; at the Port, Smith sequestered the customs, the Republic began to Oct. go to pieces and Stanley, much against his will, bade Napier stand 1842. fast till further orders.[1]

BRITISH ATTEMPT TO CONTROL THE TREK.

The British had thus intervened decisively in the affairs of the Trekkers at the vital point, Port Natal. It was, however, questionable whether they could stop short there or whether they must not go on to deal with the problems raised by the Trek in all South-Eastern Africa. Napier held that many difficulties might have been avoided had Government from the first controlled an emigration which it could not prevent, and Stanley's instructions pointed to general intervention [2] by decreeing that all Trekkers who returned to the Colony should be amnestied—a useless favour, since there were no farms there for most of them to return to. Otherwise, their communications with the Colony were to be cut off and, if they attacked the tribes, the latter were to be protected and they themselves treated as rebels.

Presuming that these far-reaching instructions could be carried out, there was much more likelihood that they would have to be applied beyond the Orange and the Drakensberg than elsewhere. The situation there was much less clearly defined than in Natal. The area was larger, communications more difficult and the European inhabitants, all of them British subjects, more turbulent. Natal had attracted the main body of emigrants, steady-going folk who intended to settle; [3] but the plains of the interior had been given over to the less civilised Trekkers and the usual trans-frontier flotsam and jetsam.

This was especially true of Transorangia, the lawless lands between the borders of the Colony and the Republic of Winburg. The two most important native powers in that part were the Griquas

---

[1] Bird, II. 63 ff., 87, 103; Chase, II. 237.
[2] Bird, II. 46, 86, 103.   [3] Cloete, *Lectures*, p. 121.

at Philippolis and the Basuto to the east of the Caledon. The Griquas
1835. had just finished a civil war.¹ Adam II had died, and Abram, his
eldest son, had fallen foul of the L.M.S. missionaries. They and
Waterboer of Griquatown had supported a younger son, Adam,
while Cornelis Kok of Campbell had helped Abram. During the
1838. strife Adam and Waterboer had divided the whole of the wide area
claimed by the Griquas along the Ramah-David's Graf-Platberg line,
a line which was to play a great part in the future Diamond Fields
1841. dispute.² Adam III finally made good his claims to Philippolis just
before the storm-centre of the Trek shifted from Natal to his
country.

Adam's neighbour, Moshesh, the Basuto chief of the Mountain,
was, however, destined ultimately to play a much greater part in
South African history than any Griqua chieftain.³ He had begun
life humbly with a mere hundred followers at Butabute in northern
Basutoland. Mantati attacks had driven him to seek refuge on
the flat-topped mountain of Thaba Bosigo farther south. There
he had taken the lead in spite of the fact that his father, Mokatshane,
still lived, and there he had rallied broken tribes, Baputi, Bamaru,
and Hlubis, the core of the Basuto confederacy. He had beaten off
Zulus, Fingos, Waterboer's Griquas, and Matabele in quick succession, and had watched with quiet satisfaction the withdrawal of the
Hlubis southward of the Drakensberg and the destruction of Dingaan. He had welcomed Boer hunters, Dr. Smith with his medals,
1833. and, above all, the Paris Evangelicals. No mere warrior, but a born
diplomatist, he was wise enough to rely on the missionaries' advice
without falling under their control. He now began to play off the
Boers against each other and against the Colonial Government with
consummate skill. It was a game he was fated to play for thirty years,
first in the hope of enlarging his borders and then of saving his land
and people. To-day the Basuto are his monument.

Moshesh's claims were wide. Northward they embraced a large
belt of territory right across to the Vaal, on the ground that the
remains of the tribes which occupied it before the *Mfecane* were now
living under his rule in Basutoland awaiting an opportunity to reoccupy it. From the point of view of Bantu law the claim was not
so extravagant as it appeared to Europeans. Westward he claimed
the valley of the Caledon, the key to the history of the relations
between the Basuto and their neighbours; for there the rains from
the eastern mountains were sufficient to enable corn to be grown
without irrigation from the *fonteins* on which the rest of the future

---

¹ On the Griquas *vide* Orpen, *Reminiscences*; Lindley, *Adamantia*; Stow, *op.
cit.*; Marais, *Cape Coloured Peoples*, pp. 32 ff.; *vide supra*, pp. 99, 135, 186.
² Bloemhof Arbitration Blue-Book, p. 30; *vide infra*, pp. 333 ff.
³ On early history of Basuto *vide Bas. Rec.*, I. 1. ff.; III. 1 ff.; Lagden, *Basutos*,
I.; D. F. Ellenberger, *History of the Basuto*.

Free State depended.[1] The bulk of the Basuto lived under Moshesh
or his sub-chiefs to the east of the Caledon, but, before either Boers
or missionaries appeared, some had begun to reoccupy lands forty
miles to the west which they or their fathers had cultivated before
the *Mfecane*.

Meanwhile, a number of Bantu, half-breed and Hottentot clans, 1833.
refugees from the lower Vaal, had arrived in the Caledon valley
under the guidance of Wesleyan missionaries. Their leaders had
asked leave to settle there of Moshesh and his rival, Sikonyela, the
two well-established Chiefs in those parts, and their missionaries
had gone through the form of buying large areas of land round their
stations at Thaba Nchu and elsewhere with a maximum expenditure
of legal language and a minimum expenditure of anything else.[2]
They then held that the lands belonged to their Society and that
their protégés, Moroko and the rest, were independent chiefs.
Moshesh and, of course, the Paris Evangelicals held that the so-
called purchase price was merely a payment to secure the usual tribal
privileges for the newcomers, who were now vassals ruling their own
people alongside the Basuto sub-chiefs. And according to Bantu law,
they were right.

As with the missionaries, so with the Boers. Moshesh held that
he had merely given them leave to graze their cattle until they were
ready to move on. Now, alarmed at the number of farmers who were
coming into the lands between the Orange and the lower Caledon,
he reminded them of this fact. But, for the moment, the matter was 1842.
not urgent because the bulk of the Boers were still in Philippolis,
where some 700 of them had leased farms from Griquas who found
them useful as purveyors of arms and brandy. To the north-west one,
David Fourie, was trying to make good his claim to a huge area 1839.
between the Modder and the Vaal round Van Wyk's Vlei which he
had 'bought' for a few score of sheep and a horse from a Bushman.
In the midst of the Europeans, half-castes and Bantu thus jostling
one another, the missionaries raised the cry that Boers, unattached
to the organised parties of Winburg or Potchefstroom, were hunting
Bushman children.[3]

Meanwhile, the situation in Griqualand was becoming impossible.
The Boers complained that their coloured neighbours stole their
cattle; they held their farms on no certain tenure, and when Adam
Kok let his people lease farms he claimed jurisdiction over the
lessees. Were they, white men, subject to Griqua law? Why were
the Griquas, emigrants from the Colony like themselves, regarded
as independent and they not? Finally, where precisely were the
Griqua and Basuto borders?

[1] Orpen, *op. cit.*, p. 173; No. 1646 of 1853, p. 49.
[2] *Bas. Rec.*, I. 5.   [3] Chase, II. 254; *Bas. Rec.*, I. 36 ff., 93 ff.

1842.   The Cape Government was step by step forced to give an answer to all these questions. Philip made a long tour of the northern L.M.S. stations, interviewed Adam and Moshesh, and came to the conclusion that the Boers were trying to secure Basutoland because of its freedom from horse-sickness. If they did that, they would drive a wedge between the Colony and Natal, which was about to become British. As in 1833, he urged that the Queen's rule be extended over Transorangia or, at the very least, treaties be made with the big chiefs, Adam and Moshesh. Napier, who took a kindly enough view of the Transorangians, laid the alternatives before Stanley with a plain hint that he himself preferred treaties, and warned all concerned not to encroach on Native lands.[1]

1842.   At this stage, to the great annoyance of Michiel Oberholster, leader of the pre-Trek Boers, Jan Mocke returned with his Three Hundred from Natal, declaring falsely that there was only a truce of six months there, and that when the Hollanders came the fighting would begin. Adam promptly demanded British protection, and Mocke, angry that two of his men should have been taken to Colesberg for trial by Judge Menzies on a charge of murder, went into laager, saying that the missionaries meant to set the tribes on him. He presently emerged and rode down to Alleman's Drift on the Orange to proclaim a republic north of the river; but he was met there by Menzies, who, acting on a hint given by Moshesh and believing that Mocke would 'exterminate' such tribes and Boers as would not swear allegiance to the new republic, proclaimed British sovereignty over the Punishment Act area, that is, all Africa south of the 25th degree and eastward of the 22nd degree of East Longitude to the Indian Ocean, always excepting the dominions of Portugal and native rulers.[2] Napier, as in duty bound, disallowed the annexation, adding privately, however, that 'colonisation' was the only true solution.[3]

Napier's position was perplexing. He had few troops; the Natalians were buying powder in Colesberg and organising an Adjunct Raad at Winburg; the withdrawal of Menzies' proclamation had emboldened Mocke, and field cornets in the north-eastern districts of the Colony had actually called out their men to help their comrades north of the Orange if they should be attacked by natives. He Jan.   therefore sent Lieutenant-Colonel John Hare to make a demonstra-
1843.   tion in force on the south bank of the Orange.[4] The presence of

[1] *Bas. Rec.*, I. 44–9; Chase, II. 255; C.O. 1450, Gov. to S. of S., Sept. 15, 1842; No. 424 of 1851, pp. 216 ff.; Macmillan, *Bantu, Boer and Briton*, pp. 195 ff.
[2] Bird, II. 56, 114; *Bas. Rec.*, I. 50; Chase, II. 258; C.O. 1374, Menzies to Napier, Oct. 16, 23 and 28; C.O. 1450, Gov. to S. of S., Nov. 7, 1842.
[3] Chase, II. 265; C.O. 1450, Napier to S. of S., Nov. 11 and Dec. 13, 1842.
[4] *Nat. Not.*, pp. 233–4; C.O. 1374, Hare to Napier, Dec. 5, 1842; Chase, II. 266, 271.

regulars quieted the uproar and Hare soon marched home, leaving detachments at Colesberg and Cradock. But disturbances soon broke out again in Transorangia. Mocke boasted that Holland had interested France and, perhaps, other powers in the fate of Natal,[1] Griquas and Basuto staked claims in all directions, Napier asked for cavalry to protect the Griquas lest they be driven into the Colony, and the missionaries clamoured for treaties for all their protégés. Stanley therefore sent Napier the 7th Dragoons, the first regular cavalry to be stationed at the Cape since the reduction of the garrison in 1817, and permitted him to sign 'Waterboer treaties' with Adam Kok and Moshesh only.[2] Both chiefs were to keep order in their dominions in return for a subsidy and send back colonial criminals to the Colony for trial. The boundaries were badly drawn. Adam's were fixed only along the Orange from Ramah to Bethulie and his wide claims northward to the Modder and eastward into Basuto territory were left undefined. Moshesh was also dissatisfied. His boundary gave him some of Sikonyela's lands and the whole of the area between the Orange and Caledon which contained many Boers, but it also cut in half the lands of Moroko and the other small chiefs, and thus excluded a large strip of good land which he claimed as his own. The whole arrangement was a *pis aller*. It might have answered in 1834, but now, beyond putting the Boers under tribal jurisdiction, it ignored all questions of finance, police and, above all, land tenure. Already, before the signing of the treaties, Oberholster had thrown himself on the mercy of the Civil Commissioner of Colesberg and found no comfort there. Now he appealed with nearly 300 of his followers to be included in the settlement which was to be made in Natal.[3] Oberholster appealed in vain; nevertheless H.M. Government was being drawn irresistibly across the Orange. Short of 'building a fort' in the Colony and leaving the Boers and the tribes to fight it out, that was the only possible solution.

Stanley had at last faced that fact in Natal. Suspecting that sinister French influences had been behind Smellekamp's recent activities at the Port, he decided to annex.[4] Napier therefore made a naval demonstration off the coast and sent Henry Cloete, Colonel Cloete's brother, to Port Natal as Special Commissioner to effect a settlement. Cloete was empowered to consult the Natalians on the form of their future local government, but to countenance neither colour bar, encroachment on native lands nor slavery. Cloete found his task a hard one. The Netherlands Government had disowned Smellekamp; but the Boer mind was still dazzled by hopes of

Nov.-Dec. 1843.

June 1843.

[1] C.O. 1362, Hare to Napier, March 9, 1843, enclosure.
[2] No. 424 of 1851, pp. 214 ff.; *Bas. Rec.*, I. 55; *Treaties* .. *1803–54*, pp. 127, 129.
[3] Bird, II. 182, 329, 349; Eybers, p. 260.
[4] Bird, II. 140, 171; Morrell, *Brit. Col. Policy*, p. 142; Uys, *Shepstone*, p. 19.

Hollander support, and had been confirmed in its faith a month before Cloete's arrival by the reappearance of the pertinacious supercargo, who had brought with him a licentiate and a schoolmaster. Smith, a Major now, had headed the party off to Delagoa Bay, and had thereby convinced the Natalians that Smellekamp had really had something important to tell them.[1] At Pietermaritzburg, Pretorius, Boshof and the harassed landdrost, Johan Zietsman, were ready to admit to Cloete what they had already confessed privately to Smith, that the republic had been a failure;[2] but the opposition headed by Commandant-General Rudolph played for time, the ubiquitous Mocke rode in from Winburg with Jan Kock, Jacobus Snyman and 600 followers to strengthen Rudolph's hands, and the republicans' wives gave Cloete their frank opinion of him and all his works. Mocke failed to secure the election of a new Volksraad and withdrew tumultously, declaring his independence of Natal; eight additional members representing the Adjunct Raad were given seats, but on learning that Cloete's powers stopped short at the Drakensberg, they too departed taking a few of the Natalians with them. The Volksraad then submitted on the terms offered and the Special Commissioner, having secured the cession of St. Lucia Bay from Panda, settled down among the moribund republican institutions to deal with the land claims and the rising tide of Zulu refugees.[3]

Aug. 1843.

Before Cloete had finished his task Napier had made way for Sir Peregrine Maitland, an Irish veteran of the Peninsula, sixty-seven years of age, shrewd enough but liable to be swayed by the advisers of the moment. Maitland was in a better position than his predecessor in that the Colony was at last paying off its debts and showing signs of prosperity, but the Trekkers were restive all along the line from Griqualand to Natal and long delays were taking place in the final settlement of the fate of the dying republic. Seeing that independence and the all-important colour bar were gone and Cloete's plans held out little hope of the security, the land and the labour that they desired,[4] the Trekkers began to leave Natal. Maitland, for his part, recognised Faku the Pondo as ruler of all from the Umzimkulu to the Umtata and from the mountains to the sea, thereby flanking Natal with yet another Treaty State and threatening the Xosas and Tembus with a tribal ally of the Colony from the rear.[5] Nearly a year passed, however, before he was able formally to annex Natal as a district of the Cape. British Natal was to be much smaller than the republic, for it was bounded by the Umzimkulu on the

March 1844.

Oct. 1844.

Aug. 1845.

[1] Bird, II. 154 ff., 169 ff., 214, 239, 256, 331; Stuart, *Holl. Afrik.*, pp. 169 ff.
[2] Bird, II. 178 ff.; *Nat. Not.*, pp. 234, 270.
[3] Bird, II. 149, 218, 256, 265, 299; *Nat. Not.*, pp. 242–4; Chase, II. 282.
[4] On Land, *vide* Bird, II. 106, 113, 123, 150, 277, 404, 436, 463. On Locations, *vide ibid.*, II. 199, 213, 282, 422, 454; *Treaties . . . 1803–54*, Appendix.
[5] No. 424 of 1851, p. 235; *Treaties . . . 1803–54*, pp. 135 ff.

south and the Tugela and Buffalo rivers on the north; the suzerainty over Panda was tacitly dropped and no mention was made of St. Lucia Bay. Natal was to be a mere detached district of the parent Colony, with its own Executive Council to be sure, but with no legislature nearer than the Legislative Council at Capetown. A few officials were appointed forthwith, notably Martin West as Lieutenant-Governor, Theophilus Shepstone as Diplomatic Agent to the Natives, and Henry Cloete himself as Recorder to administer the law of the Cape Colony in the single-judge court at Maritzburg subject to appeals to Capetown and, in criminal cases, to the check of a jury.[1]

Many of the Boers who abandoned Natal went to Winburg; others pushed on across the Vaal to Potchefstroom, where Potgieter still was. There they accepted a revised constitution, the famous April Thirty-three Articles,[2] and severed the connection between Winburg-1844. Potchefstroom and Natal. To the south they claimed a boundary along the Orange which took in Transorangia, and thus ignored Kok's claims and Napier's treaties; to the east they tried to get into touch with Smellekamp at Delagoa Bay. A small party got through with some loss and presently Potgieter followed; but the coast belt was deadly for man and beast, the country behind Sofala was no better, and the Trekkers realised that, having lost Port Natal and St. Lucia Bay, they were cut off from the sea.[3]

Meanwhile, in Transorangia, Adam Kok exercised his jurisdiction Jan. under the recent treaty for the first time by sending a European 1844. charged with murder to Colesberg. Mocke threatened war, and for the sake of peace the prisoner was released; but Oberholster declared that he would have no one in Griqualand who refused the oath of allegiance to the Queen, and joined with the chiefs in complaining that the Trekkers were trying to frighten all opponents out of the country. Jan Kock was indeed busily pressing Winburg's pretensions, and presently Potgieter himself tried to make a treaty of his own with Adam whereby Boers and Griquas should live side by side under their respective rulers, who should decide 'mixed' cases jointly. Adam, fearing to be the earthen pot beside the pot of iron, refused and asked for a British garrison. Maitland promised an inquiry, but before anything could be done Adam 'upset the apple-cart.' A Boer, Jan Krynauw, had two peccant blacks flogged by the redoubtable Commandant Kock; Adam tried to arrest Krynauw; Krynauw's friends came to the rescue, and the whole of

---

[1] Eybers, pp. 182–6, 227; Bird, II. 394, 465. The other leading officials were D. Moodie, Secretary, and W. Harding, Crown Prosecutor.
[2] Eybers, p. 349.
[3] C.O. 1382, Maitland to Stanley, July 16, 1844 (enclosures); Walker, *Great Trek*, pp. 328 ff.; *Voort. Argief.*, p. 258.

Philippolis was given over to mutual cattle-rieving and skirmishing. The Boers declared themselves under the Winburg Raad; even the pacific Oberholster was defiant, and Maitland, risking a Colesberg rising, sent up a mixed force which scattered the Boers at Zwartkopjes. Kock and Mocke fled, Oberholster's people took the oath of allegiance,[1] and Maitland, thus encouraged, determined to attempt a general settlement upon the troubled High Veld beyond the Colony's northern border.

May 1845.

The basis of any such settlement must be a fair allocation of the land between white, coloured and black. Maitland convened the Transorangian chiefs at Touwfontein and proposed a scheme which he hoped might be extended over the whole area covered by the Punishment Act. Each chief was to divide the lands he claimed into two parts, the one an inalienable reserve, the other an area in which lands could be leased to Europeans. The chiefs were to remain nominally sovereign over the whole, but in practice a British Resident would control the Europeans, send serious cases to the Colony for trial and judge mixed cases jointly with the chiefs. Half the quit-rents of leased land were to go to the chiefs and half to pay the expenses of the Resident, who was in addition to have the right to call on each chief for a given number of men for the maintenance of the peace. Such were the mutual jealousies of the chiefs and their missionaries that only Adam Kok, who was well under L.M.S. control, accepted the scheme fully.[2] Moshesh indeed accepted it in principle and Molitsane, his Bataung vassal, who was living at Mekuatling till the time should come for him to reoccupy his ancestral lands to the north of Basutoland, asked that it should be applied to him. But Moshesh was only willing to have the undisputed portion of his frontier marked out; the rest must wait. Maitland therefore had to be content with recognising Kok's lands between the Orange and the Riet as inalienable and establishing Captain Henry Warden as Resident at Bloemfontein, an ex-Griqua farm in the alienable portion between the Riet and Modder rivers.[3]

June 1845.

H.M. Government had thus planted one foot beyond the Orange. The other must needs follow, for the Touwfontein arrangement was admittedly 'the germ of future conflicts.'[4] The germ promised to develop rapidly. Moshesh contemptuously offered the Boers a small wedge of unwanted land between the Orange and the Caledon, and meanwhile pushed his outposts into the disputed lands to the west of the latter river to make room for scattered members of his clans, who, hearing of peace and prosperity in Basutoland, were flocking

---

[1] C.O. 1451, Maitland to Stanley, May 13, 1845, and enclosures in C.O. 1384; Cory, *op. cit.*, IV. 299 ff.
[2] *Treaties . . . 1803–54*, p. 189.
[3] *Bas. Rec.*, I. 88, 93, 119; Eybers, p. 261.
[4] C.O. 1334, S. of S. to Gov., Nov. 6, 1845.

to him from all sides; Fourie was in difficulties at Van Wyk's Vlei and Jan Kock was terrorising the venerable landdrost of Winburg.[1] Maitland made one more effort to establish order by bidding at his orders Warden tell the assembled chiefs that a commission was coming to hear their complaints and urge them to promise to keep the peace till it should come.[2] The commission never came, for, while March Warden yet spake, the War of the Axe broke out on the Eastern 1846. Frontier.

There had been a period of tranquillity on the Eastern Frontier during the early months of 1841, but thereafter the troubles had begun again. The Stockenstrom system steadily crumbled away. There were faults on both sides. Lieutenant-Governor Hare, who believed in coercing 'prudently and justly and judiciously,' destroyed all confidence in the Government by making such wide claims that some of the chiefs complained that Government only kept that half of the treaties that suited them best and thereby left chiefs who kept the whole worse off than their backsliding colleagues.[3] Panics and protests were the order of the day among the frontiersmen. Occasional murders were followed by demands for the annexation of Kaffirland, periodical thefts of cattle by demands for the revival of the D'Urban system. Such outbursts were expected and duly discounted by the Capetown authorities, for the fact was that all save one of the victims of murder before 1840 had been Hottentot herdsmen slain before Napier had relieved them of the dangerous duty of carrying a gun; of the ten Europeans found dead during the five years preceding September 1843, four only had, with any probability, been killed by 'foreign' Kaffirs, and one of those four had been killed on his way home from a gun-runner's haunt. The rest had been slain by Xosas or Fingos resident in the Colony, men who had ensconced themselves in inaccessible corners of farms or, now that wool was booming and labour scarce, had been invited to squat on the farms by the owners in defiance of the pass laws and the wishes of the chiefs.[4] Some of the thefts with which the tribes were automatically charged were the work of these same people or of gangs of Europeans who stole horses in the Colony and sold them in Kaffirland. Nevertheless, though Tyali was now dead, the Kaffirs stole and the native police were either too frightened of their kinsmen to interfere or else implicated in the thefts. Even Napier began to despair, and, with Sandile's permission, expelled Tola from the June Ceded Territory, posted troops once more at Fort Willshire on the 1843. Keiskamma and, by arrangement with the local chiefs, began to

---

[1] *Bas. Rec.*, I. 101 ff.   [2] *Ibid.*, I. 119.
[3] No. 424 of 1851, p. 183. Stretch's Memo. of 1846.
[4] No. 424 of 1851, pp. 61, 85, 186, 196, 202, 267, 424; Stretch's Memo.; *S.A. Comm. Adv.*, Jan. 27 and 31, 1844; Cory, IV. 355 ff.

8

build a fort, Post Victoria, between that river and the Fish. But he shrank from a full return to the D'Urban system, for that meant war.[1] As it was the pacific Kama, believing that war must come, went north for a season to seek protection from Moshesh.

The root of the trouble on the Kaffir side of the frontier was that the power of the great chiefs was waning. Sometimes the drunken Sandile tried to carry out the treaties and sometimes he did not, and,

1842. since losing the regency, Macomo had set himself against him and usurped power for himself and the councillors. Yet when all is said and done, property on the frontier had doubled in value and doubled and doubled again since the inauguration of the treaty system and, though wool explains this appreciation, wool would have been non-existent without a great measure of security.[2] There

Sept. had been little work for the garrison which enriched Grahamstown,
1844. and the small balance of beasts properly due by the tribes under the treaties had been cleared off. On the other hand the irreclaimable list was a long one, many border farms stood empty because they were not safe, a farmer named Jan de Lange had recently been killed in a scuffle with Bantu thieves in the Colony, and nothing but a show of force had induced the chiefs to give up some of the miscreants.[3]

It was under these circumstances that Maitland unexpectedly arrived on the frontier. Stanley had already talked of modifying the treaties, but, as usual, had left the Governor to use his own judgment.[4] Maitland, possibly well primed by Menzies before leaving Capetown, much more certainly impressed after his arrival on the frontier by the missionaries' picture of the growing demoralisation of the Xosas, and undoubtedly influenced by the clamour in Grahamstown, suddenly revolutionised the frontier system. He first induced the Gunukwebes and other clans in the Ceded Territory to accept new treaties. He gilded the pill by promising them annual presents, but insisted that the chiefs must hand thieves over for trial in the Colony, make good the loss of beasts traced to their kraals, restore untraced beasts which the owner might recognise in their territories and pay him for his loss of time and other expenses. They must also once more recognise the Keiskamma as the colonial boundary, remain in the Ceded Territory only on good behaviour, and allow patrols to enter and the Governor to build forts therein. He

Oct. then induced the Tembus to accept the new treaties, lined up his
1844. dragoons and imposed similar terms on the sulky Gaikas, and made alliances with Faku the Pondo and Kreli the Xosa paramount chief in the hope that they would protect travellers along the mission-road

---

[1] No. 424 of 1851, pp. 87, 134, 156 ff., 181, 228.
[2] Ibid., p. 35; Stretch's Memo.
[3] No. 424 of 1857, p. 226; but it is doubtful whether they were the real murderers (Cory, op. cit., IV. 376).
[4] Ibid., p. 268.

to Natal, prevent the landing of goods unlicensed by the Colony on their coasts and overawe the frontier tribes from the rear.[1] So, having ordered the completion of Napier's Post Victoria in the Ceded Territory and informally obtained leave from Sandile to build another fort at Block Drift on the Tyumie just within Kaffirland itself, he retired to the capital.

Several months of peace followed Maitland's settlement, but it was a delusive peace. The partial return to the pre-Stockenstrom regime had been hailed with wild rejoicings in the frontier towns, for, men said, the end of the wedge was now in and Kaffirland must soon fall.[2] Sandile, on the other hand, had agreed to the forts in the hope that, if stealing was once stopped, the colonists would have no excuse for taking his lands. The other chiefs, however, had left Maitland's presence convinced that he was a man of war—'Did you not,' they asked, 'see the swords of the dragoons?'—convinced too that some of the missionaries meant to do by force what they had failed to do by persuasion, that is, 'steal their people and be magistrates and chiefs themselves.' Patrols and forts had come again, loss of lands would surely follow, and the Xosa chiefs on both sides of the Kei allied with one another and the Tembus for a defensive war lest they 'be broke up as the Hottentots were.' The signal for that war was to be the firing of the first Kaffir hut by the troops.[3]

Sandile held out against his followers for a time; but no one paid any attention to the wrecks of the treaty system; the dragoons rode off to Zwartkopjes; possibly, as Maitland believed, Boers from beyond the Orange stirred up the Gaikas, and cattle and horse thieving began again. In the latter part of 1845 the war-party among the Gaikas gained the upper hand, set aside the regent of one clan because he dealt too hardly with thieves, killed a missionary in mistake for Theophilus Shepstone, ex-Diplomatic Agent to the Gunukwebes, and molested another missionary and a trader. Six months before the outbreak, Captain Charles Stretch, Gaika Commissioner, warned Maitland that war was coming; but the warning was not taken and, in the midst of the growing excitement, military surveyors at Block Drift, mistaking their orders, began to survey the Kaffirland bank of the Tyumie. Sandile protested and began to beat up his neighbours; troops were hurried forward on the colonial side and a clamour arose in the Colony against Hare for his weakness in abandoning Block Drift; Macomo pointedly asked if he might avoid the coming war by retiring into the Colony. Then, March followers of the dispossessed Tola rescued a comrade accused of 1846.

[1] No. 424 of 1851, pp. 227, 232 ff.; *Treaties . . . 1803–54*, pp. 131, 173–188.
[2] Stretch to Fairbairn, Nov. 7, 1844, and *Memo.* 1846; Cory, *op. cit.*, IV. 378; *Speeches . . . of the late J. M. Bowker* (1864), pp. 116 ff.
[3] Stretch, Nov. 7, 1844, and *Memo.* Stretch had warned the Governor of this as early as 1840 (No. 424 of 1851, p. 51).

having stolen an axe, and slew a Hottentot on British soil; the chiefs concerned refused to give up the murderers, and Maitland set out for the frontier with troops and burghers.[1]

This time the colonial forces struck first.[2] Indeed, Hare struck too soon. He sent a mixed and totally inadequate force straight into Kaffirland. In passing the troops fired Sandile's deserted huts. At this, the prearranged signal, the Gaikas flew at them, destroyed half their unwieldly waggon train near Burnshill and, backed by most of the Tembus, poured into the Colony. They found the colonists safely in laager; but they did immense damage to property and were so elated that, almost for the first time in these wars, they marched in the open in broad daylight till the cavalry taught them caution on the banks of the Gwanga. All the Fingos and a handful of the Xosas and Tembus supported the Colonial Government, and Maitland soon had 14,000 men in the field, by far the largest force yet assembled on the frontier. Drought hampered the transport and an attack on the wooded Amatola Mountains effected little; but the burghers of the Eastern districts led by the newly created baronet, Stockenstrom, forced Kreli, who was once more playing 'the bush' to captured cattle behind the Kei, to promise to disgorge the colonial cattle and hold himself responsible for the doings of all the Xosa clans, a return to the days when Gaika had been similarly burdened with the sins of the Zuurveld Kaffirs. Drought forced Maitland to dismiss the burghers in September. Many of them parted with the regulars on bad terms owing to the high-handed acts of some of the officers, mutual contempt for each other's methods of fighting and continual quarrels over transport; Stockenstrom, *more suo*, quarrelled with the Governor for interfering in his dealings with Kreli and, even when fresh troops arrived, no transport was forthcoming till Maitland departed from the time-honoured requisitioning and paid £2 a day for each waggon and span. Nevertheless, at the end of the year, all save three of the clans west of the Kei were registering as British subjects and busily planting their gardens in their new locations against the next fighting season.

Jan. 1847.   A force then crossed the Kei to compel Kreli to carry out his promises; Maitland made way for Sir Henry Pottinger, an East India Company man, and, since Hare was dead, Lieutenant-General Sir George Berkeley took command of the troops. Pottinger did what he could to organise the conquered territory, using the mouth of the Buffalo as the base for the advanced posts; but he was hampered by traders who supplied the enemy with ammunition, by scandalous corruption among the organisers of the largely imaginary Hottentot levies which drew on the Commissariat, and by apathy

---

[1] Cory, *op. cit.*, IV. 408 ff.; Stretch's diary and *Memo.*, 1846.
[2] On the War of the Axe *vide* No. 786 of 1847, 912 and 969 of 1848, *passim*.

on the part of the Colonists generally. After all, campaigning was a weary business, native policy was in the hands of the imperial officials and not theirs, and Maitland had announced that no farms would be given out in Kaffirland at the end of it all.[1] Even when the war blazed up again after the harvest and Sandile was proclaimed a rebel, very few burghers responded to the bait of all the cattle they could capture. But the work was done somehow, and, when Sir Harry Smith arrived as Governor, all was quiet west of the Kei.   Dec. 1847.

Smith, a dapper little man, 'electric in his every movement . . . very determined but very impulsive and theatrical,' was not the man to do anything by halves. He knew that he had behind him an Imperial Government averse to following its restless subjects round the world, for it was still 'the hungry Forties,' when the Chancellor of the Exchequer 'sat by the pool of a bottomless deficit fishing for a Budget'; but he himself had spent many years in South Africa; he knew and liked the Colonists, Afrikaner and British,, and they him; he was a first-class soldier, 'the hero of Aliwal,' fresh from his Sikh triumphs and bursting as ever with vigour and good intentions. He sprang ashore and sounded the double, and for twelve breathless months all South Africa doubled.[2]   1829–1840.

Sir Harry came as something much more than a mere colonial Governor, for H.M. Government had at last realised that its colony at the Cape had become South Africa. It had, therefore, made its Governor at Capetown also High Commissioner 'for the settling and adjustment of the affairs of the territories . . . adjacent or contiguous to the . . . frontier.'[3] Pottinger had been the first to hold this new office, but Smith was to be the first to use the powers conferred by it. His first care was for the Eastern Frontier. Everyone was agreed that the Ceded Territory and 'British Kaffirland' beyond the Keiskamma must be annexed; but the question was, on what terms? Earl Grey, the Colonial Secretary, wanted to control the chiefs in the Ceded Territory by a European officer who should command their forces and draft Kaffir 'Sepoys' as hostages to the western districts; Maitland had proposed to settle Hottentots as a 'wall of iron' along the west bank of the Keiskamma; Pottinger would have settled Europeans among the Hottentots on the lines originally proposed for the Kat River Settlement in 1829. As for 'British Kaffirland,' Maitland would have kept the Amatolas empty and ruled the tribes through European officials; Pottinger had meant the chiefs to govern under European guidance,[4] but so far no one in   Oct. 1846.

---

[1] No. 424 of 1851, pp. 32, 57, 85, 100 ff.; No. 912 of 1848, pp. 26, 51, 79, 82, 87; No. 969 of 1848, pp. 3, 39, 56; Despatch 154 of 1847 (Cape).
[2] Vide *Autobiography of Sir Harry Smith*, pp. 579 ff.
[3] No. 912 of 1848, p. 5.
[4] No. 786 of 1847, pp. 158, 195; No. 912 of 1848, pp. 1 ff., 10.

authority had publicly proposed to settle Europeans beyond the Keiskamma. Smith, however, revived D'Urban's later policy, and this time there was no Philip to say him nay. Philip still lived, but he was an old man, broken by private sorrows, robbed by death of his ally Buxton, and, in his retirement, inclined to blame the Gaikas for the war.

Smith hastened to the frontier and annexed the Ceded Territory as the District of Victoria East. In the northern half he placed the Fingos under the Rev. Henry Calderwood as magistrate. The rest of the land was soon sold and guarded by the military villages of Juanasburg, Auckland, Woburn and Ely. He then annexed the land between the Keiskamma and the Kei as the separate colony of British Kaffraria,[1] offered the chiefs their choice between the staffs of war and peace (a sergeant's pike and a tent-pole surmounted by a door-knob respectively), and received their submission.[2] A few days later he announced his terms to the boom of an exploding powder-waggon and the fluttering of torn-up paper. 'There go the treaties. Do you hear? No more treaties.'[3] Henceforward the tribes would hold the reserves allotted to them from the Queen or her representative, the High Commissioner, as Great Chief. They would still rule their people, but there would be magistrates to set aside their judgments if these were 'inconsistent with justice and humanity.' Kingwilliamstown was to be the capital; the port of East London was annexed to the Cape Colony to avoid difficulties over the customs; round each of the forts and mission stations farms were offered to Europeans and, beyond the Kei, Kreli was obliged to recognise the Queen's sovereignty over the main road to the mission stations of Butterworth and Clarkebury. So ended the long-sustained attempt to maintain territorial segregation along the line of a river, and so began the British attempt to rule black and white as inhabitants of one country.

The bare outlines of this settlement had hardly been sketched before Smith hurried northwards. He had already annexed the Stormberg area up to the Kraai river as well as the huge, unorganised territory that lay along the Orange from Ramah to the Atlantic in whose western wastes van der Stel's Namaqualand copper was about to be worked.[4]

Dec. 1847.

Dec. 1847.

---

[1] *Law and Regulations of British Kaffraria*, pp. 1 ff.

[2] The staffs of peace and war are now in the S.A. Museum, Capetown.

[3] No. 969 of 1848, pp. 24 ff., 57.   Smith was picturesque in everything he did. 'You dare to make war,' he cried to the assembled chiefs. 'You dare to attack waggons. . . . Do you see that waggon, I say? Now hear my word—Fire.' (The waggon is blown up. Their astonishment was *excessive*.) 'Ah, do you see the waggon now? And you would and shall be blown up with it if you ever again attempt to touch another; so be good and believe your father as you used to call me. . . . You *shall* be good and I *will* have peace that my people may plough' (No. 969 of 1848, pp. 51, 52).

[4] No. 969 of 1848, p. 22; No. 457 of 1850, p. 31; No. 1360 of 1851, p. 41.

He now splashed through the Orange with sixty Cape Mounted Riflemen panting in his tracks to conciliate the Boers, 'his children.' He found Warden seated at Bloemfontein surrounded by confusion. There was the usual friction between Europeans and Griquas in Philippolis, and the scuffling had begun to spread to the Basuto borderlands. The French missionaries had just occupied Koesberg to the south to strengthen the hold of a petty Basuto clan in those parts, and already they were surrounded by Boers. A few stray white men had joined Sikonyela's people, who, in defiance of their Platberg promise, had wantonly attacked a Basuto outpost in pursuance of their old feud with that tribe.[1] Smith bullied Adam Kok into abandoning his jurisdiction over Griquas outside his inalienable reserve in return for a small pension, but failed to overawe Moshesh.[2] He hurried on northwards there to find the Winburg Republic falling to pieces. The disaster to Hare's baggage train at Burnshill had inspired Jan Kock to threaten the Philippolis Griquas;[3] but Warden and his multi-coloured *posse comitatus* had chased him across the Vaal. Thereafter the heemraden had never met again at Winburg, and now two rival landdrosts were competing for the remnants of authority. But again Smith would wait for no man and posted on towards Natal.

Sir Harry was anxious to reach Natal without delay, for the Boers were drifting out of the territory to find security at Winburg or Potchefstroom, or at Potgieter's newly founded town of Andries- 1845. Ohrigstad on the road to Delagoa Bay. Whether any of them would remain in Natal depended on a satisfactory settlement of the two closely allied questions of land tenure and native policy. The Volksraad had promised two farms and one town *erf* to each married man, and one farm and an *erf* to each 'young man' who had entered the country before the end of 1839.[4] Later comers as a rule had had to be content with one farm, but Henry Cloete had found leading Boers claiming many farms, Andries Pretorius ten and Gort Rudolph no less than forty, and had had difficulty in inducing the rank and file to register their claims at all.[5] Acting on his report the new Natal Government had decided to survey farms of 6000 acres at a quit-rent of £4 for all who had occupied their places during the twelve months preceding Cloete's arrival, but of 2000 acres only for all others. Most of the Trekkers would not hear of it. It was not always easy to prove occupation, for the vital twelve months had been a time of confusion; a farm to be a farm must be 6000 acres irrespective of the quality of the ground; delay in the issue of

[1] *Treaties* . . . *1803–54*, pp. 199, 201.
[2] *Bas. Rec.*, I. 139 ff.; Orpen, *Reminiscences*, p. 169.
[3] No. 969 of 1848, pp. 61–2; No. 1360 of 1851, pp. 81 ff.; C.O. 1452, Gov. to S. of S., July 30, 1846.
[4] An *erf* is a town lot.
[5] Bird, II. 191, 271, 453; Walker, *Great Trek*, pp. 219 ff.

title-deeds and an upset price of 4s. per acre for Crown lands increased the bitterness.[1] To add to the general discontent, Zulu refugees were still pouring into a country bereft now of the colour bar, and the Boers complained that the land commission which was demarcating native reserves had unavoidably included some of their widely scattered farms therein. In any case they said that they could not live among so many natives.

1846–
1847.
Some of the Natalians had set up the short-lived Klip River Republic to the west of the Buffalo, and next year Pretorius had gone to Grahamstown to interview Pottinger on behalf of the rest. The harassed High Commissioner, in the thick of a Kaffir war and his own interminable correspondence, had declined to see him;[2] whereupon he and his followers began to quit Natal. Smith now met them trekking over the Drakensberg northwards in the greatest misery.[3] He promised 6000 acres at once to all who were entitled to them, and 6000 to others who would occupy the farms within six months and undertake not to sell or mortgage them within seven years. Some accepted the terms and others presently returned from the High Veld to Natal, where they provided a border guard and a stable population for the Klip River Division; but most of them followed Pretorius to Potchefstroom, while the Klip River republicans, finding themselves still on British soil, moved across the Buffalo into what soon became the Republic of Utrecht.

One other matter Smith settled while on Natal soil. It is not easy to decide how far he had crossed the Orange with any clear intention of annexing the country to the north of it. He himself said later on that he had come intending even to withdraw the British Resident from Bloemfontein, but that the treaty with Adam, the prayers of the chiefs and his warm reception by local Boers decided him to annex. Oberholster certainly welcomed him; Snyman told him that he could answer for 900 men and, though the Winburgers were divided, influential men told him privately that they wanted the Queen's sovereignty but could not say so openly for fear of one another. In Natal, Lieutenant-Governor West and Shepstone laid before him the not very convincing evidence they had collected on the subject of slavery in the Transvaal, perhaps in the hope that he would annex that territory, and Smith did go so far as to ask Pretorius to test the feeling of the Transvaalers. Then, thinking

Feb.
1848.
he was on firm ground, he proclaimed the sovereignty of Her Majesty over all, white, coloured and black, between the Orange, the Vaal and the Drakensberg.[4]

[1] Die Kaapsche Grensblad, Oct. 30, 1847.
[2] Grahamstown Journal, Oct. 16 and 23, 1847; Walker, Great Trek, p. 363.
[3] No. 890 of 1848, pp. 184 ff. 196, 212.
[4] No. 969 of 1848, pp. 56, 63; No. 1646 of 1853, p. 22; Eybers, pp. 270 ff.

SOUTH-EASTERN AFRICA
1835-57

Scale of Miles

0   50   100   200

British Colonies 1835-46...............
Annexations to the Cape Colony, 1847-54......
British Kaffraria..................
Orange Free State................
Transvaal (boundaries undefined).............
Bantu and Griqua States...........

Note.   The Klip River Republic was situated in the triangle formed by the Drakensberg Mountains
on the west and the two branches of the Tugela River

Pretorius was furious, for he said he had understood that Smith had wished him to sound the Winburg Boers as well. He therefore refused Smith's cheerful offer of a land commissionership in Natal and rallied his men. Potgieter refused to help; but Pretorius, relying on friends in Winburg, crossed the Vaal, filled his ranks with pressed men, and gently turned Warden out of Bloemfontein. Smith at once marched north with a strong force, scattered the Boers at Boomplaats, proclaimed the Sovereignty once more, set a price on Pretorius's head, offered Potgieter of all people the rejected commissionership, and hastened back to Capetown by way of Durban leaving Warden once more in charge.[1]

Thus Harry Smith carried Maitland's Touwfontein policy to its logical conclusion. In his person, H.M. Government planted both feet on the farther side of the Orange river.

CHAPTER IX

PARLIAMENT AND VOLKSRAAD, 1837-57

Cape Colony: Liberalism, 233; Russell, Stanley and Grey, 235; social progress, 236; municipal institutions and civilisation franchise, 237; Constitution making, 237; anti-convict agitation, 241; Parliament and Divisional Councils, 243; Separatism, 245.—Balkanisation: O.R. Sovereignty (1848-9), 245; Transvaal (1844-51), 247; Sand River Convention, 258; O.R. Sovereignty 254; Bloemfontein Convention, 254; Orange Free State Constitution, 260; Transvaal (1852-7), 264; Transvaal *Grondwet*, 267; Crown colony Natal, 269.

CAPE COLONY

HARRY SMITH'S bold but belated attempt to control the Great Trek failed to stir either Downing Street or Westminster to enthusiasm. Earl Grey, the Colonial Secretary, who had reconciled himself to the retention of Natal only by the thought that its natives would otherwise be 'exterminated,' that is 'expelled,' now coldly accepted the O.R. Sovereignty as an accomplished fact on condition that it would pay for itself,[2] and footed the bill of £1,000,000 for the War of the Axe with the remark that, as the Cape was so soon to have a Parliament of its own, it must not expect Great Britain to pay for any more of its wars. Manchesterthum was rising to its zenith and the old colonial system based on reciprocal privileges and duties was gone or going with the Corn Laws and the Navigation Acts. However

---

[1] No. 1059 of 1849, pp. 43, 61; Walker, *Great Trek*, pp. 364 ff.; Smith, *Autobiography*, pp. 596 ff.
[2] No. 969 of 1848, pp. 66-8.

8*

rapidly Colonial Secretaries might follow one another, their views and those of the British public coincided on the subject of colonies. Even Protectionists regarded colonies of settlement coldly. 'These wretched colonies,' wrote Disraeli, 'will all be independent in a few years and are a millstone round our necks.'

But ministers and people were inspired by more generous motives than those of the counting-house. They had no desire for unwilling subjects; they held as of faith, Macaulay still being in the flesh, that the attainment of British parliamentary institutions was the political end of man. As for South Africa, all Great Britain really required was the naval base in the Cape Peninsula. The rest was a burden to be borne cheerfully as long as was necessary, but not a moment longer. It was no coincidence, therefore, that the years which saw self-government achieved in North America and the way paved for it in the Antipodes by the Australian Colonies Act and the federation of New Zealand, should also have seen the Transvaalers recognised as 1852–1856. independent, the Cape granted a parliamentary constitution, most of the O.R. Sovereignty transformed into the Orange Free State, Natal cut off from the old Colony as a separate Crown Colony like British Kaffraria, and the cause of Separation from the West taken up vigorously in the Eastern Province. Nor was it surprising that, just after this fatal balkanisation had been accomplished, the ex-Governor of New Zealand, Sir George Grey, who had become High Commissioner and Governor of the Cape Colony, should have argued that since Great Britain might have to leave South Africa one day, it behoved her to set the country in order by federating it so that the parting might take place with mutual regrets[1] and with good hope that the civilisation policy of the parent Cape Colony would quickly get the better of the frontier ideas of isolated little Natal and the unstable Trekker Republics.

The Kaffir war of 1834–5 and the confusion which followed it, the beginnings of municipal government, and the desire to give the new Legislative Council a fair chance had checked the agitation for elective institutions in the Cape Colony. But that Council was not popular in any sense of the word. Its members had to be reappointed with the advent of each new Governor; it only gained the right to alter the Charters of Justice in 1844; it was frankly told by Napier that important matters were decided elsewhere.[2] Christoffel Brand in the *Zuid Afrikaan* and Robert Godlonton, now editor of the *Grahamstown Journal*, talked of an elective Assembly from time to time, Godlonton adding also a demand for Separation; Russell

---

[1] No. 1428 of 1852, p. 259; 216, April 1860, pp. 4 ff.
[2] Theal, *History*, IIb. 214; C.O. 1326, S. of S. to Gov., Aug. 8, 1838, and C.O. 1332, Jan. 4, 1844.

pleaded in the Commons for 'free and popular institutions'; but Napier, like Sydenham in Canada, had held that free local government was the first need; the Whig Melbourne Ministry fell, and it was not until the Masters and Servants Ordinance of 1842 had embodied the principles of the 50th Ordinance by ignoring colour distinctions in questions of employment and breach of contract that Fairbairn was willing to go forward once more.[1] Meanwhile, Capetown and Grahamstown meetings petitioned for an Assembly and 1841. found a powerful advocate in John Centlivres Chase, who argued that slavery being gone and municipal councils established, there was no reason why the boon should be withheld.[2]

Lord Stanley, Secretary of State to the Tory Peel, thought other- 1842. wise and, in reply to the petitions, urged all the old objections and added some new ones: the site of the capital (ever a bone of contention in South Africa), the difficulty of manning such an Assembly and devising a satisfactory non-elective portion of the legislature, the fear, justified by the event, that control would fall into the hands of the townsmen. Above all, what of the Coloured franchise and Separation ?[3]

Stanley's letter and a quarrel for official precedence between Judge Menzies and Lieutenant-Governor Hare awoke the dozing dogs of Separatism and gave Godlonton his party. The Legislative Council was purely Western till 1847, when William Cock, of Port Frances, was appointed, and the only official communication the East had with Capetown was through the Lieutenant-Governor. The latter's powers were dwindling. Governors acted over his head and relied on the weekly Grahamstown mail to keep them posted with frontier affairs, while the Legislative Council talked of dropping him from the estimates. At this the East demanded a constitution similar to that of Natal; but Maitland objected that, if this were granted, the West would let its share of the burden of Kaffir wars fall on the shoulders of the British taxpayer. On the eve of the War of the Axe, the office of Lieutenant-Governor was on the point of being extinguished,[4] and when, at the end of that struggle, the buffer province of British Kaffraria was directly annexed to the Crown, it 1847. became unnecessary and was allowed to lapse.

By this time, Russell's Whigs were in again and Earl Grey decided Nov. to risk giving the Cape parliamentary institutions.[5] The Colony was 1846.

[1] Ordinance No. 1 of 1841.
[2] Chase, *Cape of Good Hope and Algoa Bay, passim*; Eybers, p. 42; R. Kilpin, *Pioneers of Parliament* (Fairbairn, Brand, Porter, Godlonton and Saul Solomon) (*Cape Argus*, March 19–April 23, 1921).
[3] C.O. 1330, S. of S. to Gov., April 15 and 21, 1842.
[4] *G.T. Journal*, Dec. 11, 1845; C.O. 1452, Maitland to S. of S., Oct. 16, 1846.
[5] No. 912 of 1848, p. 4; No. 400 of 1846, for requests for representative government.

in a much healthier condition than it had been ten years before. Then all had been gloom with the Trekkers pouring out and the slave apprentices flocking into the towns and dorps, there to breed the measles and smallpox which slew them and the Europeans by scores. Now the tide had turned. D'Urban's economy campaign and the simplification of the fiscal system had borne good fruit; the strict collection of taxes by the Colonial Secretary, John Montagu, had enabled the Colony to wipe off its public debt and, helped by a substantial remission of the claim, to repay H.M. Government its advances towards the liquidation of the paper-money.

1838–1839.

Customs revenue rose with expanding trade; the Trekkers opened up new markets in the interior; slave compensation money and war-like stores for the Kaffir war swelled the imports, and exports moved upwards in sympathy. It is true that wine lost first place on the list for the British preference had been steadily reduced since 1825 and bad wine killed the demand for good; but faced with a failing market and a labour shortage, many of the Western farmers, like their fellows in the East, fell back on wool. Merino sheep, acclimatised in Albany on a small scale just before the war of 1834, speedily made 'gentlemen of people who only brought a spade and a check shirt to Africa,' and thus furnished Grahamstown with a surprising number of carriages; indeed, in the 'fifties wool outstripped in value all other Cape exports put together.[1] Hides and skins bulked large, guano was exported from Ichaboe Island off the Namaqualand coast and there was good hope of copper at van der Stel's Koperberg in Namaqualand. Joint-stock companies and kindred financial institutions[2] reflected the growing prosperity, and eighteen new local banks were opened in the Colony with such success that the old Loan Bank had to close its doors. Coasting trade sprang vigorously with Natal and, following on Maitland's Pondo treaty, with Port St. John's; for a time a regular steam mail service of fifty days was maintained with England; new jetties and lighthouses were built at Capetown and Port Elizabeth, and determined attempts were made to attract shipping to Port Frances (Alfred).[3] Capetown, now partly lit by gas, rebuilt its Groote Kerk, built a Roman Catholic cathedral and a military hospital, and planted a lighthouse at Mouille Point in Table Bay. In the country districts churches and villages sprang up in all directions.

1843–1846.

1837–1856.

The cause of self-government whose economic foundations were thus being laid was helped forward by the development of local liberties and responsibilities, for, as in mediæval England, Cape parliamentary institutions grew up from below. The Kaffir war of 1834 had delayed the grant of municipal institutions; but, once

---

[1] Stretch to Fairbairn, Nov. 19, 1845.

[2] E.g. Capetown Board of Executors (1838), Old Colonial Mutual Assurance Society and Grahamstown Fire and Life Assurance (1845).

[3] Lighthouses at Mouille Point (1842), Roman Rock lightship (1845), Cape Agulhas and Cape Reçife (1849–51).

that war was over, towns had been permitted, with the approval of the Governor, to elect on a simple economic franchise open to adult male British subjects of all colours Boards of Commissioners, which should have power to levy rates and take charge Jan. of their own affairs. Beaufort West, in January 1837, was the 1837. first town to take up these privileges and responsibilities. It was followed by Somerset East, George, Grahamstown and Cradock in quick succession, but it was only in 1840 that Capetown was created a municipality by special ordinance, and thus set free to replace its old-fashioned Dogberries with police patterned on Sir Robert Peel's 'bobbies.' The day of mayors, mace-bearers and full-blown city councillors was still far distant; but these Boards of Commissioners laid the foundations of that system of genuine elective local government on which the Cape Parliament was destined to rest.[1]

After the towns, the Churches. The old laws regulating the relations of the Dutch Reformed Church to the state were abrogated, the political commissioners were withdrawn and the Synod was empowered to regulate all the internal concerns of the church without regard to the Governor's approval. The Synod was to meet in 1843. Capetown every five years, a Synodical Commission was to act for it during the intervals, and the five presbyteries into which the church was now organised were to meet annually at Capetown, Tulbagh, Swellendam, Graaff-Reinet and Grahamstown. Ministers were still to be paid by the state, and the courts could deal with matters arising out of the actions of the Synod or any subordinate body; nevertheless, the most powerful ecclesiastical body in the Colony had achieved self-government.[2]

The Anglican Church also won new strength and freedom. Hitherto it had been staffed by Colonial Chaplains and controlled by the two Archbishops and the Bishop of London, but now Robert Gray was appointed Bishop of Capetown.[3] He brought many clergy with him, put new life into the thirteen existing Anglican congregations, founded the Diocesan College (Bishop's) for boys at Ronde- 1848. bosch and Zonnebloem for the sons of chiefs hard by, and fairly launched the Church of England on its missionary career in southern Africa. So greatly did his work prosper that his immense diocese of the Colony, Natal and St. Helena was presently divided, Dr. John Armstrong becoming Bishop of Grahamstown, Dr. John Colenso Bishop of Natal, and he himself Metropolitan. Similar energy was 1853. displayed by the Roman Catholics. A Vicar-Apostolic, P. R. Griffith, was appointed and, ten years later, A. Devereux became Vicar-Apostolic for the Eastern Province. Thus did the Anglicans and

---

[1] Ordinance, Aug. 15, 1836; Eybers, p. 78.
[2] Engelbrecht, *Geschiedenis*, I. 14.
[3] Locally the Church was staffed by Colonial Chaplains.

1838. Roman Catholics accept Godlonton's principle of Separation.[1] Mission societies, Moravian, L.M.S., Wesleyan, Rhenish, Berlin, Paris and the S.A. Missionary Society, flourished in and around the Colony.[2] All of them except the Moravians concentrated almost entirely on book learning, but such was their energy that Coloured and native children were in many ways better supplied with education of a sort than Europeans, many of whom in the more outlying parts, then and for long afterwards, attended the mission schools. There were good private schools in Capetown like the *Tot Nut van't Aglemeen*, a private venture of Batavian days, and the South African College, which had been founded in 1829 by the joint enterprise of British and Afrikaner colonists. On the other hand, the twenty-four 'Somerset' schools in the principal villages were going downhill. These were nominally supervised by the Bible and School Committee over which von Manger, the erstwhile 'subtle' predikant of Graaff-Reinet, presided in his dotage, while in each district centre the local predikant and a powerless schoolboard elected by subscribers watched the Scottish schoolmasters depart, the state subsidy diminish and listened to complaints by country folk that the schools did not give the kind of schooling they desired, if only because the medium of instruction was almost entirely English. For the rest, there was an elementary school at each church-place and, on the farms, itinerant teachers often of very doubtful quality and character.

Following on a report that had been prepared for D'Urban by John Bell, his Colonial Secretary, Napier turned for advice to his friend, Sir John Herschel, the famous astronomer, who, in collaboration with Thomas Maclear, the Cape Astronomer Royal, was busily surveying the southern heavens from his private observatory at Claremont near Capetown. Herschel, with Fairbairn's help, evolved the system that bears his name, whereby two classes of schools were

1839. recognised: the English-medium, classical schools, which charged a small fee to all who could not get a Government nomination, and second class schools, where education was free and Dutch was used as the medium, if desired. Local boards of subscribers were called upon to provide buildings and were permitted to supplement the teachers' meagre state salaries. The outstanding features of this Herschel System were, first, the state provision of schooling, a thing unparalleled at that time save in Prussia and one or two New England states, and, secondly, inspection in the lines that were being tentatively followed in England. Inspection, the keynote of the system, was entrusted to James Rose-Innes, the best of Somerset's Scots, who resigned his chair of mathematics at the South African College to become Superintendent-General of Education, for many

[1] C. Gray, *Life of Robert Gray*, chap. iv., vi; *Crockford's Clerical Directory*, pp. 1882 ff.
[2] Du Plessis, *Christian Missions*.

years to come, the Colony's one-man Department of Education. Two chief difficulties faced him: lack of competent teachers, a lack made worse by the recent failure of a private Normal Seminary, and the demands of philanthropists that Coloured children be admitted. He overcame the former problem by having recourse to his native Scotland, and side-stepped the latter by decreeing that all scholars must be 'decently clothed and of good deportment,' an elastic description that served to keep out such non-European youngsters as their white neighbours might object to. Presently grants were given to Mission schools and to third class schools in the country districts.[1] 1841–1843.

The primary material needs of the Colony, however, were magistrates, roads, and labour. The first were easily supplied as times improved. Stockenstrom, besides infusing an unwonted energy into the rank and file of Eastern officialdom, had made a beginning by appointing more magistrates; Napier carried on the work, and it only remained for Harry Smith, in his usual dashing style, to create ten new magistracies and two civil commissionerships at a blow.[2] Roads and labour presented greater difficulties. They were two sides of the same problem. Such hard roads as had been built since 1806, like the French Hoek Road of 1824, the Sir Lowry's Pass road over the Hottentots-Hollands in 1830 and the Queen's Road from Grahamstown to Beaufort in the 'forties, had been the work of soldiers or of convicts or of both. Either method was slow and costly, and other labour was difficult to get because farmers feared any drain on the already inadequate supply.

Since the slump of Somerset's day immigration had shrunk to the eighteenth-century scale. A few British officials remained in the Colony on their retirement; some soldiers took their discharge there; a few families ventured to land; Prize Negroes and St. Helenas helped to swell the ranks of the Coloured population; but the promising work of the Children's Friend Society, which sent out lads as apprentices, was cut short by credulous philanthropists, who were carried away by the mendacious reports of one of the apprentices, 'the boy Trubshaw.'[3] The Legislative Council then considered the question of imported labour. It discussed the rival merits of English navvies, St. Helenas and Gurkhas, while Lord John Russell for his part offered military convicts, who should finish their term on Robben Island and be liberated in Capetown. Napier persuaded him to give 1830–1839. 1841.

---

[1] Malherbe, *History of Education*, chapters iv., v.; *Quarterly Bulletin of the South African Library*, Vol. xii. No. 2, Dec. 1957, pp. 58 ff. In 1838, the Government spent £2000 on education. This rose to £7900 in 1850.

[2] At Port Elizabeth, Colesberg, Cradock and Clanwilliam (1837), Wynberg, Malmesbury, Paarl and Caledon (1839), Tulbagh, Piketberg, Simonstown, Riversdale, Mossel Bay, Richmond, Bathurst, Fort Beaufort, Stockenstrom (Kat River), Fort Peddie (Victoria East) (1848). Districts were defined in 1839 as the areas under magistrates, Divisions as those under civil commissioners. Sometimes the two areas coincided. Theal, *History*, II. 163; Proclamation, Feb. 5, 1839; No. 1056 of 1849, p. 10.

[3] No. 323 of 1840.

up the idea, and, when Stanley proposed to send out a few boy convicts, William Porter, the new Attorney-General, said Downing Street should be warned to 'commit no nuisance here.' But since the need for labour and roads was pressing, Montagu, Porter, and the

1843. Surveyor-General, Major Charles Michell, framed the 'Montagu Plan.' Trunk roads were to be built by a central board of three officials and three nominated citizens financed by a state grant, rates, and loans raised on the security of the tolls. Divisional road boards consisting of the Civil Commissioner and four elected members were to build

1848– branch roads in the same way. The firstfruits of the new policy were
1853. soon seen in the roads over the Montagu (Cradock's) Pass, Michell's Pass and Bain's Kloof, all built by convicts or free labourers imported at Government expense, for between 1844 and 1847 some 4300 labourers, mechanics and domestic servants were brought out under the Cape's first state-aided immigration scheme, and more would have been brought had not Smith's unlucky military villages swallowed up the funds.[1]

Earl Grey was thus justified in proposing and enthusiasts at the Cape in demanding free and popular institutions. The Reformers had found a powerful ally in Porter. He had won Fairbairn's confidence by refusing to follow the Governor in voting against a usury bill, Brand's by his respect for the Roman-Dutch law and opposition to Stanley's convict proposals, and popular affection by announcing in court that 'Her Majesty sent me here to prosecute, not to persecute.' Grey had ordered Pottinger to report on the situation, but it was only after the War of the Axe that Harry Smith, breathless from his gallop to the Tugela and back, asked Porter to

1848. draft a scheme. Porter's draft provided for a nominated upper house, which was in effect a continuation of the Legislative Council, and an elected House of Assembly. Sir John Wylde, the Chief Justice, alone stood out for some elective seats in the Council, while Porter himself, who always hankered after a seat in the lower house, proposed that officials should be allowed to stand for election without being held responsible to Parliament for their official acts; but all were agreed that the franchise must be low enough to admit some of Fairbairn's Coloured friends to the voters' roll. Separation they set aside, because the Cape Peninsula alone outweighed the whole Eastern Province in wealth, and decided further that the capital must remain at Capetown where dwelt one in five of the population of the entire Colony.[2]

[1] Road Report of Sept. 4, 1843; Ordinance 22 of 1843; No. 969 of 1848, p. 36; Robertson, H. M., *The Cape . . . and Systematic Colonization*; Marais, J. S., *The Cape Coloured People*. Population rose from about 54,000 Europeans and 66,000 others in 1830 to 140,000 and 210,000 in 1854.

[2] On the formation of the Cape Parliament, *vide* Kilpin, *When Downing Street Ruled*; No. 400 of 1846; 1137 and 1234 of 1850; 1362 of 1851; 57, 1427, 1581 and 1636 of 1852; 1640 of 1852–3.

Smith sent the draft to London with his blessing and granted the
right of free public meeting. All seemed to be going well when a 1849.
storm arose which very nearly wrecked the hopes of the Reformers
and threatened to split the Colony on racial lines. Like other
European Powers, Great Britain had long been accustomed to send
her more grievous criminals overseas as an alternative to hanging
them at home. Since 1788 she had sent them to Australia, but, with
the exception of Norfolk Island and Van Diemen's Land, that
continent had been closed to this particular type of assisted emigrant
in 1840. There was much to be said for the practice of transportation. Convicts were useful on public works, and ticket-of-leave men
had a better chance of making good in a new country than in the
old; but the Cape Colony preferred to rely on its somewhat inadequate local supply of convicts and had no mind to see possible
bushrangers let loose among the African and Coloured population in
a land of scattered farms. Hence, when Grey proposed to send con- Nov.
victs to Capetown provided colonial opinion approved, it was soon 1848.
made abundantly clear that opinion did not approve. Nevertheless,
Capetown heard that convicts, mostly Irishmen captured in 'Widow March
McCormack's potato-patch rebellion' of 1848, were coming in 1849.
the *Neptune*. Neither convicts nor Irishmen, the Attorney-General
always excepted, were popular in Capetown in those days, any more
than they were in the U.S.A.; a mass meeting of 5000 formed an
Anti-Convict Association; petitions to the Queen were widely
signed and thousands pledged themselves to boycott all who had any
dealings with the invaders.[1]

So far opinion in East and West was at one, and Godlonton vied
with Fairbairn and Brand, old emancipation quarrels forgotten, in
denouncing the Secretary of State. But when Smith announced that
he could not set aside his orders, a dangerous division took place.
In spite of the Governor's promise that not a convict should land
till he had received Downing Street's reply to his remonstrances, one
nominated Councillor and many field cornets resigned. The legislature had already been weakened by death and resignation, and to
save it from extinction Smith appointed three new members; whereupon a mob surrounded the Council Chamber, hustled the new
Councillors as they came out and, later in the day, smashed the
windows of the house of one and destroyed the mill of another.
Brand, bitter at his financial failure as an editor and back once more
at the Bar, and Fairbairn, who had all that intolerance to opposition
which mars the virtues of a certain type of Lowland Scot, now lost
all sense of proportion. They cut Porter for two years to come
because he would not say that the Governor could set aside his

[1] On the Anti-Convict agitation *vide* No. 217 of 1849: 104 and 1138 of 1850,
and Kilpin, *The Romance of a Colonial Parliament*, pp. 70 ff.

instructions and, when the *Neptune* entered Simons Bay, they tried to boycott the Government. The boycott was never complete, but it led to rioting in the course of which Fairbairn was assaulted in his own house, and prevented any further session of the Legislative Council for that year. Meanwhile, Smith kept his head and his word; not a convict landed and the *Neptune* sailed for Van Diemen's Land leaving intense mutual bitterness behind her. She arrived to find an Anti-Convict Association in such Australian colonies as resented Grey's well-meant attempt to send convicts once more to a continent from most parts of which they had so recently been shut out.

Feb. 1850.

At the same time, Porter's draft was returned with the approval of the Privy Council, save that the upper house was to be elective and officials were not to stand for election to the Assembly. Details were to be filled in locally and, to secure as representative a Council as possible, Smith invited the municipal councils and divisional road boards to put forward names for his consideration. He then chose the four highest on the list, three from the West: Brand, Fairbairn and Francis William Reitz, father of the future Free State President, and one from the East, Sir Andries Stockenstrom; but since the East had hitherto only been represented by a single member, William Cock, he sought to equalise the representation of the two Provinces by choosing Godlonton of Grahamstown from half-way down the list. The four Popular Members who actually headed the poll resolved to act as a party and to discuss nothing but the constitution, the one topic on which they were all agreed other than a common hostility to Godlonton, who had washed his hands of the anti-convict agitation in its later stages. Their main points were that the qualifications necessary for membership of the upper house must be reduced and the lower house be given full control of finance. In other words, they demanded responsible government and, when the Council passed on to other business, they marched out in a body after Stockenstrom, 'the Flying Dutchman,' had read his 'eleven reasons for dissent.' The Capetown municipality then asked them and Johannes Wicht, the fifth at the polls, to draft a rival constitution. This Fairbairn took to London; but Grey refused to treat him as a representative, Stockenstrom, who followed him to Downing Street, spoilt his case by a violent letter to Russell, and poor Fairbairn returned home to face financial worries and waning popularity. Nor were matters mended when Brand was passed over for the seat on the Bench rendered vacant by the death of Menzies.

1851.

Porter now drew up the 'Attorney-General's Draft' which was destined to form the framework of the constitution of 1853. This the Rump Council debated till the Eighth Kaffir War called the Governor to the frontier. The conservative Montagu, who then acted for Smith at the capital, filled up the vacancies on the Council with four Westerners of his own way of thinking and, frightened at the rumour of a Coloured rising in the West in sympathy with the Hottentot rebellion in the East, doubled the financial qualification for the franchise to exclude Coloured voters. Worse still, the Liberal Russell Feb.– ministry fell and the Tories came in; Montagu, in poor health, sailed for England to press doubtless for a nominated Legislative Council, and Smith had to make way for Sir George Cathcart as Governor. Nothing further was done till the Whigs came in once more. Then the new Colonial Secretary, the Duke of Newcastle, hastened to despatch the Order in Council which was to give the Cape its Parliament. The Legislative Council, with a life of ten years, was to be purely elective, eight members being returned for the Western Province as a single constituency and seven for the Eastern. Four members for each province were to retire every five years unless the Council were dissolved at the same time as the lower house. The West was to have a majority of two over the East in the House of Assembly of forty-six members, all of whom should sit for five years unless the House were dissolved either with or without the Legislative Council. The Governor was to summon Parliament annually at any place he chose to name, but further than that H.M. Government was not prepared to go in the direction of Separation. Finally, in spite of Montagu, the low franchise advocated by Porter and the Popular Members was adopted and, since the Secretary of State suggested that all Her Majesty's subjects 'without distinction of class or colour, should be united by one bond of loyalty and a common interest,'[1] all adult male British subjects were to be entitled to the franchise and to seek election to either house on fulfilling the conditions. Thus was the policy of legal equality based on civilisation rather than the colour of the skin carried to its logical conclusion, the policy that had been embodied in the 50th Ordinance of 1828, the Municipal Ordinance of 1836 and the Masters and Servants Ordinance of 1842.[2]

Cathcart having gone to his death in the Crimea and the Colony having greeted its new found liberties with its first issue of postage stamps, the unrivalled 'three-cornered Capes,' the Cape Parliament was opened on June 30, 1854, by the Lieutenant-Governor, Charles Henry Darling. It is easy to overestimate the liberties that had thus

Feb.– March 1852.

Dec. 1852.

[1] No. 1636 of 1853, p. 25.

[2] Eybers, pp. 45 ff. Legislative Councillors had to be at least 30 years old and possessed of £2000 in land or £4000 in movables. The Chief Justice presided over the Council. In the Assembly, Capetown had 4 seats and each of the nine Western divisions 2, Grahamstown 2 and the nine Eastern divisions 2 each. The franchise was occupation for twelve months of premises worth £25 per annum or a salary of £50 or, with board and lodging, £25. This franchise remained unchanged till 1892, when it was raised and an education test added to keep out 'blanket Kaffirs' (*vide* p. 432, *infra*).

been accorded. The Colony had by no means received the new-fangled Responsible Government that was already established in most of the British North American and Australasian colonies, but merely the traditional Representative Institutions that had been extended to British colonies of settlement as a matter of course almost from the beginning. Under that system, policy was framed by the Governor and the permanent official heads of departments responsible to the Colonial Secretary; but that policy must either be accepted or rejected by the elective Houses, which might, in the last resort, refuse supply. Such an illogical system had usually worked well enough when times and tempers were good, but when tempers and times were bad it had often ceased to answer at all.

Representative Institutions made a not-too-promising start in the Old Colony. The Reformers promptly quarrelled. Brand defeated Fairbairn for the Speakership, which the latter had regarded as his reversion, and Fairbairn, as leader of the House, attacked Saul Solomon, who had learnt journalism and negrophilism at his feet in the offices of the *Commercial Advertiser*, for delay in issuing the estimates in his capacity as Government printer. The powers of officials in the Council were rigidly restricted to Porter's disgust, and the two Houses competed for control of money bills. All, however, united in passing a bill to secure freedom of speech [1] and, in the ensuing session, legislators settled down to business. Reitz and

1855.   Wicht, two of the 'Popular' candidates of 1850, moved in favour of responsible government in the Council, and John Paterson of Port Elizabeth raised that issue in the Assembly. Paterson had mistaken his ground. Petitions poured in from the 'English' East against 'the plunder of the Colony' by the 'Dutch' West, the motion was defeated and the issue was referred to a committee. This committee, which included John Molteno, the ambitious member for Beaufort West and future first Prime Minister of the self-governing Colony, reported in favour of responsible government; but during the Session of 1856 Parliament decided to be content with representative institutions. Meanwhile, in 1855, the Legislature had created Divisional Councils elected on the now traditional 'colour blind' franchise to take over the work of the Road Boards and School Committees and, generally, to offer to the rural areas that education in local government and responsibility which Municipal Councils had long been giving to some of the towns.[2] Further, these first two sessions saw the end, for the time being, of the demand for Separation. Though Easterners had long looked upon local elective institutions as possible alternatives to more radical measures, many of them were now by no means satisfied with the Divisional Councils or with the appointment in 1854 of a Lieutenant-Governor to

---

[1] Act 1 of 1854; Eybers, p. 57.   [2] Act 5 of 1855; Eybers, p. 83.

command the troops and exercise a limited control over the Eastern civil commissioners.[1] It was natural that many of them should desire Separation. Their part of the Colony was growing in wealth as the trade with the interior developed for Port Elizabeth waggons could reach the Orange drifts two weeks ahead of those from Capetown : they felt themselves as much entitled as any Republicans or Natalians to a government which would look after their special interests; they hoped one day to absorb British Kaffraria and the by no means empty spaces of Nomansland that lay beyond it as far as the Natal border. Godlonton had come up to the first session of the Legislative Council with a complete '1820 programme,' that is, Separation, a franchise high enough to exclude natives, a vagrancy law, a modified commando system, an increased tariff and economy in the public service. His followers were strong enough to defeat responsible government with the help of Western Conservatives; but they failed repeatedly to carry Separation or the removal of the capital eastward, or even to prevent expenditure on western railways. Colesberg and Graaff-Reinet were opposed to Grahamstown rule; Hottentots petitioned against it, and gradually the agitation died away.[2] Good times, the genial influence of Sir George Grey, the new Governor, the removal of the best argument in favour of Separation by the self-immolation of the Xosas in the famous cattle-killing of 1856,[3] and Godlonton's departure on a visit to England induced all parties to give the parliamentary system a fair trial in an undivided Colony.

BALKANISATION, 1848–1857

Had Harry Smith's work stood, the Cape, the largest, most stable, and now the most politically advanced state in South Africa, must have influenced the troubled communities beyond its borders more profoundly than it actually did; but long before the Cape Parliament was in working order, Smith's hastily constructed edifice had fallen to pieces.

Europeans beyond the Colonial frontiers were stretched in a thin line from Philippolis to Durban round a solid mass of Bantu in Kaffraria and Basutoland, while the far end of the line in Natal was hemmed in between the Zulus on the one hand and the coast Kaffirs on the other. Beyond the line to the north, the Transvaalers were scattered like skirmishers among the tribes. The line was weakest at the centre in the O.R. Sovereignty. At Bloemfontein, Warden ruled with the assistance of a Legislative Council of officials 1848. and two burghers nominated for each of the districts of Bloemfontein,

---

[1] Theal, IIIb. 141.
[2] *Vide* Separation pamphlets 575, e. 908, S.A. Public Library, Capetown; *Cape Argus*, June 27, and *Grahamstown Journal*, May 16, 1857.
[3] *Vide infra*, pp. 288–9.

Winburg, Caledon River and Vaal River.[1] Civil commissioners who were also magistrates sat at each district centre, and beneath them were commandants and field cornets elected by the burghers.

Warden's authority was limited. The Europeans were under his direct rule, but the tribes were subject to him only in so far as concerned 'international' affairs or anything tending to disturb the general peace. It was a local modification of the Indian 'subsidiary' system, and Warden had to make the best of it. His main task was the definition of boundaries. To the west, along the lower Vaal, he gave the Bushmen and Koranas reserves round the Berlin mission at Pniel,[2] but he ignored the claims of the Griquas, Andries Waterboer and Cornelis Kok, to sovereign powers east of that river. He left Adam of Philippolis to shift for himself, but towards the Basuto he took a disastrously 'strong' line. Harry Smith had won Moshesh's support for the Sovereignty by telling him that he was a great chief and an ally and that arrangements would be made whereby Europeans would encroach no more. That was what a boundary meant to Moshesh: a line beyond which newcomers should not settle without his leave, while, in lands where whites and blacks were already living side by side, each race should remain under the rule of its own chiefs. He had therefore given back looted cattle to his old enemy, Sikonyela, and recognised his right to a strip of land which the Napier treaty of 1843 had cut off; but he declined to accept a line in the Caledon area between the Caledon and Orange as soon as he realised that this meant the loss of jurisdiction over his tribesmen living beyond it. He was, moreover, slow to remove his people from Sikonyela's country, and scuffling broke out. Sikonyela, Taaibosch's Koranas, and a crowd of mounted Coloured vagabonds under Jan Bloem raided the Basuto and especially their dependants, Molitsani's Bataung, in the corn-lands to the west of the Caledon. They did so once at least with the aid of white men acting under the orders of the magistrate of Winburg, who desired to clear the country for farms.[3]

As Philip's influence declined, Cape officials had departed from the old rule of regarding Adam Kok and Moshesh as the only Transorangian chiefs who need be taken seriously. They had begun to listen to the claims of the Wesleyans on behalf of the minor Caledon chiefs, partly because Moroko and Taaibosch were willing to set aside land for Europeans and partly because they overrated their strength and thought they might be a useful check on the growing power of the Basuto. Warden, an honest but easily influenced man, fell in with the Wesleyan view completely.[4] He

1848–1849.

Dec. 1848.

Circa 1845.

---

[1] No. 1360 of 1851, pp. 3 ff.; Eybers, p. 275.
[2] C. 508 of 1872, pp. 53 ff.
[3] No. 1360 of 1851, p. 24; Orpen, *Reminiscences*, p. 170; *Bas. Rec.*, I. 210 ff.
[4] No. 1646 of 1853, p. 51.

summoned a conference of chiefs, who agreed to restore cattle mutually. Moshesh performed his share of the bargain fairly well, but Sikonyela merely attacked Molitsani once more. Warden then decided to use the petty chiefs to humble Moshesh. He recognised 1849. them as independent rulers, and told Moshesh that, if he would agree to the boundaries he was about to propose, he would call off Taaibosch and Sikonyela, but if not, he would fall upon him with his Europeans and tribal allies. Letsie, Moshesh's eldest son, agreed on behalf of his father 'as a dog consents to walk with him who drags him with a riem.'

The intricate Warden Line, which the Resident laid down, cut off over a hundred Basuto villages. Some of them had only recently been occupied, but others were of old standing, and with them were cut off a great wedge of good land in the Caledon area and nearly all the corn-lands to the west of the Caledon for the benefit of Europeans or the minor chiefs. Moshesh reluctantly assented to this arrangement. Warden was thus left to maintain the Sovereignty with a corporal's guard of regulars in the Queen's Fort at Bloemfontein, burghers who were already doubtful of the advantage of holding their farms on condition that they turned out to keep the peace among Her Majesty's tribal allies, and the said tribal allies themselves.[1] And he had thrown away the support of the one chief whose friendship was worth having.

The precarious life of the O.R. Sovereignty henceforward depended on the complacency of Moshesh, the willingness of its own burghers to maintain it and of the Transvaalers to let it alone, H.M. Government's complacency and, in the last resort, the ability of the High Commissioner to support it with troops drawn from the restive Eastern Frontier. Presently all these conditions failed it and it fell.

The connection between the Sovereignty and the Transvaal was close, for many men on either side of the Vaal held that the old union of Winburg with Potchefstroom should be restored. North of the river, cattle-farmers and ivory-hunters were scattered over 100,000 square miles of country. They were still nominally British subjects, but as the nearest of them were 750 miles from Capetown they were practically independent. Their quality was different from that of the Cape and even of the Sovereignty men. Not only were they mixed with runaways, deserters and all who for one reason or another were 'agin the Government,' but such of them as were genuine Trekkers had spent twelve years in the wilderness and were, by a process of sifting, the irreconcilables of the Trek, the die-hards who had moved across the Vaal after every crisis in Natal or in the Sovereignty.

[1] No. 1360 of 1851, p. 51; No. 969 of 1848, p. 66.

Of all the die-hards, Hendrik Potgieter had trekked furthest and most often. Soon after the adoption of the Thirty-three Articles in 1844, he had moved away from Potchefstroom to get out of reach of the Punishment Act, sole suggestion of British authority in the North, and to open up trade with the indefatigable Hollander, Smellekamp, at Delagoa Bay. There, he had signed a treaty with the Portuguese, who claimed all Africa north of the 26th degree South latitude, whereby the Boers were to be allowed to settle as an independent people provided they made arrangements with the Natives.[1] These arrangements Potgieter made by acquiring what was virtually a personal gift of land from Sekwati, Chief of the Bapedi in the Lulu mountains, and founding thereon the town of Andries-Ohrigstad.[2] The Transvaalers were thus grouped loosely in two main divisions: at Potchefstroom and Magaliesberg (Rustenburg) in the south-west, where Andries Pretorius had taken the lead, and at Andries-Ohrigstad in the east where Potgieter had his headquarters in touch with the lawless folk of Buffels Rivier (Utrecht) on the Natal border and with 'Portugal' on the East Coast.

There was no constitution at first; Potgieter was Head Commandant and that was enough. Nevertheless, the Ohrigstaders claimed to be rulers of the whole Transvaal—were they not the oldest inhabitants?—and even before their trek from Potchefstroom and again immediately after their arrival in the east, some of them had petitioned that Potgieter should be chief executive officer, Head Commandant for life and full member of the Volksraad with powers to conclude treaties, summon the Volksraad and give orders to all commandants in Africa.[3]

The arrival of a strong contingent from Natal led by Jacobus Burger, ex-secretary of the Natal Raad, destroyed this incipient monarchy. Prompted by Smellekamp, this Volksraad party first got from the representative of a minor son of the Swazi King a written cession of the land on which the Ohrigstad Republic stood by way
1846. of a counterblast to Sekwati's gift to Potgieter, and then drew up a constitution more or less on Natal lines.[4] Above all they desired no executive officer at all during the Volksraad recess. Potgieter's party was stronger in the country, but his opponents had the majority in the legislature and were also possessed of a cannon. Chaos reigned. The Volksraad party practically impeached Potgieter; the Dictator tried to prevent the meeting of the Volksraad and, when it met, fourteen of his followers announced that they, as Het Volk,

[1] Engelbrecht, *Geschiedenis*, I. 43; Stuart, *Holl. Afrik.*, pp. 181–3.
[2] Buis to A.-Ohrigstad Volksraad, May 15, 1846 (Pretoria Archives).
[3] Theal, II*b* 443; *Voort. Argief.*, pp. 182, 186.
[4] *Ibid.*, p. 233; Engelbrecht, *op. cit.*, Bylage II; T. 1/25, p. 1 (Pretoria Archives).

had abolished it. Some burghers talked of abandoning the country till both parties should agree to keep the peace pending the expected arrival of Smellekamp.[1] Pretorius then tried to intervene, but he and Potgieter quarrelled so violently that no help was forthcoming from 1848. Ohrigstad during the Boomplaats campaign. At last, 'the man on the farm,' anxious for peace, made his voice heard in Cromwellian fashion in favour of a 'a man and a responsible body.' Six members from Ohrigstad met fourteen Volksraad party delegates from other May parts of the Transvaal at Derde Poort; the Potgieter faction stayed 1849. away and, with Pretorius in the chair, the assembly decided that a united Volksraad for the whole of the Transvaal should meet thrice yearly and a *Kommissie Raad* carry on during the intervals, all subject to the Thirty-three Articles. As a sop to Cerberus, the Head Commandantship for life was given to Potgeiter, but already he had sulked away northward with his friends to the Zoutpansberg.[2]

The first Transvaal Volksraad, twelve members from Ohrigstad and twelve from other parts, duly met at Krugerspost. It abolished Potgieter's office, fixed the capital at Ohrigstad, and then transferred it to Lydenburg since the village originally chosen was being abandoned because of fever and the unsuitability of its land for cattle.[3] This was no solution of the constitutional difficulty; some executive there must be and the cry was raised in the west for Pretorius as Commandant-General. In spite of the opposition of the 1850. majority of Het Volk, Pretorius took office provisionally till the Volksraad could meet. The Lydenburgers then turned out in full force, stirred up by one, Hendrick Buhrmann, a Hollander friend of Smellekamp, who had impressed them so much with the coat-of-arms and the French of his passport that some thought he was a Prince of the House of Orange.[4] Under this influence the Volksraad decided that there should be four Commandants-General: Willem Joubert in Lydenburg, Potgieter in Zoutpansberg, and Pretorius in Jan. Potchefstroom and Magaliesberg where the village of Rustenburg 1851. was about to be founded, while the burghers of Marico on the western border might choose between Pretorius and a rival local leader, who, however, soon relieved the situation by dying.

There was a risk that the turbulent Transvaalers might attack the O.R. Sovereignty where they had many sympathisers; but they contented themselves with turning back hunting parties from the

[1] Engelbrecht, *op. cit.*, I. 44, Bylage VI. and p. ix; *Voort. Argief.*, p. 267.
[2] Volksraad Minutes (Pretoria Archives); Preller, *Voortrekkermense*, III. 177; Stuart, *op. cit.*, pp. 188 ff.; *Voort. Argief.*, pp. 385 ff.; Soutter MSS.
[3] Engelbrecht, *op. cit.*, I. viii.; Stuart, *op. cit.*, p. 188; Volksraad Minutes, T. 2/25, pp. 42, 98, 113.
[4] Engelbrecht, *op. cit.*, I. 45 ; Stuart, *op. cit.*, pp. 191 ff.; Prince Hendrik of Nassau had visited Capetown in 1838.

British South, and even chasing away the explorer and artist, Thomas Baines, for daring to sketch the fourteen houses of their rising dorp of Potchefstroom.[1] The Resident in the Sovereignty thereupon urged that British rule should be extended over all Her Majesty's subjects to the north, and the Cape Executive Council actually agreed with Harry Smith that the Punishment Act ought to be extended to the Equator.[2]

July 1851.

Events nearer home soon called for Smith's undivided attention. Part of his Kaffrarian settlement was working well, part not so well. The Fingos under the Rev. Henry Calderwood in Victoria East throve amazingly and promised to become a stabilising force on the frontier, for Calderwood was experimenting along the lines on which the Cape native policy was to develop later: small quit-rents to keep the Fingos on their lands, expenditure of the money thus raised on the reserves and not on general colonial purposes, punishment of vagrants not belonging to the reserves, and rule by headmen under European control.[3] Beyond the Keiskamma, the results were less satisfactory. The Kaffrarian chiefs were indeed building the roads which would conquer their country and were eagerly competing for the good-conduct prizes which Smith offered in the hope of sharpening their appetites for Glengarry bonnets, moleskin trousers and other delights of Victorian civilisation.[4] But some of the ways of the new Great Chief perplexed the tribesmen. Why was *lobola*, the basis of their family life, the giving of the sacred cattle which legitimised the children of the wife for whom they were given, condemned as 'the sin of buying wives'? Why was witch-hunting forbidden? Were the white men in league with the witches who wrought all evil? Other things infuriated them. Magistrates, unable to apply either unsuitable colonial law or unrecognised native custom, ruled by martial law and their own good sense or, as Stockenstrom unkindly put it, 'by deprivation of law and domineering' backed by a few troops and untrustworthy Kaffir police.[5] The root weakness of the settlement was that too much was expected of the chiefs and too little given in exchange for their loss of power, while, in their midst, was the warlike prophet Umlanjeni and, beyond the Kei, the independent Kreli to point the moral. To the west were the Hottentots inspired by 'a dogged feeling . . . that they are an oppressed and ill-used race, that the word of God in the Bible tells them so' and, in the background, the Anti-Convict Agitation seeming to promise the Kaffirs that the Colonists would not support their own Government.[6] To the north was the resentful Moshesh.

---

[1] T. Baines, *The Northern Goldfields Diaries of Thomas Baines.* I. 7.
[2] No. 1360 of 1851, pp. 28, 34, 69.   [3] No. 457 of 1850, *passim*.
[4] *Ibid.*, p. 7.   [5] No. 635 of 1851, p 169
[6] No. 1428 of 1852, p, 72; Orpen, *Reminiscences*, p. 61.

Sandile the Gaika and most of the other chiefs refused to meet Oct.
Smith when summoned. Smith deposed Sandile, set up the ex- 1850.
perienced Charles Brownlee as chief and hurried back to his con-
stitution-building at Capetown. The Gaikas refused to recognise
Brownlee so long as their real chief lived, and their restlessness soon
called Smith forth again with every available man of his weak
garrison. He set up Sutu, great-widow of Gaika, in place of Brownlee,
outlawed Sandile and sent troops to rout him out. On Christmas Eve
the column was roughly handled in the Boomah Pass and, on the
morrow, the Gaikas wiped out three of Smith's costly military
villages. In all directions the tribes sprang to arms. Gaikas and
Emigrant Tembus were aided and abetted by Kreli's Galekas; some
of the Hottentots from Theopolis, Kat River and Shiloh obeyed
Willem Uithaalder's summons to strike for the independence of the
Hottentot nation;[1] the Kaffir police and even some of the Coloured
Cape Mounted Riflemen went over to the enemy. Luckily half the
Tembus retired to the Bashee; the Ndhlambi Xosas, the Fingos, the
Genadendal Hottentots and the Kat River half-breeds turned out
on the side of the Colony and, in far distant Zululand, Panda, anxious
to give his young men a chance of 'washing their spears,' offered to
sweep Kaffraria clean, an offer which called forth a panic in Natal
and an impatient refusal from Smith.

Smith struggled on, but the Colonial burghers responded badly
to his call, tribal levies from Natal failed to materialise and the first
overseas reinforcements could not reach him before May 1851.[2] By
that time serious trouble had arisen in the Sovereignty. Warden had
found that the dog at the end of his riem could bite. Sikonyela
harried Molitsani till the Bataung chief in desperation attacked a
Wesleyan station. The Resident, who already had Smith's orders to
punish Sikonyela, called up Moroko and his other allies, induced
Sikonyela to promise 300 cattle which he never paid, and then,
taking him with him, fell on the Bataung and seized much cattle.[3]
Molitsani's people promptly recompensed themselves at the expense
of Moroko; but Moshesh and Molitsani, anxious as ever to stand
well with the High Commissioner, restrained their warriors and gave
Moroko back 2500 beasts. This they did after the outbreak of the
Kaffir war had tied Smith's hands, a proof of good faith which was
ill-requited by Warden.

In the course of a scuffle with Poshuli, Moshesh's brother, in the
newly annexed Caledon lands, Warden crossed over on to Colonial

---

[1] No. 1428 of 1852, pp. 35, 43, 56; Macmillan, *Cape Colour Question*, p. 279.
On the Kaffir war of 1850–53 *vide* No. 1288 of 1850; 424, 635, 683, 1334, 1352,
1360 and 1380 of 1851; 1428 of 1852; 1635 of 1853.
[2] No. 1334 of 1851, p. 126; No. 1352 of 1852, p. 15; No. 1380 of 1851, p. 52;
No. 1428 of 1852, pp. 12, 55, 81, 246–9.
[3] No. 1360 of 1851, p. 74; No. 1646 of 1853, p. 51.

soil and thereby risked involving the Sovereignty and the Basuto in the Kaffir war, while Sikonyela and Taaibosch continued to harass the Basuto, who retaliated on the unhappy Moroko. Smith now resolved to read Moshesh a lesson and bade Warden treat Moroko as Great Chief of the Sovereignty. This frank absurdity soon became a tragedy when Warden tried to support the authority of the High Commissioner's nominee. Against the advice of friendly Boers, he called out his motley levies to humble Moshesh and drive Molitsani out of the cornlands; but the Boers, weary of these eternal Native bickerings, turned out poorly and his bands were defeated at Viervoet as they broke off to drive the cattle. Warden retired to Bloemfontein with the Platberg half-breeds and Moroko's Barolong, and, relying on a few regulars and Zulus from Natal, prepared to stand on the defensive till the Kaffir war should be ended, while Moshesh occupied the deserted lands of Moroko and the half-breeds up to the line he had always claimed and left his men free to raid the farms of those burghers who had obeyed Warden's summons.[1]

June 1851.

Soon a Boer deputation was openly bargaining with Moshesh to leave their farms alone; both the burghers and he called on Pretorius to intervene[2]; Pretorius's *Krygsraad* and *Het Volk* bade him ride south; Earl Grey, on sending further reinforcements, warned Smith that if the Sovereignty men would not support their own Government, the Queen's rule would be withdrawn after its authority had been vindicated and the allies safeguarded, and the Kaffir war dragged on its weary length.[3] The Western burghers were not called up; those of the East hung back, and Smith was forced to rely on friendly natives, volunteers and irregulars till the troops poured in.[4]

March 1852.

The loss of the *Birkenhead* notwithstanding, Smith at last had eleven battalions in the field and cleared the mountainous Waterkloof to the south of the Kat River Settlement.

But the restoration of peace in South Africa was not to rest with Sir Harry. Two commissioners, Major William Hogge and Charles Owen, had already arrived to deal with the situation outside the Colony, and presently he himself was recalled.

Nov. 1851.

Hogge and Owen found the Sovereignty revenues barely meeting civil expenses, the Natal Zulus out of hand, Fingos rationed and supplied with powder by Warden worrying the Basuto, and the Legislative Council insistent that there must be compensation for losses, withdrawal of the Queen's sovereignty over the tribes, and annexation of the rest of the country to the Cape, which was soon to have a Parliament and with whose interests those of the Sovereignty

[1] No. 1428 of 1852, pp. 113, 126, 173; No. 1646 of 1853, p. 51.
[2] No. 1428 of 1852, pp. 175–6.
[3] *Ibid.*, pp. 175, 243; No. 1646 of 1853, pp. 25, 80.
[4] No. 1635 of 1853, pp. 66, 72.

were identical.[1] The Commissioners were, however, thinking in terms of *divide et impera* rather than of annexation. Pretorius must be headed off. The Transvaalers were out of reach and it was time the fact was recognised. Pretorius had not responded to the call of the disaffected Sovereignty Boers, and the Rev. Andrew Murray the younger, who had gone up from Bloemfontein at Warden's request, found him anxious for a settlement and angry that ruffians like van der Kolff should be using his name in their raids on the farms of Sovereignty loyalists.[2] Smith withdrew the sentence of outlawry on Pretorius, who met the commissioners at Sand River. There, in spite of the threats and prayers of the Winburgers not to desert them, representatives of Potchefstroom, Magaliesberg and Lydenburg signed the Sand River Convention. According to these 'Minutes of a meeting,' H.M. Government at last guaranteed 'the emigrant farmers beyond the Vaal' freedom to manage their own affairs without let or hindrance, and promised to abstain from encroachment on their territory north of the river provided they did not encroach upon what lay to the south of it. Both parties agreed to facilitate mutual trade, extradition of criminals and free movement across the boundaries; the Transvaalers undertook to abstain from slavery, and H.M. Government assured them of the open gunpowder market which it would now deny to the tribesmen, and disclaimed 'all alliances whatever and with whomsoever of the coloured nations to the north of the Vaal river.'[3]

Jan. 1852.

So the Transvaalers won recognition of their independence after many years and Harry Smith sailed home broken-hearted knowing that, in spite of his warnings that any such step would mean a native rising from Zululand to Lake Ngami, the 'ultimate abandonment' of the Sovereignty was a settled point of Earl Grey's policy.[4] Grey proposed to withdraw because so many of the tribes and apparently of the Boers as well were opposed to the Queen's authority; but Hogge and Owen, conceiving that abandonment would be a breach of faith to all concerned, did their best to reduce the Sovereignty to order. They dismissed one or two of the least satisfactory of the officials, severely snubbed the Rev. James Cameron of Thaba Nchu, the most vociferous of the Wesleyans, condemned the Warden line and promised the Basuto a new boundary provided they kept within it and restored stolen cattle and horses. Moshesh agreed, but he failed to induce his people to disgorge, for Sikonyela was still raiding them

April 1852.

---

[1] No. 1380 of 1851, p. 67; No. 1646 of 1853, p. 14. On the Abandonment of the O.R. Sovereignty *vide* No. 1428 of 1852; 1646 of 1853; 1758 of 1854; Morrell, *Brit. Col. Policy*, pp. 299 ff.
[2] No. 1428 of 1852, pp. 153, 176, 194–5.
[3] No. 1646 of 1853, pp. 31, 36; Eybers, pp. 357 ff.; *Treaties . . . 1803–54*, p. 202.
[4] No. 1428 of 1852, pp. 202, 244–5, 253 ff.

and the magistrate of Winburg said it would be a pity to check him.[1] At last Moshesh took that duty upon himself, overran Sikonyela's country and then gave him good terms as a vassal.

At this stage, Hogge, the stronger minded of the two commissioners, died and left Owen to meet a conference of elected delegates at Bloemfontein alone. All the delegates asked for rule by a virtual Volksraad supported by an Imperial garrison and power for field cornets to effect reprisals, while half demanded also that the disputes with Moshesh be settled and that no further part be taken in intertribal quarrels. Pretorius arrived at Bloemfontein and was well received; the cry went up that Moshesh must be brought to his senses and Warden gave Baatje's half-breeds ammunition at the very July time that Moshesh was beginning to restore stock.[2] Owen dismissed 1852. him and appointed a commissariat officer, Henry Green, as Resident, while Sir George Cathcart, the new High Commissioner, set up an executive council.

On hearing that the Bloemfontein delegates had demanded such wide powers, Cathcart commented drily that the Sovereignty men had better be given independence and have done with it. In any case, he was inclined towards abandonment on any reasonable terms.[3] He was soon in a position to consider those terms. On his arrival on the Eastern Frontier, he had dismissed the useless levies, raised mounted European police, the first in South Africa, and called on the Cape burghers to turn out under threat of withdrawing the troops, a threat which he softened by offering them a share in the captured cattle. They came, took nearly 10,000 of Kreli's cattle in a Oct. few days, practically finished the war, and left the High Commis-1852. sioner free to march north to the Sovereignty with 2500 troops 'not necessarily for war but for the establishment of peace.'[4]

In reply to the usual demands by Sovereignty men for redress of grievances and compensation, Cathcart promised that these would be forthcoming and hinted for the first time publicly that the Queen's authority might be withdrawn. He was amazed at the length of the list of stolen cattle and, suspecting that all losses from whatever cause had been put down to the Basuto, obliged Green to cut it down.[5] Pressure by Green and Owen, however, coupled with the unexpectedly great cost of the expedition, impelled him to demand of Moshesh 1000 horses and 10,000 cattle within three days. After all, huge herds swarmed round Thaba Bosigo, a like amount of cattle had easily been taken from Kreli, and he could not know that the cattle were not all Moshesh's own, and that, if the fine was to

[1] No. 1646 of 1853, pp. 10, 17, 52, 85; Orpen, op. cit., pp. 156, 235.
[2] No. 1646 of 1853, pp. 57 ff., 63.   [3] Ibid., pp. 69, 70, 106.
[4] No. 1635 of 1853, pp. 104, 120, 156, 162, 167, 185.
[5] No. 1646, p. 93; Bas. Rec., II. 92–3; Orpen, Reminiscences, pp. 156, 164, 239 ff.

be paid within the time, it would have to be paid by Moshesh himself without much chance of recovering the quotas due from his subordinate chiefs afterwards. Moshesh came and asked for six days, but Cathcart was adamant. 'Do not,' said the diplomatic chieftain, 'talk of war. . . . A dog when beaten will show his teeth. . . . I will go at once and do my best, and perhaps God will help me.' On the appointed day 3500 cattle were produced, but Cathcart could not be Dec. satisfied with these. He marched straight on Thaba Bosigo to collect 1852. the balance and met with a severe check at the Berea.[1]

Moshesh was evidently surprised at Cathcart's advance, for he had discounted his threats, since 'words never kill a man,' and had meant to make terms on the verge of war, 'as H.M. Government was merciful.'[2] He now gave a diplomatic opening through which, to the general dismay, Cathcart retired. The High Commissioner had taken enough cattle to meet the bill he had presented; Moshesh delivered up some thieves immediately after the battle, and successfully restrained the cattle-thieves on his borders;[3] there was some justification at the moment for the assertion that peace reigned. In any case, Cathcart assured Moshesh that he was still the good ally of the Queen, left 300 men at Bloemfontein and hastened back to Kaffraria, there to overawe Kreli and the Kaffrarian chiefs into accepting the terms that he dictated to them. Thus, at the end of a Kaffir war which had cost the British taxpayer £2,000,000, some 2200 regulars were marking time in the Cape Colony and nearly 2500 in British Kaffraria, Moshesh was noising it abroad that he had beaten the British, and H.M. Government had decided to withdraw from the Sovereignty.[4]

A few far-sighted men might lament the unnecessary balkanisation of South Africa to which this decision gave rise, but the facts as they appeared to the Imperial Government pointed unwaveringly towards abandonment. Of all Great Britain's colonial investments, the South African were the most weary, stale, flat and unprofitable. In time of peace the colonists seemed to regard the considerable garrison as a milch cow; in time of war, with imperial troops and money flooding the country, they enjoyed a hectic prosperity except on the actual scene of operations. During those wars, each apparently more expensive and less conclusive than the last, traders sold guns and powder to the enemy at war prices; the produce and transport markets boomed and, for lack of proper support from the colonists, Governors were forced to rely on British redcoats, volunteers, tribal levies and irregulars who were all that the name implied.[5] To this

[1] No. 1646 of 1853, pp. 94 ff.   [2] Bas. Rec., III. 497.
[3] No. 1635 of 1853, p. 224; No. 1646 of 1835, p. 105.
[4] No. 1646 p. 118; Bas. Rec., II. 271.
[5] Further Papers re Kaffir Tribes, No. 1969 of 1855, p. 9; No. 1428 of 1852, pp. 252, 256; No. 1635, pp. 56, 64, et passim.

indictment the colonists could reply that native policy was controlled by the Imperial Government, which must therefore pay, and that British Kaffraria was no concern of theirs; but the Imperial authorities could still retort that they had taken over British Kaffraria to protect the frontier; that on the frontier itself farmers were much to blame for their own losses in that they encouraged Kaffirs to squat on their farms as labourers, and then seemed 'to expect troops to do duty virtually not only as police, but as herdsmen and shepherds'; [1] and that, as for the Sovereignty, they had done their best to prevent British subjects from going thither, and had only followed them up most reluctantly to secure the peace of South Africa at the wish, as they had been led to believe, of Europeans and natives alike.

Most unsatisfactory of all was the fact that the only people who seemed to benefit by the eternal wars were land speculators, who bought up the confiscated Kaffir lands. Land-grabbing on a great scale was not confined to the British colonies as the forty farms of Commandant Rudolph in republican Natal sufficiently proved; but that was no consolation at a time when speculators were busy in Victoria East, in Natal and, above all, in the Sovereignty. There, in a land which was popularly supposed in London to be fit only for antelopes, whose inhabitants could not or would not keep merino sheep, where timber for cantonments was lacking, and military stores had to be trekked up from Port Elizabeth six weeks away, H.M. Government was being asked to spend annually on troops an amount equivalent to £10 per head of white population, and this on a people many of whom sympathised with the independent Transvaalers and they with them. And for what? Missions which were said to be buying rice Christians and whose representatives were as much shopkeepers as ministers of the Gospel—clearly the Evangelical Revival was losing its grip on the English governing class in the 'fifties—and to provide shopkeepers with customers and landjobbers with security. And among the worst of the latter class were some of the officials themselves from Resident Green with his 160,000 acres downwards. [2]

This description of the Sovereignty was neither just nor complete. It was as unfair to label all those who cried out for the maintenance of British rule as speculators as it was to say that the Trekkers had trekked solely because they wanted free land and servile labour. But there was truth in the description and, in any case, the British Government had had enough of it. The European horizon had been

---

[1] No. 1635, pp. 154–5; No. 1758 of 1854, p. 20.
[2] No. 1635 of 1853, p. 222; *Further Papers*, No. 1969 of 1855, pp. 6–9; No. 1758 of 1854, pp. 23, 35, 40, 50, 72; Desp. 517, Grey to S. of S., June 26, 1855. Clerk noted one claimant who asked him to define his estate of 60,000 acres which the late 'proprietor' said had been given him by Harry Smith. The claimant was not quite certain where this estate was, but, added Clerk, 'its name very appropriately was "the Hope" ' (No. 1758, p. 50).

darkening for some time past in spite of the Great Exhibition which 1851. was to have ushered in an era of peace and plenty; Louis Napoleon's assurance from his new imperial throne that 'L'Empire c'est la paix' failed to carry conviction, and a Burmese war had hardly ended before a Russo-Turkish crisis arose which was destined to culminate in the exhausting Crimean campaign. At Cathcart's suggestion, Feb. therefore, the Duke of Newcastle sent Sir George Clerk as Special 1854. Commissioner to 'adjust' the affairs of the Sovereignty.

Newcastle had told Clerk that retention of the Sovereignty was still an open question, all the more that it was at last beginning to fulfil Grey's stipulation that it should pay its own way. Clerk, however, at once made it clear to the delegates who met him at Bloemfontein Sept. that he was bent on abandonment. These ninety-five delegates, three- 1853. fourths of whom were Afrikaners, declared that there must be no abandonment before outstanding land questions with Adam Kok had been settled, the Basuto line fixed, all native treaties cancelled, compensation paid, a guarantee given that neither the Queen's allies nor the Transvaalers would be allowed to make trouble over land claims, and full absolution granted from British allegiance.[1] Clerk was not disposed to treat these demands over-sympathetically, because he knew that though Cathcart had never seen the mass of the evidence that had been collected for Hogge and Owen supporting Moshesh's claims, he held that the Warden Line in the Caledon area was unjust to the Basuto.[2] He knew, moreover, that since the Berea battle, Moshesh had restrained the cattle thieves along his borders. Not so others. Sikonyela, Taaibosch, and Fingos under the protection of the truculent Winburg magistrate raided Basuto cattle within sight of Thaba Bosigo;[3] Sikonyela, Taaibosch and a few Europeans destroyed the Bataung reserve on Coal Spruit which Potgieter had recognised in 1838 when he had received the cession of Winburg;[4] a little later they attacked Witsi, an independent chief on the northern Basuto border. At last Moshesh could endure it no longer and fell on the Oct. disturbers of the peace. He slew Taaibosch, drove Sikonyela into 1853. exile and occupied their lands.[5] Of all their stations, the Wesleyans retained only Thaba Nchu and Platberg.

The Sovereignty delegates met once more and this time asked for Nov. 1853.

---

[1] No. 1758 of 1854, pp. 20 ff., 44 ff.

[2] *Bas. Rec.*, II. 30; Orpen, pp. 156, 241. The full case for the Basuto was first published in 1883 in Theal's *Basutoland Records*, vols. I., II., III. Vols. IV., V., VI., were prepared but never published. These are in the Cape Archives with a valuable bundle of semi-official and private letters marked *Miscellaneous Basutoland Records*.

[3] *Bas. Rec.*, II. 29; Orpen, *Reminiscences*, p. 289.

[4] *Bas. Rec.*, II. 18, 44, 50, 75; Orpen, *op. cit.*, pp. 255, 258-9. Theal calls the white men renegades: Orpen says that one of them was a member of the legislature.

[5] *Bas. Rec.*, II. 55, 76; Orpen, pp. 291.

9

a constitution under the Crown similar to that which Cathcart had rejected in 1852. Clerk, however, passed on to discuss the boundary question with Moshesh and some of the burghers. The chief made his usual statement of his past relations with Europeans and offered to compromise in the Caledon area, where his claims were weakest. The burghers rejected this, and Moshesh, learning from private conversation that they were not anxious for a definite boundary at all, claimed the whole Napier line of 1843. Clerk, finding that the Boers did indeed desire no definite boundary and were prepared to revert to the pre-annexation relations with the Basuto, simply dropped the matter.[1]

Meanwhile, the opponents of abandonment lost heart and the party of independence grew in strength. Protests by an L.M.S. conference that the Natives would suffer and similar petitions from the Cape Colony drove many waverers over to the republican side; helpers came in from the Transvaal and, at last, Clerk was able to
Jan.
1854.
summon a congress of what he called the 'well-disposed' and dismiss the rump of the original 'obstructionist' delegation. The obstructionists sent two of their number to plead their cause in London; they even 'discovered' gold at Smithfield—were not men's minds fired by the thought of the newly found gold of California and of Ballarat?—anything to give the Cape Parliament, which was to
Feb.
1854.
meet in June, time to express its opinion. It was of no avail. Clerk distributed some £50,000 of compensation money and signed the Bloemfontein Convention.[2]

That instrument, though more precise than the Convention with the Transvaalers, followed much the same lines. The 'well-disposed' tried to induce Clerk to promise that H.M. Government would make no more treaties with chiefs 'to the northward of the Orange River;' but all the Commissioner would concede was that it now had no treaties with such chiefs, always excepting Adam Kok, and had 'no wish or intention to enter hereafter into any treaties which may be injurious or prejudicial to the interests of the Orange River Government.'

The meaning of this last clause was soon made plain. The
1852.
D'Urban-Waterboer treaty had already lapsed on the death of Andries Waterboer[3] and even Adam Kok's position was not assured. For some time past, Adam's secretary had allowed Griquas to sell land in the inalienable reserve in defiance of Griqua law. The Bloemfontein Convention now bound Adam to facilitate such sales and, when he refused, Clerk and Green left him stranded. They only told

---

[1] *Bas. Rec.*, II. 94, 281, 434; Orpen, *History of the Basutos*, p. 111; Orpen, *Reminiscences*, pp. 297 ff.
[2] No. 1758 of 1854, pp. 10 ff., 24, 27, 35, 54 ; Orpen, *Reminiscences*, p. 286 ; Eybers, pp. 281 ff.; *Treaties . . . 1803–54*, p. 207.
[3] No. 1758 of 1854, p. 2.

him later of their understanding with the 'well-disposed' that Griqua lands sold to Europeans should come under Free State law, though Clerk did add that room might be found for him in British territory if he could not come to terms with the new government.[1]

Moshesh remained. Clerk intimated that the Warden Line was 'a dead horse,' but he never told him that his Napier treaty had been abrogated and, when Moshesh came to Bloemfontein to bid him farewell, avoided all mention of the boundary and rode away to- March wards the Colony with the garrison of the Queen's Fort.[2] He thus 1854. left Moshesh under the very natural impression that he was entitled to all he had held or claimed before the days of Warden, and the Free Staters believing that they were free to act in the matter of boundaries as in the days before 1843, when, as Pretorius put it, there being no law there could be no transgression.

Sir George Clerk handed over the reins of government and £3000 wherewith to 'soothe bitter recollections' to Josias Philip Hoffman and a committee of six, who found themselves rulers of some 12,000 Europeans, many of whom still regarded themselves as British subjects [3] and all of whom were cut off from the outer world and outnumbered twelve to one by the Basuto.

For the moment, however, the Free Staters' troubles came from within rather than from without. Some progress had been made under Warden. The D.R. Church of the Colony had at last followed up the Trekkers in the footsteps of Harry Smith; Andrew Murray the 1848. younger had been installed at Bloemfontein; soon ministers, consistories and schools had appeared at most of the other villages, and the Sovereignty and Natal clergy had formed the Transgariep Ring 1850. of the Church of the Colony.[4] At the capital the foundations of an Anglican cathedral had been laid and a newspaper, *The Friend of the Sovereignty*, established under Grahamstown auspices to further the march of civilisation north of the Orange and boom real estate. Bloemfontein and Smithfield were as English as Grahamstown Circa itself; but they and the other towns were tiny, some 200 one-storied 1854. houses all told, while in the countryside the farms were widely scattered; 8,000,000 acres of land remained to the Crown and, of the rest, 13,000,000 were tribal reserves and 11,000,000 alienated, in large proportion to absentee speculators. Two hundred unoccupied farms lay in a line between Winburg and Harrismith along the north-western Basuto border, broken only by the homesteads of three farmers who went into Natal annually for the winter pasture. All

---

[1] *Desp. to Sec. of State*, XXIV. (1859–62), pp. 240–1; A. 118–61 (Cape), pp. 1–17.
[2] *Bas. Rec.*, II. 99; Orpen, *Reminiscences*, pp. 312–19.
[3] Orpen, *Reminiscences*, p. 398; Burnet to Travers, Nov. 19, 1860 (*Miscel. Basuto Records*, Cape Archives); No. 216, April 1860, pp. 17, 18.
[4] Engelbrecht, *op. cit.*, I. 33, 41.

along the Basuto line there were vacant farms whose very limits had never been defined.[1]

The departure of the troops caused depression in the dorps, but, outside, the price of land actually rose, for sheep-farmers were expected from the Colony and Moshesh had shown himself eager for a settlement. In such a land, lions roamed freely among the swarming game and scattered herds. The republic was indeed almost entirely a pastoral state, dependent for corn on the Caledon valley tribes and its European neighbours north and south. Traders from the Colony ventured up sure only of a market for their gunpowder, while Transvaalers came south with meal, tobacco and dried fruits to be bartered for sheep and wool. Hard cash was scarce and becoming scarcer, for the balance of trade was against the country; recorded crime was rare, for there were no police, and where there is no arm of the law there is certainly no transgression. Besides, the tastes and upbringing of the bulk of the inhabitants did not incline them that way.[2]

From the political point of view the most serious weakness of the new state was its inexperience in the ways of settled government. The southern half of the Republic had had no European government at all till 1848; towards the end, the rule of Winburg in the north had been merely nominal, and six troubled years of Sovereignty rule had not inured the burghers anywhere to the yoke of authority, even self-imposed. Hoffman's committee made way as soon as possible for a Volksraad, which drew up the most elaborate republican constitution yet attempted in South Africa. The members rejected a ready-made constitution presented by an energetic Hollander schoolmaster; they declined to regard the Law of Moses as adequate for the occasion in spite of the eloquence of its champion who had recently been anointed 'King of the Free State' by another religious enthusiast; when South African experience failed them they fell back on a summary of the U.S.A. Constitution.[3] Under the constitution that was finally adopted, a Volksraad of twenty-nine was to be the 'highest legislative power.' Members were to be elected on an adult European male suffrage, which was open to all after six months' residence, and half were to retire every two years. A real civil executive appeared for the first time since Retief's short-lived Governorship and Council of Policy. The State President was to be elected by universal suffrage, to hold office for five years unless he were removed by a three-fourths majority of the Volksraad, to sit in that assembly but not vote, to remit sentences and declare peace

[1] No. 1758 of 1854, pp. 23-7; Orpen, *Reminiscences*, p. 97; Stuart, *Holl. Afrik.*, p. 184.
[2] No. 1758 of 1854, p. 54; *Bas. Rec.*, II. 165; *Correspondence . . .1855-7 (Cape)*, p. 20.
[3] Orpen, *Reminiscences*, pp. 308, 340.

and war subject to ratification by the Volksraad. His Executive Council was to consist of the State Secretary, the Landdrost of Bloemfontein and three Volksraad members, while his Krygsraad was to be formed by commandants and field cornets elected by the burghers, all of whom were as usual liable for service in the field. In time of war the officers in the field would elect a Commandant-General, but a permanent officer of that kind, *fons et origo* of so many troubles beyond the Vaal, the fathers of the constitution would not have. Landdrosts appointed by the Volksraad were to administer the districts and to sit with heemraden and, in criminal cases, a jury of nine to dispense justice according to 'Het Roomsch Hollandsch regt'; three landdrosts were to form the circuit court; the D.R. Church was to be the state church, and liberty of conscience and freedom of the press were to be assured.

So the constituent Volksraad dispersed leaving Hoffman to act as President under a constitution, which could be amended only by a three-fourths majority of the Volksraad in three successive sessions. Sept. Four months later, he was duly installed as first head of the Orange 1854. Free State.[1]

Away to the north, the Sand River Convention had merely 1852. recognised the obvious fact that the 15,000 Boer men, women and children 'beyond the Vaal River' were independent. The Transvaal constitution remained to be made.

It would have to be a constitution suited to a primitive society. The 5000 Boer families, and family life was the universal rule among the strapping men who married their fair-haired wives young and bred mightily, were grouped in and around three or four dorps or scattered thinly over the intervening spaces. Potchefstroom could boast of 100 houses and a Kerkstraat two miles long; but Schoemansdal, founded in 1852 as the base for the ivory traffic in the north, was fully as large, richer and contemptuous of its rival as is the way of hunters with farmers at all times.[2] Lydenburg was much smaller than either and Ohrigstad was almost deserted. Town and farm houses were rude. Andries Pretorius himself was content with a three-roomed clay house with a thatched roof among whose rafters

---

[1] Eybers, *op. cit.*, gives the Constitution as amended in 1866, pp. 285 ff.; *vide* also Theal, *History*, IV. 3 ff., 25. In 1857 the State Secretary was given a seat in the Volksraad. The first Circuit Court was very inexperienced. There were no attorneys nor advocates available, so three men, two of them English, did their best with the rules of the Cape Supreme Court, van der Linden, Grotius, Justinian, Blackstone, the Cape Statutes, the Notary's Manual and the Executor's Guide (J. M. Orpen, *Reminiscences*, p. 383. Joseph Orpen was one of the gallant three. Later in 1854 the President and Executive Council were appointed to act as court of appeal.

[2] Stuart, *Holl. Afrik.*, pp. 205–7; Engelbrecht, *op. cit.*, I. 49, civ. cvi; Engelenburg, *'N Onbekende Paul Kruger*, p. 32.

he kept his private papers and the state archives, till the achievement of independence encouraged him to import English workmen from Natal to set an example in the building of town houses at least. But, however humble the dwellings might be, each village had a substantial church built by common effort even though there might be no minister to fill the pulpit.[1]

The folk were ignorant of the affairs of the outer world; three months' schooling at the hands of an itinerant teacher completed the education of a child, as the young Paul Kruger found; but three schoolmasters had arrived from Holland in 1850, and great things were expected of them even though they threw up their hands at the local rendering of Dutch and themselves spoke too fast to be easily understanded of the people.[2] The Boers to a man—and woman—were fond of great discussions, politely inquisitive to strangers and ready to sit for hours in the study of the embarrassed minister who presently arrived from the Netherlands because they had never seen a predikant before. Their hospitality was proverbial and on it they depended for keeping in touch with one another in a country where men might trek eastward from Potchefstroom for three days before reaching a civilised habitation. Families intermarried much and it was customary for a farmer to pack his family into the waggon and set off on a solemn round of visits to relations for two or three months each year. Such book-learning as they had came to them from the daily singing of Psalms and readings in the Bible, especially in the books of Exodus and Joshua. Therein was a story which they and their fathers had enacted coming up out of the Land of Egypt, out of the House of Bondage—and their contempt for the burghers of the Cape who had remained among the fleshpots was deep—led with manifold signs and wonders through the wilderness and, at times, punished by Jehovah till at last they had entered into the Promised Land to possess it. So closely did some of them follow the historical 1849. parallel that Andrew Murray found the *Jeruzalemgangers* of Marico talking of trekking down the river Nyl which should guide them to Zion.[3]

Life in the Transvaal of those days was very simple. Skilled workmen were rare; the hard money the Trekkers had brought with them from the Colony was fast returning whence it had come or dribbling away to Natal, where they bought many of the supplies that could not be procured locally. Trade with the tribes and the Free Staters was by barter; slaughter cattle were sent down to the Cape itself, and it was on cattle that the Boers really relied. Land was plentiful,

---

[1] Stuart, *op. cit.*, pp. 213 ff.; Engelbrecht, *op. cit.*, I. 61.
[2] Engelenburg, *op. cit.*, p. 6; Engelbrecht, *op. cit.*, I. 37, 72, lxxxix ff.; Stuart, p. 210; Carter, *Narrative of the Boer War*, p. 53.
[3] Engelbrecht, *op. cit.*, I. 40, lxxxii; Stuart, *op. cit.*, p. 213.

much of it good arable land, Hollander observers noted, if only the farmers would work instead of leaving the fields to badly paid Kaffirs, who were always running away, and the gardens to their wives. Tobacco there was; oranges and peaches flourished in the south-west; game was to be had for the shooting; but when all was said and done, the Transvaal was essentially a republic of cattle-farmers.[1]

At Sand River, Pharaoh had promised to trouble the people no more, but the Promised Land was, in one respect, unhappily like the land of Egypt. It had its plagues: wild beasts, wild men, the malaria which haunted the whole country north of the Witwatersrand and slew men by scores in the Magaliesberg, and, above all, the Trekkers' own dissensions. Andries Pretorius was finding that a man's most inveterate foes are those of his own household. Some of the Winburg men had crossed the Vaal after Sand River; but the rest now taunted him with having deserted them, and Potgieter appeared in arms with his Zoutpansbergers at a great meeting of the people at Rustenburg and accused him of usurping power. The assemblage nearly came to blows, but at last the two champions were publicly reconciled, March Potgieter recognised the supremacy of the Volksraad, and all present 1852. ratified the Sand River Convention.[2]

The personal, political and religious feuds which divided the Transvaalers roughly coincided with geographical divisions. Generally speaking, Pretorius and the men of the south-west held by the Natal constitution and Retief's policy of a single republic with a strong central government, a port in the direction of Zululand and ecclesiastical independence; but nearly all the eastern Transvaalers subscribed to the Thirty-three Articles and desired local republics and incorporation with the Cape Synod. At one time it seemed that 1853. death would ease the tension, for Hendrik Potgieter and Andries Pretorius both died in the same year; but the Volksraad appointed Marthinus Pretorius and Piet Potgieter to succeed their respective fathers, and the drift towards hereditary succession was hardly weakened when young Potgieter was killed next year, for Stephanus Schoeman secured the succession by marrying the latter's widow and duly became Commandant-General of Zoutpansberg and heir also to the Potgieter feud with the house of Pretorius.

All these rancours beat upon Marthinus Pretorius, 'a gentle (almost too gentle) man of sound understanding though little developed,' according to one staunch supporter.[3] He essayed to carry out his father's policy. Having persuaded the Volksraad to give its country the ambitious title of 'The South African Republic

---

[1] Engelbrecht, I. xiv. cxlvi ff.; Stuart, *op. cit.*, pp. 216–8.
[2] Stuart, *op. cit.*, pp. 199 ff.; Engelbrecht, *op. cit.*, I. 48, lxxxix, xc, xci; Engelenburg, *op. cit.*, pp. 7, 8.
[3] Engelbrecht, *op. cit.*, I. ciii.

to the north of the Vaal river,' [1] he got leave from the Portuguese to use the road to Inhambane; but there the fly defeated him. Then, holding that Panda was still a vassal, a belief which the Zulu king

1854. apparently shared at times, he journeyed to Zululand in vain to seek an outlet at St. Lucia Bay.[2] He had little hope that the British Government would accede to his late father's request that Natal should be restored to him, but he was determined to secure as much territory in that direction as he could. The Klip River Natalians, who had crossed over into Zululand in 1848, were now organising the little republic of Utrecht on land ceded to them by Panda along the Blood river and a hunting track to the Pongola. The boundary of Utrecht to the north-west faded away into lands which had nominally formed part of the Orange River Sovereignty between the Free State Klip river and the Likwa spruit, headwaters of the Vaal. Pretorius claimed the southern branch, the Klip, as his frontier and was soon appealing to Sir George Grey, the new High Commissioner, to define his boundaries down to the sea, since the unruly folk of Utrecht were said to be asking for Potchefstroom rule. But Utrecht really sympathised with neighbouring Lydenburg, which had just secured from

1855. the Swazis a wedge of land thrust between Zululand and Swaziland far down toward the Indian Ocean,[3] and Pretorius made but little headway with its people.

He was equally unsuccessful in the Free State, where he claimed authority as the son of Andries. He had supporters in Winburg who wished to renew their old connection with Potchefstroom, disliked quit-rents and desired the free and easy polity which still held good north of the Vaal; there were also men in the Smithfield district who looked to him to settle their land disputes with Moshesh by force.

1854. His friends prepared the way and he came down to Winburg to upset the 'cripple government' of Hoffman before it was firmly established.[4] Rains and the vigilance of the landdrost of Winburg foiled him, and his rival was glad to get rid of him at the price of half the money Clerk had left to 'soothe bitter recollections.'

Pretorius now wisely decided to set his own house in order. The Transvaal Volksraad met quarterly. It was nominally supreme, but it debated in public, asked the opinion of any burghers who might be present before passing any law and was always liable to be interrupted by the tumultuary assemblage of Het Volk in arms. There was no central executive at all and the relations of the Volksraad with the Commandants-General and their Krygsraads were quite undefined. Moreover, Lydenburg, with a smaller population than

---

[1] Eybers, *op. cit.*, p. 361.   [2] Engelbrecht, *op. cit.*, I. civ.
[3] Desp. 517, Grey to S. of S., July 25, 1855; Volksraad resolution, July 21, 1855 (Soutter papers, Pretoria Archives).
[4] Engelbrecht, *op. cit.*, I. cxxxiii; Orpen, *Reminiscences*, pp. 387, 403 ff. Both Hoffman and his secretary were lame.

Potchefstroom-Rustenburg, had a majority in the legislature, which was also the court of appeal from the judgments of the landdrosts and heemraden who dispensed the 'Hollandsche Wet,' that is, van der Linden and the law of the old Colony as they remembered it. Crime was rare as in the Free State and for the same reasons; but there were no means of keeping order other than the commandos on which all were bound to serve. Revenue was precarious and drawn only from a small land tax and traders' licences till burgher rights 1855. and a farm were offered for £15 down to Europeans of good character, a qualification not too rigidly insisted upon.[1]

The utter need for some constitutional reform was emphasised at the very moment that Marthinus Pretorius took office by the controversies which raged round the question of the relations of the Dutch Reformed Church in the Transvaal with the *Niederduits Gereformeerde Kerk*, the parent church of the Old Colony. The issue was of great importance to the Transvaalers, who not only reprobated the legal equality with Europeans which that Church permitted to non-Europeans, but believed that its clergy were the spiritual sword with which Sir Harry Smith had proposed to conquer themselves in times past. They feared lest ecclesiastical union with that Church should lead to creeping and incipient political union also. Moreover, they felt that they owed their Mother Church little.[2] The Cape clergy had discountenanced the Trek; nay, more, their Synod had solemnly warned those about to trek that they would 1837. be going forth into the wilderness as a Chosen People lacking the guidance of an Aaron or a Moses and without the divine assurance of a Canaan, but none the less answerable to God and the Church for virtually denying their children baptism and other ghostly comforts. It begged them to bear the cross which God had laid upon them and to hearken to the rulers to whom God had entrusted the temporal sword.[3] Partly because they hoped to induce the Trekkers to return home before they became mere nomads, partly because they found real difficulty in recruiting their own ranks, the clergy 1843– had left them for many years to the ministrations of Erasmus Smit, 1848. Archbell, the Wesleyan of Thaba Nchu and, above all, the American missionary, Daniel Lindley of Natal. It was only after the annexation that they made any real attempt to help the Natalians or the Sovereignty men. In the eyes of the Transvaalers the clergy followed the flag. For some time past, however, either the Rev. Andrew

---

[1] Stuart, *op. cit.*, pp. 214, 216; Engelbrecht, *op. cit.*, I. 74, cii. ff. Stuart (p. 265) describes the execution of the first death-sentence in the republic. The condemned man took solemn leave of all and was then hanged by a friend.

[2] Engelbrecht, *op. cit.* I. 32; C. 1360 of 1851, p. 2; also *Verslag der Handelingen van de Algemeene Kerkvergadering . . . April 1859*, p. 40.

[3] *Die Herderlyke Herinneringen* of the Cape Synod of Oct. 1837; Engelbrecht, *op. cit.*, I. 18.

9*

1847. Murray or Synodical Commissions from the Cape had visited them,
on- baptising their children of all ages by the score and performing the
wards. other duties of their office. Meanwhile, the Transvaalers from the
first had been unremitting in their efforts to obtain a minister of their
own either from the Cape or the Netherlands. At length, after several
disappointments and believing that their desire would never be
1852. fulfilled without submission to the Cape Synod, the Volksraad
accepted the offer of a minister on those terms; but before the
decision of the Transvaal General Church Assembly had been given,
1853. a minister, the Rev. Dirk van der Hoff, arrived from Holland.
Yielding to the prayers of the dying Andries Pretorius and the
unanimous wish of the General Assembly, van der Hoff reluctantly
agreed that there should be no incorporation with the Cape Synod.[1]
Nov.   This resolution was ratified by the General Church Assembly to
1853. the fury of the Lydenburgers, who favoured incorporation and
disapproved of a Pretorius policy on principle. Smellekamp, an
object of suspicion to the Pretorius party because of his conduct in
Natal in the early days and his more recent attempts to form a
mercantile monopoly in the republic, joined with his friend, Buhrmann, and a couple of Hollander schoolmasters in attacking van der
1854. Hoff at the General Assembly.[2] At the end of a prolonged struggle
for the last word between the Volksraad, the Krygsraad, a Lydenburg
Kommissie Raad and the harassed predikant himself, the majority
resolved that their own Church, soon to be called the *Nederduits
Hervormde Kerk in de Transvaal*,[3] should be independent and that
van der Hoff should draft regulations for its governance. In the end,
Smellekamp and his schoolmaster friends had to leave the republic.
The former soon became provisional landdrost at Bloemfontein and a
further source of friction between the Potchefstroomers and the
'cripple government' of the Free State, while Lydenburg seceded
from the new Transvaal church organisation and drew up a constitution on the lines of the Thirty-three Articles of 1844, which,
however, it forbore to promulgate for the time being.[4]

Now that ecclesiastical strife had thus revealed the weaknesses of
the Transvaal's polity, Marthinus Pretorius tried to remedy the
worst of those weaknesses. In the absence of the Lydenburgers, who
Sept. refused proffered seats, he induced the Volksraad at Pienaar's River
1855. to appoint a committee to draft a Constitution.[5] He found his
staunchest supporters in Paul Kruger, a young Rustenburg field

---

[1] Engelbrecht, *op. cit.*, I. 18–23, 29, 33–4, 51 ff., 63, 67, lxxx, and Bylage
XXXV.
[2] Stuart, *op. cit.*, pp. 197, 255; Engelbrecht, *op. cit.*, I. 71, xci, cv, cxxix and
Bylage XXXV.
[3] First so named in the *Grondwet* of 1856.
[4] Engelbrecht, *op. cit.*, I. 73 ff., cii, cv, cxxix, and Bylage XLIII.
[5] Engelbrecht, *op. cit.*, I. 94, 107 ff.; Ad. T. 2/25, p. 495 (Pretoria Archives).

cornet of a dozen years' standing, and the Hollander Volksraad Secretary, Jacobus Stuart, the promoter of a land bank and colonisation company, who assisted the meeting with a French version of the United States Constitution.[1] It is noteworthy that nearly all the makers of Trekker Constitutions perused that notable document. The Rev. Aldin Grout, an American missionary, had lent the Natalians what they called the American 'law-book,' and yet, with this rigid examplar before them, they had made a Constitution of amazing flexibility. On the other hand, the framers of the Orange Free State *Grondwet*, who had had the use of Joseph Orpen's copy, feared the troubles that had plagued Natal so much that they adopted an 'entrenched' clause to prevent unduly hasty changes. Not so the Transvaalers. In spite of Stuart's precautions, they drew up a Constitution of such extreme flexibility that, to the very end of the Republic, it was a matter of hot debate whether or no the popularly elected Volksraad had the power to amend the *Grondwet* by a mere resolution. The Pienaar's River Committee recommended that *Het Volk* (the People) should still be sovereign, though it proposed no rules for the constitutional exercise of its powers, and that there should be at long last a President and also an Executive Council and a High Court, both distinct from the Volksraad, which was to be 'the highest authority.' *Het Volk* thereupon elected the younger Pretorius as President, but, in face of protests from the Zoutpansbergers, suspended the new *Grondwet* for a year.[2] At an irregular Session held in May 1856 at the newly-founded village of Pretoria, the Volksraad, which was not honoured by the presence of any Lydenburgers, made a few alterations in the draft *Grondwet* and suggested that Pretoria be the capital of the 'South African Republic,' which was, if possible, to include the Free State and stretch from ocean to ocean north of the Vaal.[3] Pretorius toured his districts beating up support and a special Volksraad and Het Volk met at Potchefstroom.

There, the original draft was substantially adopted. The burghers Dec. were to elect a Volksraad of twenty-four, all members of the State 1856. Church, half of whom should retire annually. Draft laws were to be advertised three months in advance and then to be decided by a three-fourths majority after debate by members only. The Volksraad was to appoint all civil officials on the recommendation of the Executive Council and to ratify or reject treaties, though a wide discretion was prudently left to the *Krygsraad* in times of emergency. The President, a burgher of at least five years' standing, was to be elected every five years and endowed with much the same powers

[1] Engelenburg, *'N Onbekende Paul Kruger*, pp. 21 ff.; Stuart, *op. cit.*, pp. 200 251, 263; Engelbrecht, *op. cit.*, I. 98.
[2] R. 930/55 (Pretoria Archives); Volksraad Minutes, Nov. 5–11, 1855.
[3] Ad. T. 2/25 (Pretoria Archives); Engelbrecht, I. 96.

and limitations as in the Free State. He was to be assisted by an Executive Council consisting of the State Secretary, two Volksraad nominees and a Commandant-General elected by the burghers. Appeals from the local courts were to be heard by the new High Court of three landdrosts and, in criminal cases, a jury of twelve also. The Dutch Reformed Church was to be specially safeguarded, no equality between white and black was to be tolerated in either church or state, and additional revenue was promised from a state monopoly of gunpowder, a tax on farms which was to be doubled in the case of absentee owners, transfer and market dues, and the fines of justice. Finally, Pretoria was named the capital and Potchefstroom was solaced with the title of chief town, which indeed it was.[1]

Jan. 1857.   Pretorius was inevitably elected President, the new Vierkleur flag of green, red, white and blue was hoisted, and all the duly elected officials took office, save Stephanus Schoeman of Zoutpansberg,

1855.   Commandant-General elect. He had already taken up an independent attitude by making a treaty with 'Portugal' on his own account. He now rejected the proffered post and the *Grondwet*, and thereby implicitly declared the independence of Zoutpansberg.

Dec. 1856.   Lydenburg went even further. It proclaimed its independence, and offered land and burgher rights free of charge to all desirable immigrants.[2]

The creation of British Kaffraria, Transvaal independence and the new Cape parliamentary constitution all pointed towards a self-contained government for Natal; the abandonment of the Sovereignty severed Natal's connection by land with other British territory and made its status as a detached district of the Cape anomalous and inconvenient.

Most of the Boers had gone except from the northern parts, but a considerable number of other white folk had taken their places. A few Germans had taken to market-gardening near Durban, while

1849– 1850.   Joseph Byrne and others had brought in far greater numbers of British under schemes framed more or less on Gibbon Wakefield's lines. This immigration, though less well known, had been fully as large and effective as that of the 1820 Settlers to the old Eastern Frontier, and if these Natal settlers had failed in their primary aim of supplying the Lancashire mills with cotton, they had at least formed villages at Pinetown, Verulam, Richmond and, in the north, Ladysmith. But speculators undersold Byrne, the Australian goldfields drew away many of his people and,

1856.   a full ten years after the annexation, the Europeans numbered no more than 8000 in the midst

[1] R. 1268/57 (Pretoria Archives). For Rustenburg *Grondwet*, 1858, *vide* Eybers, p. 362.
[2] Engelbrecht, *op. cit.*, I. 67, 98 ff.

of some 150,000 Bantu.[1] Nevertheless, they were a vigorous little community. Religious sects proliferated, each of them providing elementary education; associations of all kinds blossomed forth; the Natal Bank appeared, and soon six newspapers catered for the 1850. needs of the public. The lives of most of these journals were short, but the *Witness* of Pietermaritzburg and the *Mercury* of Durban were long to survive. Industries were trifling. For a time, a little 1846– cotton was available for export, but both cotton and coffee failed 1852. in face of fly and lack of labour during the rush of the picking season. Sugar, introduced from Mauritius, promised well, given 1847. more capital and labour;[2] beginnings were made with fruit and various tropical products, but for years to come the principal Natal export was the ivory of the interior. Imports, swollen by the goods of the Byrne immigrants and the needs of the garrison, largely exceeded exports; but as the Government relied mainly on customs, helped out by a native hut tax, the revenue officials made no complaint.

Government, local and central, became steadily more elaborate and less subordinated to the authorities at Capetown. Maritzburg 1846. had the honour of electing the first board of commissioners on Cape lines; it and Durban then became full-blown municipalities, and for 1854. some years county councils were formed till lack of men to fill them compelled their abolition.[3] Local justice was in the hands of chief magistrates in the principal towns and of assistants in the smaller, and, until he made way for Walter Harding and became a judge of the Supreme Court of Capetown, Henry Cloete as Recorder 1855. administered what was essentially the Cape law at the capital.[4] Lieutenant-Governors changed with bewildering rapidity, but the powers of the office grew steadily. First the council of officials was 1847. permitted to pass local ordinances,[5] whereupon an agitation for an Assembly was set on foot, which culminated in a petition of the Klip River Boers for independence after the abandonment of the neigh- 1854. bouring Orange River Sovereignty. That proposal could in nowise be entertained, but the abolition of appeals to Capetown, the opening 1855. of direct trade with England, and the approval of Lieutenant-Governor Benjamin Pine and High Commissioner Grey paved the way for complete separation from the parent Colony.[6] In 1856, Natal was created a Crown Colony by Royal Charter. Legislation was entrusted to a council of four officials and twelve members elected

---

[1] *Correspondence . . . 1855–7 (Cape)*, pp. 74, 212 ff.; A. F. Hattersley, *More Annals of Natal*, pp. 15 ff.; *Portrait of a Colony*, pp. 21–2, 61, 64–6, 102; *The British Settlement of Natal*, pp. 67, 118, 134; H. M. Robertson, *The 1849 Settlers in Natal*, I. 274, 279, 285 and II. *passim*.
[2] Holden, *History of Natal*, chapter xi.
[3] Eybers, *op. cit.*, pp. 218, 220. The County Councils lasted from 1854 to 1856.
[4] The jury system was introduced in 1852 (Eybers, p. 238).
[5] Eybers, p. 186.   [6] Desp. 517, Grey to S. of S., March 10 1855.

every four years by ballot (the first experiment of its kind in South Africa, to say nothing of Great Britain itself). The Crown retained considerable powers of veto; a modest civil list was reserved; the low franchise took no account of colour and, to the annoyance of elected members, £5000 annually were earmarked for the benefit of the natives.[1] So the Natal Legislative Council met for the first time in March 1857 and authorised the new Crown colony's first issue of stamps.

Twenty years before there had only been one civilised Government in South Africa. There were now at least eight, three of them colonial and five republican; that is, those of the Cape Colony, British Kaffraria and Natal on the one hand, and, on the other, the Orange Free State, Utrecht, Lydenburg, the Zoutpansberg and Pretorius's South African Republic. Balkanisation could hardly go further, unless Godlonton were to achieve his heart's desire of Separation.

CHAPTER X

MOSHESH AND WATERBOER, 1854–70

SIR GEORGE GREY

THE political condition of South Africa in the middle 'fifties is best described in the words of Sir George Grey's famous despatch, which is still the classic statement of the advantages of closer union and the dangers of disruption in such a country.[2] The burden of his letter is that whatever boundaries and constitutions the various states might choose to have, the native question, one and indivisible,

---

[1] *Correspondence . . . 1855–7 (Cape)*, pp. 34 ff., 218; Eybers, p. 188.
[2] No. 216, April 1860, pp. 4–10.

governed the whole situation and that, if the European states could not come together in peace, they would surely meet one another in war. After tracing the steps by which 'the dismemberment of South Africa, as far as it was then intended to carry it, became complete,' he noted the absurdity of separating the Cape Colonists from the Republicans.

'They have,' he wrote, 'the same sympathies, the same prejudices, the same habits, and frequently the same feelings regarding the native races, although marked and rapid changes in public opinion, in relation to this subject, are taking place, as also in reference to the increasing use of the English language and the adoption of English customs. . . . The only bond of union which at present holds together these states, European and native, is the High Commissioner. . . . A slight failure of temper or judgment on his part might, at any time, bring on a native war, a general rising of the natives, or a European rebellion. The defects of the system thus described appear to be that the country must be always at war in some direction. . . . Every such war forces all the other states into a position of an armed neutrality or of interference. For if a state is successful in the war it is waging, a native race will be broken up, and none can tell what territories its dispersed hordes may fall upon. Nor can the other states be assured that the coloured tribes generally will not sympathise in the war, and that a general rising may not take place. Ever since South Africa has been broken up in the manner above detailed, large portions of it have always been in a state of constant anxiety and apprehension from these causes. The smallness and weakness of the states, the knowledge that they are isolated bodies . . . has encouraged the natives to resist and dare them, whilst the nature of the existing treaties and the utter abandonment of the natives by Great Britain, to whom they had hitherto looked up, has led the natives to combine for their mutual protection, and thus to acquire a sense of strength and boldness such as they have not hitherto shown. . . . Again such petty states must be constant foci of intrigue and internal commotions, revolutions, or intestine wars. The affairs which occupy their legislatures are so small that they can raise no class of statesmen to take enlarged and liberal views. They can only inadequately provide for the education or religious instruction of their people. They can possess no able bar, no learned Judges, can have no efficient administration of justice. Trade and commerce must, therefore, necessarily languish. Their revenues will be so small that they cannot efficiently provide for their protection. Hence a new incentive is given to the surrounding native races to attack them. Life and property thus become insecure and a general lawlessness follows. . . . South Africa . . . appears to be drifting, by not very slow degrees, into disorder and barbarism. . . .'

The picture which Grey drew was intentionally dark, for he was trying to persuade a cautious Secretary of State to give him a free hand; but essentially the picture was true. The experience of four 1854– years of South African politics led him to go to all lengths to 1858. federate the British colonies and the Free State as the link between the Cape and Natal, a policy wherein he necessarily found a rival in the younger Pretorius, who also desired to secure that republic. Grey failed, and the measure of the results of his failure is the dismal history of the 'sixties in South Africa. Pretorius did indeed succeed in forming the South African Republic at the cost of a civil war; but he failed to unite it with the Free State, and the whole of South Africa sank under a wave of economic depression at a time when, from the Zoutpansberg to the Transkei and from Natal to Namaqua-Damaraland, the tide began to run strongly against the white man. The Bantu, whose numbers were increasing and whose tribal system was still in large measure unshaken, were learning European methods of warfare; many of them had guns as good as those of their opponents, for as yet breech-loaders were only beginning to find their way into South Africa and that great civiliser, the machine-gun, was not.[1] In the field the two races were never so evenly matched as in the late 'fifties and early 'sixties, and lack of discipline was by no means the monopoly of the barbarian. It was under these circumstances that the Transvaal had gradually to abandon the Zoutpansberg district, while the Free State, the central state in the South African system, became involved in a deadly struggle with the Basuto, a struggle which, as Grey foretold, drew in all other European communities and was only ended when Great Britain extended over Basutoland that authority which it had withdrawn from the O.R. Sovereignty.

1865–
1870.

Federation rather than Balkanisation was in the air when Grey came to Capetown at the close of 1854. During the past few years the German states had attempted to form a liberal federal Empire; the United States had fain accepted the desperate makeshift of the Clay Compromise rather than face disruption on the score of slavery; Earl Grey had proposed the federal solution to the Australian colonies and had envisaged a federation of the O.R. Sovereignty and the coastal colonies;[2] the Trekker republics had actually been federated for a time; the *Zuid Afrikaan*, with its significant title, had talked of an independent federal South African republic, while the Transvaal had still been nominally British soil,[3] and Saul Solomon had put federation in the forefront of his programme at the first parliamentary elections in Capetown.[4] Now Grey had come, fresh from the federation of New Zealand, to point to that policy as the one means by which South Africa might become 'a real power which may hereafter bless and influence large portions

[1] Sir George Grey had one of the earliest breech-loading rifles in South Africa (Orpen, *Reminiscences*, p. 72).
[2] Morrell, *Brit. Col. Policy*, p. 282.
[3] *Zuid Afrikaan*, April 22, 1850, and Jan. 23, 1854.
[4] Kilpin, *Pioneers of Parliament*.

of this vast continent.'[1] It was the hope of Philip uttered by a man who was in a far better position than he to carry it out.

Unlike the elderly Peninsular veterans who had preceded him, Grey was a vigorous man of forty-two, the son of a soldier who had himself been a soldier. He had since served as civilian Governor of South Australia during its early struggle for existence and of New Zealand in the midst of its difficulties with the Maoris, thus trained as no other Governor had been trained to deal with the fundamental problems of South Africa. He was prepared to take his duties very seriously. As he was never tired of explaining to the seven Secretaries of State who succeeded each other during his first five years of office, he was no ordinary Governor, but Her Majesty's High Commissioner responsible for the peace of South Africa.[2] The British colonies might be his first care, but he could not shut his eyes to what was going on beyond the Orange or even 'beyond the Vaal river.'

If federation was the goal and the need for a common native policy the main incentive to attain it, the divergent native policies of the various colonies and still more of the republics were the principal obstacles. Within the Colony itself the rule had long been *fusionnement*, that is, civil and political equality between white, coloured and black. The course pursued in overwhelming black Natal had been quite different. The British administration had found itself faced by *Circa 1846.* 100,000 Bantu within the Colony and more coming across the Tugela daily.[3] This influx, which had gone on steadily under the Republic, was in the main what happened everywhere after the Zulus or other military tribes had been defeated: the survivors of dispossessed tribes returned to their old homes as soon as they could. But something had had to be done if they were not to overrun the country altogether. The Republicans had attempted to segregate surplus natives *en bloc*; Major Smith had hinted at reserves under magisterial and missionary control; Henry Cloete had developed this idea still further, and a Land Commission, which included Theophilus Shepstone, Natal's Diplomatic Agent, set aside eight reserves of some *1846–* 1,168,000 acres in all.[4] It also proposed to station agents in each such *1847.* reserve with 'model mechanical schools,' means for training the natives in agriculture, and native police under European officers to keep order; but except for the police, this civilising plan had to be abandoned for lack of funds.[5]

Since civilisation was out of the question, Shepstone had to be

[1] *Correspondence . . . 1855–7 (Cape)*, pp. 55 ff.
[2] No. 216, April 1860, pp. 19, 25; Desp. 517, Grey to S. of S., April 9, 1855.
[3] No. 980 of 1848, *passim*.   [4] *Ibid.*, pp. 131 ff.
[5] No. 1697 of 1853, pp. 22 ff.

content with mere control. Here his early training on a Xosa mission station stood him in good stead. He shepherded 80,000 Bantu, docile from fear of Panda, into their reserves with only one show of force against a noted firebrand and, having no magistrates to help him, artificially revived the tribal system by appointing chiefs to such clans as lacked them.[1] Nearly 50,000 natives, however, remained on Crown lands or on the farms. The question of law then arose. As British subjects the Bantu were amenable to the Roman-Dutch law, which was so clearly inapplicable that the Land Commission had taken the notable step of recommending the recognition of native custom. But it was only after a long struggle with Judge Cloete, a struggle in which Porter, Attorney-General of the Cape, was called in as mediator, that Shepstone had his way.[2] Henceforward, racial differentiation distinguished Natal native policy from that of the Cape. Bantu were to be subject to native law in so far as it was not repugnant to the dictates of humanity, a law administered by their own chiefs assisted by European 'Native Magistrates' with an appeal to the Great Chief: the Lieutenant-Governor and his Executive Council. The administration of native law by Europeans marked a revolution in South African native policy, and the combination of judicial and executive functions in the hands of the Diplomatic Agent led the natives more than ever to look to Shepstone, 'Somtseu,' as the eyes and ears and mouth of the Great Chief.

June 1849.

1845- 1877.

Native law and the reserves were intensely unpopular with nearly all the handful of colonists and officials of Natal from Lieutenant-Governor Pine downwards. Earl Grey disapproved of unwieldy reserves of perhaps 400,000 acres, and Shepstone himself admitted that the existing system was so defective that it would be better to scrap them and concentrate their inmates in the empty lands down in the south-western area of the colony between the Umtamvuna and Umkomanzi. But few paid heed to Shepstone's explanation that the reserves were unsatisfactory because they were too rugged, unfurnished with magistrates and liable to lopping and paring by an administration anxious to satisfy claimants to farms.[3] The old cries which had been raised so often in the Cape against the mission stations were soon heard: the reserves drained off labour, it was dangerous to mass natives thus in the heart of the colony. Even the collection of hut tax for general revenue purposes failed to make the reserves acceptable and, to allay excitement, another commission was appointed. Composed as it was mainly of big landowners, who were avowedly interested only in land and labour, it eulogised the departed republican régime and condemned the work of Shepstone's

1852.

---

[1] No. 1697 of 1853, pp. 24 ff. On Shepstone *vide* Uys, *Shepstone*.
[2] Eybers, p. 235; Brookes, *Native Policy*, pp. 49 ff.
[3] No. 1292 of 1850, pp. 49, 198; No. 1697 of 1853, pp. 8, 22, 113, 116.

Land Commission; but the only results of its labours were to kill the wilder schemes for breaking up the reserves and to change the 'Native Magistrates' into 'Assistant Magistrates' and the 'Diplomatic Agent' into the 'Secretary for Native Affairs.'[1]

Meanwhile, Shepstone, who was perhaps already cherishing the vision of Kaffirland, Basutoland and Swaziland under Natal rule, once more took up the republican idea of segregation *en bloc*. The influx of Zulus from Panda's country emphasised the need; the prospect of empty land close by afforded the opportunity. Panda was indeed a milder ruler than either of his predecessors, for he encouraged traders, countenanced Hanoverian and Norwegian missionaries, and relaxed the bonds of discipline; but he maintained the military system and was hard put to it to give his young men an opportunity of 'washing their spears.' The Swazis had at one time furnished an outlet for superfluous energy, but since then the Zulus 1847. had driven Langalibalele's Hlubis into Natal and caused a panic by 1850. talking of a march through the colony to attack the coast Kaffirs. On the Kaffirland side of Natal lay the Amaxolo and other small clans who asked in vain to be taken over by Shepstone, and there also was Faku the Pondo, who was so disgusted at being held responsible for 1851. the cattle thefts perpetrated by uncontrollable Bushmen living in his treaty state that he ceded part of the northern area to Natal.[2] This cession was never ratified by the High Commissioner; nevertheless, Shepstone, whose original scheme for planting this part of Nomansland with Europeans had been set aside by H.M. Government on the score of expense, now proposed to lead in 50,000 Natal Zulus whom Dec. he himself would rule there as chief. Preparations for this great trek 1854. were on foot when Sir George Grey arrived at Capetown.[3]

If Natal's native policy was diverging from that of the Cape, the policy of the republics had been radically different from the first. The root of that policy lay in the frontier districts of the old Colony. There the Boers had held even more strongly than the townsmen and local officials that the natives were children of Ham, definitely inferior to *Christen mense*, divinely appointed hewers of wood and drawers of water. Retief had outlined the policy of the Trekker states when he promised that there should be no slavery, warned his men against seizing the children of unwilling Bushmen as apprentices, but proposed 'to maintain such regulations as will suppress crime and preserve proper relations between master and servant.' With independent chiefs like Moshesh, Dingaan and the rest in the early days, the Boer leaders had made treaties of friendship combined

[1] Report of Natal Native Affairs Commission, 1852–4.
[2] A. 118–61 (Cape), pp. 25–9.
[3] *Correspondence re Adjacent Territories, 1855–7 (Cape)*, pp. 13, 63–8.

sometimes with grants of land, their aim being to secure title-deeds and to occupy the open country without being flooded out by the tribes.[1] Over such chiefs they claimed no authority; but in Natal, where the Trekker native policy first had a chance of being developed fully, Panda had only been suffered to rule Zululand as a vassal of the republic. He had been bidden to keep his people beyond the Tugela and even obliged to ask leave before raiding Sapusa the Swazi. His dependence had been emphasised when the Volksraad had declared that only a joint raid was permissible in which the Republic was to have two-thirds of the proceeds.[2]

The difficulties of republican Natal had, however, been mainly internal. Some 6000 Europeans had found themselves face to face with perhaps 20,000 Bantu, whose numbers were rapidly increasing.[3] Native captains in the Republic had been ordered to report the arrival of 'foreign' natives under pain of death, and the newcomers themselves had been forbidden to build a hut on or near a Boer farm. As for the Zulus already in the country, the principle of the *Plakker's Wet* (squatter's law) had been laid down again and again. So that labour might be shared evenly, no one save the Commandant-General might have more than five native families living on his farm,

1840.   and even the apprentices captured at the battle which ended Dingaan's power were shared equally.[4] To check vagrancy and cattle thefts all free blacks had been obliged to carry passes and contract for service within a fortnight of leaving their last place, but not to contract for more than a year at any one time. No coloured person might bear firearms without a monthly permit from his master on whom fell the penalties for contravention of the rule up to confiscation and deportation for the third offence.[5] The system had been laxly administered and still the refugees had come in. Commandants had therefore been empowered to expel clans, and the Volksraad had determined on a policy of territorial segregation for 'redundant'

1842.   natives, that is, for those who were not wanted on the farms.[6] It was this policy which had given Napier final cause to reoccupy Port Natal.

The policy of the Transvaalers followed much the same lines. Potgieter had claimed all the lands and peoples that the Matabele had ruled, and dealt as overlord with the few clans living in much of that area and those who came back into it.[7] He gave reserves near Potchefstroom to the Barolong, Tawane and Matlabe, who had

---

[1] *Vide passim* J. A. I. Agar-Hamilton, *The Native Policy of the Voortrekkers.*
[2] *Nat. Not.*, pp. 135, 188, 195.
[3] Natal Native Commission, 1852; Report I. 8; Proceedings, I. 58 ff.
[4] *Nat. Not.*, pp. 37, 50, 59, 246; Bird, *op. cit.*, I. 627; Cloete, *Great Trek*, p. 55; R. 55/40 (Pretoria Archives).
[5] *Nat. Not.*, pp. 35, 38, 50, 59, 163-4.
[6] *Ibid.*, pp. 13, 36, 57, 110, 135-9, 163, 204, 246, 255, 261.
[7] Stuart, *Holl. Afrik.*, pp. 119, 213-4; R. 49/39 (Pretoria Archives).

followed him from Thaba Nchu and then, as the country filled up with Boers, moved Tawane away to Likhatlong. He settled various tribes returning from the desert in their old homes: Bakwena at Kolobeng, Bakatla at Mosega and Bangwaketse at Kanye. But over the Batlapin to the south at Kuruman he made no claims, for they had never been subject to Msilikazi; to the north he had never had any authority over the Bamangwato of Shoshong, while his successor at Potchefstroom was glad to make a treaty with Msilikazi, who undertook not 1846. to raid tribes under Boer suzerainty and kept his promise.[1] Similarly, in Lydenburg and the Zoutpansberg, Potgieter had claimed Sekwati's Bapedi in the Lulu Mountains and some of the Maguamba clans as vassals and had given them locations; but the Swazis and the Batlou remained independent, while as for Matshangana below the Lebombo Mountains, he was a potentate to be placated for the sake of the elephant-hunting on which Schoemansdal depended.

The general principles on which the Transvaalers ruled their dependent clans were to leave actual administration in the hands of the chiefs and headmen, to give them locations, which they could not alienate but even so only held on good behaviour (insecurity of tenure was the radical weakness of this policy from the native point of view); to forbid them to have guns, horses and waggons or make alliances among themselves, and to exact the labour tax, that is, labour 'at suitable wages when called upon.' Specially favoured chiefs were, however, exempted from the labour tax and given 'burgher rights,' which entailed payment of taxes in money and service with the republican forces in time of war. Natives not under a recognised chief were to enter into labour contracts before a field cornet and were to have no liquor without their master's consent.[2]

The native policy of the Transvaalers was never carried out systematically. The country was huge, the central government weak, and the borderlands, where the contact with the tribes was naturally closest, sprinkled with missionaries and scallywags, the best and the worst of non-trekker humanity. It had been so on the frontiers of the old Colony; it was so now not only along the Basuto border, but in Buffels Rivier between Natal and Zululand and in the undefined western border lands of the Transvaal, where ran the Missionaries' Road to the Zambesi. There, Robert Moffat's Kuruman was displacing Griquatown as the hunters' base, and up the Road came traders, hunters and missionaries to dispute with the republicans the control of the 'Suez Canal of the interior.'[3] Meanwhile, in the

---

[1] C. 3841 of 1884, pp. 114–5.
[2] Volksraad Minutes, Sept. 19, 1853; Andries-Ohrigstad Volksraad Minutes, April 13, 1846; Livingstone, *Missionary Travels*, chap. ii.; Chapman, *Travels*, p. 15. These rules were published in 1853, based on old custom, and elaborated in 1858 (Lokale Wetten, pp. 97 ff.).
[3] Chapman, *Travels*, chapter 1.

Zoutpansberg, some Europeans lived as savagely as the tribes; the half-breed sons of the notorious Coenraad Buis ruled Baramapulana clans in the mountains which were fast filling with natives fleeing from the Matabele, and João Albasini combined the offices of trader, chief of a Knobnose clan, blackbirder, Portuguese consul and general mischief-maker. These men and others sent out elephant-hunting parties of blacks from Schoemansdal, and naturally the blacks became good shots and kept their guns.[1]

As a body the Trekkers were no more hostile to missionaries as such than their fathers had been in the old Colony.[2] It is true that their attitude to all churches but their own was one of suspicion; 1853. the Rustenburg General Assembly decreed that none but the Dutch Reformed Church should be tolerated;[3] the *Grondwet* discouraged 1856– all churches which did not hold by the Heidelberg Catechism, and 1857. excluded Roman Catholics. But on this score their bark was worse than their bite. It was the same with the missionaries. The Nine 1837. Articles forbade any intercourse with 'allen den Sendelings genootscap van Engelant,'[4] but, though the embargo was general, it would seem that Trekkers' hostility was really directed against the L.M.S. men because of the evil they believed Dr. John Philip and his friends had wrought for them.[5] The Magaliesbergers welcomed Moravians and Hanoverians; as late as 1852, the Marico burghers were on good terms with even the L.M.S. men, the Rev. Walter Inglis and Roger Edwards, and had no objection to the Gospel being preached to natives, though some of them would have felt happier if only the missionaries would have consented to teach that the Boers were a superior race.[6]

On the other hand, the first Dutch Reformed missionaries to the Zoutpansberg found themselves very unpopular, and from the start the Transvaalers, like Somerset before them, objected to unauthorised missionaries going to the border tribes.[7] The Boers' point of view was intelligible enough. They themselves were scattered abroad among the tribes; Dr. Philip's invective was still a tradition with them, and the average missionary, especially of the L.M.S., was by no means a meek and patient evangelist. Many missionaries were men whose zeal and devotion had to make up for defective

---

[1] Hofmeyr, *Twintig Jaren*, pp. 1 ff.; A.-Ohrigstad Volksraad Minutes, Oct. 7, 1848; *Voort. Argief.*, p. 338; Volksraad Minutes, May 15 and 30, 1851, and June 15, 1852 (Pretoria Archives).
[2] On the Natal republicans' attitude to missionaries *vide Nat. Not.*, pp. 9, 11, 13, 25, 54, 58, 81, 90–1, 104, 110, 200, 210.
[3] Engelbrecht, *op. cit.*, I. 70.   [4] *Voort. Argief.*, p. 15.
[5] Engelbrecht, I. 19–23; Shaw, *Story of my Mission*, p. 504; Chase, *Natal Papers*, II. 3.
[6] Moffat, *Lives*, p. 33; Volksraad Minutes, Aug. 9, 1853; Stuart, *op. cit.*, p. 394; Livingstone, L.M.S. Kolobeng, May 26, 1849.
[7] Hofmeyr, *op. cit.*, p. 26; Eybers, *op. cit.*, p. 414.

education and knowledge of men and affairs; some were impatient of control, apt to accept native reports at their face value and inclined to take the lead in the tribe with which they were living; all of them felt that, as isolated guardians of a liberal tradition which was assuredly not valued by their white neighbours, they must speak out. And the more the missionaries spoke, the more the Boers feared that they would teach their flocks doctrines subversive of the Boer patriarchal system. They might—who knows?—even give the tribesmen guns.

The Transvaalers had long claimed a western line which included the Missionaries' Road and the Bechuana tribes along it. It was a claim that doubly threatened the missionaries, many of whom perforce combined trade with religion. They were poor men, who must make ends meet, and from the commercial point of view alone it was essential for them that the Road should be kept open. The Transvaalers' claim was challenged by David Livingstone, the most outstanding of all the notable men who have served the L.M.S. in Africa. Livingstone served his apprenticeship at Kuruman and Mabotsa, settled at Kolobeng among Sechele's Bakwena, and was soon in trouble with the Boers for giving the natives guns. He was, however, much away from 1849 onwards. discovering Lake Ngami and getting into touch with Sekeletu's Makololo on the middle Zambesi,[1] while the lands between the upper waters of the Marico and the Molopo, where his station was, became the centre of long-continued disputes. Tawane, the Barolong of Likhatlong, Potgieter's friend, had 1850. died and had been succeeded by Montsioa. Montsioa was then joined by the Rev. Joseph Ludorf, a Wesleyan from Thaba Nchu, and soon complained that Boers were demanding labour tax and taking his fonteins, on which, as in Philippolis, the life of the country depended. Andries Pretorius therefore agreed upon a new boundary. A few months later, in the absence of Ludorf but in the presence of Roger Edwards of Mabotsa, Montsioa with the other 'Molopo' chiefs 1852. recognised that the country belonged to the Transvaal as successor of Msilikazi; but whereas the other chiefs had to submit to labour tax, Montsioa was given burgher rights.[2]

The Sand River Convention defined no boundaries other than the 1852. Vaal river, and Livingstone, back at Kolobeng once more, insisted that the Road was outside the limits of the Republic. The matter was serious, for Andries Pretorius declared the Road closed and ordered all traders to go north through Potchefstroom to facilitate the collection of dues and regulate the passage of guns.[3] Then grave trouble arose with the tribes. Stirred by the news of Warden's check by the Basuto at Viervoet and then of successful cattle-raiding in

[1] Livingstone, *Missionary Travels, passim.*
[2] Bloemhof Arbitration Blue-book, p. 223.   [3] No. 1758 of 1854, p. 6.

Lydenburg by Sekwati's Bapedi,[1] Moselele's Bakatla went a-raiding on the western border and fled with the spoil to Secheli.[1] That chief had for some time past been seeking to copy Moshesh's example by gathering clans around him, and he now refused to give up Moselele. A strong commando, after due warning, attacked Kolobeng, drove Secheli out and took away some captured women and children as apprentices, while Montsioa, who had shirked his burgher duties, fled to the south-west and Ludorf retired to Thaba Nchu.[2]

Livingstone was away at the time of the attack, but his anger at the damage done to his property, whether by Boers or others, gave the affair a great publicity,[3] especially as his fame as an explorer was growing; for, in the course of the next few years, he made those journeys to Loanda and thence down the Zambesi, past the Victoria Falls, to Quilimane which revealed to the civilised world something of what lay in the centre of the Dark Continent. Relieved of his presence the Transvaalers sought to put their relations with the tribes on a more satisfactory footing. Zoutpansberg and Potchefstroom both signed treaties with the Matabele safeguarding the ivory traffic, and the Volksraad laid down general rules for the whole Transvaal forbidding the sale of arms to natives under pain of death and, to avoid all cause of offence, prohibiting barter with the tribes as on the Eastern Frontier in the old days.[4] These regulations, themselves a codification of existing customs, were expanded later, but in the absence of police they remained *une chose pour rire* in the border lands.

The first act of Marthinus Pretorius towards the tribes was friendly. He gave back his location to the defaulting Montsioa, though that chief and most of his people hesitated for a long time to return to it. There was, however, need for strong measures in the

Marginal dates:
May 1853–July 1856.
Jan. May 1853.
1858.
Oct. 1853.

[1] Van Oordt, *Paul Kruger*, p. 68.

[2] Chapman, *Travels*, chapter v.; Livingstone *Missionary Travels*, p. 118; Volksraad Minutes, Oct. 4, 1851; T. 1/25, p. 278 (Pretoria Archives).

[3] No. 1646 of 1853, p. 126; Livingstone, *op. cit.*, pp. 113 ff.; du Plessis, *Christian Missions*, pp. 252, 443 ff.
Considerable controversy has raged over this matter. The Boer patrol found Livingstone's house already broken open, probably by Secheli to get guns, etc., or by stray white men with whom the district abounded. The patrol admittedly broke open a shed and took away guns and smith's tools. On the other hand, Livingstone accused them of wholesale looting and destruction. John Smith Moffat, who had just come to the country as a missionary, reported that he afterwards saw some of Livingstone's furniture in Boer farmhouses, when the goodwives said he must not be too hard upon the patrol for taking the stuff as they were only youngsters. It would seem that the wanton damage charge can be dismissed; but, as for the looting, can any lads on active service be blamed for helping themselves to the contents of an empty house standing upon the veld in such a country? The most exemplary youths do queer things on active service, as all the world should know by now.

[4] R. 483/53 (Pretoria Archives); Leyds, *Transvaal Surrounded*, pp. 535-6; Volksraad Minutes, March 1853.

north, where Makapan beat up the Bamapela and other clans in the Waterberg, slew a certain Hermanus Potgieter against whom he had just cause of complaint, and went on the warpath. The Zoutpansberg and Rustenberg Boers formed laager; Pretorius called out a commando, and a few helpers came even from the Sovereignty. Piet Potgieter, son of the old *Voortrekker*, was killed in the attack and horse sickness dispersed the force, but not before some few of Makapan's people had been starved to death in their caverns and others 1854. shot as they ran in the open. It was a stern lesson and, until they began to fight among themselves, the Transvaalers had little further trouble with the tribesmen.[1]

The Transvaalers had, however, to face attacks from another quarter. It was popularly believed that they were slavers. The charge was not unnatural. They had migrated from a slave-owning society; some of them had objected to emancipation; the Natal Volksraad had indignantly repelled the charge on its own account, but had admitted that Potgieter, to whom most of its members were hostile, might have practised slavery in times past, though, if so, it was outside their knowledge.[2] The Slave Trade Commissioners acquitted the Boers as a body, but declared that slavery did exist in the Zoutpansberg, where Boers were in touch with Albasini and the Portuguese.[3] Portugal had forbidden slavery, but in spite of Lisbon and a British 1836. 'sentimental squadron' off the coast, Mozambique had suspended the royal decree on the grounds of 'absolute necessity' and cherished its trade in guns and ivory, black and white.[4] The Trekkers as a body were certainly neither slavers nor slave-owners.[5] Apart from lack of desire and knowledge that slaving was the surest way of calling forth British intervention, there was no need. Like those British colonists who, deprived of their slaves, fell back on indentured coolies, the Trekkers found an alternative supply. The 'labour tax' provided workers in the fields, apprenticeship the servants in the house and stables.

The apprenticeship system had been abolished in England itself 1814. only in face of the protests of many of the workmen concerned; it had been a system of old standing in the Cape Colony and had died hard there; it had existed among the Trekkers from the first on terms strictly defined by law. The laws seem to have been observed in republican Natal. There apprentices had to be *ingeboekt*

---

[1] R. 483/53 (Pretoria Archives), May 31, 1853; Orpen, *Reminiscences*, p. 397. Orpen (pp. 436 ff.) says that comparatively few were killed. Also Agar-Hamilton, *Native Policy*, p. 163.
[2] Bird, I. 623, 631, 655; *Nat. Not.*, p. 119.
[3] *Correspondence . . . 1855–7 (Cape)*, pp. 183 ff.; Hofmeyr, *Twintig Jaren*, p. 27; A.-Ohrigstad Volksraad Minutes, Dec. 15, 1847.
[4] *Correspondence . . . 1855–7 (Cape)*, pp. 186 ff.; Theal, *History*, V. 387 ff.
[5] Eybers, p. 356. Slavery was forbidden *e.g.* in 1845, 1852 and 1857.

(registered) before an official; indentures were not allowed to change hands; apprentices might not be exported, and when the harbour-master at Port Natal let two sail for Capetown he was suspended; importation was confined to members of the *Maatschappij*, and then only by leave of the Volksraad.[1] All these rules were transferred to the Transvaal and were there restated.[2] Nevertheless, after the attack on Secheli, Livingstone and other L.M.S. men accused the Boers of practising virtual slavery, and, some of them added, 'if some Power do not interfere . . . the ruin and slavery of the native tribes will inevitably follow.'[3]

In vain did the Potchefstroomers banish Edwards of Mabotsa and his colleague, Inglis, for repeating the charges and the veiled appeal to Great Britain.[4] Substantially the charges were true. Traffic in indentures, and, therefore, in apprentices did go on; the repetition of the law against it four times in quick succession tells its own tale; apprentices were traced from Lydenburg through Winburg to the north-eastern Colony itself; a Free State commission partially un-earthed a nest of blackbirders in Utrecht trading children from the Swazis and selling them in northern Natal, and would have un-earthed more had not some of the commissioners closed the inquiry just as it was becoming interesting and returned home (with a black apprentice bought on the scene of their labours) to be duly censured by the Volksraad.[5] Who then were these apprentices? Starving children, it was said, abandoned after a battle like Magongo or the fight with Secheli; children willingly exchanged for goods by their parents; prisoners in inter-tribal fights who would otherwise have been killed, or Balala, the hereditary helots of the Bechuana.[6] Maybe, said the critics, but the supply of orphans on the frontiers was singularly abundant and steady. The annals of Bushmanland in the 'twenties and, in spite of Retief's orders, of Transorangia in later days, were full of complaints about the hunting of Bushmen children by stray Boers, and the same thing had gone on under the Sovereignty, sometimes with and sometimes without official cognizance.[7] Hendrik Potgieter had reported to the Natal Volksraad a bad case of black-birding beyond the Vaal on the very eve of the second occupation of Port Natal by the British;[8] in the 'fifties there were men like Her-manus Potgieter in the northern Transvaal who 'stuck the ramrod'

Marginal dates: 1852. Nov. 1852. 1851-1858. 1855.

---

[1] Bird, I. 622, 632, 655; *Nat. Not.*, pp. 33, 42, 57, 86, 125, 130, 231; Chase, *Natal Papers*, 1. 186.
[2] Lydenburg Volksraad Minutes, May 9, 1851 (Pretoria Archives).
[3] No. 1646 of 1853, p. 116.   [4] *Ibid.*, pp. 120 ff.
[5] *Correspondence . . . 1855-7 (Cape)*, pp. 126 ff., 186 ff., 199.
[6] Hofmeyr, *op. cit.*, p. 27; Freeman, *Tour*, pp. 260, 274; Livingstone, *op. cit.*, p. 125.
[7] *Correspondence . . . 1855-7 (Cape)*, p. 126; No. 2352 of 1857, pp. 56, 102; Orpen, *op. cit.*, p. 443.
[8] *Nat. Not.*, pp. 206-8.

where it could be seen as a signal to a kraal to bring out apprentices;[1]
Marthinus Pretorius was much exercised at the doings of western
borderers, and a little later President Boshof of the Free State told 1857.
Sir George Grey that Pretorius dealt in apprentices contrary to the
Conventions and asked him to cut off the powder supplies to Potchefstroom, also contrary to the Conventions; while, by the same
post, Pretorius reported that Schoeman of the Zoutpansberg had
leanings towards slavery and made the same request.[2]

Grey probably discounted the reports written by these rival
correspondents who were on the verge of war with one another, but,
on the matter of 'virtual slavery,' his conclusion was just. It did go
on in the Free State in spite of the efforts of the authorities and the
better-class inhabitants to stop it. As to what might go on in the
Transvaal, Grey did not at this stage express an opinion.[3]

Grey's logical conclusion also could not be evaded. Either the
Republics must show that they could make their people obey their
own laws or they could not expect to be treated as governments.
Even Henry Labouchere, the Colonial Secretary, agreed that
habitual disregard of the slavery clauses would give good ground
for modifying the Conventions which galled the High Commissioner
so severely, and remarked that Great Britain had not renounced à
tout jamais the right to make treaties with the tribes specified in those
documents, but had merely indicated the 'general inclination' of its
policy. Nevertheless, he warned Grey that he must avoid making
such treaties and not even interfere as arbitrator unless both parties
invited him to do so.[4]

At first, Grey had neither the wish nor the leisure to intervene
north of the Orange. It took him a year's hard work to stop 1854–
Shepstone's great trek into Nomansland, for he held it useless to 1855.
draw off 50,000 Zulus from Natal to make room for 50,000 more and,
besides, such warlike immigrants were likely to prove ill neighbours
to the coast tribes, as in Napier's days.[5] He also had to find a definite
policy for British Kaffraria at a time when the feeble Free State
threatened to collapse on his northern border.

---

[1] Orpen, op. cit., pp. 426 ff., 485 ff., for further references.
[2] Correspondence . . . 1855–7 (Cape), p. 126; Volksraad Minutes, June 1.
1853; No. 2352 of 1857, pp. 71, 94 ff.
[3] Correspondence . . . 1855–7 (Cape), p. 126. Some years later, the Transvaal
President, M. W. Pretorius, asked the landdrost of Zoutpansberg to buy him
half-a-dozen little Kaffirs at a time when the Swazis were raiding (Aug. 16, 1864);
a few months later, Umswaas, the King of the Swazis, sent three little orphans to
the landdrost for 'his ally,' the President. These were duly inboeked to Pretorius,
who gave two white blankets for recompense (tot vergoeding)—vide Lydenburg
Landdrost's Dagboek and Contraktboek, May 12, 1865, and File T1/15 (Pretoria
Archives); Agar-Hamilton, op. cit., p. 218.
[4] No. 2352 of 1857, pp. 53, 101.
[5] Correspondence . . . 1855–7 (Cape), pp. 13, 52, 63, 177, 200.

Grey soon discovered that the common factor in all his problems in British Kaffraria, Kaffirland and the Free State was Moshesh. Moshesh was, indeed, becoming more and more the common factor in the politics of the dismembered South Africa in whose midst he sat watchful on his flat-topped mountain. He was at the height of his intellectual and political powers, no mere savage but a great man, as even the illiberal Theal stoutly avers, using diplomacy as a weapon from choice, war from necessity, and both to perfection. More than one of his sons had received his education in Capetown; one of his wives kept house in European fashion and dispensed tea and home-made sponge cake to distinguished visitors, while the chief himself, fresh from his daily tub and arrayed in the uniform of a French general and the long blue cloak which his Basuto valet so assiduously brushed, was fit to take his place at public banquets beside Special Commissioners and Presidents and embrace the embarrassed Warden in the streets of Bloemfontein.[1] His successes at Viervoet and Berea had set the tribes cattle-rieving from Lydenburg to the Molopo; he had recently absorbed the lands of Sikonyela and Taaibosch; south of the Orange he had taken Morosi, the Baputi chief of Quthing, as his vassal; he was in touch with Kreli beyond the Kei and negotiating with the Pondo Faku for the cession of much-sought-after Nomansland. He now unwittingly produced a constitutional crisis in the Free State.

The native policy of the Europeans in that area had at first been an attempt to make good a footing and, under the Sovereignty, to mark out tribal boundaries and play the smaller tribes off against the Basuto. The withdrawal of the Queen's authority had left the chiefs once more completely independent in their own lands, whatever those might be, and the republican government supreme over the rest of the country.

Hoffman, the first President, a philanthropically minded man, owed his election mainly to the fact that he alone of all the candidates was on the spot and also to the burghers' knowledge that he had influence with Moshesh.[2] Apart from the harassment caused him by Marthinus Pretorius, his main concern was with the tribal areas which chequered his state. He first pacified the Bushmen and Koranas in the Pniel reserves, who had quarrelled so violently that the Berlin missionaries had to leave, and then recognised the sovereign rights of Nicolaas, successor of Andries Waterboer of Griquatown[3] over a block of land on the Free State side of the lower Vaal. He next turned to Moshesh. That chief was conciliatory, earning merit with his missionaries by checking the liquor traffic and with the

1851–
1852.

1854–
1855.

---

[1] Orpen, *op cit.*, pp. 326, 356, 366; *Bas. Rec.*, II. 105.
[2] Orpen, *op. cit.*, p. 351.
[3] Lindley, *Adamantia*, p. 82; Theal, IV. 14–24; *vide infra*, p. 329.

Bloemfontein authorities by keeping his immediate followers quiet; but some of his dependent chiefs along the Smithfield and Winburg-Harrismith borders did much as they chose. There was also the question of the boundary itself for whose determination Clerk, before his departure, had provided a joint Free State-Basuto Commission.[1]

Hoffman visited Moshesh; but he virtually shelved the boundary issue and, a little later, told Letsie, Moshesh's son, in the presence of a large crowd, that it was impossible at the moment to go into all the claims for cattle presented by the Smithfield officials. Letsie, on hearing a test case, at once paid up in full with compensation added; whereupon local field cornets asked for a month in which to collect evidence, a month which one of them used to stir up so much trouble that Hoffman called out a commando before the fraud was discovered.[2] The commando was then disbanded and the borderers realised that there were going to be no strong measures while Hoffman was in the saddle. His opponents therefore laid hold of the fact that he had sent Moshesh, quite openly, a small keg of powder to recompense him for the salutes fired in his honour during the recent visit to Thaba Bosigo. They stirred up public opinion against him and, at last, Volksraad members trained the guns of the Queen's Fort on his house. Convinced by this infallible artillery that he was not wanted, the unhappy President resigned.[3] Feb. 1855.

Grey decided that so precarious a government must not be embarrassed lest it collapse. He therefore refrained from sending to Thaba Bosigo the British Agent whom Moshesh had been led to expect, and even withdrew John Burnet, the British Agent, from Bloemfontein to Aliwal North on the colonial border.[4] But claim and counter-claim against the Basuto ran on and matters became so strained between Moshesh and the new President, Jacobus Boshof, the 'moderate' of republican Natal, that Grey went up to the Free State. He persuaded the two parties to accept the Smithfield Treaty, which, without naming any boundary, apparently took that 'dead horse,' the Warden line, for granted and provided for mutual passes, cattle tracing and expulsion of trespassers.[5] He also had the satisfaction of hearing that Boshof had accepted the Vetberg line, which Adam Kok had just laid down between the dominions of Waterboer east of the Vaal and the lands of Cornelis Kok, and he himself solaced Adam, who was gloomily watching his original reserve of Philippolis pass piecemeal into European hands, with an annual grant.[6] Oct. 1855.

[1] *Bas. Rec.*, II. 99, 112, 121, 133; *vide supra*, p. 258.
[2] *Bas. Rec.*, II. 115, 118, 126–32; Orpen, *op. cit.*, pp. 458–61.
[3] Orpen, *op. cit.*, pp. 456 ff.; *Bas. Rec.*, II. 120, 139.
[4] *Bas. Rec.*, II. 142; Duplicate Desp. 517, April 9, 1855 (Cape Archives).
[5] *Bas. Rec.*, II. 159, 165.
[6] C. 459 of 1871, p. 48; *Correspondence . . . 1855-7 (Cape)*, pp. 71, 124.

Poor Adam might lie heavy on Grey's conscience, but the frontier affairs of the Colony were his first and gravest concern. There he was faced with the settlement which Cathcart had made at the close of the late war.[1] Cathcart had given the lands of the rebel Hottentots at Theopolis and Kat River to Europeans, established Europeans at Queenstown on the lands of Mapassas's Tembus along the White Kei, transferred the bleak Bontebok Flats from British Kaffraria to the Colony and given the loyal Fingos further lands round Oxkraal and Lesseytown. The Europeans were grouped together as far as possible and held their farms on perpetual quit-rents as a check to land speculation. Thus Cathcart proposed that the old Ceded Territory and its northward prolongation in Queenstown should form a buffer between the Colony and British Kaffraria filled with a mixed population of Europeans, Hottentots and loyal Bantu. Cathcart's policy in British Kaffraria had been different. 'Military control,' he wrote, 'and not colonisation induced me to retain Kaffraria as a separate government instead of annexing it to the Cape Colony or abandoning it.'[2] He did indeed make tiny European settlements beside the forts at Kingwilliamstown and at three or four places in the Royal Reserve round the Amatolas from which hostile Kaffirs were excluded; he also settled selected Fingos in the Reserve in villages of twenty souls and upwards, each man paying a quit-rent for his garden and *erf*; but for the rest he tried to carry out the policy which Harry Smith had decided on during the disillusionment of the war of 1850-53.[3] He held that it was useless to 'exterminate' the tribes and pile them up behind the Kei, that the colonial clamour for tribal land was unjust, and that the only policy to pursue was to leave the Kaffirs to be ruled in their reserves by their own chiefs under European guidance and to rely on time, European influence and that 'innate sense of justice and truth . . ., perhaps the only virtue they can appreciate and for which they have . . . a religious respect', to break down evil customs.[4] Hence, he even gave the Gaikas a reserve of their own albeit surrounded by the territories of more dependable tribes.

The essence of the Cathcart settlement was time and the difficulty was to make sure of the time. The Kaffrarian chiefs were still British subjects; but the Chief Commissioner and his subordinates were once more mere diplomatic agents without power, the country was really a tribal reserve, and from having had too little power the chiefs had been suddenly given too much. Grey found the troops

[1] On Cathcart's settlement, *vide* No. 1635 of 1853, especially pp. 222 ff., and *Further Papers*, No. 1969 of 1855, pp. 2 ff., 27; *Minutes . . . on Frontier Settlement (Cape)*, June 1853.
[2] *Further Papers*, No. 1969 of 1855, p. 28; *Laws and Regulations of British Kaffraria*, p. 5.
[3] No. 1635 of 1853, pp. 14, 15.
[4] *Further Papers*, No. 1969 of 1855, pp. 3, 16, 31.

1853.

vainly trying to keep the Kaffirs out of the wooded Amatolas, Pato's 1854–
men and the Gaikas intermarrying and beer-drinking with the Fingo 1855.
'dogs,' and the Fingos, an object of suspicion to the frontiersmen,
in a high state of excitement.[1] Behind them lay the independent
Kreli, paramount chief of all the Xosas, in touch with Moshesh[2]
and with the Tembus, who lay in a long line from the Indwe to the
Umtata river; behind them were the Pondos, those of Ndamazi,
Faku's son, to the west of the Umzimvubu and those of Faku himself, still in alliance with the Queen, to the east of that river. To the
north of Pondoland were Bacas, Pondomisis, Xesibes, Amaxolo and
the other little tribes of the Natal border.

Grey's first care was for defence. He had five weak battalions, one
of which was in Natal, the white Frontier Armed and Mounted
Police, which had been raised in 1852, and the Cape Mounted Rifles
which was henceforward to be a mixed European and Coloured
formation typical of the Governor's desire that folk of all races
should live and work side by side.[3] He persuaded the Cape Parliament to give £10,000 annually towards the cost of the garrison, to
increase the police to some 550 and to raise European volunteer
regiments.[4] Then, relying on his New Zealand experience and the
Imperial grant which was to help British Kaffraria through the most
critical part of its history, he began to carry out the policy which he
hoped would civilise Kaffirland as far as the Natal border.[5]

Generally speaking, that policy was the abandonment of segregation *en bloc*. Europeans and natives were to be regarded henceforth
as 'inhabitants of one country'; the power of the chiefs was to be
supplanted by that of magistrates and the country be settled as far
as possible with Europeans; in other words, instead of being a black
barrier against Kreli, British Kaffraria was to become a chequer-
board of black and white. It was Harry Smith's pre-war policy
without the 'exorbitant fines and official domineering' which Cathcart had censured.[6] Helped by the horse-sickness and cattle disease
which were sweeping off the prospective fines of justice, Grey induced
the chiefs to accept salaries instead of fines. This meant in practice
that the chiefs continued to hear the civil suits of their people, but,
having no particular interest in criminal cases, left these to the
Agents. As in the days of Harry Smith, the law lay largely at the
magistrates' discretion, for colonial law could not be applied and
native custom was not recognised. A hut tax, fines of justice and the

[1] *Further Papers*, No. 1969 of 1855, pp. 34, 35, 39; Desp. 517, May 30, 1855.
[2] *Bas. Rec.*, II. 144.   [3] Theal, IIIb. 105. 189; Cory, V. 470.
[4] No. 389 of 1858, No. 173; *Correspondence . . . 1855–7 (Cape)*, p. 8.
[5] *Further Papers*, No. 1969 of 1855, p. 38; No. 2202 of 1857, p. 61. The
Imperial grant was £40,000 till 1858, then £20,000, and so progressively less till
it disappeared in 1864. Grey had had a similar grant in New Zealand.
[6] No. 1969 of 1855, pp. 16, 36 ff., 57 ff.

Imperial grant went far towards making British Kaffraria self-supporting; good wages were offered for the making of the roads which would be as useful in war as in peace, and Grey helped forward industrial schools within and without the province and built the Grey Hospital at Kingwilliamstown to wean the tribes from witchfinding.[1]

It was not so easy to strengthen the European population in Kaffraria, perhaps a thousand all told. Cathcart had failed to get Swiss mountaineers for the Amatola area; Grey failed to get enrolled pensioners with families and was obliged to accept the offer of German Legionaries, veterans of the Crimean War, for whose settle-

1856.   ment he persuaded the Cape Parliament to vote a subsidy on condition that a fair number of families came with the men.[2] He was not in a position to pick and choose. Not only had he to carry out his new policy against the wishes of the Kaffrarian Commissioner and most of his subordinates, but there was the constant threat that war might come.[3] Neither the Colonists nor the Kaffirs regarded Cathcart's peace as anything more than a truce, and though Moshesh stood aside and let the Free State deal justly with Witsi, a noted raider in the Harrismith area,[4] he adopted the chastened chieftain into his tribe and ignored the Smithfield Treaty. In response to a scare that Kreli was coming, Grey rushed every available man to the Eastern Frontier and called on Mauritius for aid, while Moshesh claimed a line far down towards the junction of the Orange and the Caledon, where Poshuli and other minor chiefs had driven the Boers

April   into laager.[5] Luckily for Grey, the Crimean War ended and he soon
1856.   had ten good battalions; but, as if to remind him of his liabilities,
Dec.   Natal had trouble with some of its clans and was seriously alarmed
1856.   at a Zulu civil war fought out on the banks of the Tugela.[6]

So the Old Year closed in panic and the New Year dawned in madness. Prophets had arisen among the Xosas and the Tembus telling of visions of strange men from beyond the ocean, enemies of the English, who bade the tribes abandon witchcraft, sow no crops, and slay and eat fat cattle; for on the appointed day signs would appear in the sky, a whirlwind sweep the white men into the sea, and the dead heroes of the Kaffir nation arise from the earth followed by cattle and corn such as eye had never beheld. The Ndhlambis and the Galekas, Sandile's Gaikas and most of the Tembus slew and slew and, as the messengers of Moshesh came

---

[1] No. 2096 of 1856, pp. 3, 5, 7, 8, 14 ff., 34.
[2] *Ibid.*, p. 13; No. 2022 of 1857, pp. 33 ff., 59; No. 1969 of 1855, pp. 27, 72; Desp. 517, Grey to S. of S., March 10, 1855.
[3] No. 2096 of 1856, pp. 11, 22 ff.; *Correspondence . . . 1855–7 (Cape)*, pp. 96, 105; *Bas. Rec.*, II. 184.
[4] No. 2202 of 1857, p. 20.   [5] *Bas. Rec.*, II. 178, 191.
[6] Theal, III*b*. 233.

south, the madness mounted higher. For Moshesh was behind the cattle-killing.[1] He believed that war was coming between his Basuto and the Free Staters and, if war was to come, he proposed to prevent the Cape Colonists from helping the republicans by giving them something to occupy them on their own borders. He sent back to the Free State more than the tale of cattle demanded, but his people doggedly refused to give up the horses, the beasts of war, and, at Feb. that very moment, The Day dawned on the banks of the Keiskamma. 1857. The sun ran its appointed course, no wind stirred, the heroes came not, the very Xosas were not massed to follow their lead into the white man's land. Night fell, and when the chiefs called upon their warriors, they were answered by the wail of a starving people. Grey was ready with troops and food, but the mortality was frightful. No one knows how many died east of the Kei. In British Kaffraria itself the Bantu were reduced by death or dispersion from nearly 105,000 to 37,000 souls.

The Fingos and some of the other clans had abstained from the cattle-killing, but the Xosas and Tembus of the Ciskei were so 'broke up as the Hottentots were,' by their own folly, that the Cape was hard put to it to control the influx of tribesmen seeking work.[2] Grey made the most of his opportunity. He let Sandile keep part of his reserve under strict magisterial control, confiscated the lands of the other chiefs who had tried to drive their people to war, swept the wrecks of Kreli's Galekas beyond the Bashee, and began to plant the confiscated reserves with the German Legionaries. These warriors brought few women and children with them; they were neither so numerous nor so German as Grey had expected; there were far too many young officers of the Black and Tan variety. But Grey made the best of them. He kept them on full pay and therefore under the salutary restraint of military law, imported wives, principally Irish, to help to keep them in order, and, against the wishes of Downing Street, contracted with a Hamburg emigration firm to send out 4000 German peasants.[3] In the end, the Colonial Office stopped this 'questionable policy' which British Kaffraria could ill afford, but not before more than half the Germans had arrived. Thus the little colony took shape between the Keiskamma and the Kei behind the buffer of the Transkei, which the Cape police kept empty as far east as the Bashee river.

The cattle-killing had happened only just in time to relieve the situation, for two events occurred which reminded men that no state can live to itself alone, especially in South Africa, the half-way house

[1] *Bas. Rec.*, II. 184, 229–31, 241, 247, 264; No. 2202 of 1857, pp. 38–9; No. 2352 of 1857, No. 84, 86, 88, 94, 95.
[2] Van der Horst, *op. cit.*, pp. 28 ff.; Acts 22, 23, 24, 26 and 27 of 1857; Act 1 of 1858.
[3] Act 5 of 1857; No. 389 of 1858, *passim*; No. 2202, pp. 45–6.
10

1857. to the East. In August came the news of the Indian Mutiny and, without waiting for orders, Grey began to send away sorely needed troops and guns. Meanwhile, in April, Pretorius had invaded the Free State in pursuance of his policy of uniting all the Trekker republics. The rejection of the *Grondwet* by Lydenburg and Zoutpansberg had not daunted him even when Schoeman of Zoutpansberg threatened to challenge him to single combat—and God defend the right.[1] The Zoutpansberg was declared in a state of blockade and Pretorius rode·off with a few friends to attempt a Napoleonic *coup d'état* in the Free State as the successor of his father, Andries. Winburg supporters joined him, and he summoned Moshesh to a conference. The stroke miscarried. Boshof ordered him out of the country, and he went by way of Natal, leaving his Free State friends to face charges of sedition. To stop the trials and still further make good his authority, he presently invaded the Free State in force relying on his six field pieces, the knowledge that the cannon which Boshof had ordered had not yet arrived and the hope that half Boshof's men would come over to him at the first shot. The opposing armies faced one another on the Rhenoster river, but the shot was never fired. Paul Kruger, Commandant of Rustenburg, played his usual moderating part and the rival Presidents made peace. Each recognised the independence of the other; Pretorius abandoned his claim to Winburg; the Free State Unionists were fined, a penalty which was subsequently 'mitigated,' and some of the more extreme of them followed Pretorius back across the Vaal to the unfeigned relief of Boshof.[2]

Feb.   In spite of this rebuff, Pretorius made good progress in the
1858.   Transvaal. Lydenburg refused to hearken, but Zoutpansberg listened to the arguments of Kruger, acting on behalf of his President, and accepted the *Grondwet* which the westerners had recently adopted at Rustenburg.[3] The firstfruits of union were soon gathered. The Bamapela rose once more, but this time they were put down decisively by Schoeman, now Commandant-General of the South African Republic, and Kruger, who earned in this campaign a great
May   reputation for courage. The lesson of union was not entirely thrown
1858.   away. Lydenburg, which was steadily losing control of Sekwati's Bapedi, joined forces with Utrecht.

The northern republics were thus clearly moving towards union, but the Free State was more than ever divided. The considerable 'English party,' incensed at the execution of one of their number, joined the opposition, and the wretched Boshof resigned. Under

---

[1] Engelenburg, *'N Onbekende Kruger*, p. 25.
[2] No. 2352 of 1857, No. 34; *Bas. Rec.*, II. 264, 281; Engelbrecht, *Geschiedenis*, I. cxlix. On this period of Transvaal history *vide* Theal, IV*b*. and Van Oordt, *Paul Kruger*.
[3] Engelbrecht, *op. cit.*, I. 100, and *Amptelike Briewe*, pp. 21 ff.

pressure, he resumed office, but his prestige was gone and Moshesh naturally became defiant. Moshesh had checked the border cattle-rieving to appease Grey for the part he had played in the Xosa 1857. cattle-killing;[1] but now the trouble began again and the chief sent large hunting-parties westward into the belt of farms which he claimed. Boshof, with some wild idea of playing Jan Letele off against him just as the Natalians had played Panda off against Dingaan, took over that public danger of the Smithfield border as a Free State subject.[2] Letele scorned Moshesh as his inferior by birth and harried his people; Moshesh found a legitimate excuse for reprisals in Letele's depredations; and so war broke out. The burghers struck in at Thaba Bosigo, the key of Basutoland. They had reckoned without their host. The Basuto poured into the Free State and the commandos dispersed, while, in the west, the Bushmen and Koranas broke loose and Batlapin from beyond the Vaal raided both May republics.[3]   1858.

A joint Free State-Transvaal force beat the Batlapin back, took much spoil and held the Batlapin Mahura liable for crushing reparations for having sheltered his kinsfolk. The ill-success of the Basuto campaign, however, strengthened the party in the Free State which held that their republic could not stand by itself. The most convinced of all was Boshof, who, at the first reverse, called on Grey and Pretorius to come to the rescue.[4] Pretorius and Kruger arrived first, proposing to attack Moshesh unless he accepted their terms; but, in reply to petitions for republican union, they said they must await the arrival of the High Commissioner, who, in terms of his instructions, had warned them that such a union would mean June the modification of the Conventions under which both Republics 1858. enjoyed their independence.[5]

Grey soon came, but had to hurry back to the Colony immediately to expedite the despatch of further troops to India, including a thousand of the most unruly of the Legionaries whom he now sent to be shot respectably on the plains of Hindustan.[6] The British immigrants and such of the Hamburg Germans as the Secretary of State had permitted to sail were arriving and the Cape Police had been increased to 1000 strong,[7] but Grey returned to his work of mediation with his powers to enforce his decision sadly weakened. He found Moshesh boasting truly enough that he had not yet begun

---

[1] *Bas. Rec.*, II. 285 ff.   [2] *Ibid.*, 291 ff., 310; III. 123.
[3] *Ibid.*, II. 326–61; Engelbrecht, *Amptelike Briewe*, pp. 35 ff.; Agar-Hamilton, *Road to the North*, pp. 24 ff.
[4] *Bas. Rec.*, II. 353, 362, 371.
[5] No. 2352 of 1857, No. 206; *Bas. Rec.*, II. 395.   Text of proposed Transvaal, O.F.S. and Basuto treaty in Soutter's MSS. (Pretoria Archives).
[6] No. 389 of 1858, p. 37; No. 216 of 1860, p. 23.
[7] No. 357 of 1860, p. 4; No. 389 of 1858, pp. 7–9.

to fight; but he also found him so frightened of the possible union of the two Republics that he was able to induce him to sign the First Treaty of Aliwal North. By that treaty mutual claims for compensation were expunged and the Warden Line was confirmed with an extension in the Basuto's favour between the Caledon and Orange, a line which the High Commissioner himself marked out.[1]

Sept. 29, 1858.

1858–1859.
At this stage, Sir Edward Bulwer Lytton, the new Secretary of State, bade Grey report on the possibility of federating the three British colonies with a view to releasing the bulk of the Imperial garrison, and asked what the 'permanent line of policy' towards the Republics should be.[2] Grey saw his chance. He had found a strong body of opinion in the Free State in favour of federation with the Cape; federation would force the Cape to share the customs duties on goods for the Republic landed at her ports and thus show that 'prudent liberality' towards the Free State he had so often urged; Boshof would be able lawfully to get the help of the Cape burghers and field guns which he had already requested for use against the Basuto.[3] Moreover, British Kaffraria could not be annexed to the Cape without an Act of the Colonial legislature, which would hardly be forthcoming; but it could form a province of a self-governing federation, the Eastern Province and Natal could be given an otherwise unattainable autonomy and, if all the southern states united, the Transvaal republics must soon come to terms.[4] He therefore recommended a permissive Act of the Imperial Parliament empowering the colonies to take the necessary steps. He had already hinted at some such developments and had been ordered to do nothing without further instructions; but, on receipt of a formal request from Bloemfontein to appoint a commission to discuss preliminaries, he raised the question in the Cape Parliament. His hopes were speedily ended.

July 1859.
Lytton declared that Great Britain would not resume 'sovereignty in any shape or form' over the Free State, censured him for mooting the matter and presently dismissed him.[5]

From the Colonial Office point of view and especially from that of Lord Carnarvon, Under-Secretary and Mayor of the Palace to the sickly Lytton, there was nothing else to be done. This 'dangerous man,' with his revolutionary ideas that each part of the Empire might function as if it were the whole, had embarrassed the Imperial Government. He had more than once given ministers the choice between ratifying his actions and recalling him, and now ministers had taken the latter course. So, to the regret of all save possibly Pretorius, Grey sailed home.

Aug. 1859.

---

[1] *Bas. Rec.*, II. 475 ff.   [2] No. 216 of 1860, pp. 31 ff.
[3] *Ibid.*, pp. 1 ff.; No. 2202 of 1857, p. 38; No. 2352 of 1857, pp. 21, 28; No. 1969 of 1855, p. 62.
[4] No. 357 of 1860, No. 86.   [5] No. 216 of 1860, pp. 4 ff., 15, 33 ff.

Nearly a year later he came again. A change of ministry had taken July place and Newcastle sent him back to Capetown, but only on 1860. condition that no more was heard of federation.[1]

GOOD TIMES AND BAD, 1854–1870

Even if the Colonial Office had not wrecked Grey's plans, the question still remains whether South Africa was in a fit condition to be even loosely united. Great distances, mutual ignorance, local prejudices and poor means of communication were all against success; on the other hand, recent advances and the prospect of more to come might have led a less sanguine man than Grey to hope that material obstacles at least would soon be removed. World conditions and especially those in Great Britain were favourable; the advancing Industrial Revolution, the gold of California and Ballarat, war prices in Europe and presently in North America also, and the absence of serious manufacturing competition from the Continent all gave easy money and long credit to England and her colonies and even to the republics beyond their borders. The progress of banking in South Africa tells the story. In 1856 there had been seventeen local banks in the Colony, two in the Free State, and one in Natal, but as yet the Transvaal was innocent of the higher forms of finance. Six years later there were twenty-eight in the Colony; the two 'imperial' banks, the London and South African and the Standard, had arrived, and the latter had foreshadowed its policy by absorbing the local bank at Port Elizabeth and opening branches in the Free State and in Natal.

The trade of the Cape Colony flourished. Cattle and horse sick- 1854– nesses, smallpox, drought and oidium were forgotten as soon as 1859. sulphur had checked that disease in the Western vineyards. A copper boom had indeed been followed by the inevitable slump; 1854– but copper was now on a firm footing, wool, the basis of colonial 1855. prosperity, was doing well and had been reinforced by mohair in the East,[2] and, to ensure a more adequate internal supply of labour, John Molteno carried the Masters and Servants (Amendment) Act, which stiffened the law in favour of employers.[3] The Colony followed the example of self-governing Canada and, in keeping with the principles of Free Trade, abolished the British preference. The customs 1855. revenues benefited accordingly, and though expenditure on immigration, new magistracies, and a third Judge for the Supreme Court more than kept pace, no one cared so long as Grey refrained from demanding additional taxation.

[1] No. 216 of 1860, p. 38.
[2] J. Hermann, *The Jews in South Africa*, pp. 212 ff.
[3] Act 15 of 1856; Molteno, P. A., *Life and Times of Sir John Charles Molteno*, I. 62–3.

Population was increasing rapidly,[1] thanks partly to Grey's policy of assisted immigration under which more newcomers from overseas entered the Colony than at any one time in its previous history. Lighthouses were built; a breakwater was begun to make Table Bay safe during the winter months, and the Union Line instituted a monthly steam mail service of forty-two days to Devonport; Cape-

1860– town was given a local penny post, which was soon extended to the
1864. rest of the Colony, and was linked by telegraph to the naval base at Simonstown some twenty miles away; a company began to lay a telegraph line towards British Kaffraria and the wires followed the railways as they crept inland. The original railway scheme had been

1857. for trunk lines from Capetown and Port Elizabeth, but such were the mutual jealousies of Port Elizabeth and Port Frances, Grahamstown and Graaff-Reinet, that the East got no railway at all. In the

1859– West, however, one London company began a line on the 4 feet
1864. 8½ inch gauge from Capetown to Stellenbosch and Wellington, and another carried a branch from Salt River Junction down the Cape Peninsula to Wynberg.

Nor was the advance merely utilitarian. Grey encouraged the construction of the present S.A. Public Library buildings to house a museum and the existing collection of books which he enriched with his own priceless library. The Grey Institute at Port Elizabeth, grants

1858. to mission schools, the formation of the Board of Examiners which foreshadowed the examining University of 1873, the creation of elective school management boards in towns, dorps, and field cornetcies,[2] and the opening of the long-awaited Theological Seminary of the D.R. Church at Stellenbosch witnessed to the prosperity of the Colony and to Grey's interest in education.

Besides helping the Colony forward, Grey made British Kaffraria as far as it could be made from the European point of view. He was

1858. hampered by the progressive curtailing of the imperial grant, orders to use land revenues to reimburse H.M. Government for its outlay, and the fall in land revenues that ensued when the Imperial authorities put a stop to his over-ambitious immigration schemes.[3] Nevertheless, imports and exports rose, the dwindling grant at least served to fill the gap and, at one stage, he made ends meet and, incidentally, helped to ensure his own recall by drawing unauthorised bills on the Treasury. The essence of his policy was to take advantage of the

1857. clearance that had been caused by the cattle-killing of 1857 and to

---

[1] Europeans in 1854 = 140,000 and in 1865, in spite of heavy emigration, 210,000. Non-Europeans, 181,000 and 315,000. Nearly 9000 immigrants came in under the Act of 1857 between 1858 and 1862, besides more than 1000 who paid their own passages and some 700 poor children sent from Holland and 1300 Germans from Hamburg.
[2] Eybers, p. 87.   [3] *Desp. to Sec. of State*, XXIII. pp. 274, 445.

civilise the tribesmen by example. To that end, he planted among them, either in villages or on small rich farms held on military tenure, close on six thousand Europeans, including German Legionaries, their wives and specially imported German peasants. So far did the struggling little dependency advance that, in 1860, it was granted a Crown colony constitution with Lieutenant-Governor, Judge and jury complete and, sorely against Grey's will, recovered control of 1860. its port of East London from the Cape Colony.[1] The more far-reaching results of his well-intentioned policy were, however, less happy, for British Kaffraria, the Ciskei, was transformed into a chequer-board of black and white with all the resultant administrative complications, and set on the way to becoming one of the most congested, poverty-stricken and discontented regions in the whole of the future Union of South Africa. Few will regret that the British Government refused to allow him to apply his policy to the swarming Bantu in the Transkei.

Away beyond the expanse of still independent Kaffirland, Natal was exuberant. First, wool displaced ivory at the head of the list of exports, and coffee and cotton made good a modest footing; but soon sugar became king in the tropical coast-belt and in the Legislative Council. And with sugar came Indian coolies. Planters had long complained that they could not get labour. The Bantu were slow to leave their reserves, in spite of the light hut-tax, and were undependable and heavy-handed when they came. But they were better than 1852. nothing; hence an abortive attempt was made to break up the reserves. No one had yet asked seriously for the indentured coolies who were working such wonders in Mauritius and some of the Caribbean colonies as substitutes for the emancipated slaves; but now the cry was raised for them, especially as the proposed importation of destitute children from England came to nothing. Grey refused to allow Natal to have convicts, and a new law to prevent natives squatting on Crown lands or farmers keeping more than three Bantu families on any one farm was not—indeed, in the absence of police, could not be—carried out.[2] On the other hand, Grey approved of indentured Indians. Therefore, after some correspondence with the Colonial Office and the East India Company, which demanded a passage home for time-expired coolies and higher pay than the proffered six shillings a month, the Natal Council empowered the 1856. Lieutenant-Governor to make preliminary arrangements.[3]

At first the Indian Government refused[4] and the newly made Legislative Council at Pietermaritzburg tried to induce its Bantu to

[1] A. 2–63 (Cape), p. 7.
[2] *Correspondence . . . 1855–7 (Cape)*, p. 50; Natal Ord. 2 of 1855.
[3] *Correspondence . . . 1855–7 (Cape)*, pp. 30, 203 ff.; Ord. of 1856.
[4] *Selected Documents (Natal Leg. Council)*, 1857, No. 5.

work by raising the hut-tax on natives who were not working for Europeans from 7s. to 11s. annually[1] and by enforcing *isibalo*, the paid corvée on the public works. One land company even imported
1859. a few Chinese and had to send them home again. At last India agreed to allow a few coolies to go as an experiment, and, in spite of some opposition in Natal, two ordinances were hurriedly passed permitting public and private importation of British Indians.[2] Coolies, including a statutory proportion of women, were imported at the public expense and allotted to masters for three years under indenture, additional customs duties being levied to cover the cost. Masters were to pay them 10s. per month for the first year with food and lodging, rising to 12s. in the third year, and to repay Government for its outlay. At the end of his term the coolie had to re-indenture for a further year either with his old master or another and he might re-indenture for two; alternatively, he could compound at the rate of £2 10s. for each of these years. At the end of five years the coolie was free to live and work how and where he could, and men who so lived for five years were to be entitled either to a free passage home or to Crown land to the value of the passage.

Nov.   The first cargoes were disappointing; there were too few women
1860   and those of a bad type; many of the men were so unfit that they
on-
wards. had to be repatriated; the scheme cost more than had been anticipated. However, subsequent importations were more satisfactory,
1863.   and though Natal was soon faced with a deficit and the diversion of funds from public works to coolie importation, legislative councillors held that that was a light matter since the coming of the Indians benefited the exchequer and kept down the price of Kaffir labour.[3]
1864.   Indeed, a loan of £100,000 was raised to finance a 'Gibbon Wakefield' scheme of importation which should bring in 2000 coolies annually and pay for itself in the long run; the term of indenture
1865.   was definitely fixed at five years, and rules much more stringent than those in force in Mauritius and the West Indies were laid down for dealing with defaulting labourers. And already there were nearly 6500 coolies at work helping to lay the foundations of Natal's prosperity.[4]

Signs of hope and confidence multiplied in the Garden Colony.
1859– A company built a railway from the Point to Durban, the first to be
1860.   completed in South Africa, nearly two miles long; the telegraph was run from the port to the capital; roads and bridges were constructed to cope with the up-country traffic. With full Crown Colony status and the prospects of a trade boom, the machinery of government

---

[1] Ord. 6 of 1857.   [2] Ord. 14 and 15 of 1859.
[3] *Report of Emigration Commissioners (Natal), 1861; Votes and Proceedings (Natal)*, 1863, pp. 2, 17; *Natal Govt. Gazette*, 1864, pp. 279–80; 1866, pp. 467–70; *Selected Documents (Natal Leg. Council)*, 1864, No. 18.
[4] Natal Ord. 16 of 1864; Ord. 25 of 1865; Leg. Council 1 of 1872, p. 5.

was reconstructed on a more ambitious scale. A Supreme Court of 1857.
three judges was set up;[1] new magistracies were formed and official
salaries lavishly increased. But European subjects to rule were more
difficult to acquire. Settlers rejected farms on easy terms and military
tenure and, though a few Hollanders settled in New Guelderland,
assisted passages to friends and relatives of colonists produced only
2100 newcomers in eleven years. The 8000 Europeans of 1856 barely
rose to 16,000 in a decade, and masses of Crown lands passed into
the hands of speculators, who allowed the native occupants and new
arrivals to squat at anything from 5s. to 28s. a hut annually. Soon
there remained only some 4,000,000 acres of Crown and Reserve 1866.
lands, while of the 7,500,000 alienated a mere 38,000 were under
cultivation.[2] Natal thus came perilously near to being, in the unkind
words of John X. Merriman, 'a white forwarding agency in a native
territory.'

In the intervals of trouble with Transvaalers and Basuto, the Free
State progressed quietly. New magistracies were created; new villages
were founded; in many cases in the small native reserves which were
being bought up; the Dutch Reformed clergy were reinforced and
there were soon Wesleyans and Anglicans in several of the dorps,
a minister of the Separatist Reformed Church at Reddersburg and 1863.
an Anglican bishop at the capital.[3] Each church had its elementary
school, and Grey gave £3000 of his Kaffrarian grant towards the
building of the Grey College at Bloemfontein and paid for the roof
himself. As for the Transvaal, it lacked officials and police, its
revenue was small and in arrears; but it had acquired its first printing- 1860.
press and welcomed not only two new Dutch Reformed predikants, 1859–
but also a few Berlin and Hamburg missionaries and, at Goedge- 1862.
dacht in the remote and inhospitable Zoutpansberg, Alexander
McKidd, a Scot, the first Dutch Reformed missionary in the
Republic. Above all, it had at last achieved political unity. The
South African Republic and the Republic of Lydenburg had come
to terms and on April 4, 1860, a full eight years after the granting
of independence at Sand River, the first united Volksraad met at
Pretoria.[4]

The first warning that this golden age would not last for ever was 1862.
the drought. Then the Lancashire cotton mills closed; the Yorkshire
cloth weavers demanded long-staple wools instead of 'Cape shorts';

[1] Eybers, p. 242.   [2] *Correspondence* . . . *1855–7 (Cape)*, p. 34.
[3] New O.F.S. villages at Kroonstad and Boshof (1856), Bethulie and Bethlehem
(1860), Jacobsdal and Reddersburg (1861), Edenburg (1862), Rouxville (1863).
Landdrosts at Boshof, Kroonstad, Bethulie, Jacobsdal, Philippolis (1858–62).
There had been 5 magistrates in 1854; there were 10 in 1862.
[4] New S.A. Republican Landdrosts at Marthinuswesselsstroom (Wakkerstroom) and Utrecht (1859) and a new village at Nazareth (Middelburg), midway
between Potchefstroom and Lydenburg (1859).
     10*

1865–
1866. at the end of the American Civil War the United States wool market collapsed and a run on the banks took place in Great Britain. Long before this last calamity, English manufacturers and merchants and the banks had begun to shorten credit; South African importers found themselves overstocked; immigration to the Cape ceased; the exodus to New Zealand and the U.S.A. began, and men began to
1857. trek to the Republics to escape drought and taxation. The S.A.
1865– Republic had long since paid its civil servants in 'good-fors'; the
1866. Free State now began to issue paper money, and in the following year the Cape nearly resorted to the same desperate expedient, while its shopkeepers for lack of silver change were freely using tokens 'made in Birmingham,' and the Standard Bank, for the only time in its long career, declared no dividend. At the other end of Africa, the Suez Canal, with all its dreaded effects on the half-way house to India, was known to be approaching completion.[1] As the dismal 'sixties wore on everyone in the Republics and Colonies, faced with falling trade and revenue, became depressed and quarrelsome from the High Commissioner downwards. These facts go far to explain the ecclesiastical dissensions of the time, the constitutional deadlocks in the Colony and in Natal, the political extinction of British Kaffraria, and the growing confusion in the Republics which, in the Transvaal, culminated in civil war.

Churches organised on a Presbyterian basis are essentially republican in form, as James I had been quick to point out. In the nineteenth century they showed themselves to be fissile in character. Twenty years after the Great Disruption of the Scottish Kirk in 1842, a somewhat similar disaster overtook the D.R. Church in South Africa. Liberal doctrines flowing from the universities of Germany to those of the Netherlands, where so many South African predikants received their training, caused heartsearchings among clergy and laity alike. Combined with doctrinal difficulties were questions of policy. Were ministers to be appointed as hitherto by the Cape Government or to be 'called' by the congregations as the Liberals desired?—a question to which Saul Solomon, a Congregationalist, added another: Were they still to be paid by the state? Again, were ministers and elders from beyond the Colonial borders to be permitted to sit in the Cape Synod, which enjoyed its privileges under an Ordinance issued in 1843 when the Cape had been the only recognised European state in South Africa?

The western Transvaalers had already answered this last question
1853. in their own way by refusing to be incorporated in the Cape Synod. On the other hand, a minister sent by the Netherlands Society to
1858. Lydenburg took up the local cause of union with that Synod, while the Rev. Dirk Postma of the Zwolle Separatist Reformed Church of

---

[1] C. 3114 of 1882, p. 216; Amphlett, *History of the Standard Bank*, p. 202.

the Netherlands came to Rustenburg and there found many disciples, including the popular commandant, Paul Kruger.[1] Like the Free State and the north-eastern Colony, Rustenburg was full of Doppers, the 'Auld Lichts' of the Reformed Church, who were distinguished from their fellows by extreme simplicity of faith and worship and sometimes by the old-fashioned cut of their clothes. The great point of difference was that whereas the Doppers used hymns in private worship, they held that only the Psalms should be sung in church, as they were part of Holy Scripture and the hymns were not. Some of the Colonial clergy had quarrelled with them on this score, but so far van der Hoff, the minister at Potchefstroom, had avoided doing so. He hoped that Postma would be prepared to work with him.

The issue was tested at two General Assemblies. At Pretoria, Jan. Postma refused to use the hymns and, next day, fifteen men, headed 1859. by Kruger, gave notice that they had left the Hervormde Kerk and proposed to form a free *Christelyke Afgeschiedene Gereformeerde Kerk*. The conciliatory van der Hoff attended the General Assembly at Potchefstroom with his three Transvaal colleagues and ministers from the Free State and the Cape. It was there agreed to exclude Liberals by insisting that no minister should be installed in the 1859. Transvaal until his credentials had been passed by the Cape Synod, to permit each minister to decide whether or no the hymns should be used, and to give Postma the church at Rustenburg provided the other ministers might visit their supporters in the town occasionally. But after the meeting Postma and his followers refused to rejoin their old church unless the hymns were abandoned, declined to have their headquarters invaded by rival clergy, and pronounced against union with the Cape Synod. The Dopper Kerk thus went its own way and in due time, as ministers were forthcoming, formed congregations in the Free State and the Colony.[2]

The political results of this disruption in the geographically divided Transvaal were not so serious as was expected at the time. Meanwhile, the orthodox church of the Transvaal once more discussed Sept. incorporation with the Cape Synod, a policy which van der Hoff 1859. had originally favoured.[3] The prospects of this union, never good, were ruined by the action of the Liberals in the Cape Synod of 1862. That assembly first decided that ministers should observe the Church formularies faithfully, and then censured one of its members for heterodox opinions. To check the power of the Orthodox party, the

---

[1] On the rise of the Separatists *vide* Engelbrecht, *Geschiedenis*, I. 114 ff.
[2] By 1873 the *Christelijke Afgeschiedene Gereformeerde Kerk* numbered some 5000 members in 6 congregations in the Transvaal, 5 in the O.F.S., and 7 in the Cape Colony, with a Theological Seminary at Burgersdorp C.C. (1869). This last was transferred to Potchefstroom (1905) (McCarter, *Geschiedenis der Ned. Geref. Kerk in Z.A.*).
[3] Engelbrecht, *Geschiedenis*, II. 5 ff.

1862. Liberals appealed to the Supreme Court, which *inter alia* decided that extra-Colonial clergy had no right to sit in the Synod. The Cape clergy were thus left alone to carry on a long series of lawsuits which led them more than once to the Judicial Committee of the Privy Council. The Rev. Thomas François Burgers, the Liberal protagonist and future President of the Transvaal, won on points of law, but orthodoxy triumphed in the end. Ecclesiastical controversy, which found an outlet in the orthodox *Volksvriend*, edited by Jan Hendrik Hofmeyr, the future leader of the Afrikaner Bond, engendered religious zeal; the foundation of the Free Protestant Church on a Unitarian basis split the Liberals; the opening of the Stellenbosch Theological Seminary and stringent tests for clerical aspirants cut off Liberal recruits, and the Synod of 1870 was strong enough to readmit Burgers and his friends to its ranks.[1]

1865–1866. Outside the Colony the decision of the Cape Court had been decisive. The Transvaal Synod had already elected to stand by itself. Now, a Free State Synod assembled at Smithfield, while Lydenburg-Utrecht joined the Synod of Natal, till on the arrival of the Rev. Lion Cachet, a bitter opponent of Pretorius, as predikant of Utrecht, it decided to form a separate Synod of its own. The constitutional disruption of the D.R. Church in South Africa was thus completed.[2]

The Church of England underwent a somewhat similar experience.[3] The huge original diocese, already reduced in size by the consecration of Bishops for Grahamstown and Natal in 1853, was still further diminished by the creation of bishoprics at St. Helena and Bloemfontein in 1859 and 1863 respectively.[4] At this stage, Robert Gray, who had been reappointed Bishop of Capetown and recognised as Metropolitan by new letters patent in 1853, sought to strengthen the organisation of this growing Church by twice summoning Synods, a practice which the Church of England had given up long since. He thereby got into serious trouble with some of his clergy, who held Low Church opinions in contrast to the High Church leanings of himself and most of his colleagues. One of these, the Rev. William Long, Rector of St. Peter's Church at Mowbray near Capetown, twice refused to publish the summons or arrange for the election of a representative of his congregation in either Synod. He was therefore deprived by the Metropolitan's Court. The Cape Supreme Court, to a certain extent upheld Gray's action, but the Judicial Committee 1863. of the Privy Council did not. It indeed concurred with the Supreme Court that Gray's letters patent had given him no civil jurisdiction, because the Crown, having previously granted the Cape Colony

[1] Hofmeyr, *Life of J. H. Hofmeyr*, pp. 60 ff.; *Report of the Case of . . . Burgers . . . v. The Synodical Commission, 1865.*
[2] Engelbrecht, *op. cit.*, II. 18, 34 ff., and Bylage.   [3] H.C., 454.
[4] Crockford, *op. cit.*, pp. 1882 ff.; C. N. Gray, *Life of Robert Gray*, I; A. Brooke, *Robert Gray*.

representative institutions, could not regulate religion or civil rights
by the prerogative;[1] it admitted, further, that Long had run the risk
of being deprived for good lawful cause by the mere acceptance of
his benefice; but it concluded that no such cause had been shown,
since the Bishop of Capetown had no right to hold a Synod.[2]

Meanwhile, analogous trouble had arisen in Natal. There, in 1863,
Bishop Colenso, Low Churchman, mathematician, Biblical critic
and so stout a champion of the Zulus that they called him *Sobantu*,
Father of the People, had seen two of his books condemned as
heretical by the Convocation of the Province of Canterbury. Some
of his clerical brethren therefore presented him for heresy to their
Metropolitan. After a vain attempt to induce the English Bishops
to take steps, Gray reluctantly summoned Colenso to appear before 1863.
his Court at Capetown. Colenso declined to appear, contemptuously
denied that Court's jurisdiction and appealed unto Cæsar against
the sentence of deprivation. The Judicial Committee upheld him on
the ground that colonial Churches had no legal connection with the
Church of England 'as by law established,' but were simply voluntary
associations in which no one, in the absence of a specific contract,
had power to enforce obedience on another.[3] The result was a
schism in the Church in South Africa. The Natal press supported
Colenso, as also did a large section of the public, some of whom a
short while back had been angered at the sight of an Archdeacon
in a surplice in place of the traditional black gown.[4] Colenso, always
claiming to be a member of the Church of England, continued to
function as Bishop of Natal. Strong in the support of the Natal 1866.
Supreme Court and the distant Master of the Rolls, he retained his
salary and existing Church property in his little colony, and having
been confirmed by the Supreme Court in his claim to the obedience
of the local clergy, promptly deprived all who would not yield that
obedience and forbade them to officiate in the churches of his
diocese.[5] His opponents carried on as best they could amid much
petty annoyance and even some violence, which reached its peak
when they invited Bishop Edward Twells, of Bloemfontein, to conduct a confirmation and found the cathedral ankle-deep in dirty
water as the result of a gratuitous spring-cleaning.[6]

[1] *Campbell* v. *Hall*, 1774, 20 *State Trials*, 239.
[2] *Long* v. *Bishop of Cape Town*, 1863; Moore, P.C. (N.S.) 411; A. Berriedale
Keith, *Responsible Government in the Dominions*, II. 1127–8, and *The Constitutional Law of the British Dominions*, p. 433.
[3] Keith, *Responsible Government*, II. 1120, and *Constitutional Law*, pp. 434–5;
A. F. Hattersley, *Portrait of a Colony*, pp. 83 ff.; *In re The Lord Bishop of Natal*,
1864–5, 3 Moore P.C. (N.S.) 115.
[4] Hattersley, *op. cit.*, p. 82.
[5] *Bishop of Natal* v. *Gladstone*, 1866, L.R. 3 Eq. 1; XLVIII. 307 of 1867 and
454 of 1867–8: *Bishop of Natal* v. *Green*, 1868, N.L.R. 138; Hattersley, *op. cit.* p. 87;
Theal, V. 367 ff.
[6] Hattersley, *op. cit.*, pp. 83 ff.

These unhappy events gave a great impetus to the campaign for Voluntaryism, that is, the withdrawal of State grants from the minority of clergymen of various denominations who enjoyed them, a campaign that Saul Solomon, an ardent Congregationalist, was already waging in the Cape House of Assembly and the columns of the *Cape Argus* of which he had become proprietor in 1863.[1] Solomon had to wait ten long years for victory in the Cape Colony; but as early as 1869 Natal decreed that no more such grants should be made, except, of course, to incumbents who retained their existing posts.[2] In that same year, Gray and three other Bishops consecrated Dr. William Macrorie as Bishop of Maritzburg and financed him with funds which had been raised for a projected Bishopric at George in the Eastern Province of the Cape.[3] So, while George had to wait until 1911 for its promised Bishop, two rival prelates could be seen in the streets of Pietermaritzburg till the day of Colenso's death in 1883, the newer arrival, at least, anxious lest he raise his hat to a member of the wrong Church, but so quietly resolute to introduce ritualism that, before long, most people had become used to singing the canticles instead of merely reciting them. Even so, when silver candlesticks appeared on the altar of the new cathedral of St. Saviour's a full ten years later, the then High Commissioner, Sir Bartle Frere, and Lord Chelmsford, the Commander-in-Chief, walked out in protest.[4]

Two rival Bishops of the same communion in a single diocese did not end the matter; rather did they pose the problem of the legal relations of Anglican communities to the parent Church. The Crown, for its part, gave up appointing Bishops by letters patent in any of its colonies, and the Bishop of Capetown organised his followers as the Church of the Province of South Africa. In 1870 and again in 1873, Gray summoned Synods, which drew up a Constitution for that Church expressly rejecting the recent decisions of the Judicial Committee in matters of doctrine, but retaining communion with the Church of England and Anglicans the world over, acknowledging the decisions of its own Provincial Synod and, when that should meet, of the General Synod of the Church of the Anglican communion, and looking to the General Consistory of the Lambeth Conference as the final Court of Appeal. This Constitution was ratified in 1875 by yet another Synod under the presidency of William West Jones, Gray's successor, who was doubtless encouraged to go forward by the recent passing at Westminster of the Colonial Clergy Act, which defined the ecclesiastical relations of colonial Anglican clergy to

[1] W. E. G. Solomon, *Saul Solomon*, pp. 34, 64–6, 173–9; *vide infra*, p. 343.
[2] Act 7 of 1869; Eybers, *op. cit.*, p. 197.
[3] Theal, V. 368; Agar-Hamilton, *A Transvaal Jubilee*, p. 6.
[4] Hattersley, *op. cit.*, pp. 83, 90 ff.; Crockford, *op. cit.*, p. 1891.

the parent Church, but forbore to touch questions of Church property.[1]

The reality of the schism was confirmed in 1882, when the Judicial Committee ruled that though Anglicans in the colonies did not cease to be members of the Church of England simply by reason of electing their Bishops and having their own system of ecclesiastical Courts, the Church of the Province was not legally part of the Church of England by reason of its specific rejection of the Judicial Committee's findings.[2] The schism was, however, more or less healed in Natal as the white population gradually outgrew that of an English market-town, and all the more after the Archbishop of Canterbury had consecrated, in 1893, Arthur Hamilton Baynes as Bishop of Natal to succeed Macrorie, the first and last Bishop of Maritzburg; but it was only in 1910 that legislation, while recognising the distinction between the Church of England proper and the Church of the Province, gave the latter the property in Natal which had hitherto been withheld from it.[3] The schism persists to this day in the Cape, where as late as 1932 a South African Court upheld Trinity Church, Mowbray, and its companion congregations in the Cape Peninsula in their attitude of aloofness by ruling that, because their property was vested in trustees for the conduct of worship in accordance with the tenets and practice of the Church of England proper, they could not, even if they would, hand it over to the Church of the Province, save in terms of a Parliamentary Act.[4] So far were they from proposing to hand it over on any terms that, of late years, they involved the Church of the Province in crippling legal expense in their vain attempts to get possession of much of its property, notably of Bishop's Court, the seat of Robert Gray's present-day successor, the Archbishop of Capetown.[5] Nevertheless, on all the bigger issues, Gray won in the long run, for not only have many Anglican Churches overseas organised themselves as Provinces in their respective regions, that is, as voluntary associations in communion with Canterbury and each other, but all of them and the Established Church herself have revived the admirable practice of holding Synods.

The experiences of the two most influential churches in South Africa pointed the way to political self-government, but the Cape had a long way to travel before reaching that goal. The agitation of the 'fifties had died down; Christoffel Brand was in the Speaker's

---

[1] Keith, *Responsible Government*, II. 1131; C. 979 of 1874.
[2] *Merriman* v. *Williams*, 7 App. Cases 484.
[3] Keith, *op. cit.*, II. 1129 ff.; Act 9 of 1910; Crockford, *op. cit.*, p. 1884.
[4] Keith, *op. cit.*, II. 1131, and *Constitutional Law*, p. 435.
[5] Bishop West Jones was promoted to the rank of Archbishop of Capetown in 1897; *Crockford*, p. 1882.

chair; Fairbairn no longer pressed for responsible government; Saul Solomon, who was ousting him from the leadership of the Assembly, merely joined Porter in urging that officials should be allowed to stand for election as full members of Parliament.[1] Yet a parliamentary system which falls short of responsible government makes heavy demands on the tact and forbearance of all concerned. Criticism may easily degenerate into obstruction; deadlocks between the Houses, or one or both of them and the executive, are hard to avoid. All had gone well, however, so long as Grey ruled, times continued to be good and taxation remained light; but no sooner had Grey been recalled temporarily in 1860 than Molteno revived his demand for responsible government in a tone which revealed all the contempt and dislike for British authority he had conceived while serving as a burgher commandant under regular officers during the half-forgotten War of the Axe. His motion was defeated and then, in the following year, Grey being gone for good, the Easterners in their turn resumed their agitation for Separation in a more serious form than ever. Hitherto they had usually demanded separate governments for each province and a federal authority over both; but now, alarmed at a threatened export tax on wool and further expenditure on western railways and the Table Bay breakwater, they insisted on Separation pure and simple.[2]

The issues of self-government and separatism were thus both before the country when Sir Philip Wodehouse arrived as Governor. Sir Philip was a man of fifty-one, upright and able, but with a colonial experience limited to the purely official dependencies of Ceylon, Honduras and Guiana. It would have been hard for any man to live up to Grey's standard of popularity and Wodehouse was unlucky. He came with the drought and the drought only departed with him; he was faced with a growing deficit; he could not hope to be loved, if only because he had to restore the finances, in other words, to tax. He proposed to have much closer consultation among officials than heretofore so that the executive might show a united front to the Houses, to avoid military expenditure, incorporate British Kaffraria in the Colony, station an agent in Basutoland, give the Eastern Province its own Court and hold parliamentary sessions alternately at Capetown and Grahamstown. As for self-government, Newcastle, the Secretary of State, was not opposed to it in principle, but he declined to consider it so long as the Imperial Government paid for the troops.[3] Wodehouse was more downright. He regarded a self-governing colony as a contradiction in terms.[4]

1846–
1847.

1860–
1861.

Jan.
1862.

---

[1] Kilpin, *Pioneers of Parliament*; Molteno, *Life of Sir J. C. Molteno*, I. 26 ff., 71.
[2] *Grahamstown Journal*, Sept. 25 and Dec. 22, 1860; Jan. 12, 1861; *Report of Separation Debate* (*Assembly*), pp. 2, 27.
[3] A. 2–63 (Cape), pp. 3 ff., 15.   [4] C. 459 of 1871, pp. 3, 15 ff.

Here was material for misunderstanding in plenty, and the Cape constitution creaked and groaned on its way to deadlock. The Cape Parliament as a rule divided on provincial lines. The Westerners, on the whole, opposed Separation and Annexation lest they lose their predominance and be saddled with the expense caused by the withdrawal of the troops from Kaffraria. These views were shared by many Afrikaner Easterners,[1] but the 1820 Party from Albany and Port Elizabeth wished to absorb Kaffraria into a separate Eastern Province and pointed to their swelling customs revenue as a proof that they could stand alone. The Kaffrarians on the other hand had as little desire as had the Midlanders to be ruled from Grahamstown. They hoped rather to remain a distinct colony enlarged by the annexation of Nomansland (the northern half of Faku's Pondo treaty state) and the empty Transkei duly protected by the troops from Kreli's Galekas on the other side of the Bashee.

On the morrow of the cattle-killing, Sir George Grey had proposed to cut Moshesh off from the coast tribes and link British Kaffraria 1857. with Natal by planting Europeans and loyal natives in the Transkei and Nomansland. Before his recall, he had settled Fingos at Butterworth and Tembus at Idutywa in the Transkei;[2] thereafter, Robert Henry Wynyard, the acting Governor, and the frontier officials tried to intersperse whites and blacks in the lands beyond the Keiskamma. Wynyard also asked leave to plant Europeans in the Transkei, even if it did mean expense now that the disbanded Legionaries were drifting away up-country; Tembus and Peddie Fingos were desirous of moving eastward out of European control; there was a risk that the Free Staters under Pretorius might push down through Kaffirland and find a harbour at Port St. John's in Pondoland to the grievous damage of colonial customs revenues. Then Grey came back deter- 1860. mined, since all hope of solving the native problem by federation was gone, to push his native policy through Kaffirland into Natal itself.[3]

Grey prepared to drive Kreli's Galekas back behind the Umtata river and then, having induced Natal to modify its wide claims on Nomansland, told Adam Kok that he might find a substitute there for his dwindling Philippolis reserve.[4] Faku, weary of responsibility, offered to cede everything north of the 'Pondo Line'; the bickering March chiefs in those parts were willing to receive British magistrates, and 1861. Grey argued that, if Kok could be thrust into this Nomansland, his mounted Griquas would serve as 'a wall of iron' between the coast

[1] A. 2–63 (Cape), p. 15; Cape Argus, June 27, 1857; Grahamstown Journal, Aug. 24, 1861.
[2] Native Affairs Blue-book (Cape), I. No. 6 ff.; No. 2352 of 1857, p. 90; Desp. to Sec. of State, XXIII. 260, 267.
[3] Desp. to Sec. of State, XXIV. pp. 84–5, 88, 98–100, 217–23.
[4] A. 118–61 (Cape), pp. 20 ff., 34; Desp. to Sec. of State, XXIV., pp. 231 ff.; Native Affairs Blue-book (Cape), I. pp. 4 ff.

tribes and the Basuto. Thus far Grey, who finally sailed for New Zealand with a warning of woe to come if his policy were not followed out.

At first, Wodehouse proposed to follow it. The Secretary of State had approved of it all except the annexation of Nomansland and, in particular, had given him leave to colonise the Transkei and annex it to British Kaffraria provided no extra military expenditure were entailed thereby.[1] To satisfy himself on that score, Wodehouse visited Kingwilliamstown. There he speedily abandoned Grey's plans. Finding that Kreli was averse to going eastward for fear of the Pondos, he left him where he was and declined for the moment to accede to the Kaffrarians' demands for land in the Transkei, because he believed the Cape would refuse to maintain its police there and would thus throw an additional burden on the troops. What is more, he made up his mind that British Kaffraria was far too small and poverty-stricken to keep its head above water much longer, for its natives were falling deeply into debt to the swarming Cape traders, the Imperial grant was growing small by degrees and beautifully less, the Port Elizabeth firms which controlled the trade of East London paid duty at their own port and sent all the goods intended for Kaffraria overland to avoid payment of dues at East London, and the Kingwilliamstown administration 'made up of officers with high-sounding names and the smallest salaries' certainly could not pay for police of their own. Wodehouse stopped all public works and hurried back to Capetown to press annexation on the Cape Parliament.[2]

That body refused to hear of it. With an unhelpful impartiality it rejected equal representation for the two Provinces and alternate sessions and Separation, Molteno's motion for responsible government and most of the executive's inevitable proposals for new taxation.[3] But more money had to be found. The slump was upon the Colony; public works were being closed down; London would have nothing to do with projected railway construction even with government and district guarantees, and Grey's immigrants were flocking out of the country. Wodehouse had to borrow on an empty treasury as in the days of Somerset.

The Governor hoped for better things in 1864. Many new men had been returned at the Assembly general election and crops were slightly better, but the general situation was so serious that the most determined obstructionist must see that something had to be done. The deficit was large; the ending of the Imperial grant had reduced Kaffraria to helplessness; all public works other than relief works

1862.

1862–
1863.

---

[1] *Governor's Corresp.*, XXV. pp. 31, 57, 67, 72, 229, 272.   On the affairs of Nomansland and Kreli *vide* G. 53–62 (*Cape*), *passim*.

[2] A. 2–63 (Cape), pp. 4, 8, 10, 16.   [3] *Ibid.*, pp. 11 ff.

had been stopped in the Colony, and Kaffirs, under pressure of drought, were robbing on the Eastern Frontier. He summoned Parliament to Grahamstown. Western absenteeism and Eastern gratitude evoked by the establishment of the two-judge court at Grahamstown, which Smith and Cathcart had recommended, and the promise that the garrison would be brought back thither from Kingwilliamstown enabled him to carry most of his money bills at last;[1] but the inconvenience of meeting in so small and ill-equipped a town moved the majority to reject the Easterners' proposals that the capital should be transferred thither.

Before the Grahamstown Session was ended, however, Wodehouse had propounded a scheme for the settlement of Europeans in the Transkei. He proposed to raise irregular police paid by H.M. Government for five years to keep order in British Kaffraria, and to give out farms beyond the Kei. His offer led to no response, for the terms were not regarded as favourable; but the event which decided the future of the Transkei and therefore of Kaffraria had already occurred during the late session. The police had reported that Kreli meant to attack sooner or later and urged that he be driven beyond the Umtata river forthwith so that Europeans advancing to the Bashee might still have a buffer belt of territory between them and the tribes. Wodehouse had begun to move up troops before he learnt that the scare had no foundation. He realised more than that: first, that there was no logical end to such a policy until the tribes had been pushed back to the Natal border and, secondly, that the occupation of the Transkei would entail extra expense. Nevertheless, he made one more effort. He offered farms in part of the Transkei on easier terms and, to relieve the congestion in Bomvanaland, allowed Kreli to come westward across the Bashee into Galekaland. It was too late. The war scare had forced Downing Street to a decision. Orders came from London to abandon the Transkei altogether and, in Kaffraria, John Gordon Sprigg, a member of the East London divisional council, took the lead of a small but growing party which was prepared to face absorption by the Cape provided the enlarged Colony received self-government.[2]

The end came in 1865. The session of that year was the longest and most stormy thus far in the annals of the Cape Parliament, for not only was it known that the Imperial Government was considering a reduction of the Cape garrison, but over the heads of the members hung a Kaffrarian Annexation Act passed at Westminster to be made use of if they failed to pass an Act of their own. The Governor gilded the pill by proffering an increase in the membership of both Houses which would still preserve Western predominance, and even held out hopes that the lands of the Emigrant Tembus on the Indwe

[1] No. 3436 of 1865, p. 4.   [2] Ibid., pp. 1, 6 ff., 13, 23 ff.

river might become available for European settlement. In vain was the snare of the fowler spread in the sight of such experienced politicians as Solomon and Molteno. They obstructed so vigorously that Wodehouse was forced to tack his Annexation and Representation bills together.[1] The joint measure was carried and the session ended with the very relief works closing for lack of funds and Eastern farmers taking the law into their own hands against the thieving Kaffirs on the frontier. Thus, in 1866, the Cape took over British Kaffraria (Ciskei), while Natal received merely the little Alfred District and not the full half of Nomansland (Griqualand East) which she had long been claiming. On the other hand, the Transkei, hitherto kept empty by main force, was, as the frontier-minded historian Theal put it, 'allotted to barbarians.' Theal might lament that the Governor and Colonial Secretary had thus thrown away a golden opportunity of 'pushing forward the border of the white immigrants[2] without doing the slightest harm to the black immigrants; but others would rather rejoice that they had virtually saved for the tribesmen the vast bulk of the present-day Cape Native Territories that lie between the Ciskei and the Natal frontier, the one and only really extensive Native Reserve area at the disposal of latter-day exponents of the policy of racial *apartheid*.

Sept.
1866.
Wodehouse, weakened by the resignation of his Attorney-General, Porter, met a Parliament whose Legislative Council had been enlarged from fifteen to twenty-one and its Assembly from forty-six to sixty-six by the inclusion of members from British Kaffraria and the newly created constituencies within the old Colony.[3] Such was the public poverty that even the sanguine Molteno, who was now competing with Solomon for the leadership of the Lower House, refrained from raising the issue of responsible government. Trade was dead, there was the usual deficit, and expenditure was increasing as sheep-farmers and copper-miners spread further afield.[4] It was in vain that the Governor pleaded for fresh taxation. Molteno, already a large landholder, retorted by accusing the Executive of delaying the sale of Crown Lands, demanding retrenchment and seeing to it that only six months' supply was voted. He thereby forced His Excellency to borrow once more on an empty treasury.

1867.
Next year, Wodehouse duly came forward with proposals for retrenchment and, *inter alia*, a tax on wool. He also announced that the Imperial Government at last proposed to put into force at the Cape the Newcastle-Cardwell scheme for the concentration of regiments in Great Britain.[5] Colonies like Canada, New South Wales,

---

[1] Act 3 of 1865; Eybers, p. 59.   [2] Theal, V. G., pp. 46, 68.
[3] William Downes Griffith succeeded Porter as Attorney-General in March 1866.
[4] C. 459 of 1871, pp. 7 ff.
[5] *Ibid.*, pp. 1, 10; Fitzmaurice, *Life of Lord Granville*, II. pp. 21 ff.

and especially New Zealand, where British ministers were weary of finding troops to fight Maori wars undertaken by ministers responsible to the local parliament, were being asked to pay for such Imperial troops as they wanted, and Sir George Grey, once more Governor of New Zealand, was actually sending the regiments home. The Colonial Secretary, Lord Carnarvon, proposed to begin a gradual withdrawal from the Cape in 1868 and to charge more than the mere £10,000 a year voted in Grey's time for the remainder. Meanwhile, the Assembly refused to hear of the tax on wool, but sacrificed half-a-dozen magistrates on the altar of economy. Wodehouse, to achieve the same end and secure some form of government that would work, proposed to abolish the unpopular Legislative Council, to reduce the size of the Assembly and to add a proportion of official members to it.[1] The recent reform of the self-governing constitution of Jamaica in this fashion following on trouble with the negroes served as a precedent; but the bill had to be withdrawn and the alternative, responsible government, was thrown out. On the other hand, Wodehouse induced Parliament to deal reasonably with one problem which had been greatly aggravated by the recent annexation of British Kaffraria and the abandonment of the Transkei. He had before him a memorandum in which a Commission on Native Affairs condemned the whole system of passes and contracts as a nuisance to all concerned. Hence, the Native Foreigners Act was passed.[2] This measure first repealed most of the laws and regulations on those matters that had been enacted between 1857 and 1864; it then directed that passes must be carried by Native Foreigners, that is, members of tribes, other than the favoured Fingos, whose principal Chiefs lived beyond the Colonial frontiers, and, finally it provided that the Colonial Masters and Servants laws should govern contracts of service entered into by all natives whether Colonial, Fingo or foreign. This done, Parliament adjourned, while Coloured labourers trooped in from the fields to die of low fever in the towns.

The following session was quiet. Crops were better, there were rumours of gold and diamonds far to the north and, in response to 1868. Wodehouse's representations that the position of the Cape in face of the tribes was different from that of other colonies, the British Government had given up any idea of withdrawing troops for that year; on the other hand, the price of wool had fallen and a dismal year closed with an Assembly general election.[3] The new House rejected the Governor's retrenchment scheme and declined to have 1869.

---

[1] C. 459 of 1871, pp. 10 ff. On Responsible Government and withdrawal of troops *vide* also No. 181, 181 (1), 181 (2) of 1870.
[2] Act 22 of 1867.
[3] The most notable of the new members was John Xavier Merriman, son of a Bishop of Grahamstown. He was destined to sit with the break of only half a session till 1924.

either an excise on wine and spirits or an income tax; a deadlock on finance ensued between the two Houses and between both and the executive; finally, the Assembly declared that the Cape police could no longer be maintained in the new Imperial protectorate of Basutoland, whither Wodehouse had sent them in his capacity as High Commissioner, and censured the general policy of the Governor.[1]

The constitution could march no further. Wodehouse therefore dissolved the Assembly and appealed to the country to choose between his 'Jamaica' constitution and, presumably, responsible government. He and many others held that a colony which had just annexed British Kaffraria with its swarming Bantu and might soon have to take over Basutoland was to be classed with Jamaica rather than with self-governing colonies of settlement. Figures supported Wodehouse's contention, for the census of 1865, the first ever taken in the Cape Colony, and the simultaneous estimate for British Kaffraria had shown that non-Europeans in the combined areas outnumbered the Europeans by more than two to one.[2] The majority of the electorate were, however, unimpressed by statistics. They rejected twenty-two sitting members and returned Porter and Solomon to counsel a cautious advance, and Molteno and Sprigg to force the

1870. pace or, if that were impossible, to obstruct. They decided to obstruct. The drought had indeed broken at last; there was promise of a good harvest and men were beginning to take the talk of diamonds on the Vaal seriously; but there was a debt of over £1,420,000 two-thirds of which was due to Great Britain for advances to meet past deficits, the profit-producing garrison was at last being slowly cut down, and the dreaded Suez Canal, open at last, was diverting traffic from the Cape ports. In the face of all this, even Molteno shrank once more from proposing responsible government; but the Assembly threw out the Governor's constitution, rejected most of the money bills[3] and, in reply to a request for more police to keep

May order in Basutoland, resolved that the handful already there must
1870. be withdrawn. Wodehouse prorogued Parliament in despair.

The course of politics was much the same in Natal as in the Cape Colony. Natal suffered last from the depression which steadily engulfed South Africa. Her sugar was in good demand, her cotton enjoyed a brief boom during the American Civil War and, with three-fourths of her revenue drawn from customs and natives and no expenses for defence, the prehensile little colony was able to

---

[1] C. 18 of 1870, pp. 3, 33, 40; C. 459 of 1871, pp. 9, 12.
[2] Census of the Cape of Good Hope, 1865 (G. 20, 1866); van der Horst, Native Labour in South Africa, p. 39.
[3] C. 459 of 1871, pp. 14, 25, 35. The Assembly, rather than face direct taxation, relied on transfer duties, stamps, licences, succession, banknote, house and customs duties, borrowing and consolidation of the public debt.

make a brave show. But at length insects in the cotton, high freights, reviving American competition, the collapse of the world market 1866. and the stoppage of the coolie supply by the Indian Government[1] spread ruin and involved the elected members of the legislature in a prolonged dispute with the officials.

The official caste at Pietermaritzburg, 'prejudiced against the Dutch, the Cape Colony, responsible government, soldiers, non-official Natalians, and all outsiders,' was completely out of touch with the rest of the colony.[2] As soon as bad times came the elected members tried to reduce official salaries; but they were divided among themselves, the coast planters and importers seeking simply to control the existing system, the up-country members, many of them Afrikaners, demanding responsible government. The agitation for control of the finances and a poll-tax on natives to meet the deficit increased. Lord Granville, Gladstone's Colonial Secre- 1869. tary, refused on the ground that so long as the Imperial Government supplied the defences it must control policy; but he had to admit two non-official members to the executive council and see nearly all the old members returned at a general election pledged to their previous policy.[3]

The Republics meanwhile sank deeper and deeper into confusion and impotence. It is impossible to separate the history of the Transvaal from that of the Free State during this period, for not only was Marthinus Pretorius President or would-be President of both from 1860 till 1863, but Moshesh formed a compelling connecting link between them both and the other South African communities.

The failure of Grey's federation scheme had given a great impetus to that of Pretorius. Boshof resigned the presidency of the Free April State and retired to Natal, and at the end of the year Pretorius, who 1859. was on the point of achieving the union of the rival Transvaal republics, was elected in his stead by a great majority. He crossed the Vaal, pacified the rebellious men of Kroonstad by dismissing Feb. their landdrost, and took office at Bloemfontein. A small Free State 1860. plebiscite decided in favour of union with the Transvaal, and April Lydenburg-Utrecht after long negotiations threw in its lot with the 1860. S.A. Republic.[4] Republican unity seemed to be within reach at last.

Pretorius found the Free Staters a jealous folk and, like all farmers, averse to paying direct taxes. With a fair share of the customs duties levied at the ports he might have made ends meet, July but that was denied to him in spite of a personal visit to Capetown. 1862.

---

[1] *Leg. Council (Natal)*, 1 of 1872, p. 5.
[2] Martineau, *Life of Sir Bartle Frere*, II. 238.
[3] *Selected Documents (Natal Leg. Council)*, 1865 onwards.
[4] Engelbrecht, *op. cit.*, I. 101; Eybers, p. 420. On this period of Transvaal history, 1860–9 *vide* Theal, IV., and Van Oordt, *Paul Kruger*.

He was helped, however, by the recent state purchase of the Pniel
1860. reserves, and he himself bought up most of the Bethulie reserve
where Lepui had quarrelled with his French missionary. Moshesh
was a more serious problem. To relieve the friction on the border,
Grey had offered a refuge in Nomansland to Lehana, son of the
late Sikonyela, and to Jan Letele, the cattle-rieving vassal of the
Free State. Letele had declined to move because he found too good a
market for stolen Basuto stock where he was; but Lehana had gone,
1858. only to be frightened home again by Nehemiah Moshesh, who had
been hurriedly sent by his father to make a footing south of the
Quathlamba mountains lest Letele should build up a rival Basutoland there.[1] Moshesh, alarmed at the prospective union of the
Republics, repeatedly asked for an alliance with the Queen;[2] but he
refused to stop his dependants taking Free Staters' cattle till their
Government should keep Letele in order, and Pretorius's attempt to
arrange a joint court to deal with border cattle thieves was cut short
by a hurried summons from beyond the Vaal.[3]

The union of the Transvaal was as yet on paper only. The Zoutpansberg was out of reach; even in Potchefstroom men feared that
union with the Free State would endanger the Conventions which
guaranteed the independence of both republics, and the Lydenburgers were jealous of Pretorius. The latter had merely been given
six months' leave to effect union with the Free State, and now the
Volksraad decreed that he could exercise no authority in the Trans-
July vaal while he was absent and dismissed his State Secretary. He
1860. appeared to plead the cause of union; but, when the Raad decided
that no one could be President of both republics at once, he resigned
his Transvaal presidency and left Johannes Grobbelaar to act as
deputy. Grobbelaar and Stephanus Schoeman of the Zoutpansberg
then summoned *Het Volk*, declared the Volksraad defunct, reinstated the Secretary, appointed a committee to supervise the election
of a new Raad and gave Pretorius a year's leave in which to effect
union.

Pretorius resumed his interrupted negotiations with Moshesh.
That chief was the focus of a diplomatic confusion from Harrismith
to the Pondo line. Jealousies among his many sons prevented his
sending reinforcements to Nehemiah Moshesh, who was keeping
the Basuto flag flying in coveted Nomansland; but he still cherished
hopes of acquiring that territory, even though Sir George Grey had
offered Adam Kok of Philippolis an asylum there. On his western
frontier, he agreed to an inconclusive settlement with Pretorius at
the expense of Moroko of Thaba Nchu and then watched the harassed
President dash north once more to the Transvaal.[4]

[1] *Bas. Rec.*, II. 517, 526 ff., 530 ff.   [2] *Ibid.*, II. 544, 567, 602-4.
[3] *Ibid.*, II. 508, 547, 559.   [4] *Ibid.*, II. 559, 577, 582.

There Schoeman had taken Grobbelaar's place as acting-president and, though a 'revolutionist,' had summoned the old Volksraad and prosecuted the pro-Pretorius committee for sedition. A packed court passed sentence; but Kruger, determined as ever to uphold the lawful government, called out a commando against Schoeman. It was all Pretorius could do to have the sentences set aside, disband the rival commandos and arrange for the election of a new Volksraad.

So, back once more to Bloemfontein to find Grey, the one man feared of Moshesh, gone from South Africa, the Caledon farmers beginning to laager, and Moshesh himself refusing to recognise the recent boundary arrangements or withdraw his people from Winburg Dec. farms, and trying also to persuade Adam Kok, who had just sold 1861. Philippolis to the Free State, to go into Nomansland as a Basuto vassal.[1] To make matters worse the two republics quarrelled over their mutual boundary, the Transvaal claiming the Klip river as the true upper waters of the Vaal and the Free State the Likwa spruit.

Such was the confusion that had greeted Wodehouse on his arrival at Capetown. The High Commissioner talked of sending a Jan. commission of inquiry to Basutoland and even of modifying the 1862. Convention if raids by Free State subjects on friendly tribes caused a war on his vulnerable northern border;[2] but in the event he did not even send the proposed Resident to Thaba Bosigo. For the situation began to improve. Poshuli, Moshesh's brother, beat Letele and reduced him from a public danger to a mere nuisance; Pretorius bought out the remains of the Beersheba mission reserve, raised a few police and, with the support of the main body of his Free State burghers, resisted the demands of the frontiersmen in the Smithfield area to be led against the Basuto. Pretorius also pressed on the work of a commission, which presently reported that Letele in league with certain Free Staters and colonial traders was responsible for the cattle-stealing in those parts and that the Basuto had suffered more than he.[3] Thereafter Smithfield enjoyed comparative peace and the storm-centre shifted northward to the Winburg-Harrismith borders, where the Basuto were settled thickly beyond the Warden line. Moshesh played with the Free State Government while its President hastened to Capetown to enlist the services of the High Commissioner. Pretorius failed to induce Wodehouse to arbitrate the Vaal July boundary dispute, but he did secure his promise to arbitrate the 1862. Basuto line if Moshesh also invited him to do so. Moshesh forbore to reply definitely and watched troubles in both republics accumulating on Pretorius's shoulders.[4]

In the Transvaal two rival governments faced one another, for Schoeman, supported by Potchefstroom and Zoutpansberg, refused

[1] *Bas. Rec.*, II. 598, 601; III. 168 ff.   [2] *Ibid.*, III. 129.
[3] *Ibid.*, III. 113 ff., 124, 125, 131, 136.   [4] *Ibid.*, III. 173 ff., 184.

to recognise Willem Janse van Rensburg, the acting President set up by the new Volksraad. Kruger with his Rustenburgers and the men of Lydenburg chased Schoeman out of Pretoria, bombarded him in Potchefstroom just as Pretorius entered that town, and drove him and the would-be President across the Vaal. Thence Schoeman doubled on the pursuing Kruger and reoccupied Potchefstroom, while Pretorius sought to end the comic opera civil war by securing a special court to hear the rival charges of sedition. No Free State nor Natal judge would intervene in the affairs of such a state; wherefore three landdrosts and a jury passed sentence of banishment on the rebel leaders, and Schoeman, repudiating the authority of the court, dug himself in at Pretoria.

Oct. 1862.

Moshesh naturally made the most of his opportunity. Christianity extraordinary was rising to a frenzy among his people; crowded assemblies discussed the best means of expelling the white men from the good corn lands for which both races had scrambled these twenty-five years, and Moshesh, turning a deaf ear to the Free State embassies which waited on him, sent his men in to occupy the belt of farms which he had always claimed fifteen miles beyond the Warden line. Luckily, Adam Kok refused to become a Basuto vassal. He moved off on his notable trek to Nomansland losing much stock in the high mountain passes and being robbed *en route* by Poshuli and, on arrival, by Nehemiah, whom Moshesh now reinforced.[1]

Jan. 1863.

At this stage, Pretorius abandoned the Free State. A handful of Transvaalers had elected van Rensburg President and Kruger Commandant-General; the presidency of the Transvaal was thus slipping out of his grasp, and, to make sure of it, he crossed the Vaal and resigned the Free State presidency. Moshesh promptly refused to recall his raiders till Letele was disposed of, and when the Free State in desperation talked once more of federation or even annexation to the Cape and called on Wodehouse for help, he pushed his old claims to their extreme limit and claimed a line to the Vaal cutting off half the Winburg and Harrismith districts.[2]

In the Transvaal a new presidential election resulted in the return of van Rensburg. The Pretorius party refused to recognise the election on the ground that voting papers had been tampered with, and Jan Viljoen of Marico occupied Potchefstroom with his *Volksleger* in Pretorius's name. Paul Kruger, always ready to uphold the authority of the state rather than that of any individual, at once called out his little *Staatsleger*, only to be driven across the Vaal, while Viljoen and Schoeman occupied Potchefstroom and marched on his stronghold of Rustenburg. Kruger, with his back to the wall, considered that the flourishing of rifles as a means of conducting

Dec. 1863.

---

[1] *Bas. Rec.*, III. 178 ff., 194, 214.
[2] *Ibid.*, III. 184 ff., 198, 208, 234 ff.; 23719 of 1869, p. 84.

political controversy had gone far enough. He shot to kill and ended the civil war. Pretorius agreed with the triumphant Commandant-General Kruger that there should be a fresh election. This time he was satisfactorily elected, fines and banishments were cancelled; captured property was restored mutually and the prospect of something like a stable government in the Transvaal was at last attained.[1] Jan. 1864.

Meanwhile, the Free State had found its man in Jan Hendrik Brand, son of the venerable Speaker of the Cape. In his twenty-five years of office Brand was destined to make the republic. His first act was to renew the appeal to the High Commissioner for help, for Moshesh was denying the very existence of the Treaty of Aliwal North.[2] Wodehouse hastened up and awarded the Basuto a small accession of territory, but otherwise reaffirmed the Warden Line. He marked out the northern and western lines himself with great care, wrote Moshesh a stiff letter biding him adhere to the boundary laid down, and returned to Capetown pursued by Brand's thanks and the hatred of Moshesh's younger sons, Molapo and Masupha, who saw their hopes of expansion westward cut off.[3] Letsie, the eldest son and presumably his father's heir, alone was pleased for that very reason; but it remained to be seen whether Moshesh would withdraw his people behind the Governor's line. Feb. 1864. 1858.

TRIBAL PRESSURE

So far from withdrawing, the native tribes were extending their borders throughout South Africa. Kreli's Galekas were trooping into the Transkei; the Emigrant Tembus readily occupied the new lands to the east of the Indwe which Wodehouse offered them, but still held on to their old lands to the west; Sandile's Gaikas refused to budge from the remains of their Cathcart reserve, and the 40,000 Fingos, who cheerfully trekked into the heart of the Transkeian territories (Fingoland), left others of their tribe to hold the lands they had hitherto occupied within the Colonial borders.[4] European authority was represented among these tribes by agents, whose only power was to send back British subjects to the Colony for trial, while behind the border tribes lay the Pondos and the tangle of clans on the Natal border. To the north, sole barrier between them all and the Basuto were Adam Kok's Griquas in Nomansland (Griqualand East) sorely harried by Nehemiah Moshesh and his Basuto. 1864–1865.

There was also confusion along the northern border of the Colony. Over the uninviting plains of Great Bushmanland and Little Namaqualand, which Harry Smith had annexed to the Colony in 1847, and

---

[1] Theal, IV. 143 ff.; Engelbrecht, *Amptelike Briewe*, pp. 80 ff.
[2] *Bas. Rec.*, III. 250 ff., 263 ff.   [3] *Ibid.*, III. 305 ff., 310 ff.
[4] *Native Affairs Blue-book (Cape)*, II. No. 34; *Desp. to S. of S.*, XXVI., No. 99 of 1865.

also beyond the Orange on the fringe of the Kalahari desert moved Bushmen, Hottentots, Koranas, a few stray Xosas and, since in rainy seasons there was grass along the so-called rivers, poverty-stricken trek-boers from the Colony. Beyond the lower Orange was a land whose coast belt was uninhabitable desert but whose inland plateau bore grass. The southern half of this plateau was Great Namaqualand, and into it Hottentots had drifted from the Colony with their guns and horses. They and their leader Jonker Afrikaner had conquered Damaraland beyond the Swakop river and despoiled the Bantu Hereros and Damaras of their cattle. To the north of Damaraland were the Bantu Ovambo near the boundary claimed by the Portuguese of Angola. The L.M.S. had laboured among these peoples from 1805 onwards, but in the 'forties the Rhenish missionaries had taken over the work and set up their headquarters at Otyimbingue, the centre of the feather and ivory traffic. Under their guidance the Hereros prospered so much that they too acquired guns, rallied round a certain Kamaherero, and struck for freedom with the help of a few Hottentots and European traders. Christian Afrikaner, Jonker's successor, was killed; his successor, Jan Jonker, was badly beaten, and such was the turmoil that several of the mission stations were sacked and most of the Europeans forced to leave the country.[1]

Sept. 1865.

On the other side of the Kalahari, in the lands through which ran the Missionaries' Road, the Boer republics were threatened with trouble. Nicolaas Waterboer of Griquatown and Mahura the Batlapin chief of Taungs both laid claim to territory which the Free State and Transvaal regarded as legitimately theirs. In the northern Transvaal such authority as Potgieter had exercised over the Barama-pulana in the Zoutpansberg was gone; in the east, Secocoeni, son of Sekwati, and his Bapedi were indeed still vassals, but close by were the independent Swazis and below the Lebombo range was Mzila, son of Manikusa the Shangaan, master of the coast belt in spite of the Portuguese and the enemy of the Swazis and the Zout-pansberg clans.

The authority of the S.A. Republic in the Zoutpansberg, which had never been more than nominal, was represented by the landdrost and predikant of Schoemansdal and by João Albasini, who had recently added to his multifarious duties those of superintendent of the tribes, and apparently interpreted those duties to include stirring up such trouble that the ivory traffic should be diverted from Schoemansdal to Delagoa Bay.[2] For some time past the

[1] Theal, V. 96 ff., 315 ff.; du Plessis, *Christian Missions*, chapters xxi., xxxiv.; G. 50–77 (Cape), *Palgrave's Report . . . 1876.*
[2] Ba-Mangwato, *To Ophir Direct*, p. 25; *S.A.R. Staats Courant*, Dec. 4, 1864; Theal, IV. 148, 163, 211 ff.; Hofmeyr, *Twintig Jaren*; Van Oordt, *op. cit.*, chap. xviii., xix.

mountain clans and stray Europeans had been scuffling, but no serious trouble arose till a runaway Shangaan drew Mzila into the quarrel. That potentate demanded the fugitive back on pain of closing Gazaland to elephant-hunters; Albasini for reasons of his own defied the landdrost and, when Pretorius tried to still the rising storm, sent his Knobnoses on the warpath. They behaved abominably; white ruffians behaved even worse; the Baramapulana rose in arms, and July the Dutch Reformed mission at Goedgedacht had to be abandoned. 1865.

At the same moment the Transvaal's troubles with the Zulus reached their climax. The Zulus were as bitterly divided among themselves as were the Transvaalers, Cetewayo's Usutu against the Mbulazi, followers of his younger brothers. Panda, old and fat, had talked of dividing his people among all his sons, and Grey had encouraged him to do so; but he had been dissuaded by Shepstone and Pretorius, the former because he hoped thus to further his schemes for acquiring an undivided Zululand, the latter because there was more hope of getting a road to St. Lucia Bay from one chief than from many. Then two of the sons of Panda fled to the Republic and Cetewayo offered land in exchange for them. The Transvaalers gave them up on condition that there should be no shedding of blood, acknowledged Cetewayo sole heir, and received a strip of land, the so-called Blood River Territory, bounded by a line from Rorke's Drift on the Tugela to the Pongola river.[1]

It was commonly believed at Potchefstroom that the road to St. Lucia Bay had also been won, and enthusiastic friends in Holland even projected a Belgian colony at the port; but the belief was ill-founded.[2] Shepstone in person then recognised Cetewayo as heir to Panda. He refused, however, to give up fugitives who had fled to Natal soil, and the Zulu prince therefore massed his impis on the border. The Natal garrison and volunteers turned out and Sir George Grey sent up reinforcements from the Colony;[3] but the crisis passed, Panda ratified the Blood River cession and, three years later, a Trans-vaal-Zulu commission beaconed off the line. Unluckily, part of the purchase price escaped to Natal; Cetewayo mobilised once more, and, though his father reluctantly acknowledged his own share in the cession, demanded the Blood River land back. The Utrecht farmers went into laager and Kruger gathered a large commando at Wakkerstroom.[4] There he heard tidings of the great Free State-Basuto war.

During the months following Wodehouse's arbitration, Moshesh 1864. had withdrawn nearly all his people behind the new line and the

[1] A. 102–61 (Cape), pp. 1 ff.; A. 122–61, pp. 8, 13; Theal, IV. 151 ff.
[2] Engelbrecht, *op. cit.*, I. clx, clxxvi.   [3] A. 122–61 (Cape), pp. 8 ff.; 16 ff.
[4] Theal, IV. 155; Engelbrecht, *Amptelike Briewe*, pp. 99 ff.

Free Staters lined up on the border ready to occupy the country as soon as the Basuto should be gone. The tribesmen were 'desperately wound up' at the idea of parting with land, and most of the chiefs clamoured for war lest the Free State treat them as the Transvaal had treated its natives; but Moshesh himself declared he would never fight about a line which the Queen's representative had marked out.[1] He was, however, prepared to fight if a good *casus belli* could be found and, like his contemporary, Bismarck, was ready to manœuvre his foe into taking the first step. His nephew Lesoana (Ramanela) supplied the opening. He remained beyond the border sowing corn in the Harrismith area, whence he presently raided Witsi's Hoek, while far away on the Smithfield border other Basuto raided cattle.[2] Moshesh then told Brand that he knew that the two Republics were leagued with Moroko for his destruction and asked for time in which to gather his crops from beyond the line. It was the old trick which the Tembus were playing on Wodehouse at that very moment, but time was given and reparations demanded for Lesoana's misdeeds. Once the harvest was in, Moshesh determined to fight March for his full claims. The one cloud on his horizon was that Kok and 1865. Lehana had driven Nehemiah out of Nomansland; on the other hand, the Transkei was being flooded out with Bantu and in the north the Transvaalers were held by tribesmen on two fronts. June Lesoana tempted a commando to attack him; Moperi, Moshesh's 1865. brother, came to the rescue and Brand was forced to declare war.[3] The Iron Chancellor could hardly have set the stage more skilfully than had Moshesh.

Both sides were more or less equally well equipped for a short war. The Basuto could stand on the defensive on interior lines; they had guns and even home-made cannon;[4] there were white men at Thaba Bosigo to keep the guns in order; horses and food were plentiful and the mountains afforded a continual refuge. On the other hand they had no open powder market such as the Free State had, still less the ex-Confederate field-gun and rifles on which the burghers relied. Moshesh was nearly eighty years of age, failing physically and mentally, much influenced by prophets and 'killed by his sons,' who were jealous of each other and, above all, of that 'stupid sensualist' Letsie, who, like Cetewayo, aspired to the throne of an undivided kingdom. In the Free State the war had united all parties; but the burghers were outnumbered by five to one, could not keep the field for any length of time, and could expect but little aid from the Transvaal and only illicit assistance from the Colony.

The war began badly for the Republic. Lourens Wepener failed to storm Moperi's town and had to stand aside while that chief and

---

[1] *Bas. Rec.*, III. 312–17, 320, 322.   [2] *Ibid.*, III. 324 ff.
[3] *Ibid.*, III. 314, 346 ff., 357.   [4] *Ibid.*, III. xlvi, xlvii, 182, 316.

BASUTOLAND and KAFFIRLAND
1854-71

Scale of Miles

0   10 20   40   60   80   100

British Colonies as in 1854........................
The Warden Line, 1849.............................
Annexations by the Orange Free State, 1866.........
Basuto Territory annexed by Cape Colony, 1871.......

Poshuli invaded the Free State while Lesoana seized Transvaal waggons on the Natal border and, because Free Staters were sending their cattle into northern Natal, raided herds in the colony.[1] The commandos, however, soon began to gain ground and after Wepener had carried Poshuli's Vechtkop and, then, Letsie's Matsieng, the Free State showed that its policy was to be that which D'Urban had attempted against the Xosas and the Natal Volkraads had desired at the expense of the Zulus: the clearing of the country and the breaking up of the Basuto confederacy. They annexed everything to the west of the Caledon and north of the Putiatsana rivers besides all the grasslands between the Caledon and the Orange, thereby opening a corridor between the Cape Colony and what was left of Basutoland down which the Republic might reach Port St. John's in Pondoland. Thereupon, Jan Fick stormed the Berea.[2]

Wodehouse was faced with the prospect of the general war which had so long haunted Grey's imagination. Not only had the Transvaalers promised to intervene as soon as they could, but all Natal was clamouring for war with the Basuto; the soldiers from professional zeal, the Boers from a desire to help their friends, the Natal Zulus with an eye on the cattle of the despised Basuto, Shepstone in the hope of adding Basutoland to the tribal state of his dreams, and the Legislative Council in the expectation of retrieving a desperate commercial situation, as so often before, by 'a large Imperial expenditure' on troops and supplies.[3] Wodehouse felt that the time was coming when he must get that control over Basutoland which he had desired since 1862 in the interests of the peace of South Africa and, in particular, of the Cape; but for the moment his chief aim was to limit the scope of the fighting. He therefore contented himself with demanding reparations for Lesoana's raid on Natal. Moshesh was apologetic; Molapo, Lesoana's immediate superior, sent in a few cattle and there the matter rested for the moment.[4]

Meanwhile, the Free Staters twice tried to storm Thaba Bosigo. They failed and, on the death of Wepener in the second attack, settled down to besiege the key of Basutoland. Brand offered impossible terms, which Moshesh rejected; the chief told the startled High Commissioner that he had given his country into the hands of the Queen; the siege was raised, the commandos dispersed and small parties were left to patrol the Caledon.[5] Presently Pretorius and Kruger joined Fick's patrol with some 1200 Transvaalers, mostly on foot. Together they routed a force of the enemy in the open and then

Sept. 1865.

[1] *Bas. Rec.*, III. 363 ff., 373, 377, 417.
[2] *Ibid.*, 423, 439, 490. On the Basuto War *vide* No. 4140 of 1869; C. 18 and C. 99 of 1870; O.F.S. Blue-book of 1866.
[3] *Bas. Rec.*, III. 427 ff.; Memo. by R. Southey, Aug. 6, 1865 (*Misc. Bas. Rec.*).
[4] *Bas. Rec.*, III. 442 ff.
[5] 23719, p. 13; *Bas. Rec.*, III. 443, 448, 450, 493.

scattered gathering booty; but to the disgust of the Free Staters, Kruger, like D'Urban in the war of 1835, refused to permit them to 'recognise' recovered stock and treated the whole as prize of war.[1] On the other hand, Brand disappointed the Transvaalers by refusing to promise them farms in the Conquered Territory.[2] Thereafter, Pretorius could keep his men together no longer. So the Transvaalers withdrew, on horseback now, with 75 per cent. of the booty, leaving bad blood behind them and Lesoana unpunished. Pretorius hurried north with Kruger to try the effect of moral suasion on the laagered farmers, the white undesirables and the hostile tribes of the Zoutpansberg.

Wodehouse watched the growing chaos with deepening anxiety. He was indeed relieved of all serious care for the cattle claim of Natal by discovering that the claim had been overstated by 150 per cent. and already partly paid by Molapo;[3] but Cape colonists, as in the war of 1858, and Natalians had already joined in the fighting; Herschel Fingos, Kok, Lehana, and Tembus had all taken part on one side or the other; Morosi's people were flocking into the Wittebergen Reserve, the danger spot on the northern colonial frontier, and now Brand, for lack of men and money, was calling for volunteers to be paid in captured cattle and farms in the Conquered Territory. In the nature of the case, these volunteers must be mainly British subjects; therefore, Wodehouse warned the President that if he recruited British subjects, he would cut off the powder supplies. He also offered his mediation and pressed Edward Cardwell, the Secretary of State, for leave to accede to the petitions of Moshesh, Letsie and Morosi that he should annex Basutoland.[4]

The Volksraad declined the proffered mediation and, against its President's wishes, ejected the Paris missionaries from the Conquered Territory.[5] Brand then revolutionised the whole situation. He made a desperate effort to end the war and save his waning popularity by calling out two thousand men.[6] These swiftly defeated Molapo. Nehemiah thereupon deserted his father and Molapo agreed to the Treaty of Imparani, whereby he promised to hold Leribe, the northern part of Basutoland, as a vassal of the republic; the commandos began to destroy the crops and, to save his food supply, Moshesh himself signed the Treaty of Thaba Bosigo, confirming the Free State's annexations and promising compensation.[7]

March 1866.

April 1866.

[1] Information from Mr. Page of Bloemfontein, who served on the patrol. Also *Bas. Rec.*, III. 487 ff., 507; Van Oordt, *Paul Kruger*, p. 120.
[2] Burnet to Wodehouse, Oct. 28, 1865 (*Miscel. Bas. Rec., Cape Archives*); *Memoirs of Paul Kruger*, I. 110.
[3] *Bas. Rec.*, III. 517, 587, 591.
[4] *Ibid.*, III. 540; No. 4140 of 1869, pp. 13, 65.   [5] *Bas. Rec.*, III. 613 ff.
[6] Coleman to Poulteney, July 7, 1865, and Burnet to Wodehouse, Jan. 19, and March 5, 1866 (*Miscel. Bas. Rec.*).
[7] *Bas. Rec.*, III. 643, 649; Eybers, p. 320.

The treaties were a mere ruse to gain time and in no wise stilled the tumult. The Basuto showed no signs of leaving the annexed lands; the French missionaries complained of their expulsion, as Brand had known they would; the High Commissioner held the Free State responsible for the balance of the debt legitimately due to Natal, and Feb. Pretorius, angry at his exclusion from the Treaty of Thaba Bosigo, 1867. made his own peace with Moshesh [1] and tried to beat up sufficient force to restore order in the Zoutpansberg.

There was need, for after the wild doings of the white ruffians and 1865. Albasini's Knobnoses, Wodehouse had instituted an inquiry into allegations of Transvaal slavery.[2] The specific charges rested on inconclusive evidence, and Wodehouse had let the matter drop when Pretorius promised to punish the disturbers of the peace. But the guilty were still unpunished. In spite of martial law and a declaration that the state was in danger, only 200 men had responded to their President's call; next year only half the burghers called up appeared, and now Kruger had to march north to Schoemansdal with a mere 500 of the 2000 men he had demanded. There a court of three landdrosts sentenced two local heroes, who were promptly rescued by the mob, and Kruger, hearing that the tribes were rising behind him, fell back to Potgietersrust and dismissed his commando. He was June followed by most of the inhabitants of Schoemansdal, whose land-1867. drost and predikant moved to Marabastad. The mountaineers presently burnt the deserted village.

Meanwhile, farms had been allotted in the Conquered Territory; but the Basuto's crops were ripening there and Moshesh repudiated his treaty on the ground that Brand had not set aside the locations March promised to his people. The commandos went in to destroy the crops 1867. and, to save them, some of the chiefs asked to be taken over as Free State subjects. Letsie was taken over; Moperi was settled as a vassal in Witsi's Hoek; Molitsani was promised a location near Kroonstad, and the Free State took up arms to enforce the treaties of 1866.[3] July This time it was guerilla warfare, for the burghers were weary; there 1867. was no money; the chiefs kept to their mountain tops watchful to raid and, if their mountains were stormed, reoccupied them as soon as the enemy was gone; Moperi and Molapo sat still growing corn for the rest, and Moshesh and Letsie pestered the High Commissioner to hand them over to Natal since he could not take them himself, or, failing that, to cut off powder supplies equally. Wodehouse, for his part, warned Brand that if his state was to absorb so much of Basutoland, the Bloemfontein Convention of 1854 might have to be reconsidered.[4]

The Duke of Buckingham, now Colonial Secretary, was averse to

[1] *Bas. Rec.*, III. 661; Theal, IV. 230.   [2] No. 4141 of 1869.
[3] *Bas. Rec.*, III. 756, 790.   [4] *Ibid.*, 786, 799 ff.

annexation; but since 1861 at latest officials and others connected with the Colonial Office had swung round to the view that Great Britain's withdrawal south of the Orange in 1854 had been a mistake; indeed, the Radical, Sir Charles Adderley, could tell him that because this ill-judged policy had isolated Natal and left a weak debatable Basutoland between the British colonies and the Orange Free State, he should accept the Basuto's offer 'and so tend towards one British South African Government including Natal.'[1] Buckingham therefore gave way to Wodehouse's importunity and told him that he might negotiate with Moshesh for annexation to Natal provided that colony were willing and a Basuto boundary could be fixed.[2] The Makwaisberg had just fallen and Basuto refugees were pouring into the inflammable Wittebergen Reserve. Wodehouse therefore cut off powder supplies all round and offered to mediate. Brand protested, for his men had carried the Tandjesberg and part of the Kieme. It was doubtless for that very reason that the High Commissioner exceeded his instructions, took over Basutoland *sans phrase* and sent up the Cape Police.[3]

March 1868.

Some of the arguments which Wodehouse used to justify his action were as legalistic as some of those which Brand, always the advocate, used to condemn it; but there was much to be said on grounds of policy for what he had done. Brand might protest that the Free State was not exhausted and that the Basuto, short of powder, were 'on the run'; but the fact remained that, as in 1866, Thaba Bosigo still stood; the burghers could not hold the country they had overrun; in spite of cannibalism in parts of the Lesuto there was plenty of food elsewhere and the Conquered Territory itself was full of standing corn and tribesmen.[4] Moreover, as even ex-President Hoffman admitted, the land left to the Basuto by the treaties was much too limited if their tribes were to be left intact,[5] and if, as Brand proposed, they were to be broken up, that could hardly be done without sending a swarm of broken and desperate men pouring into Natal or the Colony or, worst of all, into independent Kaffirland. Colonial Governors in times past, including Wodehouse himself, had had experience of the effects of the uprooting of tribes. Wodehouse was under no illusions. He knew that the chiefs were playing double, for Molapo and Moperi had now defied the Free State and asked for British protection, but he believed he could control them and that the bankrupt republic could not. He therefore proposed to annex Basutoland and give out a belt of

---

[1] *Vide* Newcastle's comments on Sir G. Grey's despatch of Feb. 9, 1861 (C.O. 48/407) and T. F. Elliott's note on Wodehouse's despatch of July 10, 1865 (*ibid.*); C.O. 48/436; Adderley's comment on despatch No. 41, May 5, 1867.
[2] *Bas. Rec.*, III. 769, 813, 834.   [3] *Ibid.*, 813, 839, 894.
[4] 23719, p. 47; *Bas. Rec.*, III. 841, 848 ff.
[5] Burnet to Wodehouse, April 16, 1866 (*Miscel. Bas. Rec.*).

frontier farms in the Conquered Territory with British title, the proceeds of which should go to the Free State.[1]

The Volksraad preferred 'the fat acres' to the money or the proposed British 'wall of iron' along the border and, against the wishes of those many members who were prepared to trust Wodehouse's good sense, sent a deputation to London.[2] The High Commissioner was in such difficulties that he offered to resign. The French missionaries and their friends in England and France demanded full restitution; Natal intrigued for the control of Basutoland, provided the territory could be made to pay its own expenses and offer land for European settlement as in Natal itself; the Cape Parliament registered its disapproval of his policy, and the Secretary of State chided him for having exceeded his instructions. Buckingham, however, politely repelled the Free State deputation and bade Wodehouse make a settlement.[3]

Wodehouse wished to keep Basutoland as a tribal reserve under the High Commissioner as Moshesh also desired, for he had no mind to entrust it to the Cape Colony which might soon become self-governing, and still less to Natal, whose elected members, as Robert Keate, the new Lieutenant-Governor, reminded him, had a habit of taxing their own natives and would look askance at any measures intended for the benefit of the Basuto. Be that as it might, he met Keate, Shepstone and the chiefs at Thaba Bosigo, and told Moshesh that Natal would take care of him.[4] Moshesh and Letsie at once cried out that they wished to be under the Queen and not to 'go into prison'; but Wodehouse departed, disregarding the demands of Nehemiah for Nomansland and leaving Shepstone to play for the goodwill of Molapo. Soon Masupha was raiding the pro-Free State Moroko, and Morosi the Herschel Fingos; Europeans from all quarters were helping themselves to cattle, and the majority in the Natal legislature, inspired doubtless by the ambitious Shepstone, was demanding that their colony be freed from the control of the High Commissioner and permitted to take charge of all natives in South-eastern Africa.[5]

Buckingham, in despair, gave Wodehouse *carte blanche*. Wodehouse needed it, for he was faced with confusion all along the
Dec. 1867.   northern border of the Colony. In Damaraland, Afrikaner had made an effort to regain his old supremacy. He was driven off from Otyimbingue, but he sacked mission stations, drove the traders to their ships and burnt the fishing station at Walvis Bay. The Guano Islands, annexed by Great Britain between 1861 and 1866, were out

[1] C. 18 of 1870, pp. 6 ff.   [2] No. 4140 of 1869, pp. 44, 69, 78.
[3] *Ibid.*, pp. 58, 59, 90, 101; C. 18 and C. 99 of 1870, *passim*.
[4] No. 4140 of 1869, pp. 53, 56.
[5] C. S. Orpen to Halse, Nov. 25, 1868; Keate to Wodehouse, June 1868, and Surmon's diary (*Miscel. Bas. Rec.*); 23719, p. 127

of his reach; but Wodehouse sent up a gunboat and from Bismarck's 1868. new North German Confederation came an inquiry whether or no H.M. Government was prepared to safeguard the lives and property of the Rhenish missionaries. Meanwhile, the Hereros decisively defeated Afrikaner, and then the trouble spread to Colonial soil. There the Koranas harried the trek-boers and half-breeds of Great Bushmanland, and all that a special magistrate and a few police could do towards restoring order was to apprentice some of the surviving Bushmen.[1]

In the Zoutpansberg most of the farmers were in laager. Pretorius called for volunteers. He obtained fifty-three, sent Schoeman with them to the ashes of Schoemansdal and, when Makapan rose in their rear and they fell back to Marabastad, threatened to abandon the Jan. whole district. Mapela then rebelled and the devoted Kruger failed 1868. to carry his mountain with 800 men collected under pressure of martial law; powder ran short and, on a rumour that the Shangaans were coming, the force dispersed.[2] Pretorius as a last resort went up to Potgietersrust in person and prosecuted Albasini and the landdrost. Many black stories came out in the evidence; but the charges broke down on exceptions and the President had to return to Pretoria to be censured by his Volksraad for 'the wrong course of treatment of the native tribes which had hitherto been peaceable subjects.'[3]

Native troubles were not all. Complications among the Europeans themselves were looming on the horizon. Gold and diamonds had recently been discovered at three points on the Missionaries' Road, April and Pretorius had made an abortive attempt to annex the mineral 1868. areas to the west and a corridor down to the sea at Delagoa Bay on the east.[4] But at last the chaos promised to abate at its centre. Brand was sorely troubled by defaulting officials and the gilt had worn off the Basuto reparations. The farmers in the Conquered Territory complained of incessant raids; those outside it grumbled that the bulk of it was passing into the hands of speculators and had brought down the price of real estate elsewhere, and at last Brand Feb. agreed to sign the Second Treaty of Aliwal North.[5] 1869.

That treaty reaffirmed the Bloemfontein Convention, made provision for the inclusion of Molapo's Leribe once more in Basutoland and fixed the limits of the remainder along the present lines, thereby cutting off all hope of a Free State corridor to Port St. John's. Wodehouse broke the news to the chiefs, who had expected to recover the whole of the Conquered Territory and were averse to control

[1] Theal, V. 98, 321 ff., 345; du Plessis, *Christian Missions*, pp. 336 ff.; G. 50–77 (Cape); Engelbrecht, *Amptelike Briewe*, pp. 131 ff.; C. 4265 of 1884, pp. 8 ff.
[2] Theal, IV. 224 ff.; Van Oordt, *Paul Kruger*, pp. 134 ff.
[3] *Cape Argus*, Aprl. 17, 1869. [4] *Vide infra*, p. 332.
[5] C. S. Orpen to Halse, Nov. 25, 1868 (*Miscel. Bas. Rec.*); *Bas. Rec.*, V. 57 ff.; C. 18, pp. 6–17; Eybers, *op. cit.*, p. 336.

and hut tax, and passed on to allot reserves to the petty chiefs of Nomansland and negotiate in vain with the Pondos for the cession **May** of Port St. John's in the interests of colonial trade. The Free State **1869.** Volksraad ratified the treaty with only one dissentient, and he an Englishman, who wanted to let the Conquered Territory go altogether in exchange for £50,000 which would give meaning to the paper-money. Members remarked that they had not expected such good terms and reported that their constituents were well satisfied.[1] After all, honours were easy and the long-debated corn lands had been evenly shared between white and black. Pressure by Natal negrophilists and admirers in London of the Shepstone policy delayed the ratification by the Imperial Government, but at last that **March** was forthcoming. Three months later the aged Chief of the Mountain **1870.** died.[2] He had lived long enough to save his people from being 'broke up as the Hottentots were.'

John Bowker, the Governor's Agent, thus had to rely on Letsie, the new chief paramount, to keep the jealous chiefs in order. Molapo withdrew to Leribe with his people as British subjects after taking vengeance on Lesoana, who had cost him so much; Morosi retired on the same footing to Quthing; at the end of the year, after the successful collection of the hut tax through the chiefs, the simple regulations drawn up by Wodehouse to define the relative powers of the chiefs and magistrates were put into force and peace reigned once more on the troubled upper waters of the Orange.[3]

Downstream also a precarious peace had been established. In the northern Colony a mixed force captured two of the unruly Korana chieftains and sent them to the Capetown breakwater. There followed further apprenticing of Bushmen, but no one would take the farms offered on military tenure in such a country and a special **1869.** magistrate was left alone to keep order with a few police. In Damaraland, Dr. Hugo Hahn, the leading Rhenish missionary, helped by **Sept.** traders, Wodehouse and Colonial half-breeds newly settled at **1870.** Rehoboth, brought the exhausted combatants to terms. The fallen Jan Jonker Afrikaner was glad to find rest under the watchful eye of a missionary on a farm at Windhuk granted him by Kamaherero.[4] **Feb.** Finally, in the far north, Mapela made peace with Schoeman; but **1869.** the real pacification of the Zoutpansberg was made by the Shangaans and Swazis, who fell upon the clans in quick succession. In spite of this peace of attrition, Potgietersrust was abandoned because of the fever and, of all the Zoutpansberg, Marabastad alone remained to the S.A. Republic.

---

[1] C. 18 of 1870, p. 27; *Bas. Rec.*, V. 183–91.
[2] C. 18 of 1870, pp. 3, 41, 61 ff.; C. 99 of 1870, p. 3; *Bas. Rec.*, V. 236, 262, 268.
[3] *Desp. to S. of S.*, XXVII., No. 62 of 1870 and 49 of 1871; *Bas. Rec.*, V. 553 ff. Basutoland was annexed to the Cape Colony in 1871 (Eybers, p. 61).
[4] Theal, V. 100, 324; G. 50–77 (Cape), p. ii.

In that same month Wodehouse departed with the dignity and May composure which had marked his every action throughout a longer 1870. and more trying term of office than had fallen to any Governor of the Cape for many years. The most outstanding political fact of his term was that the authority of the Queen had been extended once more beyond the upper waters of the Orange river. And already a cry was going up in the colonies for an extension of that authority beyond its middle reaches along the Missionaries Road, the Road to the North.

CHAPTER XI

GOLD, DIAMONDS AND CONFEDERATION, 1861–81

DELAGOA BAY AND GRIQUALAND WEST, 1861–1871

THIS demand for a northward extension of British authority was inspired mainly by the simultaneous finding of gold and diamonds, discoveries that were destined to work a revolution in every department of South African life. Hitherto, South Africa had been an almost purely agricultural country relying on its wine, cattle and sheep, a little wheat, a few oranges, some dubious tobacco, a dwindling amount of ivory and a slowly increasing supply of wild ostrich feathers. Secondary industry there was none nor any mining worth naming other than that of copper in the wastes of the north-western Cape Colony. On the other hand, it had long been, humanly speaking, certain that the day of the miner would come, if not in the old Colony at all events in the new Transvaal. The mineral wealth of that sprawling territory had been known almost from the first. Lead, coal, salt, silver, copper and saltpetre were all to be had, and iron was abundant, notably in Lydenburg. Unlike the Bantu, however, the Trekkers had never worked that iron, but had imported it at a price from Natal, and had been so suspicious of miners and their ways that they looked askance at anyone who even suggested a search for anything so unsettling as gold. Hence, nothing had come of the Volksraad's attempts to bring in German iron and copper smelters, still less of its offer of a £5000 reward for the finding of a goldmine richer than the Lydenburg outcrops, which had been worked by Africans in times long past.[1] At last, in 1859, the Volksraad resolved to permit companies and individuals to mine on a royalty basis and, in 1866, when all South Africa was sunk to the depths of financial depression, passed the first of its many mining ordinances making, be it noted, no mention of gold other than the expression of a pious hope that it might yet be found. In the very next year, found it was and an indubitable diamond to boot; but not, alas, in the Republic. In April 1867 a solitary diamond was picked up near Hopetown in the Cape Colony just to the south of what afterwards became Griqualand West. Eight months later, Henry Hartley, a famous Albany elephant-hunter, and his companion, Carl Mauch, a German geologist, proclaimed in Pretoria that there was gold at Tati hard by the southern limits of Matabeleland and also in Mashonaland still further away to the north-east.[2]

Small though they were, these discoveries at once led to political complications by stimulating the interest which the Portuguese, Republicans and British had already begun to evince in the Missionaries' Road, which ran to Matabele–Mashonaland by way of Hopetown and Griquatown, and in Delagoa Bay, the harbour best suited to serve the prospective mines. The Portuguese, for their part, had gingerly reoccupied most of their forts on the East Coast after their destruction by the Shangaans in the 'thirties, but their hold on them was almost as precarious as that on the *prazos* of the lower Zambesi, where a few Portuguese or half-caste *capitans môr* ruled their native serfs in defiance of a royal decree abolishing the *prazo* system.[3] The gradual settlement of the hinterland by the Trekkers had somewhat stimulated their trade, notably in slaves, ivory and guns, since trade had been permitted to foreigners in 1853, and they had

1862.   hoisted their flag once more over the ruins of Zumbo, 250 miles up the Zambesi, down which Livingstone had recently voyaged to their

Nov.–   great discomfiture. Great Britain, mindful at last of Owen's annex-
Dec.   ations of 1823,[4] had hoisted the Union Jack on Inyaka Island in
1861.   Delagoa Bay on behalf of Natal. A month later, Mzila, son of Matshangana, had nominally ceded Gazaland, the hinterland of the

---

[1] Theal, IV, 240 ff.; Engelbrecht, *op. cit.*, I. civ, cixviii.
[2] G. F. Williams, *The Diamond Mines of South Africa*; Ba-Mangwato, *To Ophir Direct*, pp. 1 ff.; *Transvaal Argus*, Dec. 3, 1867.
[3] *Rec. S.E.A.*, IX. 126.   [4] *Vide supra*, p. 177.

coveted Bay, to Portugal in exchange for nominal help in a private quarrel.[1]

The Transvaal took a keen interest in Delagoa Bay, its natural port. Lourenço Marques (Espirito Santo) was in those days a small and pestilential village; nevertheless, Alexander McCorkindale, a Scot from Natal, meant to make it the base of a company which 1864. should settle immigrants in the eastern Transvaal and supply that state with gunpowder and banking facilities. This latter-day John Law had his Mississippi in the Maputa river up which he proposed to convey goods in barges and thus circumvent the deadly fly. He succeeded in planting a few brother Scots in New Scotland on the Swazi border, brought a cargo of powder to Durban where it remained for lack of money to pay the carriage up-country, and 1871. presently died at Inyaka full of confidence in the soundness of his schemes.[2]

Meanwhile, the Missionaries' Road had earned its name more deservedly than ever since John Smith Moffat, son of the famous Robert Moffat of Kuruman, had founded the first mission station in Matabeleland at Inyati near Bulawayo, Msilikazi's capital in 1859. It was soon to be even better known, however, as the Road to the North. Like Delagoa Bay, it had been in dispute before ever the gold and diamonds were discovered. David Arnot, a clever and un- 1862. scrupulous attorney of Colesberg, made up his mind, like Philip and Livingstone and afterwards Rhodes, that the British Government should advance along it to the control of the interior. He also meant to feather his nest with the proceeds of the land along that road and, naturally, preferred British title to any other; but, to do his memory justice, he cared almost as much for the winning of the game, won as he afterwards boasted without a card in his hand, as for the land itself and later on the diamonds.

Arnot began his long-sustained game of poker with the Imperial and Republican Governments in 1862. Of all the Griqua states which had bulked so large in the politics of South Africa hitherto, only Griquatown remained. There reigned Nicholas Waterboer. His sovereignty to the west of the lower Vaal was undisputed, and the Free State also recognised it over a wedge of land to the east of that river bounded by the Orange, the Vetberg line which Adam Kok had laid down between his lands and those of Cornelis Kok of Campbell in 1855, and the well-known line from Ramah on the Orange to David's Graf which had long marked the western limit of Adam Kok's Philippolis. In 1857 Cornelis made over his lands and claims on both sides of the Vaal to Adam, who passed them on to Nicolaas Waterboer some three years later. Adam had then proposed

---

[1] *Rec. S.E.A.*, IX. 115, 138.
[2] Theal, IV. 161; *Transvaal Advocate and Commercial Advertiser*, June 7, 1871.

11*

Dec.
1861.

Dec.
1862.

to sell the remains of his Philippolis reserve to the Free State and had been swindled by his agent, who sold not only them but 'the lands of the late Cornelis Kok,' admittedly not knowing where these were.[1] Adam had indeed given his agent a receipt for the purchase money, but, before moving off to Nomansland, had, on Arnot's advice, publicly denied that he had sold anything more than Philippolis.[2] Arnot then transferred his services to Waterboer and claimed Cornelis's lands on his behalf.

Arnot's claims when fully developed covered the whole of what is now Griqualand West with the southern line along the Orange from Ramah to Kheis fixed by the D'Urban Treaty of 1834; the eastern line from Ramah through David's Graf to Platberg on the Vaal agreed upon by Andries Waterboer and Adam Kok in 1838 during their war with Cornelis and Abram Kok, and the western line laid down in the Griqua-Batlapin treaty of 1842, which had been ratified by Mahura in 1864, but whose very existence was denied by the other Batlapin chiefs.[3] In support of these boundaries he held that Cornelis Kok had been a vassal of the two Waterboers, that the Vetberg line had been a mere private arrangement among the Griqua captains, that, by recognising Waterboer's sovereignty to the south of that line, the Free State had recognised Cornelis's and, therefore, Waterboer's to the north of it, and finally that Warden had acted *ultra vires* when he had issued Sovereignty land titles to the north of the line and had ceased to do so when Andries Waterboer protested.[4]

The dispute was very complicated, for the Griquas had always been a roving folk, the whole area was very thinly peopled and in Cornelis's lands to the east of the Vaal, where the famous Dry Diggings were presently discovered, farms were held on titles issued by both the Waterboers, Cornelis Kok, the Orange River Sovereignty and the Free State. It may be, as the anti-imperialist Theal asserts, that the then chaotic Cape archives contained evidence that would have upset Arnot's case, but even without that the Free State's case was strong. True, Brand's legalistic mind led him to weaken that case by claiming that the whole of the land between the Orange and the Vaal had fallen to the Free State on the abandonment of the Sovereignty in 1854, a claim which would have entitled his republic to five-sixths of Basutoland and all the Philippolis reserve which it had just gone to the expense of buying from Adam Kok III; none the

[1] G. 21–71 (Cape), pp. 42, 49, 67; Agar-Hamilton, *Road to the North*, p. 135.
[2] C. 459 of 1871, pp. 44, 74; *Colesberg Advertiser*, Dec. 23, 1862. On the Diamond Fields dispute *vide* C. 459 of 1871; C. 508 of 1872; Bloemhof Arbitration Blue-book; G. 21–71; G. 15 and 33–72 (Cape).
[3] C. 1348 of 1875 *passim*; Bloemhof Arbitration Blue-book, pp. 27 ff., 30; G. 21, pp. 91 ff.
[4] There were, in 1870, thirty-three farms with Sovereignty and 110 with O.F.S. title between the Vetberg line and the Vaal.

less, he could plead that it was scarcely reasonable to claim that Nicolaas Waterboer, ruler of a few hundred Griquas living in squalor, was the real sovereign of a vast area in which lived many Koranas, Batlapin and Europeans, in parts of which his subjects had never dwelt and over much of which neither he nor his father had exercised authority for many years, if they had ever done so.[1]. Moreover, the lands to the east of the Vaal had formed part of the Sovereignty in which both Warden and Harry Smith had merely recognised the proprietary rights of Cornelis Kok; out of it Warden had carved the Pniel reserves in which his magistrates had exercised jurisdiction; and in it the Berlin missionaries were actually living under Free State law even though Brand could not deny that the nearest landdrost was stationed well away to the east at Jacobsdal.[2]

Thus, as far as the lands to the east of the Vaal were concerned, Brand's case rested on equity, commonsense and the acts of the Sovereignty Government. He therefore declined to discuss them with Arnot. On the other hand, his claims to the Campbell Lands to the west rested solely on Adam Kok's highly questionable deed of sale. These he was willing to exchange for Waterboer's lands south of the Vetberg line or submit to arbitration. Wodehouse was willing 1864. to arbitrate,[3] but Arnot turned aside from Brand to join issue with Pretorius, who had demanded the war indemnity promised by Mahura in 1858. As agent for Mahura, Arnot refused to pay and counter-claimed a line for the Batlapin from Platberg on the Vaal up the Makwassi Spruit to the sources of the Harts and the Molopo, a line which would have pushed the Transvaal far back from the Road to the Mooi river valley in which Potchefstroom lay.[4]

Neither Government perhaps took Arnot very seriously at first; but, when the Basuto wars and the troubles in the Zoutpansberg afflicted them, Arnot stated his full claims to Griqualand West and, in spite of Brand's warning, induced a few Albany men to settle in 1867. Albania on Waterboer's side of the Vetberg line.[5] Brand, for his part tried to strengthen his position by hastily paying the balance of the Philippolis purchase money which had been outstanding for four years past, while his Volksraad refused to admit that the area south of the Vaal could be in question at all.

In the course of 1868 diamonds were found on the north bank of the Vaal near its junction with the Harts in land claimed by the Transvaal, Waterboer and Mahura. But the gold of Tati threw these River Diggings into the shade. Pretorius decided to gain control of

<hr>

[1] For the condition of the Griquas in 1870 *vide* Lindley, *Adamantia*, p. 215.
[2] For Brand's case *vide* G. 21–71, pp. 103 ff.; C. 459 of 1871, pp. 48 ff.; C. 1348 of 1875 *passim*; also G. 15–72 (Cape), p. 32; C. 732 of 1873, pp. 11, 18.
[3] G. 21–71, p. 17.   [4] Bloemhof Arbitration Blue-book, p. 81.
[5] Arnot and Orpen, *The Land Question*, pp. 307 ff.; J. A. I. Agar-Hamilton, *The Road to the North*, p. 89 *et passim*.

the Road and the gold in the interests of his bankrupt republic and to push down to the sea at Delagoa Bay. He had already stationed a landdrost at Nylstroom in the new district of the Waterberg and now asked the dying Msilikazi and Matsheng, the Mangwato of April Shoshong, to become his vassals. Without waiting for their replies 1868. he foolishly annexed a wide area to the north and west of his state, including Tati but prudently excluding the Matabele, and a strip a mile wide on either side of the Maputa river to the sea.[1]

Pretorius's anxiety to secure this new-found wealth was very natural, for the finances of both Republics were desperate and, of the two, the Transvaal's were the worse. On the eve of the Basuto wars the Free State had expelled the Standard Bank, which was squeezing the Bloemfontein Bank and thus threatening the Govern-1865. ment with 'foreign' control. The bank withdrew, taking much of the loose capital of the state with it, and thereby obliged the Volksraad to issue paper money to the local bank, which promptly trebled its own note issue. At the end of the wars £126,000 in paper were in circulation; the £5 'blueback' was worth £3; trade with the colonies was by barter only and credit to seek, and £650,000 of private debts were owing to banks and individuals in the south. The Transvaal 1869. possessed a public debt of £74,000 notes at 75 per cent. discount, a revenue which in the absence of anything like an adequate civil service just met expenditure, and the knowledge that its President had recently failed to float a public loan of £300. Many of its burghers, too, were in debt to creditors at the coast, and the Standard Bank had not even troubled to open a branch north of the Vaal. The two Republics might have issued their first postage stamps but in neither would the burghers face direct taxation; in many cases they could not, and nearly all the debts, public and private, were secured upon land. In short, the Republics were passing into pawn to the British colonies.[2]

Pretorius's hasty annexations loosed a storm. Portugal protested, Wodehouse protested, Msilikazi probably never received Pretorius's message; but Matsheng refused to become a Transvaal vassal, and on the advice of his missionary, John Mackenzie of the L.M.S., asked for British protection; the Wesleyan missionary, the Rev. Joseph Ludorf, complained once more that the Boers were taking Montsioa's fountains and made the same request;[3] philanthropic creditors in the colonies inveighed against Transvaal slavery and demanded that both Republics be annexed in the commercial inter-Aug. ests of South Africa[4] and, when Wodehouse turned a deaf ear, the 1868.

---

[1] C. 1361 of 1875, p. 33.
[2] C. 3114 of 1882, p. 216; Amphlett, *Standard Bank*, chapter iv.; Carter, *Narrative*, p. 28, quoting *S.A.R. Staats Courant*, March 9, 1868.
[3] Bloemhof Arbitration Blue-book, p. 154.   [4] No. 4141 of 1869 *passim*.

majority in the Natal legislature offered to take action themselves if they were only relieved of the veto of a supine High Commissioner.[1]

The Duke of Buckingham, who had reluctantly assented to the annexation of Basutoland, was in no mind to annex anything else except in face of 'overruling necessity'[2] and Pretorius quieted the storm by withdrawing his claims. The latter knew that he had not a leg to stand on and could hope for no support from the Free State, for the internal troubles of the Transvaal and the behaviour of its burghers during the Basuto wars had killed the Unionist party there; but he found Portugal anxious for support against Great Britain in the Delagoa Bay controversy, and was thus able to con- July clude a commercial treaty specially safeguarding the Mozambique 1869. trade in slaves and guns and defining the eastern borders of Gaza-land in such a way as to fix those of the Transvaal by implication along the Lebombo mountains. He even went so far to please his new allies as to give full civil liberty to Roman Catholics in the Republic.[3]

Pretorius still hoped to gain control of the central section of the Road and the River Diggings between the Vaal and Harts rivers. The western border of his republic had always been vague. Such 1862– authority as the Pretoria Government had exercised over the tribes 1864. in the region of the Molopo and Harts had lapsed during the civil war, and Batlapin and Koranas were actually in occupation of the diamondiferous area. Since, however, there were also a few Boers between the Vaal and Harts, Pretorius discussed matters with the local chiefs. He found the Koranas ready to accept his rule, but he failed to induce Mahura to recognise the Harts as the western boundary of the Transvaal in return for a reduction in the number of the cattle which he was said to owe as a war indemnity. Mahura preferred to Feb. pay in cattle rather than in land, and threw over Arnot as soon as he 1869. discovered that he was claiming for Waterboer part of the land be-tween the Vaal and Harts which he himself claimed. He then ap-pointed Theodor Doms as his agent. In Dom's hands the negotiations with Pretorius soon broke down.[4]

At this stage the famous diamond, 'The Star of South Africa,' was found somewhere in much-debated Griqualand and changed hands first for £11,000 and then for £25,000. The Free State hurriedly beaconed off the Vetberg Line, and Pretorius, who had just been re-elected President of the northern republic, felt secure enough to take steps to make sure of his share of the Diggings and the Road along which the gold rush to Tati was fairly setting in.[5] Australians

---

[1] No. 4140 of 1869, pp. 93, 127.   [2] *Ibid.*, p. 93.
[3] *S.A.R. Staats Courant (Supplement)*, Aug. 2, 1871, for the 1869 treaty.
[4] Bloemhof Arbitration Blue-book, pp. 89, 109 ff., 116 ff., 279 ff.
[5] T. Baines, *The Gold Regions of South-Eastern Africa*, pp. 3 ff.; 75 ff.; van der Horst, *op. cit.*, p. 125.

were coming up from Natal; representatives of London companies were at Tati and far to the north on the Mazoe, and gold had been
Nov.–
Dec.
1869.
found in the eastern Transvaal itself. He therefore proclaimed the new district of Bloemhof along the Harts river, extended the field cornetcy of Zeerust to cut the Road north of Kuruman and, a little
June
1870.
later, threw his republic open to prospectors and appointed a Natalian, Edward Button, as gold commissioner to see that the state received its due share of the value produced.[1]

By this time the diamonds had overshadowed the gold. At the New Year of 1870 there was a rush from all parts of the country to Klipdrift and Hebron in the disputed lands between the Vaal and Harts, and presently another to the old Pniel reserve on the Free State side of the Vaal. The diggers were an orderly crowd enough. Many of them had brought their families and treated the whole business as a prolonged and possibly lucrative picnic; but their very presence made the settlement of outstanding questions of jurisdiction imperative. Brand induced Waterboer to submit the question of the Campbell Lands to Wodehouse, but to the great misfortune of all concerned the High Commissioner, a stiff man but a just, was on the point of leaving South Africa and could do nothing. Hardly was he gone than Pretorius upset the apple-cart and brought intervention from the south within the bounds of possibility. At the
June
1870.
end of the Volksraad session he rushed through a diamond monopoly for 21 years to three friends. Burghers and diggers alike cried out against the scandal and the President drew back. It was too late. The diggers proclaimed a free republic at Klipdrift and Stafford Parker, an ex-able-bodied seaman of H.M. Navy, joined the ranks of South African presidents.[2]

The first attempt at a general settlement of the disputed area on
Aug.
1870.
either side of the Vaal was now made. The Free State agreed to claim no land between the Vaal and Harts, and the two Republics met their respective tribal rivals at Nooitgedacht. The conference failed. Pretorius could make no headway with the Batlapin and Barolong chiefs; Brand declined to submit the whole of Waterboer's claim to the High Commissioner; whereupon Waterboer departed and asked to be taken over as a British subject.[3] Pretorius then visited the Diggers' Republic and promised wide powers of self-government. It was of no avail. His authority was gone and Doms was busy
Aug.
1870.
offering concessions in the name of his Bantu protégés. Brand meanwhile proclaimed Free State sovereignty over the Campbell Lands and sent the Swede, Olof Truter, an aforetime policeman on the

---

[1] Bloemhof Arbitration Blue-book, p. 276; Gardner Williams, *Diamond Fields*, p. 123; Glanville, *South African Gold-Fields*.
[2] C. 459 of 1871, pp. 31 ff.
[3] *Ibid.*, pp. 36, 88 ff., 92; Leyd's *First Annexation of the Transvaal*, p. 120; G. 21, pp. 28 ff.

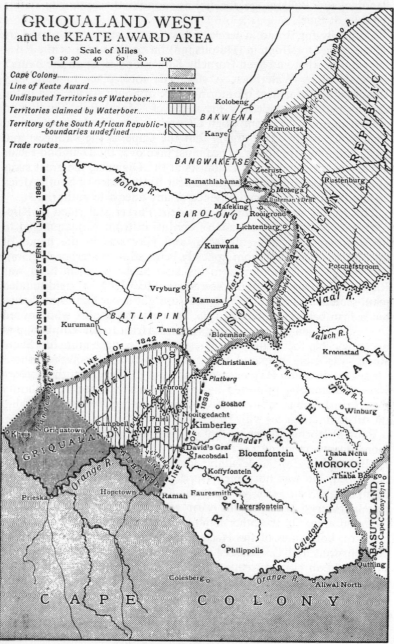

GRIQUALAND WEST
and the KEATE AWARD AREA

Scale of Miles
0 10 20   40   60   80   100

Cape Colony..
Line of Keate Award.............................
Undisputed Territories of Waterboer.......
Territories claimed by Waterboer............
Territory of the South African Republic—
—boundaries undefined.....................
Trade routes.......................................

Kolobeng

BAKWENA

Kanye   Ramoutsa

BANGWAKETSE   Zeerust   Rustenburg

Ramathlabama   Mosega
Molopo R.   Kuhrman's Drift
                    Mafeking   Rooigrond
                    BAROLONG   Lichtenburg
                                        Potchefstroom
                    Kunwana

PRETORIUS'S WESTERN LINE, 1868

                    Vryburg
                          Mamusa
        BATLAPIN
Kuruman   Taungs   Bloemhof
                                        Vaal R.
                                        Valsch R.
                                        Kroonstad
                    Christiania   Vet R.
LINE OF 1842   Platberg
            CAMPBELL LANDS   Boshof
        Hebron   Winburg
    1838   Nooitgedacht
Campbell   Pniel   Kimberley
Kheis Griquatown WEST   David's Graf
        GRIQUALAND   Jacobsdal Bloemfontein Thaba Nchu
        Orange R. ALBANY   MOROKO
                    Koffyfontein Thaba Bosigo
Prieska   Hopetown Ramah Fauresmith ORANGE FREE STATE
                        Jagersfontein BASUTOLAND
                                        to Cape Colony 1871
                        Philippolis Quthing

        Colesberg   Orange R. Aliwal North

C A P E   C O L O N Y

Emery Walker Ltd. sc.

Bendigo and Ballarat goldfields,[1] to uphold the authority of his republic at Pniel.

Unluckily for Brand, a week or two later a stone was picked up on the farm Dorstfontein (Dutoitspan) far to the south of the River Diggings in what had been Cornelis Kok's land right on the boundary claimed by Waterboer. A stampede took place to these Dry Diggings, henceforward the storm-centre of South Africa, and in the Colony petitions headed by the name of 'Moral Bob' Godlonton poured in upon the acting High Commissioner, Lieutenant-General Charles Crawfurd Hay, urging that the Cape as the strongest and most stable state in South Africa must take over the Diamond Fields in view of the numbers of Colonists at the Diggings, the great sums of money there invested and the danger to the peace of South Africa arising from the presumed absence of any adequate authority.[2]

The appeal was well timed. President Parker still ruled at Klipdrift, the memory of a decade of confusion from Namaqualand to the Zoutpansberg was still fresh, and Hay was in the hands of his officials, many of whom honestly believed in Waterboer's claims and nearly all of whom were his advocates. At their head was Richard Southey, Colonial Secretary since 1864, a rigid-minded man, secretive as Shepstone himself, upright according to his lights, but a firm believer in official rule, an early imperialist who desired to see the Queen's representatives ruling Africa to the Zambesi, and an implacable foe to the Republics, which he, once more like Shepstone, was quite prepared to bridle with the help of the tribes.[3]

Sept. 1870. Under his direction Hay warned Brand not to beacon off the Vetberg Line prematurely, protested against Truter's exercise of authority over British subjects, and bade Pretorius refrain from encroaching on tribes 'in alliance' with Her Majesty.[4]

Poor Pretorius, never a diplomatist, was becoming more and more deeply involved in controversy with the astute advisers of his Bantu rivals for the debatable lands. Their claims were now fully developed. He was not much worried by the Batlapin Jantje and Mankoroane, successor to Mahura, for at Nooitgedacht they had merely claimed lands to the west of the Harts well beyond the diamond area. On the other hand, Doms claimed for the Barolong lands on both sides of the Harts bounded to the east by the Vaal, Schoonspruit and the sources of the Marico and Molopo, on the

1837. strength of an alleged treaty whereby Potgieter had promised these lands of Tao, their ancestor, to Moroko and Tawane, the father of Montsioa. After the meeting, Ludorf, Montsioa's friend, had shown

---

[1] C. 459 of 1871, pp. 37, 92; G. 21–71, p. 18.
[2] C. 459 of 1871, pp. 62, 65.
[3] Wilmot, *Life of . . . Southey*, pp. 196 ff., 313; Froude, *Two Lectures*, p. 26; Aylward, *op. cit.*, p. 291.
[4] G. 21–71, pp. 4–7; C. 459 of 1871, pp. 38, 44.

Pretorius another alleged treaty in which the elder Pretorius recog- 1851.
nised the independence of Montsioa to the west of the Harts.[1]
Pretorius jumped at this apparent chance of disposing of Montsioa's
claims to the River Diggings and henceforward made this 'treaty'
the basis of his claims thereto. He met the chiefs once more. All
agreed to refer the boundary disputes and the question of Montsioa's
independence to the High Commissioner, and the Volksraad added Nov.
a request that the court should also determine the right of H.M. 1870.
Government to interfere in matters north of the Vaal not affecting
its own subjects.[2]

Hay did not appoint the arbitrators, because Sir Henry Barkly, the
new High Commissioner, was expected daily; but he sent John Campbell to Klipdrift with magisterial powers under the Punishment Act
over British subjects in all the territory claimed by Waterboer. A few
days later Barkly arrived at Capetown to find the impartial position
occupied by Grey and Wodehouse destroyed by Hay's action, and Dec.
Brand awaiting him in person with a proposal to refer the Campbell 1870.
Lands to foreign arbitration.[3] Brand's proposal was a foretaste of
troubles to come. It was a proposal to which H.M. Government
could not accede unless it was prepared to admit the intervention of
other Powers in a sphere over which Great Britain had long exercised
the hegemony, an intervention which might ultimately lead to the
extension to South Africa of the state system of Europe that was
changing so much for the worse as the Franco-German war swept
on.

At Klipdrift President Parker readily made way for the British
magistrate. In spite of a commission from Waterboer, which added
greatly to the gaiety of the assembled multitudes at the Diggings,
Campbell confined his authority at first to the north bank of the
Vaal river; but, following on a rush to Cawood's Hope, he extended
it to the Free State side. Brand replied by creating Truter land- Feb.
drost of Pniel.[4] At the end of the month Barkly arrived on the scene. 1871.
He persuaded Pretorius and the other claimants to the lands north
of the Vaal to submit their dispute to the ultimate arbitration of
Keate, the Lieutenant-Governor of Natal, who had been accepted
as arbitrator by Pretorius in an abortive attempt to settle the Blood
River controversy with the Zulus, and had just given great satisfac- 1869.
tion to the Transvaalers by deciding in their favour the Vaal river
boundary dispute with the Free State.[5] He also arranged for joint 1870.
administration pending the award, and tried to persuade Brand to
accept the same terms. The most Brand would concede was the
purchase of the Campbell Lands or their exchange for Albania, and,

---

[1] C. 459 of 1871, pp. 58 ff.; Bloemhof Arbitration Blue-book, pp. 150 ff., 183.
[2] Ibid., p. 165. [3] C. 459 of 1871, pp. 96, 100.
[4] Ibid., p. 132. [5] Ibid., pp. 149 ff.; vide supra, p. 313.

failing that, submission to foreign arbitration, since the Imperial Government was really a party to the cause. At this very moment divided control led to a defiance of Truter's authority; Brand sent up a commando with guns to maintain order, and Barkly despatched Cape Police to Klipdrift with the threat that he would repel force by force.[1]

April 1871.

Meanwhile diamonds had been found on the farm Bultfontein next to Dorstfontein on the Dry Diggings. Brand now offered to submit even the question of the ownership of land east of the Vaal to foreign arbitration; but Barkly refused to discuss the matter until the commando had withdrawn, and then confessed to the Earl of Kimberley, now Colonial Secretary, that he had gone too far in support of Waterboer and the diggers to draw back.[2] The noble Earl was, however, as unwilling as any of his predecessors to extend Great Britain's responsibilities in South Africa, and, though he was apprehensive of possible aggression by 'Dutch Boers and English immigrants' against natives and even of the imposition of 'republican slavery' upon the Griquas, had forbidden Barkly to annex anything that the Cape was not prepared to rule unaided.[3]

Definite steps might, however, have to be taken, for difficulties were arising between the diggers and the absentee proprietors of the diamondiferous farms at the Dry Diggings.[4] Profiting by the fact that the land grants made no state reservation of mineral rights, the proprietors proposed to reap the fruits of their enterprise to the best of their ability in the matter of licence fees. The diggers replied by rushing Dorstfontein, but presently withdrew. Then rich finds were made on the adjacent farm of Vooruitzigt. Brand promptly transferred Truter from deserted Pniel to the Dry Diggings, and the Volksraad divided the 10s. monthly licence fees between the state, the proprietors, and the elected Diggers' Committees of six in each camp, which, under the chairmanship of the government inspector, were to deal with disputed claims and other matters directly affecting the diggers.[5] So the committees made the local law and Truter saw that it was kept, no hard matter, since he was tactful and times were good—so good, indeed, that a stone was found at Colesberg Kopje also on the farm Vooruitzigt. The Kopje promptly became the 'New Rush' and, in due time, the famous Kimberley Mine.

May 1871.

Even before this last startling development, Barkly had made up his mind to annex Griqualand West if he possibly could. He had received permission to annex the lawful possessions of such chiefs

---

[1] C. 459 of 1871, pp. 133, 154, 161, 181.
[2] *Ibid.*, p. 133.   [3] *Ibid.*, pp. 65 ff., 102.
[4] Dorstfontein had been bought for £2600, Bultfontein for £2000 and Vooruitzigt presently for £6000. This last was at least certain wealth to the owner of the farm, De Beer.
[5] C. 459 of 1871, p. 184.

as desired to be taken over, provided the Cape would first undertake to incorporate such territory.[1] Southey therefore moved in the July Assembly that Waterboer's lands be annexed. In face of determined 1871. opposition on various grounds, he carried his motion by only a single vote with the amendment that nothing but what really belonged to that chief should be annexed with him. He assured the members that nothing more was intended and, at the end of the session, had the satisfaction of seeing both Houses agree without a division that the Governor should be empowered to take the necessary steps to maintain order and collect revenue in those territories pending a final settlement.[2]

In face of the first resolution Brand once more demanded foreign arbitration and sent a representative to plead his case in Downing Street and, at the close of the Bloemhof Arbitration Court which had inquired into the Transvaal claims, Pretorius made the same request. Pretorius had good cause to feel uneasy. He had done his best, even to the extent of repudiating the 'Ludorf treaty' of 1851, on which he had hitherto relied, because it did not give him all that he now wanted in the Marico area. His opponents, however, had done still better; the members of the court had failed to agree and the issue had been referred to Keate.[3] Barkly, on the other hand, frankly told Kimberley that it was useless to pretend that he was now acting in Waterboer's name at the Diggings and added that, if the Free State was allowed to absorb the richest of the Diamond Fields, it would soon outrival either of the Cape provinces in wealth and would be less likely than formerly to enter a South African confederation on terms dictated by the old Colony.[4]

Then came the Keate Award. The arbitrator decided fairly on the evidence before him; indeed, he gave a compromise decision. Setting aside the extreme claims of the Barolong, he gave them a line running from the source of the Marico river down Maquassi Spruit and the Vaal to Platberg. Besides rejecting extravagant Transvaal claims to mere unoccupied 'paper' farms, this line denied to the Republics a few genuine farms that were interspersed among Bantu kraals, some others that were held merely on native title, and the site of the projected village of Christiana, which had been hurriedly surveyed after the Diamond Fields dispute had begun. The one real blow to the Transvaalers was the loss of the embryo village of Bloemhof; but even so, that village had only been surveyed as recently as 1865. For the rest, Keate named a boundary from Platberg onwards which corresponded to that which Arnot claimed as the northern and

---

[1] C. 459 of 1871, p. 172.   [2] C. 508 of 1872, pp. 3–4.
[3] *Ibid.*, pp. 9, 16. Bloemhof Arbitration Blue-book, p. 133 *et passim*; C. 459 of 1871, p. 190; Agar-Hamilton, *The Road to the North*, pp. 67 ff.
[4] C. 508 of 1872, pp. 4, 12.

western limits of Griqualand West,[1] and, had he but known it, was the very line which appeared on the map that D'Urban had sent to London in 1834 accompanying his treaty with Andries, father of Nicholas Waterboer.[2] This gave Barkly something definite to go on. Ten days later he annexed Griqualand West and, on the morrow, proclaimed the Keate Award Line. He presently received Kimberley's letter trusting to his discretion in spite of the fact that the resolution of the Cape Parliament did not fully meet the conditions laid down; but already the Cape police had hoisted the Union Jack on the Diamond Fields.[3]

EFFECTS OF THE PRECIOUS MINERAL DISCOVERIES, 1871–4

The immediate effect of the annexation of Griqualand West and the proclamation of the Keate Line was to embitter the relations of

1871–
1872.

the Imperial Government with the poverty-stricken Republics and to throw the Free State back upon the Transvaal and Delagoa Bay. As soon as the Keate Award was known the Transvaal Volksraad altered the *Grondwet* to permit of a non-burgher standing for the presidency, obliged the unhappy Pretorius, who had after all written to thank Sir Henry Barkly for the arbitration, to resign with some of his chief officials, and promised to uphold the public and private rights of burghers in the lost lands.[4] Many burghers in both Republics clamoured for Brand as president of a joint republic and a bold push for Delagoa Bay even at the price of the Conventions; but that cautious statesman met his own Volksraad behind closed doors and quieted them with the assurance that war would be a disaster for all South Africa, and that once the truth was known in Great Britain, as it surely would be made known and not least by Englishmen in South Africa, '*alles sal reg kom,*' all will come right.[5]

The Transvaalers therefore had to seek for another President who should be more versed in diplomacy and the ways of the world than Pretorius. They found him, as they believed, in the Rev. Thomas

July
1872.

François Burgers, the Liberal predikant of Hanover.[6] Him they installed, while Brand remained at Bloemfontein to carry on a long and irritating correspondence with the officials of the Diamond Fields and Capetown on the precise position of the three beacons, Ramah,

---

[1] C. 459 of 1871, pp. 26, 90; C. 3947 of 1884, pp. 11 ff.; C. 508 of 1872, p. 26.

[2] D'Urban to Spring Rice, 26 Dec. 1834; Orpen, *Reminiscences*, pp. 149, 230.

[3] C. 508 of 1872, pp. 8, 33 ff., 49.

[4] *Ibid.*, pp. 50, 67; C. 732 of 1873, pp. 2, 31; Eybers, p. 434.

[5] C. 508 of 1872, p. 49; C. 732 of 1873, pp. 16 ff. Many Englishmen roundly condemned the annexation of the Diamond Fields, *e.g.* John Xavier Merriman, Captain Augustus Lindley, Thomas Holden Bowker, Robert Moffat of Kuruman, John Smith Moffat of Inyati and James Anthony Froude (C. 732, p. 51; C. 3841 of 1884, p. 115).

[6] C. 732 of 1873, p. 84; S. P. Engelbrecht, *Thomas François Burgers*.

David's Graf and Platberg, which should decide on which side of the line the rich Dry Diggings actually fell.[1] After long negotiations he agreed with the High Commissioner on a scheme of foreign arbitra- Aug. tion; but he fell ill at the last moment and was incapacitated for 1872. nearly a year; the acting President and, thereafter, the Triumvirate which succeeded him, reopened questions which had been disposed of, Barkly was obviously not anxious to have foreign arbitration, the promising scheme collapsed, and the Diamond Fields remained a 1873– festering sore in the body politic for three long years to come. 1876.

Economically, and in the long run politically, the gold and diamond discoveries brought good as well as evil. Certainly they brought opportunities of a fuller if more dangerous life than had hitherto been possible in agricultural South Africa. Combined with the breaking of the long drought and the eagerness of capitalists to invest in new countries during the depression in Europe, they provided money for all-important railways and other public works and helped to loosen the constitutional deadlocks in both the coast colonies.

The economic and political prospects of the Cape Colony had May– brightened rapidly throughout Hay's seven months of office. The Dec. Anglican Church of the Province of South Africa pointed the way 1870. to self-government by meeting in Synod for the first time, and the Imperial Government made up its mind that if the Colonists would not be governed, they must take up the responsibility of governing.[2] It therefore sent Barkly, experienced in the ways of the Victoria Parliament, to institute responsible government at the Cape and, thereafter, to meet the wishes of the Eastern Separationists by devising some such scheme of federal devolution in the Colony as had commended itself to Grey and Wodehouse. The Earl of Kimberley, and Gladstone behind him, also hoped that the Cape would take over Basutoland, and presently stipulated that it should assume full responsibility for Griqualand West if that territory were annexed. Looking still further ahead, they empowered Barkly to summon a conference of colonial and republican governments to discuss a general South African federation, a conference in which the autonomous Cape rather than the Imperial authority should take the lead.

The confidence of the Western Liberals in the capacity of the Colony to rule itself grew with growing revenues, and the deter-mination of Sprigg's Kaffrarians and the Midlanders not to fall under

---

[1] C. 508 of 1872, pp. 25, 28; C. 732 of 1873, p. 128; G. 15 and 33 of 1872 (Cape), *passim*; Lindley, *Adamantia*, chapter xvi; Dower, *Early Annals of Kokstad* (1902), p. 82.
[2] C. 459 of 1871, p. 14.

Grahamstown domination hardened; but opposition to responsible government from within the Colony was very strong. The Easterners were certain that their province could stand by itself now that goods were pouring through their ports to the fast developing interior, and feared more than ever to be at the mercy of a Western majority which might drain the East of money wherewith to pay for public works in the West and would undoubtedly know little, and probably care less, about the Kaffirs, who outnumbered Europeans in the frontier districts by two to one and were fast piling up once more beyond the border. They were sure of the support of the leading officials from Southey downwards and of the Western Conservatives, who, besides holding all the old objections to popular government as such, pointed to the horrors of 'Reconstruction' at the hands of carpet-baggers and Coloured voters in the conquered Southern States of the American Union, and insisted that the Basuto had asked to be taken over by the Queen and not by Molteno, that Griqualand West must be annexed first to give the diggers a voice in their own constitutional future and that, in any case, no change was necessary. Now that better times were come, they believed the existing system would work as well as it had done in the palmy days of Grey.[1]

1871.   Nevertheless, Molteno attempted to carry responsible government. The Assembly duly passed the bill which Porter drafted on his motion. This the Conservative Council threw out.[2] An Act for the annexation of Basutoland was then carried,[3] but the Assembly declined to commit the Colony to taking charge of Griqualand West. Again, very little public interest was taken in the work of a committee which discussed the possibility of 'federation' of the Cape Colony itself, that is, of devolution on a provincial basis. A few months later, that committee damned devolution with faint praise and indicated plainly that, as far as the Cape was concerned, Barkly's annexation of Griqualand West had killed the larger scheme of South African Confederation, which John Henry de Villiers, himself a member of the committee, and the Earl of Kimberley had endeavoured to launch.[4]

These very failures, however, left the issue of self-government with a clear field and, during the recess, the responsible government party gained ground. Parliament reassembled, rejoicing in a revenue double that of 1866, and this time the responsible government bill was brought forward as a Government measure. It passed both Houses side by side with another bill which at last equalised the

April 1872.

---

[1] De Kiewiet, *Brit. Col. Policy*, pp. 280 ff.; *C.H.B.E.*, VIII. 429 ff.
[2] C. 459 of 1871, pp. 168 ff.   [3] Act 12 of 1871; Eybers, p. 61.
[4] C. 459 of 1871, p. 194; C. 732 of 1873, pp. 22, 43, 97; Walker, *De Villiers*, pp. 550 ff.

representation of the two Provinces in the Assembly; in spite of hostile petitions the royal assent was given, and an Eastern request for Separation was rejected by the Queen. Barkly, faced with the task of finding a Prime Minister,[1] invited first Southey and then Porter. Both declined to serve and Solomon would only work on practically level terms with Molteno; wherefore the Governor finally invited the Lion of Beaufort to form a Ministry. Molteno prudently Dec. included Conservative and Kaffrarian elements in what was really a 1872. federal cabinet and set to work to remodel the Colony as far as might be after his heart's desire.[2]

One of Molteno's first acts was to introduce the Seven Circles Bill for the reform of the Legislative Council on the lines which had been laid down for the Assembly by Wodehouse in 1867. The proposal was to divide the whole Colony into seven circles, each returning three members, as a means of obliterating the sharp distinction between East and West, and frankly to increase the power of the rural voters against the carpet-baggers of Capetown, Port Elizabeth and Gra-hamstown.[3] The Council threw out the bill, but, after a general 1874. election, passed it and thus cleared the way for the passage in the following year of that hardy annual, Solomon's Voluntary Bill, which 1875. followed Natal's example by withdrawing state aid from the churches in the Colony. Other reforms were effected. The Colony acquired a coat-of-arms as the outward and visible sign of its new status; the appointment of the colonial born John Henry de Villiers as Chief 1873. Justice in a Colony which had hitherto received its Chief Justices from overseas in itself testified to the new powers of the Cape. New magis-tracies were set up, and the examining University of the Cape of Good Hope took the place of the Board of Examiners as the coping stone of 1873. a system of education, which had recently been strengthened by the foundation of the Gymnasium, forerunner of the Victoria College 1866. at Stellenbosch, and was now extended by that of a seminary for 1874. girls at Wellington.

With a rising revenue and expanding trade the Colony was well able to bear the financial burdens entailed by these developments. Failures there were of silk, flax and cotton; dorthesia, too, ravaged the orange and lemon orchards, and phylloxera the vineyards of the West, till the Californian ladybird and the grafting of vines on 1873.

[1] C. 732 of 1873, pp. 21 ff., 61, 71 ff., 81, 86; Act 1 of 1872; Eybers, p. 63.
[2] C. 732 of 1873, p. 141; Molteno, *Life of* . . . *Molteno*, I. 188; Walker, *De Villiers*, p. 56; Westerners: J. C. Molteno, Premier and Colonial Secretary, Dr. T. White, M.L.C., Treasurer, and J. H. de Villiers, Attorney-General; Kaffrarians: C. Abercrombie Smith (Conservative), Crown Lands and Public Works, and Charles Brownlee, Native Affairs. Easterners: Simeon Jacobs, 24 Dec. 1873–21 Aug. 1877, and Andries Stockenstrom, 22 Aug. 1877–5 Feb. 1878, Attorney General, John Xavier Merriman, 20 July 1875–5 Feb. 1878, Crown Lands and Public Works.
[3] Many of these carpet-baggers were excellent men.

American stocks overcame both pests. Wool remained the great export, with mohair steadily gaining ground, and a boom in ostriches following on their domestication and the first artificial hatching of chicks enabled prudent farmers to wipe off mortgages and all to indulge in the novelty of fencing before the inevitable slump weeded out the foolish and the unlucky. As in the good times of the 'twenties and 'fifties the state assisted immigrants. British, Belgian and German navvies were set to work upon the railway embankments, where, in the course of a 52½ hour week, they showed the Coloured folk and Natives how to shift earth and, in too many cases, less solid substances also, while German peasants made parts of the sandy Cape Flats to blossom, if not as the rose, at least as do the pumpkin and potato. Population increased rapidly.[1]

All was not so well in Griqualand West. For some time after the annexation, New Rush alone yielded stones to the value of £50,000 monthly; claims thirty feet each way were selling for £4000; iron churches, houses and canteens were springing from the bare veld, and Dutoitspan with its newspapers had already become the commercial base for the far North. Then clouds had begun to gather. Though the Diggers' Committees still sat, real power was in the hands of a triumvirate of officials, two of whom were stranded on the old River Diggings at Klipdrift. The colour bar whereunder, in republican times, no non-European might own a claim or deal in diamonds or be seen upon the streets after nine in the evening, had gone. It had never been strictly enforced, but its loss was felt at a time when New Rush had begun to attract men—and women— from all parts of the world, who debauched the native labourers and drove a thriving trade in illicit diamond buying and even in the proceeds of organised robberies.[2]

All the troubles which the Free State had been spared closed in upon the new administration. A mass meeting protested against the neglect of the Committees by the Triumvirs and burnt some canteens. Matters went from bad to worse. The diggings at the three earlier centres had deepened so dangerously that they were almost unworkable, and though a determined display of pickhandles in the hands of the more prudent section of the diggers saved New Rush by ensuring that one-fourth of each claim should be set aside as a road along which the yellow and blue ground could be carted to be sifted outside Tom Tiddler's eight acres, salvation was only for a time. These roads began to fall. So did the price of stones, by 60 per cent. in the course of six months. On the other hand working expenses and

Margin notes: 1869. 1874. Dec. 1871.

---

[1] Population rose from 181,592 Europeans and 314,789 Others in 1865 to 236,783 and 484,201 in 1875.
[2] C. 508 of 1872, pp. 31 ff.; C. 732 of 1873, p. 100.

water rose and disappointed men began to haunt the camps in a dangerous mood.

Meanwhile, opposition and very plain speaking on the value of Waterboer's rights in the Cape Assembly forced Southey to withdraw his Griqualand West Annexation Bill and, to celebrate their escape from Capetown rule, the diggers burnt some more canteens July and rioted for two happy days. The Triumvirs hastened to Dutoit- 1872. span, imposed a colour bar, provided police and detectives and prescribed lashes for Coloured diamond thieves.[1] Barkly cancelled the colour bar; but he confirmed most of the other regulations and, since the Cape Parliament had gone back on its virtual promise to take the Diamond Fields over, sent Southey north to administer the country till Crown Colony rule could be established.[2]

Her Majesty's other South African Crown Colony of Natal was prospering once more. As the gold and diamond diggings developed the demand for retrenchment died away; but a Supplementary Charter, which clearly defined the duties of the executive and legislature respectively and put the chief official salaries on a reserved list, did nothing to check the clamour for responsible government, a clamour which was swelled by the confidence bred of better times, 1873. the example of the Cape and the addition of new elected members to the Legislative Council.[3] The British ministry, however, could not give way to a demand which was often accompanied by a request for a larger garrison, and that at a time when fewer Europeans were entering the colony than were leaving it for the gold and diamond fields, among them two cotton planters from Umkomanzi, Herbert Rhodes and his delicate younger brother, Cecil John.[4] Moreover, as the white men streamed out to the Diggings, the Bantu labourers followed them and the coast planters began to press once more for Indian coolies.

The annexation of Basutoland by the Cape and even the loss of the Diamond Fields were by no means unmixed evils for the Free State. The one relieved it of its native problem, the other of an industrial problem of a most difficult kind, and both afforded it markets. Helped by the Kimberley market and the discovery of small 1870. diamond fields of its own at Koffyfontein and Jagersfontein, the republic became a farmers' and transport riders' paradise and, for thirty years to come, almost achieved the alleged happiness of having no history. Municipal Boards had been created as far back as 1856[5]

[1] Local Commissioners' Proclamation 49 of 1872.
[2] C. 732 of 1873, pp. 51, 101 ff., 108, 112, 118, 124; Proclamation 14 of 1872.
[3] Eybers, p. 198.
[4] The European population of Natal increased from about 16,000 in 1865 to 18,000 in 1875.
[5] Ordinance 8 of 1856; Eybers, p. 311.

and, in the following year, the State Secretary had been given a seat in the Volksraad. During the turmoil of the Basuto war, important measures had been carried defining more precisely the composition and duties of the legislature, regulating burgher rights, and relaxing somewhat the rigid rules that governed the alteration of the *Grondwet*.[1] Henceforward, that instrument could be amended by a three-fourths majority of the Volksraad in two successive sessions instead of three; Europeans who had been born in the Republic or who were possessed of land worth £150 and had been resident for one year or who had merely been resident for three years were to enjoy burgher rights; youths of eighteen with burgher rights might vote for commandants and field cornets, while burghers of twenty-one who had either been born in the Republic or were possessed of a small property qualification were to exercise the Presidential and Volksraad franchise. Now, soon after the close of the Basuto war, Brand set up the professional High Court on the Cape model which lack of funds and his own illness had hitherto delayed.[2] In 1874, he appointed Francis William Reitz, son of one of the Popular Members of Harry Smith's days, as Chief Justice, and in 1876 completed the Court by appointing as Puisne Judges the ex-State Attorney of the South African Republic, James Buchanan, and Melius de Villiers, brother of the new Chief Justice of the Cape Colony. New magistracies, the foundation of proper government offices at the capital, a memorial to the fallen in the Basuto wars and improvements in education, which included the formation of a normal department at the Grey College, were marks of a new vigour, while the gradual extinction of paper-money, the arrival of the Oriental Bank, and the steady growth of population witnessed to the quiet but increasing prosperity of the Free State.[3]

The Transvaal benefited less from the opening of the diamond diggings than the other states of South Africa; nevertheless, population there was increasing[4] and with it the prospect of more settled conditions, while the election of the liberal Burgers as President was a sign that the acute ecclesiastical disputes of the past were dying down, a process helped on by the arrival of further orthodox predikants.[5] Burgers himself was full of confidence. Already he envisaged an independent South African federal republic with his state cast for the leading rôle, rejoicing in 'equal rights for all civilised men' and in Delagoa Bay as its harbour 'free from the trammels of British ports and influence.' He induced the Volksraad to adopt a new flag and coat-of-arms, borrowed £66,000 at a high rate from the

[1] Eybers, pp. 285 ff., 291.   [2] *Ibid.*, p. 326.
[3] European population increased from about 12,000 in 1854 to 27,000 in 1873.
[4] European population rose from about 15,000 in 1854 to 40,000 in 1875.
[5] Engelbrecht, *Geschiedenis*, II.

Cape Commercial Bank, the one bank in the republic, wherewith to
buy up the debased paper, and dilated on the possibilities of Tati
and of the newly mined gold of Eersteling in the Transvaal itself. 1872.
When a small rush took place to the alluvial goldfields of Lydenburg,
he visited the Australians and Scots at 'Macmac' and 'New Cale- 1873.
donia,' appointed a gold commissioner, gave the diggers two seats
in the Volksraad and scandalised the straiter sect of his burghers by
striking sovereigns bearing his own image and superscription from
the nuggets with which they presented him.

The South African states were thus developing more or less
rapidly and were certainly being drawn into closer contact with each
other and with 'old Europe.' Financially, the record of the Standard
Bank tells the story.[2] This most successful of the 'imperial' banks
had swallowed up many of the local banks in the Cape Colony during
the bad times, acquired half the coin in South Africa, and prospered 1870.
so that it had become banker to the Cape Government. It had then
established itself in Griqualand West, and though the absorption of 1875.
its chief rival, the London and S.A. Bank, and its invasion of the
Transvaal were still to come, had already carried the financial
unification of South Africa far in advance of the political.

As with money, so with goods. The opening of the Capetown 1870.
docks was followed by improvements at Port Nolloth, Port Elizabeth
and East London; the Union Line and its new competitor, the Castle 1872.
Line, soon supplied a weekly mail service with a run to England of
25 days and the promise of bigger ships; the Cape Government
bought the telegraph line to Kingwilliamstown and began to extend
it, provided a daily post to Grahamstown and arranged with the 1872.
Free State for joint road and bridge building across the Orange.
Natal, for its part, had already begun to build roads and bridges and
had bought the Durban-Maritzburg telegraph. It now made expen- 1867.
sive efforts to cope with the sand bar at Durban. The attempt was on-
unavailing at the time, but one barrier to trade Natal could remove. wards.
It lowered its customs duties and so began the long rivalry with the
Cape ports for the up-country traffic on which it was becoming more
and more dependent.[3]

Then came the railways, the links of iron which were destined to
bind all South Africa together economically and politically. The
Cape bought out the private companies in the West and at Port
Elizabeth, reduced the gauge to 3 feet 6 inches, and carried on
both of these railways and a new line from East London toward the 1873–
Diamond Fields. Natal followed suit and projected a railway which 1874.

---

[1] Aylward, *Transvaal of To-day*, pp. 54, 126 ; Carter, *Narrative*, p. 562 ;
Haggard, *Cetewayo*, p. 83.
[2] Amphlett, *Standard Bank*, chapters ii., iii.   [3] Theal, V. 355.

should tap the trade of the interior, thereby inevitably promising to come into conflict with one of Burgers's most cherished schemes for the Transvaal, a Delagoa Bay railway.

Under pressure of changing conditions a few far-sighted men, other than Imperial officials, were already thinking in terms of closer union. All the arguments in favour of that step which Grey had advanced still held good, all the evils which he had foretold if it were not effected were coming to pass. J. H. de Villiers, a member of the Cape Federation Committee, and Jan Hendrik Hofmeyr, a prominent journalist, had urged that solution in 1871; de Villiers had since kept touch with Brand and other leading Free Staters, who agreed with Grey that no section of the Europeans could stand by itself in face of the tribes and were ready to consider closer union once the Griqualand West dispute was settled;[1] Burgers was 'an ardent federalist,' albeit his scheme left no room for the British connection; in the Eastern Province and in Natal men regarded federation as good business and a means of achieving local self-government.

The attitude of the Imperial authorities had also changed since Sir George Grey's time. The foreign affairs which preoccupied them forced the federal solution upon their notice: the federated German Empire based on the Zollverein, Italian unity, the Civil War fought essentially to maintain the federal U.S.A. Disraeli and Carnarvon had seen the turn of the tide within the Empire in Canadian federation; Kimberley and Barkly had considered a permissive act for South Africa and, even after the annexations of 1871 had ruined their hopes, had discussed the chances of a Natal candidate for the Transvaal presidency pledged to that policy. More recently still, Disraeli had come forward as the champion of an imperialism based on a common customs tariff, mutual defence and 'some representative council at the metropolis' to keep the parts of the Empire in touch with the centre and with each other.[2]

Foreign pressure could be expected to drive the scattered South African communities together, especially as the revolution in the balance of power in Europe might make it more difficult for Great Britain to fight their battles for them. Berlin and not Paris was now the political centre of the Continent, and German 'colonials' were

margin notes:
1859–
1871.

June
1872.

---

[1] Hofmeyr, *Life of J. H. Hofmeyr*, p. 133; Walker, *De Villiers*, pp. 51 ff., 126; C. 508 of 1872, p. 20; C. 732 of 1873, pp. 42 ff.

[2] C. 459 of 1871, pp. 12, 46, 170 ; Wilmot, *Southey*, p. 408; Buckle, *Disraeli*, VI. 410. One current of Colonial Office opinion is shown in the following minute by a permanent official. 'One great solution of the South African problem is the confederation of all these states. . . . A great blow will be struck at this possible solution . . . if the power of any of these small states was increased by the addition to it of Griqualand West. . . . Once having annexed, the feeling here will be very strong against any relinquishment. . . . A great stumbling-block will be thrown in the way of the first working of responsible government at the Cape by any difficulty of this kind from Griqualand West' (C.O. 48/463; Minutes on No. 107 of Oct. 3, 1872).

already taking a keen interest in the Transvaal and what is now Southern Rhodesia. The British monopoly of the outer world was passing; the fate of Delagoa Bay had recently been referred to the 1872. arbitrament of the French President;[1] Prussia had asked pointed 1868. questions about Namaqua-Damaraland, and however incredulous Kimberley might be of German activities in southern Africa, Barkly 1873. was satisfied that captured French mitrailleuses and attendant German officers had appeared in Pretoria.[2] Now, Disraeli took office with Carnarvon as Colonial Secretary and announced a vigorous Jan. colonial policy, which must mean, among other things, the con- 1874. federation of South Africa.

Downing Street desired a confederation which would enable it to withdraw its garrison from all South Africa save the Cape Peninsula and Natal. Garrisons had either gone or were steadily going from New Zealand, Canada and the Australian colonies, and the South African force had been reduced from 5 battalions to $2\frac{1}{2}$, the Cape Mounted Rifles disbanded, and fair warning given that part of the 1867– cost of future wars would be charged to the colonies concerned. A 1870. mere matter of a few battalions would not, however, have moved Carnarvon to press his confederation policy so strongly as he did. He was brought to the pitch of vigorous action by the need for ending the muddle in Griqualand West and still more for facing that fundamental issue of all South African life and politics—the native question.[3]

All over South Africa the tribes were increasing in numbers, the various European states were becoming responsible for their governance, and the native policies of those states were drifting further apart as they themselves were being drawn closer together. In the Cape Colony the Coloured Folk were on an absolute civil, economic and legal equality with the whites. The position of the Bantu was the same unless specially modified, and those modifications were fewer in the early 'seventies than was afterwards the case. Even in the Ciskei (British Kaffraria) the ordinary law of the Colony prevailed, though some recognition was given to native laws of marriage and inheritance, and in native cases the magistrates as a rule used commonsense and native custom.[4]

The position was markedly different in Basutoland. The Cape Parliament had been induced to annex that territory [5] in the belief 1871. that it would pay its own way, that if the Cape did not take it Natal would, and that a self-governing colony ought to control the native

---

[1] C. 1361 of 1875, p. 1. [2] Wilmot, *Southey*, p. 257.
[3] On the Carnarvon-Frere confederation campaign *vide* de Kiewiet, *The Imperial Factor in South Africa*; Uys, *Shepstone* ; W. G. Murray, *British Relations with the Transvaal* (unpublished thesis).
[4] Acts 16 of 1860 and 18 of 1864; *Report of Native Affairs Commission (Cape)*, 1883, p. 18.
[5] C. 459 of 1871, pp. 47, 67; Eybers, p. 61.

territories on its borders. The ordinary law of the Colony did not
apply to it. Under regulations issued by Barkly,[1] the Governor
legislated by proclamations, which had the force of law unless they
were repealed by Parliament to which they must be presented within
fourteen days. All men were equal before the law, but the sale of
guns to natives without a permit and of liquor under any circumstances was forbidden. Magistrates sat in open court exercising full
civil and criminal jurisdiction short of the death penalty, with an
appeal to the Chief Magistrate at Maseru and, in certain cases, to
the Governor himself. Legally the chiefs retained only minor civil
jurisdiction subject to an appeal to the magistrates, but in practice
they heard nearly all civil cases and saw their verdicts enforced by
public opinion. Beyond the issue of a handbook on Basuto customs
no official recognition was given to tribal law. The Basuto retaliated
by regarding as null and void such of the distant Governor's regulations as conflicted with that law and custom.

Apart from a handful of Cape Police and Basuto constables, the
strength of the Government lay in the character of the magistrates,
the mutual jealousies of the clans and the fact that the chiefs were
financially interested in the collection of the 10s. hut tax. But
definite attempts to civilise the tribesmen were left to the Paris
missionaries, who as ever wisely preserved as much as they could of
tribal custom as the foundation of their work, and to the Anglican
and Roman Catholic fathers who now worked beside them. By 1872,
fully 3000 Basuto could read their own language and a few English
as well. Some members of the Paris congregation at Hermon gained
so much self-confidence thereby that they seceded and for a short
time set up a church of their own, thus giving South Africa its first
experience of the newly launched Ethiopian movement, which aimed
at creating African Churches free from European control.[2]

Thereafter all remained quiet in Basutoland for some years to
come; but, in the early 'seventies, there was confusion in the adjacent
Transkeian territories from the Cape to the Natal frontier. There,
British authority was still represented by mere diplomatic agents with
some of the chiefs; but the Cape was steadily being drawn, as every
civilised community must be, into the concerns of the barbarians on
its borders. The Tembu chiefs drew small salaries from Capetown,
and Gangaliswe, the strongest of them, drew rents also from Europeans settled on the Slang and Umtata rivers. Gangaliswe, worsted
by Kreli's Galekas, offered his country to the Queen; but, when
peace had been restored by Charles Brownlee, he withdrew his offer
under pressure of his followers. Next year Joseph Orpen was sent as
resident to the Gatberg (Maclear) in Nomansland or Griqualand
East. There Adam Kok was still holding his own; but the little clans

Dec.
1871.

1872.
1873.

[1] *Native Affairs Blue-book (Cape)*, III., No. 9.   [2] Theal, IV. 340.

settled by Wodehouse were quarrelling, Nehemiah Moshesh still hankered after the Matatiele lands, and the Pondomisis and other clans to the north of the Pondo line and the Xesibes to the south of it near the Natal border had asked for British protection. Orpen restored something like order with the help of Kok and other friendly chiefs and agreed to take the Pondomisis over. The two Pondo chiefs promptly protested and repudiated the Pondo line; but when the Pondomisis resisted his control, Orpen subdued them, Shepstone fashion, with the help of his allies and fined them according to Bantu custom. It was a beginning of European authority in Nomansland.[1]

The native policy of the Republics was, as ever, radically different from that of the Cape. In neither republic was any equality admitted between black and white, and in neither could a native own land on individual title. In the Transvaal, more than elsewhere, natives were frankly viewed primarily as a source of labour. There the principle of the *plakkers wet* was maintained in theory limiting the number of native families which might squat on any one farm; an attempt was made for the first time to collect a hut tax through the 1870. headmen;[2] the authorities used the vagrancy law as a means of diverting part of the flood of good labour which drifted through on its way to the Diamond Fields, and, when the natives took to travelling in alarmingly large bodies, raised the price of passes for 1874. foreign Kaffirs fivefold. Whether or no that law was ever enforced does not alter the fact that its existence pointed to possible complications with Griqualand West on the score of labour supply.[3]

The problems of the Transvaal borderlands showed no signs of becoming simpler. The writ of the republic still ran in those parts of the Keate Award Area which were actually occupied by farmers; but, outside, land sharks stirred up the clans against one another, Burgers made treaties with Massouw, Moshette and Botlasitsi, who claimed with much justice to be Paramount Chiefs respectively of the Korana, Barolong and Batlapin, and received from them land cessions of the usual kind. The Kimberley authorities supported stronger chiefs like Montsioa and Mankoroane, who refused to recognise either those treaties or the paramountcy of their African signatories. At length Burgers repudiated the Keate Award and pro- March claimed his cessions. Barkly retorted by recognising Mankoroane as 1874. paramount chief of the Batlapin and suggesting a joint commission to beacon off the Keate line.[4]

In the Zoutpansberg, so far had the authority of the republic fallen, farmers were paying tribute to the chiefs for their lands. Secocoeni was building up a little Basutoland in the Lulu mountains

---

[1] G. 27–74 (Cape); G. 21–75 (Cape), pp. 68, 135 ff.   [2] Law 9 of 1870.
[3] Haggard, *Cetewayo*, p. 91; C. 1748 of 1877, p. 3.
[4] Agar-Hamilton, *The Road to the North*, pp. 104 ff.

of northern Lydenburg, while Bushveld fever and lack of transport for their wheat were driving neighbouring farmers back to the High Veld and sheep.[1] The Swazis were still well disposed to the Transvaal, but they turned a deaf ear to Burgers's proposals that they should become his vassals and a stepping-stone on the road to Delagoa Bay.[2] Further south, Cetewayo had long questioned the validity of the Swazi cession of land along the Pongola to the Transvaalers and, for some years past, had even played off the Natal against the republican officials in the hope of regaining the Blood River territory in which the Pretoria Government had allotted a few farms, but had not ventured to do anything more definite. Now, on the death of Panda, Cetewayo had been crowned king of the Zulus by Shepstone and had begun to revive the old military discipline.[3]

1866.

1873.

Land and warriors, the patrimony of chiefs, thus brought the white man's Governments into conflict with one another. The all-pervading influence of the Diamond Fields also spread to the tribes. As the diggings deepened into mines, the demand for native labourers grew louder and wages rose everywhere to the disgust of farmers who already resented the competition of the railway contractors as much as their fathers in the Colony had resented Montagu and his road gangs. Natives flocked from all parts to Griqualand West. Many died on the road, many were robbed on the way back, but still they came to meet men of other tribes in peace for the first time, to talk and to learn hitherto unsuspected vices. They returned to their kraals with money in their pockets and ideas in their heads, to plague their chiefs and magistrates who were already worried by the traders attracted to the native territories by the new purchasing power of the inhabitants. Most of them too came back with guns in their hands. There had been a gun traffic in South Africa *post memoriam hominum*, but never anything like the traffic of Kimberley.[4] The Free State tried to stop it on more than one occasion. Once it inadvertently went too far and was faced with what was really an ultimatum from Southey; once it had a brush with armed Basuto on its own soil, and at last Natal diggers offered to help Brand to check the nuisance.[5] For the Langalibalele crisis had arisen in their own little colony and revealed in a flash the dangers of the gun-trade and the radical weakness of the native policy of Natal.

1873.

In Natal Coloured Folk were legally equal to Europeans, but the Bantu were treated as a race apart. A monogamist Bantu could apply

[1] Aylward, *op. cit.*, p. 43.
[2] Wilmot . . . *Southey*, p. 406; *Cape Times*, Dec. 7, 1894 (article by James Buchanan).
[3] C. 1137 of 1875.
[4] Matthews, *Incwadi Yami*, p. 278; Aylward, *op. cit.*, pp. 416, 428; Leyds *First Annexation*, p. 158 (notes).
[5] *Notulen*, O.F.S. Volksraad, 1873, p. 9; *Cape Argus*, Nov. 29, 1873.

for letters of exemption from native law, and such a one exempt for
seven years and resident for twelve years in the colony could, on a
certificate signed by three European electors and countersigned by
a magistrate, apply to the Lieutenant-Governor, who might at his
discretion grant him the franchise.[1] Natives have been known to run
the gauntlet to the vote, but before 1876 none of them had even taken
out letters of exemption. The majority lived in the reserves held as a
native trust by the Lieutenant-Governor and his executive council.
There they were ruled by their own chiefs, went to the public works
in native fashion at the call of the Great Chief at Pietermaritzburg
or followed Shepstone and his sons to quell unruly neighbours.
Many of them, however, left the reserves to join their friends on the
farms or the Crown Lands, thereby escaping the *corvée*, and hundreds of refugees poured annually into Natal from outside to swell
a subject Bantu population which had latterly been increased by the
annexation of the Amaxolo in the Alfred district,[2] Natal's share of
coveted Nomansland.

Such a system could not have endured without a man like Shepstone at its head, a man who understood the 'men of the Black
House' and was implicitly trusted by them.[3] Even so the Shepstone
system had not kept pace with the times; its meagre allowance of
£5000 annually forced it to leave all civilising work to the missionaries at their forty stations; it was sufficient if it could merely control
the new generation of tribesmen which knew not Blood River nor
Magongo. Many of the elected members of the legislature were jealous
of the Shepstone monopoly of native policy, and were not above
squeezing the Natives for money or labour by levying a £5 marriage tax.

In the absence of police the laws against the sale of liquor, squatting without leave and the possession of unlicensed guns were only
enforced by fits and starts. In the year of the hated marriage tax
Langalibalele, a Hlubi chief in north-western Natal on the Basuto-
Nomansland border, was ordered to send in some of his men to have
their guns registered.[4] After some hesitation he sent in five men out
of eight named. Shepstone, busy with the coronation of Cetewayo,
did not press the matter at the moment; but rumour produced a
flutter in Natal which communicated itself to the Hlubis, Langalibalele searched native Government messengers and, when an armed
party was sent to arrest him, fled into Basutoland, the central South
African powder-magazine. A party was sent in pursuit. It was fired

1864–1865.

Jan. 1866.

1873.

---

[1] Acts 11 of 1864 and 28 of 1865 (Eybers, p. 194); Brookes, *History of Native Policy*, p. 58.
[2] *Selected Documents* (*Natal Leg. Council*), No. 25 of 1866.
[3] Martineau, *Frere*, II. 238.
[4] Colenso and Durnford, *History of the Zulu War*, pp. 17 ff. On Natal Native affairs *vide* C. 1025 of 1874; C. 1119, 1121, 1141, 1158, 1187, 1342 of 1875; G. 27–74 (Cape).

12

upon and it fled; troops, volunteers and tribal levies hurried to the scene from Natal, Nomansland, Basutoland and Capetown; Griqualand West offered help, and men in both Republics took down their rifles at the prospect of trouble with the Basuto. Molapo, however,

Dec. 1873.

handed Langalibalele over quietly; the Hlubi lands were confiscated, and the Natal volunteers carried off cattle and 'apprentices' from a small tribe which had sheltered Hlubi women. This exhibition of Zoutpansberg methods in a British colony was followed by the legal but most unsatisfactory trial of Langalibalele by the officials and chiefs who had fought against him. He was banished to Robben Island near Capetown, since there was no room for him in Natal; but the chorus of protest led by Bishop Colenso awakened echoes in

1874.

Downing Street and moved Carnarvon to order the transfer of the unhappy chief to the mainland.[1]

By producing a South African confederation for the duration of the war which never took place, Langalibalele had advertised the fact that, as in Grey's time, confederation was to be approached primarily along the line of seeking a native policy on a South African scale. Carnarvon declared his intention of inaugurating a civilising policy for the Bantu; but he showed clearly that the secondary motive which drove him forward was the need for settling the troubled affairs of Griqualand West. Southey had duly become Lieutenant-Governor of that province. He had set up an Executive

July 1873.

Council of three and a Legislative Council of three officials and four elected members to represent the 7000 Europeans in the territory. But he had been in difficulties from the first. Two of his leading officials went on leave; the public accounts were already in confusion; the indispensable police were expensive; there could be no security of tenure and no legal protection for the holders of town 'stands' and claims until the land titles were established; the Port Elizabeth syndicate which owned Vooruitzigt told him that where they had hitherto put up with shillings for diggers' licences, they now meant to have pounds. Southey determined that they should not. He not only refused to collect any more licence monies for the proprietors, but demanded a refund of those that had been collected and thereby gave rise to a long controversy, which was only ended two years later by the state purchase of the Vooruitzigt royalties for £100,000.[2] He was, however, able to deal with humbler gamblers at once. He cleared out Malays, Hindus and Chinese from their hells and expedited the departure of two American citizens with their faro tables and £60,000 of other folk's money.

[1] C. 1121 of 1875, pp. 60, 92; C. 1158 of 1875 *passim*.
[2] C. 1401 of 1876, pp. 1 ff.; C. 1342 of 1875, pp. 41, 70, 177, 180 ; Wilmot, *Southey*, pp. 236 ff.

In all this Southey had the support of the main body of the diggers, four of whom he summoned to advise him on matters directly affecting the diggings; but he soon fell foul of the land speculators and the Diggers' Committees which still sat at the four main camps. He suspended the jumping rule whereby anyone could annex a claim which had remained unworked for a week, set up a mining board with small powers and less money to cope with the land slides, and paved the way for the formation of the dreaded companies by permitting any one person to hold up to ten claims.[1] Public opinion was indeed beginning to face the fact that the deepening of the mines was making the old rule of one man one claim impossible, but there were many who resented the passing of the Diggings as the small man's paradise. The centre of opposition was the Committee at New Rush which was dominated by two men who dreamt of a diggers' republic and, when one of them was defeated at the polls, objected even to elected members on the new Legislative Council. Times were bad, the death rate was high, broken men were hanging about, and soon a clamour arose against red tape, unsympathetic officials, the lack of a colour bar, illicit diamond buying and the rest, a clamour which even the appointment of one of the two hostile leaders to the mining board failed to quell.[2]

Into this rising tumult stepped Alfred Aylward, a man of many 1874. aliases, fresh from eighteen months' imprisonment for wounding a fellow digger in cold blood.[3] He organised a Mutual Protection Society with which the land sharks began to co-operate. The sharks were becoming nervous. A land commission appointed to unravel 1872. the confusion in the overlapping land titles of Griqualand West had led to nothing more definite than talk on the part of one of its members of 'the big land swindle'; but now Southey classified the claims 1874. and proposed to appoint a special commission with judicial powers to settle such cases as might be laid before it. Some of his legislative councillors played for time, notably Arnot, member for Hay; but the High Commissioner, whose eyes were open at last, insisted on the appointment of a judge instructed to inquire into all claims whatsoever from Arnot's 800 square miles downwards.[4]

This dispute between the authorities was raging when the historian, 1874.

---

[1] Ordinance No. 10 of 1874.
[2] C. 1342 of 1875, pp. 3 ff., 108, 121; Aylward, *op. cit.*, p. 290; Wilmot, *Southey*, p. 412.
[3] C. 1342 of 1875, p. 120; Martineau, *Frere*, II. 410 ff. Sir Garnet Wolseley, who knew Aylward, said he was a most 'amusing ruffian, full of Irish stories, which he tells inimitably.' Aylward *alias* Rivers *alias* O'Brien *alias* Nelson was a Fenian. He played a stormy part at Kimberley and later in the Transvaal and Natal, wrote the best book of his time on the Transvaal (*The Transvaal of To-day*, 1878), and curiously enough died in his bed (Maurice and Arthur, *Life of Wolseley* p. 130). Probably Aylward was his real name (Uys, *Shepstone*, p. 331).
[4] C. 1342 of 1875, p. 42; C. 1401 of 1876, pp. 35 ff.

James Anthony Froude, travelled through South Africa. He was, as he said, 'a private man of letters' travelling for his own amusement, but none the less Carnarvon had asked him to go to South Africa rather than to Australia, and he reported regularly and shrewdly to his friend the Secretary of State on the prospects of confederation. Some of his speeches in the Western Province and the Free State were not calculated to calm ruffled feelings; but it was he who convinced Carnarvon that the Free State had been wronged in the matter of the Diamond Fields and that moderate men in all parts saw the reaction of native policy upon the mutual relations of the states.[1] It might be too late to withdraw from Griqualand West now, but confederation pointed to the way out of that slough and out of other sloughs as well. Carnarvon, therefore, recalled Lieutenant-Governor Pine from Natal, ordered a full inquiry into the Langalibalele case, bade Barkly press his claims in the Keate Award Area no further and encouraged him to proceed with the Griqualand West land court.[2] He then sent Sir Garnet Wolseley with wide powers to reform the constitution and the native administration of Natal,[3] and sat down to write his famous despatch to the High Commissioner proposing a round table conference in South Africa to consider a comprehensive native policy, control of the gun trade and, perhaps, confederation.[4] That done, he sent Froude to Capetown once more to help the confederation policy forward.

May 1875.

THE CONFEDERATION CAMPAIGN, 1874–81

The most serious obstacle in the way of the confederation policy was likely to be the divergent native policies of the states and colonies; but Brand was known to be liberal in these matters, Burgers was an advocate of equal rights and both Griqualand and Natal were susceptible to official pressure. The differences in the civil and criminal laws of the several territories were marked but not radical and, though the status of the governments concerned differed more markedly, Carnarvon hoped that the two Republics would be willing to step down to the level of the self-governing Cape, and he knew that Griqualand and Natal would be only too pleased to step up to it. It was a reasonable hope. The old Colony was by far the largest, most thickly populated, wealthiest and most stable civilised community in South Africa; it was the seat of the High Commissioner, in closer touch than any of the other states with England and

[1] Buckle, *Disraeli*, VI. 419; Harding, *Carnarvon*, II. 176; C. 1399 of 1876, pp. 63 ff.; Martineau, *Frere*, II. 173; Greswell, *Our South African Empire*, I. chap. 9.
[2] C. 1121 of 1875, p. 941.
[3] C. 1187 of 1875, pp. 5, 6; C. 1192 of 1875, p. 92.
[4] C. 1244 of 1875, pp. 1 ff.; C. 1399 of 1876, pp. 1 ff.

the outer world, and possessed of three ports unhampered by the sand bar of Durban or the fever-sodden hinterland of Delagoa Bay.

On the other hand there were obstacles which were more apparent to others than to Carnarvon. It is true that he was able, possessed of a high sense of duty and well informed on colonial matters; but he was so 'crotchety, nervous of being found fault with, and obstinate to a degree when he once got an idea into his head' that his colleagues called him 'Twitters.'[1] His emissary, Froude, was sent three weeks too late; Barkly's annexations had alienated the republicans, and the Free State at least was much better able to stand on its own feet than it had been a few years previously. Moreover, there was no general understanding in South Africa of the meaning of the word 'confederation.'[2] To some it meant a federation like that of Canada; to others an independent federation like that of the United States; to others again, especially in the Republics, a close alliance in which each state would keep its own laws, flag and independence. Finally, all hope of speedy success depended on the support of the suspicious Molteno ministry at Capetown.

Wolseley fired the first shot. He arrived among the Natalians and 'drowned their liberties in sherry and champagne.'[3] The local politicians and still more their wives and daughters were flattered by the entertainments and attentions of this brilliant soldier and his staff; the rival Anglican factions could take no offence when they saw their respective Bishops Colenso and Macrorie together at Wolseley's dinner-parties and the tactful General at the cathedral of neither;[4] they all hoped for a larger garrison and an Imperial guarantee for railway and immigration loans; they were appalled at Wolseley's hint that a British Delagoa Bay might be developed as a rival to Durban.[5] Besides, Natal was not in a mood to be critical. Her Government and planters—it was much the same thing—had overcome the scruples of the Indian authorities and, in spite of French and West Indian competition, had once more begun to import coolies.[6] Hence, helped by the fact that two of the most determined advocates of responsible government were absent and that another, possibly as a result of the sherry and champagne, voted for the bill by mistake, Wolseley carried 'Jamaica' reforms strengthening the official element in the legislature for five years to come.[7]

He then turned to native affairs. Natal had raised mounted police after the Langalibalele troubles. But defence was not enough.

April 1875.

1874.

---

[1] Wilmot, *Southey*, p. 270. [2] C. 508 of 1872, p. 12.
[3] Maurice and Arthur, *Wolseley*, p. 127.
[4] Hattersley, *Portrait of a Colony*, p. 91. [5] Uys, *Shepstone*, p. 111.
[6] No. 20 of 1874; *Leg. Council (Natal)*, 1 of 1872, pp. 8, 50 ff.; *Natal Government Gazette*, 1873, pp. 82, 137, 334.
[7] Maurice and Arthur, *Wolseley*, pp. 79 ff., 85; H.L. 255 of 1875; Eybers, p. 199.

Wolseley's primary aim was to avert a racial war and thus make Natal a safe member of the future federation. Lack of troops prevented him from cutting down the power of the chiefs as drastically as Shepstone and the Colonial Office desired; but he did set up a Native High Court, whose judge was to have original jurisdiction and hear appeals from the magistrates' courts, and from whose findings in serious cases an appeal was to lie to the Supreme Court. He also appointed a Commission which presently produced a handbook of native custom. Then, having abolished the marriage tax, increased the hut tax and remedied as far as might be the results of recent high-handed acts of the administration, he made way for Sir Henry Bulwer.[1]

Sept. 1875.

June 1875. Meanwhile, Carnarvon's Confederation despatch had reached Capetown.[2] It was welcomed by Westerners and Midlanders, who saw in confederation the best prospect of railway extensions, by Easterners who hoped for Separation, by those few who were annexationists at all times and places, and by those, still fewer, who agreed with Chief Justice de Villiers and Hofmeyr that confederation alone would dispose of all outstanding disputes and ward off the boundary, customs and railway wars which they saw looming ahead.[3] On the other hand, Molteno was up in arms at once against the despatch. Confederation would mean the upsetting of the balance of parties against him, the revival of the controversies East against West, expenses for defence and the loss of customs revenue to the inland states at a time when the credit of the Colony was deeply pledged for railway loans; it would involve his government in the Diamond Fields imbroglio and in Natal's tribal troubles and must *ex hypothesi* raise the whole issue of native policy.

There was another consideration which weighed heavily with Molteno. Responsible government had been hardly won; many in the Colony were still opposed to it; the appointment of his Attorney-General, de Villiers, as Chief Justice had led to an attack on the new system and, in the current session, he had been assailed by Hofmeyr and some of his own supporters in the House for hearkening to the Secretary of State too readily in the matters of Langalibalele and the possible extension of Cape authority over the Transkei and Namaqua-Damaraland. Now, with Wolseley in Natal carrying out the very changes which Wodehouse had not so long ago proposed for the Colony, came this Downing Street scheme which even suggested the names of delegates, among others, Froude, 'inebriated with the

1873.

---

[1] Eybers, p. 247; Brookes, *Native Policy*, p. 65; Murray, *British Relations*.
[2] On the Confederation campaign in 1875 *vide* Molteno, *Life of Molteno*, I. 327 ff.; II. *passim*; Hofmeyr, *Life of J. H. Hofmeyr*, pp. 120 ff.; Walker, *De Villiers*, chapter vii.; C. 1399 of 1876 *passim*, especially Froude's report, pp. 58 ff.
[3] Walker, *De Villiers*, pp. 65 ff.; C. 1399 of 1876, p. 64.

exuberance of his own verbosity,'[1] for Great Britain, Molteno himself for the Western Province and John Paterson, the high priest of Separation, for the Eastern.

The Council, by a small majority, recorded its appreciation of Carnarvon's deep interest; but on Molteno's motion the Assembly resolved that the time was not ripe for a conference, and Sprigg, the leader of the opposition, agreed that the first move must be made from within South Africa. Parliament dispersed, and on that very day Froude arrived to take part in the rejected conference. He was button-holed by the Separationists at the docks; he found nearly all the newspapers attacking the ministry; he concluded at the end of an interview that the Premier was finding excuses for a hasty action rather than defending a policy and, in spite of Barkly's warning, he redoubled the clamour by speaking at a banquet organised by the Separationists and followers of Hofmeyr.[2] He then went on to Natal, whence Wolseley had already sent envoys to take soundings at Pretoria and Bloemfontein.[3] There he heard that official Griqualand West had approved of the conference; he knew that Brand was well disposed provided the Diamond Fields question were fairly settled, that General Pieter Jacobus Joubert, acting President of the South African Republic, was willing to recommend it to his executive with 'all due caution for the particular interests' of his state[4] and, finally, that Carnarvon was thinking of a conference in Natal in which the Cape Colony might or might not take part as it chose.[5] On receipt of a cypher message from the departing Wolseley that confederation was impossible so long as Molteno was in office, Froude decided that Molteno must go. He returned to Capetown by way of the Eastern Province throwing himself as 'Royal Commissioner to the people' upon the electors for support and receiving everywhere petitions in favour of the Imperial policy.[6]

Froude's propaganda was by no means the failure that it has been the fashion to deem it. He set the tide flowing strongly against Molteno, but circumstances which he could not control arose to thwart him. Burgers had gone to Europe empowered to raise money for his Delagoa Bay railway on the security of public land and a £1 tax on each farm and non-landholding burgher. During his absence May– the Transvaal executive proclaimed a new boundary in the Keate Aug. Award Area and appointed a commission to register land claims, 1875. proclaimed the Blood River territory republican soil, gave it all out in farms and tried to tax the 15,000 Zulus living on it and, finally,

[1] Buckle, *Disraeli*, VI. 411.   [2] C. 1399 of 1876, pp. 5, 9, 64–71.
[3] *Ibid.*, p. 70; Maurice and Arthur, *Wolseley*, p. 86; Uys, *Shepstone*, p. 113; de Kiewiet, *Imperial Factor*, p. 106.
[4] C. 1399 of 1876, pp. 17 ff., 30; Hofmeyr, *op. cit.*, p. 130.
[5] C. 1399, pp. 5 ff., 33, 35.
[6] Maurice and Arthur, *Wolseley*, p. 88; C. 1399 of 1876, pp. 76 ff.

crowned Mbandine, over whom Cetewayo claimed suzerainty, king of the Swazis and induced him to sign a treaty, which, whether he understood it or not, made him a Transvaal subject.[1] Then the MacMahon Award gave Portugal all and more than all that she had asked for at Delagoa Bay; thus, though Great Britain secured a promise that the Bay should not be sold to a third party, the Transvaal was at last sure of a non-British port as soon as the fever belt could be traversed safely.[2] Burgers in Europe redoubled his talk of the Transvaal's 'golden joys,' begged for an alliance with Belgium, Portugal and Germany and for leave to send a consul to Berlin, concluded a commercial treaty with Portugal and raised a loan at usurious rates in Holland for the railway which had not yet been surveyed. All this at the very moment that Natal had arranged to build a railway to the republics.

July 1875.

Dec. 1875.

If the Transvaal promised to stand less in need of connection with its southern neighbours than formerly, Griqualand was drifting into a condition which might well make all shrink from having anything to do with it.[3] Southey suspected that wealthy men were behind the growing agitation, possibly the proprietors of Vooruitzigt anxious to force the Government to buy them out; but in any case, Aylward's Defence Association found means to arm seven companies, including one of Germans.[4] Some of the officials asked for troops, but Barkly was inclined to sympathise with the opposition and feared to send up a force which might frighten the Republics.[5] At length armed men tried to rescue a prisoner outside the court house; Aylward superintended the hoisting of the black flag and retired to the Transvaal, there to publish his own death notice, and Kimberley broke into full rebellion in the middle of a territory whose native peoples were restive, the Griquas because their lands were passing from them and the Koranas and Batlapin because most of their lands were treated as Crown lands and they themselves as ex-subjects of Waterboer. There was nothing for it, and the troops occupied the town. Sir Arthur Cunynghame, the commanding officer, however, showed his sympathy with the insurgents so strongly that Aylward was encouraged to come to life again and be acquitted with other ringleaders. The High Commissioner personally relieved Southey of his duties.[6]

June–Aug. 1875.

[1] Carter, *Narrative*, p. 562; Leyds, *Transvaal Surrounded*, p. 507; Soutter MSS., July 1, 1875 (Pretoria Archives); C. 1748 of 1877, pp. 5, 7, 23.
[2] C. 1361 of 1875, pp. 247 ff.; *Rec. S.E.A.*, IX. 263–4; Uys, *Shepstone*, pp. 116 ff.; Murray, *British Relations* (unpublished).
[3] C. 1342 of 1875, pp. 83, 200; C. 1401 of 1876, p. 3.
[4] C. 1342 of 1875, pp. 43, 70, 73, 103. There is reason to believe that some of these wealthy men proposed to offer the country to the Free State and, if it refused the offer, to set up a republic (Cunynghame, *My Command*, pp. 174, 193).
[5] C. 1342 of 1875, pp. 63, 105, 148 ff., 164 ff., 172.
[6] *Ibid.*, pp. 159, 219 ff.; C. 1401 of 1876, p. 75; Aylward, *op. cit.*, p. 290.

Nevertheless, Carnarvon was still so hopeful that he inserted a Nov. mention of his scheme in the Queen's Speech. Burgers had assured 1875. him that the Transvaal would take part in the conference, Natal had approved [1] and now the Cape Parliament was meeting for a special session. The Legislative Council voted in favour of a conference and, after a long debate, the Assembly rejected Molteno's motion condemning the 'agitation created . . . in the name of the Imperial Government.' [2] Whatever hope, however, Froude may have had of bringing effective pressure on Molteno was now destroyed by a Colonial Office despatch which cut the ground from under his feet. In that missive, Carnarvon announced that as public discussion had done all that a conference in South Africa could do, the next stage would be a conference in London. The ministerialists jumped at the opening, offered their help in the solution of the Griqualand problem and shelved the whole of the bigger scheme. The Governor flirted for a moment with the idea of an appeal to the country, but in the end decided that the petitions in favour of confederation were not strong enough to warrant a dissolution.[3] Froude for his part sailed home.

The next move came from the Free State. The *ad hoc* judge, Sir Andries Stockenstrom, son of the famous Sir Andries, gave judg- March ment in the Griqualand West Land Court. It was a judgment the 1876. soundness of whose law was not above suspicion, a judgment which left a host of questions unsettled south of the Vaal and raised new issues north of that river; but it did make clear the one point which Stockenstrom, a bitter opponent of Arnot and annexation, was resolved should be made clear, namely, that Waterboer was a mere tribal chieftain and in no sense a territorial ruler, and that he had never had any sovereignty outside Griquatown and Albania.[4] Now that the British claim had been thus weakened, Brand hurried to London to seek a settlement. He did not really want Griqualand West, partly because his republic had made all the money it had ever been likely to make by the sale of farms therein and partly because, as he frankly confessed to Carnarvon, he could never control so unruly and British a community. Terms were finally arranged with the help of Sir Donald Currie, owner of the Castle Line of steamships. The frontier was modified so as to give the Free State five farms whose owners wished to remain burghers, while the British Government promised to pay £90,000 'in full settlement of all claims' and to add a further £15,000 thereto if the Free State

---

[1] C. 1399 of 1876, pp. 19, 25, 55; *Letters of Queen Victoria*, II. 413.
[2] C. 1399 of 1876, pp. 41–3.   [3] *Ibid.*, pp. 27 ff., 48, 52–3.
[4] C. 1401 of 1876, pp. 67 ff.; *Cape Argus*, March 28, 1876; *Diamond News*, March 18, 1876; C.O. June 1880, pp. 13 ff.; Agar-Hamilton, *Road to the North*, pp. 132 ff.

12*

Volksraad should resolve within five years to build a railway that should link up with either the Cape or Natal systems.[1]

Thus was the long dispute officially laid to rest and means provided for the cancellation of the last of the Free State paper money just as the members of the London Conference began to assemble. Carnarvon, the chairman, Wolseley, vice-chairman, and Froude as representative of Griqualand West were joined by Shepstone and two elected members from Natal. Natal was the only South African state adequately represented. Brand indeed attended, but, under instructions from his Volksraad, withdrew as soon as confederation was mentioned, while Molteno, who had come to London too late to assist in the Diamond Fields settlement, refused even to appear as a witness.[2] The Conference never even discussed confederation; but, as Carnarvon remarked, its proceedings were marked by 'a singular unanimity' and gave him the information which enabled him to take the next step.

The next step was to approach confederation through the Transvaal instead of through the Cape. Carnarvon may have owed something of this idea to Shepstone intent on forming his great tribal state centring round Natal, but undoubtedly it was mainly his own. As early as 1874 he had bidden Barkly use his influence to secure the election of a well-disposed President in the expected event of Burgers's death;[3] he was well aware that the failure to secure Delagoa Bay had denied him an indirect strangle-hold on the republic, and now, with the cry for colonies rising in Germany and the Brussels Conference pointing to the coming scramble for Africa, he had become impatient. The diamonds of Griqualand were his and Natal had the necessary port; link both with the Transvaal, potentially rich in minerals, and a north-eastern confederation would be formed with which the Free State and the recalcitrant Colony must come to terms.

Carnarvon was the prophet of the event thirty years hence and, even at the moment, the state of the Transvaal seemed to favour his designs. From the first the impulsive Burgers had been regarded by the Dopper party as the elect of the townsmen and the friend of publicans and sinners in whose debt he sometimes was. Anti-British or rather anti-foreign feeling was dying down in the republic, but Burgers overstepped the mark when he imported Hollanders like the Rev. Dr. E. Jorissen, whose secular education policy was as shocking to many of the burghers as that of de Mist and Janssens had been to their grandfathers.[4] Some 300 families had already trekked beyond

Aug. 1876.

1876.

1873.

---

[1] C. 1631 of 1876, pp. 29, 70 *et passim* ; Eybers, p. 342.
[2] C. 1631 of 1876, pp. 45, 47, 67, 75; C. 1399 of 1876, p. 89.
[3] Wilmot, *Southey*, p. 408.
[4] Martineau, *Frere*, II. 165; Hofmeyr, *Hofmeyr*, p. 155; Malherbe, *History of Education in S.A.*, pp. 235 ff.

the Kalahari to escape the rule of a heretical ex-predikant; before Burgers's departure to Europe, the Doppers had ousted his attorney-general from the executive council and substituted their own leader, Paul Kruger, as additional Volksraad nominee; during his absence, they had overturned many of his reforms and marked Kruger as his successor.

On his return Burgers found that he had little hope of re-election in 1876. 1877. Taxes were coming in so badly that imported railway material had to be left upon the quay and the railway tax increased in the hope of meeting the first half-year's interest on the Dutch loan. From Durban, Port Elizabeth, Kimberley and London itself the old cries of slavery and annexation were going up, for the Natal railway was advancing northwards and the land of the Transvaal, pledged for public and private debts, was almost unsaleable. The cries were echoed within the republic by shopkeepers, many of them representatives of Natal and Cape firms, and by diggers on the Lydenburg goldfields where times were bad and fly and redwater fever were playing havoc with the transport cattle.[1]

Then came the war with Secocoeni. In spite of his guns, the Bapedi chief was not dangerous outside his reserve, but the fever and horse-sickness of his mountainous country made him difficult to subdue. He refused to pay his taxes, admit prospectors to his valleys or give up land which the Republic claimed as part of the Swazi cession of 1846, land through which Burgers's projected Delagoa Bay railway was to run.[2] The neighbouring farmers went into laager and called on Pretoria for help, while the miners practically formed a little republic and called upon Capetown and Pietermaritzburg. Burgers, on a false report that the local mission station had been burnt, took action and, to the burghers' dismay, led in person. He scored an initial success, but his Swazi allies quarrelled with the Boers over captured cattle and, on hearing that Mbeleni, Cetewayo's 'dog,' was raiding their country, went home. The commandos, mistrusting their leader, did likewise. Burgers left volunteers paid in the time-honoured fashion with looted cattle and the promise of farms to hold Secocoeni in check, and returned to face an angry legislature and a revenue falling short even of the meagre state expenditure. A special war tax was voted which there was not the remotest hope of collecting; the Cape Commercial Bank, already in low water, began to press for the repayment of loans furnished for the purchase of the paper-money and war expenses; the Postmaster-General took his salary in stamps and the Surveyor-General in land, the other civil servants went

[1] Aylward, *op. cit.*, pp. 45, 126; Haggard, *Cetewayo*, pp. 88, 190; Carter, *Narrative*, pp. 188 ff., 478 ff., 562 ff.
[2] De Kiewiet, *Imperial Factor*, p. 100.

without, and the neighbouring colonies had to finance the Transvaal mail contractor. Meanwhile, many in the colonies and in England believed that Cetewayo had stirred up Secocoeni and even meant to attack the Transvaal himself.[1] Finally, burghers were said to be passing resolutions in favour of annexation by Great Britain.

Such were the tidings, mingled with much unfair criticism of the Transvaal, which poured in upon Carnarvon. He decided that he must annex the republic to avert a general native war and further his confederation scheme. At the end of the London Conference, in reply to a business deputation of Easterners led by Paterson, he said he contemplated a Permissive Federation Act and that, as a strong hand was needed, proposed to press his confederation policy by all the means in his power.[2] Disraeli did not like the idea, for the Eastern Question was becoming critical and Paul Kruger was 'an ugly customer,' but as usual he left it all to 'Twitters.'[3] Carnarvon there-
Oct. fore commissioned the newly knighted Shepstone to annex the
1876. Transvaal provisionally if he possibly could, provided he was satisfied that a sufficient number of the inhabitants or the Volksraad desired it.[4] A week later he asked Sir Bartle Frere to go out as High Commissioner to federate South Africa and thereafter remain as first Governor-General.[5]

It is clear that Carnarvon meant to annex the Transvaal at once, but he told Shepstone that, unless he had to act immediately on arrival, he must do nothing without leave of Barkly. Unluckily for him, the departure of the supporting troops from England was delayed, Shepstone's mail-boat was wrecked on Dassen Island near Capetown, and Shepstone, on arriving in Natal, dallied for some weeks feeling the pulse of Cetewayo.[6] Meanwhile, Molteno returned home after recommending to Carnarvon a gradual unification of South Africa by means of treaties whereunder the Cape Colony should incorporate first Griqualand West and then the other outlying territories; the Free State ratified the Diamond Fields settlement; Brand and de Villiers began to draft a scheme of federation to be laid before Frere, and Carnarvon sent out the draft Permissive Bill for the comments of the various governments.[7] Frere landed at

---

[1] Aylward, *op. cit.*, p. 426; Leyds, *First Annexation*, chapter xiii.; Carter, *Narrative*, p. 563.
[2] Buckle, *Disraeli*, VI. 414; C. 1631 of 1876, p. 59; C. 1732 of 1877, p. 1.
[3] Buckle, VI. 371, 405, 411.
[4] C. 1776 of 1877, pp. 1-2; *Letters of Queen Victoria*, II. 479.
[5] Martineau, *Frere*, II. 161.
[6] Butler, *Autobiography*, p. 194; Leyds, *First Annexation*, chapter xiv., C. 1776 of 1877, p. 81.
[7] C. 1681 of 1877, p. 11; Walker, *De Villiers*, p. 129. *Cape Government Gazette*, Jan. 12, 1877; *Cape Argus (Supplement)*, Jan. 13, 1877.

Capetown to find awaiting him a minute from Barkly detailing Shepstone's plans. A fortnight later, he learned that Shepstone had annexed the Transvaal.

Shepstone had ridden into Pretoria with a few followers to be welcomed by the President as a friendly adviser with one of the state balls which so scandalised his sterner burghers. He began wisely with a sherry and champagne policy; but, after an interview with the executive council at which Kruger warned him not to tamper with their independence, he relapsed into a devastating silence. The Volksraad met, postponed the presidential election till May and ratified the peace which had just been concluded with Secocoeni.[1] Shepstone promised Burgers that he would take no action if he could carry various reforms in the constitution and the machinery of government. This Burgers tried desperately to do; but Secocoeni refused to sign the definite peace treaty, the bank declined to discount Government bills and the Volksraad set aside Carnarvon's Permissive Federation Act. It also rejected the President's proposed reforms and, with over 300 armed Boers in the street outside, cautioned him to defend its cherished independence.[2] Shepstone then declared that there was nothing for it but annexation. The Volksraad, in alarm, adopted some of the rejected reforms, created the post of Vice-President and elected Kruger to fill it, appointed John Gilbert Kotze, a Grahamstown advocate, as judge of the new professional High Court, transformed the Secocoeni volunteers into police under the ubiquitous Aylward, passed a treason law covering expressions of disapproval of the Government, set a good, if belated, example by paying taxes, and dispersed. Meanwhile, Imperial troops, Cetewayo's warriors and a representative of the Standard Bank lined up on the frontier.[3] The Zulus soon withdrew after alarming the Utrecht farmers, and Shepstone, sternly bidding them to keep quiet, took the final steps.[4] He discussed with Burgers the annexation proclamation and the President's formal protest, and then, disregarding the executive Council's offer, for what it was worth, of a treaty with the other states of South Africa for mutual protection, ran up the Queen's flag.[5]

Jan. 1877.

March 1877.

April 12, 1877.

[1] Martineau, *Frere*, II. 179; Aylward, *op. cit.*, p, 42; C. 1776 of 1877. p. 88; Leyds, *First Annexation*, p. 179.
[2] C. 1776 of 1877, pp. 110, 117 ff. ; Carter, *Narrative*, pp. 562 ff.; Leyds, *op. cit.*, pp. 180 ff.; Haggard, *Cetewayo*, pp. 110 ff.
[3] Amphlett, *History of the Standard Bank*, p. 45.
[4] J. G. Kotze, *Reminiscences*, pp. 360 ff.; Murray, *British Relations*; C. 1766 of 1877, pp. 135, 150; C. 1833 of 1877, p. 100.
[5] C. 1776 of 1877, p. 152; Carter, *Narrative*, chapter ii.; Eybers, pp. 446 ff.; Burgers, who had spent his own money in the service of the Republic, retired to the Cape Colony, where he lived in poverty till July 1878, when he was given an allowance with arrears from April 1877 (Carter, pp. 39, 569, 573; Kotze, *op. cit.*, p. 386). Burgers died on Dec. 9, 1881, *vide* S. P. Engelbrecht, *Thomas François Burgers*, p. 403.

SIR BARTLE FRERE, 1877-80

Doubtless Shepstone's desire to annex had coloured all that he had seen and heard at Pretoria, but he may well have believed that he was justified in doing what he had done.[1] The republican capital had been full of men expectant of a change, some desiring it and a few even anxious for it provided annexation were accompanied by an Act of Oblivion blotting out offences committed in the colonies. Petitions in favour of annexation had come in from townsfolk, Volksraad members had aired views in private which they would never have dared to utter publicly, and the Boers had scarcely shown a sign of offering active resistance.

Contrary to Frere's expectations, however, the annexation of the Transvaal cut the ground from under his own feet.[2] He had come with a fine Indian record behind him to carry through confederation, which he believed was near at hand, and to set on foot a comprehensive native policy at the close of the expected general native war, which was to drive all South Africans to stand together even as they had done against Langalibalele. That war might still break out, but there was now no independent Transvaal to be won over by a victory of the Imperial arms. Annexation did more. The Free State, fearing for its independence, declined to have anything more to do with confederation and, in the Western Cape Colony, a storm of protest arose against Shepstone's act. That the enthusiasts who supported the Rev. Stephanus du Toit of the Paarl in his new Afrikaans-speaking campaign should protest was only to be expected. What was much more significant was that Hofmeyr and his followers, who had hitherto supported the policy of confederation in which the Imperial Government should be the 'leader of a South African patriotism,' condemned annexation as the deathblow of their hopes.[3] For Shepstone had extinguished one of the Republics; and Froude, who himself had done much to stir the Afrikaners to political consciousness, had shrewdly noted the Republics as their 'special glory,' poor things possibly at the moment, but their own.[4]

The official attitude of the Cape was hardly more promising. Molteno, who was as suspicious of Frere as Frere of him, bluntly said that he wished to have no further concern with the Imperial policy. He was downright sulky, because, during his recent abortive visit to London, Carnarvon had forced him to promise to take steps to relieve the Imperial authorities of Griqualand West by dint of refusing to let him have Walvis Bay and Tembuland unless he did so.[5] Apart from having no inclination to help the Colonial Secretary,

---

[1] Carter, *Narrative*, pp. 26 ff., 561 ff.   [2] Martineau, *Frere*, II. 186, 193.
[3] Hofmeyr, *op. cit.*, pp. 162 ff.   [4] C. 1399 of 1876, p. 72.
[5] C. W. de Kiewiet, *The Imperial Factor in South Africa*, pp. 91 ff.

Molteno had less than no desire to burden his Colony with a virtually derelict dependency, whose population had been reduced to less than 7000 by the call of the Lydenburg gold and the pressure of the joint-stock companies which had recently been relieved of all 1876. limitation on the number of claims that they might own, whose public debt was heavy and whose people displayed no enthusiasm for absorption by the Cape.[1] However, Molteno kept his promise to the extent of carrying the Griqualand West Annexation Bill, which duly 1877. received the Royal assent;[2] but he was not unduly grieved that three years were to pass before that measure was implemented and then only after the final collapse of the Confederation policy. Plainly, one reason for this delay was that the Imperial authorities were loth to let the little dependency go so long as there was any hope of using its vote on a Confederation Conference.

On the other hand, the Legislative Council of Natal, seeing the hinterland of its colony annexed in its interests, approved of the 1877. Permissive Act. That measure closely followed the British North America Act which had federated Canada.[3] It was too elaborate for a mere enabling Act and too vague for a precise constitution, but it had an easy passage through the House of Lords. It was more roughly handled in the Commons by old-fashioned Tories, Exeter Hall men and, above all, Parnell's Irish, who practised their new obstruction tactics upon it with devastating effect. Many of its provisions were excellent; it aimed at union rather than at a loose federation and thus, in spirit as well as in many of its details, anticipated the South Africa Act of 1909, which actually effected union; nevertheless, it was still too much an Act of confederation 'as the Queen may direct.' As such it was not calculated to make Frere's task easier.

Frere, meanwhile, was feeling his way towards his civilising native policy. His prescription was a frank acceptance of responsibility, a good frontier police, firm and just rule of the tribes in reserves, a labour tax to encourage habits of industry, and no canteens. To evade responsibility was to substitute the 'gun-runner and the canteen-keeper for the English magistrate,' and, as it was, the tribes just beyond the frontier were already 'practically managed by white men, good or bad, who are not Government officials.'[4]

There were signs that the Cape meant to take up its responsibilities both beyond the Kei and in Namaqua-Damaraland. Barkly had at first merely upheld the Pondo Line and attempted to buy Port St. John's from the Pondos; but in Nomansland (Griqualand East),

---

[1] C. 1980 of 1878, p. 15; Martineau, II. 189.
[2] Act 39 of 1877; Eybers, p. 66.
[3] C. 1980 of 1878, pp. 32, 35 ff.; 195 of 1877 (text of the Act).
[4] Martineau, II. 260, 351, 356.

Adam Kok, troubled by Joseph Orpen's system of dual control, had asked either to be ruled or be left alone. The former alternative had been chosen. Kok's three districts of Kokstad, Umzimkulu and Matatiele had been placed under Orpen;[1] the claims of Nehemiah Moshesh to the Matatiele lands had been definitely rejected, and

1875. magistrates had been sent to Maclear, Qumbu, and Tsolo, the remaining districts of Griqualand East. Adam had then died, and Captain Matthew Blyth, most able of native administrators, had taken over his three districts from Orpen just in time to prevent a

1876. rising by Nehemiah. That chieftain had then been relegated to Kingwilliamstown and the Bacas of Mount Frere had been placed under Blyth's jurisdiction. Similar steps had been taken in Tembuland,

1875. where Gangaliswe had once more asked for protection. Magistrates had been appointed for the districts of Emjanyana, Engcobo, Umtata and Mquanduli, but, in deference to tribal opinion, Gangaliswe had still been recognised as chief.[2]

Tembuland and Griqualand East, two of the four big divisions of the future Cape Native Territories, were thus taking shape and there were already magistrates in Fingoland proper; but there were none in East and West Pondoland, Xesibeland, Emigrant Tembuland or in Bomvana-Galekaland, where Kreli's 12,000 warriors, cramped for room, were bickering with the Tembus and the Fingo 'dogs.'[3] The power of such magistrates as there were was little more than diplomatic, and the only share the Cape Parliament had in the system was that of making up deficits in their salaries. West of the Kei, in the Colony itself, Sandile's Gaikas still regarded Kreli as paramount chief and had, to a great extent, worked themselves free from the control of their magistrates. The tribes on both sides of the frontier were, indeed, recovering fast from the effects of the cattle-

1873. killing of 1857, many of their young men owned guns, and the death of their hero, Macomo, a prisoner on Robben Island, wounded their pride. Gaikas were even buying land from Europeans to the west of the Keiskamma and in the Waterkloof, to the anger of farmers who were debarred from buying tribal lands and still more the small farms round Kingwilliamstown which had been granted by Sir George Grey to Bantu on European tenure.[4] Soon there were complaints of cattle-stealing, and a commission under the Kaffrarian, Sprigg, reported in favour of sweeping measures for defence; but beyond sending a magistrate to Bomvanaland and passing Acts for the annexation of Fingoland and Griqualand East, the Molteno ministry did nothing for fear of expense.[5] After all, there

---

[1] Dower, *Early Annals of Kokstad*, pp. 50 ff.
[2] G. 21–75; G. 16 and 39–76; G. 12–77 (Cape).
[3] Vide *Cape Native Affairs Blue-books*, 1874 onwards.
[4] Theal, VI. 28.   [5] G. 1–77 (Cape).

had been no war these many years; there would be no war; and
then the war came, fatally delaying Frere's attempts to further
confederation.

Worried by the course of events in the Transvaal, Frere had set out Aug.
thither by way of the Eastern Frontier. He was destined for many 1877.
months to get no further than Kingwilliamstown, for on his arrival
there he learned that the Frontier Police had just crossed the Kei
into the still independent Transkei to protect the Fingos from Kreli's
hostile Galekas. He at once sent Brownlee, his Native Affairs
Minister, to summon Kreli to his presence; but that Chief, remembering how his father, Hintsa, away back in 1835, had come in under a
safe conduct and been shot while trying to escape, declined to put
himself in the power of any Cape Governor.[1] Both sides thus drifted
into a war for which the Colony was ill prepared, for its commando
system was rusty, it had nothing in the way of transport, supply or
regulations for controlling volunteers, and, since it had disbanded
its racially mixed Cape Mounted Rifles in 1870, must rely on its white
mounted Frontier Police, some eleven hundred strong under Colonel
Charles Griffith.[2] Only one of the five British regular battalions was
on the Frontier, the rest at Frere's direction being left where they
were far away from the scene of the trouble. With the Governor's
approval, Sir Arthur Cunynghame, the Imperial Commander-in-
Chief, retained this battalion within the Colony to allay panic and
repel possible invaders and, though he was *ex-officio* in command of
all the forces, Imperial and Colonial alike, left Griffiths, now Commandant-General, to do the actual fighting beyond the Kei. Backed
by Fingos and Tembus eager to possess themselves of enemy cattle,
Griffiths did this to such purpose that he had soon pushed the
Galekas back beyond the Bashee river and, believing that the trouble
was ended, allowed many of the volunteers to go home.[3] Unluckily,
Frere deposed Kreli on his own authority, suggested that Scots and
Germans be settled in Galekaland, proposed to send regulars across
the Kei, proclaimed his intention of disarming the tribesmen wholesale and forthwith began to disarm a couple of petty Galeka clans.
One of these fled to Sandile's Gaika reserve within the Colony.
Thither the police followed them and were fired on at the very
moment that the Galekas, having deposited their cattle in the safety
of distant Pondoland, poured back westward, first across the Bashee
and then across the Kei into the Cape Colony proper. There, they
were speedily joined by Tembus and Gaikas.[4]

This time the fighting was done by regulars, the Colonial Police
and expensive volunteers, partly because the commandos, who were

[1] *Vide supra*, p. 185.   [2] Theal, I. (1873–84), pp. 56, 63 ff.
[3] C. 1961 of 1878, pp. 66 ff., 177; G. 17–78 (Cape).
[4] Molteno, *Life of Sir J. C. Molteno*, II. 242 ff., 281 ff.

as averse as their Prime Minister had ever been to serving under Imperial officers, turned out badly, and partly because Frere preferred to rely on disciplined though slow-moving British troops rather than on Colonists whose frontier methods boded ill to any Bantu foemen or rebels within their reach.[1] Frere could scarcely be blamed for taking this line because memories of the Langalabilele scandal were still fresh, the agitated folk by whom he was surrounded were clamouring for drastic action, his Minister for Public Works, Merriman, had throughout displayed a disquieting bellicosity and now his Attorney-General, Stockenstrom, horrified him by averring that rebels taken in arms could be shot 'without mercy or trial.'[2] To make matters worse from his point of view, the truculent Molteno himself joined Brownlee and Merriman, the Ministers in attendance at Kingwilliamstown, and made the problem of the conduct of the war a test case between his own ideas of the powers and privileges of the Prime Minister of a self-governing colony and the authority of a nominee Governor. Barkly, for all his favourable experience of self-government in Victoria, had sometimes found Molteno something of a trial and by now Frere, with his long autocratic Indian training, had come to regard him as frankly intolerable. Matters came to a head when Molteno demanded that Commandant-General Griffiths be given a free hand to deal with the Gaika rebels. Frere would not have it so, partly because to him this was no mere police matter but a full-dress war in which extra-Colonial Tembus and Galekas were involved, and partly because he had had to call in the volunteer Diamond Fields Horse from the neighbouring colony of Griqualand West as well as two additional battalions from reluctant Great Britain. Doubtless, he wanted these British troops to build up the regular forces in South Africa with an eye to enforcing the general disarmament of the tribes, especially of the warlike Zulus; but his immediate aim was to have them so that he might settle the Kaffir war, not as Molteno chose, but as he himself chose. He therefore retorted that since the Colonial authorities had no military power, they must take orders in such matters from the Imperial Commander-in-Chief, that is, in effect, from himself as titular holder of that office.[3] Rather than submit to this dictation, the Lion of Beaufort threatened to resign. At first, Frere demurred; but, a day or two later, fully believing that the Ministry was unpopular and knowing that the Colonial forces had the Gaikas and Galekas on the run, he took a step legal though unique in the annals of Colonial self-government and dismissed him.[4] He called on the inexperienced Kaffrarian,

---

[1] Martineau, *op. cit.*, II. 201 ; C. 1961 of 1878, p. 230 ; C. 2000 of 1878, *passim*.
[2] Martineau, *op. cit.*, II. 206.   [3] Molteno, *op. cit.*, II. 297–363.
[4] Martineau, *op. cit.*, II. 202, 206, 210; Molteno, *op. cit.*, II. 337 ff. ; C. 2079 of 1878, pp. 37 ff.

Gordon Sprigg, to form a Cabinet, which the latter did forthwith, selecting exclusively Easterners like himself.[1]

East of the Kei the war was practically over, but trouble was arising with the tribes everywhere else. Secocoeni took up arms in the Transvaal;[2] Griquas and Pondos rebelled in Griqualand East; in Griqualand West the Griquas had discovered that Waterboer and Arnot had swindled them by ceding all their lands and not, as they had been led to believe, the diamond diggings only, and Stockenstrom's judgment in the Land Court had driven them into the hands of lawyers and land speculators in the effort to prove their claims.[3] Koranas and Batlapin were in like case and it only required the presence of a Xosa emissary and the attempt to levy a fine on a Batlapin chief to cause a serious rebellion which spread across the Orange to the northern border of the Cape Colony. The scuffling was soon ended in Griqualand East, but the Diamond Fields Horse had to come galloping home from the Eastern Frontier to save Griquatown and Kuruman; the fighting there was not over till November and, south of the Orange, the little war dragged on. Meanwhile, in the Ciskei, Sandile was killed after having twice asked for terms, and an amnesty was granted to the remnant of the rebels.[4] The war with Secocoeni continued.

The Kaffir war had cost the Colony the lives of sixty Europeans, £1,750,000 and a severe fright. Sprigg, urged on by Frere, therefore attempted to make a general settlement. Having established his position in Parliament against Molteno, he passed the Peace Preservation Act providing for the disarming of the tribes. He then launched an over-ambitious scheme of Colonial defence. This included the reorganisation of the Frontier Police as the Cape Mounted Rifles, the raising of mounted Yeomanry, the encouragement of Volunteer regiments as in the halcyon days of Grey, and an overhaul of the burgher militia under the Burgher Force and Levies Act, which, *inter alia*, reduced the Coloured Folk to the rank of mere levies, a poor acknowledgement of their excellent service in the old Hottentot Regiment, the Cape Corps and the Cape Mounted Rifles.[5] He met the consequent heavy expenditure by a house duty, increased customs on tobacco and spirits and, to the fury of Hofmeyr and the Western wine farmers, an excise on spirits.[6] Within the Colony the Gaika reserve was sold for farms and in the other locations the chiefs

(margin notes: Feb. 1878. ; June 1878.)

---

[1] John Gordon Sprigg, Prime Minister and Colonial Secretary; J. Miller and, Sept. 9, 1880, onwards, H. W. Pearson, Treasurer; Thomas Upington and, Jan. 28, 1881, onwards, J. W. Leonard, Attorney-General; J. Laing, Crown Lands and Public Works; W. Ayliff, Native Affairs; J. Miller, Without Portfolio Sept. 9, 1880, onwards.
[2] C. 2100 of 1878, pp. 4, 5.
[3] C.O. June 1880, pp. 10, 19; Agar-Hamilton, *Road to the North*, pp. 135 ff.
[4] C. 2144 of 1878, pp. 194 ff.; G. 17–78; G. 43–79 (Cape).
[5] Acts 7 and 13 of 1878.   [6] Martineau, II. 220; Hofmeyr, *op. cit.*, p. 147.

were replaced by magistrates, but east of the Kei there was neither annexation nor occupation by Europeans. There was, however, a great extension of European control. Galekaland, divided into the districts of Kentani and Willowvale, was united with Bomvanaland (Elliotdale) and the Emigrant Tembu lands of Southeyville and Xalanga to form the magistracy of Tembuland under Blyth; the Xesibes of the Rode valley (Mount Ayliff) were added to Griqualand East, which was consolidated under the chief magistracy of Brownlee, ex-Secretary for Native Affairs, and Nquiliso, chief of West Pondoland, was recognised as independent and given £1000 in return for
1878.   leave to build roads through his territory and the cession of Port St. John's to the Queen.[1]

The independence of the Transkeian tribes was thus rapidly passing away. It was not Frere's wish that the independence of the tribes to the north of the Colony should continue. His aim was to extend British protection over all of them up to the Portuguese borders on both sides of Africa and thus exclude the foreign intervention which he feared was coming. It would, he believed, have to
1873.. be extended sooner or later in the interests of all concerned.[2] On the West Coast, the Guano Islands had been formally added to the Colony and the whole of Namaqua-Damaraland was vaguely
1870.   regarded as a future colonial reversion. After Hahn's pacification the Rhenish missionaries and the hunters and traders had returned thither even though the game was being killed off. Troubles had soon come again. The Hottentots, poor and desperate, were reinforced by coloured vagabonds from the Colony, the Herero confederacy showed signs of breaking up, and at last the missionaries persuaded
1872.   its leader, Kamaherero, to ask the advice of the High Commissioner. Then came the Transvaal trek-boers fleeing from Burgers to the
1874.   eastern border of Damaraland. Kamaherero in alarm asked for British protection. The Cape Parliament favoured the annexation
1875.   of Walvis Bay, the one good harbour on that coast, and as much of the hinterland as might be necessary, and the Hereros at Okahandja
1877.   received a Cape magistrate; but the Kaffir war prevented any further
March   extension of control. In spite of Frere's urgency, H.M. Government
1878.   would only permit him to annex Walvis Bay.[3]

Nor were Frere's efforts to extend a protectorate over the tribes to the west of the Transvaal successful. The request of the acquisitive Shepstone and the handful of resident farmers that the Keate Award Area be restored to the Transvaal was not heeded; a mission to Lobengula, the new King of the Matabele, perished far to the north
1878.   of Bulawayo, and Sir Charles Warren had to be content with marching as far as the Molopo river receiving requests for British protection

[1] G. 43–79 (Cape); C. 2252 of 1879, p. 29.   [2] Martineau, II. 260.
[3] Theal, V. 326 ff.; G. 50–77; G. 17–78; G. 33–79 (Cape).

from most of the chiefs, disarming a few of the clans and giving the tribesmen in Griqualand West their long-delayed reserves.[1] For the rest, the British authorities continued to treat Mankoroane and Montsioa as paramount chiefs of the Batlapin and Barolong respectively on the confused Bechuana border, the happy hunting-ground of Boers, deserters and adventurers.

In the middle of 1878 Frere once more took up the question of confederation. He was weakened by the resignation of Carnarvon, but sure of the support of Sprigg and his Eastern ministry. He therefore set out hopefully for the Transvaal by way of Natal to relieve Shepstone of his duties as tactfully as might be and to investigate the affairs of Zululand. All that he had heard on the Eastern Frontier had taught him that Cetewayo was at the bottom of the troubles with the natives everywhere. It is hard to say how far that belief was justified for white South Africa was 'seeing black' at the moment; but fear of Natal's native problem was making the Cape hang back in the matter of confederation, and 35,000 Zulus subject once more to Chaka's discipline and armed with guns were a potential danger to Natal and the Transvaal borders.[2] For some time past the Natal newspapers had been full of rumours of massacres in Zululand, and missionaries of all nationalities, finding their work of no avail in face of a disapproving king and a conservative people, had been steadily abandoning Zululand, not without threats on the part of some of their followers of the wrath to come from the British side of the Tugela if the Zulus would not become Christians.[3]

The Zulus were in a resentful mood. The annexation of the Transvaal, by ringing Zululand round with British territory, had made the 'washing of spears' a still more difficult matter, for Shepstone would not allow Cetewayo even 'one little raid' upon the Swazis. Worse was to come. Hitherto Shepstone had supported Cetewayo in his claim on the Blood River land, but now that he had heard the Transvaal side of the story, he told the king that his claim was groundless.[4] Cetewayo was furious with 'that liar Somtseu.' He allowed his 'dog,' Mbeline, to raid the clans of the eastern Transvaal once more and sent men into the disputed territory to build a kraal for an induna, who should rule the Zulus living there alongside the 75 Boer homesteads. He withdrew his men on demand, but not before the farmers had laagered and Shepstone had demanded troops.[5] 1877.

The Zulus were, however, troubled as usual with civil strife and

[1] C. 2220 of 1879, pp. 34, 109 ff., 151, 235; C. 2252 of 1879, pp. 40 ff.; C. 2454 of 1879, pp. 27 ff.
[2] Martineau, II. 223 ff.; Aylward, *op. cit.*, p. 279.
[3] Colenso and Durnford, *Zulu War*, chapter xi.
[4] C. 2079 of 1878, p. 53.   [5] C. 2144 of 1879, p. 190.

Cetewayo agreed to submit his claims to an arbitration court appointed by the Natal Government. Frere assented and at once asked the unwilling Imperial Government for reinforcements to finish the Kaffir war and enforce what he was assured would be a decision adverse to the Zulus.[1] Secocoeni had risen at Cetewayo's instigation and, in response to messages from Shepstone that the king was tampering with other tribes, Frere sent a naval squadron up the coast of Zululand. The commission duly reported. It threw aside much of the Transvaal evidence and gave Cetewayo more than he had asked for. Cetewayo, *Chaka redivivus* in the eyes of his people, therefore argued that if he had been given some, he must be entitled to all that had been Chaka's. He not only built a kraal in the Blood River Territory but built another north of the Pongola near the German settlers at Luneburg. Then, without his knowledge, two runaway wives of Sirayo, a minor Zulu chief, were seized on Natal soil and carried back to be executed in Zululand. Sir Henry Bulwer, Lieutenant-Governor of Natal, demanded that the murderers be handed over; but Cetewayo, who had previously had such a one returned upon his hands, merely offered compensation and apologised. Bulwer was willing to negotiate, but Frere, taking the same line as with Kreli in 1877, insisted on having the murderers and a fine.[2]

June 1878.

Frere now arrived in Natal. He was in a better position to control the situation than before because the Natal and Transvaal correspondence was at last passing through his hands; but the Griqualand West and Northern Border scuffles were still going on and Secocoeni was unsubdued. He again asked for reinforcements and sent troops to reassure the Luneburg Germans. Then, when the Zulus on the lower Tugela interfered with military surveyors who had ignored their warnings, as at Block Drift on the eve of the War of the Axe, and ill tidings came in that the troops had retreated before Secocoeni, he concluded that nothing but the drought prevented a Zulu onslaught on Natal.[3]

Sept. 1878.

Frere determined to take the Zulu bull by the horns. To set aside the Blood River award was impossible; to enforce it *sans phrase* would mean a rebellion in the Transvaal which might spread far afield. He therefore accompanied the promulgation of the award with an ultimatum which virtually applied to the Zulus the principles of disarmament he was already applying to the coast tribes.[4] He

[1] Disraeli was unwilling to send more troops. There were 6000 already at the Cape and, as he told the Queen, there appeared to be '. . . too much eagerness on the part of the authorities to encourage war, as long as it can be carried on principally by your Majesty's British forces' (*Queen Victoria's Letters*, II. 646).

[2] On the negotiations preceding the Zulu War generally *vide* Colenso and Durnford, *Zulu War* ; Martineau, *Frere*, II. ; Worsfold, *Sir Bartle Frere*.

[3] C. 2220 of 1879, p. 354; Martineau, II. 259; *vide supra*, p. 228.

[4] Worsfold, *op. cit.*, pp. 108 ff., 118 ff. ; C. 2222 of 1879, pp. 201 ff.

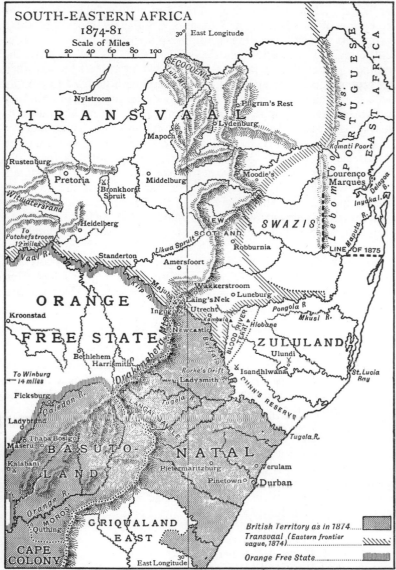

SOUTH-EASTERN AFRICA
1874-81
Scale of Miles
0   20   40   60   80   100

British Territory as in 1874
Transvaal (Eastern frontier vague, 1874)
Orange Free State

EmeryWalker Ltd.sc.

Dec.
1878.

demanded compensation for the dispossessed farmers, reparations for the Sirayo and other incidents, the observance of the promises which he had been led to believe Cetewayo had made to Shepstone at his coronation, the break-up of the Zulu military machine and the reception of a Resident in Zululand. Conflicting reports of these proposals reached the king who, in spite of the rains, set about collecting the reparations cattle, while Frere pushed on with the military preparations which he believed would at least be necessary to support Cetewayo against his own warriors if he tried to comply with his demands. In spite of friction between the civil and military officials in Natal, in spite too of arrogant young officers who talked of marching through Zululand in skirmishing order, he felt confident.[1] Hamu, Cetewayo's rival, had promised to remain neutral; the Transvaal leaders gave good advice and, though most of them and their followers declined to give active help, Piet Uys and other Boers of the Utrecht district were ready to assist against the common traditional enemy.[2] The misgivings of the British ministry had been quieted, reinforcements were due in January and, by that time, Frere hoped to be in Pretoria to cover Shepstone's retreat to England 'on leave.'

Frere had been anxious for some time past to go to the Transvaal, because the situation there was steadily worsening. All had been quiet for the first few months after the annexation. The executive councillors had kept their seats, most of the civil servants had taken the oath and, when Kruger and Jorissen set out to London to plead for independence, six Volksraad members had protested, Jorissen had gone very half-heartedly, and Kruger had declared that, if the mission was a failure, he would settle down as a good British subject.[3] There had been other hopeful signs. Shepstone had at once repealed the hated war tax and the pass fee levied on 'foreign' Kaffirs; the price of land had risen sufficiently to permit of its sale by creditors at 6d. per acre; the Standard Bank had become the Government bank and credit had been restored. Many of the Boers of the south had not been displeased at new conditions which gave them a market in the towns for their produce, and were even willing to put up with the Union Jack provided they and the blacks were ruled in the way to which they were accustomed.[4] They had waited to see how Shepstone would fulfil his promises that the Transvaal should have its own laws and legislature with the fullest possible powers, that Dutch,

---

[1] Martineau, II. 269, 282; Butler, *Autobiography*, pp. 96 ff.

[2] Martineau, II. 264, 270; Leyds, *First Annexation*, p. 245.

[3] C. 1883 of 1877, pp. 9, 23; Martineau, II. 181; Carter, *Narrative*, pp. 41, 50; Hofmeyr, *op. cit.*, p. 161; *Zuid Afrikaan*, March 2, 1878; Van Oordt, *Paul Kruger*, p. 187.

[4] '*The Times*' *History of the S. African War*, I. 59; verbal information by Mr. D. Draper, who was at that time a Transvaal burgher.

which he himself spoke to perfection, should be for practical purposes as much the official language as English, and that laws should
only be altered by competent legal authority.[1]

Had Shepstone followed his first inclination and summoned the
Volksraad, the annexation would doubtless have been ratified; but
he listened to Burgers's ex-State Secretary, who advised him against
it, and won Frere over to his way of thinking.[2] Thereafter, *more* May
suo, he let matters drift. The Treasury stinted him of money; he 1877.
stood quite alone, the usual fate of men such as he, 'silent, self-
asserting, determined to oppose all innovation and division of his
authority,' capable of ruling a tribe 'after white Zulu fashion' but
unable to deal with Boers and English or German townsfolk whose
political support, as in Natal, he made no sort of effort to win. The
Boers indeed liked him personally for his simple ways, but he
offended their legalistic minds by creating special commissionerships
unknown to the law;[3] he alienated the editor of *Die Volksstem* by
taking away the Government printing contract, alarmed Frere by
his reliance on Burgers's finance minister and drawings on Imperial
funds, and, apart from appointing his son, Henrique, Secretary for
Native Affairs, did nothing to develop the much-needed native
policy.

Carnarvon had told Kruger and Jorissen that the annexation July–
must stand, but promised to meet their wishes as far as he could Aug.
and permit the use of Dutch as one of the official languages. They 1877.
had thereupon promised to do their utmost to 'promote a feeling
of satisfaction,' asked for Government employment, and then passed
on to the Continent, where they received much sympathy but nothing
else.[4] They returned to find a changed political atmosphere. Boers,
encouraged by the clamour in the Free State and the Colony, were
complaining that their country had been annexed under false
pretences, and there was enough truth in the charge to give point to
their complaints. Kruger was not reappointed to his seat on the Nov.
executive council and thus became a free agent; Jorissen, admonished 1877.
more than once from the Bench for incompetence, was presently
retired on good terms from the post of State Attorney and sent over
to the opposition; the appointment of the Rt. Rev. Henry Brougham
Bousfield as the first Anglican Bishop of Pretoria simply reminded
the Boers that their country was now British territory.[5] Then

---

[1] C. 1776 of 1877, p. 152; Aylward, p. 391.
[2] Martineau, II. 184–6; Jorissen, *Herinneringen*, p. 34; Engelbrecht, *Burgers*
p. 367.
[3] Martineau, II. 240, 265, 305–7; Carter, *Narrative*, p. 47; Aylward, *op. cit.*,
p. 301.
[4] C. 1883 of 1877, pp. 16, 36; C. 1961 of 1878, p. 147; Van Oordt, *op. cit.*,
pp. 204 ff.; Murray, *British Relations*.
[5] C. 2144 of 1878, p. 135; Carter, *Narrative*, p. 45. For the extent of Jorissen's
legal training *vide* Jorissen, *Herinneringen*, pp. 7 ff.

Feb.-
April
1878.

Secocoeni, angry that he could only remain in his reserve as a British subject and egged on by Cetewayo, rose in arms; the Swazis refused to help so long as the Government used Zulu police, the burghers declined to turn out, the transport broke down and the campaign collapsed. Matters went from bad to worse. The post-annexation boom died away; the Delagoa Bay enthusiasts saw their hopes blighted and the Natal railway advancing but slowly; taxes came in less regularly than ever; even the annexation party cried out against Shepstone. Hence, Kruger and Pieter Jacobus Joubert,

May
1878.

armed with large petitions against the annexation, set out once more for Downing Street.[1]

Frere met the Transvaal delegates in Natal on their way home and underlined the promise of self-government which had been made to them by Sir Michael Hicks Beach, Carnarvon's successor.[2] A short week later, the time fixed for Cetewayo's acceptance of the ultimatum expired and Sir Frederic Thesiger, the new Commander-in-Chief, led four columns into Zululand. On the morrow, the Transvaalers in congress at Wonderfontein made a solemn league and covenant to regain

Jan.
1879.

their lost independence.[3] Ten days later fully 800 troops and as many tribal levies were wiped out by the Zulus at Isandhlwana. Though the Zulu rearguard was beaten off at Rorke's Drift, all Frere's hopes of reaching Pretoria speedily were ruined.[4]

Luckily the Zulus did not cross the Tugela, it may be because of their heavy losses, it may be because Cetewayo had been told by Bishop Colenso that he would get better terms if he did not attack, it may be because his Usutu and the hostile Usibebu faction, thinking the war was over, fought each other in a bloody battle, it may be, and more probably, because Cetewayo had bidden them defend Zululand to the last but in no wise to invade the Queen's territory. Nevertheless, the news of the disaster excited the tribes everywhere and, in Basutoland, Morosi of Quthing rose against the Colony.[5] On the other hand, the Transvaalers sat still, the Free Staters offered

March
1879.

help, reinforcements poured in, and Frere was able to set off cheered by the tidings of Sir Evelyn Wood's victory at Kambula. The High Commissioner found hundreds of armed Boers awaiting him in camp between Heidelberg and Pretoria. He was surprised at their insistence on independence, but he was soon on good terms with the leaders, especially with Kruger, whom he liked for his honesty and restraining influence. With Joubert, who had been agitating secretly

---

¹ Alyward, pp. 271, 347 ff.; Leyds, *op. cit.*, p. 233; C. 2144 of 1878, pp. 102, 143; C. 2220 of 1879, p. 365.
² Martineau, II. 258; C. 2128 of 1878, pp. 17 ff.
³ Martineau, II. 284; Leyds, p. 243; C. 2260 of 1879, pp. 71 ff.; C. 2316 of 1879, p. 1.
⁴ Martineau, II. 274; Colenso and Durnford, pp. 228 ff.; R. Coupland, *Isandhlwana*.
⁵ A. 17 of 1879 (Cape); C. 2318 and 2374 of 1879.

against the annexation from the first, his relations were not so good. He was, however, convinced that the real malcontents were a small minority inspired by foreign wirepullers and that the large attendance at the camp was the result of intimidation. He once more promised them self-government as part of a confederation, ordered the fuller use of Dutch as an official language, recognised a local flag and sent on to the Queen the leaders' memorial detailing their grievances and offering the alliance which was their idea of confederation. He then set about clearing up the incredible confusion in the administration. He ordered Lieutenant-Colonel Owen Lanyon, the acting administrator, to summon an executive council and temporary legislature to pave the way for a constitution-making conference and a Volksraad, and began to arrange for the railway from Capetown to Delagoa Bay by way of Pretoria and Kimberley which was to be the spinal cord of the coming federated South Africa.[1] At last the Boer laager broke up and, on the same day, Frere heard that the harassed Disraeli ministry had censured him for his Zulu policy.[2]

April 1879.

The censure from a ministry which had never expected anything more than a defensive war was accompanied by a request that he would remain in office, but it gave the signal for a renewal of the agitation against the Imperial policy.[3] Pretoria was at once filled with talk of retrocession; Frere had to return to Capetown without visiting Bloemfontein; the Free State Volksraad refused to listen to its President and voted in sympathy with the Transvaalers, and in the Colony, Hofmeyr organised another protest against the annexation, while Stephanus du Toit proposed the formation of the Afrikaner Bond on bitterly anti-British lines.[4] On the heels of all this came the news that Sir Garnet Wolseley was coming out as High Commissioner for South-East Africa, and cold instructions to drive that willing horse, the Sprigg ministry, along the road to the confederation which censure and the division of Frere's power had put definitely out of reach.[5]

Disraeli and his colleagues naturally wanted to end their South African adventure. The life of the ministry was running on; Egypt and the Clan-na-Gael in Ireland had been added to the anxieties of war in Afghanistan and strained relations with Russia; the scramble for Africa had fairly begun and German 'colonials' were advocating the colonisation of Matabeleland and the Transvaal; the British

---

[1] Martineau, II. 285 ff., 309, 321; Carter, Narrative, pp. 51 ff.; Nineteenth Century, Feb. 1881 (article by Frere); Leyds, op. cit., pp. 246 ff.; C. 2367 of 1879, pp. 54, 84 ff., 97 ff.
[2] C. 2260 of 1879, p. 109.
[3] Buckle, Disraeli, VI. 409 ff.; Worsfold, op. cit., pp. 231 ff.
[4] Hofmeyr, op. cit., pp. 164, 195 ff.; C. 2454 of 1879, p. 106; C. 2482 of 1880, pp. 37, 446 ff.
[5] C. 2454 of 1879, p. 51.

sinking fund had been suspended and the Zulu war was costing millions. That drain ended at last. Thesiger, now Lord Chelmsford, hearing that Wolseley was coming to supersede him, ploughed his way through central Zululand, losing the Prince Imperial on the way, and forced Cetewayo to a final battle at Ulundi.[1]

July 1879.

The news of Chelmsford's victory at Ulundi gave great joy to the Court and the Horse Guards where Wolseley was unpopular as a youthful thruster of forty-six, but it failed to raise the corpse of confederation from the dead. Sprigg had too much else on his hands to attempt the impossible that year. The Northern Border war had ended, but the struggle with Morosi was destined to smoulder on till the death of the chief six months later, everywhere the tribes were excited by the Zulu war and the Disarmament Act, and Sprigg himself differed from the Secretary of State on the score of policy in Griqualand West and the Transkeian territories. In the end the Colony definitely annexed Fingoland and all Griqualand East except Mount Ayliff; but Hicks Beach refused to let it have Galekaland till confederation should be achieved, and held Sprigg to part at least of the debt owing for the troops employed in the recent Kaffir war.[2] The Cape Parliament reaffirmed the Griqualand West Annexation Act of 1877, but Sprigg played for time in the hope that he might avoid taking over all the debts of the little colony and, on the main issue of confederation, declined to commit himself till he knew what Wolseley's Transvaal and Zululand settlements were to be. Hence, in spite of alarming talk in unofficial but influential quarters in London of a suspension of the Cape constitution as the surest way of attaining closer union, no definite move was made during the session.[3]

1879.

There was little hope of success whatever Sprigg might do, for South-eastern Africa was completely beyond Frere's control. Wolseley's natural jealousy had been so inflamed by Bulwer that he would listen to no advice from the High Commissioner. Rather did he send Cetewayo as a prisoner to Capetown and apply to his country the plan which Grey had long ago urged upon Panda by dividing Zululand into thirteen parts and placing the tribes where possible under scions of the houses which had ruled before the days of Chaka, on the principle that the Zulus would remain quiet once the alien Chaka system was abolished. Sometimes he appointed special chiefs: Hamu the traitor and John Dunn the gun-runner, who had deserted Cetewayo in his hour of need. The weakness of the scheme was that

---

[1] Maurice and Arthur, *Wolseley*, pp. 119 ff.; C. 2454 of 1879, p. 119.
[2] Eybers, p. 65; A. 3–80 (Cape). The Cape ultimately paid H.M. Government £150,000 out of the £259,963 claimed; Natal paid £250,000 out of £1,000,000. It is always heavy work collecting war-debts (C. 3280 of 1882, pp. 2, 15, 16, 33).
[3] C. 2454 of 1879, p. 158; Walker, *De Villiers*, p. 140.

there was no controlling power. Hicks Beach indeed hinted at a protectorate, but Wolseley adhered to his original instructions and placed residents with merely consular powers in each district.[1]

Meanwhile, in the Transvaal Lanyon was making headway in spite of his unpopularity. He reorganised the administration, collected the taxes and, until Wolseley stopped him, pressed Secocoeni hard. The new High Commissioner for South-East Africa arrived in Pretoria to find the Boers in Cromwellian fashion requisitioning powder and holding a day of prayer for the success of the independence movement. He fortified Pretoria and the principal Sept. villages, forced Secocoeni to surrender and thereupon began to send 1879. home the troops. In spite of Frere's disapproval and of local advice, he foreshadowed a rigid Crown Colony constitution what time Gladstone in Midlothian was thundering against all annexation policies.[2] In December over 6000 Boers met once more at Wonderfontein, hoisted the Vierkleur, decreed the summoning of the old Volksraad in April and decided to boycott all who co-operated with the authorities.[3] Nevertheless, Wolseley promulgated his constitution and, having seen the executive and legislative councils assemble, handed over his duties to Sir George Pomeroy Colley.

At the same moment Gladstone's Liberals took office. Gladstone April was in a difficult position. The Queen disliked him much and the 1880. idea of parting with provinces still more; she admired Frere whom so many of his followers reprobated; vested interests had sprung up in the Transvaal; a gold rush was probably coming which would reduce the Boers to a minority; retrocession, he was told, would lead to civil war; his philanthropic wing led by that redoubtable Birmingham Radical, Joseph Chamberlain, would not hear of the abandonment of the tribes; official reports were reassuring; all would surely come right if confederation and self-government were followed as the pole-stars.[4] The Cape was once more the key of the position and the dutiful Sprigg prepared to go forward; but Kruger and Joubert collogued with Afrikaner members of Hofmeyr's house in Capetown and Sprigg was forced to accept the previous question.[5] Frere's 1880. *raison d'être* was now gone and he sailed home amid a chorus of Sept.– regrets broken only by a Stellenbosch complaint about the excise; Oct. Griqualand West was at last incorporated in the Colony, the Natal 1880. 'Jamaica' constitution expired and the Cape-Basuto war began.

[1] C. 3864 of 1879; Maurice and Arthur, *Wolseley*, pp. 120 ff., 131; Martineau, II. 353.
[2] Carter, *op. cit.*, pp. 67 ff.; Martineau, II. 361; Scoble and Abercrombie, *Downfall of Krugerism*, Appendix K; C. 2482 of 1880, p. 380.
[3] Leyds, *First Annexation*, p. 262; Cf. 2505 of 1880, p. 113.
[4] Maurice and Arthur, *Wolseley*, p. 132; Morley, *Life of Gladstone*, II. 263, 266; C. 2586 of 1880, p. 12; C. 2676 of 1880, p. 46a.
[5] C. 2655 of 1880, pp. 4 ff.; Martineau, II. 346, 369; Hofmeyr, *op. cit.*, pp. 170 ff.

Spriggs had disarmed the Galekas and loyal Fingos in spite of protests from Colonists, who held it a breach of faith to take at current rates guns which, after paying customs dues, had often been bought at fancy prices. He now essayed to disarm the Basuto. Missionaries, merchants and magistrates protested; Wolseley feared it would lead to the general native war which had so long haunted the British official imagination; Lord Kimberley damned the idea with faint praise and disclaimed all responsibility.[1] As for the Basuto, they had waxed rich of late years and their chiefs disliked magisterial control; the finer points of responsible government were beyond them and they by no means appreciated the fact that since 1871 they had been ruled from Capetown and not from Windsor;[2] they had helped the Colony against Langalibalele and Morosi and could not believe that they were to be rewarded by the confiscation of their cherished guns. But Frere viewed disarmament as a necessary civilising measure like the abandonment of rapiers by European gentlemen, and Sprigg not only demanded the guns but doubled the hut tax and proposed to take part of Quthing to pay for the expenses of the late war against Morosi. The chiefs petitioned the Queen to whom they had given their country, but the handing in of guns was fixed for April 1880. At that very time died Moroko, the enemy of Moshesh; his sons began to fight for the succession and, on the other side of Basutoland, the claims of Griqualand East were in a ferment. Letsie, paramount Basuto chief, and Jonathan, son of Molapo, were willing to give up their weapons, but Lerothodi, Masupha, Joel and Lesoana, the old firebrand, all refused and drove out those who obeyed the law. Sprigg sent up the police and the War of Disarmament began.[3]

1879.

Sept.
1880.

Brand viewed the war as a rebellion and allowed the Colonial forces to use the Free State as a base, but the rising spread to Griqualand East, whose clans were stirred up by the East Pondos. In both areas the Colony was helped by friendly tribes and order was soon restored south of the Quathlamba mountains; but, in Basutoland itself, Maseru was held with difficulty, the Basuto horsemen did great execution on the Cape yeomanry at Kalabani and the inconclusive struggle dragged on.

Behind the dust and uproar in the valley of the Orange, the Transvaalers rose.[4] Colley had believed that time was on his side and had made no reforms pending the expected arrival of Sir Hercules Robinson, the new High Commissioner. Even as late as October, so

---

[1] C. 2569 of 1880, pp. 1, 3, 7, 15, 36, 45–6.   [2] Ibid., pp. 9, 11.
[3] C. 2755 of 1881, pp. 1, 38 ff., 58, 120 ff.; C. 2821, pp. 37, 69; C. 3708, p. 1. On the war generally vide C. 2755, 2821, 2964 of 1881; C. 3112 of 1882; C. 3493 and 3708 of 1883.
[4] For full and fair account of the Transvaal war vide Carter, Narrative; Morley, Gladstone, II. chapter iii. On the outbreak vide C. 2783, 2838 of 1881.

well-informed an observer as Aylward in Natal feared that the Boers would not rise. Both were wrong. The Potchefstroom officials sued one, Bezuidenhout, for his taxes and, when he proved that he had paid them, saddled him with costs and distrained upon his waggon. Nov. To the Boers all direct taxes were an iniquity and this was much worse; 1880. besides they argued that if they paid taxes willingly, they would be recognising the interloping government at Pretoria.[1] Commandant Pieter Cronje with 300 men rescued the waggon, 1500 armed men speedily assembled, and British reinforcements had to be sent up from Natal. Brand warned Sir George Strahan, the acting High Commissioner at Capetown, that the crash was coming, but the vital message, forwarded thence by post, only reached London after the War of Independence had begun.[2] The Boers assembled in thousands at Paardekraal. The old Volksraad sat once more, decreed the restoration of the Republic, named Kruger, Pretorius and Commandant-General Joubert as a triumvirate to take charge of their interests,[3] and once more offered to enter into alliance with the other South African states. Apparently the meeting went further than some of the leaders, and notably Kruger, had wished; but in any case Cronje set off to have the proclamation re-establishing the Republic printed at Potchefstroom, another party moved off to hold the Lydenburg-Pretoria road and the main body marched to Heidelberg Dec.16 to hoist the Vierkleur. They did so on Dingaan's Day just as Cronje 1880. fired the first shot at Potchefstroom.[4]

There were about 3500 British troops in all South Africa, ill-disciplined, weakened by systematically encouraged desertions, damaged in prestige by the disaster of Isandhlwana and incapable of shooting straight, for those were the days when 'Royal George' of Cambridge, Commander-in-Chief, was still able to thwart 'the damned new-fangled notions' of Wolseley or anyone else.[5] On the other hand, the military reputation of the Boers stood so low that Colley and Lanyon underrated them as a fighting force and even some of their own friends and leaders feared that they would disperse at the first check.[6] They had no cannon to speak of and so would be handicapped in siege work, but they had one very great advantage: they could shoot and they had the Westley-Richards rifle capable of killing at 600 yards. They were thus better equipped than they had ever been before and better shots than they were ever to be again.[7] They shot a British column to pieces at once at Bronkhorst Spruit, and cooped up the rest of the Transvaal garrison in Pretoria,

---

[1] Carter, *Narrative*, pp. 98 ff., 180 ff.   [2] Morley, *Gladstone*, II. 272.
[3] Leyds, *op. cit.*, pp. 265 ff.; C. 2794 of 1881, pp. 3 ff.
[4] Carter, *Narrative*, pp. 116 ff.
[5] Maurice and Arthur, *Wolseley*, p. 114.
[6] Hofmeyr, *op. cit.*, p. 172; Butler, *Autobiography*, pp. 267, 274.
[7] '*The Times*' *History*, III. 62.

Potchefstroom and the other fortified villages, while Joubert's burghers and a few unofficial Free State allies faced Colley on Laing's Nek, where the main road from Natal entered the Transvaal.

Neither side wished to push matters to extremes in face of the Basuto and Kaffir troubles; negotiations began almost at once and Lord Kimberley offered to frame a scheme of settlement if the Boers would lay down their arms.[1] This offer reached Joubert just after he had repulsed Colley at the Nek, and a more explicit offer was despatched on the very day that he checked Colley once more at Ingogo.[2] Kruger now offered to admit a commission if the troops would withdraw from the Transvaal. Not unnaturally this proposal was rejected, but Kimberley offered to appoint a Royal Commission with wide powers and bade Colley arrange an armistice.[3]

Jan.26
1881.

The Gladstone Ministry was only too anxious to find a way out of the tangle. On the one hand it was faced with concerted non-payment of rents and cattle-houghing in Ireland, a petition in favour of the Transvaal from influential Hollanders, and the fear of a rising in the Free State and possibly in the Cape.[4] Lord Granville, the Foreign Secretary, was much impressed by Bismarck's plea that white men must not fight in sight of the tribes[5] and, already, the Natal Zulus were restive at the news of the reverses to the Imperial arms. On the other hand was the ugly fact that, though the executive had annexed the Transvaal, Parliament had legislated for it and, therefore, nothing but an Act of Parliament could lawfully disannex it. But only one-third of the unwieldy ministerial party had voted in favour of retrocession; five philanthropic ministers, including John Bright and Chamberlain, had abstained from voting, and there was not the remotest hope of getting such an Act through the Houses. A compromise had to be made by which the Transvaalers should have control of their own affairs without seeming to have been excluded from the British Empire. The formula of Suzerainty would meet the case, but first there must be an end to the fighting.

Colley was anxious to relieve the beleaguered Transvaal towns and demanded an answer to his armistice proposals within forty-eight hours. His message reached Kruger only on the day after the sender had been killed at the rout of Majuba.[6] Kruger's answer was, nevertheless, favourable, and with Brand's help an armistice was arranged on the day that Potchefstroom capitulated. Kimberley now proposed that a Royal Commission should consider 'the giving back of the Transvaal subject to British Suzerainty, a Resident at the capital, and provisions for guarding native interests; control over relations with

Feb.27
1881.

[1] C. 2783 of 1881, p. 77. [2] C. 2837 of 1881, pp. 1, 6 ff.
[3] Ibid., pp. 8, 10. [4] Selborne, Memorials, II. 3.
[5] Fitzmaurice, Life of . . . Granville, II. 229.
[6] Morley, II. 276; C. 2837 of 1881, pp. 16, 23; Leyds, op. cit., chap. xix.

foreign Powers and as to frontier affairs to be reserved.'[1] The Triumvirate accepted Suzerainty, on Wood's definition, as meaning that 'the country has entire self-government as regards its own interior affairs, but that it cannot take action against or with an outside Power without the permission of the Suzerain';[2] they left much else to be settled by the coming Commission, and faced the possible loss of the tribal and gold-bearing territories to the east of the thirtieth degree of east longitude. But this possibility they prudently kept from the ears of their followers.[3] *March 21, 1881.*

The commandos dispersed, but Sir Hercules Robinson had one pressing duty to perform before he could join his fellow-commissioners, Wood and Chief Justice Sir Henry de Villiers, at Newcastle. On his arrival in Capetown, he had offered to mediate between the Colony and the Basuto. Two of the rebel chiefs were prepared to cease fighting provided they might keep their land and guns, but in spite of the cost of the war and of wholesale desertion by the burghers and yeomanry, Sprigg demanded the guns and part of Quthing.[4] Kimberley refused to allow Quthing to be touched; hence the war went on marked by costly colonial victories till the chiefs quarrelled among themselves and turned to the Governor. Robinson gave his award leaving Basutoland undiminished and promising to give back surrendered guns to 'trustworthy' warriors on payment of a licence fee. The award was generally accepted, a fine of cattle was paid and a few guns were registered; but the honours of war rested with the Basuto. And they knew it.[5] *Jan. 1881.* *April 1881.*

The failure in Basutoland, following hard upon the confederation débâcle, broke the back of the Sprigg Ministry. The final blow was given by the members from newly incorporated Griqualand West. Led by Cecil John Rhodes, now a rising power in the world of diamonds, this group demanded a railway and, when Sprigg could not give it them, turned him out in favour of Thomas Scanlen.[6] *May 1881.*

Meanwhile, the Transvaal Commission was sitting first at Newcastle and then at Pretoria. The members differed among themselves on some vital points. British reinforcements had arrived, and Wood, against the wishes of his colleagues, to the last wanted a military settlement or at least a march through the Transvaal in force before

---

[1] C. 3114 of 1882, p. 49.   [2] *Ibid.*, pp. 51 ff.
[3] Carter, *op. cit.*, p. 462. On the negotiations generally *vide* Leyds, *First Annexation*, chapter xix.; Walker *De Villiers*, chapter viii.; C. 2892 and 2998 of 1881; 3114 and 3219 of 1882.
[4] C. 2964 of 1881, pp. 5, 10.   [5] *Ibid.*, pp. 11, 17, 21; A. 44–81 (Cape).
[6] Eybers, p. 66; Hofmeyr, *op. cit.*, p. 187; Williams, *Cecil Rhodes*, p. 63. Scanlen Ministry: T. C. Scanlen, Prime Minister; Attorney-General till June 30, 1882, and thereafter Colonial Secretary; J. C. Molteno, Colonial Secretary till June 30, 1882; C. W. Hutton and, July 1, 1882, onwards, C. J. Rhodes, Treasurer; T. C. Scanlen, and July 1, 1882, onwards, J. W. Leonard, Attorney-General; J. X. Merriman, Crown Lands and Public Works, J. W. Sauer, Native Affairs; J. H. Hofmeyr, Without Portfolio till November 30, 1881.

13

evacuation; he likewise pressed for the retention of all or part of the eastern territories. The Boer leaders for their part long hesitated to accept Kimberley's interpretation of the peace terms as 'including, of course, the conclusion of treaties and the conduct of diplomatic intercourse' by H.M. Government.[1] On the other hand, the majority of the Commission decided that partition would lead to more trouble with the Boers than it was worth. Swaziland was to be independent, but the whole of the eastern districts were to be given back, provided the Queen retained her veto on native legislation and the British Resident was given full powers and a seat on the proposed Native Locations Commission, which was to hold land for the tribes, who, under the ordinary law, could hold none. Besides being an attempt to safeguard tribal interests, this bargain was an eleventh-hour effort to do the work which, apart from the tardy collection of hut-tax, Henrique Shepstone's Native Affairs Department had failed to do.

July 1881. A month after the Royal Commission had moved on to Pretoria, the Administrator was made Great Chief and native law was recognised in the courts as in Natal.[2] A few days later the Pretoria Convention was signed.

Aug. 1881. The Pretoria Convention defined the boundaries of 'the Transvaal State' on all sides for the first time, gave it 'complete self-government subject to the suzerainty of Her Majesty' and, besides embodying the points already mentioned, prohibited slavery, assured equal civil rights to all, saddled the State with a considerable share of the debt accumulated since the annexation, but, in spite of Wood's warning, made no mention of the franchise.[3] A specially elected Volksraad met at the end of September and opposed ratification so furiously that Kruger had to tell it that, if it did not ratify, there would be war again. Kimberley urged it to trust to time and experience to prove the necessity for future concessions. At last the Oct. 1881. Raad ratified 'the unsatisfactory state document . . . for the time being and provisionally.' And so the troops marched down through Laing's Nek into Natal.[4]

---

[1] C. 3114 of 1882, p. 7. On the ratification *vide* Carter, pp. 522 ff.; Leyds, *op. cit.*, chapter xx.; *Staats Courant (S.A.R.)*, Oct.–Nov. 1881.
[2] C. 3114 of 1882, pp. 19, 28, 64; Brookes, *History of Native Policy*, pp. 124 ff.
[3] Eybers, pp. 455 ff.; Walker, *De Villiers*, p. 336; C. 3219 of 1882, pp. 25, 53.
[4] C. 3098 of 1882, pp. 95 ff.

CHAPTER XII

THE SCRAMBLE, 1881-96

THE COASTS AND THE ROAD TO THE NORTH, 1881-86

'PLANTS of slow growth endure the longest,' Froude had written in the light of his South African experiences, 'and the final consummation, however devoutly to be wished, can only be brought to wholesome maturity by the deliberate action of the South African communities themselves.'[1] The Colonial Office was at last convinced that Froude was right, and three months before the battle of Majuba, Kimberley had bidden Sir Hercules Robinson make no attempt to raise the Confederation issue again unless 'it should be initiated spontaneously by the Colonies' in their own interests.[2]

The Confederation policy, so long in dying, was dead at last; the hills round Laing's Nek had echoed to the funeral volleys, and the Imperial Government was in no position to attempt a resurrection even had it wished to do so. For its prestige was far gone in the eyes of white and black alike. The long-enduring and sorely strained reputation of the handful of redcoats in which Governors had been wont to put their trust had been blown to the winds. Any future intervention in the affairs of Boers, who were satisfied that British soldiers could always be beaten, would have to be in force.

Boer contempt at one extreme was balanced by bitterness at the other. The loyalists who abandoned the Transvaal and, still more those who remained, fulminated against the power which had deserted them and, in the colonies, 'Majuba' became a word of power in moments of political excitement. Faith in the continuity of British policy had been destroyed and the attention of foreign Powers attracted to South Africa at a time when it was difficult for Great Britain to deal firmly with the Transvaal without seeming to

[1] C. 1399 of 1876, p. 83.　　　　[2] C. 2754 of 1881, pp. 3, 4.

threaten. There was for the present no hope that the Transvaalers or indeed the Free Staters would willingly enter even an economic federation, for all were suspicious, and the anti-British foreigners who flocked to Pretoria were naturally ready to play upon those suspicions in the interests of their concessions and influence. Even in Natal, Downing Street rule had given an impetus to republican feeling, and disappointed imperialists could lament that, if the British Government were to be content with Simonstown only, a republican federation would certainly be formed.[1]

For some years past there had been a vigorous thrusting of the same anti-imperial spirit in the Cape Colony against the Southey-Shepstone policy of the later 'seventies. Among the British it took the form of a 'Colonialism' inspired by Merriman's condemnation of Froude's confederation campaign as 'an agitation from abroad.'[2] So long as Great Britain looked after external defence they were well content, but intervention by the 'imperial factor' in internal matters they would not have, unless, of course, there was work to be done beyond the strength of the Colony. It was a sufficiently cynical attitude and galling to the representatives of the aforesaid factor, but the development of the same spirit among the Dutch-speaking colonists at first threatened the very British connection. The first overt signs of this spirit had appeared in 1873.[3] Hitherto the tide had run strongly in the direction of anglicisation. The Dutch of Holland was indeed the religious language, but the spoken tongue it was not nor ever likely to be. Over against it stood English with all its vigour and wealth of literature, the commercial language of half the world, whose advantages the bulk of the Cape Afrikaners and many of the Republicans also were eager that their children should have, provided it was not forced upon them. In spite of experiments by a few writers like Louis Meurant, their own spoken Afrikaans was in no sense a literary language. Again, though the divisional councils had given the country folk some training in representative institutions, those

Circa 1860.

---

[1] The editor of *Di Patriot*, the organ of the Afrikander Bond, wrote: 'We have often said it, there is just one hindrance to Confederation, and that is the English flag. Let them take that away, and within a year the Confederation under the free Afrikander flag would be established. But so long as the English flag remains here, the Afrikander Bond must be our Confederation. And the British will, after a while, realise that Froude's advice is the best for them: they must just have Simon's Town as a naval and military station on the road to India and give over all the rest of South Africa to the Afrikanders' (Hofmeyr, *Hofmeyr*, p. 198). Cp. Froude to General Bisset, July 1877: 'Create a Constitutional Dominion composed of the whole European states and if I were in Parliament I would move for a line of forts from Table Bay to False Bay. Let England keep to Table Mountain Peninsula, the only part of the country which is of Imperial service, and let the rest take its chance.'

[2] C. 1399 of 1876, p. 79; Carter, *Narrative*, pp. 4, 5, 24.

[3] On Afrikaans and the Afrikander Bond *vide* Hofmeyr, *Life of J. H. Hofmeyr*, chapter xiii.; *Union Year Book*, No. 8, pp. 14 ff. (article by J. J. Smith); L. van Niekerk, *Die Eerste Afrikaanse Taal Beweging*; *C.H.B.E.*, VIII. 857 ff.

folk had taken so little part in the general politics of the Colony that
when the Colony achieved self-government, less than one-third of
the members of the two Houses bore Afrikaner names.

The cutting of the Suez Canal diverted elsewhere the stream of
Anglo-Indians who had found favour in the eyes of the Western
Afrikaners, the discovery of the diamonds attracted British citizens
of a less prepossessing type, the Diamond Fields controversy shocked
Afrikaner national sentiment into being, and the grant of responsible government gave it new opportunities for political expression.[1]
A sign of the times was the campaign on behalf of the Afrikaans
tongue set on foot by Arnoldus Pannevis, a Hollander schoolmaster,
and the Rev. Stephanus Johannes du Toit, predikant at the Paarl.
These enthusiasts were almost a secret society at first, but during the
heat of the Carnarvon confederation campaign they founded 'Di
Genootskap van regte Afrikaners . . . to stand up for our Language, 1875.
our Nation and our People.' The association found a voice in the
newspaper *Di Patriot*, edited by du Toit's brother, Daniel François,
(*Oom Locomotief*), but it met with much opposition from upholders
of High Dutch, an opposition which was redoubled when it proposed
to translate the Bible into Afrikaans. Of all its opponents one of the
strongest was Jan Hofmeyr, a rising power in the world of journalism
and politics. Stung by Sprigg's excise, which hit the Western wine-
farmers, always his staunchest supporters, Hofmeyr began to organise
the *Boeren Beschermings Vereeniging* (Farmers' Defence Union), an 1878.
association which might easily become a political machine. Next
year he took his seat in Parliament, but the really important move
was made by Stephanus du Toit. The censure on Frere encouraged
him to publish the principles of the Afrikaner Bond on July 4, a 1879.
notable day in the history of independence.

The Bond was intended to be Pan-Afrikaner and in spirit bitterly 1880.
anti-British, although membership was open to anyone, irrespective
of national origin or political and economic affiliations, who chose
South Africa as his fatherland and sought its prosperity.[2] It aimed
at fostering national feeling, protecting the interests of farmers,
encouraging the use of Afrikaans, securing a system of education
suited especially to rural white folk, and ensuring that no harmful
principles were advocated in the newspapers. It advanced so slowly
at first, however, that by the end of 1880, it could boast only fourteen
branches in the Cape Colony and one in the Free State. The Transvaal War of Independence then gave it a great impetus. Not only 1881.
were branches formed rapidly south of the Orange, but beyond that
river also. Chief Justice Reitz and Carl Borckenhagen, the German

---

[1] Hofmeyr, *op. cit.*, pp. 142 ff.
[2] Newton, *Unification of South Africa*, I. 86 ff. ; T. Schreiner, *The Afrikander Bond*, pp. 19 ff. ; Hofmeyr, *op. cit.*, pp. 195 ff.

editor of the *Free State Express*, organised several in their republic
with the war-cry 'Africa for the Afrikaners,' and during the critical
Volksraad debates on the ratification of the Pretoria Convention,
Commandant-General Joubert presided at the inaugural meeting
in the Transvaal. After the retrocession du Toit himself went north
to Pretoria as Superintendent of Education to reverse Burgers's
bilingual policy by insisting on the use of Dutch as the sole medium
of instruction in the schools, to press for the local manufacture of
munitions, to preach a United States of South Africa under its own
flag, and to curse Brand and Hofmeyr as tools of the British.

The real strength of the Bond, however, lay in the Colony.
Hofmeyr was alarmed at the rate at which branches of his *Beschermings Vereeniging* were being absorbed by the Bond. At first he failed
to persuade his followers to take up politics, but he gradually
brought them into action on the language issue. Dutch electors in
the Albert district had petitioned in the 'fifties for the use of Dutch
in Parliament. A local branch of the *Vereeniging* had recently revived
the claim, the Dutch Reformed Church supported the appeal, and
Hofmeyr, at that time a member of the Scanlen cabinet, moved in
that sense. It was at the end of a weary session and the matter was
1882. shelved, but next year the motion was carried without opposition,[1]
and at the same time, the recommendations of a recent Education
Commission were adopted permitting the use of Dutch as a medium
of instruction in first and second class schools at the discretion of the
school committees. Thereupon the *Zuid Afrikaansche Taalbond* was
formed to press the claims of Dutch and raise the standard of its
teaching in colleges and schools.[2] Thus fortified, Hofmeyr joined
issue with the Bond, whose aims and spirit he heartily disliked.
Independence might be the ultimate destiny of South Africa, but at
the moment it spelt cutting the painter and Transvaal domination
under Kruger or Joubert, in neither of whom had he any confidence.
1883. In spite of the resistance of the *Di Patriot* party, he succeeded in
arranging a conference between the Bond and the *Vereeniging* at
Richmond. There union was effected; Hofmeyr got the upper hand
and forthwith began his long struggle to transform the aims and
spirit of the Bond in the Colony.[3]

The background of Hofmeyr's campaign was hard times in all
South Africa. During the confederation struggle all had gone well
financially; the real value of money was rising all the world over;
South Africa was full of troops and contractors; exports rose and

---

[1] Act 1 of 1882, Eybers, p. 66; Walker, *De Villiers*, p. 149. For further legislation *re* use of Dutch *vide* Eybers, pp. 133, 136.
[2] Malherbe, E. G., *Education in South Africa*, p. 414.
[3] Hofmeyr, *op. cit.*, p. 649.

imports outstripped them; the output of Kimberley diamonds increased out of all knowledge. The formation of joint stock companies in Griqualand was accompanied by heavy speculation in mining shares, the first such speculation that South Africa had experienced since the copper boom of the 'fifties; but in the confidence begotten of the boom, Kimberley was given two additional representatives; the building of the new Houses of Parliament, begun in 1875, was resumed; Capetown built a reservoir, lit its railway station with electricity, carried on its breakwater sufficiently to shelter large vessels and built a graving dock. The ocean passage to England was cut down to three weeks and railways were undertaken to Hopetown, Colesberg, and Aliwal North on the road to the Diamond Fields.[1]

As with the Colony so with Natal. European immigrants were coming in faster than they had hitherto done, and though Indians were coming in still faster and showed few signs of going home again, the little colony was confident. The cable linked it to London by way of Aden, the harbour works at Durban promised well and the railway reached Maritzburg. On the eve of the expiry of the Wolseley constitution the great majority of the legislature demanded responsible government. This Lord Kimberley was willing to give provided Natal would pay for its own defence; but a general election fought on that issue resulted in nothing more than the addition of further elected members to the Council together with two nominees especially acquainted with tribal affairs, an innovation which had been urged on a recent native affairs commission by Shepstone and Bantu witnesses. For the rest, honourable members decided to get as much control of policy as was consistent with the retention of a considerable garrison.[2] 1879–1880. 1882.

The sky was soon overcast. First, phylloxera appeared in the vineyards of the Cape; then the over-capitalised diamond companies in Griqualand West, which had latterly taken to sinking costly shafts and wasting too much of their substance in riotous litigation, called up their share capital; the banks suddenly refused to make advances on the mining securities, and diamond scrip speedily fell to half its previous value. Illicit diamond buying was rampant in spite of Acts consolidating the laws upon the subject; the fall of masses of reef made the recovery of stones difficult and working expenses burdensome. The smallpox which had wiped out many of the Javanese in 1882.

---

[1] Amphlett, *History of the Standard Bank*, pp. 59 ff.; Gardner Williams, *Diamond Mines*, pp. 220 ff.; J. Van der Poel, *Railway and Customs Policies in South Africa*, p. 8.
[2] C. 3174 of 1882; C. 3796 of 1883; Eybers, pp. 201 ff.; Brookes, *Native Policy*, p. 71. Europeans in Natal in 1878 were 22,000; Indians, 12,825; Bantu, 290,000. In 1884 they were 35,453, 27,206 and 361,766 respectively. The Imperial garrison in 1882 consisted of two battalions and a cavalry regiment.

Capetown reached Kimberley, whence it spread over the Free State, in spite of sulphur fumigation at the frontier, to die away in the mountains of Basutoland. Drought accompanied disease and presently redwater fever slew the cattle from the Colony to Zululand. Under these circumstances public works in the coast colonies languished, especially as Bantu labourers worked much more slowly than European navvies and were inclined to indulge in stick fights.

1885.   The Cape Parliament Houses were finished, but the Cape and Natal railways only struggled forward slowly towards the Orange river and the passes of the Drakensberg.

The South African states were now in the trough of such a depression as they had not known since the 'sixties and were deprived of the co-ordinating influence of the Imperial Government. The retrocession of the Transvaal was a sign that that government had decided to interfere henceforth as little as possible in the affairs of South Africa beyond the borders of its own colonies. This self-denying ordinance was unavailing. Within a short three years, owing

1884.   to a breakdown of Cape native policy, it was entangled once more in Basutoland in the heart of the South African state system; in less

1885.   than five, as a result of Transvaal restiveness and German intervention, it had annexed St. Lucia Bay, extended a protectorate over the coasts of Pondoland and taken charge of all Bechuanaland from the

1886–   borders of Griqualand West to those of Matabeleland. A little later
1887.   it had taken over the bulk of Zululand, while the Cape had annexed nearly all the Transkeian territories.

There was little in 1881 to suggest that the Cape would ever take so bold a step. Its immediate problem was how to make some definite settlement with the Basuto and to decide whether or no it was to extend its rule over Kaffirland and Namaqua-Damaraland. Its prestige was gone from Basutoland, and Joseph Orpen, the Governor's Agent, was hard put to it to maintain some show of authority by personal influence and the support of the paramount chief, Letsie, who clung to him for fear of his brothers.[1] The tribes were much divided by the jealousies of their chiefs; traders and canteen keepers along the Free State border debauched them under the eyes of the helpless magistrates; the warriors still had guns which in many cases they declined to register. Scanlen insisted that he could not restore order by force unless he was allowed to abandon all Basutoland north of the Orange, settle friendly Basuto in part of Quthing and give out the rest in farms.[2] Kimberley refused. He would have no partition and was in no mind to take charge of four-fifths of a country which had been upset by Cape ministers. Scanlen therefore

[1] C. 3112 of 1882, p. 132; C. 3708, p. 24.
[2] C. 2964 of 1881, p. 27; C. 3112 of 1882, pp. 102, 107, 124.

cancelled both the Disarmament Act and the Robinson Award, threatened to confiscate the lands of all who resisted and tried to carry out his threat.[1] Chinese Gordon came from Mauritius to reorganise the colonial forces; but he overwhelmed ministers with 1882. contradictory telegrams, found it impossible to work with Jacobus Sauer, Secretary for Native Affairs, suggested that the defiant Masupha of Thaba Bosigo should be practically independent, and finally withdrew, saying that he would not fight against tribesmen whom he admired so much. So 'the sort of a war' smouldered on.[2]

Government was in a stronger position in Kaffirland. Fingoland and Griqualand East had been annexed to the Colony; most of the 1879. other districts were under Cape magistrates; disarmament had been carried out fairly effectively and, of all the territories east of the Kei, only the two Pondolands were fully independent. A modification of the Basutoland system was being extended to both classes of dependent districts based on the gradual substitution of the power of magistrates for that of the chiefs, the civilising of the tribes and the financial autonomy of the territories.[3] Legislation was by the Governor-in-Council on the usual terms and no Colonial Act applied unless specifically stated. Hicks Beach had asked for a statutory code of laws and provision for the extension of the franchise,[4] but Sprigg would only promise the franchise when the territories should become ordinary districts of the Colony. The vote was therefore withheld and the sale of liquor forbidden.

Civil cases in which Bantu only were concerned were tried from the first according to native law, an important principle borrowed from Natal. This principle was, in the main, upheld by a strong 1883. Native Law Commission, which none the less drafted a Transkeian penal code to supersede the native criminal law.[5] The chiefs still heard petty criminal and civil cases with an appeal to the magistrates; magistrates had wide jurisdiction subject to an appeal to the Chief Magistrate or, after 1882, to the Eastern Circuit or Supreme Courts; capital charges were heard by a court of three magistrates and, after 1882, by the Circuit Court. At the same time, the Fingos, the most advanced of all the tribes, began to raise a local rate, to which the Government contributed an equal amount, and spent it on local purposes through the magistrate and headmen who met as a board quarterly. Meanwhile, Europeans had already gone into Tembuland and Griqualand without leave. A parliamentary commission, there- 1882– fore, after much bickering among its members as to the amount of 1883. land which ought to be taken, cut off large areas along the base of

---

[1] C. 3112 of 1882, p. 129.   [2] C. 3493 of 1883 *passim*.
[3] Brookes, *Native Policy*, chap. iv.   [4] A. 3–80, pp. 13 ff.
[5] *Report of Commission on Native Laws and Customs*, G. 4–83 (Cape). The criminal code came into force in 1886.

13*

the Drakensberg mountains for European settlement.[1] Thus was Sir George Grey's projected colonisation of Nomansland in a measure effected.

Hicks Beach had also proposed that Basutoland and all the Transkeian territories except the Pondolands should be united as a single dependency of the Cape;[2] but under stress of a falling revenue and the Basuto fiasco, Scanlen began to swing round to the idea of handing them all over to the Imperial Government to be administered as a South African India, and Rhodes, soon to be Treasurer, bluntly stated that the Cape ought to annex land and not natives.[3] Scanlen did not act on the letters patent empowering him to annex Tembuland, Galekaland and Port St. John's, and, after a visit to Basutoland where he found even Letsie demanding direct Imperial control, sent Merriman to London to get rid of Basutoland at least. There was

1883. nothing else to be done. On the western Basuto border the sons of the late Moroko of Thaba Nchu were at each other's throats, rival Basuto chiefs were driving opponents into the Free State, and Brand, faced as Wodehouse had been with the spread of a neighbour's war

March to his own territory, called on H.M. Government to maintain order
1884. in terms of the treaty of Aliwal North. Great Britain therefore took over Basutoland on condition that the Cape paid that territory its fair share of the customs revenue.[4] The Imperial factor had its uses after all.

On the other hand the adjacent Transkei was not abandoned. A coalition of Thomas Upington, Hofmeyr and Sprigg defeated Scanlen at the general election on this issue and, rather than face it out in the House, Scanlen courted defeat on a minor matter connected with the

May phylloxera. So, as Rhodes muttered, the Scanlen ministry 'retired on
1884. a bug' whose 'nasty legs covered the whole of the Transkeian map'; the Cape retained its hold east of the Kei, and Brand incorporated Moroko's territory in the Free State.[5]

Developments in other directions were warnings that the Bantu could not only sway the white man's policy but were capable of taking a line of their own. In this same year of 1884, John Tengo Jabavu started *Imvo zaba Ntsundu* in English and his native Xosa, the first Bantu newspaper other than a few humble missionary publications. Further, the Ethiopian movement which had first shown itself

[1] G. 66 and 92-83; G. 2-84 (Cape).   [2] A. 3-80 (Cape), p. 17.
[3] Vindex, *Political Speeches*, p. 58.
[4] Act 34 of 1883; Eybers, p. 67; C. 3708, pp. 3, 22, 25, 39; C. 3717 of 1883, p. 141; Newton, *Unification*, I. 92 ff.
[5] Hofmeyr, *Hofmeyr*, p. 246. Upington Ministry: Thomas Upington, Prime Minister and Attorney-General; Jonathan Ayliff and, from March 4, 1885, onwards, John Tudhope, Colonial Secretary; Sir Gordon Sprigg, Treasurer; Frederich Schermbrucker, Crown Lands and Public Works; Jacobus Albertus de Wet, Native Affairs.

a dozen years back in Basutoland, reappeared in a more permanent form when an African preacher, Nehemiah Tile, seceded from the parent Wesleyan body and set up his purely tribal Tembu National Church in the Transkei.[1] The Native problems of the Transvaal were, however, more immediately pressing than such things as these. Nearly all the belated reforms carried out by the Royal Commission of 1881 were not unnaturally regarded as dead letters and, so long as native legislation was subject to the Queen's veto in terms of the Pretoria Convention, the Transvaal had taken no effective steps to deal with the native problem. The Native Locations Commission had marked out some reserves within the republic and failed to mark out still more, but that was all.[2] The Government was very poor, trade was bad and, for a time, the state was hard put to it to maintain its authority over tribes within the borders. In Lydenburg, Mampuru, successor to the deposed Secocoeni, murdered that unhappy chief, defied the authorities and fled to the caverns of Njabel, chief of the Mapoch group of clans, near Middelburg. Njabel refused to give him up and for eight long months kept the commandos at bay. It was a serious matter for the Transvaal, for another failure might have results similar to those which had followed Burgers's breakdown before Secocoeni. Already newspapers were hinting that another 'Basuto' débâcle would be ruinous to the prestige of the white man in South Africa; but two thousand burghers, Secocoeni's people and dynamite finished the war at last. Mampuru was hanged for murder and Njabel's tribe was broken up.[3]

Meanwhile, trouble had arisen on the Western Transvaal border. Even before the Royal Commission of 1881 had fixed the new boundary in the Keate Award Area, Montsioa, the 'pro-British' Barolong chief of Sehuba, had fallen upon his 'pro-Boer' kinsman Machabi of Polfontein.[4] The Pretoria Convention line, a compromise between the Keate line and that desired by the Transvaalers, ran right through the lands of the chiefs who had been in alliance with Burgers, and while the ratification of the Convention hung in the balance, Moshette, the Barolong chief of Kunwana, avenged Machabi by driving Montsioa away to Mafeking. Further south on the Griqualand West border, Mankoroane, ruler of Batlapin Taungs, attacked the 'pro-Boer' David Massouw, the Korana of Mamusa, who had assisted Moshette.[5]

All these chiefs relied on European supporters, who were to be paid, in the usual fashion, in land and looted cattle. The fighting was not serious in the south and there the Pretoria Government

Marginal dates: 1881–1884. 1882–1883. May 1881. Oct. 1881.

[1] E. Roux, *Time Longer than Rope*, pp. 86, 357.
[2] Brookes, *op. cit.*, pp. 126 ff.
[3] Theal, *History*, 1873–84, II. 136 ff.; Van Oordt, *Paul Kruger*, pp. 390 ff.
[4] C. 3098 of 1882, pp. 17, 24, 36.
[5] *Ibid.*, pp. 85, 107; C. 3381 of 1882, p. 73.

July
1882.
mediated peace. Mankoroane and Massouw both gave up land on which the steady-going Gerrit Jacobus van Niekerk founded the Republic of Stellaland, where he was soon joined by farmers from the various republics and colonies.[1] In the north, however, the fighting was fiercer for many of the borderers had had a bone to pick with Montsioa since 1868. Gey van Pittius, Moshette's agent, laid waste

Oct.
1882.
the country to the gates of Mafeking and, to gain time, Montsioa became a Transvaal vassal and gave up the best of his land. There van Pittius founded the Republic of Goshen.[2]

The petty republics of Stellaland and Goshen raised big issues.

.Oct.
1881.
The Transvaal, hard pressed for money and owing the Cape no gratitude for its past selfish customs policy, had levied duties on colonial produce, a protective policy in keeping with Boer instincts, but a sinister novelty in that a tariff wall was thereby erected for the first time within South Africa.[3] The two little republics, backed by Vice-President Piet Joubert and other Transvaal officials,[4] would, humanly speaking, soon be incorporated in the Transvaal, and they straddled right across the Missionaries' Road up which the trade of the Cape must pass to the interior. Rhodes was as quick to see the danger as ever John Philip, David Livingstone and David Arnot had been in their day. He urged Scanlen to get hold of the 'neck of the bottle' by taking over Mankoroane at his own request. It was in vain that he warned him that those Transvaalers who were behind the little western republics were 'bouncing' the road to the interior.[5]

1883.
Scanlen feared Hofmeyr, who at that time looked on the hinterland as the reversion of the Transvaalers, and refused Mankoroane's offer.

Meanwhile, the scramble for Africa had begun.[6] Livingstone and

1876.
Stanley had blazed the trails; the Brussels Conference, summoned by Leopold II of Belgium, had pointed the way towards an inter-

1878.
national exploitation of the Dark Continent; Bismarck and Disraeli at the Congress of Berlin had turned the attention of diplomatists to Africa to distract it from the manifest weaknesses of the 'peace with honour.' France took the hint with such vigour that her activities in

1882.
Tunis drove Italy, which also had ambitions in that quarter, into the Triple Alliance alongside of Germany and Austria, while Leopold, deeming international action impossible and scenting a more

1879.
excellent way, formed the Congo Association and raced France with

---

[1] Leyds, *Transvaal Surrounded*, pp. 95 ff., on the Volunteers: C. 3419 of 1882, p. 67 (peace); C. 4194 of 1884, pp. 7, 8; C. 3686 of 1883, p. 51. Stellaland was proclaimed formally on Aug. 7, 1883.

[2] C. 3486 of 1883, pp. 71 ff., 80.

[3] *Staats Courant* (*S.A.R.*), Nov. 10, 1881.

[4] Agar-Hamilton, *op. cit.*, pp. 185, 189, 227, 256.

[5] Michell, *Rhodes*, I. 157.

[6] On the Scramble *vide* Scott-Keltie, *Partition of Africa*; Hertslet, *Map of Africa by Treaty*; Fitzmaurice, *Granville*, II. 314 ff.; Rose, *Development of the European Nations*, pp. 508 ff.

much success for control of the Congo basin. Soon Great Britain was fairly entangled in Egypt, Italy was established in Eritrea and the French were next door at Obock. France also wrangled with Britain for control of the Niger, carried matters with a high hand in Madagascar and put her prohibitive tariffs into force on the Gaboon. It was certain that she would enforce these tariffs elsewhere. Great Britain therefore tried to save the Congo basin for free trade by con- Feb. cluding a treaty with Portugal, which recognised Portuguese claims 1884. far up the river on both banks, declared navigation free and provided for Anglo-Portuguese control of the basin.

It was not only the mercantilist imperialism of France that free-trade England had to fear. The Great Powers of Europe and North America were all adopting a protective economic policy; the new great industries demanded the products of tropical Africa; the formation of exclusive economic blocs was visibly taking place and, into the midst of the scramble, stepped Germany clad in shining armour. Bismarck had long ago declared himself opposed to colonies and fleets,[1] but missionaries, explorers, merchants and manufacturers of the Fatherland assembled in the Frankfort Colonial Society clamoured for a German empire in Africa. The Iron Chancellor gave way. The new Triple Alliance secured his rear; Russia was friendly; colonial expansion might assuage France's grief for lost Alsace-Lorraine and, duly encouraged, add to the embarrassments of Great Britain; German colonials were bristling against the British and Australians in Fiji, Samoa, Tonga and New Guinea, a Reichstag election was near, and the 'colonials' might hold the balance. He determined to twist the Lion's tail wherever he could lay hold of it.

Bismarck found an excellent handhold for that purpose in Namaqua-Damaraland.[2] True, Walvis Bay and the Guano Islands were British and British subjects held most of the concessions on the mainland; but nearly all the missionaries were German and Germans controlled most of the trade in ivory and feathers. The coast had long been vaguely regarded as being within the orbit of the Cape, but Kamaherero's request for protection had been refused and, on 1874. the withdrawal of the Transvaal trek-boers to Angola, the Hereros had once more fallen on the Hottentots. The Cape, busy with the 1880– Basuto, had merely cut off powder supplies and left them to fight 1881. it out, and the British Government, as in 1868, had replied in non-committal terms to German inquiries on the question of jurisdiction. Robinson indeed sent a warship and Cape volunteers to defend

[1] Fitzmaurice, *Granville*, II. 337.
[2] For the Namaqua-Damaraland negotiations *vide* Fitzmaurice, *op. cit.*, II. 347 ff.; also C. 2754 and 2783 of 1881; C. 3113 of 1882; C. 3717 of 1883; C. 4190 and 4625 of 1884.

Nov. Walvis Bay; but, almost immediately afterwards, Franz Lüderitz, a
1882. merchant of Bremen, bought tracts of land further south for the
usual rifles and money from the Namaqua chieftain of Bethany and
asked for German protection. Bismarck once more asked whether
German subjects might rely on British protection and, on being
told that H.M. Government would consult the Cape, assured
Lüderitz that Germany would protect his rights to any unclaimed
May territory. The agent of the Bremen merchant promptly acquired the
1883. harbour of Angra Pequeña and the adjacent area from a local chief
Oct. and hoisted the German flag. Presently a German warship cast
1883. anchor in the bay and warned off a British gunboat.

These negotiations contributed a deeper note to the clamour rising
along the Great North Road. Van Niekerk formally proclaimed
Stellaland, arranged provisionally for its union with Goshen and
together with his puppet, Massouw, asked for Transvaal protection.[1]
The reply would depend on the nature of the proposed revision of the
1883. Pretoria Convention. Kruger had recently been elected President by
a three to one majority over Commandant-General Joubert, and
was above all things anxious to regain his republic's old status of
complete independence. His hopes were rising, for Lord Derby, the
new Secretary of State, was reported to be well-disposed. Stephanus
du Toit, General Nicolaas Smit and he therefore went to discuss
matters in London.

Derby had to deal with a Parliament and public which were
alarmed at German competition and with Exeter Hall men led by
Lord Shaftesbury and inspired by the Rev. John Mackenzie, who
were determined to resist any extension of Boer authority over the
tribes.[2] Nevertheless, he met Kruger more than halfway. Under the
Feb. unilateral London Convention, native legislation was freed from
1884. the Queen's veto, the powers of the Resident were cut down to those
of a consul and the debt reduced by a third. On the other hand, all
Europeans were to be entitled to full civil rights and equal taxation;
there were to be no vindictive tariffs nor prohibitions on the importation of British goods and, sole remnant of the substance of suzerainty,
the Transvaal was to conclude no treaty with states other than the
Free State nor with tribes to the east or west without the approval
of H.M. Government. Kruger fought hard for the Road and even
offered to neutralise it, but the High Commissioner and Scanlen
were present to stiffen Derby's back and insist that there must be a
compromise. Finally the Transvaal was given a line which included
part only of Stellaland and Goshen and, in recompense for the
exclusion of the Road, saw all mention of the hated suzerainty

[1] C. 3841 of 1884, pp. 22, 23.
[2] W. D. Mackenzie, *John Mackenzie*, pp. 173 ff., 279 ff.; J. Mackenzie, *Austral Africa*.

dropped out of the Convention.[1] So the Transvaal delegates proceeded to Holland, Berlin, Paris and Lisbon and thence home,
whither they were soon followed by a young Hollander lawyer,
Dr. Willem Leyds, who became State Attorney in place of Jorissen,
dismissed once more.

Kruger had gained much for his state including the right to use
the old title of South African Republic, but he was faced with the
difficult task of getting the Convention ratified before the end of
August. When ratified the Convention would bind the Transvaal to
appoint commissioners to guard against irregularities on its western
and eastern borders and left H.M. Government free to do likewise.
Derby, as he was fully entitled to do, at once sent the Rev. John
Mackenzie as commissioner to Bechuanaland.[2] Mackenzie first made
a treaty with Mankoroane and then rode on to Vryburg, the capital
of Stellaland. There he found the townsfolk in favour of absorption
by the Cape and the die-hards withdrawing towards the Transvaal.[3]
He took control of the government as far as he could by appointing
the Administrator, Van Niekerk, as his assistant commissioner without asking his consent, and hastened on to Goshen where van Pittius
and Montsioa were once more at war. He arrived at a fortunate
moment, for the chief had just seized Rooigrond, the headquarters
of the Goshenites, and part of the new Transvaal territory. Mackenzie
therefore declared a British protectorate over Montsioa and all that
he held, raised police and returned to hoist the Union Jack at
Vryburg.[4] Thereat there was wrath in Pretoria and dismay in Capetown, where Upington, with an empty treasury, was nervously contemplating the annexation of Bechuanaland a year hence. The High
Commissioner bade Mackenzie lower his flag, and sent Rhodes
north to supersede him and co-operate with Joubert, the Transvaal
commissioner.[5]

Rhodes arrived at Taungs at the very moment that the Transvaal **Aug.**
Volksraad unwillingly ratified the London Convention and Germany **1884.**
proclaimed a protectorate over Namaqua-Damaraland.[6] Derby and
Granville had declared that any German claim on the coast up to
the Angolese border would infringe British rights and had pressed the
Cape authorities for arguments in support of the assertion; but the
tottering Scanlen ministry, fearing to incur expense, had returned

[1] Eybers, pp. 469 ff.; Leyds, *Transvaal Surrounded*, chapter xvi; Walker, *De
Villiers*, p. 180 n.; C. 3841 of 1884, pp. 106, 145 *et passim*; C. 3947 of 1884,
pp. 40 ff.
[2] Agar-Hamilton, *Road to the North*, p. 271.
[3] C. 4194 of 1884, pp. 3, 4, 13, 17.
[4] *Ibid.*, pp. 31, 40, 44; C. 4213 of 1884, p. 31.
[5] C. 4213 of 1884, pp. 12, 13. On Rhodes *vide* Michell, *Rhodes*, I. II., Basil
Williams, *Cecil Rhodes*; Fuller, *C. J. Rhodes*; Vindex, *Political Speeches*. A full
bibliography is given by Williams, *op. cit.*, pp. 331 ff.
[6] C. 4213 of 1884, p. 45; C. 4262 of 1884, pp. 3, 11.

no answer, and when Upington at last persuaded the Assembly to resolve to annex all up to the Portuguese frontier, it was too late.[1] Bismarck had recently renewed the Dreikaiserbund with Austria and Russia and had asked Great Britain for Heligoland to guard the outlet of the projected Kiel Canal. Troubles were thickening round Great Britain in Africa and the South Seas. Gordon had gone into the Sudan 'to smash the Mahdi,' while France was pressing forward on the Slave and Gold Coasts and had joined Germany in denouncing the Anglo-Portuguese Congo Treaty. Bismarck therefore told Granville that he could not show himself friendly to England in Egypt unless England were complacent elsewhere. Granville had no choice but to agree to a joint commission in Fiji and a German protectorate over the coast of South-West Africa.[2]

Personally, Bismarck was delighted with Granville's conduct, especially as he had also secured Togoland and the Cameroons in West Africa; but with an eye to the Reichstag elections, he blustered in public and declared that friendly relations depended on the denial of the Cape's claims to South-West Africa. The danger in British eyes was that Germany might stride across Bechuanaland and join hands with the Transvaalers or move north-eastwards to link up with the Protuguese or her own agents, who were already busy in East Africa. In either case the Cape would be cut off from the interior. It was no idle fear, for when Granville cautiously asked the German ambassador in London whether there was any possible connection between Germany and the Transvaal, he was coolly told that the question was 'one of curiosity.' Nevertheless, a German survey for a railway eastward from Angra Pequeña (Lüderitzbucht) was put in hand at once.[3]

Rhodes for his part resolved to extend the authority of the Cape over Bechuanaland as a necessary step towards acquiring Matabele-Mashonaland further north as an extension of the old Colony, to exclude the nerveless imperial factor, capture the central plateau 'and let who will have the swamps which skirt the coast.'[4] He induced the Stellalanders to submit to Cape rule provided their lands were assured to them; but Vice-President Joubert, the Transvaal com-missioner, forestalled him in Goshen, by inducing Montsioa to give himself and all his lands, save a tiny reserve, into the hands of van Pittius.[5]

Sept. 1884.

Joubert then made way for the Rev. Stephanus du Toit, the apostle

[1] Fitzmaurice, op. cit., II. 349 ff.; C. 4262 of 1884, p. 1.
[2] Fitzmaurice, op. cit., II. 351, 354; Cambridge Historical Journal, Oct. 1937 (article by W. O. Aydelotte).
[3] Fitzmaurice, op. cit,, II. 355, 359 ff.; Rose, Development, p. 523; E. A. Pratt, Rise of Rail Power, p. 304.
[4] C. 4194 of 1884, pp. 88 ff.; Hole, Making of Rhodesia, p. 16.
[5] C. 4213 of 1884, pp. 93, 97, 117, 123, 137; Agar-Hamilton, op. cit., pp. 351.

of the Pan-Afrikaner Bond, who promptly hoisted the Vierkleur
and published a proclamation by which Kruger somewhat enlarged
Montsioa's reserve and annexed Goshen provisionally, subject to
the consent of Her Majesty. Kruger had signed this proclamation
as the best means of compelling the British Government to take
definite steps to end the confusion on his western border, fully intending to withdraw if any objection was made.[1] There was objection
in full measure. In the Colony the newly formed Imperial League
demanded imperial intervention and the avenging of Majuba; in
Bechuanaland Rhodes saw unexpected virtues in the imperial factor;
in London the radical and philanthropic Joseph Chamberlain called
for strong action.[2] Kruger made du Toit lower his offending emblem
and withdrew his own proclamation.[3] But already Sir Charles Oct.
Warren was on the way to uphold British interests in the interior. 1884.

Behind all the froth of the agitation there was solid ground for
alarm. The West Coast was not the only desirable site in South Africa
which invited German occupation. Apart from Port St. John's, the
long Pondo coast was still unclaimed and, beyond Natal, the coast
was open as far as Delagoa Bay. In East Pondoland, Mquikela had
long protested against the Pondo line. He now applied to Natal for
a treaty, took to cattle-rieving, threatened to prevent troops from
marching along the waggon road from the Kei to the Natal border
and proposed to levy tolls on Cape waggons. Upington therefore Sept.
annexed Port St. John's as the only means of safeguarding Cape 1884.
trade; whereupon Mquikela attacked the Xesibes and tried to open
another harbour at Port Grosvenor. H.M. Government replied by Jan.
declaring a 'warming-pan' protectorate over the whole of the Pondo 1885.
coast and warned the Cape to annex such coasts as properly belonged
to it.[4]

In Zululand the situation was more complicated.[5] There, Wolseley's
thirteen chieftains had fought among themselves and called in the
usual white assistants so freely that H.M. Government had had to
restore Cetewayo as king. His kingdom was reduced in size; Usibebu Jan.
remained independent; the Reserve of Dunn and Hlubi along the 1883.
Natal border was put under a Resident, and Cetewayo's royal powers
did not include the right to make treaties or cede land without leave.[6]

[1] C. 4213 of 1884, p. 136; C. 4251 of 1884, p. 33; Walker, *De Villiers*, p. 184;
Leyds, *Transvaal Surrounded*, pp. 500 ff.
[2] *Cape Times*, Sept. 25, 1884; Michell, *Rhodes*, I. 196; J. L. Garvin, *Chamberlain*, I. 492; III. 10.
[3] Leyds, *Transvaal Surrounded*, p. 168 (note); C. 4213 of 1884, p. 104.
[4] On Pondoland *vide* C. 2586 of 1880; C. 4590 of 1885, p. 15 *et passim*;
Fitzmaurice, *op. cit.*, II. 370; G. 3-84 (Cape), pp. 15 ff.; G. 2-85, pp. 190, 196;
Act 35 of 1884.
[5] On Zululand and the New Republic (1882-7) *vide* C. 3182, 3247, 3270, 3293
of 1882; C. 3466, 3616, 3705 of 1883; C. 3864, 4037, 4191, 4124 of 1884; C. 4274,
4587 of 1885; C. 4645 of 1886; C. 4913, 4890, 5143 of 1887.
[6] C. 3466 of 1883, pp. 105 ff., 253.

Feb. War promptly ensued; the loyal Usutu were beaten, Cetewayo was
1884. driven out to die in the Reserve, and refugees crossed over to
colonial or republican soil.[1] For some time past Natal had pressed
in vain for leave to annex Zululand, whither she proposed to send
her own 'redundant' Bantu; but H.M. Government disclaimed
authority there.[2] The Transvaal, on the other hand, was debarred
from interfering by the London Convention. There were, however,
a few Boers living in Zululand. These were now joined by Lukas
Meyer and 300 others, who called on their kinsmen to come and
restore order. Men came from the republics and British colonies
inspired by a sense of 'a holy duty' to answer the appeals of the
Zulu chiefs and rescue the frontiersmen.[3] Perhaps the empty lands
beyond the Tugela and St. Lucia Bay acted as secondary inducements; but in any case they came, divested themselves as far as
might be of their former citizenship by their own declaration, and
May secured a cession from Dinizulu, son of Cetewayo, whereunder, in
1884. return for establishing his authority, they were promised as much
land as their leaders might consider necessary for the foundation of
an independent republic.[4]

Meyer and his men crowned the Zulu prince as a vassal king and
a few days later, with the aid of the Usutu, drove Usibebu into
the Reserve. The managing committee then presented its little bill
to Dinizulu.[5] So many men had been and were still being moved
by a sense of duty that full-sized farms for all of them would have
absorbed three-fourths of Zululand. The committee compromised
for about half, organised their New Republic round Vryheid as a
capital, invited Joubert to become President and sent surveyors,
including young Louis Botha, to mark out the frontiers.[6] Those
frontiers included St. Lucia Bay, where a German in the service of
the Transvaal acquired a large cession from Dinizulu. In response
to a rumour that he meant to sell it to an agent of the indefatigable
Herr Lüderitz, a rumour presently justified by the event, H.M.
Dec. Government bethought itself of Cloete's treaty of 1843 with Panda.
1884. It annexed the Bay in the interests of Natal. The plenipotentiary of the
New Republic sought help in France, Holland and Germany, while
Vryheid, Pretoria and Berlin protested in chorus, but the thing was
done. The only potential harbour between Durban and Lourenço Marques, with the possible exception of Kosi Bay, was in British hands.[7]

[1] C. 3864 of 1884, pp. 60, 104, 190; C. 4037 of 1884, pp. 13, 41.
[2] C. 4037 of 1884, p. 117.
[3] C. 4191 of 1884, p. 58; C. 4214 of 1884, pp. 83 ff.
[4] C. 4037 of 1884, p. 83; C. 4214 of 1884, p. 69; C. 4274 of 1885, p. 2; C. 4645
of 1886, pp. 33, 48; C. 4913 of 1887, p. 7.
[5] C. 4191 of 1884, p. 56; C. 4645 of 1886, pp. 33, 46.
[6] C. 4214 of 1884, pp. 69, 83, 107; C. 4274 of 1885, p. 29; C. 4645 of 1886,
p. 47. Joubert declined the proffered presidency.
[7] C. 4587 of 1885, pp. 12, 58, 76, 80, 89, 97; Fitzmaurice, *Granville*, II. 368 ff.

The Imperial Government still proposed that the Cape should have Bechuanaland, but Cape ministers and the High Commissioner could not agree as to terms, and the arrival of Warren to head the projected expedition northward ended the discussion.[1] Rhodes persuaded the Stellalanders to offer no resistance, Kruger warned the men of Goshen to expect no help, and Warren set off with 5000 men, British and Colonial. He and Rhodes met Kruger and agreed to Jan. beacon off the Convention boundary, and an Order in Council was 1885. issued providing for the administration of justice in Bechuanaland.[2] Unluckily Warren declared martial law and tried to upset Rhodes's Anglo-Afrikaner scheme of land settlement in favour of a purely British scheme. He pushed on to Mafeking to find the Goshenites fled, and, though the High Commissioner made him revoke his proclamation of martial law, he went on beyond the Molopo to tell the chiefs that all was now under British protection as far north as the 22nd degree and westward to the 20th degree of east longitude.[3] Warren was then recalled and, because the Cape Ministry still made difficulties and many Stellalanders petitioned against absorption by Sept. the Colony, British Bechuanaland south of the Molopo was pro- 1885. claimed a Crown Colony.[4] As for the tribal men of straw, the Imperial authorities declined to treat Mankoroane any longer as a paramount chief seeing that his exiguous reserve round Taungs was a den of horse-thieves led by Scotty Smith, the Turpin of the borderlands. Massouw, Mankoroane's rival, was even less lucky, for, when he refused to pay taxes or have Transvaal beacons in his territory, Joubert and the *staats artillerie* broke up his tribe and transformed his kraal of Mamusa into the dorp of Schweizer-Renecke.[5]

Warren's expedition, spectacular though it was, cleared the air. Germany and others realised that Great Britain and her colonies had interests in the interior which they were determined to maintain and, in the course of the next few months, most of the outstanding 1885– difficulties between Great Britain and Germany were amicably 1886. disposed of. True, Gordon was slain at Khartum; Dr. Gerhard Rolfs still struggled with Sir John Kirk at Zanzibar; Harry Johnston was hard put to it to forestall Karl Peters in East Africa and, in the Pacific, Bismarck was very active in New Guinea and Samoa. But Nov. the most dangerous African questions were settled at the Berlin Con- 1884– ference. All the great Powers save the U.S.A. recognised Leopold's 1885. Feb.

---

[1] C. 4275 of 1885, pp. 9 ff. *et passim*.

[2] C. 4432 of 1885, pp. 1 ff., 25 ff., 85 ff. *et passim*. Goshenites trekked much of Warren's baggage northward at £2 a day per waggon! (Pauling, *Chronicles of a Contractor*, p. 55).

[3] C. 4643 of 1886, pp. 57, 93; C. 4588 of 1885, pp. 57, 81; C. 4432 of 1885, pp. 48, 106.

[4] C. 4588 of 1885, p. 117; C. 4643 of 1886, p. 93.

[5] Van Oordt, *op. cit.*, p. 455; Agar-Hamilton, *op. cit.*, pp. 433 ff.

Congo Free State and agreed to treat the Congo, the lower Zambesi and the Shire as free rivers and their basins as free trade areas. They also laid down rules for the Scramble. To be valid, occupation of the coast lands must be effective and duly notified to the signatory Powers, and a Sphere of Influence—blessed word—was defined as an area in which a given Power admittedly had prior rights over all others.[1]

So the Anglo-Egyptian forces abandoned the Sudan; the Italians ensconced themselves at Massowah; the Royal Niger Company made good its hold in Southern Nigeria; France declared a protectorate over the Comoros and Madagascar, and Bismarck gave up such claims as he might have had on St. Lucia Bay and the parts adjacent in exchange for concessions in the Cameroons. The Reichstag elections were safely past; he had got most of what he wanted; France showed no signs of forgoing *La Revanche* and, besides, 'the Boers were not prepared to take any proper action' in the matter of St. Lucia Bay. He proposed 'to hold rather with the English' than with the French.[2] German pressure on Great Britain ceased as suddenly as it had begun, according to plan.

Oct. 1886. The way was now cleared for the recognition of President Meyer and his New Republic. This was accorded, but the little state was deprived of its seaboard and its protectorate over Dinizulu and, next year, Great Britain annexed the remains of Zululand.[3] That territory

1887. was placed under the Governor of Natal and a Resident, one of whose first acts was to banish the rebellious Dinizulu to St. Helena.

1884. The Cape, too, summoned up courage to take part in the scramble. It relieved the Imperial Government of Walvis Bay and, in the lands to the west of Natal, annexed Galekaland and Tembuland. It also prepared to end the growing confusion on the Pondo border, where Mquikela was taking toll on the waggon road, stirring up trouble with the West Pondos and driving recalcitrants into Griqualand East.[4] Bismarck, too, was still showing himself inclined to support the claims of a couple of German traders who were settled among other concessionaires on the East Pondo coast; white men were egging Mquikela on against the Xesibes, and Harry Escombe of Natal was negotiating with him with a view to annexation. A show

Oct.– Dec. 1886. of force by the Cape was all that was necessary. The Xesibes of Mount Ayliff were annexed at last to the Colony; Mquikela's claims over Port St. John's and the road through the Rode Valley were bought out; the two Pondolands were left independent for a season

---

[1] Fitzmaurice, *Granville*, II. 371 ff.; Hertslet, *Map of Africa*, p. 20.
[2] C. 4587 of 1885, p. 80; Rose, *Development*, p. 528.
[3] Act 35 of 1884 and 3 of 1885; C. 4980 of 1887, p. 60; C. 5892 of 1890, pp. 72 ff.; C. 5143 of 1887, p. 41.
[4] On Pondoland *vide* C. 5022 of 1887; C. 5410 of 1888; G. 5 and 30–86; G. 12–87 (Cape).

with a British protectorate over their coasts, and comparative peace reigned in all the Transkeian territories.[1]

Thus the whole coast from the mouth of the Orange round to the Portuguese border south of Delagoa Bay was in British hands save the narrow belt of Tongaland, wherein lay the harbour of Kosi Bay. Inland, a great wedge of British territory had been driven between the Transvaalers and the Germans up to the boundary of Matabele-Mashonaland, the reputed region of King Solomon's Mines.

SWAZILAND AND THE NORTH, 1884–94

The connection between the port and the mines was closer than would at first sight appear. It was supplied by the Transvaal. Kruger aimed at the formation of a great independent republic north of the Vaal with a port of its own on the Indian Ocean. The recent London Convention had not given him full liberty in the sphere of external policy, for though it left him free to make treaties with chiefs to the northward, it required him to seek Imperial sanction for treaties with those to the eastward or westward. Hence, if he wished to reach the blue waters of the Indian Ocean by way of Tongaland, he must get the Queen's assent thereto.

Kruger's prospects of success in either direction were complicated by the fact that the issues were not purely political. Political divisions in South Africa were ceasing to coincide with racial. Sentiment remained as a great force, but it was yielding to economic pressure and was itself becoming a dividing rather than a uniting force among Afrikaners. The Bond had failed as a Pan-Afrikaner institution. Kruger as triumvir had been pleased to see du Toit attacking Hofmeyr, a possible presidential rival; but once he himself had been elected President with the help of his fellow-Doppers, he frowned upon an association which might be used against him in future elections and already had Joubert, his most dangerous opponent, for a patron. The Hollanders, too, worked against du Toit, the apostle of Afrikaans, and backed by public opinion forced him to resign his Superintendency of Education. The President, who liked to have a predikant in that office, failed to save him and the disillusioned du Toit went home to the Cape. With his going, the Bond flickered out in the Transvaal.[2]

Its fate was much the same in the Free State, where Brand had from the first deprecated it as a possible *imperium in imperio* and a redundant school of patriotism in a Boer republic. In the Colony, the Bond became a purely colonial institution. Its formulæ were not finally worded to Hofmeyr's taste till 1889, but he gradually gained

(margin note: 1884–1889.)

---

[1] Acts 3 of 1885 and 45 of 1887; Eybers, pp. 69, 70; G. 10 and 10*a* (Cape).
[2] E. G. Malherbe, *Education in South Africa*, p. 267.

control of it through a small *Commissie van Toezicht* and made the institution itself a training-ground in politics for the Cape country folk.[1] So the Cape Bondsmen became loyal to the Crown, jealous for the rights of Afrikaners and strong to support or overthrow ministries, while the prudent policy of Robinson, the High Commissioner, did much to sweep away the suspicions which they and colonially-minded Englishmen had entertained for the Imperial factor.

For that very reason Cape Afrikaners were suspect in the eyes of the Transvaalers. There was jealousy mingled with that suspicion. The lot of the Transvaalers had been harder than that of the Free Staters and, still more, the Colonists. They were, and they knew they were, less versed in the arts of civilisation, though their leaders believed that given time and a fair chance they could reach the same level. Now, as the task of governing his republic became more complex, Kruger found that 'sons of the soil' might indeed hold office, but the actual work of administration had to be done by others. Cape men and even Free Staters he would not have. He fell back reluctantly on educated Germans and Hollanders and thereby annoyed his burghers, who objected to being patronised by some of these men as country cousins, and infuriated Afrikaners in other parts, who asked whether they too were not sons of the soil.

The Sinn Fein economic policy of the Transvaal inflamed all these jealousies. From the first, the restored republic, regardless of its restricted home market and lack of skilled men and experience, had granted concessions and set up tariff walls in the hope of thereby becoming self-supporting. The policy had the effect of endowing it with more industries of a sort than any other state in South Africa, but it naturally failed of its main object, irritated neighbouring communities, and aroused resentment among burghers and uitlanders alike, who must pay high prices to the concessionaires, many of them Continentals, for goods which were too often imported in virtually finished form.[2]

Rival railway policies also taught the Cape and the Free State to regard the South African Republic and, to a less extent, Natal as business enemies. Now that its trunk lines had reached Kimberley, Richmond and Aliwal North, the Cape desired to carry them on to republican soil and secure free trade throughout South Africa; but the farmers of both Republics rightly feared railways as deadly competitors in the transport-riding business and possible threats to their cherished independence. Of the two, the Free State was the more inclined to meet the Cape's wishes, but the Transvaal showed that it meant to go its own way when a rush took place to De Kaap on the alluvial Lydenburg goldfields and quartz was discovered at Moodie's

---

[1] Hofmeyr, *op. cit.*, pp. 208 ff., 652; Newton, *Unification*, I. 95.
[2] Cd. 623 of 1901, *passim*; *Staats Courant* (*S.A.R.*), Oct. 11, 1881.

hard by. Since quartz called for heavy machinery, some speedy, cheap and tsetse-proof connection with Delagoa Bay, the natural harbour, became imperative. Hence, while the Portuguese gave a concession to Colonel Edward McMurdo, a United States citizen, who floated a company in London to build a railway from Lourenço Marques to the Transvaal border, the republic gave a Hollando-German syndicate the monopoly of railway construction within its own borders.[1]

Natal, which still hoped to carry its railway from Durban into the republics, found it to its interest to work with the Transvaal, its hinterland, against the Cape Colony. The Free State, on the contrary, was pulled in two directions. As an Afrikaner republic it felt that it ought to support the Transvaal; but Transvaal tariffs were disconcerting and, as a community of producers and consumers, it looked towards the Cape ports from which railways already ran to its very frontiers while the Durban line was still far away. There were indeed signs that the Free State and the Old Colony might find it possible to work together economically. The Cape had retaliated against the Transvaal, but had given Basutoland a share of the customs revenue; Rhodes was already talking of a customs union; Hofmeyr won protection for Cape produce against overseas goods, a policy which would well suit the Free State, and Rhodes obtained a rebate on the 1883–carriage of goods to the Free State equivalent to the difference 1884. between the Cape and the lower Natal duties.[2]

At one stage there was even a hope that the Transvaal would be drawn south. Its finances and the popularity of its President were 1885. both at low ebb. The Free State had rejected petitions in favour of republican union for fear of falling under the limitations of the London Convention; McMurdo's railway had foundered temporarily in the mud-flats behind Delagoa Bay; the Hollando-German syndicate showed no signs of commencing operations, and the Warren expedition had shattered any hopes that Pretoria might have entertained of a railway linking it with the West Coast. Twice Kruger asked the Cape for a customs union and once even for the Jan. extension of the dreaded Kimberley line to Pretoria, for his Govern- 1886. ment had had difficulty in raising a loan of £5000 and the Volksraad had been driven to abolish four urban seats to save expense;[3] but though Brand suggested a general Zollverein and Rhodes renewed his entreaties, the hard-pressed Upington ministry let the golden opportunity slip. It was never recovered, for when the Cape presently suggested a customs conference, Natal replied with polite

---

[1] Cd. 623 of 1901, pp. 17 ff.; C. 5903 of 1890, p. 19.
[2] Hofmeyr, op. cit., chapters xix., xx.; Van Oordt, op. cit., pp. 455 ff.; Botha, Kruger en Leyds, chap. ix., x., xi. Vide passim, J. van der Poel, Railway and Customs Policies . . ., 1885–1910.
[3] Van Oordt, op. cit., pp. 454, 457; Cd. 2479 of 1905, p. 21.

generalities and the Transvaal refused point blank.[1] For the Struben brothers, Frederick and Henry William, had discovered gold conglomerate on the Witwatersrand to the southward of Pretoria; the news had leaked out to Kimberley, and the diamond lords were rushing to the High Veld. Mining areas were proclaimed on the Rand, where, in September 1886, Johannesburg began to take shape, the great Sheba mine was opened in Lydenburg. Thus the Transvaal which had hitherto been the Cinderella of the South African family suddenly blossomed forth as the Rich Relation.[2]

Hofmeyr, the Cape Bond and Sprigg, who had taken Upington's place as Premier in a reshuffled ministry, begged Kruger to talk business and not cause bad blood among brother Afrikaners.[3] Kruger's reply was uncompromisingly businesslike. He tried to force the Free State into the economic orbit of his state. McMurdo was

Jan. 1887. advancing once more under pressure and the Netherlands Railway Company, offspring of the Hollando-German syndicate, had at length begun to build the trunk line eastward from Pretoria. Where-

Oct. 1887. fore, Kruger met Brand and offered to renew the old treaty of amity and commerce in exchange for an offensive and defensive alliance, declined to hear of a real federation and insisted that the Port Elizabeth line must be kept out of the Free State for ten years to come. Brand refused to put his burghers at the disposal of the most unruly state in South Africa, especially as the Transvaalers talked of the need of a port through which foreigners might come 'with a view to future complications.' Nor would he have his hands tied in the matter of railways. With a Bond-supported Ministry at Capetown and Robinson as High Commissioner he was less fearful of southern influences than was his brother President.[4]

Brand then joined with Hofmeyr in securing a customs conference.

Jan. 1888. The Transvaal refused to attend and the Durban Chamber of Commerce successfully repudiated the work of the Natal delegates; but the Cape and the Free State agreed upon principles. In spite of the offer of a Natal branch line to Harrismith, the Free State Volksraad, by the casting vote of the chairman, sanctioned the extension of the Port Elizabeth line to Bloemfontein.[5]

July 1888. At this crisis Brand the peacemaker died and the railway war

[1] G. 42–86 (Cape).
[2] *The Gold Fields of South Africa* (1890); Glanville, *South African Gold Fields* (1888).
[3] Hofmeyr, *op. cit.*, p. 331; G. 37–87 (Cape). Sprigg Ministry: Sir Gordon Sprigg, Prime Minister and Treasurer; John Tudhope and, from Sept. 23, 1889, onwards, Henry William Pearson, Colonial Secretary; Sir Thomas Upington, Attorney-General; Frederick Schermbrucker, Crown Lands and Public Works; Sir Jacobus Albertus de Wet, Native Affairs.
[4] *O.F.S. Orangeboek: Rapport . . . Oct. 1887*; '*Times' History of the War*, I. 95 ff.
[5] G. 8–88 (Cape); C. 5390 of 1888.

went on. Rhodes, back once more in politics after consolidating the diamond interests of Kimberley,[1] still hoped that Kruger would allow the Free State line to pass through Johannesburg and Pretoria on its way to the Zambesi and the riches of Central Africa towards which his eyes were steadily turning. Hofmeyr shared his hopes and, together, the two men defeated Sprigg's proposal to extend Kruger's bugbear, the Kimberley line, to the Transvaal frontier. Rather than have that Kruger promised that, if only the Free State line would wait at Bloemfontein till the Delagoa line was within 200 miles of Pretoria, it might then come on and he would give free trade to the Colony.[2]

So Kruger gained time and concluded a close defensive alliance March with Francis Reitz, the sometime Chief Justice and now President 1889. of the Free State.[3] Each republic was only to be bound to aid its fellow if it thought that its cause was good, but the Free State was none the less drawn politically towards the north. Economically, however, it was drawn strongly towards the south, for though Natal's delegates withdrew from the customs conference, calling on the Imperial Government to defend their interests against those of the Cape,[4] the Free State joined with the Cape in a customs union. Then McMurdo's railway stopped again and Joubert talked of blocking the Delagoa line and admitting the Natal railway. Kruger wavered once more and promised that if only the Kimberley extension were stayed till the Delagoa line was finished, he would give free trade to the Colony. He was saved by the Portuguese, who seized McMurdo's June railway and carried it on themselves.[5] Even so, Kruger was ready to 1889. discuss free trade with the British Colonies, in spite of the fact that his Volksraad, not for the last time, showed itself more unyielding than he. And then the Delagoa line reached republican soil. The reply of the South came short and sharp. A syndicate headed by Rhodes and Alfred Beit had just secured a charter for the British South Africa Company to permit of the exploitation of 'King Solomon's Mines' in what was destined to become Southern Oct. Rhodesia, and it now contracted with the Cape Government to carry 1889. the Kimberley line northward through Bechuanaland.[6] Since Kruger would not have the Cape-to-Cairo railway through his republic, it should go along the boundary drawing to it the traffic of the western Transvaal.

The financial strength of the Rhodes-Beit syndicate lay in the diamond mines of Kimberley. The process of amalgamation had begun when joint-stock companies had come into being, and had

---

[1] *Vide infra*, p. 410.   [2] Hofmeyr. *op. cit.*, p. 348.
[3] Van Oordt, *Paul Kruger*, p. 498.   [4] G. 26–89 (Cape).
[5] C. 5903 of 1890.
[6] Hofmeyr, *op. cit.*, pp. 357, 384; *B.S.A. Company Report for 1889–92*, p. 3.

1882.   been hastened by the slump and heavy falls of earth which made
         individual working an impossibility. The need for unified control of
1885.   the industry was obvious. The extension of the Diamond Trade Act
         to the whole Colony and the compounding of tribal labourers did
         something to check I.D.B.; but that evil could never be ended till all
         the South African states were prepared to work together in this and
         in other matters. Meanwhile, on the abandonment of the open pit
         system, the various companies mined and countermined each other
         underground and sought to undercut each other in the law courts and
         the diamond market.

         Two men came to the front in the struggle: Barney Barnato, an
         East End Jew, and Cecil John Rhodes, son of a Hertfordshire parson.
         In the intervals of keeping his terms at Oriel, struggling with the
         men of Goshen and drawing up a comprehensive will which endowed
         Great Britain with the most desirable portions of the earth in the
1880.   interests of humanity, Rhodes had formed the Old De Beers Com-
         pany. With the constant help of Alfred Beit and the occasional
         assistance of Lord Rothschild, he joined issue with Barnato. Barnato
         held most of the famous Kimberley mine, the richest of all the
March   diamond areas; nevertheless, Rhodes won the game. Old De Beers
1889.   and the Kimberley companies made way for De Beers Consolidated,
         which soon acquired Bultfontein, Dutoitspan, a large share in the
1891.   Free State mine at Jagersfontein and, presently, the new Wesselton
         Premier near Kimberley. It thus controlled 90 per cent. of the
         diamonds of South Africa and therefore, in view of the comparative
         exhaustion of the Brazilian alluvial areas, the vast bulk of the
         diamond output of the world.[1]

         The diamond amalgamation was not complete before the Rand
         had begun to take the place of Kimberley as the political and
         economic centre of gravity in South Africa. Rhodes was directly
         interested in the affairs of the Transvaal in that he was one of the
         founders of the Goldfields of South Africa Company, but his hopes
         were centred on the Cape Colony and 'Rhodesia' far to the north.

         Rhodes's ideas, always hazy at the edges, when fully developed
         came to this: the Imperial Government was slow to scramble for
         Africa, therefore the Colony and his companies must annex as much
         of the unclaimed interior as possible. Given that, the Transvaal and
         Natal would surely be obliged to enter the customs union. As in the
         case of the German Zollverein, that customs union might speedily
         become a political federation over which the Union Jack would float
         as the federal flag while the republics kept their constitutions and
         their own flags for local purposes. In this federation, the old Colony
         would take the lead as the base of the advance northward and the

         ───────────

         [1] Gardner Williams, *Diamond Mines*, chapters ix., x.; Amphlett, *Standard
         Bank*, pp. 65 ff.; Williams, *Cecil Rhodes*, pp. 92 ff.

possessor of the southern terminus of the Cape-to-Cairo railway and Transcontinental telegraph which were to link up with the British systems in Egypt, form the trunk lines for any coastal connections through foreign territory and tap the labour supply of Central Africa for the gold-mines.[1] So, with a suitably low tariff and a preference for British goods in the widest sense of the term, the Empire would be provided with a solid economic bloc from end to end of Africa, the core of a possible Imperial Zollverein which might even become an Imperial federation. At the last, Rhodes, like Joseph Chamberlain, was to dream of the Empire, the United States and Germany allied to police a naughty world; but his abiding hope was a federation of the British Empire. The idea of such a federation was in the air. The Home Rule Bill, improving means of communication and the Queen's Jubilee had naturally turned men's thoughts in that direction; at the first Colonial Conference, itself a sign of the times, Hofmeyr had advocated a common customs barrier round the Empire against foreign goods which would thus pay for the maintenance of the Navy, at any rate in the first instance.[2] Be that as it might, for Rhodes the first step was to secure Matabele-Mashonaland, the domain of Lobengula, which lay just beyond the northern border of the Bechuanaland Protectorate.

Under the trust deed which Rhodes had forced upon the uncomprehending Barnato, De Beers was empowered to spend its profits on the northern expansion;[3] but if the British wedge was to be driven in to the valley of the Nile or even to the shores of Lake Tanganyika, it must be driven quickly. It was Rhodes's tragedy that he must always work in a hurry in a continent where men of rival nationalities were also busy driving wedges. In the centre Leopold was rapidly transforming the Congo Free State into a Belgian preserve, and though Great Britain and Germany had defined their mutual Nov. boundaries in East Africa, the borders of German South-West Africa 1886. were still debatable and might extend far across Africa. France and Germany had also settled their outstanding disputes and recognised May– the claims of Portugal to a wide lateral belt right across Africa from Dec. Mozambique to Angola in so far as those claims did not conflict 1886. with the rights of other states.[4] Germany from the west and Portugal from the east might easily meet on the middle Zambesi; it was becoming a question too how long Portugal would respect the Shire and lower Zambesi as open rivers. Lord Salisbury had protested Aug. against the claims of Portugal to part of Matabele-Mashonaland 1887. and the shores of Lake Nyasa on the ground that British subjects were specially interested in those areas.[5] But protests were one thing

---

[1] Cd. 1897 of 1904, p. 124.   [2] Hofmeyr, *op. cit.*, p. 297.
[3] Michell, *Rhodes*, I. 184 ff.; Walker, *De Villiers*, p. 196.
[4] C. 5904 of 1890, pp. 1 ff.   [5] *Ibid.*, pp. 7, 9.

and action another. Rhodes held rightly that occupation was the surest way of making any claims good. And the Portuguese had not shone as effective occupiers of African territory hitherto.

The acquisition of Matabele-Mashonaland, however, promised to lead to trouble with the Transvaal. The Boers were an expansive people. Those who had fled from the heretical Burgers in 1873 had only recently settled down in Angola; others were now peacefully penetrating Swaziland; others again were gazing at the grasslands beyond the Limpopo and reminding one another of their old treaty of friendship with Msilikazi, Lobengula's father, and arguing that the London Convention, by omitting to close the door definitely, had implicitly left the North to them as a sphere of influence. The clause which limited the treaty-making power of the Republic to the west and east had really aimed at preserving the road to that very North for British and colonial traffic, and the un-beaconed northern boundary of the Bechuanaland Protectorate apparently cut the Transvaal off from all access to it;[1] but however that might be, signs of what was coming had already appeared.

1885.   Lobengula had not been disturbed by the proclamation of the Bechuanaland Protectorate, though he had waxed wroth when his neighbour, Khama, the Mangwato of Shoshong, had offered the Queen lands between the Shashi and Macloustie rivers which he also claimed.[2] He knew something of white men, for his kingdom had long harboured the usual European advance-guard of missionaries,

1887.   hunters, traders and scallywags. Soon concession-hunters were busy in the Protectorate and presently they clustered round the Tree of Justice at Bulawayo. Among them was a representative of the ubiquitous Rhodes and Beit who reported that Lobengula desired British protection. Had not Msilikazi, his father, long ago signed a treaty of amity with D'Urban?[3]

July   The first treaty to the point was signed by one, Piet Grobler, who
1887.   entered into an alliance with Lobengula on behalf of the Transvaal and arranged for special privileges for burghers north of the Limpopo under the jurisdiction of their own consul.[4] Robinson announced that H.M. Government was willing to define the boundary of the Protectorate so as to leave the Transvaal a window open to the north; but as the activities of the concession-hunters at Bulawayo continued unabated and the Transvaal was said to be stretching the Grobler treaty to control the granting of all concessions, he sent the Rev. John Smith Moffat, son of the famous Robert Moffat of Kuruman and now assistant commissioner at Khama's, to safeguard British interests in Matabeleland.

---

[1] C. 4588 of 1885, p. 12.   [2] *Ibid.*, p. 12.   [3] *Ibid.*, p. 22.
[4] Leyds, *op. cit.*, p. 390.

Moffat induced the king to sign a treaty pledging him not to cede territory without leave of the High Commissioner and, in spite of Transvaal protests, Robinson ratified the treaty. He also sent up the Bechuanaland Police to Fort Elebi partly as a warning to the Republic and partly to prevent strife between the Matabele and the Bamangwato in the Shashi lands.[1] Meanwhile, Grobler had been appointed consul at Bulawayo. He rashly entered the disputed territory and was slain in a scuffle with one of Khama's subordinates. It was freely stated at Pretoria that the Bamangwato had been egged on by British officials. Kruger, however, was moderate as usual, except for an attempt to invoke foreign arbitration over a trivial point at the last moment; Robinson handled the ugly business tactfully and the incident closed with the payment of compensation by Khama in person at Pretoria.[2]

Now that Lobengula's dominions were safely within the British sphere, Rhodes made haste to stake his claims therein by sending thither as his agents, Charles Dunnell Rudd, his partner in the Goldfields of South Africa Company, James Rochfort Maguire, a Fellow of All Souls, and Francis 'Matabele' Thompson, an Eastern Province man well versed in Bantu languages. Helped by Moffat and the timely arrival of prominent British officials, this curiously assorted Oct. team at last secured the famous Rudd Concession, which, in return 1888. for 1000 Martini-Henrys, 100,000 rounds, £1200 annually, and, of all things, a steamboat to ply on the Zambesi, gave its holders the monopoly of the minerals in all Lobengula's kingdom.[3] That concession was upheld by the Imperial Government and ultimately became the basis of the British South Africa Company.

It now remained for Rhodes to keep the wavering king to his bargain and float a company which could utilise the concession. The first end was achieved more or less by his agents, Maguire and Thompson, and at one critical stage by Dr. Leander Starr Jameson, who, at Rhodes's request, abandoned a lucrative practice at Kimberley to 'keep Lobengula sweet' with that elusive charm and bantering tongue of his.[4] The second objective was not attained so easily. In London, the South African Committee headed by Chamberlain fiercely attacked the wholesale concession and the guns which were to be part payment for it. Lord Knutsford, the Secretary of State, winced at the guns and was not satisfied that it was wise to let loose a gold-seeking joint-stock company in tribal country. But he was assured that natives always put up the sights as far as they would go to make the guns shoot harder and that, therefore, such weapons

[1] C. 5904 of 1890, p. 16; Michell, *Rhodes*, I. 300.
[2] C. 5918 of 1890, *passim*; Walker, *op. cit.*, pp. 202 ff.; Leyds, *op. cit.*, pp. 396 ff.; De Waal, *With Rhodes in Mashonaland*, p. 30.
[3] C. 5918 of 1897, pp. 139, 146.
[4] Colvin, *Jameson*, I. 89. Hole, *op. cit.*, p. 67.

would be less dangerous in their hands than assegais, since then, with the revival of mercantilism, the day of the chartered company had come again in Borneo, Nigeria and East Africa, he was at last induced to consider permitting the formation of a similar company under a Royal Charter in Southern Africa.[1]

Mackenzie and a strong section of the London Chamber of Commerce demanded, on the contrary, direct rule by the Crown in Matabeleland. Two distinct schools of Imperialism had taken shape in the heats of the Irish controversy. The one, the Home Rule school which included Rhodes, Hofmeyr, Sir George Grey in his old age, and all who took the 'colonial' view, held that expansion must be carried out by the self-governing colonies as active agents and initiators; the other, the Unionist, held that the Imperial Government must act and rule even though that rule might give way ultimately to colonial control. It was on Unionist principles that Warren and Mackenzie had fought Rhodes's Bechuanaland settlement and, more recently, had striven with the open sympathy of Chamberlain, the Radical supporter of Salisbury's Tory ministry, to separate the powers of the High Commissioner, who was responsible only to the Queen, from those of the Governor of the Cape, who must follow the advice of his ministers. Robinson had successfully defended his double powers at the cost of a personal quarrel with Knutsford. His term was ending, but it was confidently hoped in Capetown and in Pretoria also that he was merely going home to be reappointed. He destroyed all hope of that by his own act. On the eve of his departure he declared as his own personal opinion, but for all the world to hear, that there was no room for the action of the Imperial factor on a large scale in the internal affairs of South Africa.[2]

So Robinson sailed and Sir Henry Loch, a staunch unionist, was appointed to take his place, while Rhodes and Beit added many concessions in Bechuanaland to the all-important Rudd concession. A rival group led by Lord Gifford was, however, strongly entrenched in the Protectorate; yet another group had a footing in Matabeleland; worse still, Lobengula repudiated the Rudd concession, the usual fate of such documents, and, to appease his young bloods, executed the induna who had most markedly favoured the concessionaires.[3] Rhodes and Beit therefore joined hands with their principal opponents, made the necessary financial arrangements with De Beers, applied for a charter covering the Protectorate and what is now Southern Rhodesia, and even went so far as to offer to share

1888.

April
1889.

---

[1] C. 5918 of 1890, pp. 129, 154, 180.
[2] C. 4839 of 1886, pp. 100 ff.; C. 4890 of 1886, p. 28; C. 5488 of 1888, pp. 16 ff.; Newton, *Unification*, I. 97, 102; Walker, *De Villiers*, p. 206; Mackenzie, *Mackenzie*, pp. 416 ff.; Vindex, *op. cit.*, p. xxxi.
[3] C. 5918 of 1890, p. 201; Hole, *Making of Rhodesia*, pp. 107, 113.

with H.M. Government the cost of a telegraph line to Mafeking and to pay for a British Resident at Bulawayo, who should give moral support to their projected company.[1] That company was to carry the railway and telegraph lines northward, encourage immigration, promote trade, and 'develope and work mineral and other concessions under the management of one powerful organisation, thereby obviating conflicts and complications . . . and securing to the native chiefs and their subjects the rights reserved to them under the several concessions.' At length the charter was issued to the British South Oct. Africa Company. Two stipulations and one warning the Crown gave. 1889. The Duke of Fife, the Duke of Abercorn and Albert (Earl) Grey were to become directors to give something more than a mere financial tone to so potentially powerful an association, and the rival concessionaires, whose name was legion, must be bought out to avoid the troubles which were afflicting Swaziland; finally, the directors were reminded that, though the Charter gave them the faculty of exercising wide powers in Lobengula's dominions, those powers could only become real with that sovereign's consent.[2]

So far, so good; but the other Richmonds in the field had not been idle. England's 'most ancient ally' was making trouble on both sides of the lower Zambesi. Portugal had closed that river and seized Jan. a British ship, while Serpa Pinto was wrestling with Harry Johnston, 1888. consul at the Blantyre mission, for control of the Shire river and Lake Nyasa, not without the use of force against the Makololo.[3] Portuguese control over the eastern coast belt had somewhat improved of late, though the semi-independent *prazo* owners with their fighting tails of blacks were still a danger to the Royal authority. Pinto now proposed to push up the Zambesi and then southward down one of its tributaries to meet Colonel Paiva d'Andrada, administrator of the Mozambique Company, who claimed great concessions in Gazaland and Manica and the Mazoë valley. Soon d'Andrada was claiming that he had reasserted control over Gungunhana, king of the Shangaans in Gazaland, and over the Mashona of the hinterland up to the line of the Sabi river, who had long been vaguely regarded as Portuguese subjects and were reported never to have seen the Matabele who claimed them as 'dogs.'[4] Portugal tried in vain to bring Germany into the negotiations with Great Britain, but Salisbury ridiculed her vast claims based on forts in ruins, like Portuguese influence. He threatened to reply with force if the pro- Jan. tected Makololo were again interfered with, and followed this up 1890.

---

[1] C. 5918 of 1890, p. 195; *B.S.A. Co. Report*, 1889-92, p. 2.
[2] Eybers, *Select Documents*, pp. 559 ff.; C. 5918 of 1890, pp. 189, 224.
[3] C. 5904 of 1890, p. 13.
[4] D'Andrada, *Manica* and *Report*; C. 5904 of 1890, pp. 65, 76, 80, 223.

with an ultimatum before which Portugal fell back pending a general settlement of boundaries.[1]

The Chartered Company was thus left face to face with the Transvaal. Kruger had no particular ambitions in the North, but he earnestly desired Kosi Bay in Tongaland. To reach that port he must pass through or acquire Swaziland, whose independence had been guaranteed by the London Convention, and the lands of Mbegisa and Zambaan, two petty chieftains ruling on either side of the Maputa river between the Swazis and the Tongas. Finally, he must come to terms with Zambili, queen of the Tongas. His power to make treaties with all these chieftains was limited by the London Convention.[2]

Swaziland was surrounded on three sides by republican soil, the grazing was valuable to burghers, and Kruger naturally hoped to renew the control which his state had exercised there between 1875 and 1881. But Natal also desired to have Swaziland; wherefore one of the Shepstones and Joubert manœuvred against each other for a protectorate, while Mbandine the king gave grazing rights and concessions of the most amazing scope, variety and intricacy to anyone who would supply his wives and councillors with champagne and himself with greyhounds.[3] Once the New Republic had been recognised and Zululand annexed by Great Britain, Swaziland came to the front. Theophilus (Offy) Shepstone the younger had become agent and adviser to the harassed Mbandine, but the British Government declined to recognise him officially and suggested a joint British-Transvaal inquiry. 'Offy' and the concessionaires then elected a committee to govern the Europeans in Swaziland, and H.M. Government, seeing the hope of peace, dropped the idea of an inquiry. At the same time it took the Tongas into the British sphere by treaty and erroneously took with them Zambaan and Mbegisa.[4]

July 1887.

July 1888.

The next move in the complicated game was the absorption of the New Republic by the Transvaal as the district of Vryheid and the acquisition of the most essential Swazi concessions by the enlarged republic. The Transvaal was thus in a position to prevent any settlement in that distressful country without its goodwill. It now declared that Zambaan and Mbegisa had been included in the Tonga treaty wrongfully, and the two chiefs, protesting their independence, asked for Transvaal protection.[5] Mbandine, for his part, dismissed Shepstone and entrusted himself to one, Miller, who forwarded a request for British protection, a request which was seriously discounted by

Feb. 1889.

---

[1] C. 5904 of 1890, pp. 70, 201, 206 ff.
[2] On Swaziland vide C. 5089 of 1887; C. 5918, 6200, 6201 of 1890; on the port vide Botha, *Kruger en Leyds*, chap. xii.
[3] C. 5089 of 1887, *passim*.   [4] C. 6200 of 1890, pp. 11, 40 ff.
[5] *Ibid.*, pp. 58, 85, 110, 140.

the fact that the king granted a startling concession which virtually put the control of his foreign policy into the hands of Hermann Eckstein, a Johannesburg German and friend of Kruger. Kruger April therefore privately told Robinson that he would withdraw his claims 1889. in the north and west if he might have a free hand in the lands of Mbandine, Zambaan, Mbegisa and Queen Zambili.[1]

Kruger had good hopes of success, for the High Commissioner knew that Mbandine was playing double and had already roundly stated that Swaziland must come under the rule of either Great Britain or the Republic; but Kruger's letter reached Robinson at the moment of his departure and the later official message thus had no chance of serious consideration till the new High Commissioner, Sir Henry Loch, should arrive in December. Undeterred, the majority July of the Europeans in Swaziland declared in favour of Transvaal rule 1889. just as the Volksraad showed finally that it would have nothing to do with any customs or railway union with the colonies.[2] H.M. Government therefore revived the idea of a joint commission for which Kruger had asked; but before the members could meet, Mbandine died leaving the Queen Dowager to rule with Offy Shepstone once more as adviser. All that the commission could do, in Dec. face of a renewed request by the whites for Transvaal rule, was to 1889. set up a joint government of three to control them for four months in place of the corrupt committee of concessionaires.[3]

Loch arrived to find all the complicated issues of South African politics coming to a head. In the midst of the confusion, Bowler, a burgher of British origin, announced his intention of leading a Transvaal trek into Mashonaland. Kruger, anxious to come to terms with Great Britain, forbade the trek and, in spite of Loch's somewhat unnecessary demand that he should hold himself responsible for any violation of British territory in the north, wisely invited the High Commissioner to meet him and discuss the general situation.[4]

The ensuing conference at Blignaut's Pont was not so representa- March tive as had been expected, for, though Rhodes attended, neither 1890. Sprigg nor Reitz was present. Loch had in his hand the report of the British Commissioner to Swaziland recommending that the Transvaal should be allowed to rule the Swazi whites and annex Mbegisa's land, and in return be asked to promote British interests in the north, give free entry to South African produce, permit either the Cape or the Natal railway to cross its borders, and join a customs union with one or other of the colonies. Thereafter, the

[1] C. 5918 of 1890, p. 190; C. 6200 of 1890, pp. 116, 135, 160.
[2] Van Oordt, op. cit., p. 506.
[3] C. 6200 of 1890, pp. 105, 115, 130, 163, 204, 237, 240.
[4] Leyds, op. cit., pp. 429 ff.; C. 6217 of 1890, p. 14.

14

Republic might have a railway strip through Swaziland and an area at Kosi Bay in Tongaland subject to British rights of pre-emption. Zambaan, however, must come to Zululand.[1]

Discussion at the conference turned mainly on Swaziland and the port.[2] Loch was under orders to demand joint rule over the Swaziland Europeans and to deny the Republic sovereign rights over the railway strip through that territory. He refused to bargain for a Transvaal withdrawal in the north by giving the Republic sovereignty over Swaziland, and insisted that Kosi Bay and the railway strips must be purchased at the price of entry into a customs union. Kruger regarded withdrawal in the north as the *quid pro quo* for British withdrawal in the east, for he knew that the prospect of land in Swaziland was the only means of assuaging the disappointment of Joubert and his supporters, who were set upon a northward expansion. Rhodes at least agreed that that was the bargain, and Loch went so far as to assent to the annexation of the Little Free State on the Swazi border which Mbandine had ceded to a Transvaal official, to promise to help Kruger to make the treaties that would clear his path to the sea and, at the last moment, to recommend that he should have Mbegisa's lands and a sovereign strip through Swaziland. Kruger agreed to an extension of the life of the joint government in Swaziland and, since he could not bind himself to anything more without the consent of his executive council and Volksraad, satisfied Loch with a promise to recommend the proposed terms to his executive.

Soon Kruger was complaining that the bargain was too hard. His position was very difficult. At the Pont, he had gone as far as he could personally to accept what Loch called a provisional agreement; but though he presently admitted he had no objection to that agreement in principle and even submitted it to his executive, he soon found that it was as much as his place was worth to press it on them and still less upon his Volksraad and burghers, incensed as they were against the British by the folly of certain irresponsibles who had insulted the Vierkleur on his journey through Johannesburg to Blignaut's Pont. Loch had indeed secured some concessions for him; but the Imperial Government still refused to recognise sovereign rights over the Swazi strip and shelved the matter of Mbegisa, while Loch now sent him a signed draft of the convention, named a date for ratification[3] and proceeded to organise police to support a British commissioner in Swaziland in terms of the London Convention in case ratification should not be forthcoming.

June 1890.

---

[1] C. 6201 of 1890, pp. 5 ff.

[2] C. 6217 of 1890, *passim*, for Loch's report on the Conference and negotiations ending with the ratification of the First Swaziland Convention. *Vide* also Hofmeyr, *op. cit.*, chapter xxiii.; Leyds, *op. cit.*, chapters xxxviii.–xl.

[3] C. 6217 of 1890, p. 15.

To ease the strain Loch also sent Hofmeyr to Pretoria and, at the end of protracted negotiations, authorised him to promise that once joint rule had been established over the Europeans in Swaziland and the work of the proposed concessions court completed, the British Government would consider any other points which the Republic might raise with a desire to meet them.[1] Kruger was immensely relieved at the proposal and the executive at last gave way.[2] All mention of the doings at the Pont was omitted; everything save the Swazi-Matabeleland clauses was made dependent on the entry of the Transvaal into a customs union within six months of acquiring the port and the railway strips, and either party was left free to denounce the convention if it were not fully carried out within three years.[3] The Volksraad ratified this First Swaziland Convention as a temporary measure and intimated that it had no wish to share in the disputes pending between the British and the Portuguese.

Rhodes meanwhile made all haste to occupy Mashonaland. The immediate prospects of his Company depended on that, and all his schemes depended on his Company. It must prove itself a financial success if it was to get the funds it required from the investing public and, to do so, it must find the expected New Rand north of the Limpopo quickly. If the New Rand were found, the rush of Europeans thither would make Charterland and not the Transvaal the coming economic centre of South Africa capable of dictating, in conjunction with the Cape, the terms of the economic federation and possibly of the political federation which was to follow. A large white population would also be able to relieve the Company of the task of administration, which it naturally had no intention of retaining longer than it must, and would leave it free to build railways.[4] Given speedy development, the railways would soon pay off the debentures with which they were financed and furnish large dividends on the handful of actual shares, nearly all of which were in the hands of the Company and its friends.[5] Moreover, Rhodes proposed that only companies should be allowed to mine and, in each of them, the Chartered Company was to take anything up to 50 per cent. of vendor's scrip on flotation instead of royalties.[6] Thus, if all went well, the B.S.A. Company would become a great gold trust drawing revenue from subsidiary companies.

Finance and politics alike called for speed. Rhodes tried to form a South African board of control for his Company, but as neither

Aug. 1890.

[1] C. 6217 of 1890, p. 17. [2] Hofmeyr, op. cit., pp. 400 ff.
[3] C. 6217 of 1890, pp. 3 ff.
[4] Vindex, Political Speeches, and early Reports of the B.S.A. Company, passim.
[5] B.S.A. Co. Report, Dec. 19, 1893, p. 3, and Jan. 18, 1895, pp. 3 ff.
[6] Ibid., 1889–92, p. 18; B.S.A. Co. Annual Meeting, Nov. 29, 1892, p. 9.

Hofmeyr nor Chief Justice de Villiers would serve upon it, he gave up the idea and himself received the Company's power of attorney in Africa.[1] He was more successful in winning general support for his schemes by the judicious distribution of shares among Bondsmen and others,[2] and in arranging with three contractors who were to raise 200 Pioneers, cut a road to Mount Hampden and build forts to guard it. Jameson was sent to get the necessary leave of entry from the King. His name smelt sweet at Bulawayo, for Lobengula remembered that 'the Doctor' had cured him of his gout and that, during his last visit, a letter of commendation from the Queen herself had arrived borne by four magnificent lifeguardsmen in a bright-red coach, a letter which Jameson had tactfully reworded.[3] Now Loben-
May 1890.
gula gave his consent or, rather he did not withhold it; Frederick Courtenay Selous, the mighty hunter who was to guide the column, began to cut the Road, and the Pioneers moved up to Macloutsie. Apart from the fact that they were to be accompanied by 500 B.S.A. Company Police and a body of native labourers, the Pioneers were just such a force as had followed Lukas Meyer into the New Republic even in the matter of promised payment in gold claims and, as soon as the Company should be in a position to grant land, a farm of 3000 acres apiece.

Rhodes tried to start them off into Mashonaland at once, but Loch threatened to have the Charter cancelled if he moved them before he himself was satisfied that they could move without imperilling themselves and the peace of South Africa.[4] It was only at the end of June that they started on their 400-mile march. Loben-gula, perhaps alarmed at the size of this party of 'men to dig gold,' perhaps finding it necessary to placate his warriors, half-heartedly ordered them back; but Loch moved the Bechuanaland Police up to Fort Elebi and so secured the column a safe passage. Forts were
Sept. 12, 1890.
built *en route* at Tuli, Victoria and Charter, Salisbury was founded and the Pioneers were disbanded.[5] Meanwhile, beyond the Zambesi, on June 27, 1890, Frank Lochner had signed a treaty with Lewanika, Paramount Chief of the Barotse, by which the latter accepted British protection and gave the Company full commercial and mining privi-leges. Alfred Sharpe and Joseph Thomson then acquired similar concessions from the leading chiefs between Lake Nyasa and the frontier of the Congo Free State; but they failed to gain the rich

[1] Walker, *op. cit.*, p. 208; Hofmeyr, *op. cit.*, p. 388; Williams, *Cecil Rhodes*, p. 141.
[2] Michell, *Rhodes*, I. 276.
[3] Colvin, *op. cit.*, I. 120; Leyds, *op. cit.*, p. 425; C. 5918 of 1890, p. 237.
[4] Walker, *De Villiers*, p. 224.
[5] On the founding of Rhodesia *vide* A. R. Colquhoun, *Matabeleland*; A. Darter, *Pioneers of Mashonaland*; Hole, *Making of Rhodesia*; B.S.A. Co. *Reports*; A. G. Leonard, *How We made Rhodesia*.

copper-bearing Katanga area, which the Nova Scotian, Captain William Stairs, snapped up under their noses for Leopold II.[1]

The foundations of Rhodes's federation were now well on the way to completion. The Swazi Convention had been ratified, Mashonaland occupied and various important boundary questions apparently settled. An Anglo-German Convention gave Germany Heligoland July in exchange for Zanzibar, and a frontier in South-West Africa, which, 1890. to Rhodes's unconcealed disgust, embraced the long Caprivi Zipfel running up to the middle Zambesi. Similarly the first Anglo- Aug. Portuguese Convention left Manicaland south of the Zambesi to 1890. Portugal, but gave Great Britain Nyasaland and a Portuguese promise to build a railway from the new port of Beira to Mashonaland and to open the Pungwe river to traffic.[2]

Rhodes's base in the Colony was also secure. He had taken little part in politics from 1884 till 1888, but thereafter he had drawn near to Hofmeyr. Racialism was apparently dead; always essentially a countryman, he felt more at home with Afrikaner farmers than with British townsfolk; the aims of the Bond approximated to his own Home Rule policy; he shared Hofmeyr's views on such matters as an Imperial Zollverein, Protection and Natives. Hofmeyr, for his part, preferred the Chartered Company to the Crown in the North and showed no inclination to tax diamonds in spite of the hold on the electoral machinery which he was perfecting through the *Commissie van Toezicht*, a supervising committee manned by himself and two other Bondsmen. Sure of the support of the Bond, Rhodes joined Sauer in defeating Sprigg's schemes for local railways. Sprigg July resigned and Rhodes became Premier at the head of a cabinet which 1890. included some of the ablest parliamentarians and administrators in the Colony, notably John X. Merriman and James Rose-Innes, son of Somerset's famous Scottish schoolmaster.[3]

Rhodes's powers were thus immense. He was Prime Minister of the Colony and controller of De Beers at Kimberley, of the Goldfields Company on the Rand, and, as far as Africa was concerned, of the Chartered Company itself. He hoped that British Bechuanaland would soon come to the Colony and the Protectorate to the Company and that, if all went well, Matabeleland on one side and Manica-Gazaland on the other would be added to Mashonaland. Kruger was, of course, an obstacle, but if Gazaland were secured,

[1] *Report on the B.S.A. Company's Proceedings and the Condition of the Territories within the Sphere of its Operations, 1889–97.*
[2] C. 6212 of 1890, pp. 4 ff.; Michell, *Rhodes*, I. 287; Eybers, p. 567.
[3] Hofmeyr, *op. cit.*, chapter xxii.; Williams, *op. cit.*, chapter xiii. First Rhodes Ministry: Cecil John Rhodes, Prime Minister and Crown Lands and Public Works; Sir James Sivewright, Without Portfolio and then, from Sept. 24, 1890, onwards, Crown Lands and Public Works; Jacobus Wilhelmus Sauer, Colonial Secretary; John Xavier Merriman, Treasurer; James Rose-Innes, Attorney-General; Pieter Hendrik Faure, Native Affairs.

the Delagoa line would be cut below Komati Poort and he must come to terms. The High Commissioner was more immediately obnoxious. His multiplicity of offices and functions could alone rival those of Rhodes; he was as determined a man as Rhodes himself; it was not his wish that Rhodes was Premier, for he had asked Sauer to form a ministry first; he did not like chartered companies and was resolved that there should be no change in the status of either of the Bechuanalands until he could persuade H.M. Government to annex the Protectorate outright. He had already taken power by Order-in-Council to exercise jurisdiction there and, if he had to give up British Bechuanaland, he meant to have the Protectorate as an imperial base in close touch with Rhodes's growing empire in the North.[1]

Loch might grumble, but fortune favoured Rhodes. The Portuguese did not ratify the Convention and Salisbury declared that Great Britain's hands were free.[2] The Company's agents were already busy in Manica and now secured a concession from Mutassa, a vassal of Gungunhana the Shangaan whom the Portuguese claimed in his turn as a vassal.[3] The Portuguese champion, d'Andrada, ventured up to Mutassa's kraal. He was ignominiously arrested and sent home by way of Capetown, while the terrible Company tried to make good a treaty which it had just signed with Gungunhana himself giving it all Gazaland including Beira.[4] An East Coast port was as much a matter of life and death to the Company as it was to Kruger, for transport to Mashonaland from the south cost seven times as much as from Beira along the Pungwe river route, and with the coming of the rains, the Pioneers were short of supplies and practically cut off from the south by flooded rivers. The Company Nov. was doomed to disappointment. Great Britain signed a *modus* 1890. *vivendi* with Portugal reopening the Pungwe route; Gungunhana declared himself a subject of His Most Faithful Majesty; Jameson was arrested running guns to him on the Limpopo, and the Portuguese closed the Pungwe.[5] Rhodes sent a friend with a party of labourers to Beira to make good his entry or to get himself fired on ('they will only hit him in the leg,' said Rhodes the optimist), but no fruitful incident developed till the Portuguese rashly exposed May themselves to defeat at Massikessi in the very month that the *modus* 1891 *vivendi* ran out.[6] Parties of the Company's men at once scattered eastward seeking concessions; but Lord Salisbury called a halt,

---

[1] Walker, *op. cit.*, pp. 224, 241.   [2] C. 6212 of 1890, pp. 19, 23.
[3] *B.S.A. Co. Report*, Nov. 29, 1892, p. 6; C. 6495 of 1891, p. 218.
[4] C. 6495, p. 193, *et passim* for details of this bickering; also D'Andrada, *Manica* and *Report*.
[5] C. 6212 of 1890, pp. 7, 29; C. 6495 of 1891, pp. 115 ff., 130 ff., 162, 193; Colvin, *op. cit.*, I. 182.
[6] C. 6495, pp. 173, 234; Colvin, I. 185.

George Knight-Bruce, the Anglican Bishop of Bloemfontein, and Loch's secretary turned back a few gallant souls who were on their way 'to take Beira,' and a new Anglo-Portuguese Convention was June signed. This gave the Company Manica, but withheld Beira and found employment for an Italian arbiter for several years to come.[1]

Trouble with the Portuguese was accompanied by trouble with Transvaalers. Rhodes had gone to London at the close of 1890 to secure the deed of settlement which extended the sphere of his Company to the north of the Zambesi outside Nyasaland, and to be made much of by Society which had been fired by his enthusiasms and had just invested in Chartered shares. He returned to find that Louis Adendorff and a few other Transvaalers had obtained a land concession in southern Matabeleland from the grandson of the Chibi, a vassal of Lobengula. The concession was therefore worthless, but Barend Vorster, a noted Transvaal company promoter, took it up and, with the open support of Joubert, proposed to found a 'Republic of the North' in Banyailand, while the Portuguese consul at Capetown independently organised a Boer settlement in Manica as 'a wall of iron' between Beira and the redoubtable Company.[2] Rhodes, Hofmeyr and Stephanus du Toit, back from Pretoria a disillusioned man, beat up the Bond against the Adendorff trek and the pro-Hollander Transvaal executive with such success that Loch had to reason with prominent Bondsmen. Kruger might lament Hofmeyr's 'worship of the golden calf' but he had no mind to play into Joubert's hands or compromise his own plans in the east.[3] He condemned the trek, which thereupon wilted and presently expired in June the presence of Jameson's police and machine-guns on the banks of 1891. the Limpopo. Rhodes defeated the Manica trek with 'the silver lance.'[4]

Rhodes also defeated the High Commissioner. Loch had declared a protectorate over the Company's sphere south of the Zambesi and taken power under an Order-in-Council to legislate by proclamation, April-extend Cape law, appoint magistrates, raise revenue and generally June 1891. maintain the peace therein.[5] All this was to apply as far as possible to Europeans only, for Lobengula was still explicitly recognised as a reigning sovereign without whose leave the Company could have no jurisdiction even over white men, a jurisdiction which the Queen had advised him to leave to Jameson on the analogy of Tati.[6] Loch

[1] C. 6375 of 1891; C. 6495 of 1891, p. 264; *B.S.A. Co. Reports*, Nov. 1892, p. 16; Jan. 1895, p. 25; C. 8434 of 1897 (Manica arbitration); Hole, *Making of Rhodesia*, p. 261.

[2] Williams, *op. cit.*, p. 154; Michell, II. 31 ff.; Colvin, I. 206; Walker, *op. cit.*, p. 216.

[3] Hofmeyr, *op. cit.*, p. 417.

[4] Michell, *Rhodes*, II. 31 ff.; Williams, *Rhodes*, p. 154; Colvin, *Jameson*, II. 206; Walker, *De Villiers*, p. 216.

[5] C. 7171 of 1893, p. 1; Newton, *Unification*, I. 119 ff.

[6] C. 5918 of 1890, p. 233.

wished, and Rhodes had at first been inclined to agree, that the High Commissioner should have sole power of legislation and that actual administration should be in the hands of Imperial officials paid by the Company and debarred, as in the last days of the English East India Company's service, from embarking on trading ventures. But H.M. Government would take no responsibility, and allowed the B.S.A. Directors to legislate concurrently with its own representative by means of ordinances.[1] Henceforward, Rhodes paid little heed to the Imperial factor outside the Bechuanaland Protectorate.

The position of the Company was difficult, for strictly speaking it had power neither to rule nor grant land. This latter disability was in a measure removed by the acquisition of a land concession. Lobengula, hoping to divide the alien forces which were closing in upon him, granted a concession to Edouard Lippert of Johannesburg empowering the holder for a hundred years to grant, lease or rent land in his name in return for an annual payment. Alas for Lobengula! Lippert, a cousin of Beit, sold his concession to the Company, which was now in a position to give farms to its Pioneers and announce its success to the shareholders at their first meeting.[2]

Dec. 1891.

All was going well. The trunk line from Capetown had reached Vryburg; a subsidiary company was about to build a railway from Beira; the vendor's scrip policy promised well. But there were two flies in the ointment: the New Rand had not been discovered in Mashonaland and the tidings, which had already been indirectly announced, were now officially confirmed that the Company did not own the Rudd and other important concessions. These were owned by some of its chief directors and their friends who, on joining hands to apply for the Charter in 1889, had formed the Central Search Association with a capital of £121,000 to buy up concessions in Bechuanaland and the North, and had arranged to provide the capital for the projected British South Africa Company. As soon as they heard that the Charter would be forthcoming, the Central Searchers had agreed verbally among themselves that the future Chartered Company should have the use of their concessions in return for half its net profits. The B.S.A. Company had then come into being with a capital of 1,000,000 shares of £1, three-fourths of which were privately issued to directors and prominent supporters and the remainder held over for contingencies. Once the Pioneers had set out, the Association became the United Concessions Company, with a share capital of £4,000,000 based upon the promised 50 per cent. of Chartered profits. It agreed with the Chartered Board,

July 1890.

---

[1] Walker, *De Villiers*, pp. 207, 224 (based on Loch's *Materials*); B.S.A. Charter, § 10.
[2] C. 7171 of 1893, p. 8; Williams, *op. cit.*, p. 171; Moffatt, *Life of J. S. Moffat*, p. 261; *B.S.A. Co. Annual Meeting*, Dec. 22, 1891, p. 8.

its *alter ego*, that it should be bought out at the first opportunity with 1,000,000 specially created B.S.A. shares. On the news that the Pioneers had founded Salisbury, many of the original Chartered shares were sold in the open market at a high price and, in deference to the feelings of the 5000 new shareholders, the capitalisation was postponed till the end of 1891. Such was the news that was now 1891. broken to the shareholders. Some of them threatened legal proceedings if the arrangement were carried out. The capitalisation was postponed till the end of 1892.[1]

The news did not reassure the suspicious High Commissioner, all the more that Rhodes, who had once talked of contributing to the cost of the Bechuanaland Protectorate, was now demanding £50,000 annually wherewith to administer it, and this though the Protectorate tribes were already paying light taxes. Rhodes had so many expensive irons in the fire. He was trying to buy Delagoa Bay, taking his telegraph into Salisbury, borrowing from De Beers for the Vryburg-Mafeking railway and pressing forward beyond the Zambesi to make contact with Captain Frederick Lugard in Uganda. Would those £50,000 be spent in the Protectorate? Loch was not too sure. Jameson had recently taken charge in Mashonaland, and Loch had had to tell him that he could not levy hut tax on the Mashona subjects of Lobengula. Now 'the Doctor' was cutting down official staffs and police to the bone thereby virtually throwing the task of maintaining the peace upon the Imperial Bechuanaland Police, and talking cheerfully of empty coffers while he ran the country by tact and, on occasion, Jameson law. Twice his officials had exercised forcible jurisdiction over Mashona and, though the delinquent chiefs were admittedly public nuisances, they were none the less Lobengula's men. In any case, Loch held that conflict could have been avoided.[2]

Rhodes now met his shareholders for the first time, and assured Nov. them that no danger need be apprehended from the Matabele and 1892. that all was for the best in the best of all possible spheres.[3] But Knutsford had only acknowledged the Lippert Concession on condition that it really belonged to the B.S.A. Company and, now, Lord Ripon, Secretary of State in Gladstone's new ministry, was showing himself equally insistent and, once his attention had been officially drawn towards the unusual relations of the Company with the United Concessions, much more inquisitive than his predecessor had

[1] Vide *B.S.A. Co. Annual Meeting*, Dec. 22, 1891; *B.S.A. Co. Report*, 1899–1892, p. 2; *Report of Extraordinary General B.S.A. Co. Meeting*, Nov. 20, 1893; *Report of B.S.A. Co. Annual Meeting*, Dec. 19, 1893; *Report for 1892–94*, p. 2; *The Economist*, Nov. 18, 1893.
[2] Williams, *op. cit.*, p. 198; Gardiner, *Harcourt*, II. 190; Michell, *Rhodes*, II. 93; C. 7171, pp. 5, 10, 20, 24, 26; Colvin, *Jameson*, chapter xvii.
[3] *Report of B.S.A. Co. Annual Meeting*, Nov. 29, 1892, p. 7.

14*

been in the matter of details.[1] In view of all this, it was essential that
the capitalisation should be carried through; nevertheless, it had to
be put off till the end of 1893. And so the Company sank into debt.
Its cash and reserve of shares were almost exhausted; it was living
on a monthly subsidy from De Beers and other friends; the Beira
railway was still far from completion; the New Rand had not been
discovered in Mashonaland, and the collapse of the Australian gold
boom promised to have repercussions elsewhere. To add to Rhodes's
anxieties, his cabinet split; but the fact that distressed him most was
the crumbling of his chartered company, the keystone of the federation of the future.

A way out of the impasse was providentially indicated by Lobengula. The Matabele, though much mixed now with other tribes, still
lived for the most part in Zulu fashion grouped in kraals within
sixty miles of Bulawayo. They were a potential danger to the Europeans, a scourge to their tribal neighbours and the despair of the
missionaries, to whom, like the Zulus, they refused to hearken and
whose more docile flocks they threatened.[2] The occupation of the
Transvaal by Europeans and the formation of the Bechuanaland
Protectorate had deprived them of two of their raiding grounds and
the arrival of white men in Mashonaland had made the washing of
spears still more difficult. No political boundary had been laid down
between Matabeleland and Mashonaland, but a line had been
indicated a few miles to the west of Victoria beyond which white
men were not to go without special leave of the king.[3] The rule was
none too well observed[4] and Lobengula, who had to make the best
of the evil military system which he had inherited, had difficulty in
restraining his young men, who resented the presence of Europeans
among their Mashona 'dogs.' He turned their spears north-westward
against the Barotse; but small impis invaded Mashonaland twice,
once in the far north to collect taxes, a financial expedient for which
Lobengula apologised to Jameson, and again in the south against
the Chibi, when they passed close to Victoria. Nevertheless, as late
as June 1892, Jameson could report that his relations with the natives
were excellent.[5] But the fact remained that the Matabele were in the
way. So long as Lobengula's power stood the Company could have
no territorial jurisdiction nor ownership of land even in Mashonaland,

---

[1] C. 7171 of 1893, pp. 9, 32 ff.
[2] On the Matabele tribal system *vide* Hole, *Making of Rhodesia*, chapter iv.
[3] On the Matabele War of 1893 *vide* B.S.A. Co. *Reports*; Norris-Newman,
Matabeleland and How We got it, and *The Downfall of Lobengula*, by various
writers; C. 7171, 7190, 7196 of 1893; C. 7284, 7555 of 1894.
[4] Johan Colenbrander, the Company's agent at Bulawayo, wrote to Moffat
that white men disregarded the line and that 'old Ben...is trying to pull
straight, therefore they ought from their side to help him in cases of this sort all
they can' (C. 7171 of 1893, p. 44).
[5] C. 7171 of 1893, p. 33.

and now the interests of the Company were swinging westward June into Matabeleland. The Cape-to-Cairo railway must run along the 1892. Matabele highlands towards Lake Tanganyika, which was within reach now that the Anglo-Portuguese disputes in Barotseland had June been settled; finally the New Rand, on which the capitalisation 1892. depended, was believed to run from Salisbury to Tati through Bulawayo itself.

Rhodes had hardly been dissuaded from sending in the Pioneers to settle with the Matabele in 1890.[1] Since then the idea had grown up in Mashonaland that war must come sooner or later. That opinion was not shared by Jameson, who looked to a slow but steady absorption of the fighting Matabele into the general body of native labourers.[2] Circumstances, however, forced his hand. Early in 1893 the telegraph line was cut near Victoria and the Company's men seized cattle from the suspected Mashona culprits. The cattle proved to be royal beasts, and Lobengula had difficulty in preventing his warriors from intervening. The matter was settled amicably, but Jameson warned the king that impis which frightened away Mashona labourers might be severely dealt with.[3] Presently Lobengula complained that royal cattle in the keeping of one chieftain near Victoria had been stolen by another, and sent a small party to punish the wire-cutters and the thieves. It was turned back. He therefore sent a large force with a message that no white man should be July harmed. Having duly delivered this message, the impi began to kill 1893. Mashona and burn kraals round Victoria.[4]

Jameson was anxious to avoid the expense of war which would 'throw the country back till God knows when.'[5] He sent word to the local authorities that they must get rid of the impi peaceably and check alarmist reports. They failed, but very properly refused to give up refugee Mashona. Jameson then heard that the indunas would await him and hurried into Victoria to find the Mashona taking refuge in the hills and the Europeans, in the intervals of a cricket match, listening to speeches and at least one sermon on the text *Bulawayo delenda est.*[6] Since Mashona kraals were still burning, he concluded that there was no way out now but shooting. He wired to Rhodes that it might be necessary to march on Bulawayo and received the famous reply, 'Read Luke xiv. 31';[7] He read his Luke, decided that 1000 men would be enough, and told the indunas to draw their men off towards the border within the hour. Most of them prepared to do so, but some of the young bloods retreated slowly across the town commonage with looted cattle, attacking

[1] Michell, *Rhodes*, I. 293.   [2] Colvin, *Jameson*, I. 267.
[3] C. 7171 of 1893, pp. 42 ff.
[4] *Ibid.*, pp. 46 ff., 50, 54; C. 7555 of 1894, *passim.*   [5] Michell, *Rhodes*, II. 85.
[6] C. 7171 of 1893, p. 50; C. 7555 of 1894, p. 41.
[7] Michell, *op. cit.*, II. 85; Williams, *Rhodes*, p. 174.

kraals as they went. There they were charged by the police. Obedient
July
1893.
to the king's orders to harm no white man the warriors made virtually
no resistance; nevertheless, Jameson was told that the Matabele had
fired first.[1] He therefore reported to the High Commissioner in that
sense, arranged military details and sent a stiff message to Lobengula.[2]

Lobengula was apologetic till he heard his warriors' version of the
Victoria incident. He then returned a defiant answer, but apart from
that strove to keep the peace, if only because some of his best
regiments were in quarantine with smallpox.[3] Loch and Ripon also
tried to avert the appeal to arms[4] to the annoyance of Jameson, who
grumbled with truth that if the fighting season were lost 'our show
is burst for some time to come.'[5] Jameson spoke more truly than
perhaps he knew. He was thinking in military terms, but others were
thinking financially and had arranged that if the capitalisation could
July
31,
1893.
be effected before the end of the year, the United Concessions and
its allies would raise £170,000 on debenture for the benefit of the
B.S.A. Company.[6] From that moment it was either Lobengula's
head or the Company's. Jameson raised volunteers to be paid in
time-honoured fashion with land and claims and captured cattle;[7]
Rhodes sent up horses and equipment and set out slowly by sea for
Mashonaland, being in no mind to remain within reach of the High
Commissioner till the latter had sanctioned warlike measures; a
force of 'Johannesburg lambs' was enlisted;[8] some judicious agent-
provocateur work was done on the Matabele border, and communications between Lobengula and the anxious High Commissioner were found to be singularly defective.[9] On the day that the
last of the horses arrived, two police going in well beyond the commercial border reported that they had been fired on; Loch reluctantly
gave leave for patrols to be sent in to bid the indunas remove
Oct.
1893.
the impis which were said to be on the border;[10] a day or two later
the invaluable imperial factor was drawn in when a corporal of the
Bechuanaland Police, who was soon made lieutenant at the request
of the Company, reported that he too had been fired on near the
Macloutsie river. So the columns started, 'a regular army,' Jameson
grumbled, 'my first and I swear it shall be my last,' and Rhodes,

---

[1] C. 7555 of 1894, p. 7.
[2] C. 7171 of 1893, p. 60; *Downfall of Lobengula*, pp. 63 ff.
[3] C. 7171 of 1893, pp. 63 ff.; C. 7196 of 1893, pp. 13, 45.
[4] C. 7171 of 1893, pp. 51, 72; C. 7190 of 1893, p. 1; C. 7196 of 1893, pp. 14, 33.
[5] Colvin, I. 264.
[6] *B.S.A. Co. Report for 1892-94*, p. 2; *B.S.A. Co. Extraordinary General
Meeting*, Nov. 20, 1893. It was the only means of saving the Company, and all
that hung thereon.
[7] Cave Commission: Evidence, Aug. 7 and Dec. 17, 1919; *The Times*,
Nov. 10, 1893.
[8] Colvin, I. 295; *Williams*, pp. 174 ff.
[9] C. 7196 of 1893, pp. 22, 35 ff., 45, 48, 66 ff., 69.   [10] *Ibid.*, pp. 39, 79.

having dawdled on the road until it was too late for Loch to change his mind, ambled into Salisbury.[1]

The fighting was soon over. The machine-guns, a novelty in warfare in those days, worked wonders at Shangani and Imbembezi, and the volunteers entered the ruins of Bulawayo to find the king fled. The Bechuanaland Police meanwhile had held half the impis in the Matoppo hills and now came in with the supplies which the volunteers almost totally lacked. The campaign ended with the coming of the rains and the annihilation of Major Allan Wilson's gallant patrol. A month later it was reported that Lobengula was dead.[2] *Nov. 1893. Dec. 1893.*

So the Company's men and the Imperial police 'broke a king and built a road,' while in London the shareholders, encouraged by the rise in the price of shares at the mere rumour of war, dazzled by the prospects of 'two or three New Johannesburgs' in Matabeleland, overawed by the warning of the Company's lawyer that if the pre-Charter verbal agreement were to be set aside the Company would have no rights in Mashonaland let alone in its new conquest, and silenced by the reminder that 'we want those 170,000 golden sovereigns,' at last doubled their share capital for the benefit of the United Concessionaires, who thereupon handed over the concessions and expired in their corporate capacity.[3] The Chartered Company then raised, not £170,000, but £750,000 on debenture wherewith to pay its creditors for the cost of the campaign and to meet future expenditure. Interest thereon would first become payable in January 1896. *Nov.-Dec. 1893.*

Meanwhile, in Africa, Loch fought hard for his 'East India Company' scheme and at the very least for strict Imperial control over the Company. He was defeated. Even before the war was over Jameson had given out town stands at Bulawayo, and Rhodes, with the Cape Ministry as chorus, declared *coram populo* that his Company, having won the war single-handed, was entitled to the spoils. It was not true. As in 1890, the Bechuanaland Police had covered the advance, rushed in desperately needed supplies and done much of the work in the pursuit of Lobengula. They now had to patrol Matabeleland while the Company raised a small police force and the volunteers dispersed themselves prospecting.[4] Ripon did his best for the High Commissioner, as he always did; but Rhodes won the Cape elections, the second Irish Home Rule bill divided Lord Rosebery's *Jan. 1894.*

---

[1] C. 7196 of 1893, pp. 47, 91; C. 7290, p. 3; Colvin, I. 270; Newman, *Matabeleland*, pp. 215–16; Michell, *op. cit.*, II. 87.
[2] *Downfall of Lobengula*, pp. 2 ff., 202 ff., 214; C. 7290 of 1894, p. 8.
[3] *B.S.A. Co. Extraordinary General Meeting*, Nov. 20, 1893; *B.S.A. Co. Annual and General Meetings*, Dec. 19, 1893; *B.S.A. Directors' Report*, Dec. 19, 1893, p. 2, and *Report for 1892–94*, p. 2; *Economist*, Nov. 18, 1893.
[4] C. 7290 of 1894, p. 37; Hole, *op. cit.*, p. 326.

Liberal Imperialists from Harcourt's Radicals and, when Gladstone made way for Rosebery in March 1894, Rhodes got most of what he wanted. Under the Matabeleland Order-in-Council, Jameson became Administrator with a council of officials empowered to legislate by regulation, subject to the approval of the High Commissioner and concurrently with his proclamations and the Directors' ordinances. Provision was also made for a single-judge court. All that Loch could do was to warn Ripon to stand by for future trouble, with the Portuguese for choice.[1]

July
1894.

RHODES'S FEDERATION POLICY, 1892-96

The Matabele war made 'Southern Rhodesia', the keystone of Rhodes's federation, ready to be set in place as soon as the springs of the arch had been completed. Those springs were steadily rising. Rhodes's first cabinet administered the old Colony well; Merriman's prudent finance enabled the Cape to withstand the big bank failures of 1890, and the ensuing Bank Act promised to avert a repetition of the disaster. But a time had come when three of his colleagues, Merriman, Sauer and Rose-Innes, refused to sit any longer beside James Sivewright, whose departmental methods they could not stomach and for whom Sauer cherished a bitter hatred. Rhodes with the help of Sprigg managed to patch together another and much weaker cabinet; but the crisis cost him the services of the three malcontents as well as that of the able Sivewright and the confidence of the influential Chief Justice, de Villiers, under whom he had offered to serve and had then left in the dark till he had formed another ministry of his own.[2] On the other hand, he had strengthened his alliance with Hofmeyr by supporting the proposal that the study of both English and Dutch should be encouraged in the schools and, though Hofmeyr's attempt to defend Sivewright, a fellow Bondsman, weakened his and therefore Rhodes's hold on the Bond, that body as a whole still rallied to Rhodes's economic policy and his plans for the development of the North as the heritage of British and Afrikaner Colonists alike.

April
1893.

1892.

Rhodes's economic policy was to the taste of the Bond. He held that the time was not ripe for colonial manufactures, jeered, not altogether unjustly, at the local Capetown match factory, and pointed to Kruger's monopolies as a horrible warning; moreover, as

---

[1] *B.S.A. Directors' Report for 1892-4*, pp. 31, 35; C. 7383 of 1894, p. 9; Walker, *De Villiers*, p. 241.

[2] Williams, *Cecil Rhodes*, pp. 186 ff.; Walker, *op. cit.*, pp. 221 ff. Second Rhodes Ministry: C. J. Rhodes, Prime Minister; P. H. Faure, Colonial Secretary; Sir G. Sprigg, Treasurer; William Philip Schreiner, then from Dec. 28, 1893, onwards, Henry Hubert Juta, and then from Sept. 10, 1894, Schreiner, Attorney-General; John Laing, Public Works; John Frost, Native Affairs, and thereafter Rhodes took over that office on Sept. 11, 1893, Agriculture.

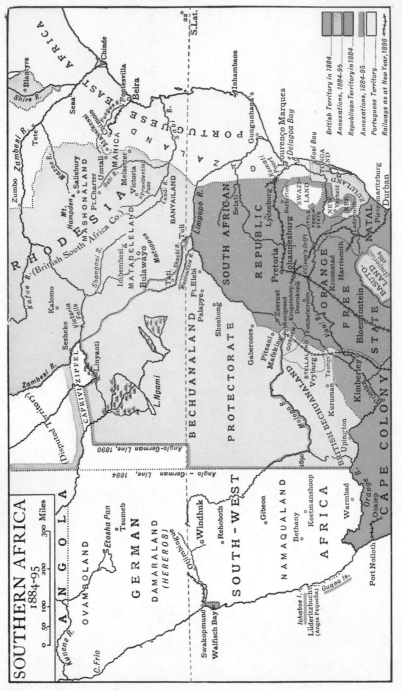

Note. Inyati is 50 miles N.N.E of Bulawayo.

one who came of farming stock himself, he protected the natural products of the country. Hasty duties on Australian mutton [1] were a curious commentary on the Imperial Zollverein which he and Hofmeyr envisaged, girding at 'this Free Trade craze' in England what time Randolph Churchill, the apostle of Tory Democracy, dilated on the desire of the British working classes to recover colonial trade; but he tried to insert in the Matabeleland Order-in-Council 1894. the Rhodes customs clause whereunder Charterland was never to go beyond the existing low Cape tariff, and was to admit South African and British goods free, thus setting the pace for the future customs union.[2] Ripon refused to have it so. Rhodes, undismayed, sent de Villiers and Hofmeyr to the Ottawa Colonial Conference, itself largely the outcome of his correspondence with the premiers of Canada and New South Wales, to discuss cable and steamship communications and Imperial reciprocity. The Liberal Government indeed gave the Australian colonies freedom to offer intercolonial reciprocity; but Ripon on behalf of Great Britain declined the offer of similar favours as economically unsound and politically impossible so long as the most-favoured-nation treaties with Belgium and the German Zollverein stood.[3] As for Imperial Federation, Rhodes had already subscribed to the funds of the Irish party to ensure that, in the event of Home Rule being granted, Irish members should be 1888. retained at Westminster as an example of federalism to other self-governing portions of the Empire. He had since given money to the 1892. Liberals with the same end in view.[4]

The difficulty of winding up the affairs of one of the banks which had collapsed in 1890 pointed to the need for one body of law for all South Africa; but the failure of Rhodes's scheme for a national teaching university at Groote Schuur in face of the opposition of the colleges outside the Cape Peninsula, and the breakdown of de Villiers' plan for a federal appeal court, suggested that federation could not be achieved piecemeal.[5] At the bottom of that question as ever lay the native problem. Rhodes knew well enough that so long as the native policy of the Colony differed so markedly from those of the Republics and of Natal there was little hope of closer union. In his salad days he had believed that an 'Indian despotism' was the best way to deal with tribal natives. He had modified his views somewhat since and now stood side by side with Hofmeyr, midway between the average Bondsman, who held quite sincerely that the only way to civilise the native was for the European to have

---

[1] Walker, De Villiers, p. 249.   [2] H.C. 177 of 1894; C. 7782 of 1895.
[3] Hofmeyr, op. cit., pp. 448 ff.; Walker, op. cit., pp. 245 ff.; C. 7553 of 1894; Wolf, Life of Lord Ripon, II. 218 ff.
[4] Williams, Rhodes, p. 133; Michell, Rhodes, I. 247; II. 47.
[5] Hofmeyr, op. cit., p. 440; Walker, op. cit., pp. 105, 213; Vindex, Speeches, p. 275,

the land and the native to learn the dignity of labour in his service, and those others like Sauer, who held that the native must be protected in his possession of the land and yet be allowed to acquire the franchise.[1] The position of the Bantu in the Colony proper was not
1879. quite so untrammelled as it had been. The vagrancy law had been
1883. stiffened; tribal natives had been deprived by law of access to liquor; Rhodes himself had helped to cut out the so-called communal
1887. tenure of land as a claim on the franchise. At the same time, however, the franchise had been extended to natives in the Transkeian territories who could qualify on the usual terms, and soon the cry was raised that 'blanket Kaffirs' were getting on to the
1892. register. Rhodes therefore raised the property qualification for all from £25 to £75 per annum, expunged the £25 salary qualification and imposed a simple education test, thus excluding not only barbarian tribesmen, but down-at-heel Europeans and Coloured folk also.[2]

Rhodes was prepared to go much further in a restrictive direction; indeed, impending differences upon native policy undoubtedly did much to produce the strain which wrecked his first ministry. In 1893, when it was rumoured that a Malay was to be elected for the Cape Division by the 'plumping' of the four votes which each elector there
Aug. alone enjoyed, he averted the danger by abolishing that anomalous
1894. privilege.[3] After the election of 1894 he added the portfolio of Native Affairs to that of the Prime Minister by statute and carried his famous Glen Grey Act. Most of the principles of that measure had already been initiated or projected, but Rhodes has the credit of systematising them and carrying them through as no other man could. Natives were to be encouraged to take land on quit-rent subject to the European system of survey and individual title, a source of expense which has deterred many natives from doing so to this day, and were to be prevented from selling or mortgaging this land without leave. The defence of this part of Rhodes's policy cost Hofmeyr the support of many Bondsmen, who were, however, reassured when the vote was withheld from such tenants and a labour tax prescribed for all non-landholding men who did not go out to work for three months in the year. Sauer and his friends resisted these last two points and the labour tax was never collected, but they approved of the system of location and native district councils under the presidency

---

[1] Williams, *Rhodes*, pp. 203 ff.; Hofmeyr, *op. cit.*, chapter xxv. For the views of a well-to-do Western Province farmer of those days, *vide* De Waal, *With Rhodes in Mashonaland*: ' If Kaffirs only knew the advantages of serving under white masters, they would gain more civilisation in one year than they do from missionaries in fifty. . . . As it is, there is now a general scarcity of labourers; Kaffirs can live so easily that they decline to be dependent on the European, They are, however, beginning to recognise their degraded position . . .' (p. 105).
[2] Acts 30 of 1887 and 9 of 1892. Eybers, pp. 70, 73.
[3] Act 16 of 1893 ; L. M. Thompson, *The Cape Coloured Franchise*, p. 7.

of officials which were to raise local rates and spend the money locally.[1]

The Act was applied first to Glen Grey district in the Ciskei, next almost immediately to four districts in the Transkei and, a little later, to yet other Transkeian territories with excellent results on the whole; but Rhodes avowedly intended that it should have an even wider application. He called it 'a native Bill for Africa.'[2] Much of the said continent was coming under his control, and more might come. He had offered to administer Uganda and the Bechuanaland Protectorate in return for Imperial subsidies; he still meant to add British Bechuanaland to the Cape Colony, and now took over the two Pondolands. West Pondoland had for long been quiet, but in East Pondoland, Sigcau, successor of the stormy Mquikela, had failed to control his half-brother, Mhlangaso. The latter first bullied Sigcau into giving trading privileges to a couple of Germans, and then rebelled and took refuge in Natal. Natal had its own designs on Pondoland; but Sigcau tried to keep on good terms with the Cape authorities and, though the German Government declined to support its traders, H.M. Government decided to annex. Once Sigcau and Mquikela had submitted to the Crown, Rhodes entered Pondoland Sept. in state and thus ended the last independent chieftainship in all the 1894. land between the Kei and the Natal border.[3]

Annexation of native territories was one thing, the achievement of federation another. The stumbling-block to any scheme of that kind was the Transvaal. Sinn Fein, the instinctive avoidance of contact with unfamiliar things, was in the ascendant at Pretoria. The Transvaal was still in the main a farmers' republic and most of its burghers desired that it should remain so, but the influx of Uitlanders, secured of their civil rights under the Convention and specifically invited into the republic by the Transvaal delegates to London in 1884,[4] was fast changing the condition of the state. The influx, small at first, had swelled to great proportions after the opening of the Rand goldfields. Many of the burghers looked askance at these men who came from the four corners of the earth to build a huge rambling city at Johannesburg where corrugated iron was beginning to be relieved by stucco and marble facings, and to develop there an industry, the like of which the world had never seen, in mines which were owned, for the most part, by overseas shareholders, controlled by European managers and miners, and worked by hordes of black barbarian labourers. And

---

[1] Act 25 of 1894; Newton, *Unification*, I. 129; Brookes, *History of Native Policy*, p. 113.
[2] Vindex, *Speeches*, p. 390.
[3] Act 5 of 1894; Eybers, p. 76; Williams, *Rhodes*, pp. 207 ff.; G. 9–94; G. 8–95 (Cape).
[4] Cook, *Rights and Wrongs of the Transvaal War*, p. 262.

in their wake came the cosmopolitan riff-raff that had corrupted Kimberley.

The Pretoria Government, hampered by the lack of railways and a slack administrative tradition, was faced with an industrial and social problem with which its small and inexperienced official staff was quite unfitted to deal. Yet it did much for the newcomers. Its gold law was liberal, far more so than that of Rhodes's Chartered Company, and if its Native Pass, Illicit Liquor and Gold Thefts laws were poorly administered, they had at least been passed in the interests of the new industry and a half-hearted enforcement of the law was nothing new in the Transvaal. Kruger, moreover, allowed a Department of Mines to come into being gradually and to discharge many administrative duties other than those directly concerned with the new industry; nor did he make any difficulty when, in 1889, the Groups which managed the mines formed the Witwatersrand Chamber of Mines, parent of the Transvaal Chamber of Mines, as a central co-ordinating body.[1] Further, he treated the white workers well, in spite of the tendency of the five thousand or so miners and other white artisans to form branches of their old United Kingdom trade unions. Trade unionism was in its infancy in South Africa, for the oldest such association, parent of the present-day Amalgamated Society of Woodworkers, had been formed only in 1881 and even the whirling labour centre of Kimberley had known nothing of the kind apart from the Knights of Labour, who, probably drawing their inspiration from the United States, had struck successfully three years later against the attempts of the companies to apply to white men the drastic methods of search for illicit diamonds that had long been applied to Africans.[2] The old President by no means welcomed these unfamiliar associations, which were British in origin and overwhelmingly British in personnel; but so far was he from seeking to suppress them, that he accepted many amendments to the mining regulations suggested by their members and refused to have employees searched for stolen gold by agents paid by the State but controlled by the Chamber of Mines, for, apart from other considerations, he was quick to see that the Uitlanders could be split along the line which divided Capital from Labour. The Uitlanders, meanwhile, found many, though by no means all of the officials eminently bribable.

Nevertheless, the Uitlanders had grievances. Some of these arose from the fact, which many of them were too slow to admit, that the Republic was politically and sentimentally an Afrikaner community whose official tongue was High Dutch. Though as much English as Dutch was used in the inferior courts, the use of Dutch in public

---

[1] *Chamber of Mines Annual Report, 1895*, p. 18; van der Horst, *Native Labour in South Africa*, pp. 129, 241.

[2] E. Sachs, *The Choice before South Africa*, pp. 137-41.

transactions was a burden to many such folk. Again, language bedevilled the education problem. In Burgers's days so many Transvaalers had been eager to learn English that preference had been
given to bilingual teachers, and when these had been lacking, uni-
lingual English-speaking teachers had been engaged. After the retrocession, the new Superintendent-General of Education, the Rev. S. J.
du Toit, had made Dutch nominally the sole medium of instruction,
but he had suffered many exclusively English-medium schools to
draw state grants, a not unreasonable concession in a country where
Boer farmhouses were often well stocked with good current English
novels. Dr. N. Mansvelt, the able Hollander who came up from
Stellenbosch as Superintendent in 1891, changed all that. He not
only founded the State Gymnasium at Pretoria, but appointed more
school inspectors and began to enforce du Toit's system. Nevertheless, he made special provision for English-medium schools, which
he allowed to draw State grants provided they devoted five hours
each week to Dutch and the history of the country and employed
teachers who could undertake that work. A good many of these
'English' schools failed to fulfil these terms and thus lost their grants,
with the result that less than half the children on the Rand went to
school at all, and far too many of those who did went to indifferent
private establishments. Other grievances were of a more material
kind. Such were the customs dues, which helped to keep up the cost
of living, and the official concessions policy, which bred hangers-on,
who bled the Uitlanders and swindled the State, notably in the case
of the monopoly of the dynamite which was so vital to the mining
industry. Above all, the Uitlanders, who paid nearly all the taxes and
made the Government rich, were denied a voice in the direction of
the policy of the State.

The vote was the monopoly of sons of the soil and favoured
individual immigrants, and, for the sons of the soil, most of the
Uitlanders entertained a contempt and lack of understanding that
was repaid in kind. Before 1882 the term of residence necessary for
acquiring the franchise had been one year. It had then been raised,
reasonably enough, to five to meet the gold rush to Lydenburg;[1]
but, though some Uitlanders demanded the vote on easier terms,
very few had even registered during the ensuing five years. Then had
come a radical change in the situation. In face of the Uitlanders'
lack of interest in his Republic's politics, Kruger warned them fairly
that while he would make no difference between them and 'old
burghers,' he would not give them the vote. He soon showed that 1889-
he had meant what he said, for the first great Rand boom alarmed 1890.
the burghers and a coincident Uitlander insult to their President and
their flag in Johannesburg infuriated them. They feared lest they be

---

[1] Eybers, p. 437; Law No. 7 of 1882.

swamped in their own republic by these foreign fortune-seekers, here to-day and openly intending in most cases to be gone to-morrow, who, if they had the power, would pile up debt in the name of development and then, when the mines gave out—and until the proving of the deep levels in 1894 there was little to show that the Rand would have a long life—would fold up their tents and silently steal away leaving the holes in the ground and the public debt to the permanent inhabitants. Worse still, the majority of the Uitlanders were British subjects and therefore suspect, for the memory of the agitation which had preceded Shepstone's annexation had not faded and some of the would-be voters seemed to think they could become burghers and still retain their British citizenship.[1] Hence, in 1890, a drastic franchise law was passed.[2] A Second Volksraad was set up to deal with the concerns of the mining areas, but it had no taxing powers and its acts were subject to review by the original Volksraad, now the First Raad. The franchise for the new House was given two years after registration and eligibility for a seat therein after four; but the vote in presidential and First Raad elections would only be forthcoming after fourteen years and, even so, there was no guarantee that the term would not be lengthened at a moment's notice. For the unicameral Volksraad legislated either by *Wet*, a leisurely process which entailed the publication of the proposed measure three months in advance, or by *Besluit*, a mere resolution carried on the spot. The High Court had twice upheld the latter practice and declared that, since the Raad was a sovereign legislature, the *Grondwet* itself was not immune from hasty alteration, and the Courts had no power of testing laws by the touchstone of a rigid constitution.[3] It was thus possible for Kruger to keep within the law by altering the law. Individuals were given the vote, but this was an act of grace and not a right.

Probably, had the franchise laws been never so liberal, few overseas men would have become burghers at the price of forgoing British citizenship; but many South Africans would have done so and their allegiance would have strengthened the Republic as a republic. But most of them, had they been given the franchise, would surely have joined Schalk Burger, Lukas Meyer, Louis Botha, Ewald Esselen and other liberally minded Boers, who, backed by Eugene Marais of *Land en Volk* and Jan Celliers of *Die Volksstem*, inveighed against the Hollanders and, at one stage, almost compelled Kruger to end the scandal of the dynamite monopoly. They would have voted Joubert into the presidential chair and that would have been the end of much of what Kruger stood for.

1884–
1887.

1892.

---

[1] J. F. Van Oordt, *Paul Kruger en die Opkomst der Zuid-Afrikaansche Republiek*, p. 473.
[2] Eybers, pp. 488, 495.   [3] Walker, *De Villiers*, p. 288.

So the franchise was withheld to make enemies, inflame grievances, give a handle to those who wished to destroy the Republic and, as the indignant Free Staters protested, differentiate the Transvaal from all other South African states on racial grounds. The root of the trouble was that the Kruger party behaved like a Chosen People towards a community which included many who were more universally recognised as such, and whose British members, under the stimulus of the new Imperialism, were beginning to suspect that they, too, had a claim to the title. A single Chosen People can usually be accommodated in a given state, but two are an embarrassment and three a disaster.

Signs of trouble to come soon appeared. Charles Leonard, a 1892. brilliant attorney from the Cape, formed the National Union. Times were bad. There was drought; the first Rand boom had broken and though the arrival of the Port Elizabeth line at the Vaal promised to reduce the cost of living, a new customs law cancelled the benefit in advance. Middle-class men and artisans therefore combined to secure equal rights and redress of grievances in an independent republic by constitutional means, while the magnates held aloof for fear of spoiling business.

The Imperial Government had no power under the London Convention of 1884 to interfere and at first had no serious wish to do so, but at length it sought to use the Swaziland negotiations as a lever to secure the franchise for the Uitlanders. Since the ratification of 1890. the first Swaziland Convention the Transvaal had secured railway strips through the lands of Zambaan and Mbegisa, but had taken no steps in regard to Tongaland, for that would commit it to joining the customs union. In Swaziland itself the joint government was not 1891– a success; the Transvaalers were not more helpful than they had to 1892. be and now threatened to enforce a taxation concession which they had acquired. Hofmeyr's promise that their wishes would be considered still stood, and Loch was so anxious to settle the matter either by taking Swaziland himself at the risk of bad blood with the Afrikaners everywhere or by letting it go to the Republic under safeguards that he twice went to London to urge the matter on Knutsford's attention. At the end of a long and dilatory correspondence with Pretoria, Ripon, Knutsford's successor, bade Loch confer with Kruger once more and, *inter alia*, raise the question of the Uitlanders.[1]

The conference took place at Colesberg.[2] It failed to settle any- April thing, and the Transvaal gave notice that the existing convention 1893. would cease in August. Loch therefore went to Pretoria to renew June negotiations. At Kruger's request Swaziland was dealt with separ- 1893. ately. The President wished to incorporate it completely in his State

[1] C. 7212 of 1893, pp. 3, 13 ff., 123 ff.   [2] *Ibid.*, pp. 137, 143, 145 ff., 152.

under republican law, but he yielded at last to Loch's insistence that, once the Swazis had issued an Organic Proclamation empowering him to rule the whites, it should be governed like a Transvaal protectorate. For the rest, he was averse to limiting his tariff to the then height of the Cape customs barrier or including the Natal railway in any agreement, but he agreed to Ripon's demand that a railway to the east of Swaziland should only be built with the consent of H.M. Government or 'under a future contemplated convention.' He failed to induce Loch to agree to any modification of the London Convention, especially with regard to the control of foreign affairs, and on his side showed himself opposed to the equality of the English and Dutch languages in his republic, attached to the dynamite monopoly and ready to offer nothing more than a selective franchise.[1]

Nov. 1893.   The Second Swaziland Convention was put into final shape and presently ratified by the Volksraad, but it never came into force. Loch's visit to Pretoria, however, profoundly affected the future course of his policy. He had been accorded a hearty welcome as the first representative of Queen Victoria, whom the Boers honoured as a great lady, to visit Pretoria since 1881. But the welcome could not hide the bitterness of party feeling. A furious presidential election had just ended. Kruger, Joubert and Chief Justice Kotze had all stood forward as candidates. There had been the possibility of a fourth candidate, for Chief Justice de Villiers had gone up from the Cape at Rhodes's suggestion to take soundings. He had, however,

1892–1893.   withdrawn, Kotze had won very few votes, and Joubert had been narrowly defeated by Kruger amid such excitement that there had been some danger of an armed protest as in times past. A commission of inquiry had declared Kruger duly elected; but Loch found that personal, religious and political rancours were still acute, and that the Bench was at daggers drawn with the Executive and Legislature. He concluded that Kruger did not command the support of a majority of his own burghers, let alone of the Uitlanders, that once the Swazi question was settled the Republic would fall to pieces, and that many of the Boers felt vaguely that Great Britain must some day reoccupy their country. If internecine strife broke out he determined, in the last resort, to step in and end it. On the other hand, a wild welcome at Johannesburg on his way home convinced him that there was no fear of the 'English republic' that Rhodes dreaded, and that the day was coming sooner than was generally expected when all the States of South Africa would, 'at their own request, be united under the British flag.'[2]

---

[1] C. 7212 of 1893, pp. 148 ff.; Wolf, *Ripon*, II. 230; Leyds, *Transvaal Surrounded*, pp. 323 ff.; Walker, *De Villiers*, p. 239.
[2] C. 7212 of 1893, pp. 153 ff.; *Cape Law Journal of* 1894, pp. 173, 269; Walker, *op. cit.*, p. 221.

Perhaps the wish was father to the thought, but Rhodes cherished the same hope and not without reason. Basutoland, the Bechuana- 1891–land Protectorate and British Bechuanaland had joined the Customs 1894. Union, Cape Bondsmen were raging against Kruger's Sinn Fein policy, the railways were advancing to put an end to Transvaal isolation. The Port Elizabeth line had reached Bloemfontein and, at May the end of the same year, Sivewright, Rhodes's right-hand man in 1891. such matters, had arranged that the Cape should lend the Netherlands Railway Company enough money to enable it to raise a large loan from Rothschild's wherewith to finish its Delagoa Bay line. In return, the Cape had been given leave to carry its own line into the Promised Land and fix the rates over the whole length to Johannesburg for three years to come; [1] hence, the first train from Capetown entered Johannesburg in September 1892 and Pretoria three months later. Soon to the west the Bechuanaland Railway Company, an offshoot of the Chartered Company, was incorporated to carry the Vryburg line to Mafeking, and the British Government agreed, much to Germany's annoyance, that no line from the west should pass through the Bechuanaland Protectorate without the consent of the Chartered Company, which would in its turn consult the Cape. [2] On the east, the Second Swaziland Convention safeguarded the approach through Kosi Bay, and Rhodes had already begun to negotiate with the Portuguese for the lease or purchase of Delagoa Bay on behalf of the Cape Colony. These negotiations were hampered by the reference of McMurdo's claims to the Berne Arbitration Court and the existence of another bidder, who may be safely located in or near Berlin; but the Chartered North was visibly taking shape under Jameson's skilful hands and the Matabeleland Order-in-Council, nearly a thousand miles of road had been built, and the east coast railway was through to Chimoio two days' ride from Salisbury. [3] Jan. In the old Colony Rhodes's base had been secured by his victory at the general election. 1894.

The Transvaalers began to fear Rhodes, 'thin, grey and haggard' though he was. As the suspicion that he was aiming at the control of their republic rose to a certainty, the rival factions drew together and cemented the defensive alliance by appointing Ewald Esselen, chairman of Joubert's election committee, State Attorney. [4] They entrenched themselves by stiffening the franchise laws. The First Raad, which had twice rejected large Uitlander franchise petitions, now codified the electoral laws in such a way that no Uitlander could acquire the full vote before the age of forty and that only at the end of fourteen years' residence for the greater part of which he

[1] Williams, *Rhodes*, p. 248; G. 5–92 (Cape), pp. 2, 5.
[2] B.S.A. *Directors' Report*, Dec. 19, 1893, p. 3.
[3] *Ibid.*, 1894, pp. 3 ff.   [4] Walker, *op. cit.*, p. 242.

would have been denationalised under an oath of allegiance which may have been modelled on that of the U.S.A., but was none the less unnecessarily galling to British subjects in a South African state permeated by British influences and surrounded by British territory. Even sons of Uitlanders born in the country fell under these disabilities unless their fathers took the oath of allegiance.[1] Then, in the course of a petty native war against Maloboch in the northern districts, the Government commandeered British subjects, who, unlike the nationals of most other states, were not exempted by treaty. Most of the men called up responded, but a few objected and thereby gave rise to complications with the High Commissioner. The Swazis moreover refused to issue the Organic Proclamation provided for by the recent Swaziland Convention and, as the life of the joint government was about to expire, Loch hurried to Pretoria.[2]

June 1894.

Loch was so convinced that civil war was coming in the Transvaal that he mobilised the Bechuanaland Police on the western border and, at Kruger's request, did not visit Johannesburg for fear of an 'incident'; but in spite of that, on his arrival at Pretoria, he was the recipient of such a tumultuous welcome from Uitlanders flourishing Union Jacks that had the President not been more level-headed than some of his advisers, the negotiations might have been imperilled. In the event, the commandeering question was settled temporarily and the life of the joint government in Swaziland extended till the end of the year; but Loch did not venture to show Kruger Ripon's despatch suggesting a five-year franchise. On the other hand, he received several Uitlander deputations, and certainly gave one of them the impression that he wanted to know how long they could hold out till reinforcements arrived by asking it pointedly how many rifles the Uitlanders had.[3] He even asked Lionel Phillips bluntly in a private talk whether they could hold out for a week, and indicated that he would have gone straightaway to Johannesburg's help if it had had three thousand rifles and ammunition. He was, however, dissuaded from going to that restive city by his pacific Imperial Secretary, Sir Graham Bower, who had no mind to see a riot under the Union Jack with the High Commissioner as chief rioter.[4] In the end, he told a National Union delegation that they must seek redress of grievances in a conciliatory spirit, and so home.

Out of these circumstances arose the legend that Loch had virtually suggested the subsequent Jameson Raid into the South African Republic. That was to go too far; but it cannot be denied that he had provided the working model, that is, an armed force on the

---

[1] Laws No. 14 of 1893 and 3 of 1894; C. 7554 of 1894.
[2] C. 8159 of 1896, pp. 1, 9; C. 7611 of 1895, pp. 5, 8.
[3] J. Scoble and H. R. Abercrombie, *The Rise and Fall of Krugerism*, pp. 149 ff., 158–9, 591 ff.
[4] Van der Poel, *The Jameson Raid*, pp. 15 ff.

Bechuanaland border to support an Uitlander rising and then the prompt arrival of the High Commissioner as mediator. He was much more perturbed at the course of events north of the Vaal than he had been in 1893 and fully believed that civil war must come if a Volksraad as intransigent as the last were returned at the coming elections in October. If war did come, a war this time not between Boer factions but between the Uitlanders and the authorities, he, as High Commissioner, intended to warn Kruger that he held him responsible for the safety of British lives and property endangered by his policy and, if the necessary protection were not forthcoming, to furnish it himself by pushing troops up the advancing western railway and arming the Uitlanders. After all, the Imperial power was the traditional guardian of the peace of South Africa, the guardian to whom its own subjects and those of other governments looked for the safety of their respective folk and investments on the Rand. Besides, he believed, as did most people in those days, that the Uitlanders were bound to win in the long run and that, if they won without British help, they might set up a republic hostile to any British-dominated federation.[1] He, therefore, pointed out to Ripon the obvious fact that the arrival of the Kimberley railway at Mafeking would make the approach to the Rand much easier, troubled poor Bower by seeking to keep rifles available for prospective Johannesburg rebels and asked the Colonial Secretary for reinforcement and instructions. Ripon vouchsafed neither, but Loch had not spoken without his book.[2] Just after his visit, Charles Leonard's brother and Johannes Wessels, leader of the Transvaal Bar, delivered fiery speeches at a mass meeting on the Rand, and Chief Justice Kotze, who had long demanded security of tenure and adequate salaries as the true safeguards for judicial independence, toured the country declaring that the Government's policy was a danger to the Republic.[3]

Others unknown to Loch were also contemplating action. The possibility of working the deep levels on the Reef had at last been 1894. proved. All along the line for thirty miles on either side of Johannesburg the gold-bearing quartz dipped down, flattening out as it sank, to a workable depth of 3000 feet and more. Most of this banket formation was so poor that gold was reckoned not in ounces but in mere pennyweights a ton; but it was consistent, calculable and well-nigh inexhaustible, there was abundant cheap coal near at hand (would the Reef ever have paid for the working without that coal?), the deep levels promised the Rand a long life and a big population

[1] Van der Poel, *op. cit.*, pp. 16 ff.
[2] Walker, *De Villiers*, p. 274; Wolf, *Ripon*, II. 227; C. 7554 of 1894; C. 7611 of 1895; A. 6–96 (Cape), Appendix, p. vi.
[3] C. 8159 of 1896, pp. 41 ff.; *Cape Law Journal* (1894), pp. 173, 269; 311–1 of 1897, p. 574.

and demanded that working costs be brought down and railway and customs issues be disposed of. A few of the mining magnates headed by Lionel Phillips, representative of the Eckstein and Beit interests, began to flirt with the National Union. They admittedly did not 'care a fig' for the franchise nor take much interest in politics for fear of irritating 'old Kruger'; but they wanted decent administration and felt that something might be done to 'improve' the Volksraad if an election fund could be raised, despite the law against it, without putting their hands into their own pockets.[1]

Rhodes's company, 'the Goldfields people,' had hinted to Phillips that he should approach the Colossus, but Alfred Beit shrewdly warned him that no good would come of that at the moment.[2] The time was, however, rapidly coming when Rhodes would be more accessible. His luck had held good up to a point. Natal had secured self-government in 1893, and the new ministry at Pietermaritzburg supported the idea of an economic union;[3] H.M. Government had proclaimed a protectorate over Uganda, and the Congo Free State had ceded a railway strip linking Lake Tanganyika with that territory. But there Rhodes's luck ran out. King Leopold hastily withdrew the priceless cession under pressure of France and the Kaiser, who threatened to summon a fresh Conference on Africa, and Downing Street bade Rhodes give up all hope of acquiring Delagoa Bay since Berlin would not let him have it even if Lisbon were willing.[4] The All-Red Route from the Cape to Cairo was thus blocked and the strangle-hold on the Transvaal averted. Further, personal inspection in company with Jameson and Hays Hammond, an American engineer from Johannesburg, convinced Rhodes that the New Rand was not to be found north of the Limpopo, and Hammond told him that unless there was a radical change politically in the Transvaal, there would be a rising. Already the Rand seethed with mass meetings, secret societies and rifle clubs; if Rhodes would help, well and good; if not, the Uitlanders would take their own line.[5] President Joseph Robinson or Barney Barnato would be no improvement on Paul Kruger—far from it—and, alternatively, a republic run by what Rhodes called the *Sydney Bulletin* Australians who were flocking to Johannesburg would be even worse.

Rhodes returned home thoughtful by way of Lourenço Marques, where his offer of help against the threatening tribes was declined, perhaps prudently, and thence through Pretoria, where he warned

June 1894.

Sept. 1894.

[1] A. 6-96 (Cape), Appendix, pp. 1 ff. This, the Cape Inquiry into the Jameson Raid, includes the Transvaal Green-book No. 2 of 1896 with a translation.
[2] *Ibid.*, pp. vi. ff.
[3] On self-government in Natal *vide* C. 6487 of 1891 and H.C. 216 of 1894; Eybers, p. 204.
[4] Gardiner, *Harcourt*, II. 311 ff.; Michell, *Rhodes*, II. 95.
[5] Colvin, *Jameson*, I. 307; Williams, *Rhodes*, pp. 354 ff.; Michell, *Rhodes*, II. 118 ff.

Kruger not to go too far lest he unite all South Africa against him. Meanwhile Jameson talked to all sorts and conditions of men on the Rand and concluded that Hammond was right. Rhodes, cautious as ever, declined to commit himself, but he realised that he might have to bargain with the Uitlanders, for if once they got railway connection with Delagoa Bay and Durban and ceased to be dependent on the Cape ports, they would hardly be content to play second fiddle in an economic federation controlled by his Cape and Charterland. Meanwhile, Jameson must drill his Rhodesian police and raise volunteers, men who might do much riding light in open country with the machine-guns which had done such execution in Matabeleland and had so greatly impressed Rhodes on his recent trek through Pondoland. The country between Johannesburg and the railhead at Mafeking was open enough.[1]

Then came the fatal Volksraad elections. Rehoboam sat in Solomon's seat and Kruger, thus emboldened, delivered a stiff defence of the dynamite monopoly and began very tentatively to arm.[2] At that, Rhodes decided to make sure of the two Bechuanalands, which would *inter alia* give him a jumping-off ground for any possible armed intervention in the Transvaal. Now that the Kimberley line had reached Mafeking, he asked Ripon to fulfil old promises and understandings by handing British Bechuanaland over to the Cape Colony and giving the Chartered Company a railway strip running northward through the Protectorate. In his eagerness to get these territories he even offered to forgo the Imperial subsidy that was to have been paid for a term of years to help to pay the cost of carrying the Cape-to-Cairo railway to Bulawayo. Ripon was noncommittal. Not so Loch, who hurried to London resolved to resign partly because he knew that he would never be able to control the course of events if the Protectorate passed from his hands into those of Rhodes, and partly because the Swaziland affair had taken a turn for the worse.[3] So far from issuing the Organic Proclamation, the Swazis had dismissed Offy Shepstone from his post as royal adviser, repudiated the Proclamation of 1890 under which the joint government functioned, and sent a deputation to London. British concessionaires urged them to stand out for the *status quo*, and Transvaalers tried to create the confusion which would entitle them to intervene under the Convention. Ripon and Loch now agreed that Swaziland must fulfil its 'manifest destiny' by passing to the Transvaal under proper safeguards for native interests.[4]

---

[1] Williams, p. 248; Colvin, II. 13; 311 of 1897, pp. 259 ff.

[2] At this time the republic had a mixed bag of 18 field-pieces and about 100 artillerymen. Some rifles and maxims were now ordered and provision made in the estimates for forts round Pretoria ('*The Times' History of the War*, I. 147).

[3] Walker, *De Villiers*, p. 255.

[4] C. 7611 of 1895, pp. 17, 21 ff.; Wolf, *Ripon*, II. 222 ff.

Kruger's East Coast port was, however, another matter. Loch had repeatedly asked for leave to help the Portuguese at Delagoa Bay in case they were attacked by the Transvaalers or by the Germans or by the French, who had a naval base on the Cape route near Cape Verde and a strong expeditionary force in Madagascar. Rosebery, the premier, feared the French; but Ripon was now convinced that the Germans, who were brutally crushing the Hereros in South-West Africa, were the enemy, and that they meant to extend a protectorate over the Transvaal. The Foreign Office hinted to Germany that the Transvaal was in the British sphere of influence and would have said much more but for strained relations with France. The Colonial Office decided to annex all that lay between Swaziland and the sea and so 'mak siccar.'[1]

Ripon persuaded Loch to return to finish the business. Kruger was to have Swaziland under the terms of the abortive Convention of 1893, but not necessarily with the consent of the Swazis. That, in Loch's opinion, was the price which must be paid to avert war between the two white peoples of South Africa. So it was arranged by the President and High Commissioner at the Volksrust-Charlestown Conference. The Pretoria Volksraad ratified the Third Swaziland Convention, and the Transvaal at once took over the territory as a protectorate.[2] The Transvaalers' satisfaction at achieving this long stride seawards was, however, short-lived. Their President addressed the Pretoria Germans on the Kaiser's birthday in terms which could only be interpreted as a confirmation of all the fears of Loch and Ripon.[3] Ripon delayed no longer. Zambaan's, Mbegisa's and the lands of the Tongas were annexed and the Transvaal was cut off from the sea.[4] It was still open to Kruger to negotiate for Kosi Bay; but he would have to deal directly with Great Britain now and, since the Wilhelmstrasse presently hinted that the inclusion of the Republic in the customs union, on which the acquisition of the port depended, would be a violation of the *status quo* which it desired to maintain, there was little chance that the negotiations would ever be resumed. Nor were they.[5]

Rhodes now took steps to force the hemmed-in republic into his economic federation 'always respecting' republican independence.[6]

Feb.
1895.

Jan.
1895.

April–
May
1895.

[1] Wolf, *Ripon*, II. 231; Walker, *De Villiers*, p. 253 (based partly on Loch's *Materials*). On Transvaal-German correspondence *vide* van Oordt *op. cit.*, p. 608.

[2] C. 7611, pp. 23, 34 ff., 42 ff.

[3] Fitzpatrick, *op. cit.*, p. 106; Botha, *Kruger en Leyds*, pp. 469 ff.; 311–1 of 1897, p. 548.

[4] C. 7780 of 1895, pp. 41 ff.; C. 7878 of 1895; Leyds, *Transvaal Surrounded*, pp. 346 ff.

[5] Walker, *De Villiers*, p. 254; Translation of *German White-book*, 1896 (Cape): Germany especially desired to maintain the commercial *status quo*, lest the Transvaal 'sink down into a province of the great "Rhodesia" . . .'

[6] Williams, *Rhodes*, p. 245.

He sailed to London to be lionised, to be made a Privy Councillor, Jan. to see his new provinces christened 'Rhodesia' and, on the morrow 1895. of Kruger's speech to the Pretoria Germans, to hear Jameson, with the Prince of Wales in the chair, prophesy a speedy South African economic federation from which political federation would surely follow.[1] That was his aim. He knew that his time was short. His heart was troubling him; he had never fully recovered from the shock of a heavy fall from his horse in 1891; his self-control was going; most of his old friends were already gone and, in their stead, were a crowd of Byzantine courtiers at Groote Schuur who shielded him from the sane breezes that blow in the outer world of facts. His power was over-great.[2] True, he had failed to get the Bechuanaland Protectorate, but he had made sure of the backing of *The Times* and *Morning Post*, and had privately gained the approval of Lord Rosebery, Gladstone's Liberal Imperialist successor as Prime Minister, to his idea of intervention by the Company's Police in support of an Uitlander Rising, always provided the Police should not move before that Rising had actually begun.[3] In South Africa his hold on the six papers of the *Argus* group was tightening, and soon the two great checks on his political action were removed. He helped to expedite Loch's departure at the beginning instead of the end of the Cape session, and to persuade Sir Hercules Robinson to return to Cape-town as High Commissioner. The change was fiercely assailed by Rhodes's opponents in South Africa, who wrongly believed that Sir Hercules was still interested in De Beers and similar companies, and queried by Chamberlain and the Unionists, who hated the 'colonial' policy for which Robinson stood. It was partly because Robinson favoured colonial rather than imperial action that Rhodes wanted him, and partly because, if trouble arose, it would be well to have a High Commissioner who enjoyed the confidence of most of the South African British and Afrikaners; indeed, Kruger himself was inclined to welcome the return of his old friend till Capetown clamour and second thoughts made him suspicious. Sir Hercules, however, had one further virtue in Rhodes's eyes. He was old and not in the best of health; hence, he would not be likely to interfere so much as Loch had done with the activities of his Prime Minister, and would yet be at hand when he was needed.[4] So Loch sailed home, and with April him, for all practical purposes, the imperial factor, while Hofmeyr, 1895. harassed by ill-health and the sight of the Bond falling to pieces,

[1] *B.S.A. Co. Annual Meeting*, Jan. 1895, pp. 19 ff.; Dugdale, *German Diplomatic Documents*, II. 366.
[2] Williams, *Rhodes*, pp. 249 ff.
[3] Van der Poel, *op. cit.*, p. 23; Sir Graham Bower's *Letters*; E. M. Bell, *Flora Shaw*, p. 177; H. Sauer, *Ex Africa*, p. 258.
[4] Williams, *op. cit.*, p. 252; Gardiner, *Harcourt*, II. 338; Walker, *De Villiers*, p. 255.

resigned his seat in Parliament. Hybris descended upon Rhodes. Nemesis and Ate would follow in due course.

The campaign to secure the inclusion of the Transvaal in the coming federation had already begun. The Delagoa Bay line was
<!-- margin note: Dec. 31, 1894. -->
finished, the Natal line was on the Transvaal border, and the expiry of the Sivewright Agreement of 1891 robbed the Cape of its power to fix through rates to the Rand. The Cape, however, still controlled the railway through the Free State and, to retain the Rand traffic, reduced its rates to Viljoen's Drift on the Transvaal's Vaal frontier. The Netherlands Company retaliated by tripling its rates over the 40 miles linking the drift to Johannesburg. The Netherlands Company, which owned the Rand end of all the lines, obviously had the whip hand; an attempted settlement at a railway conference at Capetown broke down, and the Cape administration, loading the goods on ox-waggons at the river, trekked them thence to the Rand.[1]

It paid them to do so, for the 'Kaffir Boom' in mining shares,
<!-- margin note: 1895. -->
following on the proving of the deep levels, was at its height, a boom which spread to London and Berlin and induced French investors to plunge so heavily that their country rapidly qualified for a voice in the settlement of any trouble that might arise in the Transvaal. Meanwhile, Rhodes carried a resolution in the Cape Assembly that British Bechuanaland be annexed to the Colony, and pressed for the transference of the Protectorate to the Chartered Company,[2] while Jameson in Johannesburg warned him that he must try to ride the whirlwind that was beating up there.[3] He and Alfred Beit, therefore, made their financial arrangements accordingly. Rhodes had recently told his long-suffering Chartered shareholders that there was
<!-- margin note: July 1895. -->
no need to raise new capital, but he now asked them to authorise the issue of 500,000 new shares at £3 10s. apiece.[4] Already the Company had taken steps to lay the foundations of a native administration in Charterland, and if Rhodesia were not soon off-loaded upon the Cape or upon a federation, money would be needed to finance a stable government there. Besides, the railway must be carried on from Mafeking, and interest on the Matabele War debentures would fall due at the New Year of 1896. The shares were authorised, but the issue was postponed for a season.[5]

In the middle of the year the political atmosphere in South Africa
<!-- margin note: May 1895. -->
seemed to be clearer. Robinson arrived with instructions from Ripon to play the part of mediator in the Transvaal if occasion arose, and

[1] Hofmeyr, *Hofmeyr*, p. 484; Cook, *Rights and Wrongs*, p. 51.
[2] C. 7932 and C. 7962 of 1896; Eybers, p. 76.
[3] Colvin, *Jameson*, II. 30 ff.
[4] *B.S.A. Co. Annual Meeting*, Jan. 18, 1895, p. 9; *B.S.A. Co. Extraordinary General Meeting*, July 12, 1895.
[5] B.S.A. Co. Notice, July 24, 1895.

the promise of up to 10,000 troops to back his intervention.[1] The controversy over his appointment died away, the Delagoa Bay rail- June way was formally opened in the presence of a German squadron and 1895. a much stronger British squadron alongside and, such was the good feeling of the moment, Kruger narrowly escaped the offer of a G.C.M.G.[2] But the sky soon clouded. Next week the 'cordite vote' shattered the Rosebery Ministry, Lord Salisbury's Conservatives took office, and, to the dismay of Rhodes, Joseph Chamberlain, the high priest of Unionism, became Colonial Secretary. Then, the Free State Volksraad objected to some of the terms of the customs union and talked once more of federation with its sister republic,[3] while on the Rand the National Union renewed its activities. That Union was heartened by the personal request of the new High Commissioner that Kruger should show himself accommodating; but it was weakened by the defection of some of its Labour members, who, mindful of the fate of the Kimberley voters in the days of open voting before the Cape Ballot Act, unsuccessfully demanded that a ballot clause be tacked on to the next franchise petition.[4] It was perhaps partly for this reason that the Volksraad rejected the resultant Uitlander petition after one of its members had challenged the petitioners, who this time included several leading capitalists, to 'come on and fight.'[5]

The appeal to arms came soon enough. In June 1895, the very month in which Rhodes had so pointedly raised the question of the Two Bechuanalands in the Cape Assembly, he and Alfred Beit sounded Lionel Phillips, now chairman of the Chamber of Mines, and Leonard, president of the still middle-class National Union. They found them well inclined towards the idea of outside intervention in support of an Uitlander Rising. It now remained to make sure that such intervention would be effective. Rhodes knew that Chamberlain was resolved to work for the federation of both Australia and South Africa; he had good reason to believe that he was as keen as Loch had ever been to see the Union Jack flying once more over Pretoria; he could fairly assume that he was aware that Loch and Ripon had proposed to intervene in the Transvaal in certain circumstances, and he took it for granted that, like nearly everyone else, he expected an Uitlander explosion sooner or later. Surely 'Pushful Joe' would be no less ready to act on good cause shown than his own cautious Liberal predecessor and a robust Unionist High Commissioner. The chance of finding out soon came.

---

[1] Information furnished by Sir Graham Bower, at that time Imperial Secretary to Robinson. Sidney Buxton, Under-Secretary for the Colonies, denied all knowledge of this promise.
[2] Wolf, *Ripon*, II. 228, 234.
[3] *Notulen (O.F.S. Volksraad)*, *1895*, pp. 685 ff.
[4] Rose, *Truth about the Transvaal*, p. 27.
[5] FitzPatrick, *Transvaal from Within*, p. 400.

Chamberlain indicated that he was ready to let Rhodes have the Two Bechuanalands in due time, but could do nothing about the Protectorate till he had talked with Khama and two other Bechuana Chiefs, who were coming to London to petition the Queen against handing over that territory to the Chartered Company. Rhodes therefore sent Dr. Frederick Rutherford Harris, the Company's Capetown secretary, racing off to London to counteract the Chiefs and see how Chamberlain would regard the projected Raid-Rising. During his first interview, Harris found the Colonial Secretary ready to discuss Bechuanaland, but in no wise willing to listen to hints about the Rising with external aid such as Rhodes was planning. Albert, Earl Grey, one of the Company's directors, who was 'in the know' and present at the interview, tactfully removed the unhappy secretary and himself told Chamberlain with such effect that Harris could assure Rhodes that the Colonial Secretary would do all he could to help 'provided he does not know officially of your plan.' Probably Harris did not raise the matter again at a subsequent interview, but he must have reported to his chief so cheerfully that the Company at once asked for the railway strip right through Bechuanaland, and especially for a block of land at Gaberones some hundred miles north of Mafeking with leave to station police thereon to defend the as yet non-existent railhead against 'the ferocious Bechuana.'[1]

Meanwhile, Kruger had taken a line which induced the Colonial Secretary to be much more helpful to the plotters. In August, just after the prorogation of the Cape Parliament and Harris's first interview at the Colonial Office, he had given notice that on October 1 he would close the Vaal drifts to overseas goods.[2] He thereby outraged Cape and Free State feelings and failed to smooth ruffled plumes when, in reply to warnings that he would break the London Convention if he discriminated thus against what were with few exceptions British goods, he blandly offered to set matters right by including Colonial goods in the embargo. The breach of the Convention might well lead to war, the overthrow of the Pretoria régime and, if all went well, the speedy inclusion of the Transvaal and Rhodesia in a South African federation. At this prospect, such a boom set in during September that Chartereds touched £9 for the £1 share, the Bechuanaland Railway Company proposed to raise £1,300,000 on debenture to carry the Mafeking railway northward and the B.S.A. Company guaranteed the interest on such of these debentures as were taken up at once.[3] Rhodes, for his part, took the next necessary steps. He first told the disapproving Bower the whole

---

[1] Van der Poel, *op. cit.*, pp. 31 ff.
[2] C. 8474 of 1897 for details of the Drifts Crisis.
[3] *The Economist*, Sept. 28, 1895; *B.S.A. Directors' Report*, 1894–5, p. 2.

of his scheme under the pledge of secrecy and, at his suggestion, told the High Commissioner also. Having thus ensured that Sir Hercules should be well aware of those 'damned conspiracies of Rhodes and Chamberlain,' however doggedly that official might stick to his plea of 'ignorance' to the bitter end, he next came to terms with Phillips, Leonard, Hays Hammond and his own brother, Colonel Frank Rhodes, for whom he found a job in Johannesburg. The gist of this arrangement was that Jameson should come in from the western border to assist a rising which should follow a statement of Uitlander grievances, while he himself should arm the Uitlanders and deliver the High Commissioner at Pretoria at the psychological moment. He made it clear to the 'Reformers' that all he wanted at the moment was an economic federation and that 'the rest will come in time,' but he must have wondered how folk whose interests lay in the Transvaal regarded such a consummation on the terms of one whose interests lay in the old Colony and the North. Finally, since time was running short, he decided not to wait for the leisurely transfer of Gaberones, but to press for the immediate transfer to the Company of a small area much further south around Pitsani near Mafeking itself which had been offered by Montsioa and Ikaning, two minor Bechuana chiefs who had not accompanied Khama to see the Queen. This transfer was effected at once and, on October 20, 1895, Jameson, as Administrator of the tiny cession, began to move Chartered Police thither from Bulawayo and to enrol as many as he could of the disbanded Bechuanaland Police. This done, he dashed to Johannesburg and there induced five of the leading Reformers to give him an undated letter calling upon him to come to the rescue of the women and children on the Rand.

Rhodes, meanwhile, had begun, through trusted employees at Port Elizabeth and Kimberley, to smuggle arms and ammunition to the Reformers with the utmost ingenuity but in far too small quantities. At this stage, Kruger almost delivered himself into his enemies' hands by closing the Drifts on November 1. Chamberlain, resolute to uphold the London Convention, arranged with Rhodes for joint military and financial action, saw to it that troopships on the Indian route should touch at Capetown, and sent Kruger a virtual ultimatum. While the Drifts crisis was thus rising to its climax, Chamberlain settled the fate of the Bechuanaland Protectorate. Now that Khama and his friends had indeed seen Her Majesty in a gracious audience of which their tribesmen speak with pride to this day, he with his own hand marked off nearly the whole of the vast Protectorate as reserves, but gave the Chartered Company a wide railway strip right along the Transvaal's border which linked Rhodes' new sphere around Mafeking with his older sphere south of the Zambesi. This vital strip was transferred on November 7, the very day that

15

Kruger averted war by prudently reopening the Vaal Drifts. Even so, as Harris faithfully reported, the Colonial Secretary said that Rhodes 'must allow a decent interval and delay firewórks for a fortnight.'[1]

All very well to counsel caution thus, but time was pressing harder than ever. Rhodes had indeed acquired his railway strip and had also taken over British Bechuanaland;[2] but he had also lost a golden chance of facing Kruger with the support or at least the acquiescence of the British Government and most South Africans outside the Transvaal, not least that of Hofmeyr's Bondsmen on whom his political life at the Cape had always depended. Now, the breakdown of a second railway Conference emphasised the growing economic dominance of Kruger's Republic and warned Rhodes that, if he indeed meant to have federation 'within the year,' he must rely primarily on Jameson's Police and the Uitlanders and, thereafter, such Imperial aid as might be forthcoming.[3] He received a broad hint that that support would be forthcoming up to a point when Chamberlain asked the High Commissioner for his views on the procedure to be followed in the event of a Rising 'with or without assistance from outside.' The reply, which was drafted by Bower but edited by Sir Hercules and his Prime Minister together, suggested that the High Commissioner, with the openly expressed support of the British Government, should call upon both parties to submit to his arbitration, and that the Commons should be told that large forces were in readiness to proceed to South Africa. Chamberlain, having ascertained that Rhodes shared his desire to see the Union Jack flying once more at Pretoria, gave warning that no Rising must take place without the certainty of success, because 'a fiasco would be most disastrous,' and promised that if the Johannesburgers would hoist the Queen's flag, they might choose their own Governor.[4] Then, in mid-November, came a bombshell. Grover Cleveland, President of the United States, by an unprecedented stretching of the Monroe Doctrine, threatened to intervene in a long-drawn-out frontier dispute between Venezuela and British Guiana. Chamberlain acted with his customary promptitude. Knowing that it lay with Rhodes whether there should be a Rising or no, he sent word indirectly to him and thus to the Reformers that the Rising had better take place at once before the American crisis became serious or else be postponed for some time. Then, for the first time, he told his own chief,

---

[1] Van der Poel, *op. cit.*, p. 49.   [2] Act 41 of 1895; Eybers, p. 76.

[3] On the Raid *vide* Williams, *Rhodes*; Michell, *Rhodes*, II.; Colvin, *Jameson*, II.; Hofmeyr, *Hofmeyr*; Fitzpatrick, *Transvaal from Within* (the Reformers' side of the story); S.A.R. Green-book No. 2 of 1896, translated in A. 6–96 (Cape); Nos. 308 and 311, 311 (i), 311 (ii) of 1897 (*Report of Select Committee*); C. 8330 of 1897 (A. 6–96 (Cape) without the Dutch translation); H. M. Hole, *The Jameson Raid*; G. L. Garvin, *Chamberlain*, III.; J. van der Poel, *The Jameson Raid*.

[4] Van der Poel, *op. cit.*, pp. 49, 56.

Lord Salisbury, a little of what was afoot and cabled to Sir Hercules that troopships were on their way to Capetown.[1]

Jameson, meanwhile, had done his share of the work, but the Reformers could not do theirs. Enthusiasts might still drill the rank and file who were furious enough to do anything against Kruger and his Continentals; but there was little chance of a serious rising in the midst of a boom, and at headquarters, where alone the plot was known to a handful of men, there was division.[2] Some meant business, others were plainly playing with the idea of a revolution by telegram. They prudently postponed the rising for a week because of the races which would fill their town with visitors; they boggled over the question whether the revolutionary flag should be the Union Jack or the Vierkleur, while canny Boers with one eye on the 'rest camp' at Pitsani, where the police drilled with unremitting vigour,[3] withdrew their savings from the Bechuanaland banks,[4] and Jameson fretted and fumed, fearful of discovery and apparently without any clear idea as to whether his Raid was to be the signal for the Rising or *vice versa*. At last, with open drilling going on in the streets, men, women and children fleeing the town, and the Chartered men insisting that the Rising must take place without delay, the Reformers sent an envoy to Capetown to settle the flag question with Rhodes, while the Kruger Government undertook to reduce railway rates and duties on foodstuffs, and promised to give equal subsidies to Dutch and English schools and raise the franchise and ballot questions at a special session of the Volksraad in January. Never- theless, Leonard issued a manifesto of grievances and called a mass meeting for January 6,[5] and next day, in London, it was formally announced that the long-deferred issue of the 500,000 new Chartered shares would take place on January 8.[6] But already the ill-armed Reformers had decided to postpone 'the flotation' and sent a delegation to Groote Schuur to make new plans with Rhodes and also messengers to Pitsani to stop Jameson at all costs.[7] Rhodes, relieved to be quit of a scheme which he had never liked, passed word to the High Commissioner that the Rising had 'fizzled out,' and Robinson so informed Chamberlain.[8]

Chamberlain was not surprised to hear that the Chartered people's revolution had 'fizzled,' because he had already gathered from City gossip that this might happen; but he was startled to receive a hint from Bourchier Hawksley, the Company's lawyer and no great

Dec. 27, 1895.

[1] Van der Poel, *op. cit.*, pp. 79 ff.
[2] Van der Poel, *op. cit.*, p. 79; J. L. Garvin, *Life of Joseph Chamberlain*, III. 76 ff.; C. 7962 of 1896, p. 21.
[3] A. 6–96 (Cape), pp. liii ff. *Vide* C. 7962 of 1896, p. 36, for transfer of police.
[4] Information given by H. M. Quigley, at the time bank manager at Vryburg.
[5] Fitzpatrick, *Transvaal*, p. 136; C. 7933 of 1896, p. 65.
[6] *The Economist*, Dec. 28, 1895.   [7] A. 6696 (Cape), p. lx.
[8] Van der Poel, *op. cit.*, p. 85.

admirer of Rhodes, that the latter might tell Jameson to go in and 'manipulate' a revolution. He at once cabled to the High Commissioner that anything of that sort would imperil the Charter. It was too late, for before the message could reach Capetown, the Doctor was o'er the border and awa' riding full tilt for the Rand. Jameson had long ago made up his mind that the Uitlanders would never rise if left to themselves; he knew that Rhodes's prescription was, 'Take what you can get and ask me afterwards'; he had rushed Lobengula and a High Commissioner in times past and now resolved to rush the Reformers, the Imperial factor and Kruger by going in uninvited and single-handed to force on a Rising and, therefore, British intervention. He paid no attention to frantic messages from Harris in Capetown,[1] 'on the surface a genius but, under the crust, as thick as they are made';[2] still less would he hearken to instructions from the lukewarm Reformers. Rhodes, he argued, wanted him to go in, but, as Premier of the Colony, must keep up appearances. Very well; he himself would take the responsibility. If only he could get to Johannesburg, he was sure that he could make things move (for 'the Doctor' had a wonderful way with him).[3] So he wired to Rhodes at the last moment that, unless he heard from him to the contrary, he would start. Fate and Rutherford Harris saw to it that the message reached its destination too late, and, when Rhodes wired to him to stand fast, the telegraph line had been cut south of Mafeking.[4] So Jameson rode into the Transvaal with some 500 fighting men, never realising that, though the act was his, the responsibility for it must fall upon his chief.

Dec. 29, 1895.

Thirty-six hours later, the horrified Reformers heard definitely that Jameson was coming to their rescue.[5] Putting a bold face on their difficulties, they co-opted some fifty prominent citizens to their cosmopolitan Committee,[6] prepared to proclaim a provisional government, hoisted the Vierkleur and gave out such arms as they had. Kruger withdrew his Police to the dominating Johannesburg Fort and averted possible international complications by telling the German consul at Pretoria that, if he was afraid, he could have a guard of fifty burghers in place of the marines he was anxious to bring up from Delagoa Bay.[7] He then sent Cronje, the hero of the siege of Potchefstroom during the War of Independence, to organise the defence at Krugersdorp where the road from the west climbed up the slope of the Rand.

---

[1] Van der Poel, *op. cit.*, p. 82.   [2] Colvin, *Jameson*, II. 229.
[3] So Jameson explained his action to Lionel Curtis in 1907.
[4] A. 6–96 (Cape), pp. 26, 27, cclxii.   [5] FitzPatrick, p. 138.
[6] Thirty-four of British Nationality, seventeen Afrikanders, eight United States citizens, two Germans, one Hollander, one Swiss, one Transvaal burgher and one Turk.   C. E. Vulliamy, *Outlanders*, p. 224; van der Poel, *op. cit.*, p. 111.
[7] *German White-book*, 1896 (Cape), p. 4; Walker, *De Villiers*, p. 265.

All was soon over. On receipt of definite news, the High Commissioner, counselled by his own good sense and Hofmeyr, repudiated the Raiders and ordered them back;[1] the Reformers agreed to what was practically an armistice which tied their hands for the next twenty-four hours; Jameson failed to break through at Krugersdorp and, next day, was compelled to surrender near Doornkop, knowing Jan. 2, that the High Commissioner, at Chamberlain's command, had 1896. proclaimed him an outlaw. At that very moment, *The Times*, doing its distant best for him, published the famous letter of invitation which Harris had furnished with an impossible date and its own editor had further doctored so that it should read like an express summons. A couple of days later the dejected High Commissioner arrived in Pretoria[2] at Kruger's reluctant invitation to help to clean up the mess. He brought with him, not the furious and over-cautious Hofmeyr, who had refused to come, but the anxious Bower and vehement injunctions from the Colonial Secretary to demand forthwith a five-year franchise, a less humiliating oath of allegiance, English-medium schools and full municipal rights for Johannesburg. Robinson wisely shelved these untimely demands and co-operated with the President in persuading the cornered Uitlanders to lay down their arms. This done, Kruger arrested some sixty members of the Reform Committee, issued his famous 'forgive and forget' manifesto and, after a prolonged struggle with some of his commandants who favoured drumhead court-martial and a firing party, handed over Jameson and his followers to the Imperial authorities for punishment.[3] All the Raiders, save about one hundred who were domiciled in South Africa, were quietly shipped home from Durban. With them went all hope of a peaceful federation for a generation.

[1] C. 7933 of 1896, p. 8; Hofmeyr, *Hofmeyr*, p. 490.
[2] For Robinson's policy *vide* C. 8063 of 1896, pp. 116 ff.
[3] Walker, *De Villiers*, p. 266.

CHAPTER XIII

UNIFICATION, 1896–1910

FROM THE RAID TO THE WAR, 1896–99

THE Jameson Raid revealed the risks run by a state which works through a semi-independent body like a chartered company. In Europe, the Triple and Dual Alliances already faced one another, and Great Britain, splendidly isolated, was anxiously reckoning the troops necessary to hold the Canadian frontier against the U.S.A. in case President Cleveland should carry out his threat to intervene in a long-standing Anglo-Venezuelan boundary dispute. The sudden movement of five hundred troopers seven thousand miles away set the balance of the Armed Peace a-quiver. Jameson's ride into the Transvaal called forth all the anti-British jealousies of Europe. The Pretoria Germans appealed to their government for aid, and the chiefs of the Wilhelmstrasse nervously responded. They sent an additional warship to Delagoa Bay and despatched a threatening protest to London, while the Emperor tried to beat up French and Russian support against perfidious Albion. On learning of the surrender at Doornkop, the German Ambassador in London recovered the semiultimatum unread; whereupon the Kaiser despatched his famous telegram of congratulation to Kruger as a substitute for the troops which he had at first wished to send to uphold a German protectorate over the Transvaal. Thereupon, Great Britain equipped a flying squadron, partly as a warning to the All-Highest and his enthusiastic Reichstag, partly as a precaution against American intervention on the Spanish Main. In a few days the storm subsided on both sides of the Atlantic. Great Britain came to terms with the United States; St. Petersburg sent a reassuring message to London; Portugal, the ancient ally of England, declined to have Germans in Lourenço Marques, and France intimated that in case of war her neutrality would be of the most pro-British variety and possibly something more. Soon 'My dear William' was explaining to 'Most beloved Grandmamma' that his marines had only been intended to protect the German consulate 'as they do in China and elsewhere' and in no case to have taken 'any active part in the row.'[1]

The crisis of the Raid cleared the air to this extent that the Powers now knew that Great Britain would fight rather than allow any of them to interfere in South Africa; but in South Africa itself it added immensely to Great Britain's difficulties. All the pre-Raid problems awaited solution in an atmosphere of suspicion and reviving racialism and, now, the Imperial authorities must attempt the solution themselves. Rhodes, the unofficial High Commissioner, was out of action. His office of Privy Councillor was imperilled, his power of attorney for the Company was gone and his very Charter was threatened by an angry Imperial Government and openly challenged by Sauer and Merriman, who were prepared to face that prospect of Crown colony rule in 'the North' which alone prevented Hofmeyr from joining in the attack.[2] Hofmeyr and most of his Bondsmen none the less washed their hands of Rhodes, and many Englishmen turned away from one whom they regarded as the head-centre of a bullying plutocracy which had dragged their flag in the mud.[3] Their judgment was harsh, for Rhodes, with his schemes for the good of Anglo-Saxon civilisation and therefore, in his eyes, for the good of mankind, was immeasurably more than a mere plutocrat;[4] but he was now politically impossible. Sprigg with a patchwork cabinet reigned in his stead at Capetown.[5]

[1] Lee, *Edward VII*, pp. 719 ff.; *German White-book*, 1896 (Cape); C. 7933 of 1896, p. 48; Hammann, *World Policy of Germany*, pp. 68 ff.; Dugdale, *German Dip. Doc.*, II. 368 ff.

[2] C. 8423 of 1897, p. 31.   [3] Walker, *De Villiers*, p. 269.

[4] Compare this letter from Rhodes to Harcourt written at Gwelo, on May 13, 1896, at the height of the Matabele Rebellion (Gardiner, *Harcourt*, II. 392).

'The enclosed explains my letter. It has come just as we start to try and make a junction with Buluwayo. We are 250 men and the Buluwayo column is 500. There are about 6000 natives in between us and Buluwayo and we may make a mess of it. I would be sorry to think that you thought I was "capable but not honest." I have tried to unite South Africa and no sordid motive has influenced me. . . .

                                                        C. J. RHODES.'

'May 14, We start in an hour. . . . You make one mistake—the Dutch in Africa are not all with Kruger and my action was not English v. Dutch. But we would not have the German element and the Pretoria Government must go.' *Vide* much fuller letter to W. P. Schreiner (Walker, *Schreiner*, p. 81).

[5] Sprigg Ministry, Jan. 13, 1896–Oct. 13, 1898: Sir Gordon Sprigg, Prime Minister and Treasurer; Dr. Thomas Nicolas German te Water and, from

The last state of the Uitlanders was worse than the first. All that could be expected of the Cape Colony were ministerial appeals and private Bond reminders to Kruger to remember that the condition of his republic was bound to have reactions in the Colony. In the Free State, whose burghers had lined the banks of the Vaal during the Raid with more than one anxious glance backward at the Basuto, the anti-English reaction ran strongly. Its officials, Afrikaners and Scots, corresponded with the peccant Cape in the highest Dutch of which they were capable instead of in the customary English as a protest against all things British, and Judge Marthinus Steyn easily defeated John Fraser in the race for the presidential chair from which ill-health had driven Reitz shortly before the crisis. Still less could help be expected from anyone in the Transvaal save from Kruger only. The leading Reformers were in gaol and the body of mining magnates was divided now that the more or less pro-Kruger and certainly anti-Rhodes' group led by J. B. Robinson had gone over from the Chamber of Mines to the Continental Association. The Liberal Boers had been driven into the arms of their President, who was assured of a further lease of power, immense moral prestige and an unimpeachable excuse for the rearmament which he now systematically undertook.[1]

At first Englishmen had not known what to think and even Chamberlain had taken some time to find his bearings. During the actual crisis he had urged Robinson to demand reforms in the Transvaal. Next, urged on by the still truculent Rhodes, who insisted that he must make a drive for federation, he had bidden him use 'firm language' and talked of sending large forces to the Cape and thus provide for 'all eventualities.' Having been roundly snubbed by his harassed subordinate, he had then changed his tactics, merely assuring him that he had by no means dropped the Uitlander issue and impressing on the Transvaal's Agent-General in London that, however much the rest of the London Convention of 1884 might be modified by mutual consent, Article IV must stand because it gave the Queen final control over the Republic's treaty-making powers.[2] On the other hand, he realised that the best way of avoiding the unwelcome inquiry into the genesis of the Raid which he had promised Hofmeyr would be to talk things out with the old President in a conciliatory atmosphere. He therefore invited Kruger to London with the reminder that Article IV could not be touched, and was so confident of his coming that he arranged for his passage on the

May 18, 1898, onwards, Dr. Thomas William Smartt, Colonial Secretary; Sir Thomas Upington and, from May 13, 1898, onwards, Thomes Lynedoch Graham, Attorney-General; Sir James Sivewright, Public Works; Sir Pieter Faure, Agriculture.
  [1] C. 8063 of 1896, p. 114; 'The Times' History of War in S.A., II. 66 ff.
  [2] Van der Poel, op. cit., pp. 145 ff.

Simonstown flagship.[1] Kruger accepted, but asked bluntly for a discussion of the forbidden Article. Chamberlain, in reply, cabled to Sir Hercules for submission to Kruger the substance of a long despatch defending the conduct of the British Government during the Raid and asking for redress of Uitlander grievances in general and, in especial, the grant of 'a modified autonomy' to the Rand very much on the lines that Merriman had just suggested independently. Next day, 'for reasons of policy,' he published this despatch *in extenso* weeks before it could reach Pretoria. Even so, Kruger again said he could come without prejudice to his Republic's autonomy, but he now in his turn asked plainly for compensation for the Raid, safeguards against future such incursions, the cancellation of Rhodes's Charter, the full incorporation of Swaziland, an East Coast port and a bilateral treaty in place of the Convention which was 'so injurious to the dignity of an independent "republic." '[2] All this Chamberlain accepted for discussion save only Article IV and, in spite of the opposition of many of his supporters, Kruger named the men who were to accompany him. Then came a message from a high quarter in Berlin that H.M. Government should be compelled to go to Canossa, and the realisation by the Transvaal authorities of the powerful weapon that had come into their hands by the discovery on the open veld of the saddle-bag of Captain Robert White, one of Jameson's young officers, which contained incriminating messages that had passed between the Raiders and the Reformers. Kruger, therefore, drew back, suggesting that the visit should be postponed.[3] Postponed it was— *sine die*—to the great misfortune of all concerned, for had the old President gone, he would certainly have received a great ovation from the impressionable London crowd and achieved a settlement of some at least of the outstanding questions. As it was, Chamberlain was left to silence the small group in the Commons, which pointed out that the road to Canossa lay through Pretoria itself, with the reminder that war with the Transvaal would be a serious matter and could in no case be undertaken to enforce internal reforms. He must now carry on his discussions with Kruger by letter with all the delay and chance of misunderstanding that diplomatic correspondence entails.[4]

The effect of the Raid was to scatter the political fragments of South Africa which Rhodes and economic pressure had begun to draw together. Rhodes's own base in the Colony had been destroyed; the election of Steyn portended a movement on the part of the Free State towards the Transvaal and away from the Colony; there was

---

[1] C. 7933 of 1896, pp. 19, 51, 59.   [2] *Ibid.*, p. 90; C. 8063 of 1896, p. 13.
[3] C. 8063 of 1896, p. 9; C. 8423 of 1897, pp. 15 ff.; Walker, *De Villiers*, p. 270.
[4] Cook, *Rights and Wrongs of the Transvaal War*, p. 62.

15*

no hope now of gaining the Bechuanaland Protectorate for the B.S.A. Company, some of whose directors were hurriedly resigning. But, once the first shock was past, Rhodes did not despair. Hofmeyr himself had thundered against the threat of German intervention implied in the Kaiser's telegram, time and Kruger's tariffs would surely swing the Bond over to his side once more and his fellow Englishmen would forgive.[1] He had hurried to London as soon as he could after the Raid to face the financial troubles that were crowding on his Company. Chartereds were down below the price at which the new issue of shares must be taken up, interest on the Matabele War debentures was falling due at last, and the Cape-to-Cairo railway, shut out from the line of life through the Transvaal, must be carried on through the Bechuanaland Protectorate. These difficulties were overcome and more also. Rhodes had indeed to agree that his police should be under strict imperial control; but he received assurances from Chamberlain that Uitlander grievances would not be forgotten and that as far as the Colonial Secretary was concerned, the Charter would be safe provided he withheld from the coming Committee of Inquiry certain telegrams which convicted that statesman of foreknowledge of the Raid-Rising. He then sent Lord Grey, privy to that plot, out of harm's way to organise a proper administration in Southern Rhodesia and soon followed him thither hoping that all March might yet be well in Charterland at least. Two days after his arrival 1896. the Matabele rose and slew every Rhodesian they could lay hands on.[2]

The capture of the Company's police at Doornkop and the subsequent disbanding of the Rhodesian volunteers did not cause the rebellion; they merely gave the Matabele their long-awaited opportunity. The leaders of the tribe must have known that the war of 1893 had not been of Lobengula's seeking, and they certainly knew that since the fall of their king they had had no one to look to. The head of the Company's native department was a good official, but he had to control a defective system through a handful of subordinates, some of whom were young, inexperienced and little credit to themselves or their employers, and, in the last resort, he must rely on the Matabele police, who lorded it over their fellows. But the root troubles, here as elsewhere, were land, cattle and labour. The widely scattered Mashonas, farming light granitic soil, had not felt the pressure of Europeans, especially as most of the white men had soon moved away westward; but in Matabeleland the closely grouped tribesmen had felt the pressure at once, because they favoured the heavy loams to which their fathers had been used in Zululand, and the loams covered the gold reef. These lands had been pegged out at once by white men, and the allocation of two large and

---

[1] Hofmeyr, op. cit., p. 496.　　[2] B.S.A. Directors' Report, Feb. 1896, p. 14.

little-known reserves was small compensation, since the soil of one was poor and the water supply of the other deficient. The Company, as successor of Lobengula, had then claimed all cattle as royal cattle and, pending the promised distribution, entrusted most of the beasts to the indunas to check the wholesale scramble by blacks and whites which had followed the war. The police had freely taken drafts of these animals, and when, on the eve of the Raid, the distribution was effected, few had been satisfied. Locusts had come with the white man, and now rinderpest attacked the herds; the slaughter of the newly distributed beasts by the officials in an attempt to stay the plague infuriated the tribesmen. Compulsory labour, not merely the customary labour for public purposes, but for private purposes also, was demanded by the native commissioners and their police from a stubborn and by no means fully conquered folk, who were told by their prophets that the shedding of white man's blood would alone end the prolonged drought.[1] So the Matabele slew and, when volunteers from all parts and imperial troops from the Protectorate came up, withdrew into the Matoppo Hills. Eighteen hundred men could make no lasting impression on this Matabele Basutoland, the drought and rinderpest which ravaged all South Africa made transport very difficult, the Company's funds ran low and, to the June surprise of the officials, the apparently docile Mashona rose in their 1896. rear. At last, after the soldiers had failed, the diplomatist succeeded. Oct. Taking his life in his hands, Rhodes went into the Matoppos un- 1896. armed with a few friends and induced the Matabele to submit.[2] It was the finest act of his life.

The Imperial Government insisted that the Company should keep a costly body of troops and police in Matabeleland, and the Mashona revolt smouldered on for twelve months longer; but serious fighting was over and though the Rebellion was to cost the Company close on £2,500,000, Rhodes was free to set his house in order.[3] He tried to bring men and money into the country by making lordly grants of land to development companies; he himself took up two large cattle runs; he helped Grey to staff the administration with good men drawn mostly from the coast colonies. Then, encouraged by messages from Afrikaner friends and restored in prestige by the indabas in the Matoppos, he passed slowly home to Capetown receiving ovations from the 'British' in the towns and many old Afrikaner friends at wayside stations, but sneering at the 'unctuous rectitude' of his fellow-countrymen who had taken half the earth and yet condemned his Raid.

[1] C. 8130 of 1894, p. 5; C. 8547 of 1897, pp. 5, 11, *et passim.*
[2] Vere Stent, *Incidents in the Life of Cecil Rhodes*, pp. 27 ff.
[3] C. 8060 of 1896; C. 8732 of 1898; *Report of B.S.A. Extraordinary Meeting*, Nov. 6, 1896.

From Capetown, Rhodes must go to London, there to 'face the music' of a Committee of the Commons which was to inquire into the genesis of the Jameson Raid and the past administration of his Company. The delay in the holding of this inquiry was chiefly due to Chamberlain, who would fain have averted it altogether. After the fading of his initial hopes of achieving that end by talking things over with Kruger in person, he had taken a stronger line which might have had the same result even at the cost of war. In mid-1896, he had replaced Sir Jacobus de Wet, the British Agent at Pretoria, by the much more forthright William Conyngham Greene, and had bidden one of his own subordinates prepare *The Case against the South African Republic*, despatched a staff officer to South Africa to report on the military aspects of a war with that state, horrified Bower by talking blandly of sending 'Buller and thirty thousand men' to the Cape, and only dropped his demand for the drafting thither of at least ten thousand 'with a high proportion of cavalry and artillery' in face of the united protests of the War Office, the Treasury and the High Commissioner. On the other hand, poor Bower had promised him that he would play scapegoat to Sir Hercules, if only because he held that the High Commissioner's 'innocence' was politically necessary in a divided land where Transvaalers and Bondsmen were throwing away all hope of reconciliation by hounding down Rhodes and all things British.

Then had come a series of blows which convinced Chamberlain that the inquiry must be held. First, Judge Rheinhold Gregorowski, presiding over the Transvaal High Court, sentenced four of the leading Reformers to death and the rest to two years' imprisonment, a fine of £200 and thereafter banishment for three years. The death sentences were commuted at once and, a few weeks later all the rank-and-file, save two who refused the proferred terms, were released on paying their fines and promising to abstain from Transvaal politics for three years to come. At the same time, the four leaders were also released on payment of fines of £25,000 each, fines which Rhodes and Beit to their credit paid, and either went into exile forthwith or promised to abstain from Transvaal politics for fifteen years to come. Secondly, the Pretoria authorities published the damning papers found in '*die trommel van Bobbie White*' and thereby gave a Cape Select Committee the evidence on which to condemn its ex-Prime Minister, and Chamberlain the means of extorting from Rhodes that resignation of his seat on the Chartered Board which he had refused to give in the heat of the Matabele Rebellion. Next, the Court of Queen's Bench sent Jameson and four of his officers to gaol, an imprisonment from which the former was soon released on the grounds of ill-health, but which his friends had to endure to the full and resign their commissions in the British Army into the bargain.

To crown all, Henry Labouchere, editor of *Truth*, and his fellow-Radical, Sir William Harcourt, spurred on by the vindictive Hofmeyr, fiercely attacked the Raid-Rising as a shameless financial manœuvre. There was nothing for it but to move for a Committee of Inquiry. This Chamberlain did, but the ending of the Session two days later ended the Committee for that year also.

The Committee was, however, reconstituted early in 1897, and it was this Committee that Rhodes must face. His progress through the Colony and the liberation of all except two of the Reformers gave the signal for an outburst in some of the London and colonial newspapers against the Pretoria Government as an oppressive system and a bar to the full development of the gold industry. Much of the criticism was unfair, for some of the laws had been passed for the benefit of the Uitlanders, and others might benefit them if they were well administered. A municipal law had been framed which promised to give Johannesburg some measure of control over its domestic concerns; an Education Act gave much more adequate state assistance to schools for the children of those who paid nine-tenths of the taxes; the Ballot Act, which was to come into force in 1898, would go far to weaken official pressure at elections; some eight hundred Uitlanders who had taken up arms against the Raiders had been enfranchised. But this last measure merely flicked the rest of the Uitlanders on the raw, for it was an act of grace and the hope of getting the franchise as a right was further off than ever. As it was, anxious memorials came in from enfranchised burghers begging that this extension of privilege might cease. Kruger reigned supreme in the executive, wielding great power over the expenditure of public money, virtually appointing every official in the land and, with the State Secretary, acting as 'the Government'—that word of power in South Africa—to which the rest of the executive councillors habitually referred their differences. Conservatism, moreover, ruled the Volksraad, and the Liberal opposition was apt to wilt whenever the redoubtable President entered the Raadsaal.

Much of this was galling and was naturally made the most of by many of the ultra-British Uitlanders. These disgruntled folk were by no means content that the Council of Education on the Witwatersrand, which some of their community had formed shortly before the Raid, should be doing good work for English-medium schools under the changed conditions and should be admirably seconded by a few private schools such as Roedean School for Girls. Nor were they placated when Mansvelt founded the School of Mines to relieve the Gymnasium of most of its professional courses, and hardly more so when he set up state schools, especially along the Rand, where Dutch should be introduced only gradually. What they and not a few burghers also saw and resented was that the Superintendent of

Education, himself a Hollander, should be importing numerous fellow-countrymen at the public charges to staff as many of his schools as possible. Irritation, however, was one thing, but an implied threat quite another, and in Uitlander eyes some recent legislation was positively dangerous. The Aliens Expulsion Act, approved in principle before the Raid, was now law; so was the Immigration Act, which aimed primarily at excluding paupers, persons with contagious diseases and other undesirables, but which might be used to keep out others; so were the Press Law and the prohibition of unlicensed open-air meetings, which might well be used to fetter freedom of speech and writing.[1] It is true that these Acts gave the authorities very few powers which were not exercised by a British Home Secretary, that the Expulsion Act was only used once before the war of 1899, and then, with general approval, against the murderer of Woolf Joel, that only three public meetings were prohibited, two of which were to have been in favour of the Government, that the Immigration Law was presently repealed as a technical breach of the London Convention and a nuisance to neighbouring communities, and that the Press Law was aimed at a violent and unbridled press. The Uitlanders could not foresee all this in the early months of 1897. They were naturally suspicious of such powers conferred by an oligarchic, reactionary, unicameral legislature on an executive which had a taste for meddling with the minutiæ of administration and was largely staffed by Continentals, whose lack of sympathy with British and Colonial Uitlanders was notorious.

Besides, times were bad. Railway rates, distance from the ports, the inability of the farmers to supply the needs of the growing urban population, and the restrictive economic policy of the State kept up the cost of living and, therefore, working costs in the mines. There was a lack of native labour; illicit liquor sellers played havoc with such labourers as were available; some mines were closing, others were reducing their staffs, and a stream of emigration was setting towards Rhodesia or the Cape ports; banks were shortening credit and, in the background, rinderpest destroyed the cattle, and fever and lack of food killed the poorer burghers and the natives of the Waterberg and Zoutpansberg by the score. And so it continued throughout 1897. The gold-mines, hastily organised and burdened with a rate of wages fixed during the bonanza times, felt the pinch, the development of the deep levels still fell short of the producing stage in most cases, the public revenues dwindled, the farmers, in whose interest the state was run, grew poorer every day, and the Government was driven to vote large and increasing sums for the relief of destitute burghers.[2]

---

[1] C. 8423 of 1897, pp. 44, 56, 65; Eybers, p. 505; Acts 6 of 1894 (open-air meetings) and 25, 26 and 30 of 1896.
[2] C. 9093 of 1898.

It was under these depressing circumstances that the authorities 1897. fell foul of the Bench and the Press, which, failing the unattainable franchise, were regarded by the Uitlanders as the palladia of such liberties as they enjoyed.[1] Chief Justice Kotze, as one of the leaders of the Afrikaner party, was suspect of the Continentals, as a politician he had often failed to see eye to eye with his President, and, as a jealous defender of judicial independence, he now came into conflict with the executive and the legislature. The *Grondwet* had been drawn up forty years back by men unversed in politics and living in conditions utterly unlike those of the late 'nineties. It by no means made it clear whether or no the Volksraad was a sovereign body superior to the written constitution. The Volksraad had legislated both by *wet* (statute), a process which occupied at least three months, and by *besluit* (resolution), a method which entailed no delay whatever. Much of the law touching mining, property, contract, the franchise and the High Court itself had been made by *besluite*, whose 1884– validity Kotze had more than once upheld as the work of a sovereign 1887. legislature. Fuller study of the early history of the Republic had, however, convinced him that he had been wrong, and the need for putting some check on hasty legislation impelled him to set matters right. In spite of Kruger's warning not to tamper with Jan. *besluite*, he ultimately gave judgment in a mining case against the 1897. Government and in favour of the plaintiff, Robert Brown, an American citizen. In passing, he denied the power of the Volksraad to alter existing law by *besluit* and claimed for his court the right to test laws in American fashion by the touchstone of the *Grondwet*.

The Brown judgment involved the Government in a payment of some £372,000, opened up a vista of similar judgments, threatened chaos to the laws of the Republic and the loss of much-needed capital to the mines, and imperilled delicate negotiations with the Free State. There, Steyn, the new President, stood for three principles. The first, the referendum to *Het Volk*, he had failed to carry through a Volksraad jealous of its powers; the second, economic freedom, he had in a measure achieved, for though he stood by the customs union with the Cape, he had taken over the Free State railways from Jan. the Colonial administration; the third, closer relations with his 1897. northern neighbour, he was on the point of securing. But he himself held very definite opinions on the shortcomings of his prospective allies, and now the Brown judgment startled his burghers, few of whom had any love for Transvaalers, many of whom followed Fraser in opposing entangling alliances with the North and all of whom were proud of the stability of their little state and of its courts.

[1] On the issue between Kruger and Kotze *vide* Sir J. Kotze. *The Judicial Crisis*, and Walker, *De Villiers*, pp. 287 ff.

The Transvaal executive, therefore, hurried Law No. 1 of 1897 through the Volksraad by *besluit*, denying the existence of the testing right and, in spite of the fact that the judges had been appointed for life and could only be removed after due trial, authorising the President to dismiss any of them who, in answer to his challenge, still claimed that right.[1]

The Uitlander press and its friends in the Colony supported by the Johannesburg bar, Afrikaner and British alike, took up the cudgels on behalf of judicial independence; a few wealthy Uitlanders privately guaranteed the judges against immediate want in case of dismissal, while the judges themselves, though divided on the score of the existence of the testing right, protested in a body against Law No. 1, appealed to the sovereign people and practically declared a strike. Kruger first broke the judicial strike by appointing a sixth and more amenable Judge, gave his other Judges two weeks in which to claim or renounce the testing right, and concluded his offensive and defensive alliance with Steyn. Kotze had, meanwhile, called on the Chief Justice of the Cape to come to the rescue. Before his appeal could reach Capetown, de Villiers had set out for Pretoria. There he persuaded the Judges to promise that they would not exercise the disputed testing right, on the understanding that their President would as soon as possible submit a draft law to the Volksraad establishing the independence of the Bench and providing special machinery, as in the Free State, for the alteration of the *Grondwet*. On these terms Kruger agreed to suspend the operation of Law No. 1, and so the immediate crisis passed.

March 1897.

After the Courts, the Press. The newspapers on both sides, supported either by the Government or wealthy corporations and individuals, were noisy and bitter, and the noise of the opposition organs was swelled by the anti-Kruger clamour which rolled northward from the Colony. Criticism of a President is always apt to be more disturbing to the public peace than criticism of a minister under a constitutional monarch. King and President alike symbolise the unity of land and people, but whereas all the world knows that the King can do no wrong, President Kruger was the active head of the executive and, in the eyes of many of those he ruled, could hardly do right. But to criticise his actions was to criticise all he stood for. These criticisms were all the more alarming to the isolated Pretoria Government because Kruger looked on the newspapers as the expression of the opinion of little-known Johannesburg, and also because he believed that, in spite of the failure of his hated police to find them even by dint of wading mine dams, thousands of rifles which should have been given up after the Raid were still concealed along the Reef. He had already suppressed the *Critic*, which had

[1] Eybers, p. 508.

promptly reappeared as the *Transvaal Critic* and sent a protest to Downing Street. He now took the much more serious step of suppressing *The Star*. The directors thereupon appointed a new editor, re-christened their paper *The Comet* and, in their turn, appealed to the High Commissioner against the suppression as a breach of the Convention.[1]

March 1897.

It was amid this clamour against Kruger and all his works that the reconstituted Committee of Inquiry met at Westminster. That Committee, on which Chamberlain had an honoured seat, spent much of its leisurely energies in attacking Krugerism, enlarging on Uitlander grievances and building up Rhodes as an inspired *mehrer des Reichs*. It heard Rhodes defending himself ably and pleading in extenuation his fears of German intervention; it never called vital witnesses such as the High Commissioner, now Baron Rosmead and Tafelberg, an old and dying man, Lord Grey out of reach quelling the Mashona rebellion, and Edward Fairfield of the Colonial Office, who had recently died of a stroke suspecting that he might be sacrificed to save his chief; above all, it never saw the telegrams which would have incriminated the Colonial Secretary. These Rhodes, in keeping with his arrangement with Chamberlain, refused to produce, and the Committee saw no point in pressing either him or the Chartered Company's Attorney, who would cheerfully have gone to prison rather than comply and have stayed there till the Session should end and the Committee disperse without presenting any report. Besides, the Conservative majority had no mind to smash Chamberlain and, with him, their own Administration, while the Radical, Harcourt, was intent only on destroying Rhodes and his Company and resolved to do nothing that might inculpate the High Commissioner, a nominee of the Liberal Ripon, and still less Rosebery, the one hope of the shattered Liberal party. So it let Rhodes walk off, if not with flying colours, at least so secure in popular favour that even the busmen smiled upon him.

The outcry against Krugerism rose *fortissimo* as Rhodes took the water on his way home. He landed at Capetown heralded by *The Times* as the champion who was to defeat the plot against the British connection which de Villiers, whose main ambition at the moment was to be sworn in as Privy Councillor, was said to be hatching with Hofmeyr, whom he disliked, and Kruger, who distrusted him. De Villiers' real sin was that he had often talked of returning to active political life and had latterly hinted at a moderate Anglo-Afrikaner party which he was in many ways qualified to lead. *The Times* and the Cape Progressives, who were being recruited by the newly-founded South African League from among the British in opposition to the Afrikaner Bond, meant to make Rhodes

April 1897.

[1] C. 8423 of 1897, pp. 80 ff., 130.

Premier once more if only he would 'come out as a Progressive,' break with the Bond on internal as well as on external policy, and abolish the protective duties on foodstuffs which weighed so heavily on the townsmen.[1] Rhodes would not. He still hoped to make a federation based on Anglo-Afrikaner support; he felt that it was some of the Bondsmen who had broken with him and not he with them; he would do nothing to make the breach wider; so in spite of the urgency of Edmund Garrett, editor of the *Cape Times*, a keen critic of some parts of his earlier policy and now an ardent Progressive, he took little active part in the work of the Cape session. He promised indeed to 'fight constitutionally' to win 'equal rights for every white man south of the Zambesi,' but, as soon as he could, he fled north to his Rhodesians.[2]

Meanwhile, Kruger, urged on by Steyn and other friends, took steps to restore the credit of his state which had been so sorely shaken by the judges' crisis. The mining houses, appreciative of a Government which with all its faults taxed lightly, were anxious to meet him halfway. Once the deep levels reached the producing stage the depression would pass; the Chamber had already drawn close enough to the Association to permit of a reduction of wages for African workers who were now being recruited by the recently formed Native Labour Association, and both looked to a general settlement with the authorities which would pave the way for amalgamation, a diminution in the cost of living and a reduction of white wages also. *The Comet* therefore dropped its appeal unto Caesar and resumed its old name; the High Court pronounced the decree of suppression *ultra vires* and Kruger appointed two Commissions: one under Schalk Burger to consider the needs of the gold industry and the other to overhaul the *Grondwet* and carry out the recent arrangement with the judges.

Kruger's relations with the British Government afforded an additional argument for reform. His post-Raid popularity had evaporated in the chilly atmosphere of diplomatic correspondence with a Secretary of State whom he and his advisers had always suspected of foreknowledge of the Raid.[3] Chamberlain, for his part, had so far avoided direct discussion of Article 4 of the London Convention, which limited the Republic's treaty-making powers, in

---

[1] Cook, *Garrett*, p. 137; Walker, *De Villiers*, pp. 296 ff.
[2] Michell, *Rhodes*, II. 202; Cook, *Garrett*, p. 139.
[3] Sir H. Campbell-Bannerman and Sir W. Harcourt, political opponents of Chamberlain and members of the Committee of Inquiry, were satisfied that Chamberlain was innocent of complicity; *vide* Gardiner, *Harcourt*, pp. 392, 423 ff.; J. A. Spender, *Campbell-Bannerman*, I. 191 ff.; *Cape Times*, May 16, 1926, and Oct. 24, 1922. But *vide* Garvin, *Chamberlain*, III. 30 ff.; *C.H.B.E.* VIII. 561-2.

the hope that if Kruger were left to himself, he would prove more friendly to British and colonial interests. The course of events during the past year convinced him that he must exert pressure. Hence, in the mid-April of 1897, when, faced with a bill of costs for Raid expenses at the rate of £30 for every burgher called up and, in addition, a globular £1,000,000 for 'moral or intellectual damages,'[1] he queried the former account, refused to pass the latter claim on to the Chartered Company, protested against the immigration and expulsion laws and drew attention to the Transvaal's unauthorised extradition treaties with Holland and Portugal and its adhesion to the Geneva Convention as breaches of the London Convention.[2] Just as the British Agent was presenting the despatches at Pretoria, a British squadron dropped anchor in Delagoa Bay. April 1897.

The complaint was not unreasonable if Convention rights were to be maintained and the hegemony which Great Britain had so long enjoyed in South Africa be upheld. There was much that was disquieting to a British Colonial Secretary. The Transvaal, busily surrounding its capital with forts gunned by Creusot and Krupp, was now allied to the Free State on terms which gave it a call on that republic's resources limited only by the necessity of proving that its cause was just;[3] a large section of the Bond in the Cape was advocating common action with the republicans, who had arranged to set up the federal Raad first talked of in 1889;[4] Leyds was once more on his way to Europe; fear lest Germany, France or the Transvaal should acquire an area on Delagoa Bay[5] imparted an anxious tone to the speeches in which Chamberlain wished Godspeed to Sir Alfred Milner, the new High Commissioner. Apri 1897.

Sir Alfred Milner was a Balliol man of Jowett's dispensation, a Liberal in so far as he could be identified with party politics, and a born administrator who had made his name first in the Inland Revenue and then in Egypt. He set out with the good wishes of all parties, but his reception in South Africa was more mixed. The Progressives, who had just tumultuously welcomed Rhodes, hailed him as their champion. Gone were the days when British colonials spoke with ill-concealed irritation of 'Downing Street' or asked querulously why Great Britain 'always gave way.' Chamberlain was not the man to do things by halves, and here was another man who had the reputation of meaning what he said. Surely in this year of the Diamond Jubilee, he would not give way. If the Transvaal wished to be regarded as a foreign Power, let it be treated as such.

---

[1] Fitzpatrick, op. cit., p. 287.
[2] C. 8404 of 1897, p. 4; C. 8721 of 1898, p. 1; C. 8423 of 1897, pp. 1, 41, 47, 62, 71, 110, 113, 115 ff.
[3] Van der Merwe, Steyn, I. 112; Bloemfontein Gazette Extraordinary, March 22, 1897.
[4] C.H.B.E., VIII. 566–7, 582.   [5] Ibid., 573, 576.

Already Progressives were talking of riding through the Republic with 2000 colonial troopers.[1] On the other hand, though the Bond Congress had decided not to co-operate with the federated republics, it and its British allies looked askance at a man who, with his Egyptian past and the present support of 'Pushful Joe,' reminded them too much of Frere and Carnarvon, while the arrival of British warships at Delagoa Bay and the coming of troops to a new camp at Ladysmith in northern Natal gave rise to wild rumours in Pretoria as to Great Britain's intentions.

However, the warships departed and Milner indicated that his policy was pacific. He showed, indeed, that he took a high view of British paramountcy, but he invited moderate men to help him in the task of guiding Kruger still further along the path of reform, reassured Steyn that the modest reinforcements at Ladysmith were merely a reply to Kruger's armaments, and received Steyn's promise that his help would always be forthcoming provided Transvaal independence were respected.[2] The Jubilee atmosphere engendered demonstrations of loyalty in the colonies and such good feeling in the republics that Kruger closed the public offices on the great day, released the two remaining Reform prisoners, and sent his congratulations to the Queen whose portrait adorned so many Boer *voorkamers*. Nor was the main body of the Uitlanders forgotten. Johannesburg was given its municipal council, with limited powers, but partially elected on an easily accessible franchise; the Immigration Act was repealed nominally as an embarrassment to neighbouring South African communities, but really because H.M. Government had shown that it meant business, and an appeal was promised to the courts under the Expulsion Act.

Clouds soon gathered. The Westminster Committee of Inquiry presented a report on the Raid which Chamberlain duly signed.[3] It exonerated the Colonial Secretary, the Colonial Office officials and the High Commissioner, duly sacrificed Bower, roundly condemned Rhodes as it must, found the Chartered Board innocent of complicity but scolded it for not having kept a tighter hold on the distant and uncontrollable Colossus, and postponed all inquiry into the Company's administration to a more convenient season. Next day, to the fury of Kruger who was already angry that Jameson's punishment had not been heavier, Chamberlain whitewashed Rhodes in the course of a debate in the Commons during which Labouchere and C. P. Scott, editor of the *Manchester Guardian*, had ventured on dangerous ground. Suspecting that a Radical member would read out enough of the suppressed telegrams to damn him and ruin

---

[1] Sir J. Molteno, *The Dominion of Afrikanderdom*, p. 119.
[2] Van der Merwe, *Steyn*, I. 147 ff., 153; Walker, *De Villiers*, p. 305.
[3] Nos. 380 and 311, 311 (1), 311 (2) of 1897.

the Ministry unless he gave a certificate of character to the man whom he had just condemned, he announced that though Rhodes had erred greatly as a politician, he had done nothing which reflected on his personal honour. No wonder that Kruger roared so loudly in his booming voice that passers-by in Pretoria stopped to hear what the trouble was.[1] Trouble enough. It was not the Raid that angered the old man, for that was past, but this systematic hushing-up, this 'lying in state at Westminster.' What was he to think of a Colonial Secretary who could behave as Chamberlain had done? How could he trust such a man, and how negotiate with him?[2] Yet here was Chamberlain, 'the screw merchant,' retorting to the Transvaal's request for Swiss arbitration on disputed points in the London Convention on the analogy of unfettered States that that Convention was no treaty but a mere declaration of Great Britain's intentions, and that it still included the suzerainty of 1881.[3] Milner tried to explain away the irritating claim as a matter of etymology, but it redoubled the suspicion which his own talk of paramountcy had awakened in the republicans and their friends.[4]

Then came the report of the Transvaal Industrial Commission. It left little to the imagination and it came at a bad time for revenue was falling sharply, the clamour of poor whites for loans, donkeys and mealies echoed unceasingly round the stoep of the Presidency, and the Commission's recommendations pointed to a still further loss of state income. The plea of public poverty was weakened by the conduct of the Volksraad, which chose this moment to increase the emoluments of its own members, but Kruger, alarmed at the course of events and the Uitlander agitation, drew back. He fulminated against Schalk Burger, chairman of the commission, and obtained a Volksraad committee which toned down the painfully truthful document.[5] Nevertheless, the legislature declared against further monopolies and only failed to cancel the dynamite concession by a single vote; railway rates were reduced; the Netherlands Company was obliged to give the state a larger share of its takings, and many customs duties were lowered; but other duties were raised, so that the Treasury gained by the exchange, and the proposed board of officials and mining house nominees to supervise the administration of the Gold Thefts, Illicit Liquor and Pass Laws was set aside as a

---

[1] *Daily News*, Jan. 16, 1900, quoted by E. T. Cook, *Rights and Wrongs of the Transvaal War*, p. 73.
[2] 'It was impossible to avoid drawing the conclusion that Mr. Chamberlain was Rhodes's accomplice, and that he now publicly defended Rhodes because he feared lest the latter should make statements which would be anything but pleasant hearing for the Colonial Secretary. This, at least, was the view of the matter in the Republic . . .'; *vide Memoirs of Paul Kruger told by Himself*, II. 278–9.
[3] C. 8721 of 1898, pp. 14, 21.   [4] C. 9507 of 1899, p. 6.
[5] C. 9345 of 1899, pp. 1 ff., 14 ff.

breach of the Convention, which had entrusted control of public affairs to the enfranchised burghers.

So Kruger faced the presidential election which was destined to be his last. In spite of the numerous requisitions which poured in upon him from supporters, he faced it with some trepidation. Leyds had returned home with the news that the Transvaal need not look to Europe for financial aid until it had set its house in order, and a frank warning from Chamberlain that intransigence might mean war.[1] The delay in giving effect to the recommendations of the Industrial Commission had been by no means entirely Kruger's fault. He had had to negotiate with the Netherlands Railway Company and the railway departments of neighbouring governments; difficult legal questions were involved in any dealings with the dynamite monopoly which he defended as necessary for the independence of the state, for, if it did not actually make dynamite, it could at least make cartridges. Yet his failure to carry out the report fully, coupled with a personal quarrel with J. B. Robinson, had driven the Chamber and Association of Mines together in an armed neutrality against the authorities.[2] Not only did the British Uitlanders cry out, but the French and Germans informed their respective governments that their interests were being neglected, meetings of burghers petitioned for the nationalisation of the railways and the cancellation of the dynamite monopoly, and even loyal Hollanders complained and the Volksraad showed unwonted signs of independence. Three Government measures were thrown out in quick succession and a motion to hold over the operation of the Ballot Act till after the presidential election was defeated.

Feb. 1898.
Kruger stood for re-election upon his record and fortune favoured him. Joubert and Schalk Burger split the Progressive vote, Chamberlain's known views on suzerainty played into his hands, and the slogan 'Beware of Rhodes and keep your powder dry' decided many a waverer. He was re-elected by an overwhelming majority.[3]

The old President and all that he stood for were thus entrenched. Moreover, the election had shown how little the Uitlanders had to hope for politically from even the liberal Boers. Joubert's policy had been negative, a mere disagreement with Kruger, and Burger had shown that his liberalism was of a very diluted quality. He had evaded the question of the testing right, expressed his satisfaction with the existing system of education, pronounced against any extension of the franchise, and though favouring the recent close alliance with the Free State, would not have union even with that republic, because the independent Transvaal, dominant and

[1] *Milner Papers*, I. 68, and verbal information from Lord Selborne.
[2] Fitzpatrick, *Transvaal from Within*, p. 314.
[3] *Die Volksstem*, Nov. 20, 1897; Sir D. Chaplin, *Letter-books* (unpublished).

untrammelled, was to be the centre of the united South Africa for which he was working.[1]

The first steps which Kruger took after his re-election redoubled Uitlander suspicions. Some time since, Chief Justice Kotze had not only decided that Rhodes was not so black as he had been painted and that de Villiers, by reason of his conduct during the judges' crisis, was much blacker, but also held that Kruger had broken the arrangement then made by referring the problem of safeguarding the Bench and the *Grondwet* to a Commission instead of himself introducing the necessary measure in the Volksraad before the end of 1897. De Villiers maintained that the period of grace would not be over till the end of 1898, and the President insisted that he meant to fulfil his promise; but once the election was over, Kotze declared the agreement at an end and claimed the testing right once more. The President, with the remark that the devil first invented the testing right in the Garden of Eden, abruptly dismissed him under Law No. 1.[2]

Feb. 1898.

The order of Kotze's going after twenty years of service and still more the appointment in his stead of Gregorowski, the hanging judge of the Reformers' trial, raised a storm among the Uitlanders and embittered the Legislative Council election in the Colony. Rhodes's hopes of a British federation to balance and one day to absorb the federated republics largely depended on the result of that election.[3] The old arguments in favour of the federal solution of South Africa's political problems had been reinforced by a recrudescence of trouble with the tribes during 1897 in Mashonaland, British Bechuanaland, East Griqualand and Pondoland. Moreover, Rhodesia, 'the Dominant North' was apparently qualifying for its destined rôle in such a federation. The white population of Matabeleland had doubled during the past six months; Salisbury, Umtali and Gwelo were already flourishing little towns; the Afrikaner centres of Melsetter and Enkeldoorn bade fair to follow suit; Bulawayo was revelling in a real estate boom on the strength of the arrival of the Cape-to-Cairo railway. Rhodes, encouraged by an interview with the High Commissioner, spoke enthusiastically of the coming federation and hurried away to the South about-to-be-dominated.[4]

There he had been steadily acquiring economic and social influence. In the Colony, he had vested his Groote Schuur property near Capetown in the future federal government, laid out great fruit

[1] Chaplin, *Letter-books.*
[2] Walker, *De Villiers*, pp. 316 ff.; Kotze, *Judicial Crisis.*
[3] Williams, *Cecil Rhodes*, p. 296; Vindex, *Speeches*, pp. 520–630.
[4] Williams, *Rhodes*, p. 299; *B.S.A. Co. Report*, 1896–7, pp. 56, 154.

farms at Drakenstein and organised the De Beers dynamite factory
at Somerset West hard by, and in Natal, which had just been raised
higher in the political scale by the acquisition of Zululand and
Tongaland, he had interested himself personally in the sugar industry
and, through De Beers, in the coal of Newcastle. He therefore
arranged that Harry Escombe, Prime Minister of Natal, should carry
a permissive federation bill through the Maritzburg legislature, and
himself went to work for a redistribution of seats in the Cape, which
should give the rapidly growing Progressive towns fairer representation as against the rural Bond and thus ensure the passage of a permissive federation bill for the Colony. He subscribed to party funds
and, in the words of the delighted Garrett, completed his education
as a Progressive by attacking the Bond and Krugerism in the same
breath; but he disappointed his would-be disciples once more by
slipping away to London to make sure of Southern Rhodesia, whose
fate still lay on the lap of the gods of Downing Street.[1]

Meanwhile, Milner, the High Commissioner, had unexpectedly
shown his hand. For a year he had remained studiously passive,
learning to read the Dutch newspapers, travelling round the country,
at times sorely hampered by Progressive exuberance and by no
means inclined to take seriously all the complaints which reached
him from the Rand.[2] But the handicap was too great. A reserved
and silent man, suspect as the nominee of Chamberlain, he had not
won the expected support of British and Afrikaner moderates
for his projected settlement of the Transvaal question which was
definitely to warn off foreign interlopers. Now Kotze's dismissal convinced him that the Kruger régime was hopeless. He therefore asked
leave to insist on the redress of Uitlander grievances.[3] Chamberlain
would not have it so; the foreign situation was too disquieting.
German interests were supplanting British in the Ottoman Empire;
the French, furious at British sympathy with Dreyfus, had occupied
Madagascar in force and cancelled British consular jurisdiction and
commercial privileges; French troops were moving from Lake Chad
towards the Upper Nile as Kitchener advanced along the river to deal
with the Khalifa; the scramble for spheres and coaling-stations in
the Far East proceeded while Chamberlain discoursed of the devil
and a long spoon à propos Russia, the ally of France.[4] Foreseeing
that he would not be allowed to act, Milner spoke out to the
Bondsmen of Graaff-Reinet, who had protested their loyalty overmuch. 'Of course you are loyal,' he cried. 'It would be monstrous if
you were not,' and he called on them and all like them to urge

1897.

March
1898.

---

[1] Cook, *Garrett*, pp. 139, 222.
[2] Sir W. Butler, *Autobiography*, p. 392; Walker, *De Villiers*, p. 309.
[3] *Milner Papers* I. 214.
[4] *Ibid.*, I. 222 ff.; Gooch and Temperley, *British Documents*, I. 2 ff., 34, 42 ff.,
132 ff., 333.

the Transvaal, the cause of all unrest in South Africa, to bring its institutions and still more the spirit of its administration into line with those of its neighbours.[1]

It was a fair warning, but coming when it did, it convinced everyone that the High Commissioner was the ally of the Progressive party. That party won the Council election by a narrow majority. Rhodes was now full of hope. Escombe, it is true, had been unexpectedly defeated at the Natal general election, but Natal none the less joined the customs union at last, and the Rhodes Customs Clause April was to be embodied in the new Rhodesian Order-in-Council. Under 1898. that Order the Chartered Board indeed lost its powers of legislation Oct. and must submit to much stricter imperial control than hitherto, 1898. especially in the matter of police and Native policy; but in spite of an elected minority of Rhodesians in the new Legislative Council, it still remained master in Rhodesia. Rhodes, a director once more, told the shareholders that the Rhodesians would soon have self-government and would then repay them their past expenditure on administration.[2]

The consummation of that hope and of much else depended on federation, and that again on the fate of the Cape redistribution bill. This measure passed the second reading, but two days later a vote of no confidence was carried, and Sprigg, strong in the possession of supply, appealed to the country. It was Rhodes, however, who took the lead, coming out at last as a Progressive. True, he agonised some of his friends by airing 'thoughts' which sorted ill with the pure milk of Progressivism,[3] but he at least declared that the issue was the Union Jack *versus* the Transvaal Vierkleur and roundly attacked the Bond and the Independent 'Mugwumps,' who had voted first for Redistribution and then for 'No confidence.' It was in vain. The Progressives indeed polled some fifty thousand votes, but such was the unfairness of the allocations of seats as between town and countryside that they found themselves in a minority of one in the Assembly, despite the fact that the Opposition had polled only some thirty-five thousand mainly rural votes. *Morgen* beat men, and Sprigg had to make way for William Schreiner, parliamentary leader of the Bond though himself no Bondsman, and a ministry which included, besides members of that association, the Independent, Richard Solomon, and the noted Liberals, Merriman and Sauer.[4]

[1] *Milner Papers*, I. 243 ff.
[2] Newton, *Unification of S.A.*, I. 143 ff.; C. 8732 of 1898 and C. 9138 of 1899, *passim*; *Report of B.S.A. Co. Annual Meeting*, April 21, 1898, p. 11.
[3] Colvin, *Jameson*, II. 180; Cook, *Garrett*, p. 142.
[4] Schreiner Ministry, Oct. 14, 1898–June 17, 1900: William Philip Schreiner, Prime Minister and Colonial Secretary; John Xavier Merriman, Treasurer; Richard Solomon, Attorney-General; Jacobus Wilhelmus Sauer, Public Works; Albertus Johannes Herholdt, Agriculture; Dr. Thomas Nicolas German te Water, Without Portfolio.

The Cape Parliament, under this new leadership, acted on a resolution taken in the previous session, and set an example to the rest of the Empire by unanimously voting an annual unconditional contribution of £30,000 to the Navy. The defection of a Bond member obliged the ministry to compromise on the redistribution issue on lines that were more or less satisfactory to both sides;[1] but the fact remained that, in Schreiner's hands, federation through the Cape on Rhodian lines was out of the question.

Nov. 1898. Meanwhile, the High Commissioner had been summoned to London to confer with the Secretary of State. Milner was in no hurry to achieve federation; but he held that the Transvaal must be forced to adopt a constitution at least as liberal as that of the Free State, if there was to be an end to the interstate friction which was becoming more serious as the exploitation of the gold mines proceeded. British investors and traders were not the only parties interested. The chairman of the Chamber of Mines was a Frenchman; French and German newspapers lamented that Great Britain took no steps to safeguard the financial interests on the Rand;[2] Brown, the United States citizen who had set Kruger and Kotze by the ears, held Great Britain, 'in her capacity as suzerain,' responsible for the losses he had incurred under Law No. 1 of 1897.[3] That suzerainty, real or alleged, was in any case threatened by Leyd's return to Europe as ambassador furnished with the funds for a consular service worthy of an independent republic, and Leyds claimed the Transvaal's right to arbitration on the analogy of ordinary European states.[4] Milner, for his part, was convinced that Kruger had yielded and would only yield to pressure, and the Imperial Government was now free to apply that pressure.

Aug. 1898. H.M. Government had rarely been so free. The Khalifa had been broken at Omdurman and the French headed off at Fashoda; the U.S.A., after dealing more or less justly with Spain, could hardly be censorious if Great Britain took a strong line with another recalcitrant minor state; above all, Great Britain had come to terms with Germany. The two powers had agreed to support loans to needy Portugal on the security of the revenues of her colonies in Africa and Timor. They also arranged secretly that, in the event of Portugal's defaulting, they would divide these colonies between themselves. The bulk was to go to Germany, who was now ready to let the Transvaalers shift for themselves, and the rest to

---

[1] R. Kiplin, *The Old Cape House*, pp. 88 ff.

[2] For instances *vide* Cook, *Rights and Wrongs*, p. 87.

[3] War interrupted these proceedings, but in 1902 Washington took up Brown's case. The dispute was only settled in Great Britain's favour by a special court under a French president in November 1923 (21588–24, Government Printing Office, Washington, U.S.A.).

[4] Leyds, *Correspondentie*, pp. vi. ff.; C. 9507 of 1899, pp. 7 ff.

Great Britain, including Delagoa Bay, the key to Transvaal independence.[1]

In the event, Portugal took up neither loan. Meanwhile, no one in Great Britain, other than folk interested in Rand or Chartered shares, took the slightest notice of South African affairs although Rhodes was in London to direct their attention thereto. Milner was therefore content to convince Chamberlain of the soundness of his views and assist him to write a dispatch which both men hoped would close Dec. 1898. the suzerainty debate. Without discussing its existence further, they declared that suzerainty represented the facts of the situation, and observed that, if the 1881 preamble were indeed gone, all specific mention of Transvaal independence had gone with it. At the same time, the military authorities at the Cape were ordered to prepare a Jan. 1899. scheme in case of sudden war.[2]

Rhodes, meanwhile, was still pressing forward his scheme of federation. Not only had the production of the Rand mines risen from the £7,000,000 of 1894 to some £16,000,000, but the Rhodesian mines were producing at last; the promising new township at Selukwe screened the wreckage of the slump at Bulawayo; a new issue of Chartered shares was eagerly over-subscribed and a loan raised to carry on the railway northward from Bulawayo towards Lake Tanganyika, in spite of H.M. Government's refusal to give a guarantee on Rhodes's terms. During the negotiations for this loan, however, Rhodes showed clearly that he had given up all hope of working for federation through the Cape.[3] He was willing to let the Vryburg-Mafeking line, the main security for the proposed guaranteed loan, go to H.M. Government or to Rhodesia or to a federated South Africa, but not to a colony which by its redistribution policy and the unseating of certain Progressives for corrupt practices had given Schreiner a fair working majority. In other words, he must work now through Rhodesia and the Transvaal, if only that he might get control of the 'cosmopolitan and untrustworthy' Uitlanders of the Rand and save the Boers from perishing off the face of the land as the forces of latter-day civilisation overwhelmed them.[4] For already the Poor White problem was a problem in the Transvaal.

The Uitlanders were sure of support on both sides of the water. In London *The Times*, the newly-founded *Daily Mail*, the Liberal *Daily News* and the judicious *Westminster Gazette* were alike beginning to agitate their cause.[5] In South Africa, Garrett's *Cape Times* took the same line; Rhodes added the *Diamond Fields*

[1] Gardiner, *Harcourt*, II. 461 ff.; *Milner Papers*, I. 298–9; Gooch and Temperley, *British Documents*, I. 29, 45 ff., 67, 329; Dugdale, *German Dip. Documents*, III. 38.
[2] C. 9507 of 1899, p. 28; Butler, *Autobiography*, p. 417.
[3] C. 9323 of 1899, p. 20.   [4] Cd. 369 of 1900, p. 8.
[5] Spender, *Campbell-Bannerman*, II. 126; Gardiner, *Harcourt*, II. 466.

Advertiser to the *Argus* group which ramified from Capetown to Salisbury, while Stephanus du Toit, erstwhile father of the Bond, called upon Afrikaners in his *Dagblad* to join a Colonial League in Rhodes's interests. Some months since, the jingoistic S.A. League had thrust out a branch from the Colony to Johannesburg, where its activities were presently seconded by the independent *Transvaal Leader*.

It had long been recognised by the cooler heads, and by none more clearly than the High Commissioner, that the Transvaal would give way on all points covered by the Convention, but would probably fight if internal matters, such as the franchise, were touched. The growing quarrel began to centre on that very issue. The S.A. League opened an attack on the undoubted weaknesses of the Pretoria administration. It protested against the stiffening of the press laws and the much fuller use of Dutch which Mansvelt, abandoning his sound policy of 1896, was enforcing in the public schools to check the 'unnational and unpedagogical' demand for more English. It went on with far less justification to cry out against the Expulsion Act and take up the cudgels on behalf of anyone who could claim the title of British citizen. Cape Coloured men were arrested illegally. The League ignored the courts and went direct to the acting British Agent. The authorities, in response to repeated complaints, proposed to enforce long-neglected laws against Indian traders, unpopular with all save the poorer burghers who found them cheap salesmen and easy creditors. Leaguers championed even their Asiatic fellow-subjects. A policeman, in self-defence but in the victim's own house, shot an Uitlander, Tom Edgar, who was believed to have killed a fellow-workman in a brawl. The League summoned an unauthorised open-air meeting and published a petition to the Queen.[1]

In the light of experience gained in the South Africa of the late 'seventies, Sir William Butler, the acting High Commissioner, believed that the country needed a rest cure rather than 'a surgical operation.' His opinion of Johannesburg, formed on the spot, was low. He refused to send the League's prematurely published petition to Her Majesty, counselled Chamberlain not to take the League too seriously, pointed to Rhodes as the 'sceneshaker' and, in reply to a request for proofs, furnished them with a Cape ministerial minute in support.[2] Meanwhile, two Leaguers, who had addressed the illegal open-air meeting, had been arrested. They were soon released, but an Uitlander meeting in the Johannesburg Amphitheatre was broken up under circumstances that pointed to official connivance,

Dec. 1898.

---

[1] C. 9345 of 1899 *passim*; Rose, *Truth about the Transvaal*, chapter vii; Malherbe, *History of Education*, pp. 274, 289.

[2] Butler, *Autobiography*, pp. 398, 401, 406 ff., 415.

and the policeman who had shot Edgar, was acquitted on good Feb. evidence, but with the truculent approval of the presiding judge. 1899. Thereupon the League collected 21,000 signatures for a new petition to the Queen.[1]

The rank and file of the Uitlanders were thus coming to the front as in the days before the Raid, but they were by no means a united body. A counter-petition in favour of the Government was soon furnished with 23,000 names. More to the point was the fact that the mine magnates held aloof so rigidly that the Consolidated Gold-fields, Rhodes's own Company, dismissed an employee who had taken the chair at the Amphitheatre meeting.[2] Nevertheless, financial Johannesburg had its grievances: illicit liquor, gold thefts, a tax on mining profits, the drainage concession given to a Government supporter, and difficulties which were said to be put in the way of recruiting through the Native Labour Association, a recent offshoot of the Chamber. Above all there was the high price of dynamite. When Chamberlain overcame Milner's reluctance and declared that a renewal of the dynamite concession would be a breach of the Convention, Kruger found himself faced with a possible combination of H.M. Government and the Chamber of Mines.[3]

Kruger decided to take the sting out of the attack by economic reform and a very guarded extension of the franchise. He had good reason to do so, because internal strains were once more weakening his republic as the memories of the Raid faded. The support which he had received from the Cape and the Free State during the judges' crisis had shown him that good might come out of the South after all. He therefore began to appoint to high office friendly Afrikaners wherever he could find them: Reitz, ex-President of the Free State as State Secretary, Piet Grobler as Foreign Secretary, Barend Kleynhans as Minister of Mines, and Jan Christian Smuts, a young Cape Advocate, as State Attorney. Conversely, the influence of the Continental group had waned. Leyds's work now lay in Europe, whither also the Hollander manager of the Netherlands Railway Company departed taking with him his new order of the Red Eagle and leaving his successor to hope against hope that the Transvaal might still become a 'greater Holland.'[4] Again, if Mansvelt's new Hollandising campaign in the schools drove the English to rally round the Witwatersrand Council of Education and open opposition schools, it also drove burghers to send their children to school in the Free State and the Colony, and moved Afrikaner teachers to demand an end of Hollander domination and full liberty for Transvaalers, as for Free Staters, to have English in the schools of a bilingual country.[5]

---

[1] C. 9345 of 1899, p. 185.
[2] *Ibid.*, p. 238.
[3] C. 9317 of 1899, p. 6; *Milner Papers*, I. 300.
[4] Cd. 624 of 1901, p. 44.
[5] Malherbe, *History of Education*, pp. 273 ff.

Steyn was insistent that there must be reforms, and Steyn was the indispensable ally.[1]

At this juncture a group of mining houses offered a loan of £600,000 with which to expropriate the dynamite monopoly.[2] Kruger used Lippert, the original dynamite concessionaire, as go-between and opened negotiations with these capitalists and a pair of selected Uitlanders. The London friends of this committee approved of the general terms proposed, including a five-year franchise; but they also asked that the bench be rendered inviolate and that the Government assist the mines to recruit labour, enforce the liquor laws, and admit to the executive council a financier approved by some 'independent' firm like Rothschild's to control future taxation. On these terms they were willing to support loans and discourage malicious political agitation, but on the vital point, the franchise, they declined to commit themselves until the Uitlanders as a body had been consulted.[3]

As these negotiations proceeded the general situation became easier. Chamberlain dropped the plea that the dynamite concession was a breach of the Convention, and tartly silenced the one member of the Commons who demanded strong action on the Uitlanders' behalf. Butler, moreover, had already been informed that there was no special reason to fear immediate war and was now ordered to curtail long-authorised military expenditure.[4] On the other hand, Kruger's proposals for an involved nine-year franchise, non-retrospective and lacking the vote at presidential elections on which his régime depended, were naturally condemned by the Uitlanders and their friends, all the more since he accompanied them by a determined attempt to rush a renewal of the dynamite monopoly through the Volksraad. Perhaps Kruger could not have offered a more liberal franchise at the moment, for he had to consider his stubborn Raad and still more stubborn burghers, who were convinced that Rhodes meant to have their Republic and vote them down with droves of mine employees and casual dependants.[5] His scheme might, however, have served as a basis of discussion had not the Lippert negotiations broken down. The proposals, scooped by an Irish journalist, were published prematurely,[6] the Transvaalers shrank from putting their finances under the ultimate control of a Rothschild, the parties separated with mutual charges of bad faith, and working men's meetings along the Reef demanded the capitalists' five-year franchise proposals as 'the irreducible minimum.' Milner, back once more in South Africa, noted 'the formidable proportions'

March 1899.

April 1899.

---

[1] Walker, *De Villiers*, p. 303.   [2] C. 9317 of 1899, pp. 7 ff.
[3] C. 9345 of 1899, pp. 213 ff.   [4] Butler, *Autobiography*, p. 423.
[5] C. 9345 of 1899, p. 205; van der Merwe, *Steyn*, I. 148.
[6] Fitzpatrick, *South African Memories*, p. 179.

to which this agitation had grown against a ruling caste which made
the Uitlander rank and file feel that they were 'aliens, inferiors and
suspects.'[1]

The tribes were whispering of the coming war between the white
men and the exodus of Uitlanders from the Rand had already begun,
when an attempt was made to break away from the interchange of
diplomatic notes which had brought matters to such a pass and to
return to the personal intercourse of the days of Robinson and
Loch. Though Merriman's attempt, earlier in the year, to arrange a
South African round table conference on matters of common concern had broken down, Schreiner now sent de Villiers, Chief Justice
of the Colony, to pave the way for a conference between the High
Commissioner and the two Presidents.[2] De Villiers did not see
Kruger, but at the end of a difficult task he returned to Capetown
satisfied that Schalk Burger, Reitz and Smuts would urge their
President to get rid of the dynamite scandal and give a reasonable
five-year franchise, always provided that the British demands were
fully presented once and for all. Schreiner had taken action thus
because he knew that the High Commissioner was ready to force the
pace. Indeed, on the very day that de Villiers returned from Pretoria, May 4,
Milner cabled to London his famous despatch in which he insisted 1899.
that the helotry of British subjects in the Transvaal was a matter of
South African concern and destructive of the Queen's authority
everywhere, and asserted that to win the franchise for them would
not only help them to help themselves, but would furnish a striking
proof that H.M. Government was not to be ousted from its rightful
position in South Africa by a heavily armed republic and its
republican-minded sympathisers in the Colony. Chamberlain at once
replied, detailing the sins and shortcomings of Pretoria and in-
dicating that he was prepared to press the franchise issue and,
therefore, the issue of paramountcy to all lengths.[3]

Chamberlain and Milner would have preferred to publish their
case without delay, but, in the event, they held back the publication
of their despatches while negotiations for a conference proceeded.
Steyn, though excluded from the formal conference, acted as honest
broker; Hofmeyr, Merriman, de Villiers and others deluged Pretoria
with good advice, and Milner took comfort from the thought that
Kruger must either make such a good franchise settlement that the
remaining 'nasty questions' could be discussed in 'a less thunder-
charged atmosphere,' or, by refusing to budge, justify strong measures.[4]

[1] C. 9345 of 1899, pp. 207 ff., 215 ff.
[2] 'The Times' History, I. 258; Walker, De Villiers, pp. 330 ff.
[3] C. 9345 of 1899, pp. 209 ff.; Hofmeyr, Hofmeyr, p. 536; Van der Merwe,
Steyn, I. 174; Butler, Autobiography, p. 427.
[4] C. 9345 of 1899, p. 226.

During the difficult preliminaries, the Transvaalers suffered for the absence of the suave and cautious Leyds. Reitz, confessedly no diplomatist, led Milner to talk of a one in ten chance of war by blurting out that the self-government of the Transvaal was derived not from the Convention but from its inherent rights as 'a sovereign independent state,' and, on the very eve of the Bloemfontein Conference, the Volksraad tampered with the franchise granted to favoured Uitlanders after the Raid.[1] At the Conference itself, an unhappy mixture of a semi-public discussion and a formal interchange of notes, Milner took the line which Steyn afterwards confessed was the only way to deal with Kruger: he tried to make him understand what he wanted and stuck to it. Steyn, Abraham Fischer and Smuts begged Kruger to grant the simple retrospective five-year franchise with adequate representation for the mining areas which Milner proposed; but Schalk Burger and Andries Wolmarans held that enough had been done already; a large petition came in protesting against doing anything at all, and the most that Kruger would offer was an elaborately guarded seven-year franchise which he tried to make contingent on the settlement of those other 'nasty questions': arbitration in future disputes and the incorporation of Swaziland in the Transvaal. Kruger begged Steyn not to play the tame elephant to get him into the English kraal and, in spite of Steyn's efforts, Milner declined to take up subsidiary issues till the franchise had been disposed of. The Conference ended in deadlock. A day or two later, Milner told James Rose-Innes that he could have come to terms had he been able to trust Kruger.[2] As it was, neither party trusted the other, and the High Commissioner ended the proceedings, apparently from sheer weariness, a few hours before he received Chamberlain's message urging him to let the old President talk himself out.[3] 'This Conference,' said he, 'is absolutely at an end, and there is no obligation on either side arising out of it.'[4]

Steyn returned from his leavetaking with the High Commissioner to order mausers and cartridges from Germany[5] and, at Westminster, Chamberlain startled Honourable Members, who had assembled with their thoughts more set on the suspension of the Sinking Fund than on anything approaching war, by telling them that a new situation had now arisen. Thereupon, he published the grievance and helot despatches and accompanied them by a lengthy bluebook.

A new situation had arisen with a vengeance. Coming as they did on the morrow of the abortive Conference, the despatches clanged

[1] C. 9507 of 1899, p. 32; Cd. 369 of 1900, p. 2.
[2] Sir J. Rose-Innes to the author, Dec. 12, 1931.
[3] *Milner Papers*, I. 424.
[4] Van der Merwe, *Steyn*, I. 180 ff.; C. 9404 of 1899 for details for Bloemfontein Conference.
[5] Van der Merwe, *Steyn*, I. 191.

like a trumpet-call presaging war. Clearly, however, H.M. Government as a whole had no definite warlike policy as yet. Just before the Conference Milner had indeed promised Natal defence by the whole strength of the Empire and, now, in South Africa there were rumours of an *einkreisung* of the republics and a raid from Tuli in case of hostilities; Southern Rhodesia asked for arms and, at Kimberley, De Beers began to prepare for the worst; but, for all that, the War Office continued to cut down establishments. It was only towards the end of June that it sent Butler orders to collect transport.[1]

The Imperial Government was in a difficult position. If it sent troops to South Africa it might bring matters to a head; if it waited till war had broken out, the delay might well be fatal, for the Transvaalers outnumbered the British regulars by four and, with the Free Staters, by seven to one; the young bloods were more than ready to fight if it came to the push, and many of the older men reckoned at the very least on the neutrality of the Cape Afrikaners, and some were led by their newspapers to expect European intervention. The old President was fatalistic: if war must come, let it come; better that than the loss of hard-won independence; but, on the score of foreign intervention, Leyds was consistently discouraging. With France practically bankrupt and Germany anxious to settle her differences in the Pacific amicably with Great Britain, there was little help to be looked for unless Russia made trouble for England in Asia. The best hope was either that Chamberlain and Milner were bluffing or that the Queen and the Liberals would refuse to allow the Tories to go to war. Kruger could not know the bellicose temper of the Widow at Windsor or the imperfect control which Salisbury, immersed in foreign affairs, exercised over his redoubtable Colonial Secretary; still less did he appreciate the fact that the Liberals were hopelessly divided between the Radicals, deprived now of the leadership of Morley and Harcourt, and the imperialist wing under Rosebery.[2]

Kruger's guess that Chamberlain was bluffing with his policy of 10,000 men and firmness was, at the moment, correct, for Chamberlain told Sir Henry Campbell-Bannerman as much when he tried to persuade the Liberal opposition to close ranks with the ministry on the Transvaal issue. But Milner did not bluff on principle, and it was while Wolseley was vainly urging the politicians to mobilise an army corps at once that Kruger let loose the storm by introducing his June seven-year franchise with all the features to which Milner had 12, objected.[3] Milner's account of the negotiations at Bloemfontein had 1899.

[1] Cd. 44 of 1900, p. 1; Butler, *Autobiography*, p. 440.
[2] Cd. 369 of 1900; Hofmeyr, *Hofmeyr*, p. 535; Walker, *De Villiers*, pp. 332 ff; Cook, *Rights and Wrongs*, p. 284 and chapter xxx.; W. P. Schreiner, (Assembly), Sept. 24, 1900.
[3] C. 9415 of 1899, pp. 39, 43.

16

won him the support of Rose-Innes and many Cape moderates, the manifest weaknesses of the new franchise bill won him the support of more, and the Schreiner ministry feared to speak its mind lest he call in Rhodes and Sprigg to take its place. Meanwhile, Chamberlain went far to committing H.M. Government by declaring that Britain meant to see this thing through;[1] the *Morning Post* called for an ultimatum; the Uitlander Council made wild demands; Cronje and Joubert stirred the burghers up against any concessions; Transvaalers taunted Free Staters with wishing to back out of their alliance, and early in July the Volksraad reassembled and light-heartedly created fifteen rural constituencies, more than counter-balancing the four new seats it gave to the mining areas. But already Hofmeyr and Albertus Herholdt, an Afrikaner member of the Cape Ministry, were in Pretoria to tell the Raad in secret session to look for no armed help from the Colony and to induce Kruger to modify the franchise bill and appoint a commission to deal with dynamite.[2]

The Cape delegates were assured that changes would be made in the franchise law. Schreiner hastily declared himself satisfied, Chamberlain was jubilant, and *The Times* pronounced the crisis at an end.[3] Fuller information of the proposed scheme, however, damped Schreiner's satisfaction and led Chamberlain to ask for full details before the bill was passed.[4] The Transvaal authorities de-clined to delay. The executive council resolved to give the mining areas five seats in each Raad, and the Volksraad passed the seven-year retrospective scheme in a form simpler than before, but none the less so riddled with pitfalls that Smuts, the new State Attorney, had to issue an explanatory memorandum. Milner promptly warned his chief that the franchise question was now swallowed up in the bigger issue of paramountcy, and talked privately of resigning if H.M. Government gave in.[5] H.M. Government did not give in. True, Chamberlain, supported by a full Treasury Bench, told the Commons that, though Uitlander grievances must be redressed, there must be no use of force and, what was more, accepted the principle of non-foreign arbitration on disputed points in the Con-vention and suggested a joint inquiry into the franchise law.[6] On the other hand, 2000 troops were sent to Natal, and pressure was brought to bear on Portugal to stop the passage of munitions to the Transvaal through Delagoa Bay.[7]

The struggle thereafter centred upon the joint inquiry. Rhodes,

July 27–28, 1899.

---

[1] Garvin, III. 413 ff.
[2] Hofmeyr, *Hofmeyr*, p. 543; van der Merwe, *Steyn*, I. 197 ff., 219 ff.; C. 9518 of 1899, pp. 19, 25.
[3] *S.A. News*, July 8, 1899; Hansard, 4th series, LXXIV. 1373.
[4] C. 9518 of 1899, pp. 18, 35.   [5] *Ibid.*, pp. 7, 45, 63; *C.H.B.E.* VIII. 594.
[6] C. 9518 of 1899, pp. 11, 29; Cd. 369 of 1900, p. 16.
[7] Gooch and Temperley, *British Documents*, I. 85 ff.

now President of the S.A. League and lately returned to Capetown from dining with the Kaiser and receiving an honorary degree at Oxford, declared for 'equal rights for every civilised man south of the Zambesi,' and, as in the days before the Raid, prophesied the near approach of federation provided H.M. Government stood firm. Johannesburg demanded the franchise to the strains of 'Rule Britannia,' petitions poured in from the Colony, Natal and Rhodesia praying for redress of Uitlander grievances, and the distant Canadian Parliament expressed sympathy with Uitlander aspirations.[1] Friends in London and the Colony urged the Transvaalers to accept the joint inquiry, Netherlands ministers advised the acceptance of an international commission, and Leyds bade Kruger expect nothing from the Continental Powers.[2] But Leyds also advised them to play for time by neither accepting nor rejecting this joint inquiry, while Aug. Steyn urged them to offer better terms in lieu thereof.[3] Hence, 1899. Smuts, the State Attorney, agreed with Conyngham Greene, the British agent, that there should be a five-year franchise which would carry with it the vital vote for the presidency, not less than a quarter of the seats in each Raad to the mining areas, and discussion of details of the franchise law with the British Agent. They also agreed, though less formally, on other points which were necessary to the proper working of the main agreement, and assumed that the Imperial Government would drop the suzerainty claim, interfere no more in internal matters and refer minor points to arbitration.[4]

The five-year offer in itself was, as Milner frankly said, as liberal as anything he could have asked; but experience had taught him to be on the look-out for traps, and Reitz spoilt the effect by pointing out that the franchise bill would not be submitted to the Raad till the three assumptions had been accepted as definite provisos, and this without the subsidiary advantages which Smuts and Greene had discussed. There can be little doubt that Reitz acted thus on the cabled advice of Leyds; but by so doing he had dragged that blessed word, suzerainty, out of the obscurity into which it had sunk and, in Chamberlain's eyes, asked Great Britain to give up all claim à tout jamais to intervene whether under the Convention or not.[5] Milner, observed once more that this settlement of the franchise would merely afford a better hope of agreement on other points at issue, and while Sprigg most unreasonably attacked Schreiner for permitting munitions to go through to the Free State, as he was legally

---

[1] Colvin, *Jameson*, II. 186; C. 9518 of 1899, p. 58.
[2] Van der Merwe, *Steyn*, I. 233; Leyds, *Correspondentie*, pp. 79 ff., 104, 187 ff.; Cd. 369 of 1900, p. 15.
[3] Leyds, *op. cit.*, pp. 93 ff., 106, 137.
[4] C. 9521 of 1899, pp. 44 ff.; C. 9530 of 1899, pp. 19 ff.; Cd. 43 of 1900, pp. 45 ff.
[5] C. 9521 of 1899, pp. 47, 59, 62; Leyds, *op. cit.*, p. 114.

Aug.
28,
1899.
bound to do, Chamberlain published the suzerainty despatches and taunted Kruger with dribbling out reforms 'like water from a squeezed sponge.'[1] The taunt was true, but it came ill from the man who was now called upon to reply to the five-year offer. Chamberlain once more accepted non-foreign arbitration, expressed a desire to drop the suzerainty debate, and suggested a unilateral inquiry into the franchise scheme; but he rejected the three provisos, noted that there would be other matters to be discussed after the franchise had been disposed of,[2] and, without consulting his scattered colleagues, indicated that H.M. Government might soon have to formulate demands.[3]

This 'qualified acceptance' reached Pretoria at a dangerous moment. The Volksraad was discussing one law to permit the Government to resume ownership of mine lands and confiscate the property of non-residents guilty of treason, and another cancelling the appeal under the Expulsion Act; the executive had arrested an Uitlander editor and thereby hastened the exodus from the Rand; business there was coming to a standstill and the trading centres on the coast were feeling the consequent ill effects. Milner urged Chamberlain not to let matters drag lest there be a reaction against the Imperial policy.[4] Already Lieutenant-Colonel Robert Baden-Powell was raising troops in Bechuanaland and Rhodesia, and Butler had been removed as a wet-blanket. On the other hand, the Portuguese, who had latterly been holding up munitions at Delagoa Bay, had just released them under strong German pressure,[5] Raad members were indulging in bellicose speeches, and Kruger told Steyn that if the

Aug.
31–
Sept.
1,
1899.
troops in Natal were meant for use, 'we must begin.'[6] In this tense atmosphere Pretoria read Chamberlain's reply to the five-year offer as a refusal and fell back on the seven-year proposals. H.M. Government, however, refused to go back and, failing the fulfilment of the Smuts-Greene proposals and the dropping of the provisos, reserved

Sept.
8,
1899.
to itself the right 'to consider the situation *de novo.*'[7]

Liberals in England hailed this despatch hopefully; but coming as it did with the news that 10,000 troops were to be drafted from India and the Mediterranean to South Africa, Pretoria read it as something very like an ultimatum.[8] Both sides drifted rapidly into war. Milner, against Schreiner's wishes, sent a few troops and officers to Kimberley to stiffen the town guard, and the Free State Raad

---

[1] C. 9521 of 1899, p. 63; C. 9507 of 1899; Cd. 43 of 1900, p. 14; Cook, *Rights and Wrongs*, p. 191.
[2] C. 9521 of 1899, p. 49.
[3] *Milner Papers*, I. 493; Garvin, III. 438; Hicks Beach, *Hicks Beach*, II. 104.
[4] C. 9521 of 1899, pp. 38 ff., 51; C. 9530 of 1899, p. 14.
[5] Gooch and Temperley, *British Documents*, I. 85, 88.
[6] Leyds, *Correspondentie*, pp. 109 ff.; van der Merwe, *Steyn*, I. 238 ff.
[7] C. 9521 of 1899, pp. 52, 64.
[8] *Ibid.*, p. 206; '*The Times*' *History*, I. 337, 339, 342.

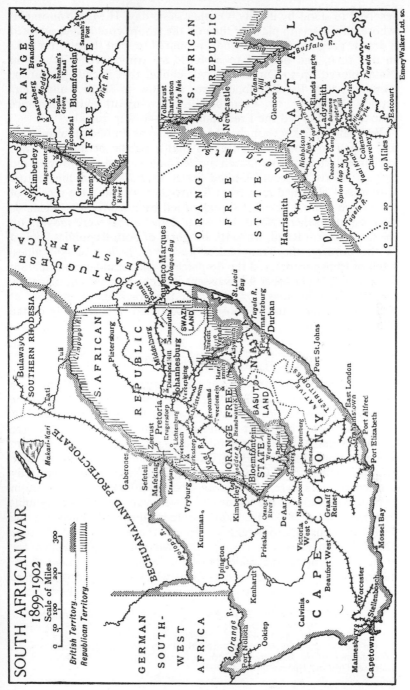

SOUTH AFRICAN WAR
1899–1902
Scale of Miles
0   50   100   200   300
British Territory
Republican Territory

Emery Walker Ltd. sc.

Sept. 22, 1899. resolved to stand by its ally. On that same day, H.M. Government, whose turn it was to play for time till the troops could land, adopted a drastic programme of demands, promised to send these to Pretoria in due time, and decided to mobilise an army corps.[1] Troops in Natal moved up to Dundee; Leyds cabled that friends in Europe wondered why the Republics were so slow to strike,[2] and Reitz replied definitely to Chamberlain's five-month-old 'grievance despatch' and urged the Free States to go to war quickly.[3]

Sept. 26, 1899. War came quickly enough. The Republicans drafted an ultimatum and began to mobilise. In face of that a pacific petition of Cape parliamentarians to the Queen availed nothing, any more than did Steyn's efforts to secure United States mediation and the mutual withdrawal of armed men from the frontiers pending the receipt of the British terms.[4] The British indeed fell back from their untenable position in northern Natal, but other detachments were moving up the Great North Road, while the burghers of both Republics flocked to the borders, the Transvaalers jeering at their reluctant allies. Lack of transport delayed the despatch of the republican ultimatum for a week.[5] On October 9 it was sent, thereby narrowly anticipating the British ultimatum. On the 12th the cracking of mausers at Kraaipan in the Land of Goshen proclaimed the beginning of the South African war.

WAR AND RECONSTRUCTION (1899–1905)

Had the British had 50,000 men on the spot, the war might have been as short as most of their war party believed and nearly all the friends of the republicans feared it would be. As it was they had little more than half that number, and of these one-third were colonial volunteers. The potential strength of the British Empire was enormous, but its striking force was neither great nor capable of rapid expansion.[6] One hundred and six thousand voluntarily enlisted regulars were with the colours, but 70,000 of them were in India and so many of the Home Army were young or physically unfit that many of the 78,000 reservists would be absorbed in bringing the field battalions up to strength. Behind the regulars stood some 120,000 militiamen and perhaps 200,000 volunteers enrolled for home service only. The majority of the regulars were drawn from the towns and all were trained on lines which developed their sense of discipline and devotion to their officers to the highest pitch,

---

[1] C. 9530 of 1899, pp. 16, 17, 38; *Milner Papers*, I. 525 ff.; Garvin, III. 463.
[2] Leyds, *Correspondentie*, p. 174.   [3] C. 9345, p. 226; Cd. 43, p. 74.
[4] C. 9530 of 1899, pp. 39, 47.   [5] '*The Times*' *History*, I. 371.
[6] On the military situation at the outbreak of war *vide* '*The Times*' *History*, II. 6 ff.; *Account of the War*, by the German General Staff (translation), I. 19 ff.; Maurice (*Official*) *History of the War*, I.

taught them to shoot somewhat better than their predecessors in the 'eighties, but apparently relied on their natural courage and patient humour to atone for repressed initiative and ignorance of big scale campaigning conditions. The Indian and Egyptian services were more workmanlike,[1] and even in the Home Army, which was detailed for the cleaning of the slate in South Africa, some of the men and still more of the officers had seen service in 'little wars' in India and Africa; but the generals were wedded to the old ways and were thrust into the field with scratch staffs; promotion was as a rule by seniority; the officers as a class were not the brains of the nation, and their peace duties and social tradition told against the scientific study of their profession. On the other hand, Intelligence was good as far as it could go for lack of funds; the field artillery was the most highly trained in the world; the mounted infantry were at that time unique in Europe; both infantry and cavalry had been taught to co-operate with quick-firers, and the use of khaki uniforms made them much less perfect targets than the *rooibaatjes* of Majuba days. The original expeditionary force was well equipped and speedily transported over six thousand miles of ocean; bitter experience soon taught the infantry to drop the Waterloo tactics which warfare against savage or semi-civilised enemies from Ulundi to Omdurman had perpetuated; the whole of the forces sent to South Africa were successfully supplied by the Service Corps on a much larger scale and for a much longer period than had been anticipated over narrow gauge, single-track railways running through a huge and difficult country many of whose people were either disaffected or actively hostile.

Probably no European army of the day, faced with this greater Spanish Peninsula would have done much better than the British did. The Boers were still a fighting people fighting on their own ground and in their own fashion, loosely organised in district commandos under their field cornets and elected field commandants, the whole under a commandant-general elected in the Transvaal for ten years and in the Free State for the period of the war. The Transvaalers had had experience of native scuffles as recently as 1898; the Free Staters were less war-hardened, but they were equally well versed in that hunting on the veld which had so much in common with their style of fighting. Apart from the commandos, there were, in the Transvaal, the Zarps, an excellently disciplined mounted police, and in each republic a small but efficient corps of state artillery with, between them, perhaps thirty old-fashioned pieces and seventy good guns, including six-inch Long Toms much heavier than the British four-point-sevens, and one-pounder quick-firing pom-poms. Guns would be difficult to replace, but the Netherlands Railway Company and the dynamite factory could supply ammunition and, when all was said

[1] The British did not use Indian or any other non-European troops.

and done, the strength of the Boers lay in their mounted riflemen. Man for man they might not shoot so well as their fathers in 1881, but they were better armed. Most of them had the clip-loaded German Mauser with a flatter trajectory and an accuracy greater than the British Lee-Metford. They relied on cover, open formation with their horses in the rear, barbed wire to hold off the infantry and deep narrow trenches as a refuge from shell-fire. But they had their weaknesses. At first the high command was poor: Joubert was old and most reluctant to take the field against Great Britain, Cronje was a bulldog with no idea of strategy and, throughout, decisions were usually taken by councils of war assisted by the circumjacent burghers, who, for their part, were apt to insist on going home when they felt so disposed, anxious at all times to keep their line of retreat open and for long totally wanting in discipline. Nevertheless, the Boers had two great advantages. They could and, once the British came up in force, must stand on the defensive at a time when rifle-fire was already deadly and the attackers had few means of countering it, for in 1899 the armoured car and aeroplane, for practical purposes, were not and the tank existed only in men's dreams. Again, while the British from first to last put 448,000 men into the field, the Boers could only raise perhaps 87,000 including cosmopolitan volunteers and colonial rebels;[1] but whereas vast masses of the British were tied to the lines of communication, the Boers, helped by 'home supply,' were able to put a much greater proportion of their strength into the firing line.

The war, 'the fight of two kopjes which lasted two years and a half,' passed through two distinct stages. The first, the period of regular warfare, ended with the annexation of the Transvaal in September 1900; the second, the period of prolonged skirmishing, which from Milner's point of view was little more than an exasperating interruption of the civil work of reconstruction, ended only in May 1902.

At the outset the Boers had over 20,000 men ready to invade the northern triangle of Natal on two sides. In that colony, the first of the drafts from India had landed and Sir George White had 13,000 British regulars and some 3000 Natal levies at his disposal. Of these, 8000 were at Ladysmith and, in deference to the local politicians and their over-confident commander, Sir William Penn-Symons, 4000 more were 'skied' further north at Glencoe. Basutoland, neutral by common consent, divided the republicans and the British in the Natal area from their friends further west. Nearly 20,000

---

[1] Some 69,000 burghers of whom more than sixty per cent. were Transvaalers, 2700 regulars, 2100 cosmopolitan volunteers and 13,300 colonial rebels (*C.H.B.E.*, VIII. 600).

other burghers were distributed along the southern and western borders of the Republics from the Basuto frontier to the Limpopo opposite Tuli. Facing them were 5200 regulars and 9000 colonial volunteers with very few guns, whose sole hope was to hold Kimberley, Mafeking, the Orange River bridge and the railway junctions south of the Orange till Sir Redvers Buller should advance with his army corps through the Colony and the Free State on his way to Pretoria. So, with the British forces standing on the defensive, the Imperial Parliament met to vote supplies, the Cape Parliament adjourned, martial law was proclaimed in Natal and the Colony north of the Orange, Chartered and De Beers shares rose appreciably on the outbreak of a war which was to clear the way for federation, and Boer columns poured across the frontiers.

At Talana and Elands Laagte the invaders learnt a respect for the British Tommy which they had not hitherto entertained, but they soon forced White back into Ladysmith and saw the road to Maritz-burg and the sea open before them. Joubert lost his opportunity. At first he would not cross the Tugela and, when he did, the troops from India were pouring up the line to meet him. In spite of Louis Botha's prayers to ride on, he fell back behind the river and closely invested Ladysmith, while on the western front the commandos sat down before Kimberley and Mafeking. Steyn was loth at first to send his men south of the Orange, for the Schreiner ministry had begged him not to do so; but at last, realising that there was no hope of Colonial neutrality, he sent them in to push their enemies back and give Cape Afrikaners a fair excuse for joining them. Within three weeks of the occupation of Colesberg, five border districts in which the Dopper element was strong had gone over almost bodily to the Republicans, and though the territory was not annexed in so many words, those of the inhabitants who joined the invaders were 'considered and treated' as burghers of the Republics.[1]

Meanwhile, the British army of invasion had landed. The bad news from Natal led Buller to change his plans. He broke up his army corps, sent a column up each of the three Cape trunk lines and led the main force himself to the relief of Ladysmith. At first all went well. Lord Methuen marched to the Modder by way of Belmont and Graspan and forced the crossing with 9000 men; but in the Black Week the whole scheme broke down. On the left, Methuen was disastrously checked at Magersfontein, Sir William Gatacre failed at Stormberg in the centre, and Buller himself on the right was defeated at Colenso. Dec. 9–15, 1899.

---

[1] On Boer Annexations *vide* Cd. 261, p. 95; Cd. 43 of 1900, pp. 99, 129, 166, 206, 217 ff.; van der Merwe, *Steyn*, II. 5. On the Rebellion *vide* Cd. 264, p. 5; Cd. 420, pp. 26 ff. For Milner's despatches of April 25–June 6, 1900, *vide* Cd. 261, pp. 5, 95, 160.

16*

These rapid reverses taught the British public that 'fifty thousand horse and foot going to Table Bay' were not enough for the work in hand. Lord Roberts was despatched as commander-in-chief with reinforcements and Kitchener of Khartum to play Carnot to his Dumouriez; militiamen were encouraged to volunteer; contingents from Canada and Australia were eagerly accepted. Pending Roberts's advance, the struggle swayed to and fro. On the British left, Cape rebels took Kuruman and, as the troops withdrew to join Roberts, were joined by a few Transvaalers who annexed Prieska, Kenhardt and Upington to the Republics. In the centre Sir John French pressed Feb. hard on Colesberg; but on the right in Natal, though the Ladysmith 1900. garrison beat off attacks at Waggon Hill and Caesar's Camp on the ridge commanding the town, Buller was defeated at Spion Kop and again at Vaal Krantz.

At length Roberts moved off with 30,000 men of the western and central forces on a wide flanking movement to cut off the Free Staters in the Colony. In response to the clamour raised by Rhodes and the Kimberley civilians, he was obliged to waste time and wear out his cavalry by relieving their town first; but, luckily for him, the contemptuous Cronje held on to the Kimberley road too long and, Feb. when he at last withdrew, was so hampered by his waggon train that 27, Roberts was able to round up him and his 4000 men at Paardeberg. 1900. It was the turning point in the first period of the war. The Free Staters trooped home from the Colony and from before Ladysmith; Buller forced the crossing of the Tugela and relieved White's weary men; Roberts broke the Free Staters at Poplar Grove under the eyes of the two Presidents, and again at Abraham's Kraal. Thereupon the commandos dispersed, Roberts entered Bloemfontein and, thinking the war over as far as the Free State was concerned, offered to allow all save the leaders to go home on parole.[1]

The offer was not unreasonable, for even before the débâcle at Abraham's Kraal both Republics had offered to make peace on the basis of continued independence; now their fighting force was reduced to less than half its strength and they were sending up S.O.S. signals to France, Germany, Russia and the U.S.A. The British Government refused to make peace on the terms proposed, but a long delay in the operations followed.[2] Kitchener crushed the Prieska rebellion, and Baden-Powell held out cheerfully at Mafeking with General Herbert Plumer waiting hard by at Sefeteli to relieve him once Sir Frederick Carrington's Field Force should come down the newly completed Beira-Salisbury railway; but Roberts's force, weary and short of supplies, was immobilised at Bloemfontein while

[1] Cd. 261 of 1900, p. 62.
[2] Van der Merwe, *Steyn*, II. 53; Cd. 261 of 1900, p. 20; Hammann, *World Policy*, pp. 91, 93; Gooch and Temperley, *British Documents*, I. 255.

the enteric bred of the muddy waters of Paardeberg swept off his men by scores and, in Natal, Buller marked time gloomily as he watched the pick of his troops departing to join the central column. The delay saved the Boers. Joubert died, the energetic Louis Botha succeeded him, and Christian de Wet brought his fellow Free Staters into the field once more by cutting up British detachments at Sannah's Post and Reddersburg. De Wet wasted time in a vain attempt to take Wepener, but 30,000 burghers, unhampered now by the waggons which had cost Cronje so dear, were ready to harass Roberts when he moved off on his long march to Pretoria.

Roberts's advance was a grand attack under unified command all along the line. On the left, Mafeking was relieved and the Griqualand May West rebellion stamped out; on the right, Buller occupied Newcastle; 1900. in the centre on the banks of the Vaal, Roberts annexed the Free State as the Orange River Colony[1] and pressed on into Johannesburg. Then, disregarding scanty supplies, de Wet's attacks on his communications and the weariness of his men disillusioned with the charms of the Golden City which they had come so far and so fast June 5, to rescue, he marched straight forward past the silent forts into 1900. Pretoria. Again there was talk of peace. Even before the fall of the capital, Steyn, Reitz and Smuts had been hard put to it to dissuade Kruger from surrendering under protest, for only 15,000 burghers kept the field and the ready money was almost gone. Now, with Botha at Diamond Hill barely covering the eastward line of retreat, the war council secretly negotiated with Roberts.[2] Good news, however, came in from de Wet, General Jacobus de la Rey threatened to set up an independent republic in the west rather than give in and, at length, the remains of the Kruger Government retired down the Delagoa Bay line. Meanwhile part of Buller's army marched north to join hands with Roberts and the rest turned westwards into the Free State, where the local commandants were quarrelling with each other. As a result de Wet had to flee to the Magaliesberg, leaving most of his followers behind in the Brandwater Basin on the Basuto border. There, Marthinus Prinsloo was captured with 4000 men and another large force under Olivier was taken near Winburg. In the last pitched battle of the war the Transvaalers were defeated at Dalmanutha and their old President, abandoning the soil of his Aug. republic from which, Antaeus-like, he had drawn his strength, sailed 1900. on a Dutch warship from Lourenço Marques to Marseilles.

The Republics were now cut off from the outer world; Roberts Sept. declared the war at an end, annexed the Transvaal and with difficulty 1900. prevented an exuberant London tourist agency from running trips

---

[1] Eybers, p. 344.
[2] Ben Viljoen, *Reminiscences*, chapter xvi.; Cd. 1791 of 1903, pp. 58, 71.

to the conquered territory. The way was apparently clear for the post-war settlement. In the Cape, the Schreiner cabinet had fallen. The Cape ministers had been anxious to deal gently with the rebels, many of whom were of the ignorant *bijwoner* type and nearly all of whom had gone into rebellion at a time when their districts had been occupied by Republicans to whom they were bound by ties of sympathy and blood. Schreiner, Solomon and Albertus Herholdt had reluctantly agreed to support Chamberlain's demand that rebels should be disfranchised; but Merriman, Sauer and Dr. Thomas te

June Water headed a party revolt which wrecked the cabinet. Sprigg once
1900. more filled the gap and, with the help of Rose-Innes as Attorney-General and Schreiner's band of Adullamites, was able to carry on without the help of the out-and-out Progressives.[1] The usual Indemnity Act was passed, special tribunals were set up to try all

Oct. accused of rebellion, theft or violence, and those found guilty of
1900. rebellion were disfranchised for five years. So the Cape Parliament was prorogued, not to meet again for nearly two years.

The Imperial Parliament, on the other hand, was dissolved although it had two more years to run. In Great Britain men had quarrelled so bitterly on the score of South African policy that some observers looked for civil war if the campaign was a long one, and in parts of Ireland men rejoiced openly at the early British reverses. At first, the Imperial Government had proposed to secure the fullest possible liberty and self-government for all alike in South Africa. In the Republics, civil administration and settled life had been restored as far as possible in the track of Roberts's advancing troops. After the annexation of the Free State, commerce and agriculture in the southern areas had begun to return to 'normalcy,' and the civil departments staffed by ex-republicans, Englishmen and Colonials had carried on under the mere supervision of the military

May authorities, but, by that time, Chamberlain had announced that the
1900. ex-republicans must prove their willingness to assist in the restoration of peace during a period of Crown Colony rule before acquiring responsible government.[2] So, while Uitlanders marched with Roberts to Pretoria to take up the reins of office dropped by the Kruger Government, arrangements were made for a nominated

Aug. legislative council in the 'Orange River Colony.' Chamberlain now
1900. induced Salisbury to appeal to the British electorate. He hoped

---

[1] Sprigg Ministry, June 18, 1900–Feb. 21, 1904: Sir Gordon Sprigg, Prime Minister and Treasurer; Thomas Lynedoch Graham, then Arthur Douglass (Feb. 19, 1902, onwards) and then Sir Pieter Faure (May 30, 1903, onwards), Colonial Secretary; Sir James Rose-Innes, then from Feb. 19, 1902, onwards, T. L. Graham, Attorney-General; Dr. Thomas William Smartt, then from May 30, 1902, onwards, A. Douglass, Public Works; John Frost, Without Portfolio; Sir Pieter Faure, then from May 29, 1902, onwards, J. Frost, Agriculture.
[2] Cd. 547 of 1901, pp. 1 ff.

·thereby to secure the ratification of his Crown Colony policy and also a reduction in the number of the hated Radical members, who had recently pressed for a renewed inquiry into the Raid on the strength of letters stolen from the office of the B.S.A. Company's solicitor and published by *L'Independence Belge*, which proved the truth of many old suspicions about the dealings of the Colonial Office with the Rhodes' group both before and after that dingy business.[1] He himself supplied the election material and the war-cry. He first told the Liberals that, if they had not encouraged Kruger by opposing him, there would have been no war,[2] and then published captured letters which had been written before the war by Merriman, de Villiers and te Water to friends in the Republics. Taken by themselves these letters substantiated many of the charges against Krugerism and Transvaal diplomacy and, though they also went far to disprove the existence of the alleged Afrikaner con-spiracy against Great Britain before the war of which so much had been and was still being made, their publication had great effect.[3] Oct. The Tories swept the country to the cry of 'Every vote given to the 1900. Liberals is a vote given to the Boers.'

For every eight votes cast for Chamberlain's policy in this Khaki Election, seven were cast against it; nevertheless, the post-war settlement was now firmly in his hands and Milner's. Both men had risked war primarily to reassert British paramountcy; but now Chamberlain, at least, was looking forward to the federation which Rhodes, in newly relieved Kimberley, had foretold would speedily follow the grant of equal rights to every civilised man south of the Zambesi and the hoisting of the Union Jack, 'the finest commercial asset in the world,' at Pretoria. Since that speech, Rhodes had busied himself with his great Oxford scholarship scheme and the search for health in England, Italy and Egypt, and had taken little active part in politics for fear of hampering the High Commissioner; but now he warned the jubilant Leaguers of Capetown that it was Krugerism which had been overthrown and not 'the Dutch,' with whom they would have to go on living after the troops were gone.[4] To the end, Rhodes clung to the hope of once more working with Afrikaners and British combined. Chamberlain apparently cherished the same expectation. In any case he issued dormant commissions which Oct. conferred the High Commissionership on Milner to be held separ- 1900. ately from the office of Governor of the Cape with which it had been associated since 1846, and empowered him to administer the Trans-vaal and O.R. Colony as soon as Roberts had departed and to

---

[1] Van der Poel, *Jameson Raid*, pp. 257 ff.
[2] Spender, *Campbell-Bannerman*, I. 233 ff., 290.
[3] Cd. 369 of 1900; Walker, *De Villiers*, pp. 336 ff., 372 ff.
[4] Williams, *Cecil Rhodes*, p. 319.

summon the intercolonial conferences which were to lead to federation.[1]

Roberts sailed home with many of his veterans, but the war did not end. Though the British held nearly all the railways, many highly mobile commandos were still at large under more or less independent leaders. De Wet suddenly emerged from the Magaliesberg and, though troops and floods prevented him from crossing the Orange, his subordinates invaded the Colony. Kritzinger approached Mossel Bay and James Hertzog pushed on to the westward of Carnarvon;[2] elsewhere, de la Rey was active in the Magaliesberg, Botha raided Utrecht and Vryheid on the one side and the Delagoa Bay railway on the other, Smuts was successful at Modderfontein, and de Wet and Steyn entered the Midlands of the Colony with 1400 men.

Dec. 1900.

Feb. 1901.

Milner had good cause to complain that matters had gone backwards during the preceding six months. The character of the struggle had, moreover, hardened. It may have been coincidence that a *Volkskongres* met at Worcester in the Western Province of the Cape to express sympathy with the Republicans in the very week that de Wet had made his first abortive attempt to cross the Orange; it was certainly disconcerting that the authorities should have sent the dreaded Australians to overawe the assembly with machine guns.[3]

It was inevitable that, with Boer commandos near Malmesbury, Colonial loyalists should form a defence force, and that, in spite of Sprigg's scruples, martial law should be extended over the whole Colony outside the ports and the native territories;[4] it was almost as inevitable that the burning of farmhouses in the ex-republics should be carried out more systematically than hitherto. How else could the British cope with burghers who were in the field one day and the next on the stoeps of their homes, each of which was a potential fort and a permanent source of information and supply? To hem in the actual commandos, Kitchener began to string out barbed wire and blockhouses along the railways. Orders were also given to destroy farms from which shots were fired or which lay nearest to any point at which the railway or telegraph line had been cut.

Dec. 1900– Jan. 1901.

Milner opposed this policy of farm-burning if only because it would make his task of reconstruction more difficult, and Chamberlain feared its political results; but Kitchener apparently agreed with de la Rey that war is 'just war' and went forward.[5] Nevertheless, he also tried gentler methods and, believing that the struggle was kept alive by a few determined leaders, organised a Burgher Peace Committee at Pretoria, formed camps to shelter Boer refugees and

[1] Newton, *Unification*, I. 172 ff.   [2] Cd. 522 of 1901, *passim*.
[3] Walker, *De Villiers*, pp. 378 ff.   [4] Cd. 823 of 1902, p. 11.
[5] Spender, *General Botha*, pp. 85, 104.

discussed terms of peace with Botha at Middelburg.[1] Apart from March other considerations, Queen Victoria had just died and her successor 1901. was anxious to close the temple of Janus at least during the coronation celebrations. News of these negotiations brought Milner hurrying northward. He would have much preferred unconditional surrender to be followed by generous treatment. Nevertheless, at the Middelburg Conference, he and Kitchener offered good terms: progress to self-government through representative institutions; no African franchise till the latter had been secured and even then the maintenance of white supremacy; £1,000,000 to meet the claims of burghers against their late governments; the prospect of a loan to farmers, the promise that no special war tax would be laid on the farms, and the trial of rebels by the courts of their own colonies. The Conference failed partly because Botha knew that his people would not yet face the loss of independence, but more immediately because, on Milner's urgent advice, H.M. Government rejected Botha's and Kitchener's plea for an amnesty to rebels. Kitchener was disappointed. 'We are now,' he remarked privately, 'carrying the war on to put two or three hundred Dutchmen in prison at the end of it. . . . I wonder the Chancellor of the Exchequer did not have a fit.'[2]

The efforts of a Cape mission to England itself were equally unsuccessful. The Bond parliamentarians were alarmed by the Worcester *Volkskongres* and other signs that Bondsmen might get out of hand and give the authorities an excuse for suppressing their organisation. They therefore commissioned Merriman and Sauer to get into touch with Hofmeyr, who had left the impossible political atmosphere of Capetown for the tranquillity of a German spa, and then to petition the Imperial Parliament for South African federation on the lines of the Australian Commonwealth Act which had just been passed at Westminster. Their prospects were not altogether hopeless. Milner could justly complain of 'the carnival of mendacity' which characterised the peace agitation in some of the colonial newspapers, and declare, with equal truth, that colonial loyalists would prefer an indefinite war to an inconclusive peace.[3] This, with the war fever raging and the coast towns full of Imperial men and money, was not surprising. But even in the Colony martial law irked the loyalists; popular sympathy with the Boers found the usual expression in the anglophobe Continental press and, in England, the Liberal Opposition, led by Campbell-Bannerman and its rising hope, David Lloyd George, was lifting its diminished head. The Liberals had recaptured the *Daily News*; Bannerman had declared for self-government as

---

[1] Cd. 1791 of 1903, p. 211. On Middelburg Conference *vide* Cd. 528, 546 and 663 of 1901.
[2] Arthur, *Life of Lord Kitchener*, II. 26.
[3] Cd. 547 of 1901, pp. 55 ff.; Spender, *Campbell-Bannerman*, I. 326.

soon as order should be re-established, and even Liberal Imperialists like Sir Edward Grey and Henry Asquith were not minded to hold out for unconditional surrender.[1] The Bond petition was indeed presented to the Commons by Sir Robert Reid (Lord Loreburn); but Hofmeyr declined to take part in a useless crusade, Merriman and Sauer were refused a hearing at the bar of the House, and their lecturing tour in the country, undertaken at a time when Lloyd George had to flee from a public meeting disguised as a policeman, had no immediate results.[2]

During the weeks that preceded the Middelburg peace negotiations, Milner had been at pains to ascertain the views of the Cape and Natal ministries on the coming settlement. Both looked forward to federation at the end of the war; Sprigg deprecated a too speedy return to self-government in the new colonies; Sir Albert Hime, Premier of Natal, asked for as much of the south-eastern districts of the Transvaal as would link Natal to Swaziland and enough of the O.R. Colony as would give Natal the Harrismith railway and a corridor to coveted Basutoland.[3] At length Milner published his dormant commission and, leaving Hime to dream of succeeding where Shepstone had failed, transferred the High Commissionership from Capetown to Johannesburg, the financial, industrial and presumably the future capital of South Africa. Some of the heads of the new departments had preceded him and he, on arrival, steadily recruited the necessary staffs. Some critics complained that he relied overmuch on young men from Oxford and employees of the mining houses, but to whom else could he turn? Outside the mining houses, men of affairs were not easy to come by and the Oxford 'kindergarten' atoned for such mistakes as it made by its energy and freshness of outlook.[4]

Knowledge of affairs, energy and freshness were all needed if the hell of the war-time republics was to be changed, if not into a new heaven, at least into the new earth which Milner planned. The destruction wrought in the tip-and-run fighting with its farm-burning and consequent concentration camps meant that everything would have to be rebuilt from the foundations upwards and built better than before. The underlying ideas of Milner's policy of reconstruction were two. First, the fighting Boers were to be pushed out

---

[1] Spender, *op. cit.*, I. 319 ff.   [2] Walker, *De Villiers*, p. 385.
[3] Cd. 1163 of 1902, p. 3.
[4] Hely Hutchinson went from Natal as Governor of the Cape; McCallum became Governor of Natal; Goold Adams became Deputy Administrator of the O.R. Colony; R. Solomon legal adviser to Milner; Wybergh, a prominent Uitlander and Leaguer, Commissioner of Mines; E. B. Sargant, Director of Education; Patrick Duncan, ex-secretary to Milner at the Inland Revenue, Treasurer. On Reconstruction *vide Milner Papers*, II. *passim*.

towards the frontiers and as many of their peaceful fellows as possible be restarted on their farms under the care of Baden-Powell's S.A. Constabulary, who were already holding the ring round Nov. Pretoria, Johannesburg and Bloemfontein. Secondly, British were 1900. to be settled on the land[1] to cut across the fatal line which had hitherto separated the urban British from the rural Afrikaners, and to set the latter a good example in new farming methods.[2] They were to be attracted in still greater numbers to the towns till they should outnumber the Afrikaners, at all events in the vital Transvaal. Given that, there might soon be a loyal British federation with the increased production that was the one means of maintaining a healthy white population above the flood of blacks. But since future production meant present outlay, the Rand was the key of the situation. The O.R. Colony could be expected to pay its way on the old simple scale, but it would have nothing over; therefore, the 'overspill' of the Transvaal gold mines must furnish the money and credit to pay for the new railways, roads, public works and education which were to 'lift' the ex-republics and make the overburdened British public some direct return for the blood and treasure it was pouring out on behalf of the Uitlanders.[3] Since the Boers' farms could not be taxed, the Rand, about to be relieved by the cancellation of the dynamite concession and the expropriation of the Netherland and Selati railway companies, must and should pay.[4] King Stork promised to be a harder taskmaster to the mine-owners than King Log.

At the moment little could be done beyond extorting permission from Kitchener for Uitlanders to return to the Rand, nominating a town council in Johannesburg and restarting three mines, a mere 150 stamps out of the pre-war 6000, but nevertheless a beginning. Then Milner sailed to England to press his views on the Colonial Secretary, to be made a viscount and to arrange the details of the Crown Colony rule which was to follow the conclusion of peace. Peace seemed to be near, for the tide ran strongly against the Boers in the early months of 1901. De Wet and Steyn narrowly escaped capture on Colonial soil; de la Rey was beaten at Lichtenburg and again at Taaibosch Spruit; Plumer took Pietersburg and with it the Transvaalers' last remaining capital and line of railway, and thereafter 'drove' the Lydenburg district; the Boers surrendered in batches, their ammunition ran low and, in the absence of de la Rey, the Transvaal leaders almost gave way. But Kruger bade them fight May on. So they fought on while Kitchener slowly enmeshed them in his 1901.

---

[1] Cd. 626, 627 of 1901.
[2] Cd. 1163 of 1902, pp. 88, 126; Cd. 1551 of 1903, p. 37.
[3] Cd. 628 of 1901; 'The Times' History, VI. 22; Milner Papers, II. 294 ff.
[4] Cd. 1163 of 1902, p. 122.

barbed wire, sent more and more of them to the prison camps in the Cape Peninsula and St. Helena, Bermuda and Ceylon, and gathered men, women and children into the concentration camps.[1]

Aug.
1900.

These camps were increasing in number, size and notoriety.[2] The first of them had been opened at Krugersdorp as a shelter for refugees, whose numbers grew after Kitchener had failed to persuade Botha to leave surrendered burghers unmolested on their farms. The refugees were soon joined by families from the destroyed farms. A year later there were forty such camps sheltering 85,000 souls, under civil administration in the O.R. Colony, military in Natal, and joint control in the Transvaal. The experiment was at first disastrous. The camps grew rapidly in size; the sites of some were badly chosen; there were the usual cases of rascally contractors, stupid officials, shortage of transport and faulty or inadequate rations; medical staffs were insufficient to cope with the epidemics of measles and pneumonia, which, as in the days of the Great Trek, raged among people who had often left their homes in poor physical condition and suffered hardship on the road, and who were in many cases unsuited by their primitive ideas of hygiene and suspicion of officials to adapt themselves to life in crowded camps. The camps were naturally denounced by the Boers and Liberals in England; but after the first breakdown the situation was saved by Anglo-Indians trained to deal with famine crowds, helpful suggestions from visiting commissions of ladies, and Milner's energy. At the end of the war there were 200,000 inmates, including some 80,000 natives in separate camps, with a death-rate down to very reasonable proportions. Botha was then able to express his thankfulness that so many of the Boers' families were in British hands, and Steyn could urge the fighting-men to go on with the war while the British looked after their families.[3] Nevertheless, the death of 4000 Boer women and 16,000 children and the policy of farm-burning of which those deaths were in large measure the indirect outcome left a deep mark on the Afrikaner consciousness. Less note has been taken of the heavy loss of life in the similar Loyalist and Native camps or among the overworked staffs in all of them.

From the military point of view, the camps were worse than useless. The British cared for the women and children while the men

---

[1] Van der Merwe, *Steyn*, II. 69; Kestell, *Met de Boeren Commandoes*, p. 158; Cd. 902 of 1902, p. 19; Maurice, *Official History of the War*, IV. 659 ff.

[2] On the Concentration Camps *vide* Cd. 608, 694, 789, 819 of 1901; Cd. 853, 893, 902, 934, 936, 939, 942, 1161 of 1902; 'The Times' History', VI. 24 ff.; Spender, I. 334 ff.

[3] Van der Merwe, *Steyn*, II. 87; Kestell and van Velden, *Peace Negotiations*, p. 83; de Wet, *Three Years' War*, p. 491. The death-rate was at its worst in June 1901.

fought and Milner, to the great comfort of the Boers, was bitterly attacked for the 'methods of barbarism,' which, in Campbell-Bannerman's words, characterised this stage of the struggle.[1] But even Liberal Imperialists agreed that the reconstruction must be left in Milner's hands. He returned to Johannesburg bringing with him a loan of £6,000,000 to be expended on administration, new rolling-stock, relief and land settlement at the end of the war. To hasten that end Kitchener drove the northern Free State, enlisted 'hands-uppers' as National Scouts in the Transvaal and as Volunteers south of the Vaal, and gave notice that all who did not surrender before September 15 would be permanently banished and the cost of maintaining their families charged against their property.[2] The threat was followed if anything by increased enemy activity. Botha raided Natal; de la Rey's New Model, a disciplined force, dominated the Western Transvaal; Smuts and his khaki-clad followers rode into the Midlands of the Colony. At that Kitchener overcame Sprigg's opposition and extended martial law to the Cape ports as the only Oct. means of stopping gun-running to the republicans. Scheepers and 1901. Kritzinger were taken and, though Salomon Maritz rode to within thirty miles of Capetown, the republicans, in spite of Smut's entreaties, failed to show themselves in strength in the Colony. It was cold comfort to the men in the south to learn that de Wet in the far- Dec. away northern Free State had rushed the Yeomanry camp at 1901. Tweefontein.

Tweefontein was the last notable Boer success. The hold of the British was tightening once more; all was quiet in the vital Rand area; the railways were working day and night to cope with the supply of troops and concentration camps and with the Uitlanders who were streaming back to Johannesburg as the mines reopened. Milner worked hard to restore the gold industry and, while Richard Solomon, his legal adviser, revised the Gold Law on conservative lines, called in Sir Godfrey Lagden from Basutoland to improve the recruiting machinery, simplify the burdensome pass system, and cause anguish to the illicit liquor sellers. But the local Bantu, with the many opportunities of earning easy money above ground that the war afforded, were shy of resuming work 3000 feet below the earth's surface.[3] Hence, Milner turned to Portuguese East Africa, always the great labour reservoir for the Rand, and concluded a Dec. *modus vivendi* whereunder the Mozambique officials agreed to help 1901. the mines to recruit Shangaans at a fee of thirteen shillings a head and, since Delagoa Bay was as much the natural port of the British Transvaal as it had been of the S.A. Republic, to maintain the

---

[1] Spender, *op. cit.*, p. 351. [2] Cd. 732 of 1901.
[3] Cd. 904 of 1902, pp. 21 ff.

pre-war proportions between the rates over the Lourenço Marques railway and those over the colonial lines.[1]

The new administration took shape in the midst of the confusion. Resident Magistrates steadily replaced the military in the occupied towns; the foundations of a four-judge Supreme Court were laid at Pretoria to receive appeals from a single-judge court on the Rand, which its members staffed in turn, and from the new three-judge court at Bloemfontein; a mass of republican *besluite* were swept away and proclamations drafted wholesale against the day of Crown Colony rule.[2] The proposed changes did not go far enough to please everyone. There was talk in certain quarters of a South African court of appeal on a federal basis and of the substitution of English law and practice, not only for the admittedly tangled law of the Transvaal, but for the Roman-Dutch law which was the basis of the civil law of all South Africa. The prudence of the new judges, nearly all Cape-trained men, and the influence of de Villiers, Chief Justice of the Cape, defeated the movement. In the main, such changes as were made followed Cape precedents.[3]

Outside the law courts, anglicisation had much freer scope. Edmund Sargant, director of education in both the new colonies, first revived the schools in the towns and then, inspired by the keenness of Boer prisoners of war for education, started schools in the concentration camps to 'make the children happy' and teach them English.[4] When the local supply of teachers ran out he imported others from Great Britain, Canada, Australia and New Zealand. Before the end of the war, 42,000 children were at school, more than had ever been so at any one time before, and most of the teachers were on excellent terms with the parents, especially with the all-important mothers. Preparations were also made for a comprehensive British land settlement. Most of the ambitious irrigation schemes drawn on an Egyptian scale by Sir William Willcocks had to be set aside on the score of expense;[5] but land boards bought large blocks of land in the new colonies and established a few settlers thereon even before the close of hostilities.

The new settlers were looked upon as forerunners of the big move that was to be made in the coming winter of 1902, the beginning of the rush that was to carry South Africa to affluence and to federation.[6] To further this latter end, Milner tried hard to suspend the

[1] Cd. 2104 of 1904, p. 189; Cd. 3564 of 1907, pp. 61 ff.

[2] Eybers, pp. 347, 515; Walker, *De Villiers*, pp. 406 ff.

[3] The Transvaal Supreme Court when completed in 1902 consisted of Sir J. Rose-Innes, Sir W. Solomon and J. W. Wessels of the Cape, and Sir W. J. Smith of British Guiana where till 1917 portions of the Roman-Dutch code survived. The president of the O.R.C. court was A. F. S. Maasdorp from the E.D. Court at Grahamstown.

[4] Cd. 1551 of 1903, p. 109; Malherbe, *History of Education*, pp. 297 ff.

[5] Cd. 1163 of 1902, pp. 37 ff.   [6] 'The Times' History, VI. 38.

Cape constitution. The Progressives' dread of partition had obliged him to give up his original plan of putting the rebellious border districts under Crown Colony rule and leaving the rest to govern itself as before. He now favoured a general suspension till federation 1900. should be achieved. There was nothing new in the idea. Lord Durham, long ago, had held that there could be no self-government in Canada without 'a decidedly English legislature,' and the Imperial authorities had taken advantage of the suspension of the constitution 1841. of rebellious French Quebec to unite that province with British Ontario. There had been hints of suspension in high quarters in London during the later stages of the South African confederation campaign in the 'seventies. Now, in spite of Chamberlain's refusal to accept the idea, Milner made no secret of his belief that a self-governing Cape would be a serious obstacle to his plans for recon-struction, federation and, above all, a comprehensive native policy while yet there was time, and that, if all the colonies were to become self-governing prior to such a settlement, South Africa might well be condemned to tread once more the weary road which in 1895 had led to the Vaal drifts and what had lain beyond them.

Therein, Milner was a true prophet. Meanwhile, at the end of the war the Transvaal and O.R. Colony would be controlled by officials supported presumably by the growing British element and by those 4500 burghers who were already fighting for the King, representa-tives of thousands whose one desire was to be let alone by British officers and Boer commandants alike;[1] self-governing Natal, ruled by the imperialistic Hime ministry and gratified by the promise of Vryheid, Utrecht and part of Wakkerstroom, would be open to pressure in the matter of Durban traffic to the Rand;[2] the Chartered Company was despairing of ever finding the new Rand in Southern Rhodesia and was deeply indebted for war expenses to the Imperial Government. But in the Cape, since Rhodes still declined the office and Jameson as yet lacked both the standing and desire to lead, the Progressives were leaderless, and Milner had no confidence in the supple Sprigg. If Parliament met, Sprigg might have to choose between reliance on the Bond and a resignation which would over-whelm the work of reconstruction in the Colony in a racial general election. Parliament had not met since October 1900; it hardly represented existing opinion; the register was out of date; Sprigg was financing himself on Governor's warrants. The constitution had thus been freely broken. It only remained to clear away the frag-ments.[3]

So Milner argued and, for some time past, sporadic S.A. Leaguers

---

[1] '*The Times' History*, VI. 43.   [2] Cd. 941 of 1902.
[3] On Suspension *vide* C. 1162 of 1902; Walker, *De Villiers*, pp. 393 ff.; *Milner Papers*, II. 569, and Index.

had demanded Suspension, but the movement never gathered weight till Rhodes headed a petition in its favour. Had Rhodes lived, March Suspension might have been carried, but he died at Muizenburg and 1902. Milner was left to push his policy single-handed. He came to the Peninsula and interviewed ministers and others, while Sprigg, bereft of Rose-Innes, who had gone to preside over the new Supreme Court at Pretoria, wavered unhappily between memories of his long parliamentary past and a present dread of the Progressives. Thomas Smartt, one of Sprigg's colleagues, now left him to head the Suspension movement; forty-two Progressive Members of Parliament May petitioned H.M. Government, and the High Commissioner openly 1902. supported their petition with a hint that Suspension was the price to be paid for the speedy withdrawal of martial law.

The inner circle conveyed the real meaning of the petition to Chamberlain. It was ostensibly Rhodes's policy: no partition of the Cape Colony, an equal voice with Natal in matters of common interest and, prior to the restoration of self-government, redistribution of seats and a new registration of voters, in other words, provision for a Progressive majority. The opposition was handicapped, for, outside the towns, the electorate was practically silenced under the weight of martial law; nevertheless, Bondsmen and Moderate Englishmen combined to defend their common privilege of making mistakes if they chose, free from official guidance. They made Sprigg's life such a burden to him that he at last declared himself against Suspension and fled to London to attend the Coronation of Edward VII and the Prime Ministers' Conference. There, the policy met its end in spite of the vigorous campaign in the Colony which produced 30,000 signatures in its favour. Hime of Natal proposed it in the name of imperial unity, and Richard Seddon, Prime Minister of New Zealand, fresh from a week's sojourn in South Africa seconded; but the Secretary of State in the chair looked on the proposal coldly. Sir Wilfrid Laurier, Prime Minister of Canada, threatened to leave the Conference if it were carried and both Sprigg and the Prime Minister of the new Australian Commonwealth supported Laurier. As a good parliamentarian, therefore, Chamberlain rejected the advice of Milner, the compleat administrator. He bade the Cape Parliament meet forthwith and promised that no special measures should be taken unless it proved recalcitrant. Thus ended Milner's hopes of a speedy 'British' federation.

In the midst of the prolonged Suspension struggle in the Cape Colony and the immense preparations for a move forward north of the Orange, 'peace broke out' as unexpectedly as it was destined to do on a later and more famous occasion. Latterly the British had March driven parts of the Free State and the Transvaal with a success which 1902. was hardly marred by de la Rey's capture of Methuen at Tweebosch.

The end had been foreshadowed when Rosebery's Liberal Imperialists Dec. demanded peace by negotiation provided the Boers made the first 1901. advances;[1] it was brought nearer when the Foreign Office declined the good offices of the Netherlands Government, but left the way Jan. open for negotiations with the Boer leaders in South Africa. British 1902. public opinion clearly favoured peace; Irish land and a Coercion Bill awaited attention, and the Balfour Education Bill promised ministers a stern struggle with the formidable Nonconformist conscience. Hence, Kitchener sounded the acting Transvaal President, Apr.9, Schalk Burger, and allowed the leaders of the two Republics to meet 1902. at Klerksdorp.

It was doubtful at first whether they would listen to talk of peace. De Wet, convinced that attack in the Colony was the only defence for republican independence, had sent Smuts to besiege Ookiep and take general command till de la Rey should come south of the Orange.[2] Steyn, again, still hopeful of complications in Europe or in Asia and long since jealous of the Transvaalers' *toenadering* with Kitchener, pleaded that time was on their side; 21,000 Boers were still in the saddle; their families were safe in the concentration camps; the supplies lacking on the High Veld were to be had in the coast colonies; a 'Rosebery Ministry' would soon come to the rescue, and if needs must, they could surrender unconditionally and thus preserve the right to rebel later with a clear conscience. So the negotiations dragged on, the Boer leaders holding out for independence, and Milner, associated now with Kitchener in the discussions, offering substantially the Middelburg terms. Meanwhile the British relieved Ookiep, Ian Hamilton drove de la Rey's country in the Western Transvaal heavily for the first time and little commandos everywhere were driven against the barbed wire and taken in detail.

In May, thirty representatives from each republic met at Vereeniging. At first Steyn and the war party held the upper hand in spite of Schalk Burger, Lukas Meyer, Botha and Hertzog; but Smuts came in with the news that all hope of a general rising in the Colony was gone; Kitchener whispered that the Tory Government would not last for ever and, though Steyn resigned the shadow of his presidency rather than give way, even de la Rey admitted that the burghers would fight no more however much the leaders might wish it. De Wet brought most of the Free Staters round and the terms were accepted by 54 votes to 6. That same night the treaty of May Vereeniging was signed at Pretoria.[3]

May 31, 1902.

---

[1] Spender, *Campbell-Bannerman*, II. 11.
[2] Maurice, *Official History of the War*, IV. 577 ff.
[3] Cd. 1096 of 1902; Cd. 1163 of 1902, p. 155; Eybers, p. 335; Arthur, *Life of Lord Kitchener*, II. chapters lv., lvi.; Van der Merwe, *Steyn*, II. 84 ff.; Kestell and van Velden, *Peace Negotiations*; Shaw, *Letters to Isabel*, p. 202.

Under the peace treaty the republicans surrendered their independence. In return the British Government promised £3,000,000 to repair the ravages of war, a large development loan free of interest for the first two years and full responsible government before any African franchise was given;[1] but beyond the private information that they would be dealt with by their own governments, no mention was made of colonial rebels. Once the commandos had laid down their captured Lee-Metfords, Crown Colony rule was proclaimed, Kitchener departed, and Milner was left with a free hand within the Crown Colonies and immense influence without them. He needed it all. Forty-five thousand Uitlanders had already returned to the Rand; but, beside the 200,000 troops, colonial volunteers and irregulars waiting to be sent away or reabsorbed in civil life, there were 32,000 Boers in the prison camps, and 110,000 more of all ages and sexes and nearly 100,000 natives in the concentration camps to be restored to what was left of their homes. It was mid-winter; grazing was scarce and the transport cattle were riddled with new or indigenous diseases; the Army drove hard bargains for much-needed supplies; crowded troop trains blocked refugee trains toiling up the single lines of worn-out railway to the High Veld; drought came in November. Nevertheless, by March 1903, the garrison had been cut down to about 30,000 men; all save 100 helpless souls had been sent home from the concentration camps, and only 1000 fighting men lingered in the prison camps overseas whence they refused to return till de la Rey in person had assured them that the talk of peace was not a trap.[2]

Jan.
1904.

Repatriation and reconstruction were helped in their early stages by an interchange of visits. Botha, de la Rey and de Wet went to London to ask for a modification of the peace treaty. They were made welcome by King Edward VII and soon won the regard of a public which counted Joan of Arc and George Washington as, in some sense, national heroes who had inexplicably taken the wrong turning; but Chamberlain they found urbanely firm.[3] They then passed on to join Steyn and Reitz on the Continent in an effort to raise funds for the Boer widows and orphans. It was a case of much cry and very little wool and, realising that 'the civilised world' to which they had appealed had lost interest in them, they returned home determined to make the best of the Treaty of Vereeniging and Chamberlain's promise of further help for distressed families.[4]

The Secretary of State had preceded them to South Africa. The auguries were hopeful. The coast colonies were enjoying a wild post-war boom; Johannesburg, flooded with newcomers, looked

---

[1] A Coloured and Asian franchise was not ruled out.
[2] Cd. 3127 of 1906, pp. 53 ff.; Cd. 1551 of 1903, pp. 1 ff.; 'The Times' History, VI. 44.   [3] Cd. 1284 of 1902, p. 7.   [4] Cd. 1329 of 1902, passim.

forward to a population of 1,000,000 within a year or two; the Cape
Parliament had belied the fears of the Suspensionists by raising its
contribution to the Navy from £30,000 to £50,000 and passing an
Indemnity Act in return for Sprigg's promise of an inquiry into the
past working of martial law, a promise but imperfectly fulfilled in
the event.[1] Martial law had been withdrawn from the colonies, old
and new, and a commission under Lord Chief Justice Alverstone
had scaled down the punishments of most of the rebels and released
others.[2] Chamberlain landed at Durban, preached conciliation, Dec.
arranged that Natal should compensate its own citizens for war losses 1902.
as its contribution to the cost of the campaign, and journeyed on to
be well received in the Transvaal by all save a few ultra-loyalists who
wanted immediate self-government.[3] He worked hard with Milner
for a fortnight hastening the settlement of claims for relief and
compensation and providing for a guaranteed loan of £35,000,000.
But he was also determined to take back something tangible wherewith to solace an over-burdened Chancellor of the Exchequer. The
mine-owners were already distressed by Milner's 10 per cent. tax
on profits, his insistence that mines should pay rates to the enlarged
Johannesburg municipality, and his unblushing talk of taking an
unwontedly large share of future mineral discoveries for the State.
Chamberlain, notwithstanding, induced a large group of firms to
promise to raise forthwith £10,000,000 as the first instalment of a
£30,000,000 loan as the Transvaal's war contribution. And so by
way of Mafeking and Bloemfontein to Capetown.[4] There, Sprigg
was dependent on the Bond, which, in the House, followed Merriman
and Sauer and, outside, took its orders once more from Hofmeyr,
while Jameson was drifting rather than climbing into the position
of leader of the Progressives. The 'callous devil' from Birmingham,
as Jameson called him,[5] made much of Hofmeyr and the English
Moderates, listened hopefully to the entirely unauthorised post-
prandial hint of a prominent Bondsman that £5,000,000 might be
forthcoming from the Colony for the war-chest, and pointedly
neglected the Progressives. He then sailed homeward without the
suggested £5,000,000, but with the knowledge that the last of the
rebels would soon be free men, though disfranchised for five years
to come.

So far, so good. But repatriation was expensive. To save time and
distress, Milner gave assistance first and asked for proofs of claims
afterwards. The £3,000,000 grant earmarked for the ex-republicans
was shared out at the rate of £25 apiece either in cash or credit, with
two shillings in the pound for losses which exceeded that amount.

[1] 'The Times' History, VI. 70 ff.   [2] Cd. 1364 of 1902.
[3] 'The Times' History, VI. 79.   [4] Ibid., VI. 87.
[5] Colvin, Jameson, II. 217.

'Protected burghers,' that is, the Hands-uppers, received an additional £1,900,000; British Uitlanders, neutrals and natives were given another £2,000,000, and close on £3,000,000 were issued in short-term loans of which the colonial governments ultimately recovered about half.[1] The financial settlement caused much bitterness. The Diehards complained, often with truth, that too many of the loaves and fishes went to Hands-uppers;[2] both accused the authorities of overcharging for the supplies which many of them took in lieu of their share of the grant. An impartial commission afterwards found that most of the prices were fair and that, for the rest, the goods had been delivered on the farms carriage-free; but this display of socialism got Milner into trouble in another quarter. In a time of dearth up-country and boom prices at the ports, he saved the burghers from the rapacity of merchants and storekeepers and drew down upon his head the anathemas of the commercial fraternity.[3]

March 1903. Worse still, after the peripatetic Government ploughs had turned over enough soil to give promise of food for the year, the harvest failed. Farmers who were hard pushed themselves and lacked both beasts and labourers refused to allow *bijwoners*[4] to return to their farms, especially as many of these tenants-at-will had been National Scouts. Relief works in the O.R. Colony and *metayer* Burgher Settlements on the farms of friendly farmers north of the Vaal did something to meet the difficulty;[5] but the relief works could be only temporary and the *metayer* colonies failed. They were private ventures, badly run, and their failure left South Africa to wrestle with the growing poor white problem as best it might. British settlement, on the other hand, proceeded but slowly. The 1400 heads of families ultimately established in the Transvaal and on the cornlands of the eastern O.R. Colony formed a useful leavening, but they could not have the social and political effects expected of the great immigration which failed to materialise.

With the coming of good rains at the close of 1903, repatriation twice carried out was accomplished. Meanwhile, drought or no drought, Milner had striven to bring about the 'lift' in other directions.[6] The guaranteed loan gave him money wherewith to pay for irrigation and forestry, new roads and a programme of railway 1907. construction which, when completed, doubled the mileage in the two provinces. Public buildings in the style that Herbert Baker was

---

[1] Cd. 3028 of 1906, pp. 53 ff.   [2] Cd. 1284 of 1902, pp. 5, 19.
[3] *'The Times' History*, VI. 48, 49.
[4] Most of these bywoners were poor whites.
[5] Cd. 1551 of 1903, p. 65; Cd. 1553 of 1903, p. 14.
[6] Of the £35,000,000 loan, £6,000,000 were used to cover existing liabilities, £14,000,000 for the expropriation of railway companies, £5,000,000 for repatriation and compensation and £10,000,000 for development ('*The Times' History*, VI. 84).

popularising rose in all directions; scientific farming was encouraged by precept, example and agricultural shows; the teachers followed the children out of the camps and by the end of 1904 more children were at school in town and dorp than even in the camps; nor were the claims of higher education in Johannesburg and Bloemfontein forgotten. Municipal councils were set up in the towns and local powers were offered to the country districts;[1] the appointment of a Lieutenant-Governor anchored the capital of the Transvaal at Pretoria, already the seat of the Supreme Court and the possessor of public offices, and Johannesburg found compensation for the disappointment of its hopes in a Water Board which gave it the prospect of a plentiful supply of water for the first time. True to his policy of autocracy tempered by consultation, Milner also established nominated Legislative Councils at Bloemfontein and Pretoria.[2] *Jan.-May 1903.*

Milner also did what he could to bring about a federation of the two northern colonies. He was Governor of both; the S.A. Constabulary and the railways, united now as the Central South African Railways, were under his control; a due share of the guaranteed loan must be allotted to the O.R. Colony. He therefore set up an Intercolonial Council, the Crown Colony version of the Republican Federal Raad, to advise him on these and other matters of common concern.[3] He even hoped that a South African educational federation might arise from the deliberations of the heads of the four colonial education departments at Bloemfontein and the subsequent Teachers' Conference.[4] This hopeful movement died away, but, in the economic sphere, Milner achieved that federation to which Rhodes had looked forward. He presided over a Customs Conference at Bloemfontein which swept away the tariff walls between the four colonies, Southern Rhodesia and the High Commission Territories and, following Canada's recent example, gave a preference to goods from the United Kingdom and offered reciprocity to other parts of the Empire.[5] *March 1904.* *March 1903.*

The Bloemfontein Customs Conference took two other momentous resolutions: first, that 'in view of the coming federation,' the native question must be handled as a whole, and, secondly, that if British tropical Africa failed to supply the labour necessary for the Rand mines, recourse must be had temporarily to indentured,

---

[1] Ord. 38 and 58 of 1903 (Transvaal); Ord. 6 and 12 of 1904 (O.R.C.).
[2] Cd. 2104 of 1904, p. 6, for history of the various councils. Legislative councils of 6 members including burghers in the O.R.C. enlarged by the addition of 4 more officials and 4 burghers in 1904, and, in the Transvaal, 16 officials and 14 others.
[3] Cd. 1641 of 1903, p. 5; Newton, *Unification*, I. 220 ff.
[4] Malherbe, *History of Education*, p. 307.
[5] Cd. 1599 and 1640 of 1903. The S.A. Customs Union arranged reciprocity with Canada in 1904, Australia in 1906 and New Zealand in 1907.

unskilled labourers from Asia.[1] The fruit of the first resolution was
the report of the Native Affairs Commission of 1903–5 which laid
down the future lines of South African native policy; of the second,
Chinese Labour.[2]

The common factor in the two resolutions was that problem of
labour which had exercised European South Africans since the far-
off days when van Riebeeck hesitated between buying Angolese
negroes, forcing the Hottentots to work by taking away their cattle,
and importing industrious Chinese. From the first, the labour supply
for the Rand mines, drawn from the Transvaal and Mozambique,
had never been over-plentiful; after the Kaffir Boom of 1895 it had
become inadequate, hampered as the industry was by intricate pass
laws and the liquor scandal, lack of systematic recruiting, haphazard
organisation of the mines themselves and the filthy conditions under
which the 'boys' had to live—or die. The Industrial Commission of
1897 had talked of a recruiting board and had got no further; the
1898.   Chamber of Mines had found Simla chilly when it mentioned Indian
coolies, and local Transvaal opinion truculent when it discussed the
rival merits of Italians and Chinese; the 100,000 natives at work on
the outbreak of war had dispersed as the mines closed down and
the Republican authorities reduced their wages from 45s. per month
with food and lodging to 20s. In the first elusive flush of victory the
1900.   Chamber had raised wages to 30s., revived the Native Labour
Association to monopolise recruiting and prevent one mine from
capturing the boys intended for another, and even cherished the
1901.   hope that kraal natives would be forced to work. The *modus vivendi*
with Mozambique, whence 75 per cent. of the labourers were wont
to be drawn, had commended the Labour Association to the favour
of the Portuguese; but Milner had also obliged the mine-owners to
carry out much-needed reforms and appointed a medical committee
which reduced the appalling death-rate to more civilised proportions.

At the close of the war only 30,000 boys were at work and barely
one-third of the available stamps falling. The natives were full of
money; they or their newly-wed wives were busy in the kraals, on
the farms or on repatriation and railway construction work; they
did not fail to note that 30s. was really a reduction of the pre-war
rate of pay; they disliked the new regulations, which bound them to
work for six months and go to the mine to which they were assigned;
they felt no serious call to go down the mines at all. In spite of the
extension of piecework and the raising of the pay to the old 45s., only
March 50,000 natives were forthcoming when the Bloemfontein Customs
1903.   Conference met. Owners, managers and engineers had for the most

---

[1] Cd. 1640 of 1903, pp. 12 ff.
[2] On Chinese Labour *vide* Cd. 1895–6–7–8–9, 1941, 1945, 1956 1986, 2025,
2026, 2028, 2183 of 1904, and Campbell, *Chinese Coolie Emigration*, pp. 160 ff.

part made up their minds that the local supply was insufficient, all the more as Natal had forbidden recruiting within her borders and 1901. was competing for the Portuguese Shangaans. Some, like the ex-Reformer, Sir Percy Fitzpatrick, frightened of Natal's Indian experience, were against the importation of the Chinese of which their friends had long spoken; but, on the other hand, indentured labour was nothing new in South Africa. The old apprenticeship system had been based upon it; Natal had imported Indian coolies since 1860; the Cape Parliament had once sanctioned the use of 1870. Chinese on the farms and, though no action had then been taken, it was now introducing Italians; in Southern Rhodesia mine-owners had tried 'Arabs,' Somalis and Abyssinians without success and were now clamouring for Chinese.[1]

A small group of men on the Rand, led by Frederic Creswell, manager of the Village Deep mine, favoured a white labour policy as the only means of saving European civilisation from dependence on black barbarism. By reorganising the internal working of his mine Creswell showed that white labour was much less expensive than had been supposed. He was, however, hampered by a strike of skilled men against unskilled European labour and by the failure of a similar experiment on four other mines; the main body of mining opinion turned against him, and the Chamber condemned his policy on the grounds that white men could not be employed on the same work alongside black and that, if the white labour policy were adopted, 48 of the 79 producing mines would be ruined and the profits on the remainder be seriously diminished. Creswell retorted that the failure of the experiment on the other mines had been due to lack of incentive to the white workers, the absence of a reorganisation of the work and opposition by financiers. He backed his assertions by an independent expert report to the effect that Europeans could supplement Africans in certain departments both above and below ground.[2]

From the Chamber's point of view the issue was simple. Nearly three hundred mining companies had been floated during the twelve months following the peace and substance must be given to them. Much money had already been spent on preliminary work. Admittedly Creswell's policy might not mean a loss on general working expenses, but it would mean a loss of profits, and if mines planned for speedy exhaustion were worked slowly, the fall in the price of shares would be serious. The Chamber's policy was, in short, to develop as much low grade ore as possible within the next five years and to find the labour wherewith to do it cheaply.[3] To Milner the

---

[1] Cd. 1200 of 1902; Cd. 2028 of 1904; *B.S.A. Co. Report*, 1900–2, p. 272.
[2] Cd. 1896 of 1904, p. 65; Cd. 1897 of 1904, pp. 403, 574 ff., 581, 612 ff.
[3] Cd. 1896 of 1904, p. 74; Cd. 1897 of 1904, pp. 120, 129, 132, 423, 438, 462, 610.

issue was still simpler. The mines were a perishing asset. Their rapid development would attract newcomers, who, as in California and Australia, would found other industries destined to flourish when the mines were holes in the ground guarded by towering dumps. In this way a great Johannesburg would make a British Transvaal which would hold the balance in a British South Africa, and this, in its turn, might go far to consolidate the Empire.[1] On the rapid development of the mines depended his whole policy of 'lift' and federation under the Crown. He fought hard against the Chinese solution, but he soon began to talk of it as the one way of attaining Creswell's ends by other means. The Chinese were to be a scaffolding which could be dispensed with as soon as a great white society had arisen within it freed from dependence on Mozambique and the tribes.[2]

During the war Chamberlain had given Southern Rhodesia permission to experiment with Asiatic labour but under such stringent regulations that the experiment had never been made. On Chamberlain's arrival in Johannesburg, Milner had suggested that importation be attempted after all; but this time the Colonial Secretary demurred strongly unless the Rand mineowners would also recruit Asiatic labour, because the Chartered Company was much too unpopular in England to permit of a sorely shaken ministry taking such a risk on its behalf alone.[3] When the Bloemfontein Conference met the general economic situation in South Africa was threatening. The harvest failed; repatriated burghers, new British settlers, overstocked storekeepers, out-of-work irregulars and those others who had flocked to the Rand were grumbling; in the coast colonies, the customary land and produce boom which had accompanied an imperial war was showing ominous signs of breaking; but all might yet be well if the mines could be set at work at full pressure. Milner reluctantly faced the fact that the labour necessary for his schemes was not to be found locally, and appointed a Labour Commission to investigate alternative sources.

The Chamber set to work to educate the public and to convince the Secretary of State that the demand for Chinese was a popular one. Sir George Farrar, an ex-Reformer, opened the campaign;[4] the Labour Importation Association took it up and made good headway in spite of the opposition of the White League, the African Labour League and the Trades Labour Council; the Boer leaders, disapproving of the proposed importation, stood aside and counselled their people to take no responsibility in the matter. Milner had meanwhile gone to London. There he refused the offer of the

---

[1] '*The Times' History*, VI. 19.   [2] Cd. 1895 of 1904, pp. 39 ff.
[3] Cd. 1200 of 1902; Cd. 2028 of 1904, p. 8; *Milner Papers*, II. 438.
[4] Cd. 1895 of 1904, pp. 8 ff.

Colonial Secretaryship on Chamberlain's resignation, but found that Alfred Lyttelton, who accepted the post, was willing to risk the Chinese. He returned to face inevitable unpopularity in a Transvaal where times had markedly changed for the worse.[1] The Civil Service and the Constabulary were retrenching; revenue was falling by £100,000 a month; broken men were drifting away from the Rand and the issue of the first instalment of the magnates' loan had been postponed.[2] Lung sicknesses were playing havoc with the labour supplies from Central Africa;[3] recruiting further afield in Uganda, Lagos and Nigeria had failed; the importation of English navvies for railway work had proved a costly failure;[4] the Indian Government had turned a deaf ear to appeals for coolies who should set natives free from the railway construction, since the Transvaal would not modify its anti-Asiatic laws;[5] the very suspension of the road and railway programme failed to swell the number of natives on the mines above 65,000; white miners struck against the use of Italians, and the employment of 1000 Europeans on unskilled work only raised the white total to 13,000. The one contribution to the solution of the labour problem which the Boer leaders had made so far was that Basutoland, Swaziland and the reserves should be broken up and the squatters' law be strictly enforced to ensure an equal distribution of labourers.[6]

Meanwhile the majority of the Labour Commission had reported Nov. that there was an actual shortage of 129,000 boys with no African 1903. supply in sight, and that in 1908 the shortage would be 365,000. The minority report queried these calculations and insisted that there must be a fixed ratio between white and black labour, but the majority report had its effect on a public which was fast swinging round in favour of the Chinese.[7] Creswell, Wilfred Wybergh, commissioner of mines, and William Monypenny, editor of *The Star*, had been obliged to resign their several offices; the Labour Importers broke up an opposition meeting at the Wanderers'; Farrar's petition, admittedly 'skilfully organised,' bore the names of three-fifths of the adult white males of the Transvaal other than Government servants; the press was unanimous; the bulk of the white miners were satisfied when they learnt that the Chinese would be kept to purely unskilled work; Boers, Southern Rhodesians and Natalians looked forward to the freeing of natives for service on the farms; guileless ecclesiastics had visions of the seeds of Christian virtue being scattered over the Celestial Empire by returning Johannesburg coolies.[8] There were dissentients. The Cape ministry protested, but

[1] S. Baldwin, *On England*, p. 189.   [2] '*The Times' History*, VI. 118.
[3] Cd. 1950 of 1904, *passim*.   [4] Cd. 1895 of 1904, p. 159.
[5] Cd. 1683 of 1903, *passim*; Cd. 2239 of 1904, p. 44; U.G. 16–1914, p. 2.
[6] Cd. 1897 of 1904, pp. 501 ff.; Cd. 1899 of 1904, p. 22.
[7] Cd. 1894–6–7 of 1904.   [8] Spender, *Campbell-Bannerman*, II. 146.

its protest was discounted by the fact that there was a general election pending in which the Coloured voters, nervous of possible Chinese competition, would play an important part, and the Progressives at least were quieted with a promise that the Chinese would be shut out from the Colony just as Indians were excluded from the O.R. Colony.[1] The Labour Ordinance duly passed the Transvaal Legislative Council and, in spite of opposition from Liberals and questionings from 'White Australia' and New Zealand, mindful of their share in winning the war, it was carried at Westminster with very few changes. The coolies began to arrive in June; by the end of the year 23,000 had come, 20,000 more were on the way and Government had long since started relief works for Europeans.[2]

Feb.
1904.

CLOSER UNION, 1904–10

The outcry against the Chinese soon died down. Gold output leapt upwards; native labour rapidly attained to the pre-war figure; the number of Europeans employed on the mines rose markedly. It must always remain a question whether this rise would have been less or greater had recourse not been had to the coolies; but, in any case, the 'overspill' from the mines made the completion of the road and railway programmes possible and, as the other Transvaal towns grew in sympathy with Johannesburg, the adult male population, potential voters, grew also and thereby improved the prospects of a British federation.[3]

These prospects were still further brightened by a Progressive victory in the Colony. There, Sprigg had at last made a false step in his egg-dance, and Jameson, leader now of a well-organised party prepared to 'vote British,' was returned to power.[4] Thanks largely to the disfranchisement of the rebels, Sprigg, Merriman and Sauer were all unseated, but Jameson had to be content with a majority of one in the Upper House and of five in the Lower. By dint of an all-night sitting and a free use of the Speaker's closure, he carried

Feb.
1904.

---

[1] Cd. 1895 of 1904, pp. 128, 229; Cd. 1899 of 1904, p. 6.

[2] Cd. 1986 of 1904, pp. 3 ff.; Cd. 2104 of 1904, p. 2; Cd. 2183 of 1904, pp. 3, 26; Cd. 2401 of 1905, p. 47; Ordinance 17 of 1904.

[3] In 1903, gold output was, £12,000,0000; in 1904, £16,000,000; in 1905, £20,800,000; in 1906, £24,600,000. The adult males on the Rand increased by 30 per cent. in twenty months and £4,000,000 worth of new buildings were sanctioned in Johannesburg alone. The average number of Europeans employed on the mines for the twelve months prior to June 1904 was 13,000. This rose to 15,000 in 1905 and to 18,000 in 1906.

[4] Jameson Ministry, Feb. 22, 1904–Feb. 2, 1908: Dr. Leander Starr Jameson, Prime Minister; Colonel Charles Preston Crewe and, from June 10, 1907, onwards, Sir Pieter Faure, Colonial Secretary; Edgar Harris Walton, Treasurer; Victor Sampson, Attorney-General; Dr. Thomas William Smartt, Public Works; Arthur John Fuller and, from June 10, 1907, onwards, Col. C. P. Crewe, Agriculture; L. L. Michell (Feb. 22, 1904–June 6, 1905), and A. J. Fuller (June 10, 1907–Feb. 2, 1908), Without Portfolio.

a bill creating twelve new constituencies mostly in urban and, therefore, presumably Progressive areas. He then relieved the disfranchised
rebels of their disabilities.[1]

For the moment the tide was apparently running strongly against
the Afrikaners; nevertheless, once the pressure of martial law had
been removed, they had begun to rally their forces. After the peace
a few die-hards had trekked away to Rhodesia or British East Africa;
others, determined to avoid the very sight of the Union Jack, had
gone into French, German or Portuguese territory, and a few
wanderers still farther afield to the Argentine, whence most of them
presently returned. As a people they had kept to the terms of the
treaty. Criticism of the authorities they were able to give in full
measure, but that was all in the game, and from the outset they had
freedom of the press and public meeting. At first they were much
divided. So little dealing would Die-hards have with Hands-uppers
that more than one predikant in the ex-Republics excommunicated
National Scouts till they should publicly confess the error of their
ways. There was bitterness against Transvaalers in the hearts of
Hertzog and many other Free Staters, whose little republic had been
ground between the upper and the nether millstones of a war arising
partly at least from the shortcomings of that Pretoria Government
which, they most firmly held, had jettisoned them in the end. Rebels
felt that they too had been abandoned. But these divisions were over-
borne by one outstanding fact. The war had undoubtedly brought
federation nearer by placing British and Afrikaners everywhere
under the same sovereign and promising them all ultimately the
same constitutional status; but it had one result which, from the
point of view of those who looked for the speedy anglicisation of
South Africa, was most disconcerting. It had taught the Afrikaners
that they were a people.

The *Afrikaner Volk* proceeded to find itself along cultural and
then along political lines. The Old Colony led the way. There
Hofmeyr, soon after his return from Europe, revived the Taalbond Jan.
to combat English with the weapon of High Dutch.[2] A little later 1903.
a much more effective armoury was discovered. Humble enthusiasts
for the spoken Afrikaans, first here, then there, began the Second
Language Campaign. In the Crown Colonies the struggle centred
upon the schools.[3] Against the wishes of the chief educational
adviser all local share in the choice of teachers and courses of
instruction had been swept away by a Government which paid all
expenses and was so set upon inculcating a knowledge of English
that it only countenanced the use of Dutch as a medium of instruction up to a maximum of five hours per week, and that by special

---

[1] Colvin, *Jameson*, II.; Act 29 of 1906.   [2] Hofmeyr, *Hofmeyr*, pp. 591 ff.
[3] Malherbe, *History of Education*, pp. 305 ff.

17

request. This attempt to out-Mansvelt Mansvelt led to a popular reaction. Opposition schools were opened in the Transvaal to preserve as much as possible of the pre-war system, Steyn and Mansvelt sent help from Holland, and soon the *Christelike Nasionale Onderwijs* committee had its own examining board and local committees, elected by parents, in control of some 200 schools in the two ex-republics. The authorities appointed advisory committees for the state schools with very shadowy powers and, to end the competition of the C.N.O. schools, Milner offered to set up local committees with an elective majority to select teachers from the Government list, provided the committees found half the expenses. Clerical influence and the financial tradition of the country were against this settlement, and so the scholastic war went on. If, in view of the excellent education provided in the Government schools and the unpopularity of some of the imported Hollander teachers, the C.N.O. movement did not achieve all that its promoters expected of it, it at least stimulated national sentiment among the rising generation.

Feb. 1904.

The Afrikaners meanwhile organised politically. Hofmeyr renamed the Bond the South African Party in the hope of winning over moderate Englishmen who disliked the old name and its associations. In the North, on the contrary, the Boer leaders held aloof from any share in the administration. Botha, de la Rey and Smuts, pleading that the time was not yet ripe for any representative institutions, declined the proffered seats on the Transvaal Legislative Council and Labour Commission.[1] Botha, however, brought the Die-hards and Hands-uppers together in conference and later, helped by the enthusiasm aroused by Kruger's funeral at Pretoria, formed the *Het Volk* party pledged to conciliation and self-government. A month later, Steyn, partially restored to health, returned home to work for self-government in the O.R. Colony.[2]

1903.

1904.
Jan.–
Feb.
1905.

Nevertheless, it was the restive British of the Rand who compelled the first slackening of the bearing rein. Ex-Uitlanders, who in the good times had called the Government timid and unenterprising, now censured it for having been wildly optimistic; others attacked it on the score of Chinese labour. Milner and Lyttelton came independently to the conclusion that a change must be made.[3] Immediate self-government was to them out of the question. Apart from the fact that nothing of the kind had been promised in the Treaty of Vereeniging, they held that the acquiescence of the Boers in British citizenship was still doubtful, that the British, 'politically inexperienced and thoughtless to a degree,' were not yet numerous

[1] Cd. 2104 of 1904, p. 9; J. C. Smuts, *Jan Christian Smuts*, pp. 92, 95.
[2] Cd. 2479 of 1905, pp. 58 ff.; van der Merwe, *Steyn*, II. 204.
[3] Cd. 2400 of 1905, pp. 1 ff.; C. 2479 of 1905, *passim*; Spender, *Campbell-Bannerman*, II. 169; *Milner Papers*, II. 520 ff.

enough to be left to themselves, and that both peoples would inevitably form parties along racial lines. On the other hand, the Balfour Ministry was tottering to its fall and the Liberals were saddled with promises whose fulfilment might thrust the solution of the Chinese puzzle on a self-governing Transvaal. Milner and Lyttelton, therefore, proposed to postpone the day of full self-government by setting up a constitution which would give the Transvaal representation strong enough, 'except where vital imperial interests are concerned, practically to direct the policy of the administration.' The change was, however, delayed till Milner was gone. He went, worn out with the work of reconstruction, whose April distinguishing mark, as he justly boasted, was 'the colossal amount 1905. which has been done in the time.'[1] The scope and quality of that work constitute his best claim to memory among South Africans.

The new High Commissioner, Lord Selborne, able, approachable, and a keen farmer, was a man who might expect to be continued in office even if the Liberals came in and whose views were yet nearly enough akin to those of his predecessor to ensure a certain continuity of policy. Be that as it might, the Lyttelton letters patent promised to circumscribe his authority considerably by providing for a unicameral legislature, one-fifth official and the rest elective on a Nov. very low European franchise, which should have full powers in all 1904. matters save the reserved list and the moneys payable to the Intercolonial Council.[2] The news of the impending change and the prospect of change to follow in the O.R. Colony had already crystallised parties in the Transvaal. The mass of the urban British accepted the Lyttelton scheme and formed the Progressive party under Farrar; but others, led by men of South African birth like Edward Solomon, Sir Richard's brother, and Henry Hull, who were hostile to the ultra-British atmosphere of the Government offices and to Johannesburg domination, had already formed a Responsible Government party and now declared that the new constitution would not march; the Labour groups drew together under Creswell; the Boers rallied to *Het Volk*, which held that any change short of full self-government was undesirable.[3] No one would listen to Milner's revolutionary proposal that the elections should be run on proportional representation lines with three-cornered constituencies. Hence, as the elections drew near, it was clear that the main struggle would be between *Het Volk*, which demanded the allocation of seats on a population basis to favour the married men and large families of the countryside, and the Progressives who held out for the automatic redistribution of seats on the basis of voters—that is, 'one vote,

---

[1] '*The Times' History*, VI. 145, 168 ff.
[2] Cd. 2400 of 1905, pp. 6 ff.
[3] Cd. 2479 of 1905, *passim*; Newton, *Unification*, I. 239 ff.

one value'—a system that would benefit the towns where, in those days, bachelors did much abound.[1]

The election never took place. The Milner-Chamberlain régime as modified by Lyttelton and Selborne was fighting against time. The hectic wartime popularity of the Tory Ministry had long since faded. The National Debt had risen sky-high, Consols were falling and Chamberlain's tariff reform campaign had rent the ministerial ranks and driven the Liberals together for the first time since Gladstone's Home Rule Bill had scattered them ten years before. The British electorate for its part, sickened by the reports of war commissions and threatened with high prices by a Government innocent of any scheme of social reform, listened once more to the renewed cry of 'Chinese slavery.' The gravamen of the Liberal charge against the system had always been that it was 'very like slavery'[2], for, though the coolies were not closely compounded as at Kimberley but merely confined to the mining properties which were often to be measured by the square mile, yet their position was peculiar in that they were specifically limited to unskilled labour. In other words, they were human machinery to be used and returned to store when no longer needed by capitalists, whose influence, in popular estimation, had increased, was increasing, and ought to be diminished all the more as they had defaulted on their war contribution.[3] Troubles, too, were arising in connection with this strange form of labour. The first arrivals were steady-going men, who spent their wages freely and thus set up a good local demand for produce; but many later comers were of a lower type and were soon complaining of knavish Chinese compound police, bullying white bosses, illegal deduction of wages and even flogging, and pointed to the failure of their employers to give the promised increase of pay. The coolies on the New Randfontein mine struck; others driven desperate by sodomy and gambling debts sought to find their way back to China, robbing and, on occasion, murdering as they went. Selborne was obliged to let the Boers of the neighbourhood have arms, station mounted police on the East Rand and warn the mine-owners that, if there were any more murders, the Chinese would have to go.

April 1905.

Dec. 1905.

Hardly had Selborne instituted his reforms than the Balfour ministry fell. The new Premier, Campbell-Bannerman, at once forbade further recruiting and presently emerged from a general election with a bigger majority than any since the days of the great Reform Bill. In that election, the cry of Chinese slavery played more than its due share in routing the Tories; on the other hand, 14,700

1832.

---

[1] 'The Times' History, VI. 160.
[2] Spender, Campbell-Bannerman, II. 145. On Chinese Labour from 1905 onwards vide Cd. 2401, 2786 of 1905; 2788, 2819, 3025 and No. 156 of 1906; Cd. 3338 of 1907, and Campbell, Chinese Coolie Emigration.
[3] Cd. 1895 of 1904, p. 230.

recently issued licences to import coolies could not be cancelled
without breach of contract.[1] Bannerman, therefore, gave leave to any
Chinese who so desired to return home, an offer of which very
few 'slaves' availed themselves, and then, to the horror of his hot-
gospellers, justified Milner's forebodings by proposing to leave the
fate of the 47,000 coolies actually on the Rand to be decided by the
Transvaalers themselves.[2]

This arrangement was almost certainly due in part to the presence
in London of Smuts, strong in the knowledge that *Het Volk* and the
Responsible Government party had come to an understanding on
the score of the Chinese and common action at the expected elections. Smuts, moreover, convinced the sympathetic Prime Minister
that the Transvaal ought to be given self-government forthwith.
Campbell-Bannerman, therefore, talked over his many hesitant colleagues and sent out the West-Ridgeway Commission to pave the
way.[3] The commissioners found mass meetings of miners convinced
by Creswell that the promised ratio between white and yellow men
had not been maintained, Selborne raising fresh police and issuing
more arms to frightened farmers, a select committee pointing to
barbed wire as the only effective check on Celestial runaways, and
Botha proclaiming the country in danger. Their chief duties, however, lay in the constitutional sphere. They proposed an allocation
of seats which they hoped would secure the even balance of parties
in the first Parliament. That was apparently all that *Het Volk*
hoped for, but the Progressives accepted the compromise only
after the High Commissioner had narrowly escaped recall for his
championship of the Lyttelton constitution. At the elections the July
British vote was split between Progressive, Labour and Independent 1906.
candidates, while Edward Solomon led the bulk of his Nationalists,
videlicet Responsible Government men, into the *Het Volk* camp. *Het
Volk* thus gained an overall majority of five in the Assembly and,
since its leader, Botha, took office with Smuts as his Colonial Secre- Feb.
tary, a majority in the nominee Legislative Council also.[4]   1907.

Opponents of the new policy feared that *Het Volk* would prove
tyrannical to the British and disastrous to Transvaal prosperity.
Many of Botha's followers, on the other hand, suspected that self-
government would be a mere sham, for bills touching Indians and
indentured labour were to be reserved, there was to be no further

---

[1] Spender, *op. cit.*, II. 228.   [2] Cd. 2788 of 1906, pp. 2, 9.
[3] J. C. Smuts, *Jan Christian Smuts*, p. 98.
[4] On grant of Responsible Government to the Transvaal *vide* Cd. 3250 of
1906. The constitution provided for a nominated Legislative Council of 15 to
become elective after four years, if desired; an Assembly of 69 (Rand 34, Pretoria 6, Districts 29) elected by Europeans in roughly equal constituencies.
Dutch could be used freely in the Houses, but English was to be the official
language. At the elections *Het Volk* won 37 seats, Progressives 21, Nationalists 6,
Independents and Labour, 5.

importation of coolies, the Labour Ordinance was to be repealed within the year, civil servants were specially safeguarded and the Land Boards were to be maintained for five years as a protection to Milner's British settlers. These mutual fears proved to be groundless. Drastic anti-Asiatic bills received the Royal Assent; Botha in the main followed the recommendations of a Crown Colony commission in reducing official staffs; the language clauses of Smuts's Education Act were moderate; the Premier, anxious to obtain the wherewithal to implement his election promises of a Land Bank and agricultural railways, was in no hurry to bid farewell to the Celestials. It was only after his return from the Colonial Conference of April 1907 that he announced that no more would be heard of the magnates' war loan, that H.M. Government had guaranteed a loan of £5,000,000 which would make the administration independent of the mining-houses, and that the coolies would go home as their contracts expired.[1] So it was done and all the more easily in that the supply of native labour had for some time past been greater than the demand. Reduced working costs, improved methods and an adequate labour supply promised a long life to the low-grade mines of the Rand from which the last Chinaman departed in March 1910.[2]

Meanwhile, a further notable new development had taken place in South African politics. Some members of the many white trade unions that had sprung up along the Rand during the past few years followed the lead of the Transvaal Miners' Association and struck in 1907 in the depth of the depression. Three hundred strikers marched to Pretoria to press their claims on the authorities and, at Smuts's request, two British regiments had to patrol the Rand to allay excitement.[3] The strikers were beaten after a three months' struggle partly because many of the more highly skilled British workers remained at work and partly because Afrikaners from the *platteland* took strikers' places at the preferred lower wages. Thus began that invasion which was destined to Afrikanerise the Transvaal trade unions so markedly in the course of a single generation. The initial effect of this flood of cheap white labour was a move by experienced white trade unionists to stem it. To that end, William Andrews, a Leicester fitter, Henry Sampson, an ex-London printer, and Peter Whiteside, a militant Australian member of the Engine Drivers' and Firemen's Union, took the lead in forming the South African Labour Party.[4]

[1] Cd. 3528 of 1907, p. 159; Cd. 3621 of 1907.
[2] Jan. 1907.   Europeans 17,000; Chinese 54,000; Natives 94,000.
    Dec. 1908.   „   18,600   „   12,000   „   150,000.
    The output of gold in 1908 was nearly £30,000,000.
[3] J. C. Smuts, *Jan Christian Smuts*, p. 101.
[4] Van der Horst, *op. cit.*, p. 241; Roux, *op. cit.*, pp. 131, 153; Sachs, *op. cit.*, pp. 47, 142–3.

The immediately significant fact, however, was that the Transvaal, far and away the wealthiest of the South African colonies, had passed under the control of Afrikaners within five years of the war of conquest. It was only a matter of time before the O.R. Colony fell May into the hands of Steyn, Hertzog and the Orangia Unie party, which 1906. they had formed to push for self-government.[1] In the Cape, again, the power of the Progressives was waning. The formation of his ministry had tried Jameson's tact, but no tact could hold his party together.[2] The rival ports, the inland towns, the Border farmers, East and West, all cherished incompatible ambitions; Merriman and Sauer had soon found their way back to the Assembly to plague the Premier, and when Jameson favoured protection to placate the farmers, he alienated the townsmen. The ministry had taken office just as the post-war slump hit the Colony with full force; the effects of the drought were presently accentuated by cattle sickness, and year by year revenue fell from the lordly £12,000,000 of 1903 to the miserable £7,000,000 of 1907. Jameson, retrenching, never drew his allowance as Prime Minister,[3] but his followers would hardly submit to an income tax or to the advances on brandy in stock which alone reconciled the S.A. Party to the excise; the farmers complained that the growing Graaff meat trust was spoiling the market for their cattle; the jealousies of the ports wrecked all Jameson's hopes of May ratifying the offer of a railway conference, which had, under pressure 1905. from Milner, set aside one-third of the Rand traffic for the Cape ports. Railways, indeed, bade fair to be a source of division rather than a bond of union unless political federation could be achieved. A second anxious conference pointed the moral; Natal was with 1906. difficulty dissuaded from leaving the Customs Union[4] and, now, the self-governing Transvaal, intent on reducing the cost of living, was certain to denounce the Customs Convention. If it did so, Natal must follow suit; economic war would ensue between the north-east and the south-west clamorous for revenue, a war in which the latter would be fatally handicapped in that the railways of the O.R. Colony, the economic ally of the Cape, were controlled by the Transvaal. What was more, the very grant of self-government to the Transvaal and the prospect of its speedy extension to the O.R. Colony must ruin Milner's federation of the two ex-Republics de par le roi, because an autonomous O.R. Colony would never suffer its appeals to go to Pretoria or be content with a mere Lieutenant-Governor instead of a full Governor. In that event, little would be left of the northern federation save the Central African Railways, the S.A. Constabulary

---

[1] On Responsible Government in the O.R.C. vide Cd. 3526 of 1907; van der Merwe, Steyn, II. 207.
[2] Colvin, Jameson, II. 237 ff.   [3] Jameson held no portfolio.
[4] Cd. 2977 of 1906; van der Poel, Railway and Customs Policies, pp. 238 ff.

and an International Council whose significance was fading now that the post-war Imperial loan was almost expended.

Selborne was as anxious as ever Milner had been to achieve federation before the colonies were free to fall upon each other, but he was prepared to try different means to achieve his end. He and some prominent members of Milner's Kindergarten had long realised that responsible government must come and ought to come, if only because the jealousies of British officials and politicians in each colony for their neighbours in other colonies proved that the Crown Colony régime was unsuited to South African conditions. It was no use waiting, as Milner had proposed to wait, till the British section was strong enough to write the federal constitution; the rivalries of the colonies were so keen that the Afrikaners could always find means to produce a deadlock. By the end of 1906 it was obvious that the British would never be in a position to dictate the constitution; rather, there was every prospect that the Afrikaners would soon be in a position to discharge that function. The parts were being reversed and it would fall to the British, fearful of 'Dutch' domination and possible secession from the Empire, to block the way to closer union.

There were, however, hopeful signs. The Cape Progressives were rapidly passing out of the 'vote British' stage; the Boers in the ex-Republics were gaining confidence in the Liberal interpretation of imperialism; Botha was big enough to see that he must carry the main body of the British with him. Lionel Curtis and Patrick Duncan, Robert Brand and Philip Kerr and other members of the Kindergarten in the Transvaal, fired by Oliver's *Alexander Hamilton*, were already debating the question of closer union;[1] Botha and Smuts discussed the formation of a federal court of appeal with the Cape Chief Justice de Villiers; the Colonial Conference approved

April 1907.

of the creation of such a court either with or without political federation. But all this was not enough. The question of closer union must be raised openly. No Afrikaner could do that without alarming the British; but the British could now do it without arousing suspicion of imperial domination in Afrikaner hearts. By making the first move, the British would 'capitalise' their position as political underdog.

July 1907.

The High Commissioner and Curtis's committee therefore drafted the famous Selborne Memorandum covering correspondence which had recently passed between Jameson and the Governor of the Cape in the matter of railways.[2] François Malan, leader of the Cape Bondsmen, agreed to support the movement towards federation

---

[1] R. H. Brand and P. Kerr, members of the Railway Board; P. Duncan, ex-Colonial Secretary; L. Curtis, ex-Assistant Col. Sec.
[2] Cd. 3564 of 1907, republished and edited by Basil Williams (1926).

which the terms of the Memorandum implied, and Jameson, whose inveterate hero-worship was fast transferring itself from the dead Rhodes to the living Botha, promised, Premier though he was, to serve under Malan on any national convention that might meet as a result of his efforts. Merriman and Sauer, suspicious of what the former termed 'the petty interference' of the High Commissioner, were against the scheme; but Malan had his way. He moved and Jameson seconded a resolution in favour of taking steps towards closer union; Hofmeyr blessed the undertaking; the Memorandum was published and South Africa fairly entered upon the final stage on the long road to federation.

The main thesis of the Selborne Review was that, since the railway interests of the various colonies were 'not only distinct but absolutely incompatible,' the alternative solutions were 'arbitration or the sword.' This potent argument in favour of closer union was reinforced by hard times, the growth of good feeling and the imminent breakdown of the Customs Union. It was driven home by signs of unwonted non-European activities, which reached their climax in the rapid spread of Ethiopianism, and by grave difficulties with Indians in the Transvaal and Natal, native unrest in Natal, stagnation in Southern Rhodesia and the approach of self-government in the O.R. Colony.

Little comment was forthcoming when, in 1902, an African, the Rev. John Dube, began to publish his Bantu newspaper *Ilanga lase Natal* at Durban, and the leading Capetown Moslem, Dr. Abdullah Abdurahman, founded his African People's Organisation (A.P.O.) not so much to defend the rights of the Coloured Folk in the Cape, which were not yet seriously threatened as to work for their extension to those folk in other parts.[1] It was a different matter with Ethiopianism. This movement had fairly got under way in 1889, when a Cape Bantu clergyman, Kanyome, had led his congregation out of the Anglican communion, and, more remarkably, a European missionary, Paul Winter, had left the local Berlin Mission station and founded the Secocoeniland Church in the Transvaal. Poor Winters's prompt ejection by his own Bantu vestry perhaps encouraged Mangena Mokoni and a score of other African ministers to secede from the Wesleyans because of their white exclusiveness and found the Ethiopian Church in the Transvaal. This new body grew so fast that in 1896 it sent the ambitious James Mata Dwane to the United States, where he arranged union with the African Methodist Episcopal Church. Back came Dwane endowed, like Dr. John Philip in days gone by, with the authority of General Superintendent to arouse jealousy among his fellow-workers in the vineyard, and then

[1] J. S. Marais, *The Cape Coloured People*, p. 276.

17*

to be put in the shade by Bishop Henry McNeil Turner. This American Negro, in the course of a short visit, ordained some sixty ministers and admitted thousands to the American Methodist Episcopal Church. This was too much for Dwane, who persuaded Archbishop West Jones and his Episcopal Synod to constitute him and some thirty of his fellow-ministers as the Order of Ethiopia within the Church of the Province.[1] Meanwhile, Bishop Levi Jenkins Coppin, first of a line of American Negro Bishops, had taken charge of the South African branch of the A.M.E. Church. That Church, far more successful than the Order of Ethiopia, soon became the largest of all the secessionist African Churches, whose numbers increased so fast from the eighteen-nineties onwards, often under American inspiration, that by 1918 there were no less than seventy-six of them. The formation of the Presbyterian Church of Africa and the breakaway from the Church of the Province, which took the resounding title of the Ethiopian Catholic Church of Zion, were followed by a rush of secessions from the Wesleyan, Scottish and American Zulu Missions and even from the Dutch Reformed Church. Many more such Churches came into being than found their way on to the official list and, had they remained united, must have aroused more suspicion among white folk than they actually did.[2] Even so, there was suspicion enough, especially in nervous little Natal, where so many of these Ethiopian Churches had their origin.

The South African Indian problem was only part of that which affected many lands washed by the Pacific and Indian Oceans. Its local roots lay in the coast-belt of Natal into which Indians had been imported steadily since 1860. As coolies, they had made the sugar industry possible and, as free men, at first with the encouragement of the authorities and then in spite of them, they had played an important part in the economic development of Natal. Ex-coolies gave the coast towns an unrivalled supply of fish, fruit and vegetables; they owned or leased on short terms land in the coast-belt which no one else would touch and made it fit for sugar-planting; they worked as domestic servants, farm labourers and petty artisans far outside the sub-tropical areas. And they increased in numbers.

As in the Cape, free Natal Indians had once been entitled to the parliamentary and municipal franchises. By 1891 they were fast gaining in numbers on the Europeans, two-thirds of them were free men and some of them had votes. Then, to induce coolies to go home at the end of their indentures, the old law offering them

---

[1] Roux, *op. cit.*, pp. 87 ff.

[2] *The South African Natives*, chap. vii, viii; J. du Plessis, *Christian Missions*, pp. 453 ff. There were nearly 1359 secessionist Churches in 1950, of which only eighty-one were officially recognized; *vide Race Relations Handbook*, chap. xxiii.

Crown land at the end of ten years was repealed, and, on achieving
self-government, Natal tried to arrange ways and means with the
Indian Government for removing her now redundant Asiatics.
Failing in this, she stiffened her laws against them. An education 1893–
test was applied to immigrants; the parliamentary franchise was 1903.
denied to all who came from states which, like India, lacked representative institutions;[1] trading licences were withheld from those
who failed to keep their books in English; coolies who neither reindentured nor went home at the end of their term were taxed £3
annually, and presently this tax was extended to their children; in
1897 it was made a criminal offence for a white man to marry an
Indian. Such was Natal's 'bitter example' which had moved the 1904.
Indian Government to refuse the Transvaal's request for coolies to
work on her goldmines.[2]

The Cape Colony contained few Indians, for it lay out of their
track, and the Free State had long ago barred its entries to Asiatics
and obliged those who were already there to wind up their businesses.
Meanwhile, Indians had found their way into the Transvaal, the
majority of them Moslem Surat traders of higher standing than
the low-caste Untouchable Madrassis who swarmed in Natal. The
Republican Government had taken steps to check this invasion by 1885.
denying Asiatics all civil and political rights, forbidding them to own
fixed property and rendering them liable to registration and residence
in special locations. But, like so many other laws in the old Transvaal,
these rules had been more honoured in the breach than the observance; the Pretoria authorities feared to go too far lest they break
the London Convention and, as it was, the grievances of British
Indians had been the subject of acrid correspondence with the High
Commissioner. During the war, British ministers and others had
given colour to the belief that all restrictions would be removed;
but even before the end of the struggle, Milner had had to suggest 1902.
that Asiatics should be registered and all, save those of the better
class, be confined to trading and residential locations.[3]

Chamberlain refused and for a long time no definite step was
taken. Throughout the Crown Colony period the officials were
haunted by the fear of embarrassing the British Raj in India where
Bengal was crying out against Lord Curzon and resorting to political
murder; but, to balance that fear, was the belief that unauthorised
Indians were being smuggled into the Transvaal and that the law
was being evaded by impersonation. An outbreak of plague in the
filthy Indian quarter at Johannesburg redoubled the popular outcry
in the towns against Indians, but H.M. Government could only
suggest that low-class Indians should be confined to locations on

[1] Act No. 8 of 1896.   [2] U.G. 12–14, p. 39; U.G. 16–1914, p. 2.
[3] On Indian grievances vide C. 7911 of 1896; Cd. 1683–4 of 1903.

1906.

purely sanitary grounds and that an education test on Cape and Natal lines be applied at the frontier.[1] The expiring Transvaal Legislative Council took the hint and prescribed finger-print registration for all unindentured Asiatics, but, at the Colonial Office's request the ordinance was held back pending the grant of responsible

1907.

government.[2] One of the first steps of the new Transvaal Parliament was to re-enact this ordinance; its next was to pass an immigration law which included an education test and thumb-print registration.[3] And already Mohandas Gandhi, a well-to-do Indian barrister in Johannesburg, had been moved by Tolstoy's interpretation of the Sermon on the Mount to throw up his practice and organise passive resistance among the Transvaal Indians, while anxious questions flashed across the wires from Simla and even Pekin. Plainly, South Africa must face Asia with a united front if it was to deal with a problem which had its roots in Natal and bore fruit in the Transvaal.

It was, however, the Bantu rather than the Indian menace which agitated Natal at the moment.[4] The Europeans of that colony were, indeed, outnumbered by their Indians, free and indentured, but they were overwhelmed by the Africans by nine to one. The war had naturally unsettled the tribes; the withdrawal of most of the troops suggested to them that the King was angry with his white children;

1904–
1908.

emissaries of the anti-European Ethiopian movement were present to point to the lesson of the stand which the Hereros and Hottentots were making against the Germans in South-West Africa. Meanwhile, for years past, conservative officials had done little more than carry on the traditional Shepstone policy of strengthening the tribal

1894–
1905.

system. Even so, their suggestions had been ignored by legislators who accompanied the steady acquisition of Crown lands in Natal proper and the European penetration of Zululand by stiffening the labour laws, punishing stock theft, increasing the squatter's tax and, finally, levying a poll-tax whose main weight fell on a people driven desperate by high rents and usurers.[5]

Feb.
1906.

The poll-tax was the last straw, and a small rising took place in Natal proper. Martial law was proclaimed and imperial troops were rushed down from the Transvaal at the request of the Natal authorities, but the local forces were strong enough to restore order. A dozen leaders were condemned to death by court-martial and, when

---

[1] Cd. 2239 of 1904, pp. 3, 37.
[2] Cd. 3308 of 1907, p. 58. Apparently the Ordinance (29 of 1906) was partially enforced at the very end of the Crown Colony régime (Cd. 3251 of 1906).
[3] Acts 2 and 15 of 1907.
[4] On Natal's native troubles *vide* Cd. 2905, 2927, 3027, 3247 of 1906; 3563 of 1907; 3888, 3889, 3998, 4001, 4194, 4195, 4328, 4403, 4404, 4585 of 1908.
[5] Acts 40 of 1894, 159 of 1899, 28 of 1902, 48 of 1903, 38 of 1905. *Vide* also Eybers, pp, 252 ff.; Brookes, *Native Policy*, pp. 74 ff.; Cd. 3889 of 1908, pp. 2, 7, 9; Evans, *Black and White*, pp. 184 ff.

Downing Street sought to stay the public executions, the Natal ministry resigned, the Australian government asked the meaning of this interference in the affairs of a self-governing colony, the ministry resumed office, the executions were carried out and a serious rebellion flared up in Zululand.[1] This time help had to be called in from the Cape Colony and the Transvaal before the rebellion was stamped out in blood. A strong local commission was appointed to overhaul the Natal native administration and found much to condemn in it; but before long, martial law was proclaimed in Zululand once more and Dinizulu, who had been restored as chief of the Usutu in 1897, was arrested for alleged complicity in the late rebellion. Miss Harriet Colenso, daughter of the famous Bishop, and H.M. Government, mindful of the fate of Langalibalele and of Dinizulu himself in earlier days, began to press for a fair trial for the son of Cetewayo.[2]

Natal, still a small and struggling colony, was plainly unfitted to rule swarms of tribesmen without danger to them, to herself and her neighbours. There was a possibility that, in default of federation, a still weaker and more heavily burdened European community might be called on to undertake a similar task. In Southern Rhodesia the memory of the pioneering past was fading as conditions became more settled and magistrates more numerous, while the Bantu indunas, as salaried officials of the Company under the control of the Native Commissioners, kept order in the kraals, collected taxes and furnished labour for the public works in the usual Bantu fashion. Meanwhile, the Order-in-Council of 1898 still held the Company responsible for administrative deficits, but it had also given the Rhodesians an elected minority in the Legislative Council. From the first, political life had centred round the closely allied questions of responsibility for the accumulated administrative deficits and the ownership of the unalienated lands. Neither the Charter nor the Lippert Concession had given the Company ownership of land, but lapse of time, 'damned iteration' and the failure of H.M. Government to define rights had bred the idea that the unalienated lands were, like the minerals, a commercial asset of the shareholders under concession from Lobengula deceased. Similarly, the Charter made no mention of a refund of the expenses of government other than the cost of public works, for, in 1889, all concerned had believed that the mineral profits would meet expenses for the short time that the Company would have to rule. These expectations had been disappointed and, since 1898, the directors had followed Rhodes in claiming that a fair proportion of past and all future deficits must ultimately fall upon self-governing Rhodesia as a public debt.

[1] Cd. 2095 of 1906, pp. 3, 25, 32.
[2] Cd. 4195 of 1908; Cd. 4585 of 1909.

The elected members had repudiated this debt, asked who really owned the lands and tried to tax the Company on the revenues drawn by it from both land and minerals. The South African War drove these quarrels underground and subjected Rhodesia to a severe strain, which it nevertheless bore so well that Rhodes was able to boast that 'this great dominant North with the Transvaal' would dictate the situation, and to prophesy that Company rule would soon end with the coming of federation.[1] The close of the war, however, found the Company robbed by death of the inspiration of Rhodes's personality, heavily in debt to the Imperial Government for war expenses, and short of revenue. The mines, which the Company had been obliged to help during the war, were shorter still of labour.[2] The war debt was presently cancelled, but Colonial Fingos proved to be more disappointing as mine-workers than the Matabele and Mashona, attempts to import extraneous labour of various kinds either failed or were disallowed, and the bulk of the labour force had to be drawn from Northern Rhodesia, Nyasaland and East Africa. As for revenue, H.M. Government refused to allow the hut-tax to be raised from 10s. to the Transvaal level of £2. Recourse was, therefore, had to a poll-tax of £1 on each male adult and 10s. on each polygamous wife.[3]

Beyond the Zambesi the Company had long ago taken over the administration of North-Eastern Rhodesia from the Imperial authorities and, in 1897, had sent Robert Coryndon as its first Commissioner to North-Western Rhodesia, where it obtained wider power of administration by a further treaty with Lewanika, King of the Barotse. It had then set up separate administrations in North-Western and North-Eastern Rhodesia,[4] but the centre of its power still lay in the south. There changed circumstances led to a change in policy. Hitherto the Company had neither mined, farmed nor traded on its own account. Its aim had been to encourage subsidiary gold-mining companies, develop the land and link the mining centres with the ports by offering railway and telegraph ventures liberal grants of land, guaranteed debentures and Imperial subsidies. In return it took the bulk of the shares in the railway companies and up to 50 per cent. of the vendor's scrip in the companies which alone were permitted to mine gold. Now, in face of the post-war slump, East Coast fever, stationary population, and the fading of their hopes of a new Rand, the Board tentatively substituted a royalty on gold for

Marginal dates: June 1901. — 1904. — 1894.

---

[1] *Bulawayo Chronicle*, June 15, 1901.
[2] *B.S.A. Co. Report*, 1898–1900, p. 9.
[3] *Ibid.*, p. 243; *Ibid.*, 1900–2, pp. 18, 72, 238; *B.S.A. Annual Meeting*, Oct. 1904, p. 10.
[4] *Barotziland-North-Western Rhodesia Order-in-Council, 1899*; (*Statute Law of N. W. Rhodesia*, pp. 20 ff.); *N.-E. Rhodesia Order-in-Council, 1900*; (*Statute Law of Northern Rhodesia, 1908–18*, pp. 37 ff.).

the 50 per cent. levy, reduced the 50 per cent. to 30 per cent. on base
metals, which, since the discovery of coal at Wankies, were being 1899.
taken seriously,[1] and left its officials with a bare majority in the
legislature. But this was not enough. The elected members not only 1903.
rejected proposals based on a report by Sir George Goldie that
they should assume two-thirds of the £7,500,000 deficit as a public
debt in exchange for one-third of the lands and minerals, but repudiated all liability for that deficit, claimed the lands for the
Rhodesians, demanded lower railway rates and a royalty on all
minerals, and talked of popular representation on the Executive
Council as a first step towards the elimination of the Company as a
ruling power.[2]

So the quarrel dragged on, exacerbated by the attempts of the
Board to raise a public loan. Then Selborne visited Rhodesia. He 1906.
found the farmers up in arms against the prospecting rights of the
favoured mining companies, individuals clamouring for the right to
mine, general resentment against the Company as a dangerous competitor, and a demand for a clear distinction between the Company's
administrative and commercial spheres.[3] So little distinction had
hitherto been drawn that practically all expenditure was still put
down to administrative account. Even so, administrative revenue
was on the point of meeting expenditure and, thus encouraged,
Rhodesians were asking for responsible government, failing that for
Crown Colony rule and, in any case, for a Royal Commission of
Inquiry. Lord Elgin, now Colonial Secretary, refused the last demand,
and the benevolent despots of London Wall, conscious of a morose
body of shareholders which still footed the bill and still waited for a
dividend, determined to regain that personal touch with the Rhodesians wherein had lain so much of Rhodes's strength. Hence in Oct.
Jameson's words, 'an avalanche of directors' descended upon the 1907.
country and brought with it a declaration of policy promising a
royalty system, freedom for individual miners, a clear division
between commercial and administrative finances and a small elective
majority in the legislature.[4]

The new Chartered policy failed to satisfy Rhodesians, for the
directors still claimed the lands under an 'accumulated title' and gave
no satisfactory reply in the matter of the deficit,[5] but it did give
a fresh direction to Rhodesian politics by reviving Rhodes's plan of
inclusion in a federal South Africa. One of the visiting directors had

---

[1] Mines . . . Ordinance, No. 19 of 1903.
[2] *B.S.A. Co. Report*, 1903, p. 17; *B.S.A. Annual Meeting*, Oct. 1904, pp. 7, 12;
Bulawayo Chronicle, Oct. 8, 1904.
[3] *Bulawayo Chronicle*, Oct. 23, 1906, *et passim*, Sept.–Oct. 1906.
[4] *B.S.A. Co. Report*, 1907, pp. 20, 27 ff.; *Proceedings of the Cave Commission*,
1919–20, 5th day.
[5] *Report of a Conference*, Oct. 1907.

frankly said that the Company would like 'a good get-out'; Jameson confessed that he had hinted to Fitzpatrick that the Transvaal should make an offer, and one elected member proposed to clear away difficulties with the ex-Republics in advance by curtailing the natives' rights to the franchise.

Dec. 1907.

South of the Limpopo the political leaders were feeling their way towards some kind of federation. Botha and Smuts might find Steyn somewhat difficult on the score of education policy, but Steyn had come back from Europe determined to work for union before an Anglo-German war swept down upon a divided South Africa;[1] in the Colony, Jameson pursued his conciliatory policy by renaming the Progressives Unionists to win over English Moderates, and by co-operating with Botha in his struggle for a better mail contract with the Union-Castle Company which had recently been formed by the amalgamation of the two old rival shipping lines. But time was running short. The Transvaal had denounced the customs convention. Responsible Government letters patent had just been issued to the O.R. Colony,[2] and now the very decision to press the federation policy forward sealed Jameson's fate.

June 1907.

Jameson's free trade and protectionist wings were at each other's throats, his budget was dismal, and he was forced to levy a 10 per cent. tax on mineral profits, in other words, on De Beers, which was already staggering under the competition of the new Premier Mine near Pretoria in which the Transvaal Government was deeply interested, the beginning of steady production in South-West Africa and the falling-off in the demand for diamonds due to a financial crisis in the U.S.A. The S.A. Party had had no desire to take office until the times should alter, but it was determined that, if federation was to come, it should not come through a Unionist Ministry which contained two Chartered directors. The party leaders decided to turn Jameson out and, at last, they beat him in the Legislative Council. 'The Doctor' appealed to the country and fought a good losing battle on the federation platform, but Schreiner, who believed that group politics were the only way of avoiding racial divisions, refused to join him in a Moderate-Unionist coalition to 'smash the Bond'; the S.A. Party was strengthened by the reinstated rebels and still further encouraged when, in the middle of the campaign, Abraham Fischer took office in the O.R. Colony with Hertzog as his Attorney-General and Director of Education. The S.A. Party carried the Legislative Council elections, and Jameson made way for Merriman

Dec. 1907.

Feb. 1908.

---

[1] Van der Merwe, *Steyn*, II. 220, 341.
[2] A Legislative Council of 11 nominees to become elective after four years if desired, and an Assembly of 38 elected on much the same franchise as in the Transvaal (11 town and 27 country members) (Cd. 3526 of 1907).

as head of a Bond-Moderate Ministry which was presently confirmed in power by the result of the Assembly elections.[1]

The self-governing constitution for the Transvaal had been passed by the Imperial Parliament avowedly and that for the O.R. Colony implicitly as steps towards the federation of South Africa from within.[2] Now, as Selborne and the Kindergarten had foreseen, the grant of autonomy to the second of the ex-Republics had made an end of the political side of Milner's northern federation, for after the O.R. Colony had received a full Governor in the person of Sir Arthur Lawley and had cut off appeals to Pretoria, all that remained of that organisation was the Intercolonial Council's vital Railway Committee. The question was how much longer the economic side of Milner's rickety structure would stand now that Natal was threatening to leave the Customs Union alongside the dominant Transvaal. Be that as it might, the mere passing of three of the four self-governing colonies, and those the largest and richest, more or less completely under Afrikaner control cleared the way for federation;[3] indeed, hardly had Merriman taken office before Smuts wrote that now was the time to push for it. Merriman jumped at the opening and even proposed that federation, 'the nearer to unification the better,' be carried by a *coup de main* on the part of the colonial parliaments without reference to that at Westminster. The cool advice of Chief Justice de Villiers to whom the correspondence was shown dissuaded Merriman from his *per saltum* tactics; but all concerned were agreed on the need for haste, for the Liberals showed signs of splitting and, if they fell, they might be succeeded by a ministry which would look less kindly than they on unification under Afrikaner auspices.[4] Preliminaries were informally arranged and, at the intercolonial railway and customs conference at Pretoria, Smuts moved six resolutions prescribing the procedure for attaining the immediate union of the four colonies and the future inclusion of Southern Rhodesia 'at such time and on such conditions' as might thereafter be agreed upon.[5] Perhaps, had the Cape and Transvaal leaders wished, a solution of the railway and customs questions might have been found; but the opportunity of fusing the economic and political sides of federation was too good to be missed, and nothing was done

May 1908.

---

[1] S.A. Party 69; Unionists 34; Independents 4. Merriman Ministry: Feb. 3, 1908–May 30, 1910: John Xavier Merriman, Prime Minister and Treasurer; Nicolaas Frederic de Waal, Colonial Secretary; Henry Burton, Attorney-General; Jacobus Wilhelmus Sauer, Public Works; François Stephanus Malan, Agriculture; David Pieter de Villiers Graaff and Henry Latham Currey, Without Portfolio.
[2] A. B. Keith, *Selected Speeches*, II. 3 ff.
[3] Southern Rhodesia was neither technically a colony nor self-governing till its annexation by the Crown in 1923.
[4] Walker, *De Villiers*, pp. 425 ff.
[5] Newton, *Unification*, II. 217 ff.; *Minutes of the National Convention*, p. 277.

beyond carrying the six resolutions and prolonging the existing railway and customs arrangements for a further year.

There were still lions in the path and no man could yet say whether or no they were chained. In spite of the agricultural revival, which had begun in 1907, the old Colony was very depressed and Merriman's financial policy at first depressed it further. Faced with a deficit of £1,000,000 he levied an income tax suitably furnished with an eye of a needle through which the agricultural camel might pass with most of its load; he retrenched; he docked the salaries of civil servants; to Hofmeyr's dismay he charged voters a fee on registration; he wrought grievous damage to the schools by throwing the whole of the deficits on the local school boards. Suffering thus, the Cape was naturally jealous of the Transvaal which, waxing fat on the proceeds of the mines, could afford to be indifferent to its less fortunate neighbours. Englishmen everywhere were crying out against the retrenchment campaign in the O.R. Colony and Hertzog's attempt to reply to Milner's policy of anglicisation by enforcing a rigid bilingualism in the schools; the O.R. Colonists, for their part, were angry that the Transvaalers should have received self-government before themselves and should then, in a time of acute depression, have presented the giant Cullinan diamond to the King; moreover, they complained that the more flexible Smuts Act made the fulfilment of their own education policy difficult.[1] Both O.R. Colonists and Natalians, particularist by tradition, feared, each from their own point of view, anything that would expose them to being swamped by the Cape or the Transvaal. Finally, in all parts of South Africa, since Sir George Grey had first suggested closer union in the eighteen-fifties, the mass of men had never looked for more than the loose kind of federation with which civilised states had experimented from the end of the eighteenth century onwards. The idea of a close union, at which Milner had hinted, was as yet confined to a few leaders.[2] Nevertheless, *The Government of South Africa* and *The Framework of Union*, two studies of existing South African constitutions and of federal systems, were being widely read and discussed in Closer Union Societies everywhere. At last, led by the Cape, the four Parliaments resolved to send delegates, representative of all parties and proportioned in numbers to the size and importance of each colony, to a National Convention.

June–July 1908.

A little later, the Administrator of Southern Rhodesia was invited to nominate three delegates without the power to vote. There was no intention of incorporating that territory as an original member of the coming union; but now that administrative revenue was at last meeting expenditure and the Company was so hard pushed for

[1] Van der Merwe, *Steyn*, II. 244.
[2] *Cp.* Milner's 'Why stop at Federation?' ('*The Times*' *History*, VI. 216).

money that it was issuing second debenture stock and calling on H.M. Government for aid, incorporation at an early date was a contingency not to be lost sight of.[1]

The High Commission Territories, that is, the Crown colony of Basutoland and the protectorates of Swaziland and Bechuanaland, though they were members of the Customs Union, were not represented. Basutoland had been under Imperial rule since 1884 and Bechuanaland since 1885, but the history of Swaziland had been more chequered. Its career as a protectorate of the S.A. Republic since 1895 had been troubled by tribal quarrels, intrigues of resident and non-resident concessionaires, interference by the High Commissioner and the constant efforts of the Pretoria authorities to incorporate it fully in the Republic.[2] In 1903 it had fallen under the rule of the Governor of the Transvaal, who had appointed a commission to cut a way through the jungle of concessions.[3] Some the commission abolished, others it reduced so as to give the tribesmen about one-third of the land, but the work was still unfinished when the territory 1907. reverted to the High Commissioner on the establishment of responsible government in the Transvaal. Many South Africans looked forward to the immediate incorporation of these territories in any federation, but the tribal inhabitants of all three shared a preference for rule by the King's officers to that of their European neighbours, who, they suspected, knew little about them save that their arms were strong and some at least of their lands good.[4]

The National Convention met behind closed doors and open windows in the killing heat of a Durban summer. It met with the Oct. knowledge present to each delegate that a colony which failed to 12, join at once must not expect to obtain ground-floor privileges later.[5] 1908. The tide flowed strongly in the direction of unification as opposed to federation. The President, Sir Henry de Villiers, fresh from a visit to Canada, and Steyn, the Vice-President, both condemned federation, but Smuts said nothing of the strong recommendation of that solution he had received from the French Canadian Prime Minister and leading Australians.[6] Nor did either of the outstanding local champions of federation attend the Convention: Schreiner because he had resigned to defend Dinizulu, Hofmeyr because he thought that unification had no chance of being carried and preferred to fight for the federal cause in the open. The five by no means outstanding Natal delegates were thus left to fight alone for federalism. They interpreted it so obviously to mean 'Natal' that the issue virtually went by default.

[1] *B.S.A. Co. Report*, 1908, pp. 22–3.   [2] C. 9206 of 1899.
[3] Newton, *Unification*, I. 232 ff.   [4] Walker, *De Villiers*, pp. 456, 463.
[5] On the work of the Convention *vide* Cd. 4525, 4721 of 1909; Sir E. Walton, *Inner History of the National Convention*; *Minutes of the National Convention*; Walker, *De Villiers*, chapters xxv., xxvi.
[6] Thompson, L. M., *The Unification of South Africa*, p. 107 and chap. v.

The Convention sat at Durban from October 12 till November 5, 1908, and then in the more equable climate of Capetown from November 23, with one short break, till February 3, 1909. During the long debates the Transvaalers had all the advantages of wealth and preparedness over their rivals. *Het Volk* and the Progressives had agreed with one another while they were yet in the way; they alone came to Durban supported by experts and armed with a constitution drafted by Smuts and the Curtis group. As a rule, therefore, it fell to them to make proposals and to the others to make amendments.

Many points were settled without difficulty, but some, like native policy and education with all its linguistic complications, were discreetly shelved; some, like the relations of the provincial governments to the central authority, were only partially settled; others almost wrecked the Convention before a compromise was reached.

The principle of legislative union under the Crown was carried at the outset. The central executive was to consist of a Governor-General appointed by the King, and ten ministers who must find seats in one or other of the two Houses within three months of appointment. Parliament was to consist of the Governor-General, a Senate and a House of Assembly, and was to enjoy the fullest powers the so-called 'entrenched' clauses which decreed the legal equality of English and Dutch as the official languages of the Union, and the maintenance of the Cape non-European franchise, and the clause which safeguarded both by demanding for their alteration a majority of the two Houses sitting together and, at the third reading, a two-thirds majority of the total membership of the two Houses sitting thus.

The composition of the Senate, which was to sit for ten years, occasioned little difficulty. Of its forty members, eight for each of the four Provinces were to be elected by the Provincial councillors and the members of the Assembly for that Province. The remaining eight were to be nominated by the Governor-General, four of them chiefly for their knowledge of 'the reasonable wants and wishes' of the non-Europeans. The composition of the vital House of Assembly, whose life was to be limited to five years at most, was another story. The twin problems of the franchise and the allocation of seats among the Provinces awakened the politician in every delegate. The High Commissioner and a few members of the Convention advocated a civilisation test for all aspirants to the vote, a principle which would have enfranchised some at least of the non-Europeans in the ex-Republics and, conversely, disfranchised poor whites. This breach with the traditions of the northern colonies and, to a less extent, of Natal was too much for the vast majority of the delegates, and it was only with great hesitation that they agreed that the Cape should retain its non-European franchise duly entrenched and that non-Europeans should be allowed to stand for election to the Cape and Natal Provincial Councils. As against these concessions, they succeeded in imposing a political colour bar to the extent of denying non-Europeans the right of sitting in the exclusively white Union Parliament.

A legend has recently found currency among those many white folk who would fain see the last of the old Cape civilisation franchise that the British authorities virtually dictated the South Africa Bill and that the Cape delegates to the Convention did not really care much about that franchise. It was not so. The British Liberal Ministers brought no pressure to bear to ensure that the dominant Europeans should treat the vast non-European majority better than most of them had done hitherto, though they might have been forgiven had they done so, seeing that the very sessions of the Convention were punctuated by demands for Bantu lands by men from all the colonies, especially from Natal, and that in Natal again not all the efforts of Schreiner, leader of the Cape Bar, could prevent the long-delayed and most unsatisfactory Special Court from sentencing Dinizulu to four years' imprisonment for his almost involuntary share in the recent Zulu rebellion. Yet, in face of all this, those Ministers merely instructed Selborne to make it clear to the Convention through de Villiers that it hoped for a general civilisation franchise and that what the Convention decided in this respect must have a bearing on the problem of the transfer of the High Commission Territories. As for indifference, it is on record that the Cape delegates fought hard for their franchise and none more resolutely than the enlightened Afrikaner, François Malan, and Colonel Walter Stanford, Schreiner's substitute,[1] that at the last the veteran Merriman would not hear of the inclusion of a prayer to Almighty God in a Constitution that embodied a colour bar,[2] and that, when the Draft Bill was published, Hofmeyr, Afrikaner of Afrikaners, saw to it that his Capetown branch of the Bond should protest for the same reason. The truth is that the Cape delegates cared immeasurably and made it clear that unless their franchise were entrenched, there would be no Union as far as the Mother Colony was concerned.

The main struggle on the allocation of seats in the Assembly lay between the Cape and the Transvaal. The Cape, whose white population was nearly as great as that of the three other Provinces put together, pressed for seats in proportion to the European population of each Province; the Transvaal, where all white men had votes and non-Europeans had none, demanded that the number of European

[1] Walker, *Schreiner*, pp. 272 ff.
[2] F. S. Malan, *Konvensie Dagboek*, p. 247.

voters be taken as the basis. In the end they agreed to take the European adult male population. The Cape received fifty-one seats but lost the seven due to its Coloured and Native voters; the Transvaal received thirty-six, and the two smaller Provinces were given seventeen apiece for at least ten years or until the total number of seats in the Assembly should reach one hundred and fifty.

The scales thus tilted against the Cape were still further weighted by the arrangements for future redistribution. The Convention adopted an Australian scheme of automatic redistribution to avoid a repetition of the fierce struggles for representation which had embittered recent Cape and Transvaal politics. The total number of European male adults in the four colonies in 1904, divided by 121, the number of seats in the first Union Assembly, gave the Union quota. If it was found after the quinquennial census that the number of white men in a given Province had increased by the amount of the quota, that Province was to be given an additional member; if it had decreased, it was to lose a member, and so in proportion. The Cape was bound to suffer heavily under this scheme, because, in 1904, its European male population had been artificially swollen by Transvaal refugees and 'birds of passage' attracted by the post-war boom. Most of these men were now gone overseas or to the Transvaal, whither the majority of still newer immigrants were going. Hence, the Transvaal stood to gain more rapidly than the Cape at the first few redistributions. Not only so, but the preference to rural areas traditional in all four colonies was perpetuated. In theory, the Judicial Commission which was to demarcate constituencies after each quinquennial census was to see to it that each contained a number of voters as nearly as possible equal to the quota of the Province in which it lay; but, in practice, it was instructed to take many modifying considerations into account, and was specifically empowered to give a preference of as much as 15 per cent. below the quota to thinly-peopled rural regions and impose a similar handicap on densely-peopled areas. In other words, the four colonies were to be united under a farmers' Constitution, which would favour the Afrikaans-speaking countryfolk against the English-speaking townsmen.

Next, the judiciary. All the colonial Supreme and High Courts and their subdivisions, such as the courts at Grahamstown, Kimberley and Johannesburg, were to form one Supreme Court organised in Provincial and Local Divisions, with an Appellate Division from which no appeal should lie to the Judicial Committee of the Privy Council save by special leave of the King-in-Council.

Further, each of the four colonies was to become a Province under an Administrator, who was to be appointed and paid by the Union Government and hold office for five years. In each there was to be a Provincial Council, elected for three years by the parliamentary voters of the Province, of twenty-five members for each of the smaller Provinces, and of a number equal to the Provincial representation in the Assembly in the case of the Cape and the Transvaal. Each Provincial Council was to elect, by proportional representation, an Executive Committee of four who should also hold office for three years and assist the Administrator. These Provincial administrations were to exercise no sovereign powers, but to discharge merely such duties as Parliament might delegate to them from time to time. The O.R. Colony was to resume its old name.

Provision was also made for the future inclusion of the Two Rhodesias and for the transfer to the Union of the governance of Basutoland, Swaziland and Bechuanaland, both on address by the Houses of the South African Parliament. With regard to the latter, H.M. Government made it clear that it could not transfer its trust unless it were satisfied as to the terms, and that unless those terms were stated at once, neither the Liberal Commons nor the country would look at any 'Constitutional Act.'[1] Selborne had to give up much of his scheme of administration by a practically independent commission, but, finally, both parties agreed to append a Schedule to the South Africa Act which more or less embodied the existing protectorate system. In especial the three High Commission Territories, on incorporation, were assured that they would not be exposed to differential duties or to tampering with tribal lands. This last was no idle proviso since Natal and O.R. Colony delegates were already asking for power to take native lands in exchange for others in Bechuanaland, and some of the Cape members wanted to annex the fertile southern strip of that area even before the transfer of the territory as a whole to the Union.[2]

Railways and the site of the capital remained. Few favoured Malan's suggestion that, on United States and Australian analogy, an artificial capital named 'Oranjestadt' should be built on the Orange river.[3] Such was the rivalry of local patriots that the Convention was threatened with disaster more than once, till at the last the capital was divided. Parliament was to sit at Capetown and the Appellate Division at Bloemfontein, at any rate, in theory, while the Executive was to be lodged at Pretoria in the massive Union Buildings on which the Transvaal was spending most of its surplus lest it be put to baser uses. Natal, on the other hand, received 30 per cent. of the Rand traffic under the railway convention for which she had been pressing since 1903, as against from 50–55 per cent. to Delagoa Bay and the remnant to the Cape ports; but to rescue the railways and harbours from the political arena, it was provided that

---

[1] Walker, *De Villiers*, pp. 449, 455 ff.; Newton, *Unification*, II. 264.
[2] Walker, *De Villiers*, p. 475. [3] Malan, *Konvensie Dagboek*, p. 269.

their budget should be separate from that of the general administration, and that they should be run henceforward 'on business principles.'

Feb.
1909. The Draft Act was naturally assailed on various grounds in each of the colonies as soon as it was published; but Hofmeyr failed to swing the Bond against it in the Cape, and three of the Parliaments accepted the Draft, though those of the Cape and the O.R. Colony April
1909. proposed serious amendments. The Transvaal legislature proposed none; but, by signing a commercial convention with Mozambique,[1] its executive aroused a storm in isolationist and jealous Natal, which had already hailed its returning Convention delegates as traitors. Nevertheless, the amendments were disposed of at a short final session at Bloemfontein from May 3 till May 11, including all save one of the twenty-three slight changes the Transvaalers now desired. The revised Draft Bill was speedily accepted by three of the Parliaments concerned and at a referendum in Natal, where the unexpectedly large favourable majority reflected the fears of the electors that unless their colony went in on the ground floor, the trade of Durban would be diverted to Delagoa Bay.

A Drafting Delegation headed by de Villiers then set off to watch over the passage of the Draft Bill through the Westminster Parliament, the only legislature that could bring the Union into being. Others, however, set out with very different intentions. Schreiner went to fight the measure in whatever lawful way he could, armed with an *Appeal to the Parliament and Government of Great Britain* which he had helped to frame. All its influential signatories and many more like them agreed with him that a loose federation was the only means of preserving the Cape's civilisation policy, that the incipient colour bar contained in the Draft Bill was 'a blot on the Constitution,' and that the paper entrenchment of the non-European franchise was 'a trap' and no safeguard at all.[2] In independent support of Schreiner went a delegation from Abdurahman's African People's Organisation, and also John Tengo Jabavu and Walter Rubusana, who were sent by the recently-formed South African Native National Conference, which was prepared to face even white adult suffrage provided the liberal Cape franchise were made attainable by non-Europeans throughout the coming Union.[3] In the event, none of these protesters were able to effect anything beyond convincing the British public that there were folk of all colours in South Africa who cared greatly for liberty and justice. Rubusana must be content to lecture up and down the country, while Schreiner himself was refused a hearing at the Bar of the House. After watching Sir Charles Dilke read the *Appeal* to the assembled Commons, Schreiner must take what comfort he could from official

[1] A. 1–1909 (Transvaal).   [2] Walker, *Schreiner*, pp. 304 ff.
[3] Roux, *op. cit.*, p. 80.

spokesmen in both Houses, who scouted the very idea that the Cape civilisation franchise would ever be thrown away and promised the African inhabitants of the High Commission Territories that, though the last word could not lie with them, transfer would never take place before they had been consulted and the Westminster Parliament had debated the issue. Meanwhile, the Drafting Delegation agreed with the urbane Colonial Secretary on a few purely formal amendments, saw the Bill go through unchanged, and learned that it had received the Royal Assent on September 20, 1909.[1] Thus did Liberals in the United Kingdom enact and like-minded men of all colours in South Africa willy-nilly accept a statute which they believed and prayed would lead to the victory of the Cape's well-tried civilisation principles throughout the Union. It was a huge political gamble, which took too little account of the strength of South African tradition and of the fear that had always lain at the back of South Africa's non-European policies; but it was a gamble that seemed to be justified. The gamblers are not to be blamed overmuch for plunging thus even though events were to prove them wrong and Schreiner right.

The sublime Burke has observed that there is a 'sacred veil to be drawn over the beginnings of all governments.' Be that as it may, the formation of the first Union ministry was attended by more than ordinary difficulty. One possible candidature for the office of Premier was ended by the death of Hofmeyr; another, when Steyn Oct. stood aside at his doctor's orders. The issue from the first really lay 1909. between Botha and Merriman. Both would have served under Steyn, but it was doubtful whether either would serve under the other. Botha had many advantages. He was an Afrikaner, Natal born and Transvaal trained, a farmer, a Liberal in the old republican days, bilingual, genial, boundlessly tactful, the representative of the dominant North. Merriman, too, was a farmer, English born, South African by adoption, with a great knowledge of men and of affairs, cultured, eloquent, imposing, the Cape Parliament with all its honourable traditions in the flesh. But he was not tactful and never had been. Jameson worked for a 'best man' Government. At first he had good hopes. He won over Schreiner, the Cape Unionists and, after great difficulty, the Transvaal Progressives, but he found Natal, economically dependent on the Transvaal, prepared to adapt its politics to its circumstances and Botha himself opposed to a coalition. Botha was hopeful of framing an electoral platform broad enough to accommodate the bulk of the British and Afrikaners who had so much in common.[2] He was anxious to have Merriman as his Minister of Finance and was on his way to Capetown to discuss

---

[1] Newton, *Unification*, II. 256 ff.; *Minutes of the National Convention*, Appendix K; Eybers, *op. cit.*, pp. 517 ff.
[2] Colvin, *Jameson*, II. 287 ff.; van der Merwe, *Steyn*, II. 236 ff.

matters when Merriman publicly declared himself in favour of existing parties. In spite of Steyn's persuasion, Botha declined to serve under his rival; wherefore Lord Gladstone, the first Governor-General, proclaimed Union and summoned Botha to office; de Villiers, newly created Baron and Chief Justice of the Union, opened the Appellate Division at Bloemfontein and promptly transferred its sittings to Capetown, and all parties rallied to the electoral combat.

May 31, 1910.

The Progressives in the Cape, the O.F.S. and the Transvaal had already formed up as the Unionist Party under Jameson to work for unity and to help Botha against his own extremists; the Natalians stood as Independents; the fast-growing Labour Party, led now by Creswell, came to a working arrangement with Botha, who renamed his combination of *Het Volk* and Nationalists the South African National Party. The Senate was formed with a substantial ministerial majority and the results of the Assembly elections were soon known. Though Steyn had failed to induce the Afrikaner parties in the various Provinces to unite, the splitting of the British vote gave Botha a majority over all other parties, a victory marred only by the personal defeat of himself and two other ministers which obliged them to find other and safer seats.[1]

CHAPTER XIV

DOMINION POWERS AND STATUS, 1910–24

Language and Colour (1910–14): problems, 539; Provincial finance and education, 540; Defence, 543; Botha-Hertzog quarrel, 544; Poor Whites, 545; Bantu Press and political organisations, 547; Natives Land Act, 549; Indians, (1908–14), 549; Colour Bar, 553; Rand strikes, 554; Southern Rhodesia (1909–15), 555.—**The Kaiser's War (1914–18):** Rebellion, 560: South-West African campaign, 563; East African campaign and overseas contingent, 565; republicanism, 566.—**Nationalist-Labour Alliance (1918–24):** death of Botha, 569; University Act, 570; growth of Nationalist and Labour Parties, 572; S.A. Party and Unionist Party fusion, 573; Simonstown Agreement, 573; industrialism and protection, 574; South African labour, 577; Indians (1914–21), 579; Bantu trade unionism, I.C.U. and Communism, 585; Rand Rising, 590; South-West Africa (1920–23), 592; Bondelswarts rebellion, 594; Southern Rhodesia (1915–24), 594; Mozambique Convention, 599; 'Civilised labour,' 602; Urban Areas Act, 602; Provincial finance, 603; Pact Ministry, 604.

LANGUAGE AND COLOUR, 1910–14

THE story of the years which immediately followed Union falls into three periods. In the first the new Union Government took up the

---

[1] S.A. National Party 66; Unionists 39; Independents 12 (Natal 11); Labour 4 (*The Round Table*, No. I, p. 101).

task which none but High Commissioners had hitherto attempted of regulating the affairs of South Africa as a whole. In the second that task was rendered immeasurably more difficult by the enormous interruption of the Kaiser's War. In the third the Union, endowed with the high but ill-defined status of a post-war British Dominion and with new powers and responsibilities in South-West Africa, found that bread-and-butter politics were for it, as for the rest of an impoverished world, a matter of life or death. Throughout this last period ran the growing realisation that the Native Question, which had ceased to be a military problem a quarter of a century before, was really the other side of the problem of the Poor Whites. The chapter ends with the fall of the Smuts Government, lineal descendant of Jameson's ministry in its later moderate phase and of Botha's conciliatory Transvaal cabinet, the accession to power of a Nationalist Afrikaner and Labour alliance, and the passing of both Rhodesias from the hands of the Chartered Company into those of the Crown.

Union, carried on a wave of good feeling, was celebrated with a great pageant at Capetown; but waves break and insubstantial pageants fade as they near the solid earth, and the opening of the first Union Parliament by the Duke of Connaught brought South Africa back to realities. The financial relations of the Provinces to the central authority, the consolidation of Provincial laws, education and bilingualism, Natives, Indians, white labour, all must be dealt with, while Southern Rhodesia and, if it might be, the High Commission Territories awaited incorporation in the Union. The work must be done by representatives of Provinces which had never acted long together either in peace or in war, and which, other than the old Colony, had had either a very short or otherwise inadequate experience of parliamentary life on the British model. And in that undertaking the lead had to be given by a ministry divided against itself.

The Botha cabinet was really federal: four ministers from the Cape, three from the Transvaal, and two from each of the smaller Provinces.[1] The contrast between Botha's amiable though vague *conciliatie* and Hertzog's rigid Free State particularism had been obvious during the National Convention. Now Botha felt that he owed his defeat at Pretoria to his colleague's education policy;

[1] First Botha Ministry, May 31, 1910–Dec. 19, 1912: Gen. Louis Botha, Prime Minister and Agriculture; Gen. Jan Christian Smuts, Interior, Mines and Defence; Jacobus Wilhelmus Sauer, Railways and Harbours; James Barry Munnik Hertzog, Justice; François Stephanus Malan, Education; Henry Charles Hull, Finance; Abraham Fischer, Lands; Henry Burton, Native Affairs; Sir Frederick Robert Moor, and, from Feb. 23, 1911, onwards, Col. Sir George Leuchars, Commerce and Industries; Sir David Graaff, Public Works and Posts and Telegraphs; Dr. Charles O'Grady Gubbins, Without Portfolio.

Hertzog refused to ease the strain by ascending the Bench and looked askance at his chief's entente with Jameson, while behind Hertzog stood his fidus Achates, Steyn, suspicious of the ministry's close connection with jingoistic Natal.[1]

Ministry and Parliament both showed their inexperience during the early sessions. Generally speaking, ministers were over-ready to share responsibility with *ad hoc* boards and refer tangled bills to select committees. They showed no inclination whatever to stand or fall by any measure; cabinet solidarity was weak; Smuts openly desired a division of functions, foreign to the British system, between the executive which should administer and the legislature which should make laws. Party cohesion had been relaxed by the very achievement of Union; the Unionist opposition, intent on helping Botha against his own left wing, rarely opposed;[2] provincialism throughout was too strong for such centripetal forces as were at work: The whole trend of events was towards a group system and a reshuffling of parties.[3]

1910–
1911.   The questions of finance and education occupied most of the first two sessions. Both were calculated to raise Provincial patriotism to fever heat. The system of Provincial government laid down by the Convention was a temporary arrangement designed to calm the fears of the smaller Provinces. Many delegates had hoped that it would soon make way for one more convenient and less reminiscent of old state jealousies on the lines of the elective Cape divisional councils. As it was, the Convention had decreed that the Provincial authorities were merely to exercise such powers as were delegated to them by Parliament and had taken elaborate precautions to exclude party politics; but it had postponed the vital question of financial relations to a more convenient season.

The ex-Colonial governments had surrendered many sources of revenue to the Union. Their successors were limited to direct taxation, which they dreaded since it must almost inevitably fall on fixed property, or to borrowing on their own credit, which entailed asking leave of the central authority. Meanwhile, pending the report of a commission under an Imperial *podestà*, the Provinces were to be maintained by the Union exchequer. Reliance on the treasury was in keeping with the traditions of the country districts outside the Cape Province, but, so long as this process went on, the Cape would be paying its own share of local expenditure through its divisional councils and school boards and part of that of the other Provinces through the Union exchequer.[4]

---

[1] Van der Merwe, *Steyn*, II. 242 ff.; H. Fremantle (*Cape Times*, Dec. 4, 1922).
[2] Colvin, *Jameson*, II. 299, 305 ff.   [3] *Round Table*, No. 15, pp. 567 ff.
[4] U.G. 11 and 14 of 1912.

This manifest injustice obliged a reluctant ministry to grasp the nettle albeit somewhat half-heartedly. It undertook to pay £ for £ on the money raised by the Provinces including that raised by the Cape local bodies, and to provide for an annual increase up to 5 per cent. for general purposes and 15 per cent. for education; but, to avoid direct taxation, the Transvaal was allowed to keep its native pass fees, though natives were under Union jurisdiction, and Natal and the Free State were given an undisguised dole of £100,000 each for the next ten years. Even so, such was the opposition that this compromise was only carried in 1913, and already the Provincial Councils had belied the hopes and intentions of their makers by organising on party lines. Next year Labour, victorious in the 1914. Transvaal Provincial elections, challenged the whole provincial system by passing *ultra vires* ordinances which conferred on select committees of the Council powers allotted to the executive.

The only function of the provincial councils which could not have been equally well discharged by divisional councils was the care of education 'other than higher.' Much had been done for the schools in the later 'nineties, and still more during the decade following by Milner's Kindergarten and Jameson's Progressives. The general tendency had been to make primary education compulsory for Europeans, to give the local public a greater share in the control of the schools and, in the Cape, a measure of financial responsibility also, and to accord fuller recognition to Dutch in the ex-Republics. In each province the traditional right of Afrikaners to select the teachers was shared by the education department, to a greater or a less degree, with district school boards and local school committees.[1]

In the Cape and Natal the question of the medium of instruction had presented few difficulties, but it was still a burning question in the northern Provinces. Selborne had relaxed the rigours of the Milner régime, and after the passing of the Smuts Education Act the *Christe-* 1907. *like Nasionale Onderwijs* schools in the Transvaal had duly entered the

---

[1] *Cape Colony* (1905–9).—Municipal and District school boards with majorities elected by the ratepayers to found new schools and enforce primary education on Europeans between the ages of 7 and 14. The Government levied a school tax on the value of fixed property through the divisional and municipal councils and made up deficits. Local committees selected, the school boards appointed, and the Director of Education, if necessary, dismissed teachers. *Transvaal* (1907).—Elective District school boards administering central funds, enforcing European education between 7 and 14, and selecting teachers, who were appointed and dismissed by the Director. *O.F.S.* (1908).—District committees with elective majorities levying fees and administering central funds, enforcing European education between 7 and 16, nominating teachers from the official list whom the Director appointed and dismissed. *Natal* (1909).—Local advisory committees elected by parents and nominal compulsion; but education was not free and all was really done by the central authority (Malherbe, *History of Education*, pp. 127 ff., 335 ff., 378 ff.).

State system. Under that Act Dutch-speaking children were not to be taught in English below Standard III, but thereafter English was to be the medium in all save two subjects and the *sine qua non* for **1905.** promotion from standard to standard. In the O.R. Colony practically all the C.N.O. schools had made terms with the Government under an agreement to which Hertzog had been a party; but then with the **1908.** coming of self-government, Hertzog had carried an Education Act prescribing education in the mother tongue up to and including Standard IV, the gradual introduction of the other language as a medium in the earlier standards and the use of each language for three of the principal subjects after Standard IV. The scheme worked ill. The British opened opposition Council schools with scant success; official explanations and even conferences on the meaning of the language clauses made confusion greater; three English-speaking inspectors, summarily dismissed by Hertzog for alleged obstruction, were awarded damages by the courts; the English-speaking Director of Education resigned on the eve of Union, and the uproar was redoubled when a council of examiners dealt strictly with teachers who failed to reach the official standard of bilingualism. 'No Hertzogism' had been the rallying cry of the Free State British in the election of 1910.[1]

Hertzog was thus the bogey of the British and the idol of the Free State Afrikaners when Parliament essayed to guide the Provinces in the way they should go in the matter of language in the schools. From the teaching point of view, mother-tongue instruction might be sound, especially in the early stages; but duplicated classes would be expensive, truly bilingual teachers were rare and separate schools would keep the two white peoples apart. Besides, what did 'Dutch' really mean in South Africa? Some said it was the tongue of the Netherlands; others a simplified form of that language; others again, and their number was growing, the spoken Afrikaans of the country, which, though still suspect of the Old Guard, was seeking to standardise its grammar and spelling under the guidance of Steyn's Suid-Afrikaanse Akademie.

The matter was entrusted to a select committee which presented two reports. The one, signed by seven members, recommended that teachers be allowed to qualify in either language and that after Standard IV the parents might choose the medium of instruction. The other, signed by the Transvaaler Christiaan Beyers alone but clearly favoured by Hertzog also, advocated mother-tongue instruction throughout and bilingual teachers. A stormy party caucus at last adopted the majority report, while, outside, Steyn thundered that, much as he had been opposed to the creation of Provincial

[1] Malherbe, *History of Education*, pp. 381 ff.; Act 5 of 1907 (Transvaal); Act 35 of 1908 (O.R.C.).

Councils, now that they had been created he meant to see their rights respected. The Transvaal acted on the report at once and the 1912. Cape followed suit, thereby in a measure giving up the long-standing parental right of choice of medium. Natal decided to adhere to this right, and the Free State adopted enough of the majority report to enable the British Council schools to come under the Provincial administration.[1]

Parliament made less rapid progress in the matter of higher education, which properly fell within its purview. At the end of the 'nineties, the Victoria College at Stellenbosch and the S.A. College at Capetown, the oldest and largest of the colleges which prepared candidates for the examinations of the University of the Cape of Good Hope, increased their staffs, limited themselves to post-matriculation classes and carried their work into more genuine university spheres than hitherto. Their example was followed by other colleges, old and new, which, on receiving recognition, were given representation on the council of the examining University of the Cape of Good Hope. Rhodes had dreamt of a national teaching university at Groote Schuur, Mansvelt of a Hollander university at Pretoria, and Alfred Beit had since given a site for a university at 1904. Johannesburg; but the really decisive step was taken by the S.A. 1905. College, which asked for a charter for itself as a separate university. Bad times and local rivalries frustrated this attempt and the examining university seemed to be entrenched more strongly than ever, when, on the eve of Union, further colleges were founded at Pretoria and 1910. Pietermaritzburg.[2] The dissipation of money and effort, the varied efficiency and size of these institutions, the impossibility of looking for research from inadequate and overworked staffs, the dehumanised tests afforded by written examinations alone, all pointed to the necessity for a change; but bill followed commission and commission 1913- bill and, beyond ascertaining what could not be done, Parliament 1914. reached no conclusion before the outbreak of the Kaiser's War.

On the other hand, the ministry carried Irrigation, Land Settlement and Defence Acts. This last was much needed, because Milner 1912. had abolished the commando system in the ex-Republics in favour of the costly S.A. Constabulary and though Botha had revived the field cornets as civil officials, he had asked H.M. Government to maintain a garrison of 30,000 men in South Africa. Constabulary and garrison had since been drastically reduced and the question of South African defence had been discussed with Richard Haldane, the British War Minister, by Union delegates in 1909 and again in 1911.

---

[1] S.C. 2–1911; Malherbe, *op. cit.*, p. 386.
[2] Other colleges were the Huguenot College, Wellington; the Diocesan College, Rondebosch; the Kimberley School of Mines, transferred to Johannesburg in 1903; Grey University College, Bloemfontein, and Rhodes University College, Grahamstown (1904).

The Defence Act of 1912 was the fruit of the Imperial Defence Conference held in London in the latter year.[1] It provided for a small Permanent Force of 2500 Mounted Police and Artillery supplemented, first, by some 25,000 men enrolled in Defence Force regiments either as volunteers or, if necessary, as conscripts between the ages of seventeen and twenty-five drawn by lot on a district basis, and, secondly, by men serving in Rifle Associations, virtually the commandos traditional to the countryside, who were free to make their own rules and choose their officers subject to ministerial approval. Unless Parliament resolved otherwise, non-Europeans were debarred from military service. The Act gave the Executive wide powers, rendered all members of the new. Force liable for service anywhere in Africa in time of war and, by a special arrangement of which little note was taken at the time, bound the Royal Naval Volunteer Reserve to serve with the Royal Navy and the Cape and Durban Garrison Artillery and Fortress Engineers to co-operate with the remains of the Imperial Garrison in any grave emergency. Christiaan Beyers, ex-Speaker of the pre-Union Transvaal House of Assembly, was appointed Commandant-General.[2]

Meanwhile, though the amalgamation of the Provincial ministerialist parties into one South African Party apparently strengthened Botha's position, internal strains and external pressure were really weakening his cabinet. Merriman, 'the humble musket-bearer in the ranks,' repeatedly opened a hot fire upon his chiefs for their Transvaal optimism, shocking to an upholder of the more modest Cape financial tradition; Beyers, resentful that he held no portfolio, harassed the ministry with his following of conservative Transvaalers; there was a widespread outcry against the concentration of the civil service at Pretoria and the increase in the cost of the public service occasioned by up-country allowances. Then the cabinet began to split visibly. The Treasurer, Hull, complained that Sauer, jealous of all Transvaalers, was running the railways without reference to his colleagues and least of all to himself, whose department, deprived by the constitution of all share in railway profits, would assuredly June have to make up any deficits. In the end, Hull resigned and Botha 1912. had to arrange the portfolios in a way which detracted from his ministry's efficiency and enhanced the power of his two Free State colleagues.[3]

The Hull-Sauer crisis was followed by much more dangerous developments. The twin rocks of offence on which the first Botha

[1] Cd. 5745, 5746 (i) and (ii) of 1911.   [2] Act 13 of 1913.
[3] F. S. Malan became Minister of Mines and Sir George Leuchars Minister of Public Works on Feb. 1, 1912.—J. C. Smuts became Minister of Finance, H. Burton Minister of Railways and Harbours, Abraham Fischer Minister of the Interior, and J. B. M. Hertzog Minister of Native Affairs in June 1912.

cabinet made shipwreck were the Premier's conception of the relations of the Union to the rest of the Empire and, closely allied thereto, Hertzog's dread lest his chief's policy of *conciliatie* might expose the tender plant of Afrikaner nationalism to the corrosion of outside influences. The old Transvaal had fought hard against those influences before 1899. During and after the war Afrikaners everywhere had shared in the struggle. There were many reasons why they should do so. Well-to-do Afrikaners felt that they must rally their folk, many of whose poorer members were going under economically. So many farmers had failed to find their feet after their uprooting during the South African war that great numbers of folk believed that the Poor Whites were the product of that disaster. This was not so; the old *lekker leven* had always been precarious and, whenever it had ceased to be possible, Poor Whites had appeared. To go no further back, many families who were virtually Poor Whites had found land and temporary salvation by joining the Great Trek and, thereafter, their kind had made shift so long as there was empty land to be had for the taking. But those halcyon days were gone; the fast-increasing number of indigent burghers had harassed Kruger in the last days of the old Transvaal and now reconstruction, scientific farming and all the paraphernalia of latter-day Western civilisation were combining with large families. and drought to drive the less efficient of the farmers under.[1] The new parliamentary system was unfamiliar to most of them; the new and complicated executive was much less accessible than the old Presidents on their stoeps. Rightly or wrongly, Afrikaners ascribed all that irked them to British influence. Their own patriotism was intensely local and instinctively protectionist, whether in matters of colour, language or economic policy. Politically they felt that they were being dragged into world affairs at the chariot wheels of an Empire for which they felt no love, while Englishmen came to them, who knew but one home, 'like Romans to a Roman province, at home everywhere.'[2] The parallel with the ancient Greeks, traders loving the sea breezes and combining loyalty to the home of their choice with affection for the mother city, would have been more just, especially if Shakespeare and the Authorised Version be admitted as a substitute for Homer; but, in any case, the straiter sect of the Afrikaners would have none of it. They objected to the preference on British goods, slight though that was; they feared what might come of Botha's attendance at the Imperial Conference; 1911. they were alarmed at his talk in London of the need for immigration and a worthy contribution to a Navy which was hard put to it to

[1] U.G. 14 of 1926, pp. 106, 111.
[2] So a widely travelled Afrikaner University colleague expressed himself to the writer.

18

maintain the necessary preponderance over that of Germany. A newspaper hint that in time of war the Union might remain neutral earned their ready approval.

Those were days when Smuts could still dismiss the discussion of Imperial affairs with something like a shrug of the shoulders; but Botha replied to *Die Volksstem's* feeler with the blunt reminder that the enemy, and not South Africans, would sit in judgment on such limited liability. During the Hull-Sauer quarrel he and Hertzog had talked over their mutual difficulties with apparently good results; but, unluckily, the Hertzogites found fresh cause of offence in his

July
1912.

sympathetic references to Rhodes—*fons et origo mali* in their eyes— on the occasion of his unveiling of the Memorial at Groote Schuur. Then, goaded by constant Unionist attacks, Hertzog twice unburdened his soul roundly, declaring that he believed in Imperialism only in so far as it benefited South Africa, that the two white peoples must be left free to develop along their own lines in two streams, and that the Union should be ruled only by pure Afrikaners.

The one speech was delivered when Botha was on the point of attending a party congress in ultra-British Natal, the other while he was on his way to take part in a bye-election at Grahamstown, another intensely English centre. Both speeches trespassed on delicate ground. They were taken to mean not only that the interests of South Africa and the Empire must clash, but that the Union was the preserve of the *ware Afrikaner* only, a term of a narrower significance then than now. To do him justice, Hertzog, like du Toit and Hofmeyr before him, always included among Afrikaners those English-speaking citizens who put South Africa first; but because he did not make this sufficiently plain and the English-speaking minority were still nervous of their future in an Afrikaner-dominated land, his recent speeches angered Englishmen and dismayed many Afrikaners. The Natal congress was not a great success, the Unionist majority in Albany was larger than ever, and Sir George Leuchars, a recent Natal accession to the ministry, resigned in protest. Botha tried to induce Hertzog to retire too, for nearly all his colleagues insisted that he must go and, when he would not, made up his mind that whatever there might be to say for two streams in

Dec.
1912.

the country, there could no longer be two voices in his cabinet. He himself resigned and reformed the ministry without including his ex-Minister of Justice.[1]

Hopes of a reconciliation were cherished for a time; but Hertzog burnt his boats in a fiery speech at Smithfield, a majority of the Free

[1] Second Botha Ministry, Dec. 20, 1912–Sept. 1919: Gen. Louis Botha, Prime Minister and Agriculture; Gen. J. C. Smuts, Defence and Finance; F . S. Malan, Education and Mines and Industries; A. Fischer, Interior; J. W. Sauer, Justice and Native Affairs; Sir Thomas Watt, Posts and Telegraphs and Public Works; Henry Burton, Railways and Harbours.

State members supported the vote of no confidence moved from the Labour bench in the Assembly, Free State constituencies were soon full of talk of a new party and demands for Botha's resignation, and Steyn urged both protagonists to stand down in favour of another *Volksvader*. At last at a S.A. Party congress, Christiaan de Wet, the Nov. Free State hero of the Anglo-Boer war, led a substantial minority out 1913. of the hall. The Afrikaners were split as decisively as were the British.[1]

At the end of the year, Botha very nearly resigned, for party, 1913. Native, Indian and European labour troubles almost overwhelmed him. The political and constitutional struggles of the two decades preceding Union had driven the native problem underground. Each colony had been free to take its own line. In the Cape the rule had remained theoretical equality between white and black. The tendency had, however, been to raise the franchise qualifications to keep out the blanket Kaffir and *pro tanto* to bring Cape practice nearer to the law of the ex-Republics. Save on a few points, native law was still unrecognised in the Colony proper; but in the Transkei it was fully acknowledged and, there, good administration and a steady exten- 1895– sion of the Glen Grey council system had given the Bantu security 1911. for their lands and training in local government. The native policy of Natal, an amalgam of embalmed Shepstonism and acquisitiveness, 1906. had produced a serious rebellion. This had been followed by an experiment on the lines which Selborne had recommended to the 1909. National Convention for the High Commission Territories, whereby a strong standing commission administered native affairs subject only to very general parliamentary control. In the Transvaal advanced 1902. natives had been relieved of the pass law after the war and, by a decision of the Courts, had been enabled to acquire land in their own right; but the mass of the Bantu in both ex-Republics were still in their pre-war condition, subject to the pass laws and heavy hut tax, unable to own land, debarred as far as possible from many avocations, and insecure in the reserves which were in some cases still unbeaconed. Some lived, where they had long lived, on the Crown lands; others were freely encouraged by farmers to settle on their farms, paying for the privilege in labour; others again, especially in the northern Transvaal where lands teeming with natives had been disposed of as farms, were permitted by farmers or land companies to remain where they were as squatters on payment of a rent, regardless of the old Squatters' Law which limited the number of such families to five for any one farm. Insecurity of tenure was the radical weakness of the whole system. There could be no finality in such a state of affairs.

[1] Van der Merwe, *Steyn*, II. 255 ff.; *Round Table*, Nos. 10, pp. 368 ff. and 11, pp. 545 ff.

1903–
1905.
The first attempt to deal with the native problem on a South African scale had been made by the Lagden Native Affairs Commission.[1] Rightly judging that land was the root of the matter, the commissioners had recommended that the Glen Grey system of individual title be encouraged without being unduly pressed; but, lest the natives acquired too much land, all save three proposed to limit their right to buy or lease to certain specified areas. For the rest, with an eye to the labour on which Milner's policy of reconstruction depended, they proposed to forbid any fresh native comers to squat on farms, to shut out undesirables from private locations, to tax all able-bodied men resident therein, to levy variable rents'on those living on Crown lands and, by means of industrial education and better facilities for travel, to awaken new needs and desires among the tribesmen. As for the franchise, they suggested that each colony should set up one or more native constituencies and debar natives from voting at ordinary elections; but they left it to the local parliaments to say whether or no natives should be eligible for seats therein. Few tangible results followed from the report at the time; the National Convention declined to touch so dangerous a subject except in so far as it concerned the Cape franchise and the future of the High Commission Territories and, in the years immediately following Union, all that had been done was to abolish the Natal standing commission and provide for the better treatment of native labourers in the larger towns.[2]

1911.

Meanwhile, non-Europeans were making their presence felt in divers ways. Abdurahman and Rubusana secured seats in the first Cape Provincial Council;[3] two years later, Dr. Pixley Seme, who in 1909 had taken the lead in forming the South African Native National Conference, started his newspaper, *Abantu-Batho*, in English and the four principal Bantu tongues; in 1912, again, a group of energetic Bantu organised the African National Council with four Provincial branches meeting annually in a National Congress to work for the extension of political rights to Africans.[4] That this new organisation did not succeed in its other chief aim of forming a united political front was largely due to Tengo Jabavu, whose jealousy of Rubusana prompted him to give no help to the new venture in his newspaper, *Imvo*, to form the rival South African Races Congress and, presently, to let the European candidate into the Cape Provincial Council by splitting the vote against Rubusana.[5] Other developments betokened the growing strain. Secret 'Ninehvite' gangs, bred of appalling social conditions, murdered freely if clumsily in the Bantu squatter-towns that fringed the wealthy Rand;[6]

[1] Cd. 2399 of 1905.
[2] Acts 26 of 1911 and 1 of 1912.
[3] Roux, *op. cit.*, p. 81.
[4] *Ibid.*, pp. 118 ff., 358.
[5] *Ibid.*, pp. 82 ff.
[6] Davidson, *Report on Southern Africa*, p. 117.

farmers, especially those along the Basuto border, revived the old complaint which had preluded the Kaffir war of 1878, that Natives free to buy anywhere were penetrating white areas rapidly, while Europeans were not allowed to buy land in the Reserves; the growing Labour Party, intent on extending the field of employment for white men and wedded to the work and wage-fund theories, demanded social, industrial and, as far as might be, territorial segregation of white and black. At last, after the failure of spasmodic attempts to eject Natives from farms, Sauer introduced his Natives Land Bill.[1] 1913. It was a curious measure to have been sponsored by so liberal a politician, even though he was virtually on his death-bed, and to have been approved of by Jabavu's Races Congress, because under it, Natives and Europeans were alike forbidden to acquire land in each other's areas, farming on shares was forbidden and, in general, steps were to be taken to get rid of rent-paying squatters altogether or reduce them to the level of labour-tenants.[2] Since the existing division of lands was manifestly unjust to the natives, a commission headed by Sir William Beaumont was appointed to mark out additional areas for them.

Had the new areas been marked off first the Act would have aroused less opposition from both black and white; as it was, the commission could not report before 1915 at the earliest and, meanwhile, native rights were seriously curtailed. The Cape was exempted by decision of the Courts because land holding was one means of acquiring the franchise, and elsewhere the executive freely used its powers of dispensation; but in the Free State natives were ejected from farms right and left under the watchful eyes of the Basuto. On the other hand, Bantu women struck successfully against the attempts of Free State municipalities to make them carry passes like their menfolk[3] and the African National Council organised a petition to the King.

As if black Africa were not enough, brown Asia had been added to the burden of the white man and that by his own act. There were comparatively few Indians in the Cape and hardly any in the Free State, but there were plenty in the towns of the Transvaal and, in Natal, they swarmed. Natal, it is true, had long talked of getting rid of her free Indians, but then tea had come to supplement sugar and induced her to import further coolies. But the days of this policy

---

[1] Act 27 of 1913.
[2] Roux, *op. cit.*, p. 83; Cabinet changes after Sauer's death, September 1913: Gen. L. Botha, Native Affairs; H. Burton, Finance; Hercules Christian van Heerden, Agriculture; Nicolaas Jacobus de Wet, Justice; Hendrik Schalk Theron, Lands; Sir David Graaff and Sir Arnold Albertus Combrink Graaff, Without Portfolio.
[3] *Ibid.*, p. 125.

were numbered. From 1907 onwards the Viceroy, Lord Minto, and his Council had contemplated ending the whole system of recruiting this semi-servile labour, evil in its effects on those parts of India where native touts harried the villages for recruits, evil too in its effects on the morals of the coolies and, still more, of those luckless women who had to accompany them, one to every three or four men. The system as a whole was not ended till 1920, but India at once told 1908. Natal that she would not be allowed to recruit any more coolies because of her recent Act, which made it harder than ever for Indians to obtain trading licences. In answer to the prayers of a Natal deputation and the request of the Colonial Office to let matters stand till the South Africa Act had been safely passed, Simla relented. Natal was allowed to recruit till 1911 on condition that Indians who had been refused licences by municipal councils might appeal to the Courts.[1]

So with their highly protected sugar flourishing, but their tea already suffering at the rough hands of Bantu labourers, the Natalians were left to face the fact that the last coolie would finish his indentures in 1916, that their Indians markedly outnumbered them, and that nearly all of them had come to stay. Indeed, to many Indians, Natal was the only home they had ever known.[2] Meanwhile, in the Transvaal, the immigration law of 1907 had 1908. been supplemented by Gold and Townships Acts, which stiffened old laws and forbade non-Europeans even to occupy land in the proclaimed gold areas which covered so much of the Rand and other townships.[3]

As the South Africa Act clearly entrusted the care of Indians to the central authority, the Union Government negotiated with Gandhi, who, still in South Africa, had linked up his passive resistance agitation with the political agitation which was raging in India. Some progress was made towards a settlement by relieving educated Indians of the finger-print test, allowing Indians who had left the country to return, and giving Indians who had refused to register another chance to comply with the law.[4] But in the main the negotiations broke down and, in spite of Gandhi's demand for equal treat-1911. ment for all, an immigration law was framed with an education test

[1] Act 22 of 1909 (Natal).
[2] In 1911 there were about 150,000 Indians in the Union. Of these, 7000 were in the Cape, 11,000 in the Transvaal, 100 (?) in the O.F.S., and 133,000 in Natal. Of the Natal Indians, some 40,000 were still under indenture and nearly 30,000 had been born in the Province. There were 98,000 Europeans and 962,000 Bantu in Natal. In 1920, the Cape parliamentary franchise was held by 2429 Indians, that of Natal by 45. In 1921, 67·27 per cent. of the Indians were Union born.
[3] On Indians (1906–11) vide Cd. 3308 of 1907; 3887, 3892, 4327 of 1908; 4584 of 1909; 5363 of 1910; 6087 of 1912, and Andrews, Documents relating to the New Asiatic Bill (1926).
[4] Cd. 3892 of 1908, p. 4; Cd. 4327 of 1904, p. 14.

and other regulations frankly aimed at 'Indians and other Asiatics.'
At this the Jews, whose numbers and nervousness were increasing,
took fright, and H.M. Government suggested that all mention of
specific peoples should be omitted.[1] This was done to the satisfaction
of the Indians and the Jews, but the Free Staters demanded much
more definite legislation and wrecked the measure.

Discussion with Ghopal Krishna Gokhale, a member of the
Viceroy's Council, then led to the informal arrangement that, if races
were not named and a few priests and professional men were allowed
to land each year, the Indians would submit to elastic tests; while
the authorities for their part, without pledging themselves, gave
Gokhale to understand that the vexatious and ineffective £3 tax on
Indians who neither reindentured nor went back to India would
disappear from Natal. The Immigration Bill was then carried at the 1913.
third attempt much on the lines proposed, empowering the executive,
subject to an appeal to the Courts, to debar anyone from entering the
Union on economic or social grounds. But the £3 tax remained
unrepealed.[2]

Uproar ensued in South Africa and Hindustan. Gandhi brought
forward his Five Points demanding the repeal of the Free State law
against the entry of Asiatics as a racial stigma, the restoration of the
old right of Indians born in the Cape to return thither, the abolition
of the £3 tax, legislation to prevent the Natal Courts from refusing
entry to the sole wife of a marriage under a polygamous code on the
ground that the marriage was really polygamous, and a reform in
the harsh administration of existing immigration, landholding and
licensing laws.

Thus set out, Gandhi's plea won the support of many Europeans
in England, India and even in South Africa; but the weakness of
his case was none the less serious. The Indians by reason of their
religion and ancient traditions were a class apart in South Africa,
despised by the Zulus as servile aliens, able by dint of a generally
low standard of life and incredible industry to undercut European
trading rivals, and, in some cases, content with truly Oriental sanitary conditions and a code of business ethics to match. The mass of
them were of low caste or of no caste; yet Gandhi was claiming the
rights of Europeanised British citizens in South Africa for men who
were 'untouchables' in their own country. The claim could not be
admitted. That, whether right or wrong, was the view taken by the
majority of South Africans of a question which was at bottom
economic. Gandhi was, however, determined that passive resistance
should continue till his Five Points were conceded and, at last, in

---

[1] Cd. 5579 of 1911; Cd. 6283 of 1912; Cd. 6940, 7111 of 1913.
[2] Act 22 of 1913. For Gokhale's speeches *vide* Andrews, *Documents relating
to the Indian Question* (1926), pp. 1 ff.

1913. protest against the Immigration Act, led an illegal procession of Indians on foot into the Transvaal by way of Laing's Nek. He and many others were lodged in gaol for their pains.

Gandhi's arrest was followed by strikes of coolies on Natal plantations, one of which was attended by loss of life and property; but he himself was soon released and a commission under Sir William Solomon, assisted by a high Anglo-Indian official, Sir Benjamin Robertson, was appointed to investigate Indian grievances. Gandhi boycotted the commission because Indians were not directly

1914. represented thereon, but the Government based an Indian Relief Act on its recommendations.[1] In spite of the fears of Natalians and Free Staters that, by analogy, the Bantu would soon ask to be relieved of the hut tax, it abolished the hated £3 tax and directed that the sole wife of a 'polygamous' marriage should be admitted and registered as monogamous.

June   By agreement with Smuts, Gandhi accepted, as 'a complete and
1914. final settlement of the controversy,' the Relief Act and a long-desired assurance that it was and always had been the wish of the Government to see that 'existing laws' were administered 'in a just manner with due regard to vested rights.' Some of his followers urged him to persist in passive resistance till they were relieved of the laws affecting trading licences, residence, landowning, and movement from Province to Province. Gandhi refused. He did, however, remind Smuts in his letter accepting the settlement of the issues raised during the late passive resistance campaign that these other questions must be sympathetically considered one day, and that nothing short of full civic rights would satisfy his fellow-countrymen. Then, having told his followers that the present Agreement was the basis from which they must work to win relief from their remaining disabilities, he sailed for India.[2]

Gandhi had only been deterred from leading another pilgrimage up the road which led to Volksrust and gaol by the outbreak of serious trouble in the world of European labour. At the time of Union, 'Labour,' to most South Africans, still meant natives or indentured coolies, and 'Industry' employment on the state railways or the gold and coal mines of the Transvaal and Natal; trades unionism was an unwelcome novelty to most of them, the syndicalism

1911. of France and Germany a name, the great British shipping and railway strikes a distant inconvenience. Nevertheless, the gulf which divided Labour and Capital along the Rand was at last becoming patent to all. Life on the Rand mines was neither so easy nor so lucrative to the employees as it had been in the days of Kruger and

[1] Cd. 7265, 7644 of 1914; Act 22 of 1914.
[2] Andrews, *Documents re New Asiatic Bill*, pp. 15 ff., 33 ff., and *The Indian Question*, pp. 12 ff.

the Cornish 'Cousin Jacks.' No man, from the mine manager down-wards, was sure of his job for long; there was, as between absentee shareholders and ever-changing staffs, little of that personal touch which could compensate the men for the non-recognition of their trade union, while silicosis (miners' phthisis) bred of the dust raised by the rock drills made life underground highly dangerous. How dangerous men realised for the first time from the reports of a com-mission appointed immediately after Union, just as the development of the mines, begun in 1904, reached its zenith and conditions of white employment became more precarious.

At first there had been little difficulty. The white men had done the skilled and semi-skilled work, the raw native the unskilled work under white supervision. That was the customary colour bar which also held good at Kimberley in the egalitarian Cape. But times were changing. Already the intelligent Chinese had had to be restricted by law to unskilled work, and now the Bantu, by no means stupid, were learning. They could not be kept at rough labour for ever. But any radical change in the division of work on the mines would have to reckon with Creswell's Labour Party, which might easily find support from some of the Hertzogites. Nearly sixty per cent. of the miners were still drawn from the United Kingdom, but they were being joined by a stream of Afrikaners, younger sons, *bijwoners*, unsuccessful farmers, the living testimony to the agricultural revolu-tion which, as yet imperfectly appreciated, was none the less taking place. Among these men moved others from countries where violence was part of political practice and even of theory.

The Labour Party was dominated by the northern trade unions. It had been organised since 1902 in the Witwatersrand Trade and Labour Council and then, since 1911, in the wider Transvaal Federation of Trades.[1] Under-represented in Parliament though this Party was, it helped to carry a Mines and Works Act whereunder regulations were issued shutting out non-Europeans from many employments, in the ex-Republics at least, on the grounds of safety, 1911. health and discipline.[2] Thus entrenched behind the so-called statu-tory colour bar and only too well aware that miners' phthisis had killed twelve of the leaders of the 1907 Rand strike and attacked the surviving five, Labour secured compensation for the victims of that dreaded disease and vainly resisted a measure which declared strikes on the state railways illegal.[3] But it was in Congress assembled at Capetown that it showed what its policy was to be. There, it was non-committal on the score of socialism, for many delegates were trade

---

[1] In 1900, trade union membership was 3836 and 11,941 in 1914 ; *Official Year Book*, No. 6, 1910–22, p. 330.
[2] Act 12 of 1911.
[3] Acts 34 of 1911 and 19 and 28 of 1912; Davidson, *op. cit.*, p. 190.

18*

unionists rather than socialists; the Northerners, wedded to colour distinctions, declined to follow the lead of those Cape unions which admitted Coloured men who were prepared to hold out for union conditions of labour; the Congress as a whole, preferring to con-

1912. centrate on the Bantu question first, in the hope that the Coloured would then be easier to handle, demanded segregation for black and white, white immigration and an end to all contracted labour. This

1913. policy was in keeping with that of the ministry, which in the ensuing session carried the Natives Land and Native Labour Regulation Acts amplifying the rules governing the recruitment of African miners and providing compensation for Africans who were injured at work on the mines. Then, appalled by the ravages of pneumonia and phthisis, the authorities put a stop to the recruitment of tropical labour for the mines from beyond the 22nd degree of south latitude.

Meanwhile, a petty quarrel between a new manager and some miners on the New Kleinfontein mine spread till it covered the whole issue of the recognition of trade unions. The Government at first

July tried to stand aside. Then, alarmed at the growing signs of violence,
1913. it hurriedly intervened with Imperial troops because its own organised forces were still only in embryo, tried to prevent a mass meeting too late and, in the ensuing riots, had to watch the troops fire on the mob. Victory lay with the strikers. They were promised reinstatement, a judicial commission, which duly found that many of their grievances were very real,[1] recognition for their unions by both Government and Chamber of Mines, and rules for dealing with future industrial disputes. The ministry, harassed by Indians and Hertzogites, also appointed one commission to consider an eighthour day and a minimum white wage on the railways, and another to investigate wages, cost of living and cognate subjects.

It was a promise of peace where there was no peace. Towards the end of the year the white coal-miners of Natal struck; Syndicalists in the Transvaal, playing on the fear that recent retrenchment was but the earnest of more to come, organised a widespread strike on the railways; the S.A. Federation of Trades brought the gold-miners

Jan. in by declaring a general strike throughout the Union. This time
1914. there was no hesitation on the Government's part, for already Basuto labourers had broken out on one of the mines. It declared martial law, called up 60,000 men on commando or in the newly organised Defence Force regiments, maintained essential services with those railwaymen who stood by their posts, and forced the leaders of the strike to surrender to de la Rey and his machine-gunners.[2]

All was over in a few days at the cost of only two lives;[3] but Smuts, that 'ruthless philosopher,' as Merriman called him, threw away

[1] Cd. 6941–2 of 1913; U.G. 55, 56–13.   [2] Cd. 7384 of 1914, *passim*.
[3] J. C. Smuts, *Smuts*, p. 133.

much of the prestige thus gained by summarily and illegally deporting nine Syndicalists to England. Parliament met with the protests of the outraged judges and the embarrassed Imperial Government ringing in its ears.[1] Many ministerialists were unwilling to stigmatise the deportees as undesirable immigrants;[2] Labourites and Unionists combined to defeat the proposal that the executive should have power to declare martial law without subsequent recourse to Parliament for an Act of Indemnity, but in face of the free use of the closure they were unable to stay the passage of the Riotous Assemblies and Criminal Law Amendment Act.[3] This measure not only prescribed penalties for those who should seek to force others to join trade unions or break contracts in public utility services, but empowered magistrates acting under special authority from the Minister of Justice to prohibit public meetings, which, in their opinion, might endanger the public peace, to arrest any speaker or listener at such meetings and, in the last resort, to order the police to fire.

The authorities refused to re-employ some of the ringleaders in the late strike, but they by no means exercised all the powers which they legally held against the rank and file. On the other hand, it was only 1914. Labour's victory in the Transvaal provincial elections and at a bye-election in the Cape Peninsula that induced the ministry to go forward with the remedial legislation promised after the July strike. They duly protected wages, gave more liberal phthisis compensation and provided for the compensation of injured workmen of all classes and colours save native miners, who were already covered, and domestic servants and farm hands;[4] but they had to jettison a measure which indeed recognised trade unions but declared strikes and lock-outs illegal till a board had duly reported thereon. Labour declined to part with the right to strike in the year which saw the Triple Alliance of transport, railways and coal preparing for battle with Capitalism in Great Britain itself.

So the Houses rose in July and members went to their homes through a countryside ravaged by the worst drought for a generation past.

The distressing course of events in the Union ruined the hopes of those who, on either side of the Limpopo, had looked for the speedy inclusion therein of Southern Rhodesia. At the time of the opening of the National Convention, H.M. Government had declined either to help the B.S.A. Company financially or to touch the question of the ownership of the unalienated lands till the end of the first term of Chartered rule should be at hand in 1914. At first, therefore, the

---

[1] A. B. Keith, *Selected Speeches*, II. 109 ff.
[2] Some of them afterwards became members of the Union Parliament.
[3] Act 27 of 1914; Cd. 7384 of 1914.　　　[4] Acts 15, 25 and 29 of 1914.

Rhodesian delegates had been inclined to dwell on the advantages of inclusion. But they soon swung round to the view that, though incorporation was Rhodesia's 'ultimate destiny,' at the moment it would mean debt and endless trouble unless terms were first made with the Company.

Besides, hope eternal was once more springing in Rhodesia and at London Wall. The small miners and farmers were prospering, the railway companies were beginning to pay their way, many creditors of the Company were exchanging their debentures for shares, and the Company's first farm, the Premier, taken up in 1907, was doing well as a training ground for settlers. Already the Board had organised a commercial branch distinct from the administrative, and now decided to seek the hitherto elusive dividend on, rather than below, the surface of the soil.

After all, whatever Rhodesians might think, the Company was 'an association formed for the acquisition of gain.'[1] It took up other farms at Rhodesdale and Sinoia, Lomagundi and Marandellas, and, realising the possibilities for cattle ranching in a country free, as yet, from the many diseases which afflicted other parts of Southern Africa, sold a large block of land in the neglected south-east to Liebig's. Jameson, too, began to talk as Rhodes had done of developments in the Bechuanaland Protectorate and beyond the Zambesi, and also of a railway which should tap the copper mines of the Katanga. Presently Selborne was making hopeful speeches in

1910. Rhodesia; Jameson himself arrived and the Duke of Connaught, fresh from the opening of the first Union Parliament, followed him.

These proofs of Imperial interest and Chartered energy were rewarded by the election of a legislature unanimously opposed to

1911. Union.[2] A new Order-in-Council promised the elected members a marked majority in future and the High Commissioner, Lord Gladstone, assured all concerned that neither the Company nor the Rhodesians should ever be summarily thrust into Union. The Board combined North-Western and North-Eastern Rhodesia as Northern Rhodesia and went forward with its new policy of encouraging immigration to Southern Rhodesia.[3] A good stamp of settler came in, the price of land rose and, with it, the value of the Company's farms along the railway, and the Company, in funds at last and fired by the

1912. enthusiasm roused by the unveiling of the memorial to its founder at Groote Schuur, elected Jameson chairman, appointed three full-time directors, entrusted the training of settlers to the new Agricultural College, farmed its estates in good earnest, and launched forth on a large scale as a cattle rancher.

---

[1] B.S.A. Extraordinary General Meeting, Jan. 1908, p. 19.
[2] Cd. 7264 of 1914, pp. 1 ff.; B.S.A. Co. Report, 1911, p. 5.
[3] B.S.A. Co. Report, 1911, p. 9; Northern Rhodesia Order-in-Council, 1911.

All this meant the opening up of the resources of the country, but it also meant that the Company, like the Dutch East India Company long ago, was now competing with its own subjects. Some of them, led by Gladstone to expect great changes when the Charter should expire, formed leagues to press for the removal of the Company, for more elective seats in the legislature, or for a Royal Commission. A fresh election was drawing near and the Board acted promptly. First, Maguire of Rudd Concession fame, and then Jameson in person hurried out with a statement of policy. They proposed to confine land settlement to a zone 25 miles wide on either side of the existing railways and of the new lines which were foreshadowed. So would the task of government be rendered easier and cheaper and so would the settlers be kept in touch with each other and with the schools.[1] But so also, some Rhodesians grumbled, would settlers be tied to the railways, which, built for the service of the mines, ran along the watershed where most of the land had already been alienated.[2] The value of the Company's holdings and even of their own would doubtless be enhanced, but newcomers, the hope of the future, would be obliged to buy at a price. There was, moreover, in their eyes, the danger that acceptance of the scheme would involve the recognition of the Company's claim to the unalienated lands as a commercial asset.

This aspect of the new policy was emphasised by a rearrangement of the native reserves effected by a Commission which did for 1914–Southern Rhodesia what the Beaumont Commission was presumably 1915. doing for the Union.[3] In the past reserves had been roughly marked out as occasion demanded. These reserves lay mostly in the south and east, the coming cattle country and, in nearly all cases, had been marked off without survey. The Commission found that native commissioners had, as a rule, vastly underestimated the areas which they were setting aside for the natives. They therefore rearranged the European and Bantu areas in such a way that 6,600,000 acres of what had been reserve land ceased to be so and 5,600,000 of other land became part of the reserves. Champions of the tribes complained that much of the old and new land was poor, but the fact remained that 40 acres were available for every native who actually lived in the reserves and that the despised sandy soils have since proved themselves the best tobacco lands in the territory. In any case the Imperial Government ratified the findings of the Commission, thus

---

[1] Cd. 7645 of 1914, pp. 31 ff.; *B.S.A. Co. Report*, 1913–14, pp. 46 ff., 67 ff.

[2] Only 8,500,000 acres remained unalienated of the 33,000,000 within the 25 mile zone. At the close of 1913, in all S. Rhodesia, the Company held some 3,851,000 acres as against 9,000,000 held by other companies and 12,000,000 held by individuals. Reserves covered about 20,428,000 acres, unalienated lands nearly 48,000,000.

[3] Cd. 8674 of 1917.

giving the tribes as far as possible security of tenure, and showed its confidence in the commissioners' sense of justice by subsequently appointing two of them to rule the great native territories of Basutoland and Uganda respectively.

The Commission's report was admittedly 'very satisfactory' to shareholders whose directors had just reasserted their claim to the unalienated lands, which were apparently worth the £7,750,000 that they asserted had been spent on the administration and development of the country. The Rhodesians were told that the claim for a refund of these deficits need trouble them no more, but that, meanwhile, the only alternative to a renewal of the Charter was incorporation in the Union.[1] Apart from other considerations, fears aroused by a recent speech by Botha that this was indeed the case and a lively March apprehension of 'the Company's displeasure' were sufficient to give 1914. the pro-Charter party an overwhelming victory at the ensuing elections. The new Council, with its large elective majority led by Charles 1915. Coghlan, voted in favour of a renewal of the Charter for ten years. This extension was duly granted by a Supplemental Charter.[2]

The B.S.A. Company had thus gained the time necessary for the maturing of its commercial schemes; it could face with comparative equanimity the claim which the Imperial Government had at last put forward to the unalienated lands on its own behalf;[3] it could, if it wished, bargain at its leisure with the Union authorities for the incorporation of Rhodesia. Possibly it had some such end in view; certainly, Botha visited Southern Rhodesia in July, 1914. But there the General heard that which brought him hurrying home to Pretoria. Austria had delivered an ultimatum to Serbia, the British fleet had disappeared into the mists of the North Sea to the strains of 'Heart of Oak,' and on the Continent the swarming battalions of the Armed Peace were forming column of route.

THE KAISER'S WAR, 1914–18

In the Union, the racialism, which had been aroused by the Botha-Hertzog quarrel, had begun to die down again. As in the days after Majuba, economic issues blurred the divisions between British and Afrikander. S.A. Party men and Unionists worked more and more closely together, especially in the months following the Rand strikes, and, with Smuts talking of a tax on undeveloped land to balance the income tax, those British who had half feared that he and Botha would use their power for purely rural Afrikaner ends were convinced of their error. Similarly, the Labour Party, strengthened by a steady recruitment of urban Afrikaners, harked back to its old

---

[1] Cd. 7645 of 1914, p. 34.   [2] *Ibid.*; Cd. 7970 of 1915.
[3] Cd. 7509 of 1914.

alliance of 1907 with *Het Volk* against 'Park Lane rule' and exchanged good offices with the Hertzogites. The war checked this hopeful development, drove the Hertzogites in upon themselves and, by reviving the racial conflict, became a war on two fronts, the foreign and the home.

Amid loyal demonstrations in the towns and the opening of subscription lists for the purchase of unprocurable machine-guns for the Old Contemptibles, the ministry at once offered to set free the Imperial garrison by itself taking over the defence of the Union. The offer was gladly accepted and the Naval Volunteers and the local Defence Force were mobilised in quick succession for the defence of the all-important Cape Peninsula; but it was only after some division of opinion that the ministry decided to send an expedition, as H.M. Government wished, to destroy the coast wireless stations at Lüderitzbucht and Swakopmund in German South-West Africa.[1]

Aug. 10, 1914.

There was, however, another side to the picture. In the country districts there was much talk of neutrality; in Pretoria, Defence Force officers from Commandant-General Beyers downwards spoke of resigning if an aggressive campaign were undertaken; in the western Transvaal there was the threat of serious trouble. Stirred by reports that Germany meant to set up a protected republic in South Africa and by the visions of a local prophet portending the fall of the British Empire, stirred also by General Jacobus de la Rey, the uncrowned king of that part of the country, burghers met in arms at Treurfontein. De la Rey frankly proposed to strike for independence, for, ever since the close of the Anglo-Boer war, he had been awaiting the opportunity and had looked to Botha and Smuts to head the movement. He was, however, dissuaded. Neither Beyers nor General Jan Kemp, another highly placed Transvaal officer, countenanced his plan and Botha convinced him that the Scriptures condemned rebellion. With a hint of better times to come, he bade his would-be followers disperse, and this they did 'amid a strange and unwonted silence.'[2]

Aug. 15, 1914.

The whole of the Defence Force was now warned to hold itself in readiness for service anywhere in Africa, nearly all the Imperial troops sailed away, the Nationalist Party Congress condemned the projected campaign, and Parliament assembled. News of the violation of Union territory by a German patrol decided many members reluctantly to support the attack on South-West Africa, and loyalty to Botha deterred even de la Rey from voting against a policy of which he heartily disapproved. So, having provided £2,000,000

Aug. 21, 1914.

---

[1] Walker, *De Villiers*, pp. 501 ff.; Cd. 7873 of 1915.
[2] U.G. 10–15, p. 6; U.G. 46–16, pp. 46, 83, 85, 102; Webb, *Oorzaken van de Rebellie*, pp. 10 ff.

Sept.
14,
1914.

for the maintenance of 15,000 troops for six months, the Houses rose.[1]

This modest estimate was soon belied by a rebellion.[2] Parliament's endorsement of the ministry's policy brought matters to a head. Beyers resigned his commission and conferred with de la Rey at Pretoria. The two men then hurried off by car towards the Defence Force camp at Potchefstroom. What their intentions were is still a matter of debate.[3] They may have proposed, as the authorities believed, to use the 1600 western Transvaalers there assembled to raise the Lichtenburg district, march on Pretoria and, thereafter, obtain arms through Salomon Maritz, who was in charge of the Union forces at Upington and in close touch with the German authorities at Windhoek; they may, as their friends declared, have been set upon less desperate courses. Be that as it may, they never reached the camp. Police patrols were on the watch along the Rand for motor-car bandits who were terrorising the neighbourhood; indeed, one of them shot a doctor who failed to stop when sum-

Sept.
15,
1914.

moned. On that same night, at the other end of the Rand, Beyers ignored a similar challenge; whereupon, one of the policemen fired and killed the unhappy de la Rey.[4] Beyers, disavowing any idea of stirring up rebellion, now joined de Wet and other leaders in calling on the Government to withdraw its troops from the German border and in organising a national demonstration against the campaign. Botha, therefore, promised to do the work himself with an expedition of volunteers and, learning of Maritz's double dealing, pushed forward loyal troops towards Upington to relieve that officer of his command. There, Maritz, strong in the possession of a treaty with the German Governor promising aid, an independent South Africa and leave to annex Delagoa Bay in exchange for Walvis Bay, with-

Oct.
1914.

drew to the German border, handed over as prisoners of war such of his men as would not follow him, and threatened to attack Upington unless he were permitted to meet Hertzog, Beyers, de Wet, Kemp and other real or supposed leaders of the rebellion.[5]

Maritz's treachery fired the train elsewhere. The Government replied by declaring martial law and commandeering men in the Transvaal to crush Maritz. A party of commandeered Transvaalers mutinied and with others like them fled to the farm to which Beyers had retired. Meanwhile, de Wet made up his mind that since Maritz was fighting, he must be helped. He addressed meetings in the northern Free State; presently, he and others tried forcibly to stop

[1] Act 3 of 1914 (Special Session).
[2] On the Rebellion *vide* U.G. 10–15; U.G. 42, 46–16; Webb, *Oorzaken*; Van der Merwe, *Steyn*, II. 293 ff.
[3] U.G. 10–15, p. 8; U.G. 46–16, p. 102; Webb, *op. cit.*, pp. 28, 40.
[4] U.G. 48–14.
[5] *Ibid.*, 10–15, p. 23; U.G. 46–16, pp. 94, 119; Webb, *op. cit.*, p. 55.

recruiting of volunteers and then occupied one or two towns, while, in the Western Transvaal, Kemp's men stopped trains and requisitioned men and material.[1] With men of opposite intentions thus moving about with arms in their hands, collision was well-nigh inevitable. Botha fell upon Beyer's commando and scattered it near Rustenburg, classic ground whereon Kruger had once ended a civil war. One wing of the rebellion was thus broken; but, in the Free State, de Wet now proclaimed his intention of getting into touch with Maritz and then marching on Pretoria to proclaim South Africa's independence. All Steyn's efforts to bring him and Beyers together in conference failed;[2] shots were fired; de Wet's son was killed, and the old general and his men began to behave with the fierceness bred of desperation. *Oct. 27, 1914.*

Outside South Africa the general situation was very grave. The German rush in the West had been stemmed on the Marne and at Ypres, but a strong German squadron had sunk British warships off the coast of Chile and, if it came eastward, there was nothing in the South Atlantic to prevent its bombarding the coast towns of the Union with incalculable repercussions in the countryside and disaster to the small expeditionary force which had already been sent to Lüderitzbucht. On the other hand, Botha soon had 40,000 men in the field, Afrikaners for the most part, led by picked officers, his old companions of the Anglo-Boer war days. He kept the predominantly British town regiments as much as possible in the background lest the struggle became a war of races; he promised all the rebels, save ringleaders and those guilty of breaches of the rules of civilised warfare, immunity from criminal proceedings if they surrendered within ten days, and then fell upon de Wet at Mushroom Valley and routed him. Thereafter it was a matter of rounding up scattered bands as mercifully as possible. De Wet was run down by troops in motor-cars on the edge of the Kalahari, Beyers was drowned in the Vaal, Kemp alone of the rebel leaders got through to Maritz. Cheered by the news that Sturdee's battle-cruisers had destroyed the German Pacific Squadron off the Falkland Islands, Botha was able to declare the rebellion over. *Nov. 12, 1914.* *Dec. 20, 1914.*

At the time it was natural to assume that the rebellion was the outcome of a conspiracy fostered by German money and intrigue. Germany had long been the traditional counterpoise to Great Britain in South Africa; German volunteers had fought manfully for the Republics in the late war; Beyers, as Commandant-General, had been made much of by the Kaiser at Berlin shortly before the war; many Afrikaners had studied at German universities or at those of Holland which had so much in common with them; a strain

[1] U.G. 10–15, pp. 27, 28, 31; U.G. 46–16, pp. 46 ff.; Webb, *op. cit.*, p. 82.
[2] Van der Merwe, *Steyn*, II. 293 ff.

of German blood ran in the veins of nearly all of them. Any such easy explanations must be set aside. There is little evidence to suggest that, at the start, there was any cut and dried conspiracy. Had there been, the outcome of the rebellion might have been very different, for Beyers and some of the other leaders were fine soldiers. Of Maritz's treachery there can be no question; but, as far as the judicial evidence goes, it would seem that Kemp, de Wet and Maritz only began to act in concert in the latter part of October and that, as late as the first days of November, Beyers aimed at nothing more definite than ousting the ministry and stopping the South-West campaign.[1] As for German intrigue, intrigue there was,[2] but the causes of the rebellion lay much deeper than anything it could have created. Opposition to the policy of invading South-West Africa brought a mass of fears, desires and prejudices to a head. Doubtless, some burghers took up arms for fear of their neighbours, others because they were told that the ministry wanted them to rebel as an excuse for withdrawing from the war, others because they thought that they were actually being called up by the authorities, others again because they believed that Steyn and Hertzog were the real leaders, a mistaken belief to which the silence of the Free State champions gave colour. Nor was the hope of *novae tabulae* wanting, for the drought was terrible, and jealousy, the besetting sin of the Afrikaners, was present in full measure among the leaders. But the prime motive forces which brought the mass of the rebels into the field were two: the longing to regain their lost independence and a very human desire to avenge themselves on Great Britain for their sufferings during the South African war. In short, England's adversity was the Afrikaner's opportunity. Underlying these motives, there was something else, a vague *malaise*, a feeling that the Afrikaners were somehow an oppressed people, oppressed by all the social, political and economic forces which, rightly or wrongly, they associated with the name of Britain. Maritz spoke for many when he announced that 'he did not want the land ruled by Englishmen, niggers, and Jews.'[3] Still, there was little bitterness against Englishmen as such. 'This,' said one old burgher, 'is a family affair between us Afrikaners. You Englishmen must keep out of it.'[4] Essentially that was so. The rebels regarded Botha and Smuts as traitors to the people, who had made terms with all that threatened their way of life and now stood in the way of independence. The ministry had lost the confidence of *Het Volk*; it must therefore resign.

From this point of view, the rising was the old armed demonstra-

---

[1] U.G. 46–16, pp. 42, 91, 102. Evidence before the Court of Inquiry was very incomplete. Many of those who knew most declined to appear.
[2] *Ibid.*, p. 82.   [3] *Ibid.*, 10–15, pp. 28, 63.
[4] Said by a burgher to one of the author's brother officers.

tion, the appeal from votes in the Volksraad to the clicking of triggers at the door of the Volksraad chamber which Henry Cloete had heard in Maritzburg in 1843 and more than one republican President since. It was the death rattle of Parliaments which had been heard more 1914. recently at the Curragh and in the Ulster of Carson and 'Galloper Smith.' From every other point of view, the *opstand* was a rebellion and to be treated as such unless the Union was to become a puritan Mexico. Twelve hundred rebels were sent home on parole, but Defence Force officers taken redhanded were court-martialled, and one of them, Jappie Fourie, was executed because he had never resigned his commission and had fired to kill to the last. When Parliament reassembled, four thousand men were still in prison awaiting sentence. A court of three judges were set up to try the more important prisoners,[1] while the bulk of the remainder were released subject to serious civil disabilities for ten years to come. The bill for rebellion losses remained to be paid, but its back was broken in the Free State, where the damage had been greatest, by the formation of the Helpmekaar Vereeniging to assist loyalists and rebels alike. It was a hopeful phenomenon.

Botha now energetically pressed forward the attack on South-West Africa.[2] In any case that attack would have been no light matter, for the territory was in area three-quarters of the size of the Union itself and, thanks to an annual grant of £1,000,000 from Berlin, was equipped with railways, roads, wireless, wells and far more arms than could be used by the 6000 soldiers, police and able-bodied men amongst its 15,000 European inhabitants. Between the ports held by the Union forces and the grassy tablelands of the interior lay some 30 miles of waterless desert; the southern approach was almost as difficult; the line of attack from behind lay across the Kalahari Desert. It was now high summer and the delay caused by the rebellion meant that Botha would have to use a larger force than had at first been intended. Parliament therefore sanctioned a loan of £16,000,000 for two years of war and in April 1915 all was ready.

Botha struck in with three columns: one from the Orange by way of Warmbad and Keetmanshoop, and two others eastward from the ports. He entered Windhoek with the Swakopmund column in May and, after an incredibly rapid march of 120 miles in a week, received July 9, the surrender of the main German force of 3400 at Tsumeb in the 1915. north of the colony. Generally speaking, the warfare had been carried on with restraint by both sides. The Germans poisoned the wells and spread land mines, but they sometimes forbore to explode the one and always gave notice of the other; hence, though 50,000 South Africans took part in the campaign from first to last, their losses were very small.

---

[1] Acts 10 and 11 of 1915.
[2] Buxton, *Botha*, chapter v.; *Union and the War*, pp. 10 ff.

Botha, conciliatory in the hour of victory as ever, gave excellent terms to the defeated Germans and returned home to fight a general election.[1]

As a party the Hertzogites had been strengthened by the rebellion and the South-West expedition. The great majority of those who had followed de Wet out of the S.A. Party congress in 1913 had been Free Staters, but, from the first, they had had the support of men in the other Provinces and had now won over more and more of those who believed that Botha was subordinating the interests of the Union to those of an Empire which was entangled at Gallipoli, threatened at the heart by the first submarine campaign and helpless to aid its Russian ally staggering under the hammer strokes of Hindenburg. Such men were numerous in the Free State and the Transvaal, where they already called themselves Nationalists; they were sure of the support of the party which was forming in the Cape round the Rev. Daniel Malan of Graaff-Reinet, and they hoped also for the help of the Labour party. But Labour was divided. It had indeed been strengthened indirectly by the Chamber of Mines' recognition of the South African Federation of Trades as a co-ordinating centre, but it had been weakened politically by the breakaway of its international socialist wing led by Bill Andrews and Sidney Bunting, which had transformed itself into the War on War Group, parent of the future South African Communist Party.[2] Creswell came hastening back from South-West Africa and secured a great majority in favour of seeing the war through, but he could not save his

Oct. 1915. Party. Electors in the towns, inflamed by the anti-German riots which had followed the sinking of the *Lusitania*, voted Unionist and almost wiped out the Labour Party in Parliament. On the other hand, the S.A. Party fared ill. Three ministers were defeated[3] and Botha's followers found themselves a minority in the Assembly dependent on Smartt's Unionists, whose support would only be forthcoming so long as they prosecuted the war. The Nationalists, who had polled 77,000 votes as against the S.A. Party's 95,000, came back as a compact group, supreme in the Free State and strong in the support of nearly half the whole rural electorate. They were now the real Opposition entitled to all the prestige that that office carries with it.[4]

---

[1] Union losses were 113 killed and 311 wounded. German officers were allowed to keep their arms and to settle in towns in the Union on parole; civil officials and reservists were permitted to remain in their homes on parole; the rank and file of the troops were interned, but were allowed to keep their arms without ammunition (*vide* Eybers, p. 570).

[2] Roux, *op. cit.*, p. 137.

[3] Two in the O.F.S. and one in a Dopper constituency in the north-eastern Cape Province.

[4] S.A.P., 54 seats; Unionists, 40; Nationalists, 27; Labour, 3; Independents, 6. In Feb. 1916, Sir Thomas Watt became Minister of the Interior, Sir Meiring Beck, Minister of Posts and Telegraphs; H. Burton, Minister of Finance till Thomas Orr succeeded him in October 1917, and Hendrik Mentz, Minister of Lands.

The war on the home front was henceforward waged with unremitting vigour. Holding, as they did, radically different views on
the rights and wrongs of the world war, the parties had no lack of
opportunity of joining battle. Beyond sending a few men to Nyasaland and Northern Rhodesia, the Union had been unable to despatch
troops far afield till the Hun had been driven from the gate, and many
men, impatient, had sailed to England or Australia to enlist on their
own account. The Government now talked of sending a force to
East Africa, including a Coloured Cape Corps, which was raised in
terms of the special resolution demanded by the Defence Act and was
destined to do excellent service in Palestine and France as well as
France as well as Africa.[1] It called, moreover, for volunteers for an
infantry brigade and five batteries of heavy artillery for service in
Europe. Other Dominion troops were highly paid, but the South
Africans, after having been discharged at the close of the South-West
campaign, were called upon to re-enlist at the British rate of pay,
the famous King's shilling a day.[2] The Unionists and Labour men
demanded the full Union rate of three shillings, the ministry proposed to make up the difference for the troops in Africa but to do
nothing for the European contingent, and the Nationalists, who were
calling for a loan to enable rebels to pay for the damage they had
done, objected to any contribution at all. The release of many rebel
prisoners on payment of fines and a promise to take no part in
politics till their terms should be completed failed to placate the
Nationalists, and Botha only silenced the Unionists and Labour men
by warning them that any division on the pay question must run upon
racial lines.

Botha's difficulties were enhanced by Smuts's departure to take 1916.
command of the heterogeneous force, which, furnished by four or
five distinct governments, was operating or, rather, failing to operate
in German East Africa. So he faced Parliament burdened with
Smuts's portfolio as well as his own and, while the Germans sought
to force their bloody way inch by inch into Verdun, carried an
Enemy Trading Act in the teeth of Nationalist opposition.[3] The one
bright spot on his political horizon was an unexpected surplus on the
revenue; but the cost of living was becoming a serious matter;
Smuts, robbed of complete victory on the slopes of Kilimanjaro,
continually asked for more money and more men to round up von
Lettow's Germans and Askaris on the bush-clad plains, and the

[1] A. Desmore, *With the Cape Corps in South Africa*; Patterson, *op. cit.*,
pp. 45, 219; *Race Relations Handbook*, pp. 534–5.
[2] By the New Year of 1916, 7500 had gone to Europe independently and
1200 were in Nyasaland-Rhodesia. By April, 600 had taken Imperial commissions, 11,000 were with the Overseas Contingent, and 24,000 in East Africa.
50,000 South Africans in all served in East Africa exclusive of Coloured troops
and many Bantu bearers, labourers and so on.
[3] Act 39 of 1916.

July
1916.

South African brigade indeed made its name at Delville Wood during the Somme offensive, but was so shot to pieces in the process that it had to be virtually reconstituted.[1] A projected rebellion, inspired perhaps by the wild doings in Dublin in Easter week and the first misleading news of the Battle of Jutland, was nipped in the bud thanks to de Wet's timely warning, but the Nationalists continued to 'fight constitutionally' and bitterly. Hertzog invited dissatisfied Englishmen to form a separate party and co-operate with his own, and his followers tried to stampede Botha's men by accusing the Premier of meditating coalition with the Unionists.

Dec.
1916.

May
1917.

Botha strove to reassure his waverers by studied coolness to the Unionists. He even cherished hopes of Afrikaner reconciliation. The stirring of Afrikaner sentiment by the unveiling of the Bloemfontein memorial to the dead of the South African War concentration camps, the death of Steyn, and the release of the last of the rebels seemed to pave the way for such a consummation. He called for a great national celebration of Dingaan's Day at Paardekraal, but the Nationalists would not dance to the piping of one who was sending a Coloured battalion to East Africa and raising a Bantu labour corps of 10,000 for service behind the lines in Europe. They held rival celebrations and, a few months later, just as the Imperial War Conference assembled, began to preach republicanism openly.

Republicanism was stimulated by many causes. Men's nerves were frayed by the long-continued war; the Nationalists looked to the cry of 'republic' to rally the older folk in the ex-Republics and the young men everywhere, who, being young, were as much inclined to go to extremes as any undergraduates; they resented the settlement of the pay question whereby the Imperial Government was to pay the South African troops the full three shillings a day in return for a Union grant of £1,000,000 to general war expenses; they listened eagerly to the talk of 'self-determination' and the 'rights of small nations' which emanated from the Downing Street of Lloyd George and the White House of President Wilson; they hoped that the fall of the Czar and the entry at long last of the U.S.A. into the war on the side of the Allies would mean favours to Republicans at the Peace Conference. True, their leaders counselled caution for the period of the war, but others were not so prudent.[2]

The Nationalists as a party found in the wool controversy an excellent means of attacking the Imperial idea along the economic line. During 1916, with armies to be clothed on an unprecedented scale, wool farmers all the world over had made fortunes. They proposed to repeat the process in 1917. The intensified German submarine campaign, however, sadly restricted the shipping available

[1] J. Buchan, *South Africa in the War*, pp. 61 ff.
[2] *Vide* South African press, *passim*.

and prevented the removal of part of the 1916 clip from South African warehouses. The British Government therefore offered to buy the whole of the 1917 clip at a price 55 per cent. higher than the pre-war rate, but none the less lower than that of the preceding year. Nationalists saw in this a British plot to use the qualified command of the sea to swindle the wool farmers. They induced many of them Oct. to reject the offer and fell upon the Botha ministry so hotly that 1917. Smartt hinted at a Unionist-S.A. Party coalition.[1]

Botha ostentatiously repudiated the very thought of a compact which would surely drive half his own followers into the Nationalist camp. He held on stolidly while the East African campaign dragged along and ill news came in from Europe of the Bolshevik revolution, the immobility of the French armies after the disastrous attack on the Chemin des Dames, the losses of the British in the mud of Passchendaele and the collapse of the Italians at Caporetto, ill news hardly compensated for by the British dash at Cambrai, the Italian Dec. stand on the Piave, and Allenby's romantic entry into Jerusalem. 1917. Recruiting, long concentrated on the overseas contingent, was becoming more difficult and Botha stilled the Unionist cry for the impossible conscription, which homogeneous Australia had rejected, only by declaring that he would have to recall the brigade from Europe to quell the consequent rebellion.[2] As it was, the Nationalists were demanding a complete amnesty for rebels, attacking him for his support of a British ministry which had seized Dutch ships carrying contraband, and opposing Smuts's departure to take part in the counsels of the Empire in London.

Mutual rancours were raised to fever heat when tidings came in that the Germans had driven through the British line opposite Amiens and the Channel ports. The South African brigade had March added to its laurels at Marrières Wood and the gunners at Givenchy;[3] –April but at home the attitude of the natives, resentful of the rising cost 1918. of living and the punishment of native strikers in Johannesburg, was so threatening and rumours of a coming Afrikaner rebellion were so insistent that Botha was obliged to call on the natives to keep the June peace and on all loyalists to stand by the authorities. At last, none 1918. too soon, relief came from the intolerable strain. Foch struck near

---

[1] *Round Table*, No. 29, p. 203.

[2] The estimated total white man power of South Africa was 685,000. Of these 136,070 enrolled for service and 76,184 went overseas. In addition, 92,837 Bantu and Coloured men served in various capacities. The percentage of Europeans who went overseas to the total white man power was 11·12 as compared with 13·48 from Canada, 13·43 from Australia, and 19·35 from New Zealand. The South African overseas effort was comparatively great, for the demands for men in East Africa were considerable and a large proportion of the Europeans were either unsympathetic or actively hostile to the Allied objects in the war (*Round Table*, No. 35, p. 496 *sqq.*).

[3] Buchan, *op. cit.*, pp. 162, 180, 272.

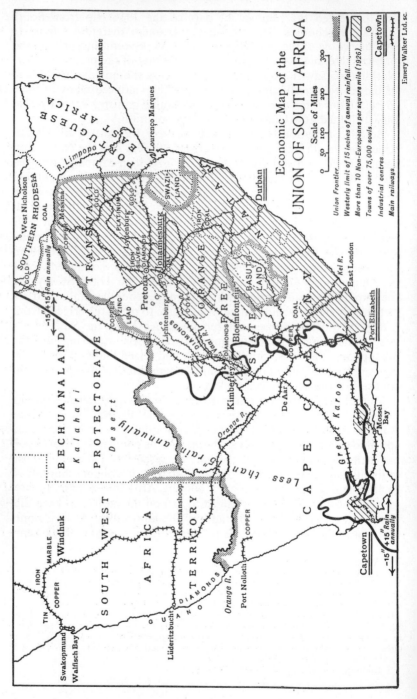

Economic Map of the
UNION OF SOUTH AFRICA

Scale of Miles
0   50   100   200   300

Union Frontier.......................
Westerly limit of 15 inches of annual rainfall....
More than 10 Non-Europeans per square mile (1926)..
Towns of over 75,000 souls........   ○ Capetown
Industrial centres........
Main railways........

Emery Walker Ltd. sc.

Rheims, the British began their tremendous thrust eastward from Nov.
Amiens and, as the forces of the Central Powers crumpled from the 1918.
Dardanelles to Scapa Flow by way of Mons and Sedan, men realised
to their surprise that the Kaiser's War was at an end.

NATIONALIST-LABOUR ALLIANCE, 1918–24

For a short time it was freely believed that the republican agitation
would cease with the gunfire. So far was this from being the case
that the Nationalists sent a delegation to Europe to demand, at the
hands of the Peace Conference, independence for all South Africa
or, failing that, independence for the ex-Republics or, in the last
resort, independence for the Free State alone. Meanwhile, Botha Dec.
had taken his seat beside Smuts on the Imperial War Cabinet. In 1918.
due time the two generals signed the Treaty of Versailles and the July
Covenant of the League of Nations not merely as members of the 1919.
British delegation, but as representatives of the Union. Then, with
a protest against the impossible penalties laid upon the fallen
Germans, they returned home to give an account of their stewardship.

Botha never lived to meet Parliament. After a short illness he died, Aug.
worn out, at Pretoria. It thus fell to Smuts alone, robbed of his 28,
tactful *alter ego*, to face all the pre-war difficulties in a more acute 1919.
form than ever and the many new problems which had arisen during
the long struggle.[1] Parliament ratified the Peace Treaty [2] and authorised the Government to accept the League's mandate for South-West
Africa, and all parties acclaimed the new Premier when he called for
a fresh start on the basis of industrial development and co-operation
between the two white peoples. The only difficulty was to define
Smuts's meaning of *co-operatie*, word beloved of Botha. The
Unionists recalled Jameson's ideal of a 'best-man ministry' and
offered to discuss amalgamation with the S.A. Party; but the call of
the blood was still strong and Nationalists and S.A. Party men diligently sought a way towards the reunion of the divided Afrikaners.

The Nationalists accepted Lloyd George's gentle repulse of their
delegation in Paris as definitely closing the question of separate independence for the ex-Republics; but if, as the British Prime Minister
claimed, the Union rested on a pact between British and Afrikaner
which could not be repudiated by one only of the parties to it, that
did not alter the fact that the South Africa Act was 'a scrap of paper'

[1] Sir Thomas Watt had recently become Minister of Public Health and
Thomas Orr acting-Minister of Posts and Telegraphs in the Botha Ministry. The
Smuts Ministry, Sept. 3, 1919–June 29, 1924, consisted of Gen. J. C. Smuts, Prime
Minister, Defence and Native Affairs; F. S. Malan, Education and Mines and
Industries; Thomas Orr, Finance and acting-Minister of Posts and Telegraphs;
Sir T. Watt, Public Works and Interior; N. J. de Wet, Justice; H. Burton,
Railways and Harbours; H. Mentz, Lands.
[2] Act 49 of 1919.

—the phrase was famous in those days—which could be modified at will by the two Houses and the Crown. Hertzog declined to give an assurance that he and his followers would join with the three other parties in cordially accepting the British connection as symbolised by the Crown; still less would he admit the truth of Smuts's contention that under its constitution the Union had no legal right to secede from the Empire. In short, in words reminiscent of Hofmeyr's softening of the early anti-British formulae of the Bond, he pointed to independence as the ideal, but left it to the people to say whether or no they would actively seek to achieve it. Attempts to reunite the Afrikaners, therefore, broke down and, as the life of both Houses would end in the following November, Smuts decided to fight an Assembly general election at once on the old party lines, trusting to the 'hearty co-operation' of the Unionists as in the past to give him a majority.

Apart from the hectic prosperity which followed the war, Smuts had few advantages in the coming struggle. The very prestige which he had gained in Europe was an offence to his opponents and the domestic record of the Botha ministry was of little help to him. The record was that of a ministry harassed by war and fear of civil war. It was by no means entirely barren. The very interdependence of the S.A. Party and the Unionists on the war issue had cleared the way for many valuable consolidating measures.[1] Something had been done for the administration of justice, more for the victims of miners' phthisis and still more for university education. François 1916. Malan had at last solved that tangled problem by abolishing the old examining university of the Cape of Good Hope, giving charters to the South African and Victoria Colleges as the University of Cape Town and of Stellenbosch respectively, federating the remaining colleges as the University of South Africa and, Liberal that he was, allocating an annual grant to the South African Native College which had been founded recently at Fort Hare in the Eastern Prov- 1918. ince, a pioneer institution for which Tengo Jabavu was diligently raising funds.[2] In the year in which this University Act came into force, the ministry had even tried its prentice hand at industrial legislation to meet new conditions; but, at the same time, it had stirred up a hornets' nest among the Indians everywhere and had, according to its enemies, shown subserviency to the gold magnates in matters of finance and lack of courage in its social legislation.

[1] *E.g.* Insolvency, Patents, Trade Marks, Mental Disorders, Railway Regulations (1916), Electoral, Deeds and Justices of the Peace laws (1917).
[2] Acts 12, 13 and 14 of 1916; Walker, E. A., *The South African College*, pp. 87 ff.; Malherbe, *Education in S. Africa*, pp. 418 ff. Further Universities were chartered: Witwatersrand, Act 15 of 1920; Pretoria, Act 13 of 1930; Natal, Act 4 of 1948; O.F. State, Act 21 of 1949; Rhodes University (including Fort Hare University College), Act 15 of 1949; Potchefstroom, Act 19 of 1950.

At the beginning of the war the main sources of revenue had been the mines and the customs. Faced with a deficit and war expenditure, Parliament had heavily increased the customs and excise, rigorously 1915. cut down the income tax exemption, taken a special levy on gold-mining profits and appropriated the sinking fund and land revenues.[1] These measures had been followed by super-income, excess profits and diamond taxes, and by drawing on the accumulated *bewaar-plaatsen* funds, that is, moneys which had been paid by the gold-mining companies for the right to work beneath the dumping-grounds that had been set aside in the early days and, having been held by the Government since 1908 pending a settlement, now amounted to some £2,000,000. Each year a deficit had been expected, 1916– but each year as loan money poured in and wool and bunkering coal 1920. poured out, a surplus had been forthcoming by dint of using all the special war levies for general purposes and charging practically the whole of the war expenditure to loan account. On the other hand, as prices and working costs rose, the deficit on the railways had mounted up and men had begun to wonder how much longer the track or even the sturdy but irreplaceable British-built engines could stand the strain. The Nationalists and Labour men, meanwhile, censured the ministry for giving half the *bewaarplaatsen* funds to the owners of the surface lands instead of keeping the whole,[2] and for reducing the amount payable by the lessees of the first six Government Mining Areas that had been leased by public tender on the Far East Rand, because the yield was so much higher than had been expected that the lessees would have had to pay into the Treasury a share falling within the steeply graded upper section of the govern- 1918. mental scale.[3]

The most costly blunder of the Botha ministry had, however, been its failure to handle the cost of living issue boldly. At the outbreak of the war, Parliament had come to the rescue of the banks and pro-ducers of gold, wool and hides and had given the executive wide powers to regulate or even undertake the supply of necessities. These powers had lain dormant till May 1916 by which time the cost of living, including rents, had risen in the larger towns to 15 per cent. above the pre-war level. A permanent Cost-of-living Commission had then been appointed to report monthly.[4] A maximum price for sugar had presently been fixed with good results; but in spite of a 23 per cent. rise in cost of living, serious sectional strikes on the Rand June and a shortage of wheat due to lack of shipping, the ministry had 1918. refused to follow the advice of the commissioners and fix a maximum

---

[1] Acts 26 of 1914 and 36 of 1917; 28 of 1914 and further Acts 1915–18; 34 of 1916.
[2] Act 24 of 1917.
[3] Act 30 of 1918. *Vide* U.G. 6 and 19–17; U.G. 1 and 4–18.
[4] Act 6 of 1918.

price for wheat. The officially recognised ' Burton loaf,' a wholesome but somewhat insipid mixture of wheat, barley, rye and maize, was a poor substitute for action and an offence to half the housewives in the land. Similarly, a Moratorium Bill, designed to control rents and the supply of labour and stores to the mines or any other industry necessary to the public welfare, had been opposed by an unholy alliance of farmers and diamond lords. Ministers had voted against each other in the Assembly and the Bill had been thrown out in another place at the end of the session in the odour of bad faith.

Such a record was not to be wiped out by eleventh-hour promises of social and economic reform, nor even by the belated passing of March the Moratorium Act.[1] Labour swept the towns at the expense of the 1920. Unionists, the Nationalists were returned as the largest single party, and the S.A. Party, the Unionists and Independents combined only gave the ministry a precarious majority of four.[2]

Condemned to carry through his reconstruction policy with Labour holding the balance, Smuts secured legislation more or less on British lines to check profiteering, speculation in foodstuffs and rackrenting, and to provide housing loans to municipalities.[3] Of 1920. other great outstanding problems, he touched only three: civil government for the South-West Africa Protectorate, currency and banking, and the administrative side of the native question.[4] In the industrial sphere, the other side of the native question, nothing was attempted nor likely to be attempted till the ministry was assured of a compact majority. There was some hope of obtaining that, for party divisions were already beginning to leave the racial line. The S.A. Party and the Unionists on the whole worked well together and the *rapprochement* between the Nationalists and Labour men was becoming closer; but national sympathy attracted many of Smuts's followers towards the Hertzogites, who in turn, farmers as most of their constituents were, shrank from the socialistic tendencies of Labour.

The stumbling-block to this *hereeniging* of the two sections of the Afrikaners was, as ever, the question of the relation of the Union to the Empire. All could agree to put 'South Africa first' and refrain from committing their country further to Great Britain, especially in the matter of the federal imperial council adumbrated by the Imperial Conference of 1917 and stoutly combated at the time by Smuts. Many S.A. Party men were willing to admit that secession,

[1] The Moratorium Act was passed in 1919 (No. 49) and extended in 1920 (No. 38).

[2] S.A.P. 41; Unionists, 25; Independents, 3; Nationalists, 44; Labour, 21. Cabinet changes: F. S. Malan, Agriculture; Col. H. Mentz, Defence; H. Burton, Finance; Sir D. Graaff, Public Works; Sir J. Graaff, Posts and Telegraphs; Sir Thomas Watt, Railways and Harbours.

[3] Acts 27, 29 of 1919, and 7 and 13, 35 of 1920.   [4] *Vide infra*, pp. 583 ff.

which had played but a small part in the recent elections, might come in time as South Africa developed as a free nation of the British Commonwealth; but few of them would agree that secession could come before the mass of both white peoples desired it. Still less were they willing to uphold 'sovereign independence' as the ideal or to admit the inherent right of a Dominion to secede. The S.A. Party Sept. and the Nationalists met in conference at Bloemfontein just after the 1920. latter had gained markedly at the Provincial elections. They failed to agree, and Smuts called on 'all rightminded South Africans' to join a new party to defeat secession and the disastrous reactions which a Nationalist victory would presumably have on overseas investors of much-needed capital.

In spite of some resistance from Natal, fearful lest the towns be sacrificed to the backveld, the moderate party long ago envisaged by Jameson came into being. The Unionists joined an enlarged S.A. Party; three of them entered the Cabinet;[1] the Senate conveniently expired through effluxion of time and the Assembly was dissolved. The Nationalists tried to push secession into the background and join Labour in fighting on the economic battleground, but the ministerialists pinned them down to the constitutional issue. At the Feb. polls the Nationalists held their own, but Labour lost heavily, and 1921. the enlarged S.A. Party was returned with a majority of 22 over all others in the Assembly and a majority in the Senate which was increased by judicious nominations.[2]

During his first year of renewed power, Smuts emphasised the Oct.– enhanced status of the Union as a post-war Dominion by taking over Nov. all War Office property in the country on the termination of the 1920. Imperial South Africa African Command. But he prudently made sure of the protection of the Royal Navy by concluding the Smuts-Churchill Agreement of December 1921 under which he guaranteed to the King's ships at all times the use of the British-built naval dockyard at Simonstown in the Cape Peninsula under the protection of Union batteries. For the rest, he devoted himself to finance rather than to legislation, for he would have to justify himself on the economic plane towards which party divisions were plainly tending.

Smuts had already taken some steps to prepare for bad times. Prior to the war, the Standard Bank, the National Bank, the Bank of Africa and the few other large corporations which practically monopolised South African banking had had a restricted right of

---

[1] Col. Deneys Reitz became Minister of Lands and Sir T. Watt Minister of Public Works and Posts and Telegraphs. The three Unionist Ministers were Patrick Duncan, Interior and Education; Sir Thomes Smartt, Agriculture, and John William Jagger, Railways and Harbours.
[2] The Nationalists held 45 Assembly seats as at the end of the Session, but Labour fell from 25 to 10, even Creswell losing his seat on the Rand.

1915. issuing notes. Shortly after the outbreak of war, Parliament had recognised notes of less than the customary £5 as legal tender anywhere and exchangeable for gold at the banks' head offices, and had later on forbidden the export of gold. That export had, however, continued, through neighbouring Mozambique mainly; but nothing serious had happened so long as British sterling, which set the pace

May for the South African pound, was pegged to the American gold
1919. dollar. Then, soon after the close of the war, the United States returned to the gold standard. The British pound at once broke away and sank; gold in the London market went to a premium on the basis of the dollar, and the diminishing percentage of working costs to yield promised a new lease of life to the low-grade gold-mines which had hitherto been troubled by the rising costs of stores and labour. On the other hand, the world demand for raw products stimulated exports, the banks gave credit freely and huge balances accumulated in London. Not only so, but gold coins were smuggled out of the country wholesale, for the banks treated sterling as if it were still at gold parity and continued to buy gold at a high premium in London and pay it out at par in the Union.

When nearly £3,000,000 in gold coins had thus disappeared, the
1920. Union Government took power to issue treasury gold-certificates as legal tender against gold and suspend redemption of these certificates should gold exceed a certain price.[1] At the same time the sole right of issuing notes was entrusted to a central Reserve Bank with limited powers of whose capital the commercial banks, sorely against the grain, were called upon to subscribe half. Gold payments were suspended just as the inevitable post-war depression struck the Union.[2] European markets, balkanised and crushed by reparations, were so helpless that Great Britain had to save South Africa by buying a large part of her 1919 wool-clip at pre-war rates, rates which were none the less nearly 20 per cent. in advance of current prices. Then the British post-war boom collapsed and the South African
1921. boom collapsed in sympathy. The panic-stricken banks abruptly shortened credit; over-stocked merchants, shopkeepers, and speculators were ruined; the premium dropped so fast that some of the weaker low-grade mines had to close down; Kimberley followed suit; produce prices fell to the damage of the farmers, and falling wages largely cancelled the benefits of falling prices in the towns. The Poor White problem, veiled by the good times, became insistent at the very moment that the Government began to talk of modifying the rent and other emergency laws of 1920, promised heavier taxation

---

[1] Act 31 of 1920.
[2] The treasury certificate clauses held good till June 30, 1923. They were then extended by Act 22 of 1923 till June 30, 1925, when South Africa returned to the gold standard; *Round Table*, No. 57, p. 190; No. 59, p. 592 ff.; *vide infra*, p. 603.

to meet the deficit which was piling up as customs and mining revenues fell away, and proceeded to cut down the war bonus in the railway and civil services. Soon the eight-hour day on the railways was threatened and the railway administration was borrowing from an exhausted Treasury to pay the interest which it had failed to find in the high and ever higher rates that were killing the export trade in coal. Labour, for its part, demanded a state bank.

Under these depressing circumstances the ministry set about industrialising South Africa in earnest. It was in industry that Smuts proposed to find room for such Poor Whites as could not obtain employment on the farms, for the attempt to re-establish them as independent cultivators of the soil had been tried too often to warrant a repetition. Before the war the exports of the Union had been almost entirely primary, that is, first, gold and diamonds, which together stood for ten-thirteenths of the total production of the country [1] and were thus the ultimate source of livelihood of the great majority of its inhabitants, and then wool, hides, feathers and mealies. The mining and luxury era had reached its zenith at the time of Union and had already been passing in 1914, for some of the older gold-mines had been already worked out, while ostrich feathers had suffered severely and diamonds had been over-produced before war had come to cause the downfall of the one and the temporary eclipse of the other.

On the other hand, Kimberley had soon recovered sufficiently to be specially taxed and the agricultural revival, much of it the fruit of Milner's Reconstruction, had made great strides. The ostriches, departing, had left behind them fences and lucerne, and wartime produce markets had boomed so vigorously that the Union had been emboldened to take its first agricultural census. Prices had fallen disastrously since the Armistice, but now the price of wool was once more rising and great preparations were being made for the export of fruit. South Africa had, in short, begun to export not merely goods of small bulk and high value in mediæval style, but goods which would fill a modern cargo ship and justify shipowners in reducing outward freights in the expectation of a homeward load. Already bunkering coal had pointed that lesson. Nevertheless as late as 1917 South Africans had still been thinking in terms of primary products and bewailing their failure to supply themselves with their own wheat.

In that year, South Africans had begun to note the new manufacturing industries which were sprouting in the forcing-house of the war. The Botha ministry had promptly held an industrial census and carried a Workmen's Compensation Act, which covered injury or death resulting from cyanide, lead or mercury poisoning. Next year, it had carried a Regulation of Wages, Apprentices and Improvers

1916.

1918.

1921.

1917.

1918.

---

[1] £49,600,000 out of a total production of £65,000,000 in 1913.

Act, which created not very effective Boards to fix minimum wages for women and young persons in such industries as the Minister might specify, and also a Factories Act on British lines, which provided for inspectors to ensure proper sanitation, ventilation and decent conditions generally.[1] At the end of the Kaiser's war, the Smuts ministry, by their Special Pensions Act, had made provision for disabled ex-Service folk, and, by their Rents Act, had set up Boards to receive tenants' complaints and oblige landlords, in certain circumstances, to reduce rents or refrain from eviction. Further, by their Housing Act, they had established a Central Housing Board and authorised local authorities to borrow Union money to finance their own or approved building schemes. Their Juveniles Act of 1921 had set up Boards to guide school-leaving youngsters into industry;[2] but the Senate had thrown out their supplementary Bills for the regulation of apprenticeship and wages on the last day of the session to the prejudice of the ministry's reputation for good faith. Meanwhile, ministers had flirted with the idea of protection since reading the report of an industrial commission shortly before the war.[3] They now talked of bounties to the steel and iron works which were to spring up near Pretoria, promised to set up a tariff board which should frame a 'scientific tariff' in place of the rough 15-20 per cent. *ad valorem* system then in vogue, and, after inspecting wares displayed to Merriman's fury in the lobby of the House, gave boot manufacturers a double measure of protection on the spot.

The industrialisation of South Africa thus tentatively undertaken was a matter of extraordinary difficulty. Here was a huge country with a mixed population of less than fifteen to the square mile, that is, less than one-thirteenth of the density of the Netherlands or the United Kingdom.[4] The centres at which population was massed lay hundreds of miles apart and could be counted on the fingers of one hand. Four-fifths of the wage-earning population were non-Europeans; three-fourths of the total population and close on half of the European population lived upon the land. In the reserves, the Bantu farmed at a mere subsistence level; native wages on the farms outside the reserves were very low and, in many parts, agriculture was not on a cash basis nor even on a wage basis.[5] Only five per cent.

---

[1] Acts 13 of 1917 and 28 and 29 of 1918.   [2] Act 33 of 1921.
[3] U.G. 10-12.   [4] U.G. 14 of 1926, p. 65.
[5] *E.g.* in Ventersdorp (Transvaal) only half a dozen farmers in the district paid cash wages of 20s.–40s. per month. Instead, farmers ploughed up 3 to 6 morgen of land for each native family on their farms and gave grazing rights. Native men worked all the year round for this, women and girls when required. In Dordrecht (Cape) some men were paid wholly in kind, that is, five sheep or one heifer every six months, with food (including an occasional meat ration), lodging, clothes and boots as required, grazing for stock and dipping for sheep. Frequently a month's service meant 30 working days (U.G. 14 of 1926, pp. 13 ff.). In short, the South African agricultural system was, in many ways, still in the fourteenth century.

of European farm-lands were actually under cultivation; wide distances enhanced the costs of collection and distribution, and, arising out of it all, was the growing problem of the Poor Whites.[1]

The industrial problem was governed, as it always had been, by the fact that the purchasing and productive power of the vast majority of the population was painfully low. The swarming Bantu had not half the purchasing power of the Europeans, who themselves numbered less than the population of many a European city; the Coloured Folk and Indians were indeed paid better than the Bantu, but their wages were always lower than those of white men in industries other than agriculture, and among white men the rates of pay for artisans in many dorps were only half or less than half those in the bigger centres; indeed, the 'spread' of wages between different industries and different districts was 'several times as great as in any other country.'[2] Yet in the principal urban areas, European artisans drew higher pay than in any European country, and even unskilled Coloured labourers drew better wages than unskilled men in such cities as Milan, Brussels and Berlin. It was not only nominal wages that were high, but real wages also, higher than in any other parts except the U.S.A., Canada and Australia, and that without any phenomenal efficiency on the part of the men who drew the wages. Moreover, the national income was low. The annual production per head of those working under European supervision was less than £100 per annum; if the reserve natives were included, it was £43; if the total population, occupied and unoccupied, were taken into account, it was only £26. In other words, while the Union's capacity to pay was that of crowded European countries like Italy, the actual wages paid to its Europeans were on the high United States and Canadian scales. Between the two there was a great gulf fixed. It was bridged by underpaying the vast mass of the workers.[3]

There were those who questioned the wisdom of the industrial policy which the ministry had adopted. Was industry, they asked, the proper haven of refuge for the Poor White, South Africa's Old Man of the Sea? Was he the kind of material out of which a successful industrialist could be made? Would it not be better to make one more effort to plant him on the land, or at least to check his manufacture by turning away from the misleading parallel of Great Britain's experiences during her industrial and agricultural revolutions and looking rather to Ireland, where security of tenure was transforming that feckless tenant-at-will, the Irish *bijwoner*, into a reasonably contented peasant?[4] For the rest, they said, encourage

[1] U.G. 14 of 1926, p. 115.   [2] *Ibid.*, pp. 11, 12, 34, 160.
[3] 96 per cent. of those of all races earning less than £500 p.a. drew less than £240 in cash; 90 per cent. drew less than £120; 80 per cent. less than £80; 54 per cent. less than £26 (U.G. 14 of 1926, pp. 26, 33, 77, 80, 264).
[4] U.G. 14 of 1926, pp. 107, 115, 167.

19

farming by keeping down the cost of living and, therefore, the cost of production, instead of bolstering up industries which contributed less than seventeen per cent. of the national income. The ministry's policy might have its advantages, but a reduction of the cost of living was not numbered among them; yet South Africa, more than most countries, must keep a watchful eye on costs of production for the world market. The self-contained U.S.A. with an enormous home market might be content to export only one tithe of its annual production, and the United Kingdom, a great trading community, could only afford to export one-third; but the Union, with its tiny and isolated home market, had to export over half. Each year, nearly all South Africa's gold, itself representing nearly one-fifth of its total income, its diamonds, much of its coal and other minerals and, above all, more than one-third of its farm produce must go overseas or be left upon the producers' hands as in the bad old days of the Dutch East India Company.[1]

The critics of the new protective policy were as voices crying in the wilderness for the majority of men of all parties were in favour of protection, those of the growing Nationalist-Labour opposition even more strongly than the ministerialists. But the social legislation which accompanied the protective laws, typified by the Juvenile Affairs Board, marked a turning-point in the history of South Africa. It was a virtual admission that the labour policy of the past two and a half centuries had been a grand mistake. Hitherto white South Africa had striven to persuade or compel black and brown South Africa to work for it, and that cheaply. Now some few white men, more far-sighted than the rest, were suggesting that low-paid labour was not cheap in the long run and that it was no good thing that the bulk of the work should be done by those whose productive powers were lowest and whose consumption, based on low wages, was low in proportion. Captain de Chavonnes and Dr. Philip had, each in his generation, pointed the same moral, and now at last men were prepared to hearken.[2] White youths relying on coloured men never learnt how to work; they would not start at the bottom of the ladder alongside of them and so had small hope of reaching the top by their own unaided efforts. 'Cheap' labour was proving to be a substitute for brains in South Africa as elsewhere, and the new census showed that the Union, for all its gold and diamonds, was a poor country overrun by middlemen.[3] The history of the farms and mines showed that in all occupations not requiring skill the scales were weighted heavily against the highly paid white man. Was that story to be repeated in the new factories?

[1] U.G. 14 of 1926, pp. 79, 159 ff.   [2] Vide supra, pp. 75, 169.
[3] U.G. 14 of 1926, p. 119.

Some men, especially in the south, held that the only way to save Western civilisation was to train European youths for the new and old industries, fix minimum wages, and admit non-Europeans to the trade unions on definite terms and thus prevent them from pulling down the European standard of life. Part of that policy had been half-heartedly adopted by the ministry. Others in the more dogmatic and nervous north demanded that since black and brown South Africa after these many years had at last learnt the dignity of labour, they must be prevented from working, at all events in competition with the white man, by the extension of the colour bar. In any case, white men realised that the problem of the non-Europeans was merely the other side of their own.

The non-European problem resolved itself into three: that of the Coloured man proper, of the Indian and of the Bantu. The first was by far the simplest. The Coloured Folk lived mainly in the western districts of the egalitarian Cape. They and their fathers had never known a civilisation other than the European. Their ideas and mode of life could make them, politically and economically, a positive source of strength to white society if properly handled, for they were, generally speaking, merely the poorer members of that society. But the main industrial development was not about to take place in the Cape Province. The necessary minerals and machinery, much of the transport and most of the capital were to be found in the Transvaal and Natal, the home of the Indians and of the Bantu. Serious trouble was threatened by the Africans. Trouble no less serious had already arisen with the Asiatics.

South Africans had hardly realised the bitterness aroused in India by the events which had preceded the Smuts-Gandhi Agreement of 1914, nor did they appreciate the meaning of many events which had happened since. India had served the Empire well during the war; she had been represented at Imperial Conferences and at Versailles; the Montagu-Chelmsford constitutional reforms were about to witness to her enhanced political status. At successive Imperial Conferences, Indian spokesmen had pressed for the removal of the disabilities laid upon their countrymen in Dominions whose ranks India had now virtually joined. No resolution had been taken on that head in 1917, Smuts merely remarking that the Immigration Act of 1913 had allayed the fears of Europeans lest they be swamped, and that other subsidiary matters could easily be dealt with. Next year both India and South Africa readily accepted the principle, a mere affirmation of existing practice, that each part of the Empire had a right to regulate the composition of its population. At the same time the Indian delegates had gathered that their request for the repeal of the Transvaal laws which restricted the right of Indians to hold or own land, *videlicet* to trade, would be sympathetically considered.[1]

1916.   It was on this point that the quarrel between India and the Union was renewed.[2] The indenture system with all its evils was almost gone from Natal and was now ending as far as Indians were concerned all the world over. In South Africa the immigration and cognate laws which had formed the main topic of the 1914 inquiries and negotiations had ceased to be a serious source of grievance. On the other hand, South Africans still wrongly believed that Indians were increasing faster than Europeans in Natal, and, probably with more justice, still evading the Transvaal immigration regulations. What was certain was that Indians had found loopholes in the Transvaal law forbidding Asiatics to own fixed property. They formed limited liability companies, which, not being individuals, could hardly be Asiatics incapable of owning land, or else they induced Europeans to buy land and mortgage it to them at cost price.[3]

Indian traders were thus spreading along the Rand and, by reason of the colour prejudice against them and their habit of sub-letting rooms to swarming families, were depreciating the property of white neighbours who already complained of their unfair competition. Be that as it might, municipal councils had latterly sought to combat the invasion by withholding trading licences from Indians as undesirables; but when the Krugersdorp magistrate upheld three Indian appeals, the city fathers had had recourse to the hitherto ineffec-

1919.   tive Gold Law of 1908. They had procured an injunction against a European who proposed to lease proclaimed land to an Indian trader. At once, applications for injunctions had come 'thick as autumnal leaves in Vallombrosa.'

Parliament, on the advice of a select committee, forbade the issue of new though not the re-issue of existing licences to Indians in mining areas, and stopped the limited liability and mortgage loopholes; but it maintained such vested rights as had arisen by those means prior to May 1919.[4] Protests against the Act poured in from India and from Anglo-India;[5] the South African Indians talked of an appeal to the League of Nations to uphold their inherent right to trade, at all events in competition with the Greeks and East European Jews who formed so large a proportion of their adversaries and whose style of life and conception of business were sometimes not vastly

---

[1] Andrews, *Documents re New Asiatic Bill*, p. 19.

[2] *Round Table*, No. 38, pp. 447 ff.; No. 46, pp. 440 ff.; No. 63, pp. 633 ff.

[3] In 1921, of the 16,000 Transvaal traders 5810 were Indians. There had been only three limited liability companies of this sort in 1913; in May 1919 there were 370.

[4] Act 37 of 1919; *Report of Select Committee on Indian Disabilities*, April 1919.

[5] 'Anglo-Indians' in those days meant the British resident, if only temporarily, in India. It now means European-Indian mixed breeds.

superior to their own, and Gandhi confessed that he could see no final solution of the land and trading problems; but, outside the Transvaal towns, South Africans were inclined to take the matter quietly, trusting to time, education, and the enforcement of sanitary regulations, however unpleasant that might be for slum landlords of all races, to raise the Indians' standard of life. In spite of bickering over the issue of trading licences as Indians penetrated the Cape ports, there was hardly any talk of repatriation there, while coastal Natal would frankly have missed her Indians had they gone; as it was the general situation was eased somewhat by the departure of 4000 poverty-stricken Madrassis, who asked an eager Government to help them home to escape the rising cost of living.[1] On the other hand, anti-Indian leagues in the Transvaal kept the agitation alive, and these leagues were presently reinforced by others in Natal, where some of the Europeans objected to the spread of Indians into farmlands outside the semi-tropical coast belt.

In the course of the quarrel the question arose as to the meaning of the 'vested rights,' which, under the Smuts-Gandhi Agreement, were to be duly regarded in the administration of then existing laws. It was a question which vitally concerned the Imperial and Indian governments, for Secretaries of State in the past had accepted unpalatable Natal and Transvaal immigration laws as the best means of ensuring fair treatment for Indians already dwelling in those colonies. The Indian authorities and many others, including the Solomon Commission, had interpreted the Smuts-Gandhi Agreement of 1914 to mean that 'no new law would be passed imposing fresh restrictions on Indians'; in other words, that the then status of Indians would be maintained.[2] The inquiries and negotiations of 1914 had turned mainly on the immigration question which was not now in dispute; but a letter written by Gandhi shortly after the con- 1919. clusion of the Agreement now came to light for the first time. It did not form part of that Agreement, but was avowedly a note on the vested rights which were to be safeguarded under the Gold Law of 1908. Therein Gandhi stated that he had not pressed for a definition of vested rights under that head lest he thereby tie the hands of his countrymen, but that, in reply to an inquiry, he interpreted them to be freedom for an Indian or his successor to live and trade anywhere in the township in which he was then established. This was the very point at issue, and the Indians, eager to gain the right to hold land, jumped at this letter and held it up as a full definition of all the vested rights that Gandhi had had in mind in 1914.[3]

---

[1] Voluntary repatriation stimulated by a state bonus took place thereafter, e.g. 2787 in 1923; 1063 in 1924; 1400 in 1925.
[2] Andrews, *Documents re New Asiatic Bill*, pp. 26 ff., 31 ff.
[3] *Ibid.*, p. 33; *Cape Times*, Jan. 22, 23 and 27, 1936.

The Indians thus laid themselves open to having rights other than those covered by Gandhi's note on the Gold Law materially reduced, and prejudiced their case before the Commission which, again assisted by Sir Benjamin Robertson, was investigating the question. That Commission recommended the encouragement of voluntary repatriation and segregation, the limitation of new licences to special Asiatic quarters, the long overdue consolidation of licensing laws throughout the Union, the strict enforcement of the immigration laws and, with one dissentient, the restriction of the right of Indians to hold farm-lands to the coast belt of Natal.[1] For the time being the ministry took no action, but at the Imperial Conference, what time the Governor-General was withholding his assent from a Natal ordinance which would have deprived Indians of the municipal franchise, Smuts declined on economic grounds to commit South Africa to the policy which had been more or less adopted by other Dominions of admitting domiciled Indians to rights of citizenship, because, after all, the Union had some 166,000 Indians and no other Dominion had more than three thousand.[2]

The Indian problem was more a matter of retail trade than of labour. The crux of the labour problem was the position to be held by the Bantu. In spite of a high infantile death-rate and the tuberculosis, syphilis and typhus which played havoc with adult natives in their kraals and still more in the slums of the towns, Europeans commonly believed that they were increasing very much faster than themselves.[3] It was a mistaken belief, for the preceding censuses of 1904 and 1911 had counted the Bantu very imperfectly with the result that that of 1921, the first reliable numbering, showed a spectacular and most misleading increase. Nevertheless, it was plain for all men to see that a great change had come over the Bantu during the first quarter of the nineteenth century. The tribal system was crumbling. Native custom was so far being modified that in

1920–1921.

1921.

---

[1] U.G. 4–21.

[2] There were 166,000 Asiatics in the Union in 1921, of whom nearly 70 per cent. had been born in the country. There were only 1200 Indians in Canada, 3000 in Australia, and 600 in New Zealand. The Indians in Natal numbered 141,000; the Europeans, who were rapidly overtaking them, 136,000. Of all the Dominions New Zealand alone gave its small Indian population complete franchise rights. Indians could acquire the federal franchise in Australia, but not the state franchise in Western Australia. They were denied both the federal and the provincial franchises in British Columbia (*British Commonwealth Relations*, p. 194). For a good account of Indians in Africa *vide* W. K. Hancock, *Survey of British Commonwealth Affairs, 1918–1936*, chap. IV.

[3] It is difficult to estimate the relative increases of the various peoples of South Africa. The census of 1911 was defective as far as natives were concerned.

	Europeans.	Coloured.	Asiatics.	Bantu.
1911	. 1,276,000	428,000 (*ca.*)	150,000 (*ca.*)	4,019,000.
1921	. 1,519,000	545,000	166,000	4,698,000.

The proportion of Europeans to others in 1921 was thus about 1 : 3·5.

some cases natives paid money instead of the sacred *lobola* cattle, committing under European influence the very 'sin of buying wives' which had horrified Sir Harry Smith in days gone by. Divided though they were, they were growing in solidarity, realising that they were the basis of society and losing faith in the white man's religion and education.

The Bantu were roughly divided into four classes: those who lived in the reserves, often in the direst poverty and always under such conditions that a great number of men had to supplement their earnings by going outside to work; those, a great number, who lived as squatters or labour tenants on European farms; the growing class of more or less detribalised natives who lived in the towns or on the farms, including those who came on short-term contracts to the mines either from within the Union or from the High Commission Territories or from Portuguese East Africa; and, lastly, the small class of educated natives who had emancipated themselves completely from tribal conditions. The threat to the European skilled labour monopoly arose from the third and fourth classes. As yet, from lack of skill and experience, native competition in manufactures was not *Circa* severe,[1] but, on the gold-mines, many natives had risen from the 1920. ranks of unskilled to those of semi-skilled labour. They had done work which should have been done by their white bosses either because those bosses would not or, in the case of some of the newly-arrived miners, could not do it. In any case, the Bantu were learning, and the inducements held out to the mine-owners to employ them on higher grade work were almost overwhelming. They throve on a wage which spelt starvation to white men; they required a smaller contribution from the management towards miners' phthisis benefit; they could be compounded; they were amenable to the criminal law for breach of contract; they had neither trade unions nor votes.

It was useless simply to shut the door in the faces of the Bantu. If their entry into industry was to be checked, they must be given alternative outlets for their energies.[2] The obvious outlet was on the land, and the idea underlying the Natives Land Act of 1913 had been territorial segregation. The work of the Beaumont Commission, which had then been appointed to set aside additional native areas, had been delayed by the war; but the mere expectation of its report had quieted the agitation against an Act which was of its nature temporary, and loyalty to the Great White King had called forth thousands of Bantu to willing labour behind the lines in Flanders and East Africa.

[1] The proportion of Europeans to others varied inversely as the size of the factories. The Bantu population increased by nearly 700,000 between 1911 and 1921. Most of the newcomers found work without displacing Europeans, whose numbers had also increased. The use of labour-saving machinery was accompanied by the employment of more men of all races (U.G. 14 of 1926, p. 102).
[2] *Vide* reports of commissions (1906–22) quoted by U.G. 14 of 1926, pp. 122 ff.

1916.   The Beaumont Report, when it did at last come, was not a hopeful document.[1] It proposed to add 22,000,000 acres to the 17,660,000 already set aside for the Bantu, that is; to allocate thirteen per cent. of the area of the Union to 4,500,000 natives and the remainder to some 2,000,000 Europeans and others. It is true that much of the land occupied by Europeans had been taken before ever the Bantu had appeared in those parts and much more while they had been temporarily absent, but a great deal had been simply occupied regardless of any claims the natives might have had upon it. Outside the Cape Province, Crown lands had been freely taken up in this way since 1913 and the natives resident thereon had been given the choice of moving elsewhere or taking service with the new owner. This process had gone so far that the Commission confessed that there was little hope of giving the Bantu large, compact blocks of land on which to develop along their own lives, because white men would not have their farms included in such areas; indeed, many of them were asking why the natives were to have the good land that the Commission actually proposed to give them.

1917.   In spite of many excellent provisions, the Native Administration Bill based on the Beaumont Report still left natives, outside their own areas, dependent on their masters and gave the executive no power to expropriate land-owners who held out for fancy prices. The Assembly divided on racial lines and the measure was shelved. Provincial Commissions [2] then traversed the same ground as the Beaumont Commission with a like result, and all that Smuts and Hertzog could suggest was that natives should be permitted to acquire land in the areas common to the various Reports and that further provision be made at a more convenient season. Beyond giving effect to the first suggestion and administering native affairs well or ill according to the system in vogue in various parts of the Union, nothing further had been done to meet the needs of the Bantu. So the men of 'the black house' lost faith in the good intentions of their rulers and, as the years ran on, the solution of the land question became more difficult.

     Meanwhile other grievances rankled. Educated natives and semi-skilled 'boys' on the mines resented the pass laws and the colour bar enforced in the ex-Republics; the mass of their fellows were harassed by low wages, the rising cost of living [3] and a sense of bewilderment at the white man's conception of law. Why should the magistrate regard as crimes so many deeds which to them were merely *delicta privata* to be atoned for by wergild? The meaning of

[1] U.G. 19, 22 and 25 of 1916.   [2] U.G. 8, 22, 23, 31, 34 and 41–18.
[3] On economic condition of the Bantu *vide* U.G. 14–26; *Cape Times*, April 12, 1926 (*At the Roots*, by W. Macmillan); S.C. 6a and 10–27. In 1918, the average yearly wage of white miners on the Rand was £355 15s. and of Bantu miners £27 10s.

debt they understood as fully as did the labour touts who traded on their knowledge; but what was a contract? Why should not a man change his mind if he wanted to?

The connection between contract and the cost of living was brought home to some of the Bantu majority, who now formed something like a trade union and, for the first time, imitated their European and Coloured fellow-workers by coming out on strike. White trade unions had long been established firmly and, since 1913, had tended to co-operate through the S.A. Industrial Federation. Most of them, and particularly those in the Transvaal, confined their membership to Europeans, but those in the more liberal Cape Province were either mixed Coloured and European or purely Coloured. Since 1913 again, most of these southern unions had become affiliated to Robert Stuart's Cape Federation of Labour Unions, which was regarded in friendly fashion by the S.A. Federation; both associations had to fear the competition of low-paid unorganised Coloured workers.[1] Thus far, however, no Bantu had formed a trade union, not so much because any legal barrier stood in their way as because the whole social and economic atmosphere was against them and the majority of European trade unionists were averse to the very idea of their so doing. Still less had they dared to strike if only because they knew that, if they did so, they would be liable to criminal prosecution under the Masters and Servants Act. Now, however, some few Bantu, thousands of whose kinsfolk had served the King well during the Kaiser's war, plucked up courage to make a stand.

The impulse came from two quarters, the one African, the other European. At Capetown in 1917, with the unobtrusive help of a local white Labour leader, the Nyasalander, Clements Kadalie, founded the Industrial and Commercial Workers' Union. This I.C.U. was not, properly speaking, a trade union, because many of its members were not wage-earners; rather was it a would-be organisation of non-Europeans against all forms of oppression and, therefore, scarcely welcomed by the few white folk who knew of its existence.[2] The decisive European stimulus came from Johannesburg. There, the War on War Group, which had broken away from the Labour Party in 1915 under Andrews, Bunting and David Jones, had presently re-named itself the International Socialist League and started its own newspaper, *The International*.[3] It now organised a handful of Bantu as the Industrial Workers of Africa and soon had the satisfaction of seeing them go into action. In May 1918, some of the white municipal employees struck at Johannesburg, refused the good

[1] Roux, *op. cit.*, p. 134.
[2] L. Barnes, *Caliban in Africa*, pp. 96 ff.; Roux, *op. cit.*, pp. 61 ff.; Sachs, *op. cit.*, pp. 157 ff.
[3] Roux, *op. cit.*, p. 138.

offices of other trade unions and obliged the City Council to capitulate. Thereupon, in June, the I.W.A. induced some hundred and fifty Bantu sanitary workers, key members of a community which lacked water-borne sewage, to 'down buckets' for higher pay. After the ensuing stench had faded away, these luckless pioneers were lawfully punished; but the Attorney-General refused to prosecute three European members of the International Socialist League and five Bantu leaders of the African National Union who were charged with inciting them to violence.[1] Immediately thereafter the white gold-miners were strong enough to oblige the Chamber of Mines to sign a *Status Quo* Agreement entrenching them in their employments as against non-Europeans.

Non-Europeans were not slow to reply to this glaring inequality of treatment. The Industrial Workers of Africa co-operated with the I.C.U. in starting an unsuccessful dock strike at Capetown and then dwindled away, while Coloured and Bantu municipal drivers came out at Kimberley, only to be defeated by white 'scabs.'[2] A much more determined reply came from Pretoria and the Rand, where, in March and April 1919, the African National Union organised mass meetings, house-to-house collections of passes and public burnings of the hated documents to the strains of 'Rule Britannia' and 'Nkosi Sikelela (God Bless),' virtually the Bantu national anthem. The usual arrests were made and the movement, which was orderly enough, was worn down by the police with the eager help of unauthorised white civilians; but George Boyes, the ex-magistrate who conducted the subsequent inquiry, bluntly told the authorities that they would have to modify the pass laws because Africans were determined to resist them.[3] Then came a bombshell. In February 1920, hard on the heels of a successful strike by white municipal employees at Durban, some 71,000 unorganised Bantu suddenly struck on the Rand mines. This upheaval was got under by white scabbing, by the diplomacy of the police who cordoned off each mine separately and falsely told the inmates that their fellows elsewhere had gone to work, and by bloodshed, when, for instance, unauthorised white civilians fired on a meeting held by the African National Union at Vrededorp, and police fired on Africans who resisted their entry into the Village Deep compound.[4]

Trouble was not confined, however, to tumultuous urban centres in the Transvaal. Early in 1920, Bantu youngsters at the Kilnerton mission institute near Pretoria and, more surprisingly, rather older theological students at the non-European college at Fort Hare rioted and even burned college buildings to enforce their demand for better food.[5] Then a much more serious affair gave further proof of the

---

[1] Roux, *op. cit.*, pp. 138 ff.   [2] *Ibid.*, p. 163.   [3] *Ibid.*, pp. 125 ff.
[4] *Ibid.*, pp. 140 ff.; Sachs, *op. cit.*, p. 156.   [5] Roux, *op. cit.*, p. 164.

growing readiness of truculent and frightened white men to shoot.
After a slow start in Capetown, the I.C.U. had spread fast throughout the Cape Province and taken firm root in Port Elizabeth. There
Masabalala, the president of the local branch, urged a peaceful
meeting of Africans to strike for higher wages. A few days later, he
was arrested by order of the Minister without a warrant and on no
specific charge. Numbers of non-Europeans therefore gathered outside the gaol asking quietly enough that he should be released on bail.
Their request was refused. Meanwhile, the now customary gang of
unauthorised white civilians had got into the police station and obtained arms. They then let fly into the crowd without orders and
the police naturally joined in. Twenty-four Africans were killed and
many others wounded as they ran. None of the ruffians concerned
was punished for this display of frontier methods in a reputedly
civilised township.[1]

Something had to be done to check these growing troubles. In
the narrower sphere of the Rand, the Native Recruiting Committee
began to issue *Umteteli wa Bantu*, a heavily subsidised newspaper
designed to keep Africans 'on the right lines.'[2] In the wider sphere of
the Union, Smuts essayed to deal with one side at least of the sorely
inflamed Native problem.[3] He set up a permanent Native Affairs 1920.
Commission to advise the Prime Minister on all matters concerning
natives, provided for the extension of the Transkeian system of
local government and taxation to all native areas, and proposed to
summon conferences of chiefs, headmen and other Bantu dignitaries
from time to time. This was a step forward in that it promised the
personal touch and solemn debate beloved of the tribesmen, and
offered them a sounder training in local government than was
enjoyed by many Europeans in the Union; but it left the vital matter
of the land untouched. The delimitation of new reserves was only
to take place after the economic and administrative relations of the
two races had been established on a firmer footing.

The response was not reassuring. Wellington Butulezi, an African,
caused something of a stir in the Transkei by prophesying that
United States Negroes were coming in aeroplanes to set Africa free[4]
and, meanwhile, a much more dangerous development of an ultra-
Ethiopian kind began to arise in the Bulhoek location near Queenstown in the Ciskei.[5] Overmuch study of the more sanguinary portions
of the Old Testament had produced some 160 native sects, all
Chosen People, nearly all independent of European control and
many duly furnished with prophets. One of these sects, the Israelites,
led by their prophet Enoch, had settled in the Bulhoek native location,

---

[1] Sachs, *op. cit.*, pp. 156 ff. ; Roux, *op. cit.*, pp. 164 ff.
[2] *Ibid.*, p. 360.   [3] Act 23 of 1920.
[4] Roux, *op. cit.*, p. 148.   [5] *Ibid.*, pp. 143 ff.

much to the annoyance of the permanent inhabitants. At first they had merely come annually as to a Zion to feast, but now the local officials unwisely treated Enoch as headman and he, repeatedly defying the law, tried to organise an anti-European conspiracy. The failure of an attempt to eject the Israelites by police, who were known to be under orders not to fire, hardened the hearts of a people who were taught that bullets could not harm them. At last, after repeated attempts to persuade them to go away, the Native Affairs Commission recommended that force be used. The Israelites charged the 800 police like Dervishes and were shot down in scores.[1] A judicial commission exonerated the authorities from blame save for their disregard of Livingstone's advice never to point a gun at a native unless you mean to shoot; but the presiding judge, Sir Thomas Graham, none the less found that the movement had been far more anti-European than religious. Be that as it might, the incident had ugly reverberations among Bantu, who, like any Nationalists, were talking of 'self-determination.' In response to a rumour that the King's veto on legislation was to be abolished, some of them asked for representation at the next Imperial Conference.

May 1921.

The stormy course of native politics awakened a new interest in the whole question among those Europeans who were frank enough to acknowledge and lament their ignorance of native customs and point of view. The University of Cape Town, after many efforts, founded a School of Anthropology primarily to study African life and languages; the University of Witwatersrand, which had recently broken away from the federal University of South Africa,[2] followed its example, and presently the study was taken up at the Pretoria University College. Unluckily, before these hopeful movements had been fairly set on foot, the whole of the social, economic and political issues bound up with the native question ran together with a crash which shook the Union to its foundations.

The ministry, suffering as had Jameson's from the internal strains set up by differences of opinion on the score of free trade and land taxing, had laid itself open to the charge that it was showing more energy in cutting down wages and war bonuses than in reducing the cost of living. It was a charge which Labour and the Nationalists were not slow to bring. Labour had done well at recent by-elections, and it was at this moment that the Chamber of Mines, in Labour's eyes the master of the Government, essayed to modify the colour bar.

Nov. 1921.

Any such modification must be dangerous to those many humble supporters of the Nationalist and Labour parties who had come to

---

[1] Report of *Native Affairs Commission*, A 4-21.
[2] Its place in that body was taken by the Potchefstroom University College (Act 19 of 1921).

seek work along the Rand without skill of any kind, and to the many more who might well follow them. Poverty had been spreading among the white folk so fast of late years, that, as far back as 1897, well-intentioned predikants had gone to the rescue by gathering as many unfortunates as they could into labour colonies at Kakamas in the Cape Colony and similar institutions in the ex-Republics. They failed, however, to make these real training grounds because the inmates had refused to move on and thus settled down as mere feckless squatters. Nor could alms-giving by the Governor-General's and Helpmekaar Funds get to the root of the matter, which was that very many of these poor folk were Poor Whites, that is, Europeans who had neither the skill to compete with more competent non-Europeans nor the will to accept low pay for rough work in competition with equally unskilled dark-skinned folk. What chance would they have of finding acceptable work on the Rand mines if the colour bar were lowered ?

Yet it was precisely the partial lowering of that colour bar that the Chamber of Mines proposed to effect on the strength of an eighteen-months-old report of a Commission, which had been appointed at a time when the low-grade mines were fighting a losing battle against rising working costs. The Commission had recommended that, in view of recent advances in medical knowledge, the recruiting of tropical labour from beyond the 22nd degree of south latitude should be permitted temporarily, mining be reorganised so as to give the labourers a longer spell on the actual 'face,' and, against the wishes of the three Labour commissioners, the unions be asked to agree to the removal of the colour bar.[1] That colour bar was of two kinds: the so-called statutory bar embodied in regulations framed under the Mines and Works Act, which then protected some seven thousand men in thirty-two occupations, and the conventional bar secured by the Status Quo Agreement whereby the Chamber, while refusing to dismiss non-Europeans already engaged on semi-skilled work, undertook not to prejudice the position of Europeans further. No action had been taken on the report at the time, for the gold premium had come to the rescue; but, now that the premium had fallen from 42s. per ounce to 19s., the Chamber felt that it must act, at all events, against this conventional bar which then protected fully four thousand men in nineteen occupations.[2] It first persuaded the unions to agree to a reorganisation of work in the mines, and then, terrified at a further rapid fall of the premium, proposed to give up the existing costly system of mining by contract and to employ non-Europeans on semi-skilled work. Dec. 9, 1921.

[1] U.G. 34-20.
[2] The price of gold fell from 104s. to 97s. 4d. in a few days. The pre-war price had been 85s. per oz.

Battle was thus joined on the ground where the most efficient of the coloured peoples pressed hardest upon the least efficient of the whites. It was a serious matter for those immediately concerned at a time when there was no scheme of industrial insurance to tide over displaced workmen. If the premium disappeared, 24 of the 39 producing mines might expect to make losses which would drive them to discharge 10,000 whites and many thousands of blacks; if the men accepted the Chamber's terms, 2000 of their weaker brethren would lose their jobs, though some of them would be reabsorbed as the richer mines recruited their full tale of native labourers. But it was also a serious matter for Labour all over South Africa. The scarcity of skilled men, the soaring cost of living and the extravagance bred of great expectations in the early days of the diamond mines of Kimberley and the gold mines of the Rand had set the standard of white artisans' pay very high. The railways had taken their cue from the mines, the engineering trades from the railways, and so it had gone till the tradition had grown up that a pound a day was the birthright of all white workers. The nearer to the Rand, the more that ambition was likely to be realised and, now, the very citadel of the Rand was threatened.[1]

Dec. 15, 1921.   The Chamber and the S.A. Industrial Federation conferred hopefully together and then adjourned;[2] but, before they could meet again, the coal-owners, thinking to save their export trade, tried to cut wages and refused the Government's offer of mediation which the men had already accepted. It was the signal for general confusion. Jan. 10, 1922.   The gold-owners gave the legal month's notice to terminate the Status Quo Agreement without prejudice to current negotiations, the Transvaal coal-miners struck, and the gold-miners, not unnaturally reading the Chamber's notice as an ultimatum, joined hands with the discontented engineering staffs and struck too. With over 20,000 Europeans and 180,000 natives thus standing idle, negotiations soon broke down. In response to Smuts's offer of mediation, the Chamber proposed a ratio of employment of one European to 10·5 natives. The Federation retorted with a demand for a population ratio of one to 3·5 enforceable by law on all industries save agriculture, and called for help against a ministry which refused to protect the white race.[3]

The cry was an answer to a hint. Just before the coal strike, Tielman Roos, leader of the Transvaal Nationalists, had bidden his people stay quietly on their farms in case of trouble, apparently to avoid spoiling the prospect of co-operation between themselves and Labour at the next elections. The prospect was a good one. The Mine Workers' Union was full of disinherited Afrikaners from the

[1] U.G. 14 of 1926, pp. 84 ff., 151.
[2] The Federation was the successor of the Transvaal Federation of Trades.
[3] On the strike *vide* U.G. 35 of 1922.

land.[1] These men formed the majority of the 'commandos' which, variously armed, paraded the Reef and flocked to a mass meeting to demand a provisional republican government, while Roos sum- Feb. moned an informal congress of Transvaal parliamentarians at 5–6 Pretoria. The Chamber then offered to retain half the men marked 1922. for dismissal pending an inquiry; but the Federation held out for resumption of work on the old terms, and so the struggle dragged on, working havoc with trade and revenue and railway receipts, while native labourers were sent home wholesale. Even were the strike to end at once these could not be speedily replaced; hence, to Feb. avoid a complete dissipation of the 'labour force,' Smuts successfully 13, appealed to the Chamber to reopen the mines. At first the response 1922. was small, for, even after Parliament had declared such organisations illegal, the commandos terrorised 'scabs'; nevertheless, many white men were anxious to return to work while work was to be had. The flow back to the mines increased daily, and Parliament, setting aside Feb. Hertzog's plea for laws forbidding the diminution of the sphere of 28, European employment, resolved by a small majority on an impartial 1922. inquiry.

The shooting stage had, however, been reached. The power-station men struck; the harassed police fired on the mob at Boksburg and, in alarm, the Federation made new proposals. These the Chamber rejected with contumely. The answer was decisive. The Council of March Action, a small group of Communists affiliated to the Third Inter- 6, national, thrust the Federation aside and let loose 'the bare-armed 1922. fighting man' to the cry of 'Workers of the world, unite for a white South Africa.' The police held out at a few vital points, but for some days most of the Rand was in the hands of revolutionaries, one of whose first acts was to attack natives in some of the compounds. The natives, however, remained quiet; burgher commandos and regiments of the recently reorganised Defence Force were hurried forward, Smuts, at great personal risk, dashed in from Capetown to take charge, and soon all was over. At the end of a desperate March struggle which cost South Africa twice as many lives as the whole 15, of the South-West Africa campaign,[2] the Federation called the 1922. strike off, the Miners' Union disowned the revolutionaries and the Chamber took back such men as it required on its own terms.

The social and industrial results of the Great Strike were far-reaching. Three white ringleaders were hanged and many others imprisoned until Smuts released them under the Strike Condonation Act;[3] the S.A. Industrial Federation collapsed, the numbers of white

---

[1] In 1910 little more than one-quarter of the white miners on the Rand had been South African born, in 1921 rather more than half.
[2] Killed in G.S.W.A., 113; on the Rand, 230 of all classes and colours.
[3] Act 29 of 1922.

trade unionists fell from some 108,000 to 81,000 in six months and so many British workers left the area that, as their places were filled by Afrikaners from the *platteland*, Transvaal labour became increasingly indistinguishable racially from Hertzog's Nationalist following.[1] Smuts appointed a Mining Industry Board to recommend future policy and, though he suffered the legal colour bar enshrined in the Mines and Works Act of 1911 to survive, set up a judicial Mining Industry Commission with whose approval the Chamber of Mines denounced the Status Quo Agreement which safeguarded the conventional colour bar. He then carried an Anti-dumping Act to protect the Union's nascent secondary industries from the competition of those of laborious Central Europe, and lastly the delayed Apprenticeship Act, which supplemented the Wages Act of 1918 by setting up committees to advise the Minister on appropriate periods of apprenticeship, the numbers of apprentices to be enrolled and the wages payable to them. By requiring in many cases that would-be apprentices must have passed Standard VII, this measure debarred from skilled trades those many non-Europeans who could not afford to pay the fees demanded by the secondary schools at which alone that standard was attainable.[2]

April 1922. The political results of the Great Strike were even more noteworthy, for Hertzog announced that the Nationalists would work with Labour at the next elections. It was the first official intimation of the coming Pact which was destined to overthrow the Smuts Ministry, a *modus vivendi* between parties both of which cherished a lively hatred for the Premier and for the Capitalism with which they identified him, both of which were deeply interested in the question of coloured labour, the one desiring it for the farms, the other fearing it as an industrial competitor, and both of which were suspicious of immigrants and averse to warlike adventures, at least outside the borders of the Union.

It was to affairs outside the Union that Smuts now addressed himself. The sanguine hopes of those who had looked to see him return from Versailles with great acquisitions of territory to the west and the far north had been disappointed. Even Botha's claim that South-West Africa must remain a province of the Union had not been realised. The Protectorate had been merely entrusted to the Union under a 'C' mandate, which empowered it to administer it as an integral part of its own territory, but included limitations which were obviously intended to safeguard the native peoples and the

Dec. 1920.

---

[1] Van der Horst, *op. cit.*, p. 242.
[2] Acts 13 and 26 of 1922; van der Horst, *op. cit.*, p. 243. Act 26 was gradually enforced with good results in such trades as building, boot, clothing and furniture-making and printing (U.G. 14 of 1926, p. 47).

duty of reporting annually to the Mandates Commission of the League of Nations.[1]

Of the 208,000 natives therein, the half who lived under tribal conditions in Ovamboland in the north were only nominally under European rule. Many of the rest (the half-breeds in the Police Zone of the south and centre and Hottentots and Bantu Hereros of Damara-Namaqualand) dwelt on some 7,000,000 acres of reserve land. The Europeans were settled almost entirely in the Police Zone, either on the grassy uplands, which, even in that land of intermittent rivers and precarious rainfall, gave grazing for cattle and sheep and permitted agriculture under irrigation, or on the tin, copper and marble mines and the diamond mines of the desert coast-belt.[2]

The 15,000 German inhabitants had been reduced by repatriation, voluntary or otherwise, to some 8000.[3] They had retained full civil rights, but, during the war, the nominated municipal and district councils with their restricted powers had been abolished and the whole country subjected to martial law. Nominated municipal councils had again been set up after the war and a High Court created, whose judge heard criminal cases with two assessors and administered Cape civil law and such German law as was not inconsistent therewith subject to an appeal to the Union appellate division.[4] The military authorities had soon made way for a civil administrator, who was now assisted by a nominated Council of Advice manned by Germans and South Africans in equal proportions and an official versed in native affairs.

These conditions could hardly last. Some 10,000 South Africans and other immigrants had settled in the country and were restive under virtual one-man rule.[5] The Germans, moreover, were still citizens of the Fatherland in a ceded colony, neither aliens in the land nor yet subjects of the Union which ruled them. Nationalists were inclined to hold that the mandate foreshadowed self-determination for these Germans, but, however that might be, there was little hope of developing the country until their position was regularised. The Government was already boring for water, and the Imperial Cold Storage Company was contemplating a big meat export through Walvis Bay; hence, as a small beginning in self-government, half the seats in the municipal councils were made elective. It was only in 1923, however, that Smuts came to terms with Berlin on the head

1919.

1920.

Jan. 1921.

1922

---

[1] U.G. 39–19, p. 10; U.G. 44–19. On South-West Africa *vide* also U.G. 34–19, U.G. 24–21 and annual reports of the Administrator.
[2] Government found 70 per cent. of the working expenses and drew 66 per cent. of the profits of the diamond mines.
[3] 6374 Germans had been sent home, including 3718 soldiers and other officials and 1433 others at their own request.
[4] Union Year Book, No. 8, pp. 988 ff.
[5] The total European population was 19,432 in June 1923.

of citizenship. Subject to ratification by the Union Parliament, German nationals were to become British subjects unless they contracted out before a given date, and German was to be an official language and the medium of instruction for German children. This was an agreement that pointed to self-government and, *pace* the League, to the ultimate incorporation of the Protectorate in the Union; but, in the event, the Smuts ministry had fallen before it could pass the necessary Act.

1924.

Meanwhile, the action of the Administrator at Windhoek had disturbed Natives throughout the Union and drawn the outraged gaze of the League of Nations upon the mandatory Power. The Bondelswarts, a Hottentot tribe whose leaders had served the Union well during the Kaiser's war, rebelled against their new rulers because they were called upon to pay a tax on the dogs without whose aid they could not maintain their life as hunters. The Administrator in person led a large force into their Reserve, killed over one hundred men, women and children with the assistance of aeroplanes, and then issued a report which failed to carry conviction. One member of the Union's Native Affairs Commission, a stout old Transvaal General, indeed applauded the Native policy of the Windhoek authorities, but the other two guardedly censured it. The Mandates Commission, while approving the conciliatory measures taken since the scuffle, condemned the Administrator's methods of conducting negotiations with the tribesmen, urged that relief be given to the poverty-stricken Bondelswarts, and called for a full report.[1]

The suspicion that Smuts was seeking to call in another Province to cancel in advance the accession of strength which South-West Africa might be expected to give to his opponents goes far to explain the vigour of the opposition from within the Union to his policy of incorporating Southern Rhodesia. Under the Supplemental Charter of 1915, the governing powers of the B.S.A. Company had been extended till October 1924 unless an absolute majority of the Legislative Council could satisfy the Imperial Government before that date that Rhodesia was fit for self-government or, presumably, the country entered the Union.[2] Railway extensions and other schemes of development had necessarily been curtailed while the Company and its subjects, white and black, bore their full share in the war. The Company worked its farms and ranches, encouraged agriculture and industries allied thereto, administered the reserve natives by a happy combination of Basutoland and Transkeian methods and waited for better times. It also expended modest sums on capital account and stood ready to make good administrative deficits. This

---

[1] *Round Table*, No. 53, pp. 171 ff.; U.G. 30–22 and 41–26; Roux, *op. cit.*, pp. 149 ff.
[2] Cd. 7970 of 1915.

last it was not called upon to do, for, taking one year with another, revenue balanced the carefully controlled expenditure.

The *raison d'être* of the Company as a ruling power was thus ceasing now that the country was beginning to pay its own way. The great majority of the elected members of the legislature, averse to union with the South, were still more opposed to the amalgamation with Northern Rhodesia, which was more than once suggested.[1] Amalgamation with the 'Black North' with its swarming Bantu and sprinkling of Europeans would indefinitely postpone the self-government which they more and more confidently expected. The responsible government movement then received a great impetus from the long-awaited verdict of the Privy Council in the matter of the unalienated lands. The Judicial Committee, to which that issue had July been referred in 1914, laid it down that these lands had always been 1918. what Rhodes himself had once called them, that is, Crown lands, but that, so long as the Company continued to rule, it was entitled to use the land revenues for the reduction of the accumulated administrative deficits and thereafter to look to the Crown for reimbursement either from the further sales of lands or otherwise.[2]

The Chartered Board at once claimed a refund of those deficits with interest and told the Rhodesians that, as the lands were no longer to be regarded as a commercial asset of the Company, they must expect no further capital expenditure by the Company on their behalf.[3] The elected members with one dissentient therefore resolved to press for responsible government. On the other hand, Milner, now Colonial Secretary, counselled delay and appointed the Cave Commission to fix the amount due to the Company from the Crown;[4] the pro-Union party in Rhodesia marshalled its forces, and the Nationalists in the Union itself raised the cry that Smuts was going 1919. to bring in a solid phalanx of Rhodesians 'to break the back of Afrikanerdom.'

There was much to be said for the incorporation of Southern Rhodesia in the Union. It was Rhodesia's traditional destiny. The country had been colonised largely from the south; its law was fundamentally the Cape law; its appeals lay to Bloemfontein; its railways, continuous with the Union system, were actually worked by the Union as far as Bulawayo; its trade lay mainly with the towns and ports of S.A.; it was a member of the Customs Union. Further, it was doubtful whether it could stand alone. Milner had pointed to finance and the swarming Bantu as the chief obstacles to autonomy. The territory was large, nearly 150,000 square miles, and most of its 33,000 Europeans were strung out along the railways. Around them

[1] B.S.A. Co. Report, 1915, p. 27; Legislative Council debates, April 1917.
[2] B.S.A. Co. Report, 1920, p. 42. [3] B.S.A. Co. Annual Meeting, Aug. 1918.
[4] Cmd. 1129 of 1921; B.S.A. Co. Reports, 1919, p. 6, 1920, p. 4.

were 770,000 natives, three-fifths of whom lived a tribal life in reserves.[1] Part at least of the Company's claim of £7,866,000 would have to be found by a country which was only just paying its way with nothing over for development or assisted immigration. Till that debt was paid the Crown lands would be beyond the reach of the Rhodesians. Again, the great mass of those lands on the high and healthy plateau along the railways had already been alienated and half the remainder was below the 'health line,' good cattle country but not so good for men and, in any case, needing heavy expenditure on roads and railways before it could be made really available.[2] The financial and native experiences of Natal, the nearest South African parallel to Rhodesia, had not been encouraging, and Natal had not harboured a corporation such as the B.S.A. Company was and would remain. For the Company controlled directly or indirectly the minerals, the railways, vast estates and the Land Bank; it held shares in most of the producing mines and in subsidiary companies of all kinds, and it was possessed of great powers and concessions in the neighbouring territories of the Bechuanaland Protectorate, Northern Rhodesia and Nyasaland.

On the other hand, many Rhodesians feared centralised Pretoria rule and the republicanism and bilingualism of the Union. They prided themselves on being a British community in spite of the Jews, Greeks and Moslems in the towns and the Afrikaners, perhaps one-eighth of the total European population, who lived in groups in the countryside. They dreaded an influx of Poor Whites into their empty acres and the free movement from the south of the bankrupts and other undesirables, whom, *mirabile dictu*, their immigration laws had hitherto succeeded in keeping out. They feared, too, the drawing off of their native labour supply to the Rand, and held with much truth that their native policy was better than that of adjacent parts of the Union. Above all, they wanted to experience self-government before going into Union and so to go, if at all, on equal terms.

The issue was settled for the moment, not in Rhodesia but in the Union, where the Hertzogites outdistanced Smuts's followers at the general election in March 1920. The pro-Union party in Rhodesia was thereby destroyed before it had gone into action and, at the general election, 12 out of 13 members were returned pledged to responsible government. Having thus secured the requisite absolute majority, they petitioned for self-government. Milner once more played for time, but the award of the Cave Commission revolution-ised the situation. The Commission fixed the amount due to the

Jan.
1921.

---

[1] There were 425,000 natives in reserves covering 19,500,000 acres, 125,000 on Crown lands and 150,000 on farms, etc.

[2] 8,360,000 acres lay within 25 miles of the railways, and 49,600,000 further away.

Company at £4,435,000 with an additional payment for the public works covered by the terms of the Charter, less the value of the extensive lands which the Company had granted to itself or to subsidiary corporations for 'consideration other than cash.'[1] With the prospective debt thus dwindling, the elected members tried again. This time they found Downing Street more amenable. Winston Churchill, Milner's successor, appointed the Buxton Committee which recommended the grant of self-government subject to rigorous safeguards for the natives, the Chartered Company and the railways.[2] Then, at the request of the pro-Unionists who had rallied after the victory of the enlarged S.A. Party at the Union elections of February 1921, Churchill asked a Rhodesian delegation to confer with Smuts in Capetown on its way to London.

The conference which followed was informal. Neither party was in a position to negotiate, but it is certain that Smuts made a strong bid for incorporation. Letters Patent based on the Buxton Report were then published.[3] The debt which Rhodesia must assume was cut down to some £1,100,000; the sale of the Crown lands was entrusted to a Crown Agent; the issue between this modified autonomy and, presumably, Union was to be decided at a referendum held before the end of October. Delegates from all the Rhodesian parties, with others from Northern Rhodesia holding a watching brief, then discussed terms privately with the Union authorities at Capetown. To the dismay of many of his own followers and the wrath of the Nationalists and Labour men, Smuts had to let Parliament rise without confiding to it the terms of the Union's offer. The Opposition objected with justice that, if the Rhodesians accepted these terms at the referendum, the Union Parliament would be faced with a *fait accompli* which it could either ratify or reject but in no wise modify, and that there was nothing to prevent the inclusion by a similar procedure of other Provinces which would still further upset the balance of black against white in an unwieldy Union. However, there was no help for it, because the Union's negotiations were involved in a dispute between the other parties to the settlement. The Company was threatening the Crown with legal proceedings unless it paid the amount of the Cave Award with interest from 1918 on the day that it should take over the government of Rhodesia, and the Crown retorted with a demand for the refund of the large sums advanced to the Company for war expenses.

Oct. 1921.

[1] *B.S.A. Co. Report*, 1920, pp. 59 ff.; Cmd. 1129 of 1921 and *Proceedings* of the Cave Commission.   The Buxton Committee presently valued the public works at £830,000.

[2] There were to be 6 Ministers, a unicameral legislature of 30, with power to add an upper house later; mining and railway bills were to be reserved for H.M. pleasure, and native affairs were, as far as possible, to be subject to the Imperial control retained under the Order-in-Council of 1898 (Cmd. 1273 of 1921).

[3] Cmd. 1573 of 1922.

At last the terms of the Union's offers to the Rhodesians and the Company were published.[1] They were accorded a mixed reception. Chartered shares rose appreciably, the leading newspapers on both sides of the Limpopo spoke well of them and Natalians regarded the wide powers left to the proposed Provincial Council at Salisbury as a welcome concession to the federal idea. Others in South Africa were less enthusiastic; indeed, the Nationalist and Labour parties were frankly hostile, for, apart from any other considerations, the Union was being asked to pay £6,836,000 to the 'great money power' for the Crown lands, railways, public works and the privilege of incorporating Rhodesians, many of whom would certainly resent the loss of an opportunity of ruling themselves for a time. And after all, the Company would still retain the invaluable minerals.

Smuts fought hard to win Southern Rhodesia. He was not offering to pay nearly £7,000,000 for a dozen Rhodesian votes in the Assembly even in the unlikely event that all would be cast in his interests. To him the Union was what the old Cape Colony had been to Sir George Grey, the most important power in Africa. Rhodesia was the railway bridge to the copper of the Katanga and much else in the far north. Already a Union trade commission was on the point of starting for Kenya, and Nyasaland and Uganda were borrowing Union railway officials thus 'giving a wider outlook to the railway policy of the Union.' Smuts visited Southern Rhodesia during the referendum campaign on the incorporation issue. While he was in the country his influence as representative of Botha's *conciliatie* and his own appeal to Rhodesians to take 'the broader point of view, the future of the sub-continent,' told in favour of Union; but once he had gone all the old fears returned, especially the fear of the Poor Whites, a fear intensified by Smuts himself, who spoke of the need of incorporating both Swaziland and Rhodesia in the Union to save the western Transvaalers from becoming *bijwoners* in their own country.

Oct. 1922.   Under these circumstances the Responsible Government Party gained a decisive victory at the referendum.[2] A financial deadlock which arose at the last moment between the Crown and the Legislative Council was averted by the British taxpayer, who performed his appointed function by providing £3,750,000 in quittance of the

[1] *Cape Times*, July 22 and 31, Aug. 1 and 22, 1922. Five Rhodesian seats in the Senate and 10 in the Assembly rising to 17, a Provincial Council of 20, a special grant of £50,000 for 10 years to make up for the loss of advantages under the Rhodes Customs Clause, a development fund of £500,000 spread over 10 years, Union railway rates, a land settlement board controlled by Rhodesians, and the promise that the Union would not take away their native labourers. On the other hand, they were asked to permit free movement across their borders and to accept official bilingualism.

[2] The majority in favour of Responsible Government was 2785 out of a total electorate of 22,000, of whom one-third were women.

amount due to the Company under the Cave Award. The Crown waived its claim to the £2,000,000 of war expenditure; the Rhodesians undertook to pay the Crown £2,300,000 for the much-disputed lands and public works[1] and, on the thirty-third anniversary of the foundation of Salisbury by Rhodes's Pioneers, 'the Colony of Southern Rhodesia' was formally annexed. Sir Charles Coghlan, Sept. long the champion of self-government, formed the first ministry and, 1923. at the ensuing elections, overwhelmed Labour and the ex-Unionist Independents.[2] In that same month, in Northern Rhodesia, the Company handed over the reins to the Crown as represented by a April Governor assisted by a Legislative Council with a minority of elec- 1924. tive members.[3]

Thus the Chartered Company passed out of the ranks of the world's rulers and presently declared its first modest dividend, while the Rhodesian Parliament met, and faced a hopeful budget, the task of finding a port more suited to its needs than Portuguese Beira, the disquieting fact that the customs union would expire at the end of the year, and the knowledge that it lacked Dominion powers and status in that the Imperial authorities had specifically retained a veto on its Native legislation.

South Africa was also considering the question of ports. The Mozambique Convention of 1909 still governed its relations with Delagoa Bay. That agreement had been concluded at a time when the Transvaal was anxious above all things to secure cheap imports and Portuguese Shangaan labourers for the mines. Now, the need for this labour was less and the need for export facilities was growing greater each year. The railway through Portuguese territory and the harbour of Lourenço Marques failed to give adequate facilities, especially to Transvaal coal, while Portuguese officialdom with a mercurial paper currency of its own was frankly an inconvenience at a port full of British and South African business men. The Union therefore denounced the Convention and asked for a share in the control of both railway and port. This the Portuguese refused to give 1922. in spite of a threat to build a rival railway through Zululand to a new port at Sordwana Bay or at Kosi Bay of famous memory. Hence, amid the jubilation of Natalians interested in the cotton areas of Zululand and expectant of a Rand market bereft of duty-free Portuguese sugar, the whole of the Convention lapsed save those clauses which permitted the Union to recruit labour in Mozambique.[4] 1923.

[1] Cmd. 1984 of 1923.
[2] At the elections Coghlan's Rhodesian Party carried 26 seats and Independents 4.
[3] *Northern Rhodesia (Legislative Council) Order in Council, 1924*; J. W. Davidson, *The Northern Rhodesian Legislative Council*, p. 18.
[4] These clauses were renewed in 1925. A new Convention was signed in 1928; *vide infra*, p. 615.

In the course of these negotiations Smuts had fallen in with the wishes of the advocates of white labour by promising to limit the importation of Shangaans to half what it had been before the Rand strike. That promise marked his return to domestic politics. Labour, Nationalism, Natives and finance were all consciously or unconsciously combining to overthrow his ministry. The artificial bulwarks of white labour on the gold-mines were weakening. After the great strike of 1922, the Mining Industry Board[1] had arranged with some success for conciliation boards in the gold, coal and power industries; but it had reported against any extension of the colour bar and recommended that, in the semi-skilled grades where racial competition was taking place, mine managers should use their discretion subject to the Chamber's ratio of one white man to every 10·5 black,

1923.   for what that was worth. Reorganisation of the mines had proceeded on these lines facilitated by a decision of the courts that the statutory colour bar was *ultra vires*.[2] Opponents of the policy complained that the freer use of non-Europeans increased the number of accidents below ground.[3] This complaint was discounted by the fact that many of these mishaps were due to rock-bursts, which naturally became more common as the mines sank deeper and the pressure of the ground above put an intolerable strain on the pillars supporting the roof of the galleries; nevertheless, from another point of view, the situation was disquieting. The use of improved machinery, the elimination of the weaker white brethren and the abolition of mining on contract undoubtedly reduced working costs[4] and increased the yield, but they did it at such a cost to the life of the mines that it was officially estimated that in 1932 half the existing mines would be worked out. If this estimate were correct, some industries more capable of maintaining a civilised society than gold and diamonds must be found and that quickly.

Smuts's opponents determined to conduct that search themselves. There was less to keep the Nationalists and Labour men apart than there had been. Transvaal Nationalist congresses might still reaffirm the principle of secession, but the Free Staters would do what Hertzog bade them do and, in the Cape, the demand for the right of secession had never recovered the vitality it had lost during the elections of 1921 in spite of Sinn Fein example and imported Irish aid. On the other hand, Englishmen were talking now of the 'Commonwealth' rather than of 'Empire' to which the obvious retort had been 'Republic.' The tactful handling of the Indian question by the

Dec.   British Government, the transfer of the defences of Durban and Cape
1921.

---

[1] U.G. 39 of 1922.   [2] *Rex* v. *Hildic Smith*, Nov. 1923.
[3] Figures for 1915–24 do not bear out this allegation (U.G. 14 of 1926, p. 121).
[4] Working costs in 1921 = 25s. 8d. per ton; in Dec. 1922 = 21s. 2d.; prewar = 17s. 11d.

Peninsula to the Union, the indefinite postponement of the abhorred
Conference which was to have defined the powers and procedure of
the Dominions in Imperial matters, the apparent solution of the Irish
question towards which Smuts had lent a helping hand, Smuts's
insistence on 'the equality of nationhood' within the Empire, the
admission by Andrew Bonar Law, a logical Canadian-born Scot and
Conservative Leader in the British House of Commons, that the
Dominions had the right to secede, all had a reassuring effect on the
minds of Nationalists. If the Irish Free State was a Dominion, what
was there to prevent South Africa becoming even as Ireland, at all
events as far as concerned constitutional status? If Canada was to
have her own ambassadors and sign a fisheries treaty with the U.S.A.
on her own account, why not South Africa also? The agreement 1922.
reached by the United Kingdom, the United States, Japan, France
and Italy at the Washington Disarmament Conference on the relative
permissible numbers of their heavy naval vessels, Great Britain's
abandonment of the Japanese Alliance and her philosophic acceptance of the cool reply given by Union ministers to her call for help
against the Kemalist Turks on the Bosphorus, Smuts's return from
successive Imperial Conferences with free hands and the assurance
that, in spite of the French and Belgians in the German Ruhr district,
there would be no great war in Europe for a generation at least, all
proved that the Union was not to be hastily committed to foreign
adventures at the call of others. And if war did come after all, the
visit of a strong British squadron suggested that it need not touch
the Union too closely.[1] There might be obvious profit in the Imperial
connection if it meant a preference on tobacco, wines and fruit and,
though that preference was not confirmed by the British Labour
ministry which took office immediately after the offer had been made,
much of the ensuing outcry arose not from Nationalists or Labour
men exultant at Ramsay MacDonald's victory, but from S.A. Party
men led by the Premier himself, who denied to the Mother of Parliaments the right of review which was universally conceded to
Dominion legislatures.

The Nationalists and Labourites moved steadily towards an
alliance. The Nationalist leaders discreetly pushed secession into
the background; the Labour chiefs declared that the 'democratic
and socialist commonwealth' was merely an 'ultimate' objective;
both, to win over those urban electors who had lost confidence in
the ministry but feared Hertzog's past too much to put him into April
office, publicly exchanged assurances that the votes cast at the next 1923.
election would not be used for cutting the painter. The Nationalists
even played up to non-Europeans. In the Western Province, where
Coloured voters were numerous, they helped to form the African

---

[1] Including the great ships *Hood* and *Repulse*.

National Bond of Coloured Folk in support of Hertzog's segregation policy, while Dr. Daniel François Malan, member for Piketberg,
telegraphed good wishes to a Bantu Conference at Queenstown in
the Eastern Province and an assurance that Africans were 'a pattern
of patriotism' and, as such, entitled to take their places 'side by side
with the Nationalists in the common political arena.' Hertzog, more
daring, sent a subscription as well as good wishes to Kadalie's
I.C.U.;[1] but he was none the less soon calling for a policy which
should protect the 'civilised labour' of Europeans and Coloured
Folk from Bantu pressure.

Feb.
1924.

Hertzog's declaration of policy committed him to finding those
'additional areas' for which the Bantu had been waiting these ten
years and without which no settlement of the Native and, therefore,
Labour problems was possible. It was full time. Councils might work
well in the Transkei and other large tribe areas, though even there
educated natives grumbled at their lack of power and the rank and
file regarded them as ingenious taxing machines; but they were useless to the 2,000,000 natives, nearly half the total, living on the farms.
From the farms and from the reserves, overcrowded by men who
had rarely been shown how to improve their wasteful methods of
cultivation, a stream of permanently detribalised folk poured into
the towns.[2] They came, and their women with them, even into towns
of the Western Province of the Cape, where hitherto there had been
few of them, thus completing the Bantu south-westward Great Trek
that had been going on long before ever van Riebeeck had landed at
Table Bay. Everywhere they threatened to pull down the Coloured
man's standard of life and, *a fortiori*, the white man's. Small and
compact cities like Durban and Bloemfontein handled the influx
well, but elsewhere there was chaos. Parliament tried to meet the
emergency by passing the Urban Areas Act, which laid down a
uniform pass law outside the Cape Province, empowered municipalities to set aside locations and assured the natives of a measure of
local self-government and security of tenure short of freehold.[3]

1923.

Most of the countryside was already in European hands. The
towns were now closed to the Bantu, except on sufferance, at a time
when the black folk were growing daily in political consciousness,
and their more advanced members, cut off by the colour bar from
many trades and industries, were falling back like any Babus on
clerical work, the ministry in native churches, journalism and agitation. Native conferences twice met under the Act of 1920 at Bloemfontein and Pretoria, on the second occasion in the old Raadsaal

1923.

[1] *The Star*, Feb. 7, 1929; Roux, *op. cit.*, pp. 191–2, 207, 363; Patterson, *op. cit.*,
pp. 47, 159–69, 212.
[2] Perhaps 300,000 by 1925 (U.G. 14 of 1926, p. 37). *Vide* Macmillan, *Complex
South Africa*.
[3] Act 21 of 1923.

itself, and yet again at the summons of the Federal Council of the Dutch Reformed Church, an organisation not hitherto identified with such a policy. These conferences complained of passes, the Urban Areas Act, and above all the existing allocation of the land which made self-development in reserves an improbability for most of them and 'differential treatment' of white and black an illusion for all; they also demanded that, since the two northern Provinces neglected their duty of educating the natives, the Union should take over full control of education. That last demand called in question the relations of the Provinces to the Union. The attempt to put those relations on a sound basis proved fatal to the decaying Ministry.

Since Union, Provincial services had been extended widely in all directions, but 'education other than higher' was still the main duty of the Provincial administrations and their main source of expense. There was much to show for the expenditure. Far more children had been brought into the schools since Union than ever before and the training of teachers had been improved out of all knowledge, but such was the Provincial demand for Union money that ministers had soon begun to dilate on the virtues of self-help. They found their audience most unsympathetic. The trend of events was all in the other direction. Even in the Cape, the stronghold of local self-government, the able but autocratic Administrator, Sir Frederic de Waal, had steadily crushed local initiative in the sacred name of efficiency. Local patriotisms, dread of centralisation, fear of un-settling the foundations of Union, and the temporary affluence bred 1916. of war had shelved the report of a commission which proposed to transfer the control of all education to the central authority and to entrust the remaining powers of the Provincial governments to fourteen large Divisional Councils.[1] The ministry refused to abolish the Provisional Councils even when the first span of life allotted to the system by the South Africa Act ended; but twice it cautiously limited its liabilities and then, faced with a heavy deficit on the general revenue and an accumulated deficit of £4,500,000 on the 1922. railways, put its foot down.[2] It drastically modified the old expansive system by giving a mere block grant amounting to 90 per cent. of the 1921 subsidy with an allowance for a 3 per cent increase yearly on the £ for £ basis. It also took away the native pass fees from the Transvaal on the ground that Native policy was a Union concern, and told the Provinces that they might find extra revenue, if they must, in heavier liquor licences.

Crushed by a financial burden which it had never been designed to bear, the Provincial system threatened to collapse. Thereafter it

---

[1] Seven such Councils in the Cape, 4 in the Transvaal, 2 in the Free State, 1 in Natal (U.G. 45–16 and 8 17).
[2] Acts 9 of 1917, 5 of 1921, and 5 of 1922.

1922–
1923.
rained Commissions. Their findings were summed up by the Baxter Commission to the effect that, since education swallowed up 75 per cent. of the Provincial revenues, the Union should provide all reasonable sums for primary and secondary education up to a limit fixed for each Province on a capitation basis, but curtail Provincial powers of taxation as a relief to the general taxpayer.[1] Nationalists inveighed against a 'merchants' report' that struck at education and indicated fixed property as the only sound foundation for local finance; Transvaal Labour rallied to the defence of free secondary education, fruit of its electoral victory in 1914; Natal bristled at the proposed limitations on Provincial freedom. Provincial elections, however, left the Free State as solidly Nationalist and Natal as nominally S.A. Party as before, and merely changed the balance of parties in the Cape and the Transvaal sufficiently to ensure that the opposing forces would cancel out in the Executive Committees and thus leave the last word with their respective Administrators. The ministry failed to come to terms with the Provincial authorities and then made up its mind to carry its Commissions' main proposals.

The prospects of success were by no means hopeless. The ministry had lost much of its prestige; it was suffering from the loss of popularity which attends an over-long tenure of office; it inevitably had to bear the odium bred of the hard times which had dogged its footsteps for the past four years. Unemployment in the Union was less than in many other parts of the world and the Kimberley mines had been reopened,[2] but times were undoubtedly bad. Farmers as a body could not get good prices and some of the diamond producers were once more in difficulties as the competition of British Guiana, Angola, the Congo and alluvial diggers in the Union itself pressed upon them.[3] Retail trade was sluggish; fires which had all the appearance of special dispensations of Providence perturbed insurance companies; business men with long and honourable careers lamented the laxity of the Union's company laws and the ease with which bankruptcy could be used as an ordinary trading weapon. Nevertheless there were signs of better days to come. Sweeping reductions in expenditure and a record traffic as the export of wool, coal and fruit recovered gave the railways a surplus which reduced their accumulated deficits to a mere £770,000. The cost of fighting a widespread plague of locusts was heavy, but the coming budget promised to be more cheerful than any since 1920. It is true that Jagger, restorer of the railway finances, resigned, a martyr to Free Trade, and Smuts's one-time effective majority of twenty-four had been reduced by by-elections to eight; but the Nationalist-Labour Pact had not yet proved itself a reality, and the ministry might still hope to carry on.

1923.

---

[1] U.G. 19 of 1923; U.G. 41 of 1923; U.G. 19 of 1924.
[2] U.G. 14 of 1926, pp. 103, 167.   [3] *Round Table*, No. 59, pp. 603 ff.

The hope was disappointed. Smuts made a belated attempt to save 1924. the situation by further protecting tenants, amending the apprenticeship laws and implementing one of the recommendations of the Mining Industry Commission of 1922 by carrying an Industrial Conciliation Act, which set up Conciliation Boards for all occupations other than agriculture and the public services, left pass-carrying Natives liable to criminal penalties for refusal to work, breach of contract or desertion, and rendered white workers who struck, save under certain conditions, liable to heavy fines and imprisonment.[1] The reply came swiftly. Andrews and his friends, who had recently renamed their International Socialist League the S.A. Communist Party, formed the S.A. Trades and Labour Council as a co-ordinating centre in succession to the shattered S.A. Industrial Federation,[2] and the loosely-allied opposition parties closed their ranks in an attack on the proposed Provincial settlement. There were those who looked to see the Smuts ministry go down fighting, but, for whatever reason, it elected to sacrifice most of its Finance Bill.[3] Amid an uproar from the Cape teachers, who were threatened with salary reductions, it passed a short Bill tiding over the Provinces financially for the time being and promised to lay down uniform scales for teachers' salaries throughout the Union. It was its last act. The loss of a test by-election at Wakkerstroom sent Smuts to the country in the very month that the Responsible Government Party swept the April board in Southern Rhodesia and the Chartered Company ceased to 1924. rule north of the Zambesi. The Provincial issue was lost sight of in the dust and heat of a purely party general election at the end of which the Pact was returned with a majority of 27 in the Assembly.[4] June Smuts, weary with seventeen years of office, handed over the reins 1924. to Hertzog, who gave seats in his cabinet to one Labour leader from the Transvaal and another from Natal.[5]

It was the end of a chapter. Men of British and Afrikaner stock stood shoulder to shoulder in the country and sat together on either side of the House. The old 'racial' lines of division were cut clean across by the economic. The re-alignment of parties was a proof that the two sections of the Europeans had realised that the issues on

---

[1] Acts 20 of 1923 and 15 and 11 of 1924; Sachs, *op. cit.*, pp. 155, 161; U.G. of 1926, pp. 47 ff.
[2] Roux, *op. cit.*, p. 206.   [3] Act 21 of 1924.
[4] Nationalists, 63 seats; Labour, 18; S.A. Party, 53; Independent, 1.
[5] Pact Ministry, June 30, 1924: Gen. J. B. M. Hertzog, Prime Minister and Native Affairs; Tielman Johannes de Villiers Roos, Justice; Dr. Daniel Francois Malan, Interior, Public Health and Education; Col. Frederic Hugh Page Creswell, Defence; Nicolaas Christian Havenga, Finance; Frederic William Beyers, Mines and Industries; Charl Wynand Malan, Railways and Harbours; Pieter Gert Wessel Grobler, Lands; Gen. Jan Christoffel Greyling Kemp, Agriculture; Thomas Boydell, Public Works and Posts and Telegraphs. An eleventh Portfolio, that of Labour, was created in 1925 and given to Walter Madeley, a Labour member. *Vide infra*; p. 608.

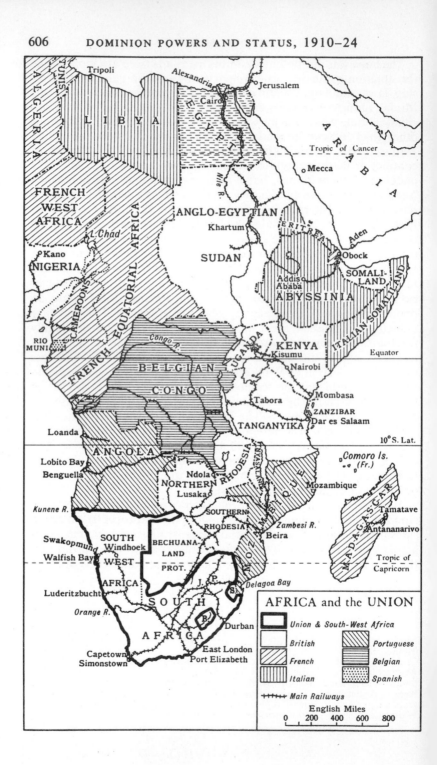

AFRICA and the UNION

which they had hitherto divided were as nothing to the issues raised
by their contact with non-Europeans. South Africans were at last
fully conscious that they stood face to face with 'black Africa and
yellow Asia.' Wherefore, the new Premier, head of a coalition
pledged above all things to the fostering of 'white South Africa,'
addressed himself to a study of that Native Question which had
exercised van Riebeeck in the beginning.

CHAPTER XV

SOVEREIGN INDEPENDENCE, 1924–39

FROM the first opponents had prophesied that if ever a Nationalist-
Labour Pact ministry were formed, it would frighten overseas capital
away from South Africa, but that its career, however nasty and
brutish, would at least be short. The prophecy was belied by the
event. The ministry which took office under General Hertzog lasted 1924–
for nearly nine years, during the first five of which the Union enjoyed 1933.
a prosperity to which it had long been a stranger.

The Pact was a more natural formation than its opponents at first
realised. Nationalist farmers and lawyers might be good Tories and
their allies Socialist townsmen; but they were as firmly united in
hostility to big business as were the American farmer-labour parties
of the day, and in hostility also to General Smuts, who in his time had
been obliged to fire upon rural rebels and urban revolutionaries.
They were, moreover, agreed upon their main political objectives: the
enhancement of the Union's international status and the safeguarding

of 'White South Africa.' Labour men, who from their leader, Colonel Creswell, downwards had fought in the late war, by no means shared their allies' desire for independence; but they could subscribe to the new Nationalist formula of 'the fullest self-determination for the Union,' while Nationalists were sufficiently socialist to favour a regulated economy which should exclude external competition and achieve something of that αὐτάρκεια without which political self-determination would have little meaning. Above all both sections were determined to check internal competition. The Nationalists held to the frontier tradition of 'no equality between white and black' even more unquestioningly than did the majority of their allies or opponents, while Labour demanded the imposition of a statutory colour bar in skilled and semi-skilled trades to replace

1923. the protective regulations that had been swept away by the courts after the unsuccessful Rand rising.[1] Finally, the two sections were drawn together by the rapid Afrikanerising of Labour, especially on the Witwatersrand gold mines. This process was to prove a source of weakness to the Labour Party in the end, since so many of its rank and file remained Nationalists at heart; but it made present co-operation easy, so easy indeed that when an eleventh portfolio, that of

1925. Labour, was created, it was given to Walter Madeley, a Labour man.

The Pact governed during two clearly marked periods. The first period began towards the close of 1924, when the world entered upon a lucid interval of recovery; the second began early in 1930 with the sudden onset of the Great Depression. Thereafter the ministry struggled on for three years more, till, in face of the grave social problems that racked the Union and the growing disorder of the

March outer world, it made way for a National ministry, a Pact on a broader
1933. basis than before, which included the great majority of Hertzog's Nationalists, nearly all Smuts's South African Party men and the remnant of Creswell's Labour following.

Good Times, 1924–30

There seemed to be no doubt about world recovery during the first
1924– halcyon period. Led by England, state after state struggled back to
1930. the gold standard, and the United States, rejoicing in the advent of 'a new economic era,' flooded Central Europe with money which furnished funds for reconstruction, reparations and the service of the American war debt. What wonder that Nationalist South Africa looked to the great republic as heir apparent to England's financial and commercial hegemony and, in a measure, modelled its economic policy on hers? Recovery helped forward and was in turn helped by a growing political stability. Democratic parliamentary institutions

[1] Van der Horst, *op. cit.*, p. 183.

might only survive in full strength in north-western Europe, the United States and the British Commonwealth, nevertheless Geneva became for those years the political centre of the world. The Locarno treaties, the admission of Germany to the League, the appointment of a disarmament commission, and the Pact of Paris gave substance to the growing system of collective security. It would be hard if the Union, thus sheltered, could not advance rapidly towards sovereign independence, all the more since the Irish Free State, least Dominion-like of Dominions, was already forcing the pace within the British Commonwealth.

The fortunes of the Union's Treasury and state railways tell the story of the good years. Nicolaas Havenga, the new Minister of Finance, at once began to remit taxation; next year he restored July South Africa to the gold standard; times were so good a year 1925. later still that honourable members voted themselves increased emoluments. True, the total public debt rose steeply while budget surpluses were cheerfully used to defray current expenses, but the dead-weight of unproductive debt was markedly reduced. Year after year the proceeds of the customs outran the sanguine estimates; the last of the good years yielded substantial surpluses both to the Treasury and the railways, and '. . . to-morrow shall be as this day, and much more abundant.'

Prosperity gave the tottering Provincial system a new lease of life. After all, the new ministry took as the basis of its proposals the Baxter Report of 1924 which had helped to bring down the Smuts cabinet.[1] Since control of education 'other than higher' had always been the sole justification for the existence of the Provinces from the administrative point of view, increased subsidies were henceforward 1925. to be paid to each of them at so much per head of the average attend-ance in their primary and secondary schools. At the same time the central government, illogically enough, relieved them of such expen-sive technical institutions as they chose to hand over, though these had no real place in that 'higher education' which had alone been en-trusted to it under the South Africa Act. This fair-weather scheme answered for the time being, but the rigid definition of the sources from which they might draw local revenue, and the fact that they were accepting one-fifth of the national revenues by way of subsidy, bound the Provinces more closely than ever to the Union Treasury.

The Pact ministry cleared the way for its main legislative pro-gramme, first, by inserting in the South Africa Act a declaration that the people acknowledged 'the sovereignty and guidance of Almighty God'[2] and, next, by issuing a Prime Minister's Circular which defined 'civilised labour' as that of folk who drew pay which would enable them to maintain 'the standard generally recognised as tolerable

---

[1] Act 52 of 1925; *Round Table*, No. 58, pp. 394 ff.   [2] Act 9 of 1925.

20

from the usual European standpoint,'[1] directed Government Departments to substitute this type of labour for the uncivilised type
as far as might be, and bade all concerned in the making of these
changes to use exclusively the Labour Exchanges attached to the
Ministry of Labour and, in cases of difficulty, to consult the Minister.[2]
The Ministry next carried a Wages Act, which embodied the main
clauses of Smuts's little-used Regulation of Wages Act and sought
to protect unorganised labour more effectively.[3] All occupations
other than the public services, domestic service and farm labour
must now either lose the right to strike by registering under the Conciliation Act of 1924 or else, at the instance either of employers or
workers, permit the Executive to fix minimum wages, the proportion
of juveniles to adults in a given workshop and similar matters on the
advice of a standing nominee Wage Board of three members to which
the Government might add one more member for the masters and
one for the men. It remained to be seen whether this Board could
recommend civilised wages that would not deny employment to
ambitious non-Europeans; but it was at least a good augury that
the first such Board got to work at once under the chairmanship of
Frank Lucas, K.C., and set a fine example of which most of its
successors were destined to fall short.[4]

In keeping with its policy of economic nationalism, the ministry
encouraged primary producers, stimulated secondary industries and
broke away as far as possible from external controls. It gave farmers
easy advances through the Land Bank, encouraged small growers
by abolishing the tobacco excise and forbidding the importation of
1925– Rhodesian 'scrap,' and in the interests of its cattle farmers, of the
1926. Transvaal especially, shut out Rhodesian and Bechuanaland Protectorate beasts of less than a given weight. It did its share in
organising the export of fruit,[5] which was already important to the
deciduous growers of the Western Cape Province and was becoming
so to the citrus growers of the Eastern Province and the Transvaal.
1925. Again, with some difficulty, it induced the diamond-producing companies of the Union to come to terms with their competitors in South-
West Africa, Angola and West Africa, and also with a buying syndicate overseas. But since it was careful not to trespass on the small
1927– man's preserves, some years passed before it set up a board to control
1928. the unexpectedly great output of the alluvial diggings near the mouth
of the Orange river, which threatened to bring down the price of
stones with a run and deprive the State of an important source of

---

[1] Circular No. 5, October 31, 1924; *vide* Official Year Book, No. 9, 1926–7,
p. 203.
[2] W. P. M. Kennedy and H. J. Schlosberg, *The Law and Custom of the South
African Constitution*, pp. 545–6.
[3] Act 27 of 1925; U.G. 14 of 1926, pp. 46 ff.
[4] Sachs, *op. cit.*, pp. 161 ff.   [5] Act 48 of 1926.

revenue.[1] Further, it extended the scope of the Workmen's Compensation Acts, amended the Miners' Phthisis Act to provide *inter alia* for the re-employment of such miners as might recover from simple phthisis and tuberculosis in the early stages. It then remembered the needs of some at least of the elderly. Realising that there was as yet neither a Poor Law nor any systematic machinery for poor relief other than such fortuitous aid as might be forthcoming from the Relief Fund, which the Administrator of the Transvaal had raised to salve the worst of the human wreckage left behind by the great Rand strike of 1922, it carried an Old Age Pensions Act. This indeed, ignored the Bantu and Indians, but made some provision for old European folk and, at a lower rate, for Coloured also.[2]

From the start, the railways had undertaken to build rolling-stock without too close a regard to costs. Presently, after more than one failure to enlist the services of private enterprise, the Government decided to set up a state-controlled, and in large measure state-financed iron and steel works at Pretoria. It had to fight its Bill 1927– through the Senate as hard as ever President Kruger had in times 1928. past fought the dynamite monopoly through his Volksraad,[3] but in due time its Iron and Steel Corporation, 'Iscor,' was producing South African steel. Other secondary industries were fostered by a 1925. protective tariff reinforced by dumping duties.[4] At the same time the preferences which had been accorded to United Kingdom goods since 1903 were cut down with the intimation that if Great Britain desired favours she must bargain for them like any other state. In the end, however, to the indignation of many Nationalists who held that South Africa owed nothing to the Navy and that, therefore, the preferences were a veiled tribute to the Imperial power, United Kingdom goods were promised most-favoured-nation treatment. A few years later the British preferences came into the foreground once more, when the Union concluded a commercial treaty for two years 1928. with the German Reich. Existing British preferences were not affected thereby, but the Union did estop itself from offering to any member of the British Commonwealth special privileges in which Germany would not share.

The ministry did not venture to submit the German trade treaty to the hostile Senate for ratification, but it defended it stoutly, partly because it believed that it portended good business, and partly also because it confirmed South Africa's release from Imperial leading-strings. One of the main concerns of the Nationalist majority of the Pact was to emphasise the Union's individuality as a national state. It was a natural policy for a party which had taken shape as a protest against Imperial entanglements and had been nurtured on a

---

[1] Act 70 of 1927 (8). [2] Act 22 of 1928.
[3] Act 69 of 1927 (8). [4] Act 69 of 1925.

fervent desire to protect and develop the distinctive Afrikaner language and way of life.[1] The ministry now took a decisive step towards this latter end. The output of Afrikaans prose and poetry was advancing steadily in quantity and, in many cases, in quality also; indeed, though English showed unmistakable signs of deterioration in the mouths of many of the rising generation of Afrikaners, Afrikaans was rapidly becoming the second language of their English-speaking contemporaries. Accordingly, in 1925, Afrikaans was recognised as an official language of the Union on an equality with English and Dutch,[2] and a grant was provided towards the cost of compiling a standard Afrikaans dictionary. Further, the branches of the Dutch Reformed Church in South Africa undertook jointly a translation of the Scriptures, which, if English, German and Czech experience went for anything, would prove the surest way of consolidating a growing language. The dictionary must necessarily be the work of many years, but the Afrikaans Bible was published with notable success in 1933.

Great advances had been made towards effective national sovereignty within the British Commonwealth during and since the war, and Nationalists, agreeing in this at least with Smuts, were anxious that the still surviving constitutional anomalies should be abolished. And they desired that their abolition should be confirmed in writing. A Convention they could appreciate, but not conventions.

The question of secession had been pushed into the background long before the elections of 1924 partly out of deference to the feelings of the Labour leaders, partly because there was no urgent need to press that issue, and in the background it remained in spite of occasional protests by Tielman Roos, Minister of Justice and leader 1925. of the Transvaal Nationalists. Hertzog indeed claimed for the Union the right of secession, but declared that secession forced upon one section of the people by the other would be 'a flagrant mistake and a national disaster.'[3] It was a view which the visit of the Prince of Wales did much to confirm among Nationalists, who, by a fortunate turn of the political wheel, had been called upon to be his official hosts. Presently, it is true, the Premier claimed the allied right of neutrality in its fullest international sense;[4] but he added that the exercise of that right could only be called for 'in the very improbable case' of Great Britain or a Dominion being declared an aggressor by the League. Improbable indeed in a world which, a month later, April accepted the Kellogg-Briand Pact of Paris and apparently envisaged 1928. henceforward only wars declared against disturbers of the common

---

[1] *Round Table*, No. 73, pp. 125 ff.; M. Roberts and A. E. G. Trollip, *The South African Opposition*, p. 10.
[2] Act 8 of 1925; Kennedy and Schlosberg, p. 111.
[3] *Cape Times*, April 29 and Nov. 17, 1925.   [4] *Ibid.*, March 9, 1928.

peace, 'public wars' which would rob neutrality in its old sense of most of its meaning.

There was universal approval of the formal separation of the 1925. Dominions Office from the Colonial Office, the 'Downing Street' anathematised by so many South African politicians, publicists and historians. But what followed evoked a storm which raged for two long years. Canada and the Irish Free State had recently defined the nationals of their respective states, and the Irish had also adopted a flag from which all reference to the Imperial connection was carefully excluded. The Pact ministry resolved to fulfil the long-cherished wishes of most of its supporters by following the example of these sister Dominions. It experienced little difficulty over the nationality clauses of its Nationality and Flag bill, once Dr. D. F. Malan, Minister for the Interior, had explained that 'Union nationals' must also be 'British subjects, a smaller circle within a larger one';[1] but it failed to secure the adoption of a flag by agreement, and when it went forward with a design of its own, not even the promise to fly the Union Jack at certain times and places could check the fierce struggle that ensued between those who insisted that the Union Jack must be incorporated in the national flag and those who would not have it at any price. Tielman Roos worked throughout for a settlement and it was an open secret that the Premier, fresh from his encouraging experiences at the Imperial Conference, was prepared 1926. to wait for a more convenient season; but Malan was determined to carry the matter through. Mercifully, on the eve of a joint sitting that was to have been followed by a referendum during which anything 1927. might have happened, a compromise was effected.[2] Two flags were adopted: the orange, white and blue of the House of Orange with the Union Jack and the flags of the two old Republics imposed upon the white, and the Union Jack itself which was to be flown officially beside the new flag at suitable points throughout the Union. Both flags were hoisted for the first time over the Parliament Houses on May 31, 1928, the anniversary of the Treaty of Vereeniging and of Union.

The flag settlement had undoubtedly been hastened by the gradual realisation of the meaning of the resolutions of the Imperial Con- 1926. ference which had taken place half-way through the controversy. Hertzog attended that Conference and achieved a great personal success by his friendly yet businesslike bearing. He returned home well pleased with the Balfour Declaration, which defined in general terms the mutual constitutional relations of the self-governing members of the Commonwealth, and still better pleased with the promise of speedy legislation to remove surviving anomalies. If, then, in the words of the Declaration, Great Britain and the Dominions

[1] *Cape Times*, May 24, 1927.   [2] Act 40 of 1927.

were 'equal in status, in no way subordinate one to another,' it followed that the Union, as a recognised state, was entitled to a flag of its own. But it followed also that a state, which was 'in no way subordinate' to another in its 'external affairs,' must see to the conduct of those affairs. From the first the Union had been represented in London by a High Commissioner and had long exchanged trade

1922. commissioners with the United Kingdom; latterly also it had sent commercial representatives to European centres. Nevertheless, even

1925. after the Irish Free State had appointed a minister of its own to Washington, Hertzog could explain that the Union did not have political envoys because their usefulness would not justify the expense.[1] The whole situation was changed by three events: the

1927. Balfour Declaration, the enhancement of the dignity of all the Dominions by the election of Canada to the Council of the League, and the long-delayed despatch of a Canadian minister to Washing-

1929. ton. A portfolio of External Affairs was therefore created and entrusted to the Prime Minister, and in due course ministers plenipotentiary were sent to Rome, Washington and The Hague.

Meanwhile, the needs and desires of neighbours nearer home, in South-West Africa, Mozambique, Southern Rhodesia and India, claimed the Union's attention. In the mandated territory a land dispute dating from the days of German administration, and quarrels between rival factions of the small group of Bastards at Rehoboth, flared up into a repudiation by the majority of these tribesmen of the agreement of August 1923 under which their Raad (Council) had accepted mandated rule by the Union. The authorities had no choice but to restore order by a show of force.[2] On the other hand, Hertzog implemented as a non-party measure and on more liberal terms the agreement which Smuts had made recently with the German Govern-

1924. ment. German nationals in the territory were now to become British subjects unless they expressed a desire to retain their old nationality; German children were to be taught in their mother tongue and, though English and Afrikaans were to be the official languages,

1925–
1926. German might be used freely in the legislature.[3] The Council of Advice made way for a Legislative Assembly of six nominees and twelve elected members, whose powers, rigidly limited for three years to come, might thereafter be enlarged at the request of a two-thirds majority.[4]

Nine-tenths of the Germans accepted naturalisation on these terms. Bitterness there was at the Union's refusal to recognise

1926. German as a third official language, at the new law which demanded from Germans and other foreign immigrants five years of probation for the franchise as against one from newcomers from the Union,

---

[1] *Cape Times*, Nov. 17, 1925.   [2] U.G. 41 of 1926.
[3] Act 30 of 1924; *vide supra*, p. 594.   [4] Act 42 of 1925.

and at the importation from Angola at heavy cost, to the Union 1928. presumably, of some four hundred Boer families whose fathers had trekked away thither from the Transvaal in the 'seventies.[1] Nevertheless, the Germans made no attempt to form a political party, but contented themselves with joining the Deutsche Bund to foster their cultural interests. The Territory prospered, increased its official establishment and borrowed freely for public works from the Union, its only money market. Hertzog, who at that time virtually claimed sovereignty for the Mandatory Power, could look forward to the day when South-West Africa would become 'an integral part of the Union . . . with the full and free consent of the people.'[2]

The Union was less successful in its dealings with Mozambique. The Convention of 1909 which had regulated mutual trade, the share of Lourenço Marques and its railway in the seaborne traffic to the Witwatersrand area, and the recruitment of Portuguese Shangaans for the gold mines had lapsed in 1923. The essential clauses had been renewed in 1925, but five years of hard bargaining passed before a new convention was signed. This agreement assured to the Portu- 1928. guese the high proportion of the Rand traffic which they had enjoyed under the old agreement, cut down the number of Shangaans who might be recruited, and, to the dismay of Rand storekeepers, held over a considerable proportion of their earnings to be spent in Mozambique territory.[3]

The vital connection with Delagoa Bay had thus been maintained at a price, but the ties which bound the Union and Southern Rhodesia together came perilously near to breaking point. After 1923. achieving self-government, Southern Rhodesia was quietly and it may be also godly governed by the veteran Sir Charles Coghlan and, after his death, by Howard Moffat, son of John and grandson of 1927. Robert Moffat the famous missionaries. Both premiers enjoyed the support of a strong Rhodesian Party majority in the single-chamber legislature at Salisbury; no noticeably ill effects followed the grant 1925. of women's suffrage, the first in Africa; revenues rose and the European population increased from some 35,000 to close on 50,000 1924– in seven years as settlers of a good stamp came in from the Union 1931. or overseas. The creation of a standing railway commission on the 1926– model recently adopted by Great Britain and a guaranteed rate of 1927. interest satisfied the British South Africa Company and other shareholders; gold, chrome and asbestos gave encouraging returns; tobacco and cattle soon ranked with gold as the staple products of the colony.

From the beginning, Rhodesians and South Africans had taken

---

[1] U.G. 21 of 1931, p. 24; *vide supra*, p. 362.   [2] *Cape Times*, July 14, 1925.
[3] Official Year Book, No. 15, 1930–32, pp. 561 ff.; Native Economic Commission, 1930–32, pp. 808 ff.

it for granted that sooner or later the colony would enter the Union. That prospect now faded steadily. Rhodesians, who had rejected Smuts's handsome terms and faced the risks of self-government rather than submit to control from Pretoria, official bilingualism and the opening of their lands to Transvaal cattle farmers and their numerous sons, were less inclined than ever to endure these things under a predominantly Nationalist ministry. British in sentiment to a degree as so many of them were, they were repelled by the reduction of the Imperial preference, the German commercial treaty, the new Union flag and nationality, and the steady advance of the Union towards sovereign independence.

Financial grievances reinforced these political antipathies. The Customs Convention, which Rhodes had always regarded as the first step towards closer union, was indeed renewed in 1925; but the Union breached the old system of mutual free trade by shutting out Rhodesian scrap tobacco and cattle below a certain weight.[1] As the Union's export of its secondary products increased, Rhodesians began to complain that the commuted payments, which the Union made on these in lieu of customs duties, were not only inadequate but a positive subsidy to Union citizens. Meanwhile tobacco growers on both sides of the border were overproducing, and the South African Government, whose tariff against overseas tobaccos was designed to be prohibitive, found it increasingly difficult to face the clamour of its own growers against the Rhodesian tobacco that was pouring across the Limpopo. When the time came for a revision of the Convention, the two governments, each anxious to protect its own primary and secondary industries, found the greatest difficulty in striking a bargain. But the Union was far and away the best market for Rhodesian tobacco, and Southern Rhodesia was the only external market in sight for the Union's manufactures with the possible exception of Northern Rhodesia, where great copper fields were being developed. Hence, the Convention was renewed for the last time. The commuted payments were indeed increased, but the importation of Rhodesian tobacco into the Union was limited strictly; each government retained the right to fix its own tariff; Rhodesians began to investigate the possibilities of a railway outlet to the West coast either through Portuguese or Imperial and mandated territory, and when the Union's Minister of Finance defended the new agreement as the bridge that should lead one day to closer political relations, told him bluntly that that day was further off than ever.

Sept. 1929.

Feb. 1930.

To balance this rebuff, the Union definitely improved its relations with the South African Indian community and the Government of

[1] Act 7 of 1925.

India behind it. When the Pact ministry took office, relations with both were strained. Natal had recently deprived Indians of the municipal franchise [1] and the right to buy or lease municipal land,[2] and though Europeans at last outnumbered the Indians in Natal and were increasing in numbers faster than they in the Transvaal, Smuts had refused on economic grounds to give them rights of citizenship. Further, because the voluntary repatriation scheme recommended by a recent Commission had not come up to expectation, he had introduced a Class Areas Bill which provided for the compulsory trading and residential segregation of Indians. This measure he had dropped; but the Pact ministry now brought it forward in a more drastic form as the Areas Reservation Bill avowedly to supplement 'the inducement which is held out to Indians to leave the country.' Shelved for the moment, it was brought forward again in the following Session amid excitement which was not allayed when the Transvaal demanded of all Indian applicants for trading licences certificates of fitness signed by the local authority.[3]

1923–1925.

1921.

1924.

1925.

1926.

At the end of protracted negotiations, the Union Government accepted the Indian Government's proposal that a Conference be held, and shelved the bill once more. Representatives of the two governments met in Capetown, where the Indians by their dignity and skill in negotiation did much to dispel the idea, which had inevitably grown up in South Africa since the cutting of the Suez Canal had separated the two lands, that the word 'Indian' connoted nothing more than an untouchable Madrassi coolie or a Surat storekeeper. In spite of grumblings from Natal an agreement was reached.[4] The Union Government withdrew its bill and undertook to finance more liberally the repatriation scheme which was only getting rid of some three thousand a year, while the Indian Government promised to do its best to make that scheme a success. Moreover, each government recognised the justice of the other's case: on the one hand the right of South Africans to maintain Western standards of life by all just and lawful means, and on the other the right of Indians domiciled in the Union to be permitted to attain to those standards if they so wished. Thus, though the Conference merely maintained the legal *status quo*, it eased the Indian problem for a time and, since it had been a direct Conference between the two governments without Imperial participation, set up a valuable precedent in Intra-Commonwealth relations. The appointment of the Hindu sage and statesman, Srinivasa Sastri, as Agent for the Government of India in the Union established another.

Jan. 1927.

Nov. 1927.

The difficulties created for the Europeans of South Africa by the presence of Indians were as nothing beside those raised by the

---

[1] Ord. 19 of 1924 and 3 of 1925. [2] Ord. 5 of 1923.
[3] Ord. 12 of 1926. [4] A. 1–27.

20*

Coloured Folk and the still more numerous Bantu. Already, in 1922, Europeans in the humbler ranks of society had risen on the Rand to check their competition by force; they and their fellows elsewhere were ready to fight as doggedly as the non-slave-owning whites of the Confederate States had fought in defence of a social system which, if it bore hardly on them, at least paid homage to their whiteness. And never more doggedly than now because of their belief, dating from the misleading census of 1921, that the Bantu were increasing so fast that they would, within measurable time, gain economic and political equality, if not predominance, and bring to pass wholesale miscegenation.

The Pact ministry drew much of its strength from the threatened classes whose standard of life Hertzog had promised to maintain at a level 'generally recognised as tolerable' by Europeans; but since the Coloured Folk also belonged to Western civilisation, the Premier now insisted that they be taken up into it 'industrially, economically and politically.'[1] Not so the Bantu with their lower standards. For them he outlined a scheme of territorial segregation and the erection of a vertical instead of a horizontal colour bar which should divide theirs from non-Bantu society. There were to be separate assignments of land and labour, two social pyramids instead of one, with freedom for every man to rise to the top of his own pyramid. Thus, as so many anthropologists desired, the decay of the tribal system would be checked, and the Bantu be encouraged to 'develop along their own lines' instead of becoming too often unhappy imitation Europeans.[2]

1924.   The omens were not good. The railway administration was already displacing Bantu labourers to make room for Europeans paid at April much higher rates; during a scuffle between the police and Native 1925. demonstrators at the Waaihoek location near Bloemfontein, unauthorised Europeans had fired indiscriminately with fatal results, and in the course of the Session Hertzog had to reprove Transvaal and Free State farmer members of both the great parties for demanding that Natives should be taxed out to work.[3] Nevertheless, the 1925. Premier launched his preliminary programme, which comprised the imposition of a statutory colour bar, the consolidation of Native taxation, and the appointment of an Economic and Wage Commission to report on the state of all sections of the community. He dealt first with the statutory colour bar, seeking to restore the situation as it had been before the Courts, three years back, had declared regulations enforcing that bar to be *ultra vires*.[4] His Mines

---

[1] *Cape Times*, March 26, 1925.
[2] On social conditions and Native legislation *vide* Brookes, *The Colour Problems of South Africa*, Macmillan, *Complex South Africa*; Robertson, *150 Years of Economic Contact*, and *Race Relations* (quarterly).
[3] *Cape Times*, June 26, 1925.   [4] *Rex* v. *Hildic Smith*, Nov. 1923.

and Works Amendment Act therefore debarred Bantu and Asiatics by law from skilled work in the mines, but in keeping with his policy of taking the Cape Coloured Folk in with the white folk in most respects, it classified that Folk together with brown-skinned Mauritians and St. Helenas as 'European' and, therefore, free to take any employment they could get. He next took steps to systematise Native taxation throughout the Union.[1]

The Native Taxation Act, which sought to effect that systematisation, relieved the Transvaal urban Natives considerably but increased the burden on all in the Cape and Natal.[2] The bulk of the taxes paid to the central government were to go into general revenue, while local taxes were to be paid to local Native councils where these existed; but the remainder of both was to be turned into a development fund which would be used in part to supplement the inadequate provision made by the Provinces for Native education.

The Bantu, as the poorest section of the community, had been hardest hit by the new protective customs tariff. The Colour Bar Bill now proposed to shut them out of a variety of the skilled and semi-skilled trades which that tariff was intended to foster. Though regulations had been framed under the original Mines and Works Act of 1911 excluding non-Europeans from such work in the mines of the Transvaal and Free State, that Act had given no authority to discriminate on racial grounds. The amended Bill did. It permitted, indeed, the issue of certificates of efficiency to Coloured men in the widest sense of the term as well as to Europeans; but it shut out Bantu and Asiatics under a statutory bar which could be extended by regulation to any district of the Union. Resisted stoutly by Smuts and the main body of the South African Party and rejected by the Senate, it was carried at a joint sitting in the following 1926. year.[3] Then, because this was not the only measure that had been rejected or amended drastically by the hostile Upper House, Hertzog pared the Senate's claws and made sure that future incoming Prime Ministers should have a friendly majority there. His Senate Act decreed that henceforward the eight nominees who had hitherto been entitled to sit for a full ten years must vacate their seats along with the thirty-two elective Senators at future dissolutions or changes of Prime Ministers.[4]

While the storm raised by the Colour Bar Bill was still raging, the Premier outlined his main segregation programme.[5] In the ensuing session he presented four interdependent measures. Of these 1926. one dealt with the Coloured Folk and three with the Natives, that is, with all who were themselves or one of whose parents had been

---

[1] Act 25 of 1926; van der Horst, *op. cit.*, p. 183; Patterson, *op. cit.*, p. 68.
[2] Act 41 of 1925.   [3] Act 25 of 1926; van der Horst, *op. cit.*, p. 183.
[4] Act 54 of 1926.   [5] *Cape Times*, Nov. 14, Dec. 2 and 4, 1925.

1845–
1877.
1905.

members of an 'aboriginal' African tribe. The Native Bills had their roots in memories of Shepstone's policy of differentiation in Old Natal and the recommendations of the Lagden Native Affairs Commission which had reported twenty years back at a time when Bantu society had been much more homogeneous than it now was. Hence the conception of the scheme was tribal and took little or no account of the many detribalised and even educated Bantu who lived outside tribal areas.

The Representation of Natives Bill proposed to deprive the Cape Bantu of access to the franchise which they had enjoyed on the same terms as Europeans since 1853, and, in exchange, to permit the Bantu everywhere, voting through their chiefs, headmen and councils, to elect seven Europeans who should sit in the House of Assembly except when Native representation was being debated, but should have no power to vote on matters of confidence unless these directly affected Natives. The second Bill projected a Native Council, partly nominated and partly elected by the constituencies defined in the first Bill, which should, under strict official control, pass ordinances binding on Natives only.

The Native Land Bill was intended to fulfil the promise made long ago in 1913 of providing more land for the Bantu. The Premier had to accept the fact that, after more than two hundred years of almost unchecked pioneering, very few large blocks of land remained on which the Union could base a self-contained Bantu society. On the other hand his problem would be simplified if the Cape Bantu lost the right to the franchise, for then they would automatically fall to the level of their fellows elsewhere and lose the right to acquire land outside Native areas in their own Province, a right which, by decision of the Courts, their franchise rights preserved to them.[1] He therefore proposed to regularise, and to extend to the Cape, the practice which had arisen in the Transvaal and Natal of permitting Bantu to acquire land in the areas common to the reports of the Beaumont Commission of 1916 and the local committees of 1918.[2] Financed by rents and other moneys accruing under the scheme, by such grants as Parliament might make and by such savings as they could themselves accumulate, they were to be free, within certain tribal limits and subject to European competition for private farms, to acquire land in the 'committee' or 'released areas.' But even if they acquired all the land in those areas, they would obtain but little additional land, since they were in occupation of most of it already. There was truth in the comment of the Transvaal Nationalist Head Committee that the scheme was 'almost impossible' unless more land were secured by the incorporation of Basutoland, Swaziland

[1] Appellate Division, 1917; *Thompson and Stilwell* v. *Kama.*
[2] *Vide supra,* p. 549.

and the Bechuanaland Protectorate in the Union.[1] As it was, the Bantu two-thirds of the total population must build their social pyramid on scattered foundations which covered in all some 12 per cent. of the surface of the Union.[2] Elsewhere they must be either landless employees or half-free labour tenants or squatters, a class which it had long been the aim of Union policy to draft into the reserves or the ranks of the labour tenants.

Finally the Coloured Persons' Rights Bill left Asians untouched, allowed Coloured men in the Cape and Natal to retain the franchise and, in the other Provinces, permitted those Coloured men who conformed to European standards of life and passed an education test to elect one European to the Lower House at the next general election. Seven years thereafter, if both Houses so resolved, they would receive the full franchise. By thus adopting civilisation as the test of political fitness this last bill enshrined the teachings of Fairbairn and Philip and Stockenstrom, Porter and Solomon, Sauer and Merriman, Rhodes and Hofmeyr, de Villiers, Schreiner and Rose-Innes, and rejected the indefinable principles of blood and race upon which the remainder of the projected code reposed.

The Premier had at last raised the Native issue in all its ramifications and braved the anger of many of his own followers, who from Tielman Roos, his Minister of Justice, downwards were utterly opposed to votes for non-Europeans and persuaded that the Natives had too much land as it was.[3] He left the four Bills lying on the table throughout the 1926 session as he had promised, and then, yielding to the demands of farmer members on both sides of the House, subjected labour tenants in the Transvaal and Natal to the very real penal sanctions and less effective safeguards of the Masters and Servants Act, which had hitherto been reserved for short-term labourers.[4] At this stage, he received the reports of the Economic and Wage Commission.[5] The majority report conveyed the warning that a Wage Board in a hurry might well put half the population, irrespective of colour, out of work in a month, questioned the wisdom of the new policy of Protection, and condemned the colour bar as bad business; the majority and minority reports both repeated that the poverty of the masses was the price·that was being paid so that those in favoured industries might draw wages approximating to the high American rates in a country whose national product only warranted pay for all on a modest Continental European scale.

Disquieted by these reports and harassed by the Flag controversy, 1927.

---

[1] *Cape Times*, Nov. 10, 1925.
[2] In round figures, Europeans, 1,680,000; Coloured, 570,000; Asiatics, 175,000; Bantu, 5,115,000 = 7,540,000 souls. Area of the Union, 302,000,000 acres [Reserves, 22,000,000; Released areas, 13,770,000].
[3] *Cape Times*, Sept. 11, 1925.   [4] Act 26 of 1926.
[5] U.G. 12 and 14 of 1926.

the ministry referred the Non-European Bills to a select committee. It next hurried through the Immorality Act, which prescribed severe penalties for such Europeans and Bantu as might indulge in illicit carnal intercourse with one another, and then turned to survey with what equanimity it might the notable growth of the I.C.U. Shortly before the great Rand strike of 1922, its leader, Kadalie, had been well received at a meeting organised in Capetown by all the local leaders and other representatives of local trade unions regardless of colour.[1] Thereafter, his organisation had gone ahead so fast that by 1925 it could claim in all parts of the Union some fifty thousand members, the vast majority of them Bantu, and had, moreover, gained the support of a young Jabavu, who had been editor of *Imvo* since the death of his father, and of the able Zulu, Allison Champion, secretary of the Native Mine Clerks' Union. In that same year he transferred its headquarters to Johannesburg and, though it thereafter lost ground in the south, it flourished in the north so vigorously that it awakened the fears of the authorities, who ordered the Criminal Investigation Department to keep an eye on it and even managed to work a good many Bantu policemen into its ranks as spies. Most northern trade unionists were either apathetic or hostile, but the S.A. Industrial Federation backed it in its demand for higher pay and, in 1927, urged all white trade unionists without much success to co-operate with an organisation that had just become affiliated to the moderate Amsterdam International.[2] The S.A. Communist Party went further and paid the I.C.U. the compliment of whiteanting it.[3] Kadalie, ill-pleased with this Red infiltration, sent delegates with many reservations to a Non-European Conference, which Dr. Abdurahman of Capetown summoned to Kimberley, a meeting, the first of its kind, which was attended by yet another son of the great Jabavu, Davidson Don Jabavu, now a Professor at Fort Hare and leader of the Cape Native Voters' Association, and by spokesmen of the African National and the S.A. Indian National Congresses.[4] There was little this assembly could do, but it was a warning that a united non-European front was not outside the bounds of possibility. Six months later, in December 1926, Kadalie began to purge the I.C.U. of its Communist members and, in due time, went overseas to present the non-European case at Geneva and perhaps also in the United Kingdom and the United States.[5]

An immediate result of the I.C.U. purge was that the expelled Communists, reinforced by the able foreign immigrant, Bennie Weinbren, began to organise the first genuine Bantu trade unions

[1] Roux, *op. cit.*, p. 206.   [2] *Ibid.*, p. 166; Sachs, *op. cit.*, p. 158.
[3] Barnes, *op. cit.*, p. 97; Roux, *op. cit.*, pp. 168-9.
[4] *Ibid.*, *op. cit.*, p. 182.   [5] *Ibid.*, pp. 171-2, 179.

on the Rand. Thereupon, Tielman Roos, the redoubtable and anti-Native Minister of Justice, went into action. He warmly supported a Native Administration Act,[1] which indeed effected valuable reforms in the sphere of civil justice and governance, but also gave 'the Governor-General,' as Great Chief on the abnormal Zulu model, wide discretionary powers over every Native in the Transvaal, Natal and the Free State. Further, Roos, who was resolved to deal drastically with anyone who put 'dangerous thoughts' into the heads of black folk, saw that the Act should also include the so-called 'hostility clause' which rendered anyone who said or did anything likely to 'promote any feeling of hostility between Natives and Europeans' liable to fine or imprisonment or both.[2]

Despite this threat, Bantu trade unions sprang up along the Rand so rapidly that the indefatigable Andrews was soon able to organise twelve of them with a total membership of three thousand into the Non-European Trade Union Federation, an association which more than trebled its membership in a twelvemonth and promised to supplant the inhospitable and chaotic I.C.U.[3] Nor was the new Federation idle, for one of its constituent unions, the Native Clothing Workers' Union, struck in May 1928 in support of Emil Sachs's white Witwatersrand Tailors' Association and thus helped to achieve a common victory, though, when it struck a little later on its own account, not a white man lent a hand and the magistrates duly punished its leaders. Kadalie, meanwhile, had effected somewhat in Geneva and Paris, but still more in London, where, on the advice of Winifred Holtby, the novelist, and other friends, he arranged that an experienced British trade unionist should be sent out to help him to disentangle the hopelessly muddled affairs of the I.C.U., which had been going downhill ever since he had expelled so many too-competent Communists in 1926. This helper duly came in July 1928 in the person of William Ballinger, by no means the kind of man Kadalie had expected; for he was an honest, downright and tactless Scot who at once set about cleaning out the Augean stables of I.C.U. finance. The amorphous organisation did not long survive the shock. Champion seceded at once and formed the separate *I.C.U. yase Natal* in his native Province, and, in the following February, Kadalie himself resigned, leaving the luckless Ballinger to shoulder the liabilities of the parent body and watch its newspaper, *The Workers' Herald*, die of inanition.[4]

Presently, in unconscious revenge, the moribund I.C.U. precipitated a cabinet crisis. The National Labour Council, whose leaders

---

[1] Act 38 of 1927.
[2] Barnes, *op. cit.*, p. 100; Roux, *op. cit.*, p. 167; Patterson, *op. cit.*, p. 32.
[3] Roux, *op. cit.*, p. 217; Sachs, *op. cit.*, p. 159.
[4] Roux, *op. cit.*, pp. 185 ff.; Sachs, *op. cit.*, p. 158.

had never been reconciled to seeing Labour men playing second fiddle in a predominantly Nationalist administration, expelled nine of the eighteen Labour members of Parliament including the ministers Creswell and Boydell. The Minister of Agriculture then refused to negotiate with the I.C.U. about a recent strike of Bantu workers at the state veterinary establishment near Pretoria. This did not, however, deter Walter Madeley, the sole pro-Council Minister, from receiving an I.C.U. deputation a little later before the Cabinet had debated the wisdom of such a step. Hertzog resigned as the easiest means of getting rid of a now unwelcome colleague, as Botha had done in his own case in 1912, and reconstituted his ministry with a Creswellite, Henry Sampson, in Madeley's stead.[1]

Nov. 1928.

Fallen thus on evil days, divided Labour was challenged by the Communists. Like the ephemeral Coloured African National Bond, the Communist Party had backed the Pact in the 1924 elections, reckoning that such support was a small price to pay for getting Smuts and his 'capitalists' out of office; but whereas the unhappy Bond, its purpose served, faded away, the Reds had increased in numbers and influence. On the other hand, they had speedily discovered that neither capitalistic Nationalists nor Social Democratic Labour loved them; indeed, the latter so regularly refused their requests for affiliation that in the end they gave it up. Thereafter, the Communist Party lost white members rapidly and, centring more and more in the Rand area, became overwhelmingly Bantu. One sign of the change was that it got into touch with Bantu sympathisers outside the Union, notably with the energetic journalist brothers, Maphutseng and Josiel Lafula, founders of *Lekhotla la Bafo* (The League of the Poor) in Basutoland.[2] Another sign was that it fell increasingly under the domination of the Moscow Comintern and, in 1928, in obedience to its ukase, adopted an ultra-red line, reorganised its newspaper, the *South African Worker*, as a predominantly Bantu journal, and appointed as editor of this, the first frankly Communist newspaper in South Africa, the uncompromising young Bolshevik, Douglas Wolton. At the same time, it became fair game for the authorities under the recently passed Native Administration Act.[3]

Feb. 1929.

The Select Committee now reported on the non-European programme. Rejecting Smuts's suggestion that the whole scheme should be submitted to a national convention, the ministry let the Land and Council Bills lie in abeyance and introduced the Native Franchise and Coloured Persons' Rights Bills at a joint sitting. Both were framed on less liberal lines than before, for now two-thirds of the representatives, who were ultimately to be allotted to the Bantu everywhere and for ten years to Coloured folk in the ex-Republics, were to sit, not in the Assembly, but in the Senate which had lingered

[1] Roux, *op. cit.*, pp. 190 ff.   [2] *Ibid.*, pp. 220 ff.   [3] *Ibid.*, pp. 206 ff., 212.

on since 1926 under sentence of inanition. The ministerial vote on the crucial Native Franchise Bill fell far short of the necessary two-thirds majority. Hence the allied Bills were withdrawn and the Prime Minister, yielding to the long-expressed wishes of Tielman Roos, made it plain that a leading issue at the forthcoming general election would be the preservation of 'White South Africa.'

The 'Black Peril' election was fought amid such a chorus of appeals **June** to the hundred-year-old traditions and policies of the Trekkers **1929.** that Sir James Rose-Innes, ex-Chief Justice of the Union, was moved to unavailing protest against this joint domination of the past and the North. It gave the Nationalists a clear majority in the Lower House, and, since the recent Senate Act now came into play, a friendly majority in the Upper. The S.A. Party, divided though it was on the score of Native policy, held its own, but Labour, split into two factions, lost more than half its seats. Creswell and a colleague were indeed given seats in what was still a Pact cabinet, but Labour was now the fifth wheel in the ministerial trek-waggon.[1] Moreover, since most of Smuts's followers were men of British stock and all Hertzog's Afrikaners, party divisions had drifted perilously near the so-called racial line.

During the general election and for some time thereafter, relations between white and black became increasingly strained. Here and **Nov.** there white mobs attacked Coloured and Bantu assemblages, and **1929.** one of them wrecked the I.C.U. Hall in Durban, the last stronghold of that dying association, with loss of life on both sides. Presently, at Durban, the totalitarian-minded Oswald Pirow, who had succeeded Roos as Minister of Justice on the latter's elevation to the Appellate Bench, led Police equipped with tear-gas against Bantu dock-labourers who were seeking to evade the payment of poll-tax. In response, however, to the downright report of Judge Daniel de Waal **1930.** and the standing Native Affairs Commission on these wild doings, the Government appointed a Commission to inquire into the state of urban Natives not only in Durban, but throughout the Union. Further, in spite of Pirow's recent successful show of force and its own parliamentary majorities, it took the prudent and unprecedented step of referring its four Non-European Bills to a Joint Select Committee of the two Houses. On the other hand, it carried a Riotous Assemblies (Amendment) Act, which gave it even wider powers than those it already held under the recent Administration Act by

[1] Second Pact Ministry, June 19, 1929–March 30, 1933: Gen. J. B M. Hertzog, Prime Minister and Native Affairs; Oswald Pirow, Justice; Ernest George Jansen, Native Affairs; Dr. D. F. Malan, Interior, Public Health and Education; Col. F. H. P. Creswell, Defence; N. C. Havenga, Finance; F. W. Beyers, Mines and Industries; C. W. Malan, Railways and Harbours; P. G. W. Grobler, Lands; J. C. G. Kemp, Agriculture; Henry William Sampson, Posts and Telegraphs and Public Works.

empowering 'the Minister' to expel from any given area or, in the case of persons not born in the Union, to deport anyone who 'in his opinion' was breeding hostility between Europeans and non-Europeans.[1] Under this new Act, Pirow promptly gave the I.C.U. its death-blow by expelling Champion from his native Natal.[2] By the end of 1931, Kadalie had retired into obscurity and his ambitious organisation, the first attempt at a Bantu mass-movement, had dispersed itself among a few isolated and short-lived trade unions. At the same time, the S.A. Communist Party committed virtual suicide. During the 'Black Peril' election, Bunting and Wolton had contested seats in Tembuland and the Cape Flats with ill success.[3] Undismayed by the openly displayed hostility and even violence of the police and white farmers in such normally law-abiding places as the Paarl and Worcester in the Western Province, the Party formed the League of African Rights. This, however, it dissolved almost at once at the bidding of the distant Comintern and allowed itself to fall into the hands of Wolton, his wife and the Lithuanian Lazar Bach and their like. These youthful zealots changed the title of *The S.A. Worker* to *Umsebenzi* (*The Worker*), enforced the most rigid discipline, and cheerfully purged their party of such 'right wing, social democratic and vacillating elements' as the veteran Bill Andrews, Bunting, Weinbren and Emil Sachs.[4] Having thus blown out the Party's brains, the Woltons, sorely harassed by the Minister under the new Riotous Assemblies Act, defied the rules they had enforced against others by sailing for their native England early in 1933, leaving *Umsebenzi* at low ebb and the Communist Party out of action for all effective purposes. Not content with these gains, Pirow then struck at Sachs, secretary of the powerful Garment Workers' Union and pioneer introducer of white women from the *platteland* into trade unions. Sachs led his union in a successful strike against a wage-cut in 1931; but when he led it out once more in the

1932. following year, Pirow thrust the Minister of Labour aside and sent in his police to the seat of the trouble at Germiston. The police precipitated conflict by trying to push scabs through the picket line and then turned their mounted section loose to the grievous hurt of many women strikers. Amid a newspaper clamour of 'Moscow' and 'Communism,' a dozen of these women were lodged in gaol and, in due time, Pirow banned Sachs and one or two other leaders from the scenes of their activities under the Riotous Assemblies Act.[5] The Minister of Justice had the satisfaction of being upheld on strictly legal grounds, first, by the Transvaal Supreme Court and then, *longo intervallo*, by the Appellate Division.

---

[1] Act 19 of 1930; Roux, *op. cit.*, pp. 201, 211.   [2] Roux, *op. cit.*, p. 201.
[3] *Ibid.*, pp. 225 ff.   [4] *Ibid.*, pp. 234, 264 ff.
[5] *Ibid.*, pp. 217 ff.; Sachs, *op. cit.*, pp. 73 ff.

BAD TIMES, 1930–34

Discretionary powers and distress were to be dominant features of the grim new world into which South Africa had passed almost without observation since the elections. Two years back, an inter- 1927. national Economic Conference had warned the world that tariffs were setting gold an impossible task in spite of the growing output of the Rand. Presently a wild speculative boom swept the United States. American money streamed westwards out of Europe; European money poured out in its wake, and then the bottom fell Oct. out of Wall Street. That disaster was followed by a rapid decline of 1929. financial stability, world trade and international good manners. It June is true that the French marched out of the Rhineland; but France 1930. and Italy were at daggers drawn, disarmament hung fire, and Hitler's Sept. Brown Shirts appeared as a serious disturbing factor in the heart of 1930. Europe.

In the Union diamonds slumped with the collapse of the American market, wool prices fell heavily to the dismay of farmers who were already afflicted by a drought which was destined to be the longest that South Africa had experienced since the dismal 'sixties, and the ministry noted a dwindling customs revenue. Scarcely realising at first what was happening, it merely began to cancel the tax remissions of the good times, took power to control the import of wheat and sought to protect unorganised workers still further and, so that it might obviate industrial disputes, amended the Wage and Industrial Conciliation Acts.[1] Further, Dr. Malan, Minister of the Interior, while refusing to yield to the clamour of extremists for the exclusion of Jews as such, achieved something of that end by carrying a Quota Act on United States lines, which fixed an immigration quota for those states of Eastern Europe from which most of the Jews were coming.[2] A year later, however, the Ministry took more decisive 1931. action. It taxed heavily in keeping with the growing depression, and began its costly but withal necessary campaign to keep the European farmers on the land. The Land Bank advanced great sums, while price fixing and quota laws placed wheat and mealies on the privileged footing long enjoyed by sugar and, more recently, by butter and cheese.

Worse was in store. While governments here and there were resorting to barter or even destroying unsaleable foodstuffs, a run on the banks, starting in moribund Austria, spread to the Bank of England. In the end an emergency National Government took control Sept. at Westminster and Great Britain went off gold. The shock split the 21, world in two: one half clinging to sterling, the other half to gold. 1931. Each government took what desperate measures it could to save

---

[1] Acts 23 and 24 of 1930.　　　　[2] Act 8 of 1930.

Nov.
1931.
itself and its people. The Union Government did as its neighbours
were doing. During a short special session, Havenga, Minister of
Finance, promised to use 'all the resources of the state' to keep
South Africa on the gold standard, and obliged the two great commercial banks to co-operate with the Reserve Bank in controlling the
outrush of capital to London. He then assumed almost dictatorial
power to regulate currency and exchange and to impose dumping
duties on goods from countries that had gone off gold, gave bounties
Feb.
1932.
to exporters, and levied a primage on imports to finance the bounties.
Three months later he demanded heavy new taxation, while the railways, in spite of the far-reaching powers which they had recently
taken to protect themselves against road competition, also confessed
to a deficit only less imposing than that of the Treasury.

It was some comfort to recall Rhodes's advice and 'look at the
comparative,' since, thanks to its gold mines, South Africa was
suffering less than most other countries. Even so, the scene at home
Sept.
1931–
March
1932.
was forbidding and abroad disquieting, for, profiting by the growing
impotence of the Western Powers, Japan had occupied Manchuria
under cover of a smoke-screen raised at Shanghai. Nevertheless, the
Pact ministry pushed on with what it could of its original plans for
safeguarding 'White South Africa' and enhancing the Union's
Oct.–
Nov.
1930.
status. Hertzog had attended the Imperial Conference which adopted
resolutions that were to be embodied in the Statute of Westminster
of 1931, and thus give legal form to the Balfour Declaration by
freeing such Dominions as might implement that Statute from the
operation of the Colonial Laws Validity Act and other Imperial
checks on their liberty of action. On his return home, he expressed
his satisfaction that at long last South Africa had achieved 'sovereign
independence' and 'finality with regard to (her) constitutional
freedom.'[1]

That last was a bold saying. Signs of coming controversy had
appeared before ever the Prime Minister had set out for London.
The question of the right of secession had emerged almost casually
from the obscurity in which it had long lain, and Hertzog, who had
always held that it was implicit in the Balfour Declaration, insisted
that the right should be affirmed. After his chief's departure, D. F.
Malan, acting Prime Minister and leader of the Cape Nationalists,
linked up that right with the right of neutrality and the divisibility
of the Crown. None of these issues were, however, pressed after the
July
1931.
Premier's return, and when the Judicial Committee, which had
hitherto been chary of entertaining South African appeals, gave
leave to a Cape Native to appeal against the application of the Administration Act to the Cape Province, Hertzog counselled caution.
A constitutional change had meanwhile linked the issue of

[1] *Cape Times*, Dec. 2, 1930, and Feb. 28, 1931.

international status with the Native problem. In accordance with a ten-year-old suggestion by Smuts, subsequent Irish, Canadian and Australian example and a resolution of the recent Imperial Conference, a new Governor-General, the Earl of Clarendon, had been Jan. appointed solely on the advice of South African ministers to repre- 1931. sent the King's Grace and in no way the British Government. It followed that, as John Mackenzie had demanded in his struggle with Sir Hercules Robinson in the 'eighties,[1] the High Commissionership 'in and for South Africa' was bestowed elsewhere, upon Sir Herbert Stanley. Sir Herbert was also 'High Commissioner in the Union of South Africa for H.M. Government in the United Kingdom,' an office corresponding to that of the Union's High Commissioner in London, who, with his colleagues from other Dominions, was now given high precedence at Court; but as High Commissioner in the old style he exercised such control as the Imperial Government still retained over Southern Rhodesia, and was responsible for the administration of Basutoland, Swaziland and the Bechuanaland Protectorate. The separation of the two offices was, on the whole, welcomed by the Bantu inhabitants of the High Commission Territories. Their High Commissioner was now definitely 'the King's man,' who should stand between them and Union influence.

There had been indications for some time past that the way of the King's men was not to be an easy one in all the lands from Capetown to Nairobi. Europeans settled among Bantu tribesmen in all that vast tract had been perturbed by a White Paper,[2] based mainly upon the report of the Hilton Young Commission of 1929 on the governance of East and Central Africa,[3] in which the British Labour ministry pointedly reiterated the warning given some years back to Kenya that in lands where few white men dwelt among many black, black interests must come first. The retort was immediate and widespread. Smuts at Oxford called for a meeting of delegates from the Nov. territories of Central, East and South Africa, which, drawing upon 1929. the Union's long experience, should show the British Government the Native policy it ought to pursue.[4] A Kenya delegation hurried to London; Northern Rhodesians and men from Nyasaland talked of joining hands with each other and even with Southern Rhodesians to escape the White Paper policy, while leading Transvaal Nationalists hopefully foreshadowed a Dixie Line drawn well to the north of the new Northern Rhodesian copper belt, which should cut off the colour bar states to the south from the colour-blind territories to the north.[5] Finally, Hertzog, in London for the Imperial Conference and in close

[1] *Vide supra*, pp. 398 ff.　　　　　　　[2] Cmd. 3573–4 of 1930.
[3] Cmd. 3234 of 1929.
[4] *Cape Times*, Nov. 4, 1929; Smuts, J. C., *Africa and Some World Problems*, p. 68.
[5] *Cape Times*, Oct. 20, 1930.

Oct.
1930.

touch with the Kenya delegation, while deprecating interference in the domestic concerns of the Union, begged that the governments concerned should consult together before any of them adopted a Native policy which differed markedly from that of the Union.[1]

The quality of the Union's Native policy was still further revealed by current legislation. Hertzog indeed declined to entertain suggestions that the Union Parliament, as a sovereign body, should amend the safeguarding clauses of the South Africa Act and then deprive the Cape Bantu of the franchise by a bare majority. But the mass of opinion behind him was set upon cancelling the value of that franchise as far as possible. It had ready to hand the report of a Select Committee, which, at the time of the first introduction of the Prime Minister's non-European programme, had recommended the extension of the male franchise of each Province to European women pending a decision on the segregation policy.[2] The ministry went even further than the Select Committee. In spite of past promises to bring the Coloured Folk over to the European side of the line, the

1930.

vote was given to European women only on the basis of the manhood suffrage which had prevailed in the ex-Republics since the days of

1931.

the Great Trek.[3] Next year, inevitably, European men were relieved of the educational and financial restrictions, which had hitherto prescribed for all in the Cape and Natal[4] and had recently been instituted in South-West Africa.[5] These were crucial acts. The frontier principle of a purely racial franchise was entrenched and extended to the Cape, the first and last stronghold of liberalism in the Union; the South Africa Act was outflanked, and by practically doubling the European vote the value of such votes as might be accorded to Bantu and Coloured men was heavily discounted.[6] Nor was this all. The weight of the non-European vote was scaled down still further in practice by a measure in terms of which such folk could, on challenge, be compelled to prove in the Magistrate's Court, either in person or by proxy, their right to be enrolled under pain of being struck off without more ado.[7]

Other measures revealed the implications of what had been done. The idea that the towns with their amenities were the preserve of

1930.

the European minority had been emphasised by the so-called Stallard Commission of 1922, which recommended that because the 'commingling' of whites and blacks was undesirable, Africans must be allowed to enter 'the white man's towns' only when they were needed to work for the said white folk and must then depart to their

---

[1] *Cape Times*, Nov. 3, 1930.   [2] S.C. 12–26.
[3] Act 18 of 1930.   [4] Act 5 of 1931.   [5] Act 22 of 1929.
[6] Registered voters, 1932: European men, 435,177; European women, 415,003 = 850,180. Coloured, 25,024 (Natal, 326); Asiatics, 1695 (Natal, 15); Bantu, 12,272 (Natal, 1) = 38,991.
[7] Act 35 of 1931; Patterson, *op. cit.*, p. 36.

own place till they were wanted again on the morrow. The Natives' Urban Areas Amendment Act now still further curtailed the right of the Bantu to move into towns and live there freely.[1] Again, after all the necessary preparations had been made for including them, no account was taken of non-Europeans at the decennial census on the grounds of expense; hence the swollen electorate must judge of the non-European programme, when next it should come forward, in the light of the 'alarmist' census report of 1921, which suggested that the Bantu were increasing so fast that they would speedily swamp the Europeans. In terms of the Administration Act of 1927, whose chief feature was the enlargement of the powers of the Governor-General over Natives, a new Native code was applied to Natal.[2] This code, inter alia, embodied a principle which had been applied by the Cape Government to the troubled Transkeian territories in 1897,[3] whereby the executive was allowed to withhold from a Native the rights of habeas corpus for at least three months and deny to the Courts all power of questioning its acts. Then, in spite of the opposition of Smuts and the bulk of the S.A. Party and the protests of the heads of nearly every Christian and Jewish church in the country, a Native Service Contract Act was passed.[4] By means of heavy fees levied on their landlords the multitudinous Bantu squatters, who lived in such rural areas of Natal and the Transvaal as might be proclaimed,[5] were to be drafted off to the reserves or be transformed into labour tenants bound to work upon their lords' lands for anything from the customary 90 days up to 180 days in each year on the days of their lords' choice. On the other hand, markedly more liberal measures were applied to the extensive and crowded Cape Native Territories. There, the Transkeian General Council, which had been formed in 1895 by the unification of the District Councils of the four more or less organised sections of those Territories, had worked so well that, from 1911 onwards, the District Council system had been extended to West Pondoland. Later, in 1927, it had been extended to East Pondoland, the last remaining area in those parts, and the Councils of the Two Pondolands had been combined in the Pondoland General Council. Now, between 1930 and 1932, the Transkeian and Pondoland General Councils were combined in the United Transkeian Territories General Council.[6] Staffed partly by European officials and partly by indirectly elected Bantu leaders, this famous 'Bunga,' sitting at Umtata, was to advise the authorities on many matters and was destined, as time went by, to acquire limited executive and legislative powers.

1931.

1932.

[1] Act 25 of 1930; Barnes, op. cit., p. 139.   [2] Proc. 168 of 1932.
[3] Walker, E. A., W. P. Schreiner, p. 99.   [4] Act 24 of 1932.
[5] No districts were proclaimed under this Act. Vide infra, p. 643.
[6] Proclamations No. 279 of 1930 and No. 191 of 1932; Kennedy and Schlosberg, op. cit., pp. 451 ff.

Meanwhile, such was the complexity of life in South Africa, there were non-Europeans whom the Government felt constrained to treat more circumspectly than its Bantu. Though the citizens of Cape-town had long been accustomed to see sedate Japanese families ashore for a few hours from the immigrant ships that were carrying them to South America, very few Japanese had availed themselves of the narrowly restricted right of entry that had been allowed them 1931. under the Immigration Act of 1913. Now, however, in view of Japan's increasing interest in the trade of Africa, her merchants, travellers and students were given much freer access to all parts of the Union other than the Free State. And since these newcomers were no longer to be classed as prohibited immigrants, they would presumably be eligible for the trading licences which were being with-held as far as possible from Indians.

Meanwhile, though it still had a majority of thirteen in an June Assembly of 148 members, the Pact ministry was failing. It had been 1931. obliged to cut the pay of its numerous employees; it could not do all that was expected of it by distressed agriculturists; it had never had the confidence of one section of Labour and was fast losing that of the other; it was itself divided, the Cape *versus* the rest, on the score of Provincial policy, that destroyer of cabinets, and the Opposition had acquired the first popular plank for its platform these many years past by calling for the abandonment of the gold standard.

The connection between gold and the Provinces was close and obvious. Even before the depression the Provinces had been making heavy weather, and now they were drifting on to the rocks. The ministry, which in its opposition days had staunchly upheld the Provincial system, swung round uncertainly towards the idea of its abolition or at the least central control of its finance tempered by 1931. administrative devolution. As for the gold standard, though the demand for sterling that had followed Great Britain's lapse had soon slackened and most of the exported capital had returned to the Union in one form or another,[1] the controversy and the closing down of some of the older Rand mines had convinced a growing number of South Africans that if present working costs were maintained, the end of the gold industry on its present scale and, therefore, the end of the South Africa they knew were plainly in sight.[2]

The Provincial problem raised big issues. In South Africa, as in all post-war parliamentary states, the legislature was fighting a losing battle with the executive. The growth of centralisation, ministerial lawlessness and the creation of administrative crimes had been most marked in the Pact's handling of the Native problem, but assuredly it had not stopped there. Rather was it spreading against a

[1] *Round Table*, No. 90, pp. 453 ff.   [2] *Ibid.*, No. 85, pp. 188 ff.

background of reviving Fundamentalism in some of the more ardently Nationalist areas of the Union, a revival which found its sharpest expression in the persecution by some of his colleagues of Dr. Johannes du Plessis, one of the finest ministers of the Dutch Reformed Church, for opinions which would have passed for the mildest liberalism in Western Europe. The Minister of the Interior, Dr. Malan, himself a minister of that Church, demanded a veto on university appointments mainly because he was dissatisfied with the meagre instruction given in Afrikaans at many of these institutions. Smuts and Jan Hendrik Hofmeyr, nephew and namesake of Rhodes's sometime friend and ally, saved for Parliament much that Malan desired to take for his office, but they had to yield to him wider powers of financial control than before, especially over the smaller universities. In such circumstances, the S.A. Party, formerly the advocate of radical reform, would not hear of the abolition of the Provinces which controlled nearly the whole of the rest of the educational machinery of the country. It demanded a clear statement of policy, but none was vouchsafed beyond a promise that no change would be made till after the next general election. Hardly had that promise been given than the rural and bankrupt Free State threw itself on the mercy of the central authority, which took it over and appointed a commission to draft a scheme of administration for such other Provinces as might give up the struggle.

1929 onwards.

1931.

1932.

   Most people, other than the more robust Nationalists, now looked for some relief to the Imperial Economic Conference at Ottawa. There Havenga upheld the high reputation which South African statesmen had long enjoyed at such gatherings, and returned home with promises of substantial advantages in the British, Canadian and Colonial markets. These were made good as soon as the Union-German treaty of 1928 had been suitably modified. On the other hand, it was presently revealed that one of his colleagues had offered subsidies to two Italian shipping companies, which would, it was hoped, further the Union's trade with West and East Africa and the Mediterranean, spur on the Union-Castle line to higher endeavour and carry away the subsidised meat which the Union was supplying to the Italian army.

July 1932.

   The Finance Minister's well-earned prestige and success could not save the tottering ministry. The Provincial struggle first inflamed the party struggle and then threatened both the great parties with disruption. In all parts of South Africa, men, by no means all of British stock, lamented the spread of discretionary rule, the marked importation of politics into the public services, the official thrusting forward of Afrikaans, which was, they held, well able now to make its own way, the slackening grip of the Lower House on the public funds for which de Villiers Roos, the courageous Auditor-General, repeatedly censured ministers and honourable members, the thrusting of the main burden of taxation on the townsfolk and Natives, and the ferocity of a party struggle which seemed to them to turn mainly on personal rivalries. These discontents found an outlet in widespread talk of a Centre Party, while in central and coastal Natal, intensely British in sentiment, federalist by tradition and hard hit by the depression, they came to a head in a movement for secession. Without going so far, the Natal members of the S.A. Party formed themselves into a distinct party pledged to federalism, and only rallied again to Smuts's standard on condition that the reunited party should work for an extension of power to all the Provinces.

Sept.–
Dec.
1932.

Party discipline and enthusiasm were fast deserting the Nationalists and it was only by dwelling on the threat which the Bantu everywhere and the 'English' of Natal portended to all things Afrikaner that they narrowly won a by-election in the combined rural and railway constituency of Colesberg. Then the S.A. Party beat them decisively at Germiston and increased its majority at a Provincial by-election elsewhere on the Rand. Realising that these majorities were against the Government rather than for his own party, Smuts called upon divided and impotent Labour to help him to carry social and industrial reforms. Forthwith a number of Labour leaders moved over to his side.

While men's nerves were thus tautly strung, Tielman Roos descended from the appellate bench and declared for a non-racial National Government and the abandonment of the gold standard. The response was immediate, especially from sections of the ministry's following; there was a renewed and unexampled flight from the South African £, and, within ten days of Roos's challenge, the Union had gone off gold.

Dec.
27,
1932.

The country soon adapted itself to the abrupt change; money once more became plentiful; the gold mines reaped a high premium and envisaged vast schemes of development, and the ministry, during its last brief moments, began to ease the burden of the recent emergency taxation. Negotiations between the Roosites and the S.A. Party failed; but, to the general surprise, Hertzog and Smuts joined hands and formed a coalition cabinet with the former as Prime Minister and the latter as second in command.[1]

March
31,
1933.

In seeking to justify this alliance to doubting followers, Hertzog pleaded that the rejection of his rival's outstretched hand would have

---

[1] Coalition Ministry: General J. B. M. Hertzog, Prime Minister and External Affairs; General J. C. Smuts, Justice; N. C. Havenga, Finance; Patrick Duncan, Mines; P. G. W. Grobler, Native Affairs; Oswald Pirow, Defence, and Railways and Harbours; J. C. G. Kemp, Agriculture; Colonel Deneys Reitz, Lands; Adrian Paulus Johannes Fourie, Labour; J. H. Hofmeyr, Interior, Education and Public Health; Senator Charles Francis Clarkson, Public Works and Posts and Telegraphs; Richard Stuttaford, Without Portfolio.

driven the Opposition into ineluctable hostility to nationalism, and Smuts urged that a party victory would have been barren and dangerous. Both could point to more compelling causes. The recent census had revealed a drift from the countryside to the towns; the 1932. Native Economic Commission had reported that large numbers of Bantu were becoming poorer and, in some parts, were faced with 'mass starvation';[1] then, to emphasise the findings of the Wage 1932–Commission of 1926 that South Africa was economically one, a 1933. Poor White Commission[2] had reported that 'nearly one-fifth of the European families in South Africa lived in dire poverty.' As if all that were not enough, storm-clouds were banking up on the horizon. At the New Year of 1933, Hitler had become master of the Reich; two months later credit collapsed in the United States; on March 27 Japan gave notice of withdrawal from the League of Nations.

This compulsion and the wave of good feeling summoned up by May the very act of coalition carried the allied parties to overwhelming 17, victory at a coupon election.[3] The new ministry could count on a 1933. very mixed and loosely compacted majority of one hundred and forty-four as against a tiny and divided Opposition of six. Havenga, the Finance Minister, secured for the state a share of the gold premium large enough to wipe out the accumulated deficit and furnish generous assistance to farmers, notably by saddling the tax-payer with part of the interest due on farm mortgages accompanied by a threat, in the true Gracchan spirit, of confiscatory action against such creditors as should demand more than five per cent. in all upon such bonds. Further, seeing that the times were dangerous, Pirow launched a five-year plan to build up his country's decayed defences. He could trust the British to look after the sea under the Simonstown Agreement, but he must provide for landward defence at least up to the line of the Limpopo and Kunene rivers. He therefore projected a striking force of 56,000 men consisting of the small Permanent Force, twenty-four Active Citizen Regiments with as many more in reserve and an Air Force of some six hundred fighters and bombers. Behind these would stand one hundred thousand riflemen, for the most part mounted, and behind those again the levy of all able-bodied white men up to the age of sixty. In the last analysis, fully 275,000 Europeans would thus be available besides numerous non-Europeans for non-combatant purposes.[4]

A movement for the fusion of the two great parties was now set on foot in rural areas. That movement detached a group from either

---

[1] U.G. 22 of 1932.   [2] *The Poor White Problem* (especially Vol. III.).
[3] Ministerialists, 144 (Nationalists, 75; S.A. Party, 61, including the Union's first woman M.P.; Creswellite Labour, 2)—Independents, 6 (Nationalists, 2; S.A. Party, 4), pledged to Coalition principles—Opposition, 6 (Labour, 2; Roosites, 2; Natal Home Rulers, 2).
[4] *Cape Times*, April 24, 1934.

wing of the ministerial phalanx. Dr. D. F. Malan, as protagonist of the Cape, had differed sharply from some of his colleagues in the late ministry on the score of Provincial policy. He had then declined office [1] and had only accepted the Coalition coupon for himself and his followers on condition that they should be free to withhold their support if Nationalist principles were jeopardised. He now held that the state had not taken nearly enough of the gold premium and, strong in the support of the Cape Nationalist Congress and much of the party press, condemned Fusion as truckling to capitalism and imperialism. At the other extreme, Colonel Charles Stallard, an independent-minded S.A. Party member from the Rand, held that the Government had endangered the gold industry by taking too much and was threatening to weaken the common front in face of the perils that overshadowed the Empire. He therefore set himself to oppose any further advance towards sovereign independence, and inevitably became the rallying centre for those men of British stock, scattered in urban centres and along the coast belt from Zululand to Port Elizabeth, who saw in Fusion at best an Afrikaner device to save Smuts from dependence on a predominantly British majority, and at worst a conspiracy to hasten the severance of Imperial ties.

1933–1934.

Feb. 1934.

Renewed discussion of status completed the hiving off of parties which Fusion talk had begun. The Union's prestige had recently been enhanced by the election of Charles te Water, its High Commissioner in London, as President of the League Assembly and the appointment of ministers at Paris and Berlin. Steps were now taken to amend the South Africa Act in accordance with the Union's international status, and to adopt certain portions of the Statute of Westminster of 1931. The debates were preceded by a welcome visit by Prince George [2] and by negotiations between Malan and Hertzog in which the former tried to entrench the right to conduct republican propaganda within the fold of the projected Fusion Party, and to secure the appointment of a locally born Governor-General as in Australia, the abolition of appeals to the Judicial Committee, the elimination of all reference to British subjects from the definition of Union citizenship, and the specific acknowledgment of the rights of neutrality and secession and the divisibility of the Crown. The Premier returned answers that were not satisfactory to the Malanites; but he had also to assure his S.A. Party allies that Fusion terms had not been prejudiced by these domestic negotiations and that neutrality, secession and divisibility were 'matters of interpretation' on which he himself and Smuts could agree to differ. [3]

1934.

The ensuing Status Act [4] affirmed the status of the Union as 'a

---

[1] Roberts and Trollip, *op. cit.*, p. 7.
[3] *Cape Times*, Feb. 16 and 19, 1934.
[2] Afterwards the Duke of Kent.
[4] Act 48 of 1934.

sovereign independent State' as defined by the Balfour Declaration
with its reminder of common allegiance to the Crown; regulated the
use of the Royal Seal which was entrusted to the Union on Irish
analogy, and proclaimed the Union Parliament the 'sovereign legislative body' without whose specific Act no future British legislation
was to apply to South Africa. Though by substituting 'Act' for
'consent' ministers had virtually amended the covering Statute of
Westminster, they accepted important amendments. The King or his
representative might still act without or even against the advice of
his Union ministers where that power was 'expressly stated or
implied,' and enjoy the 'existing conventions' which protected his
right to summon, prorogue or dissolve Parliament. Legislation
was promised to safeguard Provincial rights that might be endangered by the abolition of 'reservation for His Majesty's
pleasure.'

The passage of the Status Act was helped on by reviving prosperity
and the good temper that went therewith. The long drought had
broken, and though it had been followed by severe floods and unprecedented swarms of locusts, the public revenues were so good
that the emergency aid extended to European farmers the year before
was continued, extensive schemes were set on foot for their further
rehabilitation, and money was provided for the development of the
export of meat. As for the townsmen, taxation was reduced, the
scales of compensation for workmen's compensation and miner's
phthisis raised, help offered to municipalities for slum clearance, and
provision made for the gradual disappearance of the export bounties.
The railways launched forth on a ten-year plan for the improvement
of their main lines, while the Cape Province struggled to its feet once
more and its fellows showed hopeful signs of recovery.

At the close of this cheering Session the terms of Fusion were
published. As these were little more than an expansion of the Coalition programme,[1] the Malanites decided to maintain their identity July–
as a 'Purified' Nationalist Party, and the small Stallard group formed Aug.
a Dominion Party, which bade fair to attract urban voters who felt 1934.
that they were being taxed unduly for the benefit of the already over-
represented rural electors; but the great mass of the old Nationalist
and South African parties fused as a United Party commanding Dec. 5,
some four-fifths of the seats in the Assembly, in which the Malanites, 1934.
a mere nineteen strong, would play the necessary part of His
Majesty's Opposition.[2] It only remained for Tielman Roos to declare
his adhesion to the United Party to whose formation he had given March
the initial impetus. It was his last public act. A month later he died. 1935.

[1] *Cape Times*, June 6, 1934.
[2] The two main parties were thus the United National South African Party and
the *Gesuiverde Nasionale Party*.

DANGEROUS TIMES, 1935 ONWARDS

To Hertzog, Fusion was the natural sequel to his long and successful struggle to win equal recognition for his own people and their way of life and to convince all concerned that the ties which bound the Union to the United Kingdom were indeed 'light as air'; but he was handicapped in his attempt to weld all Europeans who truly put South Africa first into a single people by the inevitable weaknesses of a composite Ministry.[1] Those weaknesses, discernible from the start, became obvious as the enthusiasm for Fusion died away. The Cabinet was strained by personal antipathies and the rivalries of North and South, town and countryside, Liberal and Conservative, burdened by more than one politically necessary incompetent, and led by two elder statesmen who confessedly did not see eye to eye on matters of the first importance. One wing of its supporters sympathised with much that the Dominion Party stood for, while the other and larger wing was not far separated from Malan's 'Purified' Nationalists. And those Nationalists could be dangerous, for though they were only a minority party as yet, they were well disciplined and supported by the semi-secret *Broederbond*. This society had been founded in 1918 as a purely cultural association. Led by its executive committee, 'The Twelve Apostles,' which met in private amid a constant mutual inspection of credentials, it had since gone into underground politics to such an extent that it now exercised a decisive influence on Nationalist policy and, having enrolled Malan himself as a sworn member, naturally regarded his party as the best instrument for the attainment of its avowed aim of an independent and exclusive 'Kruger' republic. Hertzog openly expressed his alarm, not so much because the 'Purified' Nationalists had made a profession of republican principles necessary for party membership, as because no Afrikaner was, in his belief, safe from the machinations of 'The Twelve.' And the Prime Minister might have added that the British were even less safe, because the last publicly acknowledged *Broederbond* pamphlet had proclaimed that 'the solution of South Africa's ailments' was that *Broederbonders* should rule the land.[2]

However that might be, good times at home and increasingly dangerous times abroad gave the Fusion Ministry a much longer tenure of office than had at first seemed possible. There could be no doubt about the good times. Thanks to its gold, South Africa became

[1] Roberts and Trollip, *op. cit.*, pp. 10 ff.; C. M. van den Heever, *Generaal J. B. M. Hertzog*, pp. 600, 682; A. C. Cilliers, *General Hertzog en Hereniging*, p. 15.
[2] J. Hatch, *The Dilemma of South Africa*, pp. 46 ff.; Barnes, *op. cit.*, pp. 154 ff.; Davidson, *op. cit.*, pp. 45, 154–8; Roberts and Trollip, *op. cit.*, p. 12; G. D. Scholtz, *Dr. N. J. van der Merwe*, pp. 300–1, 304–5.

one of the very few well-to-do states in an impoverished world. Secondary industry had, it is true, outstripped the gold-mines as the Union's chief producer and was footing a larger wage bill than these had ever done, since it employed a higher proportion of well-paid Europeans; but gold represented from fifty to seventy per cent. of the annual value of the Union's exports,[1] and the mines were far more profitable to the Treasury than were the scattered secondary industries. By the New Year of 1937 the gold mines were giving the State one-fourth of its ordinary revenue and one-third of its receipts on loan account, and might have given it more had not the Treasury and Chamber of Mines agreed that the life of the vital industry must be prolonged as far as possible. Hence the companies cheerfully mined low-grade ore, which the premium had rendered payable, and spent great sums in developing the western extension of the Reef which curved away westward towards Potchefstroom. Investors were soon rejoicing in an average annual return of 25 per cent., and, as the mines throve, secondary industry and transport prospered, imports poured in, and year by year nearly every item of revenue exceeded the sanguine estimates. In spite of considerable reductions of taxation, notably of the income tax, ordinary revenue rose in four years from 1934–£34,000,000 to £43,000,000 and yielded withal a total surplus of 1938. £19,000,000. The Railway and Harbour administration, whose budget was now almost commensurate with that of the state, revelled in surpluses of like proportions.

These golden fruits were garnered at the cost of prolonged speculation such as the Rand had not known since the half-forgotten days of its heady youth. For a generation past, Rand mining, one of the most efficiently organised big industries in the world, had been a safe and predictable undertaking and the price of gold at 85 shillings the ounce had been as stable as Native money wages. Now, however, the speculative price of gold, rising as high as 140 shillings, was added to the two other variable factors: the price of stores and European wages, at a time when there was a dearth of gilt-edged securities. Consequently everyone who had cash or credit dealt in 1932– 'Kaffirs,' and within two years the Johannesburg clearing-house 1934. returns had leaped up four-fold. There was, moreover, such a rush of population to the Rand towns that all the other Provinces had to give up seats in the Assembly to the Transvaal at the quinquennial delimitation of 1938, while the building boom that started in Johannesburg and spread to other urban centres of the Union taxed the country's resources in labour and material to the uttermost.[2]

[1] In 1935 gold amounted to £71,000,000 out of a total export of just over £100,000,000.
[2] The estimated value of new building plans passed in Johannesburg rose from some £1,600,000 annually to £6,000,000 during the first half of 1937.

Meanwhile, Johannesburg the Golden, whose towering skyline and
Sept. municipal boundaries were thus changing overnight, celebrated its
1936. fiftieth anniversary with an Empire Exhibition.

Despite the pressure which bears down on ministers in times
abounding, Havenga, Minister of Finance, and Pirow, Minister of Defence and Communications, fought hard to divert as much as possible
of the golden stream to long-range purposes. Pirow applied the bulk
of his surpluses to the wiping out of deficits, writing off of dead
assets and improvement of the railway system rather than to reduction of rates, while Havenga cleared off deficits on pension and land
settlement schemes, converted war-time loans and paid off others,
chiefly oversea flotations, and financed valuable public works in-
1935. cluding the beginnings of a national system of roads. On the other
hand the Treasurer gave increased subsidies to the weaker Provinces,
more liberal phthisis compensation than ever to miners, larger
pensions to civil servants and European old-age pensioners,[1] and
unemployment insurance for the first time; while, partly to help the
farmers, he provided milk and butter at reduced rates to European
and Coloured poor folk and charitable institutions, and free milk
to European and Coloured children. Before long social services were
absorbing close on forty per cent. of the ordinary revenues, besides
considerable sums for administration, and very much larger sums
from loan account for similar objects.

Over and above all this expenditure, the Fusion ministry laboured
unremittingly to carry out its promise to foster a healthy rural
population. There was need, because though nearly two-thirds of
the Union's people were on the land, they were producing barely
one-ninth of the national income or, to put it in another way, each
worker was feeding only two persons as contrasted with forty in
mechanised New Zealand. The Ministry wrote off advances made
during the recent campaign against locusts, set up assistance boards
to compromise between farmers and their creditors, poured forth
Dec. subsidies, and concluded a barter agreement whereunder Germany
1934. was soon taking more South African wool than Great Britain herself.
It faced inevitable overproduction and the growing wrath of the
townsfolk by maintaining high internal prices for sugar, mealies,
wheat and dairy produce, and presently by carrying a Marketing Act,[2]
1937. which endowed a minister, a marketing council and such local
marketing boards as might be set up with wide powers of inquisition
and penal sanctions to carry through schemes for the disposal of
surpluses. This marketing machinery was severely criticised by
democratically-minded South Africans as a disquieting extension of
the discretionary powers of the executive, which had already been
enlarged by recent Native legislation, and a long step towards

---

[1] Act 11 of 1936.   [2] Act 26 of 1937.

authoritarian corporativism exercised through 'pressure groups.' To make matters worse the two first ventures of the marketing boards were unlucky. Drought came unexpectedly after they had compelled a wholesale export of butter and mealies, with the result that shopkeepers had to ration their customers till butter could be imported at a price, and the Natives, who had sent away much of their food supply for the year, were compelled to buy mealies at enhanced rates. 1938. Next year, however, in spite of the protests of the National Council of Women, a newly-founded Housewives' League, many women's agricultural societies, the Poultry Farmers' Association, small milling companies, the economists of the University of Cape Town, and the permanent Secretary for Public Health, boards enforced export schemes for mealies, dairy produce, tobacco, dried fruits, and, of all things, highly subsidised wheat. To sum up: within four years public 1934– expenditure had risen by fifty per cent. and, though the external debt 1938. had fallen below the figure at which it had stood at the time of Union, the total debt had more than doubled since 1910 and was increasing faster than ever.[1] Meanwhile, the Treasurer had repeatedly refused to lighten Native taxation or lower the customs tariff, which pressed most hardly upon townsmen and Natives, lest the Union's secondary industries be prejudiced.

Apart from its financial and social legislation, the Fusion ministry 1935– revised the Industrial Conciliation and Wages Acts,[2] set up a S.A. 1937. Broadcasting Council on the British model, consolidated the insolvency laws and simplified the administration of justice and, in especial, criminal procedure. In keeping also with the Coalition bargain it tided over the Provinces for yet another stage. A Coalition Commission, which had taken the problem out of the hands of the Commission appointed by the failing Nationalist ministry, had given time for the Natal devolution movement to die away. There was thus no hint of federalism in the reforms effected and, since no additional financial provision was offered to the Provinces other than power to tax incomes and persons, there was little likelihood that any of them would avail themselves of their new right to take charge of irrigation, land settlement, labour colonies and afforestation. On the other hand, increased subsidies were given to Natal and the Orange Free State, and a permanent consultative committee was set up under the chairmanship of the Minister of the Interior to co-ordinate the work of the central and provincial authorities. This done, the Fusion ministry faced the Native question.

The Joint Select Committee of the two Houses presented its

---

[1] Expenditure rose from £30,000,000 in 1934 to £45,000,000 in 1938. The debt had risen from £116,000,000 in 1910 to £263,000,000 in 1938, and by no less than £12,000,000 during 1936–38. Next year the debt rose by over £17,000,000 and was expected to rise by £24,000,000 during 1939–40.

[2] Acts 11 of 1924 and 27 of 1925.

21

long-awaited report in May 1935.[1] Opinion on the Committee had been sharply divided on many points. Three ministers—Smuts, Hofmeyr, Stuttaford—and the veteran Cape Senator, François Malan, had voted with the minority against the crucial clause which would exclude Natives from the parliamentary roll in future; Malan and Stuttaford had recorded their opinion that non-Europeans throughout the Union would have to be enfranchised speedily on a civilisation basis, and presently Smuts declared publicly against the abolition of the Cape Native franchise.[2] The report was thus in no sense a declaration of government policy; nevertheless, if the draft Bills were once adopted officially, the Ministry might hope to win this time the requisite two-thirds majority.

July 1934.   The Committee made no mention of the Coloured Folk, whose affairs were still in the hands of the Commission to which they had been referred some time back, but it reduced the three Native bills to two: a Natives Trust and Lands Bill and a Native Representation Bill. In neither was there any change of principle. The former made the Governor-General, that is, the ministry of the day, trustee of a Native Trust, which, financed as already proposed, should acquire and develop lands for Natives, acting in each Province on the advice of a board consisting of an official of the Native Affairs Department and two other members, one of whom must be a Native. The fact had to be faced that while the Bantu were to an increasing degree being shut out of 'the white man's towns' and were being debarred from buying land on their own account, none of the additional purchases of land sanctioned by the Natives Land Act away back in 1913 had yet been acquired for that luckless people, whose density in the Reserves was now eighty-two to the square mile as contrasted with twenty-one for the Union as a whole. The Joint Committee, therefore, recommended that the Native Trust should be empowered to acquire some 15,500,000 acres additional to the 22,000,000 acres of existing Reserve land, so that, if and when these purchases had been made, the Bantu would have some 37,500,000 acres out of the Union's total extent of 302,000,000 acres. It recommended further that European competition for this additional land should be reduced to a minimum and even that the Minister be authorised in certain circumstances to compel Europeans to sell land to the Native Trust.[3]

This Trust and Lands Bill was, however, also a labour Bill, the most recent and comprehensive of the series of republican, colonial and Union acts which had sought to get rid of squatters and limit the number of labour-tenants on any one farm. It therefore superseded

---

[1] Report and Proceedings: Joint Committee No. 1—1935.
[2] *Cape Times*, June 14, 1935.
[3] Act 27 of 1935; Van der Horst, *op. cit.*, pp. 302 ff.; Patterson, *op. cit.*, pp. 299, 303; Davidson, *op. cit.*, p. 49.

the drastic but hitherto unenforced Native Service Contract Act of 1932 and extended its potential operation from Natal and the Transvaal to the whole Union. In proclaimed districts, land-owners were to be obliged by steadily rising taxation either to transform their squatters into labour-tenants under the penal sanctions of the Masters and Servants Acts or to send them to some Native area. Similarly, a Divisional Council in the Cape Province or a central board elsewhere could, at the instance of the Minister or six neighbours, call upon a landowner to show cause why there should be no reduction of the number of his labour-tenants, each of whose work for his lord was to be reckoned at a full 180 days a year and not at the customary 90 with a possible maximum of 180 laid down by the Act of 1932. On the other hand, the minor provisions of that Act were retained, for Native guardians were still authorised to bind their dependants to labour in any part of the Union, and families were held responsible for breach of contract by any of their members, while official whippings for Bantu lads under eighteen years of age were now added to the penal sanctions of the Masters and Servants Act, which already restricted so narrowly their people's right to combine for economic purposes.

The Representation of Natives Bill made but meagre provision for the representation of the Bantu seventy per cent. of the Union's population. It proposed to leave the dwindling group of Bantu voters in the Cape, some 11,000 strong, upon the ordinary roll. The rest of the Cape Bantu and their fellows in other parts, voting in the four immense constituencies of the Cape Province proper, the Transkeian Territories, Natal, and the Transvaal-Orange Free State, were to elect four or, if all was going well at the end of seven years, six Europeans as additional members to the Senate, secure in their seats for seven years and endowed with a full share of such powers as still remained to the Upper House. The Cape and Transkeian con-stituencies were also to elect two additional Provincial Councillors, black or white, so long as the Cape Council retained control of Native education, public health and roads. These Councillors were to hold their seats for four years but to have no share in the election of Senators. Finally, the four huge Bantu constituencies were to return twelve Natives to a Representative Council, where they would sit beside four Natives nominated by the Governor-General and the five Chief Native Commissioners under the presidency of the Secretary for Native Affairs.

The additional Senators and Provincial Councillors and members of the Representative Council were to be chosen by electoral colleges, all of which contained a considerable proportion of members nominated by European authority, that is, by the indirectly elected Bunga in the Transkei and, elsewhere, by the 1700 salaried chiefs and

Native members of local councils, reserve boards and advisory boards. Each voting unit, whether chief, council or board, was to have as many votes as there were Native taxpayers or exempted taxpayers in its area, and must cast those votes *en bloc*. No one who had fallen under the anti-agitator clauses of the Riotous Assemblies Act of 1927 was to stand for election and, if by chance such a one found his way into the Council, he could be ejected by the Governor-General for misconduct or 'other cause' and nothing said. This elaborate system of checks and balances made very little provision for ascertaining the opinions of emancipated urban Natives, and none at all for those of the 2,250,000 Bantu, more than one-third of the whole, dispersed in the European rural areas. Even so it provided only for a purely advisory Council. Ministers and Provincial executives must indeed refer to it projected Native legislation and receive its suggestions thereon, the Treasurer must submit to it estimates of Native revenue and expenditure, and its reports must be laid upon the table of each House; but neither Parliament nor Provincial Council was under any legal obligation to pay heed to the suggestions or protests of a body whose real forerunner was not the effective Transkeian Bunga, but the Council set up under the Smuts Act of 1920, whose meetings had been pretermitted since 1930 after it had revealed too strong a taste for criticising governmental measures.

This Native legislation and another Bill reserved for a later Session were to be applied more widely than Hertzog had originally proposed, for whereas, then, the grandchild of a Native might hope to rise to the level of the European or Coloured peoples, now that Oct. 1935. privilege was to be deferred for yet another generation. Criticism was quickly forthcoming from Afrikaner and British members of the South African Medical Association, who lamented the 'obsolete native policy' which was contributing to white degeneracy by breeding a 'slave complex' in the European youth,[1] and from an Industrial Legislation Commission, British and Afrikaner once more, which damned comprehensively all 'colour bar legislation . . . as well as July 1935. uneconomic white labour policies.'[2] The Cape Native Voters' Convention and six officially summoned Bantu Conferences were indeed Sept. Oct. 1935. ready to consider the Lands Bill upon its merits, and in some cases welcomed the Representative Council either for its own sake or as a stepping-stone to something better; but with hardly an exception they condemned the abolition of the Cape Native franchise, which the Cape and Transkeian conferences feared would drive the Bantu to listen to 'anti-white propaganda, especially that generated in all Africa by the Italo-Abyssinian conflict.'[3]

These adverse comments were endorsed by Conferences of the

[1] *Cape Times*, Oct. 2, 1935.   [2] U.G. 37–1935, §§ 54, 153.
[3] *Cape Times*, July 16, 1935, and Sept. 20, 1935.

Presbyterian and Congregational churches, the Cape District Synod Aug.–
of the Wesleyan church and an All-Africa Native Convention at Dec.
1935.
Bloemfontein,[1] a federal body, which, in an attempt to form a united
non-European front, contained Bantu leaders from all parts of the
Union, Swaziland and Basutoland and, more significantly still,
representatives of the Cape Coloured African Peoples' Organisation.
Nevertheless, Hertzog resolved at first to go forward. It soon became
clear, however, that the two-thirds majority for the destruction of
the Cape Native franchise would not be forthcoming and that, if
ministerial divisions on the Joint Select Committee went for anything, the ministry would be split irremediably. Pressure behind the
scenes, the steady opposition of the All-Africa Executive, and the
resolutions of a crowded and largely European protest meeting
presided over by Sir James Rose-Innes in the City Hall at Capetown
convinced the Premier that he must give way somewhat. At the last Feb.
moment he went back to his comparatively liberal 1929 franchise 17,
1936.
proposals.[2]

In terms of the Bill thus revised, the Cape Bantu were to keep the
cherished right to the individual vote, but were to be entered on a
separate roll. Voting in three large constituencies, they were to return
three Europeans with full powers as additional members of the
Assembly; but since this representation could only be increased or
diminished by a two-thirds majority of the two Houses sitting
together, they must, humanly speaking, be content permanently
with three members in a House whose other 150 members need consider only the votes of European and Coloured constituents. All
privileges and exemptions conferred by law were to remain, but the
right to acquire land anywhere in the Cape Province was to be taken
away, for that had been secured to them merely by judgment of the
Courts.[3]

The rest of the Select Committee's Bills came forward practically
unchanged save that the scattered Bantu in European rural areas
were, after all, given a voice in the various indirect elections, Bantu
representation in the Cape Provincial Council was limited to
Europeans, and all Bantu representatives, parliamentary, provincial
and conciliar, were to be chosen at a special general election every
five years. A mere handful of members, led by Senator Malan and
Hofmeyr, Minister of the Interior, opposed on grounds of principle
and expediency.[4] The Nationalists indeed objected that the Representative Council would violate 'the supreme principle of the protection of the white man in his capacity as trustee of the natives' by

[1] *Cape Times*, Dec. 17–19, 1935.
[2] *Ibid.*, and *Cape Argus*, Jan. 25–Feb. 18, 1936.
[3] *Cape Times*, Feb. 20, 1936.
[4] *Vide* especially *Cape Argus*, Feb. 20; *Cape Times*, Feb. 27 and April 7, 1936.

consolidating the native nation,[1] but they accepted the measure as an instalment and noted that the next logical step was the political

Apr. 6, 1936. segregation of the Coloured Folk. The crucial third reading of the Representation Bill was carried by 169 votes to 11.[2]

Having thus cleared the ground, Hertzog carried the Lands Bill without difficulty.[3] Disregarding Nationalist protests against expenditure on black men while so many Poor Whites lacked land, he declared that, now that the fear of black domination was gone, it was Parliament's first duty to assist the Bantu financially and otherwise, and promised to furnish the Trust during the next five years with £10,000,000 for the purchase of land and, in spite of the mutterings of some of his own followers, with as much more as might be necessary to carry out an Act which he regarded as a final settlement of the land question.[4]

1937.   In the following year the Premier carried the third measure of his Native code. Hitherto few towns had enforced the segregation policy embodied in the Urban Areas Acts.[5] A Native Laws Amendment Act[6] now gave the Government power to oblige them to do so. Henceforward, magistrates and Native commissioners were to be free to give or withhold leave for rural or reserve Natives to go to a town to seek work, and Natives could be excluded from any proclaimed town unless they could prove to the municipal authorities that they were *bona fide* visitors, or had been engaged by the municipal council, or had been admitted by it in view of the state of the local labour market. Conversely, urban Natives, who, in the opinion of the Governor-General, were 'in excess of the reasonable labour requirements' of such a town, might be removed to land provided by the Native Trust or, if their domicile lay outside the Union, be sent home.

European South Africa, nearly one-fifth of whose members were said authoritatively to be living in 'dire poverty' and many more of whom stood in daily dread of Native competition, thus accepted, in the words of the reconstituted Native Affairs Commission, 'all the implications denoted by the term "Trusteeship"...'[7] It was well that as the law had progressively deteriorated, the quality of actual Native administration had improved steadily throughout the Union since 1910.

Hertzog's Native laws came into operation against an ugly background: a growing knowledge of the conditions under which Bantu lived in rural areas, their high death-rate, the disproportionate sentences passed in too many cases on Natives as contrasted with

---

[1] *Cape Times*, April 2, 1936.   [2] Act 12 of 1936; *Cape Times*, April 7, 1936.
[3] Act 18 of 1936.   [4] *Cape Times*, May 1, 1936.
[5] Acts 21 of 1923 and 25 of 1930.
[6] Act 36 of 1937; *Race Relations*, Nov, 1937, pp. 75 ff.
[7] U.G. 48 of 1937, p. 67.

Europeans for like crimes, and the creation of statutory criminals,
ninety per cent. of the Bantu total, by the operation of the ungraded
poll tax, the intricate pass and liquor laws, the Masters and Servants
laws and the like. These laws led to convictions at the rate of one in
fourteen of the Bantu population annually by magistrates, whose
early training had as a rule accustomed them to look through the eyes
of the public prosecutor and trust overmuch to police evidence.[1] For
some years past and on occasion with Communist encouragement,
Bantu along the Rand had repeatedly resisted the pick-up vans in
which the police swooped down on African crowds in search of
passes and the like. It was a sure sign that urban Bantu were inclined
to regard the police as enemies that some of these affairs should have
been attended by violence. The climax came in September 1937 when
police raided the Vereeniging location. In the ensuing uproar, they
lost three of their own number killed, but wounded many Africans
by rifle fire. At once white protest meetings on the local market
square and elsewhere in the North canvassed drastic action; Nationalists, already equating Liberalism with Communism, called for an
end to the propagation of Communism and 'the liberalist doctrine
of equality between black and white'; the Premier lamented 'the
deep-rooted and far-reaching hostility, perhaps organised, among
the natives towards the white man,' and even Smuts could suggest
that grievances had been put into the heads of the Bantu by mis-
guided friends. A commission of inquiry, however, presently dispelled all idea of Communist propaganda and 'widespread hostility'
and found that the trouble at Vereeniging had been due to defective
municipal administration and harsh police methods. Its findings were
confirmed by the downright report of a police commission, which
pleaded that, with so many inquisitorial laws to enforce, a South
African policeman's life could not be a happy one, but admitted that
many of the young country-bred Afrikaners, from whom the force
was now mainly recruited, lacked 'tact and consideration' and had
'an inaccurate outlook towards the urban native.'[2]

At this juncture the newly-created Native Representative Council Dec.
met for the first time, all good men, among the best of them being 1937.
the Rev. John Dube and Selope Thema, a leader of the African
National Congress and editor of *The Bantu World*, a newspaper that
had been started on business lines in 1932 by two Europeans, one of
whom was editor of *The Star*, with money lent by the enlightened
Howard Pim. The Council conducted its business with the dignity

[1] At this time from 60,000 to 70,000 Bantu were going to gaol annually for
non-payment of the poll tax, and finding themselves liable for arrears on their
release. *Race Relations*, III. 2 and 3, p. 54; V. 1, pp. 19–22; *Race Relations News*,
No. 5, pp. 5–6.
[2] *Round Table*, No. 109, pp. 196 ff.; and 110, pp. 414 ff.; *Race Relations*, V. 1,
pp. 17–18.

and political ability that had always characterised Bantu assem-
Feb. blies. A little later, the four 'Native' Senators and the three
1938. 'Native' members of the Assembly, all well chosen, took their
seats prudently refraining from identifying themselves with any one
party. Of these members the two most outstanding were John
Rheinallt-Jones, a prominent member of the liberal South African
Institute of Race Relations, and Mrs. Margaret Ballinger, the
Liberal wife of William Ballinger, himself a Senator.[1] The experience
of the first two Sessions showed that both Houses listened to all these
new members with respect, however much they may have discounted
their opinions as those of men and women speaking to a brief; but
it was unfortunate that Parliament should have rejected the
unanimous recommendation of the Representative Council that
Native education should remain with the Education Department
and not be transferred, as Government wished, to the department
of Native Affairs in the name of segregation. On the other hand, the
1937. Treasurer, noting that the proceeds of Native taxation were falling
short, a sign that the poorest section of the population was growing
poorer, handed back three-fifths instead of the customary two-fifths
1939. of the receipts to the Native development fund. Two years later he
proposed that taxes should be paid in instalments and that defaulters
might work off their sentences in private or public employ, and
offered to hand over the whole of the receipts of Native taxation to
the fund provided Native education were transferred to the Native
Affairs Department. The offer was refused.[2]

Meanwhile, a census of urban Natives had been set on foot; more
May– than one hundred middling-sized towns had been closed to in-
July dependent Natives under the Laws Amendment Act, and Lydenburg,
1938. first of all districts, had been proclaimed under the Lands Act to the
dismay of its Bantu inhabitants and the fury of many of its farmers,
who had no desire to be deprived of squatters or labour-tenants.[3]
Presently the Native Trust reported that, during the first two-and-a-
half years of its operations, it had acquired a mere fourteen per cent.
of the permissible new areas at the price of forty per cent. of the
promised £10,000,000.[4] It was told that it must be content with half
1939. the funds that it had been led to expect for the current year, though
the purchases that were being virtually forced upon it were helping
to send up the price of land throughout the Union.[5] It could not hope
for much help from Native sources at a time when Europeans in the
Central Transvaal and Transkeian territories were protesting against
the manœuvres of a Control Board which obliged Natives to pay

---

[1] Roux, *op. cit.*, pp. 302 ff., 359.   [2] *Round Table*, No. 107, pp. 678 ff.
[3] *Race Relations News*, No. 1, p. 3.
[4] From September 1936 till April 1939; *Round Table*, No. 115, p. 642.
[5] *Race Relations*, V. 3, p. 58; *Round Table*, No. 110, p. 411.

more for mealies, their staple food, than was paid by stock-breeders
or overseas consumers. ....[1] Already there were Bantu, Coloured Folk
and even Indians, who, in spite of mutual antipathies, talked of a
non-European Front against the unchecked political domination of
the white man.

The rigidly racial attitude adopted by large numbers of the
dominant Europeans during the debates on the Native Bills augured
ill for subordinate groups within the Union other than the segregated
Bantu. The Pact ministry had long ago made illicit intercourse 1927.
between Europeans and Natives a criminal offence,[2] but now, in
two successive sessions, members of the United Party introduced 1936–
bills which would have made mixed marriages a crime. Such 1937.
marriages, never common, were decreasing in frequency; hence, the
measures were shelved, but not before the Nationalist and Labour
parties, and a good many of the United Party also, including the
Minister for Native Affairs, had endorsed the principle.[3] Henceforward, the Nationalists pressed for the complete segregation of
men of colour, whether African or Asiatic, frankly on the ground
that coloured blood was bad blood and that it was shameful for
white men to live and work beside 'lesser breeds.'[4]

The Commission consisting of three Afrikaners, two men of
British stock and an able coloured Moslem, to whom the problem Aug.
of the Cape Coloured Folk had been referred in 1934, reported just 1937.
as the last of Hertzog's Native bills had become law.[5] In their
devastating report they made it clear that the Premier had been right
when, on introducing his segregation programme in 1925, he had
declared boldly that the Coloured Folk, Christian and Moslem,
'belonged with' the Europeans. They made it still more plain that
the Coloured Folk were also right when they complained that they
were 'a forgotten people' ground between the upper and nether
millstones of the official 'civilised labour' policy and cheap Bantu
labour.

The true Cape Coloured Folk constituted some three-quarters of
the group which the census distinguished as 'Cape Coloured and
other Mixed Races,' the remainder being cross-breeds of various
kinds.[6] They themselves were not, as was commonly supposed, the
progeny of Europeans crossed with Bantu, but descendants of Bushmen, Hottentots, African and Asiatic slaves and, in some cases,
though by no means in all, of Europeans. They were thus descendants
of peoples who had intermingled in the western regions of the

---

[1] *Cape Argus*, July 19, 1939; *Cape Times*, July 22, 1939.
[2] Act 5 of 1927.
[3] *Race Relations*, III. 2 and 3, p. 56; V. 1, pp. 13, 14.
[4] *Round Table*, No. 115, pp. 642 ff.   [5] U.G. 54 of 1937.
[6] Patterson, *op. cit.*, chapter II; Hatch, *op. cit.*, chap. XI, XII.

21*

Cape Colony long before the Bantu had reached those parts. Some ninety per cent. of them still lived in the Cape Province and fully one-quarter of them in their stronghold, the Cape Peninsula.[1] Never tribal, the Coloured Folk had long been civilised in Western fashion, dressing in European clothes, speaking one or both of the official languages, as good Christians as most men save for the minority, who were devout Moslems, and as keen on sports, pageants and other social events as the white folk themselves. Take them all round, they were a cheerful, happy-go-lucky people, but delicate, fragile-boned and cursed with a fecundity and mortality that rivalled those of the philoprogenitive Indians. Politically, those of them who lived in the Cape Province were far better off than the rest of the non-Europeans in the Union, because they still had access to the common parliamentary roll on the old Cape civilisation franchise, and a few of them, like Dr. Abdurahman, had long sat on the City Councils of Capetown and Port Elizabeth. Economically also, and especially in those two cities, many of them had achieved a higher standard of living than had an increasing number of the Europeans; but the mass of them were still what they always had been: low-grade urban or rural labourers or indifferent domestic servants. The majority of those who dwelt in the towns lived at or below subsistence level, while too many of those upon the farms led a squalid existence that was made more squalid by the *tot* system, whereby white farmers insisted on paying them part of their wages in so many *tots* of wine a day, a practice that drove them to the shebeens at the week-ends when no free wine was to be had. Low wages, poor housing, and the drink which made them feel 'men of men' for a short hour bred tuberculosis and other wasting diseases, while crimes of violence by 'skolly boys' fresh from intolerable conditions on the farms were lamentably on the increase in the slums.

Provision for Coloured education was defective in a country where universal primary education for Europeans was a matter only of the past thirty years. The churches, in whose hands most of it still lay, did their best with the funds and curricula provided by the state, and of late years relatively great advances had been made in the Cape Province schools,[2] where most Coloured youngsters got schooling of some sort; but, even so, they had far too few teachers and their school buildings ranged from the excellent to the highly defective. In other Provinces, conditions were worse, in the rural Free State worst of all. Very few Coloured lads could struggle as far as the Universities of Cape Town or the Witwatersrand or the non-European

---

[1] Cape, 681,000; Natal 18,500; O.F.S., 17,700; Transvaal, 50,000; Union, 768,000 in 1936; *vide* Marais, *Cape Coloured People*, chap. 9.

[2] In 1936, the Cape Province spent £523,000 on the children of 682,000 Coloured citizens as against more than £3,000,000 on those of 791,000 Europeans.

College at Fort Hare which alone opened their doors to them. Even so, unless they could 'pass for white' as many of their Folk did at the cost of cutting themselves off from their kinsmen, those who did take degrees found themselves hampered because of their colour.[1] Would-be Coloured doctors might not attend white clinics and after qualification found far too few non-European hospitals in which to practise; Coloured nurses and teachers drew only from sixty to eighty per cent. of the pay of their white colleagues, and so it went. Doubtless, it was educated folk like these who resented most bitterly of all the new white adult suffrage, but it was their humbler fellows who felt the real economic pinch. They indeed valued their admission to many trade unions alongside white men, but they were angry when those same unions would not try to get them equal pay for equal work, and blamed them almost as much as the more exclusive northern unions for the Juveniles and Apprenticeship Acts,[2] which discriminated in favour of Europeans and, by setting a well-nigh unattainable educational standard for apprentices, threatened to extinguish the invaluable class of skilled Coloured artisans. There had been moreover a marked diminution in the proportion of Coloured folk and other non-Europeans in public and private employ since the adoption in 1924 of the 'civilised labour' policy, which, thanks partly to Government example and, to say the least, lack of explanation, had too often been interpreted as 'white labour.'

The Commission's recommendations were on the whole liberal, though the three Afrikaner members favoured restrictions under some major heads. It proposed notably, with one dissentient, that the sale of liquor to Coloured persons be curtailed and that an end be made of the time-honoured *tot* system. Above all, it recommended unanimously that Coloured men throughout the Union be placed on the ordinary voters' roll on attaining the old Cape qualifications of 1892.

A Coloured National Convention at Capetown hailed the liberal sections of this report, but asked that their men and women be given the vote on the same terms as Europeans,[3] while a European and Coloured League for Social Justice began to agitate in Natal for equal political rights.[4] Nationalists, on the other hand, demanded that Coloured men be shut out of the white trade unions, and the Cape Provincial Council passed an Ordinance which empowered April municipalities to enforce segregation in public buildings, public con- 1938. veyances, places of recreation and, as the Afrikaner members of the recent Commission had recommended, residential areas also. It further put the onus of proof to the contrary on the suspected Coloured person and condemned anyone, however patently Aryan,

[1] Hatch, *op. cit.*, pp. 190 ff.   [2] Acts 33 of 1921 and 26 of 1922.
[3] *Race Relations News*, No. 2, pp. 1, 2.   [4] *Race Relations*, V. 1, p. 23.

who had married a non-European to the loss of status as a white man.[1] The Government vetoed the measure, but not before Cissie Gool, Dr. Abdurahman's daughter, and her brother-in-law, Dr. Goolam Gool, had broken away from the A.P.O., rallied many Coloured folk to their Trotskyist National Liberation League and begun to play a leading part in the organisation of a non-European United Front. Nevertheless, a little later, in the Cape Municipal Congress, representatives of the smaller towns adopted the principle of the vetoed Ordinance by a four to one majority against the spokesmen of the cities.[2]

1939.

Meanwhile, the Nationalists had made Coloured segregation one of the main planks of their platform at a general election; their four Provincial party congresses decreed a Union-wide campaign to that end, the federal council of the powerful Dutch Reformed Church voted in favour of segregation, and at the centenary celebrations of the Great Trek on the site of the Boer victory over Dingaan's Zulus, Dr. Daniel Malan dwelt on the need for a second victory now if white civilisation was to be saved. There had been a time when he had outdone the comparatively liberal Hertzog by proposing that Coloured women in the Cape be enfranchised;[3] but now he proclaimed that South Africa could never be really 'safe as a white man's country' until the civilised Coloured Folk had been segregated as completely as the Bantu. Well knowing that many of its supporters sympathised with the Nationalists, the Fusion ministry projected a scheme of residential segregation which should interfere as little as possible with existing rights, but should, in Smuts's words, 'peg the present position.' A week later part of a large and orderly Coloured protest meeting at Capetown tried to march in procession past the Houses of Parliament. It was headed off by the police, and that night the legislative capital was the scene of violence and destruction of property.[4] Everywhere an impetus was given to the attempted formation of the non-European front.

Dec.
1938.

March
28,
1939.

The Indian problem was closely allied to that of the Coloured Folk. Neither the Capetown Agreement of 1927 nor the presence of a succession of distinguished Indian Agents had reconciled the South African Indians to the ideas of segregation or repatriation, and, as they watched the progress of constitutional reform in India, they resented more than ever their own exclusion from the public life of the country which, for the vast majority of them, was the country of their birth.

[1] *Race Relations*, V. 1, p. 26; *Race Relations News*, No. 3, pp. 2, 3.
[2] Hatch, *op. cit.*, p. 200.
[3] *Die Burger*, May 1929; *Rand Daily Mail*, May 14, 1951; *Hansard (S.A.)*, 1928, col. 1659 and March 23, 1949, col. 2657.
[4] *Round Table*, No. 115, p. 648; *The Times*, March 27, 1939.

During the bad times the additional inducements held out since 1927 had failed to attract voluntary emigrants. A second Indo-Union Jan.– Conference had therefore suggested a joint inquiry into the possibility Feb. of settling South African Indians in 'countries other than India.' That 1932. joint inquiry was never held, but the Coalition ministry, with the concurrence of the Indian Government, appointed an exploratory committee which included a local Indian member. This committee March pointed to British Guiana, New Guinea and North Borneo as 1934. virtually empty lands where Indian immigrants might be more welcome than in South Africa or Mother India, but so cool was the reception of its report on either side of the Indian Ocean that no action was taken upon it.

Meanwhile, as the old fear that the Indians might swamp the Europeans in the south-eastern parts of the Union died away, something was done to improve their lot by their own efforts, the help of friends and municipal and state action, especially in Natal where most of them dwelt. A sign of the times was the formation of an Indo-European Council at Durban, on the lines of the widespread European-Bantu Councils, to seek a better understanding between the two races and uplift the Indians lest they pull down the western standards of life. A vast deal remained to be done if they were to be so uplifted, for the 'civilised labour' policy, the Apprenticeship Act and the rest bore as hardly upon them as they did upon the Coloured Folk,[1] and in addition those in the Transvaal were subject to special disabilities. Contrary to the expectation of the Capetown Conference of 1927, nothing had been done there to check the discretionary powers of local authorities to withhold trading licences from them, while, in terms of old laws dating from republican or colonial days, Indians and Coloured persons, other than those who had been specially protected in 1919 so long as they continued to trade in the same township,[2] were technically trespassing on stands in most of the towns. With the coming of the bad times, a select committee of May the Assembly decided that the legislators of 1908 and 1919 had 1930. intended that persons of colour should not occupy fixed property outside reserved areas, and recommended that areas be reserved and illegal businesses be disposed of within the next five years. Parliament acted on that report,[3] enlarging somewhat the area to which the 1932. prohibition should apply, but protecting existing businesses so long as these should remain in the hands of their then holders, and authorising the Minister of the Interior to withdraw land from the operation of the prohibitive clauses. A Commission under the chair- Oct. manship of Judge Richard Feetham was then appointed to find out, 1932. *inter alia*, how many people would be affected by the new law.

---

[1] *Race Relations*, IV. 4, pp. 89 ff.   [2] Act 37 of 1919.
[3] Act 35 of 1932.

Jan.
1935.

July–
Oct.
1935.

1936.

1937.

While the Feetham Commission pursued its baffling task, relations between Europeans and Indians became more difficult. Neither the South African nor the Transvaal Indian Congresses would have anything to do with the Commission, and the departing Agent, Kunwar Sir Maharaj Singh, himself a Christian, gave warning that the reply to fresh restrictive legislation might well be the withdrawal of his Agency.[1] At length, after the date at which illegal businesses must be disposed of had been postponed for a further two years till April 1937, that portion of the Feetham report which dealt with Johannesburg was published.[2] It found that neither the number of persons concerned nor the volume of Indian wholesale trade was as great as had been imagined, recommended for exemption a considerable area which coincided fairly well with that which the Johannesburg city council was prepared to consider, and urged that the strain of competition on European traders be eased by the readier admission of Indians into other occupations. Nearly all these proposals were embodied in the Transvaal Asiatic Land Tenure Amendment Act,[3] which went even further than the Commission on one score by accepting for the first time the principle that, given ministerial approval and in some cases municipal consent also, Asiatics and Coloured folk might not only occupy fixed property in the Transvaal, but own it.

Protection was given forthwith to illegal tenants till April 1939, but the resolutions of both Houses which were required to give life to the rest of this liberal Act were withheld. Indians, alarmed at their exclusion from the new marketing boards, became indignant when ministerialists introduced private Bills forbidding the handful of European women who were married to non-Europeans from owning land in the Transvaal, and empowering the Transvaal Provincial Council to withhold trading licences from non-Europeans who employed white people. Thanks mainly to the efforts of Hofmeyr, the divided Fusion ministry sent both Bills to select committees. These failed to report on the Married Women's Bill, but transformed the Licensing Bill into a more general measure forbidding the employment of European women by Asiatics other than Jews, Syrians, Malays, professional men, and, for so long as the Union-Japanese immigration accord of 1930 should stand, Japanese. This last exception was too much for the Assembly's sense of humour, and, amid angry protests from Delhi at the adverse distinction drawn between Indians and other Asiatics and offers from the South African Indian Congress to abstain voluntarily from employing European women, the Transvaal Licensing Bill was withdrawn. Nevertheless, the substance of both these projected measures was referred to the Murray

---

[1] *Round Table*, No. 101, p. 185.   [2] U.G. 7 of 1934 and 22 of 1935.
[3] Act 30 of 1936; *Race Relations*, III. 4, p. 86; *Round Table*, No. 116, pp. 860 ff.

Commission, which was instructed to inquire into the alleged wholesale evasions of landholding regulations in the rest of the Transvaal.
The Indians, for their part, redoubled their efforts to win full political
rights for those of their number who could attain to reasonable
financial and educational qualifications.[1] Their new Agent, Syed Sir Jan.
Raza Ali, said bluntly that unless they were given pride in being 1938.
citizens of South Africa, they would, however reluctantly, be forced
over to the non-European front.[2]

The abortive Transvaal Licensing Bill had classed Jews as Asiatics.
It was a danger which the more far-sighted members of South 1911–
African Jewry had dreaded in this land of many racial 'questions' 1913.
ever since the Union Government, in the early days, had introduced
an Immigration Bill directed avowedly at Asiatics. At that time the
Jews had formed close on four per cent. of the European population;
ten years later they had formed nearly five per cent., and fifteen years
later slightly more. They were strong in Capetown, even stronger in
Johannesburg where they formed in 1936 some seventeen per cent.
of the white population, and they controlled a high proportion of
the business of these two great cities. For the most part, however, they
were widely scattered. Some few had become farmers; many more
were storekeepers or hotel proprietors in the smaller towns and villages; the more ambitious showed a marked preference for medicine,
the law and broking. Taken as a body, they were strict Jews, anxious
to enjoy the liberties accorded to white men under the South African
sun, but swift to assert their Jewishness when these things were not
in question. Zionism flourished among them, and they gave generously to its cause.

Time was when the Jewish trader had been a popular figure in the
dorps and on the farms, but those days were past. Malan's Quota
Act of 1930 had partially closed the door against those Jews who
came from Eastern Europe,[3] whence bad times and rising *Judenhitze*
were driving them in shoals. Then, in 1933, Hitler had become
master of the Reich and thereafter Central European Jews fled to
South Africa in such numbers that they had soon outstripped the
modest Dutch and British immigration. As they came, so the agitation against them rose, especially in the dorps and smaller towns,
which were full of disappointed Afrikaners who had been driven
off the land and were dismayed to find urban trade and industry so
largely in the hands of foreigners. Had not the rebel Maritz said in
1914 that he would not have his country run by 'Englishmen, niggers
and Jews'?[4]

Amid the forming and reforming of parties at the time of Fusion,

[1] *Race Relations News*, No. 2, p. 5.   [2] *Cape Times*, Jan. 28, 1938
[3] Act 8 of 1930.   [4] *Vide supra*, p. 562.

while Nazism was gaining ground in neighbouring South-West Africa, Louis Weichardt, a barber of German extraction who had fought for the Fatherland during the Kaiser's war, began to enrol Nazi-minded Grey Shirts, who displayed the distaste for parliamentary methods and Jews so often associated with their uniform. They made little headway, for the parliamentary tradition of the country was still strong and the return of better times robbed them of much of their appeal, but they were a warning of what might well happen in a country whose dominant Europeans instinctively 'think with their blood,' form commandos readily and belong to that widespread middle class which has supplied the rank and file to fascism everywhere. It did not pass without remark that Pirow, the ebullient Minister of Defence, son of a German missionary, husband of an ardently patriotic German and a visitor to Hitler's Berlin during critical days, should presently enrol out-of-work youths in Special Service and Pioneer battalions and, a little later, call upon the middle class to develop class consciousness and organise for the defence of its own interests.[1]

1935.   For some time, no prominent politican would have anything to do with the Grey Shirts, especially after two of them had been sentenced for attempting to plant forged evidence of wrongdoing upon a synagogue at Port Elizabeth. Towards the close of 1936, however, the Government drafted an Aliens Bill and framed temporary regulations to check the Israelitish invasion. Just before these regulations could come into force, on the eve of a Cape Provincial general election, five hundred German Jews arrived at Capetown on a specially chartered steamer. Backed by a group of Stellenbosch professors, the Nationalist leaders inveighed not against undue Jewish immigration, but against Jews as Jews. Encouraged by the

1937.   effect of this anti-Semitic outcry on the Provincial election results, and well knowing that many ministerialists thought as he did, Dr. Malan called for a law which would have stigmatised Jewish aliens as prohibited immigrants and, in the tradition of the half-forgotten Cape Patriots of 1779,[2] would have debarred those in the country from accepting any paid post without official leave during the five years that must elapse before they were naturalised. Malan's demand

1937.   was rejected, but a drastic Aliens Act was carried similar to those which were being passed in many parts of the British Empire. The Quota Act was repealed and a government board was given absolute discretion to decide which individuals it would admit, other than born British subjects of the King, taking as the tests character, the likelihood of speedy assimilation, and the improbability that entry would cause unemployment. The Act made no mention of Jews, but it was well understood that it would be used primarily against them.

[1] *Cape Argus*, May 24 and June 18, 1935.   [2] *Vide supra*, p. 102.

The Jewish question, thus dragged into the forefront of party politics, set up queer cross-currents. A society˙ was formed in Johannesburg and other large towns to foster goodwill and better understanding between Jews and Christians.[1] The Transvaal Synod of the Dutch Reformed Church, taking the middle line, resolved that it dared not countenance the persecution of any section of the community, but left it to the conscience of each man to decide whether anti-Jewish movements set on foot for economic or other reasons were in the public interest.[2] The Nationalist party organisations of the Transvaal and Free State, on the other hand, excluded Jews from membership; Nationalists in conference applauded Malan when he implied that Jewish Communists were organising the rising tide of colour, and individual Nationalists and Grey Shirts encouraged Natives in the Cape, Natal and the Transvaal to boycott Jews as the common exploiters of the black man and the white.[3] In face of these developments, Pirow found it necessary to warn a country audience in the eastern Transvaal that, though he admired the Grey Shirt ideals of leadership, self-respect and discipline and was convinced that they were best for Germany, yet their introduction into the democratic Union, imperfect though the Union's democracy was, would lead to civil war.[4] Nevertheless, anti-Semitism bulked large in Nationalist politics and, though the House of Assembly rejected the measure, there was widespread electoral support for the private Bill introduced by a Nationalist to stop Jewish immigration and differentiate against Jews already in the country.[5]

April 1937.

Jan. 1938.

1939.

The truth was that by drawing apart from the Fusion alliance of Smuts and Hertzog, Malan's Purified Nationalists had set the feet of their countrymen on the path of division and exclusiveness. It was a path which attracted those many hundreds of Afrikaner undergraduates, who apparently rated the preservation of white skins higher than the dissemination of Western civilisation, for when the majority of the National Union of South African Students resolved on the motion of their Afrikaner President to admit non-Europeans from Fort Hare, the minority from Afrikaans-speaking, Nationalist and increasingly Fascist-minded seats of higher learning broke away and formed their own rival *Afrikaner Studentebond*. The Fusionists might work for national unity among white folk, but Malan and his followers were bent on keeping themselves to themselves even at the cost of perpetrating division. Smuts, a second Schreiner come to belated judgment, had foreseen something of the sort when, on the eve of Coalition, he had lamented publicly that the Union was too big, too varied in its local traditions and interests and too emotionally

---

[1] *Race Relations*, V. 1, p. 25.   [2] *Ibid.*, p. 25.
[3] *Race Relations News*, No. 2, p. 5.   [4] *The Times*, Jan. 31, 1938.
[5] *Round Table*, No. 115, p. 636.

unbalanced to function harmoniously under a single regime; he had, moreover, recalled that only a hundred years back the Trekkers had gone forth from the overgrown, loosely-compacted and spiritually divided Cape Colony to found communities of their own 'in the wilderness.' Now, however, there was no such wilderness to which the Nationalists could remove themselves from all that irked them; wherefore they were making not a physical but a spiritual Great Trek so that they might one day transform the Union itself into their Promised Land.

Two latter-day developments that troubled the Nationalists were, first, the efforts of the Bantu and their white supporters to express themselves through newspapers, and, secondly, the spread of trade unionism among folk of all colours. They had comparatively little to fear in the field of journalism, for many Bantu newspapers had been acquired, either by commercial firms or by The Bantu Press, a company in which the National Trust backed by the Government and the powerful *Argus* group of newspapers was the largest shareholder, while the Communist Bantu journal, *Umsebenzi*, having enjoyed a brief spell of prosperity during Mussolini's assault on Abyssinia, had fallen on evil days after the Duce's victory and the unsuccessful prosecution of its European editor, Edward Roux. In the trade union sphere, however, the Nationalists had more cause for anxiety. It is true that in the North those Bantu unions that were affiliated to the S.A. Trades and Labour Council never exerted much influence, mainly because many white unions excluded Africans altogether and many more insisted on segregating them in separate sections. Again, Communists and other disruptive elements ruined the non-European Trade Union Federation, which Andrews had founded in 1928, as well as many of its constituent unions; on the other hand, some of these unions were revived and others formed by leaders like the European, Max Gordon, and the Bantu ex-Communist, Gana Mkabeni. The former founded his own Laundrymen's Union and unions of African printers and bakers and, in 1938, combined these with others in a Joint Committee of which he himself was General Secretary; the latter made his Native Clothing Workers Union the nucleus of a group of unions entirely under African control.[1]

Coloured, Bantu and even Indian trade unions sprang up rapidly in the Cape Province and Natal. In the Cape, these were distributed among the three main groups of unions: first, the 'aristocratic' group consisting of the Engineers, the Typographers and so forth, secondly, the small group led by the European, Dr. Alexander Forsyth and, finally, the main body, the Cape Federation of Trades, which had been formed in 1913 by the European, Robert Stuart, who still

[margin: 1935-1936.]

---

[1] Roux, *op. cit.*, pp. 335 ff.

led it. Then came something of a revolution. First, in 1936, Sachs, who four years earlier, had been expelled from the Communist Party alongside Andrews and other stalwarts, formed a branch of his Garment Workers' Union in the Cape; but whereas in the Transvaal and Free State that union kept its members in three distinct racial sections which did not even meet in conference, here, in keeping with the liberal Cape tradition, it allowed folk of all colours to work together on free and equal terms. Next, a member of this union, the young girl Communist, Ray Alexander, and her friends captured the Cape Federation of Trades and thus drove Stuart to combine the Cape branch of the Garment Workers' Union and some constituent unions of the Federation in the separate Western Province Council of Trade Unions.[1] The Communist-led rump of the Federation retained enough energy to organise a nation-wide non-European Railway and Harbours Union; but after that effort it sank to the level of a mere committee of the predominantly northern S.A. Trades and Labour Council. Finally, the Communists extended their operations to Natal. There they found their first notable Indian recruits during the Durban textile strike of 1935 and, thus encouraged, formed European, Bantu and Indian trade unions. They did so with such success that, two years later, they had set Africans and Indians striking together at the Falkirk iron foundry in Pietermaritzburg.[2]

This proliferation of trade unions, so much of it either led or inspired by Communists, stuck in the throat of Pirow, who, as pre-Fusion Minister of Justice, had put Champion, Sachs and other leaders to the ban under various 'hostility clauses' only to see them restored to full civil rights by Smuts, his successor in that office. They positively alarmed those many Dutch Reformed Church predikants who rallied to the banner of Malan, himself an eminent Calvinist Doctor of Divinity and outstanding champion of *Ons Volk*. Two of these reverend gentlemen told the Industrial Legislation Commission of 1934, with special reference to Sachs's Garment Workers' Union, that all who demanded higher wages were downright Bolsheviks, while others of their cloth visited workshops along the Rand during the lunch hour to hold prayer meetings and inveigh against such trade unions as were not yet under Nationalist control and, above all, such as admitted non-Europeans as forces of evil, Communistic and Imperialistic organisations alien to the Afrikaner spirit and inimical to white civilisation. Presently these skirmishers were reinforced by Grey Shirts and the more recently raised Black Shirts, who were soon partially financed by the German Foreign Office. Behind them stood the *Federasie van Afrikaanse Kultur*

[1] Davidson, *op. cit.*, p. 34; Roux, *op. cit.*, pp. 337 ff.
[2] Roux, *op. cit.*, pp. 338, 364, 367.

Vereinigings (*F.A.K.*), which was founded in 1936 to serve as the nucleus of the *Nasionale Kulturraad,* whose aim was the intensive organisation of Afrikaners in every sphere. All these fighting formations were directed by the Reform Organisation which was enthusiastically financed by the Prime Minister's son, Dr. Albertus Hertzog, with £10,000 bequeathed by the late Mrs. Jannie Marais, a wealthy Stellenbosch landowner and keen Malanite, for the saving of the souls of Afrikaner workers. These Nationalist Crusaders held that if those souls were to be saved from corruption by the Jews, Communists and *Kafferboeties* who led so many trade unions, and if white civilisation itself was to be rescued from folk who ignored those colour distinctions which in their belief had been ordained in the beginning by Almighty God, Nationalists must either smash the trade unions or get control of them. Control at first seemed the better course, for this would enable the controllers to use these powerful organisations for their own political ends. Hence, they directed their attack on the Rand, the stronghold of trade unionism, and in particular against those unions which were predominantly manned by Afrikaners fresh from the backveld and therefore full of racial prejudices. Chiefest of these was the badly led white Mineworkers' Union, whose head offices the Reform Organisation actually seized on one occasion and only gave up by order of the Supreme Court. For the time being, however, the campaigners sought to gain their ends by blandishments and propaganda.[1]

While the Nationalists were thus elaborating their internal policy of segregation, the Union authorities had brought intermittent but increasing pressure on the Imperial Government to transfer to them the governance of Basutoland, Swaziland and the Bechuanaland Protectorate. Provision for the transfer had been made in the South Africa Act, a schedule had been appended thereto laying down the lines on which they should then be ruled, and the hope had been expressed by the then Under-Secretary of State that when, 'in the long distant years,' transfer took place, the transition would be so gradual, and the new law and even official personnel be so like the old, that the tribes would never know that anything had happened to them.[2] But though Union ministers had raised the question from time to time, and Europeans who lived in Bechuanaland along the railway close to the Transvaal border had petitioned that they at least should be taken over, the transfer had always been postponed. Meanwhile, beyond making up occasional deficits and stating repeatedly that there would be no transfer without discussion at Westminster and consultation with the inhabitants, white and black, the

[1] Sachs, *op. cit.,* pp. 166 ff.
[2] Newton. *Unification of South Africa,* II. 264.

distant Imperial authority had left the High Commission Territories to look after themselves.

This prolonged neglect had not been salutary. All had stagnated. Poverty, ignorance and disease were as rife there as in the general run of tribal territories and reserves in backward Africa; the soil of Swaziland and the habitable portions of droughty Bechuanaland were overgrazed, that of crowded and mountainous Basutoland heavily eroded. All had suffered during the good years from the exclusion of their light-weight cattle by the Union, the senior partner in the Customs Union to which they belonged, and Bechuanaland 1933. had suffered worst of all during the subsequent depression when its cattle export had been banned completely for two years on hygienic grounds in common with that of Southern Rhodesia, South-West Africa and the Union's Transkeian territories. Recently, however, H.M. Government had sent Sir Alan Pim to report on their condition,[1] and had begun to give more liberal financial aid.

The problem of the future of the High Commission Territories was suddenly thrust into the foreground when Vice-Admiral Edward Sept. Evans, the Acting-High-Commissioner, backed by marines and field- 1933. guns, deposed Tshekedi Khama, the able acting-Chief of the Bamangwato, for exceeding his powers. Tshekedi was reinstated upon submission, but the issue had been raised. Johannesburgers talked of transfer now that limited prospecting had at last been permitted in Native areas, Europeans in the railway blocks joined in, and Hertzog took the matter up officially. He had long ago said that he had no wish to take over unwilling subjects, but he was well aware of arguments for transfer in administrative convenience, the difficulty of coping, under divided control, with locusts and diseases that paid no heed to frontiers, the friction that might arise from having one Native policy in the Union and another in Territories that were more or less surrounded by Union territory, and the fact that, though Basuto wool and mohair went overseas, cattle and labour, the chief exports of all three Territories, found practically their only market in the Union. Many observers, in Great Britain as well as in South Africa, 1934– held that Lionel Curtis was right when he prophesied that British and 1935. Afrikaners would never settle down side by side, nor the nascent liberalism of the younger generation, which he detected at the South African universities, come to maturity, unless H.M. Government showed trust in the Union's citizens by handing over the governance of the Territories. There were, however, those who considered the price too high even for these advantages, and who noted also that the Protectorates would be a liability to the Union, that the Union was already getting all the labour that it could hope to get from them, and that transfer would make it less easy, though not impossible, to

[1] Report on Swaziland, 1932; Bechuanaland, 1933; Basutoland, 1935.

shut out their competing cattle.[1] The main body of opponents went much further. Headed by Lords Selborne and Lothian, they took the line that, since the Status Act had nullified the Schedule by abolishing 'reservation,' a new agreement must be made, and that no agreement could be made till the Joint Select Committee had reported on the Union's Native programme.[2]

The revised Native Representation and Land Bills did not commend the Union's policy to the critics, least of all to the watchful Natives in the Protectorates or to James Thomas, the Dominions Secretary. The latter announced that the Schedule would have to be re-examined in the light of subsequent constitutional changes, and that self-governing Southern Rhodesia's interest in the northern half of Bechuanaland must be borne in mind. Hertzog, who from the first had declared that he would never take over the Territories unless their inhabitants, black and white, desired it, agreed that, since it was useless to consult the Natives in their present mood, the Imperial and South African Governments should work together during the next few years to bring about a situation in which transfer could be effected 'with the full acquiescence of the populations concerned.'[3]

The Imperial Government, which had already begun to take action on the Pim reports, pressed on with its reforms. It gave grants-in-aid and large sums from the Colonial Development Fund[4] to check erosion, bore for water, carry out other development work and provide less inadequate social services; it next reinforced the small and localised Territories service with officials from other parts of the Empire, and then virtually incorporated it in its widespread and now highly trained Colonial service. At the same time it tentatively introduced indirect rule on the Nigeria-Tanganyika model. No difficulties were experienced in Swaziland, where the paramount chief and his mother, whose influence as maker of the gentle rains was great, were both ready to work with the sympathetic local officials; but Basutoland called for very careful handling lest the many chieftains should scent a plot to deprive them of the powers which had long ago been guaranteed to 'Father Moshesh' by the Great White Queen, while in Bechuanaland two proclamations were challenged by Tshekedi on behalf of the Bamangwato in the north and by Bathoen, chief of the Bangwaketsi, in the south.[5]

The challenge, especially the claim that the proclamations were in

May
1935.

---

[1] For a discussion from various angles, vide The Times, May 13 ff., 1935 Race Relations, II. 3; M. Perham and L. Curtis, The Protectorates of South Africa.

[2] Cape Times, Aug. 15, 1934.   [3] Ibid., May 24 and June 24, 1935.

[4] Grants-in-aid to Bechuanaland, 1935–38 = £402,000; to Swaziland, 1928–1938 = £326,400; Colonial Development Fund = £547,000.

[5] No. 74 and 75 of 1935.

defiance of treaty rights, was partly prompted by a desire to prove that transfer to the Union would be a breach of faith. Unfortunately for the plaintiffs, no definite treaty could be produced and, after a long hearing at Lobatsi, an able South African judge, Ernest Water- 1936. meyer, set aside their pleas in a judgment which is of importance to all protectorates.[1] He left one or two points open, but he laid it down that, in terms of the Foreign Jurisdiction Act, the decision of the Secretary of State was final when he held that, though the King did not claim 'full internal sovereignty,' he did possess 'unfettered and unlimited power' to legislate. Further, since the proclamations had made changes in Native law and custom, he ruled that the true meaning of the word 'respect' in the Order-in-Council of 1891, under which the High Commissioner exercised jurisdiction, was that full consideration must be given to that law and custom, as indeed it had been given, but not, as ·the challengers claimed, that the European authorities must refrain from interfering with them.

Meanwhile, suspicion of the Union's intentions mounted high in all three Territories. Tribesmen feared that their lands were to be overrun by the Union's Poor Whites and 'redundant' Natives; they feared the pass laws, and, those who had them, the loss of their cherished guns, the loss also of the sense of freedom that was still theirs. It was under these circumstances that Hertzog, following up June the substantial grant that had been made to the Territories by the 1936. Johannesburg Chamber of Mines for medical purposes, proposed to make them a recurrent grant of £35,000 to check soil erosion and the like. He pointed out to Nationalist critics that the Union would merely be spending money on its future estate, since he had gathered during his recent talks with the Dominions Secretary that Swaziland would be transferred in a year or two's time, Bechuanaland next and finally Basutoland, and then gave warning that, if this were not done, the Union might one day have to close its frontiers to the Terri- tories' trade.[2] In spite of the anxious assurances of the Imperial authorities that they would incur no liability by accepting Union money, the chiefs made it abundantly clear that they did not desire it, if only because, said one of them, it would not be gentlemanly to take it year by year and then to show distrust of the giver by rejecting his rule. Less highly placed tribesmen in northern Bechuanaland said openly that they would rather go under Southern Rhodesia than the Union; others from various parts declared that, if H.M. Govern- July ment abandoned them as it had abandoned the Swazis in 1894,[3] they 1936. would tighten their belts and carry on as long as they could. So the

---

[1] *Round Table*, No. 106, pp. 448 ff.; Sillery, A., *The Bechuanaland Protectorate*, p. 100; *T. Khama and Bathoen* v. *The High Commissioner*.

[2] *Cape Times*, June 12, 1936; *Cape Argus*, June 17, 1936.

[3] *Vide supra*, p. 444.

Union's offer was withdrawn and Hertzog agreed once more that the transfer must not be hurried.

1937.   Nevertheless, a year later, having carried the last of his segregation Bills, the South African Premier complained that the British Government had so far done little to secure the Natives' acquiescence, and hinted that he might soon be driven to ask the King point-blank for transfer at the risk of 'consequences of the most unpleasant character.' [1] His Union supporters, regardless of the reforms that H.M. Government had effected of late years,[2] raised the cry once more that the Territories must be taken over before they became deserts and their peoples be wasted by weakness and disease, while advocates of transfer in Great Britain, led once more by Curtis, advanced a plea of dangerously wide application that, so long as the adjacent Territories lay outside its jurisdiction, the Union could not cope with its fundamental racial problem.[3] H.M. Government stood firm, however, and assuredly Hertzog had no desire to quarrel with it in March view of the threatening world situation. In the end the hopeful course 1938.   was taken of setting up a joint advisory committee consisting of the three Resident Commissioners of the Territories and three highly placed South African officials to co-ordinate the work on either side of the interlocked frontiers.[4]

While the Union was thus showing itself reasonable in its negotiations for the transfer of the High Commission Territories, it showed itself cordial but businesslike in its dealings with Portuguese East Africa. It was in a much stronger position than it had been at the time of the signing of the Mozambique Convention of 1928 and, therefore, sought to get better terms, notably in the allocation of railway traffic and the recruitment of Bantu labour for the Rand mines. Since both governments had had to be consulted before changes could be made in railway tariffs, it had turned out that Lourenço Marques was handling more of the fast-growing Rand traffic than had been bargained for, and now that Bantu from the Union and High Commission Territories were coming forward readily, the mines were less dependent than they ever had been on Mozambique Shangaans. Perhaps to add force to its request for a revision of the Convention in this respect, the Union permitted an experimental recruitment of 'tropical' labourers from the long-forbidden regions to the northward of the 22nd degree of south latitude. Under the new Convention recruitment of Shangaans was easily provided for, most-favoured-nation agreements replaced the free lists of imports, Lourenço Marques accepted a smaller share of

[1] *Cape Times*, June 17 and July 6, 1937.
[2] *Vide* correspondence in the *Cape Argus*, July 21, 22, 24 and 28, 1937.
[3] *The Times*, Feb. 9 and 19, 1938.   [4] *Ibid.*, March 31, 1938.

the Rand traffic and, to keep the balance true, the Union was empowered to treat the Portuguese railway on the same footing as its own in the matter of goods rates.[1]

While she was thus drawing her eastern neighbour closer to herself, the Union had to watch her northern neighbour moving steadily away. Southern Rhodesia was hard hit by the falling-off of the demand for copper and other base metals from which it and Northern Rhodesia had hoped so much, and also, presently, by the banning of the whole of its limited export of cattle to the Union on the ground that disease had broken out in some of its districts. On the other hand, since it had followed Great Britain off gold, the premium stimulated its gold mines; its tobacco still went south in large quantities and was deservedly winning a footing in the British market; preferences exchanged at the Ottawa Conference of 1932 gave renewed hope. Even during the bad times its government did much to set its house in order. It bought out the mineral rights 1933. of the British South Africa Company, and, taking up the report of a Commission which had sat some years before, carried a Land 1930. Apportionment Act.[2] In spite of white Labour opposition it made large additions to the already extensive reserves, set aside smaller areas in which advanced Natives could acquire land on individual tenure, left unallotted further huge tracts mostly in dry or tsetse infested country, and earmarked the central half of the colony along the highlands and the railways for European occupation.[3] It also projected Native Councils on the lines of the Smuts Act of 1920 and, recalling old and disused laws which limited the numbers of Natives permissible on any one farm, decreed that all redundant Natives must be removed from Crown lands and European areas by the New Year of 1937. Thus, as far as concerned the land, Southern Rhodesia, faced with a far simpler problem, had done what the Union was still seeking to do, and a considerable body of its European opinion, outrunning legislation, followed the Union's example still further by demanding that Natives be deprived of the franchise.

Meanwhile, groups of Independents had taken shape, urging that Moffat's Rhodesian Party was slow to develop the country. These groups gradually drew together as the Reform Party under Godfrey Huggins, the leading surgeon of the colony, and ensured that he Sept.
1933.

[1] The proportion of Shangaans to other Bantu on the Rand mines soon fell from about two-thirds to a little more than one-quarter; *Cape Times*, Nov. 31, 1934.
[2] C.S.R. 3–26; Act 30 of 1930 amended in 1941.
[3] In round figures, European areas, 48,695,000 acres; Unassigned, 18,472,000; Reserves, 21,595,000; Native Purchase areas, 7,464,600; total, 96,226,600 acres. Europeans (1931), 50,000; Bantu 1,000,000 souls.

should take office after a narrow victory at the polls a year later. Having celebrated his success by carrying an Industrial Conciliation Act on South African lines, the new Prime Minister induced most of his own followers and the main body of the Rhodesian Party to combine in support of a 'United Party' ministry, which should be strong enough to induce the Imperial Government to relax its hold on Rhodesia's Native policy and to speak on level terms with the Union in the matter of customs. The latter object at least was speedily achieved after an overwhelming victory at a general election.[1] A conference at Capetown failed indeed to renew the Customs Convention, since each government was more determined than ever to protect its own people; but as a gesture of goodwill the Union agreed to admit a few head of Rhodesian cattle and a modicum of tobacco for a limited period. For the rest, Southern Rhodesia arranged to collect her own customs dues.[2] The Union's customs agreement with Northern Rhodesia still had another year to run, but on April 1, 1935, a customs barrier was planted on Southern Rhodesia's frontier across the Cape-to-Cairo railway and thus marked the end of a dream old as Rhodes's day of one federation from Table Bay to the Zambesi or maybe to Tanganyika.

Dec. 1934.

Feb. 1935.

Though Huggins could point to the good work of the Rhodesian Native Welfare Department and boast justly that, thanks to the state-aided mission schools, a higher proportion of Natives was receiving some sort of education than in any other British African colony, it was only after many months of persistent effort that he felt himself free enough of Imperial control to carry out his Native policy. That policy was based upon the 'gradual differential treatment of the native' in the spirit of the new trusteeship. Since the Natives were to be treated as children till there should be among them 'some regular form of religion,' he proposed to develop the reserves, overstocked and eroded as so many of them were, to revive the powers of chiefs and headmen till such times as the tribesmen were fit for 'Smuts' councils, to improve the 'economic value' of the Natives, to direct their trade into channels in which it should not 'undermine the economic structure of the white race,' and to help them to develop their agriculture 'on lines supplementary to and not competitive with that of the European.'[3]

The last part of this segregation programme had already been put into force during the depression. Ruling as it did a hard hit primary producing community, the Rhodesian Government had tried to keep up internal prices for mealies and cattle and reserve as much as possible of the home market for Europeans lest they go under.

---

[1] United Party, 24; Reform Party, 1; Labour, 5.
[2] *Cape Times*, Feb. 19, 1935.
[3] *Ibid.*, Nov. 1, 1934; April 6, 1936; March 31, 1938.

Other portions of the programme were now carried out in an emergency atmosphere. While Native families were trekking into the unfamiliar towns under stress of the bad times and the uprooting caused by the attempt to enforce the Land Apportionment Act,[1] and Rhodesians were anxiously discussing Native unrest and the danger that their Natives might learn trade union methods from their Union neighbours, a violent strike took place on some of the mines on the May Northern Rhodesian copper belt. Southern Rhodesian police were 1935. at once sent north to help the local forces and were followed, as Pirow's unsolicited contribution, by a Union aeroplane carrying a supply of tear-gas.[2]

The outbreak, precipitated by the folly of some of the Native mine police, had been due to the disintegrating effect of mining life upon raw natives, and their failure to understand a well-intentioned effort to grade the poll tax; but it was stated officially that a pre-disposing cause had been the activities of the anti-European Watch Tower movement, which, like the unhappy Israelites of Bulhoek, based its subversive doctrines on the less intelligible portions of the Old Testament and the Apocalypse.[3] Spurred on by these local terrors, Union example and the rapidly worsening world situation, the Southern Rhodesians overhauled their defence organisation and stiffened their Native laws. As in the Union, a Sedition Act pre- 1936. scribed special penalties for all who spoke or acted 'with intent to cause ill-feeling' between white and black, while the Registration of Natives and Pass Consolidation Acts, based upon the almost forgotten pass laws of Chartered days, gave the executive wide powers to limit the entry or residence of Natives in urban areas on the principle that 'the native is a visitor to our white towns for the purpose of assisting the people who live in towns, and no other native should be present.'[4] On the other hand, since the attempt to disentangle the rural Europeans and Bantu had broken down in face of inherent difficulties, short rainfall, cattle disease and lack of an adequate census, the date for complete segregation outside the for-bidden towns was postponed from 1937 till 1941.[5]

The Southern Rhodesian Premier found time amid these domestic cares to consider wider schemes. Once upon a time the Chartered 1917. Company had suggested the amalgamation, that is, the legislative union of the Two Rhodesias, and ever since the White Paper scare of 1929–30 there had been talk of closer union between those two territories and isolated Nyasaland. Now that his United Party was

---

[1] Acts 30 of 1930, 31 of 1936, and 35 of 1937.
[2] *Cape Times*, May 30 and 31, 1935 ; *Cape Argus*, May 31, 1935; Cmd. 5009 of 1935.
[3] *Vide supra*, p. 587; *Cape Argus*, Nov. 16, 1935.
[4] Acts 14 of 1936, and 34 of 1938.
[5] W. M. Macmillan, *Africa Emergent*, pp. 185 ff.

1935. securely in power and the new customs barrier had apparently ended all prospect of the incorporation of Southern Rhodesia in the Union. Huggins began to advocate the formation of a 'large economic unit' centring upon his colony and suitably favoured by tariff preferences in the British market as a return for Rhodesia's 'past sentimental efforts,' that is, presumably, the Rhodes Customs clause. This unit was to include, on the one side, the northern half of the Bechuanaland Protectorate and a railway corridor to the west coast preferably through mandated territory to Walvis Bay, and on the other Nyasaland and Northern Rhodesia or, at the very least, the Hogsback which carried most of the 13,000 white inhabitants of Northern Rhodesia, the copper mines, and the railway which he desired to see under the control of this 'Greater Rhodesia' before it became a 'black railway' like its extension in the Belgian Congo.[1]

Huggins found much support for his scheme. Thomas, the Dominions Secretary, indeed reminded him publicly that Britain was already taking seventy-five per cent. of his colony's exports besides furnishing defence for nothing;[2] but both he and his successor, Malcolm MacDonald, held out hopes of part of Bechuanaland, while Pirow, the Union's Minister of Communications, and the inhabitants of South-West Africa approved of the projected railway corridor.[3] Again, the virtual reaffirmation by the British Government of the White Paper policy in 1934[4] and the African strike on the Copper Belt in the following year had set white folk on either side of the Zambesi thinking, while in April 1935, the Governors of the Two Rhodesias and Nyasaland and the Prime Minister of Southern Rhodesia had attended a Governors' Conference, the first of its kind, at Salisbury and thus stimulated interest in closer union. Hence, in Northern Rhodesia, the seven elective members of the Legislative Council were returned at a general election pledged to work for amalgamation with Southern Rhodesia, and in Nyasaland many of the eighteen hundred white folk demanded that their territory be included,[5] lest it be grouped with the adjacent provinces of East Africa under the dreaded White Paper policy.

Rhodesians were not prepared to push yet for the 'great White Dominion' of which Nyasalanders dreamed, for that would have meant that a mere 77,000 white folk must control, not only themselves, but some 4,500,000 Africans dispersed over perhaps 488,000 square miles. Legislators from the Two Rhodesias did, however, confer in January 1936 at the Victoria Falls near the famous railway bridge that linked their territories.

[1] *Cape Times*, Oct. 20, 1934; July 10, 1935; *Journal of the Royal African Society*, Jan. 1937, p. 6.
[2] *Cape Times*, July 10, 1935.   [3] *Ibid.*, June 13 and July 10, 1935.
[4] *Northern Rhodesia Legislative Council Debates*, Dec. 1, 1934, col. 12.
[5] *Cape Times*, June 29, 1935.

The Southerners were full of confidence: last year's tobacco crop disposed of, a record gold output, base metals doing well, a loan of £250,000 triumphantly floated in London, revenue coming in most satisfactorily and, thanks to the drought, good local prices for cattle.[1] For their part, now that copper had slumped, the Northerners were inclined towards amalgamation. Both parties, moreover, were determined that the control of policy must be taken out of the hands of rapidly changing officials responsible to a distant authority which was alleged to be only temporarily interested in the Natives, and entrusted to men who had made their homes in Africa and, for lack of educational and other services, saw their children in danger of becoming Poor Whites. Nevertheless, more than one deadlock had to be resolved before a report could be adopted, with one dissentient, and a standing committee be appointed to see it through. The proposal was that, provided H.M. Government consented, a referendum should be taken in each colony on a draft amalgamation constitution based on 'complete self-government,' though hardly on the Dominion status demanded by the Southern Rhodesian Reform party.[2]

The South African Native Affairs commissioners gave their Oct. distant blessing to the scheme and animadverted strongly on the 1936. follies of 'absentee' governments in the north which hampered the new trusteeship of the men on the spot,[3] but H.M. Government declined to hear of amalgamation yet awhile.[4] Then, as the months went by a conflict of voices arose on either side of the Zambesi. Times being less good, enthusiasm for amalgamation was still widespread in Southern Rhodesia, whose Premier roundly condemned July the Imperial liberal policy in mixed colonies as 'hopelessly impractic- 1938. able and leading to disaster.'[5] On the other hand, the pro-Union party had raised its head once more and urged that Southern Rhodesia be linked with the Union as a step perhaps to the fulfilment of Rhodes's idea of one federation from Capetown to Lake Tanganyika.[6] In Northern Rhodesia indignation, stimulated by the Mineworkers' Union of the Rand, was still hot among the white miners against missions which taught trades to Natives, mining companies which gave them blasting certificates and allowed them to drive lorries, and an Imperial Government which countenanced such things;[7] but the elected members in those parts were now less eager for amalgamation. Thanks to the demand for copper in a rearming world, there was a substantial surplus; the local Imperial officials were sympathetic, and Downing Street had not only given elected members two seats on the finance committee, but had promised them

[1] *Cape Times*, March 17, 1936.
[2] *Cape Argus*, Jan. 18, 1936; *Cape Times*, Jan. 25, 1936.
[3] U.G. 48 of 1937.   [4] *Hansard*, 5th Series, cccxiii, 194.
[5] *The Times*, July 19, 1938.   [6] *Ibid.*, May 25, 1938.
[7] *Cape Times*, July 14, 1936.

equality of numbers with the official *bloc* in the Legislative Council and had, meanwhile, arranged that a nominee member should speak for African interests.[1] A depressing report by Sir Alan Pim on the social and economic condition of their Protectorate suggested that plenty of work lay ready to their hands within their own borders.[2]

March 1938. At this stage a Royal Commission under Lord Bledisloe arrived to investigate the possibilities of closer co-operation between the Two Rhodesias and Nyasaland. Southern Rhodesian ministerialists and Reformers offered to put up with continued Imperial control of Native legislation if only they might have amalgamation, though the Reformers asked that the future Greater Rhodesia should be relieved of the Chartered Company's lien upon lands and minerals in Northern Rhodesia and of the crushing Nyasaland public debt. Europeans north of the Zambesi favoured some sort of co-operation; but on both sides of the great river, missionary witnesses were often hesitant and Bantu fearful.[3] As the Commission was concluding its

Aug. 1938. labours, the British Government's proposal to settle five hundred German and Austrian Jewish families in Northern Rhodesia moved leading members of both the Rhodesian legislatures to protest that the transformation of a British colony into 'an annexe of Palestine' would be fatal to the prospects of amalgamation;[4] while the publication of an official report on the precarious condition of Nyasaland

1939. damped their enthusiasm for the inclusion of that province. After spending fully four months in Central Africa, the Bledisloe Commission recommended the speedy union of Northern Rhodesia and Nyasaland and also the acceptance in principle of the ultimate closer union of these two Protectorates with self-governing Southern Rhodesia; but it held that the immediate amalgamation of all three territories was out of the question, if only because Europeans were so few and Native policies on either side of the Zambesi so divergent. Rather did it recommend the combination of certain governmental departments, the appointment of a Commission to co-ordinate existing services and plan economic development, and the creation of an Inter-Territorial Council consisting of the Governors of the two Protectorates, the Prime Minister of Southern Rhodesia and seven other representatives of the three dependencies.[5]

While it watched with sympathy the struggle of Rhodesians to form a federation beyond its northern border, the Union strove to

---

[1] *The Times*, April 22, 1938; N. Rhodesia (Legislative Council) Amendment Order-in-Council, 1938.

[2] *The Times*, April 25, 1938; Colonial, No. 145 of 1938.

[3] *The Times*, May 25 and Aug. 28, 1938.

[4] *Ibid.*, Aug. 2, 1938. The Executive of the East African National Congress also protested against the proposed settlement of Jews in Kenya; *The Times*, Sept. 20, 1938.

[5] *Ibid.*, Oct. 12, 1938; Colonial, No. 152 of 1938; Cmd. 5049 of 1939.

maintain its own hold upon restive South-West Africa. As cattle prices fell and copper and diamond mines closed down during the bad times, the mandated territory had sunk deeper into the Union's debt. Complaints arose against the Union's customs tariff, quota laws and railway rates, and white public opinion ran strongly in favour of shaking off Union shackles and linking up with neighbouring Southern Rhodesia by means of a railway. The Legislative April Council unanimously demanded extended powers. Hertzog agreed 1932. and promised further to recognise German as the third official language, to extend to German settlers the easy naturalisation privileges hitherto reserved for Union nationals and to inquire into economic grievances.

Meanwhile, on the eve of the bad times, the Nazi-minded Brown Dec. Shirt movement had appeared, and now the Union's abandonment 1932– of gold and Hitler's victory in the Fatherland revolutionised the Jan. 1933. situation. The one event led, for the first time, to the formation of a German party, the Deutsche Bund; the other induced the non-Germans to advocate the incorporation of South-West Africa as a fifth Province so that they might share in the subsidies that were being paid to primary producers in the Union. The legislature therefore asked that no steps be taken yet awhile on its recent resolutions. Then, at the end of a trying year of increasing Nazi activities, the July– Administrator banned the Hitler Youth and Nazi organisations and Oct. 1934. expelled the leaders of both. The general election that followed immediately gave the Fifth Province or United Party the necessary two-thirds majority, whereupon it requested that the territory be incorporated. But now, burdened as they still were with the em- Jan. barrassed Orange Free State and mindful of possible difficulties 1935. with Berlin and Geneva, the Union authorities temporised. They appointed a Commission of Inquiry.

While the Commission pursued its investigations, the Nazi forces gathered strength. Unappeased by permission to reconstitute the April Youth Movement on ordinary Scout lines and acting on orders from 1935. Berlin, the recently formed Deutsche Front, which consisted mainly of newly arrived and unnaturalised Germans, obliged the cautious Deutsche Bund to amalgamate with it. The Front leaders gained the upper hand and brought pressure on all Germans, whether naturalised or not, to toe the line. Then, just as the Reich's demand for the restoration of her lost colonies became insistent, the Commission reported.[1] It found that the administration had ruled the Natives June well with the small means at its disposal,[2] providing something like 1936. indirect rule for the tribal Ovambo in the north and, where possible,

---

[1] U.G. 26 of 1936; *Round Table*, No. 104, pp. 772 ff.
[2] Europeans = 31,000, nearly half of whom were Germans, naturalised or unnaturalised; Natives = 267,000.

reserves and agricultural aid for the shattered Hereros further south. The rest of its report was less cheering. Thanks to Nazi activities and the lack of political wisdom of the various parties, the constitution had broken down, the public debt was no less than £3,500,000, and finance was desperate.

The Union Government accepted its Commission's financial proposals. It placed past loans to suspense account and demanded no interest on them, permitted South-West Africa to borrow from the Union for productive purposes, directed it to balance its budget by additional taxation if necessary, and required it to pay over to itself, whenever possible, all in excess of a fixed amount of its diamond revenues. On the other hand, since the three commissioners had differed as to the future form of government, whether administration as a fifth Province, or as a glorified Cape Division, or frankly as a predominantly Native protectorate on lines similar to those laid down in the Schedule of the South Africa Act, it decided that the present democratic constitution should be continued and steps be taken to make it workable.

Dec.
1936.
To that end the Union Government promised to recognise German as an official language, sanctioned purely cultural associations, and sought to remove the uncertainty which was hampering the economic recovery of the country by announcing that it was 'not prepared to consider the possibility of the transfer of the Mandate to another Power.'[1] It finally issued the South-West Africa Proclamation to check disruptive political activities, limiting membership of any 'public body' to British subjects, forbidding British subjects to make oath to any foreign sovereign, government or organisation, and authorising the deportation of foreigners who indulged in illegal

Apr. 2,
1937.
political propaganda. The Administrator forthwith proclaimed the three political parties of the Territory as 'public bodies.'[2]

The anxious Union authorities might hope that these resolute measures would have a quieting effect, especially as they were accompanied by an improvement in the market for diamonds, karakul and base metals. The Deutsche Bund did indeed reconstitute itself as the Deutsche Sud-West Bund and promised to obey the law; but the less tractable German leaders, continually reinforced by newcomers from the Fatherland, demanded a 'Mandate citizenship' for the territory which would have circumvented the recent proclamation,[3] while Berlin protested against the 'combative' action of the Government, and claimed that the naturalisation settlement effected by Smuts and the Weimar Republic in 1923 had been of a merely temporary nature.[4]

July
1938.
The Fusion ministry turned aside the demand of the United

[1] *Round Table*, No. 106, p. 446.   [2] *Ibid.*, No. 108, p. 864.
[3] *Ibid.*, No. 111, p. 629.   [4] *The Times*, March 16, 1938.

South-West Africa party that the Mandated Territory be incorporated for administrative purposes in the Union, and that British status be withdrawn from all naturalised British subjects who would not disclaim a dual allegiance; but, as crisis followed crisis in Central Europe and the Far East, it repeated with ever-increasing emphasis that it would defend what it held in Southern Africa 'to the bitter end.'[1]

As the life of the Coalition Parliament drew towards its close, the Fusion ministry could look back upon its record of achievement with satisfaction and forward to the general election with reasonable confidence. In the months immediately following Fusion, the Dominion Party had gained adherents by attacking the ministry's domestic policy, while the Nationalists had rallied increasing numbers with the cry of 'South Africa alone.' Presently, however, the Dominion Party had lost ground. It spoke with two voices on the Native question; its appeal to the overburdened urban taxpayer and investor rang hollow in face of abounding prosperity; all that remained to it were legalistic criticisms of those *faits accomplis*: the Statute of Westminster and the Status Acts, and the demand that South Africa should proclaim itself 'an integral and indivisible part of the British Empire,' a demand that was robbed of much of its force by Hertzog's repeated and unwonted tributes to the Royal Navy.[2] The Nationalists, on the other hand, widened their front by attacking the ministry in general and Hofmeyr in particular for their half-hearted Native policy, hesitation to segregate the Coloured Folk and tenderness towards Jews. For all that, it was only in the Cape Province, Malan's stronghold, that the Nationalists registered marked gains in seats and voting strength at the Provincial elections towards the close of 1936.

The Ministry could point to a good record of social legislation. This included the creation of a Railway and Harbours Sick Fund, provision of public employment for the poorer whites and, failing them, for Africans on railway, forestry, irrigation and anti-erosion schemes and so forth, the Blind Persons Act which gave financial aid to those who were physically or mentally unfit to earn a living, and an Unemployment Benefit Act which broke new ground by calling on workers as well as employers to contribute to the fund. The Ministry could even congratulate itself that one of the primary aims of Fusion was in process of achievement: the coalescence of the main body of the British and Afrikaners into a single South African nation. Once the British section had in a measure been relieved of fear of unalloyed Afrikaner domination, free play had been given to the unifying forces that had long been at work beneath

Margin note: May 1933– May 1938.

---

[1] *Bulletin of International News*, XV. No. 24, p. 1164.
[2] *Vide infra*, pp. 682, 691.

22

the surface. The old economic and social dividing line had been blurred as the British went on to the land in increasing numbers and Afrikaners came into the towns, and now that the vast majority of the British were South African born and bred and were intermarrying freely with the Afrikaners, the old taunt that the Englishman was only a sojourner in the land had lost its sting. The two sections therefore found that they could readily work together in the Cabinet and the Houses, display considerable unanimity over the Status Bills and still more over Native legislation, combine to demand protection for their industries, and approve, like so many isolationist Canadians, of the cautious policy of a ministry which declined to commit their country in advance to any automatic participation in the quarrels of the explosive Continent of Europe to which Great Britain was unhappily adjacent.

But though the idea of 'South Africa first' appealed to an increasing number of British South Africans, they and the Afrikaners were still far from being one people. The British had a sentimental regard for the Old Country and things British which few of their neighbours could share. Moreover, they were a political minority, and many of them did not relish the fact. At times they felt resentful because all the leading South African politicians seemed to be Afrikaners, and had an uneasy suspicion that the Afrikanerising May of the public services was being overdone; it came as a shock to 1937. them that there was hardly one man of British stock in all the long train of ministers, secretaries, advisers and the rest who attended the Coronation Imperial Conference. Malan's Nationalists naturally did their best to exploit these feelings and thus bring down the Fusion ministry.

Men of all parties joined sincerely in mourning the death of George Dec. V, but British pride and Afrikaner puritanism were shocked by the 1936. abdication of his eldest son within the year and by the circumstances which attended it. Unhappily the abdication had been preceded by protests when Edward VIII had been toasted at a state banquet, without due warning or discussion, first as 'The King' and then as March 'The King of South Africa.' It was accompanied by something like a 1937. storm over the appointment of a South African citizen as Governor-General in succession to the deservedly popular Lord Clarendon. The appointment of a Union national was a course to which the Premier had long been committed and for which he had Irish and Australian precedent, and no better man could have been chosen than Patrick Duncan, one of Milner's Scottish importations who had remained after his chief had gone home; nevertheless, quite apart from their regret at this apparent weakening of yet another Imperial link, the mass of the British joined with many Afrikaners in disapproving of the elevation to such an office of one who had spent a

lifetime in South African politics, and, at the time of his appointment, had been a minister of the Crown. In view of the republican
tradition and partisan nature of Union politics, the precedent set
was, in their eyes, most dangerous, especially as the Irish Free State
had first reduced the holder to a cypher and now, in the heat of the
abdication crisis, had abolished the office.

Parliament duly confirmed the Abdication and all that flowed
therefrom. An Abdication Act declared the facts of abdication and
succession,[1] and by a misunderstanding of the English Common
Law strengthened the theory of the divisibility of the Crown by
taking December 10 as the effective date instead of the 11th.[2] The
companion Coronation Oath Act reflected the advance that had been
made in Dominion status since the last coronation a quarter of a
century back by binding the King to rule South Africans 'according
to the statutes agreed on in the Parliament of the Union and according to their other laws and customs,'[3] a local oath which was May
presently incorporated in the collective oath which George VI took 12,
at his coronation. One more storm arose, however, before the new 1937.
King was crowned. Hertzog gave many the impression that he was
prepared to yield to the Nationalist demand for the excision of the
words 'British subject' from the definition of a Union national.
Angry protests were only stilled when the Imperial Conference, of
which he was himself a member, explained authoritatively what a
Dominion national was and defined a British subject as 'a subject
of the King in whatever part of the Empire he might live.' And to
prove that His Majesty still functioned with undivided powers as the
fountain of honour, the new Governor-General was dubbed knight.

So the Fusion ministry plodded on towards the general election
notoriously divided on such vital problems as those of the Natives,
Coloured Folk, Indians and Jews, and conscious that the tide of
prosperity was on the ebb.[4] Havenga had noted the first signs of
recession early in 1937 and had given warning that he could not go
on indefinitely providing permanent social services on the strength
of fortuitous surpluses. Then had come a series of 'Black Fridays' Mar.–
on the Johannesburg stock exchange as a result of rumours that the June
United States proposed to suspend the purchase of bullion, and 1937.
disappointment that the Imperial Conference had done nothing to
stabilise gold. After these setbacks had come the drought, and after the
drought infuriating muddles by the mealie and dairy marketing boards.

However, times were still reasonably good and Malan's Nationalists had played their cards badly. Their leaders had first disappointed

---

[1] Act 2 of 1937.
[2] The Irish Free State, on the other hand, lengthened Edward VIII's reign
in Ireland by twenty-four hours.
[3] Act 7 of 1937.
[4] For the internal political struggle *vide Round Table*, No. 106 onwards.

honest republicans and driven half the Transvaal party executive to resign by making play with republicanism but refusing to work for it here and now, and then, inspired by Dr. Albertus Hertzog, the Prime Minister's son, had alienated Labour by trying to organise a racial *Afrikaanse Mynworkers' Unie* in opposition to the recognised and already predominantly Afrikaner Mineworkers' Union. At the last moment, however, the ministry presented the Dominion party

Feb. 1938.
with a dangerous weapon. At the opening of Parliament the band played 'Die Stem van Suidafrika,' a song which Afrikaners and many British also had learned to regard as a genuinely South African anthem, as well as the time-honoured 'God Save the King.' The Premier's involved explanations aroused suspicion that he meant to substitute 'Die Stem' bit by bit for 'God Save the King,' and thus revived the bitter feelings that had characterised the flag controversy

May 1938.
ten years before. At last, however, a satisfactory official explanation was forthcoming and the mass of the British voted for the ministerialists with easy minds.

Labour came back weaker than ever; the Dominion men certainly gained on balance by their victories at East London and in coastal Natal, but were wiped out in Capetown and along the Rand, where even their leader lost his seat; the United Party was successful beyond expectation, retaining all save six of its old seats. This victory was, however, more apparent than real. The old South African Party, with its strong British urban element, now formed a much larger proportion of the strength of the Fusionists, a thing distasteful to the Nationalist-minded wing and, it was no secret, to the Premier himself; while the Sinn Fein programme of the Nationalists: anti-British connection, anti-Jew, anti-Coloured, anti-Asiatic and anti-Native, had made a wide appeal. The Nationalists came back in increased strength dominating many of the Cape districts and holding more than one-third of the seats in Hertzog's Free State. If bad times set in, there might well be a landslide in their direction in other rural areas and even in the Houses.[1]

The Fusion ministry entered upon its renewed lease of life
May 31, 1938.
disastrously. On Union Day, immediately after the elections, 'Die Stem' was played as a general salute at the military parades in most of the big towns, and, since the Governor-General was not present,
June 2, 1938.
'God Save the King' was not played at all. Stuttaford, Minister of the Interior, resigned and, to give point to this warning that there was an end to British patience, a United Party constituency on the

[1]	United Party	Nationalists	Dominion	Labour	Independents
Old House .	117	20	5	4	4
New House .	111	27	8	3	1
Votes (1938) .	445,781	259,450	57,759	43,193	30,848

Rand returned a Labour candidate at a Provincial by-election. The ministry stilled the uproar and enabled Stuttaford to return by hastily announcing that, in future, since the Union had no national anthem of its own, whenever one of the two tunes was played on suitable occasions, the other would be played too. With nerves jangled anew by the accidental drowning of 'God Save the King' in the fanfare of trumpets as the Governor-General took his seat at the opening of Parliament, the Assembly gave short shrift to a Nationalist motion that now was the appropriate moment to choose a single anthem for the Union.

This done, the ministerialists perused the Budget with what composure they might, a cheerless document seeing that the Johannesburg building boom had slackened and now, with revenue down and falling, Havenga was forced to reduce the income tax abatement and anticipate a small deficit. The Ministry itself was then involved in domestic troubles which raised big issues. One minister, Adrian Fourie, had been defeated at the elections, and, in spite of the Premier's best efforts, had failed to find a seat within the prescribed three months. He was therefore obliged to surrender his portfolio, which, after a struggle between the Cape and Transvaal members of the ministry, was given to Harry Lawrence, a young Cape lawyer to whom Hertzog had promised office. Hertzog, however, was determined to have Fourie in the ministry even at the cost of creating a twelfth portfolio, perhaps to strengthen the Afrikaner element in the cabinet, perhaps lest Fourie, who had at one time opposed Coalition strongly, might gravitate towards Malan and draw others after him. The twelfth portfolio was duly created, not without opposition in Parliament, and then one of the four Senators, who had been nominated in terms of the South Africa Act[1] mainly for his 'thorough acquaintance with the reasonable wants and wishes of the coloured races,' resigned. Without consulting some of his fellow ministers and in spite of the protests of the elected representatives of the Bantu in both Houses, Hertzog gave the vacant seat to Fourie, who lacked any such qualification. It was a blow in the face to every black man in the Union and outside it. 'The issue is simply this,' cried Hofmeyr: Sept. 'Are we going to allow non-Europeans to be made pawns in the white man's political game? One safeguard goes to-day, the next will go to-morrow.' He resigned and took with him his fellow-Transvaaler, Frederick Sturrock. After some delay, Deneys Reitz and Henry Fagan shared Hofmeyr's late offices between them, Colonel William Collins relieved Reitz of Agriculture and Robert Henderson, sole representative in the Cabinet of the all-important Rand, succeeded Sturrock as Minister without Portfolio. Meanwhile, Senator Fourie had been sworn in as Minister of Commerce and

9, 1938.

[1] *Race Relations News*, No, 3, p. 1; South African Act, § 24 (ii).

Industries, and within a week the apathy or anger of its supporters had lost the United Party four Provincial by-elections in the Transvaal to Labour and Nationalists.

Hertzog sought to restore the situation by reshuffling his Cabinet so that Pirow became Minister of Commerce and Industries as well as of Defence, and Reitz and Fourie Ministers respectively of Mines and Railways. Recovery came, however, by force of circumstances rather than political generalship. The Prime Minister and his personal followers reckoned that, in face of the dangerous world situation, they must have the backing of the British, while the latter felt that they must rally to him and his, because the often ill-natured Nationalist campaign to exacerbate exclusively Afrikaner patriotism during the centenary celebrations of the Great Trek in the latter half of 1938 had warned them that they must have friends in the Afrikaner camp, lest they become a racial minority in a world where such minorities were wont to fare badly. Meanwhile, the Nationalists had been reinforced by two new organisations born of the truculent and isolationist spirit which had pervaded the recent celebrations. The first was the *Reddingsdaadbond*, an offshoot of the *Broederbond*, which sought to further the business interests of Afrikaners in the narrowest sense. The second was the much more flamboyant *Ossewabrandwag* (The Ox-waggon Sentinel), which had been founded in the Free State by the Bloemfontein predikant, the Rev. Christian Kotze, to perpetuate 'the spirit of the ox-waggon,' in other words, the spirit of the Trekkers, and, more generally, to uphold, apply and give expression to 'the traditions and principles of the Dutch-Afrikander.' There was no notion here of imitating Hertzog and the elder Hofmeyr by accepting as Afrikaners all white folk who truly put South Africa first; the stress was not on the mind and heart, but entirely on the blood in true Hitler fashion. Nominally a cultural association like the *Broederbond* in its early days, the *O.B.* was semi-secret, bound by a stringent oath and wedded to National-Socialist ideals to the extent of accepting the *Führerprinzip*. In short, it was a thoroughly totalitarian organisation, which stood for an exclusive and intolerant Nationalism and set out to subject its fellow-Afrikaners to the peculiar brand of discipline it conceived they needed. Since it was organised on a commando basis, it had its Commandant-General, Colonel Jacobus Laas, and though Pirow soon dismissed him from his post in the Permanent Defence Force, it had soon enrolled Johannes Swart and other prominent Free Staters and, once it had spread to the Transvaal, became the most influential Afrikaner popular movement since the Great Trek itself.[1]

[1] Roberts and Trollip, *op. cit.*, pp. 73 ff.; Davidson, *op. cit.*, pp. 156, 169; Hatch, *op. cit.*, p. 41; C. R. Kotze. *Die Ossewa Brandwag*, pp. 3 ff.; A. J. H. van der Walt, *Volk op Trek*, pp. 8 ff., 19.

The *Reddingsdaadbond* and the *Ossewabrandwag* could be trusted to join wholeheartedly in hounding down anything so alien to capitalism and 'Dutch-Afrikander' traditions as trade unionism. There was need, for there were now some 216,000 trade unionists of all colours.[1] The assault was pressed most hotly against Sachs, perhaps the most prominent trade union leader of his day. Sachs, however, gave more than he got with the aid of the Courts, which thus early proved themselves stumbling-blocks to Nationalist policy. Early in 1939, he received substantial damages and costs against *Die Oosterlig*, the Malanite Port Elizabeth newspaper, and damages and an apology without going into Court from *Die Vaderland*, a nominally independent journal. His most striking victory was against some of the Nationalist predikants whose excursions into politics moved Hertzog to protest. The Synodical Commission of the *Niederduitse Hervormde Kerk*, the old state Church of the South African Republic, embodied its two-year-long investigations into 'Communism in the Trade Union Movement,' in a report that was little more than an unbridled attack on Sachs himself and his devoted Union, regardless of the fact that neither he nor many others concerned were Communists. Sachs struck back. He indeed accepted out of Court the compensation proffered by one of the reverend authors, but he was awarded £600 damages and many thousands of pounds in costs against the recalcitrant *Voortrekkerpers*, the publishers of the report. Though he was thus harassed, Sachs was at least more fortunate than Charlie Harris, secretary of the white Mineworkers' Union, who in June, 1939, was murdered on the steps of his own office by a young Afrikaner inflamed by the heady propaganda of which Albertus Hertzog's Reform Organisation was the chief source.[2]

Albertus, meanwhile, had earned a paternal rebuke for suggesting that the *Afrikaner Volk* should get together as a solid political group, and never mind 'the English.' Never would the old Prime Minister hear of any such exclusive scheme. Rather did he, and Pirow also, welcome the much more liberal suggestion of Professor Andries Cilliers of the University of Stellenbosch that the two rival sections of the Nationalist Party should, indeed, unite, but then find room for all white citizens who put South Africa first. Such a course was to both politicians the necessary preliminary to the creation of a republic. Not so to Malan. He insisted that the Republic must come before there could be any talk of reunion and comprehension.[3] Apparently, many electors concurred with Malan, for though they had to let the ministerialists win one Parliamentary by-election,

---

[1] *Report of the Department of Labour, 1938*, U.G. 51, 1939, p. 35.
[2] Sachs, *op. cit.*, pp. 56 ff., 170 ff.
[3] A. C. Cilliers, *Quo Vadis?* and *Die Stryd om Volkseenheid*, pp. 38 ff.; van den Heever, *op. cit.*, pp. 684 ff.; D. F. Malherbe, *Afrikaner Volkseenheid*, p. 35; *Die Burger*, March 6, 1939; Roberts and Trollip, *op. cit.*, pp. 17 ff.

they reduced their majority in three others. Doubtless the Nationalists approved when the authorities gave the franchise to European women in South-West Africa [1] and certainly emphasised one item of their domestic policy by presenting a monster petition in favour of Coloured segregation; meanwhile, they took heart at the multiplication of points of friction between the masterful Smuts and the increasingly dictatorial Prime Minister and a renewed demonstration of independence by the upright but difficult Hofmeyr. This latest crisis arose out of the Asiatic (Transvaal Land and Trading) Bill. The Ministry introduced this Bill to call a halt to the rapidly spreading practice of Indians in the Transvaal trading under illegal licences. The first part of the Bill 'pegged' the *status quo* till April 1941, by which time the Government hoped that it would have been able to solve this problem in consultation with the Government of India on the basis of the residential segregation which it was proposing to apply also to the Coloured Folk; the second part debarred Indians from getting new licences during the pegged period without ministerial consent. The first part went through easily enough, but by reason of its naked racialism, the second part called forth fierce protests from Hofmeyr and Leslie Blackwell, the member for Kensington on the Rand. So strongly did these two men feel on that score that they withdrew from the party caucus.

Some time back, Havenga had warned the Assembly that the loan account was swelling markedly and that since he had had difficulty in raising an internal loan, he must look overseas once more for financial aid with the knowledge that he could not reckon on getting March such good terms as in times past. Now, however, he could report 1939. that, thanks to an unexpectedly large intake of revenue, he not only had a surplus for the current year but could look forward to another for the year 1940–50. On the other hand, he intimated that though he could use part of this surplus to restore the cancelled income tax abatement, he would have to devote the bulk of it to harbours and defence.[2] On the one hand, the Government was already taking steps to transform Table Bay into a great harbour capable of sheltering very large merchant vessels and hydroplanes, thus implementing resolutions of successive Imperial Conferences that the provision of safe and adequate harbours would be an invaluable contribution to the naval and mercantile strength of the Commonwealth. On the other, now that the country had adequate air personnel and enough first and second line planes thanks to the purchase of machines on easy terms from Great Britain and, at some risk to the principle of Commonwealth interchangeability, from Germany also, the projected striking force was to be increased from 56,000 to 67,000 all

---

[1] Constitution Amendment Proclamation, No. 103 of 1939.
[2] *The Times*, Aug. 11, 1938; *Round Table*, No. 115, p. 640.

told.[1] Presumably the Minister of Defence was pushing ahead with the training of his men; in any event, he was importing British regular non-commissioned officers to smarten up the Permanent Force and was himself taking part in joint manœuvres by the Active Citizen Force and the Imperial Simonstown Squadron.

The Union Government faced the problem of supply with a comparatively easy mind. South Africa's financial resources were large; it could feed itself in a rough and ready way; it possessed minerals in great variety, and could clothe itself from its abundant hides, wool and low veld cotton. The Pretoria Steel Works, like Kruger's much criticised dynamite factory in days gone by, could turn out small-arm ammunition and, in conjunction with the widely dispersed state workshops, supply railway rolling stock. The National Road Fund, inaugurated in 1935, was giving the country good roads to supplement its railways, while the making of explosives at the De Beers dynamite factory and elsewhere presented no difficulties. Petrol, indeed, was lacking, but benzol from the Steel Works furnished a serviceable substitute and sugar alcohol a supplement, while castor oil provided an excellent lubricant. The most serious deficiencies were rubber and plant for heavy armament and internal combustion engines.[2]

Armaments presuppose policy. The Union faced that problem in three capacities; first, as a member of the British Commonwealth; then, as a member of the League; finally, and more and more consciously, as the most powerful African state in its own right south of the Sahara.

Controversy raged earliest and longest over the responsibilities arising from the first of the Union's international manifestations. At the close of 1934, Japan denounced the Washington Naval Treaty of 1922. The Dominion Party at once demanded that the Union should undertake definite commitments in a scheme of Empire defence.[3] The Nationalists, on the contrary, called for a formal assertion of the rights of secession and neutrality and a declaration that their country would keep out of all 'British' wars, and were even prepared to cede Simonstown to Great Britain as a southern Gibraltar rather than see neutrality jeopardised by the Smuts-Churchill agreement.[4] Smuts, for his part, directed the gaze of his fellow South Africans away from old Europe to Asia where great things were happening, and also to the United States with which the Dominions by their very origins had 'fundamental sympathy' and to which they must partly look for their security.[5] Hertzog declared that he was as ready as ever to co-operate with

(margin note: Jan. 1935.)

---

[1] *The Times*, Jan. 23, 1938.   [2] *Round Table*, No. 107, pp. 556 ff.
[3] *Cape Times*, Feb. 9, 1935.   [4] *Ibid.*, Jan. 31, 1935.
[5] *Ibid.*, Feb. 11, 1935.

22*

Great Britain and the rest of the Commonwealth on condition that the interests of South Africa were always 'number one,'[1] but it was Pirow who stated the ministry's policy most precisely.[2] With a reminder that Union governments of whatever party colour had always worked in close touch with the Imperial Committee of Defence and had done all that the British Government had even hinted that they should do, he stated flatly that the Union would never subscribe to a cut-and-dried scheme of Empire defence, and, recalling the rebellion of 1914 and the spirit of cautious aloofness that was now so widespread even among South Africans of British stock, gave fair warning that civil war might follow any attempt rashly to commit the Union to an overseas war. Again and again, during the months that were to come, he and Hertzog and Smuts insisted that there would be no automatic commitment as in 1914 simply because Great Britain went to war, and that in any event the decision to participate would lie with the South African Parliament. Though defence was to be one of the principal topics at the Imperial Conference of 1937, the Fusion ministry gave notice that its representatives would not come to any decision there on matters of principle affecting South Africa.

Shortly after the first outlining of policy by Pirow, however, the British Government had foreshadowed a belated scheme to bring its armaments nearer to the level of those of other Powers. Hertzog at once showed the direction in which his mind was moving. His political past had been one long struggle against Imperial entanglements, and he had driven his then colleague, Patrick Duncan, to talk of resignation by claiming that Simonstown could be treated as 'foreign territory' in the event of war.[3] Now, however, he acknowledged handsomely that Britain was South Africa's 'greatest friend and most powerful friend . . . and now that our freedom has been restored . . . the British Navy means exactly the same to me as to an Englishman . . . because the freedom of my people and my country is just as dependent upon it as England is herself. . . .'[4] Next day the German Reich restored conscription and, a little later, Italy assumed a threatening attitude towards Abyssinia.

It was then that South Africa's relations with the League of Nations began to take first place in the public mind. Hitherto, South Africans had looked to the system of collective security as a double safeguard, which, even if it could not prevent war, would at least slow down and localise its impact and bring condign punishment on the aggressor, and would also, as Smuts noted, solve for the Dominions the awkward problem of neutrality, because so long as Great Britain pursued a League policy and no member of the

Feb.
1935.

March
1935.

[1] *Cape Times*, Jan. 31, 1935.   [2] *Ibid.*, Feb. 6, 1935.
[3] *Ibid.*, Jan. 31, 1935.   [4] *Ibid.*, March 15, 1935.

Commonwealth was proclaimed the aggressor, the duty of the Union as a member of the League was clear and no question of a 'British' war could ever arise. Few had as yet realised that recourse to the League's armoury of sanctions might lead to war.

As the Italians ploughed their way through the dominions of the King of Kings excitement in South Africa mounted higher. Whichever way victory inclined, the results of the war could not fail to be evil for the Union. If the Italians were beaten again in Abyssinia, as at Adowa in 1896, the prestige of the white man would suffer in the eyes of the Bantu and Coloured Folk, who were already muttering against this most recent European aggression all the way down from Kenya to Capetown. If they won, Africans would be resentful and a strong and expansive power would be planted on the flank of the Union's aerial communications with Great Britain; its planes and askaris would threaten British tropical African colonies in which the Union was taking an increasing interest, while its submarines would not only threaten the East Coast route but might even follow southward the Italian submarines which had recently visited Union ports in the wake of the subsidised Italian merchantmen. Above all, an Italian victory would be a blow to the system of collective security, and would set a dangerous example to other dissatisfied Powers, to Germany for instance.

The Union responded at once to the suggestion advanced by Sir Sept. Samuel Hoare, the British Foreign Secretary, that a Conference be 11, 1935. summoned to consider a fair distribution of colonial raw materials as a step towards appeasement and that, meanwhile, economic sanctions should be applied to Italy;[1] indeed, her High Commissioner, the first official representative of a League member to do so, bound her to go to the limit lest Africa be left 'at the mercy of uncontrolled events.'[2] She further hailed with satisfaction the victory of the Nov. National Party at the British elections with an open mandate for 1935. foreign policy, largely on the strength of its stand for League principles. All the more severe, then, was the shock of the Hoare-Laval Dec. proposal to partition Abyssinia, a right-about-turn executed without 1935. warning and still less any consultation with the Dominions, an abrupt abandonment of the pro-League policy which the Union had learned to expect from the greatest of world powers and chief supporter of collective security. The immediate Commonwealth crisis passed with the resignation of the Foreign Secretary and the dropping of the partition proposal. Thereafter the half-hearted attempt to enforce sanctions failed, the Italians marched into Addis Ababa, and sanctions were cancelled in spite of the uncompromising opposition of the Union Government.[3] In the confusion, the March 1936.

[1] *The Times*, Sept. 12, 1935.   [2] *Round Table*, No. 101, p. 181.
[3] *Ibid.*, No. 104, pp. 855 ff.

Germans remilitarised the Rhineland, and the Führer at last raised seriously the demand for the restoration of the lost German colonies.[1] Hertzog, for his part, hurried off his Minister of Defence to London to discuss problems of rearmament and communications.

Pirow's visit to London was a sign that the Fusion ministry realised that the Union's membership of the crumbling system of collective security had become of secondary importance. Two principal rôles remained to it: its partnership in the British Commonwealth and its position as the leading African power. There was at the moment, as Pirow noted, a ninety per cent. coincidence of interest between the two,[2] but that might not always be so, and therefore, it was less than ever possible for the Union to commit itself to any rigid scheme of Empire policy and defence. Plainly South Africa proposed to stress its sovereign independence.

It was a natural policy to pursue. The Union was one of the oldest and far and away the largest and most firmly rooted of European settlements in Africa. More than 2,000,000 white men dwelt within its borders and those of dependent South-West Africa in temperate lands side by side with some 7,600,000 Coloured Folk, Indians and Bantu, whereas, in all the British territories from its frontiers to the borders of Abyssinia, there were scarcely more than 110,000 white men scattered among fully 16,000,000 of the other races and subject to all the unpredictable effects upon *homo Europaicus* of height above sea level, distance from the calming ocean, and the plunging actinic rays of the tropical sun.

Union influence had long extended far to the north. Southern Rhodesia, which contained more than half the white men in all the broad red belt beyond the Union's northern border, had been settled originally from the south; its law was still fundamentally the Roman-Dutch law of the old Cape Colony, and its appeals lay to the South African appellate division. Union troops had fought Germans and askaris in Tanganyika, and Union citizens had settled there after the war; some of the original Kenya settlers had been South Africans; the Dutch Reformed Church had missions as far north as the Sudan. The White Paper scare of 1929–30 had stimulated a 'get-together' movement from Kenya southward, and since then, the Union's Native policy had either been adapted to local uses or applauded by Europeans on both sides of the Zambesi and throughout Tanganyika and the Kenya highlands. For all that, the expectation and perhaps the desire for political expansion northward had died away in the Union as it became increasingly plain that Southern Rhodesia was set upon independent courses.

1935.

The most that the Union could now look forward to was the formation of two or three federations between its own frontier and

[1] *Vide infra*, p. 686.   [2] *Round Table*, No. 104, p. 856.

that of the Sudan, which, in the words of its Minister of Defence, should be 'linked to the Union by a common Native policy . . .' and, 'directly flowing from the common Native policy, a common defence policy.'[1] Indeed, Pirow's Defence Force was avowedly intended to help the smaller European communities in the north, especially in the event of attack by blacks or other non-Europeans. It was the one kind of war in which he could envisage the Union's taking part without hesitation, and it was he who had sent tear-gas north by carrier-plane May in the tracks of Southern Rhodesian troopers to help the Northern 1935. Rhodesian police to deal with Bantu strikers on the copper mines.

Towards the close of 1935, at the height of the Abyssinian crisis, the Union stood forth as the initiator of common action on an African scale. Its government acted as host to two Conferences, the one on health, the other on posts, telegraphs and radio communications, which were attended by official representatives from South-West Africa, the High Commission Territories, the Two Rhodesias, Nyasaland, Tanganyika, Kenya and Uganda, Portuguese Mozambique and Angola, and the Belgian Congo.[2] Next year, during the Sept. Johannesburg Empire Exhibition, it welcomed representatives and, 1936. in some cases, the heads of the same governments and of French Madagascar also to discuss transportation. This Conference adopted the South African 3 foot 6 inch gauge as the railway standard, agreed to co-ordinate roads, railways and the demarcation of air-routes, set up a permanent secretariate, and arranged to meet again in 1940 at Lourenço Marques.[3] A short year later, when the flying-boats of 1937. Imperial Airways were already making the run from England to Durban well within the week and the service of South African Airways had been extended beyond Lusaka in Northern Rhodesia to Kisumu in Kenya, Pirow made a 7,000-mile 'goodwill' flight. Taking with him Stallard, leader of the Dominion Party, but unhappily not the leader of the Nationalists who had declined the invitation, he traversed Union, Mandated, Portuguese, Belgian and British territory, conferred in Kenya with the British Parliamentary Under-Secretary for Air, and came home more fully convinced than ever that all Africa roughly up to the line of the Equator, excluding the French Equatorial Provinces but including Kenya and Uganda, was the concern of the Union, and that this vast territory could be made 'much more self-sufficient' than it was.[4]

For some time past, Malan had advocated the proclamation of a 1935. Monroe doctrine protecting 'free and peaceful South Africa' as a corollary of his desired declaration of neutrality.[5] Pirow had also

[1] *Cape Times*, Feb. 6, 1935.   [2] *Ibid.*, Oct. 16, 1935.
[3] *Round Table*, No. 105, pp. 214 ff.
[4] *Journal of the Royal African Society*, July 1937; *cf. The Times*, Feb. 6, 1936.
[5] *Cape Times*, Feb. 9, 1938.

toyed with the idea of a declaration against the powers of Asia, though his declaration would have had to be backed by force lest the Union meet an enemy who was 'too stupid to understand its con-

Aug. 1935.

stitutional position.'[1] Uplifted by the proofs of the Union's growing influence in Africa and alarmed at the bloodshed in other parts of the world, South Africans of more than one party talked of a Monroe doctrine, at all events for the southern half of their continent. These vague dreams were disturbed by the success of Italian arms and diplomacy and the growing insistence of the German demand for the old colonies; they were dispelled by the dreadful approach of a war that threatened to devastate Western civilisation in all its parts. South Africans, other than stalwart Nationalists, were steadily driven to the conclusion that the Union's best hope of security, if such could be found in an increasingly naughty world, lay in her membership of the British Commonwealth.

The Führer had put out a feeler as early as March 1935 and, in spite of the fact that H.M. Government was not prepared to discuss the transfer of any mandates,[2] had received indirect encouragement from the Union. Malan had advocated an all-round redistribution of colonies, provided that 'a special case' was made of South-West Africa, nearly all of whose European inhabitants were British subjects and more than half of them immigrants from the Union,[3] while Pirow, on the contrary, had gone so far as to admit that, if one or more of the African mandates must go back to Germany, he had rather it was South-West Africa than Tanganyika. In March 1936, Hitler put the colonial question in the forefront of his programme.[4]

Second thoughts had led Pirow and those who felt with him to change their minds, and they now shrank from the thought of seeing a totalitarian power entrenched upon the west coast a few hours' flight from the gold mines of the Witwatersrand or the great harbour and naval base in the Cape Peninsula, which was fast resuming the imperial and world importance of pre-Suez Canal days now that Italy was established in strength at so many points on the Red Sea-

July 1936.

Mediterranean route. Just after his hurried visit to London to discuss defence problems, however, Pirow raised the hopes of Berlin, embarrassed London and Pretoria, and alarmed some of the smaller colonial powers of Europe by stating that 'influential quarters in England' were convinced that there would be no peace in Europe till Germany had been given adequate colonial compensation, and that, though the restoration of Tanganyika and South-West Africa was not practical politics, he himself would like to see Germany

[1] *Round Table*, No. 99, p. 484.

[2] On the German claim to colonies see *Germany's Claim to Colonies* (Chatham House, May 1938).

[3] *Round Table*, No. 101, p. 184.   [4] *Germany's Claim to Colonies*, p. 27.

with a foothold in Africa once more, if only as a counterpoise to Italy. Which power was to provide that foothold he did not say.[1]

Pirow's indiscretion having been duly explained away, the controversy circled nearer and nearer to South-West Africa, while General Franco, with unofficial German and Italian aid, began to make head against the democratic government of Spain near the point of junction of South Africa's Atlantic and Mediterranean routes to Europe. To allay unrest in its Mandated territory and the Union, the Fusion ministry announced that it was not prepared to consider transfer to any other power.[2] A little later it stated specifically that it would not hand South-West Africa back to Germany, though, this time, Hertzog sought to render the refusal less unpalatable by expressing the hope that as soon as the conditions of the mandate had been carried out, whenever that might be, the Union and the *Reich* might agree upon the territory's future in a manner helpful to both parties.[3] *(Dec. 1936. March 1937.)*

Yet another 'indiscretion' carried the dangerous debate a stage further. The Union's High Commissioner in London, on holiday in Montreal, ventured to hope aloud that his government would be prepared to sit at a round table conference to examine the German claim to colonies and similar grievances. Amid a stony silence from Pretoria, he presently damped the ardour of Berlin by stipulating that nothing must be done to imperil the Union's security and that, of course, South-West Africa was 'quite a different question';[4] but, for all that, prominent Transvaal and Free State Nationalists gave the Germans cause to hope by declaring that, while they could not hand over a territory so full of brother Afrikaners, they would not lift a finger to defend it.[5] The Nationalist leader, for his part, looked for a friendly settlement with Germany that should leave South-West Africa in the Union's hands, and meanwhile urged South Africans to give their 'moral support' to the League or some similar organisation which might evolve a scheme that would appease the *Reich*.[6] In face of that, the Union Government stated once more categorically that it would not hand South-West Africa back to Germany.[7] *(Sept. 1937. Dec. 1937.)*

The German reply came swiftly. Their responsible officials first proclaimed the colonial question 'acute' and then announced that it had reached the stage when it could be dealt with through 'ordinary diplomatic channels.'[8] Then, while the Japanese overran province after province of China and Franco's followers and their totalitarian allies blasted their way across Spain, German troops poured up to *(March 1938.)*

---

[1] *The Times*, July 15, 1936; *Daily Telegraph*, July 14, 1936.
[2] *Round Table*, No. 106, p. 446.   [3] *The Times*, April 1, 1937.
[4] *Ibid.*, Sept. 15, 1937; *Round Table*, No. 109, p. 188.
[5] *The Times*, Oct. 15, 1937.   [6] *Ibid.*, Oct. 11, 1937.
[7] *Ibid.*, Dec. 3, 1937.
[8] *Daily Telegraph*, Dec. 7, 1937, and Jan. 27, 1938.

the foot of the Brenner Pass and into Vienna. In that same week the *Reich* put forward a definite claim to all the former German colonies and told the Union that it did not regard the naturalisation agreement of 1923 as a final settlement of the future of South-West Africa.[1]

'That challenge and the Austrian *Anschluss* rallied thousands of voters to the United Party's banner at the general election in May 1938. The Fusion ministry at once gave proof of its anxiety to keep on good terms with the *Reich* by renewing the barter agreement of 1934, but when the Germans began to press down upon Czechoslovakia, it showed more clearly than ever before where it would stand if it came to the push. The Prime Minister indeed declined to do more than promise that his ministry would do its duty and take the consequencies; but Smuts, second in command, declared that South Africa could not keep out of a general war, but must 'stand by Britain,'[2] while Pirow reaffirmed the Simonstown agreement and asked for £6,000,000 to finance an intensive three-year defence plan.[3] The Air Force was to be enlarged and the striking force mechanised; the 9·2 guns at Capetown were to be supplemented by 15-inch guns capable of holding off battleships as well as cruisers; similar armament was to be provided for Durban, the terminal point of so much of the shipping of the Indian Ocean, and the minor ports of East London and Port Elizabeth were to be fortified for the first time. Further, the railway workshops at Pretoria were to be equipped with plant for the making of motor lorries and their engines and, if need be later on, of bombs, armoured cars, tanks and heavy guns. £1,000,000 was provided for these purposes forthwith.

Sept. 1938.

Before the Minister of Defence could sail for Europe to spend this first instalment, the world was caught up in the desperate Czechoslovakian crisis. Had war come it is certain that Hertzog and Smuts, Havenga and Pirow, the inner ring of the Fusion ministry, would have tried to maintain neutrality,[4] at all events at the start, so great was the tension between the Nationalists and their opponents as the Great Trek celebrations rose towards their climax, and so widespread was the belief among men of all parties that Hitler and the Sudeten Germans 'had a case.' As it was, Hertzog refused to declare his policy beyond admitting that if Great Britain were the victim of a dangerous and aggressive attack, the Union must stand by her as a fellow-member of the League of Nations.[5]

Sept. 1938.

Sept. 24, 1938.

South Africans, with comparatively few exceptions,[6] hailed the

---

[1] *Daily Telegraph*, March 15, 1938; *The Times*, March 16, 1938.
[2] *Ibid.*, Aug. 26, 1938.   [3] *Ibid.*, Sept. 8, 1938.
[4] *Round Table*, Nos. 115, p. 638, and 117, p. 204.
[5] *The Times*, Sept. 25, 1938.
[6] The editor of the influential *Cape Argus*, Dominick McCausland, was dismissed summarily, with no reason given, after he had criticised Neville Chamberlain's policy adversely.

Munich agreement with relief and thankfulness, and their leaders, each from his own standpoint, bade them look forward hopefully. Malan called once more for a declaration of neutrality and negotiations Nov. on the colonial question with the Germans, who could hardly deny 9, 1938. that South-West Africa, the majority of whose citizens were Union-born, belonged naturally to South Africa now that they themselves had appealed to the principle of self-determination on behalf of their Sudeten kinsfolk.[1] Pirow went so far as to insist that Germany must be compensated, though he drew the line at giving her either South-West Africa or Tanganyika. Smuts, who had always believed that Oct. the League was not dead but sleeping, took the wider view and 1938. envisaged a general advance towards an assured peace now that Britain had recovered 'the moral leadership' of Europe. Returning to his original conception of the League, he called for the inclusion in its permanent machinery of a standing committee of the Great Powers which could initiate changes and tackle immediately such pressing problems as those of the colonies, currency and the function of gold.[2] The course of events in Central Europe destroyed these generous hopes. Soon the Union and all British Africa, from Nov. Bulawayo to Nairobi and Dar-es-Salaam, were filled with clamour 1938. in many tongues against the restoration of Tanganyika to Hitler's Germany, while Smuts, disillusioned, pointed not to the League but to the British Navy as 'the greatest force for peace in the world.'[3]

Pirow's visit to Europe brought home to the ministry the peril in Nov.- which the Union stood. The indefatigable minister travelled widely: Dec. 1938. to Lisbon where he arranged for civil aviation between the Rand and Loanda, to Franco's headquarters, to London, where he repeated his warning that the Union's co-operation with Great Britain must depend on community of interest and not on sentiment,[4] to Berlin at Smuts's suggestion to press for a national home for the Jews[5] and to talk trade with one of the Union's best Continental customers, and then to Rome to talk trade once more, since the Fusion ministry did not propose to renew the unpopular Italian shipping subsidy. At Brussels the principle of air reciprocity between the Union and the Congo was agreed upon, and the Belgian Premier, perhaps moved thereto by his guest's sympathy with Germany's colonial ambitions,[6] publicly recalled the fact that the integrity of the Belgian Congo had long ago been guaranteed by Great Britain, France and Germany. Back in London, Pirow disclaimed any 'colonial mission' and complained pointedly that the British public did not seem to realise that South Africa was buying more British

---

[1] *Bulletin of International News*, XV. No. 23, p. 61.
[2] *The Times*, March 16 and Nov. 7, 1938.
[3] *Ibid.*, Dec. 12, 1938. [4] *Ibid.*, Nov. 15, 1938.
[5] *The Times*, Oct. 12, 1961.
[6] *Bulletin of International News*, XV. No. 25, pp. 1183, 1209.

manufactures than any other country.[1]

On his return home Pirow found that the progress of his defence
plan had been uneven. The supply of aeroplanes was ahead of
schedule and the training of pilots and mechanics proceeding
apace; trained infantry were said to be nearly up to the number
anticipated, the undisciplined rifle associations were far above their
expected strength, and local supplies of small-arm ammunition were
coming forward well. But local supplies of heavier munitions and
material were still on paper, and the fact had to be faced that, so
long as Great Britain, rearming furiously, could spare little for
distant overseas partners,[2] the ports must make shift with the guns
they had, except Capetown, whose batteries might possibly be reinforced by the 15-inch guns of H.M. Monitor *Erebus* at anchor in
Table Bay on indefinite loan from the Admiralty. The ministry then
decided to drop all attempts to mechanise the striking force, because
land fighting was only to be expected in the unsuitable bushveld in
the northern parts of the Union or in neighbouring Southern
Rhodesia or Portuguese East Africa. It meanwhile ordered a national
register of the Union's manpower.[3]

So war, which few wanted and no one seemed able to avert, drew
nearer to a world in which the democracies were being driven by the
pressure of the totalitarian Powers to sacrifice human dignity, individual liberty and material well-being on the altar of the would-be
national, sovereign, independent State. The British Premier, Neville
Chamberlain, visited the Duce without apparent effect, and a few
weeks later the Führer annexed Bohemia and Moravia outright.
Hertzog thereupon warned the Assembly that, when it could be
inferred that a European government was seeking to dominate free
peoples and thereby endangering the liberties of the Union, the latter
might have to 'occupy itself' with the affairs of a Continent which
had been brought so perilously close by the powers of the air.[4]
It was high time that the House should so occupy itself, for,
during the next month, the Italians overran Albania, republican
resistance collapsed in Spain, the Germans made threatening gestures
in the direction of the Free City of Danzig, and the British in close
co-operation with the French allied themselves with the Poles,
guaranteed the Greeks and Rumanians against aggression, opened
negotiations with Turkey and Soviet Russia, and adopted a modified
form of conscription. In face of these ominous events, some even
of the Nationalists openly doubted the possibility of neutrality, let
alone the wisdom of secession, and the ministry, busily reinforcing

Side notes: March 1939. (twice)

---

[1] *Bulletin of International News*, XV. No. 15, p. 37.
[2] *The Times*, Nov. 17, 1938.
[3] *Round Table*, No. 115, pp. 638 ff.; *Bulletin of International News*, XV. No. 7,
p. 53.
[4] *Ibid.*, XVI. No. 6, p. 67; *Round Table*, No. 115, pp. 638 ff.

its police in excited South-West Africa, made short work of Malan's suggestion that the British guarantee to Poland had altered the situation so radically that a declaration of neutrality was called for. Hertzog retorted that, though the Dominions had been informed of April the Anglo-Polish pact, they had not been asked to approve of it, nor 12, were they bound by it; for the rest, echoing Smuts's words, he 1939. observed that Great Britain was still South Africa's best friend.[1]

'Stand by Britain.' After all, now that power politics were come again mechanised and unashamed, what other prudent course was open to a small and isolated crowned republic which possessed the Cape Peninsula, so often taken, coveted and retaken, still, as in van Riebeeck's days, the half-way house between Europe and the East, and now also the gateway to the treasure-house of the Witwaters-rand? The Union must look around for a protector in a world in which small states commonly fared worse than great, and where should it look but to the Power, which, as Hertzog generously acknowledged, had done more for it than any other Power had done or would do.[2] After all, there was nothing new in such a policy. Had not the Graaff-Reinet republicans, during the storms of the French 1795– Revolutionary wars, offered to accept George III as their protector 1796. provided they might manage their own affairs,[3] and the Natalians, when asking for independence nearly fifty years later, proposed that, 1840. in the event of an attack by sea on their republic, the Royal Navy should be free 'to interpose itself in a friendly manner or to repel the same by force'?[4] The British fleet no longer exercised the naval monarchy of those days, but Pirow, confident that the Union could give a good account of itself against an enemy once landed, still looked to it to prevent an enemy landing anywhere on South Africa's four thousand miles of forbidding coast.[5]

The ministry had already begun to take strong measures. After the Munich agreement on the fate of Czechoslovakia, Germans in South-West Africa had become truculent and, in Johannesburg, fifty persons were injured in clashes between anti-Fascists and Fascist groups egged on, the authorities believed, by foreign pro-pagandists. A little later, official German competition obliged the Government to buy a large block of land in South-West Africa, while, immediately after Hitler had annexed Bohemia-Moravia, the German minister at Pretoria warned the authorities that his country would not be responsible for the consequences if they refused a large party of German immigrants admission to the Mandated

---

[1] *Bulletin of International News*, XVI. No. 8, p. 50.
[2] *Round Table*, No. 104, p. 856. *Cf.* Smuts at Standerton. *Daily Telegraph*, Dec. 21, 1939.
[3] G. M. Theal, *Records of Cape Colony*, I. 130.
[4] J. Bird, *Annals of Natal*, I. 628.
[5] *The Times*, Jan. 23, 28, April 10, 1938.

Territory.[1] The Union Government at once called up Police reservists to guard key undertakings at South African ports and along the Rand, and a month later, foreseeing serious trouble in South-West Africa whose young men were going in large numbers to the *Reich* and returning as trained soldiers, incorporated its small local police force with its own and, in spite of Nationalist opposition, sent considerable reinforcements with machine-guns to Windhoek. In August 1939, it took over the administration of the long eastern stretch of the Caprivi Strip and made ready, in the event of war, to deal with the risings in South-West Africa and the Union itself which it knew were being planned by Nazis financed either from Germany direct, from the so-called Winter Help Fund or from local German firms and refugees whose families were at the mercy of the Führer in the Fatherland. Austria and other small states, said Smuts, had been annexed on the plea that they could not keep internal order, but the Union would never lay itself open to invasion on that ground.[2]

The prospect that an enemy might soon threaten the Union's borders drew nearer with tragic swiftness during the August of 1939, and gave a special significance to the official visit which the Portuguese President, the first head of a foreign state to tread South African soil, paid to Pretoria at the close of an inspection of his republic's African colonies. On the first of the month Great Britain mobilised her reserve fleet in reply to the calling up of the German army reservists. Three weeks later the Reich Chancellor startled the world by announcing his pact with Soviet Russia and, on September 1, sent his armies into Poland. On September 3 Great Britain and France declared war on Nazi Germany.

The outbreak of war found the Union Parliament assembled in special session to prolong the life of the expiring Senate for a few weeks. It thus obliged it to face the issue of neutrality in its most insistent form. Most South Africans agreed with Hertzog that her independent status gave their country the right to maintain neutrality, but so many of them had been repelled by Hitler's now familiar technique of aggression that they took it for granted that the ministry would elect to enter the war on the side of the Allies without question. This expectation was disappointed. Ministers were at one in resolving that the Union should fulfil its obligations, explicit and implicit, towards the League and the British Commonwealth, even to the point of defending the naval base of Simonstown; but there unanimity ended. The Prime Minister tried to settle the crucial question by simply announcing that he had decided to maintain neutrality. Smuts would not have it so. In the event, Havenga, Pirow

---

[1] *Bulletin of International News*, XVI. No. 6, p. 292.
[2] *Ibid.*, XVI. No. 9, p. 466.

and three other ministers accepted Hertzog's decision that, while denying to others the use of its territory for any purpose that would prejudice the discharge of those duties, the Union should maintain its relations towards all the belligerents unchanged and 'continue as if no war was being waged.' On the other hand, Deneys Reitz, Stuttaford and four of their colleagues agreed with Smuts's view that, though it would be inexpedient to send a force overseas as in the last war, South Africa must sever relations with the *Reich*, co-operate heartily with the Allies, and by no means follow the Prime Minister in adopting 'an attitude unknown to international law' by tempering friendship with actions that no hostile power could ever recognise as legal and proper.[1] Besides, could such a strange neutrality be enforced? Would neutral South African gunners fire in the event of a hostile attack on the British naval base at Simonstown, and could the authorities avert civil war in the streets if they refused the comfort of their ports to Allied ships or offered it to such Axis vessels as might find their way thither?

There was no question here of secession. The sufficient cause of the breakdown was an honest difference of opinion, in a time of acute crisis, between men who had never been easy partners. Hertzog was persuaded that the Polish war was a mere local affair, which in no way touched the liberties of South Africa. Smuts, on the contrary, believed that the causes of the war extended far beyond Danzig and the Polish Corridor and threatened those liberties all along the line. The last word, however, lay with the recently elected Parliament to whose decision on the issues of peace and war the leaders of all parties had long ago agreed to defer. Next day (September 4), therefore, Hertzog and Smuts submitted their rival policies to the Assembly admitting frankly and with genuine regret that the ministry was irremediably split. Had Hertzog contented himself with recommending qualified neutrality he might have gained the day, but he shocked waverers by going very near to defending Hitler's policy and, though he won the support of more than one-third of his own party and the whole of Malan's Nationalists, was beaten by 80 votes to 67.[2] Now that Parliament had spoken, the Governor-General had no choice but to refuse a belated request for a dissolution and to accept Hertzog's resignation. So the ageing Prime Minister retired after fifteen years of office admitting that Sir Patrick had acted well within his rights and, remembering the rebellion of 1914, issued an appeal to his followers, an appeal which was endorsed by Pirow and Malan, to avoid 'anything which may even savour of

[1] *The Times* and *Daily Telegraph*, Sept. 5 and 6, 1939; D. Reitz, *No Outspan*, pp. 236 ff.; Roberts, M., and Trollip, A. E. G., *The S.A. Opposition*, p. 19; *Hansard* (*S.A.*), Vol. 36, p. 3; House of Assembly Debates, Vol. 36, p. 3.
[2] *The Times and Daily Telegraph*, Sept. 5 and 6, 1939; *Debates*, Vol. 36, pp. 30–1 and 95 ff.

unconstitutional action.'[1] Smuts, backed by majorities of seventeen
in the Assembly and, presently, of eight in the reconstituted Senate,
at once formed a cabinet which included Hofmeyr and the leaders of
the Labour and Dominion parties besides most of his recent ministerial supporters.[2] The German minister to the Union was handed his
papers forthwith.

Sept.
5,
1939.

Thus did South Africa assume the ultimate responsibilities of a
sovereign independent state by going to war with the Nazi *Reich*. . . .

God protect the Land and its Peoples.

CHAPTER XVI

CIVILISATION, 1939–48

The Axis War: *Arma virumque*, 694; Reunited National Party, 698;
fall of France, 701; home supply, 704; Afrikaner Party, 707; East African
campaign, 710; invasion of the U.S.S.R., 710; Atlantic Charter, 711; El
Rezegh, 711; Pearl Harbour, 712; the New Order and the *Ossewabrandwag*,
713; Singapore, 716; sabotage, 717; Madagascar, 717; finance and controls,
718; death of Hertzog, 725; Alamein and Stalingrad, 725; end of North
African campaign, 726; Indian and Coloured policies, 727; general election,
729; dual medium, 730; Italian campaign, 730; Smuts's 'explosive speech,'
731; social services, 733; Native policy, 734; industrial problems, 734;
Nationalist activities, 735; Coalition internal strains, 739; United Nations
Charter, 742; VJ Day, 743.—**Reconstruction:** problems, 744; Nationalists
and trade unions, 748; Indians, Coloured Folk and Bantu, 749; *apartheid*
and secondary industry, 753; reconstruction, 755; South-West Africa,
759; Indian policy, 759; Smuts and U.N.O., 759; strikes and migratory
labour, 760; Nationalist advance, 765; the Royal visit, 765; uranium, 768;
South-West Africa, 769; S.A.B.R.A. and theoretical *apartheid*, 770; general
election and fall of Smuts, 772.

ALTHOUGH he had saved South Africa from what Deneys Reitz
called the shame of neutrality by bringing her into the Axis war,
Smuts held power on a precarious tenure.[3] His working majority in
the vital House of Assembly was a mere score or so and in the
reconstituted Senate a bare eight. Worse still, for all that he could

---

[1] *The Times*, Sept. 8, 1939.
[2] *Daily Telegraph*, Sept. 7, 1939. Smuts Ministry: Gen. J. C. Smuts, Prime
Minister, Defence and External Affairs; J. H. Hofmeyr, Finance and Education;
Harry Gordon Lawrence, Interior; Col. Deneys Reitz, Native Affairs; Richard
Stuttaford, Commerce and Industries; Col. William Richard Collins, Agriculture;
Senator Charles Francis Clarkson, Posts and Telegraphs; Senator Andrew
Conroy, Lands; Dr. Colin Steyn, Justice; Major Pieter Voltelyn Graham van
der Byl, Without Portfolio; Col. Charles Frampton Stallard, Mines; Walter
Madeley, Labour; Frederick Claud Sturrock, Railways and Harbours.
[3] *Bulletin of International News*, XVI. No. 19, p. 47.

reckon on the support of perhaps forty per cent. of the Afrikaner voters in the country and had included in his Cabinet six Afrikaners, two of them sons of Free State Presidents and three Republican veterans of the South African war, the great majority of his supporters in Parliament were English-speaking men drawn mainly from urban areas. Over against him stood an Opposition of sixty-seven, divided indeed between two parties but strong in the backing of the bulk of the Afrikaners in the heavily over-represented rural constituencies. Those two parties shared a common hatred of him and his so-called 'British' war, but in spite of talk of reunion in a single party, Malan's twenty-nine Purified Nationalists and Hertzog's thirty-eight stalwarts were held apart from one another by memories of mutual strife and the jealousies of their respective masterful and humourless leaders.[1] Even so, Smuts must expect determined opposition in Houses, where party divisions ran ominously close to the 'racial' line, and obstruction from Nazi-minded Black and Grey Shirts and the *Ossewabrandwag* everywhere.

Since Parliament had risen after its decisive vote on the war issue without giving him emergency powers, Smuts took such powers as he needed relying on the Courts to uphold him *ex post facto*. He ensured the quiet of the Union and South-West Africa by interning some hundreds of Germans and South African nationals and, thanks largely to appeals by Hertzog and Pirow to their followers to behave in constitutional fashion, escaped anything like the rebellion that had broken out early in the Kaiser's war.[2] He then signalled full steam ahead. Since 'the fight for Danzig' was in all probability the prelude to a fight for western civilisation in Africa, he promised to defend Imperial Simonstown and stand by the British Commonwealth, the Union's 'best friend' in a dangerous world;[3] but he nevertheless forbade medical students, women doctors and nurses to leave the country without special permission, and announced that this time no expeditionary force would be sent overseas, if only because South African soldiers would soon have plenty to do in their own continent.[4]

Meanwhile, Smuts had to raise the soldiers aforesaid. When he took stock of what he had inherited from his predecessor as Minister of Defence, he found that he had 'the plan and nothing but the plan.' Pirow had spent little more than a tithe of the large sums voted to him during the past half-dozen years, and that mainly on a single small-arms factory at the Royal Mint, Pretoria, which could turn out some twelve million rounds a year, and a train of bush-carts, which would have taken a long time to convey the guerilla bands

---

[1] *Round Table*, No. 118, p. 444.   [2] *Ibid.*, No. 117, p. 212, and No. 118, p. 438.
[3] *Bulletin*, XVI., No. 19, p. 47.
[4] *Round Table*, No. 117, p. 210, and No. 119, p. 715.

of his dreams even as far as the Union's frontiers.[1] The Permanent Force had dwindled to a mere 1350 men; the entire Defence Force, ill-trained and worse supplied, stood at about one-third its paper strength; there were no spare uniforms and scarcely any rifles in store and no organisation for putting the troops on a war-footing. The country's two home-made armoured cars were supplemented by a couple of tanks and a few guns that, with them, had survived the Kaiser's war, and neither Port Elizabeth nor East London could boast a single piece. The Navy consisted of H.M.S. A.S. *Botha*, an engineless training-ship moored permanently at Simonstown. There were a fair number of airmen, but all they had to fly with were a pair of Blenheim bombers, some three score converted Junkers and obsolete Harts and Hawker Furies and, behind these, perhaps as many even more archaic machines. Smuts lost no time in making up for the years that Pirow had eaten.[2] By the end of October 1939, he had taken over all privately owned air-training concerns and launched five major military schemes, including one for a sorely-needed corps of engineers.[3] He allowed a thousand or so Central and Eastern Europeans to enrol in a Foreign Legion, noted the offer of South African Indians to raise ten times as many men for service with the United Kingdom forces, and readily accepted the money collected by these same Indians and the Mayors of many towns to help South African sufferers from the war and send food to the British and French.[4] Volunteers of both sexes rushed into the forces and similar organisations so fast that Pirow's modest estimates were soon surpassed, and Smuts was busy arranging for the training of reservists and instructors, raising two Mounted Brigades, putting army supply on a civilian footing and providing for the training of his Air Force locally alongside part of the Royal Air Force.[5] Nor was this all. Calling to mind the many thousands of non-Europeans who had served during the Kaiser's war, he began to raise the Native Military Police to serve as stretcher-bearers, motor drivers, batmen, nurses, cooks, mechanics, boot-repairers, tailors, road and railway gangers, clerks, typists and infantrymen to guard bridges and so forth in the Union. True, none of them could rise to commissioned rank nor be armed with anything more deadly than an assegai; but Smuts promised them that this time they should all earn at least service medals and that their disabled and the dependents of their dead should receive pensions and not the mere lump sums with which

---

[1] *Round Table*, No. 118, p. 439, and No. 119, p. 713; *A Record of the Organisation of the Director-General of War Supplies (1939–1943) and Director-General of Supplies (1943–1945)*, pp. 1, 61 ff.
[2] *Round Table*, No. 119, p. 713.
[3] *Bulletin*, XVI. No. 22, p. 53, and No. 25, p. 60.
[4] *Ibid.*, XVII. No. 2, p. 118.
[5] *Ibid.*, XVI., No. 20, pp. 63 ff., and No. 22, p. 53.

their predecessors had been fobbed off in 1919. He further saw to it that, as a body, the non-Europeans should be kept in touch with the course of the war by means of an excellent bulletin published weekly by the Native Affairs Department in the two official languages and the principal Bantu tongues to supplement their own numerous weekly newspapers.[1] Southern Rhodesia also began to get into her stride. At the outset, she had prohibited the export of livestock so that she might still have frozen beef to send to the United Kingdom and, because of the unexpectedly great rush of recruits, had presently been obliged to close her recruiting-offices. She had nevertheless set up an Air Ministry to cope with her growing Air Force, taken steps to incorporate her air-training machinery with that of the Empire Air Training Scheme and, if she must face a small deficit, had none the less contributed £1,500,000 towards the cost of the war.[2]

During the early weeks of the struggle, Germany and Russia crushed Poland, Russia attacked isolated Finland, and the British Expeditionary Force took up its station beside the Belgian forces and the much more numerous French troops. Three British light cruisers drove the German pocket-battleship, *Graf Spee*, to self-destruction at Monte Video and, in general the Royal Navy kept the war at such a safe distance that South Africans scarcely realised that there was strife on the oceans until their airmen forced the crew of a German merchantman to scuttle their ship off the south coast and submit to internment. Within the Union, there was no rationing, if only because the authorities held that this would be impossible in such a highly plural and overwhelmingly illiterate society; nor was there any economic dislocation worth mentioning, because recruiting and the call of the rapidly expanding secondary industries kept down unemployment, while guaranteed markets, prices fixed by the multitudinous Control Boards, and increased demand at home and abroad reassured all producers, except possibly the fruit and sheep farmers, who must wait awhile till the Governments of the Union and the United Kingdom could come jointly to their rescue.[3]

If the red war had not yet touched South Africa, the cold war on the home front was much in evidence. True, Smuts secured his rear by winning the elections for the South-West African Legislative Assembly, thanks mainly to the fact that whereas the newly-enfranchised Germans voted Nationalist by order, the Afrikaner Nationalists voted for his United Party from fear of the Nazis.[4] In the Union itself, however, the situation was far less reassuring. There, the *Ossewabrandwag* now boasted some 300,000 sworn members, many

[1] *Round Table*, No. 119, pp. 174 ff., and No. 128, pp. 522 ff.
[2] *Bulletin*, XVII., No. 2, p. 128, No. 5, p. 330, No. 9, p. 564.
[3] *Round Table*, No. 118, p. 441.   [4] *Bulletin*, XVII., No. 5, p. 329.

of them followers of Hertzog and Havenga; Pirow was diligently and, as far as might be, secretly organising his Nazi-inspired New Order, and the *Broederbond* was not only ramifying further and further into every sphere of Afrikaner life but could claim as members all the leading Nationalist ex-Ministers, Purified and otherwise, besides perhaps three-quarters of those who had elected them and their supporters. The Opposition's first attempt to form a united front broke down mainly because the followers of Hertzog and Havenga were by no means so set on achieving a republic as were Malan and Johannes Strydom,[1] his chief Transvaal supporter. Transvaal Hertzogites, however, formed a People's Party pledged to win an immediate peace, put a stop to 'imperialist' propaganda and secure the adoption of a rule that declaration of war must be backed by a three-fourths majority in Parliament. Under this and similar backveld pressure, the rival leaders tried again and this time succeeded in forming an *Herenigde Nasionale of Volksparty* (Reunited National or People's Party) very much on Malan's terms.[2] Thus, Hertzog as parliamentary leader of the new Party and Malan as wielder of power therein were able to greet the Houses when they reopened in January 1940 with a joint statement of policy, whose purport was that, although South Africa must become a republic because that was the policy 'best suited to the traditions and aspirations of the South African people,' this republic should only be set up on 'the broad basis of rights and the national will,' must ensure equal language and cultural rights for all Europeans and should only be brought into being as the result of 'a special mandate of the electorate' and not by mere parliamentary majorities.[3]

The Assembly first rejected Hertzog's motion for an immediate peace and then passed on to finance. One of Havenga's last acts as Finance Minister had been to unpeg the sterling-dollar exchange and, as the price of gold shot up from 148s. to 168s., to offer to buy all the gold produced in the country at 150s. per ounce. Hofmeyr, his successor, had followed the same line, but had earned the hostility of the mineowners by taking the difference between Havenga's buying price and the market price as a Special War Contribution. Now, in his Budget speech, Hofmeyr estimated for a small deficit which had arisen mainly from war expenditure, the transfer of a further £90,000 of general Native tax to the Native Trust for Bantu education, increased votes for labour, health and social services, and

[1] Roberts and Trollip, *The South African Opposition*, pp. 20 ff.; A. C. Cilliers, *Volkseenheid*, p. 17; Scholtz, G. D., *Dr. W. J. van der Merwe*, pp. 398, 402 ff.; *Die Volksblad*, Nov. 6, 1939; *Die Vaderland*, Dec. 21, 1939; *Die Transvaler*, Jan. 30, 1940.
[2] Roberts and Trollip, *op. cit.*, pp. 34 ff.; *Round Table*, No. 118, p. 445; *Bulletin*, XVI., No. 25, p. 60.
[3] *Ibid.*, XVII., No. 3, p. 199; *Round Table*, No. 118, pp. 444 ff.

continued aid to the farmers, especially the fruit-farmers who were hard hit by the collapse of the overseas market and lack of refrigerated shipping.[1] This last subvention might be reduced if the demand of jam-makers for home-grown fruit came up to expectations, while wool-farmers could hope much from the United Kingdom's promise to bid at auction for their wool up to the high prices it had already paid for the Australian clip and yet leave them free to get the world price which was being forced ever higher by competing Japanese and United States buyers, a promise which induced many a wool-farmer to think less unkindly of the Smuts administration, however loudly Nationalists might condemn it as a British trap. Hofmeyr, for his part, proposed to meet the increased expenditure either from loans or from stiffer duties on luxuries, the abolition of the thirty per cent. rebate on income tax, a heavier income tax on diamond mines and an Excess Profits Duty on all concerns other than the already sufficiently burdened gold mines. The Director of the Reserve Bank promptly checked the orgy of speculation in 'Kaffirs' which broke out on the Rand by announcing that he held £112 in gold for every £100 owed to the public. Thus reassured, speculators and public together found they still had enough cash in hand to send the United Kingdom authorities £1,000,000 for the purchase of foodstuffs.[2]

Smuts used the 'guillotine' for the first time in the Assembly to carry his War Measures Act, which covered his past unauthorised assumption of emergency powers;[3] but though he then laid this weapon aside, he only checked Opposition garrulity by having recourse to all-night sittings and the suspension of standing orders for the adjournment, which enabled him as Leader of the House to insist that the business in hand must be finished before the sitting ended. By these means he carried measures dealing with rents and wines and spirits, beside an Industrial Development Act providing for a National Development Corporation, which was to furnish an initial capital of £500,000 as well as a further £4,500,000 for the purchase of shares that it might then sell to private persons.[4] He further carried an Electoral Laws Amendment Act, which cut down the period of residence necessary for registration from three months to one and directed the Judicial Commission which delimited the constituencies every five years to take into account not merely, as hitherto, the latest completed voters' roll, but the provisional roll which had not yet passed the 'objection' stage.[5] The Bill went through in spite of the protests of the Cape Coloured Folk that it dropped the compulsory registration of voters of their community

[1] *Round Table*, No. 118, pp. 445 ff.; *Bulletin*, XVII., No. 3, pp. 198 ff.
[2] *Round Table*, No. 118, p. 452; No. 119, p. 711.
[3] Act 13 of 1940 ; *Round Table*, No. 119, p. 699.
[4] Act 22 of 1940.   [5] Act 20 of 1940.

on the grounds that complications would arise, because, unlike the
Europeans, they still had to have the old Cape qualifications, and
in spite of the fierce resistance of the Opposition, who rightly saw
in it a device to reduce, however slightly, the gross over-representation of the rural areas in which their strength lay.[1]

Early in the Session, Pirow had earned an unmerciful castigation
at the hands of Smuts for venturing to defend his own lack of
performance as Defence Minister.[2] Thereafter, he had outraged
ministerialists and embarrassed friends by advocating the raising of
'storm-troopers' in true Nazi fashion to reinforce Nationalist arguments and talking loudly of 'giving a lead' if ever Union troops were
sent north even in Africa. The day was surely coming when those
troops might have to be sent, for, with the submission of Finland to
Russia and the swift overrunning of Denmark and the invasion of
Norway by the Germans, the war had begun to swing westward and
southward. Sure enough in April 1940, while the British were
straining every nerve to save the Norwegians, General Sir Archibald
Wavell, British General Officer Commanding the Middle East, paid
a flying visit to Capetown to discuss with Smuts South Africa's part
in the struggle. A week or two later, the British failure in Norway
unseated Neville Chamberlain and cleared the way for a truly
National Government, Conservative, Liberal and Labour combined,
under Winston Churchill. A short four days thereafter, Hitler swept
into the neutral and scarcely defensible Netherlands. Jeering at the
British failure in Norway, Nationalists made it clear that the fate
of the unhappy Dutch would make no difference to their policy;
but they nevertheless voted for the Prime Minister's proposal that
£100,000 be sent to help South Africa's 'cousins and friends,' whose
Queen had found refuge in the still inviolate United Kingdom. As
the Session ended, Hitler's Panzer divisions were thundering across
Belgium into France.[3]

With the reminder that Nazidom was 'something greater, more
diabolic' than the old Hohenzollern imperialism, Smuts at once
called for volunteers to man a Mobile Defence Force, whose members, distinguished by orange shoulder tabs, were to be liable to
serve for four years 'anywhere in Africa.' Thousands of young
South Africans indicated that they were ready to serve not merely
there but 'anywhere,' and so great was the response to the call that
'the General' was driven to find arms for his soldiers, and possibly
also to forestall rebellion, by calling in nearly every privately-owned
rifle in the country and requisitioning even the old cannon that had
long stood as monuments in public places. Bedding for his men he

[1] *Round Table*, No. 119, pp. 700, 708; No. 120, p. 122.
[2] *Ibid.*, No. 119, p. 713.
[3] *Ibid.*, No. 120, pp. 758 ff.; *Bulletin*, XVII., No. 10, p. 626.

found by taking thousands of blankets from the willing railway administration.[1] And so it was also in Southern Rhodesia, where a Cabinet sub-committee presided over the war-effort in almost daily session. European men and women enrolled readily as soon as the recruiting offices were reopened, gifts and interest-free loans poured into Salisbury, and Godfrey Huggins, the Prime Minister, talked of raising Native regiments for service in Africa.[2] Favoured by geography, however, the South Africans were first off the mark, for Smuts found room for some of his 'orange tabs' and a handful of planes on board an immense convoy of British troops, the first of many, that put into Table Bay on its way to the Middle-East to hold, above all, the Suez canal, the United Kingdom's vital link with India. But he did not send his men to Egypt. He sent them to Kenya, where a thin screen of British and African troops were facing the massive but still non-belligerent Italian array in East Africa.[3]

It was just in time, for events were moving with disastrous speed in far-away Europe. Late in May 1940, the Belgian King surrendered his army and thus left the British Expeditionary Force 'in the air,' while such French soldiers as ventured out of the steel and concrete death-trap of the unfinished Maginot Line were pushed off the roads by torrents of panic-stricken civilians. The British fought their way to the Channel and stood doggedly at bay behind a zareba of abandoned heavy equipment on the beaches of Dunkirk. Thence, flotillas of 'little ships' brought away nearly a quarter of a million of them, besides more than a hundred thousand other Allied troops, Frenchmen for the most part. As France began to crack, Mussolini leaped upon her and sent his planes from Abyssinia out over Kenya. Smuts at once declared war on Italy, began to intern Italians, assumed the title of General Officer Commanding the Defence Force, and hurried thousands of his men northward to defend western civilisation in East Africa.[4]

Smuts might hold that the war which had begun as Hitler's war would end as 'God's war' and that nothing could save his country if the Germans won.[5] Not so the Opposition. They were convinced that salvation for their own 'People' lay in a Nazi victory; wherefore Hertzog, as the self-appointed mouthpiece of that people, demanded that Smuts sue for peace and went almost as far as Pirow himself in justifying public demonstrations in support of this policy.[6] After the fall of Paris and the withdrawal of Marshal Petain's defeatist

[1] *Round Table*, No. 121, p. 159; *Record of the Organisation . . . of Supplies*, pp. 11, 18.
[2] *Bulletin*, XVII., No. 12, pp. 757 ff.
[3] *Round Table*, No. 120, p. 933; No. 121, pp. 147 ff.
[4] *Ibid.*, No. 121, pp. 147 ff.; *Bulletin*, XVII. No. 13, p. 826.
[5] *Ibid.*, XVII. No. 13, p. 826.
[6] *Ibid.*, p. 827; Roberts and Trollip, *op. cit.*, p. 38.

government southward to Vichy, Malan foretold the 'wonderful future' that awaited Afrikanerdom and assured his jubilant followers that the choice lay between 'a Republic or Hitler.'[1] On the surrender of the Vichy Government late in June, prominent Nationalists prophesied that the Union would make peace as soon as Smuts was gone, exulted that the British could never struggle back to Continental Europe nor even beat Hitler in their own islands and, convinced that now France had fallen, Britain must fall too, recalled the thesis which Oswald Spengler had evolved away back in 1914 that all Western Europe and, in especial, the French and British Empires were bound to decline. Humbler members of their Party sought to embarrass the authorities by hoarding coin and, when this form of sabotage failed, joined their leader in denouncing the reception of evacuee children from cruelly bombed Britain as a plot to strengthen the English-speaking element in 'their' country.[2] While the children were none the less coming, a Stellenbosch Professor, looking ahead to the day of Nationalist domination, maintained that *apartheid*, that is, the drastic separation of the racial groups one from the other was both Christian and just, undertook to prove that democracy was no match for dictatorship, and preached a totalitarianism that was to be exercised by a Leader who personified 'the People.'[3]

The imperturbable Smuts, intent on saving western civilisation, sought to keep up his countrymen's spirits by insisting that there could be no Nazi victory till 'the impregnable fortress' of Britain had been battered down. Nay, more! Determined as fully as the Anglo-American Churchill himself to draw the potentially mighty United States closer to the British Commonwealth, he broadcast on July 21, 1940, to the British and Americans, 'the two greatest free peoples of the world,' his vision of a Europe 'free in the sense of giving full scope for personal and national self-development and self-protection, each according to his own individual lines,' and also of an 'international society of free nations' furnished with something real in the way of that central control for lack of which the League of Nations had failed.[4] This said, he met the Houses in a short special session from August 24 to September 14, 1940. Though Goering's bombers were leaving hardly a house standing in vast areas of London, Portsmouth and other harbour towns in the United Kingdom, he refused to yield to the clamour that all local Germans be laid by the heels and, with the comment that 'German

---

[1] *Round Table*, No. 120, pp. 927 ff.; B. Davidson, *Report on Southern Africa*, p. 148.
[2] *Round Table*, No. 120, p. 930.
[3] Davidson, *op. cit.*, p. 147; J. Hatch, *The Dilemma of South Africa*, p. 45; O. du Plessis, *Die Nuwe Suid-Afrika*.
[4] *Bulletin*, XVII., No. 15, pp. 937 ff.

measles pass quickly,' merely interned a few South Africans guilty of intrigue and other subversive activities.[1] He then carried a War Measures Amendment Act legalising, *inter alia*, his recent unauthorised confiscation of privately-owned rifles, helped Hofmeyr through with a supplementary Budget, which levied an increased brandy excise and petrol duty to meet the immensely swollen defence expenditure [2] and, early in September, hailed with joy the gift to the United Kingdom by Franklin Roosevelt, President of the United States, of fifty old destroyers in return for the grant of naval and air bases in some of the British Atlantic colonies that covered the approaches to the Americas and the all-important Panama Canal.[3] ' It is the first portent,' he cried, 'and others will follow. . . . I see that little cloud in the sky that will become a thunderstorm.' Encouraged further by the daily news that the vastly outnumbered Royal Air Force was getting the better of the *Luftwaffe* over London, he had no mercy on Hertzog, for when that once gallant leader of Free State commandos moved for an immediate peace because the Allies, in so far as they still existed, had already lost the war, he bluntly called him a 'hands-upper,' the bitterest taunt one *oustryer* of the South African war could hurl at another.[4] Hertzog's motion was soundly defeated, the Houses rose, and Britain still stood.

Smuts could well be satisfied at the end of the first year of the war, for not only had he somewhat increased his parliamentary majority, but he had more than made good all military deficiencies. The Union now had, not the 56,000 originally contemplated, but 137,000 fighting-men organised in three Active Citizen Force divisions, three Special Rifle Defence Brigades and three Special Defence Rifle Field Forces. She had a sufficiency of planes and, like Southern Rhodesia, was giving facilities for the training of British airmen as well as her own in her superabundant great open spaces. Her Seaward Defence Force had already detected and swept a large minefield off Cape Agulhas, right on the southerly route from Europe to India, East Africa and the Suez Canal. Many formations stood behind the white soldiers. Thousands of non-Europeans from all parts of the Union and, latterly, increasing numbers from the High Commission Territories also had flocked into the Native Military Police, now renamed the Native Military Corps, and were showing themselves as keen to learn and as fully possessed of most of the qualities of good soldiers as their predecessors during the Kaiser's war or, for the matter of that, the Kaffir and Zulu wars of an earlier day.[5]

[1] *Round Table*, No. 121, p. 155; *Bulletin*, XVII., No. 19, p. 1258.
[2] *Round Table*, No. 121, pp. 155, 161; Act 32 of 1940.
[3] *Round Table*, No. 121; *Bulletin*, XVII., No. 19, p. 1258.
[4] *Round Table*, No. 121, p. 158; *Bulletin*, XVII., No. 18, p. 1194.
[5] *Round Table*, No. 121, pp. 151 ff.; S. Patterson, *Colour and Culture in South Africa*, pp. 45, 219; *Race Relations Handbook*, p. 541.

Again, European men of military age but unfit for active service were being enrolled in an Essential Services Protection Corps and somewhat younger men in the like category in the rapidly-growing semi-Military Police Reserve. Since October 1940, Smuts had recruited the National Reserve Volunteers from unfit veterans of the Kaiser's war, whose duties were to maintain internal order, guard internment camps and, if need be, prisoner-of-war camps also, and had latterly reinforced them in the larger and more vulnerable towns by the Civilian Protection Services. In short, making allowance for the multitudes of white South Africans who were either apathetic or hostile to the war effort, the percentage of the Union's Europeans who had volunteered for war service was higher than in any other Dominion. Nor were the white women behindhand. They eagerly joined the small but efficient Women's Auxiliary Air Force or the much larger Women's Army Auxiliary Services, which set men free to enlist by taking over their clerical and transport duties, and rallied in even greater numbers to the civilian South African Women's Auxiliary Service, which ran hostels and canteens and furnished hospital requirements and comforts for the troops. Dependants of service folk could look to the Governor-General's Fund, successor to the early tentative Mayor's Fund, to which the Government made substantial grants. A Civilian Defence Liaison Committee, a witness to the Prime Minister's conviction that civilians understood business better than soldiers, presided over this Jonah's gourd of a fighting force and strove to straighten out inevitable tangles in the raising, equipment and organisation of the Forces. Almost from the start, Dr. Hendrik van der Byl, chairman of Iscor, had been Director-General of War Supplies, and Thomas Stratten Director of Technical Production, while a Cabinet committee had met almost daily to advise the War Department. At the head of it all stood Smuts in his twin capacities as Minister of Defence and G.O.C. Union Defence Force.[1]

The feeding, equipment and maintenance of these fast-growing forces had been a matter of no ordinary difficulty. For lack of overseas supplies the Union had been forced back mainly on her own resources, and these were not large. The country was extensive and its population small, scattered, mixed and to a great extent backward. Given a good harvest, she could feed herself; she possessed two of the largest explosives factories in the world, and could rely also on the workshops of the state railways; Iscor and the gold and diamond mines could work wonders with her plentiful supplies of iron, copper, coal and lime.[2] But no one could gainsay the truth of

[1] *Round Table*, No. 121, pp. 147 ff.
[2] *Ibid.*, No. 121, pp. 147 ff., and No. 123, pp. 591 ff.; Proclamation No. 294 and Government Notice No. 1881 of 1939 (*Government Gazette*, Nov. 24, 1939).

the Industrial Reserves Commission's warning that so long as she relied on a mass of 'cheap' non-European labour directed by a handful of skilled and highly-paid white folk, she could never get the twelve thousand or so additional skilled folk she must have for the servicing of planes, engineering and secondary industry. Some of these were forthcoming when white trade unionists submitted to 'dilution' and lowered most of their cherished colour bars, and still more when women were called in; but the main hope of closing the gap had been disappointed, for though the recently founded Central Organisation for Technical Training had shown that it could turn out skilled mechanics by scientific methods much faster than the leisurely traditional apprenticeship machinery, it had hitherto failed to attract anything like the number of trainees that had been looked for. Nevertheless, all these things together had enabled the authorities to supply their armed forces with bombs and ordinary ammunition from their Central Ordnance factory at the Village Main, Johannesburg, to begin to furnish them with aerial missiles, trench mortars, fairly large shells, howitzers and armoured cars from the same source, and to make ready to send food to Allied Forces in East Africa and the Middle East and to pour small-arm ammunition into the Commonwealth pool, which had been formed in November 1940 by the Eastern Group Supply Conference at Delhi.[1]

Towards the close of October 1940, Smuts ventured to leave the Union for a few days. It was something of a risk, for not only was Pirow vigorously preaching the virtues of his National-Socialist New Order, but police raids on the *Ossewabrandwag* headquarters in the larger towns had revealed evidence of widespread subversive activities.[2] It was, however, a risk that had to be run, because now that Germany, Italy and Japan had signed a Tripartite Pact of Alliance, Graziani's unwieldly Italian army had rolled slowly forward from Libya across the Egyptian frontier. In face of this threat to the Suez Canal, Churchill, thinking as ever in terms of Mediterranean strategy, wanted Smuts to send his South Africans forthwith to join Wavell in Egypt. Smuts would have none of it.[3] He held that first things must come first, and to him the first thing was the saving of Kenya, Uganda and Tanganyika, where growing Allied Forces were already bickering with Italians in the borderlands of Eritrea, Abyssinia and Somaliland. So, cheered by the news that the R.A.F. had won the Battle of Britain by defeating the last of Goering's big

---

[1] *Round Table*, No. 121, pp. 150 ff., and No. 123, p. 499; *Record of the Organisation . . . of Supplies*, pp. 11, 16, 27 ff., 38 ff., 43, 48, 56, 114. During the first three years of the war, C.O.T.T. successfully posted some 16,000 of its 21,000 trainees (*Record . . .*, pp. 41 ff.).
[2] *Bulletin*, XVII., No. 24, p. 1333.
[3] J. C. Smuts. *Jan Christian Smuts*, p. 403.

23

daylight raids, he flew to Khartum. There, with Wavell's help, he convinced Anthony Eden, the British Foreign Secretary, that a full-dress attack must be launched against Italian East Africa, and then flew south to Nairobi to see how his young folk were bearing themselves and to spy out the situation on the front. He returned home after eight crowded and sometimes dangerous days rejoicing to have seen his soldiers, 'the happy warriors of the New Order,' which, whatever Pirow might prophesy, would never arise under the Swastika, but only 'under the sign of the Cross. . . . Not in mastery, but in service, not in dictatorship, but in freedom lies the secret of man's destiny. That is what these young South Africans stand for, for what I trust South Africa will stand for till the very end.'[1]

Immediately after his return, Smuts forbade the Police to belong to that subversive organisation, *Die Ossewabrandwag*, now led by Dr. Johannes van Rensburg, and noted with satisfaction that the Reunited National Party, true to the Afrikaner tradition of which it claimed to be the sole repository, was going to pieces from internal strains. Many of its younger members, resenting Hertzog's insistence on party discipline and obedience to himself as leader of the Opposition, looked for guidance to Charles Swart, his sometime political protégé, but since Fusion his bitter enemy and now van Rensburg's successor as Administrator of his native Free State.[2] Swart first tried to undermine his old benefactor in his hitherto faithful constituency of Smithfield by spreading the fantastic yarn that he had been conspiring with Smuts to bring Southern Rhodesia and, possibly, other British territories into the Union on a republican basis.[3] Having thus shaken Hertzog's faith in his Malanite allies, he took measures to bring him down. At Malan's request and under Strydom's influence, the new Party's Federal Council drafted a constitution, which indeed promised English-speaking citizens language and cultural equality, but made no mention of political equality and accepted the idea that the republic should be achieved by mere parliamentary majorities and be based on Nationalist group dictatorship. Hertzog, with some hesitation, had meanwhile drafted a much more generous scheme, which he proposed to submit to the party's Free State Congress. Before he could do so, however, the Cape Congress under the chairmanship of Adrian Fourie, another man befriended by him in times past, adopted the Federal Council's draft, the only document it had before it. More significantly still, Malan did likewise. Matters came to a head at the vital Free State Congress, where Swart and the vast majority rejected Hertzog's draft. Realising that there was here no spirit of reunion, Hertzog

---

[1] J. C. Smuts, *op. cit.*, p. 406.
[2] *Bulletin*, XVII., No. 24, pp. 1599 ff.
[3] Roberts and Trollip, *op. cit.*, pp. 38 ff., 201 ff.

walked out together with Havenga, William Brebner and Edward
Conroy. The Congress at once adopted the Council's draft with a
stiffening of the republican clauses and, in due time, the Transvaal
Congress, led by Strydom and his admirer, Hendrik Verwoerd,
followed suit and recommended that Jews be debarred from party
membership. Thereupon, in December 1940, Hertzog and Havenga
resigned their Assembly seats and then had the mortification of
seeing Swart returned at the Winburg by-election in spite of their
efforts to defeat him. Some of their followers, however, held together
under Conroy, formed themselves into the Afrikaner Party and
induced the reluctant Hertzog and Havenga to become their leader
and deputy-leader respectively in the fight against Malan's dream of
a Nationalist *Herrenvolk* republic and Smuts's 'holistic imperialism.'[1]

The Afrikaner Party made a bad start by losing to the Nationalists
the seats vacated by its two leading members. Smuts, meanwhile,
was encouraged by the splitting of the Opposition and, despite the
fact that the world had just passed through 'the darkest year in
modern history,' saw great future promise now that 'the unrivalled
resources of the United States were being turned to the Allies'
assistance.' [2] Better still, at the close of the year, Mussolini was faring
ill at the hands of the Greeks, the British had smashed six of his
capital ships at Taranto and British convoys were pouring unimpeded round the Cape to East Africa and Egypt. There, on
December 11, 1940, Wavell, reinforced by British, Indian, Australian
and New Zealand troops, attacked Graziani at Sidi Barrani and, in
the course of the next few weeks, hustled the unwieldy Italian hosts
right out of Egypt and most of Cyrenaica as far westward as
Benghazi. At the same time, a British-Indian force based on Khartum
invaded Eritrea, and at El Wak a mixed division of white South
Africans and black Gold Coasters launched, with good success, the
first serious attack on the Italians in Abyssinia. Smuts was jubilant.
'England,' he cried, 'is immeasurably stronger than before the war.
. . . When I speak of England, I take off my hat. . . . I choose the
country under which we suffered forty years ago, but which, when
we were at her mercy, treated us as a Christian nation should.'[3]
And then he challenged the Führer to invade the United Kingdom
and there decide the question which of the rival civilisations was to
survive, to fight an Armageddon from which would issue either 'a
new birth of human liberation or an eclipse of the human spirit and
the falling back into another Dark Age.'[4] Meanwhile, he gave his
National Reserve Volunteers something to do by setting them to

[1] Roberts and Trollip, *op. cit.*, pp. 46 ff.; *Die Vaderland*, Nov. 7, 8, 11, 1940;
Die Transvaler, Oct. 19 and Nov. 1, 6, 7, 15, 1940.
[2] J. C. Smuts, *op. cit.*, p. 407.   [3] *Bulletin*, XVII., No. 26, p. 1739.
[4] *Ibid.*, XVIII., No. 1, p. 51.

guard some 20,000 of the 140,000 Italian prisoners Wavell had recently rounded up.

Progress during the Session of 1941 was all that the Prime Minister could have desired. He was obliged, indeed, to use the guillotine again to overcome the objections of some of his business supporters to Madeley's semi-socialistic Workmen's Compensation Bill and, still more, to his Factories, Machinery and Buildings Works Bill, which empowered the Governor-General to issue regulations prescribing accommodation and facilities varying on a racial basis whenever the Minister might deem this necessary for 'the physical, moral and social welfare, of the workers.'[1] On the other hand, Hofmeyr had no difficulty with finance. He had been carrying on steadily Havenga's policy of repatriating the Union's overseas debts and, latterly, as wages rose, had issued Union Loan Certificates to mop up some of the resulting superfluity of cash.[2] His Budget now merely imposed some discreet additional taxation to meet the soaring cost of the war, but not more than could well be borne by a community which was just recovering from a hectic Christmas shopping season and knew that, despite the casualty lists that were beginning to creep into the papers, the war was still distant by nearly the whole immense length of Africa.

At first, war news was good. The Allied forces based on Khartum and the mixed British, Indian, South, East and West African forces based on Nairobi made good progress respectively in Eritrea and Somaliland, but further north, the balance showed ominous signs of tilting against the Allies. Wavell's small army, skied on the western frontier of Cyrenaica, had been sadly weakened, first, by the transfer of a British-Indian division to East Africa and then by the hurried despatch of further troops to help the Greeks, who were threatened by a massive German invasion by way of unready Jugoslavia. At this comparatively ill news excitement mounted in the Union, and most notably along the emotional Rand, where, in February 1941, a riot broke out after an *Ossewabrandwag* meeting in Johannesburg in which over one hundred persons, mostly men in khaki, were injured and the local Police, in many cases, obviously sympathised with the *O.B.* Smuts promptly issued a National Security Code, which prescribed severe penalties for all who possessed illicit explosives, assaulted uniformed Police, interfered violently with lawful gatherings, joined subversive and undesirable organisations, circulated inflammatory pamphlets or took part in unauthorised drilling and other military exercises.[3] On March 3, 1941, he proclaimed the *O.B.* a political organisation under this Code and ordered all public servants, including the all-important

[1] Acts 29 and 30 of 1941. [2] *Round Table*, No. 123, p. 602.
[3] *Bulletin*, XVIII., No. 3, p. 180; No. 4, p. 246.

school-teachers, to resign their membership thereof.[1] 'General' van Rensburg, who had just been tackled by Malan and Strydom for his obvious desire to control the doings of Nationalist members of Parliament, prudently ordered his followers to obey. But that did not deter Pirow, as yet unthreatened, from advertising the joys of his New Order 'under the swastika.'

Good news, however, came from Washington to offset these anxieties. Roosevelt had long realised that the demand that she should pay for supplies 'on the barrel head' was putting an intolerable strain on the indispensable United Kingdom and, after a long educative campaign, at last induced Congress to pass the famous Lease-Lend Act. That measure empowered him, as President, to give goods and services without money payment to Governments whose stability was, in his opinion, vital to the security of the United States and to accept them in return from those Governments on the same terms. Here was an assurance that the Allies would get 'the tools to finish the job,' and that without seeing the peace settlement bedevilled, as in 1919, by American demands for repayment of the 'money' they were supposed to have 'hired.' And if the United Kingdom, herself heavily bombed and her shipping harried by U-boats, was rightly one of the first beneficiaries, Smuts reckoned that his own country might look forward to sharing in the good things. This time he not only took off his hat, but threw it up in the air. 'The totalitarian dictator,' he exulted, '. . . has at last met the totalitarian forces of democracy. The end cannot be in doubt. . . . The fate and future of Western civilisation will be decided in this Armageddon.' Hitler himself . . . 'has as last convinced America. And so, in spite of herself, America is girding up her loins for the struggle. In due course she will be doing much more.'[2] To round off his prophecy, Smuts again challenged the Führer to invade the United Kingdom, telling him that, whether he failed or 'funked,' he would have lost the war.[3]

Halfway through the Session, in March 1941, Smuts flew north once more meditating upon the improved prospects of the war as a whole, but more immediately concerned to combat any idea Churchill might have of insisting that the South Africans be sent from East Africa to help the hard-pressed Wavell.[4] After a short stop at Nairobi, he went on to Cairo, where he indeed approved of the policy of helping the Greeks, but once more with the help of the sympathetic Wavell had to convince Eden and other highly-placed British officials that the East African campaign must go on. He returned full of pride in the marching and fighting powers of his white South Africans,

---

[1] *Bulletin*, XVIII., No. 5, p. 310.   [2] *Ibid.*, XVIII., No. 6, p. 377.
[3] *Ibid.*, XVIII., No. 9, p. 602.
[4] *Round Table*, No. 123, p. 602; J. C. Smuts, *op. cit.*, p. 602.

the devotion of his Coloured transport drivers and stretcher-bearers, and the coolness with which his Bantu were, if not always praising the Lord, at all events passing the ammunition under fire. As he worried through the remainder of the Session, the war news at first continued to be good. In the Mediterranean, the Royal Navy heavily defeated what was left of the Italian fleet off Cape Matapan on March 28, 1941; in East Africa, Indians stormed the strong Eritrean fortress of Kcren, South Africans and their comrades took the passable port of Mogadishu (Magadoxo) in Somaliland, and then both forces invaded Abyssinia. There, on April 5, 1941, the Transvaal Scottish headed the ceremonial entry into Addis Ababa, capital of the exiled King of Kings, and a few weeks later, the South African Brigadier, Dan Pienaar, received the surrender of the Duke of Aosta and the main Italian force. But then came a turn for the worse. The Germans drove the Allies from the mainland of Greece into Crete, and thereafter forced them to evacuate that island with heavy losses in men, ships and gear, though not before crash-landings and Allied bayonets had virtually annihilated Goering's splendidly trained and irreplaceable Parachute Corps. Worse still, Rommel and his armoured Afrika Korps slipped across to North Africa and pressed Wavell's depleted forces back to Sollum. There, Wavell stood at bay, while an Australian division held out in the isolated harbour of Tobruk in Rommel's rear.[1]

Smuts now began to send his airmen from East Africa to Wavell's aid, and when the Opposition raised the alarm that this was the prelude to sending South Africans overseas, assured them again that he would do nothing of the sort without leave of Parliament.[2] But send them to Egypt he did, a full 160,000 in all, while the war steadily became world-wide. Late in June, just before the fugitive Greek Royal family had found refuge in Capetown,[3] Hitler sent his *Grande Armée*, reinforced by unwilling Italians, clanking and rumbling into the illimitable territories of his Russian ally. 'Thank God for this,' cried Smuts, who was quick to see that Hitler, by his own act, had saddled himself with the war on two fronts which his great predecessor, Bismarck, had been so diligent to avoid. Russia, he proclaimed, must be helped to the limit, for surely South Africans could 'bless her arms and wish her all success' without for a moment identifying themselves with her communistic creed.[4] To him, Hitler was Anti-Christ, in whose existence he had never yet believed; but to Malan, 'the embodiment of all evil' was Bolshevism and its personification, Josef Stalin, head of the U.S.S.R., was now the most

[1] *Round Table*, No. 123, p. 601, and No. 124, p. 801; *Report of the Organisation . . . of Supplies*, p. 12.
[2] *Round Table*, No. 123, pp. 457 ff., and No. 124, pp. 658 ff.; *Bulletin*, XVIII., No. 11, p. 724.
[3] *Ibid.*, XVIII., No. 14, p. 931. [4] *Ibid.*, XVIII., No. 15, p. 991.

recent and unwelcome of the Allies. The leader of the Opposition did not fail to note that the scattering of Communists in South Africa, who had hitherto opposed the war, were now congratulating themselves that a Russian victory, even though it be won with the aid of 'capitalistic' armies, would redound to the benefit of workers everywhere. That was precisely what he was afraid of and, being himself a white South African born on a Western Province farm, he naturally saw workers as dark-skinned folk. He could indeed agree with Smuts that the war was 'one of the great religious wars of the world, . . . the fight between light and darkness'; but whereas to Smuts the light was that of Western civilisation, which must be kept burning with the help of whatever allies the Lord in His mercy might send, to him it was the flickering rushlight of 'white civilisation' in South Africa, which was now, in his eyes, threatened with extinction by the combined forces of Communism and Colour.[1]

The immediate danger came, however, not from Russian Communists, but from Japanese imperialists, who were swarming into the key position of Indo-China with the connivance of the Vichy Government. Smuts at once joined with the other Commonwealth authorities in 'freezing' Japanese assets and grimly watched local Japanese residents taking ship for the Far East. To balance this potential threat, good news came from the Far West.[2] There, in August 1941, on a warship 'somewhere in the Atlantic,' Churchill and Roosevelt signed the Atlantic Charter, which promised that after the war there should be a world of many freedoms, above all freedom from fear.[3]

At the moment, however, while the Germans were overrunning the industrialised Don Basin and the fertile Ukraine, Smuts's main external interest was in the North African campaign. In August 1941, therefore, he and his wife flew to see their young men and women in Egypt, she as chairman of the Gifts and Comforts Organisation and he as an elder statesmen, a veteran soldier and a newly-gazetted Field Marshal in the British Army, though still to his friends, the General, *Die Generaal*, because, as he told them, he was too old to change names, and maybe also because General was a title common to the Imperial and Republican services, whereas that of Field Marshal was not.[4] Shortly after their return from a three-day visit to Cairo, the news came in that General Alan Cunningham, who had succeeded Wavell, had driven Rommel back after a hard struggle in which the Union had suffered her first serious casualties when the 5th Infantry Brigade was almost wiped out at El Rezegh in a vain

[1] *Round Table*, No. 124, pp. 812 ff.; *Bulletin*, XVIII., No. 22, p. 1847.
[2] *Ibid.*, XVIII., No. 16, p. 1055.
[3] Cmd. 6321 of 1941; *United Nations Documents, 1941–1945*, p. 9.
[4] J. C. Smuts, *op. cit.*, p. 419.

attempt to fight its way into Tobruk.[1] That impromptu fortress was, however, relieved in the end and the fronts were stabilised along the Gazala line some thirty miles to the westward. On the other hand, Axis planes from their bases in Italy and the Balkans were making the Mediterranean such a death-trap that Malta could hardly be held and Allied shipping could only traverse its waters at great risk. Henceforward, the Allies would have to supply their forces in North Africa, the Middle East and India all the way round by the Cape of Good Hope, now once more indubitably the halfway house to the East. It was well that a few votes had not gone the other way in the crucial war division of September 1939, for had they done so, the Allies would have had to forgo the use of Simonstown for all practical purposes and thus have had no effective naval base between Freetown in Sierra Leone and Trincomalee in far-away Ceylon. They would, moreover, have lacked the comfort of the great mercantile ports of Capetown and Durban in which many thousands of their fighting-men and women were given lavish entertainment and some 6500 of their ships were afforded repairs and refreshment in the course of the first two years of the war. In default of these hospitable havens they could hardly have maintained any campaign eastward of the Cape and Gibraltar. So much depended physically on the one man who had brought South Africa into the war and kept her in it; so much depended spiritually and morally on that same man who even in the darkest days preached on the text, *Si pacem vis, para pacem*. To Smuts, no peace would be worth having unless the United States participated in its making, and he could not see her doing that unless she had been 'through the crucible of war' with the British Commonwealth with which, as Churchill put it, she was already 'somewhat mixed up.' The outstanding feature of that peace must be 'a new World Order,' for now that the day of small independent States had passed, there must be 'larger human groupings in that holistic process which fundamentally moulds all life and all history.' The prototype for such a grouping was obviously the British Commonwealth, an association in being to which the United States, sharing its ethics and political philosophy, stood far nearer than any other foreign nation.[2]

Smuts also was among the prophets. Scarcely were these words out of his mouth than the United States was thrust willy-nilly into the crucible of war. On December 7, 1941, Japanese planes with the briefest of warnings destroyed much of her Pacific fleet at Pearl Harbour in Hawaii.[3] The Union at once declared war on Japan, as well as on Roumania, Hungary and Finland, all of whom were now

---

[1] *Round Table*, No. 126, pp. 236 ff., 310; *Bulletin*, XVIII., No. 25, p. 1993.
[2] J. C. Smuts, *op. cit.*, p. 411.
[3] *Round Table*, No. 126, p. 310; *Bulletin*, XIX., No. 2, p. 75.

helpless dependants of the enemy, while Smuts, knowing that Hitler had allocated Vichy Madagascar to the Mikado, raised an additional seven thousand men and welcomed the numerous Canadians who came to train in the twenty-four South African air schools. Even so, it would be many months before the unready United States could make her weight felt in the field and, meanwhile, the Allies would have to take the immense strain of the new campaign in the Pacific and Indian Oceans. That strain was at first more than they could bear. Japanese planes followed up their success at Pearl Harbour by sinking the *Sydney*, Australia's solitary sizable warship, and also the great unescorted British battleship, the *Prince of Wales* and the battle-cruiser *Repulse*, in the Gulf of Siam. Having thus gained command of the seas westward of Panama and eastward of Ceylon, the Japanese took British Hong-Kong, invaded the American Philippines, induced a panic in urban Australia and seized bridge-heads in the Dutch East Indies and British Malaya. On the Russian front, the Germans drove far down towards the oil-bearing Caucasus and, though a desperate winter and the supplies which the British brought to Archangel at great cost to themselves enabled the Russians to push them back in places, they had established themselves on the outskirts of Leningrad and Moscow by the New Year of 1942.

At home, the struggle for the leadership of the *Afrikaner Volk* ground on. Strong in the support of many Dutch Reformed Church predikants and a growing phalanx of vigorous young men, Malan had little to fear from the visibly wilting Afrikaner Party, especially since Hertzog had made himself ridiculous by alleging that Smuts was going to lease an unspecified naval base to the United States. As a southerner, Malan felt it prudent to strengthen his hold on the north by telling a meeting of Transvaalers, whose anti-British sentiments were traditionally strong, that Germany would undoubtedly win the war and would like to see in South Africa the kind of government his party could provide, and to assure the many Poor Whites among them that they could only be really free in a republic which would give them first claim on official jobs, shield them from Jewish rapacity and magic away their perennial poverty.[1] Nevertheless, he was worried by the intrusion of rivals on his political preserves. The first of these was the New Order, which had been formed within the Party by Pirow, who claimed to be at once a good party member, a loyal Hertzogite and a friend of 'General' van Rensburg of the *O.B.* That organisation was the second of the trespassers and, in Malan's eyes, much the more dangerous of the two, for it had not only attracted into its ranks many of his own followers, but had gained such a popular hold that admirers could acclaim it as 'the

---

[1] *Round Table*, No. 124, pp. 811 ff.

greatest Afrikander association outside the Church.'[1] True, it had recently accepted the so-called Cradock Agreement by which it was to leave the political field exclusively to the Reunited National Party; but Malan thought it well to leave nothing to chance. He therefore reorganised his party on *O.B.* lines as a hierarchy of tiny cells each under a group leader and the whole under himself as Chief Leader. This done, he induced a general Party Congress at Bloemfontein, first, to accept a declaration calling on all Afrikaner organisations to co-operate in a spirit of pronounced Christian Nationalism to set up a 'Kruger republic,' which, at Pirow's suggestion, was to exercise not so much a 'democratic' as a 'resolute national' sway; then, to appoint an Afrikaner Unity Committee consisting of representatives of his Party, the *O.B.*, the *Federasie van Afrikaanse Kultur Verenigings*, the *Reddingsdaadbond* and so forth, to co-ordinate activities, and, lastly, to give him such wide powers as *Volksleier* that he could do what he chose when the general Congress was not sitting provided he reported his doings at the next session.[2]

Thus entrenched, Malan dealt first with Pirow by persuading a Transvaal Party Congress to forbid him to carry on propaganda on the ground that there was nothing Afrikaner about his National Socialist doctrines. Rather than wait to be expelled, Pirow withdrew and, with seventeen other Assembly members, formed his own New Order Party. Then, encouraged by the resignation of many officers from the *O.B.* in protest against their Commandant-General's forthright methods, Malan turned upon van Rensburg. The latter had not troubled to attend the recent Congress at Bloemfontein, preferring to spend his time as elective president of the *Afrikaanse Nasionale Studentbond* in urging the Stellenbosch undergraduates to read less and act more.[3] Meanwhile, the Unity Committee had accepted Malan's Bloemfontein scheme, but had decided that various details should be held back pending further discussion. Van Rensburg, however, published the scheme, details and all, as an Order. Backed by Strydom, Malan at once issued an ultimatum warning the *O.B.* off his political territory, stigmatising its leader as a National Socialist and threatening to expel its members from his Party unless the offending Order were withdrawn. Withdrawn it was, but van Rensburg would not yield to Malan's further demand that he should display 'positive friendliness.' Malan, therefore, struck again, giving his warm support to luckless Professor Kotze, leader of the academic wing of the *O.B.*, who had just parted company with the militants, and advising his own followers to quit the organisation. This thousands of them did, headed by Strydom and Kemp; others, like

1 *Die Vaderland*, Jan. 1941.
2 Hatch, *op. cit.*, p. 44; *Round Table*, No. 124, pp. 813 ff.
3 *Ibid.*, No. 125, p. 181; Roberts and Trollip, *op. cit.*, pp. 96 ff.

Eric Louw, who did not resign, were expelled, and the *F.A.K.* and *Reddinsgdaadbond* left the Unity Committee and formed a little front of their own.[1] The majority of the *O.B.*, nevertheless, stood firm behind their Commandant-General, continued to indulge in the conspiracy, corruption, treachery and occasional political assassination of which Malan openly accused them in the House and, in November 1941, even started a newspaper of their own, *Die O.B.* Unluckily for them, Zeesen short-wave, which had hitherto been non-committal, now came down heavily on the side of van Rensburg, thus enabling Malan to describe the *O.B.* as an 'unnational organisation' at the very moment that Smuts forbade certain classes of public servants to belong to it. In face of this two-fold assault, the *O.B.* might continue to be a power in the land, but the game was now so completely in Malan's hands that he could reject all his rival's attempts to parley. He had, in short, made sure that the campaign for the republic should be waged by his Party on more or less democratic lines and not on those laid down in München, Berlin and Berchtesgarten; but, for all that, Havenga, surveying the *disjecta membra* of the once-united Opposition, could justly lament that the Commandant-General of the *O.B.* and the *Volksleier* between them had made 'a mockery and prostitution of Afrikander unity.'[2]

To make matters worse for the divided Opposition, a split appeared in the tiny Afrikaner Party. The ageing and disillusioned Hertzog could not resist the chance of regaining some at least of his old influence and, by rushing into print, confirmed Malan's suspicions that he was flirting with Pirow and van Rensburg and went far to destroying his own deserved reputation as a statesman. Late in October 1941, he virtually subscribed to the *führerprinzip* by condemning parliamentary democracy as the ruination of the old Republics and the present cause of the impoverishment and deterioration of the *Afrikaner Volk*. He affirmed that National Socialism 'in its true character' was closely attuned to 'the spiritual and religious outlook of the Afrikander Nation'; nay, more, that it had been the corner-stone of the old Free State and still spoke to Afrikaners as 'a national tradition and custom as old as the Afrikaner nation itself.' Once it had been called into being, it would, he admitted, take on special Afrikaner shape, but it could only be called into being by 'a necessary grant of dictatorial powers.' This dangerous misreading of his country's history was too much for his fellow

---

[1] Roberts and Trollip, *op. cit.*, pp. 80 ff.; C. R. Kotze, *Die Ossewa-Brandwag*, pp. 6, 13; A. J. H. van der Walt, *'n Volk op Trek*, pp. 13, 15, 16, 21, 24; A. C. Cilliers, *Nasionale Volksorg*, pp. 67 ff.; J. S. Strydom, *Volkseenheid: op watter Grondslag?* p. 5 and Appendix; *Die Vaderland*, Oct. 8, 1941; *Round Table*, No. 124, p. 825, and No. 125, pp. 184 ff.
[2] Roberts and Trollip, *op. cit.*, pp. 87 ff., 101 ff.; *Hansard (S.A.)*, Vol. 43, pp. 1337 ff.; *Round Table*, No. 126, p. 313.

Free Staters, Havenga and Swart; for Havenga especially, who, now that he had been forced for the first time into opposition to his revered chief, quoted numberless passages from Hertzog's own speeches extolling the free white democratic institutions of the Republic that had been Jan Brand's. Since Hertzog had made himself politically impossible, his lieutenant reluctantly took his place as leader of the Afrikaner Party.[1]

The threefold splitting of the Opposition could not fail to benefit the Government, because, even if Malan's thirty-nine Nationalists, Pirow's seventeen New Order men and Havenga's nine were to combine whenever they saw a chance of bringing it down, it could reckon that its majority of eight in the Senate and its solid phalanx of eighty-nine United Party, Dominion and Labour men in the Lower House could withstand any such assault. Indeed, Smuts's Coalition had actually gained in strength since the outbreak of war by winning several by-elections in spite of the Opposition's flourishing of the Black Manifesto that had won Hertzog the general election of 1929 and the anti-Red banner that was peculiarly Malan's. The Prime Minister warned cheerful United Party Congresses that neither Afrikaners nor British could be suffered to become 'top-dog';[2] that, looking to the friendly relations that had grown up between white South Africans and brown and black warriors in East and North Africa, there must be a dropping of old ideas on the colour question 'which had brought nothing but bitterness and strife' and, that if the recent Atlantic Charter was to mean anything, there must be no more poor whitism, unemployment and similar social and economic waste after the war.[3] The implementation of this 'Smuts' Charter' must, however, await the winning of the war and, as the Allies' Black Year of 1941–2 dragged on, it became plain that victory still lay far ahead. The British in their islands were being bombed unmercifully each night and, on the high seas, their ships were falling victims to the U-boats in shoals; the fighting in North Africa was far too near the Suez Canal for comfort; in India, Congress was doing its worst to make impossible the position of the now overwhelmingly Indian Central Government and of the British-Indian defenders of their country in face of the Japanese, while these same Japanese were fast approaching Rangoon, the key to Burma, and, in mid-February 1942, having overrun Malaya, took the great British naval base of Singapore.

Such dire events inevitably had repercussions in semi-hostile South Africa. The authorities, however, replied to amateur bombing, mainly along the Rand and the Pretoria-Delagoa Bay railway, by

---

[1] *Bulletin*, XVIII., No. 22, pp. 1848 ff.; *Die Vaderland*, March 30 and April 20, 1942.
[2] *Bulletin*, XVIII., No. 26, p. 2040.   [3] *Round Table*, No. 126, p. 316.

rounding up some three hundred and fifty Police and Railway Police, many of them *O.B.* storm-troopers and many more possessed of illicit bombs,[1] and seeing to it that malefactors like the notorious ex-policeman, Robey Leibbrandt, and the woman spy, Betty Hennig, should receive stiff sentences. Against this unnerving background, Parliament met in January 1942, rejected Malan's motion for republican secession, and perused the long-delayed draft constitution for his republic, which provided for domination by Afrikaners in the narrowest sense, the use of English on sufferance, the reservation of the franchise for those who 'might be expected to assist in building up the nation,' and a State President 'directly and only responsible to God, over and against the people . . . altogether independent of any vote in Parliament.'[2] This manifesto was the signal for renewed sabotage and, during the next few months, desperadoes dislocated the vital gold industry by blowing up pylons that carried power to the Rand mines, while others in the Free State and old Trekker areas of the Cape cut telegraph and telephone wires.[3] The authorities narrowly averted an *O.B. putsch* in Durban that was to have been followed by the shooting of prominent loyalists and, haunted as they were by fear of attacks on coastal towns by planes from Japanese carriers, prescribed the death penalty for sabotage and set up Special Courts to try offenders. Undismayed, Malan celebrated the fall of Singapore by sneering at the supposed evanescence of the Russians' winter victories, justifying the search for *lebensraum* by the blameless Japanese, and moving once more for an immediate peace because the Germans were bound to win the war. Smuts turned upon him and gave fair warning that if the Japanese sought *lebensraum* in the Union, he would 'go the whole hog' and 'inspan all the forces of South Africa' regardless of colour to defend their common home, and presently declared in the University of the Witwatersrand on the occasion of the conferring of an honorary degree on the exiled Queen of the Netherlands, that, so far from winning the war, the Axis Powers could not even achieve a stalemate.[4] In April, he severed diplomatic relations with the Petain Government and sent South Africans to help other Allied forces to seize the strong naval base of Diego Suarez in Vichy Madagascar.[5] As the occupation of the rest of that vital island proceeded, tidings came of the Americans' naval victories in the Coral Sea and off Midway Island and the British repulse of heavy Japanese air attacks on Ceylon, successes which together set a term to the hitherto sweeping advance of those Asiatics towards the two Pacific Dominions and the Union.

[1] *Bulletin*, XVIII., No. 26, p. 2040; XIX., No. 3, p. 124.
[2] *Die Transvaler*, Jan. 23, 1942 (translation in *The British African Monthly*, July 1948).
[3] *Bulletin*, XIX., No. 3, pp. 124 ff.
[4] *Bulletin*, XIX., No. 6, p. 262; No. 7, p. 311.   [5] *Ibid.*, XIX., No. 9, p. 404.

During the Session of 1942, Parliament made generous provision for disabled soldiers and their dependants, and dealt with such pressing problems as banking, unemployment,[1] rents, wages, steel and industrial development. But a problem that threatened to become more pressing than even these was that of inflation as 'hot money' flowed into the Union from less secure lands.[2] Gold, the Union's chief material asset, inevitably dominated the policy of the Reserve Bank, which strove to build up a reserve fund that should pay for war-time imports and replenish commercial stocks when peace should come. Throughout the war, the bulk of the Union's gold-production had either been exported or else earmarked for the financing of imports to such an extent that, by the close of October 1941, the Reserve Bank had increased its holdings of gold by seventy per cent. and, by creating credits against the freshly-mined gold, had contributed fully four-fifths of the immensely swollen volume of current money and bank deposits. The Reserve Bank experienced some heart-searching as it contemplated this growing inflation, but it and its gold policy were by no means responsible for the whole of it. If South Africa was sick with money at the end of two years of war that had brought distress and devastation to less favoured parts of the world, much of her malaise could be attributed to the fact that her farmers had profited from high prices fixed by the Central and National Supply Boards, guaranteed markets and increased consumption at home and even, for a time, abroad, that the United Kingdom had bought most of their wool and citrus, and that local jam-makers had more than supplemented the State subsidy by their demands for soft fruit. Latterly, wheat and mealie farmers had been hit by the growing shortage of shipping, but taking it all round, agriculturalists had little cause for complaint. It was the same in other walks of life, and notably in the secondary industries that were springing up right and left and attracting to them swarms of the poorer Afrikaners and non-Europeans from the countryside. Employers were directed to pay a cost of living allowance to all folk such as these who earned less than 74s. a week, while a Commission began to consider the raising of the Bantu standard of life by the extension of social services.[3]

In face of all this, it soon became clear that, if serious inflation were to be averted, the manifold price controls would have to be supplemented by wage controls, for though the Controller of Manpower 'froze' wages in the engineering industry to check the poaching by one firm of the employees of another, he could not stop the unco-ordinated Wage Boards and the Industrial Council from screwing up wages in other concerns, nor stay the passing of a

[1] Act 17 of 1942.   [2] Round Table, No. 124, p. 816.
[3] Ibid., No. 125, pp. 177 ff.

Factory Act which made highly-paid overtime inevitable by reducing the ordinary hours of work and giving the workers holidays on full pay and other costly privileges. In spite of ministerial warnings against the risks of extravagance, South Africans indulged in an unparalleled orgy of 'spending it now' during the Christmas shopping season of 1941, an orgy to which new European and non-European recruits to industry, with unaccustomed money in their pockets, contributed more than their share.[1]

Though there had been no real shortage of consumer goods during the early months of the war, purchasing power and consequently prices had presently risen so fast that, at the New Year of 1941, a Price Controller had been appointed. A few months later, an Imports and Exports Control Board was set up to decide, *inter alia*, problems of priorities, a Purchasing Commission was established to co-ordinate purchases in the United States which was fast becoming the Union's chief source of supply, and the import of non-essentials from all dollar-using countries was prohibited.[2] Meanwhile, in spite of an Emergency Order which forbade any increase on the pre-war rate of profit, profits were increasing out of all reason, because, by adhering to that constant rate of profit, there was necessarily a widening margin between selling prices and the rising cost prices. Hence, in October 1941, the Price Controller instructed his inspectors no longer to leave it to aggrieved customers to make complaints, but to watch for and report infringements themselves, permitted only one single wholesale profit as the best means of checking evasion by the collusive and unnecessary interchange of goods between firms, and, finally, to the fury of those many shopkeepers who had sold out during the Christmas rush and would thus have to restock at enhanced prices, forbade anyone to add the same percentage 'mark up' if the cost price of their goods had risen by more than ten per cent. above the datum line of 1939.[3]

To check this dangerous inflation the Reserve Bank urged Hofmeyr to pay off external debt, to mop up surplus funds and thus, *inter alia*, to give the authorities securities with which to ensure the success of such open market operations as they might undertake. The Finance Minister needed no reminding of the wisdom of repatriating external debt and, though he was sceptical of the existence of inflation, had already begun the mopping-up process by issuing Union loan certificates. Their ready sale had encouraged him to issue, in October 1941, modest quantities of local registered stock, much larger quantities of saving bonds with a personal maximum of £5000, which were intended for those who already held the full

---

[1] *Round Table*, No. 125, pp. 173 ff.; No. 126, pp. 318 ff.
[2] *Ibid.*, No. 126, p. 321; No. 133, pp. 88 ff.; War Measures, No. 23 and 30 of 1941; *Report of the Organisation . . . of Supplies*, p. 119.
[3] *Round Table*, No. 126, p. 322.

permissible amount of the Union Loan Certificates, and the so-
called Redemption Issue, also of local registered stock, that was to
be used for the repatriation of Union loans from London.[1] The
purchase of the Redemption Issue had hung fire; but these various
checks on extravagance had together brought about a marked
decrease of overseas imports, while £2,000,000 worth of newly-
mined gold remained in the Reserve Bank in spite of the repatriation
of £30,000,000 of external debt since the outbreak of war.[2] In his
Budget speech, Hofmeyr could report a surplus of more than
£6,000,000 instead of the anticipated deficit, thanks mainly to the
unusual promptitude with which farmers had repaid state loans, a
mounting customs revenue and the record production of gold to the
tune of some £120,000,000, which would surely be taken by the
United States whose belligerency had thus far made no difference
to her insatiable appetite for the output of the Rand. He budgeted
for a small deficit, if only because war expenditure must be heavy,
and proposed to meet two-thirds of the year's outgoings by taxation
and the rest by borrowing, in spite of the competition in the loan
market of the Capetown and Johannesburg City Councils. Taxation
was to include further lessons in the virtue of saving by the levy of a
flat-rate surcharge of twenty per cent. on individual income taxpayers,
a Special Tax on profits arising from speculative dealings in land, a
General Poll Tax on all males who earned more than £250 a year,
an increased Special Contribution imposed upon the taxable income
of gold mines, stiffer Estate Duties and, to make up for the reduction
of the duty on tea and the abolition of that on knitting-wool, increased Customs and Excise Duties on petrol, tobacco and films.
The most original impost, however, was a Trade Profits Special
Levy on all profits above eight per cent. that were not already subject
to the hated Excess Profits Duty. These two levies following so hard
upon one another made Hofmeyr fully as unpopular among businessmen generally as he had long been among mineowners.[3]

Van der Byl, as Director-General of War Supplies, had exercised
an effective control on everything that fell under that head since the
early days of the war; but the first attempt to control civilian supplies
had only been made in May 1941, when restrictions on the milling
of white flour had checked the unprecedented consumption of cakes
bought at wartime charity bazaars. A little price-fixing had followed
the appointment of the Price Controller and, four months later, of
the Social and Economic Planning Council, most of whose subordinates had to cope with the vagaries of the weather, the mistaken
idea that the Union was an agriculturally 'surplus producing'
country, and the sabotaging by more than a few stout Nationalist

---

[1] *Round Table*, No. 126, p. 323.   [2] *Ibid.*, No. 127, pp. 426 ff.
[3] *Bulletin*, XIX., No. 5, pp. 124–5; *Round Table*, No. 127, pp. 426 ff.

farmers and their wives of schemes emanating from the loathed Smuts administration.[1] The Price Controller, especially, must pick his way among a maze of agricultural Control Boards, whose main aim was to keep up prices for producers by obliging them to export part of their crops at a loss and then leaving them free to recoup that loss at the expense of the would-be domestic purchasers. The hastily and ill-constructed Citrus Board had varied this programme somewhat during the near-panic that had ensued after the outbreak of war by allowing growers to put 'export quality fruit' on the local market, but as this had been picked green for export it failed to attract customers, who found that, in any event, it was priced far too high for their purses. Later on, when shipping-shortage hit the orange-growers, the Board allowed them to put up a strictly limited quantity of fruit for sale by auction, with the result that many of them sought to drive their incomes still higher by destroying part of their pick. As with oranges, so with mealies. During the first two years of the war, the Maize Control Board had clung to its traditional policy of estimating the local demand and then financing the export of the so-called surplus by a levy on what was sold in the Union. Despite warnings by mealie-traders of woe to come, it was apparently surprised when this estimated export surplus disappeared before half of it had been shipped. Then woe came. Thanks partly to a bad harvest, the total supply was so small that the output of butter, cheese and milk dwindled because of the lack of cattle-feed and the Bantu masses went hungry because they could not get enough of their staple diet.

The greatest and most persistent scandal, however, was the marketing of meat. Long wedded to a system which played into the hands of speculators and auctioneers, the Meat Control Board set a bad example to its fellows by insisting on disposal wholesale at auction, limiting the number of beasts that might be sent to the abattoirs in the larger towns, and arbitrarily varying the number of the permits of entry thereto so that buyers might be tempted to bid high while there was still a chance of getting any meat at all. Late in 1941, the Price Controller sought to ease the situation for buyers and check the rising cost of living by fixing maximum wholesale and retail prices in the larger towns. Thereupon, speculators and auctioneers withheld supplies, knowing that they could always off-load their unsold beasts in other parts of the country where prices were still uncontrolled, while many wholesale butchers, who also owned retail shops, laid themselves open to the charge that they were seeking to ruin smaller retailers, who could not carry on for so long as they, by paying more for meat than they could hope to recover across the counter, at all events for a time. Nor, while Capetown,

[1] *Round Table*, No. 127, pp. 421 ff.

Durban and Johannesburg were clamouring for meat at any price, did these gentry heed the Price Controller's command that they should share supplies with their weaker brethren. After all, business was business.[1]

At last, in March 1942, in face of these largely-engineered shortages of meat, mealies and oranges, a genuine dearth of vegetables and wheat, and a public outcry against the flocking of extravagant crowds to the Durban July Handicap, South Africa's Ascot, Smuts appointed the Minister and Secretary for Agriculture respectively as Controller and Deputy-Controller of a Food Control Organisation and, at the same time, nominated a Controller of Building Materials. Even so, the feeding of the people was still left in the hands of the Control Boards, which turned a deaf ear to those University economists who had long been urging that, as recent experience had shown, the true way to raise prices was not to restrict supplies in the manner of the old Dutch East India Company, but to pay higher wages so that a hungry populace could afford to buy all the foodstuffs that came its way.[2] The new Social and Economic Planning Council might be sketching the foundations of an economy in which there should be security and well-being for all, but the implementing of such long-term projects must be postponed to the still far-distant end of the war. Meanwhile, the tangled problems of prices and controls brooked no delay. In October 1942, therefore, Smuts took steps to co-ordinate and centralise the complex and mutually contradictory machinery of controls. He first created a Commodity Supply Directorate as the civilian counterpart of the long-established Department of War Supplies. This new Directorate was to regulate civilian supply working through a Board of Supplies and three Committees: one to co-ordinate the controls of various important commodities, another to take over certain controls from the Ministry of Commerce, and the last to ensure that manufacturers met the chief needs of the public and to advise on difficulties arising from the conflicting demands of firms which were making goods in short supply. Smuts gave the Directorate-Generalship of Supplies to van der Byl, who was to control the new Commodity Supply Directorate as well as the Department of War Supplies of which he had long been head, and to work in conjunction with a National Supplies Council under the chairmanship of the Prime Minister. In other words, subject to Smuts's final word, van der Byl was to have charge not only of war supplies, but of all civilian supplies other than food, petrol, building materials and man-power.[3]

[1] *Round Table*, No. 133, pp. 86 ff.
[2] *Ibid.*, No. 133, p. 93; Government Notice, No. 511 of March 24, 1942.
[3] *Round Table*, No. 129, p. 92; No. 133, pp. 88 ff.; War Measure, No. 146, and Government Notice, No. 200 of 1942.

There was need for some such drastic domestic reorganisation, because the war was going badly for the Allies. Their bombers might be raiding Germany more effectively, but U-boats were sinking their ships right and left, while the Germans had overrun the Crimea, stormed into the Caucasus and pressed far down towards Stalingrad on the lower Volga river. The Germans, thus drawing near to the shores of the Caspian, may have hoped to join hands with the Japanese, who had conquered all Burma, cut the Allies' communications with China, and were now lined up on the eastern frontier of India, whose Congressmen, intent only on forcing the British to 'quit India,' staged a revolution worse than any such thing since the Mutiny nearly a hundred years back and, thereby cut the communications of Wavell's defending British-Indian army for weeks on end. Nearer home, while Axis bombers were making Malta wellnigh untenable and Alexandria highly dangerous as a naval base, Rommel cut up the Allied armour at Knightsbridge, captured nearly the whole of a South African division when he overran Tobruk, which this time lacked the tanks that had enabled it to hold out the year before, and forced the Allies back to Alamein, a short hundred miles from the Suez Canal and much less from expectant Cairo.[1] It is true that Lend-Lease supplies, accompanied by United States troops, were now flowing into the Union, that losses of men at Tobruk were soon more than made up by European volunteers and a battalion of local Indians, and that, in view of the desperate situation in North Africa, the Governments of South Africa and Southern Rhodesia agreed to consult in an emergency and, meanwhile, set up a Joint South African Command under the direction of Smuts as G.O.C. Union Defence Force; nevertheless, it was now that the war came closest to Southern Africa.[2] Enemy submarines, too often well posted by South African traitors, sank ship after ship off the south-east coast; Durban was startled by at least one of the air-raid alerts that were a matter of almost hourly occurrence in the United Kingdom; Durban, again, and Port Elizabeth also had to be 'blacked-out' nightly, and a six-phase scheme for similar precautions must be framed for the other large centres. It was well that the Coast Garrison units, organised on the lines of the British Home Guard, had by this time been trained and lavishly equipped, and that coastal defences generally had been worked up to fighting pitch.

Malan was also working his followers up to fighting pitch as the events of the Black Year seemed to bring his Zeesen-sponsored Republic nearer. Elated by the Allied reverse at Tobruk and angered by the demand of the tiny South African Communist Party for a

[1] *Round Table*, No. 128, p. 517.
[2] *Bulletin*, XIX., No. 12, p. 545; No. 14, p. 638; No. 19, p. 864; No. 20, p. 914; No. 21, p. 957.

social and economic revolution that was somehow to avert similar disasters, he called in vain for a Special Session to debate the crisis. On the other hand, now that so many Pirowites and members of the *O.B.* were coming over to his Nationalist standard, he might reckon on a general rally of the divided *Afrikaner Volk* if ever it came to the push against Smuts's Coalition, which was shaken in both Houses by the restiveness of its Dominion and Labour Party members and, outside, by those many citizens who nursed grievances against its wartime civil and military administration. These critics could not go too far if only because the general election was due in 1943; but they could and did grumble with much truth that the Cabinet needed new blood, that some Ministers had too much to do and some too little and that, in any event, a Ministry of only thirteen members had no room for ornaments or passengers. Three departments drew most of the fire: the Ministries of Defence, of Finance and, lastly, of Commerce and Industries against which businessmen had chalked up an interminable score of complaints for its delays in answering applications for import permits, incalculable vagaries in priority ratings and apparent unwillingness to issue permits for goods which were high on the priority list and ready for shipment. In the background stood a populace that girded at the growing shortage of shipping and the consequent lack of many familiar commodities.[1]

Inspired by hopes of the 'inevitable' fall of Stalingrad and the Suez Canal and heartened by victory in several Provincial by-elections to the cry of 'No group-forming,' the Opposition now made such a determined effort to close its ranks that Deneys Reitz, Minister of Native Affairs and by reason of seniority Smuts's obvious deputy, was moved to blurt out that the Ministry would not resign even if it lost the coming general election. Be that as it might, while the New Order and the *O.B.* were clamouring that women be kept out of politics and immigration be barred for a hundred years to come, Malan summoned a general reunion Congress to Pretoria. Draped in the *Vierkleur*, he received a wild welcome and a renewal of his extensive powers as *Volksleier*; but that was all. It may be that Pirow and van Rensburg had failed to drag the ailing Hertzog from his retirement to further a reunion; it was certain that Malan, taking a leaf from Hertzog's book, reproved them both as untrustworthy and cowardly for pinning their hopes on a German victory. After this ill start, not all the arguments of these two suspects, nor even of the mild Havenga, that Reitz's recent outburst showed that Smuts's followers had no faith in democracy could save the assemblage from breaking up amid furious mutual recriminations.[2] Afrikaner re-

---

[1] *Round Table*, No. 128, pp. 520 ff.
[2] *Ibid.*, No. 129, pp. 90 ff.; Roberts and Trollip, *op. cit.*, pp. 139 ff.

union having thus been dismissed beyond the bounds of practical politics, Malan wooed the 'English' by playing on their accumulated discontents. Here he had small success at the moment for, at the first test, the United Party won the Hottentots-Holland by-election hands down in spite of the absence of fully one-fifth of the local electors on war service. It was perhaps some consolation to him that his hated rival, Hertzog, should have died in October 1942, an embittered and shamefully used old man.[1]

Reitz paid for his indiscretion, first, by seeing Hofmeyr, his junior, become Acting-Prime Minister when Smuts presently fell ill, thereafter, by being bidden to hand over Native Affairs to Major Pieter van der Byl, Minister without Portfolio, and, finally, by being packed off to London as High Commissioner at the first opportunity.[2] Meanwhile, Smuts had flown on his first wartime visit to the United Kingdom leaving Hofmeyr once more in charge. In the course of five busy weeks, he attended meetings of the Larger and Inner War Cabinets, the Defence Committee and multifarious special Conferences, and, intent on winning the war, addressed both Houses of Parliament at the Guildhall, broadcast an appeal to the plucky people of the Netherlands to co-operate with the United Nations after peace had come again, and at all times stressed the fact that the possession of Africa was fast becoming the dominant factor in the winning of the war.[3] While he yet spake, the tide turned abruptly, and turned primarily in North Africa. On November 2, 1942, General Bernard Montgomery and his Eighth Army began to shatter Rommel's armour around Alamein so disastrously that, but for the heavy rains that bogged down the pursuing tanks, very few of the Afrika Korps would ever have struggled out of Egypt. At the same time, the First Army, a large, incoherent and imperfectly trained Anglo-American force under the United States General, Dwight Eisenhower, was thrown ashore far to the westward in French Algeria, while on November 19 the Russians sprang a devastating surprise on the huge German army near Stalingrad. Smuts at once cabled his congratulations to 'Monty' and his men on their 'magnificent victory . . . a turning-point in this war,' since he who held the Mediterranean held the keys to Europe and could, like another Carthage, wreak vengeance on 'a recreant Rome.'[4]

Back in Pretoria and rejoiced to learn that an official inquiry attached no blame to his South Africans for the fall of Tobruk, Smuts called for 'hard fighting and good planning' to free the thousands of 'our boys' who were still prisoners in Italy.[5] He repeated his promise that he would not send South Africans overseas

[1] *Round Table*, No. 130, pp. 183 ff. [2] *Bulletin*, XX, No. 1, p. 35.
[3] *Ibid.*, XIX., No. 22, pp. 995 ff. [4] *Ibid.*, XIX., No. 24, p. 1104.
[5] *Ibid.*, XIX., No. 25, p. 1162; No. 26, p. 1209.

without leave of Parliament, and then set out his proposals for the post-war reorganisation of the British Empire for the consideration of all concerned, especially for that of the uncomprehending and suspicious citizens of the United States. With more emphasis than accuracy, he asserted that 'the old British Empire' had died about the time of the South African War and had thus made way for 'the widest system of organised freedom' there had ever been. The United Kingdom must, he admitted, continue to rule her dependencies like any Mother Country, but those scattered Colonies ought to be formed, wherever possible, into groups for better administration. Each such group should be governed by a Council manned by the United Kingdom herself, the members of that group and specially interested members of the British Commonwealth of Nations. Suitable groups should be further combined into regional groups each under a Regional Commission manned by the United Kingdom again and other governments interested regionally for security or economic reasons or both; for instance, the United States might well find a place on the Commissions concerned with the West Indies, Africa and so on. Finally, recalling the sentimental regard which so many United States citizens had for India, he proclaimed that next to winning the war, the emancipation of that great sub-continent 'without internal disruption was perhaps the greatest prize in the world.'[1]

Good news from all the fronts poured in during the early weeks of the Session of 1943. In the Atlantic, improved radar-location, more light surface craft and adequate numbers of long-range bombers were plainly giving the Allies the upper hand of the dreaded U-boats; on the other side of the world, in the Pacific, United States Marines seized the vital island of Guadalcanal, which was to be their base for 'island-hopping' along the road to Tokyo, and early in March 1943 United States warships destroyed most of what remained of the Mikado's Navy in the Bismarck Sea. Halfway between, Wavell's British and Indians smashed a full-dress Japanese assault on the Assam front just as the Russians compelled the surrender of 300,000 Germans around Stalingrad and, thereafter, began to drive the enemy away from the outskirts of Moscow and Leningrad. Meanwhile, in the January of 1943, Montgomery had taken Tripoli and chased Rommel behind the Mareth lines in Tunisia, while Churchill and Roosevelt had met at Casablanca, not so very far away, to discuss the next moves. Then the Americans, characteristically trusting to machines rather than the legs of a man, failed to stop Rommel's driving through them northward, though at the price of abandoning his wretched Italian allies. It was, however, only a respite, for on May 13, 1943, Rommel's successor and the

[1] *Life*, 1943.

entire Afrika Korps, recently reinforced to 250,000 men,were forced to lay down their arms at Cape Bon.[1]

At this stage, though her casualties, including some 13,000 prisoners, were nearing the 20,000 mark, the Union still had two full divisions and most of her Air Force in North Africa. Now that the war was 'happily moving away from Africa,' in all probability to Italy, Parliament readily agreed that volunteers should serve outside their own continent for the remainder of their original four years' term of attestation, provided that, if the war went on longer than that, they must sign on again 'for the duration.'[2] Smuts then cheered the Houses by reporting that the United Kingdom had undertaken to provide the Union with immediate supplies for railways and harbours and, later on, the equipment that would make her an even more efficient supplier of goods and materials to Allied forces in the whole Mediterranean area.[3] Next, knowing that at least one notorious mischief-maker had just been landed from an enemy submarine on the south-east coast, he proclaimed parts of Natal and the Transvaal prohibited areas and, further, told Malan that if he must move for the severance of relations with the U.S.S.R. and the suppression of domestic Communism, he should at least do so without attacking the country that was bearing the main burden of the fighting by land or referring, in passing, to the United States as 'the enemy.' The Assembly showed its concurrence by rejecting Malan's motion and passing on to consider finance and the everlasting Indian question.

Hofmeyr announced that, thanks to systematic repatriation, external indebtedness now amounted to no more than four per cent. of the country's total debt, but that because of heavy war expenditure and a dwindling revenue from the gold mines, he must budget for a small deficit. Nevertheless, he proposed to meet the cost of increased pay and allowances for the troops by savings elsewhere, to give all schoolchildren of whatever colour at least one free meal each day and, for the first time, to hand over the entire yield of the Native Tax to the Native Trust to be spent on Bantu education.[4] It was, however, the Indians and not the Bantu who claimed Parliament's attention. There were now more than 250,000 of that people, fully eighty per cent. of them South African born, and from Durban had come complaints that they were fast penetrating white areas of that city. In 1941, therefore, Smuts had appointed the Broome Commission to investigate the situation in the Transvaal and Natal and meanwhile carried a so-called 'Pegging Act' to maintain the *status quo* for two years in both Provinces. In due course the Commission had reported that the situation north of the Drakensberg need

---

[1] *Round Table*, No. 131, p. 223, and No. 132, p. 342.
[2] *Bulletin*, XX., No. 2, p. 81, and No. 3, p. 129.
[3] *Round Table*, No. 129, p. 92.   [4] *Ibid.*, No. 131, pp. 291 ff.

occasion no surprise, and that it was not serious there save in and around Johannesburg, nor serious in Natal, except possibly in Durban, where a minority of well-to-do Indians were buying real property in select white areas at an increasing rate mainly as an investment. He commented drily that Durban's city fathers had done little enough in the way of giving the Asiatic one-third of that great port's population social amenities or even decent conditions of life.[1] Smuts had, therefore, invited the Durban City Council to send representatives to a Joint European-Indian Committee, which might find a way out of the local difficulty by agreement; but the City representatives had withdrawn and the Dominion Party, whose main strength lay in coastal Natal, had fiercely criticised the very presence of Indians in the Union. Smuts, thus, had had no choice but to reappoint the Broome Commission to inquire specifically into the situation in Durban.[2]

The Indian situation was eased somewhat thereafter when a few Europeans began to talk of giving Indians some form of elective parliamentary, provincial and municipal representation, and prominent Indians gave informal assurances that their folk had no wish to penetrate white areas. Then, in April 1943, the renewed Broome Commission reported that while the mass of the Natal Indians had loyally stood by the 'gentleman's agreement' of 1927, a small minority of them had latterly been buying as much real property as they could in white residential areas.[3] Smuts promptly introduced the Trading and Occupation of Land (Transvaal and Natal) Bill to peg the trading situation in the Transvaal and the land situation in Natal for three years to come. This measure was hotly attacked by the Delhi authorities, leading South African Indians and men at both extremes of South African politics. Malan, for his part, held that it did not go nearly far enough and demanded a Union-wide Indian residential segregation, the denial of the Indians' right to vote on South Africa's domestic affairs and an end to Smuts's sacrificing of the Union's interests on the altar of 'inter-imperialism.' Hofmeyr, on the contrary, objected so strongly to the 'unnecessary' Transvaal clauses that he offered to resign.[4] Smuts would not hear of it; hence, Hofmeyr stayed and the Bill went through. So anxious was the Prime Minister, however, to find a friendly solution that he suspended the new Pegging Act and appointed a Provincial Board of Control consisting of two Europeans and two Indians under the chairmanship of a legally-trained European to divide Natal into residential areas of three kinds: first, those in which no real property deals between Europeans and Indians should be permitted;

---

[1] U.G. 39–41.
[2] U.G. 39–41, *Report of the Indian Penetration Commission*; *Round Table*, No. 131, pp. 288 ff.
[3] U.G. 21–43.
[4] *Bulletin XX*, No. 8, pp. 515 ff.; *Round Table*, No. 131, p. 290; U.G. 21–43.

secondly, those in which these should be merely restricted and, lastly, those urban areas in which they should be permitted freely.

Then, as the general election was imminent, Smuts sought to win Coloured votes by setting up a Coloured Advisory Department very much on the lines of that suspect *imperium in imperio*, the Native Affairs Department. He had misjudged his men, for the main result of his action was to give the Communists the chance of stampeding Coloured voters by telling them that this was the first instalment of segregation, and to galvanise Dr. Goolam Gool's Trotskyist Fourth International Group and its bickering rivals into activity.[1] Much more fruitful was his guarantee of nine uncontested seats to Labour and eight to the Dominion Party. The general election took place on July 7, 1943, a month earlier than had been publicly anticipated. The Pirowites boycotted the whole affair and the *O.B.*, Communists and Afrikaner men were defeated everywhere they appeared. Malan's Nationalists, a well-disciplined body whose candidatures had been approved by the *Volksleier* as well as by the Central Committee, marched to battle under the triple banners of the Black Manifesto, the Red Menace and Smuts's Shortcomings. They rather more than held their own, though with reduced majorities. By contrast, Labour and the Dominion Party won nearly all their 'guaranteed' seats, while the United Party swept the rural Cape, Transvaal and Natal and carried all save three of the urban constituencies in the Union.[2]

The Coalition had thus gained a resounding victory, but second thoughts suggested that Malan's turn might come one day. The elections had been fought in an atmosphere of warlike enthusiasm and thankfulness at the recent happy turn in the fortunes of the Allies. Never again could the ministerialists hope for such ideal conditions, whereas Malan could take comfort from the thought that nearly all their gains had been at the expense of the New Order and Afrikaner Parties, that his own Party had actually improved its position, that far fewer Afrikaners had voted for the ministerialists than in 1938, and that their abstention from voting by many electors on active service suggested that they disapproved of Smuts's policies. Now that all rival Afrikaner formations had been smashed, might not Malan hope that he would sooner or later win enough votes to give him his republic by democratic methods? However that might be, the total strength of the Opposition had fallen from sixty-three to forty-three, while that of the United Party had risen from seventy to eighty-nine and of the Coalition from eighty-seven to one hundred and five without counting the votes of the three 'Native' members and a few Independents which would usually be cast for them. Supported by such a phalanx representing nearly two-thirds of the electors who had gone to the polls, Smuts would surely be able to 'see it through.'[3]

[1] Hatch, *op. cit.*, pp. 199 ff.
[2] *Round Table*, No. 131, p. 291; No. 132, pp. 383 ff.; *Bulletin*, XX., No. 16, p. 718.
[3] Roberts and Trollip, *op. cit.*, pp. 145 ff.

Thus confirmed in power, Smuts reorganised his Cabinet by transforming the Ministries of Commerce and Industries and of Railways and Harbours into those of Economic Development and Transport respectively, and by creating the portfolio of Welfare and Demobilisation, which he entrusted to Harry Lawrence. He also ensured the appointment of Chief Justice Nicolaas de Wet as Acting Governor-General in place of Duncan, who had died on July 17 after a long illness.[1] Presently, he received a further popular endorsement of his policy at the Provincial elections in October, so far as could be judged from a contest that was so apathetic that the Afrikaner and Communist Parties took no share and the Nationalists but little outside their stronghold of the Free State. The main issue was school education and its bearing on bilingualism and, therefore, that welding of the two white groups into a single people to which Smuts and Botha before him had dedicated themselves. The vast majority of the schools were State, that is, public schools under the control of the Provincial Councils. Practice therein varied. In some, only one of the official languages was used as the medium of instruction, in others both in parallel classes, and in yet others the dual medium, that is, the use of the language which was not the children's home tongue either every other day or for half the lessons on each day. Alarmed at the spread of Afrikaans unilingualism in the schools and confirmed in their fears by a recent survey made by Dr. Ernst Malherbe, the liberal Afrikaner Director of the National Bureau of Educational and Social Research, the Coalition wished to make the dual medium universal in the public schools. The Opposition resisted the attempt on the grounds that all-pervading English would kill Afrikaans, and, still further in defiance of the facts, that the interests of the Afrikaans-speaking child would be prejudiced and education be ruined. Be that as it might, the Coalition carried most of the elections in the Cape, Natal and the Transvaal leaving the Opposition to make what they could of reduced majorities in such few seats as they held.[2]

Meanwhile, the war was going faster than ever in the Allies' favour. Early in July 1943, while the Russians were driving the enemy out of their European territories, the British, helped by the base granted to them in the Azores, were sinking U-boats by the score, and the British and Americans, equipped at last with all the planes they needed, were systematically bombing industrial centres in Hitler's *Grossdeutschesreich*, the Allies, and among them thousands of South Africans, invaded Sicily. Such was the shock that Mussolini fell. Presently, after the invaders had crossed into mainland Italy, the now friendly Government under the King and Marshal Badoglio first

[1] *Round Table*, No. 132, pp. 303 ff.; *Bulletin*, XX., No. 17, p. 178.
[2] *Round Table*, No. 133, pp. 84 ff.

signed an armistice and then, on the fall of Naples in October, declared war on Germany. Forthwith, the 'Resistance' blazed up in Italy and neighbouring France. Under these propitious circumstances, Smuts combined with the United Kingdom and United States authorities to form a Joint Supply Council for Africa and, in October, flew once more to London.[1] There, he concluded a Reciprocal Aid Agreement with the United States and, though he said less about it, a complicated agreement with the United Kingdom whereby he promised to repay its Government his country's debt of £35,000,000 by instalments and compounded for current obligations at the rate of £1,000,000 a month, provided the British would 'find' everything for the needs of his troops serving outside the Union. He was fully consulted on the preliminary negotiations and on the final terms of the Four Power Declaration of Moscow, which was issued by the United Kingdom, the United States, the U.S.S.R. and China, and, generally made himself so useful that Churchill asked him to act as Prime Minister while he himself journeyed to Teheran in November 1943 to take stock and make plans for the coming year with Stalin and Roosevelt.[2]

This signal honour Smuts declined, preferring to preach his doctrine untrammelled by the necessary reticences of high office. In mid-October at the Guildhall, he insisted that, though the defeat of Germany must be the 'first priority,' this, 'the greatest war in history should become the prelude to the greatest peace' in which 'aggression must be abjured' lest Western civilisation perish. A month later he suggested to the Empire Parliamentary Association how this might be achieved. There must, he urged his hearers, be no repetition of the fatal side-stepping and over-simplification of issues which had wrecked the peace settlement of 1919, but 'a pretty comprehensive armistice' during which to clear up the mess, and not least the mess in the British Empire. Boldly asserting that freedom, like patriotism, was not enough, he warned all concerned that, because they could not 'get away from the problem of power,' they must see to it that the United Kingdom, the United States and the U.S.S.R., the really Great Powers responsible in the last resort for the peace of the world, be given their due places in the coming international system. France, he lamented, and indeed 'the old Europe' were gone already, Germany and Japan would go in due course, and there would then remain in all Europe only the U.S.S.R., 'the new Colossus,' and the United Kingdom herself, a poor country now in material things, but rich in 'a glory and an honour and a prestige' such as no other land

[1] *Bulletin*, XX., No. 20, p. 893; *Record of the Organisation* . . . *of Supplies*, p. 6a.
[2] *Round Table*, No. 135, p. 286; J. C. Smuts, *op. cit.*, p. 432; Ministry of Information Press Release, Dec. 6, 1943 (*United Nations Documents*, . . ., p. 24).

had ever had. Facing these two from across the Atlantic would stand the mighty United States, and together this 'trinity' would hold in its hands 'the solution of present and future problems.' It therefore behoved the United Kingdom to strengthen her position in Europe by 'working closely together with the smaller democracies, which were entirely with her in outlook and way of life.' Further, 'we must look to our own household a bit' by seeking to bring the Commonwealth and Dependent Empire closer together, if only because it might not always be possible to maintain the dual system of a centralised Empire and a decentralised Commonwealth. He then repeated the proposals for the grouping of the Mother Country, her Colonies and the Dominions which he had made a few months back to American readers, a very necessary grouping in his eyes, because 'this world needs the British system . . . a mission to mankind of goodwill, good government and human co-operation, a mission of freedom and human happiness in the perils that beset our human lot.' [1]

After his return to Pretoria at the New Year of 1944, Smuts repeated the gist of this 'explosive speech,' deprecating day-dreaming about the peace that had yet to be won and insisting that this time the world would have to 'mix realism with idealism to provide leadership for freedom' and maintain forces strong enough to prevent the recurrence of anything like Nazism. The prospects of Nazi doctrines were fading in his own country as the defeat of the Axis became daily more certain. Nevertheless, the Opposition was launching a comprehensive campaign to win the elections of 1948 by stressing the danger to white South African civilisation of the slowly 'rising tide of colour,' undermining such trade unions as they did not themselves control, starting newspaper courses in politics at £5 a time and, in their eagerness to win English voters to their idea of a republic, nagging at undeniable wartime grievances, assuring English-speaking citizens that they would have nothing to fear for their cultural and language rights, and even talking of starting an English-medium anti-Semitic newspaper on the vital Rand, where Jews as a body were far from popular. Attempts were made to bridge the gulf by, for instance, the liberal editors of *The Forum* and the Nationalist *Oosterlig*; but these well-meant proposals came to nothing when Malan made it clear that only an independent republic would satisfy him. Hence, the Nationalists pegged away, encouraged by the restiveness of the Labour wing of the Coalition, which feared lest it be swamped by the United Party much as Creswell's following had been swamped by Hertzog's Nationalists in the Pact Ministry, and positively cheered by the grumbling of Dominion Party men and others in Natal that they would rather be citizens of a republic than of a Dominion, which, by reason of its membership of the

[1] *Bulletin*, XX., No. 25, pp. 1081 ff.; *The Times*, Dec. 3, 1943.

Commonwealth, must make concessions to despised and dreaded Indians.[1] Such folly by no means improved the Union's already strained relations with India and went far to cancel the good effects of Smut's offer of food to that over-populated and backward sub-continent, vast areas of which were suffering from a famine whose ravages were worsened by endemic greed, peculation and communal rivalries and the sheer difficulty of getting supplies through the maze of princely, provincial and municipal administrations.

Reinforced by many newly-elected young and vigorous men, Smuts met Parliament on January 22, 1944. At the beginning of the six-month-long Session, Hofmeyr reported a small and unexpected surplus, which he owed mainly to an increase in customs revenue arising from more plentiful shipping; but he had to budget for increased expenditure, because, though the customs might be expected to yield still more, the proceeds of direct taxation would surely dwindle and he must find £250,000 as the Union's contribution to the newly-founded United Nations Relief and Rehabilitation Administration, an additional £275,000 for Native education, and further large sums to pay for the increase of social services and their extension to the hitherto excluded non-Europeans. Additional expenditure was to be met by new taxes, notably by an alteration in the income tax, which would preclude businessmen who set up as part-time farmers from dodging the tax-collectors by writing off their farming expenses against their taxable incomes, and genuine farmers from similarly claiming as abatements the profits they had spent on the purchase of the farms of less successful neighbours.[2] In the course of the most strenuous struggle of the Session, the Government carried a measure prescribing the dual medium in the public schools and passed it on to the Provincial authorities, well knowing that lack of really bilingual teachers would forbid its implementation for many years and that, meanwhile, implementation would be obstructed doggedly by Opposition politicians and every Nationalist religious and cultural association in the land.[3] Parliament's main task, however, was the social services programme, a programme which the Prime Minister indicated was to be carried out within the framework of private enterprise, save when the State must step in to finance important basic enterprises which private capitalists had failed to support, a programme which the liberal Hofmeyr insisted must be extended to the non-Europeans.[4]

Some progress had been made of late years in the development of social services; but benefit rates were still low, there were neither national sick pay nor family allowances of any kind, nor were there

---

[1] Roberts and Trollip, op. cit., pp. 172 ff.; Die Burger, Jan. 5 and 6, 1944.
[2] Round Table, No. 135, pp. 287 ff. [3] Ibid., No. 136, pp. 383 ff.
[4] Bulletin, XXI., No. 4, p. 161.

yet old-age pensions for Bantu or unemployment cover for the vast majority of the Union's working folk. There was, however, hope that something would now be done, because Smuts had made repeated promises of a better life for all. Late in 1941, he had told his fellow South Africans bluntly that their 'race-feeling was accentuated by fear' and bade them look ahead in such matters 'not merely for generations but for centuries.' He had expounded his views more fully a few weeks later at a meeting of the liberal South African Institute of Race Relations in Capetown. Stressing the responsibility of Europeans as trustees for their non-European wards, he said frankly that in the Union the African was the worker who was 'carrying this country on his back. . . . The great problem in the world today is to adjust racial relations so that conditions of fairness, harmony and happiness will result. I think that if we were to give a holiday to all the old ideas . . . and try out . . . this principle of trusteeship, we may build up that pattern of a new South Africa, variegated unlike the pattern of any other country, but something worth having—a pattern which may be a lesson to the rest of the world.'[1] All this was in the spirit of Hofmeyr and the dignitaries of the Anglican Church of the Province, who called upon white South Africans to get rid of their prejudices; but it was a spirit to which Smuts, who so often said the right thing in relation to non-Europeans but so seldom did it, had thus far failed to give an embodiment. He had even denied the more advanced of the Bantu that very consideration which he admitted their people had earned by their services in the field. Since August 1941, when the African Mineworkers' Union had been formed in Johannesburg, similar associations had sprung up so fast that, within a few months, Madeley, Minister of Labour, had been able to take the chair at the first meeting of the non-European Trade Union Council, which claimed to represent 150,000 organised Bantu. A year or so later, however, in reply to a spate of Bantu strikes along the Rand and in Natal, Smuts issued War Measures 145 of 1942 and 1425 of 1943, the first of which rendered illegal 'all strikes by all Africans under all circumstances' and the second forbade unauthorised meetings of more than twenty persons on mine property.

The time was now come when mere repression would answer no longer, for the reports of the Social Security and Social and Economic Councils reminded the nation that it must increase production, provide more education and food subsidies for non-Europeans especially, and could not hope to make the fullest use of its country's resources till it had developed the intelligence and skill of the entire population, not merely of the 2,000,000 white folk, but, as Smuts himself justly insisted, of the whole 10,000,000 of all colours. The

---

[1] *The Basis of Trusteeship in African Native Policy* (S.A., Institute of Race Relations, pamphlet No. 2 of 1942).

debate in February 1944 revealed some party differences as to methods, but ended with such general agreement that the Government began to consider 'a people's charter' covering employment, social security, housing, public health, nutrition and education for all. To that end, it referred the Social Security Commission's Report to a Select Committee. This Committee recommended the reduction to a mere £19,000,000 of the sum of £35,000,000, which the Commission and the Finance Minister had proposed should be spent on the extension of old-age and invalidity pensions to folk of all colours. On the other hand, the House agreed that the recently appointed National Housing Commission should help to finance municipal housing schemes, and asked the authorities to lay plans for food subsidies and to consider the spending of the £20,000,000 on public health which had been recommended by yet another Commission. Thus might it hope, as Smuts put it, 'to prepare the way for a new era, for the age of man, the common man, the man, in Lincoln's homely phrase, God loves because he made so many of them.'[1]

Looking beyond South Africa's frontiers, Smuts now stated that he must consult others before acceding to the unanimous request of the Windhoek Legislature for the incorporation of their territory in the Union, but expressed the hope that his country might at last be allowed to take over the governance of the High Commission Territories, if only as a reward for its war services.[2] He next assured Southern Rhodesia and other British Dependencies further north that the Union had no desire to absorb them, but merely to strengthen wartime friendships and to co-operate for the common good. Arising out of this, he repeated his conviction that the existing Commonwealth system gave ample opportunities for mutual consultation. He passed over in silence Malan's cable to de Valera assuring him of Nationalist support in his refusal to expel the Axis Ambassadors from Dublin at Roosevelt's suggestion, but he read him a stinging lesson on commonsense and good manners for his monotonous chanting of the virtues of his 'Republic' and recurrent denigration of the invaluable Russian ally.[3] Once and only once was Smuts shaken during the Session, when, thanks doubtless to the numerous voters of German extraction, the Nationalists unexpectedly won the by-election at Wakkerstroom, which had been occasioned by the death of Collins, the Minister of Agriculture. He gave that portfolio to Jacobus Strauss and then, leaving Hofmeyr in charge as usual, set out for London in mid-April 1944 with the assurance that he would 'stand for Africa' at the forthcoming Commonwealth Prime Ministers' Conference.[4]

---

[1] *Round Table*, No. 136, pp. 380 ff.
[2] *Bulletin*, XX., No. 20, p. 893; XXI., No. 7, p. 285.
[3] *Ibid.*, XXI., No. 7, p. 285.   [4] *Round Table*, No. 136, pp. 378 ff.

By the time Smuts thus flew northward, his soldiers with their Allied comrades had plodded the length of the road to Rome and were pushing on against stubborn German resistance; the R.A.F. had fully asserted its supremacy in the German air, and the Russians had cleared the enemy out of Novgorod, Odessa and the Crimea. Well might the Prime Ministers' Conference issue a declaration expressing confidence in victory, proclaiming that no one who marched with them should be abandoned, and promising that this time there should be a world organisation of peace-loving peoples capable of striking down 'tyranny and aggression' wherever these might show their ugly heads. And well might Smuts exult in like strains when he received the freedom of that City of Birmingham which had been Joseph Chamberlain's, though he added the timely warning that if the war dragged on too long, there might be 'a cracking of civilisation' and that, in any event, it remained to be seen whether Old Europe could ever recover from her ghastly wounds.[1] The dragging-out of the war in Italy, where so many of his young men were fighting, distressed him even more profoundly than it did Churchill, because it delayed the sending of help to resurgent Jugoslavia and the consequent invasion of the Balkans that should set a term to the westward sweep of the difficult Russian ally, whom he, by this time, distrusted as deeply as did the British Prime Minister himself. In another vital area, however, the war went forward far more hopefully, for, on D Day, June 16, 1944, huge Allied forces sprang a decisive surprise on the Germans by landing in Normandy from their elaborate floating 'Mulberry' harbours. Presently yet others gained a footing in southern France. On August 23, 1944, after hard fighting, General de Gaulle's Free French soldiers marched into Paris under the Arc de Triomphe just as other Allied troops liberated Marseillés. Smuts was sped homewards with the news that, having taken Florence, the Allies were closing up to the Gothic line, the German's last fortified defences in northern Italy. Shortly after his arrival, he was cheered by news that the United States had destroyed most of what yet remained of the Mikado's Navy in the Leyte Gulf and thereby ensured the reconquest of the Philippines.[2]

Home once more, Smuts assured his audience at the Belgian and Belgian Congo Exhibition at Pretoria that he was anxious to form closer ties not only with British tropical territories, but with the Congo also as 'one of the great assets of the world.'[3] His statesmanlike courtesy, however, concealed a very real fear for the future of South Africa and western civilisation. Noting that the Union's

---

[1] *Round Table*, No. 136, pp. 336 ff.
[2] W. L. S. Churchill, *The Second World War*, VI. 158 ff.
[3] *Bulletin*, XXI., No. 19, p. 791.

casualties were close on thirty thousand, he warned his people not to expect too much too soon in spite of recent notable victories, and urged them to work harder than ever, because, even after Hitler should have fallen, they must face a long second stage of the war, this time against Japan, a stage during which they would indeed send away far less of their munitions and far fewer troops, other than airmen and technicians, but must do very much more in the way of repairing Allied shipping and keeping up the rising output of coal, which had already made their country one of the world's biggest exporters of that universally desired mineral.[1] He told the members of his own Party that, because the state of shattered Europe would be far worse than at the end of the Kaiser's war, they must not bother about frontiers or transfers of people from one government to another, but tackle first with all their might 'the problem of human salvage.' As a step towards that great end, he welcomed the United Kingdom's decision to send help to hard-pressed Greece; but he hailed with infinitely greater satisfaction the Charter for a world organisation, which the four Great Powers had just outlined at Dumbarton Oaks near Washington, a Charter that went much further than the Covenant of the League of Nations in that it proposed not merely to delay incipient wars, but to stop them 'at the start.'

South Africans might well doubt whether they would be able to fulfil the programme which Smuts had outlined if the war indeed went on much longer, because their country was by no means yet fitted to become a great source of supply. The maize situation was somewhat better, but the coming harvest threatened to be a poor one; nothing but a subsidy had induced citrus-growers to stop destroying their fruit and put some of it on the local market—at a price—and the supply of meat was so poor that, latterly, the towns had had to submit to one meatless day each week. Again, the industrial situation was unsatisfactory. Jam-making and the canning of fruit, sausages, vegetables, milk and fish had all made good progress since the outbreak of war, a progress limited only by the shortage of tin-plate; but even if these activities were to be supplemented by the dehydration of vegetables and the extraction of food-yeast from sugar-cane, they would be a poor substitute for the heavy industries which any industrialised community worthy of the name must have. Here, progress had been far slower. The engineering industries might have imported more than £1,000,000 worth of

[1] *Bulletin*, XXI., No. 19, p. 791; No. 25, p. 1077; XXII., No. 4, p. 191. The Union had been making forty-five per cent. of the Allies' total production of small-arm ammunition, when in March 1945, a terrible explosion occurred in the Grand Magazine, Pretoria. Thereafter, it cut down its production markedly. Its repair of ships was impressive throughout. (*Vide Review of the Organisation* . . . *of Supplies*, pp. 63, 116.)

24

machine tools and turned out an impressive variety of articles from assegais to X-ray vans, besides giving their additional twenty thousand employees of all colours some sort of training; but even when these had been added to the many folk who had picked up a little mechanical knowledge in the Forces, there would still be a grave shortage of really skilled workers. War industries were fairly well equipped, but the maintenance of secondary industries serving the civilian population was not what it should have been. Investment in these had long fallen to about half the pre-war level and much of their heavy equipment was now petering out. Transport was suffering so severely that, by the New Year of 1944, the authorities could scarcely replace worn-out railway tracks and overworked rolling-stock, and now that virtually all the country's buses or motor-lorries were at least five years old with no new ones in sight for some three years to come, they had been obliged to discontinue bus-services after 10 p.m. In a land of great distances and scanty communications, they were indeed fain to encourage privately-owned motor transport by the offer of a generous petrol ration, even at the risk of waste; but that did not relieve the Controller of Motor Vehicles, faced as he was with a lack of rubber and spare parts, from having to do all he could to stimulate their production and setting up depots for the stripping and reconditioning of motor vehicles of every kind.[1]

Behind it all, and largely accounting for these economic strains, lay the inflation. The Finance Minister might blandly deny that there was any such thing, but even he could not close his eyes to the fact that prices had long been rising and that the Union's effective supply of mere money had more than doubled over the past four years. So far from feeling disquiet, the Reserve Bank, like any Midas, positively gloried at the sight of this flood of money washing back and forth within the national frontiers, because it witnessed to the success of its policy of systematically buying the annual gold output at a fixed price and encouraging the commercial banks to deposit their fast-increasing takings in its coffers. The result of this policy had been to increase the Reserve Bank's gold-holdings by £50,000,000, the contents of its portfolios of foreign bills by a like amount and its investments by nearly £20,000,000. That central Bank viewed this comparatively vast accumulation with complacency, because it could always sell its gold overseas and liked to keep the balances of the commercial banks in that same universally acceptable metal; but it had apparently not realised that its so-called 'favourable' balance was due simply to the fact that there had long been far too few imports to eat away its mountain of gold. Not all the efforts of the Price Controller and his ever-growing cohorts of inspectors had served to stop the fifty per cent. rise in the price index during the four

[1] *Round Table*, No. 134, pp. 174 ff.

years of war, still less to avert the necessity of checking hoarding for the black market; nor had the prudent policy of the Director-General of Supplies, more frequent calls by ships and the consequent fuller supply of essential imports yet availed to bring down prices.[1]

Economic anxieties and the prospect of an end to the interminable war now that the Allies were nearing the German Rhine gave a sharper edge to political controversy. On the one hand Malan had latterly become more democratic than many of his prominent followers, and realising that the coming delimitation of constituencies must benefit the predominantly English-speaking urban areas, he was playing hard for the English vote even to the extent of launching *The New Era*, the promised English-medium newspaper, under the able editorship of the conciliatory Jansen. On the other hand, he was urging that, if the Union must have 'affiliation with a larger country,' it should be with what was, to him, 'the sister republic across the Atlantic,' whose soldiers were at long last playing a major part in the war and whose citizens evinced a growing interest in the economic future of his country,[2] while the Grey Shirts, the New Order and the *O.B.* waxed more vociferous and the secretive *Broederbond* more pervasive than ever. The Coalition, for its part, freely indulged in adverse criticism of 'the new despotism' bred of the exigencies of wartime, that is, the ubiquitous departmental legislation 'as the Minister may direct.' United Party men made much of unjust taxation, food shortages, incompetent Control Boards and widespread sabotage in the public services, and numbered in their ranks many folk, who, as Hofmeyr drily observed, gave a readier welcome to representatives of well advertised war subscriptions than to the less publicised tax-collectors. The Dominion Party waged its vendetta against the Prime Minister's Indian policy all the more relentlessly because the Indian problem was drifting once more towards deadlock now that the Natal Provincial Council, which Smuts had invited to supervise the implementation of his informal agreement with leading Indians, had revised residential property regulations in such a preposterous fashion that he had had to advise the reservation of the offending Ordinance and put the suspended Pegging Act into force till such time as the reconstituted Broome Commission should have explored other means of settlement. Then, while Natal Indians were clamouring that the only cure for their discontents was the restoration of the franchise, the Labour Party became intransigent. They and their supporters clung so doggedly to their civilised labour policy, the colour bar, the closed shop and the rest of it that there was small hope of inducing them to relax apprenticeship regulations or agree to such radical changes in

[1] *Round Table*, No. 133, pp. 86 ff.; No. 139, pp. 275.
[2] *Ibid.*, No. 138, p. 182.

the rates of pay as would permit of the training of low-paid non-Europeans to build sorely needed cheap houses for their low-paid brethren. Worse still, many of them, possibly taking their cue from the decision of the British Labour Party to leave Churchill's Coalition as soon as Germany had been defeated, demanded that Madeley, their own leader, should come out of the Cabinet and thus restore their Party's freedom of action.[1]

Smuts tried to give these bickering politicians something better to think of. Looking ahead and sick of party politics as ever, he told the United Party Congress, quite in the manner of Rhodes, that if South Africans meant to push their trade in the tropical North, they must improve their communications with those parts, and that if they hoped to put their own affairs on a stable basis, they must produce more, find money for extended social services, make better use of their total man-power, carry through a social 'levelling-up all round' and, generally, wake up to the fact that industrialisation, which was bringing swarms of folk of all colours into their towns, called for a radical change in their 'traditional Native policies . . . a much more profound change in the whole social and economic structure than most people had yet realised.'[2] A little later he proclaimed that the non-European problem gave 'no cause for fear or despair,' if only because the White and Coloured Folks had made such amazing progress during the past two generations and had removed one great possible source of friction by spontaneously working out a rough-and-ready scheme of residential segregation, notably in the Cape Peninsula. Some such scheme, he gave fair warning, was to be made compulsory for Europeans and Indians in Natal and be carried much further than at present in the case of the Bantu, because the flood of these Africans into the towns must be checked and their unemployed be sent back thence to the Reserves. These they would be encouraged to develop to the limit, while all who taught them subversive doctrines would be sent about their business. He then proclaimed the *Broederbond* a political organisation none of whose members could be admitted to the public service, because no man could be a member of such 'dangerous, cunning, political Fascist.' association and retain his loyalty to the State. He took as a matter of course the protests of the infuriated Malan, himself a member of the condemned society, that this attack on an organisation, which, he alleged, had done no more than had long been done by the Sons of England and the Jewish Board of Deputies, was a persecution of the *Afrikaner Volk*.[3]

In the midst of this storm, Parliament met early in 1945. Hofmeyr

---

[1] *Round Table*, No. 138, p. 182; *Bulletin*, XXI., No. 26, p. 1132.
[2] *Round Table*, No. 138, pp. 182 ff.
[3] *Ibid*., No. 138, p. 184; Davidson, *op. cit*., p. 155.

agreed with the Reserve Bank that the balance of payment was so favourable that he could cheerfully give up his recent attempt to enforce saving by those who escaped income tax, and promise that departmental committees should report on the taxation of mines and, probably, on war taxes and pre-war income tax.[1]

The House then discussed amicably enough the problems of the townward drift of the Bantu and migratory labour.[2] Thereafter, it moved out on to stormier waters, for many of Smuts's supporters concurred with much that Malan said in criticism of some aspects of the Government's domestic policy. The Minister responsible could plead justly, in reply, that the food situation was better than it had been and could even make out a case for his elaborate meat-marketing scheme; but the Minister of Welfare could not deny that disputes, mutual recriminations and agile 'passing the buck' between his department and the multitudinous municipal authorities, whose business it was to see to the actual construction, had delayed the provision of new houses. However, he made short work of it all and, with the comment that everyone would blame the Government if houses were not forthcoming, carried a Housing Act, which gave 'the Minister' drastic powers to control wages, check speculation and profiteering, and generally ensure that houses were built.[3] Finally, something of an uproar arose over public health, for here the public joined with Honourable Members in attacking no less a person than the Prime Minister himself, not so much because he had muttered that Provinces would be chary of accepting central control in a field which was primarily theirs, as because he had sneered at the 'idealistic' and 'impracticable' proposals of the Public Health Committee and thus awakened suspicion that he meant to do nothing. The uproar was only stilled when the authorities promised to push ahead with a modified scheme in which the Provinces should play their full part.

Subsequent legislation touched the Provinces even more nearly. Since 1925, the Union Government had given them fixed annual subsidies and, in addition, a proportion of the yield of the Native poll tax wherewith to pay for Native education. Now that Hofmeyr had handed over the whole of that yield to the Native Trust and was proposing to finance Native education from the general revenue, new arrangements were plainly desirable. Hence, it was agreed that the Provinces should revert to the pre-1925 footing, that is, that they should receive Union subsidies equal to half their expenditure from their own taxes, and that the Cape, Free State and Natal should receive in addition special subsidies in return for their

---

[1] *Round Table*, No. 139, pp. 275 ff.   [2] Act 25 of 1945.
[3] Act 45 of 1945; *Round Table*, No. 139, pp. 279; No. 140, pp. 376; No. 142, p. 193.

transfer to the Union of certain assigned sources of revenue. A further Act duly provided the funds necessary for Native education, and a Union Advisory Council on Education was set up with a secretariat manned by the Native Affairs Department to ensure fuller co-ordination of the work of the various Provinces.[1] The latter, assured of presumably adequate revenues and stimulation from above, might be expected to set about their task of educating the vast majority of the country's peoples much more energetically than hitherto.

Early in April, a good two months before the long Session ended, Smuts went overseas. After attending the Commonwealth Prime Ministers' Conference in London and there hearing of Roosevelt's sudden death, he went on to California to take part in the International San Francisco Conference to which he looked for the realisation of his dreams of an ordered post-war world. That ordering had recently been carried far on the economic side by the timely creation of an International Monetary Fund and an International Bank of Reconstruction and Development by the Allied Powers assembled at Bretton Woods.[2] It now remained to carry it into the political sphere. At San Francisco, however, Smuts experienced much disappointment, for not only were the Americans intent on monopolising the limelight, but the whole assemblage was so bickering and voluble that, fearing lest distant Europe should collapse while it stalled, he read it a stiff lesson on the value of time. An even more potent spur to progress came with the news that the Allies had not only overwhelmed the Germans in Italy, but had received Germany's total surrender on May 7, 1945. Thus impelled, the Conference adopted the very human preamble which Smuts had drawn up for the Charter of the United Nations and, before June was out, the Charter itself.

The Charter was a much more workmanlike piece of work than the Covenant of the League of Nations. Admitting the reality of power, as Smuts had always insisted men must, it gave the United Kingdom, the U.S.A., the U.S.S.R., France and China *ex-officio* seats on a Security Council. Armed with a far-reaching veto, which had been accorded to them in spite of the strenuous resistance of Canada, Australia and New Zealand as spokesmen of the so-called Middle Powers, these five Great Powers were to hold those seats permanently alongside a majority of representatives of smaller Powers elected from time to time by all the State members in the much less powerful General Assembly. Provision was made for the transformation of Mandated Territories into Trusteeship Territories, a provision of which all the Powers concerned availed themselves save, first, the United Kingdom, which excepted Palestine, whose

[1] Act 29 of 1945: *Round Table*, No. 138, p. 184; No. 139, p. 276.
[2] *United Nations Documents*, pp. 28 ff.

future was being debated by the visiting international Commission that had been appointed at the instance of the U.S.A. and the U.S.S.R., and Transjordan, which she herself had marked for early independence, and, secondly, the Union which had other ideas for South-West Africa. Mentioning in passing that, at the proper moment, he would ask for the termination of the mandate and the incorporation of that Territory as fifth Province of the Union, Smuts assured the Conference that his Government would meanwhile make no change in its status of its own mere motion. Finally, it was decreed that holders of Trusteeship Territories were no longer to report to the expert Mandates Commission of the dying League, but to the purely political Trusteeship Council of the United Nations Organisation.

Although U.N.O. was no more a supra-national government than had been the League, Smuts was happy to have signed a Charter that was virtually a declaration of 'war against war'; but he was justifiably affronted when Harry Truman, Roosevelt's successor, after having systematically relegated him 'to the shadows,' robbed him of the honour of making the closing speech by making it himself, and when, thereafter, the State Department abruptly denied him, who had addressed both Houses of the ancient British Parliament, the promised opportunity of addressing the two Houses of Congress.[1] He travelled home by way of Ottawa and reached London just as the over-confident Churchill was defeated at a general election by Clement Attlee's Labour Party. To deepen his dismay, tidings came that the United Kingdom and the United States had given way to the difficult Russians at the Potsdam Conference by agreeing to substitute a 'hopeless' Council of Foreign Ministers for the projected Peace Conference.[2] As he reached home, however, these setbacks were more than offset by the startling news that tottering Japan, swept off her feet by the new and devastating atom bombs which the Americans had gratuitously launched against the swarming harbour cities of Nagasaki and Hiroshima, had collapsed on August 14, 1945. True, the Russians, who had hitherto taken no part in the Pacific war, had swooped in at the last moment, if only that they might claim a voice in the Asian peace-settlement; but, at least, the fall of the Mikado's overblown Empire meant that there would be none of the long-drawn-out second stage of the war, which he had so dreaded for its possibly disastrous effects on the stability of Western civilisation.

RECONSTRUCTION

The end of the Axis war marked the end of Smuts's Coalition. The Ministry, indeed, held together until Parliament had ratified the

[1] For the San Francisco Conference *vide* J. C. Smuts, *op. cit.*; *Bulletin*, XXII., No. 13; *Chronology of International Events and Documents* (Chatham House), I; H.M. Stationery Office, 1945 (*United Nations Documents* . . ., pp. 148 ff.).

[2] *Chronology* . . ., I. No. 3, pp. 68 ff.; *United Nations Documents* . . ., pp. 193 ff.

United Nations Charter, but then Madeley handed over the Ministry
of Labour to Dr. Colin Steyn and led his own followers across the
floor of the House. At the close of November 1945, Stallard and his
dwindling Dominion Party did likewise. These friendly partings
necessitated a re-shuffling of portfolios. Sidney Waterson, for some
time past Minister of Economic Affairs, took over the department
of Mines from Stallard; Lawrence retained Welfare and added
thereto Steyn's portfolio of Justice; Clarkson relinquished Posts and
Telegrams to James Mushet, a well-known Capetown businessman,
and Dr. Henry Gluckman became Minister of Health. Backed as he
still was by a majority of fully twenty in the Assembly, without
counting the usually friendly votes of the Independents and three
'Native' members, Smuts might well hope to hold power at least till
the next general election some three years hence.[1]

It was well that this was so, because the reconstituted Ministry
must face the heavy task of reconstructing a sorely-strained country.
The repatriation of nearly the whole of the external debt could be
set against the expenditure of £536,000,000 during the war, and an
incipient post-war boom rejoiced all hearts; but other factors were
not so heartening. Swarms of service folk would have to be reabsorbed into civil life; masses of surplus war-stores must be disposed
of without wrecking the home market, thousands of houses must be
built, and, above all, help be given to the Bantu, who, amid a
universal food shortage, had seen their vital mealie crop smitten by
drought and could not look forward to anything much better in the
coming year. South Africans had known for some time past that the
transition from war to peace could not be easy.[2] Since 1943 at latest,
officals, councils and commissions had been telling them flatly that
their national economy was warped by sectional interests; they knew
that neither the Nationalists nor many of the Labour men nor even
some of the more ambitious Bantu welcomed the idea of the large-
scale white immigration, which, as in Milner's day, was the surest
means of raising the standard of living for everyone; they were being
told by the Planning Council that far more must be done to raise the
Bantu as a whole, and they had a strong suspicion that their rural
and urban industries were hampered by an 'artificial classification
of skilled workers' that did not benefit even those employees who
were truly skilled.

Most of the facts that faced South Africans were ugly. Their
isolated country, far from all the great centres of Western civilisation, carried only a small and very mixed population of some
2,600,000 Europeans, 1,100,000 Coloured Folk, 360,000 Asians and

---

[1] *Round Table*, No. 142, p. 191; *Chronology*, I., No. 10, p. 233, and No. 11,
p. 266.
[2] *Round Table*, No. 141, pp. 91 ff.; No. 142, pp. 191 ff.

8,500,000 Bantu, say, some 12,500,000 in all. And it was a poor population, for, in spite of the extravagant white standard of living, the average European income was only £125, the Coloured £25 and the Bantu £10; in short, the national income per head of all colours was a mere two shillings a day, that is, one-fifth those of the United States and Canada, markedly less than that of the U.S.S.R. and even less than those of poverty-stricken and pullulating Egypt and India. The economic and social structure was rickety, resting as it did on a low-paid, underfed and, on the whole, untrained mass of non-European labour, and depending far too much on gold and diamonds, which, together, were wont to furnish three-quarters of the value of each year's exports, one-fifth of the net national income and nearly half the State and Provincial revenues. Gold was sure of a market and, as Rhodes used to say, there would always be a demand for diamonds as long as there were women; but, although they had a knack of doing well when everything else was doing ill, both minerals were wayward. The Kimberley diamond mines had never recovered the predominance they had enjoyed before the Kaiser's war, and now that working costs were rising rapidly, it had become a question how much longer it would pay to mine vast masses of the 'pennyweight' reserves of gold ore along the Rand.[1]

If anything went seriously wrong with gold and diamonds, the farmers could never take the strain. The Union was traditionally a farmer's country, but the less said of most of its farming the better. Even before the Axis war, in spite of the boundless state aid which made agriculture the biggest system of poor relief in the land, South Africa's farmers of all colours had earned less than one-fifth of the total annual value of exports, and now, at the end of that war, most of the thirty-three per cent. of the white folk and the eighty per cent. of the others who were on the land were farming at so low a subsistence level that they earned together merely one-eighth of the total national income in money. Again, their methods were generally so archaic that one farmer could feed only one-tenth of the number that one could feed in mechanised New Zealand, and desperate soil erosion was devastating immense stretches of land in white areas no less than black. This ruination of the land was carried further by the rush of the rivers, which swept thousands of tons of good surface soil far out to sea during each rainy season, and by the steady advance of the Kalahari desert towards the Union's north-western borders. As if bad farming and unkind Nature were not enough, officialdom too often lent its deadly aid. So far from compelling farmers to mend their ways, the Department of Agriculture gave them such lavish and ill-considered help that the recipients were tempted to misuse their land for highly-priced but unsuitable crops, while the Department of

[1] *Round Table*, No. 130, p. 185.

24*

Railways and Harbours, yielding to political pressure, gave the members of this, the greatest single sectional interest, privileged rates for the carriage of their bulky produce, and thus forced more favourably situated and better run concerns of all kinds to make good the loss on this extravagant long-distance traffic. And at the end of it all, the average white farmer was earning less than £200 a year and the handful of white farm-labourers the barest of livings.[1]

Many folk saw salvation in the secondary industries, which of late years had burgeoned so vigorously that an 'occupied' population of barely 750,000 had not only been able to carry on the life of the nation, but feed and equip fully 200,000 European troops and non-European auxiliaries.[2] The Union indeed possessed many of the requisites of an industrialised country in her ample supplies of excellent coal, iron, chromium, limestone and manganese, and had reinforced her tiny minority of really skilled and intelligent workers with a fairly numerous body of semi-skilled folk of all colours, who had learned to handle machines in wartime factories or the semi-mechanised Forces; but though even the backward Bantu had shown that they could work semi-automatic machines, there was still a grave shortage of truly competent artisans. Nor was this lack likely to be supplied till drastic measures had been taken to dispel the poverty and ignorance of nine-tenths of the white folk and the over-whelming majority of the rest. For years past, the Board of Trade and the Industrial and Agricultural Requirements Commission had been pointing out that the proportion of jobs classified as skilled and, therefore, usually reserved for Europeans was probably higher than in any other industrialised country, and that the proportion of unskilled non-Europeans even to semi-skilled Europeans was also very high. These Commissions had, therefore, suggested that the crippling apprenticeship regulations be relaxed sufficiently to admit many more non-Europeans to skilled or semi-skilled trades, that the skilled labour categories be revised and minimum wage rates be readjusted gradually so that pay should tally more nearly with the differences in skill and training required for the various occupations, and that, where justified by changed conditions, the period of training be reduced.[3] Changed 'conditions' meant, primarily, the swarms of Bantu and poorer Europeans who were pouring into urban areas at the call of secondary industry in both official languages; but every-one knew that if anything like the Commissions' programme were attempted, any number of white workers and their wives, all of them voters, would cry out that legions of dark-skinned competitors were

---

[1] *Round Table*, No. 141, pp. 90 ff.; Hatch, *op. cit.*, p. 23.
[2] *A Record of the Organisation of the Director-General of War Supplies (1939–1943) and Director-General of Supplies (1943–1945).*
[3] *Round Table*, No. 130, pp. 185 ff.; No. 141, pp. 90 ff.

being enlisted to challenge their caste privileges, artificially high pay and trade union organisations. Not that non-Europeans were threatening the European stronghold anything like so seriously as most white folk imagined, for, during the past quarter of a century, the numbers of non-Europeans in secondary industry had risen only from about 117,000 to little more than 400,000, while the numbers of Europeans had risen much more markedly from some 75,000 to more than 200,000;[1] but such facts were scarcely likely to be widely known and would certainly be forgotten when it came to electing members of central and local legislatures.

Nor was this all. Thanks to misdirected fiscal, labour, transport and external trade policies, secondary industry was being carried on for the most part in small factories scattered about the countryside, very many of them turning out goods of low quality, nearly all of them run on the basis of one European to two non-European employees, and scarcely any of them able to stand without the aid of a protective system that was costing the community a round £10,000,000 each year and, thereby, keeping up the cost of living and handicapping industrialists in their search for export markets. The home market was so small that manufacturers could not face the economies that were only possible under large-scale production, and could neither afford nor get the machines that would bring down production costs. Behind it all was the problem of the water-supply, which was already hard put to it to meet existing needs and might well break down under the additional strain of expanding urban industry, ambitious irrigation works and new goldmines in the northern Free State and along the Far West Rand. It came to this: if the Union wished to industrialise herself, she could compete with heavily-industrialised rivals only by subsidising or dumping her petty exports.

Nothing but a revolution in the white folk's way of thinking could get the Union out of the impasse that was created by a declining gold-output, a spoon-fed and incompetent agriculture, a highly pro-tected industry, a gerrymandered transport system and a crippling colour bar.[2] There were indeed signs that something of the sort might take place, for an increasing number of the dominant Euro-peans had latterly learned a good deal about the weaknesses of their country's social and economic structure and were minded to remedy them. Smuts himself, three years since, had given them the opera-tive word 'trusteeship' as the guide to their policy towards their local 'colonial' liability, the non-European four-fifths of South Africa's mixed population. Not many Europeans were yet ready to go back to the old Cape civilisation policy which had worked so well for more than a hundred years, partly because those born outside the

[1] Hatch, *op. cit.*, pp. 19 ff.
[2] *Round Table*, No. 130, pp. 185 ff.; No. 141, pp. 91 ff.

Cape had had no first-hand experience of it and partly because both they and many others argued that it was one thing for the United Kingdom to give votes and even self-government to distant truly colonial peoples, but quite another for themselves to give like powers and privileges to 'colonists' who lived next door or even in their own kitchens. But any number of them agreed that they must do something on liberal lines, not only because they lamented non-European infant mortality, disease, poverty and ignorance, but felt that it was sheer folly to go on plunging, like their own Flying Dutchman, 'full sail against the wind' of world opinion.[1] They could not delude themselves with the belief that what they did in their own little corner was no one else's concern, because, plainly, whatever South Africa, the strongest African State in its own right, did or did not do concerned the British, Belgians, French, Portuguese and others who bore vastly greater responsibilities than they in the rest of black Africa, and even more the countless non-Europeans throughout the length and breadth of this second largest of the continents, and not in that continent alone. They could, indeed, plead that their Bantu enjoyed a higher standard of living than their fellows elsewhere, that their Indians were better off than their compeers in India itself, that their Coloured Folk approximated in their way of life and privileges to their own, and that day-to-day non-European administration was often much better than the laws on which it was based. They could not deny, however, that their policies were based, if not on the fear on which Smuts dwelt, at all events on a racial discrimination which pretended that material and educational advancement was all their non-Europeans were entitled to, and ignored the fact that these same 'colonial' folk were debarred from political rights and subjected to wounding slights and disabilities solely because of the pigmentation of their skins, a factor which none of God's creatures could alter. Some of them went so far as to realise that their present policies might recoil on their own heads by infecting their minds and hearts with those Nazi-inspired complexes of fear and domination which they had fought in the field, and by postponing the day when their white neighbours to the northward would even contemplate closer union with such as they, or H.M. Government dream of transferring to Pretoria the governance of the Bantu in the High Commission Territories.

Recent events on the Rand must have brought home to the British Government the risks involved in trusting white South Africans with the fate of any more folk of different colours. Transvaal Nationalists and not a few of their Dutch Reformed Church predikants staged a furious attack on the Garment Workers' Union, one of the leading trade unions on the Rand, and especially upon its

[1] R. Kipling, *The Merchantmen*. [The Seven Seas.]

secretary, Emil Sachs, an able Jewish immigrant who had been expelled from the South African Communist Party as far back as 1932 and had never rejoined it.[1] Before the Axis war, apart from some hundreds of Coloured workers, the membership of this Union both along the Rand and in the larger towns of the Cape Province and Natal had been entirely European; but during that war, labour being scarce, the Johannesburg garment workshops had taken on perhaps four thousand Coloured and Indian hands. Matters came to a head in February 1944, when Nationalist stalwarts discovered that nine Coloured women were employed in the Germiston factory. Though these women were prudently segregated in a room of their own, Nationalist champions of 'white civilisation' switched off the workshop motors, howled down the union's Branch Secretary when he came to see what the trouble was, and forced the management to dismiss the unlucky nine. When, however, the purely Afrikaner Branch Executive expelled two ringleaders in this campaign for agitation, bedlam broke loose. Nationalist newspapers sprang to the support of the three branches of the Dutch Reformed Church, which jointly set up an Enlarged Church Committee to defend 'white civilisation,' public meetings far and wide condemned the peccant Garment Workers' Union, and Nationalist members wasted days of the Assembly's time denouncing the Germiston scandal. Not content with all this, the so-called Nationalist *Hervormers* (Reformers), in private conclave, directed two women ringleaders in the recent agitation to force their way into the workshop in the hope that they would be thrown out and thus move other women-workers to strike. On the appointed day, the two women duly went back to work, and nothing happened. Nothing, that is, till March 16, 1944, when a mob of outsiders, some of them disguised as predikants and others armed with sticks, bicycle-chains and other potent arguments, broke up a meeting of some five thousand garment workers in the Johannesburg City Hall under the eyes of policemen, who maintained throughout a Gallio-like indifference. Not so Sachs. He went into action in the Transvaal Supreme Court, which, in March 1945, awarded him £300 damages and £11,000 costs against a prominent predikant. Undismayed, the disrupters formed *Die Blankenwerkersbeskermingsbond* (The White Workers' Protection Union) to carry on the work of vilification, while the Garment Workers' Union, expelling would-be trouble-makers from time to time, went from strength to strength.

Plainly, there were two radically different definitions of 'civilisation' in South Africa; yet, with the exception of the Communists, every organised party in the land clung to the colour bar. In Parliament, only a handful of ministerialists dared to follow Hofmeyr in

[1] On Sachs and trade unions *vide* L. Barnes, *Caliban in Africa*, pp. 183 ff.; Sachs, *op. cit.*, *passim*; Davidson, *op. cit.*, pp. 176 ff.

bidding white South Africans 're-examine their prejudices' and in foretelling that one day non-Europeans would be represented by their own folk, while, at the other extreme, the Nationalists fought every election on the anti-Hofmeyr platform. The vast majority of the non-Nationalist white folk more or less shared the illiberal views of the Prime Minister on the non-European issue.

The smallest, most recently arrived and, by reason of their ancient Hindu civilisation and religion, the least assimilable of the racial groups in the Union were the Indians. This 'colonial' people numbered only two-and-a-half per cent. of the total population; but they made up some thirty per cent. of that of Durban, where a few wealthy members of their community owned a fair amount of the real property. The homes of the rest of the Asiatics in that recently greatly enlarged city ranged from suburban villas that would not have disgraced Bournemouth or Surbiton down to shacks in Cato Township and Chesterville Native Township on the outskirts. Their social amenities naturally varied markedly. None of them were as yet admitted to the Durban section of the University of Natal; all were debarred even from the Workers' Education Association because whites would not sit next to them, and such of their children as went to school must put up with overcrowded classrooms. Overcrowding was, indeed, the source of most of their troubles, for such was their fecundity, as in Mother India, that in spite of a tuberculosis death-rate in Durban five times greater than that of the Europeans and a general death-rate in all Natal nearly twice as high, their birth-rate was nearly twice that of the white folk's, markedly higher than that of the Bantu, and equalled only by that of the prolific Cape Coloured Folk.[1]

The Cape Coloured Folk were the second and next smallest group.[2] The overwhelming majority of them lived in the Western Cape Province, whence they had sprung, deeply appreciating the fact that a few white men like Hofmeyr regarded them as human beings and citizens, but resenting the off-handedness of the Bantu and Indian-conscious officials in far-away Pretoria, who seemed to know little and care less about such a different folk as they at 'the shank-end.'[3] They welcomed recent increases in pay; but though few of them objected to separate schools, cinemas, bathing-places and beaches, where these existed, they all objected strongly to their displacement from many employments in favour of Europeans, which

---

[1] Hatch, *op. cit.*, pp. 224 ff.

[2] On Cape Coloured Folk *vide* Hatch, *op. cit.*, pp. 189 ff.; *Race Relations Handbook*, chap. xxi.; *Round Table*, No. 148, pp. 342 ff.; U.G. 54 of 1937; *Report . . . regarding the Cape Coloured Population of the Union.*

[3] On the presence of coloured blood in famous old Cape families *vide* de Villiers, *Geschlacht register van die Oude Kaapse Familien*; J. Hoge, *Personalia of Germans at the Cape.* [Archives Year Book of S.A. History, 1946]; *Hansard (S.A.)* May 24, 1949, col. 6433.

had gone on steadily ever since Hertzog had launched his 'civilisation policy' in 1925, and had latterly become worse after sturdy and low-paid Bantu had come trekking into the Cape Peninsula during the Axis war. That Peninsula was, so to speak, the headquarters of the Cape Coloured community.[1] Their people almost monopolised certain areas of straggling Capetown, such as the Malay Quarter, Woodstock and, above all, District Six, the Capetown slum *par excellence*, whose streets were not always safe for white folk even in the day-time because of the ubiquity of 'skolly boys,' Coloured youngsters who had run wild and were set against all authority, but which could nevertheless be traversed at all hours by clergymen, doctors, nurses and other Europeans who were known to be friendly. Further south, there were large groups of Coloured Folk in such suburbs as Newlands, Claremont and Wynberg; but throughout the length of the Peninsula, as the industrial and white residential areas spread, so the poorer Coloured Folk found themselves being squeezed further and further out on to the sandy Cape Flats, only to find that the available land there had been bought by European individuals or syndicates. Those of them who could risk it had to buy land at high prices, usually on the costly instalment system, which meant that failure to pay led to frequent evictions and the subsequent re-sale of the same plot. Hence, ramshackle, semi-rural settlements proliferated on the outskirts ranging from fairly respectable Kensington down to slums of the worst kind. One of the latter was the scattering of hovels in the swamps beyond Wynberg, whose squalor was, however, relieved by the efforts of Dr. Oscar Wolheim, the Afrikaner Warden of the Cape Area Flats Distress Association, and his devoted assistant, Miss Mary Attlee, sister of the British Labour Prime Minister, who made their institution a civilising centre and found that even skolly-boys, like Boy Scouts the world over, responded to sympathy and the offer of something interesting and harmless to do. Still further south again, numerous Coloured Folk lived in the bush behind Fish Hoek, driven thither by the servitude forbidding non-Europeans to live on the farm on which that sea-side suburb had recently been built. Nevertheless, the Coloured Folk could still qualify for the old Cape franchise, attend the more civilised Universities, get schooling that was in too many cases barely passable by reason of overcrowding and lack of teachers, but was in an increasing number of cases very good, and also run their own newspapers and political organisations.

Politically, the Coloured Folk were much divided, not only in the Cape Peninsula but in other large centres like Port Elizabeth and East London. Shortly before the general election of 1943, Smuts had galvanised their politicians into activity by setting up the dreaded

[1] *Round Table*, No. 148, p. 342.

Coloured Advisory Board, which many of them took to be the first step towards segregation. In due course, these politicians had split into three mutually distrustful groups. First, Dr. Goolam Gool, a Trotskyist, organised the Anti-Coloured Advisory Department Committee and, strong in the support of *The Guardian* newspaper, made it the rallying-centre of the Non-European Unity Movement. His extremism, however, drove moderates to break away from the Teachers' League of South Africa and form a Teachers' Educational and Professional Association of their own. This association worked with the second political group, which was headed by George Golding. That patient politician, backed by his group's newspaper, *The Sun*, led his fellow-moderates out of the old-established African People's Organisation and proposed to work with the authorities, even to the length of accepting the Coloured Advisory Council and Department. The third group consisted of the more extreme members of the A.P.O. Led by Bennie Kies, editor of *The Educational Journal*, it started its own newspaper, *The Torch*, joined hands with the radical Teachers' League, and showed itself to be so anti-European that it did not trouble to explain the justice of its cause even to sympathetic white folk.[1]

The folk who felt the pressure of the expansive Europeans most severely were the Bantu, seventy per cent. of the Union's population.[2] It had been so in the old frontier days when the struggle for land and waterholes had been cut across by the white man's demand for Native labour; it was so now, in the industrial age, with the difference that the struggle had been transferred from the open veld to the factories and poorer quarters of the rapidly-growing towns. The vast majority of the Bantu, and especially the warlike and conservative Zulus, were what their ancestors had always been: tribal pastoralists and scratch-farmers, poor, underfed, prone to disease, superstitious and ignorant of the white folk's ways. The Bantu could, indeed, boast a small but increasing intelligentsia and a much larger body of detribalised or semi-detribalised families; but even the most advanced of them were fain to admit that their people as a whole would need European leadership until the far-off day when their decaying tribal system should have been completely dissolved and they themselves been given their rightful place on the land and in the urban areas. The bulk of them lived either in the Reserves or on European farms; a substantial number of their menfolk found intermittent homes of a sort in the goldmining compounds along the Rand, and a rapidly increasing minority dwelt in townships, locations or shanty towns as near as was permissible to their places of

---

[1] Hatch, *op. cit.*, pp. 193 ff.; Roux, *op. cit.*, p. 366; *Round Table*, No. 148, p. 343.
[2] *Ibid.*, No. 148, pp. 340 ff.

work in the so-called 'white man's' towns. Their infantile and general death-rates had never been counted precisely, but it was known that both were grim and that their tuberculosis death-rate was seven times that of the Europeans. Their educational facilities varied greatly. Most of their schools were financed by missionary societies and State grants, which, thanks mainly to Hofmeyr, had latterly become so liberal that the Union was spending far more on Bantu education than any of her neighbours. Even so, barely one-third of their children were going to school at all, and most of those who did found that the schools could not take them far enough to gain admission to apprenticeship for skilled trades or to such universities as drew no colour bar.[1]

Of all the peoples of South Africa, the Bantu had had the longest experience of the policy of segregation or, as it was beginning to be called, _apartheid_, that is, separation. In days long gone by even the Cape Colony had regarded them as foreigners who were only to be admitted on terms; indeed, it was only since the eighteen-forties that Europeans, whether republican or colonial, had attempted to rule them as members of their own communities. On the other hand, one or two Governors, Dutch and British, backed by a few of the more far-sighted missionaries, had experimented with a policy of separation by creating Reserves near the frontiers of the rapidly expanding Cape Colony and Natal, that is, territorial refuges in which Bantu and half-caste Griqua tribesmen could be Christianised and civilised while the tide of white settlement swept round but not over them. No Governor and no missionary pursued this humane policy more vigorously than Sir Philip Wodehouse and Dr. John Philip, and none earned a more sinister reputation in the pages of pro-colonial historians. It could hardly have been otherwise, because their policy cut dead across the desires of acquisitive frontiersmen, Afrikaner and British. Yet, in their day when Queen Victoria was young, there had been land and to spare for all to make a policy of _apartheid_ practicable. Now it was not so. After a full century of scarcely checked white land-grabbing, most of such Reserves as existed were small and scattered; indeed, the only large solid blocks, other than the High Commission Territories, lay in the Cape's Ciskei and Transkeian Territories and Natal's Zululand. Many of the Reserves contained good land, but all suffered from primitive farming, heavy overstocking, grievous soil erosion and human overcrowding so severe that, by 1945, they were carrying more folk than ever before and failing to support them.[2] Only some forty per cent. of the Bantu dwelt therein, and others had little chance of finding a livelihood there unless farming methods were revolutionised. Nor was there

[1] Davidson, _op. cit._, p. 127; _Round Table_, No. 148, p. 341.
[2] Sachs, _op. cit._, p. 116.

much real hope of markedly extending the Reserves, because so many white folk either refused to make land available for 'Kaffirs' or else demanded unconscionable prices.

In 1945, some fifty per cent. of the Reserve population of, say, 3,250,000 were away at any one time, either on European farms or in domestic service or in secondary industry. Those on the farms were paid either in cash or in kind or in both and, in addition, were often allowed to run a few head of stock and farm a small patch for themselves; but, in any event, they lived as poorly paid serfs of their white lords, who complained loudly that they could never get enough of them.[1] The farmers' chief competitors for Bantu labour were industry and the goldmines. The pull of industry was especially strong, because Hofmeyr's enlightened policy and the doubling of wages during the past two decades offered those Bantu who went to urban areas much better economic conditions and often better social conditions also than they had ever had before.[2] It was the goldmines, however, that exerted the steadiest, though not, as was commonly believed, the most powerful attraction. In 1945 or thereabouts, the Rand mines drew only some 140,000 of their 300,000 Native labourers from the Union as against 50,000 from the High Commission Territories, 80,000 from Portuguese Mozambique and 25,000 from the tropical North, nearly half of these last from far-away Nyasaland. But wherever they found their labourers, the mines would take only the young and reasonably healthy. These men, the pick of their race, were well cared for physically; but they were carefully segregated in compounds and, though they were free to go out into the town, were separated from their wives and children. They thus grew up to be neither bachelors nor family men, neither truly urban nor rural workers, but just 'boys,' whatever their age, who must be content to receive food, lodging and from £3 to £4 each month as contrasted with the £70 to £120 received by their white fellow-workers and, because they were Bantu, must look for no advancement to skilled and well-paid jobs.[3]

Contrary to general belief, the Bantu were not going to urban areas very much faster than were the poorer white folk from the countryside; indeed, between 1921 and 1946, the proportion of Bantu to the total rural population had fallen only by one-ninth, while that of the Europeans had fallen by no less than two-fifths, or, to look at it from another angle, whereas in 1921 the total numbers of urban Europeans had been 847,508 and of Bantu 587,000, twenty-five years later they were 1,794,312 and 1,719,312 respectively. Nevertheless, the mines and industry between them had seen to it

---

[1] Davidson, B., *op. cit.*, pp. 45 ff.; Robertson, H. M., *South Africa, Economic and Political Aspects*, p. 39.
[2] *Ibid.*, p. 209; S. van der Horst, *Native Labour in South Africa*, p. 263.
[3] *Round Table*, No. 141, pp. 95 ff.

that the Union should have close on 2,000,000 more or less urbanised Bantu on its hands.[1] This raised in a pressing form the problem of migratory labour, a system that had begun on the Diamond Fields in the eighteen-seventies and had since been maintained by the Rand mineowners and successive Native Mine Wages Commissions on the theory that the Bantu were farmers who came to town for a spell and then went home to the Reserves till they were needed again.[2] Now, however, a growing number of officials and businessmen were beginning to ask whether the goldmines, a wasting asset, were to be suffered to stand in the way of more lasting and beneficent developments in other directions and, by their example and pervasive influence, to tempt secondary industry also to base itself on migratory labour.

Critics attacked the system of migratory labour all along the line. It was, they claimed, wasteful of time, money and energy in that these thousands of Bantu had to walk or be carried by train, bus or plane to the scene of their labours and then go back the same way; it was, they argued, anti-social, for if the worldly-wise rulers of the Belgian Congo held it undesirable that more than five per cent. of the men should be absent from a given area at any one time, it must be disastrous for the Union to permit the absence of nearly six times as many; nor, they observed, did these migrants become really skilled workers, because the colour bar was against their promotion in the mines. Worse still, while these able-bodied men were forgetting whatever farming they had ever known, their holdings suffered at the hands of the women, youngsters and older folk, while their temporarily deserted wives were tempted into evil courses and the unchecked youngsters ran wild; in short, the system was destroying the very tribal system to which many Europeans were anxious to confine or restore the Bantu. Yet the remedy was plain. Recruitment for the mines on which the country so largely depended must, indeed, be hampered as little as possible; but those same mines must not be allowed to stand in the way of better Bantu farming, higher Bantu wages and a more thorough industrialisation of the whole community; the Reserves must be rendered capable of supporting a larger number of families by improved methods of farming and the erection of factories in or near their few little towns, and white employers must be encouraged to follow the excellent example of Iscor by providing not merely bachelor compounds, but family accommodation at places of work.[3]

The multitude of more or less detribalised Bantu suffered many

---

[1] Davidson, *op. cit.*, p. 78.

[2] U.G. 28 of 1948, *Report of the Native Laws Commission, 1946–8.* [Fagan Commission].

[3] Davidson, *op. cit.*, p. 97; U.G. 28 of 1948, pp. 49 ff.; *Round Table*, No. 141, pp. 94 ff.

disabilities. The authorities refused to recognise their numerous trade unions and made it a crime for them to strike; they bore the full weight of the complex colour bar, were liable in many cases to penalties heavier for them than for others, and must endure frequent and sudden raids by unsympathetic policemen, who were seeking to enforce the pass and liquor laws for breach of which Bantu furnished an utterly disproportionate and misleading number of each year's 'criminals.' Moreover, they were to an increasing degree regarded as 'foreigners,' who had no business in the 'white man's towns' unless they were ministering to the needs of those who had a recognised right to be there. Those of them who were not so engaged were apt to be treated as 'redundant' members of society to be packed off to their 'homes' in the Reserves at the Back-of-beyond-fontein in the Never-never Land, and even those who were so 'ministering' must go to their own place at the end of the day's work. Their 'own place' was for most of these Bantu, as for so many similarly situated Coloured Folk and Indians, in the locations, Native townships and shanty-towns that sprawled on the outskirts of the white man's towns. The quality of these urban appendages varied enormously. Long-established Ndabeni near Capetown and New Brighton near Port Elizabeth fell little short of the Bloemfon-tein Location, which was probably the best of all, while some of the newer mixed settlements along the Rand, such as Alexandra, Pim-ville, the Western Native Township and 'the snob township' of Orlando, were respectable enough. But most of the agglomerations of dwellings in the outer marches of the wealthy Rand, and notably the 'controlled' squatters camps at Jabavu and Moroka, were as foul as miserable Windermere wallowing in the intermittent floods on the Cape Flats or the illegal squatting settlements on the farms that ringed Pretoria round.[1]

In spite of their many handicaps, most of the folk in these dreary townships were decent, hard-working and cheerful. Nor were they lacking in public spirit. During the Axis war, Bantu barrow-boys from some of these areas sold bread, cakes and coffee at the factory gates to fellow Africans who had no other means of getting something to eat. At the end of the war, the local authorities prosecuted some of them for this breach of municipal regulations and only desisted when the dusky vendors paraded outside the City Hall with their cafés-de-move-on adorned with protesting placards. Again, the folk of Alexandra and Moroka would have raised town guards to control disorderly elements had not this same unsympathetic Johannesburg City Council stopped them, while twice during the war the workers of Alexandra had defeated the attempts of a bus company to raise

---

[1] Davidson, *op. cit.*, pp. 89, 118 ff.; U.G. 28 of 1948, p. 5; Hatch, *op. cit.*, p. 151; van der Horst, *op. cit.*, pp. 270 ff.

fares by walking the twenty miles to and from work each day till a utility company took over the services—at the old fares.[1]

Most of the non-European 'dormitories' throughout the Union suffered from overcrowding and rack-renting, because the Africans and Coloured owners of the stands (freehold plots) mortgaged them heavily, as a rule to European individuals or Building Societies, and then sought to meet their liabilities by packing in far too many tenants. Nor could the inhabitants readily find homes elsewhere, as the 15,000 folk, who marched out of swarming Orlando and Alexandra under the leadership of Mpanza Sofazonka, discovered when they tried to found Moroka on the opposite hillside. The Labour Johannesburg City Council promptly sent policemen to pull down the shacks and only deigned to recognise the new shanty town after the crowd, led by its womenfolk, had stoned the hated invaders and killed two of them. As if callous City Fathers and heavy-handed policemen were not enough, jealous white neighbours and young blackguards of their own stock added to the woes of the non-European hangers-on of white society along the Rand. Just as Capetown's District Six had its Coloured skolly-boys, so these Rand slums had their *Tsotsies*, successors of the aforetime violence-loving *Amalaita*, gangs of youths who maintained such a reign of terror that few white folk, other than the Police, dared venture on to their raiding-grounds after dark. The most permanently dangerous situations arose, however, at places like Newlands and West Dene, where Poor Whites were separated only by a road from the Bantu of New Clare and the mixed population of Sophiatown. These Europeans, fresh from the backveld and resentful of the comparative prosperity of their despised dark-skinned neighbours, were apt to shoot at sight, frontier fashion, in times of excitement; but, in justice, it must be said that little more could be expected of harassed and ignorant white folk, who knew that the Police had driven away thousands of the Bantu who had joined the crowd outside the Johannesburg City Hall intent on welcoming Smuts on his return from the San Francisco Conference, and knew also that white society as a whole, at all events in those parts, by no means recognised that the large and growing population of permanently urbanised Bantu families were morally entitled to freehold tenure of land and houses and, in general, to a chance of advancement in the towns which were now their only homes.[2]

In face of all this, South Africans tackled the task of reconstruction with mingled thankfulness and apprehension. They at once began to demobilise their forces and soon found that most of the discharged service folk were as ready to go back to their old jobs

---

[1] Davidson, *op. cit.*, pp. 122–3; Hatch, *op. cit.*, pp. 53, 156.
[2] Davidson, *op. cit.*, pp. 117 ff.; Hatch, *op. cit.*, pp. 59, 153.

as their employers were to have them, and that neither masters nor men were unduly grieved that the newly-instituted War Stores Disposal Board was getting rid of surplus stock so slowly, because this left a clear field for the sale of their current production.[1] Some of the weakest factories were closed without appreciably swelling the ranks of the unemployed; but though many of those that survived suffered somewhat from lack of raw materials and so forth, the vast majority promised to pull through, always provided that white trade unionists would continue to put up with wartime dilution by folk of other colours.

Major Gideon van Zyl having been installed as Governor-General to preside over the reconstruction, Parliament met early in 1946 to continue the good work. The Assembly first raised the salaries of Ministers and Members, gave the Leader of the Opposition a salary, and then passed on to the Budget. This provided for considerable tax-relief in spite of a marked drop in goldmining revenue, handed over £300,000 of Native pass fees to the Transvaal Provincial Council, and found large sums for ambitious schemes of social security. Parliament refused to set up a Ministry of Food or to institute rationing, but it did sanction the appointment of a Director of Supplies, who, with powers much greater than those of the Food Controller, was to have charge of commodity, export and import controls under the supervision of the Minister of Economic Development.[2] It further passed a Silicosis Bill, which gave generous compensation to those of the thirty thousand European and three hundred thousand Bantu mineworkers who might fall victims to that dread disease, and then established a Social Welfare Department to co-ordinate the work of the Departments concerned and a National Health Department to implement the recent Public Health Amendment Act.[3] Next, with the warm support of the predominantly rural Opposition, it created a Soil Conservation Board, as well as a Wool Board to carry out the agreement reached by the London Conference of 1945 for the disposal of accumulated Commonwealth stocks of wool. The Assembly, however, evinced far less unanimity when the Government announced that, while it could not itself undertake nor even sanction any major scheme of immigration until all South Africans had found homes, it would not stand in the way of private organisations that might wish to bring in skilled workers and would assuredly welcome all immigrants of 'the right type.' Then, while an unprecedented stream of newcomers began to pour into the country, the House quarrelled bitterly over the Aliens Affairs Bill, which

---

[1] *Record of the Organisation of . . . Supplies*, p. 124.
[2] *Govt. Gazette Extraordinary*, No. 3561, Oct. 26, 1945; War Measure 75 of 1945.
[3] *Round Table*, No. 144, pp. 395 ff.; Acts 24, 47, 51 and 53 of 1946.

empowered the authorities to send back to Germany those Germans in the Union and South-West Africa who had been listed by a Special Commission for deportation. This, thundered Malan, was to punish members of a nation whose only crime was that it had lost the war, whereas the real enemy of Christian civilisation in South Africa was Russian Communism.

Much of the time of this busy Session was taken up by the problems of South-West Africa and the Indians, both of which were destined to embroil the Union with the newly-founded United Nations Organisation. In the Mandated Territory, the two so-called 'South African' parties had drifted apart during the war, but were now at one in demanding Union nationality and the ending of doubts as to the status of their Territory, while the Germans, who had been disfranchised during that war and now realised that South-West would never go back to the Fatherland, also desired Union nationality and, further, the incorporation of their Territory in the Union. Early in the Session, a young Nationalist moved that the Territory become the fifth Province of the Union, arguing that U.N.O. had no more right to determine its destiny than had the now defunct League of Nations. Smuts replied that South-West Africa would soon be given representation in the Union Parliament and that he would press for incorporation; but should he fail in this, he would maintain the *status quo* by administering it under the Mandate and reporting to the Trusteeship Council. Forthwith, in May 1946, the Windhoek Legislative Assembly unanimously asked for incorporation. The authorities at once held an informal and not altogether satisfactory referendum among the non-European and unrepresented majority. The result of this inquiry, which omitted the 56,000 tribesmen of the tropical north, was said to be that 208,850 favoured incorporation and that 35,520 rejected it, the bulk of the dissident minority being the Hereros, the aforetime Bantu *herrenvolk* of those parts, and the Damaras, their dutiful dependants.[1]

Meanwhile, deadlock had been reached on the Indian problem. On the one hand, European and Asiatic spokesmen in Natal had failed to come to terms and, on the other, Smuts had declined to accept Nehru's suggestion that the issue be referred to a round-table conference. The one practicable proposal that Parliament had before it was the report of the second Broome Commission to the effect that Indians be given a 'loaded' franchise and critical Delhi be invited to send a mission to see the facts for itself. Hence, because the Pegging Act of 1943 was on the point of expiring by the efflux of time, Smuts introduced the Asiatic Land Tenure and Indian Representation Bill.[2] This he justified as the best that could be got under

---

[1] *Round Table*, No. 144, pp. 336 ff.
[2] Act 28 of 1946; *Chronology*, II., No. 6, p. 175.

the circumstances, and even Hofmeyr accepted it as a fair temporary solution with the promise of better things to come. In terms of this measure, the position of the Transvaal Indians was left much as it was, but that of the Natal Indians was in many ways improved. First, Asiatics and non-Asiatics were forbidden to agree between themselves to transfer real property in any part of Natal, unless the Minister gave them leave or the property lay in one of the many 'exempted areas' which were to be free from all restrictions. These areas were to be defined so generously that some of them might be expected to become purely Indian and, meanwhile, all of them together might satisfy the ambitions and absorb the superfluous cash of these few wealthy Indians who were the most persistent penetrators of white residential areas. Secondly, though the Bill did not restore to Natal Indians the full franchise of which they had long since been deprived, it did give them and the Transvaal Indians representation by one nominated Senator and another elected by themselves on a separate communal roll, and by three white Assembly members similarly elected. Natal Indians were also to elect two members to their Provincial Council, both of whom might be Indians.[1]

The Bill was resisted fiercely within the Assembly by the Dominion and Nationalist parties, which clamoured that these unassimilable Indians had no claim to any political rights whatever, and more unexpectedly by Madeley and two other Labour members. Madeley even led one of these die-hards into the Nationalist ranks, where he himself soon died; but the rest of his followers rallied to the steady-going Rand chemist, John Christie, and helped the ministerialists to carry the measure.[2] Opposition outside the Houses was much more widespread. In Natal, the left wing of the Indian Congress had recently formed an Anti-Segregation Council and won forty-six of the seats on that Congress's Executive Council, twelve of them for Communists. Thus impelled, the president of this Natal Congress therefore joined with Dr. Yusuf Dadoo, the radical leader of the Transvaal Indian Congress, to inveigh against Smuts's 'spurious offer of a sham franchise' and 'diabolical attempt to strangulate Indians economically and degrade them socially.' In far-away India, even moderate men like Srinavasa Sastri, sometime High Commissioner at Pretoria, could condemn the Act as 'hellish,' and the much less temperate Delhi Government, now almost entirely Indian, severed trade relations with the Union to the grave inconvenience of South African farmers, who found themselves short of Indian jute-bags, and to the detriment of some Indian shopkeepers in Durban and a few Transvaal towns, who were subjected to

[1] *Round Table*, No. 143, pp. 287 ff.
[2] *Ibid.*, No. 143, p. 291; Sachs, *op. cit.*, p. 51; Roux, *op. cit.*, p. 372.

sporadic boycott, and still more to Durban's Indian importers.[1] When the measure became law in June 1946, India withdrew her High Commissioner from the Union, and the All-India Congress Committee called upon the Viceroy to use his influence at Pretoria and assured the South African Indians of its support. Thus encouraged, many of those Indians organised passive resistance and *hartals*, and, by ostentatiously trespassing on European-controlled ground in Durban, exposed themselves to rough handling by gangs of young white toughs.[2]

Late in May, Smuts set off once more on his travels leaving Hofmeyr in charge. Scenting trouble from those many United States citizens, who demanded the abolition of imperial preferences without showing any intention of lowering their country's own high tariffs in exchange, he broadcast from London his abiding faith that the British Commonwealth would stand so long as its world-wide communications held good, and that by reason of its sense of humour and other assets of 'an imponderable kind,' could serve as 'a governor in the middle,' which would prevent the two giants, the United States and the U.S.S.R. from disrupting 'our world.'[3] He then attended the Paris Peace Conference, urged the Dutch and Belgian Parliaments to help in bridging the not yet impassable gap between the eastern and western halves of Europe, and then, after a hurried visit to Switzerland, sailed for New York to attend the meeting of U.N.O. at Flushing Meadows.[4] There, he suffered his first international set-back these many years. Both in committee and General Assembly, his Indian policy was furiously attacked by Mrs. Pandit, Nehru's vigorous and eloquent sister, and Alexei Vyshinsky, spokesman of the U.S.S.R. It was in vain that the leading British representative proposed that the question of U.N.O.'s competence to touch a purely domestic matter be referred to a panel of six jurists, or that Smuts, with the passing remark that charges of discrimination came ill from the sister of a Brahman and denials of liberty from a latter-day Russian, suggested that it be referred rather to the International Court, which might send a fact-finding Commission to South Africa. Mrs. Pandit and Vyshinsky blandly side-stepped both suggestions and induced the overwhelming majority of the General Assembly to demand that Indians be treated in conformity with the 'gentleman's agreements' concluded between the Indian and South African authorities from 1927 onwards and the supposedly relevant but unspecified clauses of the Charter, and to request that progress be reported to itself at its next Session. No one

[1] *Round Table*, No. 143, p. 292.
[2] *Ibid.*, No. 145, p. 32; Y. M. Dadoo, *Five Months of Struggle*; *Chronology*, II., No. 6, p. 167; No. 12, pp. 349, 351, 357–8; No. 13, pp. 380–1.
[3] *Chronology*, II., No. 11, p. 317.   [4] *Ibid.*, II., No. 20, pp. 610, 622.

said a word about the limited franchise that had been granted to the Indians. Nor did South-West Africa fare better in what was, to Smuts, a mere cockpit of 'emotion, passion and ignorance.' Vyshinsky, with much justice, questioned the adequacy of the so-called Native referendum in that Territory; Mrs. Pandit prophesied that incorporation would mean 'permanent helotry' for non-Europeans, and the majority, setting aside a Danish-American amendment that the General Assembly had too little information to warrant its taking a decision, rejected incorporation out of hand and demanded that the Mandate be superseded by United Nations Trusteeship.[1]

Smuts flew home smoothing his ruffled plumes to find even the most liberal white South Africans seething with indignation at the stream of 'unjustifiable odium' that had thus been poured upon them by Hindus and Communists of all people. Some indeed joined the fair-minded Hofmeyr in pointing out that neither the Indian question nor other similar issues could any longer be treated as their country's purely private concern, and in excusing local Indians for appealing to Delhi over the head of a South African Government that refused to recognise them as full citizens; but most people simply stressed the domestic nature of the issue. The leader of the Opposition pressed Smuts to come out of U.N.O. altogether. He told him frankly that he would support him if he declined to report to the Trusteeship Council and treated South-West Africa in such a way that it would make no difference whether she were incorporated or no, but that otherwise he would accuse him of permitting outside interference. Expanding his ideas, Malan rejected all thought of submission to Trusteeship, demanded that the Mandated Territory be given representation in Parliament with a status equal to that of a Province, clamoured for the immediate repeal of the 'undesired and futile' Indian franchise, insisted that there be no Conference with India other than one that aimed at getting rid of the Indians lock, stock and barrel, and finally called for a Joint Committee to go into the whole issue. Smuts, whose self-respect had been doubtless restored by the expert Lord Hailey's approval of his Native administration in South-West Africa, was by no means inclined to accept Malan's offer.[2] Convinced as he was that his little country had been the victim of false propaganda at Flushing Meadows and alarmed at the bickering and wild talk in General Assembly and Committee, he preferred to suspend judgment on the 'young and inexperienced' United Nations Organisation. Meanwhile he renewed his old promise that he would administer South-West Africa as

[1] *Round Table*, No. 145, p. 33, and No. 146, pp. 133 ff.; *Chronology*, II., No. 22, pp. 720 ff.; No. 23, p. 756; No. 24, pp. 790, 793.
[2] *Round Table*, No. 146, p. 198.

hitherto under the Mandate and report to the Trusteeship Council, and gave an assurance that he would seek no agreement with Delhi on Indian legislation. This said, he appointed an Indian Advisory Board to watch over Indian interests and even proposed that Natal should restore the municipal franchise to her Asians. Running true to form, white Durban rejected this liberal suggestion out of hand.[1]

Trouble with the urban Bantu was now added to Smuts's burden. The spate of strikes which had greeted his drastic anti-Bantu War Measures of 1942 and 1943 had died down, and thereafter all had seemed to be going well. Few of the Bantu trade unions had accepted the offers of the Labour Party on the Rand and the white South African Labour and Trades Council to admit to their ranks all *bona fide* unions whatever their colour, but by the end of the Axis war, there were fully fifty Bantu trade unions on the Rand, the chief of them being the African Mineworkers' Union. These unions were organised in three groups: first, those controlled by orthodox Communists; secondly, the Workers' Industrial League under Trotskyist leadership, and, finally, those which had rallied to the Bantu chairman of the non-European Council of Trade Unions, who was presently forced by Communists to make way for a fellow-countryman, John Marks, secretary of the African Mineworkers' Union.

Towards the close of the 1946 session, Smuts hopefully appointed a strong Commission under Judge Henry Fagan, an ex-Nationalist politician of liberal views, to report on the pass laws, the position of the Bantu in urban areas and industry, and the pressing problem of migratory labour. He arranged also with the Board of Trade that there should be a National Institute of Personal Selection and Research under Dr. Simon Biesheuvel, an Afrikaner even more liberal than Judge Fagan, which should pick out Bantu mineworkers who were fit for promotion to posts of some little responsibility. He naturally welcomed the proposal of the Calico Printers' Association, a large Lancashire cotton combine, to erect a textile factory at Kingwilliamstown in the heart of the Ciskei, an overwhelmingly Bantu area in the Eastern Cape Province, for here was a promise that jobs might now be taken to Africans rather than Africans be brought to the jobs however little industrialists and their white employees elsewhere might relish such competition by low-paid 'colonials.'[2]

Then came a setback. On the Rand, the chief whirlpool of migratory labour where white miners were talking of a strike for higher pay, thousands of members of the African Mineworkers' Union struck in August 1946. Because their union was not recognised by

[1] *Chronology*, III., No. 2, p. 50; No. 3, p. 79.
[2] *Round Table*, No. 142, pp. 194 ff.

the authorities, the strikers had no means of collective bargaining other than by showing themselves in the streets. This large numbers of them did by marching to the Johannesburg City Hall in orderly fashion to demand the permits that would take them home. The police drove them back to their compounds with some loss.[1] This strike, the biggest since the Rand Revolution of 1922, involved over 70,000 Africans from first to last, flaring up now in this mine and now in that with frequent clashes with the police, who were sometimes called in to drive the strikers down the mines and then, when they refused to come up again, sent down to rout them out. After perhaps a dozen strikers had been killed either by rifle fire or trampling in the crowd, the strike petered out. Thereafter, while police and managements were quietly coming to terms with white miners, who had staged an equally illegal strike at Blyvooruitzig, and even Hofmeyr was refusing the request of the Anglican Synod of Johannesburg that he should recognise the African Mineworkers' Union, the authorities carried off masses of documents from the Communist headquarters in Johannesburg and Capetown and indicted some fifty Europeans, Indians and Bantu for conspiracy under the Riotous Assemblies Amendment Act in that they were alleged to have incited the strikers. This charge had to be withdrawn for lack of evidence, but most of the accused pleaded guilty to breach of War Measure 145, which made it a criminal offence for Bantu to strike, and were duly given short terms of imprisonment.[2] A few months later, the authorities, with somewhat greater success, charged the members of the National Executive of the S.A. Communist Party with sedition. They can scarcely have been surprised when the Native Representative Council, affronted by the recent unequal justice meted out to black and white strikers and long dissatisfied with its existing powers, should have turned a deaf ear to the Prime Minister's talk of entrusting it with the administration of the Reserves and even of recognising Bantu trade unions by suspending its own sittings *sine die*.[3] Presently, in June 1947, this Council refused to take part in the election of a 'Native' member to the House of Assembly.

Meanwhile, the political tide had begun to turn against Smuts. True, he had maintained his party's voting strength in the House, but the fact remained that the Nationalists had won four of the eight by-elections since 1943. Now, in January 1947, thanks mainly to non-Nationalist European and Coloured voters who nursed economic grievances against the United Party administration, they had won the seat at Hottentots-Holland, a mixed rural and urban constituency

---

[1] *Round Table*, No. 145, p. 93; Davidson, *op. cit.*, pp. 106–7; Roux, *op. cit.*, pp. 340 ff.; Sachs, *op. cit.*, p. 61.
[2] *Ibid.*, p. 61; Roux, *op. cit.*, pp. 348–50.   [3] *Round Table*, No. 148, p. 341.

not far from Capetown, in a contest which Smuts had made a test of confidence in his Indian and South-West African policies. Then came a further Nationalist victory at Wolmaranstad in the Transvaal, which encouraged the divided Opposition to talk once more of forming a united front and Havenga to draw so close to Malan that Christie, in alarm, suggested that there should be an electoral pact between his Labour Party and the ministerialists. In the wings, as it were, Stallard's Dominion Party was plainly fading away, for it sought to hold neither its solitary seat outside Natal at East London North nor a presumably safe seat at Durban, and failed miserably in a three-cornered contest in Zululand in which the Nationalist candidate, the moderate and likeable Jansen, was also defeated.[1]

While the United Party was thus shaken, the Labour Party worried, the Dominion Party dying and the Nationalists justifiably hopeful, there came a welcome break in the clouds of political controversy when King George VI, Queen Elizabeth and their two daughters accepted the veteran Prime Minister's invitation to visit South Africa. 1947. The 'pleasant holiday,' which Smuts had promised them, turned out to be two months of desperately hard work during which the Royal visitors travelled fully ten thousand miles by land through the Union, the High Commission Territories and Southern Rhodesia at the height of the southern summer, a strain which undoubtedly shortened His Majesty's life. The fears expressed in many parts of the English-speaking world that Royalty's sojourn in such a divided and republican-minded country might be attended by untoward events proved to be groundless, because, however seriously South Africans took their politics, they were a courteous and hospitable folk who could lay aside their differences on occasion. The nearest approach to anything of the kind was the absence, on principle, of most of the Nationalist members of both Houses on the occasion of the presentation of the Loyal Address; but this was more than made up for by their eager attendance on February 21, 1947, at the opening of Parliament by the King in person.

Capetown, whose inhabitants of all colours dearly loved a pageant, set an example by its dignified welcome, while the local exuberance of Port Elizabeth was so stunted in the press that jealous Durban skilfully organised the loudest loyal uproar of the tour, an uproar louder even than that of mercurial Johannesburg. The welcome at Afrikaner centres was quieter. Ultra-Nationalist Stellenbosch, bedecked with the Union tricolour to the exclusion of the companion Union Jack, maintained the silence which many explained as an Afrikaner mark of respect; equally Nationalist Bloemfontein, however, evinced an urbane pleasure when the Royal visitors called on the widow of the late President Steyn, and Nationalist Pretoria was

[1] *Round Table*, No. 146, pp. 197 ff.; No. 147, p. 298; No. 149, p. 506.

gratified when they attended the Groote Kerk on Palm Sunday, delighted when His Majesty spoke admiringly of the Voortrekkers, and
genuinely touched when he restored the late President Kruger's
massive Bible to the old statesman's heirs. Everywhere, folk flocked
in often from great distances, prominent among them, in the Transvaal especially, commandos of *oustryers* of the South African war
wearing their republican medals. Thousands, again, waited for hours
simply to see the White Train go by and were delighted when the
King, as he often did, ordered an unscheduled 'whistle stop' so that
he might speak to them. The non-Europeans were frantic with joy,
for was not this their King, great-grandson of Queen Victoria the
Good, still to them a living reality? Whole populations seemed to
have turned out in the High Commission Territories, while in Durban
as at Ladysmith, Natal Indians defied the boycott proclaimed by their
local Congress leaders and swarmed around the Royal family cheering and singing *Die Stem van Suid Afrika*, virtually the Afrikander
national anthem. Always there were the excited children of all sorts,
sizes, colours, tongues and political affiliations, and so it was in the
High Commission Territories further north in Southern Rhodesia.

Before the visit was over, Smuts had taken his visitors to his
'church' at the top of Table Mountain where one could get away
from party politicians and see things far below in perspective.[1] It was
a weary party that sailed home, as they had come, on the great battleship, H.M.S. *Vanguard*; but that weariness had its recompenses, for,
if the visit could have no effect on the course of local politics, the
visitors had learned much, and the peoples of the Dominion, who
still honoured their fathers and mothers, had seen the Crown in the
flesh as the head of a happy family. As the *Vanguard* faded away
below the northern horizon, Smuts told the Senate that British rule
was 'a safer guarantee of universal peace than the hitherto most
disappointing United Nations Organisation.'[2]

Behind all the ceremonial and rejoicings, Parliament had been
busy with finance rather than legislation. Necessarily so, because the
world's economic state was grave and the Union's prosperity less
assured than it had been hitherto. During and since the war, South
Africa had repatriated almost the whole of her external debt,
accumulated large sterling balances and dollar holdings and, thanks
mainly to her comparative freedom from trade restrictions and the
ready sale of her gold in New York, had paid for extravagant purchases from the United States without having to draw on the
sterling pool. At the same time, the policies of the Reserve Bank
and commercial banks had almost quadrupled her supply of money
over the past eight years. All this, however, depended in the last

[1] *Round Table*, No. 147, pp. 207 ff.
[2] *Chronology*, III., No. 10, p. 288; No. 11, p. 320.

resort on the goldmines, which had to set against the virtual doubling of the price of gold during that period an almost threefold rise in working costs.[1] Then, in June 1946, had come the first warning. By that time the Union had indeed compounded her Lend-Lease debt to the United States on favourable terms, but she had had to find nearly £60,000,000 for U.N.R.R.A., the International Bank and the International Fund.[2] These heavy outgoings, together with continued lavish importations, abruptly reversed the balance of payments and in nine short months drained away three-fourths of the Reserve Bank's holdings of gold.

In spite of these ominous signs and the heavy cost of subsidising grain for local consumption during the prevalent drought, Hofmeyr could show a surprisingly good surplus and risk presenting 'a rich man's Budget.' There was something for nearly everyone in his tax remissions of some £15,500,000, which included cheaper postage and petrol, gentler treatment for the harassed goldmines, and the abolition, first, of the Special Trade Profits Levy and then of the even more widely detested Excess Profits Duty, which had too often been dodged by nimble-witted businessmen, who had taken the hints dropped by a couple of the Finance Minister's colleagues that they should 'salt away' their profits till these could be paid out as dividends in happier days.[3] An important addendum to the Budget was furnished by Smuts. Rather than follow the example of Southern Rhodesia, Australia and some other members of the Commonwealth by cutting down the importation of costly United States goods and thus curtailing dollar expenditure, he induced the House to sanction a gold loan of £80,000,000 to the United Kingdom. He justified the loan as 'good business' on the plea that South Africa might as well devote her 'substantial gold reserve' to reconstruction as leave it lying idle, and thereby help the struggling United Kingdom, and, through her, the whole sterling *bloc*. Good business the loan certainly was, for though it would only yield South Africa interest at one-half per cent., it could be recalled in whole or in part if ever her gold reserves fell below the £100,000,000 mark, and was to be repaid in any event at the end of three years during which nearly half of it would have been spent on the purchase of South African foodstuffs, fruit and wine.[4] This last stipulation won the approval of the largely rural Nationalists, whose leader was by no means averse to keeping his country's best customer on her feet; even so, the loan failed to achieve one of its avowed ends, because such money as it mopped up was soon more than replaced. New money poured in from June 1947 onwards, either in the form of dollars drawn from London by

[1] *Round Table*, No. 149, p. 509; No. 154, pp. 182 ff.
[2] *Chronology*, III., No. 11, p. 320.   [3] *Round Table*, No. 147, pp. 301 ff.
[4] *Ibid.*, No. 149, p. 509; *Chronology*, III., No. 20, p. 610.

South Africans in exchange for the sterling proceeds of local deals in shares or real property at inflated prices, or of funds brought in by well-to-do immigrant British income tax dodgers, whose extravagance reflected little credit on themselves, their new country or their old.[1]

While the Union's supply of mere money thus surged upwards once more and the tide of immigration from the United Kingdom and other parts of Europe mounted ever higher, Nehru fell foul of Smuts. At the end of an acid correspondence in which he had failed to induce him to resume relations with India on his terms, the Pundit called upon the General Assembly of U.N.O. to insist that South Africa bow to its recent resolutions on the local Indian problem and respect those clauses of its Charter which covered 'fundamental freedoms without distinction of race, language and religion.'[2]

Irritated though Smuts was at this prospect of further trouble with an international body of which he had expected so much and from which he had received so little, he flew to London in November 1947 to witness the wedding of Princess Elizabeth, the Heiress Apparent, and Philip, Duke of Edinburgh, and to take his seat on the so-called 'Half Conference,' that poor substitute for the traditional Imperial Conference, which consisted merely of the British Ministers concerned, Mackenzie King, Prime Minister of Canada, and the High Commissioners of the other Dominions, including newly-promoted India and Pakistan. He perused with pleasure the General Agreement, which had recently been signed at Geneva by the United Kingdom, the Dominions, Southern Rhodesia and newly-self-governing Ceylon, providing for the reduction or even the abolition of specific margins of imperial preferences in exchange for the lowering of tariff walls by the United States and other highly protected countries.[3] Then, having taken seizin of the little Marion and Prince Edward Islands some fourteen hundred miles off the Union's southeast coast,[4] he returned home to hear the good news that the United States was offering financial aid to depressed Europe in terms of the recently launched Marshall Plan, to hail hopefully the suggestion of Ernest Bevin, the British Foreign Secretary, that splintered Europe be integrated, to take preliminary steps towards the working of his country's 'considerable uranium reserves,' and to discuss defence with the Union's military leaders and Montgomery, the victor of Alamein and now Chief of the Imperial General Staff. Defence bade fair to become a pressing problem, not only to keep Communism out of Africa, but to enable the Commonwealth to maintain itself

---

[1] *Round Table*, No. 154, p. 183.
[2] *Chronology*, III., No. 16, p. 468; No. 20, pp. 606-7.
[3] *Round Table*, No. 150, p. 622.
[4] *Chronology*, III., No. 23, p. 704; IV., No. 1, p. 20.

in the 'entirely new alignment of world power' that was being brought about by the severance of the Communist East from the capitalistic West, an end which could only be achieved by an organisation which should include not only the states of the Commonwealth, but also the United States, 'the mainstay of the Western group,' and the truly democratic European Powers. Thus might there be 'a new birth of time' and the salvation of 'our Western civilisation.'[1]

At the New Year of 1948, Smuts visited South-West Africa and, true to his repeated promises, offered its Legislature wider powers and the Territory itself representation in the Union Parliament; but he declined to commit himself one way or the other to the demand that South Africa should help its dependency to carry its railway northward into tropical Ovamboland, or accede to the widespread desire of Southern Rhodesians that their railway system should be linked with Walvis Bay by way of the Bechuanaland Protectorate. This done, he returned home to prepare for the coming general election and, as the first step, reshuffled some ministerial portfolios leaving Education to Hofmeyr, but transferring Finance to Frederick Sturrock, and entrusting the Interior to Harry Lawrence, Transport to Waterson and Economic Development to Mushet.[2]

In spite of the recent growth of Nationalist strength, in the Free State and Cape Province especially, Malan and Havenga had very little hope that their electoral pact would give them the thirty additional Assembly seats they must have to give them a majority, and even the sanguine Swart could counsel them merely to work for victory five years hence. The United Party, whose main strength lay in the Transvaal, Natal and the Cape, had an electoral pact with Christie's Labour Party, but nothing of the sort with the Dominion Party, which, with a belated sense of humour, now renamed itself the South African Party, and still less with the anti-Christie group of Labour men who rallied to a Natal zealot as the Centre Party.

The Ministerialists stood upon their not wholly defensible record. The Opposition accepted the challenge and summoned to its aid an unpredictable mass of supporters, who, like it, were not concerned overmuch with the Western civilisation on which the Prime Minister set such store, but almost exclusively with the preservation of the little pocket of white civilisation in South Africa. In short, Malan and Havenga showed that their main aim was to succeed where van Reibeeck and so many of his successors had failed by achieving *apartheid*, that is, segregation writ large, the permanent physical, mental and, as far as might be, spiritual separation of the four great racial groups in the Union each from the other, partly to preserve the racial purity of each, partly to do away with the friction that

[1] *Chronology*, III., No. 23, p. 704; No. 24, p. 743.
[2] *Round Table*, No. 151, p. 667; *Chronology*, IV., No. 2, p. 57.

25

arose from intermingling and partly to give each the chance of developing along its own lines in its own appointed place.

The theory of *apartheid* had been worked out during the past couple of years principally by Professors at Stellenbosch, 'the heart of intellectual nationalism.' A group which included Dr. Theophilus Dönges, future Minister of the Interior, Dr. Ernest Jansen, ex-Speaker and future Minister of Native Affairs and Governor-General, Dr. Nicolaas Diederichs, Professor Werner Eiselen future Secretary of Native Affairs, Professor Andries Cilliers, Professor Bernardus van Eeden, Colonel Stallard leader of the Dominion Party, and others had met at Stellenbosch in 1947 and there formed *Die Suid-Afrikaanse Buro vir Rasse Aangeleenthede* (the South African Bureau of Race Relations). Their primary aims were to counteract the work of the liberal Institute of Race Relations, to conduct research into racial problems and to advise thereon. Taking it for granted that white prejudice on the score of colour was unalterable, they worked out a well-reasoned case for *apartheid* based on European supremacy. It was no mere blue-print for oppression, but in many ways an idealistic programme for the protection of the interests of each racial group and the fostering of goodwill and co-operation between them by the complete segregation of each group, including, of course, the white folk. Such segregation, the authors observed truly, would merely make compulsory a process that was already far advanced on a more or less voluntary basis, for nearly all the inhabitants of the Union were averse to the mixing of the races, some of the Christian Churches practised the traditional social segregation, and Indians and Bantu, if not the Coloured Folk also, understood residential segregation well enough. For the rest, S.A.B.R.A. looked forward to an ultimate federation of 'racial States' within the Union and subject to its Government, though beyond assuming that the Reserves were somehow to become the 'fatherland' of the Bantu majority, it did not indicate where the other races were to find the areas in which they were to 'develop along their own lines,' whatever those lines might be. Some of its members realised that the Reserves were inadequate; indeed, Eiselen and Cilliers proposed that the Union's eight million Africans should be pushed bodily northward of the Limpopo river, though they did not say whether this should be into Southern Rhodesia or the Belgian Congo. Diederichs, on the other hand, hoped merely to stave off the Bantu flood as long as possible and, meanwhile, to act on the principle that 'the corner-stone of Nationalist doctrine was that races which differed funda-mentally and naturally must be kept apart from each other to the advantage of both.' Nevertheless, it was he who led the attack on liberalism, in his eyes the worst enemy of the non-Europeans, which 'for the sake of the material and industrial benefits' of the white folk sought to deny to other peoples 'the right of their own society and their own fatherland' in which they could develop as 'independent' nations. Here, S.A.B.R.A. could reckon on the support of very many of those Europeans who were not directly interested in mining or secondary industry; but it was less assured of this when it gave frank warning that, when *apartheid* had been achieved, white folk would have to do much more of their own work and face an unwelcome wholesale immigration, if they were to get the necessary skilled workers, servants and so forth.[1]

The *apartheid* policy had been summarised for election purposes in a pamphlet, whose authors recommended the idea as a product of 'the experience of the established European population . . . based on the Christian principles of justice and reasonableness,' and proposed to prohibit mixed marriages, to set up a body of experts in non-European affairs, and to empower the authorities to supervise 'the moulding of the youth' and forbid 'destructive propaganda' carried on by outsiders against the Union's handling of its racial problems. They laid special stress on the position of the Cape Coloured Folk midway between the Europeans and the Bantu, urging that, on the one hand, they be protected against Bantu competition and encouraged to make Christianity 'the basis of their lives' and that, on the other, they be segregated in every possible way. Politically, they were to be represented in the Upper House by a white Senator nominated for his knowledge of their affairs, but were to forgo 'the present unhealthy system' of the common roll and be placed on a roll of their own and elect to the Assembly three Europeans, who, however, might not vote on motions of confidence, declarations of war or changes in the political rights of non-Europeans. They were further to elect in the same way three Europeans to the Cape Provincial Council as well as all the elective members of a Coloured Representative Council for the Cape Province, who were to sit beside a few white officials under the chairmanship of the head of the Coloured Affairs Department. Thus might the Cape Coloured Folk look forward to having, within their own, as yet, unspecified areas, their own Councils and their own police managed by themselves 'within the framework of the existing Councils with higher authority.'[2]

In his election manifesto of April 21, 1948, Malan naturally made the most of the Government's shortcomings; but he dropped all his more or less anti-British and anti-Semitic talk, and did what he could to reassure doubters by undertaking to look after the interests of ex-Service folk, offering to help the anti-Communist forces if ever

[1] *Round Table*, No. 152, pp. 814 ff.; No. 153, p. 33; Hatch, *op. cit.*, pp. 28 ff.; Patterson, *op. cit.*, p. 218; Davidson, *op. cit.*, p. 27.
[2] *The National Party's Colour Policy*; Hatch, *op. cit.*, pp. 37 ff.

Russia became aggressive, and promising to put his scheme for a republic into cold storage during the life of the coming Parliament. But though he made no mention of the political gains he hoped to secure for his own party by the segregation of Coloured voters, he did not conceal the fact that the fear against which Smuts had so often inveighed lay at the back of his own *apartheid* policy by asking whether the European race meant to 'maintain its rule, its purity and its civilisation' or merely be content to 'float along' till it vanished without honour 'in the black sea of South Africa's non-European population.' He called upon the white folk to save themselves 'without oppression and with (due regard) to the natural rights of non-Europeans to a proper living and their right to their own development in accordance with their own requirements and capabilities.' He proposed that, for a start, the Bantu be deprived of all representation in Parliament and the Cape Provincial Council.[1]

Less moderate politicians than Malan gave this appeal to racial pride and exclusiveness a personal turn by concentrating their attacks on Hofmeyr, whom they accused of condemning South Africa to become the home of 'a coffee-coloured race' by reason of his advocacy of full political equality for non-Europeans, regardless of the fact that little enough of that kind of thing had happened during the long century of that equality in the old Cape Colony. The Prime Minister, moreover, a party tactician far inferior to his rival, had played into Malan's hands. Thrice since the end of the war he had deprived himself of likely supporters by making it more difficult for Coloured voters to register, especially those many who feared to face intimidation at the hands of policemen who so often served as registration officers, and now, on the eve of the poll, he recognised the new State of Israel with unnecessary haste and thereby threw away the votes of many English-speaking voters, who had no love for Jews of any kind and a bitter hatred of the gunmen of Palestine who were murdering British soldiers right and left.[2] In the event, Malan's Nationalists and Havenga's Afrikaner Party men narrowly won the general election on May 26, 1948, to their own surprise and to the dismay particularly of those Ministers and their wives who had confidently left their belongings in their official residences while they went campaigning and now had to ask their unlooked-for successors for a few days' grace in which to take them away. Christie's Labour Party retained a mere six seats, the little Central Party failed to win any, the remains of Stallard's South African Party were wiped out and the United Party fared ill.[3] Smuts's

[1] *Round Table*, No. 152, pp. 815 ff.
[2] Acts 40 of 1945, 46 of 1946 and 50 of 1948; L. Thompson, *The Cape Coloured Franchise*.
[3] *Chronology*, IV., No. 11, p. 369.

followers indeed polled some 150,000 more votes than their principal opponents, but they had done so only by registering overwhelming majorities in the comparatively few urban constituencies, while those opponents had gained far more seats in the over-represented rural areas, albeit with small majorities. The upshot was that the allied Opposition parties held a tiny majority of five in the vital House of Assembly. The Nationalists had won twenty-five seats from the United Party and the Afrikaner Party seven; together, they had driven that party from virtually every Afrikaans-speaking constituency in the country and, in the anti-British Transvaal, had seen Smuts himself deprived of his seat at Standerton which he had held for a quarter of a century. Though they did not know it, they had almost driven Smuts out of public life, for he was so shocked by his defeat that he thought seriously of giving up politics and was only induced to find himself a safe seat in Pretoria East by the thought of the defeated Churchill still marching on and, more certainly, by the pleadings of Senator Andrew Conroy.[1]

Smuts resigned forthwith, just as Judge Fagan presented his report on migratory labour, the Bantu pass laws and the rest. Whether Smuts would have implemented what might have been an epoch-making report will never be known. It was certain that his successor would not. Malan made haste to announce his Ministry and at once showed that his policy of *apartheid* was to be applied to white politicians on a linguistic and cultural basis. Ignoring the un-broken seventy years' sequence of mixed English and Afrikaans-speaking ministries in the old Cape Colony and the Union, he observed that co-operation had not yet gone far enough to warrant his forming such a ministry himself. Therefore, to guide a House which was more nearly divided than ever before along Afrikaner *versus* British lines, he chose colleagues who were all Afrikaners and, although sufficiently bilingual, all primarily Afrikaans-speaking. He himself became Prime Minister and Minister of External Affairs, and entrusted the portfolios of Finance once more to Havenga, sole representative in the Cabinet of the Afrikaner Party on which he was dependent for his majority.[2]

Smuts found much consolation for the descent of 'this blight . . . this Broederbond Government' upon South Africa in his simultaneous, unanimous and, to himself, unexpected election as Chancellor

---

[1] *Chronology*, IV., No. 14, p. 499; J. C. Smuts, *op. cit.*, p. 512; *Round Table*, No. 152, pp. 814 ff.

[2] The remaining members of the Ministry were Dr. Ernest George Jansen, Native Affairs; Johannes Gerhardus Strydom, Lands; Paul Oliver Sauer, Transport; Charles Robberts Swart, Justice; Dr. Eric Louw, Economic Development and Mines; Dr. Theophilus Ebenhaezer Dönges, Interior and Posts and Telegraphs; Stephanus Petrus le Roux, Agriculture; François Christiaan Erasmus, Defence; Barend Jacobus Schoeman, Labour and Public Works; Albert Jacobus Stals, Education. (*Chronology*, IV., No. 11, p. 369.)

to his old English University. Stressing the fact that Cambridge had thus paid a compliment to the whole of the British Commonwealth which he had served so long and so well, he flew to England on the morrow of the poll to be installed and, with a glance at the recent Russian-inspired *coup d'état* in democratic Czechoslovakia, to bid his hearers beware of Communism. But he bade them put first things first, and to him 'the greatest task for the world' was the salving of shattered Europe now so fatally partitioned between the Powers of the East and the West. 'The battle for Europe has begun,' he cried, 'and must not end before final victory is attained.' With this trumpet-call, he passed on to receive an Honorary Doctorate of Laws in the University of Leyden in his ancestral Netherlands, and thence returned home to salvage what he could of Western civilisation in his own country.[1]

CHAPTER XVII

COMMUNISM, COLOUR AND THE COURTS, 1948-55

MALAN AND HAVENGA

IMMEDIATELY after taking office Dr. Malan made haste to thank his supporters and, in especial, those many English-speaking electors

[1] J. C. Smuts, *op. cit.*, pp. 513, 521; *Chronology*, IV, No. 12, p. 409.

who had voted for him. He sought to remove lingering doubts by promising equal rights to all white South Africans and disavowing all thought of isolation far more specifically than ever before. He recognised South Africa's partnership in the comity of nations, undertook to retain membership of the United Nations Organisation so long as that body did not interfere in his country's domestic affairs, and freely acknowledged the Union's 'particularly friendly relations' with the United Kingdom and other members of the British Commonwealth with all of whom he proposed to co-operate so long as that did not prejudice his country's status and freedom of action as 'a sovereign independent State.' Recalling that the prickly Nehru's India was now a full member of the Commonwealth, he expressed the opinion that this co-operation could be attained better by making 'independent contacts' with this member or that than by taking part in 'discussions at general and all-embracing Conferences.' Finally, in the hope of securing peaceful mutual relations and co-operation at home, he reaffirmed his conviction that it was only under a system of *apartheid* that non-Europeans could enjoy 'a greater independence and feeling of self-respect . . . as well as . . . better opportunities for free development in accordance with their nature and abilities,' and Europeans could feel sure that 'their identity and their future' were protected.[1]

Thus far an honest and humane Prime Minister. Unfortunately, what he and his colleagues did was not so reassuring. They at once stopped the training of Bantu artisans, warned would-be immigrants that they would have to conform to the regulations much more strictly than hitherto, permitted public servants once more to join the *Broederbond* and *Ossewabrandwag*, appointed 'Grievance Commissions,' which reinstated in the Police and other services without loss of seniority those 'poor people' who had been the 'victims' of the late Administration, and moved their opponents to wrath and their own followers to an outburst of hero-worship by releasing Robey Leibbrandt and four other notorious traitors, who had been imprisoned during the recent war for treason and sabotage.[2] The Minister of Defence, Erasmus, began to re-arm the backveld against the Communist peril which was as yet non-existent in those regions, and went far to destroying the morale of the fast-dwindling armed forces by his scarcely disguised racialism. For instance, when advancing years obliged General Pierre van Ryneveld to resign from the office of Chief of the General Staff, he set aside his obvious successor, Major-General Edward Poole, the Deputy C.G.S., on the grounds that his Intelligence Department had reported adversely on the doings of the Nationalist Party during and since the Axis war

[1] *Round Table*, No. 152, pp. 816 ff.; *Chronology*, IV., No. 12, pp. 420–1.
[2] *Ibid.*, IV., No. 12, p. 421.

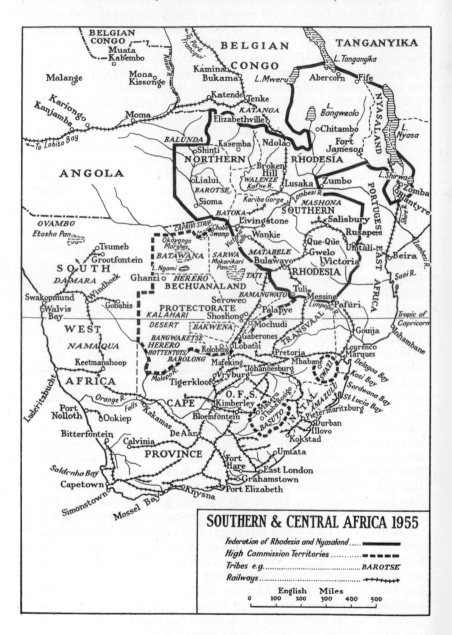

SOUTHERN & CENTRAL AFRICA 1955

Federation of Rhodesia and Nyasaland .....
High Commission Territories ....
Tribes e.g. .... BAROTSE
Railways ....

English   Miles
0   100   200   300   400   500

and that he himself had, thereafter, allowed it to destroy various office files.[1] Poole was shipped off out of harm's way to distant Berlin as head of a Military Mission and the vacancy filled by a good Afrikaner, General Len Beyers.

Depending as Malan did on the Afrikaner Party for his small majority in the Assembly and a bare half of the votes in the reconstituted Senate,[2] his tenure of power was precarious. Moreover, he himself was a man of seventy-four by no means in the best of health and well aware that, when he should be gone, there would be a fierce struggle for the succession between the veteran but indispensable Havenga and, probably, three much younger and more downright men: first, the Free Stater, Swart, Minister of Justice; secondly, Dönges, the leading Cape Nationalist after himself and now Minister for the Interior, and, lastly, and perhaps the strongest candidate of all, Strydom, leader of the Transvaal Nationalists and Minister of Lands. Be that as it might, Parliament met on August 6, 1948, and at once faced the problem of finance.

'Lucky Havenga's' good fortune had held to this extent that the country was outwardly prosperous and he himself heir to a surplus of £8,500,000, which was due mainly to the recent payment of many arrears of income tax. Beneath the surface, however, all was not so well. True to tradition, the outgoing Finance Minister had left him free to present his own Budget; but neither Hofmeyr nor his colleagues had been able to enforce that diminution of imports which alone could have checked the drain on the gold reserve or close the dangerous 'dollar gap'; indeed, such had been the continuing orgy of dollar spending that the Union had had to draw on the sterling pool to meet her trading deficit.[3] There was, indeed, still much money in the banks, but some £100,000,000 of this was unstable 'hot money.' Again, such had been the blow to confidence given by the unexpected Nationalist victory that fully £200,000,000 had been withdrawn since Malan took office. Meanwhile, the total cost of dollar imports stood well above the value of the new annual gold production, and the statutory limit of the Reserve Bank's gold-cover had almost been reached. When this should have sunk to £100,000,000 there might be nothing for it but to recall the recent gold loan to the United Kingdom in whole or in part, unless indeed the situation could be saved by the reimposition of import controls. This Havenga was loth to do. In the event, it was only in November 1948 that he reluctantly prohibited the importation of certain luxury goods, fixed the amount of the dollar-exchange for the year beginning in July 1948 at a mere fifty per cent. of that for the past year and, though he did allow additional quotas for the importation

---

[1] *Chronology*, IV, No. 17, p. 587. [2] *Ibid.*, IV., No. 15, p. 532.
[3] *Round Table*, No. 152, pp. 814 ff.; No. 154, pp. 182 ff.

25*

of some capital goods and other essentials, took retrospective action against those greedy traders who had rushed in as many such imports as they could before controls should come again.[1] Point was given to this warning that the Union's currency was by no means so 'hard' as many folk had supposed by the fact that the adverse trade balance for the year just ended was the largest in the country's history. Despite these ominous signs, the Budget contained many tax-remissions, notably to individual income-tax payers, but it also provided for the heavy additional expenditure that arose from the increased pensions and allowances prescribed by the Smuts administration and, for the rest, left Indians wondering whether they were to get either benefit and the Bantu in no doubt whatever by withholding both.[2]

Apart from the repeal of the recently-granted Indian representation in Parliament and the Natal Provincial Council, the output of legislation was slight.[3] Rather did Ministers have recourse to that departmental legislation 'as the Minister may direct,' which their predecessors had tended to relinquish in their last days. By these means they abandoned Native housing schemes and plastered post offices, booking offices and suburban railway coaches in the hitherto comparatively immune Cape Peninsula with *apartheid* notices in both the official languages and, now that there were so many Bantu in those parts, in more than one African tongue bidding folk of the various colours to use only those facilities that were set apart for them.[4] When, however, enthusiasts urged that all Bantu be driven into the Reserves, the Minister of Economic Affairs revealed the fundamental weakness of the whole *apartheid* policy by warning them that if they did any such thing, secondary industry must collapse. Nevertheless, Malan showed that he meant to go ahead with that policy, for when Smuts asked him whether he would respect the entrenched clauses of the South Africa Act when it came to abolishing what remained of Bantu parliamentary representation, he replied that he would take high legal advice as to whether or no those clauses had been rendered nugatory by the sovereignty granted to the Union Parliament by the Statute of Westminster of 1931.[5] Then, as a step towards *apartheid*, he dropped Smuts's recent attempt to induce Union and Provincial authorities to employ at least more Coloured Folk and circularised all Departments bidding them substitute Poor Whites for Bantu.[6] Meanwhile, Dönges warned future immigrants that they would be selected by a 'more discriminatory

---

[1] *Round Table*, No. 154, pp. 184 ff.; *Chronology*, IV., No. 21, p. 738.
[2] *Round Table*, No. 153, pp. 92 ff.
[3] Asiatic Laws Amendment Act (Act 47 of 1948).
[4] *Round Table*, No. 153, p. 32.   [5] *Ibid.*, No. 153, p. 35.
[6] Patterson, *op. cit.*, pp. 69 ff.; *Chronology*, IV., No. 19, p. 658; *Race Relations Summary*, 1949–50, p. 61.

process' than hitherto, and that, while the authorities would honour their obligations to such of them as had already booked passages and to the wives and families of newcomers who had already arrived, they would spend no more public money on the provision of transport and see to it that no more special immigrant ships should sail after the end of the year.[1]

Ministers then turned their attention to external affairs. Malan first pointedly affirmed the Union's rights of neutrality and secession, which few denied, and then eagerly assured John Costello, the new Prime Minister in Dublin, that if he made the Irish Free State a republic, South Africa would recognise the new State and give it reciprocal rights of citizenship, provided that this step was not regarded as a precedent applicable to other states outside the Commonwealth.[2] He also approved officially of the Council of Foreign Ministers' plan to place Italy's late African colonies under either British, French or Italian Trusteeship, and suggested the formation of a Pan-African Alliance which should forward the salvage of Europe and ensure to Africans the blessings of Western civilisation and immunity from Communism.[3] Having reasserted his claim that the Indian problem was purely domestic and his country's right to incorporate South-West Africa, he explained that he was set, not upon full incorporation, but merely on the 'closer integration,' whose details he had discussed with the rival United and Nationalist parties in the Mandated Territory.[4] This done, he appointed Charles te Water as South Africa's 'roving ambassador of goodwill' and, before the Session was ended, sent his Minister of Economic Affairs upon his travels.

Before setting out, Eric Louw explained to all and sundry that his country was not against immigration as such, that it was applying restrictions to all alike, and that, in any event, it could not absorb large numbers of newcomers at the moment. He followed this up with a fair and reasonable account of the principles of the *apartheid* policy, but spoiled it by alleging that most of the South African Indians' grievances were 'all moonshine' and that not one in thirty of these Asiatics cared a straw about the United Nations' agitation on their behalf. Having thus assured himself of a hesitant welcome, this brash young man took his seat at the Conference of Commonwealth Prime Ministers in London and the General Assembly of U.N.O. in Paris. At neither did he effect much; but he did tell the assembled Prime Ministers, at his chief's direction, that South Africa held by the Commonwealth of her 'own free will and not under pressure' and, as his own contribution, that she would continue to do so only on the basis of 'South Africa first.' Malan, for his part,

---

[1] *Chronology*, IV., No. 16, p. 560; No. 22, p. 771.
[2] *Ibid.*, IV., No. 23, p. 808.   [3] *Ibid.*, IV., No. 17, p. 587.
[4] *Ibid.*, No. 20, p. 709.

intimated that he could wish to see his High Commissioner in London raised to the rank of Ambassador, and that he would rather leave U.N.O., that 'menace to liberty,' than subject South-West Africa to its Trusteeship Council.[1]

Meanwhile, the necessarily involved *apartheid* programme had hung fire. One powerful opponent was, indeed, removed when Hofmeyr died on December 3, 1948.[2] A difficult colleague he may have been, but he had also been the most outspoken South African champion of civilisation since Schreiner. Hence, his passing was an irreparable blow to the dwindling forces of liberalism and almost more than Smuts could bear, following so swiftly as it did the deaths of his own eldest son and his industrial right-hand man, Dr. Hendrik van der Byl. Worse still, from the purely practical point of view, the passing of such a loyal and indefatigable helper as Hofmeyr left Smuts to hold the fissiparous United Party together almost single-handed, because the rest of his late colleagues were so far from rich and so busied with finding their feet again in their aforetime everyday avocations that they could not spare much time for politics.[3] But if these things promised to help Malan, others threatened to baulk him. It was not so much that the Annual Assembly of the Baptist Union and the Anglican Bishops of the Church of the Province condemned his policy as a scheme for giving the white folk 'the exclusive benefits of Western civilisation,' as that, on the very day of Hofmeyr's death, Havenga dug his heels in.[4] The Finance Minister and his little Party, on whom success depended, refused to have anything to do either with the abolition of the Bantu franchise or the relegation of Coloured voters to a separate roll till there was a far more 'adequate majority' in favour of such measures than that which they and the Nationalists possessed. In spite of the Prime Minister's assurances that 'high legal authority' indeed held that the Statute of Westminster had freed Parliament from all need to conform to the procedure laid down in the entrenched franchise clauses of the South Africa Act, in spite also of Strydom's vehement insistence that resistance to *apartheid* was as treasonable as refusal to bear arms in the country's defence, Havenga stood his ground and obliged Malan to face the fact that he could not go much further with his cherished policy until either he or the times did alter.[5]

Held up thus on the main front, Malan nevertheless showed what was in his mind by forbidding citizens of India and Pakistan to fly over Union soil without special passes, and telling the recalcitrant Native Representative Council that, because it had been a failure, it must make way for local councils enjoying some small measure of

---

[1] *Chronology*, IV., No. 14, p. 499.
[2] *Round Table*, No. 154, p. 103; *Chronology*, IV., No. 23, p. 809.
[3] J. C. Smuts, *op. cit.*, p. 576.   [4] Sachs, *op. cit.*, p. 63.
[5] Hatch, *op. cit.*, p. 62; *Chronology*, IV., No. 23, p. 809.

autonomy.[1] A pair of his colleagues then showed that they were far more resolutely opposed to freedom of thought, word and movement than he. First, Dönges stopped Dr. Gungathura Naiker and another radical leader of the S.A. Indian National Congress from attending a meeting of U.N.O., and Sachs of the hated Garment Workers' Union from going to Europe to take his seat in the Trade Union Congress by confiscating their passports. A little later, however, he burned his fingers when he tried to get possession of Sachs's renewed passport and unseat Ballinger, who had just been elected to the Senate by the Bantu, on the grounds that he was not a Union National. In due time, the Appellate Division upheld the new Senator and allowed Sachs's appeal with costs.[2] The Minister of Education then cut down drastically the grants for the feeding of Bantu schoolchildren, that is, for those who needed it most, on the plea that they should be encouraged to become self-supporting,[3] and next in quick succession, withdrew the five medical scholarships awarded by the Government to Bantu students at each of the liberal Universities of the Witwatersrand and Capetown. His restoration of three to each in face of protests did not satisfy the two bodies of undergraduates, who promptly subscribed the money for the remainder. He then tried vainly to induce these two 'colour blind' Universities to become as officially pure white as were the Nationalist Afrikaner Universities of Stellenbosch, Bloemfontein, Pretoria and predominantly 'Dopper' Potchefstroom, and, in his zeal for the ultra-Calvinist theory of Christian National education which had its fountain-head at the last-named seat of learning, relieved its authorities of the conscience clause and thus set them free to apply religious tests to applicants for teaching posts.[4]

After passports, Senators, schoolchildren and Universities came trade unions. Doubtless Schoeman, Minister of Labour, had held by his promise not to meddle with their domestic affairs;[5] but others had plainly suffered from no such inhibitions. On September 16, 1948, a white mob broke up a meeting of some three thousand members of the Garment Workers, who were listening to Sachs's report on a highly favourable wage award made by impartial arbitrators. Protests to the Minister of Justice did not earn even a reply. Rather did that eminent Free Stater leave it to Schoeman to appoint a Commission consisting of a retired Magistrate and the Magistrate of a petty dorp in his own Province, whose legalistic and small-town ideas of the proper functions and aims of urban trade unions could be trusted to impel them to busy themselves with indicting the Garment Workers' Union for its lawful exercise of discipline by expelling *Hervormer* troublemakers during the past few

---

[1] *Chronology*, V., No. 1, p. 20.   [2] Hatch, *op. cit.*, p. 64; Sachs, *op. cit.*, p. 80.
[3] Hatch, *op. cit.*, p. 67; Davidson, *op. cit.*, pp. 86–7.
[4] Hatch, *op. cit.*, p. 66.   [5] *Chronology*, V., No. 4, p. 119.

years rather than with investigating the recent outrage. In spite of protests by the S.A. Trades and Labour Council, these magistrates wasted a year and £5000 of the taxpayers' money by ignoring most of the aggrieved union's evidence and accepting that of its foes, of whom the chief was an expelled 'imbecile,' others of them folk who had simply been expelled from the union with no reflection on their sanity, and nearly all members of the Action Committee of the hostile *Blankebeskermingsbond*. Their report was virtually a vicious attack on Sachs and his union, including the accusation that Sachs had entertained delegates of various colours in his own home. They found, indeed, that the 'imbecile' witness had been guilty of a crime by inciting to and participating in the uproar under review; but this did not convince the Minister of Justice that there was sufficient evidence to warrant his prosecution. On the other hand, their report assuredly moved the Minister of Labour, who recalled that Sachs had been a Red in days long gone by, to warn the House of Assembly that the authorities might be compelled to interfere in trade union domestic matters, because some eighty of those unions, European and Coloured, were dominated by Communists.[1]

This scarcely-veiled threat was a direct incitement to Albertus Hertzog and his friend, Dr. Diederichs, to smash or, preferably, gain control of trade unions. These two men had long been paying special attention to the white Building Workers', Transport Workers' and Mineworkers' Unions. This last-named powerful body had struck a couple of years back in an unsuccessful attempt to get rid of its General Secretary, who worked under a closed shop agreement in alliance with the Chamber of Mines. In February 1947, some six thousand of its members, calling themselves the United Mineworkers' Union, had struck again ostensibly to oust the dominant clique, but really to get control in the interests of the Nationalist Party. Smuts had tried to smooth the trouble over by appointing a Commission to hold fresh elections. In the event, the bulk of these elections were held, under Government auspices, only after Malan has assumed power. Then, a Committee of out-and-out Nationalists was returned under whose guidance the Mineworkers' Union ceased to be a force in the genuine trade union movement.[2]

There now came a reminder that intolerance and racialism were not monopolies of the white folk. At Durban in January 1949 a Zulu lad slapped a young Indian shop assistant in the course of an alter-cation. He was himself assaulted by the latter's Indian master out-side and was badly cut when his head was smashed through the shop window in full view of a crowd of Zulus and Indians waiting for a bus. At the sight of blood, the Zulus, who had long nursed grudges real and imaginary against Indians, 'went berserk' and the Indians,

[1] Sachs, *op. cit.*, pp. 179 ff.
[2] *Ibid.*, pp. 171 ff.

who had no love for Zulus, retaliated. During the ensuing sporadic fighting many on both sides were injured and much property was destroyed before police and hurriedly drafted troops could restore order. The rioting broke out again next day with the Zulus as a rule taking the offensive determined this time 'to be rid of Indians' once and for all, and the Indians as a body clamouring for protection here, there and everywhere all at the same time. On the other hand, some of the wealthier Indians, whose purchase of European property had brought their community into ill odour with their white neighbours, and whose arrogance had offended many of their humbler co-religionists, fired at Zulus from the windows of their swiftly-moving cars. When, however, the authorities had at last got the rioting under, the Indian rank and file again became 'truculent, provocative and aggressive.' Indeed, the trouble spread to Pietermaritzburg, where the manager of the Native Administration Department complained that the local Indians were provoking the Zulus, who, left to themselves, had no wish to make trouble, and even to far-distant Johannesburg, whence the Transvaal Indian Congress demanded that the white South African Defence League be forbidden to clamour for the expulsion of all Indians. Malan stationed troops in the disturbed areas, especially in Durban, and then appointed a Judicial Commission of Inquiry. This Commission duly exonerated the authorities from all blame for not having foreseen the utterly unexpected outbreak, and then recorded that three hundred buildings had been destroyed and seventeen hundred damaged, and that 147 persons had been killed and 1087 injured, more than half of them Zulus. In view of the wide publicity given by the local Indian press to alleged Zulu atrocities, it is well to record that the final comment was made by the Courts which presently gave three Indians heavy prison sentences for culpable homicide.[1]

It was against this stormy background that Parliament met. The Speech from the Throne foreshadowed, first, co-operation as far as 'the particular interests' of South Africa were concerned with the North Atlantic Treaty Organisation, which had recently been formed for mutual defence by the United Kingdom, the United States and several democratic Western European states; then, steps to control Communism and, finally, the fostering of a better understanding with U.N.O., an understanding that was scarcely bettered by Louw's truculent reminder that the Union would no longer report on South-West Africa. Having appointed a Commission to report on the whole policy of *apartheid*, the House turned to finance.[2] In his Budget speech, Havenga scouted the idea that the country was heading for bankruptcy seeing that it still held £50,000,000 in gold besides a

---

[1] *Chronology*, V., No. 2, pp. 54–5; No. 6, p. 183; No. 8, p. 264; No. 11, p. 368; U.G. 36–49, *Report of the Committee of Enquiry into Riots in Durban.*

[2] *Chronology*, V., No. 4, p. 119; No. 7, p. 223; No. 8, p. 254; *Round Table*, No. 155, pp. 288 ff.

statutory gold reserve of £36,000,000; but the goldmines, with their dwindling output, were failing him; he had had the greatest difficulty in raising a domestic loan and that almost entirely by institutional subscriptions, and he had to confess, to Smuts's fury, that he had already recalled £15,000,000 of the recent gold loan to the United Kingdom to help South Africa balance her payments. Faced as he was with the problem of reducing overseas payments by more than half, he proposed to lengthen the list of prohibited imports, apply a new system of controls to all imports from overseas, and curtail drastically the transfer of funds to non-dollar areas. This was by no means the end of the story. So fast did exchange of all kinds drain away that, before the Session ended in June 1949, a six-month ban had had to be put on the importation of all consumer goods save those that had been shipped from the United Kingdom or ordered from the United States in conformity with the exchange control regulations before the end of that month, the Director of Imports and Exports had been empowered to cancel any document he might have issued, and yet more of the gold loan had been recalled from the United Kingdom.[1] Meanwhile, the Reserve Bank had re-verted to its old policy of mopping up superfluous cash by calling on banks, insurance companies, building societies and the like to find £1,000,000 wherewith to finance a Corporation, which should accept funds seeking short-term investment and re-invest them in Government stocks, Municipal stocks and Treasury Bills with re-discount facilities afforded by itself.

Some slight advance was meanwhile made towards *apartheid*. Racial complications were intensified in post offices and on the railways, Indians were offered a larger bribe to leave the country, the Native Representative Council was told that it would not be summoned again, and the vexed question of racially mixed trade unions was referred to a Commission. Next, the Mixed Marriages Act prescribed criminal penalties for those very few Europeans and Cape Coloured Folk who might marry one another, and the Unemployment Insurance Act deprived the Bantu of benefits.[2] Two purely political measures promised to have more far-reaching effects. The first of these enabled Germans to recover the citizenship of which they had been deprived during the Axis war, while the second, the South-West African Affairs Amendment Act, went as near as well could be towards incorporating the Mandated Territory by giving the 26,000 European voters gross over-representation in the Union Parliament through two elected Senators and two more nominated for their knowledge of the wants and wishes of the unrepresented non-Europeans, and six white Assembly members elected at the rate

---

[1] *Chronology*, V., No. 5, p. 152; No. 11, p. 368; No. 12, p. 403.
[2] Acts 41, 53, 55 and 56 of 1949; *Round Table*, No. 156, pp. 288 ff.

of one for every four thousand voters as contrasted with nine thousand in the Union.[1]

No one could tell how the cat would jump in South-West Africa, though knowing as he did the political proclivities of the newly-enfranchised electors in those parts, Schoeman could boast confidently that the Ministry would soon be able to 'take the Hottentots off the white man's roll.' Malan was not so gratuitously insulting as his colleague, but he nevertheless regarded his Party's victory in the Provincial general elections as a further mandate for his *apartheid* policy.[2] Thus encouraged, he set out for London in April 1949, to attend the Commonwealth Prime Ministers' Conference, where he voted with a readiness tinged maybe with envy in favour of allowing Nehru's new Republic of India to retain her seat in 'the Club.' Thence he went on to The Hague and, thereafter, to Berlin, where he watched the Allies wearing down Russia's attempted blockade of that much-divided city by their amazing air-lift, and so back to Capetown to be congratulated by Smuts on the success of his mission, to admit cheerfully in reply that the Commonwealth was indeed remarkably adaptable and, probably because that was so, to renew his promise that he would make no move towards a republic during the life of the existing Parliament.[3]

Shortly before the expected end of the Session, Smuts in his turn set off for England with the remark that he hoped that the extraordinarily liberal treatment meted out to the new India would be regarded as exceptional.[4] On arrival, he was perhaps faintly amused to see te Water, the Union's Ambassador-at-large, newly returned from a tour of the two Rhodesias, the British East African dependencies, Egypt, Greece, Italy and Spain, taking a leaf from his own book by expressing his Government's desire, first, to co-operate with all European States that had territories in Africa and, then, to reinforce the recent North Atlantic Treaty Organisation with a network of regional security agreements which should include African and Mediterranean alliances.[5] Be that as it might, he himself scarcely concealed his distaste for recent events in India and Pakistan, and warned a meeting of London journalists and a more academic audience in the Cambridge Senate House that things were happening in Asia that might soon make disquieting developments in the West look like 'small potatoes.' He, therefore, urged the drifting United Kingdom to pull herself together and, as holder of the key position in the world, save the hope of the future by encouraging co-operation

---

[1] Act 23 of 1949; Hatch, *op. cit.*, p. 68; *Round Table*, No. 155, p. 292; No. 156, p. 387.
[2] *Round Table*, No. 155, p. 291.
[3] *Chronology*, V., No. 9, pp. 273, 279, 286–7, 290; No. 10, p. 329.
[4] *Ibid.*, V., No. 10, p. 329.
[5] *Ibid.*, V., No. 13, pp. 433, 439, 443.

between the Commonwealth, the United States and democratic Western Europe.[1]

Things were indeed happening, and not only in restive Asia. Smuts had sailed in the almost universally held belief that the serious work of the Session was over. Events soon showed that he had by no means taken the measure of opponents who were prepared to use the machinery inherited from the Westminster Parliament and to ignore its spirit. No sooner was he safely below the horizon than the Session was prolonged for a month, Dönges unexpectedly had his South African Citizenship Bill moved to the top of the Order Paper, and Malan insisted that that drastic measure be passed if only because republican India's retention of her membership in the Commonwealth had for ever destroyed 'the idea of a super-state' and, with it, 'the common status of Commonwealth countries.'[2] In theory, there was much to be said for what the Ministry proposed. Until recently, the only domestic nationality known to the law of the United Kingdom, the Dominions and the Colonies had been that of 'British subject,' which conferred a valuable common status on all the King's subjects the world over however precisely each member of the Commonwealth might have specified the qualifications which British subjects must have before they could acquire immigration, franchise and similar rights in its territory. Latterly, however, Canada, the most loosely-hung and isolationist of the Dominions, had drawn a fairly sharp distinction between British subject and Canadian citizen, and now the United Kingdom, of all states, had outdone her. The recent British Nationality Act, by decreeing that British subjects in the Mother Country and her Dependencies were to have merely the novel status of 'citizens of the United Kingdom and Colonies,' had reduced the status of British subjects to secondary rank and emptied it of most of its hitherto highly prized content. True, if any Dominions desired, its nationals could remain British subjects as before. Australia and New Zealand did so desire, but the newly created Dominion of Ceylon adopted the new British formula.[3] It was scarcely to be expected that the Nationalists would refrain from following the Canadian, British and Sinhalese precedents; but few people imagined that they would surpass them with such utter logic and vindictiveness.

Dönges's Citizenship Bill was crashed through in the course of one short week, in spite of huge protest meetings in most of the towns.[4] All amendments were rejected; the guillotine was used for the first time in the Senate, and used so ruthlessly in the Assembly that many clauses were never debated at all. Even so, the measure was only

---

[1] *Chronology*, V., No. 12, p. 392.   [2] *Ibid.*, V., No. 12, p. 403.
[3] *Round Table*, No. 152, pp. 826 ff.; No. 154, pp. 196 ff.
[4] *Ibid.*, No. 156, pp. 383 ff.; *Chronology*, V., No. 13, p. 446; Act 44 of 1949.

carried by the votes of two Independents from Natal. Its author might exult that the Union now had the most up-to-date and constitutionally correct nationality law in the Commonwealth, but it assuredly had the most isolationist. Malan's own Nationality and Flag Act of 1927, which had carefully described Union nationality as a small circle within the great circle of British subjecthood, had gone by the board; the very title of Union national had made way for that of South African citizen, and nothing remained of the old common status but the oath of allegiance to the King which must be taken by would-be citizens. This citizenship could be acquired in one of three ways; first, by birth or descent from a Union national; secondly, by registration in the case of citizens of another member of the Commonwealth or the newly-proclaimed Republic of Ireland; thirdly, in the case of aliens, by naturalisation. The essential change was that whereas any British subject had hitherto been able to acquire South African nationality by a mere two years' residence in the Union, now he must register, a long and cumbrous process which involved five years' residence, application to the Minister and the fulfilment of various requirements customarily demanded only of 'other aliens' prior to naturalisation.[1] One such obstructive requirement was the 'adequate knowledge' of the privileges and responsibilities of a South African citizen, a requirement altogether too suggestive of the esoteric knowledge of the intricate United States Constitution sometimes demanded by Southern registration officers intent on keeping Negroes off the voters' roll.

To sum up: the only difference between the registration of a British subject and the naturalisation of an alien was that the former must wait for five years before registering and the latter must wait six and, in addition, advertise his application. But there was more in it than even this, for the Minister was given dangerously wide discretionary powers. He could not, indeed, touch immigrants who had been registered before the Act came into force; but he could summarily deprive of citizenship all who had registered thereafter and all naturalised aliens whatever, and that not necessarily by judicial process. He might and, in some cases, must ask a Court or a Commission to decide whether a citizen had been guilty of an offence which would render him liable to deprivation in terms of the Act, though he was not bound to accept its findings and, still less, to act on them. In short, in numberless cases, 'the Minister' alone could decide who should and who should not be South African citizens. Finally, the Act broke faith with those numerous recently arrived British immigrants, who now found that they must wait for the franchise more than twice as long as they had justifiably expected. That, however, was not the least of the virtues of the Act in the eyes of a Minister set upon the

[1] *Chronology*, V., No. 17, p. 592; *Hansard (S.A.)*, 1949, col. 7578.

perpetuation of Nationalist domination *quocunque modo*, for the long wait must keep nearly all of them off the voters' roll until after the next general election, presumably four years hence. It was a dodge that naturally moved the Leader of the Opposition to wrath. Fresh from his latest European crusade in defence of Western civilisation, Smuts promised to repeal at the first opportunity a measure so reminiscent of the franchise manœuvres of Kruger's isolated little republic in its last days.[1]

Towards the close of this stormy Session, Erasmus disbanded the Cape Corps and gave notice that Coloured men would never again be allowed to serve in a combatant capacity, but only as servants of white soldiers.[2] He then set off for London to solicit the gift of a couple of destroyers, to discuss with Canadian Ministers the co-ordination of his country's arms production with that of the United Kingdom and other leading Western Powers, and to attend the unofficial British Commonwealth Relations Conference at Bigwin Inn, Ontario.[3] He celebrated his return home by depriving Smuts without thanks of his half-forgotten wartime post of Commander-in-Chief of the Union Defence Force.[4] With a good-humoured shrug of his shoulders, his victim retaliated by proclaiming his Nine Points of Policy, which included the maintenance of the Constitution as laid down in the South Africa Act, the fostering of a united South African nation and of freedom and dignity for the individual, the promotion of the Western way of life and European leadership combined with justice and—no Republic. Having discharged this broadside, the indefatigable veteran, ignoring the coronary thrombosis, which, unknown to his family, was already troubling him, dashed off to London to attend the dinner in honour of the seventy-fifth birthday of his old friend, Dr. Chaim Weiszmann.[5]

The Minister of Finance was scarcely slower off the mark in his quest of the Golden Fleece. He had need to find it, because what with the continued importation from North America of a much bigger proportion of a greater volume of goods at prices much higher than in pre-war days, the Reserve Bank's gold and exchange had dwindled to a mere £60,000,000 and was like to dwindle still more unless the influx of fresh capital could be quickened.[6] He at least convinced the suspicious authorities of the International Monetary Fund that he had not been dealing in the open gold market without leave, and thus gained permission to go on selling

[1] *Chronology*, V., No. 14, p. 481; J. C. Smuts, *op. cit.*, p. 521; Davidson, *op. cit.*, p. 162.
[2] *Government Gazette*, April 17, 1949; *Cape Times*, April 19, 1949.
[3] *Chronology*, V., No. 12, p. 403.
[4] *Ibid.*, V., No. 20, p. 628; J. C. Smuts, *op. cit.*, p. 521.
[5] *Chronology*, V., No. 22, p. 759; J. C. Smuts, *op. cit.*, p. 521.
[6] *Chronology*, V., No. 15, p. 516.

semi-processed gold under additional safeguards; but however greatly this concession might reassure the goldmining companies, it did not do away with the need for continued austerity. He next learned at the Conference of Commonwealth Finance Ministers, the first of its kind, that the interests of dollar-using Canada were very different from those of her 'sterling' fellow-members, and then, having recalled the balance of the famous gold loan and promised to pay for imports from the sterling area in gold, was obliged to follow the United Kingdom's lead and devalue the long overrated South African pound from 4.03 to a mere 2.80 dollars.[1] Thus shaken, he sailed for New York where his best hopes lay. Alas! maybe because of his hectoring and vote-catching manner, more certainly because he had just had to devalue, and most certainly because general prices in that part of the world were rocketing while the price of gold remained obstinately stationary, he failed to secure an increase in the selling price of that universally desired metal. Nor would he accept a United States loan because of the strings attached thereto. All he could do was to borrow £26,000,000 from other foreign sources and go home knowing full well that devaluation must send general prices still higher, but hoping that this rise might help his country in the long run.

On landing Havenga found that something of the sort was indeed happening. It was true that working costs were going up on the goldmines and thereby hitting the newly discovered goldfields in the northern Free State, one or two of which had failed to live up to the deservedly high reputation for probity established by the Rand mines by reporting fabulously rich strikes, which had been found either to have been 'salted' or to be far less promising than they had been said to be for company promoting purposes; but to offset these regrettable incidents, devaluation was enabling the Rand mines to give their white miners something of the rise in pay and other advantages they had long been demanding. He himself soon found that, after concluding one-year trading agreements with Japan and various sterling Governments, his country's financial position had at last improved so markedly that import control allocations for the first half of 1950 could be fixed thirty per cent. higher than those for the year just ending. It all might have been worse.[2]

To complete the tale of South African notabilities who went on their travels, the Minister of Economic Affairs set off to attend a meeting of U.N.O. preceded by an official statement that 'in the interests of efficiency' the Union would no longer report on South-West Africa.[3] On his arrival at New York, Louw told a meeting of reporters that his Government was resolved to keep the control of its own country and the Mandated Territory in the hands of 'representatives

[1] *Chronology*, V., No. 18, p. 617.
[2] *Ibid.*, V., No. 18, p. 634; No. 20, p. 689.   [3] *Ibid.*, V., No. 14, p. 481.

of European culture,' lest it fall into the hands of 'a black proletariate with strong Communist backing.' Then, after enduring the usual exaggerated attacks by Indian spokesmen and seeing the General Assembly adopt a Franco-Mexican motion that the Union be called upon to make a settlement with India and Pakistan, he made the now customary reply that the Indian problem was one for South Africa alone and stalked out in protest.[1] South Africa, however, had not heard the last of South-West, for the issue was raised at the next Session of the General Assembly a few months later by the Rev. Michael Scott. This saintly Anglican clergyman, who had recently busied himself much with the affairs of the Basuto, had now taken up the case of the Hereros. These Bantu tribesmen, at one time the dominant folk in South-West Africa, had suffered grievously at the hands of the Germans. Those of them who had not fled to the Bechuanaland Protectorate had indeed been given Reserves by the Union authorities, but nothing like as much as they held their increasing numbers entitled them to. The Union Minister concerned had tried to stop Scott's going to lay the Herero's grievances before the Trusteeship Committee by demanding his passport; but Scott had eluded him by flying from Southern Rhodesian soil.[2] On his arrival, the Committee resolved to hear him without seriously examining his credentials in spite of the protests of the leading United Kingdom representative and of Jooste, the Union's Ambassador at Washington, who now represented his Government in U.N.O. Jooste explained temperately and clearly that his Government would report no more because its past voluntary gesture of goodwill in so reporting had simply led to unwarranted overseas criticism of its policy, and, during Scott's hearing, pleaded that the General Assembly had no power to establish a right of petition by inhabitants of the Mandated Territory. This said, he withdrew in protest on instructions from his Prime Minister, who declared that U.N.O. was suffering from 'interference mania,' blamed it for admitting 'agitators' of the Scott type who had side-stepped their country's lawful government, and refused either to place South-West Africa under Trusteeship or to give any account of the recent raising of that Territory to self-governing status.[3] Undeterred by this outburst, the Trusteeship Committee first adopted the Indians' perennial proposal that the Union be called upon to place South-West Africa under Trusteeship and report as usual, and then, reverting to Smuts's rejected suggestion of 1946, resolved that the legal aspects of the problem be referred to the International Court of Justice at The Hague.[4]

Away in South Africa itself, the implications of *apartheid* were

[1] *Chronology*, V., No. 10, pp. 332, 335.   [2] *Ibid.*, V., No. 23, pp. 8 ff.
[3] *Ibid.*, V., No. 23, p. 799; *Round Table*, No. 158, p. 186.
[4] *Chronology*, V., No. 24, p. 841.

being debated not without heat and dust. Dönges, encouraged by the formation in Natal of an Indian Nationalist Party which insisted that Indians owed their sole allegiance to the Union, promptly demanded stiffer regulations and drastic steps to reduce the numbers of Indians to a minimum.[1] The far more humane Jansen, Minister of Native Affairs, thinking in the tribal terms that came naturally to a white Natalian, foreshadowed the residential segregation of Europeans and Bantu in rural areas and, thereafter, the sorting out of the latter into their respective and decaying tribes.[2] Presently, Eiselen, the newly-appointed Secretary for Native Affairs, said that while he did not expect to see a great and compact 'Bantustan' in his day, he would do his best to win the confidence of the tribesmen and push ahead with the constructive side of the *apartheid* policy.[3]

Eiselen was like to have hard work to do so, because if the Bantu were not to be admitted to the towns, they must be given bigger Reserves. Yet, here were Ministers claiming that because the flow of Bantu to the towns was too great, it was not worth while even trying to buy any more of the additional land promised to them by Hertzog's Native Lands and Trust Act, and Nationalist Congresses in the Cape and the Transvaal gravely debating widespread demands that land already acquired by the Native Trust should be bought back for white occupation. Then, perhaps in reply to the clamour of the *Ossewabrandwag* and New Order for the implementation of the positive side of the policy, the authorities closed twenty-one towns, including Johannesburg and Pretoria, to all Bantu who were not engaged in mining or a few other occupations, and transferred to the Rand local authorities the power to register Bantu and issue passes to them, which had hitherto been exercised by the Native Affairs Department. The Krugersdorp Bantu showed their disapproval of this last measure by killing four policemen at the cost of one of their own number killed and a few others wounded by rifle-fire. Nor was this the only trouble on the Rand, for at about the same time there were disturbances at Newlands, New Clare and Randfontein.[4] Swart, Minister of Justice, ordered an inquiry; but when he remarked that he did not know what the Bantu had to riot about, he was answered by the Leader of the Opposition and the spokesmen of many Churches. Smuts told him that the Government had squandered their country's greatest asset, the goodwill of her workers, by 'dinning into those vast labour masses . . . that they were a menace to European civilisation'; the General Assembly of the Presbyterian Church, the Annual Conference of the Methodist Church and the

---

[1] *Chronology*, V., No. 14, p. 481; No. 10, p. 329.
[2] *Ibid.*, V., No. 21, p. 725; Davidson, *op. cit.*, p. 27.
[3] Davidson, *op. cit.*, pp. 27 ff.; Hatch, *op. cit.*, pp. 35, 85 ff.
[4] Sachs, *op. cit.*, pp. 62 ff.; *Report of Commission*, U.G. 47 of 1950; *Chronology*, V., No. 21, pp. 725–6.

Wynberg Ring of the Dutch Reformed Church condemned *apartheid*, while, at Johannesburg, the Christian Council of South Africa, representing all the Christian Churches other than the Roman Catholic and Dutch Reformed Churches, foretold that even the idea of trusteeship which underlay the *apartheid* policy could only be *ad interim* and must in the end give way to the more generous conception of partnership.[1]

Towards the close of this year of stress, on Dingaan's day now tactfully renamed *Helderdag* (Heroes' Day) to avoid wounding the feelings of every Bantu in the land, South Africa's leaders and perhaps one in ten of her white people assembled to dedicate the Voortrekker Monument. This massive edifice stood well against blue sky and white clouds on a hill near Pretoria. Its interior was, however, far finer than its exterior, for there was told the story of the Great Trek in marble bas-reliefs excellent in execution and even more admirable in spirit in that there was no trace of bitterness against the British nor, more surprisingly, the Zulu enemy. The ceremony was marked by a message of goodwill from the distant King, fine speeches in Afrikaans by Malan and Smuts and in English by Judge Cyril Newton-Thompson, grandson of that leading resident of Grahamstown, who, on behalf of his fellow-townsmen, had presented a Bible to the Uys Trekkers as they passed through his little town on their way to 'the wilderness' more than a hundred years ago. The Prime Minister and Newton-Thompson spoke mainly of the past; but the Leader of the Opposition, as his manner was, spoke more of things to come, warning his hearers, so many of whom were of Trekker stock, against blindly following the example of their forebears, who had been fatally given to bickering even in face of a common peril.[2]

In spite of Smuts's appeal for unity, the bickering went on, at all events among the Europeans. On the other hand, the stresses of the policy of *apartheid* were beginning to drive the other peoples closer together. Natal Indians and Zulus, who had fought one another not so many months back, might find it hard to co-operate, and Cape Coloured Folk, in Natal again, might petition that they be not compelled to share the same railway carriages with such as these; but in the Cape Colony, where the rival Coloured factions had hitherto spent more time and energy in quarrelling with one another than in fighting Malan, even Golding's moderate Coloured People's National Union, some 85,000 strong, at last gave up all attempts to co-operate with the authorities, the Coloured Advisory Council resigned in protest against the *apartheid* policy, and a Convention of Coloured Folks' Organisations in Capetown not only upheld its action but resolved to form strong Coloured trade unions. Natal Indians had

[1] *Chronology*, V., No. 20, p. 689; No. 22, p. 759; Sachs, *op. cit.*, pp. 62 ff.
[2] *Chronology*, V., No. 24, p. 838; *Round Table*, No. 158, pp. 183 ff.

long presented a more united front than any other racial group, but they were far away in every sense from the Cape Coloured Folk and, for obvious reasons, found it hard to co-operate with the Bantu. That people, the crux of the non-European problem, were a much-divided folk. Even those 200,000 or so of them who were organised in trade unions suffered from that weakness, and, though some of them had struck successfully from 1940 onwards, taken as a whole they were not making much headway because of mutual jealousies and lack of a co-ordinating centre. Now, however, the recently organised anti-European Youth Movement had galvanised the long-quiescent African National Congress into such vigorous life that Dr. Alfred Xuma, president of that Congress, could arouse enthusiasm among its members when he told them with truth that Dingaan, the villain of the Voortrekker Monument dedication, had, with all his faults, been a defender of African freedom and bade them stand firm like him in their own struggle for liberty. There was need to stand firm and get together, for the old frontier troubles were flaring up throughout the purlieus of the Rand: tribesmen against tribesmen, Basuto against their Zulu civil guards, non-Europeans of all sorts against trigger-happy Poor Whites, tribesmen against policemen, always with Bantu women well to the fore. Meanwhile, the Minister of Justice found in the Bantu, whom his police were arresting wholesale for breach of the peace and liquor laws, a welcome supply of compulsory labour wherewith to supplement the dirt-cheap compounded Bantu workers on the farms of many of his rural supporters. Had he not recently opened a Convict Labour Station, which had been built at Leslie near Pretoria by the local Farmers' Association Labour Supply Company at the cost of £12,000 to house just such labour, and remarked that he hoped to open many another?[1]

The Nationalist and Afrikaner rank-and-file, like most other white South Africans, thought of *apartheid* in terms of the Bantu, but the Prime Minister, as a Western Province man, thought of it primarily in terms of the much less numerous Cape Coloured Folk. As a fair-minded man, Malan was ready to give as well as take, and knew that thus far he had given the Coloured Folk and Indians virtually nothing and the Bantu very little beyond additional funds for education. On the other hand, as a practical politician, whose long-term *apartheid* policy depended on a permanent Nationalist majority, he was only too well aware that the two most obvious steps towards that end were the exclusion of 'Native' representatives from Parliament and the relegation of the Cape Coloured voters to a separate

---

[1] Hatch, *op. cit.*, p. 67; Davidson, *op. cit.*, p. 45; Sachs, *op. cit.*, p. 114, *Cape Times*, Sept. 3, 1949; Scott, M., *A Time to Speak*, pp. 169 ff.

roll with merely token representation. Backed by Dönges, he therefore made one more desperate effort to overcome Havenga's 'commendable obstinacy,' which had hitherto prevented him from doing either the one or the other. The Minister of the Interior argued in his glib fashion that Coloured voters would be much better off on a separate roll, because they would then be saved from exploitation by rival European parties at election times; but Malan himself pleaded far more frankly that there was no hope of winning certain Western Province seats before they were so segregated. It was no use. Havenga was by no means convinced that all 'high legal authority' was agreed that the entrenched clauses no longer held good and, in any event, was resolved not to tamper with any non-European parliamentary rights until he had been authorised to do so by 'a clear expression of the will of the people.' There was nothing for it but to mark time. Hence, on December 12, 1949, the Prime Minister and his indispensable ally issued a joint statement to the effect that no legislation involving the entrenched clauses would be introduced during the coming Session.[1] 'Patience and shuffle the cards.'

CENTRAL AFRICA

The course of events in the Union since Malan's assumption of power had given a great impetus to the movement towards the closer union of her northern neighbours, the Two Rhodesias and Nyasaland.[2] Shortly before the recent war, the Bledisloe Commission had counselled delay, and the long struggle itself had inevitably ruled out the possibility of further progress towards amalgamation. True, in April 1943, when it was clear that the Allies were winning, Sir Godfrey Huggins, the recently knighted Prime Minister of Southern Rhodesia, had gone so far as to suggest that these three territories be formed into one economic *bloc* and the East African dependencies into another; but three years later, when Germany was at last collapsing, even he reluctantly accepted the Bledisloe Commission's main positive suggestion that there should be merely a kind of executive federation, somewhat on the lines that were being followed in East Africa. Hence, in April 1945, a Central African Council was established at Salisbury consisting of the Governor of Southern Rhodesia in the chair, the Governors of the two trans-Zambesi Protectorates, and four members from each of the three territories including the Prime Minister and three other Ministers from Southern Rhodesia and the leading unofficial members of the Legisla-

---

[1] *Round Table*, No. 157, pp. 88 ff.; No. 159, pp. 282 ff.; *Chronology*, V., No. 24, p. 838. On exploitation of Coloured voters *vide* Long, B. K., *In Smuts's Camp*, pp. 128 ff.
[2] Cmd. 8233 of 1951, para. 32; Colonial, No. 191 of 1945 and No. 210 of 1947.

tive Councils of Northern Rhodesia and Nyasaland. This Council was purely consultative, for though it was equipped, like its East African counterpart, with a permanent Secretariate and various joint Services, it lacked the Central Legislative Assembly which promised to make the latter a so much more effective organ of governance.[1] Nor did the new Council hold out to Southern Rhodesians any hope of that freedom from Westminster control which so many of them ardently desired.

Huggins knew that there was no prospect of getting beyond this halfway house till his colony had struggled back to a peace footing, and he was hampered in the task of achieving even this limited aim 1946. by seeing his United Party do so badly at a general election that it would find itself in a minority if the Liberals and two rival Labour parties ever combined. Some factors, however, favoured him. Agriculture and, above all, tobacco were doing well; gold output from the five hundred small and scattered mines was rising fast, and secondary industry had arrived. On the other hand, there was a vast deal to be done, primarily the reinstatement of ex-Service folk in civil life and the accommodation of newcomers who poured in so fast that, in face of the lack of houses and the white folk's lavish demand for servants, he had to provide for the selection and limitation of the numbers of immigrants by the Aliens Act of 1946.[2]

This demand for servants was a reminder that the fundamental problem for Southern Rhodesia, as for the Union, was the Native question. There were, however, differences of approach. White Southern Rhodesians did not speak of *apartheid* and flattered themselves, as a rule justly, that their relations with their swarming Bantu were better than those of the average white South African. Admittedly, most of them were far less liberal on this score than their Prime Minister and a few of his fellow-politicians; but many of them were keenly interested in Native education and social welfare, pleased when a Commission inquired into the social and economic aspects of trading by and with Africans, talked hopefully of the day when there should be a Central Board of Co-operative Organisations in each Reserve and also model Native townships, which should be self-contained in the matter of shops, banks, amusements and so forth and be connected by good roads with the towns in which their inhabitants worked. Meanwhile, these good folk positively applauded Huggins when he obliged wealthy Bulawayo and Salisbury to clean up their squalid Native locations.[3] Nevertheless, others less liberal demanded that the Bantu be segregated in their comparatively

---

[1] *Bulletin*, XXII., No. 10, p. 458; Colonial No. 191 of 1945 and No. 210 of 1947.
[2] *Chronology*, II., No. 9, p. 259; No. 15, p. 458.
[3] Davidson, *op. cit.*, pp. 233, 236.

extensive Reserves and all Bantu women be shut out of the towns to discourage their menfolk from coming thither. Huggins did, indeed, carry an Urban Areas Act, which, as in the Union, decreed that Africans must live in their own separate locations; but he would not hear of barring them out of the white man's towns completely, for, as he observed tartly, they came to those towns because the white folk asked them to work for them and, without their labour, white society could not exist for five minutes. Take them all round, white Southern Rhodesians were not intolerant; but they had their colour bars all along the line, regarded the towns as the white man's preserves, and were so deeply persuaded that their Colony was 'a white man's country' that they were startled when Huggins warned them that it might be 'awkward' if ever they lost 'the flying start' he had given them over the Africans.[1]

The Bantu had no illusions. However diligently the Prime Minister and his like might preach the doctrine of 'parallel development' for black and white, the mass of them regarded the existing system as one of white domination buttressed by the colour bar. And no wonder. No Bantu had security of tenure outside the comparatively extensive Reserves; urbanised Africans must live in such locations as there were and, even after the recent spring-cleaning, none of these was anything like so good as the best in the Union; no African could legally take part in collective bargaining, because such as they were not officially regarded as employees; no African could get a commission in the admirable and overwhelmingly Matabele British South Africa Police, and none of their Chiefs were now much more than subordinate officials, who must suffer their traditional functions to be performed by white civil servants. The Bantu of Southern Rhodesia could hope for better things in the political sphere than their fellows in the Union, because their colony had inherited the old Cape civilisation system and therefore offered full political rights to all adult British subjects of either sex and any colour who could fulfil certain economic and educational requirements. In practice, however, only some four hundred of them had the vote, partly because the vast majority of their people were too poor to qualify and partly because the eight thousand or so 'incipient voters' who could have done so were held back by apathy or the fear that if they got on the roll, they would have to pay income tax. For the rest, only the Southern Rhodesian Labour Party angled for their support and, even so, proposed to segregate them in a separate branch of its organisation, while, as in the Union, a good many white citizens had long demanded that the civilisation test be abolished and all non-Europeans be entered on a separate voters'

[1] Davidson, *op. cit.*, pp. 225, 232; *Legislative Assembly Debates*, Nov. 30, 1944.

roll. Huggins admitted frankly that it might come to that one day, but for the moment successfully resisted the demand.[1]

Huggins drove his restive team forward and was rewarded by confirmation in power at the general election of September, 1948, which gave his United Party twenty-four seats as against the six shared by the Liberals and Labour.[2] He at once sought to better the lot of Africans in commerce and industry, launched an ambitious four-year plan of railway construction and other public works, opened negotiations with Portugal for the improvement of Beira, his country's natural but most inadequate port, and signed an interim customs agreement with the Union on whose harbours and railways Southern Rhodesia was still so dependent.[3] Then, dropping into the background the idea, with which he had been toying, of asking for Dominion powers and status, he took up once more his schemes for Amalgamation.[4] He advocated first, the union of the three Central African territories; next, 'a partnership with the Union,' which would, in a measure, realise Rhodes's dream and, finally, since he was convinced that there was 'going to be a United States of Africa as sure as the sun comes up,' a federation of all the British territories in the continent. He held that Central Africa could not hope to survive unless it formed itself into a single economic *bloc* and must consolidate itself politically if it were to resist the fatal southward pull of Malan's Nationalist Union. He, therefore, hoped to follow the example of the aforetime South African colonies, who had solved their political and economic problems simultaneously by effecting Union, and if he had any doubt as to the fundamental importance of economics in any scheme of Amalgamation, the experience of the English, the Scots, the Old Thirteen, Canadians, Bismarck's Germans and the Australians was there to teach him better, to say nothing of the present counsel of Sir Miles Thomas, an old friend and projector of ambitious schemes of development. Plainly, a single Government could at least ease the inter territorial competition of Southern Rhodesia's farms, mines and Que-Que steelworks and Northern Rhodesia's lead, zinc and copper mines for Wankie coal and Nyasaland's man-power, and could, moreover, inspire the increased confidence that would attract local and, still more, overseas capital for the financing of extensive irrigation schemes and the huge hydro-electric plants that were to be fed by the water-power of the Kafue river, a northern affluent of the Zambesi, and the Kariba Gorge both well below the Victoria Falls.

Huggins believed that the prospects of amalgamation were better

[1] Davidson, *op. cit.*, pp. 235 ff.; *Round Table*, No. 155, pp. 227 ff.
[2] *Chronology*, IV., No. 15, p. 532; V., No. 18, p. 618.
[3] *Ibid.*, IV., No. 21, p. 737; V., No. 1, p. 20.
[4] *Ibid.*, IV., No. 13, p. 465; *Round Table*, No. 155, pp. 230 ff.; No. 159, pp. 222 ff.

than they had ever been, for, not only were his Southern Rhodesians getting used to the idea, but their prospective partners beyond the Zambesi were rising nearer to them on the constitutional plane. Little-considered Nyasaland was rising the more slowly of the two Protectorates, but one Indian and two African nominees now sat in her Legislative Council beside the five officials and the four European nominees, who, since 1907, had constituted the Legislative Council, while the vast African majority was learning to handle day-to-day affairs through their three elective Provincial Councils and many lesser organs of local government.[1] Progress in Northern Rhodesia had been far more rapid. There, since 1939, four elective members of the Legislature had sat also on the Executive Council, mixed nominee and elective African Urban Advisory Councils had been created in the Copper Belt, and Urban African Courts had been at work in such towns as there were. Next, at the instance of Sir Stewart Gore-Browne, a landowner who represented one of the northern districts, the Advisory Council system was extended to the whole Protectorate, and Regional Councils, partly elected by them and partly nominated by tribal authorities, were set up in each Province.[2] Then, in 1945, the Legislative Council was reorganised so drastically that its official majority disappeared.[3] Henceforward, it was to consist of six officials, five unofficial nominees of whom three were to speak for Africans, and eight other members, who, because Africans were merely British protected persons and therefore unable to get the vote like British subjects, were elected in effect by the scattering of European farmers and businessmen, a few Indians, the highly-paid white employees of the mining companies and state railways, and the wives of such of them as were married. Next year, an African Representative Council drawn from the Regional Councils met for the first time to speak for all the Africans in the land. Finally, in 1948, a further marked advance was registered. Arthur Creech Jones, the Labour Colonial Secretary, directed, first, that the new Representative Council should elect two Africans to the Legislature and, secondly, that the Legislature should include among the members it sent up to the Executive Council one of those who had been nominated to speak for Africans, that one or two of the unofficial members thus sent up should be responsible for groups of departments without themselves becoming Ministers, and that the opinions of all four of them together should carry the same weight in the Executive as in the Legislative Council.[4]

There could be little doubt that the individual unofficial opinion that would count for most would be that of the able Roland Welen-

[1] Nyasaland (Legislative Council) Order-in-Council, 1907, and 1938.
[2] *Legislative Council Debates*, Sept. 17, 1942, col. 148 ff.
[3] N. Rhodesia (Legislative Council) Order-in-Council, 1945.
[4] *Chronology*, IV., No. 16, p. 553; *Round Table*, No. 159, p. 221.

sky, a sometime Southern Rhodesian engine-driver and now the elected member for Broken Hill, the dominating personality in the Protectorate's trade unions and, since the death in 1945 of Sir Leopold Moore, who had been for many years the most influential of the elective members, the leader of the unofficial members in legislature and executive alike.

The colour bar was as rigid in both Protectorates as in most parts of Africa south of the Zambesi. Voluntary residential segregation was the practice in those comparatively small areas in which folk of the various races worked side by side; but in contrast to Southern Rhodesia and the Union, Africans held the vast bulk of the land and Europeans must be content with what were virtually white Reserves. Both Protectorates, and Nyasaland in especial, were reservoirs of labour for territories further south.[1] Whereas, however, overwhelmingly agricultural Nyasaland had neither industrial colour bars nor trade unions, Northern Rhodesia had both on her state railways, the big lead and zinc mine at Broken Hill, the even more important copper mines contiguous to those of the Belgian Katanga and, latterly, in uranium mines hard by. These rich mines, which made Northern Rhodesia such a desirable member of a Central African federation, were owned for the most part by British and United States shareholders. Some of the mining companies relied on semi-segregated male labour, but others gave their African employees tied cottages for themselves and their families and sometimes also garden patches in which they could grow fruit and vegetables for sale within their compounds. Whichever course they followed, however, they only paid them some £5 a month in addition to rations, in contrast to anything from £100 to £300 a month to their white miners, the highest such wages in all Africa.[2] Mainly because of this wide disparity in rewards, the miners of both races were apt to be restive, especially the white men who remembered that the price of copper had fallen catastrophically during the early 'thirties. In 1942, white miners on the Nkana and Mufulira copper mines struck successfully for increased pay; whereupon, some fifteen thousand Africans struck and only went back to work after the police had killed seventeen of them and wounded sixty-five others.[3]

That African strike, failure though it was, marked a turning-point. On the one hand, the white miners, quick to see the writing on the

---

[1] In 1935, nearly one-fourth of Nyasaland's wage-earners were at work outside their Protectorate. In 1942 about one-third of Northern Rhodesia's able-bodied males were employed outside its borders, some 50,000 of them in Southern Rhodesia; *Report of the Committee on Emigrant Labour*, 1935; *Native Administration and Political Development* ... Report by Lord Hailey ... 1940–42, pp. 255, 277.
[2] Spearpoint, F., *The African Miner on the Rhodesia Copper Mines*, pp. 38 ff.; Davidson, *op. cit.*, pp. 242, 251
[3] Davidson, *op. cit.*, p. 248.

wall, extorted an agreement from the companies that they would not employ Africans on skilled or semi-skilled jobs throughout the Copper Belt, and, on the other, the companies set about encouraging African trade unions and similar elective organisations, which might bridle the monstrous regiment of a handful of over-paid, highly privileged and strategically placed white miners and, at the same time, enable their Government to qualify for grants under the Colonial Development and Welfare Act, none of which the United Kingdom would make to any territory that did not give trade union facilities impartially. At the companies' request, the Colonial Secretary at once sent out an adviser, who soon organised a number of African peasant co-operative associations, while they themselves allowed African miners to choose committees of 'boss-boys' and tribal representatives. Three years later they went a step further. Impressed by an effective African strike on the railways and the skilful negotiation of a housing and wages agreement by the African Milling Employees' Union at Bulawayo, they summoned another expert from the United Kingdom to advise on the formation of African trade unions.[1] The first result of this policy was the creation of the African Shop Assistants' Union, and the second the Dalgleish Commission, which recommended that Africans be admitted to certain skilled and semi-skilled jobs. Welensky knew only too well that Africans would one day get the education that had hitherto enabled Europeans to keep ahead of them. Hence, while admitting frankly that no laws could stop Africans from forming trade unions if they wanted them, he and his followers sabotaged the Dalgleish Report.[2] Having thus presumably safeguarded the privileged position of the white folk and their children's children, Welensky demanded either self-government for Northern Rhodesia or else closer union with colour bar and autonomous Southern Rhodesia.[3]

Huggins could thus be reasonably assured of Welensky's support in his campaign for Amalgamation; but, quite apart from the strong likelihood of African opposition, he was not certain of the general backing of his own white fellow-citizens, and by no means confident that any political party at Westminster, and least of all Attlee's Labour administration, would approve of his aims.[4] It was not so much that British Parliamentarians might doubt the ability of the white folk, a mere three per cent. of the population, to carry the physical and financial burden of the projected state; it was rather that they would remember what had happened after the withdrawal of

[1] Davidson, *op. cit.*, pp. 246 ff.; Cmd. 8235 of 1951, p. 35.
[2] *Northern Rhodesian Debates*, May 6, 1946, col. 56, *East Africa and Rhodesia*, Aug. 1946.
[3] *Northern Rhodesian Debates*, Nov. 25, 1943, col. 152 ff., and Aug. 28, 1945, col. 56, 109.
[4] *Vide, The Colonies: The Labour Party's Post-war Policy* (*1943*), p. 3.

Imperial control from Natal in 1893, from the Union in 1910 and even from his own colony in 1923. They might, therefore, hesitate to risk the clamping down of the colour bar on yet another such 'white man's country' in the heart of a Black Continent in which they ruled some 60,000,000 other watchful Africans.

In spite of these lions in the path, Huggins gave the signal to go forward. Hence, in February 1949, his friend, Sir Miles Thomas, took the chair at the Victoria Falls Conference, a virtually private meeting which was attended by himself and the Finance Minister for Southern Rhodesia and, without the knowledge of the Colonial Secretary, by Welensky, "the Napoleon" of Broken Hill, and other European legislators for the two Protectorates. There was no African representation. At Huggins's suggestion, the Conference substituted a scheme for a loose federation for the originally contemplated close Amalgamation, and agreed that Africans should have some representation in the Upper and less powerful House of the Federal Parliament. It then adjourned, proposing to meet again later on to consider a detailed plan drafted by a committee of experts, which should be voted on at a referendum and, if carried, be submitted to His Majesty. So far, so good; but though no formal report was issued for the time being, it was widely known that Welensky had talked of Central Africa as the coming 'eighth Dominion' and scouted the very idea of an African plebiscite as 'fantastic,' and even Huggins had said that Africans must put up with rule by a 'benevolent aristocracy' for a good while. Many Africans, therefore, and notably the powerful Barotse in Northern Rhodesia, showed that they were as doggedly opposed to the new Federation as to the old Amalgamation, and asked Huggins whether he would drop his policy of parallel development in favour of the comparatively liberal policies of the two Protectorates.[1]

The British authorities now stepped in. Creech Jones visited Central Africa and, holding as he did that the new Central African Council met all immediate needs, told Huggins and Welensky repeatedly that he was opposed to federation. He declined to recognise the projected committee of experts, though he readily agreed to answer any constitutional questions submitted to him by the Governor and, since the needs of the three territories might well have changed with changing conditions, promised to consider proposals for constitutional change laid before him in due form. Meanwhile, he frankly warned his hearers that H.M. Government could not 'transfer its trust and neglect its solemnly pledged duty towards Africans.'[2] Then, after discussion with the unofficial nominee members of the Northern Rhodesian Executive Council he agreed that where those members were unanimous on any matter affecting Africans, the

---

[1] *Round Table*, No. 155, pp. 230 *sqq.*; *Chronology*, No. 4, p. 119; No. 5, p. 191.
[2] *Ibid.*, V., No. 8, p. 253; No. 9, p. 289.

26

Governor should, always saving his reserved powers, accept their advice, provided that the nominee representing African interests should have kept in close touch with the elected African members of the Legislative Council throughout and should have actually voted with the other unofficial members of the Executive Council.[1] Having thus left Huggins and Welensky in no doubt as to his attitude towards Federation, he travelled home by way of Tanganyika, where he sought to impress on all concerned the meaning of his party's conception of trusteeship.

Creech Jones had hardly reached Westminster when the Governor of Northern Rhodesia reported that differences had arisen between the forceful Welensky and another nominee on his Executive Council. Since it was desirable that this body should work smoothly, he asked leave to demand that nominee's resignation and, if this were not forthcoming, to replace him. Leave was given, the recalcitrant nominee was unseated and his place was filled by a pro-federation member. In face of this success for the federalists, it was well that the British Labour Ministry should have made its opposition to their policy crystal clear. This task was entrusted to the Minister for Commonwealth Relations, Philip Noel-Baker. He echoed Creech Jones's advice that the three territories concerned should make the most of the Central African Council, refused to commit himself to giving Southern Rhodesia that part of the Bechuanaland Protectorate, which it was claiming on the strength of the still unrevoked promise that the United Kingdom had made to Rhodes's Company in far-off days before the disastrous Jameson Raid had altered the whole situation, and, finally, paid no heed to the adoption by the Northern Rhodesian Legislative Council of Welensky's motion that H.M. Government ought to take the lead in achieving federation, a motion on which the official members had abstained from voting and which the four European 'Native' and African members had opposed.[3]

Under these circumstances, Federation necessarily marched so slowly that the disgusted Huggins was soon accusing the Imperial authorities of having caused a deadlock by their ignorance of African conditions, distrust of local officials and desire to see immediate African representation in the coming Federal Parliament for which Africans were not yet fitted. In his wrath, he even went so far as to threaten that, if Federation were withheld, he would go back to his old policy of demanding Dominion powers and status for his own colony.[4]

[1] *Round Table*, No. 159, p. 221; information kindly furnished by Mr. Creech Jones.
[2] *Round Table*, No. 159, p. 222.
[3] *Ibid.*, p. 224; *Chronology*, V., No. 24, p. 827; VI., No. 1, p. 19.
[4] *Ibid.*, V., No. 24, p. 837.

APARTHEID

The British Government might hesitate to give a decision about the fate of the Bechuanaland Protectorate, but the South African Prime Minister had no such inhibitions. Malan promptly protested that to bring Southern Rhodesia in as a co-partner in the settlement would be a breach of the 'solemn agreement', which he alleged had been made at the time of Union, that the 'disposal' of the territory should be a matter exclusively for the British and South African authorities. Neither the fact that there never had been such an agreement nor a saving sense of humour deterred him from calling from amid the ruins of the old Cape civilisation system for the transfer to the Union of the governance of the High Commission Territories. However, with a fellow feeling for Attlee's precarious hold on power and with Smuts's warm approval, he presently promised not to press this issue till the United Kingdom should have a more stable administration.[1]

Doubtless Malan had made his demand because he knew that all was not well in the Territories. In Basutoland there had been many ritual murders during the past few years, an atavistic 'strike-back' surprising in so predominantly Christian a community.[2] After six highly-placed Basuto had been executed and eight others imprisoned for this crime, an expert Cambridge investigator reported that the backsliding had been caused by the feeling of insecurity bred of the multiplication of Chiefs and Tribal Authorities in an anachronistic and rickety society, and he might have added also by the puzzlement of Protestant Africans at the zeal evinced for their conversion by newly-arrived French Canadian Roman Catholic missionaries.[3] Certainly a sense of insecurity pervaded the very highest quarters in the little land, for recently the Queen Regent had sent a petition to the King with a covering letter from the Rev. Michael Scott begging her 'father, protector and defender' to send 'children from the home of the saviour of our nation, Queen Victoria the Good,' to take the places of the numerous Union nationals in the civil services of the three Territories, whom her people feared because they came from a country whose Government was set on proclaiming a republic, 'a thing which we Basuto detest.'

There was trouble also in the Bechuanaland Protectorate. Tshekedi Khama, the masterful ex-Regent of the Bamangwato with whom the authorities had had trouble in times past, was away in England.[4] There also was Seretse Khama, his nephew and lawful heir to the chieftainship. Seretse had recently married an Englishwoman. One

---

[1] *Round Table*, No. 158, pp. 121 ff., 185; No. 165, p. 91; No. 166, pp. 140 ff.; *Chronology*, VI., No. 1, p. 20; VI., No. 8, p. 248.

[2] Davidson, *op. cit.*, p. 220; *Round Table*, No. 158, p. 185.

[3] Davidson, *op. cit.*, pp. 221 ff.; Cmd. 8209 of 1951, *Report on the Recent outbreak of 'Diretlo' Murders in Basutoland.*

[4] *Vide supra*, p. 661.

section of the Bamangwato *kgotla* (tribal assembly) refused to accept Seretse's bride as Queen and the other demanded the return of Tshekedi. Gordon Walker, who had succeeded Baker as Secretary of State for Commonwealth Affairs, was possibly anxious to placate white South African opinion and more certainly fearful of faction fighting by notoriously quarrelsome tribesmen. He, therefore, made difficulties about letting either the ex-Regent or the Chief return home and, finally, refused to recognise Seretse as Chief for five years to come, forbade him to visit his tribe during that period, and directed the District Commissioner and a small tribal Council to act as the Native Authority in the Bamangwato Reserve.[1]

Besides making the point that nothing much had happened in the High Commission Territories as a result of Hertzog's pre-war promise of co-operation, Malan noted justly that all three were parts of South Africa geographically, racially and, as members of the South African Customs Union, economically also, and that the removal of such political anomalies would enhance the Union's prestige and self-respect. He went too far when he asserted that it was 'unheard of' for a sovereign state to have territories subject to an external authority embedded in its body;[2] but he was nearer the truth when he said the British had neglected to develop liberal elective institutions in any of them. In Swaziland, there was indeed little room for such reform under the mild autocracy of Sobhuza II; in Bechuanaland such schemes were still only on paper, and in Basutoland, the most advanced of the three, the authorities had merely encouraged a few producers' co-operative societies, had made no use of the superabundant 'intellectuals' and had scarcely touched the tribal system on whose Chiefs and Councils they depended for the maintenance of indirect rule and the struggle against soil-erosion and the like. True, there was the long-established *Pitso*; but that purely advisory Native Council contained a majority of Chiefs and met only once a year, while only one of the nine District Advisory Councils, whose main task at their annual meetings was to elect the minority to the *Pitso*, had as yet been allowed to vote by ballot. Malan was, however, on much less sure ground when he complained that he could not organise his country's defence unless he had control of the Territories, and on ground very much weaker still when he asserted, like so many of his fellow-citizens, that the Union got nothing in return for all it gave them and could do far more than the existing authorities to conserve the headwaters of the Basutoland rivers on which vast stretches of the Union depended.[3]

The British had an answer to much of all this. They could point out that Basutoland and Swaziland sent peas, wheat, wool and asbestos to the Union in exchange for finished goods, raw materials,

---

[1] Cmd. 7913 of 1950, White Paper.   [2] *Chronology*, VII., No. 17, p. 531.
[3] *Round Table*, No. 158, pp. 121 ff., 185.

dairy produce and cattle, and that Bechuanaland sent all her fat beasts to the Rand. Coming and going across the frontiers was two-way traffic, Transvaal farmers trekking into Swaziland for the winter grazing and Territory Natives flocking to the Rand mines and Free State and Transvaal farms. Health services, again, had been much improved and educational facilities raised at least to the level of those in the rural parts of the Union; much was being done for forestry, irrigation, water-boring and ranching in Bechuanaland, for land-settlement in Swaziland, where there was good hope of coal, iron and hydro-electrical power, and for soil and water conservation throughout nearly the whole of vital Basutoland. The fact was that the Territories and the Union were interdependent, and if, as some South Africans threatened, the Union ever tried to enforce transfer by an economic blockade, she would find her own miners and farmers suffering as well as the tribesmen.[1]

Nevertheless, the British were in a quandary. They had no wish to hold permanently three Territories which were a small but chronic source of expense and an embarrassment in their dealings with Pretoria; still less did they wish to affront South Africa. On the other hand, they knew that the inhabitants dreaded transfer; they realised that the Schedule appended to the South Africa Act safeguarding those inhabitants after transfer meant little now that the Union had become fully sovereign, and that if they thrust those inhabitants under such an illiberal Government, they and the millions of other Africans further north, for whom they themselves were also responsible, would be gravely unsettled. Finally, they felt that they could not very well go back on the promises, old as the days of Union, that the Africans should be consulted before transfer were effected. The harassed Secretary of State, therefore, played for time by promising to discuss the matter with Malan whenever he might so desire and then pushed on with the development of the three Territories.

Meanwhile, Malan busied himself with matters of wider import. He negotiated successfully with the Anglo-American Atomic Energy Commission for the production of uranium from his country's gold-mines, acceded to the agreement reached at Paris by the Powers concerned for technical co-operation in Africa south of the Sahara and incidentally got rid of Marshall Clarke, the able but now unwanted General Manager of Railways, by sending him to represent the Union on the Central African Transport Board, which had been set up under this Paris Agreement.[2] He then despatched his Minister of Transport to Colombo, where, in January 1950, the Conference of Commonwealth Finance Ministers debated a possible peace treaty with Japan and resolved that the best means of combating Communism in South-East Asia was to foster the economic well-being

[1] *Round Table*, No. 166, pp. 140 ff.   [2] *Ibid.*, No. 159, p. 285.

of the swarming and poverty-stricken masses of those parts.[1] In spite of recognising the independence of Indonesia, he refused to countenance the Chinese Communist Government[2] and then, turning to Commonwealth affairs, indicated that he was as dissatisfied as any Canadian Liberal with the King's official title, which republican India's retention of her place in 'the Club' had rendered unsuitable and, while assuring Smuts that he would consult the electorate before writing 'Republic' into the Constitution, suggested that the next step should be the substitution of an elective President for the nominee Governor-General.

Malan's sufficiently startling proposal was made amid a display of totalitarianism by the authorities great and small. Angered by the 'odium' poured from overseas on the *apartheid* policy, Erasmus blurted out that though there was to be no regular censorship, the Minister concerned could not be expected to ensure that 'slanderous messages' sent by newspaper correspondents should reach their distant editors.[3] Dönges banned a couple of Soviet journals [4] and, infuriated by the Appellate Division's defeat of his latest attempt to confiscate Sachs's passport, was scarcely dissuaded by more cautious colleagues from introducing a Bill giving him the desired powers. He contented himself with merely reducing the validity of passports from five years to one. Further down the scale of authority, the Transvaal Provincial Council virtually transferred to school inspectors the right hitherto exercised by parents of deciding which was their 'home language' and thus of determining which schools their children should attend.[5] Further down still, policemen, many of them Poor Whites in a badly paid service, were earning an evil name for their manhandling of non-European convicts and accused persons who found themselves in their gaols or even in their clutches in the open. The worst cases came from Natal. A white constable killed Milton King, a West Indian seaman, in the street at Durban and was fined no more than £10, apparently because King had drawn his knife; but in this case, the victim's island government extracted compensation. Magistrates at Tugela Ferry 'reluctantly' sentenced three white policemen to fines of £1 or seven days for subjecting Bantu suspects to electric shocks and other abominations, and at New Hanover sentenced another, this time to several years' imprisonment, for murdering a Zulu lad by the mediæval water torture. The Minister of Justice had to confess that, over the past two years, fifty-two policemen had been punished departmentally and close on three hundred and fifty others fined by the Courts for violence and assault upon non-Europeans under arrest. If the above-mentioned cases

[1] *Chronology*, VI., No. 2, pp. 38 ff.   [2] *Ibid.*, VI., No. 12, p. 392.
[3] *Ibid.*, V., No. 23, pp. 779 ff.   [4] *Ibid.*, VI., No. 6, p. 287.
[5] Hatch, *op. cit.*, p. 66.

were at all typical, Swart could have added that they had usually received light sentences.[1]

Immediately after the opening of the Session on January 2, 1950, the Ministry showed that if it was not yet ready to emulate Nehru by proclaiming a republic, it could at least imitate isolationist Canada by abolishing the appeal to the Judicial Committee of the Privy Council, a dead-letter this fifteen years.[2] Then, in his Budget speech, Havenga announced that though there was a surplus of £1,500,000 instead of the small anticipated deficit, he must ask for an increase in postal and telegraphic charges and the petrol duty to cover the deficit which he foresaw at the end of the coming year. He next gave the good news that an agreement recently concluded with the United Kingdom and the influx of capital from Switzerland, the United States and elsewhere had strengthened the country's financial position so markedly that some controls could be lifted with the hope of yet more to follow. Meanwhile, he proposed to reinforce the dollar reserves by requiring that payment for diamonds exported elsewhere than to the United Kingdom should be paid for in that currency, noted that, thanks to the marking up of the value of gold reserves after devaluation, the mines had already made a profit of £1,700,000 on sales at a premium, and expressed the hope that the Governments concerned and the President of the International Monetary Fund would permit them to sell at least half their output at these enhanced prices. Before the end of the Session, he could report further general improvement and look forward to still better things from the progress of industry and the working of the Free State goldfields, assuming that the latter could find labour and water and keep working costs down.[3]

All was not so well, however, on some other sections of the ministerial front. Erasmus had fallen foul of Beyers, who had resigned his post as Chief of the General Staff either because, as the Minister said, there had been differences between them over arrangements for the ceremonial opening of Parliament or, according to Beyers, because Erasmus had undermined discipline by moving strategic units as he chose, appointing, promoting and transferring officers of his own mere motion and creating jobs for political friends. This quarrel subsided when Beyers departed and General de Wet du Toit took his place, but discussion of the affairs of the Transport Department revealed an even more disquieting situation. There, the costly *apartheid* policy of suiting the type of employment and consequent pay to the colour of the recipient's skin was sending up

---

[1] Hatch, p. 159; Davidson, *op. cit.*, p. 120; Patterson, *op. cit.*, pp. 225–6; U.G. 47 of 1947; *Report of Penal and Prison Reform Commission.*

[2] Act 16 of 1950.

[3] *Round Table*, No. 158, pp. 185; *Chronology*, VI., No. 7, p. 220; No. 8, p. 248; No. 15, p. 511.

working costs against railways and harbours, which must cope as best they might with obsolete rolling-stock, inadequate facilities and a rapidly rising wages bill that already ran away with fully two-thirds of their takings. Nor was much economy likely so long as the so-called Grievance Commission could compel the Minister to carry out periodical purges at the instance of the disgruntled.[1]

If Defence and Transport were in a bad way, the United Party, Smuts's 'child' was showing signs of going to pieces as its creator at last began to sink under the burden of overwork. Jacobus Strauss, the acting leader of the Party, a comparatively young Johannesburger who had once been Smuts's private secretary, found that his followers were divided into three groups; first, Smuts's devoted followers who were ready to back him through thick and thin; secondly, Dr. Colin Steyn and a few others whose allegiance was much cooler, and, lastly, a group which included Sir de Villiers Graaff, Marais Steyn and a number of the younger men who rallied to Harry Oppenheimer, son of Sir Ernest, one of the chief Liberal influences in Southern Rhodesia. The Oppenheimer group was influential, because it had the support of a number of wealthy men who had joined with its leader to raise a non-party fund wherewith to finance some of the United Party's activities and, in especial, its information service and, more generally, to organise the defence of 'freedom of speech, language and worship and the fundamental rights of man as recognised by the Member States of the United Nations.' Meanwhile, it was the only group on which Strauss, who was himself not outstandingly liberal, could rely to put up a stiff resistance to the *apartheid* policy, if only because it feared that that policy would prejudice the interests of the finance, commerce and industry in which so many of its members were engaged. The rest of the Party consisted of men who did not care much either way, and of others who so far approved of the policy in their hearts that they could expel a colleague from the caucus for advocating equal rights for folk of all colours.[2]

In face of so feeble an Opposition, Malan had little difficulty in carrying fairly drastic legislation on *apartheid* lines. The first such measure was an amended Unemployment Insurance Act,[3] which deprived of allowances such lower-paid persons, Coloured Folk for the most part, as refused to accept 'suitable employment,' which might mean hated farm work. The second was the Immorality Amendment Act,[4] which extended the penalties hitherto reserved for Europeans who had carnal intercourse with Bantu to all such as had similar intercourse with non-Europeans of any kind. The third was the

---

[1] *Round Table*, No. 159, pp. 282 ff.; *Chronology*, VI., No. 3, p. 87; No. 4, p. 116.
[2] Hatch, *op. cit.*, pp. 108 ff.; Davidson, *op. cit.*, pp. 111 ff.
[3] Act 41 of 1949.   [4] Act 21 of 1950.

Population Registration Act, which decreed that, after the compilation of a national register, every individual over sixteen years of age must carry an identity card specifying *inter alia* the holder's racial origin.[1] The Opposition resisted this last measure half-heartedly, not so much because it would reduce all who had one-sixth 'black blood' to the level of non-Europeans, as because it was an additional pass law which would assuredly be applied first to the Cape Coloured Folk, so many of whom were physically indistinguishable from White Folk. The real opposition came from Nationalists and one stout United Party man, Sarel Tighy of Johannesburg West, who objected that the measure was 'a White Kaffir Act' in that it would compel Europeans to carry what was to all intents and purposes a pass.[2]

Then came the Group Areas Bill.[3] This Bill, the logical sequel of the Registration Act and the most downright *apartheid* measure of the Session, had a rougher passage, if only because it was vague and gave 'the Minister' far too much discretion. There was to be wholesale compulsory segregation based on the division of the country into definite areas for exclusive occupation by this racial group or that, an admittedly gradual process, which was, however, to be speeded up by a semi-judicial Land Tenure Advisory Board that would have power to send its inspectors, interpreters and policemen into any dwelling, whether by day or by night, and that without notice. On the strength of the reports of these subordinates, the Minister could evict a man from his home or place of work or both without being obliged to find him alternative accommodation, and thus force him to sell at knock-down prices. Dönges, who sponsored the Bill, assured the House that the proclamation of an area would usually call for the prior approval of Parliament and, with an eye on the already protesting Nehru, gave warning that he would not tolerate outside interference on behalf of any racial group in the Union. Strauss blandly admitted that his Party approved the Bill in principle and that he himself, so far from seeking to repeal it, would merely try to make it 'workable and equitable'; but when he asked that it be sent to a Commission, and the Oppenheimer group pleaded that it be at least postponed because in its existing form it would gravely prejudice industry, the Prime Minister replied that it must go through, otherwise non-Europeans would never be able to live 'with proper pride' or enjoy any measure of local self-government. Go through it did after brief discussion, the *apartheid*-minded Durban members characteristically taking a line of their own and abstaining from voting.

[1] Act 30 of 1950; *Round Table*, No. 159, pp. 282 ff.; *Chronology*, VI., No. 5, p. 143.
[2] *Round Table*, No. 158, p. 184; *S.A. Hansard*, March 9, col. 2685.
[3] Act 41 of 1950.

26*

The most serious storm of the Session arose over Swart's Suppression of Communism Bill.[1] Relying on the precedents of strong anti-Communist measures recently adopted by the United Kingdom and several other members of the Commonwealth, the Minister of Justice asked for almost dictatorial powers to deal decisively with anyone who was even faintly tinctured Red. The Minister was to be authorised to black-list any Party or present member of a banned association and, thereby, forbid such person to be a member of Parliament, Provincial Council, public body or other organisation, while the Governor-General was to be empowered to ban any newspaper or publication suspected of Communistic tendencies and to send his agents into premises there to ask questions. If anyone were proved to have attended an unlawful meeting during the period of his prosecution, he would be 'deemed' to be a member of that meeting or a supporter of its cause and would have to give proof to the contrary. There was to be no appeal against a proclamation which declared an organisation unlawful or an individual to be either a supporter thereof or a 'deemed' Communist. The penalty for furthering the interests of a banned organisation was to be anything up to ten years' imprisonment, and for defying the Minister's ukase up to three years.

Such a totalitarian measure might have been expected to sting the Opposition into resolute resistance. It did no such thing. Strauss, divided between an ardent desire for the eradication of Communism and fear for civil liberties, merely suggested that the Bill be held back while the Government sought to remove the evil conditions in which Communism flourished. Swart would have none of it. He retorted that the S.A. Communist Party was working for 'an independent Native republic' as a step towards 'a workers' and peasants' republic,' and threatened to move for a Committee to investigate the records of various persons and organisations and thus, maybe, avert the risk of imprisonments without trial.[2] On that same evening of June 14, 1950, white policemen did what they could to prove *apartheid* orthodox by heavy-handed blows and knocks administered without provocation or warning to members of an orderly procession of Coloured Folk, who were parading in Parliament Street just outside the Houses in protest against the Bill. The half-dozen injured having been removed, Swart accepted the assurance of the recently elected Communist 'Native' member, Sam Kahn, that his Party had dissolved itself a few days since; but he did not accept his challenge to set up a Judicial Committee to investigate his charges of conspiracy, which Kahn hotly denied. The Bill, rushed through in a mere thirty·hours by ruthless use of the guillotine, became law on the last day of the Session. Swart was thus enabled to try his new

[1] Act 44 of 1950.   [2] *Chronology*, VI., No. 12, p. 393.

weapon by 'naming' Kahn and a few fellow-Communists, and by seeking to oust from their seats the mildly Socialist 'Native' Senator, William Ballinger, and Margaret, his able Liberal wife. He learned at once, however, that where there are Judges, the way of the totalitarian is hard, for the redoubtable Appellate Division foiled him all along the line.[1]

The background of the Session was enlivened by sporadic and widespread non-European unrest. This began mildly enough with the death of two Bantu and the injuring of a few others in a tribal stick fight in northern Natal. Later incidents were far more serious, for on two occasions many were injured when policemen and local Poor Whites fired on non-European rioters, who returned the fire, amid the blazing houses of New Clare on the dingy outskirts of Johannesburg.[2] Scarcely had the police let go most of the hundreds of Bantu whom they had rounded up during these affairs for questioning than they had to intervene in a Bantu fight in the Benoni location. Swart believed that these disturbances were caused by the Bantu vagrants who swarmed in the purlieus of the Rand and, therefore, held military detachments in readiness to help the police and even projected a mechanised police section to deal with rioters, while the Prime Minister lamented that the Bantu were dissatisfied with what the authorities had done for them since the war, Smuts thundered that their changed attitude was intolerable, and even the patient Jansen could induce the Senate to reject a motion for the ultimate enfranchisement of non-Europeans by declaring that this would 'sound the death-knell for the white race.'[3] The agitated Johannesburg City Council naturally followed such a lead by prosecuting a couple of hundred African proprietors of cafés-de-move-on, who had banded together to bake bread for sale to their hungry compatriots in shops and factories.[4]

In face of such doings, the Council of Action of the African National Congress refused to co-operate further with the authorities and joined hands with the hitherto aloof S.A. Indian National Congress to organise protest demonstrations in the Transvaal. Swart, scenting trouble from the Communists who were prominent in both organisations, authorised the Rand magistrates to forbid meetings on or around Labour Day; nevertheless, the two Congresses held a protest meeting in a Rand township on that very day, stoned the police as they approached and saw eighteen of their supporters killed and thirty wounded.[5] The consequent Commission admitted indeed that most of the police had behaved correctly, but so far from joining

---

[1] Hatch, *op. cit.*, pp. 60, 129 ff.; *Chronology*, VI., No. 12, pp. 393 ff.
[2] *Ibid.*, VI., No. 3, p. 87; No. 4, p. 116.
[3] *Ibid.*, VI., No. 4, p. 116.   [4] Hatch, *op. cit.*, p. 133.
[5] *Chronology*, VI., No. 9, p. 277.

with the Minister of Justice in complimenting them as a body, recorded that some of the younger constables had been too harsh. It found that the disturbances had been due to the bursting forth of long-pent-up feelings, especially against the police, that grievances real and imaginary had been inflamed by Communists, and that a good many Bantu were opposed to control either by the Government or other white folk. On the other hand, it paid tribute to the solid core of decent law-abiding Africans in the Rand townships. As if to prove the truth of the Commission's testimonial, the African People's Congress and the Transvaal and Natal Indian Congresses jointly organised a Freedom Day protest against the whole policy of *apartheid*. They gained but little support from the distant and faction-ridden Cape Coloured Folk, whose doctrinaire and anti-white non-European Movement deprecated this first attempt to stage a national political strike because it was sure to break down and thereby discredit their campaign; but, for all that, they carried through their protest on June 26, 1950, without any untoward incidents.[1]

The Ministerialists and, doubtless, the Opposition also could congratulate themselves that the Suppression of Communism Act had been passed, because almost before the ink of the Governor-General's signature thereon was dry, North Korean Communists had invaded South Korea from which the scanty United States garrison was contemplating withdrawal. After some hesitation because of the remoteness of the scene of the conflict, Malan had fallen into line with the comparatively few members who answered the call of the United Nations General Assembly for a combined Crusade against the invaders by sending a fighter squadron to Korea and directing his service chiefs to report on means for expanding and modernising the Union's armed forces.[2] While the Reds, who had been prominent in the recent Rand disturbances and demonstrations, were rejoicing at the early successes of the Korean Communists, the Union drifted deeper into difficulties with India. A few months earlier, to Nehru's annoyance, Pakistan had lifted her section of the trade ban which Undivided India had placed on the Union in 1946, and had even accepted Malan's invitation to help him arrange the agenda for a round-table conference between the three Governments concerned. The Indian Prime Minister, whose representatives at Lake Success had long been demanding this very thing, relented sufficiently to permit of his joining in these discussions.[3] Then had come the introduction of the Group Areas Bill. At this threat to enforce residential segregation on South African Indians, Nehru had refused to take any further part so long as the measure was being

[1] *Chronology*, VI., No. 13, p. 432; Hatch, *op. cit.*, p. 165.
[2] *Chronology*, VI., No. 13, p. 432; No. 15, p. 511; No. 16, p. 546.
[3] *Ibid.*, VI., No. 4, p. 116, No. 12, p. 391.

rushed through. Taking its cue, the S.A. Indian Congress called for intervention by the Powers assembled in the Philippines to consider the affairs of South-East Asia and Pacific lands and, further, appealed to U.N.O. to outlaw the Union because of her 'Fascist and racial tendencies.'[1] Towards the close of the year, in spite of the now customary protest by Dönges, a great majority of the U.N.O. delegates accepted the proposal moved by Mrs. Pandit, the Indian Ambassador to the United States and representative of her country at Lake Success, that the text of the Group Areas Act be circulated, that India, Pakistan and South Africa be urged once more to push ahead with the round-table conference, that if agreement were not reached speedily a Mediation Commission be appointed, and, finally, that the Union be asked to refrain from putting the new Act into force while negotiations were proceeding.[2]

Malan paid no attention to the resolutions of the General Assembly; but he and his more prudent colleagues damped down the agitation for wholesale and immediate *apartheid*, which had been stimulated by a drastic scheme to that end recently submitted by the Congress of the Federated Dutch Reformed Churches and supported by a couple of Commissions, which urged that, when this had been achieved, all Indians should be 'repatriated.' Having pointed out as frankly as Huggins himself that the Union's dependence on non-European labour rendered anything of the sort unworkable, he nevertheless promised to canalise the townward flow of Bantu, to send as many as possible back to their 'homes' in the Reserves, and to teach them to make the best use of their land. Jansen, for his part, promised the Bantu an improved tribal system, which should lead up to a Central Council for all of them in exchange for representation in Parliament.[3] On the other hand, Eric Louw, who had shown that he very well knew the weaknesses of the *apartheid* policy, called upon the Afrikaner Party to fall into line with the Nationalists and at least put the Cape Coloured voters on a separate roll. He was reminded pointedly by Havenga that he and the Prime Minister had promised to let the Coloured issue stand over for at least a year.[4]

The time was drawing near, however, when even the most pointed of Havenga's reminders would avail little. One by one, Malan saw the obstacles to his essential policy falling away. Hofmeyr was gone, Smuts for all his toughness could scarcely last much longer, and now a turn of events in South-West Africa put the game into his own hands. The International Court, to which U.N.O. had submitted the legal aspects of the South-West African dispute, ruled unanimously in July 1950 that the Territory was still under Mandate, that the

[1] *Chronology*, VI., No. 11, p. 351.
[2] *Ibid.*, VI., No. 22, p. 736; No. 23, p. 765; No. 24, pp. 795, 798.
[3] *Ibid.*, VI., No. 8, p. 248. [4] *Round Table*, No. 159, p. 282.

Union, therefore, could not change its status without leave of U.N.O. and that it was still open to the Union to place it under Trusteeship. It ruled further by a six to one majority, that the Union was still bound by international obligations arising from the Mandate to send in petitions from the inhabitants and to report on its administration.[1] Malan doggedly refused to 'saddle' South-West Africa with these judicially-imposed burdens; but Smuts, in what was almost the last of his public pronouncements, reminded him that refusal to report would damage their country's international reputation. The plea fell on deaf ears and the South-West African general elections went forward. These were fought solely on the locally popular platform of *apartheid* and refusal to report to U.N.O. Thanks almost entirely to the solid pro-Nationalist votes of the three thousand recently enfranchised Germans, they gave Malan's Party fifteen as against three United Party seats in the Windhoek Legislative Council besides all the four new Senators and six Assembly Members in the Union Parliament. Malan and Havenga together thus had a majority of twelve in the Lower House and of four in the Senate, where they would no longer be dependent on the Speaker's casting vote; but the really significant fact was that Malan now had an independent majority of his own and could beat down Havenga's resistance to the political segregation of the Coloured Folk. Once those voters were safely out of the way, he might hope to carry the half-dozen Western Province constituencies in which they now had a decisive voice and thereby ensure the permanent majority of his dreams.

Smuts knew this also only too well and realised that Malan's victory meant at least the indefinite postponement of the drawing together of the two white groups for which he and Louis Botha had worked so hard and so long. Haunted by this grim knowledge, he died quietly at the age of eighty on the evening of September 11, 1950, at his beloved farm, Doornkop, on the Irene estate near Pretoria. Malan at once offered to give his remains a state funeral, but the family preferred a great military funeral. They scattered Smuts's ashes on a rocky hill behind his rambling farmhouse where he used to sit so often.[2]

Robbed of Smuts's masterful leadership, the fissiparous United Party could be expected to make less effective resistance than ever to Malan. It indeed elected Strauss as his successor more or less unanimously, but with so little enthusiasm that one or two of its members suggested that he should make way for Havenga as leader of a rejuvenated Moderate Party. Nothing came of this by no means unreasonable proposal, if only because the leader of the Afrikaner Party was busy making the best terms he could with his triumphant

---

[1] *Chronology*, VI., No. 11, p. 354; No. 14, pp. 473 ff.
[2] J. C. Smuts, *op. cit.*, p. 273.

ally. He induced Malan to leave Bantu representation untouched. but had to agree publicly that the Coloured voters should be segregated during the coming Session. The Prime Minister sought to soften the blow by increasing the moderate element in his Cabinet. He gave the portfolios of Mines and Education respectively, to Johannes Viljoen and the Speaker, Jozua Naude, both of them admirers of Hertzog and Havenga; but he balanced these concessions by inducing the cautious Jansen to resign so that he might prepare himself to take over the Governor-Generalship at the New Year, and giving his portfolio of Mines to Dr. Hendrik Verwoerd, an ardent disciple of the Transvaal extremist, Strydom.[1] He then went straight ahead.

The Speech from the Throne on January 19, 1951, indicated that the coming Session would be strenuous. Strauss at once observed in passing that the marked falling-off of British immigration during the past year had been balanced by an influx from Italy, Germany and the Netherlands of newcomers more congenial to ministerialists. He then begged Malan to call a halt to racial legislation and concentrate on economics and defence now that the Korean war was broadening out so fast that Dönges had just urged the Commonwealth Prime Ministers' Conference to enrol Germany, Italy, Spain and Japan in a world-wide line-up against aggressive Communism.[2] The Prime Minister turned his request aside by assuring him that the Government fully intended to continue giving help in Korea, and the Minister of Defence not only gave details of his preparations in the event of war, but reminded him that problems of transport in Southern and Central Africa had recently been discussed at Johannesburg by the United Kingdom, France, Portugal, Belgium and all the states and territories south of the Sahara. Havenga then painted a comparatively cheering picture of the economic situation, which had improved so much of late that many controls on essential consumer goods were gone and others going. He foretold immediate relief from credits arranged by the banks and the substantial loan advanced by the International Bank for Reconstruction and Development towards the cost of electric power plant and transport. Pointing to the long-run benefits that should accrue from the agreement recently concluded with the United Kingdom and the United States for the extraction of uranium from South Africa's slimes and gold mines, he had little difficulty in carrying supplementary estimates which were calculated to yield a substantial surplus at the end of the current year. Thereafter, he easily carried the regular Budget, which effected a few changes in taxation and foreshadowed a much larger surplus, the whole of which was to be carried to loan account.[3]

The Session was indeed strenuous. No less than ninety-one Bills

[1] *Chronology*, VI., No. 21, p. 706.   [2] *Ibid.*, VII., No. 3, pp. 68, 77.
[3] *Ibid.*, VII., No. 3, pp. 78, 82; No. 7, p. 206.

were introduced and of these seventy-three were carried covering a field as wide as insurance, rents, pensions, public holidays and, in face of much public criticism, provision of pensions for parliamentarians and the raising of their salaries from £1000 to £1400 a year. Prefaced by Malan's assurance that he regarded the Middle East as the Union's first line of defence, the Defence Act Amendment Bill went through with the support of the Opposition in time to strengthen the hands of the Minister of Defence on the eve of his departure for defence talks in London.[1] Other measures carried the *apartheid* policy further. Verwoerd had in his hand the report of an Industrial Legislation Commission, which recommended that although the evidence had been 'overwhelmingly' against racial segregation, trade unions should be organised on that basis because 'other witnesses' insisted on it. He, therefore, provided for the racial segregation of merchant seamen by his Merchant Shipping Bill. Bantu builders fared even worse. Progressive members of white trade unions had proposed that Bantu be trained as skilled workers to build cheap houses for their low-paid kinsfolk on condition that they be accorded full trade union rights and be not allowed to undermine white standards. Their reactionary fellows had refused, however, to hear of 'Kaffirs' being thus favoured and, even though emergency regulations withheld trade union privileges from the Bantu in question and fixed their maximum wages at half that of Europeans, had boycotted the whole affair. The Minister of Labour now introduced his Native Building Workers' Bill, which would permit Africans to build houses for Africans only and yet safeguard white standards. The Opposition did not object to the scheme as a whole nor yet to its regulation by an Advisory Board and consultations between the Minister and his colleagues, but it at least protested that once more everything seemed to be left to 'the Minister ' backed by fines and imprisonment, and asked where the extension of the legal colour bar, hitherto limited to the mines, was going to end.[2] This measure having been duly carried, Verwoerd's Bantu Authorities Bill at last got rid of the Native Representative Council and fulfilled Jansen's promise by substituting for it a pyramid of purely tribal institutions. First, there was to be the Chief and his Council in each tribal area; then, Regional Councils, consisting of members chosen, subject to ministerial disallowance, to control two or more of those areas; next, similarly selected Territorial Councils, each to control two or more Regional Councils and, finally, 'Native' Senators elected by the tribal and ministerially-controlled Regional Councils. It was a rigid system, which offered little room for the swarms of detribalised Bantu and set up a precedent that might make it easier for Ministers

---

[1] Act 44 of 1951; *Round Table*, No. 164, p. 293.
[2] Hatch, *op. cit.*, p. 80; Sachs, *op. cit.*, pp. 164–5.

to claim the right to tamper with the free election of 'Native' Members to the Lower House.[1]

It was to Assembly elections that the Prime Minister now directed his attention. There, straight ahead, were the Cape Coloured voters strongly entrenched behind the South Africa Act, the Great Redan which he must storm if he were to win through to his Sebastopol of a presumably permanent majority. He trained his heaviest artillery upon it forthwith. In terms of the Separate Representation of Voters Bill,[2] the Coloured Folk in the Union were to be represented by one additional nominee white Senator, but the Cape Coloured voters were to be put on a separate roll and given little more representation in the Assembly than that left to the Cape Bantu in 1936. The Coloured voters in the Cape, together with the twelve hundred or so in Natal, were to elect four Europeans to the Lower House with full powers other than a voice in the election of Senators. Those in the Cape Province were also to elect to the Provincial Council two Special Representatives, who might be Coloured men. There was to be, in addition, a Coloured Affairs Council consisting of eight elective Coloured members, three Coloured members nominated respectively for Natal, the Free State and the Transvaal and three non-voting white officials representing the Cape Provincial Council and the Departments of Welfare and Labour, the whole under the chairmanship of the head of the Sub-Department of Coloured Affairs in the dreaded Department of Native Affairs. If this drastic measure were carried, it would sweep away almost everything that still survived of the old Cape civilisation franchise.

The South Africa Act of 1909, the outcome of a hard-fought compromise, had endowed the Union with a constitution as flexible as that of the United Kingdom, save for two clauses which had been 'entrenched' as the only means of inducing the reluctant Cape to come in, a voluntary entrenching which resembled the self-imposed safeguards against hasty alteration embodied in the old Free State's republican constitution. One of these clauses provided that the legal equality of the two official languages should never be touched, and the other that no voter in the Cape Province be disfranchised by reason only of his race or colour, unless the relevant Bill were carried, not by the mere majority of each House sitting separately, but by a majority of the two Houses sitting together, and, at the Third Reading, by a two-thirds majority of the total membership of those Houses once more sitting together. The legal and moral sanctity of this Union bargain had been affirmed again and again by leaders of all parties, including Malan himself. When Parliament petitioned

---

[1] Act 68 of 1951; Hatch, *op. cit.*, p. 80; Sachs, *op. cit.*, p. 164.
[2] Act 46 of 1951; *Chronology*, VII., No. 4, p. 108; *Round Table*, No. 162, pp. 135 ff.

the British Parliament to extend the Statute of Westminster to South Africa, Hertzog and Smuts had both seen to it that the Petition should include a request that the entrenchment should be left intact; when the consequent Status Act was passed, the Coalition Government had stated that the situation remained unaltered and, later on, Jansen, the present Governor-General, had ruled from the Speaker's chair that this was indeed so.[1] In 1937, however, the Appellate Division had found in the course of a cursory judgment that, since the passing of the Statute of Westminster and the Status Act, the Courts had had no power to question the validity of any Act that had been passed, printed and promulgated.[2] Inspired by political ambition, Malan had then turned right round, laid hold of that judgment and declared war on the Coloured voters. Supported by some 'high legal authority' at least and well aware that he could not get the necessary two-thirds majority in the existing Parliament, he had long proposed to carry his Bill by ordinary parliamentary procedure, arguing that, by cancelling the validity of the entrenched clauses, the Statute of Westminster had left the now sovereign South African Parliament free to pass measures by any procedure it chose.[3]

The question was, could the Bill be carried legally by the procedure the Prime Minister proposed? If it were so carried and the procedure was proved to be illegal, a deadly blow would have been dealt to the South Africa Act, the measure that had brought the Union into being, the nearest approach to a written constitution South Africa had. It would lie with the Speaker to rule in the first instance whether Malan was in order or no. The successful Nationalist candidate for that office, who notoriously shared the Prime Minister's views, came down on the ministerial side and thereby ensured the passing of the Bill.[4] Malan then insisted that the measure did not fall within the scope of the entrenched clause because it neither disqualified nor diminished the rights of any individual Coloured voter, each of whom would still have a vote, though, to be sure, those voters would have less relative power as a group in that they would no longer be able to sway the issue in this constituency or that. When Strauss threatened to appeal to the Courts if the Bill were carried by the procedure proposed, he retorted that, if the Courts declared the Act invalid, they would be undermining the sovereignty of Parliament and claiming for themselves a function that belonged exclusively to the legislature.[5] Thereafter, accusing the Opposition, on the one hand, of stirring up race hatred and, on the other, assuring English-speaking

---

[1] *Round Table*, No. 167, pp. 224 ff.; Hatch, *op. cit.*, p. 72; D. V. Cowen, *Parliamentary Sovereignty and the Entrenched Clauses.* . . .
[2] *Round Table*, No. 163, pp. 292 ff.; No. 167, p. 224; Ndhlwana *v.* Hofmeyr, 1937, A.D. 229.
[3] *Round Table*, No. 162, pp. 140 ff.   [4] *Hansard (S.A.)*, April 11, 1951.
[5] *Ibid.*, April 17 and March 8, 1951.

Natal that the entrenched dual language clause was in no danger from him, he piloted the Bill through by the ordinary procedure. All Strauss could do was to promise to embody a Bill of Rights in the South Africa Act.[1]

Some such guarantee of personal liberties might well be called for in a merely nominal democracy that was rapidly becoming totalitarian. The Minister of Justice led the way down the slippery slope. Finding that his Suppression of Communism Act did not give him all the powers he wanted, he carried an amending Bill which enabled him to deal departmentally, as he deemed fit, with anyone who at any time and in any place had laid himself open to ministerial suspicion of having been even the mildest of Communists or Fellow Travellers.[2] His colleagues made haste to follow. First, they cut off the B.B.C. news, though not its entertainment, and gave the monopoly of the transmission of news to the more amenable S.A. Broadcasting Corporation. Next, the Minister of Education threatened to withhold the customary state grants from those voluntary cultural societies which would not undertake to exclude non-Europeans either as performers or onlookers. He was, maybe, surprised when some of them politely bade him keep his money rather than agree to deprive such folk of a chance of acquiring the civilisation which in most parts of the world was the passport to full citizenship, and was possibly nonplussed when the City Fathers of Capetown, Coloured men among them, told him that in such matters they could draw no distinction between human beings of different hues, who were, after all, ratepayers. Again, the Minister of the Interior proclaimed that new passports were no longer to be the property of the holders but of the Government, which was to be free to cancel them at any time. Dönges followed up this ukase by refusing to issue passports to numerous non-European students who wished to pursue their studies in India and elsewhere overseas, by driving the head of the Pretoria National Physical Laboratory to resign her post by withholding, for no cause shown, the passport which would have enabled her to study the latest results of atomic research in the United Kingdom, and by impelling the British Medical Association to refuse the invitation to attend the Medical Association Conference at Johannesburg by declining to guarantee the admission to the Union of non-European members or wives.[3] Swart then did his best to hasten the ministerial stampede by magnifying the scare, which Albertus Hertzog had started, that on a given day non-European delivery boys were going to poison the Free State's milk supply, by alleging that there was shortly going to be a wholesale poisoning of water supplies and

---

[1] *Chronology*, VII., No. 8, p. 238; *Round Table*, No. 163, pp. 292 ff.
[2] Act 50 of 1951; Hatch; *op. cit.*, p. 63; Davidson, *op. cit.*, p. 34.
[3] Hatch, *op. cit.*, pp. 64 ff.

destruction of power plants.[1] He possibly found relief by black-listing the redoubtable Sachs; nevertheless, though he could justly boast that none of the three hundred or so persons whom he had 'named' under the Suppression of Communism Acts had succeeded in their appeals, he could not deny that the Courts had latterly given many major decisions against the authorities. Indeed, one of his ardent supporters was so shocked by this judicial intransigence that he urged the Prime Minister in the columns of the official organ of the *Reddingsdaadbond* to make it illegal for Judges to carry on thus and to dismiss any who did so, just as President Kruger had dismissed his Chief Justice long ago.[2]

Meanwhile, the position of the trade unions was becoming increasingly insecure. Three organisations claimed to speak for the 400,000 Europeans and the million or so non-Europeans who were members of unions; first, Stuart's group in the western Cape Province; secondly, the Communist-led rump of the Cape Federation of Labour and, lastly, the S.A. Trades and Labour Council, whose headquarters were in Johannesburg. This notable Council, the one really national Centre in the land, claimed a total membership of about 130,000 in its affiliated unions. Probably because it was a co-ordinating rather than a policy-making organisation, it had no colour bar, but allowed any union to apply for affiliation and left each of them free to settle its own racial problems. Further, despite the fears of the Minister of Labour, it showed few signs of associating itself too closely with Christie's Labour Party, because its Communistic members regarded it as reactionary, its Nationalist members condemned it as Communistic, and its United Party members agreed with Ministers that trade unions should keep out of politics.[3]

The racial policies of the trade unions varied widely. Many of the larger unions, especially those connected with mining, and some of the less important craft guilds also maintained a rigid colour bar, though some of them followed the Engine-drivers' Union in favouring a separate African co-ordinating Centre. Others of the larger unions were less exclusive, those in the Transvaal tending towards parallel development by the formation of separate branches within the same union for Europeans, Coloured Folk and Africans respectively, and those in the Cape inclining towards the admission of folk of all colours to the same union on equal terms. Most of the members of Sachs's Garment Workers' Union in the Cape and Natal were already non-Europeans, and even in the Transvaal the numbers of such members were increasing so fast in the parent body that their six hundred shop-stewards could work towards the integration of workers irrespective of colour and condemn *apartheid* in their annual

[1] Hatch, *op. cit.*, p. 88.   [2] *Inspan*, August 1951; *vide supra*, p. 471.
[3] Sachs, *op. cit.*, pp. 188 ff.

Conferences. Some three-score other Transvaal unions were beginning to take the same line.[1]

There was, however, another side to the picture. For some years
past, Nationalist-inclined Afrikaners had been pouring from the
platteland into many trade unions along the Rand, especially into
the dozen or so which consisted of railway and harbour workers
under firm ministerial control. They had poured above all into the
white Mineworkers' Union. This once-powerful organisation had
fallen from its high estate. It was now little more than a tool in the
hands of the Nationalist Party and was, moreover, in such serious
financial trouble that its Executive Council had recently contemplated
taking action against its Finance Committee. One cause for this
embarrassment was now revealed. Shortly after taking office, the
Minister of Labour had signalised his virtual assumption of command of the anti-trade-union campaign by organising the *Geko-
oordeneerde Raad van Verenigings* as a rival to the Trades and Labour
Council, and seeking to attract thereto dissident members of the Iron
and Steel, white Mineworkers and other unions. Presently, Albertus
Hertzog made a dead set at the Builders', Mineworkers' and Garment
Workers' Unions. He and another member of the executive of the
Mineworkers' Union became directors of *Die Werkerspers*, which
published its three newspapers through *Die Voortrekkerpers*, an
equally new creation, which boasted among its directors the Ministers
of Justice and the Interior. These journals accused trade union leaders
and, in especial, the hated Sachs of Communism and other misdemeanours so unwarrantably that they were repeatedly forced to pay
damages and costs either in or out of Court. At last Sachs and Peter
Huyser, the Afrikaner national organiser of the Building Workers'
Industrial Union, obtained such heavy damages against *Die Werkerspers* that that firm could not possibly pay them, because its debts,
mainly to the Mineworkers' Union, amounted to £2000 and its paid-
up capital to a mere £7. Thereupon, Sachs obtained an order of the
Court for its liquidation and started proceedings with only slightly
less success against *Die Voortrekkerpers*. This final shock sent the
white Mineworkers' Union over the precipice. Some fifteen thousand
of its more ardently Nationalist members broke away, formed the
rival *Afrikaner Mynwerkers Unie* and joined the dozen or so other
tame unions which had rallied to the ministerially-sponsored *Geko-
oordeneerde Raad*.[2]

This display of *apartheid* in the trade unions sphere impelled non-
Europeans to strike back as best they could. As long ago as December
1950, the African National Council had set aside the impracticable

---

[1] Davidson, *op. cit.*, pp. 183 ff.
[2] *Ibid.*, pp. 187 ff.; Sachs, *op. cit.*, pp. 186 ff.; *Rand Daily Mail*, Aug. 22,
1951.

idea of demanding the repeal of all discriminatory legislation and resolved rather to launch a campaign of mass disobedience eighteen months hence on April 6, 1952, the very day on which white South Africans would be celebrating the tercentenary of the coming of van Riebeeck and, with him, white civilisation to the far end of Africa. It, further, adopted the motion of its president, Dr. James Moroka, that 'all peoples, irrespective of nationality or colour, who have made South Africa their home and who believe in the principles of democracy and equality of men, are South Africans, and, as such, entitled to live a full and free life on the basis of the fullest equality.' [1]

It was an African who had sketched the plan of campaign and uttered the war-cry, but it was an Indian who made the first move. This was Manilal Gandhi, a younger son of the Mahatma, manager of his recently murdered father's settlement at Phoenix near Durban and editor of the local weekly, *Indian Opinion*. Inspired by the doctrine of *satyagraha*, which his late father had evolved and practised in his half-forgotten campaign against the discriminatory laws of the Transvaal and the Union,[2] Manilal, from April 1951 onwards, proceeded to defy petty local segregation rules and even to trespass on forbidden Free State soil. The authorities ignored him; but as memories of mutual faction-fighting died away, his example helped to bring Indians and Bantu so much closer together that the S.A. Indian National Congress and the African Native Congress could join hands to organise resistance.[3] The introduction of the Separate Representation of Voters' Bill won them some support even from the undecided Cape Coloured Folk. True, some of the more energetic and sensitive members of that Folk, disheartened at having been degraded from the proud status of British subjects to that of Union citizens and fearing still further reduction to the level of mere 'Coloured persons,' were beginning to leave the Union for the freer atmosphere of the United Kingdom or even for that of comparatively libertarian Southern Rhodesia, where they might at least have a better chance of 'passing as white.' At the other extreme, the Coloured non-European Unity Movement, backed by the All-African Convention, jeered at all talk of political strikes as being hypocritical and urged that the proper course was to withhold co-operation from the authorities and, meanwhile, build up a united non-European front. Nevertheless, despite its preference for the boycotting of sports meetings to political strikes, Golding's right-wing Coloured People's National Union made common cause with the more or less Communistic Franchise Action Committee and, with the help of some members of the Coloured A.P.O., the African Native Congress and the S.A. Indian National Congress, organised frequent demonstrations against the

---

[1] Hatch, *op. cit.*, pp. 167 ff.; Davidson, *op. cit.*, pp. 197 ff.
[2] *Vide supra*, pp. 524, 551 ff.   [3] *Round Table*, No. 170, p. 131.

Separate Representation of Voters Bill. The most impressive of these demonstrations took place in Capetown in March 11, 1951, and was almost immediately followed by a fairly successful one-day strike.[1]

Europeans now organised a far more widespread mass protest. Early in the year, a relative of Jacobus de la Rey, the famous western Transvaal General of South African war days, himself a Commandant, and 'Sailor' Adolph Malan, a noted airman, had founded the War Veterans' Action Group to which ex-Service men and women flocked from all parts of the Union. So far was it from having a liberal attitude on the non-European issue that it was destined to exclude Coloured Folk and Bantu from its Alamein Day celebrations; but it was united in its determination to be done with the Malan administration and thus to deliver its country from the totalitarianism against which its members had so long fought in the field. It presently changed its name to that of the Torch Commando, converged in scattered commandos on Capetown and there, bearing torches, conducted a huge mass-meeting on the Parade Ground outside the Castle and a procession through the principal streets of the city in protest against the procedure by which the Separate Representation of Voters Bill was being carried. The Commando's own proceedings were orderly, but those of some of the casual Coloured Folk who had tagged along behind it in its march were not. These folk, trooping home to the slums of District Six, found themselves faced in Church Square, under the shadow of the Groote Kerk, by teams of young policemen, who had been trained to break up mobs and had been brought in specially from the countryside to show their prowess. They did, and for the second time during this disastrous Session, the Mother City was the scene of scarcely excusable violence by the guardians of law and order. The police charged without warning, and, equally without warning, used their truncheons on the heads or other parts of the anatomy of anyone they could get at.[2] It was diligently noised abroad that the crowd had been trying to destroy the Groote Kerk, a rumour well calculated to induce Nationalists, if inducement were needed, to vote for the virtual disfranchisement of Coloured Folk.

Demonstrations by Europeans and non-Europeans alike were not the only adverse comments on the legislative and administrative records of the Government. Such was the world-wide torrent of criticism that Strauss, on a visit to London, was moved to beg the British public to trust the Union and regard her problems with sympathy. Others reacted in quite another fashion. Ministers railed against the 'unfairness' of overseas comment, especially that by

[1] *Cape Times, Die Burger, Rand Daily Mail*, March 9, 1951; *Rand Daily Mail*, May 8, 1951.
[2] *Round Table*, No. 164, pp. 390 ff.; Cape newspapers, *passim*, May 29, 1951, onwards; *Hansard (S.A.)*, May 29 and June 20, 1951.

United Kingdom newspapers; the staid Governor-General lamented that 'the fires of racial prejudice' were being kept alive by political strife and dangerous influences that sought the destruction of democratic principles, and the Prime Minister, the apostle of *apartheid*, ended a broadcast appeal for unity and tolerance all round by warning overseas critics that, if they went on accusing white South Africans of oppressing non-Europeans, he would be driven to proclaiming a Republic, though not unless he were sure of the support of 'a reasonable number of English-speaking citizens.'[1] Several other Ministers accused the Torch Commando of being Communist-inspired on the analogy of the totally distinct Springbok Legion, which was indeed under Communist leadership. Malan was particularly angry with the Commando because among its members were five retired Judges as well as four Generals, who were making their backsliding yet more 'improper' by finding fault with their country's Defence Force. This at a time when Anglo-Egyptian relations in the Sudan and the Suez Canal Zone were so strained that Union military officers had had to go north to take counsel with General Sir Brian Robertson, the British Commander-in-Chief Middle East, and thereafter to attend a Pan-African Defence Conference at Nairobi. But if Malan could not quell his external enemies, he could at least make more certain of defeating his domestic foes. This he did in September 1951 by persuading Havenga to formally combine his Afrikaner Party with his own Nationalist Party, a fusion which would incidentally strengthen the moderate element among his own followers and check Strydom and other zealots who were pressing him, in season and out of season, to proclaim a completely independent Republic.[2]

NKRUMAH, SERETSE KHAMA AND FEDERATION

On the eve of curtailing the political privileges of the Cape Coloured Folk, Malan, who not so long ago had blamed the British Government for having been too slow to endow the High Commission Territories with elective institutions, protested that it was going too fast and too far in that direction in the Gold Coast. Like other West Africans, the people of that colony had been much longer in touch with western Europeans than any other Africans south of the Sahara and, thanks to their unhealthy climate, had few white folk in their midst. After quelling post-war social, industrial and political disturbances, the British Government had given the Gold Coast a near approach to self-government based on adult suffrage.[3] The

[1] *Chronology*, VII., No. 12, pp. 368-9; No. 18, p. 562.
[2] *Round Table*, No. 164, p. 391; *Chronology*, VII., No. 17, pp. 531-2.
[3] Colonial, No. 248 and 250, Oct. 1949.

Convention People's Party did so well at the ensuing elections that the authorities released its leader, Dr. Nkwame Nkrumah, who had been imprisoned for starting a campaign of civil disobedience, and, in February 1951, gave him a seat on the Council of Ministers as Minister without Portfolio and Leader for Government Business. The South African Prime Minister was shocked deeply and the Leader of the Opposition only slightly less so by this elevation of a Negro to so high an office, and by the hope expressed subsequently by James Griffiths, the British Colonial Secretary, that the Gold Coast would soon become a Dominion. Malan condemned what the United Kingdom had done as 'unrealistic' and, with far more justice, complained that if she were, of her own mere motion, to follow up the recognition of India, Pakistan and Ceylon as three Dominions by the admission of Gold Coast as another, she would radically change the 'whole complexion and character' of the Commonwealth, which had rested hitherto on 'specific common interest and sufficient homogeneity of cultural and political outlook' and, worse still, would unwittingly help U.N.O. to kill that Commonwealth, a disaster which he for one would regret.[1] Gordon Walker, Secretary of State for Commonwealth Relations, tried in vain to placate him by observing truly that his Government's policy of giving self-government by instalments was well known and that the Dominions had always been consulted before any addition had been made to their number. Malan retorted by switching the debate to the future of the High Commission Territories, declaring that however anxious he might be to settle the problem of transfer by agreement, he might have to make it an election issue and would never accept African refusal as a veto on transfer.[2]

This pronouncement was ill-hearing to a Secretary of State who had just finished a tour of the three Territories assuring their inhabitants that they would not be transferred till they and the British Parliament had been consulted and seeking to straighten out the Bamangwato tangle. All three peoples reiterated their dogged objection to transfer and the Bamangwato asked that Seretse be sent back to them as Chief.[3] Without committing himself on that score, Walker went homewards by way of Capetown, where, at a public dinner, Malan good-humouredly twitted him with his Government's hesitation to hand the Territories over. He passed it off with a laugh, but, back once more in Downing Street, he refused to let Seretse go home unless the tribal *kgotla* asked for his return. Nor would he allow Tshekedi to go home. Thereupon, pro-Seretse mobs attacked Tshekedi's followers so fiercely that the Bechuanaland Protectorate

[1] *Round Table*, No. 163, pp. 219 ff.; *Chronology*, VII., No. 5, p. 134.
[2] *Ibid.*, VII., No. 18, p. 562.
[3] *Ibid.*, VII., No. 4, p. 107; No. 5, p. 134.

Police, reinforced by fifty Southern Rhodesian troopers, had to arrest many of them. Impressed by this uproar and the consequent appeal from South African Bantu organised in the African National Conference that the British public should compel its Government to allow both men to return, Walker gave Tshekedi at least liberty to go where he would. When, however, on the ex-Regent's return, the tribesmen refused to hold the *kgotla* that was to have debated the advisability of that step, he banished him from the Bamangwato Reserve and, presently, hurried out to the Territories once more, if only to calm those Bechuana Chiefs who were asking that both Tshekedi and Seretse be allowed to return untrammelled.[1] All that came of these comings and goings was that a formal and ineffective Native Authority was set up in Swaziland, and the Bechuana were assured that there was no truth in the rumour that their country was to be partitioned between the Union and Southern Rhodesia. The Bamangwato were left under their makeshift Native Authority.

Meanwhile, Huggins had been busied with many things since the British Government had imposed a check on his federation schemes at the close of 1949. In the course of the next few months, he had welcomed a United Kingdom High Commissioner to Salisbury, and had visited Lisbon to discuss the running of an oil pipe-line from Beira to Umtali and to sign a treaty with the Portuguese and British authorities for the improvement of the harbour works at Beira and the inadequate single-track railway to that port.[2] Returning home, he quieted the clamour for wholesale immigration to maintain white civilisation in his colony by pointing out that white immigrants were already pouring in at the rate of 16,000 a year, and added the warning that, though many of these were English-speaking South Africans, not a few were Nazi-minded Afrikaners whose influence on the rising generation could scarcely be good. He also managed to shelve a Native Land Husbandry Bill, which aimed at stemming the rush of Bantu into the towns by obliging each urban African male of full age who earned more than a given sum either to give up his cherished cattle in his Reserve or to work for a European farmer for sixty days each year. On the other hand, fearing to lose ground politically, he had to swallow what he frankly called the 'tactless' Electoral Amendment Act of 1951 in order to placate those many white folk who insisted that Africans were so barbarous that they would never be fit to take part in political life for a hundred years to come. He himself would have preferred to have merely a sound educational qualification which would have given the vote to many poor but intelligent Africans, but, as it was, he was obliged to leave the existing educational qualification untouched, and to see the

[1] *Chronology*, VII., No. 12, p. 369; No. 14, pp. 412, 426; No. 15, p. 464.
[2] *Ibid.*, VI., No. 12, p. 392.

economic qualifications pushed up to such a height that the franchise was well nigh inaccessible to those comparatively few Africans who might wish to earn it. All that he had been able to save was the common roll, for what that was now worth, the roll which Southern Rhodesia had inherited from the parent Cape Colony.[1]

On his return early in 1951 from the Commonwealth Prime Ministers' Conference in London and renewed discussions of the Beira pipeline in Lisbon, Huggins first coped successfully with a Cabinet crisis and then surveyed the general situation. Business was booming and such had been the confidence instilled into home and overseas investors by the mere talk of Federation that more than a thousand new companies with considerable capital had been launched during the past year, and now the Economic Co-operation Administration was offering to lend up to £8,000,000 for the construction of railways in Central Africa generally and the development of copper and cobalt mining in Northern Rhodesia.[2] Meanwhile, an Inter-Territorial Hydro-Electrical Power Commission had recently recommended the harnessing of the waters of the Zambesi at the cost of £74,000,000.

The Salisbury authorities were not so well satisfied with the course of events north of the Zambesi. There, little Nyasaland was indeed jogging along much as usual, but Northern Rhodesia, whose mines and scattering of secondary industries were flourishing, was moving fast into new and possibly dangerous waters. During the past couple of years, African trade unions had sprung up so fast that, in 1951, nine of them had been able to combine to form the Northern Rhodesian African Mineworkers' Union. This new and inexperienced organisation now made a fatal mistake. It agreed with the white Mineworkers' Union that Africans must be paid at white rates for all jobs they might take over from Europeans and be provided by the companies with houses and other amenities on the white level. It was an agreement which threatened to block Africans' economic and industrial advancement far more effectively than even the Colour Bar Agreement, which the white Union had extorted from the companies in 1942, because no management would dream of offering 'equal pay for equal work' until the work of Africans had indeed become equal to that of Europeans. That would take a long time to achieve and, meanwhile, the recent agreement could not be changed without the concurrence of both parties to it. Undismayed, the African Mineworkers' Union, now 25,000 strong, promptly affiliated with the Miners' International and gained a marked rise in pay, while African Teachers, Railway Workers and

---

[1] The property qualification was raised from £150 to £500, and that for income from £100 to £240.
[2] *Chronology*, VII., No. 14, p. 411.

Hotel and Catering Workers formed unions, which thrust out branches all over the Protectorate. Nevertheless, though seven such trade unions with a total membership of more than 30,000 could hold a Trade Union Congress before 1951 was out, the redoubtable Welensky, at that time champion of privileged white workers and their families, had shown how little hope there was of a relaxation of the industrial colour bar by hinting in the columns of *Die Burger*, the leading Nationalist Afrikaans Capetown morning paper, that the British Government did not really care for the fate of white Central Africans, and that the ideal Native policy for the coming Federation would be something between the United Kingdom's White Paper policy and the *apartheid* policy of the Union.[1]

At this stage, Federation passed out of the realms of wishful thinking into the sphere of practical politics, for James Griffiths and Gordon Walker, the newly-appointed Secretaries of State for the Colonies and for Commonwealth Relations respectively, swung the British Labour Government round in favour of the idea. Griffiths at once arranged with Huggins and other local politicians that the Central African Council and the Governments directly concerned should nominate a purely official Exploratory Conference, which should sit in London and there draw up a scheme for discussion. In due time this Conference reported. Prefacing its recommendations with the long-delayed Report of the Victoria Falls Conference of 1949 and surveys of the geographical, historical and economic conditions and of the Native policies of the three Central African territories,[2] it suggested that a Federal Government, headed by a Governor-General, should be entrusted with such matters as defence, economic planning, railways, higher education, civil aviation and Customs, and that there should also be a unicameral Federal Parliament of thirty-five members, that is, seventeen for Southern Rhodesia, eleven for Northern Rhodesia and seven for Nyasaland. Three of the members from each territory were to represent African interests. Those interests were to be further safeguarded by the allocation of everyday Native affairs to the territorial authorities, the maintenance of the responsibility of the two Protectorates to the British Government and, an idea that would never have occurred to any parliamentarian, the appointment as member of the Federal Cabinet of a Minister of Native Affairs, who should be responsible, not to the Federal Parliament, but to that at Westminster.

Armed with this basis for discussion, the two Secretaries of State set out for Central Africa to talk things over with all concerned before attending the projected further plenary Conference. They found Africans everywhere protesting that the scheme was too heavily

[1] *Chronology*, VII., No: 6, p. 171.
[2] Cmd. 8233, 8234 and 8235 of 1951.

weighted in favour of the white folk and, in Southern Rhodesia, a group of *apartheid*-minded Afrikaners, organised in the curiously named Democratic Party, demanding resistance to Communism, the maintenance of white supremacy and the speedy grant of Dominion powers and status to their Colony.[1] Digesting these radically opposed opinions, the two Ministers took their seats, on September 20, 1951, at the resumed Victoria Falls Conference, which, besides the usual local European delegations, included the two Europeans and four Africans who represented Native interests in the Legislative Councils of Northern Rhodesia and Nyasaland. Sitting behind closed doors under the chairmanship of the Governor of Southern Rhodesia, this Conference echoed the slogan of 'partnership,' which the Colonial Secretary had picked up on his way south, and, disregarding the dissent of its African members, accepted the Exploratory Conference's scheme with three notable additions: first, that land and the political advancement of Africans should be matters solely for the territorial authorities; secondly, that the Protectorate status of the trans-Zambesi territories should be maintained, and, lastly, at Huggins's suggestion, that there should be a common voters' roll.[2]

The proposals of this Conference had a very mixed reception. Huggins, faintly scornful, called the assemblage 'a mothers' meeting' bent on placating the black folk, and then, having startled his white Southern Rhodesians by warning them that if the two Protectorates sent Africans to the Federal Parliament, their Colony must do likewise, set about getting rid of the projected independent Minister of Native Affairs, whose position would be so anomalous that it would wreck the whole scheme. The Africans, for their part, were disquieted. The two Northern Rhodesian Africans who had attended the recent Conference refused to work for Federation until the blessed word 'partnership' had been defined and applied to their country, while humbler folk speaking through the mouths of their traditional leaders condemned the whole thing as mere white man's work. The Northern Rhodesian and Nyasaland African Congresses, strong in the backing of the younger educated folk as well as of older conservatives, told the Colonial Secretary that Federation was out of the question, not because it was Federation, whose intricacies they could no more explain than could the average United Kingdom voter, but simply because it was a scheme that would put them at the mercy of white Southern Rhodesians, who might take away their highly-prized land and then push them into a rigid Amalgamation after all. Like any Gold Coasters, they demanded universal suffrage, an increase of African representation in their respective Legislative

[1] Hatch, *op. cit.*, p. 238.
[2] *Chronology*, VII., No. 18, p. 543; No. 19, pp. 572–3.

Councils, and, generally, the extension of democratic elective methods on equal terms with Europeans to all urban, district, provincial and Protectorate affairs. So far as they could speak for their fellow-countrymen, that was what Africans meant by 'partnership.'[1]

MALAN AND THE COURTS

While British Secretaries of State were facing criticism from Bantu in Central Africa, South African politicians were once more under fire at Lake Success. There, an Indian delegate attacked the Group Areas Act as an attempt to drive Indians out of trade, the one thing left to them now that they had been denied 'the most elementary' political and social rights, and, despite the fact that it was his own Prime Minister who was obstinately blocking the scheme, persuaded the General Assembly to go back to the proposal which it had made some two years back of appointing a Three Power Commission of Good Offices to arrange a round-table Conference between India, Pakistan and the Union. Further, the General Assembly impelled Dönges to walk out in protest by discussing South-West Africa, albeit without hearing the Chiefs of those parts because the authorities had refused to give them exit permits. In due time, Dönges, who had meanwhile forbidden the Rev. Michael Scott to return to South Africa, reappeared and delivered his soul. He warned his hearers that if they persisted in meddling in his country's domestic affairs, the Union would retaliate, challenged Scott's right to speak for the Hereros and others, and, with the support of the British Attorney-General, declared that it set a bad precedent to invite Chiefs to appear before the 'vindictive' Trusteeship Committee. Nevertheless, the General Assembly by a large majority once more urged South Africa to place her Mandated Territory under that Committee. Scott, for his part, requested that a report be sent to the Chiefs of South-West Africa, since he might not now go to them nor they come to him.[2]

South African and British delegates might hold that the United Nations' demands were too condemnatory to do any good, but dark-skinned folk in South Africa believed that good might come of a downright condemnation of *apartheid*. Accordingly, at the New Year of 1952, the Joint Planning Council, which had recently been formed by the African and S.A. Indian National Congresses, resolved that there should be a mass disobedience movement against unjust laws.[3] It was with this threat looming in the background that Parliament assembled some six weeks later. It had to listen to a mixed financial story. A loan from Swiss banks repayable either in

[1] *Chronology*, VII., No. 20, p. 622.
[2] *Ibid.*, VII., No. 1, p. 22; No. 2, pp. 49, 51, 56; No. 3, p. 97.
[3] *Round Table*, No. 170, p. 131.

instalments or as a whole within eighteen months had eased the general situation, while a United Kingdom-United States loan would finance further uranium production; but such was the Union's dependence on gold and diamonds that these two products together had contributed nearly one-fourth of the past year's value of exports, and gold had had to be called upon to square the heavy adverse balance of payments. In spite of the record expenditure for which he must budget, Havenga expected to have a surplus instead of the anticipated deficit a year hence, a surplus which would be almost entirely due to recovery of tax payments in arrear.[1] Then came the douche of cold water. The Finance Minister announced that import controls must come again thereby diminishing the yield from customs duties, and that unless he could achieve an increase in the price of gold, sharply rising working-costs must reduce income tax payments by the Rand mines. He proposed to make good this falling-off by speeding up the collection of tax payments in arrear, reducing the primary abatement on income tax, levying a new tax on all companies other than the gold mines, raising postal and telegraphic charges, imposing an excise on sweets and soft drinks and increasing the excise on films and the duty on beer. Loan expenditure must go up by over £75,000,000, but little more than half of this would be financed by fresh borrowing. Finally, as the easiest means of fulfilling his promise to the United Kingdom to maintain the value of sterling, he asked leave to authorise the Reserve Bank to transfer £10,000,000 of its gold reserve to the Bank of England as payment in advance of the anticipated higher British earnings in South Africa. The Minister for Economic Affairs, for his part, gave warning that in order to maintain a sound economic position and carry out promises of economy made at the recent Commonwealth Finance Ministers' Conference in London, the sum available for the purchase of overseas goods would be cut down by more than a third.[2]

Again the Session proved to be a full one. Most of the seventy-seven measures, including the much criticised Defence Amendment Act, mainly concerned Europeans;[3] but many others touched non-Europeans first and foremost. Such were notably the Group Areas Amendment Act, the Criminal Sentences Amendment Act, which prescribed flogging for certain offences, and the Bantu Urban Authorities Act,[4] which rounded off the Bantu Authorities Act of the previous Session by creating a Bantu local authority in each Native location, village or other area as far as possible on a tribal basis, but giving such authorities less power than their counterparts in the Reserves and leaving them all well and truly under the control of

---

[1] *Round Table*, No. 167, pp. 282 ff.; *Chronology*, VIII., No. 7, p. 205.
[2] *Ibid.*, VIII., No. 6, p. 176; No. 7, p. 205.   [3] Act 62 of 1952.
[4] Act 65 of 1952.

Europeans in the towns and cities directly concerned.[1] This attempt to re-tribalise the Bantu was, however, of less immediate moment than the campaign to segregate the Coloured voters politically. Four of these voters had duly challenged the validity of the Separate Representation of Voters Act in the Cape Supreme Court. When that Court, bound as it was by the finding of the Appellate Division in 1937 on which the Prime Minister relied, upheld the Act, they promptly appealed. The Appellate Division, the highest Court in the land, consisting of Chief Justice Albert Centlivres and Justices Leopold Greenberg, Oliver Schreiner and the two recent Nationalist creations, Frans van den Heever and Oscar Hoexter, listened to argument for a week. A full month later, just as the van Riebeeck tercentenary celebrations were rising to their climax, it delivered its detailed and devastating judgment to the effect that the Act in dispute was 'invalid, void and of no effect,' because it had been passed by a procedure that took no account of the still relevant entrenched clauses.[2]

Before ever he had seen the detailed judgment, Malan refused to accept a decision by which mere nominated Judges called in question the legislative sovereignty of the freely elected representatives of the people. Backed by the Speaker, he not only rejected Strauss's demand for a debate, but accused him and his United Party of renewing imperialistic attacks on nationalism by daring to make it and, worse still, of denying Parliament's right to manage its own affairs. He forthwith gave notice of a Bill that should place the sovereignty of Parliament beyond question and protect the Courts from the 'danger' of being tempted to 'test' the validity of its Acts.[3] Strauss, seconded by the Torch Commando, at once summoned all good citizens to the defence of the Law and Constitution by every legitimate means; huge crowds in Johannesburg and Durban demanded that the Ministry resign, and Government supporters and their opponents in impulsive Pretoria assaulted one another so violently that the police had to step in. A much more significant event presently took place in the Pretoria location. There, on April 6, 1952, thousands of Bantu came together and pledged themselves as 'an oppressed people' to carry on 'a relentless struggle' for the repeal of unjust laws on lines laid down by the African National Congress with the support of the S.A. Indian National Congress and Coloured Folk's organisations. It was the first overt sign of the coming Resistance movement, but for the moment the active battle was waged by white men. Strauss and his followers joined with Christie's Labour men in a United Front to get rid of a Ministry which had broken promises repeatedly

[1] Acts 33, 38 and 65 of 1952.
[2] *Round Table*, No. 167, pp. 224 ff.; *Chronology*, VII., No. 21, p. 652; VIII., No. 7, pp. 204 ff.; *vide Cape Times*, March 21, 1952, for full text of judgment.
[3] *Chronology*, VIII., No. 7, pp. 204 ff.

made to the Coloured Folk by leaders of all parties and not least by Malan himself, and to restore the rights of the people under that law which Nationalists were defying and, therefore, threatening to breed anarchy.[1] All Strauss got for his pains was a suave assurance from Dönges that the Government merely desired to 'protect' the Courts from the risk of being packed, as in the United States, a civil warning from Havenga that he stood with Malan in this matter, an accusation from Louw that he and his were committing a species of economic sabotage by working up a constitutional crisis that would scare away capital, and a grave reproof from the Prime Minister himself that he was setting a bad example to Africans and Indians by consorting with the Labour Party and the Torch Commando.[2]

Late in April, Dönges introduced the measure that was to put the Appellate Division in its place. According to this High Court of Parliament Bill, any document that had been 'enrolled' as an Act since the coming into force of the Statute of Westminster of 1931 was to be deemed an Act and be respected as such by whatever procedure it had been passed.[3] The new 'Court of Law' was to consist of all the members of both Houses sitting together under a President nominated by the Governor-General. The President was to appoint a Judicial Committee consisting of ten members of the Court who need not be lawyers, and that Committee deciding by a bare majority was to report to the Court, which, voting in its turn by a bare majority and subject to no appeal, could confirm, vary or overturn the judgment or order of the Appellate Division under discussion. Thus, Parliament in another form passing upon its own handiwork could review future judgments and also past decisions by which the Appellate Division had declared any Act invalid since December 1931. The Speaker set aside Strauss's demand that, because entrenched clauses were involved, the Bill must be passed by the appropriate procedure and, thereafter, the Government forced the measure through by all the many means of compulsion at its disposal. Strauss promised to test the validity of the new Act in the Courts and to apply to them meanwhile for an injunction restraining officials from taking action under any order prejudicial to the rights of Coloured voters that the High Court might issue. Forthwith, a Cape Malay voter took the matter to the Cape Supreme Court.[4]

While Parliament was thus preparing to assert its judicial superiority to the Appellate Division in certain spheres of law, Natalians recalled that their fathers would never have gone into the Union unless the rights of the English language had been entrenched

---

[1] *Round Table*, No. 167, pp. 124 ff.; *Chronology*, VIII., No. 8, p. 235.
[2] *Ibid.*, VIII., No. 8, p. 235; No. 9, p. 266.
[3] Act 35 of 1952; *Round Table*, No. 167, p. 226; No. 168, pp. 380 ff.; *Chronology*, VIII., No. 9, pp. 264 ff.
[4] *Round Table*, No. 169, pp. 91 ff.

27

as firmly as those of the Cape Coloured voters. Some of them, including many members of the Torch Commando, talked openly of seceding from the Union or of demanding, at the very least, a new National Convention to overhaul and buttress the threatened Constitution.[1] Their alarms were justified by recent ministerial doings, especially those of the Minister of Justice. Towards the close of the Session, Swart had invoked the Suppression of Communism Acts to oust the Communist, Sam Kahn, from his seat as one of the 'Native' members in the Assembly and to deprive the erstwhile Communist, Sachs, of his office as secretary of the multi-racial and far too independent Garment Workers' Union. He was confirmed in his naughty ways by the increased majority with which the Nationalists won the by-election at Wakkerstroom hard by the northern border of agitated Natal.

The first practical comment on these doings came from Africans. For some weeks past, meetings of Bantu up and down the country had been listening to detailed plans for defiance of specified discriminatory laws by selected volunteers from the larger centres. After reminding one such big assemblage at Port Elizabeth that they must hate oppressive laws and not any particular political party, Moroka speedily found three thousand volunteers and, together with four other leaders, set them an example by defying Swart's command that they should resign their offices. Three weeks later, towards the end of July, thirty-six Africans went into the Port Elizabeth railway station through the entrance marked 'For Europeans only' and were duly arrested, while, away on the Rand, other Africans and a few Indians met the same fate by entering the Boksburg location without permits. Thus, as the Session ended, the Resistance began.[2]

The Resistance was deliberately on a small scale at first; indeed, at the end of the first month, only some eight hundred persons had been arrested for formal 'defiance,' scarcely more than those who had been run in during that period for the casual breach of curfew and *apartheid* regulations.[3] Even so, it caused a stir. Strauss condemned the campaign, Swart threatened suitable legislation to cope with it, and the *O.B.*, while still leaving its members free to join the Nationalist Party, resolved to reorganise itself and press for a party-less 'Kruger' republic. The *Ossewabrandwag's* resolution was not, however, so much a counterblast to the Resistance as to the so-called 'Natal stand,' that is, the adoption by a representative Conference of the recommendation of the Council of the United Democratic Front, which had recently been formed in Natal, to work with the United Front for the defeat of Malan at the next general election.

[1] *Round Table*, No. 167, pp. 226 ff.; *Chronology*, VIII., No. 15, p. 483.
[2] *Round Table*, No. 170, pp. 133 ff.; *Chronology*, VIII., No. 9, p. 266.
[3] *Round Table*, No. 174, p. 134.

Swart, ignoring this challenge, preferred to cut off the head of the Resistance by arresting Moroka and three other leaders of the African and Indian Congresses on the charge that their share in the movement had brought them within the definition of Communism as laid down by his Suppression of Communism Acts.[1] Then, late in August, the new High Court of Parliament went into action. Though it had been reduced to the level of a mere Nationalist Party caucus by the abstention of all the Opposition members, it reversed the decision of the Appellate Division on the validity of the Separate Representation of Voters Act.[2] The Cape Supreme Court at once riposted by declaring the High Court of Parliament Act itself invalid because it had not been passed by the 'entrenched' procedure. Malan was furious at this set-back, coming as it did amid the unwelcome publicity given to the Resistance by leading English-medium newspapers. He accused the United Party, the Labour Party, the Torch Commando and the Resistance of having formed an unholy alliance to his hurt, called upon South Africans to choose between 'the life and death of the people,' appealed to the two European sections to stand together, insisted that it was a lie to say that South Africans oppressed their Natives, and declared that it was time the Government 'protected' its Africans from the United Nations Organisation. The Ministers of Labour and Justice, for their part, suggested that the law should be so amended that the authorities could 'get at' the instigators of the Resistance, and Swart, meanwhile, gave his police a surely superfluous hint to go 'slightly beyond the limits of their powers in isolated cases.'[3]

The rapid spread of the Resistance went far to justify Swart's anxiety. Few Indians and still fewer Coloured Folk had hitherto taken part in a movement which was thoroughly Bantu in inception and execution and was significantly supported as vigorously by African women as by their menfolk. Confined at first to small groups or even individuals in the larger towns, it had appeared presently in smaller centres; but in nearly all of them, it had generally been carried through by decent church-going people, who often preceded defiance with prayer-meetings and never resorted to violence unless the police first used their truncheons. Nearly all these passive resisters had achieved their purpose of going to gaol for increasingly lengthy periods rather than pay the ever heavier alternative fines.[4] The movement inevitably attracted the attention of U.N.O. Malan might justifiably tell caste-ridden India that she should mend her own religious and social manners before she endangered the peace

[1] Chronology, VIII., No. 16, p. 509; No. 17, pp. 532–3.
[2] Ibid., VIII., No. 17, p. 534.
[3] Ibid., VIII., No. 17, p. 534; Round Table, No. 169, p. 91; No. 170, p. 134.
[4] Ibid., No. 169, pp. 88, ff.

by attacking South Africa for her differential treatment of her non-Europeans; nevertheless, India, with the support mainly of other Asians and Africans, staged a long and bitter debate thereon, and induced the General Assembly to appoint a Commission to go into the whole matter and ask the Union to modify its Group Areas Act. Malan, with a passing reproof to the critical British Labour Party for meddling in his country's concerns, damned U.N.O. as 'a hopeless failure,' while his Minister for Economic Affairs flamboyantly asserted that the provision of admirable social amenities for Africans at the Vereeniging Steelworks was symbolic of what was being done in all parts of South Africa, and his representative at Lake Success gave fair warning that the Union would refuse to recognise the recently-appointed Commission.[1]

Whatever the authorities might assert and propose, an unofficial development was taking place in South Africa, which, in so far as it portended the creation of a genuine Liberal Party, was perhaps the most hopeful that had taken place since the achievement of Union. The Rt. Rev. Ambrose Reeves, Anglican Bishop of Johannesburg, four 'Native' members, several of the staff of the University of the Witwatersrand and a handful of others began to advocate a return to the well-tried Cape civilisation policy.[2] It was a trumpet-call that was answered by similar groups in Capetown, Kimberley and Pietermaritzburg and was, doubtless, blessed by the dead and gone William Schreiner; but the Ministerial reply was quite otherwise. Swart and Schoeman, who preached openly that 'the People' meant the white folk, saw no need for giving mere non-Europeans a better status and scouted the very idea of an inter-racial discussion; rather did they propose to stamp the Resistance out. Havenga, for his part, with a strange blindness to the facts, tried to show that Swart's recent arrests had had nothing to do with that movement and, in all good faith, wildly over-estimated the number of organised Africans who repudiated it altogether.[3]

At this stage on October 18, 1952, in the well run Bantu township of New Brighton near Port Elizabeth, police arrested two Africans, not for taking part in the Resistance, but for theft. During the ensuing riot, eleven persons, four of them Europeans, were killed and twenty-seven injured.[4] In response to the immediate imposition of a curfew and other emergency measures, the African National Congress called for a one-day strike at New Brighton. A week or two later, while police were advising Europeans to avoid certain roads in those parts, and white traders, warned by friendly Natives, were

[1] *Chronology*, VIII., No. 19, pp. 599 ff.; No. 20, p. 636; No. 21, p. 666; No. 22, pp. 696 ff.; No. 24, p. 753.
[2] *Ibid.*, VIII., No. 19, p. 600.   [3] *The Times*, Oct. 8, 1952.
[4] *Chronology*, VIII., No. 20, p. 636.

leaving their homes in the adjacent Ciskei, riots broke out in East London and along the distant Rand in the course of which two Europeans and seven Africans were killed and more than a hundred injured in clashes with the police.[1]

Though these wild doings had little enough to do with the Resistance, they distressed Moroka and other African leaders lest they bring that movement into disrepute, and moved Strauss to ask for a special Session or a Judicial Commission of Inquiry. Malan refused to grant either, and joined with Swart in blaming the Resistance on the African and S.A. Indian National Congress, Pundit Nehru and, inevitably, the Communists.[2] Swart, who shared the Prime Minister's belief that the recent riots had been anti-white, promised to enforce measures under extended powers as drastic as any that the Kenya authorities were taking against the anti-European Mau-Mau rebellion among the Kikuyu around Nairobi. As a foretaste, a proclamation made it an offence punishable by a maximum of three years' imprisonment or a fine of £300 either to incite Africans to break the law or to permit or address a meeting of more than ten Africans. This challenge was taken up by Europeans. Patrick Duncan, son of a late Governor-General of the Union, resigned his official post in Basutoland and announced his intention of taking part in the Resistance, and a score or so of white folk successfully courted arrest in Capetown and Johannesburg by breaking *apartheid* regulations or addressing illegal African meetings.[3]

It was now that the Courts asserted themselves once more. In mid-December, the Appellate Division unanimously rejected the Government's appeal against the invalidation of the High Court of Parliament Act by the Cape Supreme Court.[4] This time the Prime Minister accepted the verdict, but announced that he would make the quarrel between the Legislature and Judicature an issue at the next general election. Then, as if to show that the law was the law for non-Europeans as well as for Ministers of the Crown, the Transvaal Supreme Court sentenced Moroka and his African and Indian colleagues, whom Swart had arrested some time back, to nine months' imprisonment for breaches of 'statutory Communism,' which, it remarked sardonically, had nothing to do with Communism as generally understood. It then suspended the sentences for two years on condition that none of the defendants was convicted under the Suppression of Communism Acts during that period of grace.[5] The even-handed Appellate Division took the same merciful course when

---

[1] *Chronology*, VIII., No. 22, p. 693. [2] *Ibid.*, VIII., No. 22, p. 693.
[3] *Round Table*, No. 169, p. 89; No. 170, pp. 135 ff.; *Chronology*, VIII., No. 23, 719 ff.; No. 24, p. 751.
[4] *The Times*, Nov. 14, 1952; *Chronology*, VIII., No. 22, p. 693; *Round Table* No. 169, p. 94.
[5] *Chronology*, VIII., No. 23, p. 720.

it rejected Sachs's appeal against a recent sentence of six months' imprisonment for having attended meetings in Johannesburg in contravention of those statutes.[1] Encouraged by this partial success, the Minister of Justice forbade the president of the Transvaal branch of the African National Congress to attend any meeting in the Johannesburg magisterial district or to reside therein for six months to come.

Regardless of this warning from the highest judicial quarter that to defy the law, whatever its nature, was to play with fire, the Resistance gathered weight and speed. There was, indeed, no other practical way in which unarmed and virtually voteless Europeans could combat laws which they regarded as unjust. Force would be useless while the white folk possessed all the weapons, organisation and communications, and a sit-down strike was out of the question, because the strikers would lack stores of food to carry them over and could not be sure that the police would allow such a strike to be bloodless. As it was, the authorities refused the request of many Africans to form a Civic Guard of their own to protect life and property, and went ahead with the stamping out of the Resistance.[2] During the short special Session which was called in January 1953 to pass supplementary estimates to tide over till after the general election three months hence, they carried a Public Safety Act,[3] which empowered 'the Minister' to suspend all save a very few common or statute laws whenever the country or any part thereof was in danger. The Government could issue public safety regulations wherever such laws were suspended, though it would have to allow these to lapse if Parliament refused to sanction them. Even so, such refusal would in no way invalidate any action taken under those regulations nor prejudice any 'right, privilege, obligation or liability acquired, accrued or incurred' thereunder. Readily assured by Swart's explanation that this purely deterrent measure was necessitated by the recent riots and the threats of the chairman of the Torch Commando to 'bring the country to a standstill,' the majority of the Assembly rejected Strauss's not unreasonable proposal that Parliament should be summoned whenever a state of emergency had been proclaimed. So, amid protests by Africans and Indians in the larger centres and Swart's furious assertions that newspapers were waging a 'horrible lying campaign' against his cherished measures, the Bill went through with only nine dissentients.[4] In face of that, de Villiers Graaff, leader of the United Party in the Cape Province, promised that his Party would limit the validity of the new Act to one year only and provide that Parliament must be summoned within thirty

---

[1] *Chronology*, VIII., No. 24, p. 751; *The Times*, Dec. 13, 1952.
[2] *Chronology*, IX., No. 1, p. 26.   [3] *Ibid.*, IX., No. 3, p. 88; Act 3 of 1953.
[4] *Chronology*, IX., No. 4, pp. 118–19.

days of the proclamation of an emergency. To round off the creation of this virtually totalitarian régime and reveal still more clearly the feebleness of the United Party as an Opposition, the House passed, without a division, the Criminal Law Amendment Act, which not only prescribed stiffer penalties for certain existing crimes committed under given circumstances, but made it an offence to incite anyone to break the law as a step in an organised campaign of defiance, to give financial aid to defiance organisations or even to publish reports which could be interpreted as incitements to defiance.[1]

One further significant measure, though of a very different kind, was duly passed. It was in keeping with the Prime Minister's well-known desire for a Republic and also with constitutional propriety that the Royal Style and Titles Act should have followed the precedent set by the new Dominion of Ceylon, and described Her Majesty, Elizabeth II, merely as 'Queen of South Africa and of her other Realms and Territories . . . Head of the Commonwealth.'[2] This done, Malan went to the country.

The Nationalists took the field for the general election ruffled by two more judicial rebuffs. The Appellate Division ruled that non-Europeans must have substantially the same railway waiting-room facilities as Europeans,[3] while the Cape Supreme Court reserved judgment on Swart's attempt to keep Brian Bunting, Kahn's Communist successor, from taking his seat in the Assembly as one of the 'Native' members. In the event, Bunting took the seat to which he had been elected, but was promptly ejected under the Suppression of Communism Acts.[4] Meanwhile, Malan had won the elections. That had not been difficult, because his own party had principles and stood by them, whereas his chief opponents had drifted so far to the right since the death of their old leader that even their policy on racial issues differed from that of his Nationalists only in degree. Their defeat was well-nigh assured by the uninspiring platform on which they stood: the maintenance of existing African representation in Parliament, the treatment of the Coloured Folk as an 'appendix' of the whites, the mere amendment of segregation and anti-miscegenation laws so that they should not cause hardship, a stiffening of prohibitions against Indians in the matter of miscegenation and immigration, and the holding of a round-table conference with India and Pakistan to further the 'repatriation' of South Africa's Indians. Virtually disregarding these side issues, Malan went straight forward to carry the two key positions, whose possession would, he hoped, at last make South Africa safe for the white man and his civilisation and settle once and for all the quarrel between Parliament

[1] *Chronology*, IX., No. 3, p. 88; No. 5, pp. 150–1.
[2] *Ibid.*, IX., No. 5, p. 151. [3] *Ibid.*, IX., No. 7, p. 203.
[4] *The Times*, March 24, 1954.

and the Courts. He concentrated, therefore, on *apartheid* as a matter of 'life or death' to the people and on the supremacy of the *Volkswil* as expressed by a lawfully elected legislature. He and his naturally made the most of recent developments in various parts of British Africa from the elevation of Nkrumah to the office of Prime Minister of the Gold Coast to the disastrous Mau Mau rebellion in Kenya, and, further, showed themselves solicitious for the interests of 'the youth,' the electors of the not distant future. None was more solicitous on this score than Malan himself, who was assured by the assembled undergraduates of Stellenbosch that where he led, young South Africa would follow, and then joined with them in rejoicing in the material prosperity of their country and the rosy prospects of an *apartheid* policy that was based on 'a mighty act of creation.'[1]

The general election resulted in a substantial Nationalist victory, though once more on a minority of the votes cast. Their Party now had ninety-four seats instead of only eighty-five, while the United Party's strength had fallen from sixty-four to fifty-seven and that of the Labour Party, robbed of its leader by the sudden death of Christie, from six to five.[2] Malan now had a majority of twenty-nine including the six members from South-West Africa and, as far as seats went, a further popular mandate. Such a victory naturally stirred the Pretoria undergraduates to enthusiasm as they paraded the streets of their city waving the *Vierkleur* and vociferously cheering a leading Nationalist when he held out to all white youngsters of eighteen years of age the immediate prospect of the franchise. Nevertheless, when the shouting and the tumult died, the depressing fact became crystal clear that the Prime Minister still lacked the two-thirds majority that he must have before he could put the Coloured voters on a separate roll in the only way the Appellate Division would sanction.

Desirous as he was of a friendly settlement of the constitutional crisis, Malan called on a dozen or so members of the United Party, other than Liberals or Leftists, to give him his two-thirds majority.[3] Meeting with no response, he then sought to calm English-speaking citizens by assuring them that the equality of the two official languages was in no danger, and reminding them, with a strange forgetfulness of many similar and now broken promises to the Coloured Folk, that this equality was 'in any case entrenched in the minds and convictions of all responsible sections in the country.' His assurances failed to carry universal conviction and the formation of predominantly English-speaking parties went on. The first such

---

[1] *The Times*, March 6, 1953.
[2] *Ibid.*, April 18, 1953; *Chronology*, IX., No. 8, p. 235; *Round Table*, No. 171, pp. 288 ff.
[3] *Ibid.*, No. 171, p. 290; *Chronology*, IX., No. 9, p. 280.

movement resulted in the formation of a Liberal Party pledged to restore the old Cape civilisation system, the second and, at the moment, more influential in the organisation of the by no means Liberal supporters of the 'Natal stand.'[1] The leader of this latter venture was the veteran Natal Senator, George Heaton Nicholls, who announced his resignation from the United Party on the morrow of the general election, because he believed that 'the unfruitful and sordid marriage' celebrated at the time of Union had broken down and the division between the two white races was complete and final. Now that the United Front had failed to unseat Malan, he proposed to form a Union Federal Party, which should aim primarily at preserving the rights of English-speaking people in terms of the Union bargain and thus make a wider appeal at home and overseas than a purely isolationist Natal movement could possibly do. Inspired doubtless by memories of the fight for federation put up by Schreiner and Natal Ministers forty years back, and also by the elaborate federal scheme propounded by Arthur Keppel-Jones, a young history lecturer in the University of the Witwatersrand, he proposed to end the current 'religious war' by partitioning the Union, in the first instance, into the old Trekker and still overwhelmingly Afrikaner areas, that is, the Transvaal, the Free State and certain frontier districts of the Cape Province, which should become a republic within the Commonwealth, and the remaining more or less English-speaking areas, which should retain their old traditions and allegiance to the Crown. These two areas were to be loosely federated. He did not explain what was to be the fate of the numerous folk who would inevitably find themselves on the wrong side of the frontier, nor did he define his policy towards non-Europeans beyond promising that each one of them would be able to find self-expression through appropriate governmental organs with powers 'commensurate with his degree of civilisation.' He was content to plead that his scheme would permit the planning of civilisation 'without the distraction of party politics' and the handling of non-European policy in conformity with 'the traditions of the separate sections.'[2]

The formation of the two new Parties shook the United Party, especially in the Transvaal, where its numerous Jewish members were naturally attracted by the Liberals. Strauss might argue that the policies of both Parties were as impracticable as that of the Nationalists, but he was so little minded to see his followers drifting away to one or the other that he sought to rally his men by reaffirming his election programme.[3] He managed thus to stop the rot for the

[1] *Round Table*, No. 171, p. 291; *Chronology*, IX., No. 10, p. 318.
[2] V. Bartlett, *Struggle for Africa*, pp. 78 ff.; A. Keppel-Jones, *Friends or Foes?*; *Round Table*, No. 171, p. 291; *Chronology*, IX., No. 9, p. 281; No. 10, p. 318.
[3] *The Times*, June 19, 1953; *Chronology*, IX., No. 10, pp. 318 ff.

moment; but the Torch Commando, denied the victory over Malan which had been its main *raison d'être*, began to go to pieces. Few of its rank-and-file showed signs of joining the Liberal Party, which they regarded as dangerously pro-Native; but many, and notably the Natalians among them, were attracted by Nicholls's programme. Meanwhile, numbers of its more conservative members, headed by de la Rey himself, resigned from an organisation which they now regarded as a mere Jingo retort to Nationalist sectionalism and, by reason of its close affiliations to the Union Federal Party, a denial of the great conception of the union of the two white races. Undismayed, the Torch Commando Congress, dominated by Natalians, resolved to carry on in Natal at least and to back the U.F. Party in its demand that a referendum be held in Natal before ever that Province was included in a republic.[1] Ministerial comment was not slow in coming. Louw, angry that these developments in the Garden Province had already adversely affected the country's loan funds and currency resources, brought home to the businessmen and industrialists, who did much abound in the ranks of the Torch Commando and the Federalists, their utter dependence on the home market for the sale of their sugar and, in particular, on Durban's through traffic to the Rand by announcing that he could give Natal neither loan facilities nor import permits until it had shown clearly where it stood in relation to the Union. Presently, in face of protests by local businessmen and some of his own colleagues, he tried to explain his threat of an embargo away, but Swart was more downright. He told the Natal Provincial Council, in reply to its request for an assurance that there should be a referendum, that the English could 'never really co-operate' until they had been persuaded by 'pure logic' to accept a republican polity.[2]

Accompanied by Havenga and leaving Strydom to act as Prime Minister, Malan set out late in May 1953 to attend the Commonwealth Prime Ministers' Conference and, in spite of the objections of some of his die-hards, to please English-speaking South Africans by gracing the new Queen's Coronation. While in London, he begged the British public to examine the sources of their South African news carefully, because that news was often 'so overwhelmingly contaminated by political bias' and by hatred of anyone or anything that was not purely British that it might well give rise to 'another Ulster' at the far end of Africa. He should in justice have added that such an Ulster would have been impossible without the threat of a South African 'Republic of Ireland'; but, be that as it might, he travelled home leisurely by way of the Netherlands, where he told

[1] *Round Table*, No. 173, p. 52; *Chronology*, IX., No. 9, p. 281; No. 10, p. 318; No. 11, p. 340.
[2] *Ibid.*, IX., No. 11, p. 340.

the good folk that South Africa naturally looked to them to provide many of the immigrants she so sorely needed.[1] Back in Pretoria, he first scolded the British Labour Party yet again for interfering in his country's affairs, and then claimed that the title 'Head of the Commonwealth' had no more than a symbolic meaning and denied that the Monarchy was a 'permanent part' of the Union's constitution. Finally, he echoed his arch-enemy, Nehru, by proclaiming boldly that if the desire to break away arose solely from the hope of winning more freedom, he himself would be against any such step, because the Commonwealth gave South Africa 'the greatest freedom' anyone could desire. This confession of political faith may have warmed the heart of the Union's visitor, the Prime Minister of Australia; but Robert Menzies must have doubted the depth of his host's affection for the Commonwealth by the steps he took to make it well-nigh impossible for Indian wives to join their husbands in South Africa.[2]

Shortly before the opening of the first Session of the new Parliament, the Minister of Native Affairs, anxious to please the Zulus who had thus far taken no part in the Resistance, bought for them, at their request, European farms on which were graves of former Zulu Chiefs.[3] Other manifestations of official policy were less gracious. There was no call for any, one way or the other, at the German mission school near Lichtenberg in the western Transvaal, where African pupils burned the Principal's house and other buildings as a protest against unsatisfactory conditions; but the police took the lead in Johannesburg when they raided offices and houses of members of the Communist-dominated Springbok Legion, the Civil Rights League, and the Society for Peace and Friendship with the Soviet Union, and also of the African National Congress, whose president, Chief Luthuli, was forbidden by the Minister of Justice to enter certain areas or address meetings therein during the next twelve months.[4] It was the police, again, who arrested three Indians just before the start of a meeting that had been called in Johannesburg city to protest against the proposed ejection of close on 20,000 non-Europeans from their homes on the outskirts of the western extension of that sprawling city, and, after the meeting had begun, marched into the hall and arrested one of the Joint Secretaries of the S.A. Indian National Congress, because he was taking part in the meeting in defiance of Swart's overworked ban under the Suppression of Communism Acts.[5]

This round-up had scarcely been completed when Parliament met

[1] *Chronology*, IX., No. 12, p. 371.
[2] *Ibid.*, IX., No. 14, p. 447; IX., No. 18, p. 564.
[3] *The Times*, Aug. 24, 1953.
[4] *Chronology*, IX., No. 10, p. 318; No. 12, p. 340; No. 13, p. 418.
[5] *Ibid.*, IX., No. 13, p. 418.

on July 3, 1953. On the previous day, Malan had announced that he would hold a Joint Session of the two Houses as a 'gesture of goodwill' and a 'first attempt' to settle the 'so-called constitutional issue,' and that he would hold a similar Session to validate the disputed Separate Representation of Voters Act.[1] The projected Amendment Bill was intended to remove all doubts about the validity of Acts such as those which had granted white adult suffrage in 1930 and 1931, to give 'legislative certainty' to the clause of that Act which guaranteed the equality of the two official languages, and to confer on the Courts 'by specific and express legislative provision' and for the first time 'the testing right . . . in certain matters.' Thus might the whole problem be solved 'outside party politics.' There can be no doubt that, quite apart from his natural desire to outflank the Judges, Malan genuinely desired a friendly settlement; but none of the Opposition groups was willing to help him to achieve either end and thus betray the Coloured voters in return for the mere further entrenchment of the dual language clause and the legal enactment of a right which the Appellate Division held was already theirs and entrenched already. They, therefore, opposed a Bill whose aim was the validation of the original political segregation measure so doggedly that, though they could not stop it from passing through nearly all its stages, they always denied it the necessary two-thirds majority. Then, the Third Reading, which had been postponed more than once, was at last put off for a full two months because of the sudden death of Dr. Karl Bremer, Minister of Health and Social Welfare.

After having been calmed by the assurance that recent talks between the Prime Minister and Leader of the Opposition had been merely exploratory and inconclusive at that, the House turned to finance. In his sober Budget speech, Havenga announced that expenditure must rise from the current £210,000,000 to no less than £233,000,000 during the coming year, if he were to find the money to meet the cost of the consolidation of certain cost-of-living allowances as part of the basic salaries of civil servants, increased bonuses to pensioners, the maintenance of bread subsidies at the existing level, larger University subsidies and the heavy bill for a widespread campaign against locusts. In spite of the fact that there were many tax payments outstanding and, thanks to a record revenue, a surplus of some £14,000,000, he proposed additional taxation, notably on everything that had to do with motor transport. He hoped thereby to make an end of day-dreams and inflation, and to aid the Reserve Bank in its efforts to give public investment a chance by checking private demands for funds to finance industrial and similar development. He could not, however, gainsay his anxiety at the speed

[1] *Round Table*, No. 172, pp. 388 ff.

with which the Loan Estimates had leaped up from £75,000,000 to £92,000,000, chiefly because of the money needed by the railways and the plant for the extraction of motor-spirit. He expected to raise most of this alarming sum from the funds of the Public Debt Commissioners, and a further £24,000,000 from voluntary domestic and external loans and so forth; but the rest he must get by means of compulsory loans at four per cent., which would be repaid in five years' time and the interest thereon be taxed as a whole in the year of repayment. This novel compulsion was to take the form of a general savings levy on all adults who earned more than modest incomes, a percentage addition to individual basic income tax and surtax payments, and a small addition to income tax payable by companies other than those engaged in goldmining.[1]

The House then proceeded to carry further anti-non-European measures. Replying to the Industrial Legislation Commission, which had recently recommended that Native trade unions be recognised officially and given a limited right to bargain collectively, the Minister of Labour asserted that it would be 'race suicide' to permit them to do anything of the sort, because such unions could be used as political weapons. He therefore piloted through his Native Labour Bill, which indeed set up elaborate machinery for the settlement of African labour disputes, but gave the Africans no share in its working save through nominees and that at the lowest level,[2] and, moreover, made permanent Smuts's war measure rendering Native strikes and lock-outs of Natives criminal offences. This Act was followed by Swart's Reservation of Separate Amenities Bill which circumvented a recent decision by the Appellate Division by making it legal to provide separate and not necessarily equal facilities and amenities for white folk and others on the state railways and elsewhere.[3] Prefacing the introduction of the Bill by jeers at the 'theoretical so-called liberalism' which condemned those separate facilities that had always been customary in South Africa, and by warning Honourable Members that anything like the recent 'disgusting' marriage of the late Sir Stafford Cripps's daughter to a black African would be 'the end of their country,' Swart explained that, while no Government would wish to be unfair to non-Europeans, equal facilities were 'impossible and impracticable.'[4] Its corporate conscience having thus been eased, the United Party merely proposed to move amendments and, in the event, let the Bill through virtually unchanged.

Lacking effective defenders in Parliament, non-Europeans took their own line. At one extreme, some sixty Bantu attacked Native

[1] *Round Table*, No. 172, pp. 393 ff.; *Chronology*, IX., No. 14, p. 448.
[2] Act 48 of 1953; *Daily Telegraph*, Aug. 5, 1953.
[3] Act 49 of 1953; *Chronology*, IX., No. 17, p. 541.
[4] *The Times*, Aug. 7, 1953.

policemen and white municipal officials who invaded the Klerksdorp location and, though a few of their own number were wounded, killed one official and two constables. At the other extreme, a decorous Coloured deputation warned the Prime Minister that their people's self-restraint might give way if he persisted in trying to segregate them politically, and a Conference of Coloured People's Organisations gave weight to that warning by appointing a committee to draft a scheme of resistance to the hated Separate Representation of Voters Amendment Bill.[1] Nevertheless Malan could observe with truth that at least a minority of the Coloured Folk were willing to accept his policy and, with less accuracy, that few of them were serious in their opposition. Meanwhile, he could ask what he himself and the non-Europeans had to hope or fear from the new Liberal and United Federal Parties.

Malan could reasonably reckon that, between them, the new Parties would weaken the United Party by drawing away members from its opposite wings, while it was almost inconceivable that any of his Nationalists would go over to an organisation so tainted with imperialism as was Nicholls's U.F.P., and still less to Liberals, who, in the eyes of many of them, were scarcely distinguishable from Communists. Both Parties published their programmes in mid-August 1953.[2] The United Federal Party, recalling one of Rhodes's dreams, proposed a Constitution which it hoped would in all probability induce the predominantly English-speaking Eastern Province of the Cape, possibly the Two Rhodesias and Nyasaland and, conceivably, the adjacent Belgian and Portuguese territories to join their projected loyalist area. It probably lost sight of the fact that, if the traditionally separatist Eastern Province indeed wished to do so, it must claim a right of secession which would give the three northern and markedly Nationalist districts of Natal herself an equally good claim to break away and rejoin the Transvaal from which they had only been separated at the end of the South African war. However that might be, non-Europeans would surely ask what prospects of political advancement there would be for them, and here, as might have been expected of a scheme drawn up by a scattering of white Natalians hereditarily well versed in the art of jockeying dark-skinned folk off the voters' roll, that their progress was likely to be even slower than that of Pirow's famous bush-carts. True, their standard of living and economic opportunities were to be improved very gradually; Africans who reached a high degree of civilisation were to be relieved of the pass laws, and all were assured of 'sympathetic administration' under 'a fair and equitable' system of social and residential segregation, 'wherever possible on a voluntary basis'; but as for political privileges, non-Europeans must wait patiently

[1] *Chronology*, IX., No. 16, p. 510.   [2] *Round Table*, No. 173. pp. 48 ff.

till, in due time, they could be given 'group representation' on local government bodies in urban areas, while even those of them who passed 'suitable tests of a high standard' must wait again till they were admitted to the common roll. This last concession was to be the outcome of 'a long-term policy to be taken in steps over a considerable period of years ... subject always to due safeguards against the disproportionate representation of any one section of the non-European population.'[1]

What now of the Liberals? Their Party, small, corporately poor and physically scattered, would seem to be at a disadvantage compared with the Federalists, who were mainly concentrated in southern Natal; on the other hand, this very dispersion gave promise of growth in that the Party had more than one root and, being thus in touch with many and very different parts of the Union, might serve to rally liberally-minded men and women on a national scale and even to influence members of other Parties, just as British Liberals were influencing many Labour men and Conservatives. Again, on the face of it, its bold demand for a return to the old Cape civilisation policy all along the line might prove far more attractive to non-Europeans than the Federalists' ultra-cautious programme. But it was by no means certain that it would be so.[2] Less worldly-wise than Moroka and his friends, the Liberals were not ready to let adult white suffrage stand and work for a non-European franchise on terms, but demanded that white adult suffrage be abolished and a general franchise on a common roll be offered to all Union citizens of full age, who had passed Standard VI after some eight to ten years' schooling and either possessed real property worth £500 or earned £250 a year or had otherwise shown themselves worthy of political privilege and responsibility. This idea that the franchise was something to be earned would make small appeal to the more democratic wing of the Cape Coloured Folk or the rank-and-file of the African and S.A. Indian Congresses, who were set on the adult suffrage that was already enjoyed by Nehru's Indians and Nkrumah's Gold Coasters and was held out to themselves by Communists. As it was, African voters of the Cape Western constituency had elected two Communists successively to 'Native' seats in the Assembly, and there was no guarantee that others would not follow their example. Nor was the Party's non-committal attitude towards the Resistance such as to commend it to countless Africans and Indians.

As far as white folk were concerned, however, the Liberals would undoubtedly draw like-minded supporters away from the United Party. That fissiparous organisation was already weakened by the restiveness of some quarter of its members against Strauss's feeble leadership, and by the virtual revolt of Bailey Bekker, chairman of the

[1] *Round Table.*, No. 173, p. 51. [2] *Ibid.*, No. 173, pp. 54 ff.

Party in the Transvaal, and four other members, who had either resigned or been expelled from the Party caucus.[1] Although this tiny conventicle of protestants had accepted the principles of *apartheid* and asked only that Malan should come out more strongly than he had yet done in favour of preserving the rights of the English language and the Commonwealth connection, Swart could still jeer at the United Party as a whole as 'the servant of the British Empire' and, in so far as it had tried to follow the course marked out by Botha, Smuts and Hertzog, the would-be destroyer of the soul of the Afrikaner. In his eyes, the first aim must be the preservation of that soul, leaving the 'remnants of imperialism' to rally round the Federalists or the Liberals if they chose. In Strauss's eyes, on the contrary, the first aim must be the salvation of his own Party. Hence, while stalwart Nationalists from many parts were forming an association to press for an independent republic, he saw to it that the United Party should carry more than one vote of confidence in himself, though not without ominous adverse votes and abstentions.[2]

With courage in a measure restored, the United Party faced the oft-postponed Third Reading of the Separate Representation of Voters Amendment Bill on September 16, 1953. At once, a Natal Labour member surprised his hearers by moving that the Bill be discharged, that the original measure be reintroduced and that, after its Second Reading, it be referred to a Joint Select Committee.[3] The Prime Minister would have none of it. He insisted on a division, but failed to get the two-thirds majority by sixteen votes.[4] Swart thereupon secured the First Reading of his Appellate Court Bill. To the dismay of not a few Free State ministerialists and some Nationalist newspapers, this proved to be a frontal attack on the Appellate Division. With the avowed intention of getting the Cape Coloured voters off the common roll, the Minister of Justice proposed that the Appellate Division be divided into three sections: first, a Court of Civil Appeal; secondly, a Court of Criminal Appeal and, thirdly, a Court of Constitutional Appeal. The two first sections were to be staffed by the Chief Justice and as many Justices of Appeal as the Governor-General might appoint, but they were to have no 'testing rights' or power to hear appeals in cases which involved the validity of Acts or Provincial Ordinances. The third section was to consist of a President and four Justices of Appeal appointed by the Governor-General, who might, however, when he deemed it expedient, designate any Judge or acting-Judge of the Supreme Court to serve either as President, substitute Justice or additional

[1] *The Observer*, Aug. 30, 1953; *Round Table*, No. 173, pp. 53 ff.
[2] *Chronology*, IX., No. 18, p. 574; No. 21, p. 701.
[3] *Daily Telegraph*, Sept. 17, 1953.
[4] *Chronology*, IX., No. 18, p. 574; *Round Table*, No. 173, pp. 102 ff.

Justice, or simply to fill a vacancy. This third section of the Court would alone be empowered to hear appeals that involved the validity of Acts or Ordinances. There was in no case to be any right of further appeal. In face of this Bekker and his followers promptly urged the Prime Minister to accept the Natal member's rejected proposal, and this Malan did. He and Havanga managed to silence the 'young lions' of their Party behind closed doors and, early in October 1953, held another Joint Session, the second of the year. As almost the last act of the Session, Swart's Bill was withdrawn, and a Bill to revalidate the Separate Representation of Voters Act was introduced and then referred to a Joint Select Committee. After the House had risen, that Committee was transformed into a Commission and held its first sitting in Pretoria some three weeks later.[1]

While Malan sought thus for an agreed settlement, Pirow, from the wings, castigated Government and Opposition alike for their failure to evolve a real Coloured policy, and warned them that the only alternatives were racial assimilation or the creation of a distinct Coloured race in a fifth Province, while the Nationalist Administrator of the Transvaal showed plainly that he could wish for a censorship that should preserve the morals of Africans.[2] The Minister of Labour, for his part, gloried in the fact that the authorities had already banned thirty-three former Communists from trade union activities, boasted that they would continue to do so, and, further, threatened to introduce an Industrial Conciliation Bill that should oblige Europeans and others to have their separate trade unions and might even empower the Minister to decree that certain kinds of work should be done only by certain racial groups.[3] The Anglican Bishops of the Church of the Province tried to raise the debate to higher levels by condemning the immorality of assigning a particular racial group to a position of permanent inferiority;[4] the Transvaal Congress of the United Party celebrated its recent qualified victory in Parliament by passing with acclamation yet another vote of confidence in Strauss, and then, as if to remind Swart that there were still Judges in South Africa, the Courts went into action once more. The Transvaal Supreme Court annulled the conviction of the former president of the S.A. Indian National Congress and four other non-Europeans for breach of the Suppression of Communism Acts, while the Appellate Division sought to check Swart's over-free wielding of his scourge by holding that nothing in those Acts deprived of his right to be heard any person who was liable to be affected by the Minister's acts thereunder, that the vital words in these Acts,

---

[1] *Round Table*, No. 173, p. 105; *Chronology*, IX., No. 19, p. 612; *The Times*, Sept. 30, 1953.
[2] *The Times*, Sept. 22, 1953.   [3] *Ibid.*, Sept. 24, 1953.
[4] *Chronology*, IX., No. 21, p. 701.

'in the opinion of the Minister,' implied that the said Minister had taken reasonable steps to form that opinion, and that the mere presence of the name of a person on the list of members of an unlawful organisation by no means entitled the Minister to issue an order against him or her, because that person might have severed all connection with it before ever either Act had come into force.[1]

Meanwhile, the closing weeks of the Session had been disturbed by a recrudescence of Zulu-Indian animosities. At Cato Manor near Durban, Africans had looted and burned several Indian shops after one of their lads had been killed by an Indian-owned bus while trying to board it in motion. Twenty-six of them were arrested, all Durban was put on the alert, and police reinforcements were sent in with orders to shoot any African caught looting. Trouble with the Indians inevitably involved inter-Dominion friction, because behind the Natal Asiatics stood Nehru's India, a fellow-member of that Commonwealth to which Malan clung for all his increasingly cautious talk of a republic. Scenting Delhi-inspired trouble at Lake Success, Malan proposed that the members of the Commonwealth should together 'drive' the meddlesome United Nations Organisation back within the limits of its Charter, and then draft a Charter of their own providing for the civilisation of Africans, the protection of Africa from Asiatic penetration and the exclusion of the forces of militarism and Communism from the entire African continent. Nehru retorted by protesting against the recent exclusion from the Union of the Indian wives of Indian residents, to which Malan rejoined first by accusing him of being South Africa's 'greatest enemy' and then by refusing to support India's claim to take part in the projected political conference on Korea, because she had given no help in those parts and had even collected £20,000,000 within her own borders to finance the Resistance against his policy of *apartheid*.[2]

This wordy warfare was duly transferred to Lake Success. There, in reply to the customary Indian attacks, Jooste, the Union's permanent delegate and Ambassador at Washington, explained that the recent withdrawal of the right of Indian wives and children to join Indian husbands and fathers in South Africa was simply the withdrawal of a privilege which they alone had enjoyed, and observed that India apparently preferred making political capital in U.N.O. to seeking a way out of the complications arising from the *apartheid* policy in consultation with the Union and Pakistan at Pretoria.[3] Unimpressed, the majority resolved that this very round-table conference, which India was blocking, should be held and, on the strength of the recommendations of the Commission of Good Offices

[1] *Chronology*, IX., No. 23, p. 771; No. 24, p. 808.
[2] *Ibid.*, IX., No. 16, pp. 509 ff.; No. 19, p. 612; *The Times*, Aug. 12, 1953.
[3] *Chronology*, IX., No. 20, pp. 662 ff.

that a similar conference of all South Africa's races should also go into the whole tangled problem, further resolved with many important abstentions that this Commission should continue to urge the Governments directly concerned to come to terms and, failing compliance, report to U.N.O. at its next session. It followed up these resolutions, the Union alone dissenting, by appointing a small committee to investigate the position of South-West Africa in the light of the Mandate, and by once more requesting the Union to forward petitions from its inhabitants as well as regular reports. It was in vain that the leading United Kingdom representative objected that the Commission of Good Offices was an illegal body and denied that the Declaration of Human Rights had created any legal obligations whatever, and that Jooste accused that Commission of being anti-European and guilty of numerous untruths and half-truths of which he gave sufficient instances. Against the votes of the United Kingdom, the four more or less white Dominions, France, Belgium, the Netherlands, Greece, and Colombia, the delegates adopted by nearly four to one a motion sponsored by India and sixteen other nations that the Commission should carry on and invite the Union to co-operate.[1]

U.N.O. thus held by its opinion that, despite Jooste's protests, the *apartheid* policy was something more than a mere matter of domestic concern, and found that the United States Department of Commerce for once agreed with it to the extent of lamenting that 'current political and racial tensions in the Union constituted the most important single deterrent to foreign investment.' Luckily for South Africa, the International Bank had confidence enough to warrant its lending her a substantial sum, repayable by instalments within ten years, to finance railway improvements and electrical development.[2] This welcome *ad hoc* aid could, however, neither conceal the fact that the general flow of capital from overseas had almost ceased and that the Reserve Bank's holdings of gold and foreign exchange were draining away fast, nor justify the Minister of Economic Affairs in fixing the value of import permits for the coming year at more than fifty-five per cent. of that for the year just past. The Minister of Finance, on the other hand, took a more optimistic view. He believed that the self-denying course adopted by the recent Commonwealth Prime Ministers' Conference had indeed led to freer trade and greater convertibility of currencies. To carry on the good work, he pleaded strongly for an increase in the price of gold on the ground that present attempts to maintain a fixed price in terms of the depreciated United States dollar drained reserves and thus checked the 'liquidity' of other countries. He therefore proposed to renew the gold guarantee of £50,000,000 to the United Kingdom at the

---

[1] *Chronology*, IX., No. 21, p. 703; No. 22, p. 740; No. 23, p. 777; No. 24, p. 814.
[2] *Ibid.*, IX., No. 17, p. 541; No. 23, p. 731.

risk of substantial drawings on the Union's gold and dollar reserves, and announced that import permits would soon be issued for use in any currency desired, though admittedly a big switch back to dollar imports would force the Union to rectify its balance of payments by favouring sterling imports once more.[1]

The year closed with Strauss assuring the United Party Congress that he would fight to the last against a republic, and Malan giving the northerners, Swart and Strydom, a broad hint that there might be strong southern competition for the Succession when he should be gone by voluntarily making way for Dönges as leader of the Nationalist Party in the Cape Province.[2] Then, stung by the election of two Africans to the undergraduate Representative Council in the University of Cape Town, he proposed to appoint a Commission to recommend a fair way of ending this 'mingling' of the races in the Universities of Cape Town and the Witwatersrand, and thus to oblige those seats of learning to draw the racial distinctions that were already drawn in most of the schools that sent them their students. The Minister of Education gave him eager support. He, indeed, admitted that the task of sorting out the six per cent. or so of non-Europeans from those Universities would take time, promised that there should be neither legislation nor positive orders on that score, and disavowed all thought of interfering with academic freedom; but he, nevertheless, gave the University authorities a veiled warning that, if they did not comply, he would cut down to the permissible limit the state grants on which they were dangerously dependent and thus make it hard for them to maintain their institutions at the present level.[3] It was in keeping with this policy of cultural *apartheid* that the Prime Minister should have told Africans from the High Commission Territories and Southern Rhodesia that though they might at long last come to the Union for higher education, they must go either to non-European Fort Hare or to the University of Natal's non-European Medical School at Durban.[4]

Malan's concession to African students from the High Commission Territories, limited though it was, was all the more welcome because it was markedly different from the policy he was threatening to pursue towards the Territories themselves. Soon after Churchill's Conservatives had taken office at Westminster after their narrow electoral victory in October 1951, he had warned the new Prime Minister that unless transfer were effected within a reasonable time, he would treat the inhabitants of those Territories as 'foreigners.' The only immediate outcome of this interchange had been an agree-

---

[1] *Chronology*, IX., No. 20, p. 659; *Round Table*, No. 173, pp. 105 ff.
[2] *Chronology*, IX., No. 22, p. 738; *The Times*, Nov. 20, 1953.
[3] *Chronology*, IX., No. 24, p. 809; *The Times*, Sept. 2 and Nov. 3, 1953.
[4] *Chronology*, IX., No. 23, p. 772.

ment to publish the lengthy correspondence on the subject.[1] Now, however, in 1953, Malan revived the controversy at the annual Free State National Party Conference. Mindful that many of his hearers keenly desired possession of neighbouring Basutoland and Bechuanaland, he told them that, since he was 'in a hurry,' the problem of transfer must be settled within the next five years without any of the assurances which some were demanding that Africans should thereafter have a say in South African affairs. 'We cannot,' he said, 'accept conditions of this nature. We are doing seven times as much for our Natives as Great Britain for her African Coloured peoples. So far as self-government for the Natives is concerned, England should come to learn from us, not we from England.'[2] The excitement of the occasion might be permitted to account for Malan's platform arithmetic, and hope deferred for his unsubstantiated assertion that the local British officials were systematically stiffening the backs of their Africans against transfer; but it could not be denied that he had made fair points, first, by gibing at the slow progress of self-government in the Territories, and, then, by arguing that if the British authorities pushed millions of protesting Africans on either side of the Zambesi into a dreaded Federation, they could not claim that the promised consultation with Africans in the Territories carried with it an African right of veto in the matter of the transfer.

The High Commission Territories were, however, not the only parts of black Africa in which British policy failed to conform to the standards of the Prime Minister of white South Africa. Frankly alarmed that Nkrumah should have been promoted from the rank of Leader of Government Business to that of Prime Minister of the Gold Coast, Malan gave a solemn warning that this 'forcing' of something perilously like self-government on Negroes must fail; nay, more, that the mere example was dangerous, because 'anyone with common-sense' must realise that if the rest of the black Africans got such powers and privileges, they would drive the white folk and their leadership out of all Africa south of the Sahara. Already, he noted, Africans in Northern Rhodesia were demanding what the Gold Coasters now had.[3]

After having loosed these salvoes against the British in Africa, Malan once more turned his batteries on U.N.O. He deprecated, indeed, all talk of the Union's leaving that highly-censorious organisation; nevertheless, he accused it of having caused unrest in South Africa, of failing in its primary task of giving peace to a troubled world, and of having interfered so persistently in domestic matters that even the French delegate had recently walked out. The

[1] Cmd. 8707 of 1952.
[2] *Chronology*, Vol. IX., No. 20, pp. 659 ff.; *The Times*, Oct. 22, 1953.
[3] *Chronology*, Vol. VIII., No. 5, p. 15.

wish possibly being father to the thought, he prophesied that U.N.O. would go to pieces if it did not reform itself radically. Doubtless, the moderate Governor-General shared his Prime Minister's belief, if not his wish; but he was more specifically aggrieved that the Western nations seemed to be concerned only with retaining the favour of 'the eastern and non-white world' and not at all with the building up of a new Western nation at the far end of Africa. The Nationalists, for their part, seemed to have no care for world favour, European or other, for they were unremitting in their endeavours to 'stamp out' the Resistance, even though the Africans, anxious for co-operation with Europeans, remained quiet on the whole. The Minister of Justice gave them a lead by bidding the prominent local Indian, Dadoo, to resign from no less than fifteen organisations to which he had never belonged. Then, early in December 1953, the Resistance took an unexpected turn, when white folk took part in it for the first time. As good as his word, young Patrick Duncan, on crutches, led seven Europeans, fourteen Africans and eighteen Indians, including Manilal Gandhi, into the Germiston Native location and there held an unlawful meeting.[1] All were arrested and duly punished.

As if the Resistance with its alleged taint of Communism were not enough, scarcely less dreaded Liberalism showed its head unmistakably when the newly-formed Liberal Party held a National Conference and fought its first election in a well-to-do and almost solidly United Party municipal constituency in Johannesburg. The candidate was defeated partly at least because his U.P. opponent borrowed his programme; but he none the less polled nearly thirty per cent. of the votes cast and moved friendly local papers to warn the United Party that he had shown it 'the red light.' Thus encouraged the Liberals decided to hold another Conference shortly and, in due time, to contest other Rand municipal seats, Provincial seats for Sea Point and the Cape Flats, and even the 'Native' seat in the Assembly from which the Communist, Brian Bunting, had recently been ejected under the Suppression of Communism Acts. Their Natal Provincial Congress meanwhile asked their Administrator to provide better health services and compulsory education for all, especially for non-Europeans, and to give non-Europeans the municipal franchise. Significant of the educative influence that Liberalism in action could have on others, this modest advance impelled Nicholls to assure all concerned that his Union Federal Party likewise stood for 'the direct representation of Africans by Africans within the walls of Parliament,' though he did not add that this was a matter for the far-distant future. Even the United Party was driven to showing itself more liberally-minded than for many a long year, though the chief immediate effect of that welcome change was to impel a pair of

[1] *The Times*, Dec. 8, 1953.

frontier-minded Natal and Ciskei Members to resign from the Caucus and drift away in the direction of the five rebels in Bailey Bekker's newly-formed Independent United Party.[1]

Meanwhile, at the close of 1953, a number of Protestant religious leaders had made a stand which they hoped would have a more far-reaching influence on inter-racial relations than the doings of the politicians. The three branches of the Dutch Reformed Church, working through the Federal Missionary Council, summoned a Conference of Protestant churchmen to discuss South African Christians' problems in their multi-racial land with special reference to the Christianising of non-Europeans. Besides representatives of the principal English and Afrikaans-speaking Churches, the Conference was attended by those of the Swedish, Finnish, Norwegian, Swiss and London Missionary Societies.

Differences of opinion were revealed on the score of the *apartheid* policy, not least among members of the three Dutch Reformed Churches. Many of these good men pointed out that none of the Afrikaans-speaking Churches admitted that all peoples were equal in every respect. They maintained that, although the Nationalist Government rejected the idea as impracticable, total *apartheid* was the only course which their Churches held to be in conformity with the teachings of Scripture, that differentiation on the grounds of colour need not mean discrimination against non-Europeans, and that discrimination, in its turn, did not imply the denial of human dignity. Many others, however, went much further; indeed, they more or less expressed the widespread Afrikaner self-congratulation that their traditional practice of *apartheid* in racial matters had saved them from mingling their blood with that of dark-skinned folk and, to that extent, had enabled them to preserve their own civilisation. They honestly believed that the demand for racial equality all along the line was a defiance of that God who had shown plainly that He wished peoples and nations to become and remain distinct by dividing light from darkness, the waters from the dry land and one thing from another so that He might make a world, and who, though He had made of one blood all the nations of men, had scattered abroad the builders of Babel who tried to hold mankind together. Themselves members of Churches with fine missionary records, they held that their first duty was to Christianise non-Europeans and help them to build up their own self-governing Churches so that no race or nation be robbed of the chance to make its own special contribution to the unfolding of Christian truth. There was even a considerable minority which asked why, if there were to be racial Churches, there should not be class Churches also.

Markedly different views were, however, put forward by three

[1] *The Times*, Jan. 29, 1954.

leading Dutch Reformed Church divines. The Moderator of the D.R. Church in the Transvaal claimed that *apartheid* was based on principles as well as on practical considerations, and insisted that though the Church must always protest when violence was threatened to the truth of God's word, it must remember that the State had also been specially instituted by the Almighty and must never presume to dictate to it what its final racial policy should be. A less Erastian attitude was revealed by the Professor of Theology in the University of Pretoria, who maintained that, although *apartheid* was justified and, indeed, rendered necessary by the actual situation in South Africa, it had no Scriptural authority behind it. The third of these speakers, Dr. Barend Keet, one of the most influential and best loved men at the Stellenbosch Theological Seminary, would have none of such appeals to practical considerations and existing conditions. Supported by the Anglican Archdeacon of Johannesburg, a leading Wesleyan Minister and a minority of his own Communion, he told the Conference that while he admitted gladly that the success and growing independence of the non-European Churches were proofs of God's blessing on them, the real reason for their formation and maintenance was 'colour feeling.' He gave warning that acceptance of present reality as the best that could be had was a denial of the Christian ideal, and pleaded that it was full time that the Church, in obedience to the teaching of the Master, led the State, not towards further *apartheid*, but towards unity.[1] The Conference therefore agreed to invite non-Europeans to its next meeting and broke up; but a postscript to its findings was provided a little later by the Anglican Bishop of Johannesburg, who urged that the Church should do much more than it was doing to create an atmosphere in which Africans could grow up to become responsible human beings.

CENTRAL AFRICAN FEDERATION

The course of events in the High Commission Territories was such that the Prime Minister of the Union might well have reckoned that his best chance of getting control of them lay in the possibility that the British Government might weary of its responsibility. In Basutoland, tribesmen and even Chiefs were perpetrating so many ritual murders, usually to get 'medicine' powerful enough to produce good crops, that the local authorities condemned the evil practice at *pitsos* (meetings) throughout the country, held an 'anti-medicine month,' and started a pilot scheme on some hundred thousand acres which might prove that better crops could be ensured by community effort than by hole-in-corner magic.[2] In the Bechuanaland Protectorate, the miserable affair of Tshekedi and Seretse Khama dragged

[1] *Round Table*, No. 174, pp. 161 ff.; *The Times*, Jan. 29, 1954.
[2] *The Times*, Sept. 22, 1953, and March 23, 1954.

on. Lord Salisbury, the new Secretary of State for Commonwealth Relations, indeed allowed the ex-Regent to go home and be formally readmitted to his tribe on condition that he took no part in Native administration; but he told Seretse in the presence of a Bamangwato delegation that he must not return till his tribesmen had elected a new Chief, who must be neither himself nor Tshekedi. He tried to soften the blow by offering him an official post in distant Jamaica, but this the unhappy young man refused, while in the forbidden land of his fathers Bamangwato killed three policemen and tumultuously affirmed their loyalty to him and no other. So threatening was the situation and so averse were the tribesmen to electing a new Chief, that the District Commissioner and his *ad hoc* African Council, who were still in temporary control of the Reserve, postponed the *kgotla* that was to have made the election till after the ploughing season.[1] At last, in May 1953, Lord Swinton, Salisbury's successor, and Harry Hopkinson, Minister of State for the Colonies, decreed that the Bamangwato chieftainship must remain vacant and the administration be taken over by Rasebolai Kgamane, the senior member of the tribe eligible for that office.[2] At the same time, they undertook to spend £16,000,000 over the next four years on Basutoland, so that the most coveted of the three Territories might become agriculturally self-supporting, to see what could be done in the way of developing the coal, iron and hydro-electrical potentialities of Swaziland, and, besides encouraging beef-production in Bechuanaland, to give that Protectorate grants-in-aid for extended administrative services.[3]

While the British Government was thus trying to make the High Commission Territories less dependent on the Union, white federalists on either side of the Zambesi were once more seeking to make their country strong enough to withstand the southward pull of their great neighbour. Huggins cannot have been as confident as he had been a year or so back that his Southern Rhodesia could play the leading part he had marked out for it in a federal Central Africa, for times were not so good as they had been. He had been obliged to postpone plans for development, to stock-pile extensively, to lengthen the period of military service, and to cut down the influx of immigrants by one-third lest the swarms of newcomers wreck the social services. Not only so, but he had had to shoulder a large deficit and look forward to shouldering one still greater unless the drought broke. As it was, he had been obliged to tax heavily and insist that dollars be earned by the sale of the entire gold-output on the free market, where the best prices could be obtained.[4] On the other hand,

[1] *Chronology*, VIII., No. 7, pp. 194–5; No. 9, pp. 251–8; No. 22, p. 693; IX No. 10, p. 295.
[2] *Ibid.*, IX., No. 10, p. 307.   [3] *Ibid.*, VIII., No. 19, p. 586.
[4] *Ibid.*, VIII., No. 9, p. 247.

he was loth to draw back now that the political atmosphere at Westminster was so much more favourable to federation than it had ever been in the days of Attlee's Labour administration.[1] On a visit to London with the Governors of the three Central African dependencies to discuss the Report of the latest Victoria Falls Conference, he had found the Secretary of State for Commonwealth Relations well-disposed, and Colonel Oliver Lyttelton, the energetic Colonial Secretary, positively enthusiastic. This son of the Colonial Secretary who had sanctioned Chinese labour on the Rand mines in Milner's time was resolved to further the cause of Federation by all means in his power. He, therefore, not only bade the Governors of the two Protectorates invite spokesmen of their African Representative and Protectorate Councils to meet him in London forthwith, but arranged that the next Conference should be held in London in April, that is, three months earlier than had been originally proposed, so that he might have a draft scheme embodying safeguards for Africans in good time before the subsequent Conference in July.[2] Hence, the Governor of Northern Rhodesia called upon white and black to recognise that each other's races had a right to homes in their common country, and Huggins, as president of the newly-founded Central African Association, summoned his followers to a campaign for a federation that should be fair to all concerned.

The London Conference of April 1952 was by no means so representative as Huggins, at least, had hoped. The two Secretaries of State headed a strong United Kingdom delegation, and he himself and other prominent local politicians brought with them representative groups of Europeans from their respective territories; but the only Africans present were two from Southern Rhodesia, whom he had nominated on his own authority without consulting their fellow-countrymen. In spite of the dissent of these two Africans, the Conference adopted a draft scheme, which in the main confirmed earlier proposals, but amended them in two important respects by proposing, first, that two Africans should be elected to the Federal Parliament by a process which it forebore to define and, secondly, by suggesting that a scarcely more practicable Advisory African Affairs Board should take the place of the anomalous independent Minister as champion of African interests.[3] This Board represented a desperate attempt to protect Africans from being overridden by a virtually white electorate, which would, for a long time to come, have the last word politically and, as experience of the Union had shown, could not be limited even by the most elaborate of paper safeguards and entrenchments. It was to consist of a Chairman appointed by the Governor-General, the three Territorial Secretaries of Native Affairs,

---

[1] *The Times*, Oct. 31, 1951   [2] *Chronology*, VIII., No. 5, p. 139.
[3] *Ibid.*, VIII., No. 9, p. 247; Cmd. 8573 of 1952.

and one European and one African, none of whom was to be a member of any legislature, nominated by the Governor-General from each of the three Territories. Its duty would be to register objections to any measures that discriminated against Africans, though, to be sure, in certain circumstances, His Excellency could ignore those objections.

The Conference's draft scheme had a mixed reception on both sides of the equator. In London, spokesmen of the African Congresses of the two Protectorates poured scorn on 'the professed safeguards,' which they feared would never stay the extension northward of the Southern Rhodesian colour bar, while representatives of seventeen African organisations assembled at Bulawayo warmly endorsed the objections advanced by the two African delegates to the recent Conference.[1] The Colonial Secretary, lamenting this public criticism, insisted that 'partnership' was the only possible solution, but nevertheless refused to give the Imperial Parliament a chance of debating the Federation Bill in all its parts. Rather did he tell the Commons that after a further Conference in July had ratified the draft scheme, the Houses would be faced with a mere Permissive Bill empowering Her Majesty to set up the Federal Constitution by Order-in-Council.[2] Huggins grumbled truly enough that the projected Advisory Board would wreck the whole scheme, the leader of the Rhodesia Party called for the linking up of the High Commission Territories with Southern Rhodesia and, thereafter, perhaps the federation of the enlarged State with the Union, while away in Capetown one ebullient parliamentarian boldly demanded that Southern Rhodesia herself be incorporated in the Union before Federation could be achieved. Malan, however, turned this last suggestion aside with the reasonable observation that the initiative must come, not from him, but from Southern Rhodesians, who had rejected a somewhat similar proposal made by their own Prime Minister shortly after the Axis war.[3]

Meanwhile, overseas notabilities were invading the Zambesi lands. First came Attlee to put Labour's point of view to the Salisbury Rotarians and visit the local Native township, and then Henry Hopkinson, Churchill's Minister of State for Colonial Affairs, to proclaim that Federation would create 'a great new bastion of British Power,' whereas failure to achieve it speedily would give rise to 'bitterness and frustration, depression and despair.' The impressionable Minister affirmed also that the scheme approved by the recent London Conference covered all interests concerned, confessed his inability to find out what Africans were really thinking, and alleged, though without giving instances, that they were being subjected to a good

[1] *Chronology*, VIII., No. 9, pp. 247, 258.   [2] *Hansard*, June 25, 1952.
[3] *Rhodesia Herald*, June 27 and July 1, 1952; *Chronology*, VIII., No. 5, p. 151.

deal of intimidation. He was at once taken to task for talking thus airily by the Blantyre Mission Council, some Northern Rhodesian missionaries, the Established Kirk of Scotland, the British Council of Churches, and the noted historian and anthropologist, Margery Perham, who lamented that ill will was mounting against the white man in Britain's African dependencies, to go no further afield, and urged that the British should educate Africans and work with them in genuine partnership.[1]

European opinion in Central Africa was deeply divided. On the one hand, the newly-formed Capricorn Africa Society advocated large-scale immigration and the creation of a true partnership between black and white.[2] On the other hand, Sir Ernest Guest's Rhodesia League and the even more extreme White Rhodesia Council clamoured that Federation would undermine the white man's position, and asserted in true frontier fashion that Europeans on the spot knew much better than did distant officials and politicians at Westminster, who must pander to 'a large mass of ill-informed opinion in the United Kingdom.'[3] Many white trade unionists, most of the Afrikaner voters who already formed one-fifth of Southern Rhodesia's electorate, and large numbers of the universally enfranchised European housewives looked askance at a Constitution that would admit one or two Africans to the Federal Parliament and might lead to the industrial advancement of Africans and, therefore, to African competition with the rising generation of white folk. In Northern Rhodesia, Welensky undoubtedly spoke for many of his fellow trade unionists and their wives when he inveighed against the unlucky Advisory Board, maintained that the best way to deal with African demands for admission to skilled trades was to 'guarantee the security of the white man,' and expressed his firm belief that failure to achieve immediate federation would lead to a 'head on clash' between white and black extremists.[4] As if to give point to his words, clashes did occur, though they had little enough to do with politics. First, the Wankie Colliery embarrassed every owner of a chimney in Central Africa by raising the price of coal markedly and without warning, and then, in October 1952, some thirty-seven thousand members of the African Mineworkers' Union struck for a rise in pay similar to that which had recently been accorded to white miners. These Africans stood firm for three weeks with excellent discipline, while European employees kept essential services going, and only went back to work after they had been promised that their case would be submitted to an independent

[1] *Chronology*, VIII., No. 16, p. 492; No. 17, pp. 515, 521; *The Times*, Dec. 8, 1952.
[2] *Greater Rhodesia*; *The Times*, May 30, 1951.
[3] *Ibid.*, Nov. 13, 1952, and Jan. 1, 1953.   [4] *Ibid.*, Dec. 27, 1952.

British arbitrator. In January 1953, an eminent Cambridge economist recommended a substantial increase of pay, albeit less than the strikers had asked for, and observed that all would not be well on the Copper Belt until Africans were allowed to attain to 'positions of greater responsibility and importance.'[1]

Meanwhile, Huggins, Welensky and other leading politicians had joined Lyttelton, the Colonial Secretary, Lord Salisbury, now Lord Privy Seal, and Lord Swinton, Salisbury's successor as Secretary of State for Commonwealth Relations, at the final Federation Conference in London.[2] This time there were no Africans present, because Huggins had brought none from his colony, and the Legislative Councils of Northern Rhodesia and Nyasaland had failed to induce any of their African members to attend. The Conference had before it the recommendations of a Civil Service Commission that a Central African customs union be created and that many governmental departments be federated.[3] After sitting throughout January 1953, it resolved that the Two Rhodesias and Nyasaland should be federated around Salisbury as the capital for the time being under a Governor-General appointed by the Queen, an Executive Council and, at least at the start, a unicameral Federal Parliament of thirty-six members.[4] Certain matters of common concern were to be entrusted to the Federal authorities, but many others, and especially those touching Native interests, were to fall to the Territorial authorities, while yet others were to be subject to concurrent Federal and Territorial legislation with the proviso that, in cases of conflict, the Federal law was to prevail. Southern Rhodesia should elect fourteen members of the Federal Parliament, Northern Rhodesia eight and Nyasaland four; but there were also to be three specially elected Africans from each of the three Territories, as well as three Europeans to speak for African interests, one of whom was to be nominated for Southern Rhodesia and one elected for each of the Protectorates. Further safeguards for African interests were provided by the retention of their Protectorate status by both of the Territories north of the Zambesi and the creation of a Standing Committee of the Federal Assembly to discharge the duties that would have fallen to the much-criticised Advisory African Affairs Board. This Committee was to consist of a chairman nominated by the Governor-General and armed with a casting-vote, the three European members of the Assembly charged with the care of African interests, and one African for each of the three Territories elected by those same European

[1] *Chronology*, IX., No. 3, p. 87.
[2] *The Times*, Jan. 1, 1953; *Chronology*, IX., No. 1, p. 5.
[3] Cmd. 8671, 8672 and 8673 of 1952.
[4] Cmd. 8753 of 1953; *Report of the Conference on Federation*, Cmd. 8754 of 1953. *The Federal Scheme*; *The Times*, Jan. 9 and Feb. 6, 1953; *Chronology*, IX., No. 4, p. 105.

members and the six African members of the Federal Assembly. It was, however, permissible to doubt whether a mere Committee of the Federal Parliament would prove to be an improvement on the independent Advisory Board. If it did its duty, it would be quite as likely as the rejected 'loose-head' Minister or Board to produce 'head-on clashes' between the authorities at Westminster and those on the spot, most of whose electors wanted Federation largely because it promised to free them from interference by British officials and parliamentarians. And if, as it well might, the Committee forced a dissolution, what chance would its members stand of re-election? However that might be, the Constitution was not to be immutable, for it could be changed at any time, subject to reservation for Her Majesty's pleasure, by a two-thirds majority excluding the Speaker, and was in any event to be overhauled by the United Kingdom, Federal and Territorial Governments together not earlier than seven years nor later than nine years after it had been put into operation. This was, however, cold comfort to the African ninety-seven per cent. of the population of the future Federation, because, whereas in the neighbouring Union a two-thirds majority was necessary before any changes adverse to non-European Cape voters could be made, here no changes favourable to actual or potential African voters could be effected without that majority.

It remained to be seen whether the two northern Territories could maintain their Protectorate status in the coming Federation. Meanwhile, vocal African opinion showed itself dead against a scheme which it held was being forced upon the country. In Northern Rhodesia, the president of the African Congress and eight hundred of his followers ceremoniously burned the Federation White Paper as a sign of 'bitter opposition' to the whole affair, and threatened that its forcible imposition would be followed by unrest 'perhaps of the worst kind.'[1] From Nyasaland, three chiefs, sponsored by the Rev. Michael Scott, set out for London to support that protest and, if it might be, to 'see the Queen.' Lyttelton brusquely declined to let Her Majesty be troubled, made light of the chiefs' arguments, rejected the appeal against haste made by the well-informed International Confederation of Free Trade Unions, and then turned and rent Griffiths, his Labour predecessor, for moving the rejection of the scheme.[2] Strong in the backing of nearly all the national newspapers, he told the Commons that the Government took full responsibility for pressing on with the 'liberal' scheme and, in addition to enumerating the now familiar arguments for speed, asserted that the recalcitrant Northern Rhodesian African Congress was retailing as 'indigenous' the 'prefabricated' objections sent to

[1] *Chronology*, IX., No. 7, p. 202; IX., No. 3, p. 80.
[2] *Ibid.*, IX., No. 7, p. 193; *The Times*, March 21, 1953.

them from the United Kingdom. Thanks to these arguments, a split in the Labour ranks and a three-line whip, he gained the Commons' approval of the Federation scheme by 304 to 260 votes before the end of April 1953.[1]

The next step was for the men on the spot to say whether or no they too would accept the Federal scheme. At the referendum in Southern Rhodesia, while Huggins was manfully trying to convince Africans that Federation would mean partnership and not repression, two-thirds of the eighty per cent. of the electors who went to the polls voted in favour of the proposals.[2] In Northern Rhodesia, most of the European members of the Legislative Council were cheered by the news that the International Bank was advancing a large sum for railway construction, and that their Barotse at least had promised not to oppose the coming Constitution, provided it preserved their rights under the late King Lewanika's concession to the Chartered Company long ago, and that the Federation Order-in-Council would recognise that their country was still to be a Protectorate.[3] The Legislative Council therefore accepted the Federation White Paper by seventeen votes against the four cast by the two African members and the two Europeans who represented African interests. There was, however, some opposition outside the legislature. The Northern Rhodesian African Congress thought at first of adopting Michael Scott's suggestion that it ask the British Government to drop Federation and substitute the partition of the two Protectorates into one European and two African states very much on the lines that Gore-Browne had long been advocating; but it decided finally merely to start a campaign 'as in the Union' against the colour bar in Government offices, hotels, restaurants and shops.[4]

While this campaign was being waged good-temperedly enough, events took an ugly turn in Nyasaland. There, Scott and the Paramount Chief Mwase induced the Council of Nyasaland Chiefs, of which the latter was president, and the Nyasaland African Congress also to appeal to the United Nations against Federation.[5] One of the Chiefs, Gomani, went much further by calling on his people to start civil disobedience. When he refused to withdraw this advice, he was suspended from his office as a Native authority. He, his sons and Scott thereupon fled to neighbouring Portuguese East Africa. All were promptly arrested, and Scott was sent back to Nyasaland to be proclaimed a prohibited alien and deported by air to his native England.[6] In face of this drastic step, Mwase and four other Chiefs resigned their offices as Native Authorities, though, to be sure, fifteen of the hundred others who carried on promised to support Federation,

[1] *Chronology*, IX., No. 7, p. 194.
[2] *Ibid.*, IX., No. 8, p. 234.
[3] *Ibid.*, IX., No. 6, p. 177; No. 9, p. 278.
[4] *Ibid.*, IX., No. 9, p. 279.
[5] *Ibid.*, IX., No. 8, p. 232.
[6] *Ibid.*, IX., No. 11, p. 339.

however little they might like it.[1] Meanwhile, the Christian Council of Northern Rhodesia, which represented all save the Roman Catholic and Dutch Reformed Churches, expressed regret that the United Kingdom authorities were still going forward while African opinion remained so strongly opposed, and asked for a declaration of the rights of all men in the coming Federation as well as the promise of a greater share for Africans in educational, industrial and political life. Scott, on landing in England, warned his fellow-countrymen that they were running the risk of teaching Africans to regard all white folk, even missionaries, as hostile aliens.[2]

The Colonial Secretary was apparently ready to run that risk. Pooh-poohing the extent and genuineness of African opposition, dilating on the economic benefits that would accrue from Federation, and pleading that his Government was 'morally bound' to the other Governments concerned, he defeated numerous Labour amendments and induced the Commons to pass the Third Reading of his Rhodesia and Nyasaland (Constitution) Bill by a majority of twenty-three. The Lords made no serious difficulty and, in mid-July 1953, Her Majesty duly signed the necessary Order-in-Council.[3]

This news was greeted with less unrest than had been expected. There was, indeed, little or none apart from a few sporadic disturbances in Nyasaland, which involved the death of six Africans, the serious injury of seven and the arrest of many more; but, as against this, urban Africans at Blantyre lamented such breaches of the peace and formed a Nyasaland African Progressive Association friendly to the authorities.[4] Meanwhile, political parties began to take shape with an eye to the coming Federal and Territorial elections, while the Queen Mother and Princess Margaret were visiting the Rhodes Centenary Exhibition at Bulawayo, which celebrated past achievement, and laying the foundation-stone of the multi-racial Rhodesia University College at Salisbury, the first tangible proof that 'partnership' might bring good to black as well as white. On August 7, 1953, Huggins, the newly-knighted Sir Roland Welensky and Sir Malcolm Barrow, the leading European politician in Nyasaland, easily induced their recently formed Federal Party to accept a definition of 'partnership,' which combined a not unreasonable amount of *apartheid* with Southern Rhodesia's traditional Cape liberalism. That hitherto vague term was now to connote harmonious relations between folk of all races, a recognition that Europeans and Africans had distinctive and complementary parts to play and must expect to be rewarded in accordance with their competence therein, that each race must develop along its own lines and accept different facilities and amenities so

---

[1] *Chronology*, IX., No. 12, p. 373.   [2] *The Times*, June 26, 1953.
[3] *Chronology*, IX., No. 13, pp. 401, 418; No. 14, pp. 436, 447.
[4] *Ibid.*, IX., No. 18, p. 573.

long as their respective masses remained so far apart in culture and, finally, that special privileges would be withdrawn and special political representation be diminished as full political rights were gradually extended to those who became civilised.[1] The Party as a whole expressed the hope that there would be informal rather than compulsory residential segregation. It resolved, further, that economic though not social equality be assured to assimilated Africans, while its three leaders claimed to have the support of leading members of the Federal Party in the Salisbury Parliament and certainly had that of the Southern Rhodesian press for their proposal that Africans should be eligible for party membership. The leaders then announced that their aim was to foster good racial relations, encourage selective immigration and hasten the day when they might realise one of Rhodes's dreams by admitting other African states to their Federation. Lastly, so that the best men might be elected to the Federal Parliament, they urged that unnecessary party politics be avoided at the outset and, above all, that elections for the Territorial legislatures be not fought on the same platform as those for the Federal House.[2]

It was perhaps natural that able politicians should see no need for rival parties, but it was too much to ask that no such parties be formed, especially in a land where most of the electors were of either British or Afrikaner stock. Almost at once, a Progressive Party appeared on the Copper Belt with a policy even more liberal than that of the Federal Party itself. This development caused Huggins little anxiety, because although the Progressives criticised his partner, Welensky, for his anti-African proclivities, they proposed to confine their activities to their own Protectorate.[3] Not so John Dendy Young's Confederate Party. Young himself was a dogged opponent of Federation; his right-hand man, an ex-Southern Rhodesian Finance Minister, was a warm advocate of Gore-Browne's scheme for the partition of the two Protectorates into European and African states; four of his other most prominent followers were members of the predominantly Afrikaner Democratic Party, which was so fresh to the world of politics that it had not yet had time to fight an election, and many of the rank-and-file were recently arrived Nationalists from the Union.[4] The Confederates appealed to all 'moderate racial elements' to sink their differences, work for the good of the Federation and pursue 'a sound liberal and progressive Native policy'; but, when it came to the point, this ostensibly reasonable programme turned out to be one of almost unadulterated *apartheid* based on the idea that practices and principles which had been evolved in the

---

[1] *The Times*, Aug. 14, 1953; *Chronology*, IX., No. 9, p. 280; No. 17, p. 540.
[2] *Ibid.*, IX., No. 13, p. 417.   [3] *The Times*, June 26 and Aug. 14, 1953.
[4] *Ibid.*, Oct. 19, 1953.

28

United Kingdom were in no wise applicable to Africans, who, its framers alleged, were probably 'politically the most immature people in the world.'[1] As if the Confederates' programme was not enough to horrify Huggins, they ignored his suggestion that the Federal and Territorial battlegrounds be kept distinct as far as might be. The Party proposed to campaign on one and the same platform at all times and in all places, and though it had been formed in Southern Rhodesia, directed its main attack upon Northern Rhodesia, where it hoped to profit from the fear of 'the Black North' entertained by so many of the privileged miners and railwaymen and their wives. Its vice-president and principal candidate in that region therefore impressed upon disappointingly small audiences in the mining towns that there must be compulsory residential segregation, none of the replacement of white workers by black which they said falsely was the aim of the Federal Party, and above all no common voters' roll which would lead one day to an exclusively African Parliament. Their distant leader backed them manfully from south of the Zambesi, finding no difficulty in quoting the dead Smuts in support of *apartheid* and, quite in the manner of Malan and Heaton Nicholls, promising to guarantee permanent white civilisation in Central Africa, to create African states within the Federation ultimately, and to encourage Africans, always safely segregated on their own voters' roll, to develop to the fullest extent politically and economically in their own areas.[2]

Huggins made ready to fight these importers of the Union's least enlightened policies all along the line. Resigning his leadership of the Southern Rhodesian United Party in favour of the equally liberal Reginald Garfield Todd, he called upon his Federal Party, on the one hand, to stand firm against enthusiasts who demanded equal rights for all civilised men straight away and, on the other, to resist the Confederates and other extremists whose *apartheid* notions would riddle politics with race hatred.[3] Then, on September 4, 1953, Lord Llewellin arrived as Governor-General designate and, for a start, took the oath as President of the Rhodesia and Nyasaland Appeal Court. Three days later, as the first step towards the creation of an Interim Federal Government, Huggins himself was sworn in as Prime Minister and Minister of Finance, Defence and External Affairs, a temporary accumulation of offices reminiscent of that which the devoted Duke of Wellington had shouldered in the far-off days of William IV. Todd, for his part, became Prime Minister of Southern Rhodesia.[4] So far, so good; but now a storm beat up. Lyttelton summoned to London the Governor of Northern Rhodesia,

---

[1] *The Times*, June 26, 1953; *Chronology*, IX., No. 13, p. 418.
[2] *The Times*, Aug. 19 and 24, 1952; *Chronology*, IX., No. 18, p. 573.
[3] *Ibid.*, IX., No. 16, p. 509.   [4] *Ibid.*, IX., No. 18, p. 572.

'the Napoleon of Broken Hill,' Geoffrey Beckett, an elected member who held the portfolio of Agriculture, John Moffat, one of the European nominees who represented African interests, and the two African members of the Northern Rhodesian Legislative Council to discuss with him constitutional changes in their Protectorate. The Conference did not march. It began badly when the Colonial Secretary brusquely told the Africans that he would only inform them whether or no British protected persons, such as they and their fellows were, could get the franchise on the same terms as British subjects when he visited their country later in the year, and insisted that, meanwhile, the sole business before the meeting was his constitutional proposals. These were, first, that because the Federal authorities would relieve the Territorial administrations of many of their duties, the number of officials in the Executive Council should be cut down from seven to five, and that each of the four unofficial members be given a portfolio so that they might form a Government Front Bench in the legislature. Secondly, membership of the Legislative Council was to be enlarged from twenty-three to twenty-six by reducing the number of official seats from nine to eight and increasing those held by white elected members from ten to fourteen and those held by Africans from two to four and maybe, later on, to five.[1] White and black alike would not hear of it. The two Africans complained that the reforms would not go 'even halfway' to giving them what they wanted, lamented that over the years the white settlers had wrested power after power from the Imperial authorities, and gave notice that they would ask their Governor to summon a special Session of the African Representative Council to go into the whole matter. Welensky and Beckett, from the other extreme, grumbled that Africans were being given too much, that the balance would be left with the official members, and that the way would be paved for a common voters' roll in place of the existing carefully devised machinery for representation on a racial basis.[2] So the meeting dispersed. On their return home, the two white recalcitrants persuaded their elective fellow-members to reject the proposals, and to request their Governor to urge the Colonial Secretary to come out to them at latest before the opening of the next Session of the Legislative Council in November.[3]

Hard on the heels of this deadlock in one Protectorate came a last desperate attempt by opponents of Federation in the other to avert their fate. All had been quiet in Nyasaland since the local African Congress had called off the passive resistance campaign and resolved to co-operate with the authorities; but now Michael Scott handed U.N.O. a letter in which eighty-three Chiefs begged that the

[1] *Chronology*, IX., No. 18, pp. 562–72; *The Times*, Sept. 1, 1953.
[2] *Chronology*, IX., No. 19, p. 595.   [3] *Ibid.*, IX., No. 22, p. 737.

International Court be invited to give an advisory opinion as to whether or no the Protectorates were sacred trusts which could not be handed over by one administering authority to another.[1] In spite of the warm support of the Indian representative, nothing came of this appeal and Federation went forward unimpeded. The Constitution came into force on October 23, 1953, sixty-four years after the granting of Rhodes's Charter; the Interim Government took office next day and speedily assumed control of external affairs. Huggins could not accede to the wish of an influential group which called for a truce to debates on Native affairs for three years during which a Commission should frame a workable Native policy, because there was little chance of any such truce now that the United Rhodesia Party had emerged from its recent voluntary withdrawal, joined hands with some members of his own old Rhodesia Party, and begun to campaign for the Territorial elections in Southern Rhodesia.[2] On the other hand, things promised at first to go well in Northern Rhodesia, where the Chamber of Mines promised to institute very shortly a non-contributory pension scheme for all its employees, and the little Progressive Party dissolved itself lest it split the Liberal vote and let in the Confederates.[3]

At this stage, Welensky tried to force the Colonial Secretary to withhold his constitutional reforms till after he had visited the country. He and another elected member resigned their portfolios, all the elected members refused to co-operate further, Beckett thundered that there must be an end of domination by the British Parliament, politicians and public opinion, while Welensky himself, on moving the rejection of the reforms in the Legislative Council, prophesied a 'first-class row' if Lyttelton would not stay his hand and, therewith, appealed to the electorate. Alas! Welensky's motion was rejected and then the distant Colonial Secretary made an end of this storm in a Copper Bowl by explaining in unwontedly conciliatory tones that he had never meant to suggest that there should be any immediate change in the franchise arrangements, and by promising that there should be none during the next five years or so. On the other hand, he refused to change his scheme unless the Government and all parties so desired, and only promised to visit Lusaka in January 1954 to talk things over with the elected members and also to meet the African Representative Council.[4] Hence, resignations were withdrawn and co-operation resumed and the voters everywhere sallied forth to the hustings.

The Federal general election of December 15, 1953, was virtually a straight fight between the Federal and Confederate Parties. It

---

[1] *Chronology*, IX., No. 20, p. 663.   [2] *Ibid.*, IX., No. 20, p. 646.
[3] *Ibid.*, IX., No. 20, p. 658; No. 21, p. 700; *The Times*, Oct. 23, 1953.
[4] *Chronology*, IX., No. 24, p. 796; No. 22, p. 737.

resulted in a crushing defeat for the latter, which received little more than one-third of the votes cast in Southern Rhodesia in spite of the many presumably sympathetic Afrikaners on the roll, barely one-fifth in Northern Rhodesia, where its hopes had run high, and scarcely any in more conservative Nyasaland. Next day, Huggins announced his Federal Ministry with himself as Prime Minister, Welensky, that notable ex-engine driver, most appropriately as Minister of Transport, Donald MacIntyre and John Caldicott as Ministers of Finance and of Health and Agriculture respectively, and Barrow as Minister of Internal Affairs till the coming New Year, when he would hand over his portfolio to Julian Greenfield, who would hold it together with his present portfolio of Justice.[1] Scarcely was the Federal Party thus triumphantly confirmed in power than Lyttelton paid his promised visit to Lusaka. There, he repeated his assurances to the elected members, suggested that constitutional issues were merely secondary, and urged all concerned to make it their first business to devise a system in which Europeans would run no risk of being swamped and Africans would not feel that they were afflicted by 'political arthritis.' This timely tiding over of an awkward crisis doubtless enabled the United Rhodesia Party to win all the seats in the Southern Rhodesian territorial elections save four that went to Independents, and ten seats in Northern Rhodesia as against the two won by Independents.[2] Thus it was that, on February 3, 1954, the Governor-General could open the first Session of the Federal Parliament with a quiet mind and words of hope.

THE FEDERATION

The Federation took the water on a fairly even keel, but its helmsmen were at once faced with the problem of keeping it running freely. That problem arose out of the very nature of a federal system. As its name implies, a federation is the result of a treaty concluded at a given moment to meet the needs of that moment. Since its makers are rarely prophets, they cannot provide infallibly in advance for the strains that must arise from changing circumstances, ensure that administrations and peoples unaccustomed to co-operation with one another will always work together for common ends, or resolve conflicts between old territorial and new federal loyalties.

In all three Territories, officials gave the lead by grumbling with true departmental patriotism at the speed with which the Federal Government was taking over their authority, their functions and many of themselves. Again, each Territory nursed fears, suspicions and jealousies of its neighbours and the central authority. Many

[1] *Chronology*, IX., No. 24, p. 808; X., No. 1, p. 28.
[2] *Ibid.*, X., No. 2, p. 55; No. 3, p. 87; No. 5, p. 153; *The Times*, Jan. 29, 1954.

Southern Rhodesians resented the continuance of Colonial Office control over the two Protectorates, while many black Northern Rhodesians and Nyasalanders were by no means minded to see Southern Rhodesia's comparatively rigid colour bar extended north of the Zambesi. Educated Africans and most of the Europeans in the Protectorates did not see why their Territories should not have the measure of self-government that Southern Rhodesia had long enjoyed; nearly all Africans in those parts, the semi-independent Barotse above all, dreaded lest white newcomers should take their cherished lands; the more vocal black Nyasalanders still resented the very idea of federation and the fact that the standard of living of their people was so much lower than that in the other Territories; black Northern Rhodesian miners fretted against the obstacles thrown in the way of their advancement by extravagantly paid and highly privileged white miners and their wives, all armed with the votes that were denied to themselves because they were still merely 'British protected' persons. Northern Rhodesians, white and black, were however agreed that their mines, one of the chief sources of the national revenue, should never be 'milked' for federal purposes.

Pledged as they were by their Prime Minister to a policy of 'partnership,' the Federal authorities set great store by the nascent multi-racial Rhodesia University College. Its creation would be an outstanding proof that that policy was a reality. The Inaugural Board appointed as temporary Principal, William Rollo, a downright and liberally-minded Glasgow Scot and Professor of Classics in the old-established multi-racial University of Cape Town, the premier University in Africa south of the Sahara. It presently reported that, after having consulted the British, Federal and Territorial Governments, it had come to terms with the University of London, which was willing to take the College into a special relationship provided it approved of its constitution and programme of development. Entrance qualifications were to be fairly stiff, though there was good hope that French might be substituted in some cases for the Latin which many schools in the Federation were not yet competent to teach adequately, and the Board expected that though Europeans must lead in the College, as elsewhere, fully one-third of the students should be Africans in three years' time with more to follow. Multi-racial the College was to be, but because it would be situated in a European area in Salisbury, it would rest with the Southern Rhodesian and not with the Federal Parliament to decide whether or no the Land Apportionment Act of that Colony should be so amended as to permit of Africans living within its precincts. The Board hoped to start the Faculties of Arts and Sciences by May 1956 at the latest and, thereafter, those of Agriculture and Medicine.

A few months later, it found a permanent Principal in Dr. Walter Adams, Secretary of the Inter-University Council for Higher Education in the Colonies.[1]

Territorial and racial differences revealed themselves during the debates on the Income Tax Bill, the first important measure to be laid before the Federal Parliament. This Bill merely provided machinery for the assessment and collection of a Federal income tax, leaving specific financial proposals to be made in the forthcoming Appropriation Bill. At once, Southern Rhodesians, who had long paid income tax in their own Colony, demanded a reduction in the rate of taxation, while Dendy Young, the Confederate one-man Opposition, and the African Members from the Protectorates protested against the increase of their existing burdens by so unwelcome a novelty. Some of the Africans even raised the cry of 'no taxation without representation,' demanding, in short, that British-protected persons, such as they and their fellows were, should not be called upon to pay till the colour bar had been abolished and they themselves had been included in the common voters' roll. The Bill went through, but before the Appropriation Bill could be introduced, something of a split had occurred in the Confederate Party. Dendy Young, the only begetter of that organisation, and his right-hand man were indeed re-elected Leader and Deputy-Leader respectively, but a round dozen members resigned mainly because they resented the influence which Afrikander Nationalists were gaining in the Party.[2] The Minister of Finance then introduced the Appropriation Bill, intimating that £70,000,000 would be spent under the Federal Development Plan during the next three years. Of this, £30,000,000 would be devoted to communications and £4,400,000 to education, notably to new schools for European and Coloured children, but not for African youngsters, who were a Territorial responsibility. The Bill, income tax and all, had a quiet enough passage after the Prime Minister and Welensky had stressed the economic advantages of federation, and pointed to the confidence in their new State shown by its citizens, who had subscribed a loan of £4,000,000 in a couple of hours, and those of the United Kingdom, who had oversubscribed one of £10,000,000 in five minutes.[3]

The succeeding measure, a Deportation Bill, had a much rougher passage, if only because it was a reminder of the half-gale that had rocked the Federation at its launching. First, Africans had struck in quick succession at Bulawayo and Wankie. They had gone back to work as soon as armed police had hurried in, but their strikes had been a hint to European trade unionists that they should see to their

---

[1] *Federation Newsletter*, April 14, 1954.
[2] *South Africa*, June 19, 1954.
[3] *Federation Newsletter*, Sept. 25, 1954.

own interests betimes. Hence, in May 1954, delegates representing perhaps twenty thousand workers organised in fifteen trade unions and local committees had dissolved the Trade Union Congress of Rhodesia and formed the far more comprehensive Trade Union Congress of the Federation. A week or two later, the white firemen in Southern Rhodesia had struck under the leadership of Charles Taylor, a new arrival in the country, and had induced many of their northern comrades to join in. The movement had become so serious that the authorities had proclaimed a state of emergency and arrested Taylor, because they were convinced that he was bent on transforming the Railway Union into a militant force that should wreck the legal machinery for industrial negotiation. In due course, after the High Court had refused Taylor's application for a stay of proceedings, they had deported him as a prohibited immigrant.[1] In the ensuing excitement, the Council of the new Trade Union Congress had shown that it inherited a good deal of the colour bar policy of its predecessor, for though it had agreed that the standard of living of Africans ought to be brought nearer to that of Europeans, it had insisted, doubtless under Northern Rhodesian inspiration, that all workers of whatever colour must try to attain to the white man's standard of living and workmanship, and that all learners and apprentices must face the training programme laid down for Europeans.[2]

The Deportation Bill now sought to give the Minister concerned wide powers to deal summarily with strikers and, further, to send Union-born Africans, who were serving long terms of imprisonment, back to their own country, there to complete their sentences. It might be, as the Minister pleaded, that the powers he was asking for were very similar to those wielded by the British Home Secretary, and that the gaols had all they could do to accommodate the country's own prisoners without housing others; what his Parliamentary critics boggled at was that those powers were excessive, unless he simply meant to use them for strike-breaking, and that 'returned' African convicts could hardly expect considerate treatment in Swart's South Africa. Nor did those critics stand alone. The Council of the new Trade Union Congress, mindful of Charles Taylor's fate, demanded that prospective deportees of his kind be given full public trials, and, in the Commons, Labour members protested so vigorously that the Colonial Secretary had to remind them that no African convict would be sent back to the Union without reference to his Office.

Greenfield, the comparatively liberally-minded Minister of Home Affairs, next introduced his Immigration Bill. Some measure of this sort was very necessary, because the existing population was small for the size of the country, only some 6,876,000 souls all told. Of

[1] *The Times*, June 7, 1954.   [2] *Chronology*, X., 11, p. 356; 16, p. 536.

these 220,000 were Europeans, 26,400 Asians and Euro-Africans, that is, mixed-breed Coloured Folk, and 6,630,000 Africans. Nor was the white population increasing really fast, for though some 16,700 Europeans had arrived during the past year, the great majority of them from the United Kingdom, Ireland and South Africa, at least 14,500 had left for good.[1] Under these circumstances various big undertakings were hard put to it to get the men they needed. The railways especially were in difficulties. They could indeed rejoice that the United States Foreign Operations Administration had lent them £3,500,000 for development; but they had to lament a desperate shortage of skilled men because young white Rhodesians fought shy of taking service with them. Union nationals and local Africans were alternative sources of supply; but the Railway administration was not keen on taking the many South Africans who applied, and positively averse to training African firemen, as one of the African Members for Nyasaland suggested. Rather than have recourse to such desperate remedies, the Minister of Transport, Sir Roy Welensky, proposed to offer free passages to Dutch, West German and Scandinavian recruits.

Something on a much larger scale was plainly necessary. This the Immigration Bill sought to provide.[2] The underlying idea was to bring in as many Europeans as possible on a selective basis and, above all, as many British as might be, so that the Federation should indeed become the 'great British bastion' envisaged by its advocates. To that end, certain classes of British immigrants were to be offered assisted passages. At the same time, since there were immigrants and immigrants, Greenfield made it crystal clear which kind the authorities wanted and which they did not. First, entry was to be denied to all, who, in the Minister's opinion, were unacceptable either on economic grounds or because their standards and habits of life were frankly impossible, all who might become an expense to the public, all idiots, epileptics, criminals, prostitutes and homosexuals, and all who were either suspected of being Communists or refused to swear that they were not such. In making his decision the Minister was to rely, *inter alia*, on official reports from any Government. Secondly, the Bill differentiated specifically against two classes of would-be newcomers: first, Africans from the Union, who must face stiffer obstacles than hitherto lest they lead local Africans along undesirable paths, and, secondly, Asians from any source, who were as difficult to fit into the Western scheme of things in the Federation as in any other mixed society in Africa. These last were to be shut out altogether, unless they were ministers of religion, teachers, or wives of persons already resident in the country. In general, a fact-finding committee was to take counsel with the Immigration Boards and

[1] *Federation Newsletter*, Nov. 1, 1954.   [2] *Ibid.*, Aug. 16, 1954.

28*

decide how many immigrants could be absorbed in the light of the houses and jobs available. At once there were protests from many quarters. Noting that Europeans could move freely, many Africans objected that the new obstacles put in the way of Africans from the Union would isolate them from their southern brethren to whom they were being more and more closely drawn by social, cultural and economic ties; Nyasalanders of all colours condemned the branding of any particular race as prohibited or undesirable; ministerial supporters in Nyasaland, again, asked that professionally and technically trained Asians be admitted 'according to need'; many local Europeans and Africans backed the Nyasaland Asian Convention when it begged that selective Asian immigration be permitted, and, in Parliament itself, Europeans from many parts spoke well of Asians. In the event, the Bill went through, but only after the anti-Communist clause had been dropped, mainly because the Prime Minister declared that there was no such thing as a Communist Party in the Federation and that such few Reds as trickled in soon saw unsuspected virtues in capitalism.[1]

Huggins could by no means treat African ambitions thus airily. Two African Members moved that everyone be treated on the same footing in public places, notably in post offices, on the railways and the like. Some Europeans objected that such a step towards social integration would be against the wishes of nearly all white folk and of many black, while others gave warning that if money were spent on providing such equal facilities, it must be at the expense of hospitals, schools and, above all, Native housing on which fully £6,000,000 would have to be spent during the next few years if the Federation were to stand.[2] The Prime Minister told the movers bluntly that their humbler brethren could not be given the treatment desired till they had been 'cleaned up . . . a bit,' warned them that if the motion were carried, the white folk would be alienated and the clock be put back 'at least ten years,' and counselled patience because he simply had not got the money to educate and elevate the black masses, whose 'abject poverty' was the root of the trouble. In the end, an amendment was carried pledging the authorities to do the best they could; but that did not deter the President of the Northern Rhodesian African Congress from accusing Huggins of having written off 'partnership' from the Federal Constitution, and boasting that the time would come when Africans would 'run that Parliament or some other.' Sure enough, the African Congresses in the two Protectorates agreed to unite as a step towards the formation of a single Federation-wide Congress which should hasten that far-off event.

Many Europeans did indeed resent the nationalistic attitude of

[1] *Nyasaland Times*, Aug. 6, 1954; *Federation Newsletter*, Sept. 25, 1954; *Rhodesia Herald*, July 31, 1954.   [2] *Ibid.*, June 24, 1954.

African Members in Parliament and, still more, of the African Congresses in the Protectorates. They agreed heartily with their Prime Minister when he reminded Africans that they had been given a good position in the Central Legislature, and warned them that any attempt to form a Party on a racial basis would inevitably drive Europeans to resist.[1] Nevertheless, Huggins could not shut his eyes to the fact that inter-racial relations were deteriorating, nor deny the truth of the charge brought by African Members and Dr. Alexander Scott, Independent Member for Lusaka, that this was largely the fault of white folk, who knew or ought to know better. Nor could he pronounce the distant Commonwealth Relations Conference assembled in Pakistan entirely wrong when it denounced segregation as a confession of failure, and foretold that Europeans would vanish from Africa if they did not recognise that the majority of the voters in that continent would one day be Africans.[2]

Europeans descended from plain speaking to downright quarrelling, and that on Territorial lines of division. Since the federal scheme had been 'put across' to the white electors primarily by the argument that it would make possible the production of hydro-electrical power on a great scale, there was a certain sardonic appropriateness in the fact that the bone of contention was the siting of the first great plant. The choice lay between an installation on the Kafue river in Northern Rhodesia and another in the Kariba Gorge below the Victoria Falls in Southern Rhodesia. Welensky and his fellow-Northern Rhodesians naturally held that the Kafue project should have priority, partly because it would first and foremost serve their mines, which were making such a heavy contribution to the Federal exchequer, and partly because they believed that the issue had been settled in their favour a few months back, when the Prime Minister and the then Governor of their Protectorate had jointly stated that this scheme should be put in hand first, provided the money could be found. This statement of policy they regarded as a binding contract, and pointed out that a good deal of exploratory work had been done and considerable sums expended on the strength of it. The Southern Rhodesian Premier, Garfield Todd, would not have it so. He urged that the rival scheme should have priority, because, although it was the more costly of the two, it could probably be finished first, was capable of easy expansion, and could readily be made capable of providing power to the mines and so forth in Northern Rhodesia as well as to the industries of his Colony. Be that as it might, Welensky gravely rebuked. poor Todd for his parochialism, and Parliament, in May 1954, decided in favour of the Kafue project.[3]

[1] *Optima*, May, 1954.
[2] *Rhodesia Herald*, June 26, 1954.   [3] *The Times*, May 10, 1954.

In the event, the first such work to be put in hand was in neither of the quarrelling Rhodesias, but in little-considered Nyasaland, where a drainage scheme was launched in June to make some ten thousand acres of swamp around Lake Shirwa available for rice-growing.[1] Then, six months later, Huggins dropped his bombshell. He bluntly moved that the Kariba project be put in hand first after all, and added that a French expert was coming shortly to make a final technical appraisal. He explained that the so-called contract of 1953 had been merely a joint statement of what he and the then Governor had mistakenly believed to be possible, and adduced in justification of his change of plan the fact that the two big mining groups were not only moving their head offices from the Copper Belt to Salisbury, but approved warmly of 'Kariba first.' Welensky, whose local patriotism rarely blinded him to facts, admitted reluctantly that the necessary £54,000,000 would only be forthcoming for a fully proved project, which the Kariba scheme was and that on the Kafue was not. The motion was hotly opposed by Scott and Guillaume van Eeden, respectively Independent Members for Lusaka and Kafue itself, and the four Africans from the Protectorates; nevertheless, it was carried by a four to one majority.[2] Then the fat was in the fire. The indignant Mayor of Lusaka appealed unto Caesar by petitioning Her Majesty to see to it that the Kafue project be given priority, and the Northern Rhodesian Legislative Council, disregarding Huggins's offer to talk things over with a committee from those parts at once and, thereafter, to explain matters to a public meeting in Lusaka, grumbled that they could have carried out their pet scheme even without Federation, presumably by 'milking' the mines for local purposes, and expressed 'disappointment and disgust' at its summary shelving.[3]

The shadows that thus gathered round Lusaka became inspissated gloom as the limelight swept by and focused on Nyasaland. Perhaps it mattered little that, in the Commons, a Labour Member, fresh from a visit, should have expressed her inexpert enthusiasm for the brilliant future that awaited the Cinderella of the Federation; but it was quite another matter when a leading British firm spoke hopefully of controlling the waters of the Shire river and Lake Nyasa, improving communications, and erecting a hydro-electricity plant, which might decide the British Aluminium Company to work the adjacent bauxite deposits. Not only so, but an investment consultant to the United States Foreign Operations Association, who was touring the Federation at the invitation of the Prime Minister, waxed lyrical over the prospects of this undertaking and the possibilities of

---

[1] *Federation Newsletter*, June 3, 25, 1954.
[2] *Ibid.*, June 3, 1954; *The Times*, March 2, 3, 9, 12, 1955.
[3] *Chronology*, XI., 6, p. 196.

spinning and weaving elsewhere in the Protectorate.[1] The less pre-possessing of Cinderella's elder sisters could only hope that she would not be ignored by the representative whom private American investors were thinking of stationing permanently in Central Africa.

Finally, even before the Kafue *versus* Kariba battle had reached its climax, the unpredictable Northern Rhodesian Independent, van Eeden, had challenged the very structure of the Federation. In the hope of easing racial tensions, he virtually revived Gore-Browne's scheme of partition by proposing that Southern Rhodesia and the southern and wealthier half of his own Territory should become a Dominion, and the remainder a Protectorate under Imperial governance. There would, of course, be no social equality between Europeans and the rest in his Dominion, but home-born 'advanced' Africans were to be permitted to progress industrially after passing prescribed tests and even ultimately to achieve 'legislative equality.' Such Africans, however, and Europeans also would be granted the vote only after meeting property, financial and educational require-ments, and enfranchised Africans would have to give up their special land rights and other 'protective' privileges. Dauti Yamba, a Northern Rhodesian African Member, supported the idea, provided the projected Protectorate were divided into two independent 'States'; but Scott and several other European Members condemned it as 'bad tactics . . . irresponsible,' and smacking too much of Con-federate and even Nationalist ideology. The redoubtable President of the Northern Rhodesian African Congress rejected the scheme outright, mainly because it proposed no safeguards for the quarter of a million Africans who would be left in the 'Dominion.' In due time, the Federal Party Executive, with only two dissentients, expelled van Eeden. Undismayed, the champion of partition de-clared that he would form a Party of his own quite distinct from the Confederates, make his plan the main issue at the next Federal general election, and, in any event, look forward to seeing its being seriously considered when the Federal Constitution came up for revision in seven years' time.[2]

SOUTHERN RHODESIA

Whatever the future might hold for the Federation, each of its component parts had a political life of its own. The Southern Rhodesian Parliament began its career as a subordinate legislature by resolving that its Colony should henceforth be known as 'the State of Southern Rhodesia,' because the title of Territory was

---

[1] *Federation Newsletter*, Dec. 13, 21, 1954, and Jan. 20, 1955; *The Times*, March 15, 1955.
[2] *Ibid.*, Dec. 22, 1954; *Sunday Times*, Jan. 9, 1955.

beneath the dignity of a self-governing community.[1] Its Prime Minister, Garfield Todd, had meanwhile signalised his assumption of office by observing that the Protectorates ought not to be under Colonial Office control. Then, remembering his liberalism, he atoned in a measure for having thus caused a stir among Africans north of the Zambesi by assuring his own Africans that he would spend a round £2,000,000 each year on their housing and betterment generally.[2] Herein he had the support of his Minister of Native Affairs, Patrick Fletcher. The latter was, however, considerably less liberal than his leader. He held that the established segregation policy was plain common sense and took a poor view of African potentialities. He refused to allow Africans to take tickets for state lotteries, decreed that they should carry identity cards Union-fashion complete with photographs, and would not hear of them taking part even in municipal politics without a direct mandate at a general election. He admitted, indeed, that they should be allowed to rise in the world economically, but only by means of well-controlled organisations in urban areas and not through trade unions, which they were by no means fit to run. Above all, he was as resolute as Verwoerd, his opposite number in the Union, that no Africans should have freehold tenure even in Local Government Areas, and was by no means pleased when his Prime Minister proposed to permit this form of tenure even in white urban areas.[3]

The Prime Minister had offered to make this last concession as a step towards ending a skirmish in which his Government had become involved with Africans and trade unionists simultaneously. The colour bar being what it was, a British-trained African lawyer was finding it hard to practise at home, despite the backing of some of his fellow-lawyers in the distant United Kingdom. Todd's trouble, however, had arisen over another and even more prominent African. This was no less a person than Masotsha Hove, a Member of the Federal Parliament, who wished to join the local Guild of Journalists on its formation. The organisers were willing to admit him; but the authorities invoked the Industrial Conciliation Act, which, as in the Union, withheld recognition from African trade unions, and refused to register their Guild, unless they amended its Constitution to exclude Africans. While the organisers hesitated, yet another British-trained African lawyer was admitted to the Southern Rhodesian Bar amid the cheers of fellow-countrymen outside. At that the authorities gave way, registered the Guild with its Constitution unamended, and promised to make it easier for African lawyers to become barristers of the High Court by leasing land to them in European areas, if the

[1] *Federation Newsletter*, April 30, 1954; *The Times*, April 23, 1954.
[2] *Ibid.*, July 2, 1954; *Daily Express*, May 13, June 1, 1954.
[3] *Federation Newsletter*, April 14, 1954; *Rhodesia Herald*, June 14, 1954.

Minister concerned and the Bar Association agreed that this was essential to their practice.[1]

The Land Apportionment Act would have to be amended if this promise were to be carried out, non-European members ·of the Rhodesia University College be allowed to live on its site in a white area of the capital, and multi-racial hotels and clubs be permitted. Since that Act was based on the principle of racial residential segregation, the Minister of Native Affairs moved that African barristers be given irrevocable permits entitling them to have offices in European areas, that such clubs and hotels be sanctioned in certain circumstances, and that African members of the College be allowed to live within its precincts. At once there was an outcry that Southern Rhodesia, where not so long ago Africans had not been suffered to walk on the footpath, was becoming another Gold Coast, and that however innocuous a multi-racial hotel might be, a similar club might easily suffer a blameless debate to degenerate into a highly reprehensible dance. Poor Fletcher had to agree that his hotels should be available only to Africans born outside the Federation, that his clubs must confine themselves to religious, welfare and cultural activities, and that African undergraduates, post-graduates and families of African members of the staff might indeed live on the College site, but not the families of those *in statu pupillari*. Even so, the municipal councils of metropolitan Salisbury and frontier Umtali protested, four thousand citizens signed the *ad hoc* Segregation Society's hostile petition, and a Minister and five other ministerialists voted against the amendments. Nevertheless, these were carried by a three-fourths majority.[2]

This qualified victory for liberalism proved that by no means all the white folk in Southern Rhodesia or, for the matter of that, in the Protectorates also felt themselves driven to seek a fugitive and cloistered existence behind the shelter of the colour bar. If further proof were needed, it was furnished by the widespread approval that greeted the inaugural meeting in Salisbury of the Inter-racial Association under the chairmanship, most appropriately, of the temporary Principal of the coming multi-racial University College, who had signalised his appointment by a whole-hearted affirmation of the multi-racial ideal. This organisation, reinforced by its quarterly journal, *Concord*, set itself to work for an integrated society on a civilisation basis, essentially similar to that which had once been the glory of the old Cape Colony from which the Two Rhodesias were sprung.[3] The new Association was soon reminded, however, that there were still plenty of colour-bar-minded Rhodesians of more than one colour, especially of the artisan class. It sponsored a conference

[1] *Rhodesia Herald*, June 12, 14, Oct. 26, Nov. 1, 1954.
[2] *Ibid.*, May 11, 1954; *The Times*, May 27, 1954; *African Weekly*, May 12, 1954.
[3] *Ibid.*, May 26, 1954; *Concord*.

in the capital of representatives of a score of European and African organisations concerned with the employment of Africans in one way or another, and was delighted to find that the majority favoured multi-racial trade unions; but it was dashed when a few of the Africans expressed the fear that this might lead to the neglect of their interests, and a good many of the Europeans said bluntly that Africans stood small chance of apprenticeship in the building industry, which, with the possible exception of printing, was the only walk of life in which they were as yet seeking skilled employment. For all that, the local branch of the African Artisans' Union was emboldened to ask the authorities to provide more of their kind with instruction through apprenticeship and similar institutions.[1]

Training of Africans on a big scale was becoming an urgent matter, because fully half of the five hundred thousand black employees in Southern Rhodesia were working in urban areas, and it could not be long before the great majority of these would have become urban dwellers completely cut off from the land. The Prime Minister, therefore, took a tentative step towards the recognition of their many hitherto unrecognised trade unions. In terms of his Native Industrial Workers' Union Bill, avowedly an interim measure, conditions of service would still be regulated by Native Labour Boards; but henceforward registered African trade unions were to have direct representation on those Boards under independent chairmen. There were, however, to be no Industrial Councils yet awhile, African trade unionists were forbidden to strike, and all of them, like other trade unionists, would still be subject to the Peace Preservation Act, which many folk regarded primarily as an engine for strike-breaking. This measure won fairly general approval, but there were those who thought it did not go far enough and others who feared it was going too far. For instance, on the one hand, the secretary of an Industrial Council dreaded lest separate African trade unions should breed racial friction, and, on the other, James Young, a visiting representative of the International Conference of Free Trade Unions, urged that Africans be recognised as full-blown 'employees,' since the best way to teach responsibility was to give responsibility. The Bill, at the Prime Minister's suggestion, was referred to a Select Committee.[2]

While African trade unionists were thus looking forward to the recognition of their trade unions, African businessmen began to get together. For a start, in September 1954, delegates from nearly every district in Mashonaland attended the inaugural Conference of African Chambers of Commerce.[3] But these be matters for townsfolk

---

[1] *African Weekly*, Aug. 18, 1954; *Rhodesia Herald*, July 20, 1954.
[2] *Ibid.*, July 20, 29, Oct. 13, 1954; Jan. 26, 1955; *Federation Newsletter*, Nov. 1, 1954; *Manchester Guardian*, Dec. 17, 1954; *African Weekly*, Oct. 20, Nov. 17, 1954.
[3] *Ibid.*, Sept. 29, 1954.

and, meanwhile, the countryside and its relationship to urban life demanded attention. There was need, because some ninety per cent. of the Africans were only part-time farmers, and the land, the country's greatest asset, was imperilled by the fourfold increase of African population and the thirty-five-fold increase of cattle during the past half-century.[1] The indefatigable Todd, therefore, carried his Native Land Husbandry Bill, which aimed at dividing the population into urban and rural groups and encouraging good farming in the Reserves. He then promised Africans the security of tenure they desired in two of their existing townships and, to the ill-concealed anxiety of his Minister of Native Affairs, undertook to consider the setting aside of areas near their places of employment in which Africans could buy land and build houses on freehold tenure. Finally, he tried to meet African demands that they be allowed to elect Africans to the Southern Rhodesian Parliament in the same way as they were elected to the Federal Parliament, by promising to have the franchise examined speedily either by a Select Committee or a Royal Commission.[2]

Southern Rhodesia, as a mere subordinate member of a federation, could have no external policy of her own. None the less she had external problems. Her scattering of Indian shopkeepers and so on were scarcely more popular there than in most other parts of British Tropical Africa and, behind them, lay Nehru's watchful and resurgent India. The Minister of Native Affairs thus had some ado to allay the fears of an Honourable Member lest Africans, who accepted scholarships from the Delhi Government for study in India, might pick up ideas about 'social science' that would not be in keeping with British traditions, and might inspire them to subversive activities in African schools. Fletcher told him that the authorities were Laodicean on that score; none the less, the said authorities invoked the Subversive Activities Act to ban *Nehru in India* lest it 'engender feelings of hostility' between two or more sections of the community, and this though it was an Indian officially-published information 'documentary.'[3] Nor were Africans always much more welcome than Indians. In Fletcher's opinion, Africa was become a 'happy hunting-ground for political self-seekers' who tried to 'cash in on ignorance,' and the two Protectorates in especial were the haunt of leaders who spent too much of their time in stirring up discord in Southern Rhodesia. Wherefore, he saw to it that Harry Nkumbula and Kenneth Kaunda, respectively President and General Secretary of the Northern Rhodesian African Congress, should be sent straight back to Lusaka on their arrival in Salisbury. To make

---

[1] *Rhodesia Herald*, Jan. 6, 1955.
[2] *Ibid.*, Aug. 9, 28, 1954, and Feb. 8, 1955; *African Weekly*, Aug. 11, 1954.
[3] *Ibid.*, Aug. 14, 1954.

assurance doubly sure, George Davenport, his colleague for Justice and Internal Affairs, pushed through the Inter-territorial Movement of Persons Bill, which would keep out 'agitators from the north' of whatever race, and that in face of a petition by local Asians praying His Excellency to withhold his assent, because their fellows beyond the Zambesi would have to get a permit if they wished to enter Southern Rhodesia.[1]

Thus the new 'State' pulled through the first year of federation, somewhat unsteadily perhaps, but on the whole moving in a Liberal direction. After seven years of effort, the Rt. Rev. Edward Paget, Bishop of Mashonaland, had failed to found a Rhodesian branch of the Y.M.C.A., because whites blankly refused to foregather with blacks. Nevertheless, he was making one more effort to launch his scheme either on a Federal or, failing that, a narrower Southern Rhodesian scale. He was doubtless encouraged by signs of a slackening of the colour bar in other directions. The Africans, who had long found all headmasters for Village Settlement Schools, were now promised that some of them should soon be appointed to like offices in the much larger African urban schools, which had hitherto been a European monopoly.[2] Better still, the Secretary of Rhodesia's fairy godmother, the Beit Trust, opened an extension of the Remedial Exercises Clinic,[3] which had been begun as a one-woman venture by Mrs. Molly Clutton-Brock at her husband's mission station at St. Faith's, Rusape, where, to the scandal of some and the admiration of others, white volunteers worked in the fields beside black men at black men's wages under a black overseer. It was a thing almost unheard of in Africa. If the experiment were at all widely repeated elsewhere, 'partnership' would indeed have been achieved, and there would be no need for shrewd and expert visitors like Professor Kenneth Kirkwood, holder of the Rhodes Chair of Race Relations at Oxford, to suggest that white folk who could not or would not live up to that ideal should be helped to quit the country.

NORTHERN RHODESIA

In Southern Rhodesia the colour bar was little more than an embarrassment; in Northern Rhodesia it bade fair to become a burden. It is true that, early in the year, Africans in the Copper Belt gained a qualified victory. After vainly protesting in due form, they picketed the butchers' shops, not without intimidation and abuse, till shopkeepers agreed to serve them over the counter like everyone else and not send them round to a mere side-wicket or even to the

[1] *Rhodesia Herald*, Aug. 25, 1954; *The Times*, Sept. 2, 1954.
[2] *Sunday Mail*, Nov. 7, 1954.
[3] *African Weekly*, Nov. 3, 1954; *Rhodesian Herald*, Jan. 22, 1955.

back-door. At once, however, local Europeans cried out against this interference with 'democratic freedom,' and the Legislative Council made it an offence to watch or beset any place with intent to stop anyone doing what was lawful thereat, stipulating only that no offender should be prosecuted without the written sanction of the Attorney-General. The distant Colonial Secretary had to quiet hostile critics in the Commons; but even the Liberal, John Moffat, and Harry Franklin, European representatives of African interests in the Lusaka Legislature, supported the measure, and, lest Africans should think that picketing was the only path to trouble, the Director of African Education warned Africans that they might be dismissed if they yielded to the temptation to become 'politician teachers.'[1]

At this stage, in May 1954, Lyttelton, the Colonial Secretary, arrived hard on the heels of the new Governor, Sir Arthur Benson. Both were promptly told by the Euro-African Society that unless the Coloured Folk, for whom it spoke, were given a definite place in society as the separate community they had always claimed to be, they would throw in their lot with the Africans and adopt their way of life. Lyttelton replied that other minorities would demand similar recognition if the request were granted, but His Excellency promised to arrange a meeting shortly to talk things over.[2] A week or two having gone by, the Society repeated that it would carry out its threat unless the promised meeting were held within the next six months. Africans then made their protest in their own way. On two successive Sundays, members of the Northern Rhodesian African National Congress took their seats in the Dutch Reformed Church at Broken Hill to see whether they would be suffered to remain by a congregation which notoriously shared the *apartheid* prejudices of the South Africa from which so many of its members had recently come. On each occasion, they left quietly when asked to do so; but when the elders called upon the police to 'stop Africans from coming into the church,' the latter replied that they could do nothing unless there was a breach of the peace.[3] After the Church and State, the market-place. The Urban Advisory Council at Lusaka forbade the brewing of Native beer, whereupon the Women's League protested. Receiving no answer, the League protested to the District Commissioner and organised a demonstration near the local African market. The crowd of two thousand or so dispersed quietly, but a similar demonstration by men and women in the neighbourhood was broken up by the police, who used tear-gas, made baton charges and arrested several of the demonstrators. Three of these were given stiff sentences, and the Governor had to assure an agitated Legislative Council that the authorities could and would deal firmly with disturbances of this

---

[1] *African Eagle* (Lusaka), May 11, 1954; *Rhodesia Herald*, June 19, 1954.
[2] *Central African Post*, June 23, 1954.　　[3] *Manchester Guardian*, Oct. 2, 1954.

kind.[1] On the other hand, there were many folk to whom 'partnership' was more than a meaningless word, for the curriculum in African schools was calculated to encourage racial co-operation; Europeans gave ready help to Africans in such activities as Scouting, Guiding, football, boxing and Red Cross training; African lads in one Secondary school gave more than six pounds to the swimming-bath fund at a European school in the capital, and, from overseas, the United Nations' Children's Fund sent the Federal Authorities more than £14,000 for health centres, hygienic units, midwifery services and the training of the necessary personnel.[2]

Meanwhile, the authorities had begun to show where they stood. Early in the Session, John Gaunt, member for Midlands and Territorial chairman of the Confederate Party, resigned from that Party. He had never been enthusiastically in favour of Federation, and now moved that Northern Rhodesia should demand immediate self-government, safeguard permanent white supremacy in European areas, and appoint a Select Committee to inquire into the constitution, finances and doings of the African National Congress. He withdrew his motion, however, on being assured that the authorities had their own sources of information and knew how to deal with breaches of the peace.[3] The House then agreed to a motion by John Roberts, Member for Health, Land and Local Government, that its right course would be to seek self-government as a member of the Federation and, if the public so desired, petition Her Majesty to grant similar powers to the Federation as a whole.[4] Presently it passed an Inter-Territorial Movement of Persons Bill, similar to that which had just been passed by the Southern Rhodesian legislature, to prevent the diversion of incoming Asians northward into its Protectorate.[5] The Executive, for its part, deported James Singala, President-General of the Nyasaland African National Congress, who had ventured to enter Lusaka after having been proclaimed a prohibited immigrant, and next banned a number of publications which had emanated directly or indirectly from suspect India.[6] Finally, the High Court, for its part, sentenced Nkumbula and Kaunda, respectively President and Secretary of the local African National Congress, to a couple of months' imprisonment apiece for being in possession of forbidden literature. These sentences, passed on men who had recently been summarily sent home from Salisbury, were resented by their fellow-Africans, two thousand of whom assembled outside the Court, some of them wearing black arm-bands as a sign of mourning,

[1] *Central African Post*, June 16, 28, 1954.
[2] *African Weekly*, Sept. 18, 1954; *East Africa and Rhodesia*, Sept. 30, 1954; *Rhodesia Herald*, Aug. 16, 1954.
[3] *Ibid.*, June 14, 1954.   [4] *Federation Newsletter*, Aug. 16, 1954.
[5] *Central African Post*, Nov. 17, 1954.
[6] *Rhodesia Herald*, July 27, 1954.

and re-affirmed their resolve to struggle on towards their 'ultimate goal.'[1]

There was, however, a more pleasing side of the medal. The Legislative Council showed no sign of yielding to those Europeans who clamoured for a 'show down' on the land question, because the allocation to Africans of all but a paltry 3,000,000 of the Territory's 200,000,000 acres denied to white folk the expansion that was their due.[2] The Member for Commerce and Industry uncompromisingly told the assembled Lusaka Chamber of Commerce that it must mend its manners towards dark-skinned customers in its shops, and Harry Franklin welcomed Europeans, Euro-Africans and Africans to the inaugural meeting of an association he had formed on the lines of the Inter-racial Association in Southern Rhodesia.[3] Best of all, John Moffat carried the Legislative Council with him, against the solitary vote of John Gaunt, in favour of dispelling all fear of domination by a single racial group, of approving the Colonial Secretary's promise to hold the balance true in contentious matters, and of enabling everyone to progress as fast and as far as they could regardless of creed or colour. The local African National Congress hailed these Moffat Resolutions as the beginning of 'an epoch,' adopted them as the basis of its policy, and resolved to constitute itself a political party on the assumption that the franchise would have been extended to Africans by 1959 at the latest; the distant *Manchester Guardian* commented drily that much trouble might have been averted had they been introduced three years earlier, and the Governor marked his approval by nominating Moffat as one of the European Members for African Interests in the Federal Parliament.[4] Gaunt, on the other hand, showed his resentment. Just after the end of the Session, he announced that he would form his own Dominion Party, which, holding aloof from the Confederates and by no means supporting the demand for the dismemberment of the Federation recently proposed to the Federal Parliament by van Eeden, would seek to carve out black and white 'States' therein and refuse to countenance anything like a common voters' roll.[5]

More immediately important than what Gaunt threatened or Moffat proposed was what the white Mineworkers' Union might do. This was far and away the most powerful of all the European unions, for it could claim at least five thousand members, whereas none of the other white unions had much more than one thousand and a good many far fewer. Similarly, its rival, the African Mineworkers' Union was over twenty-five thousand strong and thus fully five

[1] *The Times*, Jan. 13, 1955; *Pretoria News*, Jan. 14, 1954.
[2] *Central African Post*, June 25, 1954.
[3] *Ibid.*, Nov. 20, 1954.
[4] *Rhodesia Herald*, July 30, 1954.
[5] *Ibid.*, Aug. 18, 20, 1954; *African Weekly*, Aug. 25, 1954.

times stronger as far as numbers went than any of its fellows.[1] The point at issue between these two big unions and, of course, the mine-owners was how far, if at all, Africans were to be allowed to trespass on the white man's field of work. Negotiations had been dragging on for some time, when, shortly after the launching of the Federation, Sir William Lawther, President of the National Union of Mine-workers in the United Kingdom and Secretary of the International Mineworkers' Federation, had taken the chair at a joint meeting at Kitwe. Under his mediating influence, both unions had agreed that they had a common responsibility to raise the standard of living of every mineworker and win recognition of the Africans' right to advance in industry; but both had also renewed their recent promise to demand equal pay for equal work.[2] Some African miners promptly struck against that fatal proviso which would debar their advance-ment for ever and a day; then, having made their protest, they went back to work and left it to the mineowners to make the next move.

The two big groups, the Rhodesian Selection Trust and the Anglo-American Company, made no comment on their white employees' description of their bloated salaries as 'wages,' which enabled them to maintain the fiction that their trade unionism was a genuine off-shoot of the British; but they said outright that the traditional British principle of 'the rate for the job' was plain nonsense under highly artificial Central African conditions.[3] Both groups argued, with con-siderable African support, that Africans could never be advanced till certain European jobs had been simplified and subdivided so that they might fill them. It would be disastrous for all concerned, they held, to pay full white rates to Africans as things were. They there-fore proposed to frame scales of pay that should take into account the different circumstances in which Europeans and Africans were employed, to safeguard Europeans, to maintain white leadership, to limit the numbers of Africans who would be advanced during the next five years, and to discuss the whole business again later on. At one stage, there was good hope of a settlement, for the white miners had long been willing to let Africans take European jobs on absolutely the same terms as themselves, and now the mineowners were pro-posing to train Africans for fuller responsibility in 'intermediate' jobs right outside the white man's field of work. Unhappily, the white miners ruined everything. Claiming that they were only following 'accepted trade union principles,' they went back to their old refusal even to contemplate a subdivision of jobs and insisted that the fixing of two parallel wage-scales, one higher than the other, would not be in 'the interests of organised labour.'[4]

---

[1] *Federation Newsletter*, Nov. 4, 1954.
[2] *Ibid*, June 9, 1954.   [3] *Economist*, 8 Jan., 1955.
[4] *East Africa and Rhodesia*, July 29, 1954.

Disappointed though it was at this breakdown, the Northern Rhodesian Chamber of Mines promised its Africans a long-service non-contributory pension scheme and liberal annual leave with pay, and the Government, late in July, appointed a Board of Inquiry under Sir John Forster to find out what, if anything, stopped Africans from advancing as far as they could, to set out the basis on which men were taken into the industry, and to make recommendations with due regard for the interests of the workers and the welfare of the Territory and the Federation. The Board pursued its labours against a background of sporadic African strikes. First, the African General Workers' Union struck to extort double pay for African bricklayers. Some weeks later, just as the ten thousand strikers were trailing back to work, the African Government Workers' Union downed pens and, then towards the end of October, the African Trades Union Congress, with very small success, called for a widespread supporting strike. By the time the Board of Inquiry reported, these troubles were dying away. The Board condemned the 'rate for the job' as a permanent barrier to African advancement, and observed that white miners and their families would have ample time in which to readjust themselves, seeing that the mineowners had promised that no white man should lose his job to a black fellow-worker. The Rhodesian Selection Trust accepted the Report at once. Not so the white Mineworkers' Union. It refused to budge an inch.[1]

The Selection Trust tried to break the deadlock by proposing that Africans be allowed to prove that they were worth the rate for a given job, and even by offering to accept the principle of 'equal rates for work of equal value,' if the white miners in their turn would agree to amend the existing schedule of occupations and minimum rates to which they had recently agreed and thus give Africans a chance of doing such work as they might be fit for in the 'European field.'[2] The next move was made, however, by the African miners. At the New Year of 1955, nearly all of them, say, 35,000 all told, struck, not against the colour bar, but for a soaring increase of pay. They threatened to stay out till a new wage-structure was forthcoming, and stay out they did, while white miners had to do 'Kaffir Work' for the first time in their lives, though not at Kaffir wages. The mineowners issued an ultimatum and, after the strike had gone on for a further month, dismissed the 32,000 strikers who had ignored it and began to take on new hands. Before long they could congratulate themselves that they had about one-third of the customary African labour force at their disposal, and that production was fully

---

[1] *Federation Newsletter*, Nov. 18, 1954; *The Times*, Nov. 4, 1954; *Manchester Guardian*, Nov. 18, 1954.
[2] *The Times*, Dec. 6, 1954.

two-thirds the normal; nevertheless, the vast majority of the strikers doggedly stood to their guns, strong in the belief that as soon as the mineowners realised that they must pay them higher wages, they would insist on making fuller use of their abilities.[1] At this juncture, to the unconcealed annoyance of Huggins and Welensky, who resented outside interference, the National Union of Mineworkers in the United Kingdom sent the strikers £1000 by the hands of Ronald Williams, Labour M.P. for Wigan and its legal adviser. While Williams was advising the strikers on benefit rates, back pay and other problems arising out of the strike, the white miners reiterated their resolve to resist African 'inroads' to the last ditch. Their leaders went much further by conferring with those of the South African Mineworkers' Union in Salisbury with a view to resisting the said inroads and advised their followers to vote on that issue. The result was a shock to them, because a majority of the rank-and-file voted in favour of letting Africans have some relatively skilled white jobs. At the same time, the mineowners offered to open certain jobs to Africans, the Anglo-American Company going so far as to promise that the numbers of Africans thus employed should never be more than one-twentieth those of the Europeans. Hence, early in March, the strikers called off their three-month-long strike. They were taken back to a man.[2]

The white miners' leaders were contemptuous of what they regarded as a betrayal of their interests. Thus, it was in a mood of mingled righteous wrath and devotion to extreme trade union principles that they agreed with their *apartheidgesind* opposite numbers from the Rand to form a liaison committee that should decide, *inter alia*, how far Africans should be permitted to advance. All was not plain sailing, however. The more the copper-mining rank-and-file saw of the southerners, the less they liked them. It was well enough that they should warn them that, if they wished to maintain white supremacy, they must let Africans have as few of their jobs as possible or, preferably, none at all; it was all to the good that they should have given them £5000 to help them in their struggle to maintain that supremacy; it was intelligible that the Secretary of the South African Union should count his country lucky because it had a Nationalist Government to protect white men against 'unfair' African competition; but it was by no means so well that that Secretary and his companions should try to dictate policy. There was no blinking the fact that the Rand unionists were predominantly Afrikaner and under the thumb of the Nationalist Party leaders. The majority of the copper-miners had no desire to see too much of

[1] *Daily Telegraph*, Jan. 10, 1955; *The Times*, Dec. 6, 1954, Jan. 6, 1955.
[2] *Ibid.*, Feb. 17, 1955; *Manchester Guardian*, Feb. 1, 1955; *Sunday Mail*, Jan. 23, 1955; *Federation Newsletter*, Feb. 15, 1955.

such influences in their country and, by the same token, voted in yet another ballot in favour of guarded African advancement.[1]

As the trade unions' *mariage de convenance* grew cold, Welensky waxed warm. Sir Roy was, of course, no copper-miner, but he was the most outstanding trade unionist in the Federation, a loyal Northern Rhodesian, and a dogged opponent of interference whether from the distant United Kingdom or the neighbouring Union. It was significant that his constituents, the lead and zinc-miners of Broken Hill, should have grumbled that they were 'fed up' with South African interference; it was of first-class importance for all Africa that he himself should then have proclaimed the faith that was in him. For him, the solution of the racial problem lay in letting the African advance as far as he could. 'We Europeans,' he roundly declared, 'have nothing to fear. . . . The best way to lose our lead would be to sit back, hedge ourselves around with so-called protective regulations and do nothing about our own advancement.'[2]

NYASALAND

If white Northern Rhodesian copper-miners were one of the Federation's most anxious problems, politically-minded African Nyasalanders were the other. They had quieted down somewhat since Federation had become an accomplished fact, but they were still implacably hostile to the new polity into which they had been dragged willy-nilly. Chief Gomani, one of the most prominent of the dissenters, died in May 1954 and was committed to the grave by a Dutch Reformed Church predikant, who praised his devotion to his people as highly as Lord Hailey had once praised his virtues as a Chief. Other leaders survived, however, and a group of them, Chiefs and African Members of the Nyasaland Legislative Council and the Federal Parliament, duly presented their Petition of Right to the Colonial Secretary on his arrival almost at the moment of Gomani's death. Unimpressed by Lyttelton's cheery but vague talk of increasing the number of African nominees in their Territorial legislature, they asked that that number should be raised from three to ten, thus giving the black folk parity with the Europeans and Asians together, and that those Members should be elected under a 'proper franchise' and should themselves choose those of their group who were to have seats on the Executive Council. So much for politics. Now for the education on which black Africans rightly set such store. They asked for adult education, more schools of every

---

[1] *Manchester Guardian*, Feb. 1, March 7, 1955; *Union News*, May 2, 1955; *The Times*, Feb. 4, April 16, 21, 22, May 3, 4, 1955.
[2] *Ibid.*, April 27, May 4, 1955; *Rhodesia Herald*, Nov. 18, 1954.

kind, the removal of the age-limit which kept far too many of their children out of the Primary Schools, and the appointment of Africans as headmasters of all Senior Primary Schools. Turning to higher education, they urged that Africans be encouraged to stay at their universities until they had qualified, that more scholarships be awarded for study overseas, and that the authorities see to it that their schools were given staffs competent to teach the Latin and other subjects that all students must have before they could enter the Rhodesian University College. All too well aware that the Prime Minister of the Federation, who was also in Nyasaland, had first observed that the local legislature was none of his business, Lyttleton replied as reassuringly as he could, and returned home to face attacks by Labour Members, notably on the practice of sending uniformed police to take notes, South African fashion, at meetings of the Nyasaland African National Congress. Having weathered the tail-end of the storm, he resigned office in July 1954. After all, the Federation, to whose formation he had so powerfully contributed, was settling down on its foundations, and the first and biggest of the much-to-be-desired hydro-electrical power installations was passing beyond the blue-print stage. It was time for him to resume his duties as Chairman of Associated Electrical Industries, which he had given up a year or two back in order to become Colonial Secretary. In due course, he took his seat in 'the Other Place' as Viscount Chandos of Aldershot.[1]

Alan Lennox-Boyd, Lyttleton's successor, at once proclaimed that the only permissible bar in the Commonwealth was that of 'civilisation.' It was in keeping with this enlightened pronouncement that the first multi-racial District Council in Nyasaland should have met with the District Commissioner in the chair; but even though this welcome advance was accompanied by the opening of one African Secondary School and the planning of another, it was too slight to satisfy African leaders. Anxious to carry their talks with Lyttelton further, they invited his successor to visit their Territory.[2] They had cause for disquiet. In Salisbury, the Southern Rhodesian Premier openly deplored the fact that the status of the Protectorates stood in the way of the Federation's chances of obtaining self-government, and, in the Federal Parliament, van Eeden was beginning to talk of taking the pick of the Federal territory for the tiny European minority and leaving the remainder to the rest; at home, newly-arrived tea-planters were clamouring for that Amalgamation of the three Territories in a centralised polity which Africans had always feared would be the next step to Federation; in the Federal Parliament, Sir Malcolm Barrow, their leading politician and Minister

[1] *The Times,* July 29, 1954; *Daily Telegraph,* Sept. 11, 1954.
[2] *Pretoria News,* Feb. 1955.

of Commerce and Industry to boot, was calling for a selective white immigration which must threaten their cherished lands. In this demand, Sir Malcolm had the enthusiastic backing of the white Convention of Associations and the newly-formed Land-owners' Association. The members of these two organisations already controlled more than half the freehold land in the Territory, and yet they clamoured for more, dwelling in frontier fashion on the virtues of the white men and the failings of the black, and, in passing, insisting that the invasion of Nyasaland by 'foreign' Africans must be controlled, because though only some four hundred such had come within the past twelve months, their kind formed more than two-thirds of the population in the Southern Province alone.[1]

Maybe the Africans were unduly nervous, but it was understandable that the Nyasaland African National Congress should have accused the Federal authorities of most unwarrantably scheming to treat their Protectorate as mere conquered territory, should have condemned all talk of Amalgamation, a Federal Dominion and the rest, and should have demanded that Nyasaland be withdrawn from the Federation forthwith and be given self-government. Critics might retort that Congress wanted to run before it could walk; nevertheless, its demands were supported in the Commons by a couple of Labour Members, one of whom had recently visited its country. The harassed Imperial authorities played for time, pointing out justly enough that it was only five short years since Africans had first been nominated, let alone elected, to the Legislative Council. In February 1955, however, under increasing pressure, they proposed substantial constitutional reforms.[2] These satisfied no section of the community. Europeans most reluctantly accepted the raising of African representation in the Legislative Council from three to five in the hope that there would be no further changes before the Federal Constitution came up for revision in 1958 or, preferably, for a full ten years. Asians objected that if they must vote on a common roll with Europeans, the latter, who had hitherto had a fixed proportion of five seats to one, would win all six seats. Politically-minded Africans were furious that the franchise was still to be withheld from them and the method of selecting African Members to remain unaltered. Crowded African meetings warmly supported their Members and the Central Executive of the African National Congress in rejecting the whole scheme as 'entirely inadequate,' demanding parity of representation between their two-and-a-half million fellow-tribesmen and the nine thousand others, white and brown, and insisting on the free election of Africans to the Legislature

[1] *Federation Newsletter*, Nov. 16, 1954; *East African Review*, May 27, 1954.
[2] *Rhodesia Herald*, Feb. 10, 1955.

and the immediate grant of self-government.[1] Educated Africans may have welcomed talk of hydro-electrical, irrigation and allied projects in their Protectorate, but the mass of the black men were unimpressed by what was, in their eyes, a mere matter for white folk. At all events, Congress did not shift its ground, for it presently accused the Archbishop of Canterbury himself of showing his approval of the hated Federation by the mere fact that he had come to institute therein the new Church of the Province of Central Africa.[2]

Thus stood the Federation at the dawn of the second year of its life. Progress in the vital field of inter-racial relations had admittedly been uneven: encouraging in Southern Rhodesia, less encouraging in frontier-minded Nyasaland, and assuredly least encouraging along the Copper Belt in Northern Rhodesia. Nevertheless, progress there had been. In the Federal Parliament, at least, legislators had become less parochially-minded, African Members were plainly giving up all idea of forming a party of their own, Dendy Young, the Confederate one-man Opposition, had established a reputation as a fair-minded though vigorous critic, Sir Roy Welensky, deputy Prime Minister, was revealing possibly unsuspected powers of statesmanship, and Sir Godfrey Huggins, now Lord Malvern, still presided over the national destinies with increasing deafness but unimpaired geniality. Whatever Gaunt, van Eeden and Nyasaland Congressmen might threaten, each in his degree, the Federal Constitution remained unshaken and the country's credit stood high at home and overseas. Much would have to be done before the white folk could lay aside the colour bar and, turning their backs on the *apartheid* policy of their South African neighbours, set their Federation on the way to fulfilling the hopes of its projectors by becoming 'a great British bastion' in Central Africa. If ever they made up their minds to do so, and there was no valid reason why they should not, they would have made their own avowed policy of 'partnership' a living reality to the untold advantage of the Federation and all Africa.[3]

THE UNION

The manful attempt by many members of the Conference of Protestant Churchmen towards the close of 1953 to lift the racial issue out of the dust and heat of party controversy had no perceptible effect on the South African authorities. The Prime Minister, now nearing his eightieth birthday, and the Minister of Native Affairs

---

[1] *Rhodesia Herald*, 10, 11 Feb., 1955.   [2] *The Times*, April 1955.
[3] Progress by the end of 1958 had been disappointing on the whole.

announced that the *apartheid* programme would go forward; many of their followers jeered that the United Party proved, by its very talk of economic integration of the races, that it really wanted the despised 'partnership' that was so much spoken of in the new Federation of Rhodesia and Nyasaland, and, just after the opening of the Session at the close of January, 1954, Verwoerd declared that, however sadly some local authorities under liberal influences had failed to control the trek of Africans into urban areas, the Government at least had in no way permitted integration and was resolved as ever to push ahead with its separatist policy.[1]

After the inevitable defeat of Strauss's motion of no confidence, the Minister of Finance introduced his Budget. Havenga announced that thanks to his grave warning a year back against the danger of overspending and also the savings he had since forced upon the public, he had a surplus of £15,000,000. This he proposed to transfer to loan account, thus bringing up to a round £32,000,000 the total contributed to that account from revenue during the past and current years. He then foretold another surplus of £15,000,000 at the end of the coming financial year even after making large tax concessions. These included the abolition of most of the recent special taxes, an increase in the primary abatement on income tax, rebates on the cost of new plant and housing for employees, a reduction of the farmers' taxes to make up for a slight drop in the fixed price of mealies, and repeal of the duty on imported tyres and the excise on soft drinks. True, he cast a passing shadow over his rosy picture by reminding the banks that they must still 'ca' canny' in the granting of credit; but he let the sun shine once more when he reported that private savings and the national income had both increased most satisfactorily and that, in general, the country had pulled through the worst of the post-war years. Not only had it made good enormous wartime shortages, but it had steadily industrialised itself, constructed huge hydro-electricity power plants and, in spite of tardy delivery of rolling-stock by some British firms, had completed the re-equipment of its railways on a comprehensive scale. Henceforth, capital expenditure in all these fields would diminish and the fruits of investment be garnered, notably from that devoted to the extraction of oil from coal, which would reduce the demand for foreign exchange wherewith to pay for costly petroleum imports. He agreed warmly with Harry Oppenheimer that such financial difficulties as remained were purely temporary and that, within four years at the most, gold and uranium from the Rand and the new Free State mines would send up the country's purchasing power by at

[1] At this very moment, the liberal Dr. E. H. Brookes showed in his *South Africa in a Changing World* that the authorities were dangerously simplifying a complex social and ideological problem, which was by no means unique.

least £100,000,000 with more in sight. This being so, he hinted broadly that there might be a lifting of some of the import controls, which had *inter alia* helped light and medium British cars to drive the much more expensive and cumbersome American vehicles off the roads, though he warned the less efficient industrialists that they might have small cause to rejoice when those controls should indeed be gone.

Passing on to the basic problem of gold, Havenga expressed pained surprise that anyone should have even dreamed of devaluation, all the more that the recent reopening of the London gold market on the recommendation of the Commonwealth Finance Ministers would surely widen the area in which sterling could pass freely. For the rest, he told South Africans that they must still sell their gold exclusively through the Reserve Bank, which could, however, sell in the open market if it could get better prices there than in London, and begged them not to imagine that anything of all this would raise the official price of gold, a consummation which he himself had indeed hoped for, but had never really expected.

Some of the measures that were carried thereafter had little directly to do with *apartheid*. Such were the Suppression of Communism Amendment Bill, which circumvented a recent decision of the Appellate Division by restoring to the Minister of Justice power to have his way with no more said by simply 'deeming' a person to be or to have been a Communist, and a short Bill which amnestied all who had been convicted of treason during the recent war.[1] Again, the racial issue was only raised indirectly by the South-West Africa Administration Bill, which, to the ill-concealed dismay of many of the local inhabitants, virtually completed the administrative absorption of the Mandated Territory by transferring control of its Native affairs to Verwoerd's Department in Pretoria.[2]

Subsequent measures were, however, inspired by full-blooded *apartheid*. The most crucial of these was a revised version of the Separate Representation of Voters Bill. This was based on the report of the Select Committee to which the unlucky measure had been referred at the close of the preceding Session. Apart from a memorandum submitted by S.A.B.R.A., very little of the voluminous evidence received by that Committee had been in favour of the political segregation of the Cape Coloured voters; nevertheless, the Committee virtually recommended that the old Bill should be reintroduced, with the addition of provision for an Advisory Council of Coloured Affairs consisting of nominees and elective members. The revised measure, the Separate Representation of Voters Validation and

---

[1] *Daily Telegraph*, Jan. 30, 1954; *The Times*, March 24, 1954.
[2] *Daily Telegraph*, Jan. 30, 1954; *Pretoria News*, April 21, 1954.

Amendment Bill, was given its First Reading at a Joint Session in the middle of May 1954, after Malan had threatened to revive Swart's dormant Appeal Court Bill if he did not get his two-thirds majority. At the Second Reading, Malan rejected Bekker's suggestion that a compromise might be made by allowing existing Coloured voters to remain on the common roll and enrolling future such voters separately. This he did on the plea that the matter was urgent, because in half-a-century's time the Coloured voters, who now numbered only some 40,000, would outnumber the European in the Cape Province by some 2,000,000. He threatened, further, to seek a fresh mandate at the forthcoming Provincial general election if he did not have his way, excusing his thus dragging the Provinces into national politics on the ground that they had a say in the election of Senators, and tried hard to prove that not all the Coloured Folk were against him. Nevertheless, he failed to get the required majority. Finally, at the Third Reading early in June, he accepted Bekker's plan and gave a warning that 'if the European people were to be saved, it must be in this generation.' Alas, the majority still fell short by nine votes, one of Bekker's followers voting with the Opposition and thereafter rejoining the United Party.[1]

The next measure, Schoeman's Industrial Conciliation Bill, fared scarcely better. The Minister of Labour might avow that he would always mete out justice to Africans, but he also held that mere economic theories must give way to racial survival. To safeguard that 'first priority' and to round off his already very considerable control over Africans in industry, he now sought to provide that all industrial disputes be referred to a Board nominated by himself. So far from acceding to the oft-expressed desire of 'Native' Members that all Bantu workers, and not merely the select few, be dignified with the name of 'employee,' his Bill would shut Africans out of all trade unions, oblige Coloured and Indian unionists to separate themselves from their European fellows, withhold registration from multiracial unions, empower the Minister to allocate occupations on a racial basis, and incidentally hit the moribund Labour Party severely by forbidding either trade unions or employers' associations to affiliate themselves to any political party.[2]

By thus enforcing economic *apartheid* on racial lines, Schoeman plainly hoped to make an end of Bantu trade unionism and hasten the attainment of his Party's end of reducing all trade unions of whatever colour to the lowly level of State or, more accurately, Nationalist controlled organisations concerned solely with the social and cultural interests of their members. This latter goal seemed to be within

---

[1] *Round Table*, No. 176, pp. 420 ff.; *Chronology*, X., No. 10, pp. 330 ff.; *Rand Daily Mail*, May 20, 1954.
[2] *Round Table*, No. 176, pp. 419 ff.

reach, because ever since they had split a year or two back over this very question of admitting non-Europeans, the two hundred thousand or so organised trade unionists had remained divided into four main groups, in spite of the efforts of their more far-sighted leaders to win their allegiance to a single co-ordinating body. At last, however, with the aid of a mission from the Trade Union Council in the United Kingdom, those leaders managed to induce representatives from all the groups to form a Trade Union Unity Committee, which, alarmed lest new industries should go elsewhere to work under 'more practical laws,' condemned Schoeman's industrial *apartheid* and projected Conciliation Board by overwhelming majorities. In face of this 'expert' opposition, the Minister had his Bill referred to a Select Committee after the Second Reading.[1] At once, three of the trade union groups: the South African Federation of Trade Unions, the S.A. Trades and Labour Council, and the Western Province Federation of Labour Unions agreed to a merger in which unions that had Coloured or Indian members were to be included. Their decision was hailed by Labour politicians as 'a wonderful step towards unity.' It did not, however, go the whole way, for not only did the Amalgamated Engineering Union hold aloof, but they themselves explicitly excluded unions that had Bantu members. It may be that they took this line because, as Nationalists were swift to suggest, they believed that Africans distrusted mixed trade unions, but by taking it they went far towards supporting the Government in that denial of elementary trade union rights to the African majority which moved the International Confederation of Free Trade Unions to protest to the International Labour Organisation.[2]

Verwoerd, the Minister of Native Affairs, more fortunate than Malan and Schoeman, had the satisfaction of carrying three measures, all of which fundamentally aimed at giving his own Ministry and that of Labour vastly increased powers to check agitation even at the cost of silencing legitimate criticism and driving Bantu opposition dangerously underground. The Native (Urban Areas) Consolidation Bill, the first of the three, authorised the Minister, after a public hearing and in consultation with the European Local Authority concerned, to curtail the extent of Bantu urban residential areas and order the removal of 'redundant' Africans therefrom. In certain cases, Africans were to have consolidated passes in place of the multiplicity of easily mislaid documents they had hitherto carried; on the other hand, for the first time, Africans from the High Commission Territories would have to get a special pass if they wished to work in urban residential areas. Taken together with existing

---

[1] *Survey*, No. 95, pp. 10 ff.; *Chronology*, X., No. 9, p. 297; *South Africa*, May 15, 1954.
[2] *Survey*, No. 95, pp. 10 ff.; *Rand Daily Mail*, June and Nov. 1, 1954.

legislation, the new Act gave the authorities very full power to control
the entry of non-Europeans into urban areas and, conversely, to
direct Africans towards the white man's farms. Verwoerd's second
measure, the Native Tenant and Land Amendment (Squatters) Bill,
logically enough dealt with those farms.[1] There was to be no limit
to the number of full-time Bantu labourers; but there was assuredly
to be drastic 'elimination' of squatters, that is, Bantu living on
farms in return for paying rent but, in most cases, doing no work
for the farmers. No Bantu would be forced to work for anyone,
but displaced squatters would be offered jobs by the Labour Bureaux.
They would, if they found such jobs distasteful, be offered work
elsewhere.

Verwoerd's third and most controversial measure was the Natives
Resettlement (Western Areas) Bill.[2] This was a whole-hearted
application of *apartheid*, which would empower him to restrict the
right of residence in the sprawling non-European township of
Alexandra on the northern outskirts of Johannesburg to those whose
work lay in adjacent parts of that great city, and also to remove
perhaps as many as 60,000 non-Europeans, Bantu for the most part,
from the Western Areas. These so-called 'black spots' consisted of
the townships of Sophiatown, Martindale and New Clare. When
they had been built as temporary or emergency locations a generation
earlier, they had been separated from white Johannesburg by wide
open spaces; but since then, Europeans, mostly Afrikaners, had
flooded across these and even ringed the townships round. Since
these voters with their backveld prejudices could not abide the propinquity of human beings of another colour, it was obvious that the
latter would have to go further out to the projected location of
Meadowlands some twelve miles from the centre of the city.[3]

Verwoerd presented his Bill as a measure for 'slum clearance' and
made much of rack-renting by Bantu freeholders, who admittedly
packed as many tenants as possible on to their stands; but though
perhaps one-fifth of the doomed Western Areas were undoubted
slums, the remainder ranged from the usable to the eminently
respectable. Taken as a whole, these Areas were certainly no worse
than the 'temporary shelters' or 'controlled squatters' camps,' which
had been planted on the open veld between 1904 and 1948 and,
though repeatedly condemned, still constituted the only homes of
some 130,000 folk.[4] Regardless of these considerations, Verwoerd
pressed his Bill, promising compensation for displacement where
necessary and assuring the involuntary evacuees that they should

---

[1] Act 18 of 1954; *Observer*, June 20, 1954.
[2] Act 19 of 1954.
[3] *The Times*, May 24, 1954; *Observer*, May 2, 1954.
[4] *Daily Telegraph*, Jan. 10, 1955; *Industrial Review of Africa*, Sept. 1954.

29

have their own churches, shops, schools and so forth to be run by themselves, and might even have their own houses, though only on a comparatively precarious leasehold and not on the freehold which many of them enjoyed. Finally the Bill empowered the Minister to short-circuit the Johannesburg City Council by carrying out the projected Great Trek through a nominee Native Resettlement Board responsible to himself. Indeed, Verwoerd refused the offer of the City Council, which approved of the removals in principle, to see to everything provided no one was moved before new houses were ready for them. Suspecting that Council of liberal tendencies, he preferred, as he said, to take the 'democratic' course of handing the task over to his nominee board, which was free to incur what expenses it chose and to send the bill to the City Fathers.[1]

The Bill was stoutly opposed, chiefly because it gave dictatorial powers to 'the Minister' and lacked the consent of the people most directly concerned. Verwoerd was, indeed, fain to accept one amendment, which provided that a thousand stands should be set aside in Meadowlands on which Africans might build houses better than those the authorities were planning, houses capable even of finding room for their suites of furniture, radio sets and motor cars; but another amendment he proposed himself to the effect that uprooted Africans who still desired freehold tenure could get it in the overcrowded Reserves, the nearest of which was some hundreds of miles distant from the Witwatersrand. The United Party members of the Johannesburg City Council and leading local Anglican clergymen condemned the Bill, to which some Nationalists, without sharing the fear of their fellows who foresaw bloodshed when the removals should begin, retorted by asking how Africans could be expected to co-operate when their minds were being thus poisoned.[2]

The Resettlement Act duly took its place beside other Nationalist legislation aimed at the retribalisation of the Bantu, though the authorities must wait for the report of the Tomlinson Commission, which for two years past had been investigating the social and economic condition of the Reserves, before they could propose reforms therein and thus give their policy of *apartheid* even the semblance of justice.[3] Verwoerd, however, was in no mind to waste time waiting. He at once took the longest step yet towards retribalisation by filling in the details of the Bantu Education Act.[4] That measure, which had been passed during the previous Session, was ostensibly intended to put free education up to Standard II within reach of thousands of Bantu children who were getting no schooling

[1] *Round Table*, No. 176, p. 419; *Manchester Guardian*, Oct. 5, 1954.
[2] *Die Volksblad*, March 20, 1954.
[3] *Round Table*, No. 176, p. 418.   [4] Act 47 of 1953.

at all. To achieve that end, it provided that the Native Affairs Department should take over Bantu lower education from the Provinces and Churches and Missionary Societies, which had furnished it hitherto. On a given date, the Primary Schools were to be converted into Governmental or Tribal Authority Schools. Thereafter, no one might have a Bantu school other than one of these unless it had been officially registered, and the Minister might withhold registration if he 'deemed' that the said school was not in the physical, mental or moral interests of the children. Finally, the Minister could issue regulations and prescribe penalties for the breach thereof; for instance, a fine of £50 or, in default, imprisonment for six months for running an unauthorised school or admitting Bantu youngsters to such an illegal institution.[1]

The governmental grants paid for Native education had risen steadily year by year till now the authorities could claim that they were spending £7 a year on each Bantu child in school, though, if account were taken of those very many who did not go to school at all, the real expenditure per head was nearer £2 13s. 4d. Hence, Havenga in his Budget speech in 1954 had announced that the grant would be fixed at £6,500,000 and that anything in excess of that figure would have to be found by the Bantu themselves.[2] Many would hold it to be doubtful justice to ask the poorest in the land to pay for what they so sorely needed and thus save the pockets of the Europeans, who could afford to pay nearly £44 a year for the schooling of each of their own children, and to be disingenuous if it were assumed that the whole of the grant was paid by white taxpayers, for though few Africans paid income tax for obvious reasons, nearly all paid a special poll tax, all of them felt the burden of indirect taxation, and all by their cheap labour helped to create the wealth in which, on the Finance Minister's own showing in the same speech, the white folk were revelling.[3] However that might be, Verwoerd sought to justify his policy by insisting that Africans valued what they themselves provided more highly than what was merely given to them, and defended the Act against United Party critics on the ground that it was based on legislation enacted from 1923 onwards under Smuts's administrations to prevent Communists and the like spreading subversive doctrines in schools under the wing of the clergy. He carried an amendment fixing an early date for transfer of the schools, and then announced that he would in due time, first, assume direct control over all Bantu secondary and industrial schools, and, a little later, over all Bantu teacher training schools, so that more teachers might be trained more cheaply than hitherto. All these schools

[1] Act 47 of 1953, § 9.
[2] *Round Table*, No. 176, pp. 416 ff.
[3] *Rand Daily Mail*, Feb. 2, 1955.

would be controlled at the outset by his ubiquitous Department and, even after they had been placed under that of his projected regional or territorial Bantu Authorities, would still be subject to its general supervision. He expressed the hope that after transfer the ecclesiastics and their lay helpers would still carry on the actual work of teaching and running the boarding-houses in accordance with regulations laid down by him, though on grants cut by a quarter. He announced that, of course, no institution which refused to accept the new terms could expect any financial help, and left his hearers wondering whether the Act was to be extended to South-West Africa over whose Native affairs he had just assumed control.[1]

Early in June, while amendments to the Bantu Education Act were being passed by the Assembly, Verwoerd elaborated his views in the Senate. He honestly believed that if economic integration could be said to exist simply because Africans were employed in factories and on the farms, 'then the asses, oxen and tractors were also integrated because they, too, were indispensable.' It therefore came as no real surprise that he should have told Honourable Senators that there was no place for Africans in the European community 'above the level of certain forms of labour.'[2] The rest followed from this assumption. Bantu education must, he insisted, 'stand with both feet in the Reserves and have its roots in the spirit and being of Bantu society.' To him, Africans were tribesmen, and so that they should remain tribesmen, he would see to it that they no longer got an education that drew them away from their own community and raised false hopes by showing them the 'green pastures of European society' in which they would never be permitted to wander. The whole aim of the Act was, he explained, to 'transform education for Natives into Bantu education.' He then proceeded to show wherein the distinction lay. 'Bantu education' in African Primary schools was to mean simply the three R's learned through the medium of the mother tongue, together with a knowledge of English, Afrikaans and 'the cardinal principles of the Christian religion.' Such schooling would equip the youngster to 'meet the demands which the economic life of South Africa would impose upon him'; in other words, it would teach him that he was never to have a future in white society and yet enable him to understand orders in either or both of the official languages. He reminded teachers that though there was no limit to the educational heights to which the pick of their pupils might one day attain, they must no longer teach the rank-and-file as if they were destined to go even as far as Standard VI.[3] To make sure, all white teachers were to be removed from Bantu Primary schools and, the Minister hinted broadly, most of the

---

[1] *Round Table*, No. 176, pp. 416 ff.
[2] *Pretoria News*, June 7, 1954; *Rand Daily Mail*, July 19, 20, 1954.
[3] The lower limit for would-be apprentices.

teachers would in future be women, because they understood little children better than men could and were, he implied, cheaper.[1]

The Act, which was to ensure that 'Bantu education' should henceforth conform to 'the broad national policy,' was duly passed, and then officially-appointed examiners showed what that education was to be even in scarcely attainable Standard VI. Their history and geography papers reeked of decomposing tribalism and suggested that young Africans needed to know little more in those fields than details about the officially-coveted High Commission Territories and the names of leading members of the Union Ministry and Native Affairs Department.[2] Verwoerd then announced that children in the primary and secondary schools alike must provide their own pens, exercise-books and so forth under pain of exclusion, and that though children in the sub-standards and primary schools would be under the supervision of their teachers for the customary four-and-a-half hours each day, those in the sub-standards at least would have only three of actual schooling. By this arrangement, teachers and class-rooms would be enabled to cope with two shifts daily, and, since the schools would not be equipped for recreation, the toddlers assisted by their parents were to fill in the rest of their full shift of four-and-a-half hours by keeping classrooms and grounds tidy. As for schools on farms and mining and industrial premises, African grown-ups were to build the walls by leave of the owners. The Department would then supply the doors, windows and roofs, but if the owners withdrew their consent, these movables would be taken away. Save by leave of 'the Minister' none but children of bona-fide workers in the mine or factory concerned or children of approved residents on the farm might attend, a highly selective scheme which might lead to poor results seeing that in many cases only a small proportion of the children already attending such schools fell under those heads.[3]

Such an Act and such a programme so swiftly following the Re-settlement Act aroused widespread opposition, lay and clerical, local and overseas. Roman Catholics and Presbyterians were up in arms at once; the Anglican Archbishop of Capetown condemned the 'terribly dangerous' fear that inspired recent Nationalist legislation; the Principal of the non-European College of Fort Hare lamented the 'sentence of death' passed on mission schools; Judge Feetham, late of the Appellate Division, foresaw serious encroachments on religious freedom; the United Transkeian Territorial Council, the famous *Bunga*, hotly criticised the official exposition of the 'New Deal' for Bantu education, and the distant *Manchester Guardian* saw the Education Act as a device to 'minimise English influences and encourage Afrikander influences among the Bantu, . . . to humiliate

---

[1] *Education for Ignorance*, pp. 15 ff.
[2] *Sunday Times* (Johannesburg), Nov. 21, 1954.   [3] *Ibid.*, Nov. 21, 1954.

the Englishman and exalt the Afrikander in the State's approach to African life.'[1] Indeed, almost the only important churches to support the Education Act were the various branches of the Dutch Reformed Church, which approved of its 'back to the kraal' spirit and may be hoped to profit by the hamstringing of rival Missions.[2]

None criticised the Education and Resettlement Acts more vigorously than Ambrose Reeves. Anglican Bishop of Johannesburg, in whose diocese lay the Rand with its crowded Bantu schools, and Father Trevor Huddlestone of the Community of the Resurrection, who not only condemned Verwoerd's 'educational pattern' as un-christian, but faced the loss of the great Church of Christ the King and numerous mission and educational centres when the clearance of the Western Areas should have been effected. These two in especial drew the fire of defenders of the new educational policy. Highly placed officials stigmatised their protests as the outcome of 'ignorance, prejudice and hysteria.' They declared that the Bantu child was to be given a better chance to 'develop gradually so as to be of service to his people,' prophesied a golden age when the pro-jected Bantu School Boards should have given parents a bigger say in the administration of the schools, promised that there should soon be a four-year course up to Standard II for all African children whose parents desired it,[3] held out the hope of much fuller facilities for technical and industrial training and, finally, gave an assurance that none of the two hundred existing Secondary schools should be closed.[4] Verwoerd, meanwhile, explained his scheme at *indabas* of Chiefs and Headmen in the Free State and Transvaal, accusing 'most of the English churches' of having far less real interest in Bantu welfare than had a Nationalist Government which had given Africans more posts in their own areas than any of its predecessors, alleging that they were angry simply because the state subsidies, 'the milk of the cow,' would flow in their direction no longer, and, forgetful perhaps of the distinction which he himself had recently drawn between education for Africans and 'Bantu education,' in-sisting that education was everywhere the same and its purpose the same.[5]

Home from the backveld, Verwoerd made it plain that under his régime there should be little of that freedom for teachers which is the life of education.[6] He warned Bantu teachers that they would not be allowed to publish in newspapers unfavourable comments on any Government Department, School Committee and so on, nor

---

[1] *South Africa*, June 5, 1954; *Contact*, Sept. 1954; *Rand Daily Mail*, May 19, 1954; *Manchester Guardian*, May 22, 1954.
[2] *Round Table*, No. 176, p. 417.   [3] Thus ensuring them bare literacy.
[4] *Survey*, No. 93, p. 12.
[5] *Rand Daily Mail*, Nov. 15, 16, 1954; *The Times*, Nov. 16, 1954.
[6] *Education for Ignorance*, p. 13.

identify themselves with any political party, nor become members of a Native Advisory Board or other local authority without leave of their School Board and 'the Minister.' He told them that they would be liable to trial for misconduct by their School Board without legal representation, that they must live in a school hostel if required to do so by that Board, and must realise that an increase of salary was not a right, but an act of grace on the part of the Minister, who would require a Departmental report on the applicant's industry, discipline, punctuality, efficiency and conduct before making up his mind. Even then, he would have to see whether he could find the money.

So much for teachers. Now for owners of the schools. Verwoerd sent to each ecclesiastical organisation in a Bantu township a circular and subsidiary documents, which set out the terms on which it would be suffered to carry on its work. Each was bound by law to confine itself to missionary work, but if any of them, like the representatives of 'a certain church,' obviously the Church of the Province, went beyond their proper sphere, the authorities could cancel the lease which it had granted. Further, if the Minister 'deemed' that the lessee was using the site for an unauthorised purpose, or that either he or his representatives anywhere were doing anything that might lead to a breach of the peace and a worsening of relations between races or between the Bantu and 'governmental persons or bodies,' he could cancel the lease without compensation at three months' notice. New schools were to be in the hands of the Department and not those of an ecclesiastical organisation, and no one who was not an African might live on such a leased site without ministerial leave. Recipients of the circular were to inform the Minister before the end of the year whether they proposed to lease their schools, carry on with a reduced subsidy, or frankly close their doors.[1]

Some Churches and Missionary Societies, headed by the various branches of the Dutch Reformed Church and the Swedish Lutheran Mission, accepted the new terms cheerfully; others, like the Congregationalists and Methodists, hoping that they might still have a right of entry for religious purposes, reluctanty acceded thereto, and the London Missionary Society resigned itself to leasing to the Minister its great Tiger Kloof Native Institution at Vryburg for twenty years. The general response, however, was an outburst of protest. Churches so different as the Roman Catholic, the Seventh Day Adventist and the United Jewish Reformed Congregation in the Transvaal resolved to carry on without state aid, and, as a personal contribution, the Bantu novelist, James Ngubane, offered to wash lavatories part-time at the Ohlanga Institute near Durban and thus

[1] *Survey*, No. 95, p. 15.

help it to fulfil the liberal intentions of its Bantu founder, John Dube. The American Board of Missions, however, gave notice that it must close its hundred schools and, after Verwoerd had declined its offer to run its teacher training centre of Adams College in Natal for five years, resolved to close that also at the end of the coming year.[1]

The Anglican Church of the Province, the Church most suspect of the authorities, failed to present an entirely united front. Its leaders, white and black, refused to have anything to do with Verwoerd's 'fantastic' scheme for training Africans merely as members of 'an uncivilised society'; but its Archbishop and all save one of its Bishops sitting in Synod at Umtata resolved that, as a choice between 'two grievous evils,' they should lease to the Department their schools other than those that were also used for Church purposes, lest the teachers lose their jobs and the children get no education save that of the streets.[2] This course was followed in the main, though the Bishop of Pretoria decided to keep open the Grace Dieu Secondary School in Pietersburg, leaving the authorities concerned to close, if they must, St. Cuthbert's School in the Transkei and the African Teacher Training College and High School at Modderfontein in the Free State.[3] The dogged Bishop of Johannesburg took a line of his own. Strongly supported by his clergy, he resolved to close his twenty-three schools with their ten thousand pupils at the sacrifice of £45,000 in land and buildings, but at the same time to use such of these schools as were held in freehold for parochial purposes and to organise vigorously the training of Sunday School teachers, Scouts and leaders of other youth and adult organisations.[4] Huddlestone went his own way in his more limited sphere. He had known that he was a marked man ever since, in June 1954, a hundred armed police had invaded a big multi-racial 'Resist Apartheid Conference' which he was addressing in Johannesburg, and had taken the names and addresses of all present on the plea that they were investigating a case of treason.[5] Nevertheless, regardless of the fact that the Minister of Justice had been deaf to protests by Labour Members against that 'act of provocation,' he now faced a big meeting summoned by the Education League and, under the eye of numerous uniformed policemen, set on foot an organisation to raise money to save St. Peter's School near the Priory of his Order in Rosettenville. Encouraged by the call of the distant *Observer* to

[1] *Rand Daily Mail*, Oct. 14, 15, Nov. 23, Dec. 13, 1954; *The Star*, Oct. 11, 1954; *Pretoria News*, Jan. 8, 1955; *Die Transvaler*, Oct. 22, 1954; *Natal Mercury*, Oct. 27, 1954; *The Drum*, Dec. 1954; *E. Province Herald*, Oct. 23, Dec. 11, 1954; *The Times*, Dec. 10, 1954.
[2] *Ibid.*, Oct. 17, 24, 26, 1954; *Chronology*, X., No. 22, p. 741; No. 23, p. 774; *Rand Daily Mail*, Nov. 11, 1954.
[3] *Ibid.*, Nov. 22, 24, 1954.   [4] *Ibid.*, Nov. 22, 1954.   [5] *Ibid.*, June 28, 1954.

men of goodwill to subscribe to that fund, he presently set about collecting £10,000 in the Union and overseas to finance fourteen Church Family Centres for recreation and other out-of-school activities.[1]

The *Observer* was only one of many allies gained by the Churches and Missionary Societies. Virtually all the English-medium newspapers in South Africa and many of the leading journals in the United Kingdom rallied to their side; the Archbishops of Canterbury and York declared that the time had come to speak out against the new Hitlerism in the Union; the Society for the Propagation of the Gospel called for prayers for the struggling Churches in South Africa, a call that was answered most appropriately on Dingaan's Day by practically every congregation of the Established Church. Others gave more tangible help. While a Special Group of the British Council of Churches appealed for men and money to help Sunday schools, youth organisations, and so forth, the S.P.G. at once sent the Church of the Province £25,000, of which it earmarked £6000 for Family Centres in the Johannesburg Diocese, and speedily collected a further £12,000 and sent two delegates to take counsel with religious leaders in South Africa.[2] At the close of the year, the British people showed the Bishop of Johannesburg, who had come to their country to make his appeal in person, that they were as ready as their ancestors in slave emancipation days to put their hands in their pockets in a good cause.

This was too much for the Nationalists, all the more because Harry Oppenheimer condemned their policy as an attempt to slow down economic progress for the sake of an ideology, and overseas newspapers reminded them that some of their allies, like Portugal and Belgium, by no means shared their views on the colour issue.[3] Verwoerd, reserving his choicest invective for the Bishop of Johannesburg, denounced this torrent of criticism as 'unworthy, unchristian,' and warned Bantu parents that if they kept their children away from his schools in obedience to the Cape African National Congress, they would risk seeing them shut out for good. There was, indeed, some justification for his excitement, because, fanned by his threat of a 'Jim Crow' existence for Africans, the Resistance was flaring up once more. Notably, Bantu and other non-Europeans were inviting all political parties and scores of other organisations to send delegates to a Congress of the People, which should frame a Freedom Charter, and, sure enough, the Liberal Party had accepted that invitation so that it might implement its recent resolution to co-operate with the African National Congress in pressing for the

[1] *Rand Daily Mail*, June 29, Dec. 13, 1954.
[2] *Church Times*, Oct. 22, 1954; *Pretoria News*, Nov., 1954.
[3] *Rand Daily Mail*, June 21, 1954.

repeal of all discriminatory legislation and the ultimate granting of adult suffrage.[1]

Naturally, the Nationalists defended their policy, some with the utmost politeness, like Gerhardus Jooste, High Commissioner in London, who pleaded that the Europeans were simply asserting their 'inalienable right to . . . a future as a nation'; others at least courteously, like Eiselen, Secretary for Native Affairs, who claimed that the Bible taught 'the basic inequality of human beings' however fully God of His grace might deign to treat them on the Last Day as equal before Himself; some bluntly, like Eric Louw, Minister of Economic Affairs, who insisted that in all Africa south of the Sahara the interests of the white man should be the 'paramount consideration,' and others downright brusquely, like Strydom, Minister of Lands, who boasted that the white man would 'fight to the death' to maintain the dominance he had enjoyed in South Africa for three hundred years. Mindful of the Commission which had long been investigating the affairs of the Press with special reference to messages sent overseas by correspondents, Strydom also gave warning that the authorities would take prompt steps against any newspaper that sought to undermine that dominance in the present 'unexpected and unparalleled' situation, and, with an eye to the Red Peril, announced that foreign-born Communists would be deported and, once their connection with Communism had been proved 'beyond reasonable doubt,' certain publications would be prohibited.[2]

Strydom and Verwoerd, at least, went beyond words to acts. As 'a purely precautionary measure,' the former forbade his Police to associate with 'named' Communists of whom there were now close on six hundred, and both invoked the Suppression of Communism Acts, first, to debar ex-Chief Albert Luthuli, President-General of the African National Congress, from attending public meetings or leaving the magisterial district of Lower Tugela for two years to come, and then to send two other Africans back to the Transvaal, there to report regularly to specified officials, because their presence in East London was 'inimical to the peace, order and good government' of their fellows in that region.[3]

Under the growing stress of the times, non-Europeans tended to fare badly. It was not so much that otherwise decent white folk too often turned a blind eye on their many fellows who assaulted men

---

[1] *Pretoria News*, May 31, 1954; *Chronology*, X., No. 23, p. 774; *E. Province Herald*, June 28, 1954; *The Times*, Nov. 25, 1954.

[2] *Survey*, No. 93, pp. 6 ff.; No. 94, pp. 5 ff.; No. 95, pp. 5 ff.; *The Times*, Aug. 18, Sept. 21, 1954; *Natal Daily News*, Aug. 28, 1954.

[3] *Survey*, No. 93, p. 7; *Rand Daily Mail*, July 12, 13, 1954; *India News*, July 17, 1954.

of darker hue in the streets, but that non-Europeans could not always be sure of even-handed justice in the Courts. Doubtless it was all in order that the Secretary-General of the African National Congress should be given three months in the Kroonstad Regional Court for having attended a meeting of half-a-dozen persons after having been forbidden to do so, and that his successor should have been arraigned under the Suppression of Communism Acts, especially as the former was released on bail and allowed to appeal and the latter was let go after the charges had been withdrawn. But what was to be said of justice when a Coloured man in Natal was sentenced to death for having raped a white woman and, a few days later in the same Province, a middle-aged European was merely given nine months hard labour for having similarly outraged an Indian girl, who had duly borne a child, the learned Judge perpending that the white miscreant had 'a poor background' and that, anyway, Indian girls were given to marrying young. Even worse was the acquittal at Groblersdal in the Transvaal of a European who had forced carnal intercourse on a Bantu girl, and the sentencing of his victim to four months' imprisonment, though in this case the scandal was so great that the Minister of Justice was fain to remit the punishment a week or so before the period expired.[1]

Nevertheless, there were still Judges in South Africa. The law at least was with the Cape Supreme Court when it dismissed an appeal by the Communist, Sam Kahn, an aforetime 'Native' Member in the Assembly, against his conviction for having attended a social 'gathering,' a vague term which their Lordships forebore to define. It was assuredly even more completely with the Appellate Division when it reversed that decision a few months later on the very ground that there was no authoritative definition of that blessed word either in the Suppression of Communist Acts or anywhere else.[2] No appeals went forward, however, from the Transvaal Supreme Court, when Judge Nicolaas de Wet set aside a ruling by the Chairman of the Land Tenure Advisory Board that the Transvaal Indian Congress should not be heard publicly against a proposal to demarcate Group Areas in Johannesburg, nor from Judge William Ramsbottom's judgment against the Transvaal Law Society with no allowance of costs for trying to expel Nelson Mandela, an African attorney, who had been convicted of taking part in the Resistance. There could in the nature of things be no appeal when Judge Leslie Blackwell of the Witwatersrand Division of the Supreme Court, at a moment's notice, expelled Special Branch detectives from a meeting in Johannesburg of the non-European Congress of the People, which they had invaded under

[1] *Natal Mercury*, Aug. 19, 1954; *Natal Witness*, July 21, 1954; *The Times*, Oct. 12, 1954; *New Statesman*, Sept. 18, 1954; *Star*, July 13, 1954.
[2] *The Forum*, Dec. 1954.

a 'strong suspicion' that named Communists and other undesirables were present in defiance of the law.[1] Undismayed, Swart began to extend the duration of his ban from the now customary two years to five, while a leading Transvaal Nationalist newspaper cried out against the sacrifice of white supremacy to mere money-making as 'a premature surrender which must result in suicide.'[2]

Businessmen and Bantu were increasingly perturbed as the authorities pushed ahead with the Western Areas clearance scheme and foreshadowed others of a like nature. Official notice was given that thousands of Africans were to be shifted from Apex near Brakpan on the Far East Rand to make room for factories and so forth, while Eiselen, of his own mere motion, talked to S.A.B.R.A. of a gradual removal from the Cape Western Province of some 78,000 Bantu who had trekked in of recent years and, by their superior physique, cheerfulness and comparative freedom from drunkenness, were competing for employment unfairly with Cape Coloured Folk, whose home that region was.[3] As for the Western Areas, Verwoerd warned all those who should ignore an order to move or, worse still, offer organised resistance that they would be guilty of an offence. In spite of the housing-shortage for folk of all colours along the Rand, he announced that when the first removals began in Sophiatown in February 1955, the houses would be bull-dozed, because, although these were of the better kind, they lay close to those of Europeans. Bantu, Asiatic and Coloured bachelors were to go to similar houses at a safe distance; but Bantu families must leave, most of them the Minister believed, well pleased to exchange rack-rented shacks for admittedly better dwellings, as ready as their children to be 'dumbfounded' by the 'stout' dustbins with which each house was provided, and willing to set off their slightly higher train-fares to and from work against the lower rents they would have to pay. Lest Verwoerd's hopes were destined to disappointment, however, the authorities, on the eve of the first removals, prohibited public meetings in the Western Areas and put the principal leaders of the African National Congress to the ban.[4]

Towards the close of the year, the Conference of World Churches met at the University of the Witwatersrand and showed how deeply Christian men could be divided on the issue of *apartheid*. This, the first multi-racial Conference of its kind to be held in the Union, was summoned by the Dutch Reformed Church to discuss first and foremost 'the extension of the Kingdom of God in multi-racial South Africa.' Of the delegates from forty-two Protestant Churches,

[1] *Rand Daily Mail*, July 26, Sept. 1954.
[2] *Die Transvaler*, June 24, 1954.
[3] *Chronology*, XI. No. 2, p. 60.
[4] *Rand Daily Mail*, Jan. 7, Feb. 10, 11, 25, 1955.

Missions and Societies, fifty-six were Coloured Folk, Indians and Africans. These sat discreetly in their own section of the hall; but it must have been the multi-racial character of the delegates and the variety of the Churches they represented that moved the Governor-General to observe in his opening speech that there were already some twelve hundred and fifty African Churches and sects in the Union, and the end was apparently not yet. Physical segregation was, however, cut across by divisions of a far more fundamental kind. Members of the Dutch Reformed Church deprecated the preaching of 'a social gospel,' because Christ did not come to deliver men from 'social, economic and political slavery, but from the slavery of sin.' Tacitly rejecting this comfortable doctrine, the Anglican Archbishop of Cape Town lamented rather the failure of the Churches to withstand the assaults of aggressive Islam, not least in his own Diocese, while the Bishop of Bloemfontein, recalling the almost complete absence of Reserves in the Free State, dwelt on the dangers likely to arise from a landless, rightless and dispossessed folk, who did not feel that they belonged to the community. In the event, despite some protests from Dutch Reformed members, the great majority condemned racial segregation and pleaded that all should be given access to the franchise; but, on the crucial issue of *apartheid*, Dutch Reformed Church members and, significantly, some non-Europeans also voted in favour, and the Anglicans and mass of the non-Europeans voted adversely. Some declined to commit themselves, but all were united in calling on the Government to find an additional £10,000,000 a year for the education and social training of Coloured Folk and Indians and in arranging that multi-racial Conferences be held every third year.[1]

The report of the Holloway Commission, which had long been inquiring into the problem of non-European students at the Universities of Cape Town and the Witwatersrand, was not calculated to console Verwoerd and his fellow-Nationalists for the inconclusive findings of the Conference of World Churches. Many of those who had given evidence had been opposed to the exclusion of such students, the more knowledgeable of them pointing out that it would cost fully £200,000 to transfer even two hundred additional students to the non-European College at Fort Hare, and that the Fort Hare experiment itself was by no means a success in that it bred frustration and resentment in the hearts of its segregated inmates. The Commission found that, however desirable segregation might be in principle, it could not be applied to all Universities; hence, although it recommended that non-Europeans be concentrated either at Fort Hare or the non-European section of the University of

[1] *Rand Daily Mail*, Dec. 10, 1954.

Natal at Durban, it made an exception in the case of post-graduates.[1]

Meanwhile, a sufficient number of the electors had shown themselves so well pleased with the official policy that they had given the Government a resounding mandate at the Provincial general election in August 1954. The Nationalists swept the Free State, gained an overwhelming majority in the Transvaal, slightly improved their position in Natal, and for the first time secured a majority in the Cape.[2] Possibly, it was by way of celebrating this victory of their employers that the Police seized likely documents in the office of the left-wing newspaper, *Advance*, and also in the homes of its editor and staff;[3] undoubtedly it was the realisation that Malan had been confirmed in power that prompted most of the political parties in South-West Africa to show their hands. Many of the electors in those parts disliked the increasing interest which the South African Parliament was showing in their affairs, resented talk by South African Nationalists of incorporating their Territory as a fifth Province of the Union, dreaded lest their labour supply be drawn off to the expanding mines along the Rand and elsewhere, and were downright worried because the Union's Minister of Defence, accompanied by senior officers of his own Department and that of Native Affairs, should have recently watched Air Force manœuvres over the Caprivi Strip.[4] The jubilant local Nationalists, however, urged the Germans, who had voted solidly for them at the past Parliamentary general election and still held the balance, to abandon the idea of seeking to save some shred of independence by forming a party of their own; rather let them take a more active part in politics as good Nationalists —looking forward to the day when there should be a single Republic south of the Limpopo and Kunene rivers in which they might clear non-Europeans off lands in white areas once the Group Areas Act had been extended to their Territory.[5] The Nationalists further submitted 'propositions' to Malan, claiming that now that the Mandate was dead and gone, South-West Africa and the Union had become 'one people and territory' as far as the outer world was concerned, and that their Territory had become sovereign by sharing the sovereignty of the Union. They were somewhat dashed by Malan's curt reply that all good Nationalists had known this for a long time past; but they took comfort from the thought that even their local United Party rivals and at least one leading newspaper of that persuasion on the Rand were going so far in their direction as to ask the Pretoria authorities to drop all idea of incorporation, to continue to

---

[1] *Rand Daily Mail*, May 6, 1954; *Pretoria News*, May 13, 1954, and Feb. 2, 1955.
[2] *Chronology*, X., No. 17, p. 566.   [3] *Ibid.*, X., No. 17, p. 567.
[4] *Windhoek Advertiser*, April 23, May 7, 1954; *Rand Daily Mail*, June 2, 1954; *The Times*, June 23, 1954.
[5] *Die Suidwester*, Nov. 6, 1954; *Central African Post*, Jan. 17, 1955.

give economic aid, and to make an undisputed end of the Mandate by endowing South-West Africa either with self-government or, alternatively, an independent status in a federal relationship with the Union.[1]

Air Force manœuvres over the Caprivi Strip were only one outcome of the Union's growing concern for the defence of Africa south of the Sahara and the exclusion of Communism therefrom. Within the Union, Malan and Erasmus had long desired to see the Imperial naval base at Simonstown subjected to joint control by the United Kingdom, the United States, France, Belgium and Portugal under a chairman from their own country. In the wider field, both hoped for a Western Indian Ocean Treaty on the lines of N.A.T.O. and S.E.A.T.O. to head India and the U.S.S.R. off from Africa and, more immediately, to fill the defence 'gap,' which was widening in the Middle East and, above all, in the vital Suez Canal Zone as Western Powers gradually 'quit Africa' under pressure of Arab nationalism and anti-colonialism. Both men saw fertile fields for the propagation of Communist doctrines in Mau-Mau-ridden Kenya and swarthy and unstable Abyssinia, to say nothing of Pretoria, the Rand and Basutoland in the heart of their own country; they feared, moreover, that Nkrumah in the Gold Coast and Nehru in India might well be overthrown by Red revolution.

Defence talks began in Capetown with Paul Reynaud, ex-Prime Minister of France, and were presently carried further by Erasmus in conference at Dakar with representatives of the United Kingdom, France, Belgium and Portugal. A few months later, Erasmus discussed them in greater detail with the British Ministers directly concerned. He did not claim that any precise plan for joint African defence had been evolved in these London talks; but he could report that agreement had been reached on most points, that he himself had bought much-needed equipment for the Union's armed forces, and that he could hope that the problem of Simonstown would soon be solved, if only because highly-placed naval officers at that base were reassuring on that score and possibly suspected, as did others, that in these days of atomic warfare, Simonstown, the 'stout little yard,' as the British C.-in-C. South Atlantic affectionately called it, was not so valuable to the United Kingdom as it once had been.[2]

---

[1] *Windhoek Advertiser*, Aug. 27, 1954; *Chronology*, X., No. 17, p. 567; *Survey*, No. 96, p. 7.

[2] In July 1955, it was agreed that the Simonstown base should be returned to the Union by March 31, 1957, at latest, the Union paying the United Kingdom £750,000 in three instalments. British personnel was to be withdrawn gradually, and the Union in return undertook to continue the recruitment of non-European staff with no differential pay based on colour. The base was to be included in the new South African ' area ' under a South African flag officer, free in peacetime from executive control of the British C.-in-C. South Atlantic Station in whose sphere the South African area would fall. British and Allied Navies were to have the use of the base even when the Union was a non-belligerent. . . . *The Times*, July 5, 1955; *White Paper*, Cmd. 9520 of 1955.

Meanwhile, Erasmus could congratulate himself that as soon as the British had fulfilled their promise to hand over their huge wartime ammunition dump, at least one potential hotbed of Communism within the Union would have been eliminated.[1]

One of Erasmus's chief preoccupations was how to fit the High Commission Territories into his defence scheme, for now that jet-bombers could reach the great concentration of mines and industries along the Rand in half-an-hour from the Limpopo frontier, he held it to be highly dangerous that those Territories should be 'blind spots' in his network of radar defence.[2] It might have been suggested that he should have tried to reach some co-operative arrangement with the British authorities similar to that under which the Territories and his own country had long been included in a single customs union; as it was, he made the most of his not altogether tenable argument. By so doing, he sought to give additional weight to the demand which Malan was once more making, with the general support of all political parties, for the speedy transfer of the governance of the Territories in terms of the South Africa Act. The British reply came short and almost sharp, for Churchill repeated the promise, old as that Act, that the local Africans must be consulted first, and expressed the hope that Malan would not press the issue, seeing that there could be no question of transfer 'at the present time' nor of summary transfer at any time without a breach of 'trust.'[3] This was bad enough, but far worse to Malan's mind was the threat of many British Labour Members never to permit transfer while racial discrimination persisted in South Africa. Nationalist newspapers thereupon 'discovered' Basutoland as a breeding-ground of Communism and the missionary control of its education as an obstacle to the imposition of Verwoerd's scheme of 'Bantu education' in their own land; some Nationalists, recalling the successful infiltration in Kruger's days, tried to acquire land and business concessions in Swaziland, and a few zealots even urged their Prime Minister to seize all three Territories without more ado. Malan, however, prudently turned a deaf ear to such sabre-rattling and merely assured all concerned that his patience was almost exhausted.[4]

One of the stock charges brought by South Africans against the British, with the somewhat incongruous support of the Anti-Slavery Society, was that they had let the Territories stagnate. The British could not altogether deny this; but they could plead that they had latterly done, and were still doing, a good deal to put them in

[1] *Survey*, No. 93, pp. 5 ff.; *The Times*, Sept. 14, 1954; *Daily Telegraph*, Oct. 3, 1954.
[2] *Survey*, No. 94, p. 4.
[3] *Chronology*, X., No. 8, pp. 241–2, 258–9.
[4] *Ibid.*, X., No. 17, pp. 567, 602; *Manchester Guardian*, Nov. 10, 1954; *Daily Telegraph*, Sept. 16, 1954.

better economic and social shape with the aid of U.N.O. and similar agencies and their own Colonial Welfare and Development money. They were even now proposing to build two Teacher Training Institutions and six Secondary Schools in Basutoland, whence a highly educated African research officer was about to take up one of the new Bantu scholarships at Oxford, to enlarge the Bamangwato College and make it available to all children in Bechuanaland, and to start post-matriculation courses in all three Territories so that Africans might aspire to enter the Rhodesia University College in Salisbury. The Bechuana hoped much from the 'water hunt' financed by British taxpayers in their dry and thirsty land, and were rejoiced at the opening of the Lobatsi abattoir, the first major industry to have been established in those parts. Many of them, again, were encouraged by news of talk in Mafeking, Pretoria, Windhoek and London of a railway running through their territory and linking the Rhodesian system with some port on the coast of the Mandated Territory. Such a line was projected by the South-West Railway Exploration Company, which had recently been formed in London, and would, if constructed, surely reinforce the pull to the North that was already being exerted by the marketing of so many Bechuana cattle in the Rhodesias and the Belgian Congo. It might even lead to the 'affiliation' of their Protectorate with the new Central African Federation and thus do away with all risk of its transfer to the Union. It was a solution of an old problem which appealed notably to Tshekedi Khama, who, for all that he was now only a private citizen, was still a power in the land.[1]

These advances were in line with the policy advocated by the *Observer*, whose editor, disappointed at the patent failure to 'mollify South Africa by agreeableness' and irritated by Malan's insistence that he had a 'moral duty' to take over the Territories, suggested that the United Kingdom and United States should together tell the Union flatly that if it tried to gain its ends by forceful means, such as economic blockade, they would buy no more of its gold, wine and wool and would, meanwhile, develop the Territories politically on Parliamentary lines.[2] Here the editor touched upon the weakest side of the British administration. The Imperial authorities, holding, as they did, that it was 'unwise to hasten,' had done scarcely anything in that direction since they had taken over the Territories in 1868, 1885 and 1903 respectively. True, as early as 1898, they had given Basutoland a National Council for the discussion of domestic affairs and had recently made it one-third elective; again, in 1920, they had set up a European Advisory Council in Swaziland to sit alongside

---

[1] *Federation Newsletter*, Sept. 17, 1954; *Windhoek Advertiser*, Sept. 14, 1954; Tshekedi Khama, *Bechuanaland and South Africa*, p. 14.
[2] *Observer*. Dec. 5, 1954; *Chronology*, X., No. 17, p. 602.

the *Liquoquo*, the Paramount Chief's traditional council, and formed both African and European Advisory Councils in Bechuanaland. These Bechuanaland Councils had latterly taken to holding joint sessions at regular intervals, but neither they nor any of the other institutions were anything like the Executive and Legislative Councils which Lord Hailey had long since said the Territories ought to have on the analogy of other British African dependencies.[1] Doubtless, fuller use of the Advisory Councils and the creation of a hierarchy of Village and Tribal Councils might one day lead to these high things; but progress towards real self-government was bound to be slow, because the Territories were bound economically so closely to the Union and their other neighbours that the Executive must have the last word in determining their external relations.[2]

In Swaziland, some tentative advance was being made by the Paramount Chief, who had recently created a National Treasury and Native Courts to be followed, perhaps, by a network of Standing Committees drawn from the *Liquoquo* and the Councils of the subordinate Chiefs;[3] but nothing of the kind had yet been attempted in divided Bechuanaland, nor yet in Basutoland. In that Crown Colony the Resident Commissioner and Queen Regent, European officials and multitudinous Chiefs, educated Africans, white folk and black folk had long been drifting further and further apart; indeed, the only indigenous political advance had been unofficial, when, in 1952, some educated Africans had formed the Basutoland African Congress to press for a Legislative Council with a strong elective element and were now demanding that the Territories should never be transferred without 'the express consent' of their peoples. Meanwhile, however much Nationalist clamour might tend to drive the various groups closer together, there remained in all three Territories the fundamental weakness of Dualism, that is, joint rule by tribal authorities and European officials. This system was least unsatisfactory in Swaziland, because there the power of the Paramount Chief was still a reality; but it worked ill in Basutoland, where the authority of the Queen Regent was severely limited by that of the many and jealous subordinate Chiefs, 'the Sons of Moshesh,' each of them tenacious of his rights and strong to make trouble with the backing of his loyal followers. It remained to be seen what would come of the inquiry into the whole problem which the High Commissioner had recently entrusted to a Commission under the chairmanship of Sir Henry Moore.[4] The situation was, if possible, even worse in Bechuanaland, for there there was no Paramount Chief, but only the eight big Chiefs, each in his own Reserve and each

---

[1] Lord Hailey, *Native Administration in British Tropical Africa*, V. 140.
[2] *Anti-Slavery Society Reporter*, May 1954.   [3] *The Times*, April 15, 1954.
[4] *The Friend*, Jan. 12, 13, 1955.

suspecting that his tenure of office was precarious since the recent
appointment of a District Commissioner as Native Authority in the
Bamangwato Reserve, the largest of all, and the subsequent super-
cession of Seretse Khama, the lawful heir to the chieftainship, by
Rasebolai Kgamane. Leading Bechuana, like Tshekedi, suspected
that the elective Local Councils of which officials talked were a device
to hold them back and, at the best, would give them powers no greater
than those enjoyed by fellow-Africans in the Union's Reserves. They
demanded rather the concurrent creation of Executive, Legislative
and Local Councils, arguing that the United Kingdom authorities
could find out what the people thought about transfer more easily
from a semi-elective Legislative Council than from white officials, or
Chiefs suspect of yielding to official pressure, or a more or less
tumultuary *Kgotla* drawn, if that were possible, from the whole
Protectorate.[1]

Nationalists, who freely criticised the British for their administration in the High Commission Territories, resented the fact that their
own governance of non-Europeans was criticised with equal persistence by U.N.O. They and most other white South Africans thus
found it a welcome relief when that institution showed marked signs
of relaxing its pressure. Possibly it did so because it was weary of
waging an inconclusive campaign against stubborn South African
resistance backed by protests from the United Kingdom and other
colonial Powers at interference in domestic affairs; be that as it
might, the very order of the agenda for the Session beginning in
September was eloquent of boredom with the tiresome wrangle,
for though South-West Africa was moved from near the bottom to
second place, Indians and *apartheid* appeared low down.[2] There was
indeed some plain speaking about *apartheid*, but no one attempted
to initiate a full dress debate thereon. Rather did the General
Assembly quietly accept the advice of the Rev. Michael Scott and
his tribal clients that a Committee of Experts should show the Union
the many ways in which U.N.O. and its specialised agencies could
help it to solve its racial problems. It might have been expected that
there would be the usual lengthy and acrimonious discussion of
Indians, more especially because Malan had just bracketed Nehru
with Communism as his country's peculiar peril, accused him of
trying to drive the white man out of Africa by encouraging the
Resistance, and impelled him to close the office of India's High Commissioner at Pretoria, thus putting the coping-stone to the trade
embargo which his country had been maintaining against South
Africa for eight years past.[3] In the event, this customary war of words

[1] T. Khama, *op. cit.*, pp. 9 ff.
[2] *The Times*, Oct. 27, 1954; *Survey*, No. 96, pp. 3 ff.
[3] *Chronology*, X., No. 9, pp. 296 ff.; No. 10, p. 419.

was averted after a usually truculent Latin American had asked what good had come of all the mutual recrimination, and the leading South African delegate, in reply, had stated that his Government was willing to resume direct negotiations with India and Pakistan.[1] Having decided to invite the three Governments directly concerned to follow that course, the General Assembly passed on to South-West Africa and, by the attention it bestowed on it, showed that one Johannesburg newspaper had been unduly optimistic when it asserted that the affairs of the Mandated Territory were no longer a matter of international concern. The point at issue was a proposal to ask the International Court for an advisory opinion as to whether the General Assembly must agree unanimously on questions arising from reports and petitions from that Territory, as South Africa insisted it must, or whether it could do so by a mere two-thirds majority, thus circumventing the Union's inevitable veto. In the end, despite South African protests, the General Assembly resolved to seek that opinion; whereupon, a South African delegate, affirming that his Government was 'proud of its administration,' gave much more information thereupon than had been forthcoming since Pretoria had ceased to report seven years back.[2] As if to reward the speaker for his courtesy, the General Assembly invited his country to join with the United Kingdom, the United States, France, Belgium, Canada and Australia in the planning of an international agency to discuss the peaceful use of atomic energy.[3]

This recognition by the most ecumenical of its critics that their country could be a power for good in the world enhanced the satisfaction which South Africans felt at an assurance from their High Commissioner in London that, in spite of the acid tone of some of the British newspapers, they had more friends in the United Kingdom than they suspected.[4] Again, nearly all of them were delighted to welcome the European tourists, who were flocking to 'Sunny South Africa' in response to the reduced fares demanded by the Union-Castle Company during the off-season. On the other hand, though one eminent tourist, Prince Bernhard of the Netherlands, could wax enthusiastic at the rosy prospects the Union held out to immigrants, not all South Africans could claim that immigration was what it should be or deny that the outward flow was ominous; indeed, during the past year, only 16,257 Europeans had come to take up permanent residence and of these little more than one-third were British, while more than 10,000 had left the country for good, fully three-fourths of them for Rhodesia.[5] On the other hand, though

---

[1] Survey, No. 96, pp. 4, 7.
[2] Ibid., No. 96, pp. 6 ff.; Observer, June 13, 1955.
[3] Survey, No. 96, pp. 3 ff.   [4] Ibid., No. 93, p. 5.
[5] Ibid., No. 93, pp. 5, 8; South Africa, June 26, 1954.

men might come slowly, money was coming fast from the United States and Switzerland, thus witnessing to overseas confidence in the Union's economic stability.[1] That confidence was confirmed by news of a record export of gold and oranges and a very satisfactory export of uranium. The chemical industry was flourishing; a successful trial had been made of extracting the oxygen from air as a step towards converting coal into petrol and by-products, and new factories were going up so fast that secondary industry could be sure of retaining the proud position it had won since the war of being the largest single contributor to the national income. Industrialists, keen on yet further expansion, were talking of founding something like an Industrial Bank on the model of the successful *Handelsinstituut*; but they were worried because, for all the increasing efficiency of their undertakings, they were obliged to call in non-Europeans to give them the semi-skilled labour they must have, while those of them who owned textile, clothing and pottery factories along the Rand had had to offer Bantu employees wage-incentives.[2] The money thus put in circulation did at least increase the purchasing power of the non-European majority and could be well afforded by a business community, which had been accorded a five per cent. increase in import quotas a few months back and was now being relieved of many other controls. Looking back, men could see that the turning-point had come in 1949, when Havenga had set up the National Finance Corporation to find uses for idle funds that could not be invested readily in the ordinary way, and now Dr. M. H. de Kock, chairman of that unique institution, could report that, thanks to a recent improvement in the balance of payments on capital and current accounts, deposits therein actually exceeded £100,000,000.

With money to burn, South Africans of varying colours laid plans to beautify their already lovely country and commemorate their several pasts. The Government proposed to spend lavishly on the National Parks and the Art Gallery that was to mark the coming centenary of the administrative capital; the African National Congress, reasonably enough, talked of raising memorials to dead Bantu heroes; the local Irish, with the aid of the Dublin authorities, set about collecting money for a monument to Irishmen who had fallen on the Republican side during the South African War and, perhaps partly as a counter-blast, Strauss's Committee displayed equal zeal in finding the wherewithal for an equestrian statue of Smuts to be placed beside that of his old friend, Louis Botha, on the slopes of Meintjes Kop to which Nationalists were once more talking of transferring the seat of Parliament.

All was not so well, however, below the surface. It could not be

[1] *Optima*, Sept. 1954.
[2] *Survey*, No. 93, pp. 9 ff.; No. 95, p. 3; No. 96, pp. 6, 17.

so while the so-called Union remained the 'Land of Contrasts.' The fundamental and pressing question was what the non-Europeans in general and the Bantu in particular had to hope from any of the political Parties. Plainly, they had less than nothing to hope from Bekker's little splinter group, which accepted *apartheid* with a few illusory modifications, usually voted with the Nationalists and had appropriately begun to call itself the Conservative Party. They could scarcely expect more either from Heaton Nicholls's Union Federal Party, which relegated their political advancement to a distant future and hedged it round with if's and an's, or from the Labour Party, which was, indeed, becoming more liberal, but was numerically weak. Far and away their best hope lay in the new Liberal Party, whose strength in the two Houses together now rivalled that of the Labour Party. It is true that African votes cast for the Nationalist candidate in the Transvaal-Free State Senatorial election suggested that an increasing number of the Bantu in those parts approved of *apartheid*, but none the less, the stalwart Liberal, William Ballinger, had been triumphantly returned once more. His wife, even more Liberal than he, had been returned unopposed to the Assembly by Cape Eastern; the Liberal, Walter Stanford, had carried the Transkei, and the left-winger, Lee Warden, though he had been debarred from addressing public meetings and was still awaiting his fate at the hands of the Minister of Justice as a suspected Communist, had none the less been returned for Cape Western in succession to the avowed Communist, Miss Ray Alexander, who had recently been ejected from the Assembly before she could even take her seat.[1]

Despite these welcome successes, the Liberals were still too weak to sway the course of politics, all the more that death had robbed them of the veteran lawyer, Douglas Buchanan. Thus, the fate of the non-Europeans still lay in the hands of the two major Parties. The policy of the Nationalists they knew only too well; that of the United Party they were now to learn. Early in 1954, Strauss had asked a Committee in each Province to pave the way for a 'big step forward' by re-examining their Party's non-European policy. The omens were not good for, while the Committees yet sat, a leading United Party Senator told the non-Europeans bluntly that it would be a long time before his Party would desire their direct representation in Parliament.[2] In the event, the Transvaal, Free State and Natal Committees did not go an inch beyond the Honourable Senator, and even the Cape Committee, in what was traditionally the most Liberal of the Provinces, recommended that the political advancement of the non-Europeans should come a poor second to their economic development and that, in any event, political privileges

---

[1] *South Africa*, Jan. 1, 1955. Warden was allowed to take his seat.
[2] *Rand Daily Mail*, July 12, 1954.

should only be granted to them with the 'substantial agreement of the European community.'[1] Thus ill-supported, Strauss failed to swing the subsequent Provincial Congresses in the three northern Provinces, and found the atmosphere of the Cape Congress so chilly that he virtually ignored the non-European issue and sought to warm the hearts of his hearers by trumpeting the advantages of membership of that 'mutual protection society,' the British Commonwealth, denouncing the very idea of a Republic, and accusing the Nationalists of having split the European community into two camps by their 'exclusiveness and clannishness.'[2]

Shortly before the United Party Conference met at Bloemfontein in mid-November, white South Africans were angered by the tactlessness of the Speaker of the Pakistan Parliament, who, for all that he was the guest of the Union authorities, urged the Moslems of Capetown to join hands with the Bantu and 'fight' for their rights no matter what the consequences.[3] Even without this open challenge to white supremacy, the result of the Conference was a foregone conclusion. Strauss, an Emperor without his legions, made but a sorry performance. After pleading for more immigrants to strengthen the position of the white folk, he frankly abandoned all hope of his 'big step forward' in favour of 'certain forward-looking steps' suggested by the Cape Committee in its less conservative moments. European leadership must be maintained; but seeing that, as even Verwoerd admitted, African labour was indispensable, he advised that Africans must be given a more definite and secure place based on the Western way of life. Whether or no racial discrimination were an evil depended, he averred, on the way in which it was enforced and the motives for its enforcement. An industrial colour bar there must be to protect the white man's standard of living, a bar that was not, however, to be maintained by legislation, but by collective bargaining with Africans through works committees and in no wise through trade unions which few of them yet knew how to run. He upheld 'the rate for the job' as fiercely as any Northern Rhodesian copper-miner, and showed his utter abhorrence of miscegenation by declaring that he would never repeal the Mixed Marriages Act. He proposed, however, to relieve 'deserving' Africans by simplifying the pass laws, and to appoint a Minister of Health who should sweep away slums, permit freehold tenure in African villages and locations, and undertake town and regional planning on a comprehensive scale; but the nearest he got to attacking the ministerial policy was to suggest that the laws governing municipal control over Africans should be suitably amended in the light of the Fagan Report. He then handled

[1] *Survey*, No. 93, p. 11; *Chronology*, X., No. 3, p. 773.
[2] *Ibid.*, X., No. 23, p. 773; *Survey*, No. 93, pp. 4 ff.; *The Times*, Sept. 16, 1954; *Daily Telegraph*, Sept. 23, 1954. [3] *Ibid.*, Sept. 23, 1954.

the political problem most gingerly. Accepting the principle of the measures which had virtually disfranchised the Cape Bantu in 1936, he none the less wished to see the Acts themselves referred to a Select Committee; he was prepared also to consider the revival of the Native Representative Council with increased powers, and to advance non-Europeans politically; but, before they could earn the franchise, the Bantu, at least, must serve a long apprenticeship for democracy in a hierarchy of institutions similar to those which were apparently soon to be set up in their urban areas and Reserves. He finally proposed that 'advanced' Bantu be given special individual votes in the Colleges that elected 'Native' Senators and that the number of the said Senators be raised from four to six. After two days' debate, the Conference adopted this uninspiring programme. It even showed itself bolder than its leader by resolving that the better-run Bantu trade unions should be recognised *de facto* as well as Bantu works committees.[1]

The Bantu were soon to realise what this programme portended. First, the overwhelmingly United Party Provincial Council at Pietermaritzburg decreed that there should be no inter-racial sport in any institutions under its control in Natal. Next, at the opening of Parliament late in January 1955, Strauss and his followers revealed their attitude towards non-European political aspirations and their own jealousy of the Liberals, who might draw away the more enlightened members of their Party, by refusing to perform the customary courtesy of formally introducing the newly-elected and Liberal 'Native' Members to either House. This they left to the Labour Party. Again, a day or two later, Strauss condemned as 'unrealistic and utterly unacceptable' a motion by the Labour Leader that the eight 'Native' Senators be directly elected, and that the Africans of the Free State, Transvaal, Natal and, possibly, South-West Africa also be given 'Native' representation in the Assembly. Lastly, Strauss went back on his own record by declining 'to renew his promise to reinstate the Cape Coloured voters, if they were removed from the common roll.' Small wonder that Strydom should have remarked acidly that the sooner the United Party went to pieces the sooner there would be a more healthy atmosphere.[2]

Non-Europeans knew only too well what they had to expect from the Nationalist Party, because the policy of that Party, unlike the feeble time-serving of the official Opposition, was clear-cut and based on intelligible principles. Further, they could see that Nationalists were practising what they preached in that they had at least begun to carry out those parts of their *apartheid* policy which

---

[1] *Survey*, No. 95, pp. 14 ff.; *Rand Daily Mail*, Dec. 1954 ; *The Times*, Nov. 19, 1954.
[2] *Rand Daily Mail*, Feb. 8, 1955; *Observer*, Dec. 5, 1954.

apparently favoured Europeans, and were showing in their legislation and administration that their ideal was not the parliamentary tradition which they had inherited from the United Kingdom by way of the old Cape Colony, but the Republican tradition of the Trekkers, that is, a paternal Government based on the votes of Europeans and ready to override the Courts themselves if they tried to thwart the will of *Het Volk*. Finally, they could discern no division in a Party all of whose members supported their leader's policy enthusiastically.[1]

It was well for the Nationalists that their Party was so closely knit, because it was now subjected to the strain of a change of leadership. There had been talk of Malan's possible retirement ever since he had unexpectedly stood down from the leadership of the Cape Nationalists in favour of Dönges and, latterly, men had begun to wonder who should be his successor. Some thought that it would be Dönges himself, able, resolute and still comparatively young, but they reflected that the dominant Transvaalers would not accept another Cape man if they could help it. Many more believed that the steady-going and likeable Havenga would be called upon to carry on for a time, for they believed that the Prime Minister wished that this should be so, and they knew that Havenga was an excellent Finance Minister, who had sometimes been acting Prime Minister, a power in the Free State and the only member of the Cabinet who had fought for the Republics during the South African War. On the other hand, they realised that 'Klassie' was seventy-two years old and not in the best of health, and suspected that he was not popular with some of his younger colleagues, because he had been leader of the now defunct Afrikaner Party and was much less enthusiastic than they for a Republic outside the Commonwealth. At one time many had fancied the chances of Havenga's fellow Free Stater, Swart; but he had gradually fallen out of the running, and now political tipsters were freely naming the Transvaaler, Strydom, as the most likely winner. Like Malan, Smuts and Hertzog, Strydom was a Cape-born man. He had gone north after the collapse of the ostrich-feather boom shortly before the Kaiser's war, had practised as a lawyer and captained the Pretoria Rugby Fifteen, and had then reverted to farming, taken to politics and found a safe seat in the Assembly for Waterberg. He had enjoyed an unimpeachable Nationalist reputation since the day when he, alone of Transvaal Nationalists in the Lower House, had joined with Malan in rejecting Coalition and Fusion. Still comparatively young and abounding in vigour, his hopes of the succession were strengthened by the fact that he was Director of the *Voortrekkerpers*, whose publications from *Die Transvaler* downwards profoundly influenced all good Nationalists,

[1] *The Times*, Jan. 12, 1955.

leader of a go-ahead group in the Cabinet which included Eric Louw and Verwoerd, sometime editor of *Die Transvaler*, and virtual master of the Party caucus.[1]

Malan, meanwhile, kept his own counsel and carried on as if he were not even contemplating any decisive step. It was not until mid-October that he took the plunge. After unveiling the famous statue of President Kruger, which had been removed from the station approach to a far more appropriate position in the middle of Church Square almost under the shadow of the Volksraad buildings, he announced that he would resign the leadership of the Party in six weeks' time. A few days later, at George, he explained that he was going because it was wise to make way for a younger man betimes, and begged his followers in no wise to form groups within the Party or hearken to zealots who would fatally bar the door to the 'English' by setting up a purely Afrikaans-speaking Republic.[2] South African Jewry thereupon paid him its highest honour by inscribing his name in its Golden Book as a recognition of his 'contribution to better racial understanding in South Africa.' At last, on November 30, 1954, the Nationalist caucus met in the Volksraad at Pretoria to elect a Party Leader. It duly nominated Havenga and Strydom, who was returning hot-foot from Europe, his first trip overseas. The former, however, stood down as soon as he saw that he had no chance. His absent rival was elected unanimously. Havenga declined to address the excited crowd in Church Square, which was acclaiming the Transvaal's victory over the South with frantic brandishing of the *Vierkleur* and singing of the old Republican *Volkslied* round Kruger's statue. Rumour has it that he muttered that a people usually got the Government it deserved; but History must be content to record that he withdrew from political life to his Free State farm openly saying, 'I am finished.'[3]

Malan at once resigned the office of Prime Minister, and Strydom returned on the very evening of his triumph to be invited by the Governor-General to form a Ministry. This he did without delay. Havenga, of course, and Malan, who had now resigned his seat for Dec. Piketberg, were not included, but the other Ministers were given 1954. office with a minimum of reshuffling. Besides becoming Prime Minister, Strydom took the portfolio of External Affairs; but because he confessedly knew little of overseas affairs, he proposed to hand this over to Eric Louw, who would hold it together with that of Finance, which he now inherited from Havenga. Sauer, a friend of the ex-Finance Minister, a Cape man possessed of a sense of humour that

---

[1] *Survey*, No. 95, p. 3; *Round Table*, No. 178, p. 187.
[2] *Ibid.*, No. 177, p. 82; *Survey*, No. 93, pp. 1 ff.; No. 96, p. 12.
[3] *Round Table*, No. 178, p. 188; *The Times*, Nov. 30, Dec. 1, 1954; *Daily Telegraph*, Dec. 1, 1954.

was possibly not welcome to some of his dourer colleagues and a not altogether successful Minister, had to transfer his portfolio of Transport to Schoeman and take that of Lands in exchange. There were, however, some surprises. First, no room had been found for Diederichs, the Party's economic expert; secondly, the Ministry of Posts and Telegraphs had fallen to the lot of the Party's Chief Whip, Jan Serfontein, a Free Stater, who could, in his new position, be trusted to 'protect' farmers from wage-fixing as valiantly as in his old; thirdly, an appointment which caused some murmuring, Schoeman's portfolio of Labour was given to Johannes de Klerk, who had indeed been a useful member of the Transvaal Executive Committee and a successful organiser of election campaigns as Secretary-General of the Party, but who was also the new Prime Minister's brother-in-law and not yet a Member of either House.[1]

The general effect of these changes was to transfer the balance of power from the Cape to the Transvaal, to give the Strydom group the last word in the Cabinet and to entrust the fortunes of the Union to a man who was far more extreme than Malan had ever been. 'The Lion of the North' was brisk, stocky, easily moved to wrath and given to hitting back hard, but he had his virtues, for he was patently sincere and honest, without any trace of 'slimness.' What he said he meant, and that he tried to do. In some ways, indeed, he was unhappily limited, for he knew little of the outer world and, with the 'clannishness' of his kind, had, of his own choice, few acquaintances outside Nationalist circles. To counterbalance these deficiencies, however, he had a great inner source of strength. Like his friend, Verwoerd, he was a devout *Dopper* of the straitest Calvinistic persuasion, married to a daughter of the *pastorie*, given to quoting Scripture even more freely than his clerical predecessor, and utterly convinced that the *Afrikaner Volk* had a 'divine mission' to uphold white civilisation in Southern Africa.

Strydom speedily told the country what it must expect of him. Though he had made no secret of his belief that the 'English' could never really co-operate with the Afrikaners until both groups were citizens of one Republic, he promised that there should be no major move towards the creation of such a polity during the life of the present Parliament, and that when the change was made, it would only be after a plebiscite or special general election. It would then remain for the Nationalist Party to decide whether or no the Republic

[1] Strydom Ministry: J. G. Strydom, Prime Minister; E. H. Louw, Finance and External Affairs; C. R. Swart, Justice; Dr. Hendrik Frensch Verwoerd, Native Affairs; F. C. Erasmus, Defence; B. J. Schoeman, Transport; Albertus Johannes Roux van Rhyn, Economic Affairs and Mines; Dr. T. E. Dönges, Interior; Johannes Hendricus Viljoen, Education and Forestry; Jan Johnathan Serfontein, Posts and Telegraphs; S. P. le Roux, Agriculture; Jozua François Naudé, Public Health; Johannes de Klerk, Labour; P. O. Sauer, Lands and Irrigation. *Chronology*, X., No. 24, p. 807; *The Times*, Dec. 4, 1954.

should remain within the Commonwealth. Seeing the future, as he did, as a struggle between Nationalism and Liberalism, he proposed to develop the nation along Christian-National lines, to which end Parliament would relegate the Cape Coloured voters to a separate roll with mere token representation and determine the relations between itself and the Judiciary.

The new Prime Minister had latterly dropped his open anti-semitism, and now assured the 'English' that, though he looked forward to the day when the two official languages should have made a 'merger,' they would have fair play in the Republic for their language and other rights and that he himself would seek skilled immigrants without any anti-British bias. He intimated that he would seriously consider the enfranchisement of European youngsters of eighteen, but told the Indians and Bantu bluntly that, because there was no halfway house between *baaskap* and equality, they need not look to him for votes. He further reminded the Bantu that they would be given a more practical education suited to their needs and be 'guided towards maturity' by being taught to achieve self-sufficiency in their own 'homeland.' He undertook to build up the South African Navy, defend Simonstown and push ahead with Malan's projected Pan-Southern African Defence Organisation, to encourage the creation of industries in or near the predominantly African areas of the Transkei, Natal and the eastern Transvaal and to secure the speedy transfer of the governance of the High Commission Territories. Meanwhile, he would follow the path of *apartheid* to the end.[1]

Thus did Strydom give notice to the peoples of the Union that they were to be held to the course which their political masters had marked out.

*   *   *   *   *

Postscript.—Before his death in August 1958 Strydom had carried out much of his policy, notably the transference of the Cape Coloured voters to a separate roll by dint of the wholesale packing of the Senate to get the requisite two-thirds majority. He was succeeded by Verwoerd, who enfranchised the white juveniles and then secured a narrow majority in favour of a republic at a referendum in which the Cape Coloured voters were disfranchised for the occasion and the predominantly Nationalist voters of South-West Africa were allowed to take part, although they were not Union citizens. On 31 May 1961 South Africa became a republic, at Verwoerd's own choice outside the Commonwealth, under the presidency of Swart, her last Governor-General.

[1] *Round Table*, No. 178, p. 189; *Survey*, No. 95, p. 4; *Chronology*, XI., No. 8, p. 267; *Pretoria News*, Dec. 21, 1954; *The Times*, Dec. 13, 1954; *Observer*, Dec. 5, 1954.

SELECT BIBLIOGRAPHY OF BOOKS TO WHICH REFERENCES ARE GIVEN IN THE TEXT

A. BRITISH PARLIAMENTARY PAPERS.

The Session during which each paper was printed is indicated, *e.g.* 1857–8, and the volume for that Session into which it was bound by order of the House concerned, *e.g.* XVI. For a comprehensive list, 1797–1935, *vide C.H.B.E.*, VIII. (2nd ed.), 917 ff.

1814–15, XIII, 916, *Treaty between Great Britain and the United Netherlands, 1814.*

1819, II, 539, *Select Committee on Poor Laws,* 1819.

1821, XIV, 45, *Expense of conveying settlers.*

1826, XXIII, 438, *Papers re British coinage order,* 1825.

1826–7, XXI, 42, *Papers re Prize Slaves* ; 202, *Papers re Slaves* ; 470, XXI, *Papers re S.A. Commercial Advertiser.*

1826–7, XXI, 282, 406, *Commissioners of Inquiry on Cape government and finances.*

1829, V, 300, *Commissioners of Inquiry on Cape trade, harbours, etc.* ; XXV, 335, *Reports from Protectors of Slaves.*

1830, XXI, 8, *Order-in-Council consolidating Slave laws* ; 584, *Commissioners of Inquiry on Native tribes.*

1830–1, XVI, 230, *Measures for helping Slaves.*

1835, XXXIX, 50, 252, *Papers re Native Inhabitants.*

1835, L, 278–II, *Papers re abolition of slavery,* 1834.

1836, I, 471, *Bill for punishment of offences within certain territories adjacent to the Cape.*

1836, VII, 538, *Report of Aborigines Committee* ; XXXIX, 279, *Correspondence re death of Hintsa.*

1837, VII, 238, 425, *Further reports of Aborigines Committee* ; XLIII, 503, *Papers re Kaffir War.*

1840, XXXIII, 323, *Report on Children's Friend Society.*

1846, XXIX, 400, *Applications from the Cape for Representative Government.*

1847, XXXVIII, 786, *Corresp. re Kaffir Tribes.*

1847–8, XLII, 980, *Corresp. re Natal* ; XLIII, 912, 969, *Papers re Kaffir Tribes.*

1849, XXXVI, 1056, *Corresp. re Kaffir Tribes* ; 1059, *Papers re Natal* ; XLIII, 217, *Papers re Convicts.*

1850, XXXVIII, 104, 1138, *Papers re Convicts* ; 1137, 1234, *Corresp. re Representative Assembly* ; 1288, *Papers re Kaffirs* ; 1292, *Corresp. re Natal.*

1851, XIV, 635, *Select Committee on Native Tribes* ; XXXVII, 457, *Appointment of Sir H. Smith as Governor* ; 1360, *Corresp. re Orange River Sovereignty* ; 1362, *Papers re Representative Assembly* ; XXXVIII, 424, 1334, 1352, 1380, *Corresp. re Kaffir Tribes.*

1852, XXXIII, 1427, *Papers re Representative Assembly* ; 1428, *Corresp. re Kaffir Tribes.*

1852–3, LXII, 1697, *Corresp. re Natal* ; LXVI, 1581, 1636, 1640, *Corresp. re Cape Constitutional Ordinances* ; 1635, *Corresp. re Kaffir Tribes* ; 1646, *Corresp. re Orange River Sovereignty.*
1854, XLIII, 1758, *Corresp. re Orange River Sovereignty.*
1854–5, XXXVIII, 1969, *Further corresp. re Kaffir Tribes.*
1856, XLII, 2096, *Grey and the O.R. Territory,* 1855–6.
1857, Sess. 1; X, 2202, *Further papers re Kaffir Tribes.*
1857, Sess. 2, XXVII, 97, *Corresp. re Grant for civilizing Native Tribes.*
1857–8, XL, 389, *German immigration* ; 2352, *Corresp. re Kaffir Tribes.*
1860, XLV, 216, 357, *Recall and reappointment of Sir G. Grey.*
1862, XXXVI, 293, *Correspondence re Natal.*
1865, XXXVII, 3436, *Corresp. re annexation of British Kaffraria.*
1866, XLIX, 476 and 3661, *Corresp. re Bishoprics of Cape Town, etc.* ; (Not printed : 3689, Judgment of the P.C. upon the Bishop of Natal.)
1867–8, XLVIII, 454, *Judgement in Bishop Colenso v. Dean of Maritzburg.*
1868–9, XLIII, 4140, *Corresp. re Moshesh* ; 4141, *Corresp. re alleged kidnapping in Transvaal.*
1870, XLIX, C. 18, C. 99, *Corresp. re Treaty of Aliwal North.* ; 181, 181—I, 181—II, *Corresp. re Responsible Government at the Cape and withdrawal of troops.*
1871, XLVII, C. 459, *Corresp. re Cape Colony.*
1872, XLIII, C. 508, *Corresp. re Cape Colony.*
1873, XLIX, C. 732, *Corresp. re Cape Colony.*
1874, XLV, C. 1025, *Papers re Kaffir outbreak in Natal.*
1875, H.L., XIV, 255, *Papers re Natal Constitution* ; LII, C. 1244, *Proposals for S. African Conference* ; C. 1342, *Papers re Langalibalele* ; C. 1348, *Papers re Griqualand West boundary* ; LII, C. 1342—I and LIII, C. 1121, 1141, 1158, *Papers re Kaffir outbreak in Natal* ; LXXXIII, C. 1361, *Corresp. re Delagoa Bay.*
1876, LII, C. 1399, *Proposal for S. African Conference* ; C. 1401, 1631, *Corresp. re Griqualand West* ; C. 1401–1, *Corresp. re Natal.*
1877, LX, C. 1681, *Corresp. re Griqualand West* ; C. 1732, *Corresp. re Confederation Bill* ; C. 1748, *Transvaal Native affairs :* C. 1776, 1883, *Papers re annexation of Transvaal.*
1878, LV, C. 1961, 1980, 2000, *S. African Corresp.* ; LVI, C. 2079, 2100, 2144, *Further S. African Corresp.* ; C. 2128, *Corresp. re Kruger and Joubert.*
1878–9, LII, C. 2220, 2232, 2342 ; LIII, C. 2252, 2260, 2316, *S. African Corresp.* ; C. 2318, *Disturbances in Basutoland* ; C. 2367, *S. African Corresp.* ; LIV, C. 2374, *Papers re Zulu and Basuto Wars* ; C. 2454, *S. African Corresp.*
1880, L, C. 2482, 2505; LI, C, 2584, 2586, 2655, 2676, *S. African Corresp.*; C. 2569, *Corresp. re Basutoland;* LI (148), *Report on Griqualand West Land Question.*
1881, LXVI, C. 2740, 2783, *S. African Corresp.* ; C. 2754, *Instructions to Sir H. Robinson* ; C. 2755, 2821, *Corresp. re Basutoland* ; LXVII, C. 2837, *S. African Corresp.* ; C. 2892, *Instructions to Transvaal Commissioners* ; C. 2964, *Corresp. re Basutoland* ; C. 2998, *Convention of Pretoria.*
1882, XXVIII, C. 3114, 3219, *Report of Transvaal Commissioners* ; XLVII, C. 3098, 3381, 3419, *Corresp. re Transvaal* ; C. 3112, 3175, *Corresp. re Basutoland* ; C. 3113, *S. African Corresp.* ; C. 3174, *Instructions to Sir H. Bulwer.*
1883, XLVIII, C. 3493, 3708, *Corresp. re Basutoland* ; C. 3796, *Corresp. re Natal* ; XLIX, C. 3466, *Corresp. re Cetewayo* ; C. 3486, 3686, *Corresp. re Transvaal.*

1884, LVI, C. 3855, *Corresp. re Basutoland* ; C. 4190, *Corresp. re Angra Pequeña* ; LVII, C. 4036, *Corresp. re Bechuanaland* ; C. 3841, 4194, *Corresp. re Transvaal* ; C. 3914, 3947, *Corresp. re Convention of London* ; LVIII, C. 3864, 4037, 4191, *Corresp. re Zululand.*

1884–5, LV, C. 4227, *Instructions to . . . Warren . . . re Bechuanaland* ; LV, C. 4442, *British and German spheres* ; LVI, C. 4263–4589, *Corresp. re Basutoland* ; LVI, C. 4590, *Corresp. re Pondoland.*

1884–5, LVI, C. 4214, 4274, 4587, *Corresp. re Zululand* ; C. 4262, 4265, *Corresp. re Angra Pequeña* ; LVII, C. 4213, 4252, 4275, 4432, 4588, *Corresp. re S.A. Republic.*

1886, XLVIII, C. 4643, 4839, 4890, *Corresp. re S.A. Republic* ; C. 4645, *Corresp. re Zululand.*

1887, LIX, C. 4956, 5237, *Corresp. re Bechuanaland* ; LXI, C. 4913, 4980, 5143, *Corresp. re Zululand* ; C. 5089, *Corresp. re Swaziland.*

1888, LXXIV, C. 5390, *Corresp. re Customs and Railway Conference* ; C. 5488, *Corresp. re High Commissionership* ; LXXV, C. 5524, *Corresp. re Bechuanaland.*

1888, LXXV, C. 5410, *Corresp. re Pondoland* ; LXXV, C. 5331, 5522, *Corresp. re Zululand.*

1889, LXIII, C. 8773, *Charter of the B.S.A. Company.*

1890, LI, C. 5903, *Corresp. re Delagoa Bay Railway* ; C. 5904, *Corresp. re Portuguese claims in Mashonaland* ; C. 5918, *Corresp. re Bechuanaland and B.S.A. Company* ; LII, C. 5892, *Corresp. re Zululand* ; C. 6200, *Corresp. re Swaziland* ; C. 6201, *Sir F. de Winton's Report on Swaziland.*

1890–1, LVII, C. 6212, *Corresp. re Anglo-Portuguese Convention* ; C. 6217, *Corresp. re Swaziland Convention* ; C. 6487, *Corresp. re Responsible Government in Natal* ; C. 6495, *Corresp. re Portuguese East Africa* ; XCVI, C. 6375, *Treaty of Lisbon.*

1893–4, LX, 216, *Corresp. re Responsible Government in Natal* ; LXI, C. 7171, 7190, 7196, 7290, *Corresp. re B.S.A. Company, Mashonaland, Matabeleland* ; LXII, C. 7212, *Corresp. re Swaziland* ; C. 7284, *Corresp. re death of two Indunas at Tati.*

1894, LVII, 177, *Corresp. with B.S.A. Company re Customs* ; C. 7383, *Papers re administration of Matabeleland and Mashonaland* ; C. 7554, *Petition from British subjects in S.A. Republic* ; C. 7555, *Sir F. Newton's Report on Matabele affray.*

1895, LXXI, C. 7611, *Corresp. re Swaziland* ; C. 7633, *Corresp. re British residents in S.A. Republic* ; C. 7780, 7878, *Corresp. re Tongaland* ; C. 7782, *Corresp. re Customs and Railway Agreement (Rhodesia)* ; C. 7911, *Papers re British Indians in S.A. Republic.*

1895, LXXI, C. 7637, *Papers re British sphere north of the Zambesi.*

1896, IX, 380, *Report of Select Committee on (the Jameson Raid).*

1896, LIX, C. 7932, *Transfer of British Bechuanaland to Cape Colony* ; C. 7933, 8063, *Corresp. re disturbances in S.A. Republic* ; C. 7962, *Corresp. re Khama and future of Bechuanaland* ; C. 8060, *Instructions to Col. Martin re B.S.A. Company's territories* ; C. 8130, *Report of Matabeleland Land Commission* ; C. 8159, *Papers re commandeering of British subjects in S.A. Republic*; XCVII, C. 7926, 8105, *Anglo-American correspondence re arbitration on Venezuela-British Guiana boundary*; C. 7972, 8012, 8016, 8194, 8195, *Correspondence and Papers re Venezuela-British Guiana boundary.*

1897, IX, 64, 311, 311–1, 311–2, *Reports from Select Committee on South Africa* ; LXII, C. 8380, *Report of Cape Select Committee on Jameson Raid* ; C. 8423, *Corresp. re imprisonment of Reformers* ; C. 8434, *Papers re Manica Arbitration* ; C. 8474, *Papers re closing of Vaal*

Drifts ; C. 8547, *Col. Martin's Report re B.S.A. Company's Native administration*; CII, C. 8439, *Treaty with Venezuela re Boundary with British Guiana.*

1898, LX, C. 8721, *Corresp. re S.A. Republic* ; C 8732, *Corresp. re administration of B.S.A. Company* ; C 8773, *B.S.A. Company's Territories* ; C. 9093, *Report on the Trade, Commerce and Gold Mining Industry of the S.A. Republic.*

1899, LXIII, C. 9138, *Papers re B.S.A. Company* ; C. 9206, *Corresp. re Swaziland* ; C. 9323, *Corresp. re extension of railway to Lake Tanganyika* ; LXIV, C. 9317, *Corresp. re explosives monopoly in S.A. Republic* ; C. 9343, *Corresp. re S.A. Republic's claim for Raid damages* ; C. 9345, *Papers re British subjects in S.A. Republic* ; C. 9404, 9415, 9518, 9521, 9530, *Corresp. re Bloemfontein Conference and reforms in S.A. Republic* ; C. 9507, *Corresp. re Status of S.A. Republic*; CXI, C. 9499, 9500, *Venezuela Case re Venezuela-British Guiana Boundary*; C. 9501, 9533, *Award re Venezuela-British Guiana Boundary.*

1900, LVI, Cd. 35, *Corresp. with the Presidents* ; Cd. 43, 261, 420, *Corresp. re S. Africa* ; Cd. 44, *Corresp. re defence of Natal* ; Cd. 264, *Corresp. re Cape rising* ; Cd. 369, *Corresp. re recent political situation in S. Africa.*

1901, XXIV, Cd. 626, 627, *Reports of S. African Land Settlement Commission* ; XXXV, Cd. 623, 624, 625, *Report of Transvaal Concessions Commission* ; XLVII, Cd. 522, *Kitchener's despatches* ; Cd. 546, 582, *Corresp. re Middelburg Conference* ; Cd. 547, *S. African Corresp.* ; Cd. 663, *Negotiations between Botha and Kitchener* ; XLVIII, Cd. 628, *Report on Transvaal and O.R. Colony's finances.*

1901, XLVII, Cd. 461, *Corresp. re stoppage of resistance* ; XLVII, Cd. 528, *Papers re Middelburg negotiations.*

1902, LXVII, Cd. 893, *Report on Concentration Camps by Mrs Fawcett's Committee* ; Cd. 903, 1163, *S. African Corresp.* ; LXVIII, Cd. 819, 902, *Reports on Refugee Camps* ; LXIX, Cd. 823, *S. African despatches* ; Cd. 904, *Papers re Native legislation in Transvaal* ; Cd. 941, *Corresp. re addition of territory to Natal* ; Cd. 1096, *Corresp. re Boer terms of surrender* ; Cd. 1162, *Papers re Suspension of Cape Constitution* ; Cd. 1200, *Corresp. re S. Rhodesian labour supply* ; Cd. 1284, *Papers re Boer Generals* ; Cd. 1329, *Corresp. re appeal of Boer Generals to civilised world*; LXIX, Cd. 1364, *Report of Martial Law Commission.*

1903, IV, 189, *Loan and War Contribution Bill* ; XLV, Cd. 1463, *Further Corresp.* ; Cd. 1552, 1586, *Papers re Finances* ; Cd. 1531, 1536, 1635, *Papers re British Central Africa.*

1903, XLV, Cd. 1551, 1553, *Papers re Transvaal and O.R. Colony* ; Cd. 1599, 1640, *Papers re Bloemfontein Customs Conference* ; Cd. 1641, *Papers re Intercolonial Council* ; Cd. 1683, *Papers re Indian coolies*; LXXXVII, Cd. 1528, Anglo-Venezuelan Protocol for settlemen of claims, 7 May 1903.

1904, XXXIX, Cd. 1894, 1896, 1897, *Reports of Transvaal Labour Commission* ; LXI, Cd. 1895, 2104, *Corresp. re Transvaal and O.R. Colony*; Cd. 1898, 1899, 1986, 2183, *Corresp. re Transvaal labour* ; LXII, Cd. 2028, *Corresp. re proposed introduction of Chinese into S. Rhodesia.*

1904, XL, Cd. 1789, 1790, 1791, 1792, *Report of Commissioners appointed to inquire into the S.A. War.*

1905, LV, Cd. 2399, *Report of S.A. Native Affairs (Lagden) Commission* ; Cd. 2400, 2479, *Papers re constitutional changes in Transvaal* ; LVI, Cd. 2239, *Corresp. re British Indians in Transvaal.*

1906, LXXIX, Cd. 2905, 2927, 3027, 3147, *Corresp. re Native disturbances in Natal* ; Cd. 2977, *Pietermaritzburg Customs Convention* ; LXXX, Cd. 2788 ; *Corres. re labour in Transvaal mines* ; Cd. 3250, *Transvaal Letters Patent* ; Cd. 3251, *Transvaal Asiatic Law Amendment Ordinance.*

1907, LVII, Cd. 3338, *Report of Transvaal Foreign Labour Department* ; Cd. 3526, *O.R. Colony Letters Patent* ; Cd. 3528, *Corresp. re Transvaal and O.R. Colony* ; Cd. 3564, *Papers re Federation (the Selborne Memorandum).*

1908, LXXII, Cd. 3888, 3998, 4001, 4004, 4194, 4195, 4328, *Corresp. re Natal Native Affairs* ; Cd. 3889, *Report of Natal Native Affairs Commission*; LXXIII, Cd. 3887, 3892, 4327, *Corresp. re Transvaal Asiatic legislation.*

1909, LX, Cd. 4525, 4721, *Report by delegates to S.A. National Convention* ; LXI, Cd. 4587, *Mozambique Convention.*

1910, LXVI, Cd. 5099, *Corresp. re referendum in Natal* ; Cd. 5363, *Corresp. re Asiatic legislation.*

1911, LII, Cd. 5579, *Corresp. re Union Immigration Bill (Asiatics).*

1912–13, LIX, Cd. 6087, *Corresp. re Transvaal Gold and Township Law* ; Cd. 6283, *Corresp. re Asiatic Immigration Bill.*

1913, XLV, Cd. 6941, 6942, *Corresp. re employment of Regulars in Rand disturbances.*

1914, XLIX, Cd. 7112, *Report of Commission on Witwatersrand disturbances* ; Cd. 7265, *Report of Indian Inquiry Commission* ; LIX, Cd. 7348, *Corresp. re General Strike* ; Cd. 7264, *Corresp. re S. Rhodesian Constitution* ; LX, Cd. 7509, *Corresp. re ownership of land in S. Rhodesia.*

1914–16, XLV, Cd. 7645, *Corresp. re continuance of the B.S.A. Company's Charter* ; Cd. 7873, *Corresp. re expedition against German South-West Africa* ; Cd. 7874, *Report re Rebellion* ; Cd. 7970, *B.S.A. Company's Supplemental Charter.*

1917–18, XXIII, Cd. 8674, *Papers re S. Rhodesia Native Reserves Commission.*

1921, XXIV, Cmd. 1129, *Papers re (Cave) Commission on money due to B.S.A. Company* ; Cmd. 1273, 1471, *First* and *Second Report of (Buxton) Committee on Rhodesia.*

1922, XVI, Cmd. 1573, *S. Rhodesia Responsible Government Letters Patent.*

1923, XVIII, Cmd. 1914, *Corresp. re B.S.A. Company in N. and S. Rhodesia* ; Cmd. 1984, *Agreement re position of B.S.A. Company.*

1924, XXVI, Cmd. 2220, *Memo. re Germans in South-West Africa.*

1928–9, V, Cmd. 3234, *Report of (Hilton Young) Commission on closer union in East and Central Africa.*

1929–30, XXIII, Cmd. 3573, *Memo. on Native policy in East Africa* ; Cmd. 3574, *Conclusions of H.M. Government on closer union in East Africa* ; XXXI, Cmd. 3487, *S. African treaty of commerce with Germany* ; Cmd. 3495, *S. African convention with Mozambique.*

1930–1, XXXVI, Cmd. 3676, *S. African-Mozambique commercial agreement.*

1931–2, VII, Cmd. 4114, *(Pim) Report on position of Swaziland.*

1932–3, X, Cmd. 4368, *(Pim) Report on position of Bechuanaland Protectorate.*

1934–5, VII, Cmd. 4907, *(Pim) Report on position of Basutoland.*

1935, VII, Cmd. 5009, *Report of Commission on Disturbances in the Copper Belt*; Colonial No. 150, *Report on Labour Conditions in N. Rhodesia.*

1938, Colonial No. 145, *(Pim) Report on position of Northern Rhodesia*; Colonial No. 152, *(Bell) Report on position of Nyasaland.*

1939, Cmd. 5949, *Report of the Rhodesia-Nyasaland (Bledisloe) Royal Commission.*

1945–47, Colonial No. 191 *and* 210, *Inter-Territorial Organization in East Africa.*

1950, XIX, Cmd. 7913, *Statement on Succession to the Bamangwato Chieftainship.*

1951, X, Cmd. 8209, *Report on ' Diretlo ' murders in Basutoland*; Cmd. 8233, *Report of Conference on Closer Association*; XXVI, Cmd. 8235, *Comparative Survey of Central African Native policies.*

1952, XXIV, Cmd. 8573 ; *Draft Federal Scheme, May* 1952; IX, Cmd. 8671, *Report of the Judicial Commission*; Cmd. 8672, *Report of the Fiscal Commission*; Cmd. 8673, *Report of the Civil Service Preparatory Commission*; XXIII, Cmd. 8707, *H. C. Territories: History of Discussions with the Union.*

1953, Cmd. 8753, 8754, *Report of the Conference on Federation.*

1955, Cmd. 9520, *Exchange of Letters on Defence . . .*

B. UNION OF SOUTH AFRICA PARLIAMENTARY PAPERS.

1911, S.C. 2, *Report on Public Education.*

1912, U.G. 10, *Report of Commission on Trade and Industries*; U.G. 11 and 14, *Reports of Financial Relations Commission.*

1913, U.G. 30, 31 and 37, *Reports of Public Service Commission*; U.G. 55 and 56, *Report of Witwatersrand Disturbances Commission.*

1914, U.G. 12, *Report of Economic Commission*; U.G. 16, *Report of Indian Enquiry Commission*; U.G. 48, *Report of Commission re deaths of General de la Rey and Dr. Grace.*

1915, U.G. 10, *Report on the Rebellion.*

1916, U.G. 19, 22 and 25, *Report of Native Land (Beaumont) Commission*; U.G. 45, *Report of Provincial Administration Commission*; U.G. 42 and 46, *Minutes* and *Report of Judicial Inquiry into the Rebellion.*

1917, U.G. 6 and 19, *Report* and *Proceedings of State Mining Commission*; U.G. 8, *Minutes of Provincial Administration Commission.*

1918, U.G. 1, *Report of State Mining Commission*; U.G. 4, *Agreement re Modderfontein Areas*; U.G. 8, 22, 23, 31, 34 and 41, *Reports of Provincial and other Commissions on Native Lands.*

1919, U.G. 34, *Report re administration of South-West Africa for 1918*; U.G. 39, *Treaty of Peace (Versailles)*; U.G. 44, *Corresp. re Mandate for South-West Africa.*

1920, U.G. 34, *Final Report of Low Grade Mines Commission.*

1921, U.G. 4, *Report of Asiatic Inquiry Commission*; U.G. 16 and 34, *Interim Reports of Unemployment Commission*; U.G. 24, *Report of Commission on Government in South-West Africa*; A. 4, *Report of Native Affairs Commission re ' Israelites ' at Bulhoek.*

1922, U.G. 17, *Report of Unemployment Commission*; U.G. 30, *Report on Bondelzwarts Rising*; U.G. 35, *Report of Martial Law Commission*; U.G. 39, *Report of Mining Industry Board*; White Papers (1) *Corresp. re defence of Cape Peninsula (Simonstown Agreement)*; (2) *Corresp. re transfer of Imperial War Department property.*

1923, U.G. 19, *Report of Financial Relations Commission*; U.G. 41, *First Report of Education Administration Commission*; White Paper, *Corresp. re terms for inclusion of Southern Rhodesia in the Union.*

1924, U.G. 19, *Second Report of Education Administration Commission.*

1926, U.G. 14, *Report of Economic and Wage Commission*; U.G. 41, *Rapport van die Rehoboth Kommissie.*

1927, S.C. 6A and 10, *Reports of Select Committee on Native Affairs.*

1928, U.G. 33, *Report of University Commission.*

1931, U.G. 21, *Report of the Mandates Commission*; U.G. 39, *Report of the Indian Penetration Commission.*

1932, U.G. 22, *Report of Native Economic Commission*; unofficial *Report of the Carnegie Commission on the Poor White problem, 1932-3.*

1934, U. G. 7, *Report of Transvaal Asiatic Land Tenure (Feetham) Commission, Parts I and II.*

1935, U.G. 22, *Report of Transvaal Asiatic Land Tenure (Feetham) Commission, Part III*; Joint Committee No. 1, *Report on Native Representation*; U.G. 37, *Report of the Industrial Legislation Commission.*

1937, U.G. 48, *Report of the Native Affairs Commission for 1936*; U.G. 54, *Report of the Cape Coloured Population Commission*; U.G. 54, *Report re Cape Coloured Population.*

1939, U.G. *Report of the Indian Penetration Commission.*

1941, U.G. 39, *Report of the Indian Penetration Commission.*

1943, U.G. 21, *Report of the Second Indian Penetration Commission* (Durban).

1948, U.G. 28, *Report of the Native Laws Commission.*

1949, U.G. 36, *Report of the Commission of Enquiry into Riots in Durban.*

1950, U.G. 47, *Report of Commission of Inquiry into evidence by Natives (on the Rand).*

1954, U.G. 20, 21, *Report (on) the Subject Matter of the Separate Representation of Voters Validation and Amendment Act.*

C. BRITISH PARLIAMENTARY DEBATES.

Prior to 1813, these are given in *Cobbett's Parliamentary History* and *Parliamentary Debates*; thereafter in *Hansard's Parliamentary Debates*. References below indicate series, volume and column.

Motion *re* expenses of Cape, 1795-1802; June 11, 1804, *Cobbett's Parl. Hist.*, II, 610.

Question *re* capture of Cape; April 16, 1806; *Cobbett's Parl. Debates*, VI, 753.

Lords. Debate on emigration to Cape; July 12, 1819, *Hansard*, 2, XI, 1549.

Wilberforce on slavery at Cape; July 25, 1822, *Hansard*, 2, VII, 1783.

Debate *re* Somerset's conduct; December 7, 8, 1826, *Hansard*, 2, XVI, 303, 320.

Cape petition for responsible government; June 8, 1827, *Hansard*, 2, XVII, 1168; and May 24, 1830, 2, XXIV, 1005.

Motion *re* treatment of aborigines; July 14, 1835, *Hansard*, 3, XXXIX, 549.

Albany petition; July 10, 1838, *Hansard*, 3, XLIV, 114.

Lords. Debate on Cape petition; June 21, 1842, *Hansard*, 3, LXIV, 272.

Cape Dutch petition *re* representation; June 2, 1848, *Hansard*, 3, XCIX, 249.

Lords. Petitions *re* Legislative Council; February 6, 1851, *Hansard*, 3, CXIV, 156.

Lords. Question *re* Sir H. Smith's policy; May 20, 1851, *Hansard*, 3, CXVI, 1153.

Cape petitions for representative government; June 4, 1851, *Hansard*, 3, CXVII, 399.

Lords. Motion for committee on Cape representative government; July 15, 1851, *Hansard*, 3, CXVIII, 694.

Question *re* recall of Sir H. Smith; February 9, 1852, *Hansard*, 3, CXIX, 251.

Re Orange River Territory; May 9, 1854, *Hansard*, 3, CXXXIII, 52.

Re German Legion at Cape; May 22, 1857, *Hansard*, 3, CXLV, 753.

British Kaffraria Annexation Bill; February 16, 1865, *Hansard*, 3, CLXXVII, 312.

Lords. *Re* Colonial Bishoprics; June 18, July 13, 1866, *Hansard*, 3, CLXXXIV, 503, 787.
Re Cape Town railway; June 15, 1866, *Hansard*, 3, CLXXXIV, 501.
Re S. African Confederation; March 3, 1871, *Hansard*, 3, CCIV, 1275.
Lords. *Re* Cape responsible government; March 8, 11, 1872, *Hansard*, 3, CCIX, 1621, 1747.
Re S. African Confederation; May 28, 1872, *Hansard*, 3, CCXI, 806.
Re Cape responsible government; July 29, August 8, 1872, *Hansard*, 3, CCXIII, 24, 698.
Re Delagoa Bay, Basutoland, etc.; February 21, 1873, *Hansard*, 3, CCXIV, 790.
Re Zulu War, March 14, 17, 24, 25, 27, 28, 1879; *Hansard*, 3, CCXLIV, 931, 1038, 1503, 1606, 1864, 1865, 1991; March 31, 1879, 3, CCXLV, 20; May 27, 1879, 3, CCXLVI, 1364.
Re Basuto Disarmament, May 25, 1880; *Hansard*, 3, CCLII, 451.
Annexation of Transvaal; August 7, 1877, *Hansard*, 3, CCXXXVI, 545; August 15, 1878, 3, CCXLII, 2061.
Lords. *Re* Frere's Salary, June 10, 1880; *Hansard*, 3, CCLII, 1579.
Lords. *Re* Zulu campaign, September 2, 1880, *Hansard*, 3, CCLVI, 1025.
Re Basutoland, January 20, 1881, *Hansard*, 3, CCLVII, 1065.
Annexation of Transvaal, January 21, 1881, *Hansard*, 3, CCLVII, 1109.
Lords. *Re* Transvaal Triumvirate, February 21, 1881; *Hansard*, 3, CCLVIII, 1345.
Re Transvaal negotiations, March 4, 1881; *Hansard*, 3, CCLIX, 326.
Lords. *Re* Transvaal peace arrangements, March 31, 1881; *Hansard*, 3, CCLX, 249.
Re Transvaal rising, July 15, 20, 25, 1881; *Hansard*, 3, CCLXII, 1009, 1368, 1756.
Re Cetewayo, August 16, 1881; *Hansard*, 3, CCLXV, 149; April 17, 1882, *Hansard*, 3, CCLXVIII, 756.
Lords. *Re* Angra Pequena, May 12, 1884; *Hansard*, 3, CCLXXXVIII, 3; June 19, 30, 1884, *Hansard*, 3, CCLXXXIX, 787, 1653.
Re Bechuanaland, November 13, 1884; *Hansard*, 3, CCXCIII, 1655.
Re Stellaland, May 1, 1885; *Hansard*, 3, CCXCVII, 1279.
Lords. British missionaries in East Africa, May 28, 1889; *Hansard*, 3, CCCXXXVI, 1224.
Lords. *Re* Delagoa Bay, July 9, 1889; *Hansard*, 3, CCCXXXVII, 1793.
Lords. *Re* Portugal and East Africa, May 16, 1890; *Hansard*, 3, CCCXLIV, 1094.
Re Anglo-German Agreement Bill, July 24, 25, 28, 1890; *Hansard*, 3, CCCXLVII, 743, 917, 1077.
Lords. *Re* Swaziland, August 4, 1890; *Hansard*, 3, CCCXLVII, 1713.
Lords. *Re* Anglo-Portuguese African treaty, June 11, 1891; *Hansard*, 3, CCCLIV, 135.
Re Swaziland, May 4, 1893; *Hansard*, Series 4, XII, 131.
Re Matabeleland, November 9, 1893; *Hansard*, 4, XVIII, 537.
Re Rhodes and Cape hinterland, January 12, 1894; *Hansard*, 4, XX, 1446.
Re African companies, March 15, 1894; *Hansard*, 4, XXII, 391.
Matabeleland and Mashonaland Agreement, July 31, 1894; *Hansard*, 4, XXVII, 1480.
Re Transvaal, August 17, 18, 1894; *Hansard*, 4, XXVIII, 1466, 1490.
Re Swaziland, August 18, 1894; *Hansard*, 4, XXVIII, 1507.
Re Transvaal and Swaziland, February 6, 1895; *Hansard*, 4, XXX, 133.
Re Swaziland, March 14, 1895; *Hansard*, XXXI, 1064.
Appointment of Sir H. Robinson, March 28, 1895; *Hansard*, 4, XXXII, 426.

Swaziland affairs, March 29, 1895; *Hansard*, 4, XXXII, 487.
Lords. Personal explanation by Lord Loch, May 1, 1896; *Hansard*, 4, XL, 313.
Lords. *Re* Trial of Jameson, July 2, 1896; *Hansard*, 4, XLII, 516.
Select Committee on Jameson Raid, July 30, 1896; *Hansard*, 4, XLIII, 1057.
Select Committee on Brit. S. Africa, August 11, 1896; *Hansard*, 4, XLIV, 566; January 21, 28, 29, February 5, 1897; *Hansard*, 4, XLV, 171, 762, 801, 1417
Africa and European Powers, April 2, 1897; *Hansard*, 4, XLVIII, 425.
B.S.A. Company, February 8, 1898; *Hansard*, 4, LIII, 79.
Lords. *Re* Bloemfontein Conference, June 8, 1899; *Hansard*, 4, LXXII, 597.
Re Bloemfontein Conference, June 8, 1899; *Hansard*, 4, LXXII, 636.
Transvaal. Explanation by Chamberlain, July 6, 1899; *Hansard*, 4, LXXIV, 40.
Cape. Statement by Chamberlain, July 25, 1899; *Hansard*, 4, LXXV, 278.
Lords. S.A. crisis, October 17, 1899; *Hansard*, 4, LXXVII, 3.
S.A. crisis, October 17, 18, 19, 25, 27, 1899; *Hansard*, 4, LXXVII, 60, 181, 254, 600, 765.
Lords. *Re* Butler's despatches, February 1, 1900; *Hansard*, 4, LXXVIII, 244.
Jameson Raid Committee, February 20, 1900; *Hansard*, 4, LXXIX, 599.
Concentration camps, June 17, 1901; *Hansard*, 4, XCV, 573.
Martial Law in S. Africa, April 24, 1902; *Hansard*, 4, CVI, 1208.
Lords. *Re* peace terms, June 2, 5, 1902; *Hansard*, 4, CVIII, 1086, 1510.
Lords. *Re* British settlers in S. Africa, July 15, 1902; *Hansard*, 4, CXI, 219.
Cape Constitution, July 29, August 6, 1902; *Hansard*, 4, CXII, 23, 810.
Lords. Chinese labour, February 11, 12, 1904; *Hansard*, 4, CXXIX, 965, 1141.
Chinese labour, February 16, 17, 22, 1904; *Hansard*, 4, CXXIX, 1501, and CXXX, 26, 631.
Lords. Chinese labour, March 4, 18, 21, 1904; *Hansard*, 4, CXXXI, 167, and CXXXII, 4, 117.
Lords. *Re* Transvaal Labour Ordinance, August 11, 1904; *Hansard*, 4, CXL, 196.
Lords. Chinese labour, February 27, 1905; *Hansard*, 4, CXLI, 1277.
Selborne's appointment as High Commissioner, March 6, 1905; *Hansard*, 4, CXLII, 491.
Lords. *Re* Transvaal and O.R. Colony, February 26, 27, 1906; *Hansard*, 4, CLII, 706, 906.
Lords. *Re* land settlement in Transvaal, March 27, 1906; *Hansard*, 4, CLIV, 1019.
Lords. *Re* Transvaal Constitution, July 31, 1906; *Hansard*, 4, CLXII, 611.
Lords. *Re* British settlers in S. Africa, November 14, 1906; *Hansard*, 4, CXLIV, 1382.
Lords. *Re* Transvaal and O.R.C. Constitutions, December 17, 1906; *Hansard*, 4, CLXVII, 939.
Re Transvaal and O.R.C. Constitutions, December 17, 1906; *Hansard*, 4, CLXVII, 1063.
Lords. *Re* Chinese labour, June 27, 1907; *Hansard*, 4, CLXXVII, 56.
Lords. *Re* Indians in Transvaal, May 19, 1908; *Hansard*, CLXXXIX, 35.
Lords. *Re* S.A. Federation Convention, February 16, 1909; *Hansard*, 5th Series (Lords), I, 3, 9, 20, 31.
King's Speech—S.A. Constitution, February 16, 1906; *Hansard*, 5th Series (Commons), I, 13.
Lords. S. Africa Bill, Royal Assent, September 20, 1909; *Hansard*, 5th Series (Lords), III, 1.

Re S. African Union Bill, July 27, 1909; *Hansard*, 5th Series (Commons), VIII, 1023.

Lords. *Re* S. Africa Constitution, February 31, 1910; *Hansard*, 5th Series (Lords), V, 4, 7, 13, 16, 30.

Re Union of S. Africa, June 27, 1912; *Hansard*, 5th Series (Commons), XL, 572.

Re Rand strike, July 7, 8, 14, 31, 1913; *Hansard*, 5th Series (Commons), LV, 35, 242, 879 and LVI, 801.

Lords. *Re* Indians in S. Africa, July 3, 1913; *Hansard*, 5th Series (Lords), XIV, 1507.

Re Union of S.A. Indemnity Bill, February 12, 1914; *Hansard*, 5th Series (Commons), LVIII, 353.

Lords. King's Speech—Rebellion in S. Africa, November 11, 1914; *Hansard*, 5th Series (Lords), XVIII, 17, 32.

Re S. Rhodesia Native Control Bill, December 20, 1927; *Hansard*, 5th Series (Commons), CCXII, 368.

Re the Rhodesias, February 20 and July 13, 1928; *Hansard*, 5th Series (Commons), CCXII, 1281 and CCXIX, 2649.

Lords. *Re* S.A. Protectorates, July 26 and December 13, 1933; *Hansard*, 5th Series (Lords), LXXXVIII, 1121 and XC, 466.

D. WORKS.

ABBOTT, W. C., *The Expansion of Europe.* 1925.

AGAR-HAMILTON, J. A. I., *The Native Policy of the Voortrekkers* 1928.
„ „ *A Transvaal Jubilee, being a History of the Church of the Province of South Africa in the Transvaal.* 1928.
„ „ *The Road to the North* 1937.

AMERY, L. S. (general editor), ' *The Times* ' *History of the War in South Africa, 1899–1902.* Seven volumes. 1900–9.

AMPHLETT, G. T., *The History of the Standard Bank of South Africa, Limited, 1863–1913.* 1914.

ANDREWS, C. F., *Documents relating to the New Asiatic Bill.* 1926.
„ „ *Documents relating to the Indian Question.* 1926.

ANGOVE, J., *In the Early days : Reminiscences of Pioneer Life in the S.A. Diamond Fields.* 1910.

ARNDT, E. H. D., *Banking and Currency Development in South Africa, 1652–1927.* 1928.

ARNOT, D., and ORPEN, F. H. S., *The Land Question of Griqualand West.* 1875.

ARTHUR, SIR G., *Life of Lord Kitchener.* 1920.

AYLWARD, A., *The Transvaal of To-day.* 1878.

AUTHORITY, published by, *A Record of the Organisation of the Director-General of War Supplies (1939) and Director-General of Supplies (1943–1945).* 1945.

BAINES, T., *The Gold Regions of South-Eastern Africa.* 1877.
„ „ *The Northern Goldfields Diaries of Thomas Baines, 1869–72.* Three volumes. 1946.

BALLINGER, W. G., *Race and Economics in South Africa.* 1934.

' BA-MANGWATO,' *To Ophir Direct, or the South African Goldfields.* 1868.

[BARNARD, LADY ANNE], *South Africa a Century Ago.* 1st edition. 1901.
2nd „ 1924.

BARNES, L., *The New Boer War.* 1932.
„ „ *Caliban in Africa.* 1930.

BARROW, JOHN, *Travels into the Interior of Southern Africa.* Two
    volumes. 1801.
BARTLETT, V., *Struggle for Africa.* 1953.
BEAZLEY, C. R., *Prince Henry the Navigator.* 1908.
BELL, K. N., and MORRELL, W. P., *Select Documents on British
    Colonial Policy, 1830–60.* 1928.
BENT, J. T., *The Ruined Cities of Mashonaland.* 1892.
BEYERS, C., *Die Kaapse Patriotte, 1779–91.* 1929.
BIRD, J., *The Annals of Natal.* Two Volumes. 1888.
[BIRD, W.], *The State of the Cape in 1822.* 1823.
BLOK, P. J., *Geschiedenis van het Nederlandsche Volk*, VI, VII. 1907.
BLOMMAERT, W., *Het Invoeren van de Slavernij aan de Kaap (Argief-
    Jaarboek vir S-A. Geskiedenis*, I). 1938.
BOTHA, C. G., *The French Refugees at the Cape.* 1919–23.
      ,,   ,,   *Early Inferior Courts of Justice (S.A. Law Journal*,
    1921); *Early Cape Land Tenure (ibid.*, 1919); *The Dispersion
    of the Stock Farmers . . . in the 18th Century*, and *Prices in the
    18th Century (S.A. Journal of Science*, 1923).
BOTHA, P. R., *Die Staatkundige Ontwikkeling van die Suid-Afrik-
    aanse Republiek onder Kruger en Leyds.* 1926.
BOYCE, W. B., *Notes on South African Affairs from 1834 to 1838.* 1838.
British Commonwealth Relations (ed. A. J. Toynbee). 1934.
British Central Africa. Fabian Colonial Bureau pamphlet. 1951.
BROOKE, A., *Robert Gray, First Bishop of Cape Town.* 1947.
BROOKES, E. H., *The History of Native Policy in South Africa from
        1830 to the present day.* 1924.
    ,,   ,,   *The Colour Problems of South Africa.* 1934.
BROWNLEE, C., *Reminiscences of Kaffir Life and History.* 1896.
BRYCE, JAMES, (LORD), *Impressions of South Africa.* 1899.
BUCHAN, JOHN, *The History of the South African Forces in France.* 1920.
BUCKLE, G. E., and MONYPENNY, W. F., *The Life of Benjamin
    Disraeli, Earl of Beaconsfield*, Vol. VI. 1920.
Bulletin of International News (Chatham House, July 1923–June
    1945 onwards). 1923–45.
BURCHELL, W. J., *Travels in the Interior of Southern Africa.* Two
    volumes. 1822–4.
BUTLER, SIR W., *Autobiography of Sir William Butler.* 1911.
BUXTON, EARL, *General Botha.* 1924.

CACHET, F. L., *Die Worstelstryd der Transvalers.* 1899.
Cambridge History of the British Empire, Vol. VIII. 1936.
CAMPBELL, P. C., *Chinese Coolie Emigration to Countries within the
    British Empire.* 1923.
CARTER, T. F., *A Narrative of the Boer War.* 1900.
CASILIS, J. E., *The Basutos.* (translation) 1861.
CATON-THOMPSON, G., *The Zimbabwe Culture.* 1931.
CHAPMAN, J., *Travels in the Interior of South Africa.* Two volumes. 1868.
CHASE, J. C., *Natal Papers.* Two volumes. 1843.
    ,,   ,,   *The Cape of Good Hope and Algoa Bay.* 1843.
Chronology of International Events and Documents. (Chatham 1954
    House). onwards.
CILLIERS, A. C., *General Hertzog en Hereeniging* 1940.
    ,,   ,,   *Die Stryd om Volkseenheid.* 1941.
CLAPHAM, J. H., *An Economic History of Modern Britain*, I. 1930.
CLOETE, HENRY, *The History of the Great Boer Trek* (edited by
    W. Brodrick-Cloete). 1900.

COLENBRANDER, H. T., *Gedenkstukken der Algemeene Geschiedenis van Nederland*, XXIII. 1914.
COLENSO, F. E., and DURNFORD, E., *The History of the Zulu War and its Origin.* 1881.
COLQUHOUN, A. R., *Mashonaland.* 1893.
COLVIN, I., *The Life of Jameson.* Two volumes. 1923.
COOK, E. T., *Rights and Wrongs of the Transvaal War.* 1901.
„   „   *Edmund Garrett. A Memoir.* 1909.
CORY, SIR G. E., *The Rise of South Africa.* Five volumes.   1910–30.
COWEN, D. V., *Parliamentary Sovereignty and the Entrenched Clauses of the S.A. Act.* 1951.
COUPLAND, R., *Wilberforce.* 1923.
Crockford's Clerical Directory, 1951–52. 1952.
CUNNINGHAM, W., *An Essay on Western Civilisation in its Economic Aspects.* Two volumes. 1904.
CUNYNGHAME, A. T., *My Command in South Africa, 1874–8.* 1879.

D'ANDRADA, J. C. P., *Manica, being a Report and Protest of the Affairs occurred at Manica.* 1891.
DADOO, Y. M., *Five Months of Struggle (Indian Passive Resistance, June 13–November 13, 1946).* 1946.
DARTER, A., *The Pioneers of Mashonaland.* 1914.
DAVIDSON, B., *Report on Southern Africa.* 1952.
DAVIDSON, J. W., *The Northern Rhodesian Legislative Council.* 1947.
DÉHERAIN, H., *L'Expansion des Boers au XIX Siècle.* 1905.
„   „   *Le Cap de Bonne-Espérance au XVII Siècle.* 1909.
DE KIEWIET, C. W., *British Colonial Policy and the South African Republics, 1848–72.* 1929.
„   „   *The Imperial Factor in South Africa.* 1937.
DE KOCK, M. H., *Economic History of South Africa.* 1924.
DE WAAL, D. C., *With Rhodes in Mashonaland.* 1896.
DE WET, C. R., *Three Years War.* 1902.
DORNAN, S. S., *Rhodesian Ruins and Native Tradition (S.A. Journal of Science, 1915).* 1915.
DREYER, A., *Die Kaapse Kerk en die Groot Trek.* 1929.
DUGDALE, E. T. S., *German Diplomatic Documents, 1871–1914,* Vols. II, III. 1929.
DU PLESSIS, J., *Christian Missions in South Africa.* 1911.
DU PLESSIS, I. D., *The Cape Malays.* 1944.

EDWARDS, I. E., *The 1820 Settlers in South Africa.* 1934.
„   „   *Towards Emancipation.* 1942.
ELLENBERGER, D. F., and MACGREGOR, J. C., *History of the Basutos.* 1912.
ENGELBRECHT, S. P., *Geschiedenis van die Niederduits Hervormde Kerk in Zuid-Afrika.* Two volumes. 1920–25.
„   „   (editor), *Paul Kruger's Amptelike Briewe, 1851–77.* 1925.
„   „   *Thomas François Burgers.* 1933.
ENGELENBURG, F. V., *'N Onbekende Paul Kruger.* 1925.
„   „   *General Louis Botha.* 1929.
EVANS, MAURICE S., *Black and White in South East Africa.* 1916.
EYBERS, G. W., *Select Constitutional Documents illustrating South African History, 1795–1910.* 1918.

FITZMAURICE, LORD E., *Life of the Second Earl Granville.* Two volumes. 1905.

FITZPATRICK, (SIR) J. P., *The Transvaal from within.* 1899.
„ „ „ *South African Memories.* 1932.
FOUCHÉ, L., *Die Evolutie van die Trekboer.* 1909.
„ „ *Het Dagboek van Adam Tas* (text also in English). 1914.
„ „ *Mapungubwe.* 1937.
FREEMAN, J. J., *A Tour in South Africa.* 1851.
FRIPP, C. E., and HILLER, V. W. (editors), *Gold and the Gospel in Mashonaland.* 1949.
FROUDE, J. A., *Two Lectures on South Africa.* 1880.

GARDINER, A. F., *Narrative of a Journey to the Zoolu Country.* 1835.
GARDINER, A. G., *Life of Sir William Harcourt.* Two volumes. 1923.
GARVIN, J. L., *The Life of Joseph Chamberlain.* Three volumes. 1932–34.
GERMAN GENERAL STAFF, *The War in South Africa from October 1899 to September 1900* (translation). 1904–6.
GEYER, A. L., *Das Wirtschaftliche System . . . am Kap, 1785–95.* 1923.
GIE, S. F. N., *Geskiedenis van Suid-Afrika,* Vol. I. 1924.
GODEE-MOLSBERGEN, E. C., *De Stichter van Hollands Zuid-Afrika. Jan Van Riebeeck.* 1912.
„ „ *Reizen in Zuid-Afrika* (Linschoten-Vereeniging). Three volumes. 1916–22.
GOLDMANN, C. S., *South African Mines.* . . . . Three volumes. 1895–6.
GOOCH, C. P., and TEMPERLEY, H. W. V., *British Documents on the Origins of the War,* I. 1927.
GOODFELLOW, D. M., *A Modern Economic History of South Africa.* 1931.
GRANT, P. W., *Considerations on the state of the colonial currency . . . at the Cape.* 1825.
GRAY, C. N., *Life of Robert Gray, Bishop of Capetown.* Two volumes. 1876.
GREEN, J. E. S., *Rhodes goes North.* 1936.
GRESWELL, W., *Our South African Empire.* 1885.
GREY, EARL, *The Colonial Policy of Lord John Russell's Administration.* Two volumes. 1853.

HAGGARD, (SIR) H. RIDER, *Cetewayo and his White Neighbours.* 1882.
HAKLUYT, R., *The Principal Navigations . . . of the English Nation.* Two volumes. 1599.
Hakluyt Society, Publications of the, Vols. LVI, LIX. 1877–80.
HALFORD, S. J., *The Griquas of Griquatown.* 1950.
HALL, R. N., *Great Zimbabwe.* 1904.
„ „ *Pre-Historic Rhodesia.* 1909.
„ „ and NEAL, G. W., *The Ancient Ruins of Rhodesia.* 1902.
HANCOCK, W. K., *Survey of British Commonwealth Affairs, 1918–1936.* 1937.
HARDINGE, SIR A., *The Life of Henry Howard Molyneux Herbert, Fourth Earl of Carnarvon.* 1925.
HARRIS, JOHN, *Collections of Voyages,* I. 1705.
HARRIS, W. CORNWALLIS, *The Wild Sports of Southern Africa.* 1839.
HATCH, J., *The Dilemma of South Africa* 1952.
HATTERSLEY, A. F., *More Annals of Natal.* 1936.
„ „ *Later Annals of Natal.* 1938.
„ „ *The Natalians.* 1940.
„ „ *Portrait of a Colony. The Story of Natal.* 1940.
„ „ *The British Settlement of Natal.* 1950.
HEADLAM, C., *The Milner Papers, 1897–1905.* Two volumes. 1931–33.

HEERES, J. E., *De Overgang der Kaapkolonie van Nederland in Engeland's bezit.* 1897.
HELLMAN, E. (editor), *Handbook of Race Relations in South Africa.* 1949.
HENDERSON, G. C., *Sir George Grey.* 1907.
HERRMAN, L., *The Jews in South Africa.* 1930.
HERTSLET, L. and E., *The Map of Africa by Treaty.* Three volumes. 1909.
HICKS BEACH, LADY VICTORIA, *The Life of Sir Michael Hicks Beach.* Two volumes. 1932.
HODGSON, M. L., and BALLINGER, W. G., *Indirect Rule in Southern Africa (No. 1) : Basutoland.* 1931.
    "   "   "   " *Britain in Southern Africa (No. 2) : Bechuanaland Protectorate.* 1932.
HOERNLE, R. F. A., *South African Native Policy and the Liberal Spirit.* 1939.
HOFMEYR, J. H., *The Life of Jan Hendrik Hofmeyr.* 1913.
    "   " *South Africa.* 1931.
    "   " and others, *Coming of Age.* 1930.
HOFMEYR, S., *Twintig Jaren in Zoutpansberg.* 1890.
HOGE, J., *Geskiedenis van die Lutherse Kerk aan die Kaap (Argief-Jaarboek vir S-A. Geskiedenis,* II). 1938.
HOLE, H. MARSHALL, *The Making of Rhodesia.* 1926.
    "   " *The Jameson Raid.* 1930.
HUNTER, M., *Reaction to Conquest.* 1936.
HUTCHINSON, H., and NANKIVELL, J. W., *South Africa. Its Land and Its Peoples.* 1934.

ISAACS, N., *Travels and Adventures in Eastern Africa.* Two volumes. 1836.

JEPPE, C., *The Kaleidoscopic Transvaal.* 1906.
JOHNSTON, SIR H. H., *A History of the Colonisation of Africa.* 1905.
JORISSEN, E. J. P., *Transvaalsche Herinneringen.* 1897.
Journal of the Royal Institute of International Affairs. 1922 onwards.

KEANE, A. H., *The Gold of Ophir.* 1901.
KEITH, A. BERRIEDALE, *Selected Speeches and Documents on British Colonial Policy, 1763–1917.* 1918.
    "   " *Responsible Government in the Dominions.* Two volumes. 1928.
    "   " *The Constitutional Law of the British Dominions.* 1933.
KELLER, A. G., *Colonization.* 1908.
KELTIE, J. SCOTT, *The Partition of Africa.* 1895.
KENNEDY, W. P. M., and SCHLOSBERG, H. J., *The Law and Custom of the South African Constitution.* 1935.
KEPPEL–JONES, A., *Friends or Foes?* 1950.
KESTELL, J. D., *Met de Boeren Commandoes.* 1903.
    "   " *Through Shot and Flame.* 1903.
    "   " and VAN VELDEN, D. E., *The Peace Negotiations between the Governments of the S.A. Republic and the O.F. State, and the Representatives of the British Government.* 1912.
KHAMA, TSHEKEDI, *Bechuanaland and South Africa.* 1955.
KIDD, DUDLEY, *The Essential Kafir.* 1904.
    "   " *Kafir Socialism.* 1908.

KILPIN, R., *The Old Cape House.* 1918.
  „   „ *Pioneers of Parliament* (*Cape Argus*, March 19–April
      23). 1921.
  „   „ *When Downing Street Ruled* (*Cape Argus*, Feb. 16 on-
      wards). 1924.
  „   „ *The Romance of a Colonial Parliament.* 1930.
KOTZE, (SIR) J. G., *Documents and Correspondence relating to the
      Judicial Crisis in the South African Republic.* 1898.
  „   „   „ *Biographical Memories and Reminiscences.* 1934.
KRÜGER, D. W., *Die Weg na die See* (*Argief-Jaarboek vir S-A.
    Geskiedenis,* I). 1938.
KRUGER, S. J. P., *The Memoirs of Paul Kruger . . . told by himself.*
    Two volumes. 1902.
LAGDEN, SIR G., *The Basutos.* Two volumes. 1909.
LANGER, W. L., *The Diplomacy of Imperialism, 1890–1902.* Two
    volumes. 1935.
LAURENCE, SIR PERCEVAL, *The Life of John Xavier Merriman.* 1930.
LEE, SIR SIDNEY, *King Edward VII. A Biography,* I. 1925.
LEIBBRANDT, H. C. V., *Précis of the Archives of the Cape of Good
      Hope :* (i) *Van Riebeeck's Journal,* three
      volumes (1897); *Journal, 1662–70* (1901);
      Journal, 1671–4 and 1676 (1902); *Journal,
      1699–1732* (1896); *Letters Despatched
      from the Cape, 1652–62,* three volumes
      (1900); *Letters Despatched, 1696–1708*
      (1896); *Letters and Documents Received,
      1695–1708* (1896); *Memorials, 1715–1806,*
      two volumes (1905–6); *The Defence of
      William Adriaan Van der Stel* (1897);
      Resolutien . . . 1652–62 (1898). 1897–1902.
  „   „   *Rambles through the Archives . . . 1688–1700.* 1887.
  „   „   *Slachter's Nek Rebellion, 1815.* 1902.
LEIPOLDT, C. L., *Jan van Riebeeck.* 1936.
LEONARD, A. G., *How We Made Rhodesia.* 1896.
LEONARD, C., *The Political Situation in South Africa, 1885–1895.* 1903.
Letters of Queen Victoria, The. Second Series, II., and *Third
    Series,* II.; edited by G. E. Buckle. 1926 and 1931.
Letters received by the East India Company, III., IV. 1899–1900.
LEYDS, W. J., *The First Annexation of the Transvaal.* 1906.
  „   „ *Eenige Correspondentie uit 1899.* 1919.
  „   „ *The Transvaal Surrounded.* 1919.
  „   „ *Tweede, Derde* and *Vierde Verzameling* (*Correspon-
    dentie*). 1930–34.
LICHTENSTEIN, H., *Travels in Southern Africa in the Years 1803 to
    1806* (translation). 1812.
LINDLEY, A. F., *Adamantia, the Truth about the South African
    Diamond Fields.* 1873.
LINSCHOTEN, J. H. VAN, *The Voyage of J. H. v. L. to the East Indies*
    (Hakluyt Society). 1885.
LIVINGSTONE, D., *Missionary Travels and Researches in South
    Africa.* 1857.
LLOYD, A. C. G., *The Birth of Printing in South Africa.* 1914.
LONG, B. K., *Sir Drummond Chaplin.* 1952.
LORAM, T., *The Education of the South African Native.* 1917.
LOVELL, R. I., *The Struggle for South Africa.* 1934.

McCARTER, J., *Geschiedenis der Nederduitsche Gereformeerde Kerk in Zuid Afrika.*   1876.
MacCRONE, I. D., *Race Attitudes in South Africa.*   1937.
McDONALD, J. G., *Rhodes : a Life.*   1927.
MacIVER, D. RANDALL, *Mediæval Rhodesia.*   1906.
MACKENZIE, JOHN, *Austral Africa.* Two volumes.   1887.
MACKENZIE. W. D., *John Mackenzie.*   1902.
MACLEAN, J. (Ed.), *A Compendium of Kafir Laws and Customs.*   1866.
MACMILLAN, W. M., *The Cape Colour Question. A Historical Survey.*   1927.
    „   „   *Bantu, Boer and Briton. The Making of the South African Native Problem.*   1929.
    „   „   *Complex South Africa.*   1930.
    „   „   *Africa Emergent.*   1938.
MACNAB, R., *The Emergence of Afrikaans as a Literary Language (Journal of the Royal Society of Arts,* No. 5000, Vol. CV).   1957.
MALHERBE, E. G., *Education in South Africa, 1652–1922.*   1925.
MALHERBE, D. F., *Afrikaner Volkseenheid.*
MANNING, H. T., *British Colonial Policy after the American Revolution, 1782–1820.*   1933.
MARAIS, J. S., *The Cape Coloured People, 1652–1937.*   1939.
    „   „   *Maynier and the First Boer Republic.*   1944.
MARQUARD, L., *The Peoples and Policies of South Africa.*   1952.
MARTIN, A. D., *Doctor Vanderkemp.*   1931.
MARTINEAU, J., *The Life and Correspondence of Sir Bartle Frere.* Two volumes.   1895.
MATTHEWS, J. W., *Incwadi Yami.*   1887.
MAURICE, SIR F. B., and ARTHUR, SIR G. C. A., *The Life of Lord Wolseley.*   1924.
MAURICE, SIR J. F., and STAFF, *History of the War in South Africa, compiled by direction of H.M. Government.* Three volumes.   1906–8.
MAY, H. J., *The South African Constitution.*   1949.
MEURANT, L. H., *Sixty Years Ago.*   1885.
MICHELL, SIR LEWIS, *The Life of the Rt. Hon. Cecil John Rhodes.* Two volumes.   1910.
MILLIN, S. G., *Rhodes.*   1933.
MOFFAT, J. S., *Lives of Robert and Mary Moffat.*   1885.
MOFFAT, ROBERT, *Missionary Labours and Scenes in Southern Africa.*   1842.
MOFFAT, R. U., *Life of John Smith Moffat.*   1921.
MOLEMA, S. M., *The Bantu, Past and Present.*   1920.
MOLTENO, SIR J. T., *The Dominion of Afrikanderdom.*   1923.
MOLTENO, P. A., *Life and Times of Sir J. C. Molteno.* Two volumes.   1900.
MOODIE, D., *Specimens of the Authentic Records . . . and The Records or a series of official papers relating to . . . the Native Tribes of South Africa,* Parts I, III, V.   1838–41.
MOODIE, D. C. F., *The History of the Battles and Adventures . . . in Southern Africa : to 1880.*   1888.
MORLEY, JOHN (LORD), *Life of William Ewart Gladstone.* Two volumes.   1903.
MORRELL, W. P., *British Colonial Policy in the Age of Peel and Russell.*   1930.
NEWTON, A. P., *Select Documents relating to the Unification of South Africa.* Two volumes.   1924.
NEWTON, LORD. *Lord Lansdowne. A Biography.*   1929.
NORRIS-NEWMAN, C. L., *Matabeleland and How We Got it.*   1895.

ORPEN, J. M., *History of the Basutos of South Africa.* 1857.
    „   „   *Reminiscences of Life in South Africa.* 1908.
OWEN, W. F. W., *Narrative of Voyages to . . . Africa.* 1833.
PATTERSON, S., *Colour and Culture in South Africa.* 1953.
PAULING, G., *Chronicles of a Contractor.* 1926.
PAYTON, C. A., *The Diamond Diggings of South Africa. . . .* 1872.
PERHAM, M., and CURTIS, L., *The Protectorates of South Africa.* 1935.
PERKINS, DEXTER, *The Monroe Doctrine, 1868–1907,* Baltimore. 1937.
PETERS, C., *The Eldorado of the Ancients.* 1902.
PHILIP, JOHN, *Researches in South Africa.* 1828.
PHILLIPS, R. E., *The Bantu in the City.* 1938.
PIROW, OSWALD, *James Barry Munnik Hertzog,* Capetown. 1957.
PLAATJE, S., *Native Life in South Africa. . . .* 1916.
PRELLER, G. S., *Dagboek van Louis Trigardt, 1836–8.* 1917.
    „   „   *Piet Retief.* 1920.
    „   „   *Voortrekkermense.* Three volumes. 1918–20–22.
    „   „   *Voortrekker Wetgewing. Notule van die Natalse
    Volksraad, 1839–45.* 1924.
PRESTAGE, E., *The Portuguese Pioneers.* 1933.
PRETORIUS, H. S., and KRÜGER, D. W., *Voortrekker-Argiefstukke,
    1829–1849.* 1937.
PYRAH, G. B., *Imperial Policy and South Africa.* 1955.

*Race Relations. Official Journal of the S.A. Institute of Race
    Relations* (quarterly, November 1933 onwards).   1933 onwards.
Race Relations News (monthly, July 1938 onwards).   1938 onwards.
RAPHAEL, L. A. C., *The Cape-to-Cairo Dream.* 1936.
REITZ, D., *Commando.* 1929.
    „   „   *Trekking On.* 1933.
    „   „   *No Outspan.* 1943.
REYBURN, H. A., *Studies in Cape Frontier History (The Critic,*
    October 1934, January, April and July 1935). 1934–5.
ROBERTS, A. W., *Some Reflections on Population. (S.A. Journal of
    Science,* 1926.) 1926.
ROBERTS, M., and TROLLIP, A. E. G., *The South African Opposition,
    1939–1945.* 1947.
ROBERTSON, H. M.,   *150 years of Economic Contact between White
                    and Black (S.A. Journal of Economics,*
                    December 1934 and March 1935); *Some
                    Doubts concerning Early Land Tenure at the
                    Cape (ibid.,* June 1935); *The Cape of Good
                    Hope and 'Systematic Colonization' (ibid.,*
                    December 1937); *The 1849 Settlers in Natal.*
                    I, II *(ibid.,* September, December, 1949);
                    South Africa. Economic and Political Aspects
                    (1957). 1934–57.
ROBSON, W. H., *New Light on Lord Castlereagh's Diplomacy (Journal
    of Modern History,* III, No. 2, June 1931). 1931.
ROGERS, H., *Native Administration in the Union of South Africa.* 1933.
ROSE, E. B., *The Truth about the Transvaal.* 1902.
ROSE, J. HOLLAND, *The Development of the European Nations,
    1870–1900.* 1908.
Round Table, The, (published quarterly). 1910 onwards.
ROUX, P. E., *Die Verdedigingstelsel aan die Kaap . . . 1652–1795.* 1925.
ROUX, E., *Time Longer than Rope.* 1948.

ROYAL INSTITUTE OF INTERNATIONAL AFFAIRS, *United Nations Documents, 1941–1945.* 1946.

SACHS, E. S., *The Choice before South Africa.* 1952.
S.A. NATIVE RACES COMMITTEE. *The South African Natives.* 1909.
SAUER, H., *Ex Africa* . . . 1937.
SCHAPERA, I., (editor), *Western Civilisation and the Natives of South Africa.* 1934.
    „   „   „   *The Bantu-speaking Tribes of South Africa.* 1937.
    „   „   „   *Apprenticeship at Kuruman being the journals and letters of Robert and Mary Moffat, 1820–1828.* 1951.
SCHOFIELD, J. F., *Zimbabwe : Critical Examination of the Building Methods employed. (S.A. Journal of Science, 1926.)* 1926.
SCHOLTZ, G. D., *Dr. W. J. van der Merwe.* 1944.
SCHREINER, T. L., *The Afrikander Bond.* 1901.
SCOBLE, J., and ABERCROMBIE, H. R., *The Downfall of Krugerism.* 1900.
    „   „   „   „   *The Rise and Fall of Krugerism.* 1900.
SCOTT, M., *A Time to Speak.* 1958.
SHAW, LORD, *Letters to Isabel.* 1921.
SHAW, W., *The Story of my Mission in South-Eastern Africa.* 1860.
SHEPHERD, R. H. W., *Lovedale* . . . 1940.
SILLERY, A., *The Bechuanaland Protectorate.* 1952.
SMITH, A., *Report of the Expedition for Exploring Central Africa.* 1836.
SMITH, SIR HARRY, *The Autobiography of Sir Harry Smith.* 1903.
SMITH, J. J., *The Evolution and Recognition of the Afrikaans Language. (Official Year Book of the Union of South Africa, No. 8.)* 1927.
SMITH, E., *The Blessed Missionaries.* 1950.
SMITH, E. W., *The Life and Times of Daniel Lindley, 1801–80.* 1949.
SMUTS, J. C., *A Century of Wrong* (translation). 1899.
    „   „   *Africa and Some World Problems.* 1930.
    „   „   (junior), *Jan Christian Smuts.* 1952.
S.A. Congress of Democrats, *Education for Ignorance.* 1954.
S.A. Institute of Race Relations, *A Survey of Race Relations.* 1949–52.
S.A. Liberal Party, *Contact.* 1954.
S.A. Native Races Committee, *The South African Natives.* 1909.
SPARRMAN, A., *A Voyage to the Cape.* Two volumes (translation). 1786.
SPEARPOINT, F., *The African in the Rhodesian Copper Mines. (Journal of the Royal African Society.)* 1937.
SPENDER, H., *General Botha.* 1919.
SPENDER, J. A., *The Life of the Rt. Hon. Sir Henry Campbell-Bannerman.* Two volumes. 1923.
SPOELSTRA, C., *Bouwstoffen voor de Geschiedenis der Nederduitsch-Gereformeerde Kerken in Zuid-Afrika.* Two volumes. 1906–7.
STAVORINUS, J. S., *Voyages to the East Indies* (translation). 1798.
STENT, VERE, *A Personal Record of some Incidents in the Life of Cecil Rhodes.* 1925.
STOCK, J. L. W., *The New Statutes of India (S.A. Law Journal).* 1915.
STOW, G. W., *The Native Races of South Africa.* 1910.
STUART, J., *De Hollandsche Afrikanen en hunne republiek in Zuid Afrika.* 1854.

THEAL, G. M., *Basutoland Records.* Three volumes. 1883.
    „   „   „   „   Three unpublished volumes in the Cape Archives.

THEAL, G. M., *Belangryke Historische Dokumenten.* Three volumes.
1896–1911.
„   „   *Documents relating to the Kaffir War of 1835.*   1912.
„   „   *History and Ethnography of Africa, South of the
          Zambesi, before 1795.* Three volumes.   1910.
„   „   *History of South Africa since 1795.* Five volumes.
          I–IV (1908); V (1910).   1908 and 1910.
„   „   (editor), *Records of the Cape Colony, 1793–1827.*
          Thirty-six volumes.   1897–1905.
„   „   (editor), *Records of South-Eastern Africa.* Nine
          volumes.   1898–1903.
„   „   *Willem Adriaan van der Stel and other Historical
          Sketches.*   1913.
THOMPSON, G., *Travels and Adventures in South Africa.*   1827.
THOMPSON, L. M., *The Cape Coloured Franchise.*   1949.
„   „   *The Unification of South Africa 1902–1910.*   1960.
TINDALL, B. A., (editor), *James Rose Innes. Autobiography.*   1949.
TROLLOPE, A., *South Africa.*   1878.

Union of South Africa and the Great War, 1914-18. Official History   1924.
UYS, C. J., *In the Era of Shepstone.*   1933.

VAN DEN HEEVER, C. M., *Generaal J. B. M. Hertzog.*   1946.
VAN DER HORST, S., *Native Labour in South Africa.*   1942.
VAN DER MERWE, J. P., *Die Kaap onder die Bataafse Republiek, 1803–6.*
1926.
VAN DER MERWE, N. J., *Marthinus Theunis Steyn.* Two volumes.   1921.
VAN DER MERWE, P. J., *Die Noordwaarste Beweging van die Boere
          voor die Groot Trek (1770–1842).*   1937.
„   „   „   *Die Trekboer in die Geskiedenis van Kaap-
          Kolonie (1657–1842).*   1938.
VAN DER POEL, J., *Railway and Customs Policies in South Africa,
          1885–1910.*   1933.
„   „   „   „   *The Jameson Raid.*   1951.
VAN OORDT, J. F., *Paul Kruger en de Opkomst der Zuid-Afri-
          kaansche Republiek.*   1898.
„   „   „   *Who were the Builders of Great Zimbabwe?*   [1906].
VAN RIEBEECK SOCIETY PUBLICATIONS: I. *The Reports of Chavonnes
and his Council, and of Van Imhoff, on the Cape, 1717 and
1743,* (1918); II. *Life at the Cape in the Mid-Eighteenth Cen-
tury, by O. F. Mentzel,* (1919); III. *The Memorandum of Com-
missary J. A. de Mist,* (1920); IV. *A . . . Description of the Cape
. . . by O. F. Mentzel, Part I.* (1921); V. *Collectanea,* (1924);
VI. *A . . . Description of the Cape . . . by O. F. Mentzel, Part
II.* (1925); VII. *The Diary of the Rev. Francis Owen, 1837–8,*
(1926); VIII. *The Wreck of the Grosvenor, 1782,* (1827);
IX. *Die Dagboek van Hendrik Witbooi, 1884–1906,* (1929);
X., XI. *Travels in Southern Africa, by Henry Lichtenstein,
1803–6,* (1928 and 1930); XII. *Journals of O. Bergh and I.
Schrijver, 1682–9,* (1931); XIII. *Louis Trigardt's Trek across
the Drakensberg, 1837–8, by C. Fuller,* (1932); XIV. *The early
Cape Hottentots, 1688–95,* (1933), XV. *The Journals of H. J.
Wikar and Jacobus Cornelius Janz, 1760–91,* (1934); XVI.,
XVII. *Travels and Adventures in Eastern Africa, by Nathaniel
Isaacs,* (1936 and 1937); XVIII. *D. G. van Reenen se Joernal,
1803,* (1937); XIX. *Duminy Dagboeke, 1793–1810,* (1938);

XX, XXI. *Diary of Dr. Andrew Smith, 1834–6*, I., II. (1939–40);
XXII. *Buck Adams' Narrative, 1843–8*, (1941); XXIII. *W. S.
van Ryneveld se Aanmerkingen over de Verbetering van het Vee,
1804*, (1942); XXIV. *M. D. Teenstra ; De Vruchten mijner
Werkzaamheden, 1830*, (1943); XXV. *O. F. Mentzel's Description of the Cape*, Part III., (1944); XXVI. *South African
Journal of J. S. Dobie, 1862–3*, (1945); XXVII., XXIX. *Chronicle
of Jeremiah Goldswain, 1819–36*, I., II., (1946 and 1949);
XXVIII. *Journals of J. T. Rhenius and C. F. Brink, 1724–62*,
(1947); XXX. *Journals of Andrew Geddes Bain, 1826–46*,
(1949); XXXI. *Journals of the American Missionaries, 1835–8*,
(1951); XXXII. *Die Konvensie-dagboek van F. S. Malan,
1908–9*, (1951); XXXIII. *Die Dagboek van H. A. L. Hamelberg,
1855–71*, (1952); XXXIV. *Source Book of the Wreck of the
Grosvenor*, (1953); XXXV. *Narrative and Journal of Gerald
McKiernan in German South-West Africa*, (1954); XXXVI.   1918
Andrew Smith and Natal, (1955).   onwards.

VARIOUS AUTHORS. *The Cape Coloured People To-day.*   1942.
VILJOEN, B., *My Reminiscences of the Anglo-Boer War.*   1903.
' VINDEX,' *Cecil Rhodes. His Political Life and Speeches.*   1900.

WALKER, ERIC A., *Historical Atlas of South Africa.*   1922.
„   „   *Lord de Villiers and his Times. South Africa,
              1842–1914.*   1925.
„   „   *The S.A. College and the University of Cape
              Town, 1829–1929.*   1929.
„   „   *The Frontier Tradition in South Africa.*   1930.
„   „   *W. P. Schreiner, a South African.*   1937.
„   „   *The Great Trek.*   1938.
WALKER, I. L., *The Civilised Labour Policy and the Displacement
of Non-European Labour.*   1935.
WALKER, O., *Kaffirs are Lively.*   1948.
WALLIS, J. P. R., (editor), *The Matabele Mission . . . 1858–1878.*   1945.
„   „   „   *The Matabele Journals of Robert Moffat,
1829–1860.* Two volumes.   1945.
WALTON, SIR E. H., *The Inner History of the National Convention
of South Africa.*   1912.
WESSELS, SIR W. J., *History of the Roman-Dutch Law.*   1908.
WILLE, G., *Principles of South African Law.*   1945.
WILLIAMS, BASIL, *Cecil Rhodes.*   1921.
„   „   *The Selborne Memorandum on the Union of South
Africa.*   1925.
WILLIAMS, GARDNER F., *The Diamond Mines of South Africa.*   1902.
WILLS, W. A., and COLLINGRIDGE, L. T., *The Downfall of
Lobengula.*   1894.
WILMOT, A., *Monomatapa.*   1898.
„   „   *The Life and Times of Sir Richard Southey.*   1904.
WILSON, G., *The Economics of Distribution in Northern Rhodesia.*   1941.
WOLF, L., *Life of the First Marquess of Ripon.* Two volumes.   1921.
WORSFOLD, W. BASIL, *Sir Bartle Frere. A Footnote to the History
of the British Empire.*   1913.
„   „   *Sir Bartle Frere.*   1923.

Unpublished Post-graduate Theses

AGAR-HAMILTON, J. A. I., *Early Republican Constitutions in South Africa.*
Transvaal University College.

DE KIEWIET, C. W., *The Northern Border, 1803–46*. University of the Witwatersrand.

DENYSSEN, H. D., *The Labour Problem in Natal, 1852–74*. University of Cape Town.

GRIEVE, C. S., *The Policy of H.M. Government towards Europeans beyond the Colonial Borders, 1830–46*. University of Cape Town.

MATHESON, D. D., *The Origin and Status of the New Republic*. Transvaal University College.

MOLTENO, C., *British Policy towards the Natives beyond the Colonial Frontiers, 1830–45*. University of Cape Town.

MURRAY, W. G., *British Relations with the Transvaal, 1874–81*. University of Oxford.

PITMAN, B. P., *John Fairbairn*. University of Cape Town.

SMIT, G. J. J., *The Native Policy of the Cape Colony, 1853–71*. University of Cape Town.

STEYN, H. P., *Brits-Kaffraria, 1853–66*. University of Cape Town.

TURNER, L., *The Cape and the Trafalgar Campaign*. University of the Witwatersrand.

VAN DER POEL, J., *Moshesh, 1858–70*. University of Cape Town.

INDEX